PROFESSIONAL GARDE MANGER

A Comprehensive Guide to Cold Food Preparation

LOU SACKETT | JACLYN PESTKA

•CONSULTING AUTHOR•

WAYNE GISSLEN

PHOTOGRAPHY BY J. GERARD SMITH

WILEY

JOHN WILEY & SONS, INC.

Senior Acquisitions Editor	Mary J. Cassells	Senior Designer	Carole Anson
Senior Developmental Editor	Julie R. Kerr	Cover Designer	Howard Grossman
Project Editor	Michele Traeger	Cover & Interior Photography	J. Gerard Smith
Editorial Assistant	James Metzger	Graphics Supervisor	Clint Lahnen
Editorial Assistant	Jenni Lee	Illustration Creation	Cheryl Grubbs
Production Editor	Barbara Russiello	Graphics Processing & Imaging	Brent Savage
Production Manager	Micheline Frederick	Executive Media Editor	Tom Kulesa
Marketing Manager	Margaret Barrett	Media Consultant	Lydia Cheng
Compostion & Text Design	Mauna Eichner, Lee Fukui		

This book was set in 10/12 Din by Mauna Eichner and Lee Fukui and printed and bound by RR Donnelley & Sons Company. The cover was printed by Lehigh Phoenix.

This book is printed on acid free paper.

Library of Congress Cataloging in Publication Data:

Sackett, Lou
Professional garde manger : a comprehensive guide to cold food preparation / photography by J. Gerard Smith ; Lou Sackett, Jaclyn Pestka, Wayne Gisslen (consulting author)
p. cm.
Includes bibliographical references and index.
ISBN 978-0-470-17996-3 (cloth)
1. Cookery (Cold dishes) 2. Quantity cookery. I. Pestka, Jaclyn. II. Gisslen, Wayne. III. Title.
TX830.G58 2010
641.7'9--dc22

2009053273

Printed in the United States of America

10 9 8 7

This book is dedicated to the memory of Linda Cohen.

Contents

3 Simple Salads and Tossed Salads 56

4 Cold Vegetables and Fruits 76

Recipe Contents

Note: Recipes in italic are variations.

2 | Sauces and Dressing

3 | Simple Salads and Tossed Salads

4 | Cold Vegetables and Fruits

5 | Complex Salads

6 | Cold Seafood

7 | Cold Meats

8 | Cold Soups

9 | Garde Manger Sandwiches

10 | Cold Hors d'Oeuvres

11 | Cured and Smoked Foods

12 | Sausages

13 | Pâtés, Terrines, and Charcuterie Specialties

14 Cheese and Other Dairy Products

15 Mousselines

16 Aspic and Chaud-Froid

17 | Condiments, Embellishments, and Décor

Appendix: Basic Preparations

Preface

The specialized field of garde manger is unique among the culinary arts for the broad spectrum of career opportunities it encompasses. Although frequently an entry-level job, garde manger work at its highest level demands extensive education and training, as well as technical mastery and artistic talent.

Now, more than ever, the development of specialized skills is key to career advancement. In today's food service, owners and managers look for employees with more to offer. Mastery of garde manger work and, ultimately, the ability to create and direct a garde manger department make any chef more employable.

ABOUT THE AUTHORS

Professional Garde Manger is the much-anticipated new addition to Wayne Gisslen's *Professional* series. Co-authors Lou Sackett and Jaclyn Pestka are pleased and honored to have worked with Wayne in creating this book.

Lou Sackett is a culinary educator and food writer whose career includes more than fifteen years teaching culinary arts at secondary and post secondary levels, as well as owning and operating a nationally acclaimed restaurant. Among her contributions to this book are salads and vegetable preparations, hors d'oeuvres, and aspic and chaud-froid work. Her experience in preparing and selecting fine cheeses is showcased in this book's dairy chapter. Lou is the team's primary writer and food stylist.

Jaclyn Pestka is a nationally acclaimed restaurant chef originally specializing in world cuisines. She is currently executive chef of Channels Food Rescue, a nonprofit organization that fights hunger and offers food-service workforce training to adults. Her career as a post-secondary chef instructor led to in-depth exploration in garde manger and expertise in charcuterie work. She is widely known for her superb artisan sausages, pâtés, and smoked foods created in both traditional and contemporary styles. Her goal is to pass on her extensive knowledge of the charcutier's art with clearly explained theoretical information and detailed, step-by-step procedure instructions.

Consulting author **Wayne Gisslen** is the author of the bestselling series of culinary books that includes ***Professional Cooking***, ***Essentials of Professional Cooking***, ***Professional Baking***, and ***Advanced Professional Cooking***, all published by Wiley. A graduate of The Culinary Institute of America, he has written and worked extensively in the field of culinary arts, with experience as a restaurant chef, test kitchen supervisor, and food and beverage consultant.

GOALS OF THIS BOOK

Professional Garde Manger is designed for culinary students and instructors, and working chefs wishing to hone their skills in cold foods preparation. It is appropriate for both beginning and advanced courses in garde manger, as a supplement to a basic culinary arts text for the specialized coverage of garde manger work, and for use in the study of catering and banquet service.

The initial goal of this book is the development and refinement of skills. ***Professional Garde Manger*** is designed to transition the mid-level culinary student or working chef into the more challenging, upper-level work of the culinary specialist.

A secondary goal is to show the many facets of traditional and modern garde manger work. What, exactly, is garde manger? What kinds of dishes and products does the garde manger department produce? What are the specialized skills needed for success? This book provides answers to these questions.

The ultimate goal of this book is to thoroughly prepare culinary students, cooks, and chefs for the specialized work of the garde manger. With careful study and practice, users of this book will succeed in preparing cold dishes for à la carte restaurant service as well as hors d'oeuvres, appetizers, main dishes, accompaniments, and decorative pieces for banquets and buffets—meeting professional standards and exceeding customer expectations.

ORGANIZATION OF THIS BOOK

Professional Garde Manger introduces the most important preparations in the garde manger's repertoire. It begins with the history of garde manger, essential to understanding its traditions and concepts.

To every extent possible, ***Professional Garde Manger*** presents a linear progression of information. Earlier chapters cover fundamental subjects needed to progress to more advanced topics. Basic recipes precede more complex ones. In the few cases when the subject matter or recipes require information or skills presented later in the book, the reader is referred ahead.

The book's organization also accommodates today's most prevalent post-secondary culinary school course structure. Thus, the book's first 15 chapters mesh seamlessly into a 15-week course of study, or can be combined to accommodate a shorter course. Advanced topics, in Chapters 16 through 18, offer additional challenges for longer courses, advanced courses, or independent work. It is not essential to follow exactly the chapter order. Once basic concepts are mastered, the instructor may teach in whatever order suits the program.

A WEALTH OF RECIPES AND VARIATIONS

Professional Garde Manger offers more than 375 recipes and 400 variations appropriate for use in the culinary classroom and professional kitchen.

The recipes were chosen to present a variety of dishes from all areas of the North American and European garde manger repertoires. Many recipes can be considered a foundation on which the developing student can build and elaborate. Others are appropriate for the intermediate level, while some are advanced.

Most recipes are supplemented with one or more *recipe variations*. Each suggests ways in which the recipe can be modified to create a new dish similar to the recipe on which it is based. Variations include: substituting one main ingredient for another; changing a seasoning, sauce, or accompaniment; changing a cooking method; or a combination of such modifications. Some variations simplify a recipe, while others make it more challenging.

VARIATION

TERRINE GRANDMÈRE
[grahn-MARE]
GRANDMOTHER'S TERRINE

Replace the Madeira with 2 oz (60 mL) reduced red wine. Replace all of the chicken livers and 12 oz (340 g) of the lean pork butt with trimmed pork liver. Replace 4 oz (120 g) of the pork fatback with trimmed smoked bacon.

The Professional Recipe Format

The recipes in this book are written in a professional recipe format that reflects the manner in which professional chefs both think and work. They are suited to the operations of a contemporary à la carte restaurant, in which modular food components are prepared ahead of time and then synthesized into finished dishes when the customer order is placed.

Finished dish recipes demonstrate the final presentation of a dish, whether a plated presentation for á la carte service or a platter presentation for buffet service. Finished dish recipes are designated with the "knife and fork" symbol.

Component recipes give thorough instructions on how to prepare and hold the various elements that make up a finished dish. Some are main components, while others are subsidiary components, such as aspic jewels added to the plate to enhance the main component. Component recipes are designed to be used in many other contexts: as stand-alone dishes or combined with other component recipes to create completely new dishes. This reflects the modular nature of today's restaurant cooking. The section titled "How to Use This Book" (p. xxviii) contains additional information on the professional recipe format.

Stunning Visuals and Dynamic Illustrations

Because identification, technique, and presentation are of great importance in garde manger work, ***Professional Garde Manger*** features more than 700 illustrations, including 140 photos and drawings of equipment and food products, 450 technique photos and drawings, 100 finished dish presentations, and 50 *unique plating blueprints*. No other book includes both step-by-step plating instructions *and* color photos or plating blueprints for virtually every finished dish.

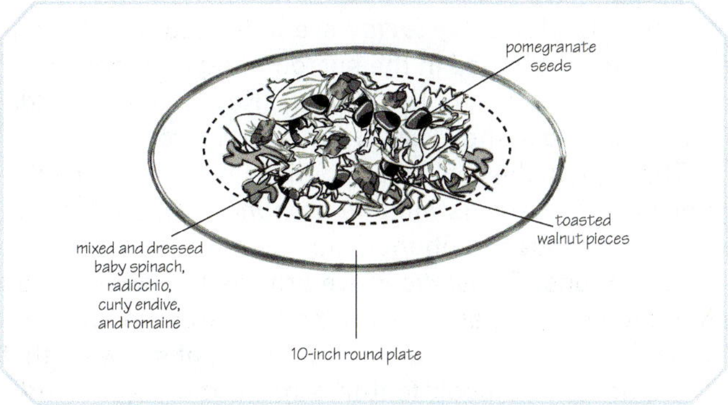

UNIQUE TOPICAL COVERAGE

In addition to the advanced subjects of aspic and chaud-froid work, condiments, garnishes and decorations, and buffet planning, preparation, and execution covered in Chapters 16 through 18, ***Professional Garde Manger*** features unique topical coverage not offered in other books.

The extensive coverage of charcuterie (Chapters 11 through 13) is specifically designed to lead the beginning garde manger student through each procedure in a clearly explained, step-by-step manner to ensure both true understanding of the subject and a safe, successful product.

Also unique is thorough coverage of vegetables and fruits, including a separate chapter on cold vegetable and fruit preparations (Chapter 4), as well as a chapter on vegetable- and fruit-based complex salads (Chapter 5).

Finally, ***Professional Garde Manger*** not only includes basic information on making simple fresh cheeses but also extends coverage of cheese making for higher-order understanding of the ripening and aging processes.

FEATURES OF THIS BOOK

Following the proven model of ***Professional Cooking*** and ***Professional Baking***, ***Professional Garde Manger*** emphasizes both *understanding* and *performing*. Thus, each chapter initially focuses on theory. Procedures directly follow theory, with emphasis on mastering skills. The book contains many features designed to make learning easier.

Prerequisites and Learning Objectives

Because garde manger is an advanced field of study, students should have mastered basic culinary theory and skills before undertaking it. For this reason, each chapter begins with a list of *prerequisites* detailing the knowledge and techniques needed for understanding the chapter's concepts and successfully completing its recipes.

PREREQUISITES

Before studying this chapter, you should already

- Have read "How to Use This Book," pp. xxviii–xxxiii, and understand the professional recipe format.
- Know how to perform basic meat, poultry, and seafood preparation and cooking methods.

Each chapter also includes a list of *learning objectives* alerting students to the important concepts and techniques they will master. After studying a chapter and practicing its techniques, students are encouraged to refer back to the chapter objectives and evaluate the level of mastery they have achieved.

After reading this chapter, you should be able to

1. Explain the difference between simple salads and complex salads.
2. Prepare each type of complex salad presented in this chapter in accordance with food safety practices.

Sidebars and Procedure Boxes

For clarity, the main text of each chapter covers the basic concepts essential for success: the "need-to-know" information. More complex information and other related topics that support the text are presented separately, in concise *sidebars*. For example, scientific principles are explained in *"The Science of . . ."* sidebars and historical facts are presented in *"The History of . . ."* sidebars. General sidebars appear throughout as well.

The Science of Ripening

The processes by which ripening occurs are complex. Many involve the enzymatic breakdown of various molecules. However, one of the most important factors

The History of "French" Dressing

In France, the classic simple salad of leafy greens is always tossed with some form of simple vinaigrette. In the 1880s, European chefs introduced

Procedure boxes highlight key preparations in detail, step by step, with accompanying photos or illustrations. Recipes utilizing and reinforcing a particular procedure directly follow the procedure box. By first *learning*, and then *doing*, the student acquires a solid foundation of knowledge and expertise.

Procedure for Cleaning Salad Greens

With the exception of commercially pre-cleaned products, all salad greens must be thoroughly washed, drained, and dried before they are consumed.

1. **Separating**
   Remove the leaves from the core or the stems (A) and discard any unusable parts. Do not tear or cut the greens into pieces before washing, as the absorption of excess water leads to wilting and decay.
2. **Washing**
   Thorough washing of salad greens is of the utmost importance. Consuming a mouthful of grit along with a bite of salad is an unpleasant experience. Washing also removes foreign matter such as insects and bits of packaging. The water used for washing salad

Guidelines boxes also provide important summaries of related practices needed to implement procedures and recipes correctly.

Guidelines for Food Safety for Mayonnaise

To avoid the dangers of food-borne illness, observe the following food safety guidelines when preparing or using mayonnaise.

- **Use pasteurized egg yolks.**
  In mayonnaise, the eggs remain raw, so harmful microorganisms are not killed by heat.
- **As pasteurized yolks are sold frozen, thaw them under refrigeration and then bring the refrigerated yolks to room temperature quickly.**
  To avoid bacterial growth, yolks should spend as little time as possible at room temperature.
- **Sanitize all tools and containers.**
  Even if made from pasteurized yolks, mayonnaise is still a good breeding ground for bacteria that, in high concentration, may contaminate it during production and storage.
- **Keep mayonnaise refrigerated until it is needed.**
  Limit to 1 hour or less the amount of time house-made mayonnaise remains in the temperature danger zone (41°–135°F/5°–57°C/in Canada: 40°F–140°F/4°C–69°C).).
- Label house-made mayonnaise with the time it was made as well as the date.
- Discard refrigerated house-made mayonnaise after 48 hours, even if it appears to be still good.

Emphasis on Terminology

Garde manger work includes many specialized terms. This book has features that enable readers to correctly use and properly pronounce this terminology.

Each chapter's ***key terms*** are indicated in bold magenta color, explained in the surrounding text, and listed for review at the end of the chapter. Key terms are additionally defined in the *glossary* for easy reference.

Throughout the book, most foreign language terms and many scientific terms include *pronunciation guides* that enable the reader to phonetically sound out the correct pronunciations. *Translations* are provided when a foreign language word is part of a recipe title. Additionally, the CulinarE-Companion™ recipe management software that accompanies this book features more than 1,000 *audio pronunciations* of select terms and recipe names, reinforcing correct pronunciation.

RESOURCES TO SUPPORT THIS BOOK

CulinarE-Companion™ Recipe Management Software, with Video Demonstrations

A revised and enhanced version of Wiley's recipe management software accompanies this book and now *includes video instruction to enhance and reinforce learning*! These new video demonstrations offer students and instructors the chance to preview, review, practice, and prepare necessary skills at any time.

All recipes from the book are included in the software—even including some bonus recipes not in the book—plus a range of useful features for adapting and manipulating recipes to suit individual needs. With this software, you can:

- Add, edit, modify, and print recipes, adjust portion sizes or yields.
- Create and organize shopping lists.
- Resize recipes in U.S. or metric measures.
- Search recipes by main ingredient, cooking method, and cuisine type.
- Calculate nutritional analyses of recipes.

Instructor's Manual and Computerized Test Bank

The **Instructor's Manual** (978-0-470-25399-1) is a chapter-by-chapter guide to presenting the material in ***Professional Garde Manger***. Each chapter contains:

Chapter Prerequisites and Objectives (reprinted from the chapter for your convenience).

Chapter Outline and Overview, with page numbers for easy reference to the book. Outline heads correspond to the heads presented on each chapter's PowerPoint slides. Under each section head there is a brief overview of the section.

Instructor's Notes provide advice from the hands-on chef instructors who wrote and evaluated this book. These include:

- Curriculum planning ideas, such as suggestions for expanding the chapter or combining it with other chapters to create units of study that fit your curriculum
- Tips for explaining the material to address various learning styles
- Troubleshooting production pitfalls, including ways to prevent errors that can occur in the laboratory or production kitchen
- Suggestions for modifying the chapter material to accommodate classes or individual students working at varying skill levels
- Tips for encouraging and motivating

Answers and Definitions include briefly stated answers for the chapter's Questions for Discussion and short definitions of the chapter's key terms, with references to pages where material is more fully explained.

Student Study Guide Solutions provide concise answers to the questions in the **Student Study Guide**.

Computerized Test Bank

The *Test Bank* has been specifically formatted for **Respondus**, an easy-to-use software program for creating and managing exams that can be printed to paper or published directly to Blackboard, WebCT, Desire2Learn, eCollege, ANGEL, and other eLearning systems. Instructors who adopt ***Professional Garde Manger*** can download the test bank for free.

Additional resources also can be uploaded into your LMS course at no charge. To view and access these resources and the test bank, visit www.wiley.com/college/gisslen, select ***Professional Garde Manger***, click on the Instructor Companion website link, and then click on LMS Course Student Resources—or contact your Wiley representative for more information.

PowerPoint Slides

Ready-to-use **PowerPoint** slides effectively reinforce your lectures. The PowerPoints can be downloaded from the book's website at www.wiley.com/college/gisslen.

Student Study Guide to Accompany Professional Garde Manger

This companion study aid is a valuable tool for reinforcing the theory and practice of garde manger techniques. For each chapter in ***Professional Garde Manger***, the **Student Study Guide** (978-0-470-28473-5) offers exercises to test comprehension, understanding, and retention of the material. Each set of exercises opens with key term definitions that must be mastered for successful communication in the garde manger kitchen. Additional work includes multiple-choice, short-answer, fill-in-the-blank, and culinary math problems related to garde manger work. (Answers are included in the **Instructor's Manual**.)

Book Companion Website

A robust companion website contains information for both students and instructors, and is available at www.wiley.com/college/gisslen.

How to Use This Book

Professional Garde Manger is a valuable tool for the working chef, but is primarily designed for the intermediate-level culinary student. The subject matter is organized in a logical progression from basic preparations to more complex preparations. Advanced topics are covered at the end. Within each chapter, theory and understanding are discussed first, followed by information on ingredients, an explanation of basic procedures, and, finally, recipes. If you are new to the subject of garde manger, it is advisable to follow the order of the book.

To successfully prepare the recipes presented in this book, you must study and understand the basic procedures used in making them. In fact, there are two important things you should do to enhance your learning and make your course of study more beneficial:

1. Before you begin a chapter, review the chapter prerequisites. Know the fundamental information upon which the chapter is based and make sure that you have mastered the required skills.
2. Before you prepare any of the recipes, make sure you are familiar with the professional recipe format in which they are written and that you understand how each recipe works.

CHAPTER PREREQUISITES

You are expected to have previously mastered a wide variety of culinary fundamentals prior to your garde manger course. You have most likely already taken courses in basic knife skills, cooking techniques, and sanitation, and even perhaps baking fundamentals.

Garde manger success depends on a sound foundation of culinary knowledge and food preparation skills, and each of its many different subspecialties has different technical requirements. For this reason, a list of prerequisites is presented at the beginning of each chapter. As much as possible, this book is organized so new information builds on previously learned information. Thus, a chapter prerequisite may refer you back to a previous chapter. However, in a few cases you will be referred to a later chapter for special techniques.

Chapter prerequisites alert you to basic knowledge and skills you should possess before proceeding.

PREREQUISITES

Before studying this chapter, you should already

- Have read "How to Use This Book," pages xxviii–xxxiii, and understand the professional recipe format.
- Know basic meat and poultry cuts, and be proficient at fabricating them.
- Be familiar with various spices, and know how to toast and grind whole spices.
- Be proficient at clarifying stock.
- Have read Chapter 11, "Cured and Smoked Foods," and understand the use of curing mixtures.
- Have read Chapter 12, "Sausages," know the various types of pork fat, and be proficient at preparing standard-grind forcemeats.
- Know how to work with gelatin if you will be preparing pâtés en croûte, or have read ahead to Chapter 16, "Aspic and Chaud-Froid," pages 630–663.

THE PROFESSIONAL RECIPE FORMAT

The recipes in this book were written by professional chefs for professional chefs—and especially for culinary students who aspire to become professionals. These recipes reflect the manner in which food is prepared in the *à la carte commercial kitchen*. For this reason, the recipes may look different from other recipes with which you have worked. However, after reading the following recipe information and working with the recipes, you will begin to think about food preparation in a new, more organized, and professional way.

Modular Cooking

The professional cooking process is modular. Each finished dish contains a number of component preparations, most of which are made ahead of time. Take, for example, a chicken salad sandwich. With each order, the line chefs cannot begin poaching chicken, making mayonnaise, washing lettuce, and baking rolls. For efficiency, the chicken salad must be premade, the lettuce previously cleaned and dried, and the rolls already baked, cooled, and sliced. Each of these premade elements is a module, or *component*, of the finished sandwich. To create the finished dish, the components are simply combined.

Component Recipes

For each component requiring any type of complex preparation there is a written recipe, in this book referred to as a *component recipe*. The most important component recipe in a finished dish is called the *main component recipe*. In our chicken salad sandwich, the main component recipe is the chicken salad recipe. Recipes for other components of lesser importance are called *subsidiary component recipes*. In this book, main component recipes are typically placed in close proximity to the finished dish recipes that feature them. However, in some cases you will be referred to another chapter to find component recipes.

In more complex preparations, the main component recipe may comprise yet other component recipes. For example, to prepare the chicken salad, you must use two additional component recipes: poached chicken and mayonnaise. However, in a typical food-service operation the poached chicken and mayonnaise recipes are not used solely for the chicken salad. One advantage of modular food preparation is each component recipe usually can be used to make other dishes.

Finished Dish Recipes

A recipe that explains how to assemble component recipes into a finished dish is a *finished dish recipe*. These finished dish recipes are identified by the knife and fork icon by the recipe title. Finished dish recipes help you learn how each particular garde manger preparation is properly presented and served.

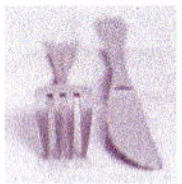

The knife and fork icon identifies recipes for finished dishes.

One characteristic of a typical finished-dish recipe is that its ingredients list is largely composed of component recipes. In this book, the ingredients of a finished dish recipe are entitled "components." To prepare a finished dish recipe, you must first prepare all of its component recipes.

In garde manger work, finished dishes are grouped into two categories by service type: plated dishes and platter presentations.

1. A **plated dish** consists of a single serving of food, intended for one diner only, and presented on a plate from which the diner directly eats. Garde manger plated dishes may be assembled *à la carte* (one-at-a-time to order), or they may be set up ahead of time, *banquet style*.

2. A **platter presentation** is intended to serve two or more diners. Multiple servings of food are presented on a single tray or other vessel; to serve, the food is transferred from the platter to individual plates.

COMPONENTS

1 Kaiser roll
1 fl oz (30 mL) *Mayonnaise (p. 41)* or commercial mayonnaise
4½ oz (125 g) *Classic Chicken Salad (p. 159)*, made with chopped chicken
1 leaf (¼ oz/7 g) Green-leaf lettuce or romaine lettuce
3 slices (1½ oz/45 g total) Vine-ripe tomato

External Garnish

2 Pimiento-stuffed olives

In each recipe's ingredients list, component recipes are easily recognized because their titles are printed in blue.

Finished dishes are also categorized by their place in the meal. All finished dishes have been classified as one or more of the following:

1. Hors d'oeuvre
2. Appetizer
3. Lunch main course
4. Main course
5. Buffet presentation

TERRINE DE CAMPAGNE *[tair-EEN duh kahm-PAHN(yuh)]*

COUNTRY TERRINE

Fig. 1: Foreign recipe titles include phonetic pronunciation guides and English translations.

TERRINE DE CAMPAGNE

WITH MUSTARD AND CORNICHONS ***APPETIZER***

Fig. 2: When the title of a finished dish is similar to that of its main component recipe, the finished dish is identified by including the names of its sauce or accompaniments in the title. Here, mustard and cornichons.

The Anatomy of a Professional Recipe

Professional recipes have five main elements:

1. Title
2. Yield
3. Ingredients/components list
4. Procedure
    a. Preparation
    b. Holding
    c. Final assembly
5. Variations, if any

CLASSIC CHICKEN OR TURKEY SALAD

LUNCH MAIN COURSE

Yield:
1 qt (1 L),
about 1¾ lb (840 g)
Portions:
varies according to application
Portion size:
varies according to application

Fig. 3: Yields are expressed in a variety of ways.

The Recipe Title

The title of a recipe has two main functions: to describe the dish and to distinguish it from all others of its type. As well, a recipe title should make the dish sound enticing.

In ***Professional Garde Manger***, recipe titles are in English unless the dish has a foreign name that is in wide, common use. Foreign recipe titles include phonetic pronunciation guides and English translations (Fig. 1). Audio pronunciations for many of these foreign recipe titles are also available as part of the CulinarE-Companion™ recipe management software that accompanies this book.

Sometimes the title of a finished dish is very similar to the title of its main component recipe. In this case, the finished dish is typically identified by including the names of its sauce or accompaniments in the title (Fig. 2).

The Recipe Yield

A recipe's yield is the amount of product the recipe makes. Yield may be expressed in weight, volume, count (number of units), or number of portions, including portion size. Keep in mind that *yields may vary slightly to significantly*, depending on variations in ingredients, accuracy of measuring, and the manner in which preparation methods are applied (Fig. 3).

The yield of each component recipe is planned within the context of the typical classroom kitchen. Most component recipes are written with a yield of four servings, which is enough food for tasting by a class of 20 students. Some component recipes are written to accommodate the volume of a particular vessel, such as a standard-size terrine form; if your vessel is of a different volume, adjust the ingredient amounts accordingly. Preparations typically made in large quantity, such as sausages and soups, are written in the smallest reasonable yield. If you need larger yields, you can easily scale up most recipes using your culinary math skills or the accompanying CulinarE-Companion™ recipe management software.

Finished dish recipes normally have a yield of 1 serving, because that is how they are typically assembled during *á la carte* restaurant service.

Platter presentation recipes are written in a yield that makes sense for both tasting purposes and within the context of the dish.

Recipe Ingredients/Components

The recipe ingredients are the materials from which any dish is built. Careful measurement of ingredients is essential for success, particularly in more complex preparations such as cured foods and emulsified forcemeats. In this book, ingredient measurements are primarily expressed in weight, with volume and count measurements used when appropriate. Both U.S. standard and metric measurements are given.

In some cases, you will need nonfood ingredients, such as doilies or sandwich picks, to complete your presentation. These are included in the ingredients/components lists under the heading "Supplies." In some recipes, ingredients are divided under other headings for clarity.

Recipe Procedure

The procedure section of each recipe contains directions in numbered steps. When a single step requires multiple actions, for clarity, that step is further broken down into substeps.

Recipe procedures are further broken down into stages, reflecting the manner in which food is typically premade, stored, finished, and served.

PREPARATION

Preparation is defined as all the work that can be done to a particular dish ahead of time without compromising its final quality. Because garde manger dishes are served cold or at room temperature, often, many of their components can be prepared well in advance. Some can be completely prepared ahead of time.

The preparation stage can usually be done on the same day as service, or sometimes as early as several days in advance. (The holding section provides the information you need to judge how far in advance preparation can begin.) In more complex recipes, many of the ingredients lists include component recipes. In these cases, prepare those component recipes first. Once all component recipes are prepared, and all raw materials are fabricated, preparation is complete.

CHICKEN SALAD ON A KAISER ROLL

LUNCH MAIN COURSE

Yield:
1 sandwich, 4½ oz (125 g) filling

COMPONENTS

1 Kaiser roll
1 fl oz (30 mL) *Mayonnaise (p. 41)* or commercial mayonnaise
4½ oz (125 g) *Classic Chicken Salad (p. 159)*, made with chopped chicken
1 leaf (¼ oz/7 g) Green-leaf lettuce or romaine lettuce
3 slices (1½ oz/45 g total) Vine-ripe tomato

External Garnish
2 Pimiento-stuffed olives

Supplies
2 Frilled sandwich picks

Nonfood ingredients are listed as Supplies.

Procedures for component recipes are typically divided into preparation and holding.

PROCEDURE

PREPARATION

1. Combine the mayonnaise and seasonings.
2. Taste and correct seasoning.
3. Blend the dressing with the remaining ingredients.
4. Refrigerate ½–1 hour, then taste and, if necessary, correct the seasoning and adjust the texture with more mayonnaise.

HOLD

If made with commercial mayonnaise, store refrigerated in a freshly sanitized, covered container up to 4 days; with housemade mayonnaise, store up to 2 days.

HOLDING

Holding is the proper storage of components and fabricated raw materials during the time between preparation and final assembly. Because you are working with professional recipes, basic food safety and sanitation knowledge is assumed. Keep in mind that *holding is an option*; it is not mandatory. However, instructions for holding must answer three essential questions:

1. At what temperature should the items be stored?
2. How long can the items be stored?
3. Are there any special instructions for storage?

The answer to the second question, giving the length of time for storage, is your clue to how far ahead preparation can begin.

When preparing platter presentations in buffet work, it frequently is necessary to do the final assembly of the platters quite some time before service. Thus, there is usually a second holding phase after final assembly.

FINAL ASSEMBLY

In garde manger work, the *final assembly* of a dish involves combining all components and fabricated raw materials to create the dish in its finished form.

In *à la carte* service, final assembly is all the work that is done to a particular dish after the customer order is placed. In this book, the final assembly of plated dishes is sometimes further divided into two phases: finishing and plating.

- *Finishing* consists of any last-minute preparation, such as tossing salad greens with a dressing, or toasting bread for a sandwich. Not all final assembly involves finishing. (Note: Finishing can also refer to the final work done on a previously prepared component, such as the unmolding and slicing of a terrine.)
- *Plating* is arranging the food on the plate. The recipes in this book give very specific directions for arranging food on the plate. These directions include special terms used by chefs and food stylists to clarify plating directions. By following the plating directions carefully, you should be able to create plates that look exactly like the photo or blueprint that accompanies the recipe. Knowing how to correctly follow plating instructions is an important skill because the best food-service establishments insist on precise plating for consistent presentation.

In this book, finishing and plating directions are planned to take no longer than 15 minutes. Use this as a guideline as to when to begin the final assembly of your plated dish.

A Note About U.S.–Metric Conversions

In this book, recipe ingredient amounts are expressed in both the U.S. and metric systems. When working with the recipes, use one system or the other; do not alternate between the two systems. Each is designed to be self-contained.

You may notice that the given ingredient amounts are not always exact equivalents, U.S. to metric. When appropriate, metric amounts have been rounded up or down to avoid the use of odd numbers and decimals and, thus, make recipe scaling easier. In most recipes, 1 oz is represented by 30 g rather than 28.3 g. Metric amounts have been determined on a case-by-case basis, according to the demands of the recipe. For example, in most recipes ¼ oz equals 7 g. However, you may notice one or two recipes in which ¼ oz equals 8 g; this is because in these recipes a little more, rather than a little less, ingredient is needed. Oven temperatures and lengths are treated similarly. When spacing cheese straws on a sheet tray, 1 inch equals 3 cm. However, when cutting out the center of a puff pastry bouchée, more precision is needed. In this case, 1 inch equals 2.5 cm.

PROCEDURE

PLATING

1. Fill the cucumber cup with a rosette of tarragon mayonnaise and place it on the back left of a cool 10-in. (25-cm) plate.
2. Mound the micro greens next to the cup.
3. Overlap the galantine slices leaning on the micro greens.
4. Scatter an arc of aspic jewels on the plate to the right of the galantine slices.
5. Serve the bread in a basket lined with a linen napkin.

The procedure for finished dish recipes is often divided into finishing and plating steps and includes detailed instructions for arranging the plate.

In buffet service, final assembly refers to the arrangement of food on platters, trays, or other presentation vessels. Recipes in this book refer to the final assembly of platter presentations simply as *presentation*. If the main component of the platter requires fabrication, the head *finishing and presentation* may be used.

Recipe Variations

Many recipes in this book include variations. Recipe variations are guidelines for modifying the existing recipe to make another dish that is similar to, yet different from, the original. Most variations are ingredient-driven, replacing one set of ingredients with another. Some change the seasonality of the dish by replacing ingredients available in one season with those of another. Some variations change the ethnicity of a dish, allowing you to make dishes representative of many different world cuisines. Yet other variations change the presentation of a dish.

YOUR GARDE MANGER BUFFET

For students, the last two chapters are an essential tool to synthesize the skills and information acquired during your garde manger course. As a grand finale, your chef instructor may challenge you to plan, prepare, and serve a buffet of cold dishes. Chapter 18 covers basic information that will help you do so. For example, use the section on buffet calculations to determine the quantity of food you will need and to accurately cost and price your buffet. Backwards planning will help you correctly schedule preparation and service. Use the sample menus provided, or create your own. Chapter 17 includes information on décor work that can enhance the visual appeal of your buffet.

For working chefs, the recipes and ideas presented are intended to spark your imagination and hone your skills. Newly energized, you can improve your everyday preparations, and produce more creative menus for special events, especially the all-important buffets that are the hallmark of garde manger work.

VARIATIONS

TARRAGON CHICKEN/TURKEY SALAD

Replace the scallions with ½ oz (15 g) chopped shallots. Add 2 tbsp (30 mL) chopped fresh tarragon.

CHICKEN/TURKEY SALAD WITH WALNUTS AND GRAPES

Omit the scallions. Add 4 oz (120 g) halved seedless grapes and ½ oz (15 g) toasted walnut pieces.

CURRIED CHICKEN/TURKEY SALAD

Sauté 2 tsp (10 mL) Madras curry powder in ½ fl oz (15 mL) safflower oil until fragrant. Cool and add to the dressing. Hydrate ½ oz (15 g) currants in 2 fl oz (60 mL) port wine and then cool. Add to the salad along with ½ oz (15 g) toasted slivered almonds.

Recipe variations typically substitute one set of ingredients for another to create a dish similar to, yet different from, the original.

Acknowledgments

The creation of a truly comprehensive first edition book on a subject as broad in scope as garde manger requires more than a single author, or even a team of authors. Writing ***Professional Garde Manger*** required a multitalented support team comprising a dynamic publisher, far-thinking acquisition editors, hardworking developmental editors, a meticulous copyeditor, a creative design team, a fine photographer with top-notch assistants, numerous researchers, technical advisors, scientific advisors, culinary advisors, chef instructor manuscript reviewers, food shoppers, recipe testers, kitchen assistants, washers-up, gofers, and patient friends with shoulders to lean on when the going got rough.

To acknowledge each and every person who contributed to this project would leave little room for the subject material. However, the following individuals and groups deserve special mention.

Chef Jim Switzenberg of Harrisburg Area Community College in Pennsylvania facilitated the connection that got this project off the ground. During recipe development, Chef David Haynes of Adams County Tech Prep in Gettysburg, Pennsylvania, lent his tools, commercial smoker, and lots of good advice. Chef Michael Kalanty of the California Culinary Academy in San Francisco was a valuable resource for information on breads and pastries, and has been an enthusiastic supporter from the beginning.

One of the most challenging aspects of creating a culinary book is the food photography because it requires so many different talents and efforts. Before the first photo can be taken, skilled professionals must source, purchase, and store the food, find the perfect serviceware, and prepare the many components of each dish. The photographs here are the result of two major photo shoots.

For the Minneapolis shoot, we'd first like to thank Meg Gisslen who graciously opened her home to our crew of chefs and nearly a hundred pounds of meat as we focused on the charcuterie and cold meats chapters. Rick Elsenpeter of Lund's Market was instrumental in the sourcing and procurement of the meats and fish needed for the photo shoot. Thanks, also, to Chefs Rick Forpahl, David Eisenreich, Lynn Wolkerstorfer-Isakson, and Megan Grzeskowiak for their fine work in preparing the pâtés, sausages, cured foods, aspic and chaud-froid dishes, and other preparations completed that week.

Dauphin County Technical School in Harrisburg, Pennsylvania, was the site of another marathon photo shoot. We thank DCTS Director Dr. Kevin Lacey, Assistant Director Ms. Toni Arnold, and Principal Dr. Peggy Grimm for making it possible, and Ms. Madeline Bowman for facilitating the event. Special thanks to Chef Robert Biddle, Director of Culinary Arts, for hosting the event and to Chef Ann DeAngelis Refford for her help. Guest chefs who contributed to this shoot include Adam Eyer, Jillian Weisenreider, Jake Wysocki, Lennise Watson, Suzanne Brozoskie, and David Haynes and his Adams County Tech Prep student helpers. DCTS Culinary Arts students did an enormous amount of work, including preparation and cleanup, and exhibited maturity and professionalism far beyond the realm of high school students. Many thanks to them. Heidi Hart provided many of the plates and other serviceware that enhanced our presentations, and lent a hand with food preparation as well. Specialty food products were provided by Brogue Hydroponics of Brogue, Pennsylvania, and DiBruno's House of Cheese, Philadelphia, Pennsylvania. Thanks to the seafood department at Wegman's in Camp Hill, Pennsylvania, for sourcing our fish and shellfish.

The beautiful photographs that make this book so visually compelling are the work of photographer Jim Smith. In addition to his skill and artistry as a photographer, we'd like to thank him for his constant optimism and good humor that made long days on the set fly by quickly and kept morale high. We acknowledge his professionalism and personal fortitude during a difficult time. Thanks also to Jim Smith's assistants Jeremy Grubard and Mike Vasiliauskas.

The updated and enhanced CulinarE-Companion™ is a result of a coordinated team effort. Thank you to Lydia Cheng and Tom Kulesa for their consultation in reviewing, conceptualizing, and coordinating its development. Thank you to project editor Michele Traeger for coordinating all of the editorial efforts. We are also grateful to the many beta testers who took time to test CulinarE-Companion. Their feedback was instrumental in the development and completion of the software. Thanks also to Chef Jean Vendeville of Savannah Technical College for his review and input for the audio pronunciations.

Working on ***Professional Garde Manger*** has been a true pleasure due to the many talented professionals at Wiley. Publisher JoAnna Turtletaub had the vision to put this author team together. Her impeccable taste and good judgment are evident throughout the book. Thanks to editor Melissa Oliver for her work in the early phase. Many heartfelt thanks to editors Mary Cassells and Julie Kerr for managing a million details, ruthlessly editing lengthy content, and moving this massive project along. Thanks to Madeleine Perri for an excellent copyediting job and to Mauna Eichner and Lee Fukui for designing and composing this beautiful book. The production and creative team, including Micheline Frederick, Barbara Russiello, Harry Nolan, and Carole Anson, surpassed our expectations in producing a book that is literally a work of art. Also thanks to Wiley's Indianapolis team who have prepared the files for printing: Brent Savage, color photos and imaging; and Cheryl Grubbs, the illustrator.

Finally, and most importantly, we'd like to acknowledge and thank the hundreds of culinary students we've worked with over the years. In teaching them, we've also taught ourselves—by finding answers to their questions, by anticipating their mistakes and troubleshooting their failures, and by celebrating their successes. From them we've learned that what's obvious to the instructor is not always obvious to the student and, thus, to look at our material with the fresh eyes of the beginner. We hope this makes a better book.

REVIEWERS

Much of the scientific information in ***Professional Garde Manger*** was fact-checked by experts in the field of food science. Thanks to Lisa J. Mauer of Purdue University for making sure the information is correct and up to date. Sketches for illustrations of scientific concepts were done by Elizabeth Johnson, environmental biologist with The Nature Conservancy (and expert prep cook).

Professional Garde Manger was shaped by the opinions and ideas of the chef instructors who graciously reviewed the manuscript. Their valuable feedback helped us produce a book that truly meets the needs of the market. They are:

Mike Artlip
Kendall College
Chicago, IL

Robert W. Beighey
Sullivan University
Louisville, KY

Valentina Columbo
Le Cordon Bleu Las Vegas
Las Vegas, NV

Jonathan Deutsch
Kingsborough Community College
Brooklyn, NY

David Eisenreich
Hennepin Technical College
Brooklyn Park, MN

Rick Forpahl
Hennepin Technical College
Brooklyn Park, MN

Keith Gardiner
Guilford Technical Community College
Jamestown, NC

Wendy Gordon
Rockland Community College
Suffern, NY

Brian Hay
Austin Community College
Austin, TX

Robert Hudson
Pikes Peak Community College
Colorado Springs, CO

Melodie Jordan
Keystone College
La Plume, PA

Kevin Lane
Alaska Culinary Academy
Seward, AK

Jim Switzenberg
Harrisburg Area Community College
Harrisburg, PA

Chris Thielman
College of DuPage
Glen Ellyn, IL

Lynn Wolkerstorfer-Isakson
Hennepin Technical College
Brooklyn Park, MN

Wiley CulinarE-Companion™ Recipe Management Software

Supporting chefs throughout their careers, ***CulinarE-Companion*** includes all recipes from ***Professional Garde Manger*** plus *50 bonus recipes, audio pronunciations, illustrated procedures*, and *technique videos*. Create shopping lists, resize recipes, perform metric conversions, and analyze nutritional content of ingredients and recipes. Add your own recipes, photos, and videos, and create your own cookbooks.

The software downloads and installs effortlessly on your computer's hard drive. It runs locally from your hard drive—so no need for an Internet connection. Once installed, ***CulinarE-Companion*** is yours to keep and never expires! At no additional cost, use the registration code and instructions included with your new copy of ***Professional Garde Manger***, to install yours today.

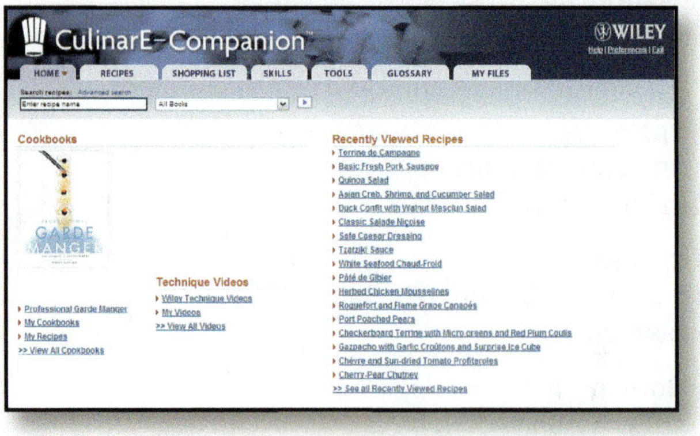

The Homepage

- View recipes—click on "Professional Garde Manger" under "Cookbooks."
- With improved search functionality, search recipes by recipe name or even part of a name, and search by variation.
- View recipes, procedures, and technique videos—organized by kitchen skill: click on "Skills" tab.
- Click "Glossary" tab to access definitions from ***Professional Garde Manger's*** glossary plus hundreds of additional defined terms and audio pronunciations.

Recipe List

- Refine your search by course, cuisine, main ingredient, primary cooking method, or dietary considerations.
- Add recipes to your shopping list, as well as export and print recipes.

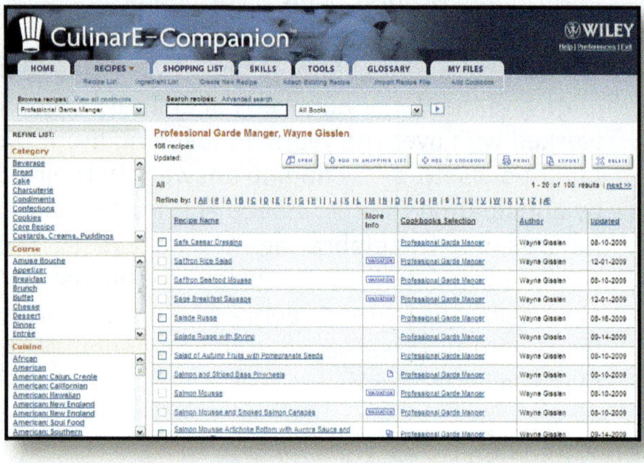

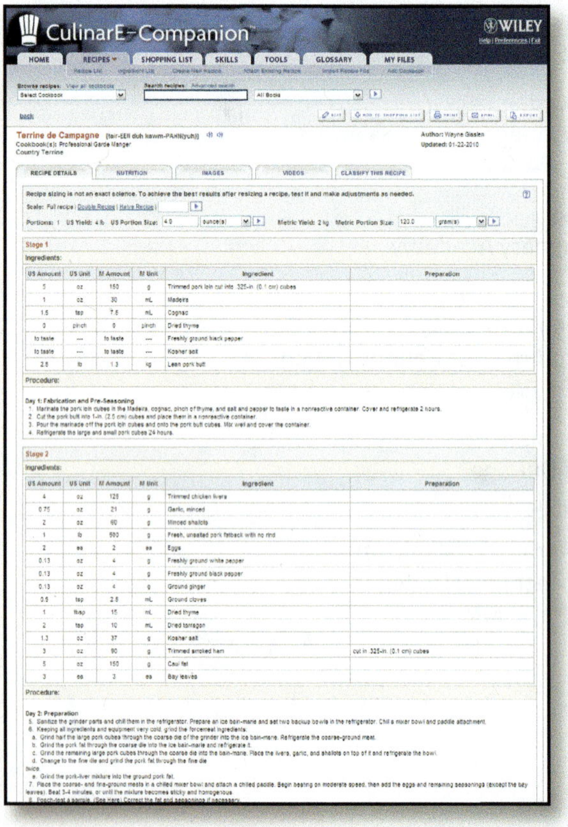

Recipe Screen

- Resize recipes, perform metric conversions, show recipe notes, variations, and more!
- Referenced procedures and recipes are easily accessible by simply clicking the relevant item.
- View photos of plated dishes: click the "Images" tab; view related technique videos: click the "Videos" tab; or add your own photos and videos.

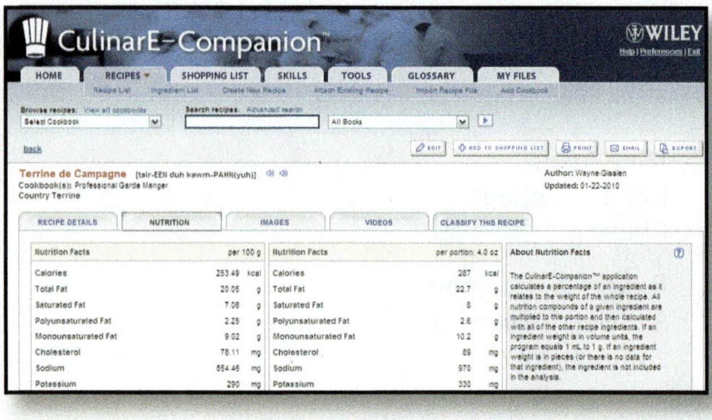

Nutritional Information

- View important nutritional information for ingredients and recipes.
- Nutritional information calculates automatically for all recipes, even new recipes you add, by clicking "Create New Recipe."

PROFESSIONAL
GARDE MANGER

Chapter 1

PREREQUISITES

Before reading this chapter, you should have already learned

- About basic food-service equipment.

The Garde Manger Profession

The world of professional food service embraces many specialized fields of work. One of the most respected is garde manger, or cold foods preparation. The earliest form of garde manger work was food preservation. The culinary term *garde manger* is derived from the French language and literally translates as "keep to eat." Predecessors of modern garde manger chefs developed techniques to make food last longer and taste better. They discovered the processes of salting, drying, and smoking and used these to store perishable meats and fish for weeks and months without refrigeration. From scraps and trimmings, they created rustic sausages and hearty meat pies. Faced with excess milk, they turned it into cheese.

As the craft of garde manger developed, so did its products. Cured and smoked foods acquired subtle flavors and silken textures. Sausages became rich and refined, and meat pies became elegant *pâtés en croûte*. Plain, fresh curds were variously cultured, ripened, and aged to become hundreds of unique cheeses. As preservation became less crucial, fresh foods were added to the repertoire. Salads and cold vegetables, and the dressings and sauces that enhance them, became garde manger specialties. Cold appetizers and main dishes became elegant works of culinary artistry. The garde manger chef today is in charge of all types of savory dishes that are served cold.

After reading this chapter, you should be able to

1. Recount the history of the garde manger profession from early food preservation to modern times.
2. List the 12 attributes and characteristics of a successful garde manger chef.
3. List and define the 6 types of service.
4. Identify various types of food-service operations that provide opportunity for garde manger work.
5. Identify large and small equipment used for garde manger work.
6. Design a restaurant garde manger service line and set up a garde manger station.

THE HISTORY OF GARDE MANGER

The garde manger profession began with the need to preserve food.

Food Preservation in Prehistory

The practice of food preservation is much older than the term *garde manger*. Long before humans created organized societies, they already knew how to preserve food. In medieval times, manors and castles were equipped with underground larders, or cold food storage rooms. On French estates, the larder was called the *garde manger*. Thus, one meaning of the culinary term ***garde manger*** is "a place in which cold foods are prepared and stored." Another meaning is "the person in charge of cold foods preparation and preservation." A third meaning is "the craft, or profession, of cold foods preparation." Garde manger, with all three of its meanings, is now part of culinary English, and is pronounced gahrd mawn-ZHAY.

The first dependable method of preserving food was drying it. Perishable moist foods, such as meat and fish, were made less perishable by placing them in the sun to dry. Adding salt to the food, either by soaking it in seawater or rubbing it with mineral salt mined from the earth, helped foods dry faster and keep longer without spoiling. While the foods were drying, they were sometimes hung from poles over a smoky fire to keep away insects and animal predators. Humans soon learned that smoke made these foods taste better as well.

Farm families were early practitioners of garde manger. They developed better drying techniques and began to use other flavorings, such as herbs, spices, wine, and beer, along with salt. They discovered that tough meats could be tenderized by chopping or grinding them into little pieces, and that adding lots of fat, salt, and spices to their ground meats made them keep longer and taste good, too. It was on the farm that the art of fine cheese making was developed and refined.

Classical Cuisine and Culinary Competitions

Cold platter presentations and *pièces montées*, or showpieces, of classical cuisine are a mainstay of modern culinary competitions. Plate presentation and team buffet presentation are additional categories. Culinary competitions and salons were conceived as a vehicle for top chefs to promote their restaurants and for hotels and caterers to promote their operations. Culinary competitions allow chefs the opportunity to create artful showpieces and improve their technical skills. Creativity is stimulated beyond the level of day-to-day work. Competitions are a good place to learn new ideas and skills, and they offer the opportunity for networking with other garde manger chefs.

Garde Manger in the Classical Cuisine Period

During the Middle Ages and the early Renaissance, foods prepared for the aristocracy were overly elaborate and heavily spiced. In the mid-1600s the taste of European food, and the style in which it was served, slowly began to change. This can largely be credited to La Varenne, the first French chef to break with the Italian-influenced medieval tradition. La Varenne stressed the importance of natural flavors, lighter sauces, and fresh vegetables. At the same time, new ingredients from Asia, the Middle East, and the Americas were added to the European larder.

This lighter, more modern style of cooking resulted in new dishes and new opportunities. Salads of leafy greens with vinaigrette dressings took their place among the heavier cooked foods and became the standard accompaniment to roasted meats. More refined cold dishes combined meat, poultry, or fish with vegetables. The role of the garde manger expanded from food preservation to the preparation of all cold foods for the table. The garde manger staff moved out of the basement and into the kitchen.

The evolution of French cuisine from La Varenne through Escoffier is frequently referred to as the ***classical cuisine*** period of French cooking. For more information on the chefs of classical cuisine, refer to the sidebar on page 6.

The Ten Commandments of Nouvelle Cuisine

1. Avoid unnecessary complications.
2. Shorten cooking times.
3. Shop regularly at the market.
4. Shorten the menu.
5. Don't hang or marinate game.
6. Avoid too-rich sauces.
7. Return to regional cooking.
8. Investigate the latest techniques.
9. Consider diet and health.
10. Invent constantly.

Henri Gault and
Christian Millau, 1973

In the late 1800s, grand hotels such as the Waldorf-Astoria in New York and the Stanford in San Francisco brought in French chefs. These chefs created a new style of cooking called ***continental cuisine***, which can be described as a combination of classical French cuisine with North American ingredients and taste preferences. Later, it incorporated Italian cuisine elements as well.

One of the most prominent features of continental cuisine was the lavish cold buffets prepared and presented by the garde manger department. The popularization of the formal cold buffet increased work opportunities for garde manger chefs. By the time of Escoffier's death in 1935, the profession of garde manger chef had developed into its modern form.

Garde Manger in Nouvelle Cuisine

Just as La Varenne is credited with the transition to classical cuisine, ***Fernand Point*** [fair-nahn PWA(N)] is for *nouvelle cuisine*. This new and radically different style of French cooking emerged in the late 1960s and became world famous in the early 1970s. Point's culinary philosophy included seeking simplicity and perfection in all of his dishes, openly sharing knowledge and techniques, and exploring new ideas.

Nouvelle cuisine literally translates as "new cooking." Chefs developed a fresher, lighter, and more imaginative style of French cooking, inspired by the guidelines later called "The Ten Commandments of Nouvelle Cuisine" (p. 4). One influence on the garde manger chef was the new practice of plating food in the kitchen. Previously, most fine-dining French restaurants sent food to the table in platter presentation, to be portioned onto plates by the servers. Now, garde manger chefs began to create intricate plate presentations that included individual food portions formed in molds.

As nouvelle cuisine chefs traveled the world, they began to add international influences—both techniques and ingredients—to their dishes. Later chefs expanded on this principle to create new hybrid cuisines that mixed French cooking with Asian or Latin American ingredients. In the 1980s, this hybrid cooking style came to be known as ***fusion cuisine***. The adoption of international ingredients influenced garde manger work and expanded the garde manger repertoire. Garde manger chefs began adding soy sauce and sesame oil to classic vinaigrette formulas. Japanese sushi and sashimi (pp. 227, 228) prompted experimentation with raw seafood. Mexican-style salsas took their place alongside classic relishes and vegetable coulis. Spare Asian plate presentations were emulated.

Garde Manger in the Twenty-First Century

It can be said that increasing globalization and the ongoing experimentation of successive generations of chefs is making it impossible as yet to define any one particular modern style.

Contemporary Advances in Garde Manger

By the end of the twentieth century, the art of garde manger had seen several important advances. At the same time, one of its traditional functions, the fabrication of meat and poultry, had become virtually obsolete.

By the 1980s, virtually all food-service meat and poultry was being fabricated in packing houses or by meat and poultry purveyors. Today, meat and poultry products arrive in restaurants prefabricated and prepackaged, and they typically go straight to the hot line. Some chefs disagree that the change to prefabricated meats was an advance. However, the elimination of in-house meat

The Pastry Connection

There are many similarities between garde manger work and pastry work. For example, both require patience and attention to detail, along with skilled handwork and a keen eye.

- **Mathematics and science:** Both involve formula ratios and accurate scaling. Vinaigrettes, mayonnaise, and forcemeats involve emulsification, as do icings and cake batters.
- **Shared ingredients and techniques:** Gelatin is used in glazes for cakes and tarts, as well as in chaud-froid and aspic work. Fruit is essential to dessert work and features prominently in garde manger.
- **Bread and pastry work:** Canapés, bruschette, and croûtons are based on bread. Savory tartlets and barquettes, puff pastry bouchées, and savory profiteroles made from choux paste are used for appetizers and hors d'oeuvres. Modern plate presentations use savory tuiles and unsweetened choux décor items.
- **Artistic ability:** Both cold desserts and cold savory dishes rely on their visual appeal to entice. A highly developed sense of color and design is important.

fabrication effectively freed the garde manger chef to spend time on more creative work.

A definite advance was the change of status accorded to cold foods. In the 1980s, growing concern with healthful eating made salads much more popular. Instead of listing only one or two salads on the menu, entire sections were dedicated to salads, both appetizer and main course portions. With the influence of European and Asian cuisines, menus began to feature complex salads that included cold seafood, poultry, and meat as well as cold vegetables and leafy greens. Charcuterie products, such as smoked meats and fish, and pâtés and terrines, have become popular appetizers and lunch entrées.

An Expanding Workforce

As North American society becomes more multicultural, food-service operations and garde manger departments, in particular, benefit from the diverse talents and strong work ethic of immigrants from around the world. The garde manger department of hotels and large restaurants is a virtual United Nations of ethnicities. Today's cold appetizers, hors d'oeuvres, and buffet dishes frequently exhibit the influence of world cuisines. A modern North American buffet or cocktail party is as likely to include sushi, empanadas, and samosas as shrimp cocktail or quiche.

Star Chefs of Classical Cuisine

Pierre François de la Varenne, known simply as ***La Varenne*** [lah vah-REN], is considered the founder of modern French cuisine. This chef is credited as the first to use roux as a thickener, and to refine the technique of dough lamination to make an early form of puff pastry. He lightened and simplified European cooking and popularized fresh vegetables and herbs. In 1651 La Varenne wrote an important cookbook, *La Cuisinier François*, which contains recipes still in use today.

Marie-Antoine Carême

Marie-Antoine ***Carême*** [kah-REM] was a great innovator of European cuisine. Carême rose to culinary stardom around 1800. Although he worked exclusively as a cook in aristocratic households, Carême's writings influenced restaurant cooking as well. He is most famous for his *pièces montées* (p. 666),

(continues next page)

THE SUCCESSFUL GARDE MANGER CHEF

Today, you have the opportunity to specialize, or focus your career, on one particular branch of the culinary arts. However, even if you think garde manger will ultimately be your career specialty, you should spend time working on the hot side as well. Experience in baking and pastry is also a plus. Once you have gained some well-rounded work experience, you can then settle in to a career in garde manger.

The field of garde manger requires a specific set of talents, skills, and personal characteristics. While many of these attributes are the same as those for chefs in other culinary fields, some are unique to garde manger.

Attributes and Characteristics of a Successful Garde Manger Chef

Successful garde manger chefs have these attributes and characteristics:

- *Basic training and general experience:* A garde manger chef must be thoroughly grounded in the basic culinary principles and skills of European and North American cuisines. Because garde manger encompasses virtually all techniques used in hot foods cooking, experience in general restaurant and catering work is beneficial.
- *Formal culinary education:* Today's competitive entry-level job market makes a culinary school education virtually a necessity. Many top-level operations no longer consider job applicants without some type of academic or technical degree.

- *Manual dexterity:* You must be good with your hands. Much garde manger work involves handling tiny food dêcor items and placing them accurately on small pieces of food. Dexterity can be improved by practicing work tasks and by doing dexterity exercises. Special tools, such as food-service tweezers, are also of help.
- *Physical stamina:* Food service is highly physical, tiring work. Garde manger chefs are frequently on their feet for long hours and may have to lift and carry heavy objects. Joint pain in your hands or becoming chilled easily may make garde manger work a challenge.
- *A well-developed sense of taste:* Garde manger chefs need a sensitive palate. Because cold temperatures dull taste receptors, cold foods are more difficult to evaluate and season. Smoking tobacco or ingesting chemical food additives may damage your sense of taste.
- *Artistic ability:* Garde manger dishes depend strongly on visual appeal. A sense of color and design is important. The most successful garde manger chefs have innate artistic ability.
- *Mathematical ability:* You must be able to quickly and accurately scale formulas up and down, and make weight-volume conversions. Bad math often results in failed products and can even be dangerous. When working with curing compounds, a miscalculation in the formula ratio can make customers seriously ill. In the business of garde manger, you must cost recipes and price menu items. When planning banquets and buffets, you must determine per-person food costs. For all types of service, you are expected to keep labor cost percentages in line.
- *Knowledge of food management and sanitation:* Foods served cold are even more susceptible to infestation by harmful pathogens than hot foods. Garde manger chefs must be doubly vigilant about sanitation, and must thoroughly understand and enforce safe food-handling practices.
- *Good interpersonal skills:* Garde manger involves teamwork. To succeed, you must be able to follow instructions, accept constructive criticism, help and support coworkers, and help maintain morale. To lead a team, you must lead by example and take responsibility for the success of your team.
- *A sense of urgency:* Time is money. Be aware of labor costs, and accomplish all tasks as quickly as possible without being sloppy or careless. Be aware of deadlines, and meet them with time to spare. Motivate the rest of your team to have the same sense of urgency.
- *Attention to detail:* Small but important details can make or break the success of a garde manger preparation. For example, the ingredients for a mayonnaise must be at room temperature, or it will not properly emulsify. To be a successful garde manger chef, you must be willing and able to sweat the details.
- *The ability to organize and plan:* Organizing garde manger events requires ordering food ingredients, presentation serviceware and equipment, linens, and props. The buffet table layout must be planned ahead on paper or with a computer program to accommodate the flow of service and to make it visually attractive. Individual platters must be planned using sketches, cutouts, or computer graphics. Prep lists and work schedules must be planned and posted.

or elaborately constructed food centerpieces. Classic garde manger presentations of carved fruits and vegetables, aspic and chaud-froid work (Chapter 16), and ice carvings owe their beginnings to the work of Carême.

Georges-Auguste Escoffier
Courtesy Adjointeà la Conservation du Musée Escoffier de l'Art Culinaire

Georges-Auguste *Escoffier* [eh-SKOFF-yay] further simplified French cuisine in the late 1800s and early 1900s. He identified the basic cold sauces used in garde manger work and named the many garnitures used in cold foods presentation. Escoffier also created the brigade system still used in large kitchens today. Escoffier recognized garde manger as a specialized type of work that is significantly different from hot foods cooking, and he physically separated the garde manger station from the hot line. He placed meat and poultry fabrication among the responsibilities of the garde manger department.

OPPORTUNITIES IN GARDE MANGER

Almost every food-service business serves cold foods. Large operations, such as hotels and institutions, have entire departments in charge of cold foods preparation and service, while smaller operations have garde manger sections staffed by one or two chefs and assistants. Alternative garde manger career choices include artisan food production, food product research and development, and food styling.

As a garde manger chef, the type(s) of service you must master depend on the needs of the operation in which you work. (See Table 1.1 for an explanation of the different types of service.) Accomplished garde manger chefs are comfortable working all services.

TABLE 1.1 | Six Basic Types of Service

1. À la carte service	Customers order dishes individually from the menu, and the dishes are prepared to order.
2. Banquet service	Plated foods are served to large numbers of guests at one time. Cold dishes are typically plated ahead of time but may be sauced and garnished at the last minute.
Family-style banquet service	Food is served on platters to each table, and guests are expected to serve themselves.
3. Buffet service	Platter presentations of food are placed on display for service to large numbers of guests. Buffets frequently include food-based showpieces and other edible decorations.
Buffet hors d'oeuvres or stationary hors d'oeuvres	Hors d'oeuvre trays are presented on small tables.
Cafeteria service and food bar service	Specialized forms of buffet service that utilize permanently installed heating and refrigeration equipment.
4. Passed service or butler service	Attractively arranged platters or trays of single-bite portions of food are passed, or carried, around the service area where guests are standing or informally seated away from tables.
5. Room service	Foods on covered plates are placed on trays or carts for delivery on premises.
6. Take-out service or take-away service	Foods are packed in disposable containers for pickup or delivery. Picnic baskets and box lunches are variations of this service style.

Courtesy iStockphoto.

Garde Manger in Restaurants

In a small restaurant there is frequently only one garde manger chef on duty during a particular service. In larger restaurants you may have one or more additional chefs with you on the cold line. Unless a party or banquet is scheduled, in restaurants all garde manger service is à la carte.

Restaurant kitchens are typically small and crowded. Therefore, you should expect a restaurant garde manger service line to be compact, and you should not be surprised if it is quite close to the hot line. While this can be inconvenient, it also has benefits. Tight quarters allow for handing off (see sidebar on p. 9). Compact kitchens also make cross-training easier and more prevalent. For example, on a slow night the garde manger chef can watch and learn the sauté station, and vice versa.

To become a successful restaurant garde manger chef, you must be fast at finishing and plating and turn out plates that are consistently neat, clean, and uniform in appearance. While a career in restaurant work is not for everyone, it is both exciting and rewarding. The skills you acquire in a restaurant setting will serve you well in other branches of garde manger.

Garde Manger in Catering

Catering involves serving large numbers of guests with a planned menu of dishes. Different service styles are utilized for various types of events, including passed or butler service, buffet service, and banquet service (see Table 1.1 for details). While the garde manger staff participates in all of these service styles, buffet work gives the garde manger chef the true opportunity to shine.

In buffet work, the garde manger chef primarily works on platter presentations. Platter presentations must be especially attractive and artfully arranged. For large buffets serving hundreds of guests, platters may be set up and replenished on a service line dedicated solely to buffet work. The garde manger department is generally responsible for the edible decorations, such as aspic and chaud-froid showpieces, ice carvings, and fruit and vegetable arrangements, which give each buffet its special character.

Handing Off

Handing off is one way that co-operation between the hot side and the cold side can enhance a menu. For example, "grilled" salads have become popular in recent years. To turn out a grilled chicken Caesar salad, a cook on the hot line grills a marinated chicken breast. At the same time, a garde manger cook finishes and plates a Caesar salad. The hot line then hands off the chicken to the garde manger cook, who slices and arranges it on the salad.

Garde Manger in Hotels

Hotel food service offers the largest variety of job opportunities because hotels typically encompass many dining venues, virtually all of which include garde manger positions. On its premises, a large hotel might have:

- A fine-dining restaurant serving lunch and dinner
- A casual restaurant serving breakfast, lunch, and dinner
- An established breakfast/brunch buffet
- A bar, pub, or tavern serving sandwiches and bar food
- A snack bar or coffee shop open 24 hours
- A room service kitchen
- A catering department offering services ranging from hors d'oeuvres, buffets, and banquets to break service and box lunches

Large hotels offer a range of experience. You might be hired to work the salad station in the casual restaurant, then join the garde manger staff of the catering department, and finally earn a position in the fine-dining restaurant.

Garde Manger on Cruise Ships

In essence, a cruise ship is a floating hotel. Garde manger chefs working on cruise ships have all the advantages of hotel chefs plus free travel. Because cruise ships are well known for their lavish and extensive buffets, the garde manger department is an important part of their culinary staffs. Many of the world's finest garde manger chefs work for cruise lines. As a member of a cruise chip garde manger team, you have the opportunity to learn from them.

Garde Manger in Institutional Cooking

Institutional cooking is food service for large groups of repeat customers, as in college cafeterias or hospital service. As the people who live or work in institutions have become more sophisticated and food-conscious, the operations that prepare and serve their food are finding it necessary to meet the demand for fresher, tastier, and more contemporary food. Institutional feeders must offer a large variety of food choices. They may utilize a menu cycle, a sequence of menus that changes daily over an established number of days before reverting to the first menu and beginning the cycle again.

Garde manger chefs working in medical institutions prepare food for a special-needs population. Thus, they may need extra training in both sanitation and nutrition. Hospitals and other medical facilities utilize both cafeteria-style buffet service and room service.

Garde Manger in Private Clubs

Club food service combines restaurant cooking and catering with the repeat customer aspect of institutional food service. The garde manger chef in a private club can expect to do cold line turn-out work and to plan and execute banquets and cold buffets. Club members sometimes take a strong interest in the club's operations and frequently express opinions about the menu, food quality, and kitchen operations. Thus, club chefs must be customer-oriented and have superior interpersonal skills.

Garde manger chefs working in clubs have frequent down-time during slow seasons. This allows them time to practice and develop ideas for culinary competitions. Many clubs enthusiastically support their chefs' efforts to compete and win.

Garde Manger in Retail Stores

Until recently, it was unusual for a retail food store or supermarket to hire a professional chef for food preparation. Today, however, the retail sale of ready-to-eat foods is one of the fastest-growing sectors of food-service business. This trend is providing garde manger chefs with a wide-open field of opportunity.

Preparing cold dishes and charcuterie items for retail sales is creative and satisfying work. While larger stores operate with standardized recipes and set menus, many small operations encourage their chefs to use their imagination in creating new and unique signature dishes.

Courtesy iStockphoto.

Artisan Food Production

An ***artisan*** is a skilled craftsperson who makes products primarily by hand using traditional methods. Therefore, ***artisan foods*** are high-quality, traditional-style, handmade food products. Artisan charcuterie products are among the most successful of the artisan enterprises. Handmade sausages, pâtés, terrines, confits, and rillettes are now sold in high-end retail stores and online. Cured and smoked seafood products are equally popular. Bottled sauces and condiments are low-risk products that sell well and are easy to store and ship. Artisan cheeses are challenging to produce but rewarding to sell.

Chefs who choose to go into artisan food production must do adequate research to know and abide by local, state, and federal regulations. However, owning and operating a small food-production facility enables you to make your own schedule and work on your own terms. Some small-scale entrepreneurs have grown into large and profitable corporations that sell their products worldwide.

Product Testing and Development

Many of the characteristics of a successful garde manger chef are also required for the testing and development of industrially produced food products. Large food-production corporations need trained chefs to work in their product-development divisions. Good math skills, attention to detail, organizational skills, and the ability to work independently are essential qualities for product testers. Developing new products requires imagination, technical skills, and a sensitive palate. Many chefs with garde manger training go on to work in industrial food testing and development.

Food Styling

Flip through any magazine, or spend a few minutes watching television, and you will see scores of advertisements for restaurants and prepared food products. Colorful and artistically arranged dishes in photos and on television shows and in movies are the work of food stylists.

Experienced garde manger chefs often make the transition into food styling. Artistic flair, combined with food-production skills and organizational abilities, enables them to set up food shots for both still photography and film. Freelance food stylists work when they choose and sometimes get to travel to shoots in faraway places. Stylists working for magazines and food production corporations earn job security and benefits.

GARDE MANGER FACILITIES AND EQUIPMENT

When you enter the field of garde manger, the design of the facility and the equipment you use depend on the type of operation you join. The purpose of this section is to familiarize you with the basic large and small equipment you will encounter in both garde manger preparation and turn-out.

The Garde Manger Prep Kitchen

The basic preparation of most garde manger products and dishes is no different than the preparation of foods served hot. The same stoves, ovens, broilers, steamers, grills, and refrigeration units are also found in the garde manger prep kitchen. In large operations, where hundreds or even thousands of guests are served, high-volume equipment such as steam-jacketed kettles and tilt-table braziers are used as well.

Garde manger subspecialties, such as charcuterie work and cheese making, require their own specialized preparation equipment, both large and small (discussed in the appropriate chapters). Because of the special nature of these crafts, it is advisable to keep their preparation work separate from other, standard garde manger preparation. At right is the floor plan of a garde manger prep kitchen designed with a dedicated charcuterie preparation area.

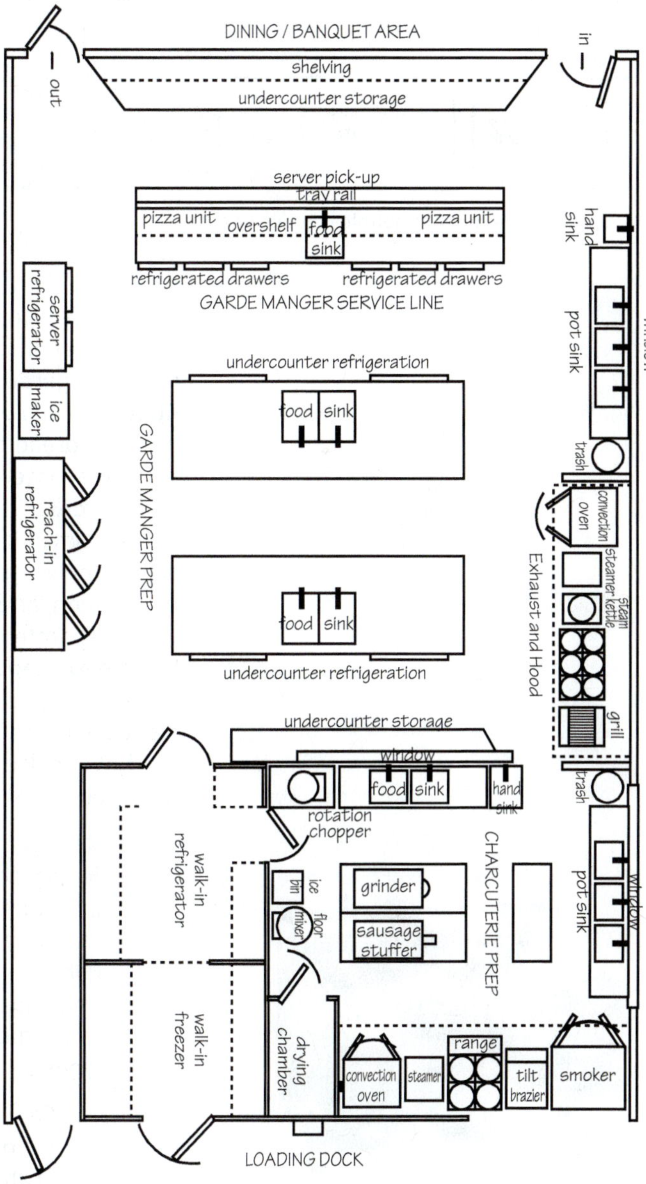

The floor plan of a garde manger prep kitchen designed with a dedicated charcuterie preparation area

The Garde Manger Service Line

A ***service line*** is a row of large food-service equipment units selected and arranged for the fast and efficient turn-out of food. Service lines may be single or double.

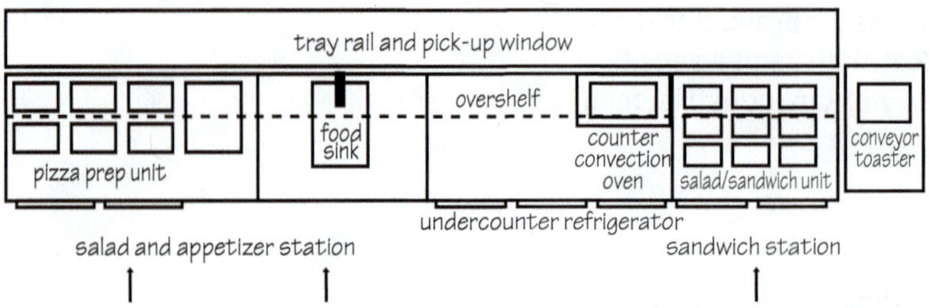

A typical garde manger single-service line

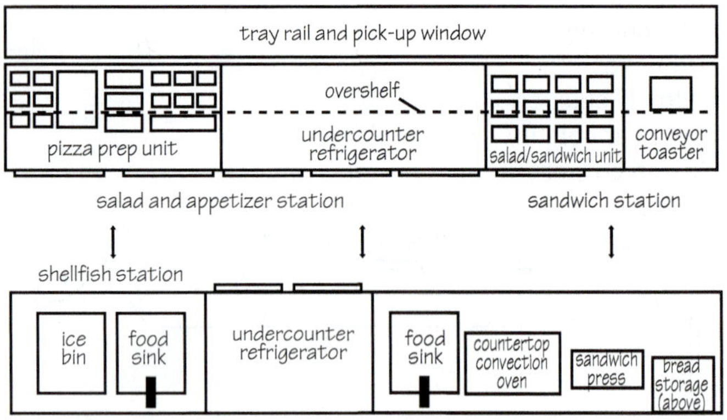

A typical garde manger double-service line

- A ***single-service line*** consists of one row of equipment with a pickup window situated above one or more of the equipment units. Cooks and chefs working a single-service line work facing that row of equipment only.
- A ***double-service line*** consists of a front line and a back line running parallel. The cooks and chefs stand in the corridor formed by the two lines, which is typically about 36 inches wide. By simply turning toward the front or the back, they are able to utilize several equipment units and work spaces without taking extra steps. Typically, the front line is used for plating food and contains the window where finished plates are picked up. The back line is for finishing the food components (and on a hot line typically contains the cooking equipment). On a garde manger double-service line, the back line might contain refrigeration for larger food items and workspace for cold foods that require last-minute assembly.

Stations

A ***station*** is a portion of a service line dedicated to turning out one particular type of preparation. In a large, midlevel restaurant with a high-volume lunch business, the garde manger line typically includes a sizable cold sandwich station fitted with one or more sandwich/salad units, several conveyor toasters (p. 13), multiple bread bins, and possibly one or more sandwich presses (p. 13). There may be a large salad station as well as a station dedicated to cold appetizers and entrées.

In a small kitchen, the garde manger service line may be so compact it consists of only one station. All of the cold dishes, regardless of type, come out of that station, and one cook is expected to work it successfully.

If separate menus for different services are featured, the service line must be able to adapt to the changeover. For example, the sandwich/salad unit that stores sandwich fillings at lunch must accommodate the cold appetizer garnishes at dinner and the fruit compotes and cereal toppings at breakfast.

Let's look at the large equipment with which garde manger service lines are fitted.

Refrigeration Units for the Garde Manger Line

Refrigeration equipment has two main functions: to keep prepared foods cold during the service, and to ensure the refrigerated foods are fast and easy to access. On the service line, speed is of the utmost importance. For this reason, it is important to choose correctly configured refrigeration equipment, and to arrange your food ingredients in the equipment in a logical and orderly fashion (see sidebar, p. 13). The following are types of refrigeration units for the garde manger front line:

Sandwich/salad units and *pizza prep tables* are available in widths from 27 to 72 inches (69 to 183 cm). These are designed with refrigerated cabinets below and a cold bain-marie configuration on top. Their design includes a cutting-board work surface the width of the unit. The bain-marie top can be fitted with hotel pans of many sizes,

Sandwich/salad unit fitted with overshelf
Courtesy Unified Brands.

such as quarter-pans, sixth-pans, eighth-pans, and sixteenth-pans, useful for various garnishes and sauces and dressings in squeeze bottles. Pizza prep tables are a good choice for high-end restaurants because their wider work surface accommodates the larger plates typically used in fine dining.

Undercounter refrigeration units are more useful than upright units, because they provide needed workspace on top. They are available in various widths, typically ranging from 30 to 72 inches (76 to183 cm). These are standard-equipped with a single interior shelf. However, they may be modified by the manufacturer to be more efficient. Custom-fitted *sliding drawer frames* are designed to hold hotel pans of various sizes, which keep prepared foods in good shape and easy to reach. *Bun tray racks* or *pan slides* hold multiple sheet trays or hotel pans without crushing their contents. If the garde manger department turns out plated desserts, there should be at least one refrigeration unit dedicated solely to dessert components. (If dessert components are stored in the same refrigerator as savory items, undesirable flavors and aromas can permeate them and make them unfit to serve.)

The Art of Improvising

In a perfect world, all service lines are fitted with brand-new, state-of-the-art equipment. Unfortunately, the real world is rarely perfect. Many small, independent restaurants cobble together used equipment purchased at auction or from distress sales. It might take years before a restaurant is profitable enough to afford an equipment refit.

Smart garde manger chefs know how to make the best of such situations. For example, you can rig a small cold bain-marie for garnishes by placing sixteenth-pans in a deep hotel pan full of ice. You can create a bun tray rack for an existing refrigerator by cutting down an old rolling pan rack to size. Catering equipment can be pressed into service on the line.

Improvisation is great, but make sure all modifications meet sanitation guidelines and comply with health code regulations in your area.

Worktables and Overshelves

On the garde manger service line, stainless-steel worktables provide additional workspace and fill gaps between refrigeration units. They are available in several widths and many lengths. Optional features include undershelves, drawers, and backsplashes.

An *overshelf* is a multi-tiered shelf unit designed for attachment to a worktable or refrigeration unit. Overshelves create the window where finished plates are placed for pickup by servers.

Optional Heating Equipment

A few items in the garde manger repertoire require crisping, warming, or heating before they are served.

Countertop convection oven

A *countertop convection oven* is used for toasting croûtons for canapé bases and to accompany dips and spreads, for toasting sandwiches, and for heating slices of quiche and other savory pastries.

A *conveyor toaster* works continuously and discharges the finished toast directly onto the work surface. *Commercial pop-up toasters* work in the same manner as domestic toasters.

Conveyor toaster
Courtesy of Lincoln Foodservice, LLC.

A *sandwich press* is a specialized heating unit designed for making panini and Cuban sandwiches.

A *commercial toaster oven* can take the place of both a toaster and a convection oven. However, this equipment is rather large and generates a lot of external heat. It is most appropriate for large service lines in high-volume operations.

A *microwave oven* is of limited use on the garde manger line because microwave heating has adverse effects on bread and pastry items. However, it is handy for taking the chill off sauces, cold vegetables, and other cooked foods that should be served at room temperature.

- **Additional Line Equipment**
  Basic items common to both hot and cold lines are needed.
  - A *hand sink* for sanitation purposes.
  - A small *food prep sink* for fresh water to thin a sauce or for rinsing produce in an emergency.
  - *Bread bins* or bread drawers for Pullman loaves and rolls.
  - A covered *trash can* and a receptacle for soiled equipment.
  - Additional storage for nonrefrigerated food ingredients and non-food items.
  - Adequate storage space for customer bags and take-out containers if take-out service is offered.

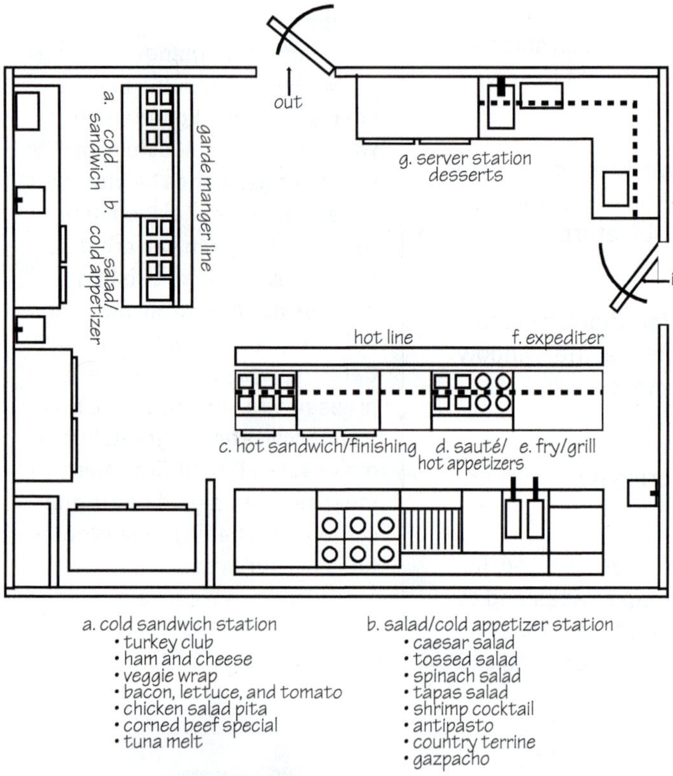

Restaurant line map with garde manger dishes

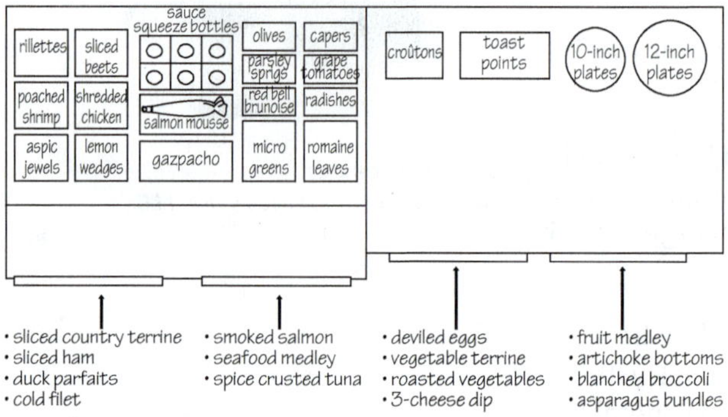

A typical cold appetizer station line map

Map Making

The head garde manger chef must know how to make the menu work within the parameters of the existing service line. An entry-level garde manger cook must know how to set up the assigned station properly. Both responsibilities are made easier with the use of maps.

- **The Line Map**
  A ***line map*** defines the boundaries of each station and indicates which menu items come out of each. The menu designer must make certain the menu is feasible for turn-out. It is important that the line stations can properly accommodate ingredients storage and that workspace is adequate. The stations must be properly aligned to create ***flow***, or a logical and fluid progression of movements, especially if dishes are to be handed off from one station to another.
- **The Station Map**
  A ***station map*** lists the components of each dish the station must turn out and indicates the place where each of these components is stored. In order for the line chefs and line cooks to quickly and efficiently turn out the menu, their stations must have the correct *mise en place*. If ingredients are in the wrong place, valuable time will be lost in searching for them.

Each time the menu changes, or if you devise a better plan, you must rework your line maps and station maps. While drawing line maps and station maps is additional work, maps make set-up fast, easy, and consistent, and they help ensure quick and efficient turn-out.

Small Equipment for Garde Manger

Virtually all of the small equipment items used for general food-service preparation and turn-out are also used for garde manger. However, some specialty tools are specific to garde manger work. Some of these tools were adopted from baking and pastry, while others were designed specifically with garde manger in mind.

In this section, tools for general garde manger work are illustrated and identified. Tools and equipment used in garde manger subspecialties such as charcuterie, cheese making, and advanced décor work are presented in the appropriate chapters.

Cutting Tools and Equipment

Table 1.2 identifies some of the cutting tools and equipment used in the garde manger kitchen.

TABLE 1.2 Cutting Tools and Equipment

	Tools and Equipment
Knives	 paring knife;  turning/fluting knife; Thai decorating knife (not shown);  narrow flexible boning knife;  smoked salmon knife
Shears	 poultry shears; 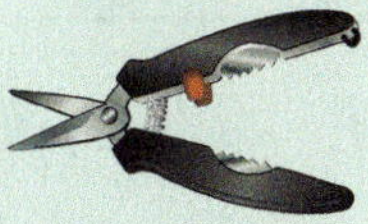 lobster shears; 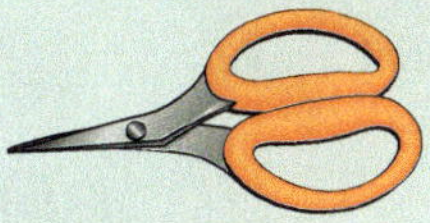 kitchen shears
Mollusk tools	 oyster knife;  clam knife; 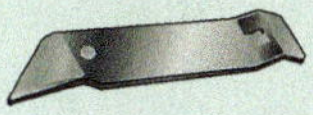 bottle opener (used for oysters)
Zest tools	 microplane grater;  zester;  stripper/channeler
Fruit tools	 corer; 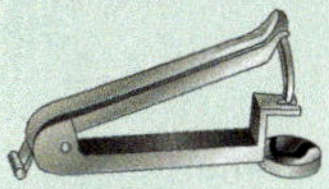 pitter
Slicers	 pickle slicer; 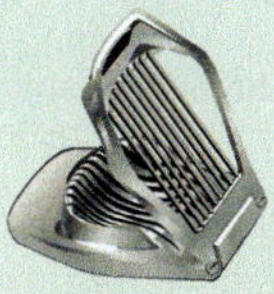 egg slicer;  egg wedger; 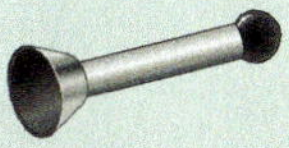 egg top cutter;  quail egg cutter; 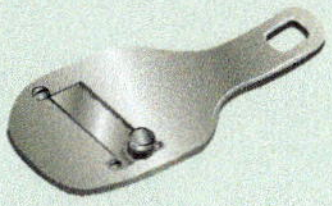 truffle plane; 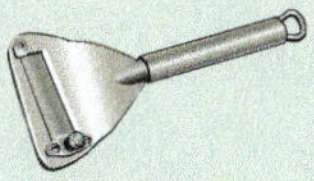 cheese plane

(continues)

TABLE 1.2 Cutting Tools and Equipment *(continued)*

	Tools and Equipment
Cutters	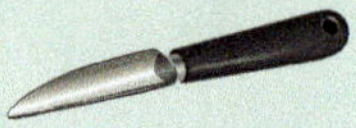 *V*-shape cutter 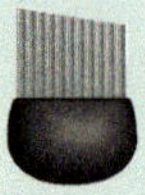 crinkle cutter 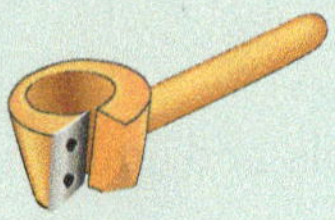 vegetable frill maker 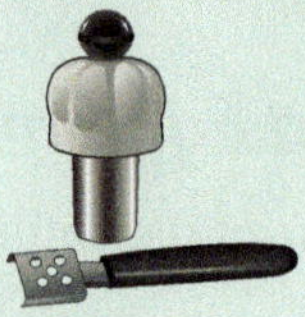 cylindrical vegetable cutter 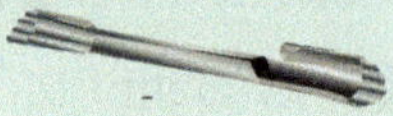 gouge
Specialty slicers	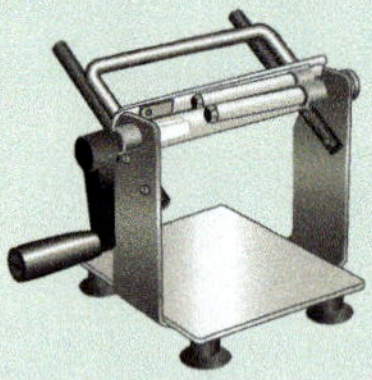 vegetable sheeter 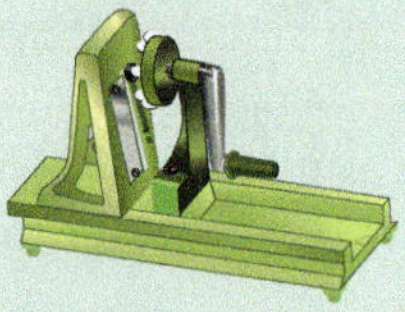 turning slicer 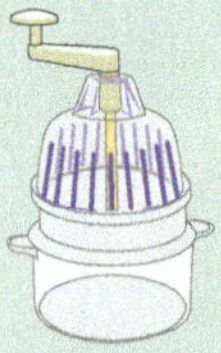 spiral slicer
Individual geometric cutters	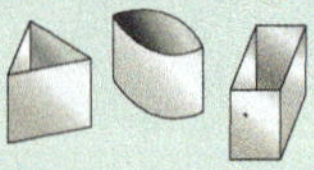 triangle, leaf, rectangle; many other shapes available
Representational cutters	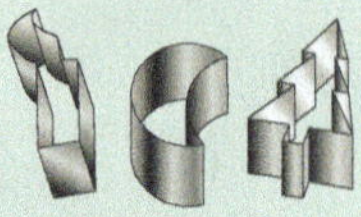 many shapes available
Cutter sets	 geometric hors d'oeuvre cutter set; many other shapes and sizes available
Mandolines	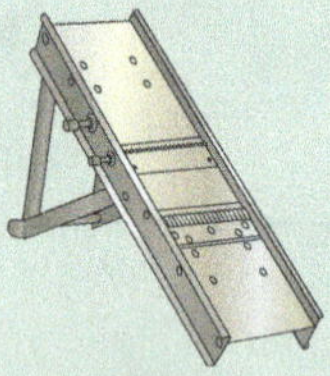 mandoline  swing mandoline 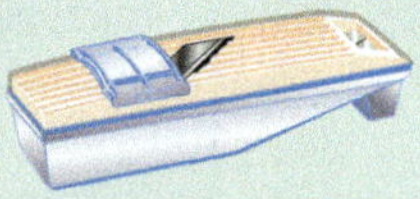 Asian mandoline
Processors	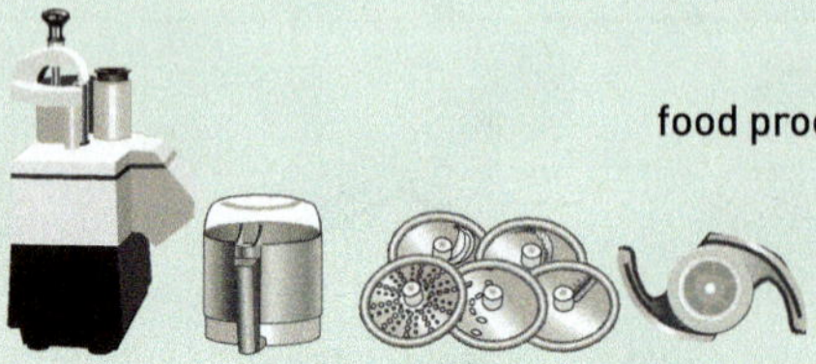 food processor with various cutting blades

Shaping Tools and Equipment

Table 1.3 identifies shaping tools and equipment used in the garde manger kitchen.

TABLE 1.3 Shaping Tools and Equipment

	Tools and Equipment
Stainless-steel and plastic scoops	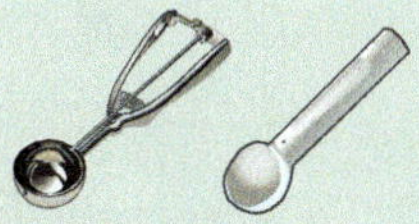 spherical are most common; other shapes available
Parisiennes	 various sizes round, oval fluted, oval, double
Butter tools	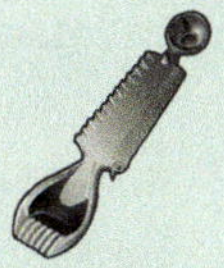 curler 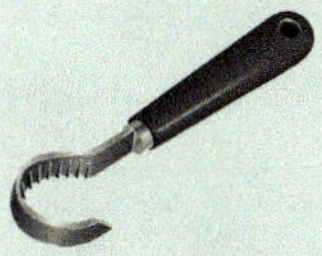 serrated curler 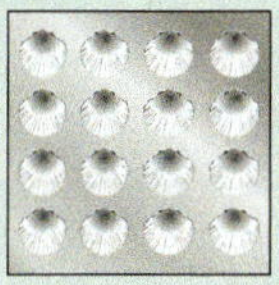 butter form
Individual stainless-steel molds	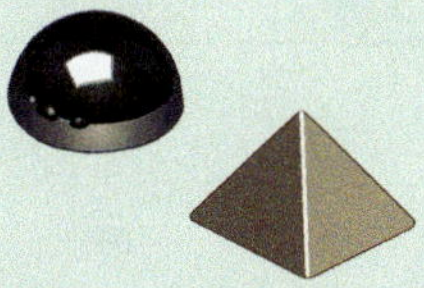 demi-spheres, pyramids shown, also timbales, brioches, savarins
Entremet forms	 ring 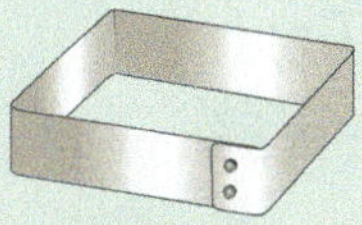 square  rectangle
Pans	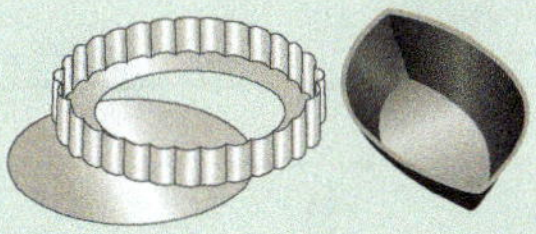 tartlet, barquette
Modular molds, frames, and extractors	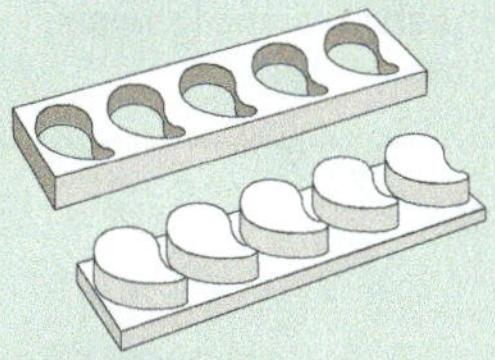 comma-shaped shown; also round, hexagonal, tear-shaped, square, oval, triangle, others
Silicone molds	demi-spheres, pyramids, cylinders, savarins (not shown)

Application Tools

Table 1.4 identifies some of the application tools used in the garde manger kitchen.

TABLE 1.4 Application Tools

	Tools
Brushes	 pastry brush 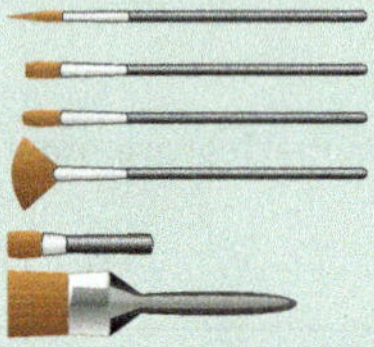 paintbrushes  straight spatula 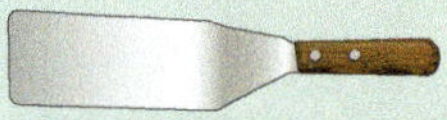 offset spatula
Tweezers	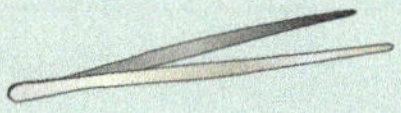 food-service tweezers 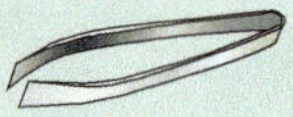 angled fish tweezers 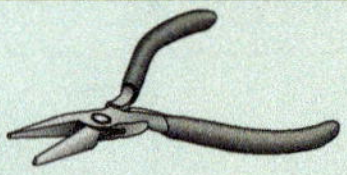 needlenose pliers
Droppers and bottles	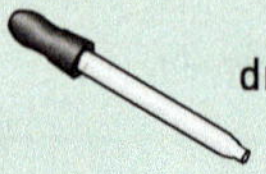 dropper 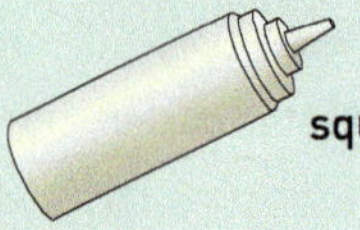 squeeze bottle 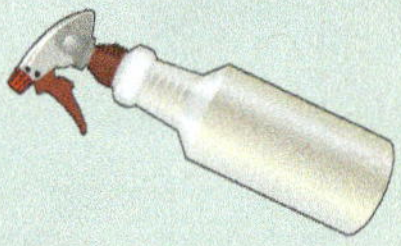 spray bottle
Pastry tools	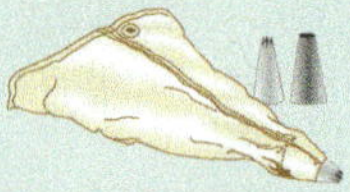 pastry bag and tips 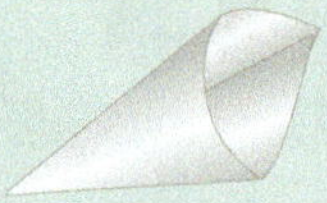 piping cone

Straining Tools

Table 1.5 identifies some of the application tools used in the garde manger kitchen.

TABLE 1.5 Straining Tools

	Tools
Strainers	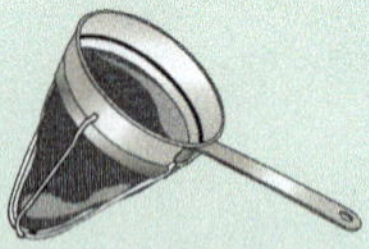 mesh strainer or fine-mesh strainer (*chinois*)
Sieves	 drum sieve (*tamis*)
Fruit and vegetable tools	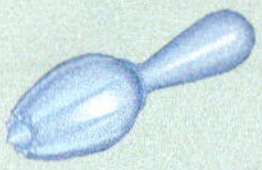 lemon reamer, lemon strainer (not shown) 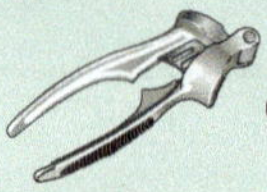 garlic press  potato ricer
Mills	 manual food mill; grinder food mill attachment (not shown)

TERMS FOR REVIEW

garde manger (place, person, or craft/profession)
classical cuisine
continental cuisine
Fernand Point
nouvelle cuisine
fusion cuisine
La Varenne
Carême
Escoffier
handing off
catering
institutional cooking
artisan
artisan foods
service line
single-service line
double-service line
station
line map
flow
station map

QUESTIONS FOR DISCUSSION

1. Explain the origin of the term *garde manger*, and list its three meanings.
2. Discuss early methods of food preservation. Explain how food preservation evolved into the craft of garde manger.
3. Name the three most important chefs of the French classical cuisine period, and list their accomplishments. How did each of these chefs influence garde manger?
4. Discuss nouvelle cuisine. List its Ten Commandments, and explain how these guidelines changed French cooking. What was its impact on garde manger?
5. List and discuss the 12 attributes and characteristics of a successful garde manger chef. Which of these qualities do you already possess? How will you develop those you lack?
6. List and define the six basic types of service.
7. Discuss opportunities in garde manger food service. Choose one or more garde manger career options you think you would enjoy. List both the pros and cons for your choice(s).
8. Draw a garde manger service line map for a cold appetizer menu. Draw a station map for one of the stations on your line.

Chapter 2

PREREQUISITES

Before studying this chapter, you should have already learned

- To prepare a meat or seafood *glace* (highly reduced stock).
- To identify and use fresh and dried herbs.
- To identify and use whole and ground spices.
- To handle and prepare eggs and dairy products according to food safety guidelines.

Sauces and Dressings

Most dishes prepared by the garde manger department are enhanced by some type of sauce. In some cases, the sauce is an integral part of the dish, as it is in salads and sandwiches. In other dishes, such as cold roast meats or pâtés and terrines, the sauce is served on the side. No matter how it is used, the sauce is an important element of any finished dish. Because garde manger primarily involves cold foods, the sauces on which we focus are those served cold or at room temperature.

By definition, a ***sauce*** is a fluid accompaniment to solid food. A cold sauce that has a pronounced acidic flavor is often called a ***dressing***. Dressings usually enhance salads, although they are sometimes used on sandwiches and as dips.

Two major types of sauce are fundamental to garde manger work: vinaigrette and mayonnaise. We begin this chapter by learning about these two basic sauces. Then we go on to study dairy-based cold sauces and cold sauces based on fruits and vegetables.

After reading this chapter, you should be able to

1. Explain the chemistry of cold emulsions.
2. Prepare a successful vinaigrette by hand as well as in a mixer, blender, or food processor.
3. Repair a failed or broken vinaigrette.
4. Prepare mayonnaise by the traditional handmade procedure as well as in a mixer, blender, or food processor.
5. Repair both failed and broken mayonnaise by several methods.
6. Prepare cold sauces based on dairy products.
7. Prepare cold sauces based on fruits and vegetables.
8. Use and store vinaigrettes, mayonnaise, and other cold sauces in accordance with food safety guidelines.

INTRODUCTION TO EMULSION SAUCES

The two fundamental sauces in garde manger work, vinaigrette and mayonnaise, are both ***emulsions***, which can be described as uniform mixtures of two normally unmixable substances. When mixed together uniformly, using the correct technique, these substances become *emulsified*.

It is well known that oil and water do not readily mix, making the preparation of these sauces a challenge. Oil and vinegar are the two main ingredients in both vinaigrette and mayonnaise. Because water is the primary component of vinegar, if you combine vinegar and oil in a container they form separate layers, with the watery vinegar on the bottom and the oil on the top. If you mix them together simply by stirring, they will quickly separate and settle into their original two layers. The challenge is to get the two liquids to stay mixed. Much of the explanation of how to make these sauces is focused on this challenge.

Vinaigrette is an example of a ***temporary emulsion***, which is also called an ***unstable emulsion***. A properly made vinaigrette stays emulsified for some time, but eventually the oil and water separate. Mayonnaise, on the other hand, is a ***permanent emulsion***, also called a ***stable emulsion***. A properly made and stored mayonnaise stays emulsified indefinitely.

Because of the different characteristics of vinaigrette and mayonnaise, they require preparation techniques that have slight, but important, differences. Vinaigrettes are somewhat simpler in composition than mayonnaise, so these serve as a good introduction to creating emulsions and are covered first. After you master the procedure for making temporary emulsions, you can then learn the permanent emulsion techniques for making mayonnaise.

Traditional Proverb

"Let the salad maker be a spendthrift for oil, a miser for vinegar, a statesman for salt, and a madman for mixing."

VINAIGRETTES

Whether used as a dressing for leafy greens, tossed with cooked vegetables and other ingredients to make complex salads, or as a marinade, at least one type of vinaigrette can be found in every garde manger mise en place.

At their most basic level, ***vinaigrettes*** are simple mixtures of vegetable oil, salt, and vinegar. These ingredients have been used to enhance salad greens since ancient times, when humans first learned to press oil out of olives and to make wine from grape juice. In modern commercial food service, we rely on prepared mixtures of oil and vinegar combined in specific ratios. This ensures our preparations are consistent from day to day. Such a mixture is called a vinaigrette, or vinaigrette dressing.

The traditional formula for vinaigrette specifies using 3 parts oil to 1 part vinegar. Modern oil-to-vinegar ratios are more likely to be 4 to1 or even 5 to1, depending on the flavors of the ingredients and on the vinaigrette's intended use. This change is because many of today's vinegars are quite strong in flavor. When determining a vinaigrette's oil-to-vinegar ratio, you should follow the dictates of your own palate—but remember to include salt in the mixture before tasting. Salt modifies the taste of the vinegar by reducing the impact of its acid.

Before preparing a vinaigrette, select ingredients that will produce both the desired flavors and the body, or degree of thickness, you want to achieve. Your choice of ingredients can greatly influence these characteristics.

Making Artisan Wine Vinegars

To make traditional artisan wine vinegar, the grape juice of choice is placed into wooden barrels, where it undergoes basic alcoholic fermentation to become wine. A microscopic organism called ***mycoderma aceti*** is introduced into the wine and causes an additional ***acetous fermentation***. This process, combined with oxidation, changes the alcohol in the wine into ***acetic acid***. Both the natural flavors present in the wine and the flavors produced by the barrel give the resulting vinegar its particular taste profile.

TABLE 2.1 Vinegars and Other Acid Ingredients

Vinegars	Made From	Characteristics	Uses/Types
Wine	Wine grapes	Sold as red or white wine vinegar	Chardonnay, Merlot, Zinfandel, sherry
Aged wine	Wine grapes	Dark color, full body, deep flavor from concentration	Balsamic vinegar
Rice	Rice wine or fermented rice	Low acid content, mild and slightly sweet flavor	Japanese rice vinegar, Chinese rice vinegar
Malt	Grain	Rich brown color, moderate acidity, subtle sweetness	Fish and chips, traditional cream dressings
Cider	Apple cider or mash of apple peels and cores	Highly acidic at full strength; typically sold in diluted form Pronounced apple flavor and honey-gold color; also unfiltered artisan versions	American and British dressings
Fruit	Fermented fruit juice, such as berries, pineapple, or coconut	True types are rare and expensive Commercial types are made from other vinegars flavored with fruit juice	Simple and complex salad dressings
Flavored	Vinegar infused with herbs, spices, flowers, fruits, or aromatic vegetables	Depends on the ingredients used	
Distilled white	Corn, potatoes, or wood	Tasteless, highly acidic	Pickling
Acids	**Made From**	**Characteristics**	**Uses/Types**
Verjus	Fresh juice of unripe wine grapes	Tart but not sour	Sauces, poaching liquids, vinaigrettes
Citrus juices	Lime, lemon, or grapefruit juices	Highly acidic (oranges are sweeter and milder; team with more acidic ingredients)	
Vegetable and fruit juices and purées		Acidic in nature	An acid component in vinaigrettes (often thickened in a reduction before use)

Ingredients for Vinaigrettes

Acid Ingredients for Vinaigrettes

The acid component is generally considered the primary flavor of a vinaigrette. Most vinaigrettes are named after their acid component, as in "balsamic vinaigrette" or "cider vinaigrette."

Vinegars may be processed from many foods, each of which lends its own special flavor, color, and acidity level. The sources for vinegars are as diverse as apples and rice. Also, vinegar is no longer the only type of acid ingredient for vinaigrettes. Fruit juices, vegetable juices, and *verjus* [vair-ZHOO] (p. 23) are other intriguing options. See Table 2.1 for a list of ingredients that may be used as the acid component of a vinaigrette formula.

Storing Vinegars

Due to their high acid content, vinegars are self-preserving and keep for extended periods without refrigeration. Keep bottles tightly closed in a cool, dark place.

Oils for Vinaigrettes

Oil in a vinaigrette contributes richness and a smooth mouthfeel, and it binds the dressing to the food being dressed. The flavor of the oil in a vinaigrette is often a secondary issue. The garde manger chef may choose to use a bland oil to

TABLE 2.2 | Oils

Oils	Made From	Characteristics	Uses/Types
Olive	Olives from the Mediterranean and California	Range of flavors, colors, and textures	Classic choice for vinaigrettes
Corn	Germ of dry field corn	Light, mild flavor	Cooking, salad oil
Peanut	Peanuts	Mild but distinctive flavor	Asian dressings, sautéing, deep-frying
Soybean	Soybeans	Off-flavors make it less desirable as a salad oil	Frying
Safflower	Seeds of the safflower plant	Colorless, mild flavor, light texture, winterized (does not become cloudy when refrigerated)	Frying (high smoke point), salad oil
Sunflower seed	Sunflower seeds	Mild flavor, light yellow color, considered healthful	
Canola (rapeseed oil)	Rapeseeds	Pale color, mild flavor, considered healthful	
Refined sesame	Raw sesame seeds (refined by heat process)	Clear color, bland and light flavor	Cooking, salad oil
Asian-style roasted sesame	Roasted sesame seeds	Strong flavor, dark color	Seasoning
Nut oils	Various tree nuts (walnuts, hazelnuts, almonds)	Rich texture, strong taste, perishable (keep refrigerated)	Simple and complex salads, finishing sauces
Flavored oils	Infused with herbs, spices, or aromatic vegetables, truffles	Depends on ingredients used	Dressings, table condiments
Olive Oil Type	**Oleic Acid Content**	**Olive Type/Press**	**Characteristics**
IOOC extra-virgin olive oil	No more than 0.8%	Not fully ripe olives	Soft, mellow flavor; deep green color; full-bodied texture
IOOC virgin or superfine olive oil	1–1.5%	Riper olives	Slight pungent flavor; yellow-green/golden color, light body
IOOC olive oil or pure olive oil	Higher than 3.3%	Refined by natural process to remove bitterness and reduce acidity level	Bland, flavorless; often blended with 5–25% virgin olive oil
Blended olive oil		May contain other oils.	Questionable quality
Olive pomace oil		Extracted from olive oil pressing using chemical solvents	Inferior flavor, considered unhealthful
Unfiltered olive oil		Unstrained virgin or extra-virgin oil	Thick texture, cloudy appearance, full flavor, highly perishable

Demystifying Olive Oil

Most nations follow the standards of the International Olive Oil Council (IOOC), which uses the term *virgin* in the grading of olive oil. To be classified as a ***virgin olive oil***, an oil must be made completely from olives and must be extracted by purely physical processes that do not include heat or chemicals. ***Extra-virgin olive oil*** is the top grade of virgin olive oil. The IOOC grades in Table 2.2 are based on the amount of oleic (oil-derived) acid present in their composition; they do not necessarily indicate quality or freshness.

highlight the flavor of the acid component and the other seasonings. However, some oils are stronger in flavor. If a flavorful oil is used in a vinaigrette, the acid component and the other seasonings must be carefully chosen to complement it. Texture must also be considered when choosing an oil. Full-bodied oils with a heavy texture can overwhelm delicate greens and are best used only on sturdy greens or in composed salads using cooked vegetables and other hearty ingredients. Thinner, lighter oils complement delicate greens. See Table 2.2 for a list of recommended salad oils for vinaigrettes.

STORING OILS

Like all fats, vegetable oils are perishable. When oil goes bad, it acquires an acrid odor and a rank, nasty flavor that is hard to describe but unmistakable once experienced. Oil in this state is called ***rancid***. The three major enemies of oil are *oxygen*, *heat*, and *light*. Oxygen rapidly combines with fats and causes decomposition. The best way to keep oil fresh is to prevent its exposure to oxygen. Use the following points to protect oils:

- Keep bottles tightly closed, and store them away from heat.
- Transfer valuable, highly perishable oils from half-empty bottles into smaller bottles to minimize the oxygen inside. Consider storing fine, expensive artisan oils using an oxygen replacement system such as those used to preserve wine in open bottles.
- Plastic can transfer off-flavors to delicate oils. Keep fine oils in dark glass or nonreactive metal containers; do not keep them in squeeze bottles for prolonged periods.
- Keep fine oils under refrigeration and bring to room temperature just before use.

Artisan Olive Oils

An artisan olive oil made by a small producer is ideal for dishes where the oil plays a starring role. These oils offer a wide range of flavors, textures, and colors. For example, Spanish and French oils are usually lighter in flavor, texture, and color, while Italian oils are usually fruitier and more full-bodied, with a darker color. Early-harvest oils are pressed from greener olives, resulting in a green color and subtly bitter flavor complemented by lower acidity. Late-harvest oils are pressed from riper olives and have a lighter, more golden color and a soft, mellow flavor. Most artisan oils are not blended. A single bottling usually comes from a single olive grove.

Aromatics for Vinaigrettes

A number of aromatic vegetables are commonly used to flavor vinaigrettes. They may help make vinaigrettes more stable when finely minced or pulverized (see p. 28). See Table 2.3 for the most popular aromatics for vinaigrettes.

TABLE 2.3 Aromatics

Aromatic	Preparation	Flavor/Texture	Characteristics
Shallots	Raw, finely minced	Mild yet distinctive flavor	Retain sweet flavor; do not dilute the flavor or body of the vinaigrette
Scallions	Chopped, minced	Mild, light flavor; attractive green color	Green part of scallion discolors quickly; add just before serving
Garlic	Crushed to paste; pressed in garlic press; pulverized; finely minced; cooked	Lightly crushed cloves provide a milder flavor; roasted or braised puréed garlic adds rich, subtle flavor and thickens or stabilizes an emulsion	Complements hearty greens and starchy vegetables
Fresh ginger	Finely minced; pressed in garlic press; juiced	Pungent; adds Asian flavor profile	Found in many Asian vinaigrettes
Citrus zest	Removed with zester or swivel peeler, then finely minced	Tangy	Adds pungent essential oils that boost flavor and aroma; good for low-acid vinaigrettes

Herbs and Spices for Vinaigrettes

Herbs and spices are the finishing touch that makes vinaigrettes distinctive. Your choice of herbs or spices is virtually unlimited and is based on the intended style and use of the vinaigrette (see Table 2.4).

TABLE 2.4 Herbs and Spices

Herb/Spice	Preparation	Flavor/Texture	Characteristics
Fresh herbs	Mince	Bright, lively flavor	Bright green color and fresh flavor destroyed by acid; add just before serving
Dried herbs	Rehydrate by steeping in liquid (acid component) to release flavors; add directly to vinaigrette	Strong flavor; mellow vinaigrette for several hours to bring out herb flavors	Add dried herbs sparingly; judge final flavor after several hours of mellowing
Spices	Steep whole spices in acid or oil; add ground spices directly to vinaigrette		Use in specialty vinaigrettes and fusion cuisine; do not add pepper to vinaigrettes, as the flavor becomes bitter

Condiments for Vinaigrettes

A number of prepared sauces and seasonings are used to flavor vinaigrettes. Some contribute to stabilizing the emulsion as well (see Table 2.5).

TABLE 2.5 Condiments

Condiment	Preparation	Flavor/Texture	Characteristics
Mustard	Prepared mustards can be used as is; dry mustard must be hydrated before mixing	Piquant flavor and stabilizing effect	Add to the acid base at the beginning of preparation
Tomato products	Tomato paste or tomato sauce	Sweet and tangy flavor; deep red color	Vegetable fiber helps hold the emulsion
Worcestershire sauce	Good addition to composed salads that include meat	Bold flavor; dark color	Anchovy protein in sauce aids in holding the emulsion

Protein Ingredients for Vinaigrettes

Protein ingredients add distinctive flavor and help stabilize the vinaigrette's emulsion. Table 2.6 describes the proteins most commonly used in vinaigrettes.

TABLE 2.6 Protein Ingredients

Protein	Flavor/Texture	Characteristics
Anchovy paste	Adds subtle umami flavor	Enhances the flavor of the other ingredients
Egg yolk (pasteurized raw or hard-cooked)	Yields thick, creamy vinaigrette when added at beginning of preparation	Too much yolk creates a sour-tasting mayonnaise rather than a vinaigrette
Dairy products (sour cream, crème fraîche, heavy cream)	Thick, light in color, creamy in flavor	Add fresh cream at the end of preparation or the acid will curdle it
Glace	Highly reduced meat, poultry, or seafood stock; adds savory base flavor	All vinaigrettes; useful to dress salads with protein component; a flavor liaison between protein and other salad ingredients

Once you understand the basic principle of creating an emulsion, as explained later in this chapter, and, further, understand how to use emulsifying agents to make your vinaigrettes more stable, you can then use your imagination to prepare signature vinaigrettes.

Understanding Vinaigrette Emulsions

A more precise definition of an emulsion is a mixture of two normally unmixable fluids in which one of the fluids is broken up into tiny droplets and dispersed in the other. The liquid broken into droplets is called the ***dispersed phase*** of the emulsion. The other liquid, which surrounds all those droplets, is called the ***continuous phase***. In a standard vinaigrette, the vinegar is the dispersed phase and the oil is the continuous phase. Thus, the vinegar is broken into tiny droplets during mixing and evenly distributed throughout the oil.

A well-made vinaigrette is cloudy and thick (as shown on p. 29). It is thicker than either oil or water because the tiny droplets get in each other's way as they circulate throughout the mixture, much as starch particles get in each other's way when they are cooked in a sauce in order to thicken it. Most important, the vinegar and oil can no longer be seen individually but instead are combined into a uniform mixture. The mixture is now called an ***emulsified vinaigrette***. An emulsified vinaigrette coats salad greens and other ingredients evenly and uniformly.

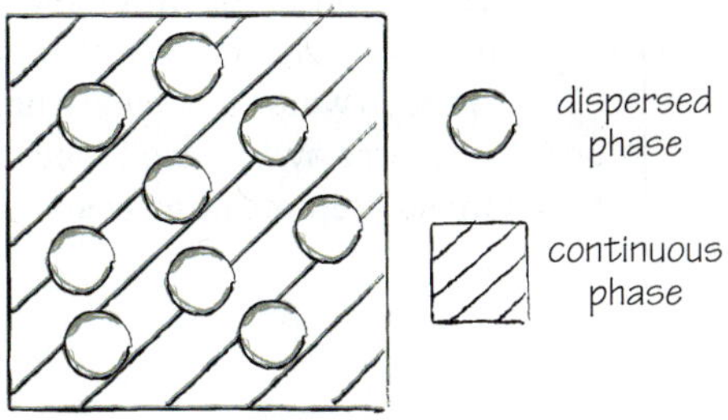

Dispersed and continuous phases of an emulsion

Broken Emulsions

Because a vinaigrette is a temporary or unstable emulsion, sooner or later the vinegar and oil will separate. As the water droplets circulate in the mixture, they bump into each other and, because of their polar attraction (see sidebar, p. 28), they combine into larger droplets. These larger droplets, in turn, combine with other large droplets. Gradually, the droplets become large enough to separate completely from the oil and form a separate layer on the bottom of the container. When this happens, we say the emulsion is ***broken***.

Stabilizing Emulsions

To make a vinaigrette emulsion last longer, chefs have two useful techniques:

- Making the droplets smaller
- Adding stabilizing ingredients

CREATING SMALLER DROPLETS

In a vinaigrette, the smaller the droplets of vinegar, the longer it takes for them to recombine and separate. So, making smaller droplets increases the stability of the emulsion.

Two conditions are necessary to form smaller droplets:

1. **More energy is needed during mixing.** During mixing, the chef must use enough energy to break the surface tension to make smaller and smaller droplets (see sidebar, p. 28). An electric mixer, a blender, or a large industrial homogenizer exert more energy than a handheld whip.
2. **Ingredients must be at the proper temperature.** It is harder to break up droplets at cold temperatures. At warm temperatures, the droplets move around in the mixture more rapidly, making it more likely that they will hit each other and recombine. The best temperature is 60–80°F (16–27°C), or roughly room temperature.

The Science of Polar Molecules and Surface Tension

Water is made up of ***polar*** molecules. One side of the molecule has a slight positive charge and the other side a slight negative charge, like the two poles of a magnet. Because opposite charges attract, water molecules are strongly attracted to each other. Visualize water beads on glass.

Surface water molecules cling tightly to each other and form a kind of elastic sheet. This force is called ***surface tension***. It is surface tension that enables water bugs to walk on the surface of a lake, for example.

The reason water and oil are normally unmixable is because water molecules are strongly attracted to each other and, thus, force away the oil molecules. For this reason it is difficult to break water into droplets and then further break those droplets into yet smaller droplets in order to disperse them into another fluid.

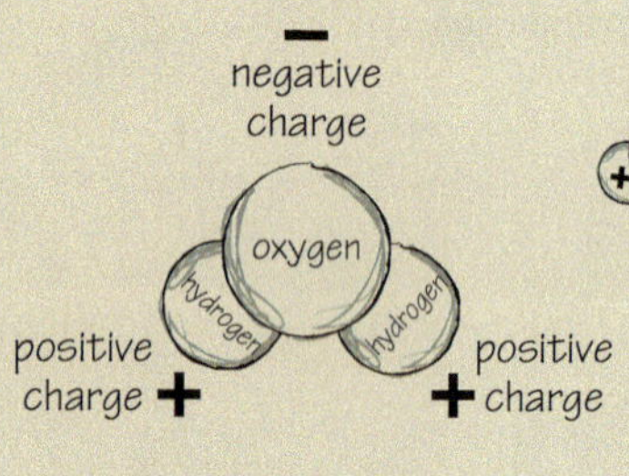

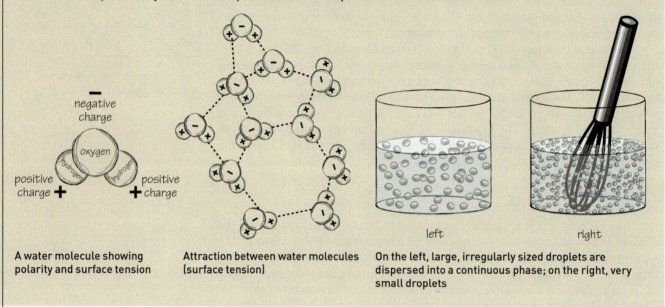

A water molecule showing polarity and surface tension

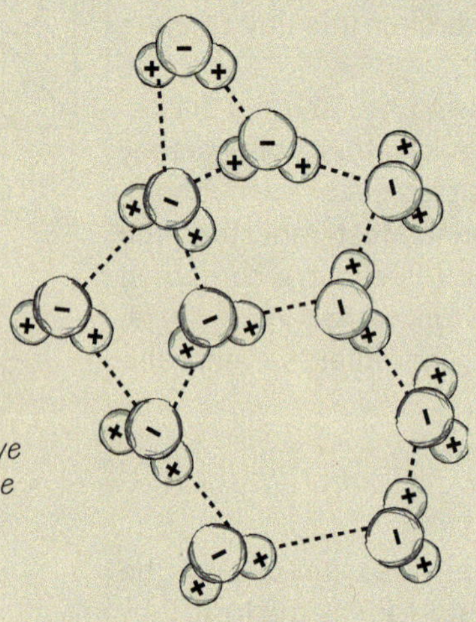

Attraction between water molecules (surface tension)

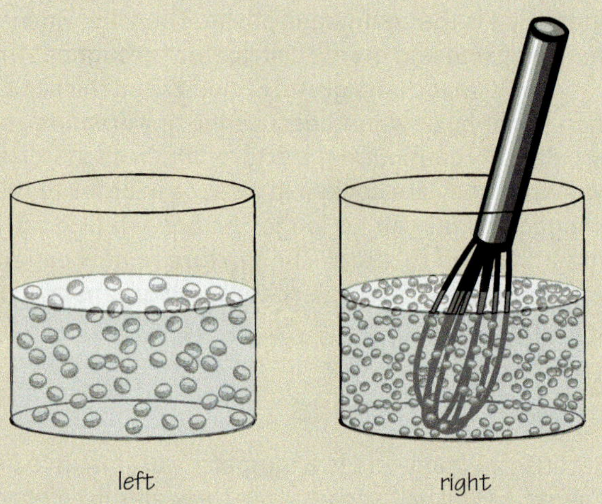

On the left, large, irregularly sized droplets are dispersed into a continuous phase; on the right, very small droplets

ADDING STABILIZING INGREDIENTS

Anything that keeps water droplets from bumping into each other can help stabilize the mixture. An ingredient added to an emulsion to prevent droplets from combining is called a ***stabilizer***.

Fine particles of solids in the mixture can help stabilize the emulsion because they get between the droplets, preventing them from hitting each other. Many ingredients, including powdered spices and finely chopped herbs and aromatics, are useful not only for flavoring the vinaigrette but also for stabilizing the emulsion.

Other stabilizing ingredients work much more effectively and, under the proper conditions, can keep a mixture in emulsion for an indefinite period. These are called ***emulsifiers*** (see sidebar, p. 38).

The lecithin in egg yolks is one of the most effective emulsifiers for vinaigrettes. Other emulsifiers available to the garde manger chef include the milk proteins, particularly ***casein***, in dairy products, and the gelatin protein in *glace* (p. 26). These are true emulsifiers because part of the molecule dissolves in water and part of it in oil (see sidebar, p. 38).

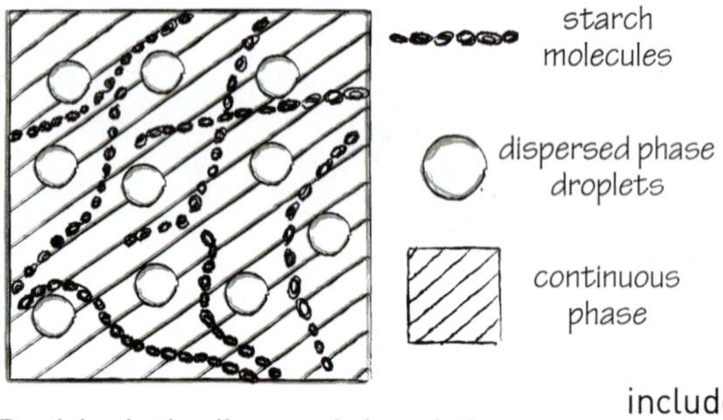

Particles in the dispersed phase help keep droplets of water from coming together and merging

Vinaigrette Mixing Methods

For small amounts of vinaigrette, a bowl and a whip are the best tools to use. For larger amounts, it is easier to use electrically powered mixing equipment, such as a mixer with the whip attachment, an immersion blender, or a blender or food processor.

Basic Procedure for Making Vinaigrettes

1. Have all ingredients at room temperature.
2. Assemble equipment: a stainless-steel mixing bowl and a whip.
3. Combine the vinegar and seasonings in the bowl.
4. Whip until frothy (A).
5. Whip in the oil in a thin stream (B).
6. Taste and correct the flavor balance.

Procedure for Making Vinaigrettes in a Blender/Processor

1. Have all ingredients at room temperature.
2. Assemble equipment: either a blender or a food processor with the bowl and blade in place.
3. Combine the vinegar and seasonings in the blender jar or in the food processor work bowl.
4. With the blender or food processor running at high speed, pour the oil in a thin stream through the lid opening or feed tube.
5. Taste and correct the flavor balance.

Balancing and Seasoning Vinaigrettes

While it is important to master the technique of preparing a well-emulsified vinaigrette, it is equally important to be able to evaluate the vinaigrette's flavor balance. Keep in mind the following:

- Acid is a strong, fundamental taste that can easily overwhelm more subtle flavors.
- Salt balances the effect of acid on the palate.
- Sweet ingredients, such as sugar, honey, or fruit juices, also balance the effect of the acid component.
- Blend the fundamental flavors so they complement each other and the food the vinaigrette will dress.

When tasted alone, in high concentration, a vinaigrette may taste sufficiently tart and well seasoned. However, when it is mixed with other foods, the resulting dish can taste bland because the vinaigrette's flavor is diluted. The best way to judge a vinaigrette's seasoning and its acid-oil balance is to dip a piece of clean, dry lettuce into it and taste the two together.

All vinaigrettes benefit from a ***mellowing period***. During this period, the aromatic ingredients in the mixture release their volatile oils, and the flavors of the acid ingredients, oil, and seasonings have time to marry. Mellowing time ranges from a half-hour or so, if the aromatics are minced fine, to several hours, if the vinaigrette contains dried seasonings or crushed aromatics. Once the mellowing period is done, taste the vinaigrette again and make any necessary adjustments.

A broken vinaigrette

Holding and Storing Vinaigrettes

Vinaigrettes should be applied to foods at room temperature for several reasons. Room temperature is the point at which the flavors are most pronounced and at which the oil has its best mouthfeel. In addition, vinaigrettes stay in emulsion for a longer time at room temperature. While vinaigrettes must be stored under refrigeration for food safety reasons, they must be returned to room temperature before use. Once refrigerated, they become thick and viscous, and their flavors become muted. Avoid shaking or mixing the vinaigrette until it has reached room temperature, because this may cause it to come out of emulsion. If this happens, it can be put back together by the methods described on page 31.

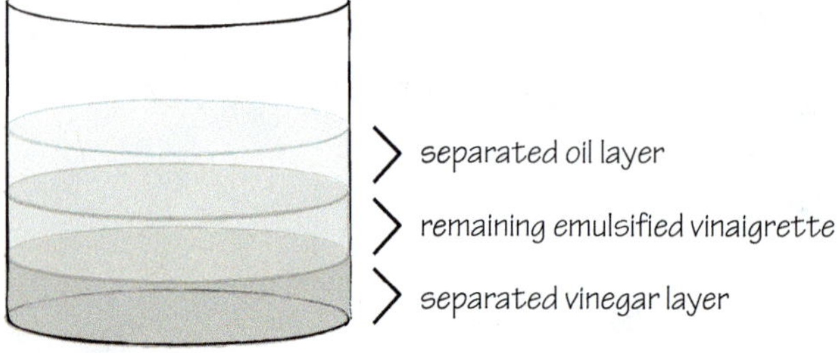

After time, the water droplets in a vinaigrette will be attracted to others of their own kind; when this happens, the watery vinegar and the oil separate, and the vinaigrette is said to be broken.

Repairing Broken Vinaigrettes

No matter how powerful the agitation with which the ingredients in a vinaigrette are combined, the oil and vinegar will eventually separate and the vinaigrette will ***break***, or come out of emulsion (see photo and drawing at left). Chefs call this a ***broken vinaigrette***.

Fortunately, a broken vinaigrette can be fixed easily by any one of three methods (see Table 2.7).

TABLE 2.7 Methods to Fix a Broken Vinaigrette

Method 1	Place the room-temperature broken vinaigrette in a blender and blend at high speed. The powerful action of the blender blades in the tight confines of a blender jar will put almost any broken vinaigrette back into emulsion. (Food processors are less efficient in doing this because their bowls are larger and their action is not as strong.)
Method 2	Start a new batch of vinaigrette and whisk the room-temperature broken vinaigrette into the new vinegar base along with the oil (see photo). Of course, this will result in having twice as much vinaigrette as you originally intended to make.  Vinaigrette repair, Method 2
Method 3	If time allows, wait for the broken vinaigrette to come to room temperature and completely separate. Ladle off the oil and begin again.

Classic French Vinaigrette

The best-known and most frequently used vinaigrette dressing is based on a specific combination of flavors from classical French cuisine. The formula for a classic French vinaigrette includes red or white wine vinegar, Dijon mustard, salt, minced shallots, a hint of garlic, and a light-colored, light-textured olive oil.

The History of "French" Dressing

In France, the classic simple salad of leafy greens is always tossed with some form of simple vinaigrette. In the 1880s, European chefs introduced vinaigrettes to American restaurants. Before that time, most Americans were familiar only with English-style cream-based salad dressings. The classic French vinaigrette composed of vinegar, olive oil, salt, Dijon mustard, shallot, and garlic became known in the United States as *French dressing*.

In the 1950s, industrial food producers began to manufacture a highly spiced, sugary-sweet mixture of vegetable oil and distilled white vinegar colored red from both paprika and tomato, and they labeled it "French dressing." This product remains on supermarket shelves today.

To avoid confusion, it is best to avoid the term *French dressing* and instead use the word *vinaigrette* when referring to the classic French formula.

RECIPES

CLASSIC FRENCH VINAIGRETTE

Yield:
8 fl oz (240 ml)
Portion size:
varies

INGREDIENTS	U. S.	METRIC
Minced shallot	½ oz	15 g
Minced fresh garlic	⅛ oz	4 g
Dijon mustard	½ fl oz	15 mL
Kosher salt	to taste	to taste
Red or white wine vinegar	2 fl oz	60 mL
Pure, golden olive oil (not extra-virgin)	5 fl oz	150 mL

PROCEDURE

PREPARATION

1. Mix ingredients using the Basic (p. 29) or Blender/Processor (p. 29) Procedure.
2. Taste and correct the seasoning.

HOLDING

Store in a freshly sanitized squeeze bottle or nonreactive container at room temperature up to 3 hours or refrigerated up to 1 week. Bring to room temperature before using.

VARIATIONS

SHERRY VINAIGRETTE

Replace the red or white wine vinegar with sherry vinegar.

WALNUT VINAIGRETTE

Omit the garlic; reduce the mustard to 1 tsp (5 mL); use white wine vinegar; replace the olive oil with walnut oil.

HAZELNUT VINAIGRETTE

Omit the garlic; reduce the mustard to 1 tsp (5 mL); use white wine vinegar; replace the olive oil with hazelnut oil.

HERBED VINAIGRETTE

Add minced fresh herbs of choice; reduce hold time to 24 hours.

TARRAGON VINAIGRETTE

Replace the red or white wine vinegar with tarragon vinegar.

TOMATO VINAIGRETTE

Replace the mustard with 2 fl oz (60 mL) canned tomato purée; reduce the vinegar amount to 1 fl oz (30 mL).

CREAMY VINAIGRETTE

Omit the garlic. Replace the vinegar with fresh lemon juice. Replace 2 fl oz (60 mL) of the oil with crème fraîche or sour cream, added at the end of mixing.

ROQUEFORT VINAIGRETTE

Replace the mustard with ½ oz (15 g) softened Roquefort cheese.

AMERICAN CIDER VINAIGRETTE

Yield:
8 fl oz (240 ml)
Portion size:
varies

INGREDIENTS	U.S.	METRIC
Minced shallot	¼ oz	7 g
Kosher salt	to taste	to taste
Granulated sugar	1 tbsp	15 mL
Cider vinegar	2 fl oz	60 mL
Corn oil	6 fl oz	180 mL

PROCEDURE

PREPARATION

1. Mix ingredients using the Basic (p. 29) or Blender/Processor (p. 29) Procedure.
2. Taste and correct the seasoning.

HOLDING

Store in a freshly sanitized squeeze bottle or nonreactive container at room temperature up to 3 hours or refrigerated up to 1 week.

THICK MUSTARD VINAIGRETTE

Yield:
8 fl oz (240 ml)
Portion size:
varies

INGREDIENTS	U.S.	METRIC
Minced shallot	½ oz	15g
Minced fresh garlic	¼ oz	7g
Dijon mustard	2 fl oz	60 mL
Poultry glace	2 tbsp	30 mL
Brown sugar	1 tsp	5 mL
Kosher salt	to taste	to taste
White wine vinegar	1½ fl oz	45 mL
Pure, golden olive oil (not extra-virgin)	5 fl oz	150 mL

PROCEDURE

PREPARATION

1. Mix ingredients using the Basic (p. 29) or Blender/Processor (p. 29) Procedure.
2. Taste and correct the seasoning.

HOLD

Store in a freshly sanitized squeeze bottle or nonreactive container at room temperature up to 3 hours or refrigerated up to 1 week.

VARIATIONS

GREEN PEPPERCORN MUSTARD VINAIGRETTE

Add 1 tbsp (15 mL) drained, chopped green peppercorns after emulsifying.

HONEY-MUSTARD VINAIGRETTE

Replace the brown sugar with up to 1 fl oz (30 mL) strong-flavored honey.

BALSAMIC VINAIGRETTE

Yield:
8 fl oz (240 ml)
Portion size:
varies

INGREDIENTS	U.S.	METRIC
Minced shallot	½ oz	15 g
Freshly minced garlic	¼ oz	7 g
Kosher salt	to taste	to taste
Balsamic vinegar	2 fl oz	60 mL
Extra-virgin olive oil	3 fl oz	90 mL
Safflower or canola oil	3 fl oz	90 mL

PROCEDURE

PREPARATION

1. Mix the ingredients using the Basic (p. 29) or the Blender/Processor Procedure (p. 29).
2. Taste and correct the seasoning.

HOLDING

Store in a freshly sanitized squeeze bottle or nonreactive container at room temperature up to 3 hours or refrigerated up to 1 week.

LEMON VINAIGRETTE

Yield:
8 fl oz (240 ml)
Portion size:
varies

INGREDIENTS	U.S.	METRIC
Minced shallot	¼ oz	7 g
Kosher salt	to taste	to taste
Granulated sugar	to taste	to taste
Fresh lemon juice	2 fl oz	60 mL
Pure, golden olive oil (not extra-virgin)	3 fl oz	90 mL
Safflower or canola oil	3 fl oz	90 mL

PROCEDURE

PREPARATION

1. Mix ingredients using the Basic (p. 29) or Blender/Processor (p. 29) Procedure.
2. Taste and correct the seasoning.

HOLDING

Store in a freshly sanitized squeeze bottle or nonreactive container at room temperature up to 3 hours or refrigerated up to 1 week.

VARIATIONS

LIME VINAIGRETTE

Replace the lemon juice and zest with lime juice and zest.

GRAPEFRUIT VINAIGRETTE

Replace the lemon juice and zest with grapefruit juice and zest.

TROPICAL VINAIGRETTE

Prepare Lime Vinaigrette, but replace half the lime juice with pineapple juice; add 1 tbsp (15 mL) mango purée; omit the sugar; optionally, add 1 tsp (5 mL) minced Serrano chile.

SAFE CAESAR DRESSING

Yield:
8 fl oz (240 ml)
Portion size:
varies

INGREDIENTS	U.S.	METRIC
Egg	1	1
Water	½ fl oz	15 mL
Kosher salt	to taste	to taste
Fresh lemon juice	1½ fl oz	45 mL
Minced anchovies or anchovy paste	1 tbsp	15 mL
Minced garlic	¼ oz	7 g
Grated Reggiano Parmesan cheese	1½ oz	45 g
Pure, golden olive oil (not extra-virgin)	3 fl oz	90 mL

PROCEDURE

PREPARATION

1. Place the egg, water, and half the lemon juice in a stainless-steel bowl. Whisk vigorously, then whisk over a hot bain-marie until the mixture thickens slightly and reaches 140°F (60°C).
2. Whisk over an ice bain-marie until the mixture reaches room temperature.
3. Scrape the egg mixture into a blender and add the remaining lemon juice, anchovies, garlic, and cheese. Blend.
4. With the blades running, pour the oil through the blender top opening to create an emulsion.
5. Taste and correct the seasoning, adjusting lemon juice and salt to taste.

HOLDING

Refrigerate in a freshly sanitized squeeze bottle or nonreactive container for 24 hours only.

ASIAN VINAIGRETTE

Yield:
8 fl oz (240 ml)
Portion size:
varies

INGREDIENTS	U.S.	METRIC
Garlic clove, peeled	¼ oz	7 g
Fresh ginger	2 oz	60 g
Rice vinegar	2½ fl oz	75 mL
Granulated sugar	2 tsp	10 mL
Chinese or Japanese soy sauce	½ fl oz	15 mL
Scallion, minced very fine	½ oz	15 g
Kosher salt	to taste	to taste
Peanut oil	5 fl oz	150 mL

PROCEDURE

PREPARATION

1. Using a juice extractor or garlic press, juice the garlic and ginger.
2. Combine the garlic and ginger juice, vinegar, sugar, soy sauce, scallion, and salt.
3. Add the oil using the Basic (p. 29) or the Blender/Processor Procedure (p. 29).
4. Taste and correct the seasoning.

HOLDING

Store in a freshly sanitized squeeze bottle or nonreactive container at room temperature up to 3 hours or refrigerated up to 1 week.

VARIATIONS

SICHUAN VINAIGRETTE

Replace the white rice vinegar with Chinese red vinegar; add Sichuan hot chile paste to the acid components to taste.

MISO VINAIGRETTE

Add 1 tbsp (15 mL) red or white miso to the acid components; adjust sugar to taste.

POPPY SEED DRESSING

Yield:
8 fl oz (240 ml)
Portion size:
varies

INGREDIENTS	U.S.	METRIC
Minced shallot	½ oz	30 g
Honey	½ fl oz	15 mL
Kosher salt	to taste	to taste
Dry mustard	1 tsp	5 mL
Black poppy seeds	1 tbsp	15 mL
Raspberry vinegar	2 fl oz	60 mL
Fresh lemon juice	½ fl oz	15 mL
Safflower oil	4 fl oz	120 mL

PROCEDURE

PREPARATION

1. Mix the ingredients using the Basic (p. 29) or the Blender/Processor Procedure (p. 29).
2. Taste and correct the seasoning.

HOLDING

Store in a freshly sanitized squeeze bottle or nonreactive container at room temperature up to 3 hours or refrigerated up to 1 week.

RASPBERRY VINAIGRETTE

Yield:
8 fl oz (240 ml)
Portion size:
varies

INGREDIENTS	U.S.	METRIC
Minced shallot	¼ oz	7 g
Kosher salt	to taste	to taste
Raspberry vinegar	2½ fl oz	75 mL
Raspberry purée	½ fl oz	15 mL
Safflower oil	5 fl oz	150 mL

PROCEDURE

PREPARATION

1. Mix the ingredients using the Basic (p. 29) or the Blender/Processor Procedure (p. 29).
2. Taste and correct the seasoning.

HOLDING

Store in a freshly sanitized squeeze bottle or nonreactive container at room temperature up to 3 hours or refrigerated up to 1 week.

VARIATIONS

PEAR VINAIGRETTE

Replace the raspberry vinegar with pear vinegar and the raspberry purée with pear nectar.

CRANBERRY-WALNUT VINAIGRETTE

Replace the raspberry vinegar with red wine vinegar and the raspberry purée with 1 fl oz (30 mL) sweetened cranberry juice concentrate. Replace the safflower oil with walnut oil.

POMEGRANATE-WALNUT VINAIGRETTE

Replace the raspberry vinegar with red wine vinegar and the raspberry purée with 1 fl oz (30 mL) unsweetened pomegranate juice. Add 1 tbsp (15 mL) sugar. Replace the safflower oil with walnut oil.

MAYONNAISE

Fine house-made mayonnaise is one of the glories of the cold kitchen. Considered *the* mother sauce of garde manger work, mayonnaise is the basis of hundreds of dips, spreads, and dressings.

Mayonnaise is a cool permanent emulsion sauce classically made from vegetable oil, vinegar, and egg yolks. Mayonnaise can be made thick enough to bind the elements of a composed salad, or it can be made thin enough to pour as a sauce. A mayonnaise can act as a bland base for other stronger and more highly seasoned ingredients, or it may be boldly flavored enough to stand on its own.

Mayonnaise to be used as a sauce is prepared so as to have a nappé consistency similar to that of a classic velouté sauce. ***Nappé*** consistency is thick enough to coat a cool, clean, metal spoon yet thin enough to flow on the plate.

Ingredients for Mayonnaise

The basic ingredients of classic mayonnaise are egg yolks, oil, salt, and vinegar (see Table 2.8). However, many chefs prefer to use lemon juice instead of vinegar.

The History of the Name

The origin of the term *mayonnaise* is disputed. Carême believed the sauce should be called *magnonaise*, a term derived from *manier*, meaning "to manipulate" or "to stir." The *Larousse Gastronomique* asserts that the word is a corruption of *moyeunaise*, derived from archaic French *moyeau*, or "yolk." Yet others believe *mayonnaise* was named in honor of the French military victory over the city of Mahon in 1756.

TABLE 2.8 Mayonnaise Ingredients

Ingredient	Type	Characteristic
Egg yolks	High-quality pasteurized yolks	To comply with food safety regulations
Vinegar	Almost any type (see p. 23)	Avoid strong-flavored vinegars and dark-colored varieties
Lemon juice	Fresh-squeezed juice	Lends a light, fresh flavor
Vegetable oil	Almost any type (see p. 24), depending on the use of the mayonnaise	Oil should be fresh, with no signs of rancidity
Mustard	Dry mustard or prepared mustard	Adds a piquant flavor; is added to the yolk-acid base; helps form the emulsion
Salt	Fine ground	Add a small amount to the yolk-acid base at the beginning of preparation; more salt can be added when the mayonnaise is finished; whenever salt is added, allow time for it to dissolve
White pepper		If pepper is used, make sure it is finely ground white pepper so the mayonnaise will not be discolored

Understanding Mayonnaise Emulsions

As for vinaigrette, mayonnaise preparation depends on vigorous agitation and on the oil being beaten into the water base very slowly. When making mayonnaise, begin adding the oil to the base literally one drop at a time.

Unlike a vinaigrette emulsion, a mayonnaise emulsion is permanent. It is strongly stabilized by the addition of egg yolk, an ingredient that contains lecithin, a powerful emulsifier (see the sidebar and figure on p. 38).

Because in mayonnaise the permanent emulsion is achieved without the application of heat, mayonnaise is frequently called a *cold emulsion sauce*. However, *cold* is not technically the correct term. To create a successful mayonnaise emulsion, all ingredients must be at just about room temperature—around 70°F (21°C). Remove the egg yolks from the refrigerator or freezer far enough ahead to reach the proper temperature by the time you are ready to begin preparation. If your oil is refrigerated, bring it to room temperature as well.

To achieve a light, fluffy texture in your mayonnaise, it is necessary to have sufficient water in the emulsion. You can add water to the acid base, or you may add water while incorporating the oil.

The speed and power with which the oil droplets are dispersed into the watery base also play a part in creating a light and fluffy texture. In a correctly prepared mayonnaise, when approximately one-third of the oil has been incorporated into the watery base the mayonnaise visibly thickens to the point where it clings to the blades of the whisk and will ***ribbon***, or form thick bands on the surface, when it falls back into the bowl. At this point the emulsion has "caught," and you are said to have a ***caught emulsion***. Once the emulsion has caught, add the oil more quickly and whip it in more gently. If you continue beating too hard and adding oil too slowly, you will end up with a ***tight mayonnaise***, which is overthickened and oily. Extremely tight mayonnaise has an unpleasant greenish color and feels greasy on the tongue.

Many chefs finish each batch of mayonnaise by stirring in a few drops of boiling water. This raises the temperature of the mayonnaise by a degree or two, thus setting the emulsion by slightly firming the egg proteins. The extra water also counters surface evaporation, which can result in unwanted oil droplets on the surface of the mayonnaise. The amount and type of extra liquid you add depends on the desired thickness and flavor of the finished sauce.

The mixture clings to the blades of the whisk and ribbons on the surface when it falls back into the bowl.

Thick mayonnaise and nappé mayonnaise

The Science of Emulsifiers

Egg yolks contain lecithin in large quantities, which is why egg yolks are so useful for emulsifying sauces like hollandaise and mayonnaise.

Lecithin is related to fat and has an electrical charge at one end that is attracted to water. The long tail of the lecithin molecule dissolves in the oil droplets, and the charged end sticks out of the oil droplet and attracts water molecules. In other words, an oil droplet coated with lecithin is attracted to water more than to other oil droplets.

Many protein molecules work in a similar way, forming long chains of amino acids. Some segments are attracted to water and some to oil.

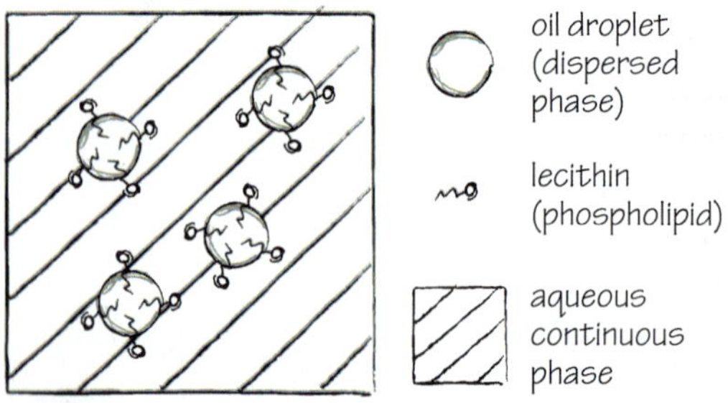

A permanent emulsion is achieved when one end of long, slender lecithin molecules dissolves in the tiny droplets of oil, while the other end is attracted to water. Thus, each oil droplet is surrounded by water. The separated oil droplets do not join to form larger droplets that float to a separate layer.

Failed mayonnaise

Mayonnaise should be prepared at least a few hours in advance of serving, and it should be refrigerated until it is needed. This cold rest further stabilizes the emulsion. The product also thickens a little more as it rests. However, once a mayonnaise has been refrigerated, it must be handled carefully. If cold mayonnaise is beaten or even stirred vigorously, it can easily break. Gently fold in seasonings or other ingredients to cold mayonnaise. Better yet, if time allows, bring the mayonnaise to room temperature before mixing.

Guidelines for Preparing Mayonnaise

When deciding on the amount of watery ingredients to add to a mayonnaise, keep the following facts in mind:

- The higher the proportion of oil, the thicker the mayonnaise will be.
- The higher the proportion of water-based ingredients, the thinner the mayonnaise will be.
- By adjusting the amount of water-based ingredients, you can create a thick mayonnaise to use as a sandwich spread or a salad binder, or a thinner, nappé mayonnaise to use as a sauce.

Mayonnaise Mixing Methods

Small amounts of mayonnaise can be made easily by hand. For larger amounts, it is more efficient to use electrically powered mixing equipment.

Troubleshooting Mayonnaise

Because the preparation of mayonnaise is somewhat difficult and the chemistry behind it is complex, you should understand what can go wrong and how to repair it.

Failed Mayonnaise

There are two main reasons for a mayonnaise emulsion to fail:

1. The ingredients were too warm or too cold.
2. The oil was incorporated too quickly.

If the watery ingredients and the oil do not successfully emulsify, the result is a ***failed mayonnaise***. The yolk–acid base may remain thick and opaque, with the oil clearly visible in translucent streaks and swirls. Sometimes the ingredients combine into an opaque mass but appear as a thin liquid and will not thicken properly no matter how much the mixture is beaten.

Broken Mayonnaise

If a properly emulsified mayonnaise comes apart and the oil and liquid separate, the result is a ***broken mayonnaise***. A mayonnaise emulsion breaks for three basic reasons.

Procedure for Making Mayonnaise (Traditional Method)

A

B

C

1. Have ready a small amount of boiling water. Yolks, vinegar or lemon juice, and oil should all be at room temperature.
2. Whip the yolks, vinegar or lemon juice, and salt in a bowl until light and frothy.
3. While whipping vigorously, begin adding room-temperature oil, 1 drop at a time, until the emulsion begins to catch (A).
4. Gradually slow the speed of whipping to stirring, and increase the rate at which you add the oil (B). When the mixture becomes very thick (C), stir in a few drops of lemon juice, vinegar, or cool water, and then resume adding oil and liquid until the desired texture is achieved.
5. Taste and correct the seasoning, adding salt, more vinegar or lemon juice, and finely ground white pepper if desired.
6. Stir in a few drops of boiling water (D).
7. Refrigerate 1 to 2 hours.

D

Procedure for Making Mayonnaise (Blender/Food Processor Method)

1. Have ready a small amount of boiling water. Yolks, vinegar or lemon juice, and oil should all be room temperature.
2. In the blender jar or processor bowl, blend or process yolks, vinegar or lemon juice, and salt until light and frothy.
3. With the blade running, pour in oil through the top opening or feed tube in a very thin stream. As the emulsion catches and the mixture becomes thick, begin adding oil faster and faster.
4. When the mixture becomes very thick, add a few drops of lemon juice, vinegar, or cool water, and then resume adding oil and liquid until the desired texture is achieved.
5. Taste and correct the seasoning, adding salt, more vinegar or lemon juice, and finely ground white pepper if desired.
6. Pulse in a few drops of boiling water.
7. Refrigerate 1 to 2 hours.

Broken mayonnaise

1. Too much oil was added to the yolk–acid base.
2. At some point, the oil was added too quickly.

If a finished, successful mayonnaise breaks when additional ingredients are added to it:

3. The finished mayonnaise was whipped or vigorously stirred while cold.

Repairing Failed or Broken Mayonnaise

While a failed or broken mayonnaise can be frustrating, there is no need to throw it away. If the mayonnaise failed or broke due to temperature issues, first slowly bring the mayonnaise (and any repair ingredients) to 70°F (21°C) by letting it stand at room temperature. See Table 2.9 for steps to repairing mayonnaise.

TABLE 2.9 Method to Repair Failed or Broken Mayonnaise

Traditional Double-Batch Repair	1. Start with a new set of yolk, acid, and salt. 2. Whip the failed/broken mayonnaise into the new yolk–acid base 1 drop at a time (A). 3. Add the proper amount of new oil (B). 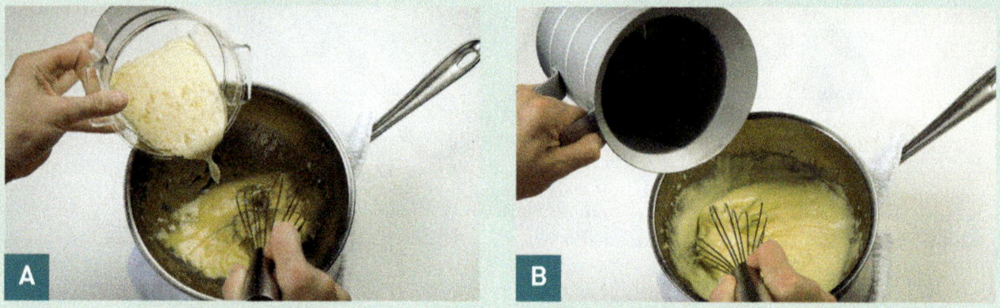
Single-Batch Repair	1. Ladle off the oil from the separated mayonnaise and reserve. 2. Bring the base and oil to room temperature. 3. Vigorously whisk the yolk–acid base, and carefully whisk in the removed oil, drop by drop, until the emulsion catches. 4. Proceed as usual.  Allow the broken mayonnaise to stand until the oil separates from the yolk base.
Blender Repair	1. Place the failed/broken mayonnaise in a blender and blend at high speed to reemulsify. 2. Adjust the texture of the resulting mayonnaise with more liquid.

Guidelines for Food Safety for Mayonnaise

To avoid the dangers of food-borne illness, observe the following food safety guidelines when preparing or using mayonnaise.

- **Use pasteurized egg yolks.**
  In mayonnaise, the eggs remain raw, so harmful microorganisms are not killed by heat.
- **As pasteurized yolks are sold frozen, thaw them under refrigeration and then bring the refrigerated yolks to room temperature quickly.**
  To avoid bacterial growth, yolks should spend as little time as possible at room temperature.
- **Sanitize all tools and containers.**
  Even if made from pasteurized yolks, mayonnaise is still a good breeding ground for bacteria that, in high concentration, may contaminate it during production and storage.
- **Keep mayonnaise refrigerated until it is needed.**
  Limit to 1 hour or less the amount of time house-made mayonnaise remains in the temperature danger zone (41°–135°F/5°–57°C/in Canada: 40°F–140°F/4°C–69°C).
- Label house-made mayonnaise with the time it was made as well as the date.
- Discard refrigerated house-made mayonnaise after 48 hours, even if it appears to be still good.

RECIPES

MAYONNAISE

Yield:
8 fl oz (240 ml)

Neutral Mayonnaise

If the mayonnaise you are making is for the entire garde manger department to use as needed, you should make a ***neutral mayonnaise***, one having no particularly assertive flavors. Thus, use a mild-flavored oil, such as safflower oil or canola oil. Mayonnaise intended for a specific preparation may be made from a more flavorful oil such as olive oil or a nut oil.

INGREDIENTS	U.S.	METRIC
Pasteurized egg yolk	1 fl oz	30 mL
Kosher salt	to taste	to taste
White wine vinegar	1 tsp	5 mL
Dry mustard	¼ tsp	2 mL
Finely ground white pepper	pinch	pinch
Bland-tasting vegetable oil	6 fl oz	180 mL
White wine vinegar	1 tsp	5 mL

PROCEDURE

PREPARATION

Follow the Traditional or Blender/Food Processor Procedure on page 39.

HOLDING

Refrigerate in a freshly sanitized, covered container up to 48 hours.

CLASSIC MAYONNAISE SAUCES

For each of the following preparations, add the listed ingredients to 12 fl oz (360 mL) mayonnaise.

SAUCE AURORE *[oh-ROAR]*

1 fl oz (30 mL) canned tomato purèe, fresh lemon juice to taste, thin with half-and-half

SAUCE MOUTARDE À LA CRÈME *[moo-TARD ah la KREM]*

2 tsp (10 mL) fresh lemon juice, 2 tbsp (30 mL) Dijon mustard, 2 fl oz (60 mL) heavy cream

SAUCE RAIFORT *[ray-FOR]*

2 tbsp (30 mL) prepared horseradish, 2 fl oz (60 mL) heavy cream

SAUCE RAIFORT AUX NOIX *[ray-FOR oh NWA]*

2 tbsp (30 mL) prepared horseradish, 2 fl oz (60 mL) heavy cream, 1½ oz (45 g) toasted chopped walnuts

SAUCE RÉMOULADE *[ray-moo-LAHD]*

2 tsp (10 mL) Dijon mustard, 1 tbsp (15 mL) chopped sour pickles, 1 tbsp (15 mL) nonpareil capers, 1 tbsp (15 mL) minced parsley, 1 tbsp (15 mL) minced tarragon, 1 tbsp (15 mL) minced chervil, and 1 tsp (5 mL) anchovy paste

SAUCE RUSSE *[ROOCE]*

2 fl oz (60 g) combined cooked lobster roe and tomalley, 2 tbsp (30 mL) red caviar, 1 tbsp (15 mL) fresh lemon juice, 1 tsp (5 mL) Dijon mustard

SAUCE TARTARE *[tahr-TAHR]*

When preparing mayonnaise, replace the raw yolk with cooked yolks; ¼ oz (7 g) minced chives

SAUCE ANDALOUSE *[ahn-dah-LOOZ]*

2 tbsp (30 mL) canned tomato purée, ¼ cup (60 mL) minced roasted red bell pepper

SAUCE VERTE *[VAIRT]*

¼ cup (60 mL) *each* blanched, refreshed, squeezed dry, and puréed spinach and watercress, 1 tbsp (15 mL) *each* blanched, refreshed, squeezed dry, and puréed parsley, chervil, and tarragon

SAUCE SUÉDOISE *[sway-DWAZ]*

2 fl oz (60 mL) unsweetened cooked apple purée, 1 tbsp (15 mL) prepared horseradish

MAYONNAISE CHANTILLY *[shahn-tee-YEE]*

Whip 4 fl oz (120 mL) heavy cream to soft peaks and fold in.

AÏOLI *[EYE-uh-lee]*

In a mortar, crush together ½ oz (15 g) minced, freshly peeled young garlic, ½ tsp (3 mL) kosher salt, 2 tsp (10 mL) minced lemon zest; add 1 cup (240 mL) Mayonnaise (p. 41) made with olive oil, and fresh lemon juice to taste.

ROUILLE *[roo-EE]*

Prepare Aïoli, but add 1–2 tsp (5–10 mL) cayenne or hot paprika to the mortar mixture.

The History of Commercial Mayonnaise

Today, commercially made mayonnaise is so widely available that it is hard to imagine a time when mayonnaise was considered a special-occasion food. In 1912, Manhattan delicatessen owner Richard Hellman began marketing a shelf-stabilized mayonnaise packed in jars. Now, hundreds of brands of commercial mayonnaise are available.

Using Commercial Mayonnaise

Food safety issues, perishability factors, and budgetary concerns are major factors that drive most food-service operations to use commercial mayonnaise. Commercial mayonnaise is made with artificial stabilizers and preservatives, and all brands are pasteurized during production. This keeps commercial mayonnaise emulsified and allows it to be safely refrigerated for many weeks. While all commercial mayonnaise is made thick enough to stand up on a spoon, some brands are thicker than others. When a commercial mayonnaise is intended for use in bound salads (p. 158), where thickness is a desirable quality, you should choose a brand labeled "heavy" or "extra-heavy."

CONTEMPORARY MAYONNAISE-BASED SAUCES AND DRESSINGS

For each of the following preparations, add the listed ingredients to 12 fl oz (360 mL) mayonnaise.

TARTAR SAUCE

1 tbsp (15 mL) minced sour pickles, 2 tsp (10 mL) nonpareil capers, 1 tbsp (15 mL) minced shallot, 1 tbsp (15 mL) chopped hard-cooked egg white, 1 tbsp (15 mL) sieved hard-cooked egg yolk, sugar to taste

FINES HERBES MAYONNAISE

1 tbsp (15 mL) each minced fresh parsley, tarragon, chives, and chervil, 1 tsp (5 mL) minced fresh thyme leaves

RUSSIAN DRESSING

2 fl oz (60 mL) bottled chili sauce or ketchup, 1 tbsp (15 mL) sweet pickle relish, 1 tbsp (15 mL) prepared horseradish, 2 tbsp (30 mL) minced shallot, 2 tbsp (30 mL) minced pimiento, 2 tbsp (30 mL) minced chives

THOUSAND ISLAND DRESSING

Russian Dressing (above) with the addition of 3 tbsp (45 mL) chopped green bell pepper, 2 tbsp (30 mL) chopped hard-cooked egg white, 2 tbsp (30 mL) sieved hard-cooked egg yolk

GREEN GODDESS DRESSING

2 tsp (10 mL) tarragon vinegar, 2 tsp (10 mL) minced anchovies, ¼ cup (60 mL) minced scallions, 2 tbsp (30 mL) minced parsley, 1 tbsp (15 mL) minced tarragon, 1 tbsp (15 mL) minced chives, 2 fl oz (60 mL) heavy cream

LOUIS DRESSING [LOOEY]

2 fl oz (60 mL) bottled chili sauce, 2 tsp (10 mL) prepared horseradish, 1 tsp (5 mL) Worcestershire sauce, 3 tbsp (45 mL) minced California green olives, 1 tbsp (15 mL) minced tarragon, 2 tbsp (30 mL) minced chives

ROQUEFORT DRESSING

⅓ cup (80 mL) French Roquefort cheese, 2 fl oz (60 mL) half-and-half

BLUE CHEESE DRESSING

⅓ cup (80 mL) crumbled blue cheese, 1 tsp (5 mL) sugar, 1 tbsp (15 mL) white wine vinegar, 2 fl oz (60 mL) heavy cream

ROASTED RED BELL PEPPER MAYONNAISE

½ cup (120 mL) roasted red bell pepper purée

CURRY MAYONNAISE

2–3 tsp (10–15 mL) curry powder sweated in 1 tbsp (15 mL) vegetable oil and cooled, 1 tbsp (15 mL) fresh ginger juice, 2 tsp (10 mL) honey, 1 tbsp (15 mL) fresh lime juice

GINGERED MAYONNAISE

The juice of 2 oz (60 g) fresh ginger, peeled and expressed in a juicer or through a garlic press

CHIPOTLE MAYONNAISE

¼–½ oz (8–15 g) canned chipotle chiles en adobo, minced fine, pinch sugar

MUSTARD MAYONNAISE

¼–½ oz (7–14 g) Dijon mustard, pinch sugar

ANCHOVY MAYONNAISE

¼ oz (7 g) anchovy paste, pinch sugar

ANCHOVY-MUSTARD MAYONNAISE

¼ oz (7 g) anchovy paste, ¼ oz (7 g) Dijon mustard, pinch sugar

CREAMY TARRAGON MAYONNAISE SAUCE

¼ oz (7 g) minced shallot, 1 oz (30 g) minced fresh tarragon leaves, 2–3 fl oz (60–90 mL) half-and-half (enough to achieve a pourable consistency)

LEMON MAYONNAISE SAUCE FOR SEAFOOD

1 tbsp (15 mL) minced lemon zest, ½ fl oz (15 mL) fresh lemon juice, 2–3 fl oz (60–90 mL) shellfish stock (enough to achieve a pourable consistency)

BÉARNAISE MAYONNAISE

1 fl oz (30 mL) white wine vinegar, 1½ fl oz (45 mL) white wine, 2 tsp (10 mL) minced shallot, 1 tsp (5 mL) dried tarragon, (all reduced to 1½ fl oz (45 mL) and cooled), ½ oz (15 g) minced fresh tarragon leaves

TONNATO SAUCE

2 oz (60 g) Italian canned tuna in olive oil, ½ oz (15 g) best-quality anchovy filets, ½ fl oz (15 mL) fresh lemon juice, 2 tsp (10 mL) minced lemon zest, 2 tsp (10 mL) nonpareil capers (all puréed in a mortar or food processor), 3–4 fl oz (90–120 mL) cool veal stock or veal *cuisson* (enough to achieve a pourable consistency)

DAIRY-BASED SAUCES

Many of the most popular North American salad dressings, cold sauces, and dips are based on dairy products.

Dairy-based dressings and sauces may be made from fresh cream or from fermented dairy products (p. 563), such as sour cream, crème fraîche, yogurt, or buttermilk. Sour cream and crème fraîche are thick enough to make a sauce of nappé consistency. However, sometimes mayonnaise is blended into these sauces to add body and richness. Fresh cream, buttermilk, and most yogurts need additional thickening. Dressings based on fresh cream, buttermilk, and most yogurts need additional thickening, such as mashed hard-cooked egg yolks or a cooked starch base, as in Old-Fashioned Boiled Dressing (p. 46).

To function successfully as a salad dressing, a dairy-based sauce must be seasoned with an acid ingredient. Traditional cream dressings are flavored with malt vinegar or cider vinegar. Citrus juice and zest are also welcome additions. Many savory dairy-based sauces are also flavored with a little sugar or other sweetener. Take care that the sweet-acid-salt flavors are in balance. Fresh herbs, condiments, and even cheeses and vegetable purées may be used to enhance dairy-based dressings.

RECIPES

MIAMI MUSTARD SAUCE

Yield:
8 fl oz (240 ml)

INGREDIENTS	U.S.	METRIC
Dry mustard	1 tbsp	15 mL
Water	1 tbsp	15 mL
Minced shallots	1 tbsp	15 mL
Dijon mustard	2 fl oz	60 mL
Sugar	2 tsp	10 mL
Finely ground white pepper	½ tsp	3 mL
Mayonnaise	3 fl oz	90 mL
Sour cream	4 fl oz	120 mL
Salt	to taste	to taste

PROCEDURE

PREPARATION

1. Combine the dry mustard and water to make a smooth paste.
2. Add the remaining ingredients and whisk until smooth.
3. Refrigerate at least 30 minutes to allow the mustard to hydrate and the flavors to meld.
4. Correct the salt.

HOLDING

If made with commercial mayonnaise, refrigerate in a freshly sanitized, covered container up to 1 week; with house-made mayonnaise, up to 48 hours.

(Variations on next page)

VARIATIONS

CREAMY TARRAGON MUSTARD SAUCE

Add 2 tbsp (30 mL) chopped fresh tarragon.

CREAMY TOMATO MUSTARD SAUCE

Decrease the sugar to taste after adding 2 tbsp (30 mL) canned tomato purée.

CREAMY DILL MUSTARD SAUCE

Add 2 tbsp (30 mL) chopped fresh dill.

CREAMY HORSERADISH SAUCE

Omit the mustards and water. Add 1½ fl oz (45 mL) prepared horseradish.

HORSERADISH CREAM

Omit the mustards and water. Reduce the amount of mayonnaise by 2 fl oz (60 mL). Reduce the amount of sour cream by 1 fl oz (30 mL). Add 2 fl oz (60 mL) prepared horseradish. Fold in 6 fl oz (180 mL) unsweetened whipped cream.

BUTTERMILK RANCH DRESSING

Yield:
8 fl oz (240 ml)

INGREDIENTS	U.S.	METRIC
Mayonnaise	2 fl oz	60 mL
Sour cream	2 fl oz	60 mL
Granulated onion	1 tsp	5 mL
Granulated garlic	1 tsp	5 mL
Finely ground white pepper	pinch	pinch
Sweet paprika	pinch	pinch
Dried thyme	pinch	pinch
Dried powdered sage	pinch	pinch
Celery seeds	¼ tsp	1 mL
Cider vinegar	2 tbsp	30 mL
Sugar	1 tbsp	15 mL
Worcestershire sauce	dash	dash
Hot pepper sauce	dash	dash
Minced scallion	2 tbsp	30 mL
Buttermilk	3 fl oz	90 mL
Kosher salt	to taste	to taste

PROCEDURE

PREPARATION

1. Whisk together the mayonnaise, sour cream, granulated onion and garlic, pepper, paprika, thyme, sage, celery seeds, vinegar, sugar, Worcestershire sauce, hot pepper sauce, and scallion.
2. Whisk in the buttermilk and correct the salt.

HOLDING

Refrigerated in a freshly sanitized, covered plastic container up to 5 days.

SWEET YOGURT DRESSING FOR FRUIT SALAD

Yield:
8 fl oz (240 ml)

INGREDIENTS	U.S.	METRIC
Plain whole-milk yogurt	7 fl oz	210 mL
Honey	1 fl oz	30 mL
Minced lemon zest	1 tbsp	15 mL
Poppy seeds	1 tsp	5 mL
Pure vanilla extract	1 tsp	5 mL
Fresh lemon juice	to taste	to taste

PROCEDURE

PREPARATION

1. Mix the ingredients together using a whip.
2. Taste and correct the seasoning, adding more honey and/or lemon juice as desired.

HOLDING

Refrigerate in a freshly sanitized, covered container up to 5 days.

OLD-FASHIONED BOILED DRESSING

Yield:
about 10 fl oz (300 mL)

INGREDIENTS	U.S.	METRIC
Half-and-half	6 fl oz	180 mL
Egg yolks	2	2
Cornstarch	2 tsp	10 mL
Kosher salt	2 tsp	10 mL
Sugar	2 tsp	10 mL
Dry mustard	1 tsp	5 mL
Finely ground white pepper	¼ tsp	1 mL
Cider vinegar	2 fl oz	60 mL
Unsalted butter	1 tbsp	15 mL

PROCEDURE

PREPARATION

1. Prepare a hot bain-marie and an ice bain-marie.
2. Scald the half-and-half and hold hot.
3. Whisk together the yolks, cornstarch, salt, sugar, mustard, pepper, and vinegar. Whisk in the hot half-and-half.
4. Place the bowl over simmering water in the hot bain-marie and whisk until thick.
5. Taste and correct the seasonings, and then whisk in the butter.
6. Transfer the bowl to the ice bain-marie and cool to room temperature, whisking occasionally.

HOLDING

Refrigerate in a freshly sanitized, covered container up to 5 days.

TZATZIKI SAUCE

APPETIZER

Yield:
8 fl oz (240 ml)

INGREDIENTS	U.S.	METRIC
English or Kirby cucumber	6 oz	180 g
Salt	to taste	to taste
Fresh lemon juice	½ fl oz	15 mL
Light, golden olive oil	1 fl oz	30 mL
Thick whole-milk yogurt	6 fl oz	180 mL
Minced very fresh garlic	½ oz	15 g
Chopped fresh dill	½ oz	15 g
Finely ground white pepper	pinch	pinch

PROCEDURE

PREPARATION

1. Trim and peel the cucumber. Use a spoon to scrape out and discard the seeds.
2. Grate the cucumber into a strainer and press on it to remove as much liquid as possible.
3. Mix the cucumber with some salt and allow to stand at room temperature about 15 minutes.
4. Combine the lemon juice and olive oil in a small bowl. Whisk in the yogurt a little at a time. Add the garlic and dill.
5. Squeeze the cucumber in your hand to remove the remaining liquid. Add it to the yogurt mixture and stir to combine.
6. Taste and correct the salt. Season with pepper.
7. Place the tzatziki in the refrigerator and allow to mellow for at least 30 minutes.
8. Taste and correct the seasoning again, adding lemon juice and/or salt as needed.

HOLDING

Refrigerate in a nonreactive, covered container up to 24 hours.

COLD SAUCES MADE FROM VEGETABLES AND FRUITS

Sauces made from fruits and vegetables were not commonly featured on formal menus until the end of the twentieth century. The growing interest in world cuisines as well as the demand for lighter, lower-calorie dishes now make salsas, relishes, chutneys, and vegetable and fruit purées important elements in the garde manger repertoire. Because they are primarily used as condiments, relishes and chutneys are covered in Chapter 17.

Salsas

Salsa is one of the most popular and widely used cold sauces in North America. Salsa accompanies Mexican and Mexican-American dishes and is an ingredient in many standard sandwiches, sauces, dips, and appetizers. Modern Caribbean cuisine features salsas made from mangos, pineapples, guavas, and many other tropical fruits. Southwestern cuisine includes salsa combinations such as black beans and corn, and roasted peppers and nopal cactus.

Bottled salsas, called ***cooked salsas***, are typically made from tomatoes, onions, garlic, and various types of chiles, as well as natural and artificial thickeners, stabilizers, and preservatives. ***Salsa fresca***, or ***fresh salsa,*** is made from tomatoes or other soft, juicy vegetables or fruits that have not been cooked, other than sometimes a brief blanching in order to remove the skins. Ingredients fabricated into small dice and simply tossed together are correctly called a fresh, or uncooked, relish. When traditional salsa ingredients are prepared this way, the sauce is called ***pico de gallo*** [PEE-koh day GAH-yoh]. A traditional salsa made from firm, ripe avocadoes is ***guacamole*** [gwa-kah-MOH-lay] (covered in Chapter 4).

The main ingredient (tomatoes, or another fruit or vegetable) of a fresh salsa is flavored with aromatic vegetables such as onions or scallions and sometimes a hint of garlic. Fresh chiles give heat, while fresh herbs add a bright flavor. Citrus juice is added if needed.

Ideally, fresh salsas are made by grinding chopped vegetables together in a mortar into a rough but pourable purée. A sturdy bowl and potato masher or mallet can also be used. Pulsing chopped vegetables in a food processor is useful for making large quantities, but avoid rapid processing, which incorporates too much air and creates an unpleasant, frothy texture. Blenders should not be used.

Fresh salsas do not hold well because the vegetables and fruits in them are perishable and can become limp and watery in a short time. The raw onion and garlic in the mixture oxidize quickly, and can taste old after only a few hours. Thus, salsas should be made in small quantities and prepared at the last possible moment.

Procedure for Making Fresh Salsa

1. Place chopped chiles, onions, and other aromatic vegetables in a mortar or heavy bowl and add approximately half of the salt.
2. Using a pestle, potato masher, or mallet, pound the aromatics into a rough paste (A).
3. Add the tomatoes (or other main ingredient vegetable or fruit) to the aromatics paste, and pound or grind into a rough purée (B).
4. Taste and correct the salt.
5. Balance the acidity with citrus juice, if needed.
6. Stir in chopped fresh herbs (C).

A

B

C

Vegetable and Fruit Purées

Many vegetables and fruits can be puréed to a saucelike consistency by grinding them into a pulp. This pulp is then usually strained through a sieve or food mill for smoothness. This is called puréeing, and the resulting product is a ***purée***.

The term *purée* can also be applied to smooth mixtures of foods of varying thickness other than vegetables and fruits. A puréed sauce made from a vegetable or fruit is more specifically called a ***coulis*** [koo-LEE].

Coulis

Many soft-textured fruits, such as ripe berries, peaches, and mangos, are soft enough to be ground into a purée without cooking. Fruit skins are usually removed before the fruit is ground. Blanching and refreshing (p. 96) and roasting or charring (p. 109) are the most common techniques for loosening the skin.

A coulis can be used as an ingredient in a more complex preparation, but it is frequently used as a sauce in its own right. A fruit coulis can be sweetened with sugar or enhanced with a spirit or liqueur. A vegetable coulis used as a sauce is lightly seasoned with salt and may be flavored with aromatic vegetables such as shallots, garlic, or ginger. A savory coulis may be enhanced with an acidic ingredient such as vinegar or citrus juice, or enriched with a flavorful oil.

Commercial Frozen Fruit and Vegetable Purées

One of the drawbacks of fruit and vegetable coulis is the labor involved in preparing them. Peeling, seeding, puréeing, and straining these foods take time and attention. The inconsistency of fresh produce, particularly for fruits, is also problematic.

Today you can purchase high-quality, commercially prepared fruit and vegetable purées. They are available frozen, usually in half-liter jars and in 2-kilo tubs. Although costly, they keep for months in the freezer and minimize labor.

Procedure for Making Vegetable or Fruit Coulis

1. If necessary, skin the vegetable(s) or fruit by blanching and refreshing (p. 96), roasting or charring (p. 109), or paring.
2. Trim and discard cores, hulls, seeds, and unripe areas.
3. Chop the vegetable(s) or fruit into small pieces (A). (The smaller the pieces, the less air will be incorporated by the action of the blender or processor, resulting in a smoother, better-textured sauce.)
   a. Place the vegetable or fruit in a blender or food processor, and pulse until it becomes a smooth pulp (B). Do not overload the machine. Work in batches if necessary.
   b. Alternatively, place the vegetable or fruit in a small, nonreactive bowl and grind to a pulp with an immersion blender. Avoid incorporating air into the pulp.
4. Transfer the pulp to a food mill, strainer, or drum sieve set over a bowl. Strain the pulp by forcing it through the sieve (C).
5. If necessary, thin the purée to the desired texture.
6. Season the purée as desired.

A

B

C

Cooked Vegetable Purée Sauces

Firm vegetables cannot be made into a smooth purée when in their raw state. They must be cooked first to soften their fibers. Once cooked, they are puréed in the manner described on page 49. In fact, the preparation of cooked vegetable purée sauces is virtually identical to that of cold vegetable purée soups (see Chapter 8).

When preparing purées of green vegetables, it is important to preserve their attractive green color when you cook them. Green vegetables are typically blanched *à point* (p. 101) and refreshed in order to preserve their color. Orange and orange-red vegetables may be blanched or poached. Starchy vegetables, such as potatoes and winter squashes, are rarely used to make cold sauces because their thick texture and heavy mouthfeel are unpalatable when cold.

Cold purée sauces made from cooked vegetables are usually flavored with aromatic vegetables and enriched with flavorful oils. Because the appeal of these sauces lies in their freshness, it is best to make them in small quantities and serve them as quickly as possible.

RECIPES

FRESH TOMATO SALSA

APPETIZER

Yield:
8 fl oz (240 mL)

INGREDIENTS	U.S.	METRIC
Serrano chile, minced	⅛ oz	4 g
White onion, finely chopped	1 oz	30 g
Garlic, minced	⅛ oz	4 g
Salt	to taste	to taste
Vine-ripe tomato, chopped	6 oz	180 g
Chopped cilantro	1 tbsp	15 mL

PROCEDURE

PREPARATION

Follow the Procedure for Making Fresh Salsa on page 48.

HOLDING

Serve immediately, or refrigerate up to 8 hours.

(Variations on next page)

VARIATIONS

ORANGE-TOMATO SALSA
Add ¼ cup (60 mL) seeded, membrane-free orange segments and 1 tsp (5 mL) minced orange zest to vegetables and pound; continue with Fresh Tomato Salsa recipe.

PINEAPPLE SALSA
Substitute fresh pineapple pulp for the tomatoes.

MANGO SALSA
Substitute chopped ripe mango for the tomatoes. Balance the flavor with fresh lime juice to taste.

AVOCADO-TOMATO SALSA
Toss ½ cup (120 mL) diced firm-ripe avocado with kosher salt and lime juice; add to Fresh Tomato Salsa.

SWEET CORN SALSA
Add 3 oz (90 g) cooked fresh corn kernels after step 3 (see Procedure for Making Fresh Salsa, p. 48).

PICO DE GALLO
Toss Fresh Tomato Salsa ingredients together rather than pounding into a purée.

GREEN SALSA

APPETIZER

Yield:
8 fl oz (240 mL)

INGREDIENTS	U.S.	METRIC
Tomatillo, husked and washed	5 oz	150 g
Serrano chile, minced	½ oz	15 g
White onion, chopped	2 oz	60 g
Minced garlic	1 tsp	5 mL
Salt	to taste	to taste
Tomatillo, husked, washed, and chopped	1 oz	30 g
Chopped cilantro	1 tbsp	15 mL
Sugar	to taste	to taste

PROCEDURE

PREPARATION

1. Poach 5 oz (150 g) tomatillos in barely simmering water for 6–8 minutes until they are soft and olive-green in color. Refresh in ice water.
2. Drain the tomatillos well and purée them in a blender or food processor.
3. Place the chile, onion, garlic, and salt in a mortar or small stainless-steel bowl. Using a pestle or mallet, pound the vegetables until they are thoroughly mashed.
4. Add the chopped raw tomatillo and pound lightly to release the juices.
5. Stir in the puréed tomatillo and the cilantro.
6. Correct the salt and balance with sugar, if necessary.

HOLDING

Refrigerate in a freshly sanitized, covered container up to 3 days.

VARIATION

GREEN SALSA WITH AVOCADO
Add 3 oz (90 g) firm-ripe avocado cut in ⅜-inch (10-cm) dice.

BASIC TOMATO COULIS (SAUCE)

Yield:
about 1 pint (500 mL)

INGREDIENTS	U.S.	METRIC
Vine-ripe tomatoes	1¼ lb	600 g
Garlic	¼ oz	7 g
Shallots	½ oz	15 g
Olive oil	1 fl oz	30 mL
Salt	to taste	to taste

PROCEDURE

PREPARATION

1. Follow the Procedure for Making Vegetable or Fruit Coulis on page 49. Blanch and refresh the tomatoes to remove the skins.
2. Flavor the coulis with the juices of the garlic and shallot, pressed through a garlic press.
3. Whisk in the olive oil.
4. Season the coulis with salt.

HOLDING

Refrigerate in a covered, nonreactive container up to 12 hours.

VARIATION

ROASTED TOMATO COULIS

Skin the tomatoes by charring them on a grill or under a broiler.

TAPENADE

APPETIZER

Yield:
8–10 fl oz (240 mL), 10–12 ounces (300 g)

INGREDIENTS	U.S.	METRIC
Pitted European black olives, preferably Niçoise	4 oz	120 g
Drained capers in brine	2 oz	60 g
Drained, best-quality oil-packed anchovies	1½ oz	75 g
Young garlic, optional	½ oz	15 g
Extra-virgin olive oil, preferably artisan	4–6 fl oz	120–180 mL

PROCEDURE

PREPARATION

1. Place the olives, caper, anchovies, and (optional) garlic in a small food processor, and pulse to a coarse purée.
2. Pulse in the oil through the feed tube, adding just enough to achieve the desired consistency: less oil for a spreadable paste, more for a sauce.

HOLDING

Store in a freshly sanitized, nonreactive container at cool room temperature up to 3 hours. Refrigerate up to 7 days. Bring to cool room temperature before serving.

RED PLUM COULIS

Yield:
about16 fl oz (500 mL)

INGREDIENTS	U.S.	METRIC
Sugar	4 oz	120 g
Water	4 fl oz	120 mL
Ripe, red-flesh plums	1 lb	0.5 kg
Fresh lemon juice	to taste	to taste

PROCEDURE

PREPARATION

1. Combine the sugar and water in a small saucepan and bring to a boil. Cool to room temperature.
2. Blanch, refresh, and skin the plums using the procedure on page 96.
3. Cut the plums into quarters. Remove and discard the pits.
4. Place the plums in a food processor fitted with the steel blade. Pulse the machine to chop the plums, and then run the machine briefly to grind them into a smooth purée to a pourable consistency.
5. Transfer the plum purée to a bowl. Stir in enough sugar syrup to sweeten and thin the purée to a pourable consistency.
6. Balance the flavor with lemon juice.

HOLDING

Refrigerate in a covered container or squeeze bottle up to 24 hours.

VARIATIONS

GOLDEN PLUM COULIS

Replace the red-flesh plums with yellow-flesh plums.

PEACH OR NECTARINE COULIS

Replace the plums with ripe peaches or nectarines.

SPICY MANGO SAUCE

Yield:
about 8 fl oz (240 mL)

INGREDIENTS	U.S.	METRIC
Ripe mango (12 ct.)	1	1
-or-		
Frozen mango purée, thawed	5 fl oz	150 mL
White part of scallions, chopped	½ oz	15 g
Seeded, minced Scotch bonnet chile	1 tsp	5 mL
Salt	to taste	to taste
Water	2 fl oz	60 mL
Sugar	to taste	to taste
Fresh lemon juice	to taste	to taste

PROCEDURE

PREPARATION

1. Pit and skin the mango and cut it into ½-in. (1.5-cm) dice.
2. Place the mango, scallions, chile, and a little salt in a blender and purée, adding just enough water to loosen the blades.
3. Taste and correct the flavor balance. (If the mango is very tart, add sugar, and then balance the salt; if the mango is sweet, add lemon juice, and then balance the salt.)

HOLDING

Refrigerate in a covered, nonreactive container up to 8 hours, or freeze up to 2 weeks.

RED BELL PEPPER PURÉE

Yield: *about 1 pint (½ L)*

INGREDIENTS	U.S.	METRIC
Red bell peppers	2 lb	1 kg
Fresh lemon juice	as needed	as needed
Light golden olive oil	2 fl oz	60 mL
Salt	to taste	to taste
Water or an appropriate stock	as needed	as needed
Vinegar of choice (optional)	as needed	as needed

PROCEDURE

PREPARATION

1. Roast the peppers directly over a gas flame or on a grill until the skin is blackened all over. Immediately wrap the peppers in foil and allow them to steam in their own heat until cooled to room temperature.
2. Scrape all of the blackened skin off of the peppers. Do not wash them. Remove the stem, seeds, and membranes.
3. Place the pepper flesh in a blender with some lemon juice, the oil, and a little salt. Purée the pepper flesh until smooth.
4. Transfer the purée to a nonreactive container.
5. If necessary, thin the purée to the desired consistency with water or stock.
6. Taste and correct the seasoning, adding additional lemon juice or optional vinegar as needed.

HOLDING

Refrigerate in a freshly sanitized, nonreactive, covered container up to 3 days.

VARIATIONS

ROBUST ITALIAN RED BELL PEPPER PURÉE

Replace the light olive oil with dark-green extra-virgin olive oil; add the juice pressed from ¼ oz (7 g) garlic.

CREAMY RED BELL PEPPER PURÉE

Thin the purée with half-and-half instead of water or stock. Omit the additional vinegar.

TERMS FOR REVIEW

sauce
dressing
emulsion
temporary emulsion
unstable emulsion
permanent emulsion
stable emulsion
vinaigrette
mycoderma aceti
acetous fermentation
acetic acid
virgin olive oil
extra-virgin olive oil
rancid
dispersed phase
continuous phase
emulsified vinaigrette
broken
polar
surface tension
stabilizer
emulsifier
casein
mellowing period
break
broken vinaigrette
nappé
neutral mayonnaise
ribbon
caught emulsion
tight mayonnaise
lecithin
failed mayonnaise
broken mayonnaise
cooked salsa
salsa fresca/fresh salsa
pico de gallo
guacamole
purée
coulis

QUESTIONS FOR DISCUSSION

1. Explain why vinegar and oil don't easily mix together.
2. Define the term *emulsion*, and explain how you would create an emulsion when making a vinaigrette.
3. What is a cold emulsion sauce? Why is this term inaccurate? Explain the temperature requirements for making a successful vinaigrette or mayonnaise.
4. List the procedure steps for the traditional vinaigrette mixing method and for the blender/processor method.
5. Name the two basic emulsifiers and, for each, list two ingredients in which they are found.
6. What is the traditional ratio of vinegar to oil in a vinaigrette? How has this changed, and why?
7. Name three basic types of acid ingredients you might use in a vinaigrette, and suggest a complementary oil for each.
8. Name and define the three basic grades of olive oil identified by the IOOC. Explain the difference between a commercially produced olive oil and an artisan oil.
9. Explain the factors you would take into consideration when balancing the vinegar-oil ratio and the seasonings in a vinaigrette.
10. Why is mayonnaise considered the mother sauce of garde manger work?
11. List and explain three food safety guidelines that must be followed when preparing house-made mayonnaise.
12. Describe a tight mayonnaise, and explain what went wrong to make it tight.
13. Explain how to achieve a very thick mayonnaise and describe its uses; explain how to achieve a nappé mayonnaise and describe its uses.
14. List two reasons why a mayonnaise might fail; list two reasons why a mayonnaise might break.
15. List and explain three methods for repairing a failed or broken mayonnaise.
16. List and describe five classic mayonnaise sauces.
17. List and describe five modern North American sauces, dressings, or dips derived from mayonnaise.
18. List and describe two North American dairy-based sauces.
19. Compare and contrast the preparation of the two basic types of salsa.
20. Compare and contrast the preparation of coulis and cooked vegetable purée sauces. Include the various ways in which the vegetables are fabricated and cooked.

Chapter

3

PREREQUISITES

Before reading this chapter, you should already

- Have read "How to Use This Book," pages xxviii–xxxiii, and understand the professional recipe format.
- Know basic sanitation procedures for products served raw.
- Know state and local regulations for food-service glove use.

Simple Salads and Tossed Salads

Salads made from leafy greens are among today's most popular foods. Salad greens were once considered a seasonal item because they were available for a short time only in the spring and then again in the cool early fall months. Now most salad greens can be enjoyed year round. Yet each type of green still has its optimal season, or time of year, when it is most readily available. In its season you will find the flavor and texture of that particular salad green is at its best. Garde manger chefs can emphasize the seasonal nature of greens by creating light, delicate salads in the springtime, featuring colorful, robust salads in the summer, and offering rustic combinations of sturdy greens in fall and winter.

Everyone knows that salads are healthful. In addition to providing high amounts of vitamins and minerals, salad greens provide a wealth of the essential dietary fiber lacking in many modern diets. If tossed with vinaigrette dressing, salads contribute additional vitamins from the vinaigrette's acid component as well as the healthful nutrients found in vegetable oils. Green salads are a favorite of health-conscious customers, people on weight-loss regimens, and anyone who prefers to eat lightly.

After reading this chapter, you should be able to

1. Explain the differences between simple salads and tossed salads.
2. List the five salad greens flavor groups and identify the greens that belong to each.
3. Discuss the advantages and disadvantages of the market forms in which salad greens are available.
4. Recognize signs of quality in salad greens.
5. Properly store, clean, and fabricate salad greens.
6. Prepare salads using à la carte, tableside, family-style, and banquet procedures.
7. Create salads that are attractive, well balanced, and seasonal.

Mixed Green Salad with Classic French Vinaigrette, a simple salad

Salads in History

Both the composition of salads and their place in cuisine have changed significantly through the centuries. Medieval and Renaissance diners enjoyed simple green salads as accompaniments to large joints of roasted beef and game. By the time of John Evelyn's *Acetaria: A Discourse on Sallets* (1699), which advised dressing greens with Lucca olive oil, vinegar infused with flowers and herbs, and crystalline sea salt, salads were virtually identical to many served today. By that time, however, they had fallen out of favor with the English upper classes.

Not so in the American colonies. Thomas Jefferson's diaries record his growing numerous native and European salad greens and serving them dressed with imported oils and vinegars. Salads never lost favor with the French. Then and now, in France no serious meal is considered complete without a vinaigrette salad served after the main course.

In the 1920s, Californians began serving green salads as appetizers. Also at that time, Americans started tossing green salads with mayonnaise-based dressings. Today green salads are served as appetizers, side dishes, and even entrées. No matter how served, a green salad is always appreciated.

SALADS MADE FROM LEAFY GREENS

One reason for the popularity of salads is that there are so many kinds. In this chapter we focus on salads made primarily from leafy greens. Other, more complicated salads made from raw and cooked vegetables, fruits, grains, legumes, or various protein foods are classified as ***complex salads***. These are covered in Chapter 5.

Simple Salads

A salad of leafy greens tossed with a vinaigrette dressing and having few or no garnishes is known as a ***simple salad***. In formal European dining, simple salads are served after the main course in order to refresh the palate. In more casual meals they are also served as side dishes, frequently accompanying grilled or roasted meats. In American dining, simple salads may be served as appetizers. However, when lots of garnishes are added to a leafy greens salad, or when dressings other than vinaigrettes are used on it, we can no longer correctly call it a *simple* salad.

The dividing line between a simple salad and a complex salad is a bit subjective. Some chefs believe adding a cherry tomato or a few toasted nuts to a green salad places it in the realm of a complex salad. Others tolerate a few garnishes on a green salad and still call it a simple salad. However, most agree that a green salad tossed with a creamy or mayonnaise-based dressing is not a classic simple salad. Nor is a green salad topped or tossed with numerous vegetable garnishes correctly called a simple salad even if it is dressed only with vinaigrette. For these types of salad, Americans have created a different name: the tossed salad.

Steakhouse Tossed Salad with Buttermilk Ranch Dressing, a tossed salad

Tossed Salads

A green salad mixed or topped with a variety of brightly colored vegetable garnishes, typically served with the diner's choice of dressing, is known as a ***tossed salad***. As an alternative to vinaigrette-type dressings, a tossed salad may be served with a dairy- or mayonnaise-based dressing. Tossed salads function as a light starter to be eaten before a substantial main course. Served in large portions, a tossed salad is sometimes called a *dinner salad* and served as a light entrée.

SALAD INGREDIENTS

The term *greens* does not accurately describe all salad options available. From magenta radicchio to ivory-colored Belgian endive, today's salad greens come in many colors, enabling the garde manger chef to create attractive simple salads without resorting to bright-colored garnishes. Adding to variety, leaf shapes range from tiny, spoon-shaped mâche leaves to ruffled lolla rossa to spiky frisée. Textures are even more varied. Chefs can choose from soft and tender butter lettuces, crunchy head lettuces, crinkly spinach, delicate micro greens, and firm chicories. Finally, each salad green has its own unique taste.

Salad Greens: The Five Flavor Groups

Chefs often group vegetables by their botanical genus and species name. For instance, the term *brassica* is used to group some greens of the cabbage/mustard family. Usually, though, it's more helpful for chefs to categorize salad greens according to similarities in taste, texture, and appearance. Because taste is subjective and traditions vary, it is likely you will find some greens categorized differently by different chefs. The following lists will be helpful when choosing and combining leafy greens to make tasty and interesting salads.

Lettuces

Loose-leaf lettuce appears as large bunches of broad, ribbed leaves with ruffled edges. Its flavor ranges from mild to bland depending on its source, and it has a delicate texture that wilts easily. It is available in green-leaf and red-leaf varieties.

Oak-leaf lettuce consists of small bunches of slender, delicate leaves with a distinctive oak-leaf shape. Its mild flavor is pleasantly fresh and slightly herbal. Standard oak leaf is pastel green, while red oak leaf has russet to burgundy leaf tips.

Romaine or **cos** has large, elongated bunches of loosely formed heads with large, deep-green leaves and large pale-green ribs. Romaine is full-flavored, crunchy, sturdy, and long-keeping. Romaine hearts are the heads stripped of the outer leaves, leaving only the pale inner leaves; these are usually sold in a three-pack.

Boston lettuce comes in medium- to large-sized round heads with delicate, cupped leaves. It ranges from bright green outside to pale green in the middle to ivory-yellow at the heart. It is quite perishable. Boston lettuce's soft texture and mild, buttery flavor are best enhanced with thin, light dressings.

Bibb lettuce or **limestone lettuce** has small to very small heads with flared or cupped leaves fading from dark green at the tips to creamy white at the base and forming a tight, creamy-white heart. Bibb is delicate in texture and quite perishable. It has a mild, subtle flavor.

Lolla rossa

Lolla rossa comes in small, loose heads of ruffled leaves that are pale green at the base and deep burgundy-red at the tips. It has a moderately sturdy texture, a fluffy mouthfeel, and a delicate flavor.

Mâche [MAHSH] is also called *lamb's lettuce, lamb's tongue, field lettuce,* and *corn salad*. It consists of small, delicate deep-green oval leaves on slender stems. It has a very tender texture and a delicate, nutty flavor.

The History of Iceberg Lettuce—Tossed, Shredded, and Wedged

In the 1920s, American horticulturalists developed a type of lettuce that could withstand unrefrigerated rail shipping from the West Coast to the East. These sturdy, round heads of crisp-textured, bland-flavored lettuce were named *Iceberg*, possibly because of their rock-hard texture or because they were packed in crushed ice for the trip. By the 1950s, most Americans considered Iceberg to be *the* lettuce. In fact, many Americans were unaware that any other kind of salad green existed. Iceberg lettuce's round shape inspired some anonymous pantry cook to cut it into wedges, like a cabbage, and serve it on a plate drizzled with a thick, mayonnaise-based dressing. This "Wedge of Iceberg" salad was a prominent feature of the American dining scene well into the 1960s, and it is still found on some deliberately old-fashioned, or "retro," menus.

Iceberg is the generic name for commercially grown crisp-head lettuce. These large, firm heads have crisp, cupped leaves largely composed of water. Its crunchy texture is its best attribute; its high water content and the large-scale commercial conditions under which it is grown result in a flavor that ranges from bland to tasteless.

Spinach and Beet Greens

Curly spinach has dark-green, deeply crinkled leaves with large veins and coarse stems; both veins and stems must be removed before eating. The crevices in spinach leaves capture dirt, so careful washing is necessary. The unique texture gives spinach a fluffy mouthfeel without crispness.

Curly spinach

Flat-leaf spinach is similar to curly spinach, but without the crinkles. It is easier to clean than curly spinach, but lacks its mouthfeel.

Flat-leaf spinach
© iStockphoto.

Baby spinach consists of small, delicate, rounded leaves; its short, tender stems need not be removed. It has a mild flavor. It is usually sold prewashed and dried; the higher cost is offset by its resulting ease of preparation.

Baby Swiss chard has small, slightly ruffled leaves, and is available in both dark green and vivid red. It is noted for its earthy flavor. It is usually sold prewashed and dried.

Baby beet greens are instantly recognizable as small, pointed, dark-green leaves with bright-red stems and veins. They have an earthy flavor that is an acquired taste. Highly perishable, they are among the first greens to deteriorate.

Baby beet greens
© iStockphoto.

Brassicas

Baby kale consists of small, slightly elongated deep-green leaves with a little ruffle at the tips. It has a sturdy texture and mild cabbage flavor.

Baby collards have small, rounded medium-green leaves. They have a sturdy texture and a sweet, mildly cabbage-like flavor.

Tatsoi [taht-SOY] has small, rounded and cupped, deep-green leaves with white stems and veins. It has a delicate, slightly crisp texture with a warm flavor and a slight peppery bite.

Cabbages of full size are rarely used in fine dining salads. However, fine-shredded European and Asian cabbages can be added to casual salad mixtures. Red cabbage is often included in green salads for color.

Spicy Greens

Watercress has small to tiny rounded, dark-green leaves on prominent stems. Its leaf texture is delicate, but the stems are crunchy. Large stems tend to be tough and should be trimmed. Watercress has a cool, peppery flavor. Wild cress can be very sharp in flavor; cultivated watercress is grown in flooded man-made beds and is milder in taste.

Garden cress is sometimes called *upland cress* or *field cress*. It is grown on dry land and has larger leaves than watercress, with a milder flavor.

Arugula [ah-ROO-goo-lah] (also *rugula, rocket, roquette*) has elongated leaves with a sculpted, oak-leaf shape emerging from tough, prominent stems. Dark green in color, it has a pungent, "hot," spicy flavor. Rarely used alone, it adds a powerful punch when combined with other greens. Take care when cleaning, as it can be sandy.

Mizuna [mee-ZOO-nah] (technically *mini-mizuna* or *Japanese mini-mustard*) is distinctive in appearance, with tiny, jagged dark-green leaves on prominent stems. It has a peppery, mustardy flavor and a fluffy mouthfeel.

Baby mustard greens are small, dark-green, rounded leaves with a warm, spicy-bitter flavor and delicate texture.

Baby turnip greens are similar to baby mustard greens, but they have earthy flavor overtones.

Bitter Greens

Curly endive is also called *chicory*. It consists of elongated bunches of long, narrow leaves that are ruffled at the pointed tips. The outside leaves are dark green with white veins. Inside, the leaves form an ivory-colored core. The texture ranges from sturdy to tough, while flavor ranges from slight bitterness in young specimens to considerable bitterness when overgrown.

Frisée [free-ZAY] is a variety of curly endive. The low, compact bunches have delicate, feathery, pointed leaves. Good-quality specimens are almost completely ivory in color, with a slight greening on the outside leaves. Frisée has a mildly bitter flavor and a ruffled texture.

Belgian endive [awn-DEEV] is also called *witloof chicory*. Its small, bullet-shaped heads have smooth, crunchy, pointed leaves. Heads of good quality have ivory leaves with only slight yellowing at the tips. Green tips are a sign of improper growing practices. Belgian endive has a sophisticated, mildly bitter flavor.

Escarole [ESS-ka-roll] appears as large, elongated bunches of broad, thick, ruffled leaves. The exterior leaves are pale green with prominent, pale ivory ribs, while the interior leaves are pale ivory to yellowish-white. Escarole has a sturdy to tough texture and a bitter flavor.

Radicchio [rah-DEE-kee-oh] is unmistakable, appearing as small to medium-size rounded heads of magenta leaves with prominent creamy-white veins. Radicchio has a sturdy texture and mildly bitter chicory flavor.

Treviso [tray-VEE-so] has pigmentation similar to radicchio, but the head is like a small, flared romaine. Its color is slightly more brownish-magenta than radicchio, and sometimes shows freckling. Both its texture and flavor are similar to radicchio.

Dandelion greens have elongated, medium-green leaves with jagged, notched edges. The original French name, *dent de lion* [dahn duh lee-OHN], or "lion's tooth," comes from its leaf shape. Wild dandelion must be harvested young and small, while its distinctive, bitter flavor is still palatable. Cultivated dandelion is larger and milder in flavor.

Dandelion greens
© iStockphoto.

Sprouts
© *iStockphoto.*

Immature Salad Greens

In addition to traditional salad greens, today's garde manger chefs make use of new forms of salad greens and vegetables that have come into wide availability only in the last few years.

> ***Sprouts*** are the first shoots produced from a plant seed. They are harvested before any true leaves have formed. Sprouts from virtually any vegetable plant are edible, and all are packed with nutrients. Mung bean or soy sprouts are used in Asian cooking and salads, while mild alfalfa sprouts and peppery radish and mustard sprouts are often added to contemporary salads.
>
> ***Micro greens*** consist of the stem and the first true leaves that form after a plant has sprouted. Micro greens have a lacy texture and a flavor reminiscent of the mature plant, but much more delicate. They may be harvested from lettuces and herb plants as well as from other vegetable plants, such as corn shoots and pea shoots.
>
> ***Baby greens*** are the young, immature leaves of standard lettuces and other salad greens. While they are usually blended into prepared salad mixes, baby greens are also available packaged individually. Many vegetables, such as cabbages and turnip greens, are marketed as salad greens in their "baby" form only but are used as cooking vegetables when fully mature.

Greens Mixes

Proprietary greens mixes, or brand-name mixtures of salad greens, are now widely available in many forms. These are called "proprietary" because each producer has its own blend. Perhaps the best known is a mixture called ***mesclun*** [MEHZ-klun], a mixture of baby lettuces, young arugula, and immature red chicory that originated in Provence, a region of southern France. Mesclun marketed in North America may even include such nontraditional greens as mini-mizuna or baby bok choy.

Another popular greens blend is called ***spring mix***. This blend can contain virtually any baby green or specialty green, depending on the formula used by the producer.

Most greens mixes are sold prewashed and dried, ready for immediate use.

Fresh Herbs and Edible Flowers

The leaves of fresh herbs add a pronounced flavor accent to salad greens. The choice of herb to add to a salad depends on the flavors of the other greens as well as the seasoning of the vinaigrette. Fresh herbs for salads may be gently torn into little pieces or cut into chiffonnade. Tiny herb leaves, called ***pluches*** [PLOOSH], may be added whole.

The petals of ***edible flowers*** are a wonderful addition to simple salads, adding attractive bursts of color and, in many cases, a distinctive and unusual flavor. Brightly colored pansy petals, delicate miniature orchids, and peppery nasturtium blossoms are popular edible flowers. Herb flowers lend an attractive appearance as well as a hint of herbal flavor. If the flowers are meant to be eaten as part of the salad (as opposed to being used as a garnish), they are usually pulled apart into petals and the interior organs discarded. Care must be taken to acquire flowers raised specifically as food items to avoid the risk of contamination by herbicides and pesticides.

Edible flowers
© *iStockphoto.*

PURCHASING SALAD GREENS

Salad greens are produced in several ways. Each production type has advantages and disadvantages. The informed chef chooses the type that suits the demands of both the operation and the season.

Market Forms

Conventionally Grown Greens

By far the best way to obtain salad greens is to purchase them in their natural season directly from a local truck farmer or specialty grower. Greens eaten only hours after harvest have superior flavor and texture, and they contain almost their entire original nutrient content. Such greens have a distinct local flavor derived from the particular qualities of the area's soil and climate. Small growers often choose to plant more exotic and flavorful varieties than do large commercial growers. Such greens are quite perishable. Be sure to refrigerate these greens as soon as they arrive.

Commercially grown greens may be raised in open fields or under cover in hoop houses. They are comparatively low in cost, consistent in quality, and available virtually year-round. Commercially grown greens are rapid-cooled after picking and typically last longer than local greens.

Organic salad greens are grown by methods that comply with the U.S. Department of Agriculture (USDA) guidelines for organic produce (p. 78). They are grown without the use of chemical fertilizers, herbicides, and pesticides, and their seeds have not been genetically modified. The effects of chemicals used in growing salad greens are direct and potentially dangerous to human health. For this reason, many customers prefer salads made with organic greens.

Hydroponic Greens

Hydroponics is the practice of growing plants in water-based nutrient solutions, normally in climate-controlled greenhouses. Hydroponic systems allow growers to raise and harvest delicate food plants throughout the entire year. Salad greens thrive under hydroponic growing conditions. However, many chefs believe they lack flavor. Most hydroponic lettuces are sold in "living" form.

"Living" Greens

Salad greens and herbs sold with their roots intact are marketed as ***"living" greens***. These are packaged with their root ball submerged in a shallow well of water. A few specialty producers market herbs and baby greens in flats of soil, ready for the chef to harvest with scissors. The big advantage of such greens is their freshness. If rooted lettuces are stored in a few inches of fresh water, they will keep for many days or even weeks, in some instances. The disadvantages of these products are their high cost, the storage space they require, and, in the case of hydroponic living greens, the environmental impact of their packaging.

Precleaned, Prefabricated Greens

Increasingly popular with consumers and food-service operations alike, packages of pre-cleaned and cut salad greens save a lot of labor. However, due to

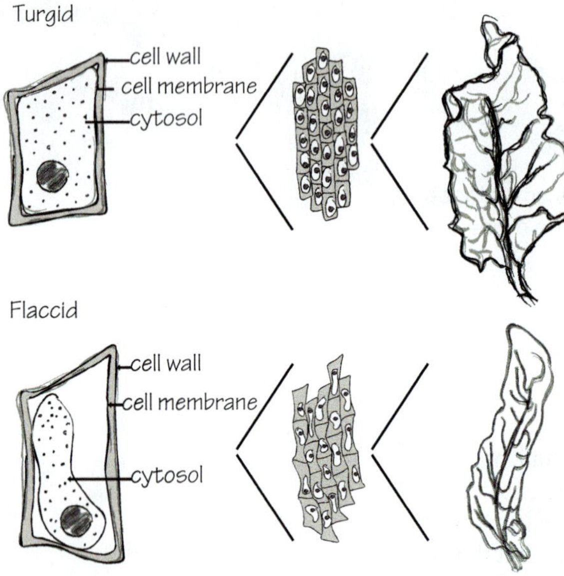

Vegetable cells, turgid and flaccid

intensive handling, they are more perishable than fresh conventional greens. Further, they can pose health risks from bacterial and viral contamination. In recent years, several outbreaks of food-borne illness have been traced to pre-cleaned greens. Finally, certain customers may have allergic reactions to the antioxidants often used on pre-cleaned greens.

Packaged, pre-cleaned, and prefabricated greens must be strictly rotated, used quickly, and carefully inspected for wilting and spoilage. The time involved in picking through such mixes can be more labor-intensive than washing and fabricating conventional greens.

Quality Evaluation of Salad Greens

The most important quality to look for in any type of salad green is freshness. A perfectly fresh salad green is ***turgid*** (the opposite of flaccid, or wilted; see illustration and photo at left). In other words, its cells are full of water. Its leaves stand upright when the bunch is picked up, and each leaf breaks cleanly when pulled apart. The leaf edges show no signs of softening, flattening, or disintegration. A fresh salad green is vividly colored and has no bruising or brown discoloration, called ***rust***, where it was cut at harvest. Lettuce heads should be firm and relatively heavy, indicating sufficient moisture content and proper maturity.

Wilted greens (left) and turgid greens (right)

Maturity is another quality factor. Avoid purchasing big, overgrown lettuce heads or long, spindly bunches of loose greens. Extreme overmaturity is a state described as ***bolted***, in which a lettuce or other type of green develops long, thick stems, grows tall, and has flattened or even inverted leaves. Such specimens are tough and have a strong, often bitter flavor.

CLEANING, FABRICATING, AND STORING SALAD GREENS

Salad greens are among the most perishable foods in the professional kitchen. Correct handling during fabrication is essential to minimize waste and ensure a quality product.

Storing Unprepped Salad Greens

Most salad greens must be stored between 38°F and 42°F (3°C and 6°C) and under conditions of moderate humidity. Very large food-service operations maintain separate refrigeration units specifically dedicated to salad greens and other leafy vegetables. However, most food-service operations just use the warmest spot in the walk-in (normally near the door and away from the compressor) to store salad greens.

It is best to keep commercially grown salad greens in their original containers as long as possible. These containers are manufactured for proper storage. Greens obtained from a farm or purchased loose are best stored in bus tubs, arranged in shallow layers and kept covered with damp kitchen towels. Living greens and stemmed greens keep longest if stored upright with their roots or freshly cut stem ends in a few inches of water and their tops covered with damp towels. Remove any rubber bands or twist-ties, as they cause bruising.

Before storing, also remove any visibly wilted or decaying leaves, which can cause further decay. With the exception of pre-cleaned, prefabricated products, salad greens should not be stored in sealed plastic bags because trapped moisture and respired gases can speed the deterioration of the greens.

Procedure for Cleaning Salad Greens

With the exception of commercially pre-cleaned products, all salad greens must be thoroughly washed, drained, and dried before they are consumed.

A

B

C

1. **Separating**
Remove the leaves from the core or the stems (A) and discard any unusable parts. Do not tear or cut the greens into pieces before washing, as the absorption of excess water leads to wilting and decay.

2. **Washing**
Thorough washing of salad greens is of the utmost importance. Consuming a mouthful of grit along with a bite of salad is an unpleasant experience. Washing also removes foreign matter such as insects and bits of packaging. The water used for washing salad greens may be treated with a commercial vegetable sanitizer, a product that kills a broad spectrum of food-borne pathogens and that may remove or neutralize pesticides and herbicides. Some operations treat salad greens with antioxidant solutions that prevent browning. These should be used in small and carefully measured quantities, as some people are allergic to these substances.

    - Completely submerge the greens in cold water. Gentle swishing or up-and-down agitation of the water (B) helps loosen and dislodge dirt particles, after which the water should be left undisturbed for a few minutes so the particles sink to the bottom. Curly spinach, arugula, and any other salad green that appears very dirty may need repeated washing in several changes of water.
    - Slightly wilted greens benefit from a longer soaking in water that has been chilled with the addition of ice. After 10 to 20 minutes, the cell walls will regain a measure of turgidity and the greens will crisp up. Drain the greens after about 20 minutes to prevent the leaves from becoming waterlogged.

3. **Draining**
Drain the salad greens without delay to prevent them from becoming waterlogged and to prevent loss of flavor and nutrients through leaching.

    - Lift the greens out of their washing water into a colander (C) or perforated pan rather than draining the sink. If the sink is drained while the greens are still in it, the greens will settle onto the bottom and become recontaminated with particles of dirt.
    - Do not pour the greens and the wash water into a colander. You will only pour the soil that has been removed back onto the greens.

4. **Drying**
Drying greens properly is essential for maintaining quality. Moisture remaining on greens has two destructive results. First, the greens become soft and soggy, and the decay process is

(continues)

(continued)

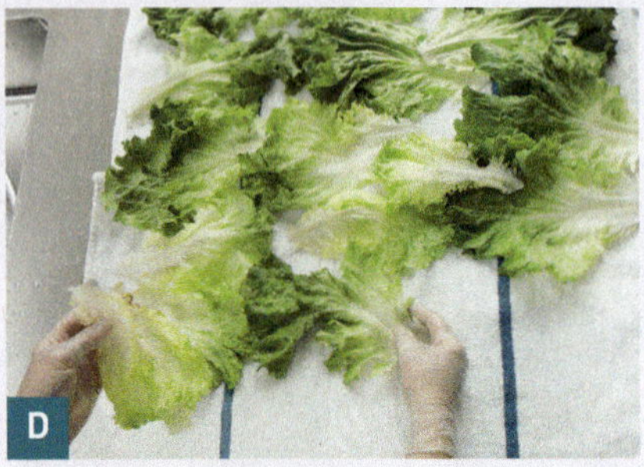

hastened. Second, the moisture prevents the dressing from properly adhering to the leaves. The outcome is a mess of bland, soggy greens sitting in a pool of watery, diluted dressing.

- A salad spinner is the most effective drying means. Electrically powered commercial spinners quickly and gently dry many pounds of greens at one time. Wet greens are placed in the central basket of the machine. The machine spins the basket at a rapid speed. The moisture is physically forced to the outside of the chamber and runs down into the bottom of the machine. Machine-dried greens can be stored for a day or two in perforated plastic bags.
- Instead of a commercial spinner, you can dry salad greens in kitchen linen after shaking them as dry as possible in a colander. Lay out clean, dry kitchen towels or aprons on a work surface, spread the greens in a single layer (D), and gently roll the greens in the towels (E). Place in a clean, dry bus tub or hotel pan and immediately refrigerate them. Within an hour or two, the linens will absorb excess moisture and the greens will be ready to serve.

Storing Prepped Salad Greens

Once salad greens are cleaned and dried, they should be used as quickly as possible. However, fresh, properly washed and dried sturdy greens will last several days in the refrigerator. If refrigerated for more than 24 hours, check for moisture. If still a little wet, rewrap in dry linen. Once the greens are nicely dry, transfer them to perforated plastic bags; they can usually be refrigerated in these bags for a few days longer.

Fabricating Salad Greens

Most greens must be fabricated into bite-sized pieces that are easy to eat using only a fork. If the central vein of a lettuce leaf is thick, discolored, or bitter, it may be removed during fabrication.

Fabricate greens as close to service time as possible. Once fabricated, the greens have more open surface area exposed to oxygen and moisture, and they decay more rapidly. Refrigerate fabricated greens in a freshly sanitized, thoroughly dried container covered with a damp towel. It is best to fabricate soft and delicate greens, such as Boston and Bibb lettuces, to order.

The two fabrication methods most commonly used for salad greens are tearing and cutting.

Tearing salad greens

Tearing

The classic method of reducing salad greens into bite-sized pieces is to tear the leaves. This must be accomplished without twisting, crushing, or bruising the leaves, and is somewhat time-consuming. In the past, cutting with old-fashioned carbon-steel knives discolored the leaves, which is the reason for the old rule never to cut salad greens. Today, tearing greens is still the preferred fabrication method in fine-dining restaurants, as it does the least damage to the cell structure of the leaves and gives salads a handcrafted appearance.

Cutting

For speed and efficiency, sturdy greens, such as iceberg and romaine, may be fabricated by cutting. Using a stainless-steel knife, you can quickly stack and cut the greens into bite-sized squares or shreds. Iceberg lettuce may be shredded on an automatic slicing machine.

Cutting salad greens

Misting greens with dressing in a spray bottle

FOUR METHODS OF PREPARING SIMPLE AND TOSSED SALADS

Simple salad preparation varies according to the service style used by the individual food-service operation.

À la Carte Salad Preparation

In fine-dining restaurants, simple salads are always prepared to order by placing the greens in a work bowl and tossing them with a light coating of the specified dressing. The goal in dressing salad greens is to coat each individual leaf with a light film of dressing, so each bite is perfectly balanced in flavor.

To maintain proper portion control, garde manger chefs must become skilled at estimating the proper amounts of both greens and dressing. For speed of preparation and good control of application, vinaigrettes and other dressings are typically kept in large squeeze bottles. To lightly coat whole, delicate leaves of lettuce for an arranged presentation, garde manger chefs occasionally put light, thin dressings into spray bottles and mist the greens with the dressing. While greens are being tossed with the dressing, small pieces of nonjuicy garnish ingredients are sometimes added and mixed in. Salads may be tossed and plated with a gloved hand or with tongs. They may be completed with the addition of a simple garnish.

a. To dress a salad à la carte, squeeze a small amount of dressing onto the greens.

b. Use a gloved hand or tongs to gently toss the greens with the dressing.

c. Mound the greens on the plate.

Measuring Portions for à la Carte Salads

Portion control is an essential skill for any food-service professional. In a well-run establishment there are strict portion control guidelines for all food products, including salad greens and dressings. For both accuracy and costing purposes, salad greens portions are correctly expressed in units of weight. However, for the garde manger chef making salads to order during a busy à la carte service, weighing each portion is simply not practical. Instead, chefs usually portion salad greens by eye, estimating the correct volume amount that equals the prescribed weight amount.

To accurately measure salad greens by eye, practice by weighing out the correct amount of various types of greens. Take note of the volume amount that represents the most commonly used weight of the greens used in your salads. Test yourself from time to time to make sure your estimates remain accurate.

Guidelines for Creating Superior Simple Salads

- **Simple salads require the best ingredients.** In addition to using the freshest greens, you must also search for the best and freshest garnishes and vinaigrette ingredients. The off-flavor of a low-grade vinegar or a slightly rancid oil might be hidden in a more complex salad, but such poor ingredients are instantly noticeable in a simple salad.
- **For each salad, choose greens and garnish items whose textures, flavors, and colors complement one another.** Delicate micro greens added to a winter salad based on hearty chicories would be overwhelmed in both flavor and texture. Adding julienne carrots to a radicchio salad would result in an unpleasant clash of colors. Adding Asian mung bean sprouts to a Provençal mesclun mix makes no sense in terms of ethnicity.
- **Match the texture and flavor of the dressing to the character of the greens.** Sturdier greens can stand up to rich, thick vinaigrettes, while delicate greens need a lighter, thinner dressing. For example, Belgian endive is excellent dressed with a thick mustard mayonnaise, while tender Boston lettuce is best with a lemon vinaigrette. Mild, subtly flavored greens do well with nonvinegar acid components and thus marry well with citrus or verjus vinaigrettes.
- **Combine greens, dressings, and garnishes with care and discretion.** Flavors may be compounded or contrasted. To compound flavors, the vinaigrette for a salad containing nutty-flavored mâche might contain walnut oil, and the salad could be garnished with toasted walnut pieces. To contrast flavors, imagine a slightly bitter radicchio salad dressed with a sweet port-wine vinaigrette and garnished with pear slices poached in port.
- **Enhance flavor with a little freshly ground pepper added at the last minute.** Fine-dining restaurants maintain the custom of sending a peppermill to the table when the salad course is served. Although black pepper is traditionally served, white pepper is an interesting alternative that works well with some greens.
- **Salads must be served on cool plates.** Because restaurant kitchens are often warm, most operations keep salad plates chilled during service. Chilled plates acquire a film of condensation when moved to the warm air, so be careful not to leave unsightly fingerprints in the condensation on the plate rims.
- **Plan your salad in the context of the meal in which it will be served.** A simple or tossed salad must complement the menu's cuisine style. If served as part of a set menu, the salad must connect the previous course to the one after it. It must not repeat the flavors or ingredients featured in the other courses. If wine is an important part of the meal, avoid a vinegar-based dressing; choose one based on mild citrus or verjus instead.

Tableside Salad Preparation

Although the practice is less popular today, tableside preparation of simple salads is a classic way to create excitement and present a high-quality product at the same time. In North America, tableside salad making is most commonly associated with the Caesar salad. However, in European restaurants the after-entrée salad is often presented in this manner. Greens, dressing ingredients, and garnishes are wheeled to the table on a ***gueridon*** [GEH-ree-don], or service cart. Guests may confer with the captain as to the type of oils, vinegars, and seasonings used in the dressing. The dressing is mixed in the bottom of an attractive wooden salad bowl, and the salad greens are tossed with the dressing before being plated, garnished, and served.

Family-Style Salad Preparation

Featured in casual restaurants that cater to large parties of guests, family-style salads are sent to the table in large bowls with the guests' chosen dressing in a cruet or service boat on the side. Guests serve and dress their own salads.

Banquet-Style Salad Preparation

For both banquet service and in budget and midlevel restaurants, undressed salads are plated and garnished ahead of time. Dressings may be placed in portion cups set on the plates or served separately in cruets or sauceboats. The salad plates are placed on trays, covered with plastic film, and refrigerated until needed.

When setting up plated salads ahead of time, you should avoid adding perishable garnishes such as cut tomatoes or onions, as they deteriorate quickly and may make the other ingredients soggy or give them off-odors. Crisp garnishes such as bacon or croûtons become soggy in the refrigerator. These types of garnishes should be added just before service.

A Savory Addition

In Europe, the after-entrée vinaigrette salad is often served directly onto the dinner plates during family meals. Diners mix their salads with the remaining concentrated sauce or *jus* from the main course, essentially adding *glace* to the vinaigrette and a savory flavor to the salad.

RECIPES

MIXED GREEN SALAD WITH CLASSIC FRENCH VINAIGRETTE

*APPETIZER**

Yield:
1 portion
Portion size:
about 3 oz (90 g)

INGREDIENTS	U.S.	METRIC
Cleaned romaine, torn into bite-sized pieces	1 oz	30 g
Cleaned leaf lettuce, torn into bite-sized pieces	1 oz	30 g
Cleaned Boston or Bibb lettuce leaves	1 oz	30 g
Classic French Vinaigrette (p. 32), in squeeze bottle	1½ fl oz	45 mL
Cherry tomato halves	5 pieces	5 pieces

**or served after a main course*

PROCEDURE

FINISHING

1. Place the romaine and leaf lettuce in a work bowl.
2. Gently tear the Boston lettuce and add it to the bowl.
3. Squeeze the vinaigrette over the top. Toss to coat the greens with the dressing.

PLATING

4. Mound the greens on a cool 10-in. (25-cm) plate.
5. Arrange the cherry tomato halves around the salad.

VARIATIONS

Any type of sturdy green or mixture of greens may be substituted for the romaine. Garnish options include carrot curls and radish flowers.

ROSETTE SALAD WITH LEMON VINAIGRETTE

APPETIZER*

Portions: 1
Portion size: *about 3 oz (90 g)*

INGREDIENTS	U.S.	METRIC
Whole cleaned Boston lettuce leaves	1½ oz (approx.)	45 g
Whole cleaned Bibb lettuce leaves	1½ oz (approx.)	45 g
Lemon Vinaigrette (p. 34), pushed through a fine-mesh strainer and placed in a spray bottle	1 fl oz	30 mL
Minced chervil	1 tbsp	15 mL
Minced lemon zest	1 tsp	5 mL

**or served after a main course*

PROCEDURE

FINISHING

1. Place the lettuce leaves in a work bowl.
2. Spray with vinaigrette on both sides (A).

PLATING

3. Starting with the largest leaves, arrange the lettuce leaves on a cool 10-in. (25-cm) plate in an alternating concentric pattern, like the petals of a rose (B).
4. Spray with a little more vinaigrette.
5. Sprinkle with chervil and lemon zest.

A

B

VARIATION

Tuck a few small leaves of cleaned lolla rossa or baby red-leaf lettuce into the rosette for color.

AUTUMN GREENS WITH POMEGRANATE-WALNUT VINAIGRETTE

APPETIZER

Portions:
1
Portion size:
about 3 oz (90 g)

INGREDIENTS	U.S.	METRIC
Cleaned baby spinach	1 oz	30 g
Cleaned radicchio, torn into bite-sized pieces	½ oz	15 g
Cleaned heart of curly endive, torn into bite-sized pieces	½ oz	15 g
Cleaned romaine, torn into bite-sized pieces	1 oz	30 g
Pomegranate-Walnut Vinaigrette (p. 36)	2 fl oz	60 mL
Toasted walnut pieces	2 tbsp	30 mL
Pomegranate seeds	1 tbsp	15 mL

PROCEDURE

FINISHING

1. Place the greens in a work bowl.
2. Toss with the vinaigrette.

PLATING

3. Mound the greens on a cool 10-in. (25-cm) plate.
4. Sprinkle with the walnuts and pomegranate seeds.

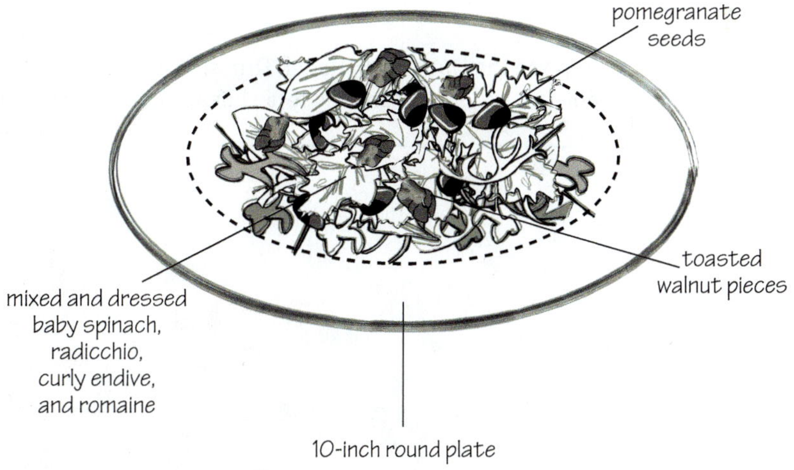

STEAKHOUSE TOSSED SALAD WITH BUTTERMILK RANCH DRESSING

APPETIZER

Portion:
1
Portion size:
about 4 oz (120 g)

INGREDIENTS	U.S.	METRIC
Cleaned iceberg lettuce, torn into bite-sized pieces	1½ oz	45 g
Cleaned romaine, torn into bite-sized pieces	1½ oz	45 g
Buttermilk Ranch Dressing (p. 45), in squeeze bottle	2 fl oz	60 mL
Red onion, separated into rings	1 slice	1 slice
Julienne carrot	2 tbsp	30 mL
Peeled cucumber	5 slices	5 slices
Radish, sliced thin	1	1
Grape tomato or cherry tomato halves	2 pieces	2 pieces

PROCEDURE

FINISHING

1. Place the greens in a work bowl.
2. Toss with the dressing.

PLATING

3. Mound in an 8-in. (20-cm) salad bowl or on a cool 10-in. (25-cm) plate.
4. Top with the garnish vegetables.

VARIATIONS

Replace the Buttermilk Ranch Dressing with Blue Cheese Dressing (p. 43), Russian Dressing (p. 43), or virtually any other American-style dressing.

GREEK SALAD

Replace the Buttermilk Ranch Dressing with Lemon Vinaigrette (p. 34); add 3 Kalamata olives, 1 oz (30 g) crumbled feta cheese, and 1 dolma (stuffed grape leaf) to the garnishes.

SPINACH, MUSHROOM, AND BACON SALAD WITH POPPY SEED DRESSING

APPETIZER

Portions:
1
Portion size:
about 4 oz (120 g)

INGREDIENTS	U.S.	METRIC
Stemmed, de-veined, and cleaned curly spinach, torn into bite-sized pieces	2 oz	60 g
Very fresh white mushrooms, sliced thin	1 oz	30 g
Poppy Seed Dressing (p. 35), in squeeze bottle	2 fl oz	60 mL
Red onion, separated into rings	1 slice	1 slice
Crisp-cooked bacon, crumbled	⅓ cup	80 mL
Grape tomato or cherry tomato halves	7 pieces	7 pieces

PROCEDURE

FINISHING

1. Place the spinach and mushrooms in a work bowl
2. Squeeze most of the dressing over the top and toss together.

PLATING

3. Mound the salad on a cool 10-in. (25-cm) plate.
4. Top with the garnishes.
5. Squeeze the remaining dressing over the top.

VARIATIONS

Replace the Poppy Seed Dressing with Thick Mustard Vinaigrette (p. 33) or Roquefort Vinaigrette (p. 32).

CONTEMPORARY CAESAR SALAD

APPETIZER

Portion:
1
Portion size:
about 4 oz (120 g)

INGREDIENTS	U.S.	METRIC
Pale inner romaine leaves, cleaned, torn into bite-sized pieces	4 oz	120 g
Safe Caesar Dressing (p. 34), in squeeze bottle	2 fl oz	60 mL
Reggiano Parmesan cheese, in block (optional)	¼ oz	7 g
Garlic Croûton Cubes (p. 703)	½ cup	120 mL

PROCEDURE

FINISHING

1. Place the romaine in a work bowl.
2. Squeeze the dressing over the top.
3. Toss to coat well.

PLATING

4. Mound the salad on a cool 10-in. (25-cm) plate.
5. Optional: Using a cheese plane or a swivel peeler, shave shards of cheese over the salad.
6. Scatter the croûtons over top.

VARIATIONS

GRILLED CHICKEN CAESAR DINNER SALAD

Double the salad ingredients and place on a cool 12-in. (30-cm) plate; season and grill a 4-oz (120-g) boneless chicken breast; slice diagonally and fan over the top of the salad.

The History of Caesar Salad

During Prohibition in the United States, wealthy southern Californians frequently traveled south of the border to Tijuana, Mexico, to dine and legally drink alcohol. A popular Tijuana restaurant was owned by an Italian named Caesar Cardini. As the story goes, on the busy July 4, 1924, weekend, Cardini was running low on regular menu items, so he bluffed his way into culinary history by concocting a "special" tableside salad from hearts of romaine lettuce, eggs, and the Italian pantry staples on hand. Thus, Caesar salad was born. Customers were encouraged to pick up the long romaine leaves with their fingers to eat them. This only added to the mystique of Caesar's new salad.

Although Cardini tried to keep his dressing recipe secret, restaurants in Hollywood and throughout Los Angeles soon began serving their versions of Caesar salad, most of which included mashed anchovies in the dressing. According to Cardini, the original Caesar salad had no anchovies but rather acquired its faint anchovy flavor from Worcestershire sauce. Today the Caesar salad—complete with anchovies—is one of North America's most popular dishes.

SPRING GREENS WITH RASPBERRIES AND RASPBERRY VINAIGRETTE

APPETIZER*

Portions:
1
Portion size:
about 4 oz (120 g)

INGREDIENTS	U.S.	METRIC
True spring mix, or a combination such as baby romaine, baby red leaf, baby oak leaf, baby beet greens, mâche, young dandelion, and chervil, cleaned if necessary	2 to 3 oz	60 to 90 g
Raspberry Vinaigrette (p. 36), in squeeze bottle	1½ fl oz	45 mL
Raspberries	1 oz	30 g

**or served after a main course*

PROCEDURE

FINISHING

1. Place the greens in a work bowl.
2. Squeeze the vinaigrette over the top
3. Toss gently, adding most of the raspberries once the greens are lightly coated.

PLATING

4. Mound the salad on a cool 10-in. (25-cm) plate. Garnish with the remaining raspberries.

TERMS FOR REVIEW

complex salad
simple salad
tossed salad
sprouts
micro greens
baby greens
proprietary greens mix
mesclun
spring mix
pluche
edible flowers
hydroponics
"living" greens
turgid
rust
bolted
gueridon

QUESTIONS FOR DISCUSSION

1. Explain the seasonal nature of salads both in the past and in the present. List several greens that might be used in a spring salad, in a summer salad, and in an autumn salad.
2. Explain the difference between a simple salad and a tossed salad.
3. Name the five salad greens flavor groups, and list three greens that belong to each group.
4. Describe the signs of quality you would look for when purchasing salad greens.
5. Name three market forms for salad greens, and discuss the advantages and disadvantages of each.
6. Outline the steps that must be followed when preparing salad greens, including the two main methods of fabrication.
7. List and describe the four methods of salad preparation, and explain the advantages and disadvantages of each.
8. Discuss the factors you would take into consideration when creating your own signature green salad.

Chapter 4

PREREQUISITES

Before reading this chapter, you should already

- Have read "How to Use This Book," pages xxviii–xxxiii, and understand the professional recipe format.
- Be able to identify standard vegetables and fruits, and to evaluate them for quality.
- Know how to properly store standard vegetables and fruits in order to retain quality.
- Be able to fabricate standard vegetables and fruits, including the use of classic cuts.
- Be able to prevent enzymatic browning of vegetables and fruits using various techniques.

Cold Vegetables and Fruits

Vegetables and fruits are the raw materials with which many types of garde manger preparations begin. In addition to salads, many sandwiches and virtually all side dishes are based on vegetables, while fruits accent a variety of savory dishes.

The opportunity to work with farm-fresh vegetables and fragrant, ripe fruits is one of the true pleasures of garde manger work. Vegetables and fruits enhance both the texture and the nutritional value of your dishes. Their bright colors are indispensable in creating attractive plate and platter presentations. Because many fruits and vegetables are seasonal, they create variety when used to accent your menu.

This chapter helps you explore more deeply than you may have done in your introductory classes to acquire knowledge and skills for vegetable and fruit preparation. We focus on methods most frequently used for cold presentations and introduce advanced techniques for vegetable and fruit fabrication. The recipes in this chapter feature vegetables and fruits in starring roles.

After reading this chapter, you should be able to

1. Preserve texture, color, flavor, and nutrients when cooking vegetables and fruits for cold service.
2. List the six changes that occur during the fruit-ripening process.
3. Identify specialty vegetables and fruits, and fabricate them for various garde manger preparations.
4. Prepare vegetables to be served cold by the steaming, blanching, poaching, stewing, braising, roasting, and grilling methods.
5. Cook vegetables to the appropriate degree of doneness for various garde manger applications.
6. Manage the ripening of fruits through proper purchasing and storage.
7. Create attractive fruit platters.

VEGETABLES IN GARDE MANGER WORK

Virtually every type of vegetable is used in modern North American garde manger work. In addition to standard European and North American varieties, vegetables from Asia and Latin America also have entered today's garde manger repertoire. Identification of these standard and specialty vegetables is covered in most introductory cooking texts, which can be supplemented with an up-to-date produce buyers' guide.

Many of the vegetable fabrication and cooking techniques you have already learned also apply to vegetables for garde manger. Later in this chapter, you will learn specialized garde manger methods and techniques for standard and specialty vegetables. First, however, it is useful to look at the ways in which cold vegetable dishes are classified.

Organic Produce

Forty years ago, organic produce was available only in health food stores and on farms where it was grown. Today, almost every supermarket has an organic produce section. Featuring organically produced foods on your menu is a sign of quality that will enhance the reputation of your operation. It is fortunate that organic produce is relatively simple to identify.

In order for the USDA to recognize a vegetable or fruit as ***certified organic produce***, it must:

- Be grown without the use of chemical fertilizers, pesticides, and herbicides
- Not be subjected to biotechnology or irradiation
- Not be fertilized with reprocessed sewage
- Come from a farm that is certified organic

USDA organic seal

APPLICATIONS FOR COLD VEGETABLES

In addition to their use as components of many other types of garde manger preparations, cold vegetables are also featured as dishes in their own right. These are most frequently served as appetizers or as accompaniments to cold main dishes. Because vegetable-based salads are also served in these situations, you may be wondering about the difference between the two. Generally speaking, if a dish consists of *whole, intact* cold vegetables or a *single type* of cold vegetable, it is considered a ***cold vegetable dish*** even if it is sauced with a salad dressing. If a *mixture* of cold cooked vegetables is tossed with a salad dressing, the dish is usually considered a complex salad. However, there are exceptions to this rule.

Cold vegetable dishes are divided into three categories:

1. **Cold vegetable appetizers**
   Cold cooked vegetables are frequently served with vinaigrettes or other salad dressings, but they may be served with sauces other than salad dressings. For example, cool roasted vegetables may be sauced with their pan juices. Many vegetable stews are excellent served at room temperature. They may be accompanied by bread or served in a pastry shell.
   The versatile cold vegetable dip is also a popular appetizer. Guacamole (p. 117), Hummus (p. 118), and Baba Ghanoush (p. 119), for example, are often served as hors d'oeuvres or appetizers. Vegetable dips are typically served with chips or crackers but may also be accompanied by raw or lightly cooked cold vegetables.

2. **Cold vegetable side dishes**
   In formal European dining, it is a rule that hot main dishes are served with hot side dishes, and cold main dishes are served with cold side dishes. Therefore, cold vegetables figure prominently in buffet work, in which a selection of cold vegetable side dishes typically adds color and freshness to the display. In casual dining, cold vegetable sides are sometimes served with grilled and fried foods.

3. **Cold vegetable entrées**
   Entrées composed solely of cold vegetable preparations are less common than hot vegetable entrées. In buffet work, including one or more vegetarian entrées is a thoughtful touch.

UNDERSTANDING VEGETABLES

Before you go on to more specialized work with vegetables, let's review vegetable basics and introduce new information that will enhance your understanding of vegetable identification and preparation.

In culinary terms, a ***vegetable*** is a plant part that is prepared and served as a savory (nonsweet) food. This definition also includes many foods such as beans and tomatoes, which in the botanical sense are fruits (p. 83).

To correctly select and serve vegetables, you must have a thorough understanding of the major culinary vegetable classifications and know when particular vegetables are in season.

Culinary Classifications of Vegetables

Because so many types are available, it is helpful to classify vegetables into groups. Classifications are also helpful when substituting one vegetable for another, because vegetables in the same group are usually similar in many ways, and are often interchangeable.

Because vegetable types are so varied, and because people have different goals for their classifications, there is no set vegetable classification system on which everyone agrees. You may find that vegetables are classified differently in other texts. In Table 4.1, we divide vegetables into nine groups. However, you will discover that some vegetables belong in more than one group, and others do not fit neatly into any group at all. Although the classifications used here are purely culinary, not scientific, when appropriate, botanical family names are used.

TABLE 4.1 Vegetable Family Groups by Culinary Use

Leafy Greens	Lettuces, spinach, field greens, mustard greens, chard, leafy chicories, the edible greens of root vegetables (such as turnip and beet greens), leafy members of the brassica family (such as kale and collards)
Brassicas	Cabbages, cauliflower, broccoli, Brussels sprouts, leafy cabbages such as kale and collards
Cucurbits	Cucumbers, zucchini and other summer squashes, winter squashes, pumpkins
Nightshade fruits	Tomatoes, peppers, eggplants
Legumes	Beans and peas, including seed pods such as green beans and snow peas as well as seeds such as lima beans
Alliums	The onion family, including scallions, leeks, shallots, and garlic
Stems and Shoots	Celery, fennel, asparagus, artichokes (actually flower buds rather than stems)
Roots and Tubers	Carrots, beets, the turnip family, radishes, potatoes
Asian and Exotic	A general classification for vegetables that are relatively new to mainstream Western cooking, such as tropical tubers, avocados, Asian brassicas, fiddlehead ferns, sprouts, etc.

Vegetable Characteristics

Understanding the ways in which vegetable characteristics develop will enable you to handle each vegetable in the correct way.

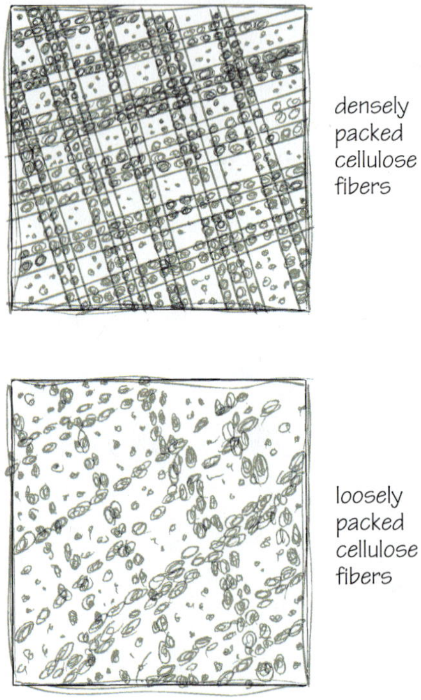

Cellulose in vegetable cell structure

Vegetable Textures

Vegetables are composed of several types of cells whose structure is primarily formed of ***cellulose***, or plant fiber. The amount and type of cellulose in the cell walls and the amount of water and pectin (a sugar derivative) within the cells determines the vegetable's texture.

Chefs typically divide vegetables into three texture groups.

1. Hard vegetables, such as carrots, rutabagas, and winter squashes
2. Firm vegetables, such as green beans, turnips, head cabbage, and corn
3. Tender vegetables, such as zucchini, eggplant, cucumbers, and tomatoes

The texture of a particular vegetable is also influenced both by its state of maturity and its state of freshness. Mature vegetables (those that have grown to full size) are typically firmer than vegetables harvested when young and small. Fresher vegetables (those that are used within a short time of harvest) typically have a higher internal water content and thus are heavier and crisper than vegetables that have been stored for long periods.

Waxed Produce

Commercial growers combat moisture loss in many fruits (apples), and vegetables that are botanically fruits (slicing cucumbers, plum tomatoes), by applying a thin coat of edible wax to their surfaces. These products are called ***waxed produce***. Produce that appears shiny and feels slick to the touch has most likely been waxed. While not harmful, wax is not a desirable dietary component and also contributes an unpleasant mouthfeel to foods coated with it. For this reason, waxed produce should be peeled before being served.

Vegetable Colors

Vegetable colors are created by the presence of ***plant pigments***. Three main pigment groups are responsible for vegetable colors:

1. ***Chlorophyll*** in green vegetables
2. ***Carotenoids*** in orange and orange-red vegetables
3. ***Flavonoids***
   a. ***Anthocyanins*** in purple and purple-red vegetables
   b. ***Anthoxanthins*** in most white vegetables

In some vegetables, one pigment dominates. In others, two or more pigments combine to create color.

You should already know that certain substances and cooking methods adversely affect vegetable pigments. For example, acidic ingredients destroy chlorophyll and turn bright green vegetables an unattractive olive drab color. Many white vegetables are susceptible to enzymatic browning. It is your challenge to preserve or heighten vegetable colors in your preparations.

When deciding how a particular vegetable should be cooked, consider the color of the part you are actually going to cook. For example, although most eggplants are purple and artichokes are green, these are only the skin colors. The bulk of these vegetables—the part that is cooked and eaten—is white, and should be handled in the manner of white vegetables.

Vegetable Nutrients

Vegetables are among our most healthful foods, as they are typically low in fat, high in fiber, and contain important vitamins and minerals. Different vegetable types have different amounts of vitamins and minerals in differing proportions. When you offer customers a wide variety of interesting vegetable dishes, you not only enhance their dining experience but also improve their diets.

FRUITS IN GARDE MANGER WORK

While fruit preparations are most closely associated with the pastry kitchen and are frequently served for dessert, fresh fruit is also an important element of garde manger work. As are vegetables, virtually all of the world's fruits are now available to the garde manger chef and can be researched though the same sources.

APPLICATIONS FOR FRUITS AND FRUIT DISHES

The garde manger department utilizes fruits in many ways. Often, garde manger fruit preparations bridge the gap between sweet and savory foods. For example, a poached pear may be used as a dessert component or served as an accompaniment to a cold roast or charcuterie item. When preparing fruits for use in savory applications, the challenge is to bring out the basic flavor of the fruit without making it overly sweet.

Garde manger fruit preparations can be divided into six categories:

1. **Fruit platters**
When served at breakfast or brunch, thoughtfully arranged platters of perfectly cut fresh fruit add a welcome note of freshness and color to a meal typically heavy on proteins and starches. Giving guests several seasonal fresh fruit options with their morning meal is a courtesy they will remember.

2. **Fruit salads**
Fruit salads, covered in Chapter 5, are equally appropriate as morning fare, lunch entrées, or appetizers in casual meals.

3. **Fruit accompaniments**
Both fresh fruits and cooked fruit preparations are used to accent plates and platters. Fresh fruit frequently complements cheese trays. A few slices of tart, ripe plum or a wedge of pear make appropriate garnishes for charcuterie items. Hams are frequently paired with fruit: Prosciutto is typically served with melon or figs, while cold baked hams are often accompanied by pickled peaches or baked pineapple rings. Fruit compotes and preserves accent sandwiches and cold meats.

4. **Fruit décor**
The bright colors and interesting shapes of fresh fruits make them particularly appropriate for decorative use. For this purpose, small fruits such as berries, kumquats, and clusters of grapes may be left whole.

Heirloom Vegetables

By 1970, many of our best-loved vegetable and fruit cultivars were virtually extinct due to industrial agriculture. In the late twentieth century, independent horticulturists, small vegetable growers, and home gardeners banded together to save as many traditional vegetable and fruit cultivars as possible. These old-fashioned cultivars became known as ***heirloom*** vegetables and fruits because their seeds had been handed down from past generations who saved them from one year to another. While these specialty vegetables are available in season only, and demand a higher price, their superior flavor is unmistakable.

Guidelines for Preparing Fruit Platters

- Fabricate and arrange fruits in such as way as to make them easy to serve and easy to eat. Guests should be able to neatly serve themselves from the platter without causing the arrangement to collapse.
- Alternate shapes and colors on the platter.
- Create height on the platter by using a tall fruit centerpiece, such as a whole pineapple or a melon basket, and then arranging the cut fruit in a cascading flow from the center to the edge.
- Treat fruits that may discolor from enzymatic browning with a coating of citrus juice or an ascorbic acid solution.
- Don't prepare fruit platters too far ahead of time, and add particularly perishable fruits at the last possible minute before serving.
- To preserve the presentation appearance throughout the duration of a buffet or reception, have backup fruit fabricated and ready to replenish, or prepare several smaller platters to exchange as necessary.

Fruit display
Courtesy Dreamstime.com. © Alan Smith.

However, for décor work, fruit is most often fabricated by carving it into representative or abstract shapes. Simple fruit décor, such as the Apple Bird (p. 716), is covered in Chapter 17.

5. **Fruit baskets**
Fruit baskets consist of whole, small, unfabricated fruits that can be eaten out of hand and do not require constant refrigeration. Apples, pears, peaches, plums, grapes, oranges, tangerines, and bananas are the most common fruits included. Garde manger chefs in retail stores are responsible for assembling fruit baskets for sale as gifts. In hotels, fruit baskets may be offered as guest amenities. In some cases, the pastry department may be called on to provide cookies or other sweets for inclusion in a deluxe fruit basket.

6. **Fruit displays**
Because of their attractive appearance, fruits are frequently grouped into attractive containers and used as a centerpiece or display item, much in

Guidelines for Making Fruit Baskets

- Pack the bottom of the basket with tissue paper or raffia to cushion the fruit and create a full appearance.
- Wash all fruit in a sanitizing solution and dry completely before packing it in the basket.
- Arrange larger, sturdier fruits on the bottom and smaller, more delicate fruits on top.
- If cookies or other sweets are included in the basket, they should be individually wrapped in plastic or cellophane.
- Enclose the finished basket in a cellophane wrapper tied with a bow. If a card is to be included, attach it in a prominent place where it will be seen.
- Don't seal basket wrappers or attach cards with staples, as they pose the food safety threat of physical contamination.

the same manner as cut flowers. Fruits may be stacked free-form in their containers or held in place with florist wire. Whether a fruit display is featured on a buffet table or as a freestanding display, it must be monitored carefully for freshness. While not intended for consumption, fruit for displays should nonetheless be washed in produce sanitizing solution, as some guests inevitably help themselves.

UNDERSTANDING FRUIT

A ***fruit*** is the reproductive organ, specifically the ovary, of a seed plant. When we speak of fruit in the culinary sense, we mean those plant ovaries that have *fleshy pulp sweet enough to be served as a dessert*. However, many vegetables are botanically classed as fruits. Tomatoes, squash, and avocados are good examples.

When fruit reaches its full size, it is considered mature. For most vegetables, maturity is the optimal point at which harvesting and consumption should occur. However, most fruits (including those classed as vegetables) undergo an additional phase of development that makes them better to eat. This phase is called ripening.

Ripening is the process by which a mature fruit completes its life cycle. Six important changes occur during ripening.

1. Skin color changes, usually from green to a warm color such as yellow, orange, red, or violet.
2. Acid content decreases.
3. Sugar content increases.
4. Texture softens, and its flesh becomes juicier.
5. Characteristic aroma develops.
6. Characteristic flavor develops.

When all of these changes are complete, the result is a ***ripe fruit***.

The challenge to farmers, shippers, purveyors, and chefs alike is to get fresh fruit to the table at exactly the point of perfect ripeness. If you don't immediately serve a fruit that has reached perfect ripeness, it will continue to ripen to the point where its texture becomes unpleasantly soft and its flavor begins to wane. Overripe fruit can no longer be served in its natural state but can sometimes be processed into a purée for use in fruit soups or sauces, for frozen desserts, and in baking. The natural progression of ripening leads to ***decay***. Sooner or later, the fruit's flesh softens to a mealy or mushy texture and finally disintegrates. Both its skin and flesh turn an unattractive brown color, and its flavor and aroma become unpleasant. When fruit reaches the decay stage, it can no longer be used.

Decay is hastened by physical stress, such as when an apple is dropped on the floor and becomes bruised or broken open. At the site of the bruise, ripening happens quickly and decay begins, even under an intact skin. Decay can also be caused by the invasion of microbes, such as bacteria and molds. If bacteria or mold is growing within a particular piece of fruit, it can easily and rapidly be transferred to other fruits stored in the same container through skin imperfections. The old saying "one bad apple spoils the whole barrel" is really true. That's why it is necessary to take the time to ***cull***, or pick out, fruits that show signs of spoilage.

The Science of Ripening

The processes by which ripening occurs are complex. Many involve the enzymatic breakdown of various molecules. However, one of the most important factors is the action of a simple hydrocarbon gas called ethylene. ***Ethylene gas*** triggers several enzymatic processes. As fruit ripens, the ethylene gas it produces causes the fruit to go into a frenzy of biochemical activity and creates the changes listed on this page. These changes make the fruit as attractive to the eye and as luscious to the palate as possible in order to attract people or animals to eat it and, thus, distribute its seeds over a wide area to ensure survival of the species.

Growers, shippers, and purveyors have learned to control the production and presence of ethylene gas in order to manipulate ripeness in many fruits. This allows them to extend the season of fruits and makes it possible for consumers to purchase fruits far out of their normal seasons. However, with few exceptions, fruits allowed to ripen naturally and harvested in season are far superior to fruits subjected to artificial ripening.

Seasonality

While most fruits are now available year-round, a few types are still markedly superior when used in season. Melons, berries, and stone fruits such as peaches, plums, and cherries harvested fully ripe from local sources should be featured throughout their respective seasons. Apples and pears are best in late summer and through the fall. Tropical fruits are a good choice for winter menus, replacing local fruits that are unavailable at that time of year.

PURCHASING, STORING, AND MANAGING PRODUCE

Experienced garde manger chefs know that purchasing good produce is more than half the battle. Vegetables and fruits harvested at the proper stage of development and handled correctly by the purveyor are a pleasure to prepare and serve. Once you have selected high-quality produce, you must then store it properly and use it quickly. Many types of fruit, and some vegetables, require special management.

Judging Quality

Choosing the best produce depends not only on sight but also on the senses of smell, touch, taste, and even hearing. When purchasing vegetables and fruits, evaluate their:

- **Appearance.** Fresh and fully mature produce has intense color. Avoid pale colors and multiple blemishes. Unless a vegetable or fruit is intended for display, imperfectly sized or shaped specimens are perfectly usable. Vegetables should be of medium size and slender for their type. The optimal size of fruits depends on their intended use.
- **Feel.** Insist on touching the vegetables and fruits you buy. The weight and feel tell a lot about the inner texture. Produce should feel heavy in relation to size, signifying adequate internal water content. Produce, even tender items, should also feel firm to the touch.
- **Aroma.** Truly fresh vegetables not subjected to prolonged refrigeration and displayed at room temperature have a distinct, natural aroma. Ripe fruits are especially fragrant.
- **Sound.** When split or broken open, fresh vegetables are crisp. You should hear a distinct snap. Some fruits should also sound crisp.
- **Taste.** Taste vegetables and fruits during your purchase evaluation. Even vegetables usually served cooked should have natural sweetness and juicy mouthfeel when tasted raw.

Judging Ripeness

When evaluating fruits for quality, ripeness is also a consideration. Fruits purchased underripe may never properly ripen. However, in some cases it is necessary to purchase underripe fruits ahead of time and manage their ripening in-house. Either way, these three characteristics help determine whether a fruit is ripe:

1. **Strong aroma:** Your very best clue as to whether a fruit has reached its optimal state of ripeness. A ripe fruit has a powerful and unmistakable scent that clearly says "apple" or "peach" or whatever the fruit may be. Always judge aroma at room temperature.
2. **Yielding texture:** A signal of ripeness in many fruits. With the exception of fruits that are supposed to be hard and crisp (such as apples), fruits that are optimally ripe give when gently pressed, especially around the stem or stem scar. The amount of give determines the stage of ripeness.
3. **Color development:** A sign of ripeness in some fruits but not in others. Refer to a produce buyer's guide for the color development of individual fruits.

Storing Produce

Wholesale produce received directly from a purveyor arrives packed in the proper containers for storage and should be kept in those containers until you are ready to fabricate it. The temperature at which produce should be stored varies according to type. Most vegetables and many fruits keep well when refrigerated at about 38°F (3°C). However, with fruits (and some of those vegetables that are botanically fruits), you must take ripening into consideration.

Managing Ripening

Some fruits ripen only if they are still on the plant. Berries and melons are examples. If held at room temperature after picking, they may soften in texture and become a little juicier. However, they will not ripen any further. Thus, you must purchase these fruits ripe, or nearly ripe, and monitor them for decay.

Other fruits, such as peaches, bananas, and tomatoes, can ripen even after harvesting, provided they were properly mature when picked and are held under

Guidelines for In-House Produce Management

- To prevent underripe fruit from ripening, store under refrigeration.
- To prevent ripe fruit from becoming overripe or decaying, store under refrigeration.
- To allow underripe fruit to ripen at a natural rate, store in an open container at 55°–70°F (13°–21°C).
- To speed the process of ripening underripe fruit, place a cut-open apple with the fruit in its carton and wrap the carton in a sealed black plastic trash bag; store at 70°–80°F (21°–27°C). Check twice per day.
- Don't refrigerate bananas, as low temperatures cause their skin to turn brown.
- Gently turn refrigerated berry pints and half-pints upside down to relieve pressure on the bottom berries.
- Cull fruit packages daily to prevent the spread of decay.
- Store uncut potatoes, onions, garlic, and shallots at cool room temperature.
- For best flavor and texture, avoid refrigerating tomatoes and avocados.
- Store asparagus and other costly stem vegetables standing upright with cut stem ends in 1–2 in. (2.5–5 cm) water. Drape a clean, damp towel over the tips.

the proper conditions. A few fruits actually benefit from being picked underripe and ripened off the plant: Pears become mealy and mushy if ripened on the tree, while avocados ripen *only* after they are harvested. These fruits require careful managing to ensure they are at their proper stage of ripeness when served. Following the guidelines on page 85 will help you serve fruit at its proper ripeness and avoid waste.

Storing Fabricated Produce

Once a vegetable or fruit is peeled or cut, its inner plant tissue is exposed to oxygen. This leads to rapid deterioration through dehydration, loss of volatile flavor compounds and nutrients, bacterial invasion, and, in some cases, enzymatic browning. For this reason, most fabricated vegetables should be used as quickly as possible. Fruits to be served raw should be fabricated at the last possible moment. Those subject to enzymatic browning should be brushed with lemon juice.

If you must hold uncooked, fabricated produce for longer than an hour or so, keep it moist by storing between clean, damp towels in freshly sanitized, covered containers. Some fabricated uncooked vegetables are stored submerged in water. Potatoes and artichoke hearts are stored in this manner. Vegetables for crudités (p. 87) are held submerged in ice water to crisp them. However, do not keep crudité vegetables in water longer than a few hours because they will become waterlogged and may lose nutrients.

Storing Cooked Vegetables

Cooking can destroy or dissolve out some nutrients from vegetables and fruits. On the other hand, cooking is a useful technique to temporarily halt or slow the deterioration of flavor, texture, color, and nutritional content. Cooking also stops the activity of enzymes that break down the texture of raw produce. For this reason, chefs often choose to cook many vegetables, and some fruits, as a way of holding them.

Once vegetables are cooked, refreshed, and drained, they must be kept relatively dry to prevent nutrient loss and to further discourage microbial growth. Cooked vegetables should be kept in freshly sanitized, covered containers lined with clean, dry, lint-free towels to absorb moisture. Tender vegetables should be placed in shallow layers so they don't squash under their own weight. Most cooked vegetables may be stored at 3°–38°F (1°–3°C) three to four days. If you have excess cooked vegetables that will not be used within three days, your best bet is to freeze them right away. Although there will be some loss of texture, the vegetables will remain safe to serve and can be used in soups or purées.

In garde manger work, fruits to be cooked are usually poached. Poached fruits are best held refrigerated in their *cuisson* (p. 98), or poaching liquid.

FABRICATING PRODUCE

Most vegetables and many fruits require fabrication before they can be cooked or served. Four basic steps are involved.

1. **Washing.** All produce must be washed before fabrication to remove insects, soil, and pathogens or chemicals. Even produce that is to be peeled should be washed so the flesh isn't contaminated during peeling.

   Wash vegetables and fruits by immersing in cool, chlorinated tap water or produce-sanitizing solution (especially when preparing for high-risk populations). Gently scrub vegetables to be served with skin intact (radishes, baked potatoes). Vegetables with lots of nooks and crannies (broccoli, cauliflower) should be soaked in water 5–10 minutes. Don't allow porous fruits, such as strawberries, to soak for longer than a few minutes, as they can become waterlogged. Very delicate raspberries and blackberries should be washed only with a gentle mist of food sanitizer and then immediately blotted dry on kitchen towels.

2. **Trimming.** Most vegetables and fruits have at least one naturally tough, fibrous, or discolored part that must be removed before cooking or eating. In fruits, stem and blossom ends normally must be removed. Stems and shoots have a tough ***healed end*** where they were cut during harvesting. This should be trimmed away. The fibrous central cores of certain vegetables and fruits, such as tomatoes and strawberries, should be removed.

   Large or hard seeds (as of peppers, cucumbers, and melons) should be cut or scraped out along with the membrane. The tough healed end of edible stems (broccoli, asparagus) should be trimmed away. The prominent center vein of leafy vegetables (kale, cabbage) should also be trimmed.

3. **Peeling.** Classically trained chefs peel virtually all vegetables and fruits to ensure good appearance, consistent texture, and even cooking. Peeling is also recommended because today many produce items are coated with wax. A swivel peeler is typically used. Vegetables with tough skins are peeled with a flexible boning knife using a technique called ***pelée à vif*** [peh-LAY ah VEEF], or *skinned alive*.

   Some produce items require yet other peeling methods. Tomatoes and peaches are blanched and refreshed to loosen skins. Beets and peppers are often roasted first.

4. **Cutting into shape.** Once washed, trimmed, and peeled, most vegetables and fruits are then cut into appropriate shapes. The possibilities for creating interesting and unusual shapes are almost limitless.

Pelée à vif

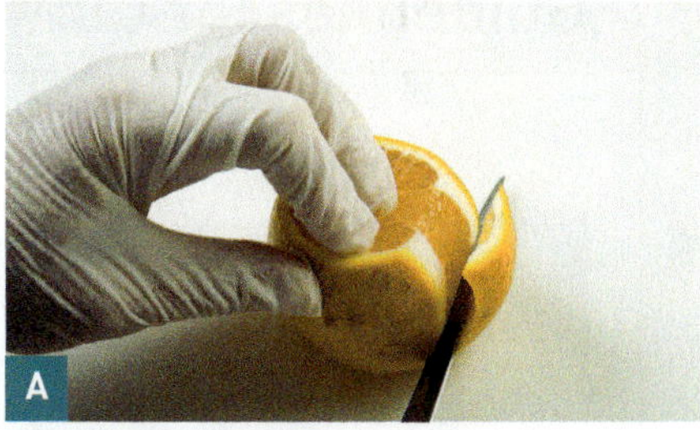
A

Cutting downward in a curving motion, slice off the peel, leaving only the orange's flesh.

B

The orange can now be sliced or cut into segments having no membrane.

C

Slicing the orange

PREPARING VEGETABLES FOR RAW SERVICE

You can do little to improve the flavor or texture of vegetables to be served raw. Thus, when purchasing them, insist on the best and freshest. The most appropriate vegetables for raw service are those harvested slightly immature. In fact, the classic French raw vegetable dish, ***crudités*** (kroo-dee-TAY, p. 89), is traditionally served only in spring and early summer, when vegetables are young. If you must serve crudités composed of mature vegetables, you may wish to blanch and refresh (p. 96) the firmer ones to an al dente (p. 91) texture. Although not traditional, it is better than serving tough, fibrous raw vegetables.

Crisping Raw Vegetables

You can replace some lost moisture and firm the texture of most vegetables by immersing them in ice water after they have been peeled and fabricated. This procedure is called ***crisping***.

Guidelines for Cutting Vegetables and Fruits

Pare the skin of the pineapple.

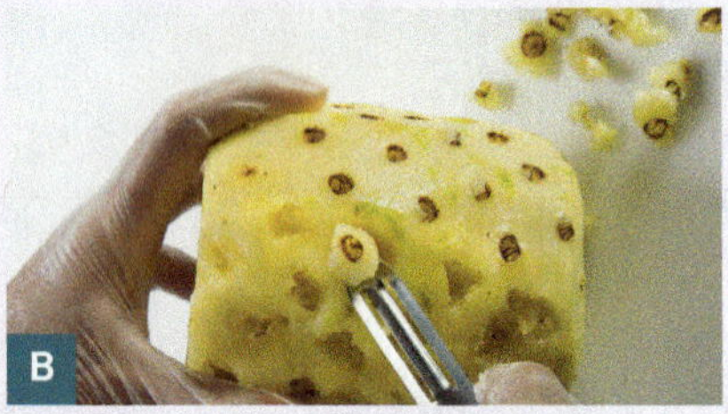

Remove the eyes with the tip of a swivel peeler.

1. Cut produce into precise, uniform shapes. Carelessly cut vegetables and fruits not only look unprofessional but also cook unevenly.
2. When deciding how to shape a particular item, keep in mind the cooking method to be used. Rounded vegetables are ideal for sautéing as they roll around in the pan for even cooking, while those cut into large, flat slices are best for grilling. Whole pears poach more quickly when cored and most quickly when quartered or sliced.
3. Vegetables and fruits for garnishes or side dishes should contribute visual interest to the plate by adding a contrasting shape. For a scallop dish, shape contrast can be created by cutting carrots into bâtonnets or juliennes rather than rounds. Melon cut into parisiennes contrasts nicely with pineapple cubes.
4. Vegetables or fruits that will be mixed together in a salad or medley should be roughly uniform in size. This looks best and makes eating easier. Soft vegetables, which are likely to shrink when cooked, should be cut slightly larger than firmer vegetables that will retain their original size after cooking.

In operations that use large quantities of pineapples and apples, a corer is a useful tool. *Courtesy Vacu Vin, Inc.*

A cherry pitter quickly removes the cherry's central seed while leaving the cherry intact. *Courtesy OXO.*

Procedure for Crisping Vegetables

1. Fabricate the vegetables as desired.
2. Prepare a container of ice water large enough to immerse and hold the vegetables.
3. Immerse the vegetables in the ice water from 30 minutes to 1 hour.
4. Drain the vegetables in a colander and remove any remaining ice cubes.
5. Place the vegetables in a freshly sanitized plastic container lined with clean, lint-free towels to absorb excess moisture.
6. Cover the vegetables and refrigerate until needed.

Hold crisped vegetables for the shortest possible time.

CRUDITÉ BASKET WITH THREE DIPS

BUFFET

Yield:
about 2½ lb (1.25 kg) vegetables plus 1½ pt (0.75 l) dips

Portions:
varies

Portion size:
varies

INGREDIENTS	U.S.	METRIC
⅜ × ⅜ × 4-in. (1 × 1 × 10-cm) carrot bâtonnets	4 oz	120 g
Celery hearts with leaves, about 4-in. (10-cm) lengths	4 oz	120 g
Broccoli florets	4 oz	120 g
Cauliflower florets	4 oz	120 g
Belgian endives, leaves separated	4 oz (2–3 heads)	120 g (2–3 heads)
Red bell pepper, cut in ⅜ × 4-in. (1 × 10-cm) strips	6 oz	240 g
Yellow bell pepper, cut in ⅜ × 4-in. (1 × 10-cm) strips	6 oz	240 g
Radish Tulips (p. 716)	12 pieces	12 pieces
Kale leaves	5 oz	150 g
Green or white cabbage	1 lb	0.5 kg
Curly parsley	2 oz	60 g
Grape tomatoes, washed	5 oz	150 g
Three-Onion Sour Cream Dip (p. 570)	½ pt	240 mL
Roasted Red Bell Pepper Mayonnaise (p. 43)	½ pt	240 mL
Garlic-Herb Cheese Spread (p. 594)	5 fl oz	150 mL
Half-and-half	3 fl oz	90 mL
Unwaxed cucumbers, seeded, cut in ⅜ × ⅜ × 4-in. (1 × 1 × 10-cm) spears	5 oz	150 g
Supplies		
4-in. (10-cm) bamboo skewers	36	36

PROCEDURE

PREPARATION

1. Fill a large, freshly sanitized tub half full of ice water.
2. Place the carrots, celery, broccoli, cauliflower, endive leaves, peppers, and radish tulips in the water and set a sanitized plate or lid on top to keep them submerged. Refrigerate at least 2 hours and up to 6 hours.
3. Line a 10-in. (25-cm) diameter basket with the kale leaves.
4. Set the cabbage, rounded side up, in the basket. Use a skewer to make 36 holes, ½-in. (1-cm) deep, in the cabbage at ½-in. (1-cm) intervals (A).
5. Drain the vegetables and blot them dry on clean kitchen towels.
6. Impale all of the radish tulips (B), all of the tomatoes, and 6 each of the broccoli and cauliflower florets on the skewers. *(continues)*

A

B

PROCEDURE *(continued)*

7. Insert the base of the skewers into the holes in the cabbage (C).
8. Arrange the remaining vegetables between the skewers. Mound the broccoli and cauliflower florets and insert the long-cut vegetables upright between them (D). Use the parsley to fill in around the edges of the basket and to cover any open spaces.
9. Refrigerate the basket until needed.
10. Place the Three-Onion Dip and the Red Bell Pepper Mayonnaise in serving dishes.
11. Place the cheese spread in a food processor fitted with the steel blade. Thin the spread to dipping consistency by adding half-and-half through the feed tube while pulsing the blade. Pour the cheese dip into a serving dish.

C

D

HOLDING

Refrigerate, covered with clean, damp towels, up to 6 hours.

PRESENTATION

12. Place the basket on the serving table and arrange the bowls of dip in front of it.

VARIATION

Vary the vegetables and the dips as desired. While not technically crudités, al dente blanched and refreshed cooked vegetables may be used. Refer to Chapter 2 for vinaigrettes, dressings, mayonnaise sauces, and dairy-based sauces that may be used as alternative dips.

COOKING VEGETABLES AND FRUITS

While in garde manger work some vegetables and many fruits are frequently served in their raw state, cooking these foods properly is an important skill to master. In fact, when working with vegetables and fruits, you must understand what *proper cooking* actually means. Unlike meat cookery, in which doneness is specified by customer order and determined by temperature, cooking vegetables and fruits for cold service requires judgment and discretion.

Doneness

Four factors determine the correct doneness to which a vegetable or fruit should be cooked:

1. **Intended use:** Vegetables and fruits to be used in salads are often cooked more lightly to retain a crunchy texture. However, vegetable stews such as Ratatouille (p. 105) and fruits in compotes are cooked until tender. Vegetables and fruits for purées must be cooked soft.
2. **Cooking style:** If you are making an Asian dish, vegetables and fruits should be lightly cooked and crisp-textured. In French cuisine, they are cooked to a more tender texture. In Eastern European and American Southern cuisines, vegetables are cooked to a soft texture. Poached fruits should also be cooked soft.
3. **Customer preference:** Some customers appreciate crisp, lightly cooked vegetables and fruits, while to others these would be undercooked. If customer plates are returned to the dish room with uneaten produce, reevaluate the doneness.
4. **Vegetable maturity or fruit ripeness:** *When cooking vegetables, maturity trumps all other factors.* No matter the type of dish you are making or the cooking style in which you are working you must cook a vegetable according to its texture. If vegetables are more mature, and thus more fibrous, than expected, you may have to change your cooking plans or return them to your purveyor.

   In fruit, *ripeness determines cooking doneness*, or whether to cook at all. Underripe fruit is best for moist-method cooking and not-too-ripe fruit for dry-method cooking. Perfectly ripe fruit is best served raw.

Because of these variables, it is impossible to state that one particular doneness is universally correct for all vegetables or fruits. Thus, you will prepare various produce items at varying states of doneness for different uses. Chefs recognize three basic levels of doneness for vegetables and fruits:

1. ***Al dente*** [ahl DAYN-tay]: This literally translates as "to the tooth." Although it is usually used to describe pasta, North American chefs apply the term to vegetables as well. Al dente vegetables are cooked just enough to lose their raw taste while retaining their crunchy texture.
2. ***À point*** [ah PWAN]: This literally translates as "to the point," or food cooked to the point of perfection. *À point* vegetables are cooked to a texture that is tender but with just a little resistance to the bite. Green vegetables prepared this way lose their raw, grassy taste, and their natural sweetness becomes more pronounced.

Overcooked and Undercooked Vegetables

An overcooked vegetable or fruit is one cooked to a softer texture than the chef wants to achieve. *Overcooked* typically describes an item that has a limp and discolored appearance and a mushy mouthfeel.

An undercooked vegetable or fruit is one cooked to a harder texture than the chef wants to achieve—or than the customers prefer. *Undercooked* typically describes an item that is tough, fibrous, and difficult to chew. When chefs do not take a particular vegetable's state of maturity, or a fruit's state of ripeness, into account, and neglect to taste their finished product for texture, the result is frequently undercooked vegetables.

Overcooked vegetables were once quite common. Today the problem is often the exact opposite. Many chefs now undercook vegetables in an attempt to achieve crispness and vivid color. In doing so, they sacrifice flavor and mouthfeel for appearance.

3. ***Fork-tender***: Some cold vegetable and fruit preparations are cooked to complete tenderness, such that they can be cut with the side of a fork.

Primary Cooking Methods

Whether cooking produce for use in complex salads, cold appetizers, or for garnish and décor work, these seven methods are those typically used in garde manger work:

1. **Pressure steaming**
2. **Boiling/blanching**
3. **Poaching**

The methods listed above are covered in depth in the next section. Note that pressure steaming and boiling/blanching are the most frequently used methods for vegetables, and poaching for fruits. Although the remaining four methods listed below are used less frequently, they can produce excellent results.

4. **Stewing.** This produces tender vegetables or fruits in which the flavors of the sauce and of the produce combine. When stewing vegetables or fruits, be mindful of the texture of the various items being stewed, adding each at the appropriate time.
5. **Braising.** Braised vegetables and fruits should be very tender and have a deep, complex flavor from both the cooking medium and the initial browning. Braising begins with sautéing in a flavorful fat. The moist part of the braising process usually consists of simmering in stock, a lightly acidic *cuisson*, or, for fruit, a light syrup. The pan is covered to create the steam that cooks the exposed part of the food.
6. **Roasting/steam roasting.** Tender-textured vegetables and fruits are dry-roasted in a manner similar to meats. Steam-roasting, with basting or a covered pan, is necessary for firm and hard items.
7. **Grilling.** Today, garde manger chefs frequently use grilled vegetables in salads, sandwiches, terrines, and other composed cold dishes. Grilled fruits make unusual garnishes or accompaniments. As it is a dry-heat method, grilling is used only for tender vegetables and fruits. However, grilling can be used as a secondary cooking method to finish pre-cooked items.

Pressure Steaming

To steam means to cook food completely surrounded by water vapor at a temperature of 212°F (100°C) or higher. There are two ways to steam foods:

1. **Stovetop steaming:** Done in a compartmented pan on a stove burner. While stovetop steaming is common in Asian restaurants, in Western cuisines it is more typically utilized in home cooking.
2. **Pressure steaming:** A specialized, high-temperature form of steaming used in professional kitchens. Pressure steaming is the ideal way to efficiently and quickly soften vegetable fiber while preventing acid concentration.

A ***pressure steamer*** is a commercial steam cooker specially built to quickly generate steam and hold it efficiently. Pressure is expressed in units called ***PSIs***, or "pounds per square inch." Steam begins when water boils at 212°F (100°C). However, when held at 5 PSI, steam reaches 227°F (108°C), and at 15 PSI it reaches 250°F (121°C). Thus, foods steamed under pressure get hotter and cook more quickly. For this reason (and because you can't see inside a pressure steamer), it is easy to overcook the food you are steaming. Due to product variations, it is often necessary to check the doneness of a batch of food before the specified cooking time has elapsed. This poses no problem, because commercial pressure steamers are designed to have almost instantaneous recovery (p. 95). Even if you have to open the door to check the doneness of the food inside, when you re-close the door the original temperature and pressure return within a few seconds.

In garde manger work, pressure steaming is almost always followed by refreshing, reviewed on page 95.

Procedure for Pressure Steaming Vegetables

A

B

1. Place a solid hotel pan in the bottom of a pressure steamer to collect drips. Turn on the steamer and wait for the ready indicator to come on.
2. Fill a large bowl or tub halfway with equal parts ice and water. Place it near the steamer.
3. Prepare freshly sanitized, lidded storage containers lined with clean, dry kitchen towels. Have ready a spider or perforated lifter.
4. Spread uniformly fabricated vegetables in perforated hotel pans in layers no more than 2 in. (5 cm) deep.
5. Load one or more pans of food into the steamer (A) and set the timer for slightly less time than you estimate the food will need to cook.
6. When the timer goes off, check the food's doneness by tasting a sample item. If necessary, continue steaming until the food reaches the desired doneness. (If you need to cook additional batches, record the total cooking time but deduct 5 seconds of recovery time for each time the door was opened.) Remove the pan(s) from the steamer.
7. Refresh the vegetables by *immediately* transfering them into the ice water. Stir to evenly distribute them. Potatoes, and other porous foods such as beets and winter squash, should be slightly undercooked and allowed to cool in the pans rather than refreshing them.
8. When the refreshed vegetables are thoroughly cold, drain them and place in the towel-lined containers to blot dry (B).

STEAMED CHILLED SNAP PEAS WITH GINGERED MAYONNAISE DIP

BUFFET

Yield:
1 lb (0.5 kg)
Portions:
varies
Portion size:
varies

INGREDIENTS	U.S.	METRIC
Sugar snap peas	1 lb	0.5 kg
Red-leaf lettuce	2 oz (3 leaves)	60 g (3 leaves)
Gingered Mayonnaise (p. 43)	8 fl oz	240 mL
Minced parsley	⅛ oz (1 tbsp)	4 g (15 mL)
Pink pickled ginger, chiffonnade	¼ oz (2 tbsp)	4 g (15 mL)

PROCEDURE

PREPARATION

1. Remove the stem ends from the snap peas and pull off the strings.
2. Follow the Procedure for Pressure Steaming Vegetables on page 93 to cook the snap peas al dente.

PRESENTATION

3. Line a 14-in. (35-cm) tray with the lettuce leaves.
4. Place the mayonnaise in a 10-fl oz (300-mL) serving bowl and place it in the center of the tray.
5. Sprinkle a ring of parsley around the edge of the mayonnaise.
6. Sprinkle a ring of pickled ginger just inside the parsley ring.
7. Arrange the snap peas around the bowl.

Boiling and Blanching

BOILING

Boiling is the next best option to pressure steaming. Boiling is cooking food completely submerged in water at 212°F (100°C). Boiling is a penetrating method and, thus, an efficient tenderizer. However, boiling is also a violent cooking method, because at the boiling point water molecules move around very quickly. This is apparent when you look at the roiling, bubbling action of water at the boil. Because this violent motion can easily break up delicate foods, boiling is not used for foods with delicate textures.

BLANCHING

Blanching is boiling a food for a short period in order to partially cook it or to fully cook it to a firm texture. Today, most chefs use the term *blanching* to describe boiling vegetables in water to an *à point* or al dente texture, and then stopping the carryover cooking by refreshing them. The term *boiling* is used almost exclusively for starches such as potatoes and pasta.

Vegetables and fruits are blanched for three basic reasons.

1. **To remove skins or peels.** To remove the skin from a tomato or a peach, blanch it for a few seconds and then immediately refresh it. The skin slips off easily, and the flesh remains raw.
2. **For par-cooking.** Firm or hard vegetables are sometimes blanched to partially soften their texture before another cooking method is applied. You might blanch cauliflower before baking it in a gratin. Blanching also stops enzymatic browning and removes undesirable strong flavors from vegetables such as turnips.
3. **To pre-cook** for cold service or for reheating. For this purpose, vegetables are fully cooked, usually *à point* or al dente.

Succession Blanching

Blanching several types of vegetables in the same water is called ***succession blanching***. When succession blanching, you should begin with mild-flavored vegetables and proceed in order of flavor strength. For example, blanch snow peas first, then carrots, then Brussels sprouts. Proper succession blanching helps prevent the transmission of flavors and odors from one vegetable to another.

REFRESHING

To quickly and efficiently stop the process of carryover cooking in steamed and blanched foods, they must be transferred immediately after cooking into a large vessel containing ice water. This technique is called ***refreshing*** or ***shocking***.

Proper refreshing quickly lowers the temperature of the food to near the freezing point, ensuring it retains the same texture when cold as when the cooking was completed. It also preserves bright colors that are easily destroyed by prolonged exposure to heat.

For maximum efficiency, an ice bath for refreshing should be about 50% ice and 50% water, measured by volume. Product must remain in the refreshing water only until thoroughly cold throughout, usually no more than 10 minutes. Once cold, the product should be drained thoroughly, and it is often blotted on clean kitchen towels to remove excess moisture.

Recovery Time

When a cold or room-temperature food is added to a hot cooking medium, the food lowers the temperature of the cooking medium. The time it takes to compensate for this drop in temperature and to regain the original cooking temperature is referred to as ***recovery time***.

When a gallon of water boils on a high heat burner and you add a pound of refrigerated raw green beans to it, the cold temperature of the beans lowers the temperature of the water. The stove burner works to raise the water's temperature back to the boil. If it takes 45 seconds to restore the water to the boiling point, the recovery time is 45 seconds.

During recovery time, the beans are no longer boiling but rather simmering. Problems can occur when recovery time is too long. For example, longer cooking time at a lower temperature is likely to discolor the beans. To prevent such problems, you have three options:

1. Cook fewer green beans at a time, so the beans' temperature will not lower the water temperature as much.
2. Use more boiling water, for the same result.
3. Use a more powerful heat source, so recovery is faster.

Procedure for Blanching and Refreshing

1. Using the rough formula of 1 gal (4 L) water to 1 lb (0.5 kg) product, bring the water to a rapid boil in a saucepan or stockpot. If available, use a pot with a blanching basket. If blanching multiple batches, have additional boiling water ready at hand.
2. Prepare a large bowl or tub halfway filled with equal parts ice and water. Place it near the range. When refreshing a large volume of produce, have extra ice at hand.
3. Prepare freshly sanitized, lidded storage containers lined with clean, dry kitchen towels. If you do not have a blanching basket, have ready a spider or perforated lifter. Tongs may be used for small amounts of product.
4. Drop the appropriate amount of product into the boiling water (A). (Except in the case of green vegetables, you may cover the pan until the water recovers the boil.) Cook at a rapid boil until the product becomes vivid in color (B) and its raw smell begins to disappear. Taste-test a sample and evaluate the doneness. (When blanching to remove skin, a few seconds is usually sufficient.)
5. When the product reaches the desired texture and flavor, immediately lift it out of the pot and drop it into the refreshing water (C). Stir to evenly distribute.
6. When the refreshed product is thoroughly cold, drain it, remove any ice clinging to it, and place in the towel-lined containers.

Note: Boiled potatoes should not be refreshed.

BROCCOLINI PINZIMONIO FOR TWO [peen-tzee-MOH-nyoh]

APPETIZER

Portions:
2
Portion size:
4 oz (120 g)

INGREDIENTS	U.S.	METRIC
Broccolini	8 oz	240 g
Unfiltered extra-virgin olive oil	2 fl oz	60 mL
Fresh garlic, peeled	¼ oz (1 clove)	7 g (1 clove)
Fine sea salt	to taste	to taste
Aged balsamic vinegar	½ fl oz	15 mL
Grape tomatoes	2 oz (6 pieces)	60 g (6 pieces)
Crusty Italian bread	6 oz	180 g

PROCEDURE

PREPARATION

1. Trim the healed ends of the broccolini and remove any wilted or discolored leaves.
2. Follow the Procedure for Blanching and Refreshing, page 96, to cook the broccolini al dente.
3. Blot the broccolini dry on clean kitchen towels.

HOLDING

Refrigerate the broccolini wrapped in clean, dry, lint-free towels up to 24 hours.

FINISHING AND PLATING

4. Pour the oil into a 4-oz (120-mL) shallow dip dish or ramekin.
5. Force the garlic through a garlic press into the oil.
6. Stir in the salt and vinegar.
7. Place the dish on the left side of a cool 12-in. (30-cm) plate.
8. Arrange the broccolini on the right side of the plate.
9. Cut an *X* into the grape tomatoes and arrange them on the broccolini stems.
10. Serve the bread on a separate plate or in a napkin-lined basket.

VARIATION

Replace the broccolini with peeled broccoli rabe or peeled broccoli spears.

Poaching Vegetables and Fruits

Poaching is cooking food completely submerged in a flavorful liquid at a low temperature. Poached vegetables and fruits may be used to good advantage in garde manger work. Poaching is normally used for vegetables from the white, orange, or purple-red color groups, and for firm-textured or under-ripe fruits. Green vegetables are poor candidates for poaching because low, slow cooking discolors them. Ripe fruits should not be poached, as they become mushy or grainy. Foods that float or that may turn brown should be weighted so they stay submerged (see procedure below for the technique).

In this section, we focus on poaching techniques and ingredients that are specific to vegetable and fruit cookery.

CUISSONS

The French culinary term for a flavorful poaching liquid is ***cuisson*** [kwee-SOH(N)]. Vegetables are typically poached in stock, vegetable broth, or seasoned water. Sometimes a flavorful fat, such olive oil or a nut oil, is added as an enrichment, giving the vegetable a luscious mouthfeel. Fruits are typically poached in a light syrup consisting of 2 parts liquid to 1 part (or less) sugar. Poached foods for cold service should not be cooked in *cuissons* containing large amounts of butter or other semisolid fats, because these can contribute a greasy mouthfeel.

Frequently, a *cuisson* for vegetables and fruits is seasoned with an acidic ingredient, such as lemon juice or wine. Keep in mind that acids act to firm vegetable fibers and can significantly prolong cooking times. If an acidic ingredient is used, use a nonreactive cooking vessel. Do not use acids when cooking green vegetables, because acids turn their pigments from bright green to olive green. (Whole artichokes are an exception: acid prevents the white artichoke heart from darkening.)

Procedure for Poaching Vegetables and Fruits

1. Combine the *cuisson* ingredients in a saucepan or brazier just large enough to hold the *cuisson* and one batch of product. (If the *cuisson* is acidic, use a nonreactive pan.) Bring the *cuisson* to the boil.
2. Prepare a round of parchment paper of the correct size to cover the surface of the *cuisson*. Have ready a plate that will fit into the pan and cover most of the surface of the *cuisson*. Prepare an ice bain-marie large enough to hold the poaching pan.
3. Drop the fabricated fruits or vegetables into the *cuisson* and adjust the heat so that when recovery is complete, the *cuisson* maintains a gentle simmer. Place the parchment on the surface and set the plate on top of it.
4. Simmer until the product reaches a texture slightly under the desired doneness. Test by removing the plate and inserting a paring knife into a sample.
5. Remove the pan from the heat and set it into the ice bain-marie.
6. When the *cuisson* and the product are cold:

   Refrigerate the product in its *cuisson* in a freshly sanitized, nonreactive covered container.

   –or–

   Remove the product from the *cuisson* and store it appropriately.
7. Thicken or reduce the *cuisson* as desired.

PORT POACHED PEARS

Yield:
about 12 oz (360 g)
Portions:
4
Portion size:
3 oz (90 g)

INGREDIENTS	U.S.	METRIC
Lemon	1	1
Firm pears	20 oz (4)	600 g (4)
Imported red port	12 fl oz	0.75 L
Water	12 fl oz	0.75 L
Sugar	12 oz	360 g

PROCEDURE

DAY 1

1. Squeeze half the lemon into a bowl of cold water large enough to hold the pears.
2. Peel the pears, cut them in half lengthwise, and remove the cores.

3. Follow the Procedure for Poaching Vegetables and Fruits on page 98, making a port wine syrup *cuisson* using the port, water, and sugar.
4. Steep the poached pears for 24 hours in the port syrup.

DAY 2

5. Remove the pears from the port syrup. The finished pears will be a rich, deep ruby-red color.
6. Reduce the syrup as desired to make a sauce or glaze. Season the sauce or glaze with the remaining lemon.

HOLDING

Refrigerate in a freshly sanitized, covered container up to 5 days.

COOL LEMON CARROTS

SIDE DISH

Yield:
about 1 lb (500 g)
Portions:
4–6
Portion size:
3–4 oz (85–120 g)

INGREDIENTS	U.S.	METRIC
Young carrots	1 lb	500 g
Lemon	1	1
Shallots, sliced thin	½ oz	15 g
Pure golden olive oil	1 fl oz	30 mL
Salt	to taste	to taste

PROCEDURE

PREPARATION

1. Trim and peel the carrots. Cut them into rounds ¼-in. (1-cm) thick.
2. Use a swivel peeler to remove the lemon zest in 1 or 2 strips. Juice the lemon.
3. Place the carrots in a sauté pan just large enough to accommodate them with about 1 in. (2 cm) headroom. Add water to cover. Mix in the lemon zest, shallots, oil, and salt. (Do not add the lemon juice at this time.) Cook at a simmer until the carrots are just al dente.
4. Raise the heat and allow the *cuisson* to reduce/evaporate until nearly gone. Stir frequently.
5. Season the carrots with lemon juice and more salt, if needed.
6. Open-pan cool.

HOLDING

Refrigerate in a freshly sanitized, covered container up to 5 days.

VARIATION

MOROCCAN CARROTS

Omit the shallots. Toss the finished carrots with 1 tsp (5 mL) each ground cinnamon and ground cumin, ¼ oz (7 g) minced garlic, and ½ oz (15 g) chopped parsley.

POACHING À BLANC

Vegetables susceptible to discoloration are sometimes poached in a special *cuisson* called a *blanc*, meaning "white." A ***blanc*** consists of water, oil, lemon juice, salt, and a flour slurry. Artichokes and cauliflower are two vegetables frequently cooked in a *blanc*. Poaching in a *blanc* is called ***poaching à blanc***.

Procedure for Poaching à *Blanc*

1. Prepare iced refreshing water or an ice bain-marie large enough to hold the saucepan you will use for cooking the vegetables.
2. Assemble the following ingredients:

Water for cooking	2 qt (2 L)
All-purpose flour	1 oz (30 g)
Additional cold water	3 fl oz (90 mL)
Light olive oil	1½ fl oz (45 mL)
Fresh lemon juice	1½ fl oz (45 mL)
Salt	1 tsp (5 mL)

3. Prepare the *blanc*:
   a. Bring the cooking water to a boil in a nonreactive saucepan.
   b. Place the flour in a small bowl and whisk in the additional cold water to make a thick **slurry**, or starch paste. Whisk in the oil, lemon juice, and salt.
   c. Whisk the slurry into the boiling cooking water.
4. Add the vegetables and wait for the *blanc* to recover a brisk simmer.
5. If necessary, weight the vegetables with a plate or nonreactive lid to keep them submerged.
6. Simmer the vegetables until they reach the desired doneness. Check their texture by inserting a knife into them.
7. Remove the vegetables from the blanc and refresh them in the ice water.

   –or–

   Place the saucepan in the ice bain-marie until the vegetables and *cuisson* reach room temperature.
8. Drain the vegetables and blot them dry on clean, lint-free towels.

BABY ARTICHOKES POACHED À BLANC

Yield:
about 1 lb (0.5 kg)
Portions:
varies
Portion size:
varies

INGREDIENTS	U.S.	METRIC
Lemon	1	1
Baby artichokes	1½ lb	0.75 kg
Water for cooking	2 qt	2 L
All-purpose flour	1 oz	30 g
Additional cold water	3 fl oz	90 mL
Light olive oil	1½ fl oz	45 mL
Fresh lemon juice	1½ fl oz	45 mL
Salt	1 tsp	5 mL

PROCEDURE

PREPARATION

1. Prepare acidulated water using half of the lemon.
2. Fabricate the baby artichokes following steps 1 through 4 on page 112. As you trim each artichoke, rub it with the remaining lemon half and drop the artichoke into the acidulated water.
3. Cook the artichokes according to the Procedure for Poaching à *Blanc* on this page.

HOLDING

Refrigerate in a freshly sanitized, covered container lined with towels up to 5 days. Bring to room temperature before serving.

BABY ARTICHOKES CÔTE D'AZUR

[koht duh-ZOOR]

APPETIZER

Portions:
1
Portion size:
6 pieces, about 5 oz (150 g)

INGREDIENTS	U.S.	METRIC
Baby Artichokes Poached à Blanc (p. 101)	6	6
Classic French Vinaigrette (p. 32), in squeeze bottle	1 fl oz	30 mL
Red Bell Pepper Purée (p. 54), in squeeze bottle	5 fl oz	150 mL
Thick Aïoli (p. 42), in pastry bag fitted with a large star tip	1 fl oz	30 mL
Chervil or flat-leaf parsley	1 pluche	1 pluche
Crisp baguette	3 oz	90 mL

PROCEDURE

FINISHING AND PLATING

1. If the artichokes are cold from refrigeration, warm them to room temperature in a microwave oven on low power for a few seconds.
2. Toss the artichokes with the vinaigrette.
3. Squeeze a pool of red bell pepper purée onto a cool 10-in. (25-cm) plate.
4. Arrange 6 artichokes on the plate in a spoke pattern with the stems in the center.
5. Pipe a rosette of aïoli in the center of each plate.
6. Place the chervil pluche on the rosette.
7. Serve the baguette on a separate plate or in a napkin-lined basket.

VARIATION

BABY ARTICHOKES TONNATO

Present the artichokes on a pool of Tonnato Sauce (p. 43) garnished with tomato filets, capers, and black olives.

POACHING À LA GRECQUE

In the days before refrigeration, garde manger chefs used a classic *cuisson* that includes salt, acidic ingredients, and vegetable oil to both cook and preserve vegetables at the same time. Called ***poaching à la Grecque***, this technique produces al dente vegetables that are slightly pickled and thus have a tangy taste.

VEGETABLES À LA GRECQUE

[ah-lah GREK]

SIDE DISH

Yield:
about 2 lb (1 kg)
Portions:
6
Portion size:
5 oz (150 g)

INGREDIENTS	U.S.	METRIC
Cauliflower, cut in 1-in. (2.5-cm) florets	8 oz	240 g
Carrot, cut in 2-in. (5-cm) bâtonnets	8 oz	240 g
Peeled small boiling onions (X cut in root end)	6 oz	180 g
Raw artichoke bottoms (p. 113), quartered (see Note)	6 oz	180 g
Pure golden olive oil	4 fl oz	120 mL
White wine vinegar	2 fl oz	60 mL
Small peeled garlic cloves	1½ oz	45 g
Bay leaves	2	2
Fresh thyme	¼ oz (4 sprigs)	(7 g) (4 sprigs)
Small dried red Italian chile	1	1
Water	as needed	as needed
Kosher salt	to taste	to taste
Sugar	to taste	to taste
Black peppercorns	2 tsp	10 mL
Coriander seeds	1 tsp	10 mL
Zucchini, with skin, cut in 2-in. (5-cm) bâtonnets	6 oz	180 g
Fresh thyme leaves	¼ oz	7 g
Fresh oregano leaves	¼ oz	7 g

Note: Frozen, cooked artichoke bottoms may be used. If already tender, add them along with the zucchini.

PROCEDURE

DAY 1

1. Combine the cauliflower, carrot, onions, artichokes, oil, vinegar, garlic, bay, thyme, and chile in a nonreactive saucepan just a little larger than the volume of the vegetables. Add water to the level of the vegetables and bring it to a brisk simmer.
2. Lightly season the *cuisson* (p. 98) with salt and a pinch of sugar.
3. Tie the peppercorns and coriander seeds in cheesecloth sachet and bury the sachet in the *cuisson*.
4. Cook the vegetables at a brisk simmer about 10 minutes, or until they are al dente.
5. Transfer the vegetables and their *cuisson* to a freshly sanitized nonreactive container. Mix in the zucchini.
6. Cool the vegetables to room temperature and then refrigerate them, covered, for at least 12 hours and no longer than 24 hours.

DAY 2

7. Thoroughly drain the *cuisson* from the vegetables into a large nonreactive sauté pan or brazier. Discard the bay leaves and spice sachet.
8. Reduce the *cuisson* to a dressing by boiling it over high heat to about 4 fl oz (120 mL) liquid. Cool it to room temperature.
9. Taste the dressing and correct the acid-oil-salt balance.
10. Mix the drained vegetables with the dressing and the thyme and oregano leaves.

HOLDING

Refrigerate up to 2 hours. To hold up to 2 days, reserve the fresh herbs and add them just before service.

PRESENTATION

11. Mound the vegetables in a serving bowl or add to a plate presentation.

Stewed, Braised, Roasted, and Grilled Vegetables

Stewing produces tender vegetables or fruits, during which the flavors of the sauce and the produce combine. Braised vegetables and fruits should be very tender and have a deep, complex flavor from both the cooking medium and the initial browning. Tender-textured vegetables and fruits are dry-roasted in a manner similar to meats. Steam-roasting, with basting or a covered pan, is necessary for firm and hard items. Garde manger chefs frequently use grilled vegetables in salads, sandwiches, terrines, and other composed cold dishes.

BRAISED LEEKS VINAIGRETTE

APPETIZER OR SIDE DISH

Yield:
about 1 lb (0.5 kg)
Portions:
4
Portion size:
1 leek, about 4 oz (120 g)

INGREDIENTS	U.S.	METRIC
Leeks	2 lb (4 large)	1 kg (4 large)
Pure golden olive oil	1 fl oz	30 mL
Minced yellow onion	2 oz	60 g
Peeled, minced carrot	1 oz	30 g
Peeled, minced celery	1 oz	30 g
Minced garlic	¼ oz	7 g
Fresh lemon juice	½ oz	15 mL
Kosher salt	to taste	to taste
Poultry Stock (p. 749)	1 pt	0.5 L
Fresh thyme	¼ oz (2 sprigs)	7 g (2 sprigs)
Thick Mustard Vinaigrette (p. 33), at room temperature	8 fl oz	240 mL

PROCEDURE

PREPARATION

1. Prepare the leeks as illustrated on page 116. Tie the stem end of each leek with kitchen string.
2. Heat a sauté pan large enough to hold the leeks, add the oil, and lightly brown the leeks over moderate heat on all sides. Remove them from the pan.
3. Add the mirepoix vegetables and sauté them over low heat until they are softened and beginning to brown. Stir in the garlic.
4. Return the leeks to the pan and add the lemon juice, a little salt, and the stock. Cover the pan and cook at a brisk simmer about 12 minutes, or until the leeks are soft enough to insert a knife in them with no resistance.
5. Carefully remove the leeks to a perforated half-hotel pan set over a drip pan. Gently press on the leeks to help them drain.
6. Reduce the leek *cuisson* to 2 fl oz (60 mL). Add the liquid that drains from the leeks to the *cuisson* as it reduces.
7. Scrape the reduced *cuisson* into a bowl and whisk in the vinaigrette.
8. Transfer the leeks to a solid half-hotel pan and carefully remove the strings.
9. Pour the vinaigrette over the leeks. Cover the pan and marinate the leeks at least 2 hours. Turn them gently once or twice for even marination.

HOLDING

Refrigerate up to 5 days. Bring to room temperature before serving.

COOL RATATOUILLE

[rah-tah-too-EE]

APPETIZER OR SIDE DISH

Yield:
1 qt (1 L), about 1½ lb (0.75 kg)
Portions:
4–6
Portion size:
5–8 fl oz (150–240 mL),
4–6 oz (120–180 g)

INGREDIENTS	U.S.	METRIC
Eggplant	12 oz	360 g
Pure golden olive oil	2½ fl oz	75 mL
Kosher salt	to taste	to taste
Small zucchini, cut in ¾-in. (2-cm) dice	10 oz	300 g
Yellow bell pepper, cut in ¾-in. (2-cm) squares	10 oz	300 g
Chopped yellow onion	5 oz	150 g
Minced garlic	½ oz	15 g
Tomato concassé	1 qt	1 L
Bay leaf	1	1
Dried basil	½ tsp	3 mL
Dried thyme	¼ tsp	1 mL
Dried tarragon	½ tsp	3 mL
Extra-virgin olive oil	2 fl oz	60 mL
Red wine vinegar	to taste	to taste

PROCEDURE

PREPARATION

1. If using small, thin-skinned eggplants, trim the ends and cut them into 1-in. (2.5-cm) dice. If using a large standard eggplant, peel before dicing.
2. Heat a large sauté pan very hot, add 1½ fl oz (45 mL) pure olive oil, and sear the eggplant dice on all sides. Season with a little salt. Transfer to a large nonreactive saucepan.
3. Add ½ oz (15 mL) pure olive oil to the sauté pan, lower the heat, and sear the zucchini and peppers. Add them to the saucepan.
4. Add the remaining pure olive oil to the sauté pan, lower the heat, and add the onion. Sauté a few seconds, and then add the garlic and concassé. Add salt and bring the mixture to the boil.
5. Pour the tomato concassé over the vegetables. Add the dried herbs and mix gently.
6. Partially cover the pan and simmer the vegetables in the sauce until they are just tender.
7. Cool the ratatouille to room temperature and remove the bay leaf.
8. Stir in the extra-virgin olive oil. Season the ratatouille with a little vinegar if it tastes flat. Balance the salt.

HOLDING

Hold at cool room temperature up to 4 hours. Refrigerate up to 5 days. Bring to room temperature before serving.

PRESENTATION

9. Mound the ratatouille in a serving bowl or add it to a plate presentation.

ROASTED SUMMER VEGETABLE MEDLEY

SIDE DISH

Yield:
about 2 lb (1 kg)
Portions:
8
Portion size:
4 oz (120 g)

INGREDIENTS	U.S.	METRIC
Slender zucchini	8 oz	240 g
Slender yellow summer squash	8 oz	240 g
Small, slender eggplants	12 oz	360 g
Red bell peppers	10 oz	300 g
Yellow bell peppers	10 oz	300 g
Small sweet onions	8 oz	240 g
Firm plum tomatoes	10 oz	300 g
Chopped fresh garlic	½ oz	15 g
Pure golden olive oil	8 fl oz	240 mL
Kosher salt	to taste	to taste
Fresh thyme sprigs	¼ oz	7 g
Fresh tarragon sprigs	¼ oz	7 g
Fresh oregano sprigs	⅛ oz	3 g
Freshly ground black pepper	to taste	to taste
Red wine vinegar	to taste	to taste

PROCEDURE

PREPARATION

1. Preheat an oven to 425°F (215°C).
2. Fabricate the vegetables:
   a. Trim the zucchini and yellow squash. Cut each in half widthwise and then in half lengthwise to make quarters.
   b. Trim the eggplants and cut them into shapes similar to but slightly larger than the squash. Make sure each piece has skin on it.
   c. Remove the core, seeds, and membranes of the peppers and cut them into slabs of the same size as the squash pieces.
   d. Trim and peel the onions and cut them into wedges about the same thickness as the squash pieces. Secure each wedge together with a toothpick.
   e. Blanch and refresh the tomatoes to remove the skins. Make sure the tomatoes remain raw and firm. Remove the cores.
3. Place the vegetables and garlic in a half-hotel pan and toss them with the oil, salt, and lemon juice. Add the herb sprigs.
4. Roast the vegetables 15–20 minutes, stirring gently at 5-minute intervals, until the vegetables are lightly browned at the edges.
5. Cool the vegetables to room temperature.
6. Taste the vegetables and season them with pepper, vinegar, and more salt if necessary. Remove the herb sprigs and toothpicks.
7. If necessary, drain off excess cooking liquid into a sauté pan and reduce it to a light sauce. Cool the sauce and pour it over the vegetables.

HOLDING

Hold at room temperature up to 3 hours or refrigerate up to 2 days. Reheat and then cool to room temperature before serving.

PRESENTATION

Present the vegetables in a serving bowl or as part of a plate presentation.

Procedure for Steam Roasting Vegetables

1. Preheat a standard oven to a minimum of 400°F (200° C) or a convection oven to a minimum of 375°F (190° C).
2. Spread appropriately fabricated vegetables in a hotel pan in one layer. If the vegetables will not be peeled after roasting, toss them with salt, other desired seasonings, and oil. Add a small amount of water or a flavorful liquid to the pan according to your judgment. Cover the pan with a lid or a double layer of aluminum foil.
3. Place the vegetables in the preheated oven and steam roast to the desired doneness. Test the vegetables by inserting a knife into them. When done, they should show little resistance.
4. When the vegetables are cooked almost to the desired texture, uncover the pan and, if necessary, gently stir to redistribute the oil and seasonings. Continue roasting until the vegetables' exterior surfaces have acquired the desired brown color.
5. Open-pan cool the vegetables and then peel them.

   –or–

   Open-pan cool the vegetables. Add acidic flavorings if desired, and correct the seasoning.

ROASTED BEETS

Yield:
about 12 oz (360 g)
Portions:
varies
Portion size:
varies

INGREDIENTS	U.S.	METRIC
Beets, stems and greens removed	1 lb	0.5 kg
Water	as needed	as needed

PROCEDURE

PREPARATION

1. Preheat an oven to 400°F (200°C).
2. If necessary, sort the beets according to size in order to roast similar size beets together.
3. Scrub the beets under cool water and place them in a half-hotel pan with about ½-in. (1-cm) water. Cover the pan with foil, place it in the oven, and bake the beets according to size and desired doneness. Medium size beets cook to al dente texture (for carpaccio) in about 30 minutes. For tender beets bake about 45 minutes, or until they show little resistance when tested with a sharp knife.
4. Remove the foil (A) and cool to room temperature.
5. Trim the stem and root end of each beet and pare away the skin (B).
6. Fabricate the peeled beets as desired. For carpaccio, slice al dente beets paper-thin on a mandoline.

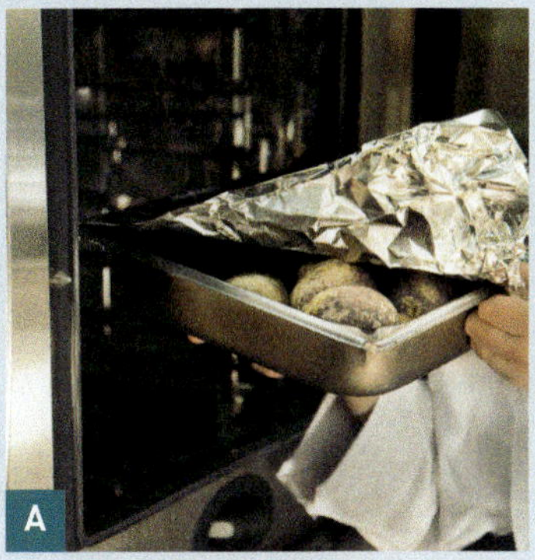
A

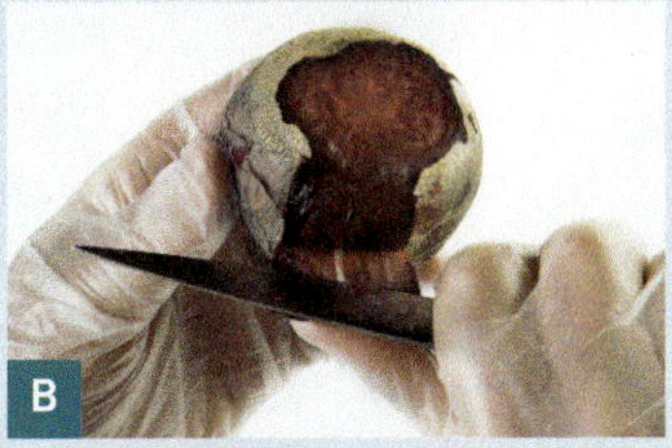
B

HOLDING

Cover and refrigerate up to 5 days.

GRILLED SUMMER VEGETABLE MEDLEY

SIDE DISH

Yield:
about 2 lb (1 kg)
Portions:
varies
Portion size:
varies

INGREDIENTS	U.S.	METRIC
Extra-virgin olive oil	4 fl oz	120 mL
Peeled whole garlic cloves	½ oz	15 mL
Kosher salt	to taste	to taste
Small, slender eggplants (see Note)	12 oz	360 g
Small, slender zucchini	10 oz	300 g
Small, slender yellow summer squash	10 oz	300 g
Red bell pepper	8 oz	240 g
Yellow bell pepper	8 oz	240 g
Sweet onion	12 oz	360 g
Lemon juice, red wine vinegar, or balsamic vinegar	to taste	to taste
Freshly ground black pepper	to taste	to taste
Fresh thyme leaves	⅛ oz	3 g
Fresh basil leaves, chiffonade	¼ oz	7 g

Note: If using large, standard eggplants, peel them before slicing.

PROCEDURE

PREPARATION

1. Fabricate the vegetables:
   a. Trim the stem and blossom ends of the eggplant(s) and cut into long, oval slices ⅜-in. (1-cm) thick.
   b. Trim the stem and blossom ends of the zucchini and yellow squash. Cut them lengthwise into ⅜-in. (1-cm) slabs.
   c. Remove the stem, core, and seeds of the peppers and cut them into rings ½-in. (1-cm) thick. Trim any membrane adhering to the inside of the rings.
   d. Peel the onion and cut it into ½-in. (1-cm) slices. Separate the slices into rings.
2. Place the oil in a large bowl. Force the garlic through a garlic press into the oil. Alternatively, crush the garlic with the flat of a chef knife blade and add it to the oil. Season the oil with salt.
3. Preheat a grill to high heat.
4. Toss the vegetables in the oil to coat them well.
5. Grill the vegetables slightly less done than if they were to be served hot. As they finish grilling, remove them to a half-hotel pan to cool.
6. Season the vegetables with lemon juice or vinegar. Correct the salt and season them with pepper.

HOLDING

Hold at cool room temperature up to 3 hours. If necessary, refrigerate up to 3 days. Bring to room temperature before serving.

PRESENTATION

Arrange the vegetables on a serving platter and top with the fresh herbs. Alternatively, utilize as part of a plate presentation or as a sandwich internal garnish.

Special Vegetable Fabrication and Cooking Techniques

A few vegetables are so unusual or complex in structure that they require special techniques for both fabrication and cooking.

Roasted Peppers

Roasted peppers are not actually roasted but, rather, *char-peeled*. They are either grilled or broiled in order to remove their skins and slightly soften their flesh while giving them a subtle, smoky flavor. Roasted peppers are tasty and colorful additions to salads and sandwiches, and make attractive garnishes and décor items.

Procedure for Preparing Roasted Peppers

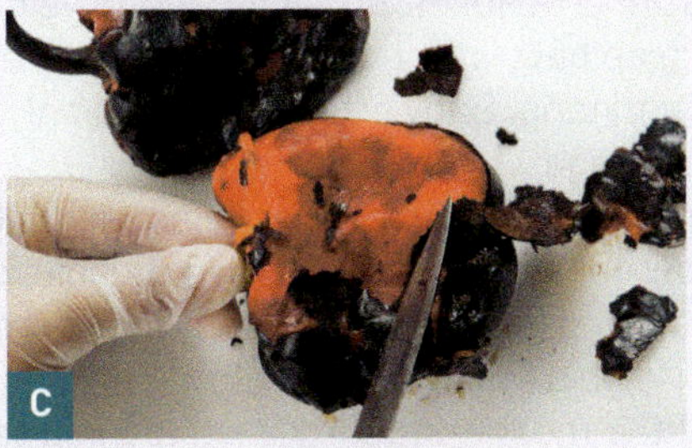

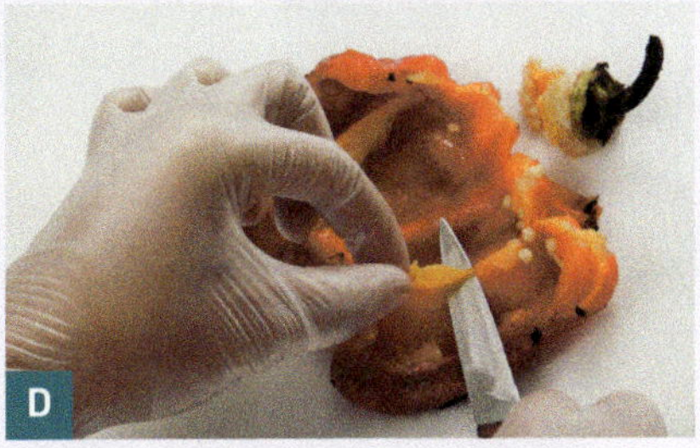

1. Preheat a grill or broiler to the highest setting.
2. Prepare for steaming the peppers after grilling: Use a pouch made of aluminum foil, a heavy-duty plastic bag, or a hotel pan with a lid.
3. Place a manageable number of peppers on the grill or under the broiler and cook them, turning often, until the skins are blistered and mostly charred (A). Do not allow the peppers to burn through to the flesh.
4. Immediately transfer the peppers into the steaming pouch, bag, or pan (B). Allow the peppers to steam in their own carryover heat just until they collapse. Do not steam them until they are soft and flaccid.
5. Spread the peppers to cool.
6. Lay 2 pieces of parchment paper on a work surface. Prepare a freshly sanitized container to hold the fully fabricated peppers.
7. To clean the peppers, put on food-service gloves. (This is especially important when cleaning roasted chiles.)
8. Place the peppers on one of the parchment sheets. Using a paring knife, scrape and pull off the charred skin (C). Transfer each peeled pepper to the other parchment sheet as you work. When all peppers are peeled, roll up and discard the parchment containing the charred skins.
9. Change to a fresh pair of gloves and wipe the knife.
10. If the peppers are to be stuffed, make a slit in one side of each pepper and carefully remove the seed ball and membranes without tearing the pepper or dislodging its stem. Be sure to remove all the seeds. Transfer each pepper to the container after it has been cleaned.

    –or–

    Remove the stem and core of each pepper and open it out flat. Remove the seeds and membranes (D). Cut into desired shapes. Transfer the peppers to the container.

Don't Rinse Roasted Peppers!

It is a mistake to rinse roasted peppers under running water while peeling them. Rinsing not only washes away valuable flavor compounds and nutrients but also causes the pepper flesh to become waterlogged. In most preparations, the few flecks of charring that remain on unwashed peppers add to the rustic look of the finished dish and should not be considered a flaw. If the peppers are to be used as a garnish or décor element, charred bits can be wiped away with a clean, damp towel.

Artichokes

Artichokes are complex vegetables,with their tasty flesh hidden deep within an armor of overlapping leaves and protected by tiny, sharp spines. In the center of the artichoke is the hairy ***choke***, a crown of inedible, fibrous spines. Once the many inedible parts are removed, proportionally little of the artichoke is left to eat. In fact, the edible part can be as little as 30%.

This edible portion is called the ***artichoke heart***. It consists of the cup-shaped ***artichoke bottom*** and the tender, edible interior leaf bases. In addition, the thick stems of large artichokes have edible cores. The edible flesh of an artichoke is pale yellow or white. Green or purple parts are fibrous and are not eaten.

Once cut, artichokes quickly discolor due to enzymatic browning. To slow this browning, immediately rub the cut surfaces with lemon or drop the artichokes into acidulated water. Cook artichokes as soon as possible after fabrication to stop enzymatic browning. Pressure steaming is the best cooking method because it is fastest. When boiling artichokes, weight them with a plate or lid to keep them submerged in the cooking water. Artichoke hearts and bottoms are often poached *à blanc*.

BABY ARTICHOKES

Baby artichokes are small, immature artichokes, so young they have not yet formed a hairy choke in the center. A true baby artichoke weighs no more than 2 oz (60 g) and is no more than 2 in. (5 cm) long. Baby artichokes need only to be trimmed following steps 1 through 4 on page 112.

Many so-called baby artichokes marketed in North America are actually the small, fully mature artichokes that grow on the lower part of the artichoke plant. They weigh up to 5 oz (150 g) and are as long as 3½ in. (9 cm). They have a small choke and are fabricated and cooked in the same manner as large artichokes.

Pages 111–114 illustrate some of the most frequently used techniques for fabricating artichokes.

Procedure to Prepare Artichokes for Stuffing

1. Using a serrated knife cut off the artichoke stem flush with the base. Drop the stem in acidulated water and rub the cut base with a lemon half.
2. Cut off the top third of the artichoke and discard it. Rub the cut surface with the lemon.
3. Using scissors, snip off the spiny top of each leaf (A).
4. Gently press open the artichoke's leaves to reveal the choke. Using a demitasse spoon or parisienne scoop, scrape out the hairy choke (B).
5. Immediately rinse the artichoke's interior under cold water, shake dry, and squeeze in some lemon juice. Hold the artichoke in acidulated water until ready to cook it.
6. Cook the artichoke in lots of rapidly boiling water (C), weighted down so it stays submerged, until the bottom is knife-tender. Alternatively, cook the artichoke in a pressure steamer.
7. To judge doneness, pierce the bottom of the artichoke with a paring knife (D). If the artichoke will be baked or otherwise further cooked, it should show slight resistance to the knife. If it will be served with no further cooking, there should be no resistance to the knife.
8. Lift the artichoke out of the cooking water, pour the water out of the center, and immediately refresh in ice water until cold throughout.
9. Gently squeeze the water out of the cooled artichoke and drain it upside-down on a rack set over a sheet tray.

Procedure to Prepare an Artichoke Heart

1. To remove the artichoke's outer leaves, bend each leaf back until it breaks just above its fleshy base (A). Do not snap the leaves off below the fleshy base. Stop removing leaves when you reach the tender inner cone of pale-colored leaves.
2. Cut off the top two-thirds of the leaf cone (B) and rub the exposed surfaces with a lemon half.
3. Using a flexible paring knife, cut off the bottom ¼-in. (0.5-cm) of the stem, then pare away all of the stem's fibrous green skin and flesh (C). Leave only the pale, whitish interior. Rub the cut surfaces with lemon as you work.
4. With the flexible paring knife, trim away the fibrous outer flesh of the artichoke base, leaving only the pale, whitish interior (D). Rub the cut surfaces with lemon.
5. Cut the artichoke heart in half lengthwise and rub the cut surfaces with lemon. Insert the point of the knife just under the hairy choke and, cutting in an arc, slice under it (E). Pull the choke away from the bottom and discard it, then drop the cleaned artichoke heart half into the acidulated water. Repeat with the remaining half. Note: If whole artichoke hearts are needed instead, follow step 4 of Procedure to Prepare Artichokes for Stuffing (p. 111).
6. Boil (F) and refresh the artichoke hearts, or poach them *à blanc* (see the recipe directions on p. 101).

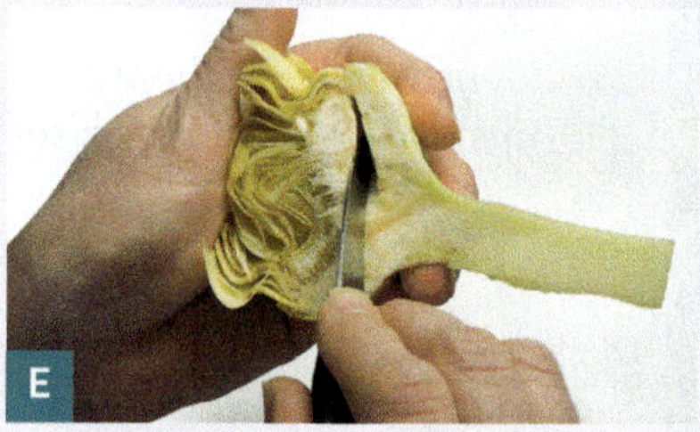

Procedure to Prepare an Artichoke Bottom

1. Cut off the artichoke stem flush with the base (A).
2. To remove the artichoke's leaves, bend each leaf back until it breaks just above its fleshy base (B). Do not snap the leaves off below the fleshy base. Remove enough leaves so only the inner leaves with tender, pale bases remain.
3. Cut the leaves off of the artichoke bottom (C) and discard them.
4. Using a flexible paring knife, pare away the fibrous green flesh of the base (D), leaving only the pale, whitish interior. Rub the cut surfaces with lemon.
5. Using a parisienne scoop, scrape out the hairy choke (E, F) and rinse the bottom under cold water. Immediately drop the artichoke bottom into acidulated water.
6. Poach the artichoke bottoms *à blanc* (see recipe directions on p. 101).

A

B

C

D

E

F

Procedure to Prepare Sliced Artichoke Hearts

1. Prepare artichoke hearts through step 5 of the Procedure to Prepare an Artichoke Heart (p. 112).
2. Using a sharp chef knife, cut the hearts into thin slices (A). Immediately drop the slices into heavily lemon-acidulated water.
3. Pan-steam the artichoke hearts just al dente in a small amount of salted, lemon-acidulated water (B).
4. Open-pan cool.

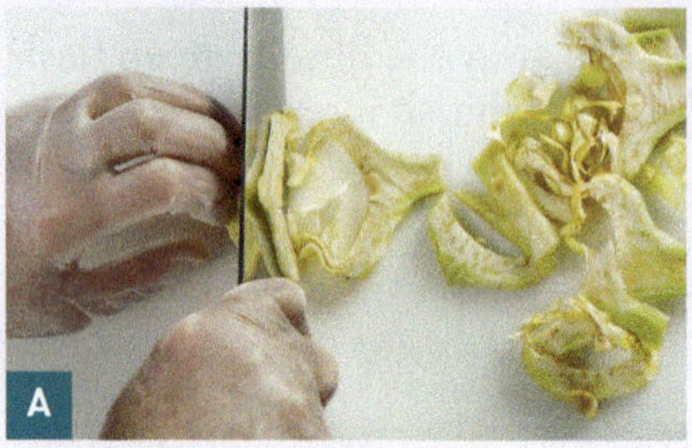
A

B

Asparagus

While today it is available virtually year-round, in the Northern Hemisphere asparagus is seasonal to spring. Fresh, local asparagus has an intense flavor and tender texture not found in distance-shipped asparagus.

Slender shoots of asparagus are called ***pencil asparagus***, because their diameter is the size of a pencil or smaller. Both standard asparagus and thick, ***jumbo asparagus*** have a fibrous outer skin on the lower part of the stalk that must be removed with a swivel peeler to ensure even cooking. White asparagus shipped from Europe has very fibrous skin and must be peeled deeply.

Cook asparagus immediately after peeling it. Alternatively, hold the peeled stalks refrigerated between clean, wet towels until cooking time. Asparagus can be cooked by steaming, boiling, or grilling.

Procedure for Asparagus Fabrication

1. To remove the fibrous stalk base, hold each end of the asparagus spear and bend it gently (A). The spear will break at the place where it changes from tough to tender. Do not cut the stalk ends with a knife.
2. Using a sharp swivel peeler with a narrow opening, lightly scrape the asparagus spear beginning about 1 in. (2.5 cm) from the tip and gliding the peeler toward the base (B). To keep the spear from breaking, lay it flat on the work surface.

A

B

Broccoli

Texturally, broccoli can be considered two vegetables in one. Each stalk of broccoli consists of a thick, meaty-fleshed stem and a lacy, open crown. The classic presentation for broccoli is fabricated into ***spears*** consisting of peeled stem and crown. It is more common today to serve only the ***florets***, or crown pieces, which are favored for their distinctive shape and texture. Nonetheless, broccoli stems are delicious in their own right, with a mild flavor and tender texture under the thick, fibrous skin. Because of this skin, broccoli stems must be peeled before they are cooked or eaten raw.

Procedure to Prepare Broccoli Spears

1. Using a paring knife, trim the hard, healed end of the broccoli stalk. Slide the knife under the skin and pull it toward the crown (A). The skin of a mature broccoli head usually peels away from the flesh. If it does not peel away easily, pare the skin with the knife.
2. Cut lengthwise through the main stalk and branched stems to make slender, even-sized spears (B).

Procedure to Prepare Broccoli Crown or Florets

1. To make a broccoli crown, cut the stalk just below the place where it branches out (A).
2. To create florets, cut farther up the stalk (B).

The cylindrical stalks of peeled broccoli stem may be cut into rounds, ovals, bâtonnets, or juliennes. All these shapes make interesting additions to salads, soups, stir-fries, and other composed dishes. Peeled stems may also be cooked soft and puréed to become the base for soups and sauces.

Procedure to Prepare Broccoli Stem Shapes

1. Peel the broccoli stalk and trim it into a rough cylinder. It can then be fabricated into rounds, ovals (shown here), bâtonnets, or juliennes.

Leeks

Leeks are well known for capturing sand and soil within their many layers of flesh. This is not a problem in preparations where the leeks are to be cut into slices or pieces, because they can easily be separated and washed. However, when you are presenting leeks whole, a special fabrication and cleaning method must be used.

Procedure to Prepare Whole Cleaned Leeks

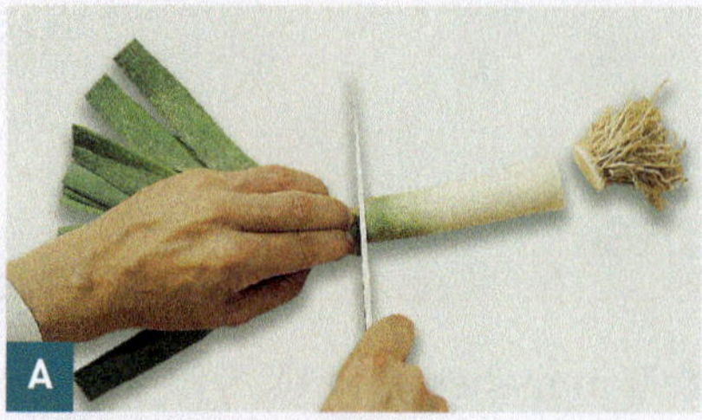

1. Cut the leek at the point where the flesh changes from pale green to dark green (A). Reserve the dark green tops for stock. Trim about ¼ in. (0.75 cm) of the leek's root end.
2. Cut vertically through the stalk about ½ in. (1 cm) from the root end (B).
3. Fan open the leek's layers (C) and wash under cool running water.

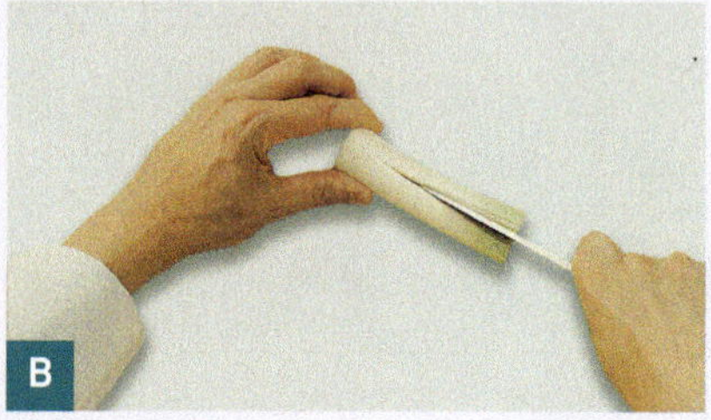

ADDITIONAL VEGETABLE RECIPES

GUACAMOLE AND CHIPS FOR TWO

APPETIZER

Portions:
2
Portions size:
4 oz

INGREDIENTS	U.S.	METRIC
Chopped sweet onion	2 oz	60 g
Minced fresh garlic	¼ oz (1 tsp)	7 g (5 mL)
Minced Serrano chile	¼ oz (2 tsp)	7 g (10 mL)
Kosher salt	to taste	to taste
Whole firm-ripe Western avocado, cold	10 oz	300 g)
Small lime wedge	2	2
Vine-ripe tomato, small dice	2 oz	60 g
Chopped cilantro	¼ oz (2 tbsp)	7 g (15 mL)
Green-leaf lettuce	1 leaf	1 leaf
Plain tortilla chips	4 oz	120 g

Note: For large-quantity preparation of guacamole, the mashed onion, garlic, and chiles may be prepared up to 1 hour ahead and refrigerated. The avocado may be diced and tossed with lime juice ½ hour ahead and refrigerated. Combine and finish at the last minute.

PROCEDURE

FINISHING AND PLATING

1. Combine the onion, garlic, chile, and salt in a mortar or shallow bowl. Mash with a pestle or the back of a spoon to release the juices.
2. Peel and dice the avocado. Add the avocado dice to the mortar.
3. Squeeze the juice of one lime wedge over the avocado. Use a fork to lightly mash the avocado and combine it with the onion mixture. Do not overmash or overmix.
4. Stir in the tomato and half the cilantro.
5. Taste and correct the salt-lime balance.
6. Place the lettuce leaf on the front center of a cool 12-in. (30-cm) plate.
7. Mound the guacamole on the leaf and sprinkle it with the remaining cilantro. Place the remaining lime wedge beside the guacamole.
8. Arrange the chips in an arc behind the guacamole.

HUMMUS

APPETIZER

Yield:
1 pt (0.5 L)
Portions:
4–8
Portion size:
2–4 fl oz (60–120 mL)

INGREDIENTS	U.S.	METRIC
Middle Eastern sesame paste (drained of oil)	½ oz	15 g
Fresh garlic, minced	¼ oz	7 g
Canned chickpeas, with liquid	15 oz	450 g
Fresh lemon juice	1 fl oz	30 mL
Kosher salt	to taste	to taste
Pure golden olive oil	4 fl oz	120 mL
Chopped parsley	¼ oz	7 g
Paprika Oil (p. 685), in squeeze bottle	1 fl oz	30 mL
Pita bread, cut in wedges	8 oz	240 g
–or–		
Flatbread crackers	6 oz	180 g
Supplies		
12-in. (30-cm) paper doily	1	1

PROCEDURE

PREPARATION

1. Place the sesame paste and garlic in a food processor fitted with the steel blade.
2. Drain the chickpeas and reserve the canning liquid. Reserve 1 oz (30 g) of the drained chickpeas for garnish.
3. Add 14 oz (420 g) drained chickpeas to the processor with half of the lemon juice and some salt. Grind to a rough purée.
4. With the processor running, alternately add the olive oil and some of the canning liquid to make a light, emulsified mixture.
5. Taste and balance the seasonings with more lemon juice and salt.

HOLDING

Refrigerate in a freshly sanitized, covered container up to 2 days.

PRESENTATION

6. Place the hummus in an 18-fl oz (0.5-L) serving bowl and smooth the surface.
7. Sprinkle a line of parsley around the edges of the hummus and arrange the chickpeas on it.
8. Shake the paprika oil and drizzle it decoratively over the surface of the hummus.
9. Place the bowl on a 14-in. (35-cm) tray lined with a doily.
10. Arrange the pita or flatbread crackers around the bowl.

BABA GHANOUSH

[bah-bah-gan-OOSH]

MIDDLE EASTERN EGGPLANT DIP

APPETIZER

Yield:
1 pt (0.5 L)
Portions:
4–8
Portion size:
2–4 fl oz (60–120 mL)

INGREDIENTS	U.S.	METRIC
Young, slelnder eggplant	2 lb	1 kg
Fresh garlic, minced	½ oz	15 g
Chopped sweet onion	2 oz	60 g
Chopped fresh green chile (preferably Italian or Serrano)	½ oz	30 g
Kosher salt	to taste	to taste
Pure golden olive oil	3 fl oz	90 mL
Freshly ground black pepper	to taste	to taste
Freshly toasted, ground cumin	½ tsp	5 mL
Sweet Hungarian paprika	½ tsp	5 mL
Chopped flat-leaf parsley	½ oz	15 g
Vine-ripe tomato, cut in ⅜-in. (1-cm) dice	4 oz	120 g
Fresh lemon juice	to taste	to taste
Pita bread, cut into wedges	8 oz	240 g
Supplies		
12-in. (30-cm) paper doily	1	1

PROCEDURE

PREPARATION

1. Preheat a charcoal or gas grill, or a broiler, to high heat.
2. Grill the eggplants according to the Procedure for Preparing Roasted Peppers (p. 109) until they are blackened and soft through. Cool. Do not wrap or cover them.
3. Place the garlic, onion, chiles, and some salt in a mortar or heavy bowl. Pound the vegetables with a pestle or mortar to release their juices.
4. Slit the eggplants lengthwise and scrape the flesh onto a cutting board. Discard the skins. Coarsely chop the eggplant and scrape it into a bowl.
5. Combine the pounded vegetables, eggplant, oil, tomatoes, and seasonings.
6. Allow the mixture to mellow at room temperature for about 30 minutes.
7. Taste and correct the seasoning.

HOLDING

Refrigerate in a freshly sanitized, covered container up to 2 days. Bring to room temperature before serving.

PRESENTATION

8. Mound the Baba Ghanoush in an 18-fl oz (0.5-L) serving bowl.
9. Place the bowl on a 14-in. (35-cm) tray lined with a doily.
10. Arrange the pita bread triangles around the bowl.

THREE MIDDLE EASTERN DIPS WITH GRILLED PITA (FOR TWO)

APPETIZER

Portions:
2
Portion size:
4½ fl oz (135 mL), plus 3 oz (90 g) bread

INGREDIENTS	U.S.	METRIC
Hummus (p. 118)	3 fl oz	90 mL
Baba Ghanoush (p. 119)	3 fl oz	90 mL
Tzatziki Sauce (p. 47)	3 fl oz	90 mL
Pure golden olive oil	1 fl oz	30 mL
8-in. (20-cm) pita breads (2 pieces)	6 oz	180 g
Supplies		
8-in. (20-cm) paper doily	1	1

PROCEDURE

FINISHING AND PLATING

1. Make sure the hot line has a grill preheated to high heat.
2. Place the dips in three 3-oz (90-mL) ramekins garnished as directed in the recipes. Place the ramekins together in the center of a doily-lined 12-in. (30-cm) plate.
3. The hot line brushes the pitas with oil on both sides and grills them until the exteriors are grill-marked and slightly crisp but the interior is still soft.
4. When you receive the grilled pitas from the hot line, place them on a cutting board and cut each into triangular wedges.
5. Arrange the pita wedges around the ramekins.

ASPARAGUS BUNDLE TOURANGELLE

APPETIZER

Portions:
1

Portion size:
3 oz (90 g) asparagus, ½ oz (15 g) ham

INGREDIENTS	U.S.	METRIC
Peeled, blanched, refreshed asparagus *(à point)*	3 oz	90 g
Classic French Vinaigrette (p. 32), in squeeze bottle	½ fl oz	15 mL
Smoked ham, thin sliced	½ oz (2 slices)	15 g (2 slices)
Fresh goat cheese, room temperature	¾ oz	25 g
Chopped fresh tarragon	¼ oz	7 g
Freshly ground white pepper	to taste	to taste
Freshly toasted Croûtons for Leeks (p. 703)	1	1
Carrot Essence (p. 691), in squeeze bottle	4 fl oz	120 mL

PROCEDURE

FINISHING

1. Blot the asparagus dry on a clean, lint-free towel and place it in a wide bowl.
2. Squeeze the vinaigrette over the asparagus and roll it to coat each spear with the dressing.
3. Place the ham slices on the work surface, overlapping at the short ends.
4. Spread the goat cheese on the ham slices in an even layer. Sprinkle with one-third of the tarragon.
5. Arrange the asparagus at one end of the overlapping ham slices with tips extending over both edges.
6. Roll the ham around the asparagus to form a bundle.

PLATING

7. Place the croûton in the center of a cool 10-in. (25-cm) oval plate. Place the asparagus bundle on the croûton and press it gently so it stays in place.
8. Squeeze the carrot essence around the bundle.
9. Garnish with the remaining tarragon.

ARTICHOKE VINAIGRETTE

APPETIZER

Portions:
1
Portion size:
1 large artichoke, EP about 3 oz (90 g), plus 3 oz (90 g) bread

INGREDIENTS	U.S.	METRIC
Large globe artichoke, about 12 oz (360 g), prepared for stuffing (p. 111), pressure steamed or boiled, refreshed, and drained	1	1
Thick Mustard Vinaigrette (p. 33), in squeeze bottle	4 fl oz	120 mL
Very fine julienne lemon zest	1 tbsp	15 mL
Lemon wedge	1	1
Crisp baguette	3 oz	90 g

PROCEDURE

PLATING

1. If the artichoke is cold from refrigeration, place it in a microwave and bring it to cool room temperature by heating it on low power for a few seconds only.
2. Hold the artichoke upside-down and gently squeeze to remove excess water.
3. Place the artichoke in the center of a cool 10-in. (25-cm) plate. Open the leaves to hold the vinaigrette and ensure an attractive presentation.
4. Squeeze half of the vinaigrette into the center of the artichoke. Squeeze the remaining vinaigrette over the leaves and onto the plate well.
5. Scatter the lemon zest around the plate well.
6. Place the lemon wedge on top of the artichoke.
7. Serve the baguette in a napkin-lined basket or on a side plate.

NAPOLEON OF SUMMER VEGETABLES

APPETIZER

Portions:
1
Portion size:
about 5 oz (150 g)

INGREDIENTS	U.S.	METRIC
Grilled Summer Vegetable Medley (p. 108), zucchini, yellow bell pepper, eggplant, onion, yellow squash, red bell pepper, fabricated to fit puff pastry squares	3 oz (each)	90 g (each)
Garlic-Herb Cheese Spread (p. 594), in pastry bag with large star tip	2 oz	60 g
2½-in. (6-cm) squares baked puff pastry	4	4
Basic Tomato Coulis (Sauce) (p. 52), in squeeze bottle	2 fl oz	30 mL
Bright Green Basil Oil (p. 686), in squeeze bottle	½ fl oz	15 mL
Peeled cherry tomato	¼ oz (1)	7 g (1)
Fresh basil	⅛ oz (1 sprig)	3 g (1 sprig)

PROCEDURE

PLATING

1. If the vegetables are cold from refrigeration, warm to room temperature in a microwave oven on low power.
2. Assemble the napoleon:
   a. Pipe a flat ½-fl oz (15-mL) rosette of cheese spread on one of the puff pastry squares and place it on the work surface.
   b. Arrange the zucchini and yellow bell pepper on the square.
   c. Place another square on top so the corners do not match the corners of the first square. Press gently to firm the napoleon.
   d. Pipe another flat ½-fl oz (15-mL) rosette of cheese spread on this square.
   e. Top with eggplant and onion.
   f. Place another square on top so the corners do not match the corners of the second square. Press gently to firm the napoleon.
   g. Pipe another flat ½-fl oz (15-mL) rosette of cheese spread on this square.
   h. Top with yellow squash and red bell pepper.
   i. Place the final square on top so the corners do not match the corners of the third square. Press gently to firm the napoleon.
   j. Pipe a hollow rosette of cheese spread in the center of the top square.
3. Use an offset spatula to place the napoleon in the center of a cool 10-in. (25-cm) plate.
4. Squeeze the coulis around the plate well.
5. Squeeze dots of Basil Oil on the coulis around the napoleon.
6. Cut an *X* in the bottom of the cherry tomato and place it on the rosette. Stick the sprig upright out of the rosette.

VARIATION

NAPOLEON OF SPRING VEGETABLES

Replace the Garlic-Herb Cheese with fresh goat cheese or mascarpone. Replace the Grilled Summer Vegetables with cool steamed asparagus, cool steamed snow peas, and Carrot Ribbons (p. 382). Replace the Tomato Coulis with Beet Oil (p. 687); replace the Basil Oil and basil sprig with Bright Green Chervil Oil (p. 686) and a chervil sprig.

ADDITIONAL FRUIT RECIPES

FRUIT KEBABS WITH MINTED YOGURT SAUCE

APPETIZER

Portions:
8
Portion size:
about 5 oz (150 g)

INGREDIENTS	U.S.	METRIC
Ascorbic acid powder	¼ oz	7 g
Cold water	1 qt	1 L
Unwaxed Red Delicious apple	8 oz (1 large)	240 g (1 large)
Firm-ripe nectarines	8 oz (2 small)	240 g (2 small)
Ripe pineapple	1 lb (¼)	0.5 kg (¼)
Cantaloupe or honeydew melon	14 oz (¼)	420 g (¼)
Strawberries	6 oz (8 large)	180 g (8 large)
Large red or green seedless grapes	3 oz (8 large)	90 g (8 large)
Sweet Yogurt Dressing for Fruit Salad (p. 46) with chopped fresh mint instead of poppy seeds	8 fl oz	240 mL
Supplies		
8-in. (20-cm) wooden skewers	8	8

PROCEDURE

PREPARATION

1. In a nonreactive container, dissolve the ascorbic acid powder in the water.
2. Quarter and core the apple, then cut each quarter in half. Place in the ascorbic acid water.
3. Cut the nectarines in quarters and remove the pits.
4. Trim the pineapple (p. 88) and cut the pineapple flesh into 1-in. (2.5-cm) cubes.
5. Peel the melon and cut the melon flesh into 1-in. (2.5-cm) cubes.
6. Hull the berries.
7. Thread 1 piece of each type of fruit onto each skewer. If necessary, trim the fruit pieces for an attractive appearance.

PLATING

9. Fill a 10-fl oz (300-mL) ramekin or sauce dish with the yogurt sauce.
10. Arrange the skewers on a rectangular serving tray.

HOLD

Wrap the tray in plastic film and refrigerate up to 12 hours.

VARIATIONS

Vary the fruit as desired.

APPLE AND CHEDDAR PLATTER WITH WALNUTS

BUFFET APPETIZER

Yield:
about 1 lb (½ kg) fruit,
16 oz (0.5 kg) cheese,
5 oz (150 g) nuts

Portion Size:
1⅓ oz (45 g) fruit,
1⅓ oz (45 g) cheese,
½ oz (15 g) nuts

Portions:
10

INGREDIENTS	U.S.	METRIC
Ascorbic acid powder	¼ oz	7g
Cold water	1 qt	1 L
Granny Smith or other green apples	6 oz (1)	180 g (1)
Red Delicious apples	12 oz (2)	360 g (2)
Golden Delicious apples	6 oz (4)	180 g (1)
Small kale leaves	2 oz (3 or 4)	60 g (3 or 4)
Yellow cheddar cheese, 1 × 2 × ⅛-in. (2 × 5 × 0.33-cm) slices	8 oz	240 g
White cheddar cheese, 1 × 2 × ⅛-in. (2 × 5 × 0.33-cm) slices	8 oz	240 g
Apple bird (p. 717)	1	1
Large, shelled walnut halves	5 oz	150 g

PROCEDURE

PREPARATION

1. In a nonreactive container, dissolve the ascorbic acid powder in the water.
2. Core the the green apple, one of the red delicious apples, and the yellow delicious apple. Cut the cored apples into even wedges about ⅜ in. (1 cm) thick. As you work, place the apple wedges in the acidulated water.
3. Cut off the top and bottom of the remaining red delicious apple to make a socle (p. 183).
4. Place the apple socle in the water.

PLATING

5. Place the apple socle in the center of a 14-in. (35-cm) round tray.
6. Arrange the kale leaves around the base of the apple to make a frill.
7. Drain the apple wedges and blot dry.
8. Arrange a ring of apple slices around the socle, alternating red, green, and yellow slices.
9. Arrange a ring of cheese slices around the apples, alternating white and yellow slices.
10. Arrange the walnuts around the rim of the tray.
11. Set the apple bird on top of the apple socle.

HOLD

Cover the sliced apples with plastic wrap directly on their surfaces, then wrap the entire tray. Refrigerate no longer than 2 hours.

VARIATION

Vary the types of apple and the types of cheese as desired.

TERMS FOR REVIEW

certified organic produce
cold vegetable dish
vegetable
cellulose
plant pigments
chlorophyll
carotenoid
flavonoid
anthocyanin
anthoxanthin
waxed produce
heirloom
ethylene gas
fruit
ripening
ripe fruit
decay
cull
healed end
pelée à vif
crudités
crisping
al dente
à point
fork-tender
pressure steamer
PSI
succession blanching
refreshing
shocking
recovery time
blanching
poaching
cuisson
blanc
poaching *à blanc*
slurry
poaching *à la Grecque*
choke
artichoke heart
artichoke bottom
pencil asparagus
jumbo asparagus
spear
floret

QUESTIONS FOR DISCUSSION

1. List the three basic vegetable textures and give two examples of each.
2. Explain how vegetable texture is developed.
3. Discuss vegetable colors. Include in your discussion the plant pigments responsible for various vegetable colors and how vegetable colors are affected by cooking.
4. Explain how you would use your five senses to evaluate vegetables and fruits for purchase.
5. List the six changes that occur during the fruit ripening process.
6. Explain the qualities to assess in determining whether a piece of fruit is at its perfect stage of ripeness.
7. How would you store a case of underripe peaches needed for an event scheduled in two weeks?
8. How would you store a case of underripe peaches needed in two days?
9. List and describe the four steps in vegetable fabrication. Explain potential food safety problems that can occur during vegetable fabrication, and what steps you would take to avoid them.
10. Explain why even fruit that will be peeled must be washed. How would you wash fruit that is to be served raw?
11. Compare and contrast blanching and pressure steaming as applied to vegetables for cold service.
12. List the three stages of doneness for vegetables. Explain the factors you would take into consideration when deciding to what doneness you would cook a particular vegetable.
13. Describe how you would fabricate and cook the following vegetables for cold service:
    - zucchini
    - carrots
    - beets
    - green beans
    - artichoke bottoms
    - roasted peppers
    - asparagus
14. List some techniques you would use when preparing fruit platters.

Chapter 5

PREREQUISITES

Before studying this chapter, you should already

- Have read "How to Use This Book," pp. xxviii–xxxiii, and understand the professional recipe format.
- Know how to perform basic meat, poultry, and seafood preparation and cooking methods.

Complex Salads

Salad is a broad term encompassing a staggering variety of dishes, making it difficult for chefs to agree on the correct way to classify the various types. In Chapter 3 you learned about simple salads and tossed salads, both made primarily from leafy greens. In a wider sense, *salad* refers to virtually any mixture of cold foods that is enhanced with a tart, tangy sauce or dressing.

Among the many types of salads are those made up of raw or cooked vegetables or fruits, salads based on starches or legumes, and salads based on protein foods. Some salads combine all three. We call these dishes ***complex salads***.

A bowlful of crisp, colorful vegetables glistening with a tart vinaigrette, a side of creamy potato salad, an array of cool seafood in lemon mayonnaise, and a mixed antipasto with olive oil and balsamic vinegar are all examples of complex salads. These inviting dishes are an indispensable part of both American and European cuisines.

After reading this chapter, you should be able to

1. Explain the difference between simple salads and complex salads.
2. Prepare each type of complex salad presented in this chapter in accordance with food safety practices.
3. Plate arranged salads in the bedded, mounded, flat, molded, and stacked presentation styles.
4. Use specialized garde manger tools to prepare contemporary arranged salads.
5. Create your own signature complex salads following the guidelines given in the chapter.

UNDERSTANDING COMPLEX SALADS

Because complex salads can be prepared and presented in many ways, there are several ways to classify them.

Classifying by Presentation Style

Complex salad in a mixed presentation

Complex salad in an arranged presentation

One way to classify complex salads is by basic presentation style: mixed presentation or arranged presentation.

1. ***Mixed presentation***. In this style, all of the ingredients are mixed together with the dressing and mounded on a plate or platter. A salad made in this manner is called a *complex salad in mixed presentation*. Sometimes this type of salad is placed on a lettuce liner leaf or on a bed of torn or cut leafy greens. Additional garnish elements may be arranged on top.
2. ***Arranged presentation***. In this style, each of the various elements is dressed or seasoned separately and then all are assembled together on the plate in an attractive, artful composition. This is called a *complex salad in arranged presentation*. The five styles of arranged presentation are covered later in this chapter.

Classifying by Role in the Meal

Alternatively, complex salads can be categorized into several subclassifications based on their traditional role in the meal.

SALADS BY ROLE

Complex side salads: used as side dishes

Bound protein salads: used at center of plate or as sandwich fillings

Complete salads (vegetable, starch, protein): used as appetizers or entrées, depending on size

Fruit salads: used as breakfast, brunch items

Salads consisting of vegetables, legumes, grains, or starches that are typically served as accompaniments are referred to here as ***complex side salads***. Coleslaw, potato salad, and three-bean salad are typical complex side salads. Salads composed primarily of diced meat, poultry, or seafood mixed with a thick dressing are traditionally served center of plate on a bed of lettuce with garnishes. We call these preparations ***bound protein salads.*** They can also be used as sandwich fillings. Chicken salad, ham salad, and egg salad are good examples.

Complex salads consisting of an equal mixture of vegetables, starches, and proteins contain the three elements of a complete entrée. These are called ***complete salads*** because they provide a complete and balanced meal. Vegetarian complete salads may include dairy products, nuts, soy protein, or legume/starch combinations that provide both substance and nutritional balance.

Another category of complex salad is ***fruit salads***. These salads are primarily based on fresh fruit, although they may have other ingredients as well.

In the next section, we examine complex salads classified by role in order to learn how they are prepared. We'll also learn about variations within each type.

Liner vs. Bed

One or two whole pieces of plain lettuce placed under a complex salad are called ***liner leaves***. (top photo,above). A layer of dressed or plain lettuce pieces placed under a complex salad is called a ***bed of greens*** (see photo, p. 165).

Complex side salad

Bound protein salad

Complete salad

Guidelines for Complex Salads Food Safety

Complex salads with protein-based ingredients or egg-based dressings require extra diligence with regard to food safety. In addition to normal safe food-handling practices, be sure to follow these special guidelines when preparing and serving complex salads.

- Wear food-service gloves, and be sure to change gloves between tasks.
- Prevent cross-contamination by thoroughly sanitizing your hands and all equipment before proceeding to assemble a protein element (cooked or ready-to-eat) with any raw ingredients and dressing.
- When using leftover items to make complex salads, make sure they are still fresh and wholesome at the time of use. The discard date of the complex salad must be based on the discard date of the leftover ingredients and not the salad itself.
- Open-pan cool rice, potatoes, pasta, and other starchy salad components, and limit the cooling time to less than 1 hour.
- Never combine a new batch of a complex salad with an older batch.

Green Vegetables in Complex Salads

Green vegetables pose a particular problem when you include them in complex salads. When either raw or cooked green vegetables come into extended contact with an acidic dressing, they lose their bright green color and take on a less appealing olive drab color. However, to be most flavorful, complex salads (especially those that contain potatoes, legumes, or grains) need time for their flavors to mingle with the dressing and mellow. You must decide whether to preserve color at the expense of flavor, or vice versa.

To preserve the bright color of the green vegetables, dress the salad just before service. Alternatively, you can keep the green vegetables separate from the main part of the salad and then mix them in to order. If, on the other hand, you want to infuse green vegetables with the flavor of their dressing, you should mix the salad well ahead of time and allow the vegetables to absorb the dressing. Of course, the vegetables will discolor, but they will also become very flavorful.

Onions in Complex Salads

Raw onions are one of the most perishable ingredients in a complex salad and deteriorate in a very short period. Within a day, or even within hours, deteriorating raw onions can harm both the texture and the flavor of a complex salad. This is because most types of cut raw onions tend to water out (see below) and acquire off-flavors rather quickly.

Shallots and scallions have a milder flavor and contain less water than onions. This makes them good choices for use in complex salads. However, they will still lose quality if mixed with the salad ingredients and stored for more than a few hours. Fabricate and add the onion component to each day's batch at the last minute before service.

Complex Side Salads

Complex salads without a protein component are most often served in small portions as a side dish. Because most salads are cold foods and most entrées are served hot, chefs often wonder when it is appropriate to serve a complex salad as a side.

In formal cuisine, hot accompaniments are served with hot foods and cold accompaniments with cold foods. Thus, in formal dining, complex side salads should accompany only cold entrées, such as cold roast meats and cold poached seafood. For this reason, they are traditionally served as part of cold buffets and on cold entrée plates.

In today's more casual dining, these rules have been relaxed to a certain extent. Now complex side salads are sometimes paired with hot entrées, most commonly fried, grilled, or smoke-roasted foods. For example, potato salad is a favored accompaniment for fried chicken, and coleslaw is an appropriate side dish for barbecue brisket. Garnish-size portions of complex side salads are frequently used to accompany fried, grilled, or baked appetizers. You might serve broccoli slaw with a savory pastry turnover or gingered bean sprout salad with fried wontons to add a light, fresh taste. Complex side salads frequently accompany sandwiches in order to fill up the plate and add value to the dish.

There is practically no limit to the combinations you can put together to make interesting complex side salads. The four types of complex side salads are:

1. Raw vegetable side salads
2. Cooked vegetable side salads
3. Pasta side salads
4. Grain and legume side salads

Guidelines for Removing Excess Water Content

Some raw vegetables ***water out***, or release moisture, when mixed with dressings and allowed to stand. This happens because the salt in the dressing attracts and absorbs water from inside the vegetables' cell walls, diluting the dressing and making the salad loose and watery. Vegetables with high moisture content and soft cell walls, such as cucumbers, are particularly prone to watering out. Firm vegetables that are young and fresh also tend to water out. Use judgment to decide whether to treat vegetables by one of the following methods before combining them with other ingredients and dressings.

- *Salting:* After fabrication, toss vegetables with a little kosher salt and place in a colander or on towels to drain for a short period. The salt will draw out excess water. You'll probably need to reduce the amount of salt in the recipe for which the vegetables are intended.
- *Scalding:* This method is used on sturdy vegetables such as cabbage, carrots, turnips, celery, and celery root. Loosely pack the fabricated vegetables in a colander. Pour an equal volume of boiling water over the vegetables, tossing them with tongs as you pour. Rinse the vegetables under cold water and then drain them. Gently squeeze the water out of the vegetables and blot them dry with towels.
- *Pre-dressing:* Toss the fabricated vegetables with some of their intended dressing or with a neutral-flavored vinaigrette. Let stand at room temperature up to 1 hour. The vegetables will exchange some of their water content for the dressing through the process of osmosis (p. 411). This adds to their flavor as well. Transfer to a colander to drain.

Raw Vegetable Side Salads

Their crunchy texture and elemental flavor make raw vegetables excellent ingredients for side salads. Review Chapter 4, pages 84–85, to ensure vegetables meet the criteria for palatability in their raw state.

CUCUMBER SALAD

SIDE DISH

Yield:
about 1 qt (1 L), about 24 oz (720 g)
Portions:
6–8
Portion size:
4–5 fl oz (120–150 mL), 3–4 oz (90–120 g)

INGREDIENTS	U.S.	METRIC
Large, slender cucumbers (see Note)	2 lb	1 kg
Kosher salt	1½ tsp	7 mL
Slivered sweet onion	5 oz	150 g
Sugar	2 tsp	10 mL
Corn oil	3 fl oz	90 mL
Cider vinegar	1 fl oz	30 mL
Ground white pepper	pinch	pinch

Note: If the cucumbers are very young and slender, with few seeds, they may be sliced into rounds and not seeded.

PROCEDURE

PREPARATION

1. Peel the cucumbers and trim the ends.
2. Slice in half lengthwise and scrape out the seeds.
3. Slice the cucumbers into thin crescents.
4. Toss the cucumber slices with the salt, put them in a colander placed over a tray, and set a plate on them to weight them gently.
5. Allow to drain in the refrigerator 1 hour.
6. Blot the cucumbers with towels to remove surface moisture and excess salt.
7. Place them in a bowl with the onion.
8. Mix the cucumbers first with the sugar, then the oil, and then the vinegar.
9. Taste and correct the seasoning.

HOLD

Refrigerated in a covered container up to 8 hours.

PLATING

10. Using tongs or a slotted spoon, lift the solids out of the liquid dressing.
11. Place in individual dishes, or add to a plate as a component.

VARIATIONS

HERBED CUCUMBER SALAD

Add chopped or minced fresh herb of choice, such as dill, tarragon, chervil, etc.

CREAMY CUCUMBER SALAD

Omit the oil. Refrigerate the salad for 1 hour, then drain and fold in 4 fl oz (120 mL) thick sour cream or crème fraîche. Optionally, add ½ oz (15 g) minced fresh dill.

ASIAN CUCUMBER SALAD WITH MISO

Cut the cucumbers lengthwise into quarters before seeding and slicing. Replace the onion with scallions cut very thin on a sharp diagonal. Replace the dressing ingredients with 4 fl oz (120 mL) Asian Vinaigrette (p. 35).

CAROTTES RAPÉES [kah-ROT rah-PAY]

SIDE DISH

Yield:
about 1 qt (1 L), about 24 oz (720 g)

Portions:
6–8

Portion size:
4–5 fl oz (120–150 mL), 3–4 oz (90–120 g)

INGREDIENTS	U.S.	METRIC
Peeled young carrots	1¼ lb	1 kg
Thick Mustard Vinaigrette (p. 33)	5 fl oz	150 mL

PROCEDURE

PREPARATION

1. Use a mandoline to fabricate the carrots into fine julienne.
2. Toss the julienne carrots with the vinaigrette.
3. Taste and correct the seasoning.

HOLD

Refrigerated in a covered container up to 8 hours.

PLATING

4. If necessary, drain excess liquid from the carrots.
5. Place in individual dishes, or add to a plate as a component.

VARIATION

CARROT SALAD WITH CURRANTS

Rehydrate ½ oz (15 g) currants in 2 fl oz (60 mL) port wine. Toss the currants and their liquid with the carrots and vinaigrette.

CREAMY COLESLAW

SIDE DISH

Yield:
1 qt (1 L), about 24 oz (720 g)
Portions:
6–8
Portion size:
4–5 fl oz (120–150 mL), 3–4 oz (90–120 g)

INGREDIENTS	U.S.	METRIC
White or savoy cabbage	1½ lb	750 g
Mayonnaise (p. 41), or commercial	10 fl oz	300 mL
Sugar	2 tsp	10 mL
Cider vinegar	1 tbsp	15 mL
Celery seeds	1 tsp	5 mL
Dried thyme	pinch	pinch
Carrot, trimmed and peeled	3 oz	90 g

PROCEDURE

PREPARATION

1. Bring 2 qt (2 L) water to the boil.
2. Remove any tough or discolored outer leaves of the cabbage.
3. Quarter the cabbage lengthwise and cut out the core.
4. Cut the cabbage across the grain into very fine shreds.
5. Place the cabbage in a colander and pour the boiling water over it, tossing with tongs as you pour (see photo).
6. Immediately refresh under cold running water, then press and squeeze the cabbage very dry.
7. Mix the mayonnaise with the remaining seasonings.
8. Mix together the cabbage, carrots, and dressing. Allow to mellow in the refrigerator 30 minutes.
9. Taste and correct the seasoning.

HOLD

Refrigerate in a freshly sanitized, covered container up to 3 days.

PLATING

10. Place in individual dishes, or add to a plate as a component. Garnish as desired.

VARIATIONS

MYSTERIOUSLY GOOD COLESLAW

Add ½ fl oz (15 mL) very fresh prepared horseradish to the dressing.

RED CABBAGE SLAW

Use red cabbage. Add 4 fl oz (120 mL) cider vinegar to the boiling water in step 3. Omit the vinegar from the dressing.

OLD-FASHIONED COLESLAW

Replace the mayonnaise with Boiled Dressing (p. 46).

BROCCOLI SLAW

Replace the cabbage with 1 lb (½ kg) peeled broccoli stems fabricated into fine julienne in a food processor or with a mandoline.

TOMATO-BASIL SALAD

SIDE DISH

Yield:
1 qt (1 L), about 2 lb (1 kg)

Portions:
6–8

Portion size:
4–5 fl oz (120–150 mL), 4–5 oz (120–150 g)

INGREDIENTS	U.S.	METRIC
Minced fresh garlic	¼ oz	7 g
Extra-virgin olive oil, preferably unfiltered artisan type	3 fl oz	90 mL
Ripe local tomatoes or vine-ripe tomatoes	3 lb	1.5 kg
Kosher salt	to taste	to taste
Sweet onion, diced fine	2½ oz	75 g
Balsamic vinegar	to taste	to taste
Freshly ground black pepper	to taste	to taste
Fresh basil leaves	1 oz	30 g

Note: The tomato water that drains from the tomatoes may be used for soups, sauces, etc.

PROCEDURE

PREPARATION

1. Combine the garlic and olive oil and allow to stand at room temperature about 30 minutes.
2. Bring at least 1 gal (4 L) water to a rapid boil.
3. Prepare an ice bain-marie.
4. In batches, blanch the tomatoes 1–2 seconds only and immediately refresh (A).
5. Core and peel the tomatoes (B).
6. Cut the tomatoes half horizontally and gently pull out the seeds (C).
7. Cut the tomato flesh into 1-in. (3-cm) chunks (D).
8. Put the tomatoes in a large colander and gently toss them with a generous amount of salt.
9. Spread the tomatoes in a shallow layer (E) and allow to drain at room temperature about 30 minutes (see Note).
10. Toss the tomatoes with the garlic oil.
11. Taste, and add more salt if necessary.

A

B

C

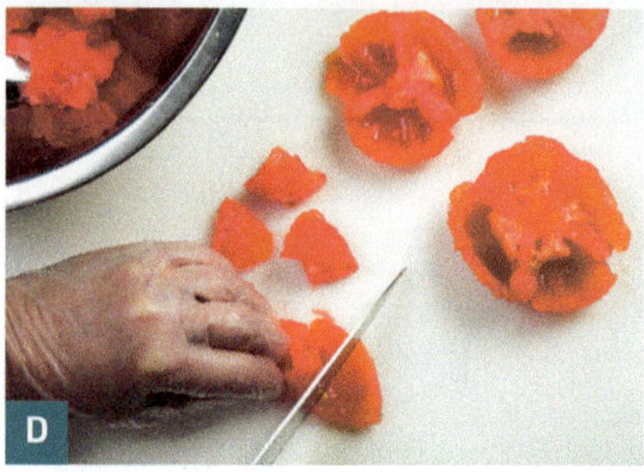
D

E

F

PROCEDURE

HOLD

Store cool room temperature, covered, up to 3 hours.

FINISHING

12. Toss the tomatoes with the onion and season with vinegar and pepper.
13. Pull the basil into small pieces and toss into the tomatoes (F).

PLATING

14. Spoon the salad and its dressing into individual dishes.

    Alternatively, use a slotted spoon to lift the salad onto a plate as a component teamed with other foods.

VARIATIONS

TWO-COLOR TOMATO BASIL SALAD

Replace half the red tomatoes with yellow tomatoes.

TOMATO SALAD OREGANATA

Replace the basil leaves with fresh oregano leaves.

HEIRLOOM TOMATO COCKTAIL

Replace the standard tomatoes with peeled whole red, green, and yellow cherry or grape tomatoes. Serve in a martini glass with a Parmesan Thin (p. 695).

VINEGAR SLAW

SIDE DISH

Yield:
1 qt (1 L),
about 24 oz (720 g)
Portions:
6–8
Portion size:
4–5 fl oz
(120–150 mL),
3–4 oz (90–120 g)

INGREDIENTS	U.S.	METRIC
White or savoy cabbage	1½ lb	750 g
American Cider Vinaigrette (p. 32)	8 fl oz	240 mL
Celery seeds	½ tsp	3 mL
Sweet onion, sliced very fine	3 oz	90 g
Carrot, trimmed and peeled	3 oz	90 g
Cider vinegar	to taste	to taste

PROCEDURE

PREPARATION

1. Remove any tough or discolored outer leaves of the cabbage.
2. Quarter the cabbage lengthwise and cut out the core.
3. Cut into very fine shreds.
4. Mix the cabbage with half the vinaigrette. Allow to soften at room temperature 1 hour.
5. Transfer the cabbage to a colander and press firmly to extract all moisture.
6. Mix with the remaining vinaigrette, onion, and carrot.
7. Taste and adjust the tartness by adding more vinegar to taste.

HOLD

Refrigerate in a freshly sanitized, covered container up to 3 days.

PLATING

8. Place in individual dishes, or add to a plate as a component.

VARIATION

PEPPER SLAW

Omit the carrot; add 2 oz (60 g) each fine julienne red, yellow, and green bell pepper. Add freshly ground black pepper to taste just before serving.

Mellowing Time for Salads

Most complex salads, especially starch-based salads, have not yet achieved their best flavor and texture immediately after they are prepared. Complex salads need time for the solid ingredients to absorb some of the liquid ingredients, and for the flavors of all the ingredients to mix and mingle. They must rest for a time after assembly and before they can be properly evaluated for seasoning and mouthfeel. This is referred as *mellowing time*. After the mellowing of the salad is complete, retaste and fine-tune its seasoning level and make sure it has the proper amount of dressing. The necessary mellowing time varies from one product to another.

Cooked Vegetable Side Salads

Vegetables not normally consumed raw make wonderful complex salads, provided they are properly cooked before they are combined with the other salad ingredients. In most cases, vegetables should be lightly cooked, tending toward the al dente side of doneness. However, to be palatable with such light cooking, the vegetables must be tender and fresh before they are cooked. Take care to preserve or heighten the natural colors as well as flavor and texture when cooking (pp. 91–95).

GREEN BEANS VINAIGRETTE

SIDE DISH

Yield:
1 qt (1 L),
about 24 oz (720 g)
Portions:
6–8
Portion size:
4–5 fl oz
(120–150 mL),
3–4 oz (90–120 g)

INGREDIENTS	U.S.	METRIC
Fresh, young green beans	1½ lb	750 g
Thick Mustard Vinaigrette (p. 33)	6 fl oz	180 mL
Fine slivered shallots	2½ oz	75 g
Kosher salt	to taste	to taste

PROCEDURE

PREPARATION

1. Trim the stem end of the green beans. Unless the pointed tips are wiry or discolored, leave them intact.
2. Blanch the beans *à point* (p. 91), refresh, and blot dry in towels.
3. Toss with the vinaigrette and the shallots.
4. Taste and season with salt if needed.

HOLD

Store refrigerated up to 3 hours only. If held longer, the beans will still taste good, but they will be discolored.

PLATING

5. Place in individual dishes, or add to a plate as a component.

VARIATIONS

HARICOTS VERTS VINAIGRETTE

[AH-ree-ko VAIR]

Replace the green beans with haricots verts (small French grean beans). Remove the tips.

CREAMY GREEN BEAN SALAD

Reduce the Thick Mustard Vinaigrette (p. 33) to 4 fl oz (120 mL) and add 2 fl oz (60 mL) crème fraîche.

GREEN BEAN AND ROASTED PEPPER SALAD

Reduce the green beans to 1¼ lb (625 g). Mix in 1 cup (240 mL) julienne roasted red bell peppers (p. 109).

TRICOLOR BEAN SALAD

Reduce the bean quantity to 1 lb (500 g). Replace the Mustard Vinaigrette with Balsamic Vinaigrette (p. 33). Replace the shallots with 3 oz (90 g) sliced sweet onion. Add 6 oz (180 g) filet of tomato cut into coarse julienne.

GREEN BEAN AND GOLDEN BEET SALAD

Reduce the green beans to 1 lb (500 g). Mix in 12 oz (360 g) roasted and peeled golden beets cut into long, slender bâtonnets. Add ⅛ oz (4 g) fresh tarragon leaves just before serving.

ROASTED BEETS IN MUSTARD VINAIGRETTE

SIDE DISH

Yield:
1 qt (1 L), about 2 lbs (1 kg)

Portions:
6–8

Portion size:
4–5 fl oz (120–150 mL), 4–5 oz (120–150 g)

INGREDIENTS	U.S.	METRIC
Red beets	2 lb	1 kg
Thick Mustard Vinaigrette (p. 33)	8–10 fl oz	240–300 mL
Sugar	to taste	to taste
Kosher salt	to taste	to taste
Slivered red onion	2 oz	60 g
Minced parsley	¼ oz	7 g

PROCEDURE

PREPARATION

1. Roast the beets as instructed on page 107.
2. Cool, peel, and cut into thin wedges.
3. Toss the beets with 3 fl oz (90 mL) of the vinaigrette.
4. Taste and add some sugar if necessary.
5. Allow the beets to mellow at room temperature 1 hour.
6. Adjust sugar and salt if needed.
7. Mix in the onions and enough vinaigrette to give the beets a thick coating.

HOLD

Refrigerate in a freshly sanitized, covered container up to 6 hours. If onions are held out, the salad may be refrigerated up to 3 days.

PLATING

8. Place in individual dishes, or add to a plate as a component.
9. Garnish each serving with parsley.

VARIATIONS

BEETS IN CRÈME FRAÎCHE

Reduce the Mustard Vinaigrette to 3 fl oz (90 mL). Fold in 4–6 fl oz (120–189 mL) crème fraîche after 1 hour mellowing.

BABY BEETS IN MUSTARD VINAIGRETTE

Replace the red beets with a variety of baby beets either roasted or, if peeled, steamed. Replace the onion with minced shallot.

GOLDEN BEETS IN MUSTARD VINAIGRETTE

Replace the red beets with golden beets.

CHOGGIA BEETS IN LEMON VINAIGRETTE

Replace the red beets with chioggia beets. Rather than cutting them in wedges, slice thin to show their ring pattern. Slice the red onion into rings. Replace the Mustard Vinaigrette with Lemon Vinaigrette (p. 34).

MINTED THREE-PEA SALAD

SIDE DISH

Yield:
1 qt (1 L), about 24 oz (720 g)
Portions:
6–8
Portion size:
4–5 fl oz (120–150 mL), 3–4 oz (90–120 g)

INGREDIENTS	U.S.	METRIC
Fresh peas in the pod	1½ lb	750 g
Sugar snap peas or snow peas	5 oz	150 g
Pea shoots	2 oz	60 g
Mayonnaise (p. 41), made with lemon juice	4 fl oz	120 mL
Minced lemon zest	1 tbsp	15 mL
Fine ground white pepper	dash	dash
Chopped mint leaves	¼ oz	7 g
Fresh lemon juice	to taste	to taste

PROCEDURE

PREPARATION

1. Shell the peas.
2. String the snap or snow peas and cut in half on a sharp diagonal.
3. If necessary, tear the pea shoots into 2-in. (5-cm) lengths.
4. Blanch the snap/snow peas al dente, refresh, drain, and blot on towels.
5. Pan-steam the peas in a little salted water *à point* (p.91), refresh, drain, and blot.
6. Mix the lemon zest into the mayonnaise.
7. Fold in all of the pea products along with the mint.
8. Taste and correct the seasoning, adding lemon juice as necessary.

HOLD

Refrigerate in a freshly sanitized, covered container up to 4 hours.

PLATING

9. Place in individual dishes, or add to a plate as a component.

VARIATIONS

If fresh peas are unavailable, substitute 8 oz (240 g) frozen peas.

If pea shoots are unavailable, omit them and change the recipe title to Minted Pea Salad. You may add 2 oz (60 g) radish sprouts or alfalfa sprouts for texture.

TARRAGON THREE-PEA SALAD

Replace the mint with chopped tarragon.

Potato Salads

The garde manger chef can create unusual and attention-getting potato salads that add recognition value to the plate. To do so, use various types of potato and combine them with interesting supporting ingredients, dressings, and garnishes.

CHOOSING POTATOES FOR POTATO SALAD

As you should already know, potatoes are classified according to texture. The texture type you choose ultimately determines the texture and mouthfeel of your potato salad. It also influences the cooking method you should use.

- The traditional choice is an all-purpose potato having a texture midway between waxy and mealy. Such a potato will retain its shape after cooking, yet soften enough to blend with the dressing. All-purpose potatoes may be boiled or steamed in their jackets, or skin-on, and then cooled, peeled, and diced.
- If you choose to use mealy potatoes, such as russets, fabricate them before cooking. For best texture, cook them by steaming or poaching. Avoid using aged russets, as they are quite expensive and tend to fall apart when mixed.
- New potatoes are very waxy and, although they have a pleasant, slightly sweet flavor and hold their shape well, they tend to remain separate from the dressing and don't bind nicely. If you want to make a new potato salad, it's best to mix some cooked, diced russets or all-purpose potatoes into the mixture so it binds together.

Procedures for Making Potato Salads

Traditional Method

When properly done, this method results in cooked potatoes with a dry, light-textured flesh that readily absorbs and mixes with the dressing.

A

1. Scrub the unpeeled potatoes under cold running water.
2. Sort the potatoes by size. Cook potatoes of similar size together at one time.
3. Cook the potatoes by one of the following methods:

   Place the potatoes in a pan, cover with cold water, and bring to the boil (A). Cook at the boil until the potatoes are just tender when pierced with a knife. Drain.

   –or–

   Place the potatoes in one layer in a perforated hotel pan. Steam under pressure until just tender when pierced with a knife.
4. Open-pan cool the potatoes to lukewarm.
5. Peel the potatoes and cut into slices or dice.
6. Refrigerate just until the potatoes reach 38°F (3°C)—see sidebar.
7. Mix the potatoes with the dressing.

8. Add the remaining salad ingredients. Taste and correct the seasoning.
9. Refrigerate and allow the salad to mellow for the specified time.
10. Evaluate the seasonings and mouthfeel, and correct if necessary.

Prefabrication Method

This method results in potatoes that cook more evenly and quickly and that cool faster. It can be used with commercially processed peeled potatoes.

1. Scrub the potatoes under cold running water.
2. Prepare a large pan of cold water.
3. Peel the potatoes, placing each peeled potato into the water to prevent enzymatic browning.
4. Dice or slice the potatoes as desired, returning the pieces to the cold water as you work (A).
5. Prepare a pressure steamer, or bring a large quantity of salted water to the boil.
6. Drain the potatoes.
7. Cook the potatoes by one of the following methods:

   Place a single layer of potatoes in a perforated hotel pan and steam them until just tender (B).

   –or–

   Briskly simmer the potatoes in salted water until just tender. Drain.
8. Open-pan cool the potatoes to room temperature.
9. Refrigerate just until the potatoes reach 38°F (3°C).
10. Mix the potatoes with the dressing.
11. Add the remaining salad ingredients. Taste and correct the seasoning.
12. Refrigerate and allow the salad to mellow about 1 hour.
13. Evaluate the seasonings and mouthfeel, and correct if necessary.

Safety Factors for Mayonnaise-Based Salads

Potato and other starch salads almost always taste better if the starch is mixed with the dressing while the just-cooked starch is still warm. This is because the starch absorbs more of the flavorful dressing. However, in a food-service setting, it is difficult to do this and still meet health regulations for chilling the mixture to a safe temperature within the required time.

If you are able to meet all safety regulations for chilling foods and to monitor and log temperatures and times for each batch, you might try mixing warm starches with dressing and then chilling. Otherwise, be safe and chill all ingredients before mixing.

ALL-AMERICAN POTATO SALAD

SIDE DISH

Yield:
1 qt (1 L), about 2 lb (1 kg)

Portions:
6–8

Portion size:
4–5 fl oz (120–150 mL), 4–5 oz (120–150 g)

INGREDIENTS	U.S.	METRIC
Mayonnaise (p. 41), or commercial	6 fl oz	180 mL
Prepared yellow mustard	2 tsp	10 mL
Bread-and-butter pickle juice	½ fl oz	15 mL
Bottled hot sauce	dash	to taste
Celery seed	pinch	pinch
Kosher salt	to taste	to taste
Sugar	to taste	to taste
Fresh ground white pepper	to taste	to taste
All-purpose potatoes	1½ lb	750 g
Peeled celery, diced fine	1 oz	30 g
Scallions, sliced fine on the diagonal	1 oz	30 g
Bread-and-butter pickles, diced fine	1 oz	30 g
Chopped parsley	¼ oz	7 g

PROCEDURE

PREPARATION

1. Combine the mayonnaise with the condiments and seasonings.
2. Either before or after cooking, cut the potatoes into ¾-in. (2-cm) dice.
3. Prepare according to either method of the Procedures for Making Potato Salad (pp. 142 and 143).
4. If necessary, crush a few of the potatoes to thicken and bind the dressing.

HOLD

Refrigerate in a freshly sanitized, covered container up to 2 days.

PLATING

5. Place in individual dishes, or add to a plate as a component.

VARIATIONS

OLD-FASHIONED POTATO SALAD

Replace the mayonnaise with Old-Fashioned Boiled Dressing (p. 46).

SOUTHERN POTATO SALAD

Replace the bread-and-butter pickles with sweet pickles and increase the sugar; add 1 oz (30 g) finely diced red bell pepper.

SCANDINAVIAN POTATO SALAD

Replace half the mayonnaise with sour cream. Replace the bread-and-butter pickles with dill pickles. Omit the mustard, celery seed, and hot sauce. Replace the scallions with red onions. Add ½ oz (15 g) minced fresh dill.

SMASHED POTATO SALAD

Using a potato masher, crush all the potatoes, adding 2 fl oz (60 mL) sour cream for a smooth consistency.

EGG POTATO SALAD

Prepare All-American or Southern Potato Salad, but reduce the potatoes by 4 oz (120 g) and add 2 diced hard-cooked eggs.

REDSKIN POTATO SALAD

Reduce the all-purpose potatoes to ½ lb (240 g) and add 1 lb (0.5 kilo) Red Bliss potatoes, scrubbed but not peeled (may use any variation).

FRENCH POTATO SALAD

SIDE DISH

Yield:
1 qt (1 L), about 2 lb (1 kg)
Portions:
6–8
Portion size:
4–5 fl oz (120–150 mL), 4–5 oz (120–150 g)

INGREDIENTS	U.S.	METRIC
All-purpose potatoes	1½ lb	750 g
Kosher salt	to taste	to taste
White wine	2 fl oz	60 mL
Thick Mustard Vinaigrette (p. 33)	6 fl oz	180 mL
Slivered shallots	1½ oz	45 g
Chopped parsley	¼ oz	7 g

PROCEDURE

PREPARATION

1. Cut the potatoes into ¾-in. (2-cm) dice.
2. Prepare according to the Prefabrication Method of the Procedures for Making Potato Salads, page 143.

HOLD

Store at cool room temperature up to 2½ hours. Refrigerate up to 2 days, but bring to room temperature to serve.

PLATING

3. Place in individual dishes, or add to a plate as a component.
4. Garnish each serving with parsley.

VARIATIONS

ITALIAN POTATO SALAD

Replace the Thick Mustard Vinaigrette with Balsamic Vinaigrette (p. 33). Replace the shallots with sweet onions. Add 1 oz (30 g) each julienne roasted red, yellow, and green bell pepper.

MEDITERRANEAN POTATO AND MUSSEL ENTRÉE SALAD

Add 6 oz (180 g) steamed, shelled mussels, 2 oz (60 g) finely diced roasted red bell pepper, 2 tbsp (30 mL) chopped parsley. Serve in tomato shells on lettuce leaves.

CREOLE POTATO SALAD

Replace the Thick Mustard Vinaigrette with Classic French Vinaigrette (p. 32), but use Creole mustard when making it. Add 2 tsp (10 mL) prepared horseradish, 1 tsp (5 mL) sugar, 1 oz (30 g) finely diced celery, and 1 oz (30 g) finely diced green bell pepper.

GERMAN POTATO SALAD

SIDE DISH

Yield:
1 qt (1 L), about 2 lb (1 kg)
Portions:
6–8
Portion size:
4–5 fl oz (120–150 mL), 4–5 oz (120–150 g)

INGREDIENTS	U.S.	METRIC
All-purpose potatoes	1½ lb	750 g
Kosher salt	to taste	to taste
Apple cider vinegar	2½ fl oz	75 mL
Sugar	2 tbsp	30 mL
Prepared brown mustard	1 tsp	5 mL
Water	3 fl oz	90 mL
Rindless smoked slab bacon, diced fine	3 oz	90 g
Yellow onion, chopped medium	5 oz	150 g
Celery, peeled, diced fine	1½ oz	45 g
Caraway seeds	½ tsp	2 mL
All-purpose flour	1 tbsp	15 mL
Corn oil	2 to 4 fl oz	60 to 120 mL
Freshly ground black pepper	to taste	to taste
Chopped parsley	¼ oz	7 g

PRODUCTION

PREPARATION

1. Peel the potatoes and cut into ¾-in. (2-cm) dice.
2. Boil the potatoes in salted water *à point* (p. 91).
3. Drain the potatoes and spread in a hotel pan to cool slightly.
4. Whisk together the vinegar, sugar, mustard, and water. Set aside.
5. Over low heat, sauté the bacon until rendered and almost crisp.
6. Add the onion, celery, and caraway seeds to the fat in the pan.
7. Sauté until the onions and celery are tender but not brown.
8. Add the flour and stir over low heat for few seconds, then whisk in the vinegar mixture along with a little salt.
9. Simmer briskly 1–2 minutes, or until the mixture thickens.
10. Whisk the corn oil into the pan to make about 10 fl oz (300 mL) emulsified dressing. (The amount of corn oil needed depends on the amount of bacon drippings produced by the bacon.)
11. Taste and correct the seasoning to make a sweet-salty-tart dressing. Make sure to add enough salt and vinegar to balance the sweetness.
12. Toss the potatoes with the hot dressing.
13. Season with pepper.
11. Cool to room temperature and allow to mellow 30 minutes.
12. Taste and reevaluate the seasonings and mouthfeel. Make necessary corrections.

HOLD

Refrigerate in a freshly sanitized, covered container up to 3 days.

FINISHING

13. Warm each serving in a microwave oven for a few seconds only.

PLATING

14. Place in individual dishes, or add to a plate as a component.
15. Garnish each serving with parsley.

VARIATION

GERMAN-AMERICAN POTATO SALAD

Replace the caraway seeds with celery seeds. Add 2 fl oz (60 mL) finely diced pimiento.

SALADE RUSSE [suh-LAHD ROOCE]

RUSSIAN SALAD

SIDE DISH

Yield:
1 qt (1 L),
about 2 lb (1 kg)

Portions:
6–8

Portion size:
4–5 fl oz
(120–150 mL),
4–5 oz (120–150 g)

INGREDIENTS	U.S	METRIC
Red beets	½ lb	250 g
Young, slender carrots	½ lb	250 g
All-purpose potatoes	¾ lb	360 g
Kosher salt	to taste	to taste
Fresh peas in the pod	½ lb	240 g
–or–		
Frozen peas, thawed	3 oz	90 g
Classic French Vinaigrette (p. 32)	3 fl oz	90 mL
Mayonnaise	8 fl oz	240 mL
Chopped shallot	½ oz	15 g
Minced lemon zest	1 tbsp	15 mL
Fine ground white pepper	to taste	to taste
Fresh lemon juice	to taste	to taste
Minced parsley	¼ oz	7 g

PROCEDURE

PREPARATION

1. Roast the beets as instructed on p. 107.
2. When they are cool enough to handle, peel the beets and cut into ⅜-in. (0.75-cm) dice.
3. Toss with 1 fl oz (30 mL) vinaigrette.
4. Peel the carrots, cut into ⅜-in. (0.75-cm) dice, blanch *à point* (p. 91), refresh, drain, and blot dry.
5. Toss with 1 fl oz (30 mL) vinaigrette.
6. Peel the potatoes, cut into ⅜-in. (0.75-cm) dice, boil in salted water al dente, drain, and spread to cool 5 minutes.
7. Toss with 1 fl oz (30 mL) vinaigrette.
8. Shell the peas and pan-steam in a little salted water.
9. Refresh and blot dry.
10. Mix the mayonnaise with the shallots, lemon zest, and pepper.
11. Fold in the vegetables. Season with lemon juice and salt, if needed. Allow to mellow in the refrigerator 1 hour.
12. Reevaluate and correct the seasoning.

HOLD

Refrigerated in a freshly sanitized, covered container up to 3 days.

PLATING

13. Place in individual dishes, or add to a plate as a component.
14. Garnish each serving with chopped parsley.

Pasta Side Salads

Salads based on pasta are a recent addition to the complex salad repertoire. Fifty years ago, the standard mayonnaise-based macaroni salad was the only pasta salad typically encountered in North America. However, this changed after Americans discovered the great variety of Italian pasta shapes. Cool pasta salads made with various shapes and dressings soon followed.

The scores of pasta shapes, colors, and flavors available today allow for the creation of an unlimited number of interesting and unusual pasta salads.

Guidelines for Making Pasta Salads

- Boil the pasta in a large amount of heavily salted, rapidly boiling water, and cook it only until it reaches an al dente texture. Don't add oil to the water, because this makes the surface of the pasta slick and prevents the dressing from clinging to it.
- Avoid refreshing the pasta under running water. Doing so washes off the surface starch that causes the pasta to cling to its sauce or dressing, and also makes the pasta soggy. Instead, drain the pasta well, turn it out into a wide, shallow pan, and toss it with a little of its intended dressing so the pasta cools quickly and absorbs the flavorful dressing rather than plain water. (See food safety sidebar on p. 143.)
- Match the size and shape of the other ingredients to the size and shape of the pasta, just as you would when creating hot pasta dishes. Pasta salads prepared in this manner are pleasing to the eye and have a good mouthfeel.
- While it's thrifty to use leftover boiled pasta for pasta salad, keep in mind that cold pasta doesn't absorb and bind with dressing very well. When using cold leftover pasta, plunge it into boiling water for a second, drain it, and then proceed.

Procedure for Making Pasta Salads

1. Bring a large quantity of salted water to the boil. Use a ratio of 1 gal (4 L) water to 1 lb (2 kg) pasta.
2. Drop in the pasta, stir well, and boil to al dente.
3. Drain in a colander.
4. Immediately transfer the pasta to a hotel pan and mix it with some of the dressing to keep it from sticking together (see safety sidebar on p. 143 regarding mixing warm ingredients with mayonnaise dressing).
5. Open-pan cool, and then chill.
6. Add the remaining ingredients and dressing.
7. Taste and correct the seasoning.
8. Refrigerate and allow the salad to mellow for the specified time, usually about 1 hour.
9. Evaluate and correct the seasoning if necessary.

TRADITIONAL MACARONI SALAD

SIDE DISH

Yield:
1 qt (1 L), about 24 oz (720 g)
Portions:
6–8
Portion size:
4–5 fl oz (120–150 mL), 3–4 oz (90–120 g)

INGREDIENTS	U.S.	METRIC
Elbow macaroni	8 oz	240 g
Kosher salt	to taste	to taste
Mayonnaise (p. 41), or commercial	6 fl oz	180 mL
Prepared yellow mustard	½ fl oz	15 mL
Bottled hot sauce	dash	dash
Worcestershire sauce	dash	dash
Sugar	2 tsp	10 mL
Cider vinegar	1 tsp	5 mL
Peeled celery, ¼-in. (0.6-cm) dice	1½ oz	45 g
Red onion, chopped medium	¾ oz	25 g
Scallions, chopped medium	¾ oz	25 g

PROCEDURE

PREPARATION

1. Prepare according to the Procedure for Making Pasta Salads (p. 148).

HOLD

Refrigerate in a freshly sanitized, covered container up to 3 days.

PLATING

2. Place in individual dishes, or add to a plate as a component.

VARIATION

ROSE'S DELUXE MACARONI SALAD

Add ½ cup (120 mL) cooked drained red kidney beans, ½ cup (120 mL) cooked corn kernels, 1 oz (30 g) each small diced red and green bell pepper, and ½ cup (120 mL) cooked, crumbled bacon.

CHINESE-STYLE PEANUT NOODLE SALAD

SIDE DISH OR APPETIZER

Yield:
1 qt (1 L), about 1 lb (500 g)
Portions:
6–8
Portion size:
4–5 fl oz (120–150 mL), 2–2½ oz (60–75 g)

INGREDIENTS	U.S.	METRIC
Fresh Chinese lo mein noodles or fresh linguine	9 oz	180 g
Kosher salt	to taste	to taste
Asian Vinaigrette (p. 35)	3 fl oz	90 mL
Trimmed, peeled carrot	2 oz	60 g
Trimmed, peeled broccoli stems	2 oz	60 g
Julienne red bell pepper	2 oz	60 g
Peanut oil	½ fl oz	15 mL
Crushed red chile	½ tsp	3 mL
Minced shallots	¾ oz	22 g
Minced garlic	¼ oz	7 g
Peanut butter	1½ fl oz	45 mL
Chinese soy sauce	½ fl oz	15 mL
Chinese red vinegar	1 fl oz	30 mL
Sugar	1 tbsp	15 mL
Poultry Stock (p. 749)	2 fl oz	60 mL
Shredded scallions	1 oz	30 g
Chopped roasted peanuts	1 oz	30 g
Chopped cilantro	¼ oz	7 g

PROCEDURE

PREPARATION

1. Boil the noodles al dente in salted water, drain, and shake dry.
2. Toss with 2 fl oz (60 mL) of the vinaigrette and allow to mellow at room temperature 1 hour.
3. Use a mandoline or food processor to cut the carrot and broccoli into very fine, long shreds.
4. Separately blanch the carrots and broccoli al dente, refresh, drain, and blot dry.
5. Toss with 1 fl oz (30 mL) Asian Vinaigrette.
6. Warm the peanut oil, red chile, shallots, and garlic in a small saucepan until they sizzle.
7. Add the peanut butter, soy sauce, vinegar, sugar, stock, and just enough water to make a thin sauce. Simmer about 5 minutes, then cool to room temperature.
8. Taste and correct the seasoning.
9. Toss the noodles with the sauce and shredded or julienne vegetables, including scallions.
10. Correct the seasoning and texture; add more stock or water if the sauce tightens too much.
11. Refrigerate and allow to mellow 30 minutes.
12. Reevaluate and correct as necessary.

HOLD

Refrigerate in a freshly covered container up to 8 hours. Bring to room temperature to serve.

PLATING

14. Mound each portion on a cool 10-in. (25-cm) plate.
15. Garnish each serving with chopped peanuts and cilantro.

VARIATION

GRILLED CHICKEN PEANUT NOODLE ENTRÉE SALAD

Top each serving with a 4 oz (120 g) boneless chicken breast that has been marinated in Asian Vinaigrette, grilled, and sliced on the diagonal.

BROCCOLI ROTINI SALAD

SIDE DISH OR APPETIZER

Yield:
1 qt (1 L), about 24 oz (720 g)
Portions:
6–8
Portion size:
4–5 fl oz (120–150 mL), 3–4 oz (90–120 g)

INGREDIENTS	U.S.	METRIC
Italian rotini pasta	4 oz	120 g
Kosher salt	to taste	to taste
Balsamic Vinaigrette (p. 33)	5 fl oz	150 mL
Small broccoli florets, blanched, refreshed, drained	6 oz	180 g
Roasted red bell pepper, cleaned, cut in ⅜-in. (1-cm) dice	½ c.	120 mL
Pitted brine-cured black olives, halved	1 oz	30 g
Sweet onion, chopped	1½ oz	45 g
Grated Reggiano Parmesan cheese	1½ oz	45 g

PROCEDURE

PREPARATION

1. Prepare according to the Procedure for Making Pasta Salads (p. 148).

HOLD

Refrigerate in a freshly sanitized, covered plastic container up to 8 hours. For longer keeping, hold out the broccoli and add just before service.

PLATING

2. Place in individual dishes, or add to a plate as a component.

VARIATIONS

BROCCOLI AND SAUSAGE ROTINI ENTRÉE SALAD

Add 4 oz (120 g) cooked, sliced Italian sausage.

FARFALLE AND ARTICHOKE SALAD

Replace the rotini with farfalle (bowties) and the broccoli with sliced artichoke bottoms prepared as on page 113. Replace the Balsamic Vinaigrette with Lemon Vinaigrette (p. 34). Omit the olives. Slice the remaining vegetables rather than dicing or chopping.

Grain and Legume Side Salads

Grains and legumes make interesting and unusual side salads. Scores of rice varieties, wild rice, wheat varieties, barley, buckwheat, quinoa, corn products, dried beans, dried peas, and lentils all can be turned into delicious side salads. A welcome break from the ordinary, grain and legume ingredients add flavor, texture, and a powerhouse of nutrients to the entrées they accompany.

It is difficult to generalize about procedures and techniques related to various types of grain and legumes because there are so many options and so many possible cooking methods. Keep the following guidelines in mind.

Guidelines for Making Grain and Legume Side Salads

- Cook grains and legumes for salads so they are tender, yet firm enough so as not to disintegrate when mixed with dressing. While overcooked grains and legumes have an unattractive appearance, undercooked grains are unpleasantly chewy, and al dente legumes are notoriously difficult to digest. While all have different cooking requirements, many grains and legumes rely on carryover cooking to further tenderize their interior starch without splitting or bursting their exterior surfaces. Before preparing a large batch of a particular grain or legume salad, try a smaller test batch to perfect your procedure.
- Pre-dress grains and legumes before they harden in the refrigerator so they absorb flavorful liquids and don't dry out the finished salad. (See safety sidebar on p. 143.)

Legumes for Salads

Dried beans	Red kidney, pinto, rosa, borlotto, navy, pea bean, cannellini, flageolet, fava, lima, black-eyed pea, and many other rare and heirloom cultivars
Dried peas	Chickpeas, split green peas, and yellow peas
Lentils	Green, brown, French green, Indian pink (masoor dal), and other special cultivars

Grains for Salads

Rice	Long-grain white, long-grain brown, jasmine, basmati, brown basmati, pecan or popcorn rice, Asian red rice, Asian black rice
Wheat and wheat-like grains	Bulgur, cracked wheat, wheat berries, triticale
Grain-like pastas	Couscous, Israeli couscous, fregola
Miscellaneous grains	Buckwheat, millet, barley, quinoa

TUSCAN WHITE BEAN SALAD

SIDE DISH OR APPETIZER

Yield:
1 qt (1 L), about 2 lb (1 kg)
Portions:
6–8
Portion size:
4–5 fl oz (120–150 mL), 4–5 oz (120–150 g)

INGREDIENTS	U.S.	METRIC
Dry Italian cannellini beans, soaked overnight	8 oz	240 g
Bay leaf	1	1
Sage	2 sprigs	2 sprigs
Thyme	1 sprig	1 sprig
Extra-virgin olive oil	2 fl oz	60 mL
Lemon Vinaigrette (p. 34)	4 fl oz	120 mL
Red onion, ⅜-in. (1-cm) dice	2 oz	60 g
Peeled celery, ⅜-in. (1-cm) dice	2 oz	60 g
Minced lemon zest	2 tbsp	30 mL
Chopped parsley	¼ oz	7 g
Freshly ground black pepper	to taste	to taste

PROCEDURE

PREPARATION

1. Drain the beans and place them in a small saucepan. Add just enough water to cover by 1 in. (3 cm).
2. Bring the beans to the simmer, skim, and add the bay leaf, sage, thyme, and oil.
3. Simmer partially covered, checking water level often, about 30 minutes, or until the beans have just become tender but are not soft or falling apart. Add water as necessary.
4. Season the beans lightly with salt during the last 5 minutes of cooking.
5. Cool the beans in their broth to room temperature.
6. Strain the broth into a sauté pan, pick out and discard the herbs, and reduce the broth to a glaze, scraping the sides of the pan with a rubber spatula.
7. Scrape the glaze into the beans.
8. Mix the beans with the remaining ingredients and allow to mellow at room temperature 1 hour.
9. Taste and correct the seasoning.

HOLD

Refrigerate in a freshly sanitized, covered container up to 2 days; bring to room temperature to serve.

PLATING

10. Place in individual dishes, or add to a plate as a component.

VARIATIONS

SICILIAN WHITE BEAN SALAD

Replace the salt with anchovy paste. Replace the celery with fennel. Add 1 oz (30 g) red bell pepper cut in ⅜-in. (0.75-cm) dice.

ITALIAN CECI BEAN SALAD

Replace the white beans with chickpeas. Add additional water. Extend the cooking time as necessary.

FRENCH LENTIL SALAD

SIDE DISH

Yield:
about 1 qt (1 L),
about 26 oz (780 g)
Portions:
6–8
Portion size:
4–5 fl oz
(120–150 mL),
3–4 oz (90–120 g)

INGREDIENTS	U.S.	METRIC
French (Le Puy) green lentils	8 oz	240 g
Water	as needed	as needed
Poultry Stock (p. 749)	8 fl oz	240 mL
Extra-virgin olive oil	2 fl oz	60 mL
Smoked slab bacon, in one slice	1 oz	30 g
Whole garlic cloves, smashed and peeled	2	2
Fresh thyme	1 sprig	1 sprig
Yellow onion, in one piece	2 oz	60 g
Clove	1	1
Sherry Vinaigrette (p. 32)	3 fl oz	90 mL
Chopped shallot	1½ oz	45 g
Chopped parsley	½ oz	15 g
Red bell pepper, cut brunoise	1 oz	30 g

PROCEDURE

PREPARATION

1. Place the lentils in a saucepan with water to cover to twice their depth. Bring to a simmer, then drain off the water.
2. Add fresh water and repeat.
3. Repeat again, draining well after the last simmer (see Note).
4. Add the stock, oil, bacon, garlic, and thyme to the pan.
5. Stick the clove into the onion and add it to the pan, along with enough water to cover by ½ in. (2 cm).
6. Bring to the simmer and cook partially covered, checking the water level often, about 10–20 minutes or more, until the lentils are tender but not soft. Add water if necessary.
7. Taste and add salt if necessary.
8. Prepare an ice bain-marie.
9. Cool the lentils to room temperature by placing the pan in the ice bain-marie.
10. Drain and discard the cooking liquid. Pick out and discard the whole seasonings and bacon.
11. Toss the lentils with the vinaigrette and shallots and allow to mellow at room temperature 1 hour.
12. Correct the seasoning.

Note: Blanching the lentils removes some of their earthy taste.

PROCEDURE

HOLD

Refrigerate in a freshly sanitized, covered container up to 4 days.

FINISHING

13. Mix parsley into each serving.

PLATING

14. Place in individual dishes, or add to a plate as a component. Top each portion with a sprinkling of brunoise red bell pepper.

VARIATION

WARM LENTIL SALAD WITH FRENCH GARLIC SAUSAGE

ENTRÉE

Gently heat 6 oz (180 g) lentil salad in a microwave oven and serve warm on a bed of lettuce topped with 4 oz (120 g) grilled sliced French Garlic Sausage (p. 502) and crusty bread.

TABBOULEH

[tah-BOO-leh]

MIDDLE EASTERN WHEAT SALAD

SIDE DISH

Yield:
1½ pt (750 mL), about 24 oz (720 g)

Portions:
6

Portion size:
4 fl oz (120 mL), about 4 oz (120 g)

INGREDIENTS	U.S.	METRIC
Coarse-grain bulgur wheat	5 oz	150 g
Boiling water	12 fl oz	360 mL
Kosher salt	1 tsp	5 mL
Fresh lemon juice	1½ fl oz	45 mL
Extra-virgin olive oil	3 fl oz	90 mL
Minced garlic	⅛ oz	3 g
Toasted and freshly ground cumin	pinch	pinch
Chopped parsley	2 oz	60 g
Red onion, chopped medium	3 oz	90 g
Vine-ripe tomato, ⅜-in. (1-cm) dice	4 oz	120 g
Freshly ground black pepper	to taste	to taste

PROCEDURE

PREPARATION

1. Place the bulgur in a bowl, add the salt, and pour the boiling water over top.
2. Stir to combine.
3. Allow to the water to absorb into the bulgur while the bulgur cools to room temperature.
4. Mix the garlic and cumin into the vinaigrette.
5. If necessary, squeeze out extra moisture from the bulgur and combine it with the lemon juice, olive oil, and remaining ingredients.
6. Allow to mellow at room temperature 30 minutes.
7. Taste and correct the seasoning with salt and pepper. If necessary, adjust the taste and mouthfeel with more lemon juice and olive oil.

HOLD

Store covered at cool room temperature up to 3 hours. Refrigerate about 5 hours more.

PLATING

8. Place in individual dishes, or add to a plate as a component.

QUINOA SALAD

[KEEN-wah]

SIDE DISH

Yield:
1 qt (1 L), about 24 oz (720 g)
Portions:
6–8
Portion size:
4–5 fl oz (120–150 mL), 3–4 oz (90–120 g)

INGREDIENTS	U.S.	METRIC
Quinoa	8 oz	240 g
Water	14 fl oz	420 mL
Safflower oil	2 tsp	10 mL
Kosher salt	1 tsp	5 mL
American Cider Vinaigrette (p. 32)	3–4 fl oz	90–120 mL
Cooked corn kernels	3 fl oz	90 mL
Carrots, diced ¼ in. (0.5 cm), blanched and refreshed	2 oz	60 g
Spinach leaves, steamed, refreshed, blotted, and rough chopped	4 oz	120 g
Red onion, medium chopped	1 oz	30 g
Fresh lemon juice	to taste	to taste

PROCEDURE

PREPARATION

1. Wash the quinoa under cool running water for 5 minutes, or until surface foam subsides. Drain.
2. In a small saucepan, bring the water to the boil. Stir in the quinoa, oil, and salt, and cover the pan. Simmer over medium heat 15 minutes, or until the water has absorbed and the quinoa is al dente. (When fully cooked, the germ sprout appears as a *C*-shape curled around each kernel.)
3. Turn out into a half-hotel pan and spread out to cool.
4. While still warm, toss with the vinaigrette.
5. Cool to room temperature.
6. Mix with the remaining ingredients.
7. Taste and correct the seasoning.
8. Allow to mellow at room temperature 30 minutes.
9. Reevaluate and correct as necessary.

HOLD

With spinach and onions, refrigerate up to 8 hours. If spinach and onions are held out, hold refrigerated in a freshly sanitized, covered container up to 3 days.

PLATING

10. Place in individual dishes, or add to a plate as a component.

Uncooked quinoa (left) and cooked quinoa (right)

VARIATION

ANDEAN QUINOA SALAD

Add 2 tsp (10 mL) minced garlic and ½ tsp (3 mL) ground cumin to the vinaigrette. Replace the carrot with cooked sweet potato. Replace the spinach with roasted, peeled poblano chile. Add 1 oz (30 g) crumbled fresco cheese.

COOL CUCUMBER RICE SALAD

SIDE DISH

Yield:
1 qt (1 L),
about 24 oz (720 g)
Portions:
6–8
Portion size:
4–6 fl oz
(120–180 mL),
3–4 oz (90–120 g)

INGREDIENTS	U.S.	METRIC
Long-grain white rice	7 oz	210 g
Water	10 fl oz	300 mL
Kosher salt	1 tsp	5 mL
Vegetable oil	1 tsp	5 mL
Cucumber	7 oz	210 g
Lemon Vinaigrette (p. 34)	4 fl oz	120 mL
Chopped scallions	1 oz	30 g
Sour cream or crème fraîche	4 fl oz	120 mL
Finely ground white pepper	to taste	to taste
Additional salt	to taste	to taste

PROCEDURE

PREPARATION

1. Cook the rice:
   a. Preheat a standard oven to 400°F (200°C).
   b. Place the rice in a heavy 1-qt (1-L) saucepan with a tight-fitting lid.
   c. Rinse the rice under cool water, swishing it with your hand, until the water changes from opaque to clear.
   d. Drain.
   e. Add the water, salt, and oil.
   f. Cover, bring to the simmer, and cook about 12 minutes.
   g. Transfer the pan to the oven and bake 15 minutes more.
   h. Remove the pan from the oven and let rest undisturbed at room temperature 15 minutes more.
2. Fabricate the cucumber:
   a. Peel the cucumber, trim the ends, slice in half lengthwise, and scoop out the seeds.
   b. Cut into ⅜-in. (1-cm) dice, salt lightly, and roll up in a clean, lint-free towel to drain.
3. Mix the salad:
   a. Scrape the rice out into a half-hotel pan and spread out to cool.
   b. While still warm, toss in the vinaigrette.
   c. Cool to room temperature.
   d. As soon as the rice reaches room temperature, mix with the cucumber, scallions, and sour cream. Season with pepper and additional salt if needed.

HOLD

Refrigerate up to 5 hours. (Rice becomes hard and grainy under prolonged refrigeration.)

VARIATIONS

COCONUT RICE SALAD

Replace the water with canned unsweetened coconut milk. Omit the oil. Add ½ oz (15 g) chopped pickled ginger.

SAFFRON RICE SALAD

Add ½ tsp (2 mL) crushed saffron threads to the rice cooking water. Replace the cucumber with cooked peas and/or ⅜-in. (1-cm) lengths cooked asparagus.

Complex Main Course Salads

Bound Protein Salads

Bound protein salads are made from diced or chopped meat, poultry, eggs, or seafood with a small amount of vegetable ingredients and mayonnaise or another thick dressing. This type of salad is referred to as *bound* because the thick dressing binds, or keeps the main food items glued together. When a well-made bound salad is picked up with a disher or portion scoop, it stays together in a cohesive mass that is firm enough to hold its shape on a plate. Bound protein salads such as chicken salad, tuna salad, shrimp salad, and egg salad may be served as the centerpiece of a cold entrée plate or used as a sandwich filling.

Guidelines for Preparing Bound Protein Salads

- The cooked protein item should be fresh, moist, and tasty in its own right. While it is acceptable to recycle leftover cooked meats and poultry into bound protein salads, check carefully for quality and freshness.
- Keep the accent vegetables to a minimum, and cut them very small. Customers perceive the celery, onion, peppers, and other vegetables in these salads as filler and consider a salad with a high ratio of these accent vegetables to be of poor value.
- Fabricate the protein item in a size appropriate for the salad's intended use. If a salad is to be served as a plated entrée, the item can be cut into fairly large dice. However, for sandwiches it should be chopped into small pieces so the salad binds tightly together and stays neatly in the roll or bread.
- To improve the flavor of a bound protein salad, try mixing an appropriate glace into the dressing. Some poultry glace whisked into the dressing for a chicken salad or some seafood glace into the dressing for a shrimp salad acts as a liaison between the protein and its sauce, and it gives the finished salad a powerful flavor boost.
- If served in plated presentation, the bound salad should be placed on a bed of greens or on a *liner leaf*. A leafy greens liner adds lightness and crunch, gives color to the plate, and makes the plate look more full. Appropriate garnishes also add welcome texture and color.

CLASSIC CHICKEN OR TURKEY SALAD

LUNCH MAIN COURSE

Yield:
1 qt (1 L), about 1¾ lb (840 g)
Portions:
varies according to application
Portion size:
varies according to application

INGREDIENTS	U.S.	METRIC
Mayonnaise (p. 41), or commercial	6 fl oz	180 mL
Sugar	1 tsp	5 mL
Cider vinegar	1 tsp	10 mL
Kosher salt	to taste	to taste
Finely ground white pepper	to taste	to taste
Poultry glace (optional)	2 tsp	10 mL
Diced or chopped cooked chicken or turkey	20 oz	600 g
Peeled celery, ¼-in. (0.5-cm) dice	3 oz	90 g
Chopped scallions	1 oz	30 g
Lettuce and other garnishes	as needed	as needed

PROCEDURE

PREPARATION

1. Combine the mayonnaise and seasonings.
2. Taste and correct seasoning.
3. Blend the dressing with the remaining ingredients.
4. Refrigerate ½–1 hour, then taste and, if necessary, correct the seasoning and adjust the texture with more mayonnaise.

HOLD

If made with commercial mayonnaise, store refrigerated in a freshly sanitized, covered container up to 4 days; with housemade mayonnaise, store up to 2 days.

PLATING

5. Place the salad on a lettuce leaf on a cool plate and add garnishes.

   –or–

   Use as a sandwich filling.

VARIATIONS

TARRAGON CHICKEN/TURKEY SALAD

Replace the scallions with ½ oz (15 g) chopped shallots. Add 2 tbsp (30 mL) chopped fresh tarragon.

CHICKEN/TURKEY SALAD WITH WALNUTS AND GRAPES

Omit the scallions. Add 4 oz (120 g) halved seedless grapes and ½ oz (15 g) toasted walnut pieces.

CURRIED CHICKEN/ TURKEY SALAD

Sauté 2 tsp (10 mL) Madras curry powder in ½ fl oz (15 mL) safflower oil until fragrant. Cool and add to the dressing. Hydrate ½ oz (15 g) currants in 2 fl oz (60 mL) port wine and then cool. Add to the salad along with ½ oz (15 g) toasted slivered almonds.

CLASSIC SHRIMP SALAD

LUNCH MAIN COURSE

Yield:
1 qt (1 L),
about 20 oz (600 g)
Portions:
varies according to application
Portion size:
varies according to application

INGREDIENTS	U.S.	METRIC
Raw shrimp (medium to small most economical)	2 lb	1 kg
Shellfish Stock (p. 750)	2 qt	2 L
Mayonnaise (p. 41), preferably made with lemon juice	6 fl oz	180 mL
Chesapeake-style seafood seasoning	1 tsp	5 mL
Minced lemon zest	1 tbsp	15 m
Fresh lemon juice	to taste	to taste
Sugar	to taste	to taste
Peeled celery, ⅜-in. (1-cm) dice	3 oz	90 g
Chopped scallions	1 oz	30 g
Lettuce and other garnishes	as needed	as needed

PROCEDURE

PREPARATION

1. Poach the shrimp in the stock according to the procedure on page 195. Make shrimp glace by reducing the *cuisson*.
2. Peel and slice, dice, or chop the shrimp according to their size and intended use.
3. Mix the mayonnaise with the shrimp glaze and seasonings.
4. Taste and correct the seasonings.
5. Mix together the shrimp, dressing, and vegetables.
6. Refrigerate ½–1 hour, then taste and correct the seasonings and texture.

HOLD

Refrigerate in a freshly sanitized, covered container up to 2 days.

PLATING

7. Serve on a liner leaf or bed of lettuce with garnishes.
   –or–
   Use as a sandwich filling.

VARIATIONS

CLASSIC LOBSTER SALAD

Replace the shrimp and stock with two 1¼-lb (550-g) cold-water lobsters, steamed, chilled, and shelled. Use 2 tsp (10 mL) shellfish glace made from the lobster shells or from another source.

CLASSIC CRAB SALAD

Replace the shrimp with 1 lb (500 g) cooked crabmeat, carefully picked over. Omit the stock. Use 2 tsp (10 mL) shellfish glace from another source.

CURRIED SHRIMP SALAD

Proceed as for Curried Chicken/Turkey Salad, page 159.

SCANDINAVIAN SHRIMP SALAD

Replace half the mayonnaise with sour cream. Omit the Chesapeake seasoning. Add a little white pepper. Add ½–1 oz (50–30 g) minced fresh dill. Increase the sugar.

ASIAN CRAB SALAD

Prepare classic crab salad, omitting the celery. Add 1 tbsp (30 mL) chopped pickled ginger and 1 tsp (10 mL) soy sauce.

HAWAI'IAN SHRIMP SALAD

Replace the Chesapeake seasoning with 1 tsp (10 mL) soy sauce. Replace the celery with chopped fresh pineapple.

TRADITIONAL TUNA SALAD

LUNCH MAIN COURSE

Yield:
1 qt (1 L), about 2 lb (1 kg)
Portions:
varies according to application
Portion size:
varies according to application

INGREDIENTS	U.S.	METRIC
Mayonnaise (p. 41), or commercial	7 fl oz	225 mL
Sweet pickle relish	1 fl oz	30 mL
Prepared yellow mustard	2 tsp	10 mL
Worcestershire sauce	½ tsp	3 mL
Bottled hot sauce	to taste	to taste
Water-packed white tuna	28 oz can	800 g can
Peeled celery, ⅜-in. (1-cm) dice	3 oz	90 g
Chopped scallions	1 oz	30 g
Chopped parsley	¼ oz	7 g
Lettuce and other garnishes	as needed	as needed

PROCEDURE

PREPARATION

1. Combine the mayonnaise with the relish, mustard, Worcestershire sauce, and hot sauce.
2. Drain the tuna very well, place in a bowl, and flake it apart.
3. Mix with the mayonnaise, celery, scallions, and parsley.
4. Taste and correct the seasoning.
5. Refrigerate ½–1 hour, then taste and correct the seasonings and texture.

HOLD

Refrigerate in a freshly sanitized, covered container up to 3 days.

PLATING

6. Serve on a liner leaf or bed of lettuce with garnishes.

   –or–

   Use as a sandwich filling.

VARIATIONS

EGG TUNA SALAD

Replace 5 oz (150 g) of the tuna with 5 oz (150 g) or about 1 cup (240 mL) chopped hard-cooked egg.

MEDITERRANEAN TUNA SALAD

Replace the dressing ingredients with 8 fl oz (240 mL) Balsamic Vinaigrette (p. 33). Omit the celery and add 2 oz (60 g) brunoise red bell pepper and 3 tbsp (45 mL) nonpareil capers.

TRADITIONAL EGG SALAD

LUNCH MAIN COURSE

Yield:
about 1 qt (1 L), 2½ lb (1.25 kg)
Portions:
varies according to application
Portion size:
varies according to application

INGREDIENTS	U.S.	METRIC
Mayonnaise (p. 41), or commercial	6 fl oz	180 mL
Prepared yellow mustard	1½ fl oz	45 g
Sugar	2 tsp	10 mL
Celery seeds	½ tsp	2 mL
Finely ground white pepper	to taste	to taste
Bottled hot sauce	to taste	to taste
Worcestershire sauce	½ tsp	3 mL
Hard-cooked eggs, shelled	18	18
Kosher salt	to taste	to taste
Finely chopped scallions	1 oz	30 g
Lettuce and other garnishes	as needed	as needed

PROCEDURE

PREPARATION

1. Make the dressing: Mix the mayonnaise, mustard, sugar, celery seeds, pepper, hot sauce, and Worcestershire sauce.
2. Separate the whites and yolks of the eggs.
3. Chop the whites and crumble the yolks into them.
4. Toss with a little salt.
5. Blend in the dressing and scallions.
6. Allow to mellow in the refrigerator 1 hour.
7. Taste and correct the seasoning and texture.

HOLD

Refrigerate in a freshly sanitized, covered container up to 2 days.

PLATING

8. Serve on a liner leaf or bed of lettuce with garnishes.

   –or–

   Use as a sandwich filling.

VARIATIONS

DILLED EGG SALAD

Omit the celery seeds, hot sauce, and Worcestershire sauce. Replace the yellow mustard with Dijon mustard. Reduce the scallions to ½ oz (15 g). Add 2 oz (60 g) minced fresh dill.

PENNSYLVANIA DUTCH SWEET EGG SALAD

Increase the sugar to 1 tbsp (15 g). Add 1½ fl oz (45 mL) sweet pickle relish.

Complete Salads in Mixed Presentation

Complete salads are based on a protein item and include substantial amounts of several vegetables, one of which is often a starch. They are called *complete* because they offer all the elements of a nutritionally balanced meal. When the protein element of a complete salad totals at least 4 oz (120 g) and the salad fills a 10-in. (25-cm) or larger plate, the salad can be served as a casual dinner entrée. In slightly smaller size, a complete salad becomes a luncheon entrée, and at about half size, it's just right as an appetizer. Salads that include both vegetables and a protein item but no starch element can be considered complete if they are accompanied by bread. Complete salads can be served in both mixed and arranged presentations.

Many complex side salads, such as vegetable, pasta, grain, and potato salads, can be transformed into complete salads by adding a complementary protein item. For example, if sliced grilled chicken breast is added to the Broccoli Rotini Salad on page 151, the dish may be considered a complete salad and can be served as an entrée. Thus, many of the guidelines, techniques, and procedures listed previously apply to complete salads as well.

INSALATA DI FRUTTI DI MARE

[een-sah-LAH-tah dee FROOT tee dee MAH-ray]

ITALIAN SEAFOOD SALAD

APPETIZER

Yield:
1 qt (1 L), about 2 lb (1 kg)

Portions:
4 lunch servings, 6 appetizer servings

Portion size:
8 fl oz (240 mL), 8 oz (240 g) or 5 fl oz (150 mL), 5 oz (150 g)

INGREDIENTS	U.S.	METRIC
Lemon	½	½
Court bouillon (p. 194)	1 pt	500 mL
Small shrimp, in shell	8 oz	240 g
Calamari tubes, cleaned, cut into ⅜-in. (1-cm) rings	6 oz	180 g
Dry-pack sea scallops, trimmed and sliced	6 oz	180 g
Farm-raised mussels, in shell, cleaned and soaked 30 minutes	1 lb	500 g
Lemon Vinaigrette (p. 34), made with extra-virgin olive oil only	6 fl oz	180 mL
Shallots, slivered	¼ oz	7 g
Tomato filet, coarse julienne	2 oz	60 g
Chiffonnade basil leaves	½ oz	15 g
Boston lettuce leaves	4 oz	120 g
Crusty Italian bread	12 oz	360 g

PROCEDURE

PREPARATION

1. Place the court bouillon in a nonreactive saucepan, squeeze the lemon into it, and bring it to a simmer.
2. Drop in the shrimp and poach them just until pink and loosely curled. Using a slotted spoon, remove the shrimp to a half-hotel pan.
3. Drop in the calamari and poach it a few seconds, or until it becomes opaque in color. Remove to the hotel pan.
4. Drop in the scallops, poach a few seconds or just until opaque, and remove to the pan.
5. Pour about 2 fl oz (60 mL) bouillon into another saucepan. Add the mussels, cover the pan, and steam the mussels just until they begin to open. Uncover the saucepan, lift out the mussels to the hotel pan, and strain the liquid back into the rest of the bouillon.
6. Peel the shrimp and return the shells into the pan of bouillon.
7. Simmer the shells in the bouillon 20 minutes.
8. Strain the resulting stock, return it to the saucepan, and reduce it to a glaze.
9. Shell the mussels and remove any beard filaments.
10. As the stock boils down, add to it any liquid that comes out of the various seafood items.
11. Whisk the cooled glaze into the vinaigrette and add the shallots.
12. Mix the seafood into the vinaigrette.

(continues)

PROCEDURE *(continued)*

13. Taste and correct the seasoning.

HOLD

Refrigerate in a freshly sanitized, covered container up to 6 hours. To hold up to 2 days, keep the seafood and vinaigrette separate.

FINISHING

14. Mix the tomato and basil into each portion just before serving.

PLATING

15. Place a lettuce leaf on a cool 10-in. (25-cm) plate.
16. Mound a portion of the salad and its dressing on the leaf.
17. Serve a portion of the bread in a basket.

VARIATIONS

CALIFORNIA SEAFOOD SALAD

In step 14, add ½ diced firm avocado. Replace the basil with ¼ oz (4 g) each chopped parsley and chopped cilantro.

ASIAN SEAFOOD SALAD ON NOODLE NEST

Replace the Court Bouillon aromatics with ginger and scallion. Replace the Lemon Vinaigrette with Asian Vinaigrette (p. 35). Replace the shallots with scallions and add 5–6 oz (140–180 g) blanched and refreshed snow peas. Serve on a Crispy Noodle Nest (p. 707).

MINNESOTA DUCK AND WILD RICE SALAD

APPETIZER OR LUNCH MAIN COURSE

Yield:
1 qt (1 L), about 2 lb (1 kg)

Portions:
4 lunch servings,
6 appetizer servings

Portion size:
8 fl oz (240 mL), 8 oz (240 g) or
5 fl oz (150 mL), 5 oz (150 g)

INGREDIENTS	U.S.	METRIC
Wild rice	4 oz	120 g
Water	as needed	as needed
Kosher salt	as needed	as needed
Long-grain white rice	5 oz	150 g
Cranberry-Walnut Vinaigrette (p. 36)	8 fl oz	240 mL
Dried cranberries	1 oz	30 g
Boneless, skin-on duck breast	12 oz	360 g
Freshly ground black pepper	to taste	to taste
Chopped red onion	3 oz	90 g
Toasted, chopped walnuts	½ oz	15 g
Watercress, large stems removed	6 oz	180 g

PROCEDURE

PREPARATION

1. Cook the wild rice:
   a. Rinse the wild rice and place in a small saucepan with 1¼ qt (1.25 L) salted water.
   b. Simmer about 40 minutes, or until al dente and the ends of the grains have begun to split open.
2. Cook the long grain rice:
   a. Rinse the long-grain rice until the water runs clear.

PROCEDURE

  b. Place the long-grain rice in a heavy 1-qt (1-L) saucepan with about ½ tsp. (3 mL) salt and 10 fl oz (300 mL) water. Cover and bring to the simmer. Cook over low heat 15 minutes, then remove the pan from the burner and allow the rice to steam in its own heat until the pan is cool.

3. Steep the cranberries in 8 fl oz (240 mL) boiling water until hydrated. Drain.
4. Drain the wild rice, shake it dry, and toss it with the warm cooked rice and about 3 fl oz (90 mL) vinaigrette. Cool to room temperature.
5. Prepare the cracklings:
   a. Remove the skin from the duck breast. Cut the skin into fine julienne.
   b. Place the duck skin in a small sauté pan and cook over low heat until the fat renders out and the skin turns into crispy cracklings.
   c. Transfer the cracklings to a paper towel and season with salt. Reserve.
6. Prepare the duck breast:
   a. Season the duck breast with salt and pepper and pan-sear it to a rare doneness.
   b. Cool the duck breast to room temperature.
   c. Slice the duck breast ⅜ in. (0.75 cm) thick, and then cut each slice in half lengthwise to make coarse julienne.
7. Mix the salad:
   a. Add the duck and its juices to the rice mixture.
   b. Add the remaining ingredients except the cracklings and watercress.
   c. Toss with more vinaigrette to bind and season.
   d. Allow to mellow at room temperature for ½ hour.
   e. Taste and correct both mouthfeel and seasoning, adding more vinaigrette if necessary.

HOLD

Refrigerate in a freshly sanitized, covered container up to 8 hours. Hold the cracklings lightly covered at cool room temperature.

FINISHING

8. Crumble some of the cracklings over each portion and toss to combine.

PLATING

9. Place a bed of watercress on a cool 10-in. (25-cm) plate.
10. Mound a portion of the salad on the cress.

VARIATION

MINNESOTA TURKEY AND WILD RICE SALAD

Replace the duck with diced roast turkey dark meat.

Fruit Salads

Fruit salads may be presented either mixed or arranged. The more casual mixed fruit salad is typically prepared ahead of time and is fast and easy to present. Arranged fruit salads are plated to order and, in many ways, resemble a fruit platter. The difference, however, is that an arranged fruit salad is presented in its dressing, while a fruit platter has no dressing but may have sweet dips or sauces served on the side.

Guidelines for Preparing Mixed Fruit Salads

- Choose fruits whose flavors, textures, and colors complement one another.
- Fabricate fruits into pieces of the same general size, making sure each piece will fit easily on a spoon. Fabricating fruits into many shapes creates visual interest.
- Create a theme by using mixtures of seasonal fruits, tropical fruits, or specific types of fruit.
- Choose a dressing that complements the fruits' flavors. For example, sweet fruits are best mixed with a tart, tangy dressing, while acidic fruits taste best with a sweeter dressing.
- Because fabricated fruits are highly perishable, prepare fruit salads at the last possible minute before serving. If you must prepare fruit salads ahead of time, store under refrigeration, and don't plan to hold them long.
- Fruits subject to softening and enzymatic browning should be held out of bulk prepared salads and added just before serving. The same holds true for crisp or crunchy garnishes, such as toasted nuts, that soften in contact with fruits and dressing.

WALDORF SALAD

APPETIZER OR SIDE DISH

Yield:
1 qt (1 L), about 2 lb (1 kg)
Portions:
4–6
Portion size:
5 fl oz (150 mL), 5 oz (150 g) or 8 fl oz (240 mL), 8 oz (240 g)

INGREDIENTS	U.S.	METRIC
Apple cider	8 fl oz	240 mL
Thick *Mayonnaise (p. 41)*, or commercial	10 fl oz	300 mL
Fresh lemon juice	1 tbsp	15 mL
Kosher salt	to taste	to taste
Finely ground white pepper	to taste	to taste
McIntosh or other juicy, sweet apples	2 lb	1 k
Peeled celery hearts, ⅜-in. (1-cm) diced	6 oz	180 g
Toasted walnuts (see Note), broken into small pieces	4 oz	120 g
Minced parsley	½ oz	15 g
Red-leaf lettuce leaves	4–6	4–6
Additional McIntosh or other apple	1 5-oz	1 150-g
Fresh lemon juice, in squeeze bottle	to taste	to taste

Note: If preparing the salad more than 1 hour prior to service, leave out the walnuts and add just before serving.

PROCEDURE

PREPARATION

1. Place the cider in a small sauté pan and reduce over moderate heat, scraping with a heatproof rubber spatula, to a glaze. Cool to room temperature.
2. Scrape the cider glaze into the mayonnaise and mix in the lemon juice, salt, and pepper.
3. Peel and core the apples, then cut them into ½-in. (1-cm) dice.
4. Immediately mix the apples into the mayonnaise along with the celery, walnuts, and half the parsley.
5. Taste and correct the seasoning.

HOLD

Refrigerated in a freshly sanitized, covered container up to 2 days.

PLATING

6. For each serving, place a lettuce leaf on a cool 10-in. (25-cm) plate.
7. Using the appropriate portion scoop, place the salad in the center of the leaf.
8. For each serving cut 5 apple slices from the additional apple, squeeze lemon juice on them, and fan them across the stem end of the lettuce leaf.
9. Sprinkle the salad with the remaining parsley.

The History of Waldorf Salad

One of America's best-known fruit salads is the Waldorf salad. Its invention is credited to Oscar Tschirsky, the famous maître d'hôtel of Manhattan's Waldorf-Astoria hotel during the 1890s. Known as "Oscar of the Waldorf," Tschirsky published a cookbook containing a recipe for a mayonnaise-based salad consisting of little more than apples and celery. Soon, the salad was copied in hotel dining rooms and restaurants across America. Toasted walnuts were a later addition, appearing in the 1920s.

TROPICAL FRUIT SALAD IN A PINEAPPLE BOAT

APPETIZER OR BRUNCH MAIN COURSE

Yield:
about 1¼ qt (1.5 L), 2 lb (1 kg)
Portions:
4
Portion size:
about 12 fl oz (240 mL), 5 oz (150 g)

INGREDIENTS	U.S.	METRIC
Baby pineapples	2 ½ lb (4)	1.2 kg (4)
Ripe mangoes	12 oz (1)	375 g (1)
Ripe papaya	12 oz (1)	350 g (1)
Kiwi fruit	6 oz (2)	180 g (2)
Small star fruit	4 oz (1)	120 g (1)
Navel orange	12 oz (1 large)	350 g (1 large)
Firm-ripe banana (see Note)	5 oz (1 large)	150 g (1 large)
Tropical Vinaigrette (p. 34), reduce oil to 2 fl oz (60 mL)	4 fl oz	120 mL

Note: If preparing ahead of time, leave out the banana and add to order.

PROCEDURE

PREPARATION

1. Place a cutting board inside a full sheet tray.
2. Place each pineapple on its side on the board and slice off the top quarter.
3. Using a flexible knife, cut around the inside of each pineapple's shell to release much of the flesh.
4. Remove the core from each pineapple and discard.
5. Use a parisienne scoop to remove the remaining pineapple flesh and hollow out the cavity of each boat.
6. Wrap and refrigerate the boats until needed.
7. Fabricate the fruit to your discretion following the guidelines on page 166.
8. Place the fruit in a bowl.
9. When finished, scrape any juices accumulated on the board and in the sheet tray into the bowl with the fruit.
10. Mix the vinaigrette into the fruit.

HOLD

Refrigerate in a freshly sanitized, covered container up to 24 hours.

PLATING

11. Place a pineapple boat on a 9-in. (23-cm) rectangular or oval plate and fill it with a portion of fruit.

VARIATIONS

Virtually any tropical fruit may be substituted or added.

THAI TROPICAL FRUIT SALAD IN PINEAPPLE BOAT

Add 2 tbsp (30 mL) very finely minced fresh lemongrass and 2 fl oz (60 mL) coconut cream to the dressing.

SUMMER FRUIT SALAD WITH POPPY SEED YOGURT DRESSING

APPETIZER OR BRUNCH MAIN COURSE

Yield:
about 1 qt (1 L), 2 lb (1 kg)
Portions:
4–6
Portion size:
5 fl oz (150 mL), 5 oz (150 g) or 8 fl oz (240 mL), 8 oz (240 g)

INGREDIENTS	U.S.	METRIC
Sweet Yogurt Dressing for Fruit Salad (p. 46)	8 fl oz	240 mL
Firm-ripe peaches or nectarines	8 oz	30 g
Firm-ripe plums, any variety	7 oz	270 g
Blueberries, picked over for stems	½ pt	250 mL
Blackberries	½ pt	250 mL
Raspberries	½ pt	250 mL
Mint	4–6 sprigs	4–6 sprigs
Supplies		
Cocktail napkin or 5-in. (13-cm) doily	4–6	4–6

PROCEDURE

PREPARATION

1. Prepare an ice bain-marie.
2. Place the dressing in a bowl near your work surface.
3. Blanch the peaches or nectarines and plums for 1–2 seconds and refresh immediately.
4. Remove the skins.
5. Cut the flesh into ¾-in. (2-cm) cubes and place them directly into the dressing.
6. Scrape any accumulated juices into the bowl.
7. Gently fold in the berries.

HOLD

Refrigerate as briefly as possible and no more than 4 hours.

PLATING

8. For each portion, spoon the fruits and dressing into a 10-oz (300-mL) wineglass or glass bowl.
9. Place on an underliner plate lined with a cocktail napkin or doily.
10. Garnish with a mint sprig.

VARIATION

Add or substitute other spring or summer fruits, such as strawberries, melon balls, etc.

STRAWBERRY SALAD WITH BLACK PEPPER BALSAMIC DRESSING

APPETIZER OR SIDE DISH

Yield:
slightly less than 1 qt (1 L), about 1 lb (480 g)

Portions:
4–6

Portion size:
5 fl oz (150 mL), 2½ oz (75 g) to 7 fl oz, (200 mL), 3½ oz (100 g)

INGREDIENTS	U.S.	METRIC
Small strawberries, preferably local in season	1 qt	1 L
Black peppercorns	1 tsp	5 mL
Balsamic Vinaigrette (p. 33), garlic omitted	3 fl oz	90 mL
Boston lettuce leaves	2–3 oz (4–6)	60–90 g (4–6)

PROCEDURE

PREPARATION

1. Wash, dry, and hull the berries.
2. Place in a bowl.
3. In a small mortar or heavy bowl, crush the peppercorns coarse.
4. Sift the pepper to remove the fine particles.
5. Using a rubber spatula, gently toss the berries with the vinaigrette and peppercorns.
6. Refrigerate at least 30 minutes, stirring occasionally.

HOLD

Refrigerate no more than 4 hours.

PLATING

7. For each portion, line a cool 8-in. (20-cm) plate with a lettuce leaf.
8. Mound the salad on the leaf.

VARIATION

If small, local berries are not available, use commercial berries. Halve, quarter, or slice the berries as appropriate.

SALAD OF AUTUMN FRUITS WITH POMEGRANATE SEEDS

APPETIZER OR BRUNCH MAIN COURSE

Yield:
about 1 qt (1 L), 24 oz (750 g)
Portions:
4–6
Portion size:
5 fl oz (150 mL), 4 oz (120 g) to 8 fl oz (240 mL), 6 oz (180 g)

INGREDIENTS	U.S.	METRIC
Pomegranate-Walnut Vinaigrette (p. 36)	8 fl oz	240 mL
Unwaxed Golden Delicious apple	5 oz	150 g
Unwaxed Red Delicious apple	5 oz	150 g
Firm-ripe Bartlett or Anjou pear	5 oz	150 g
Ripe figs, any type	3 oz	90 g
Green seedless Thompson grapes	4 oz	120 g
Red Flame grapes	4 oz	120 g
Pomegranate	½	½
Red-leaf lettuce	2–3 oz (4–6 leaves)	60–90 g (4–6 leaves)

PROCEDURE

PREPARATION

1. Place the vinaigrette in a bowl near the work surface.
2. Core the apples and cut them into ¾-in. (2-cm) cubes.
3. Immediately add the apples to the vinaigrette and stir to coat them.
4. Peel and core the pear and cut into ¾-in. (2-cm) cubes.
5. Stir the pears into the vinaigrette.
6. Trim the figs, cut into sixths or eighths, and add to the bowl.
7. Cut the grapes in half and add to the bowl.
8. Break the pomegranate half into pieces, pull out the seeds, and separate them from the pith.
9. Add the pomegranate seeds to the bowl and gently toss all ingredients together.
10. Refrigerate at least 30 minutes.

HOLD

Refrigerate no longer than 4 hours.

PLATING

11. For each portion, line a cool 8-in. (20-cm) plate with a lettuce leaf.
12. Using a slotted spoon to portion the fruit, so excess juice is left behind, mound the salad on the leaf.

MELON AND PROSCIUTTO WITH LEMON-THYME SORBET

APPETIZER

Portions:
1
Portion size:
about 5 oz (150 g) plus 3 fl oz (90 mL) sorbet

INGREDIENTS	U.S.	METRIC
Ripe honeydew or Crenshaw melon, in one piece	8 oz	240 g
Very thinly sliced Italian prosciutto, cut into 1 × 4-in. (3 × 10-cm) ribbons	1 oz	30 g
Lemon-Thyme Sorbet (p. 713)	3 fl oz	90 mL
Lemon-thyme leaves	½ tsp	3 mL

PROCEDURE

FINISHING

1. Cut the melon into long, slender, 1-in. (2.5-cm) wedges.
2. Peel each wedge and cut it in half crosswise
3. Wrap each melon wedge in a prosciutto ribbon.

PLATING

4. Arrange the melon in a circular pattern on a cold 10-in. (25-cm) plate, leaving a 2-in. (5-cm) space in the center.
5. Scoop the sorbet into the middle.
6. Sprinkle the melon with the lemon-thyme leaves.

VARIATIONS

MELON AND PROSCIUTTO WITH PORT WINE SORBET

Replace the Lemon Thyme Sorbet with Port Wine Sorbet (p. 713).

FIGS AND PROSCIUTTO WITH PORT WINE SORBET

Replace the melon with ripe figs and adjust the presentation accordingly.

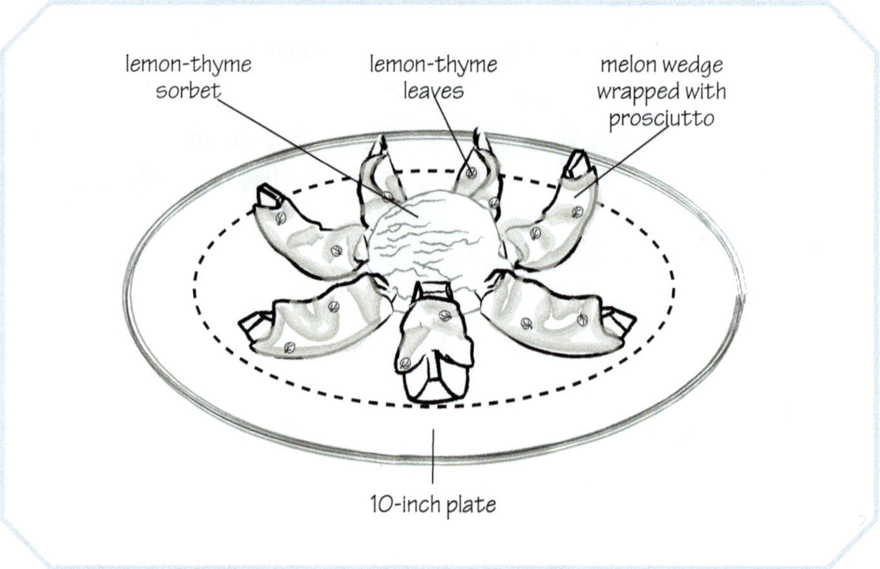

UNDERSTANDING ARRANGED SALADS

A complex salad in arranged presentation, or ***arranged salad***, is a complex salad consisting of several separate food elements placed on the plate in a precise, planned design. Another term for an arranged salad is *composed salad*, a direct translation of the French *salade composée*. European and North American cuisines include quite a few classic and well-known arranged salads, such as Salade Niçoise and Cobb Salad. In addition, modern garde manger chefs are constantly creating new salad combinations, arranged in striking, contemporary designs. Indeed, the possibilities for creating spectacular constructions are virtually limitless. However, it is important to remember that when you are creating arranged salads, as with any dish, flavor must come before presentation. No matter how fantastic an artfully arranged salad might appear, its true worth is measured by its taste.

At the simplest level, an arranged salad has a minimum of three elements:

1. A main food item
2. A secondary food item that is often a base, such as a liner leaf or bed
3. A garnish

An elementary example of an arranged presentation is a scoop of chicken salad presented on a lettuce leaf liner and garnished with cherry tomato halves. However, a modern day arranged salad may be composed of many more than three elements, often comprising several main and secondary food items, several garnishes, and one or more separate sauces or dressings that may be used for plate painting, as in the photo on page 186.

Basic arranged salad

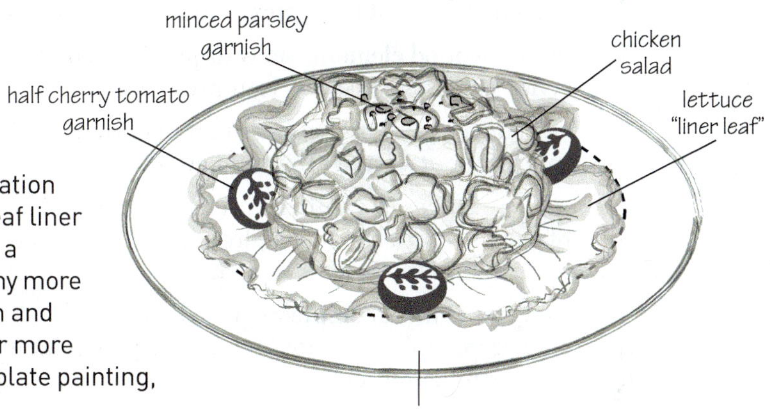

Constructing the Plate

Some arranged salads are relatively simple in design and easy to plate, while others are complicated and challenging to assemble. Although it is difficult to describe all the many procedures for arranged salads, some basic guidelines apply to the majority of arranged salads.

Contemporary arranged salads may be classified into the following five presentation styles:

1. Bedded
2. Mounded
3. Flat
4. Molded
5. Stacked

Bedded Presentations

Among the most common and traditional arranged salads are those based on a bed, or layer, of salad greens. A salad presented in this manner is said to be a

> **Plate Painting**
>
> A new and technically challenging presentation style in which sauces and dressings are used to create artistic designs on the plate is called ***plate painting***. Before attempting to prepare the salads in this chapter that include plate painting, you should read the information on pages 714–715. Special tools used for plate painting are pictured on page 18.

bedded presentation. *This is different from placing one or two whole lettuce leaves under a complex salad as a liner.* A bed of greens is literally a simple salad used as a component of a complex salad. As such, the bed salad is usually tossed with its own dressing before it is placed on the plate. To increase visual interest, you can create height on the plate by mounding the greens rather than laying them flat on the plate. Make sure the texture of the greens for the salad bed is sturdy enough to hold the toppings without becoming flattened or wilted. Also make sure the flavor of the greens complements the toppings used.

Guidelines for Preparing Arranged Salads

- Present arranged salads on plates large enough to accommodate all elements without crowding. Keep in mind that mounded and stacked presentations will be taken apart by the diner, and room is needed to spread them on the plate.
- Unusually shaped plates, such as squares and rectangles, can help achieve a striking presentation. While most arranged salads have plenty of colorful ingredients and show best on white plates, some arranged salads benefit from presentation on a plate of a contrasting color.
- Make sure the food elements on your plate are solidly constructed so the plate can be transported by tray service or arm service and your presentation will arrive at the table intact.
- Keep the convenience of the diner in mind. Make sure the customer can eat the salad neatly and easily, and without a lot of effort and attention.
- Do not place sauces or garnishes on the plate rim. This breaks both the rules of presentation and the rules of good sense. The philosophy of plate presentation considers the plate rim the frame and the plate well the canvas. Sauces and garnishes on the rim often end up on diners' sleeves.
- All the elements must complement each other, and all must serve a purpose in the final synergy of the dish. For example, you should not add a particular element because of its color without considering its flavor, texture, and general appropriateness to the theme of the dish.

The Language of Plate Presentation

Restaurant chefs use trade-specific terminology when writing instructions on how to arrange a plate presentation. Here are some of the terms with which you should be familiar:

Plate rim: The raised outer edge of the plate. The rim serves as the frame for the composition created when the food is arranged on the plate.

Plate well: The main part of the plate inside the rim.

Front of the plate: The part of the plate intended for placement nearest the diner.

Back of the plate: The part of the plate intended for placement farthest from the diner.

O'clock: A directive that indicates a specific place on the perimeter of the plate well that corresponds to the numerals on a standard clock. For example, 12 o'clock is at the back of the plate, while 6 o'clock is at the front of the plate.

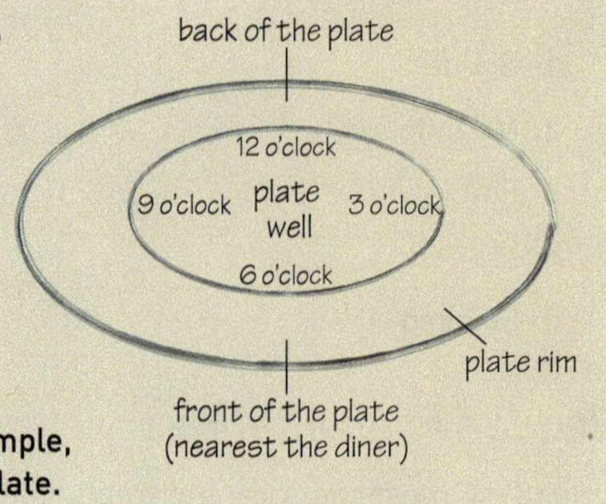

HOLLYWOOD COBB SALAD

LUNCH MAIN COURSE

Portions:
1
Portion size:
about 10 oz (300 g)

INGREDIENTS	U.S.	METRIC
Torn iceberg lettuce	1 oz	30 g
Torn romaine lettuce	1½ oz	45 g
Watercress, large stems removed	1½ oz	45 g
Classic French Vinaigrette (p. 32), made with white wine vinegar and 1 tsp (5 mL) sugar	3 fl oz	90 mL
Cooked chicken breast, cut in ⅜-in. (1-cm) dice	1½ oz	45 g
Tomatoes, seeded and cut in ⅜-in. (1-cm) dice	2 oz	60 g
Crisp-cooked crumbled bacon	½ oz	15 g
Crumbled blue cheese	½ oz	15 g
Hard-cooked egg, coarse chopped	1½ oz	45 g
Small radish tulip (p. 716)	1	1

PROCEDURE

FINISHING AND PLATING

1. Toss the greens with just enough vinaigrette to coat lightly.
2. Mound the greens in a volcano shape on a cool 10-in. (25-cm) plate.
3. Toss the chicken with just enough vinaigrette to coat.
4. Toss the tomatoes with just enough vinaigrette to coat.
5. In the order listed, arrange the garnishes in vertical stripes around the greens mound to look like lava flowing from a volcano.
6. Place the radish tulip on top.
7. Serve the remaining vinaigrette in a small sauceboat.

VARIATION

VEGETARIAN COBB SALAD

Replace the chicken with cooked chickpeas. Replace the bacon with soy bacon bits.

HAZELNUT BAKED GOAT CHEESE SALAD

APPETIZER OR LUNCH MAIN COURSE

Portions:
1
Portion size:
about 8 oz (240 g)

INGREDIENTS	U.S.	METRIC
Cylinder of goat cheese, about 1½ in. (4 cm) in diameter and ¾ in. (2 cm) tall	1 oz	30 g
Flour	as needed	as needed
Egg wash	as needed	as needed
Finely chopped and sifted hazelnuts	1 oz (about)	30 g (about)
Spray pan coating	as needed	as needed
Untoasted baguette croûton, 1½ in. (4 cm)	½ oz	15 g
Clarified butter, melted	1 Tbsp	30 mL
Spring mix baby lettuces	3 oz	90 g
Hazelnut Vinaigrette (p. 32)	2 fl oz	60 mL
Edible nasturtium blossoms	2	2
Chervil pluches	1 tbsp	15 mL

PROCEDURE

PREPARATION

1. Dust the cheese with flour.
2. Coat the cheese with egg wash.
3. Roll the cheese firmly in the hazelnuts so they adhere well.
4. Place the coated cheese on a rack and refrigerate uncovered at least 1 hour.

HOLD

Refrigerate the cheese in a closed container with parchment between layers up to 3 days. Refrigerate all other ingredients up to 3 days.

FINISHING

5. Preheat a countertop oven to 400°F (200°C).
6. Spray a sizzle plate with pan coating and place the hazelnut-crusted cheese and the croûton on it.
7. Brush the cheese and croûton with clarified butter.
8. Bake about 5 minutes, or until the hazelnuts are golden and the bread croûton is crisp.
9. Toss the lettuce with just enough vinaigrette to coat lightly.

PLATING

10. Mound the lettuce on a cool 10-in. (25-cm) plate.
11. Place the cheese on the croûton and then set it on top of the greens.
12. Drizzle the remaining vinaigrette on the cheese and greens.
13. Pull the petals off the nasturtium blossoms and scatter them over the greens.
14. Sprinkle the chervil over the greens.

VARIATIONS

HAZELNUT BAKED GOAT CHEESE SALAD WITH RASPBERRIES

Replace the wine vinegar in the Hazelnut Vinaigrette with raspberry vinegar. Replace the nasturtium petals with fresh raspberries.

CORN-CRUSTED BAKED GOAT CHEESE SALAD

Replace the hazelnuts with tortilla chip crumbs. Replace the Hazelnut Vinaigrette with American Cider Vinaigrette (p. 32) made with a touch of ground cumin. Place a dollop of Fresh Tomato Salsa (p. 50) between the cheese and the croûton. Replace the chervil with cilantro.

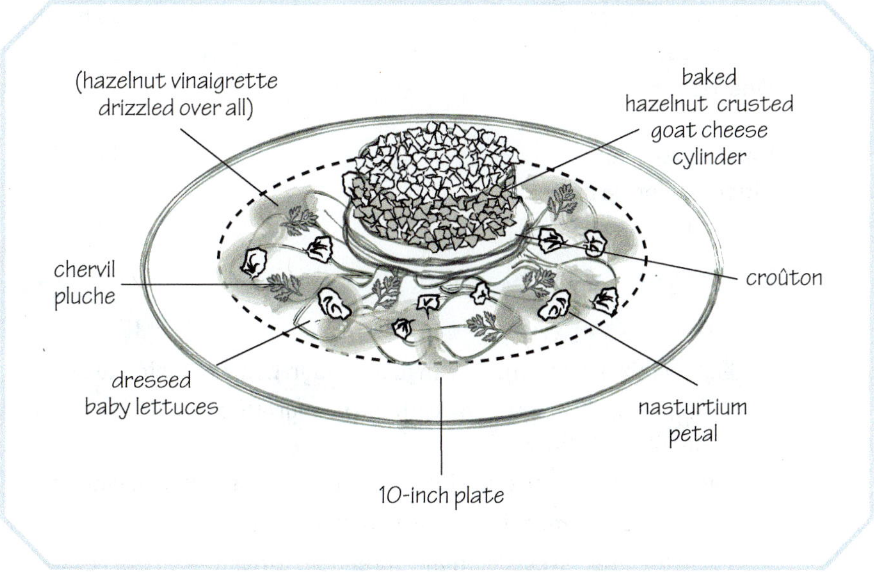

CRAB LOUIS IN AVOCADO [LOO-ee]

LUNCH MAIN COURSE

Portions:
1
Portion size:
10–12 oz (300–360 g)

INGREDIENTS	U.S.	METRIC
Dungeness crabmeat, picked over	3 oz	90 g
Louis Dressing (p. 43), in squeeze bottle with large opening	3 fl oz	90 mL
Romaine lettuce, shredded	3 oz	90 g
American Cider Vinaigrette (p. 32)	1 fl oz	30 mL
Firm-ripe California avocado, chilled	4 oz (½)	120 g (½)
Fresh lemon juice	as needed	as needed
Kosher salt	to taste	to taste
Vine-ripe tomato	1 oz (3 wedges)	30 g (3 wedges)
Hard-cooked egg	1 oz (½)	30 g (½)
Pitted California black olive	1	1
Minced parsley	1 tsp	5 mL

PROCEDURE

FINISHING AND PLATING

1. Lightly mix the crabmeat with just enough Louis dressing to bind it.
2. Toss the shredded romaine with the vinaigrette and bed it in the center of a cool 10-in. (25-cm) plate.
3. Peel the avocado, coat it with lemon juice, and sprinkle it with salt.
4. Mound the crabmeat in the cavity of the avocado.
5. Place the filled avocado on the shredded romaine with the pointed end toward 2 o'clock.
6. Arrange the tomato wedges in a fan next to the avocado.
7. Place the egg at the base of the fan.
8. Place the olive in front of the egg.
9. Place a dot of parsley on the crabmeat.
10. Squeeze flourishes of dressing around the plate well.

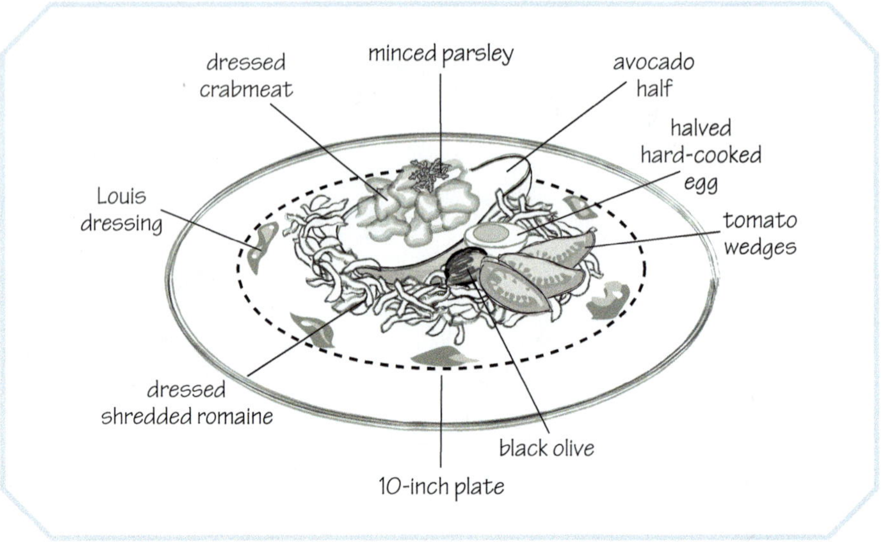

Mounded Presentations

In a **mounded presentation**, an assortment of complex salads is arranged together on a plate in separate piles. Be sure to choose salads that are complementary in flavor and work together to express a theme. In addition, carefully consider the placement of each item in an effort to create an attractive combination of colors and textures.

CLASSIC SALADE NIÇOISE [suh-LAHD nee-SWAHZ]

LUNCH MAIN COURSE

Portions: *1*
Portion size: *about 12 oz (350 g)*

INGREDIENTS	U.S.	METRIC
Romaine lettuce leaves, tops only	3 to 5	3 to 5
Mediterranean Tuna Salad (p. 161)	5 fl oz	150 mL
French Potato Salad (p. 145)	4 fl oz	120 mL
Green Beans Vinaigrette (p. 139)	about 4 oz	about 120 g
Vine-ripe tomato	3 wedges	3 wedges
Hard-cooked egg wedges	3	3
Niçoise olives	5	5
Oil-cured anchovy fillet, halved lengthwise	1	1
Minced parsley	½ tsp	3 mL
Brunoise red bell pepper	1 tsp	5 mL
Classic French Vinaigrette (p. 32)	2 fl oz	60 mL

PROCEDURE

PLATING

1. Place the romaine leaves on a cool 10-in. (25-cm) plate in a spoke pattern.
2. Mound the tuna salad, potato salad, and green bean salad on the leaves in the center of the plate.
3. Arrange the tomato wedges and eggs between the salads.
4. Garnish the plate well with the olives.
5. Arrange the anchovy halves in an *X* pattern on the tuna salad.
6. Place a dot of parsley at the intersection of the *X*.
7. Place a dot of red bell pepper on the potato salad.
8. Serve the vinaigrette in a small sauceboat or ramekin.

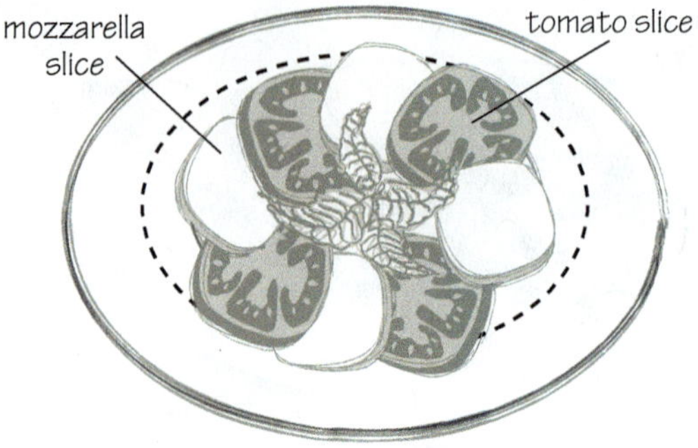

Flat Presentations

The ***flat presentation*** style is open to several interpretations. Some include salads assembled from sliced solid foods as well as salads made from spreads, dips, and purées. Usually presented on an oversized plate, this type of salad sometimes appears as though the food elements have been applied to the plate with a brush or a palette knife.

INSALATA CAPRESE

[een-sah-LAH-tah kah-PRAY-zay]

TOMATO MOZZARELLA SALAD

APPETIZER

Portions:
1
Portion size:
about 10 oz (300 g)

INGREDIENTS	U.S.	METRIC
Bright Green Basil Oil (p. 686)	2 fl oz	60 mL
Very fresh garlic, freshly minced	½ tsp	2 mL
Fine ground sea salt	to taste	to taste
Chopped fresh basil	¼ oz	7 g
Firm-ripe local tomato (see Note)	8 oz	240 g
Fresh Cow's-Milk Mozzarella Cheese (p. 592) or purchased	2½ oz	75 g
Balsamic vinegar (optional; see Note)	to taste	to taste
Basil	⅛ oz (1 small sprig)	3 g (1 small sprig)
Crisp Italian bread	3 oz	120 g

Note: The best tomatoes for Caprese are highly acidic; for such tomatoes, no vinegar is needed. For best presentation, choose tomatoes that are the same diameter as the cheese.

PROCEDURE

PREPARATION

1. Combine the oil, garlic, and salt.
2. Allow to mellow at room temperature at least ½ hour.
3. Blanch, refresh, and peel the tomato as directed on page 136.
4. Core the tomato and cut horizontally into 4 even slices, reserving the rounded ends for another use.
5. Lay the slices on paper towels and salt lightly. Cover with more towels and press gently to remove excess moisture.

PLATING

6. Taste the tomatoes for acidity (see Note).
7. Cut the mozzarella into 4 slices.
8. Arrange the tomato and mozzarella slices in an overlapping circle on a cool, deep-welled 10-in. (25-cm) plate.
9. Spoon the basil oil over top and allow to mellow another 10 minutes or so, occasionally basting the salad with the oil from the edge of the plate well.
10. If the tomatoes lack acidity, drizzle with a little balsamic vinegar (see Note).
11. Place the sprig of basil in the middle of the salad.
12. Serve the bread in a basket.

(Variations on next page)

VARIATIONS

CAPRESE CON MOZZARELLA DI BUFALA

Substitute imported Italian bufala mozzarella for the cow's-milk mozzarella.

TWO-COLOR CAPRESE

Use an equal number of red and yellow tomato slices.

CAPRESE CON CIPOLLE

Place thin slices of sweet onion between the tomatoes and mozzarella.

BEET CARPACCIO

[kahr-PAH-choh]

APPETIZER

Portions:
1
Portion size:
about 10 oz (300 g)

INGREDIENTS	U.S.	METRIC
Roasted and peeled red beets (p. 107)	6 oz (2 small)	180 g (2 small)
Balsamic Vinaigrette (p. 33), made with extra-virgin olive oil	3 fl oz	150 mL
Freshly ground black pepper	to taste	to taste
Very thin sliced shallot rings	½ oz	15 g
Italian fontina cheese, cold (see Note), from the block	1 oz	30 g
Bouquet of mâche or microgreens	½ oz	15 g
Bright Green Parsley Oil (p. 686), in squeeze bottle	½ fl oz	15 mL
Crisp Italian bread	3 oz	90 g

Note: The fontina must be chilled in order for it to be firm enough to cut with a cheese plane.

PROCEDURE

PREPARATION

1. Using a mandoline, slice the beets paper-thin.

PLATING

2. Dip each beet slice in the vinaigrette and arrange the slices in overlapping concentric circles on a cool 12-in. (30-cm) plate.
3. Grind pepper over the beets.
4. Scatter the shallots over top.
5. Using a cheese plane, shave paper-thin slices of fontina over the beets.
6. Arrange the bouquet of mâche or microgreens in the center of the plate.
7. Drizzle the parsley oil around the edge of the plate well.
8. Serve the bread in a basket.

VARIATIONS

TWO-COLOR BEET CARPACCIO

Use an equal number of red and golden beet slices.

BEET CARPACCIO PARMIGIANO

Replace the fontina with Reggiano Parmesan cheese.

The History of Beet Carpaccio

Carpaccio is a famous dish, originally made with raw beef filet, that dates from the 1920s. In the 1980s, garde manger chefs began to play with classic concepts and to change the ingredients in well-known dishes. By substituting beets for the beef, they created a vegetarian version of Carpaccio that has become a popular salad. Beets are especially suitable for Carpaccio, in part because their deep, red color mimics that of raw beef.

AVOCADO-PAPAYA PINWHEEL

APPETIZER

Portions:
1
Portion size:
about 9 oz (270 g)

INGREDIENTS	U.S.	METRIC
Small, ripe papaya, with seeds	4 oz (½)	120 g (½)
Tropical Vinaigrette (p. 34), in squeeze bottle	2 fl oz	60 mL
Firm-ripe Western avocado, chilled	4 oz (½)	120 g (½)
Spicy micro greens	¾ oz	20 g

PROCEDURE

FINISHING

1. Peel the papaya and reserve 1 tbsp (15 mL) of the seeds.
2. Cut the papaya into long, slender slices.
3. Coat the papaya slices with some of the vinaigrette.
4. Peel the avocado and cut into similar slices.
5. Coat the avocado slices with some of the vinaigrette.

PLATING

6. Arrange the papaya and avocado in an alternating pinwheel pattern on a cool 10-in. (25-cm) plate, leaving about 1 in. (3 cm) of space in the center.
7. Toss the micro greens with a little vinaigrette and mound in the center.
8. Drizzle any remaining vinaigrette over the fruits.
9. Garnish with a sprinkling of papaya seeds.

VARIATION

AVOCADO-MANGO PINWHEEL

Replace the papaya with a small, firm-ripe mango. Garnish with toasted black sesame seeds.

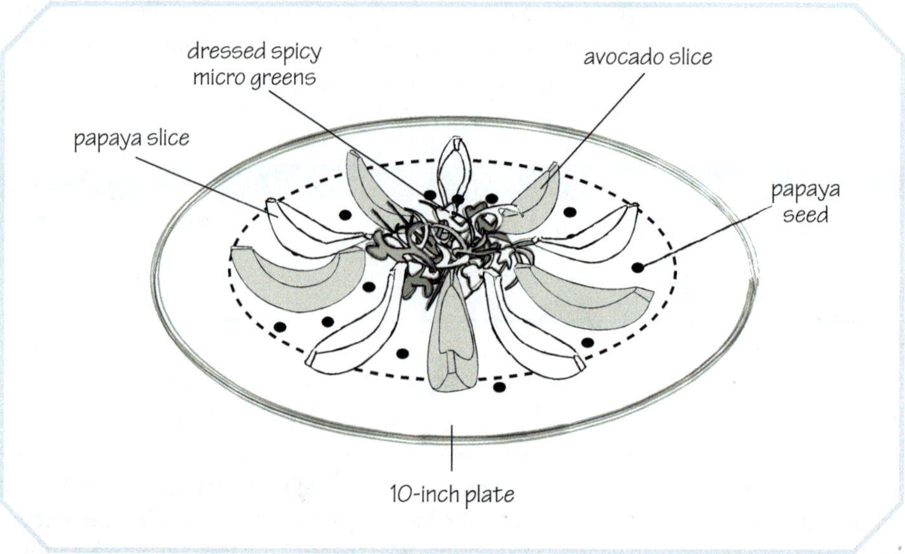

Molded Presentations

Far removed from outmoded 1950s-style gelatin molds, molded foods today represent the cutting edge of professional food presentation. In a contemporary ***molded presentation***, foods are compressed into attractive shapes by pressing them into a food-service-grade form, such as those illustrated in Table 1.3 on page 17.

Contemporary molded salads may be composed of virtually any ingredients, as long as the ingredients are bound with a sauce or dressing thick enough to hold them in place once the form is removed. Salads with firm and relatively long-keeping ingredients may be packed into multi-unit forms during preparation. Once chilled and set, the shaped foods are unmolded and transferred to plates with a spatula. Salads that have more perishable ingredients, such as avocadoes or fresh fruit, are typically molded to order.

Molded salads may serve as a component of other salad presentations. They frequently act as a socle or plinth in a stacked or plumed presentation. A ***socle*** (SOCK-el) is a molded base in any of several shapes, and a ***plinth*** is a square or rectangular block that serves as a base.

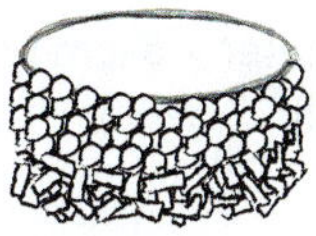

A.
layered salads molded in entremet ring

B.
salad molded in pyramid form topped with mounded and pluche garnishes

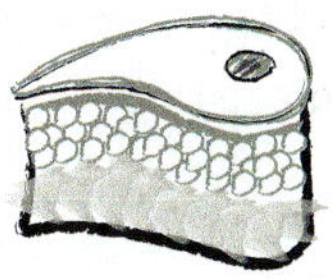

C.
layered salads molded in a teardrop form with "dot" garnish

D.
salad molded in a hemisphere form on croûton socle with rosette and sprig garnish

ASIAN CRAB, SHRIMP, AND CUCUMBER SALAD

APPETIZER

Portions:
1
Portion size:
6 fl oz (180 mL), about 6 oz (180 g)

INGREDIENTS	U.S.	METRIC
Starch-free pan coating spray	as needed	as needed
Hawai'ian Shrimp Salad (p. 160), made with chopped shrimp	2 fl oz	60 mL
Asian Cucumber Salad with Miso (p. 133)	2 fl oz	60 mL
Red tobiko caviar	¼ oz	7 g
Asian Crab Salad (p. 160)	2 fl oz	60 mL
Gingered Mayonnaise (p. 43), in squeeze bottle	½ fl oz	15 mL
Small cooked, peeled shrimp	¼ oz (1)	7 g (1)
Cucumber butterfly (p. 716)	1	1
Soy Glaze (p. 690), in squeeze bottle	½ fl oz	15 mL
Asian Vinaigrette (p. 35), in squeeze bottle	2 fl oz	60 mL

Note: This dish requires an entremet ring, illustrated on p. 17; alternatively, a round cutting tool may be used.

PROCEDURE

PLATING

1. Spray the inside of a 2½-in. diameter × 2-in. tall (6-cm diameter × 5-cm tall) entremets ring with pan coating and place it in the center of a cool 10-in. (25-cm) rimless plate.
2. Pack in the shrimp salad, then the cucumber salad (A, B).
3. Sprinkle all but ¼ tsp. (3 mL) tobiko near the rim where the salads meet the ring (C).
4. Pack in the crab salad (D).
5. Squeeze in the mayonnaise and smooth the top with an offset spatula (E). Lift the ring.
6. Top the salad with the shrimp curled around a cucumber butterfly.
7. Squeeze a fine-line ring of soy glaze around the salad about ½ in. (1.25 cm) away from it. Squeeze a pool of Asian vinaigrette in the plate well; the glaze ring should stop it from flowing under the salad.
8. Dot the remaining tobiko in the center of the shrimp.

A

B

C

D

E

AMUSE-BOUCHE PROVENÇAL

APPETIZER

Portions:
1
Portion size:
2½ oz (60 g), plus garnishes

INGREDIENTS	U.S.	METRIC
Tapenade (p. 52)	1 oz	30 g
Tomato-Basil Salad (p. 136), made with finely diced tomatoes	1 oz	30 g
Mediterranean Mayonnaise (p. 41), made with olive oil, in squeeze bottle	½ fl oz	15 mL
Niçoise olive	1	1
Red Bell Pepper Oil (p. 687), in squeeze bottle	¾ fl oz	20 mL
Bright Green Basil Oil (p. 686), in squeeze bottle or dropper bottle	½ tsp	2.5 mL

Note: This dish requires an entremet ring, illustrated on p. 17; alternatively, a round cutting tool may be used.

PROCEDURE

PLATING

1. Place a 2-in. (5-cm) diameter × 1¼-in. (3-cm) tall entremet ring or round cutter in the center of a cool 8-in. (20-cm) plate.
2. Spoon the tapenade into the ring and pack it down.
3. Spoon the tomato-basil salad into the ring and pack it down.
4. Squeeze the mayonnaise into the ring and smooth the top with a small offset spatula.
5. Use a clean, dry towel to blot up any oil that appears around the base of the ring, and then lift off the ring.
6. Place the olive on top.
7. Squeeze an arc of red bell pepper purée onto the plate around the cylinder.
8. Squeeze 5 dots of basil oil inside the arc.

Stacked Presentations

In this presentation style, large, flat pieces of food are stacked one on top of the other to create a tall, tower effect. These solid pieces may be cemented together with bound protein salads, thick sauces, spreads, or mousses. To provide a crunchy element, croûtons, wafers, or pastry layers may be included in the construction. Salad greens usually appear in these presentations as lacy tangles or plumes extending from the top.

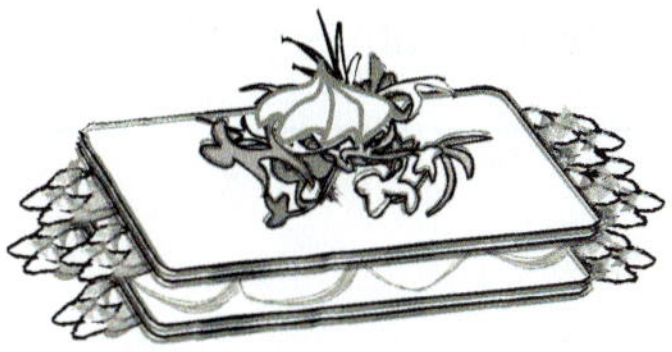

A.
"Napoleon" style stacked presentation topped with micro greens, rosette and pluche garnish

B.
cylindrical stacked presentation topped with micro greens

THREE-BEET ROQUEFORT SALAD TOWER

APPETIZER

Portions:
1
Portion size:
about 7 oz (210 g)

INGREDIENTS	U.S.	METRIC
Steamed, peeled red beet (p. 107), cut in 2 round slices 3 in. in diameter × ⅜ in. thick (8 cm in diameter × 0.75 cm thick)	1½ oz (2 pc).	45 g (2 pc)
Steamed, peeled golden beet (p. 107), cut in a round slice 3 in. in diameter × ⅜ in. thick (8 cm diameter × 0.75 cm thick)	¾ oz (1 pc)	23 g (1 pc)
Sherry Vinaigrette (p. 32), in squeeze bottle	1 fl oz	30 mL
Roquefort Mousse (p. 598), in pastry bag with large star tip (do not freeze)	3 fl oz	90 mL
Very fresh red onion, chopped fine	½ oz	15 g
3½-in. (9-cm) Phyllo squares (p. 707)	3	3
Baby golden beet, steamed, cooled, peeled	½ oz (1)	15 g (1)
Mâche or microgreens	½ oz	15 g
Beet Oil (p. 687), in squeeze bottle	½ fl oz	15 mL

PROCEDURE

FINISHING

1. Toss the red beet slices with a little vinaigrette.
2. Toss the yellow beet slice with a little vinaigrette.

PLATING

3. Pipe a dot of roquefort mousse in the center of a cool 10-in. (25-cm) plate and place a phyllo square on it.
4. Place a yellow beet slice on the phyllo square, pipe a thin circle of mousse on top, scatter with half the onions, and press another phyllo square on top.
5. Repeat with a red beet slice, the remaining mousse and onions, and the third phyllo square.
6. Place the remaining red beet slice on the top phyllo square.
7. Toss the greens with the remaining vinaigrette and mound them on top of the tower.
8. Place the baby beet on top of the greens.
9. Squeeze dots of beet oil around the plate well.

VARIATIONS

BEET AND ROQUEFORT SALAD TOWER

If golden beets are not available, use all red beets. The baby beet may be replaced with a parisienne-cut roasted beet.

BEET AND HAM MOUSSE TOWER

Replace the Roquefort Mousse with Ham Mousse (p. 264).

TERMS FOR REVIEW

complex salad
mixed presentation
arranged presentation
liner leaf
bed of greens
complex side salad
bound protein salad
complete salad
fruit salad
water out
arranged salad
plate painting
bedded presentation
plate rim
plate well
front of the plate
back of the plate
o'clock
mounded presentation
flat presentation
molded presentation
socle
plinth

QUESTIONS FOR DISCUSSION

1. Explain the difference between a simple salad and a complex salad.
2. List the five types of complex side salad and give two examples of each type. Suggest some main dishes these might accompany.
3. Explain the vegetable preparation term *water out*. List and describe the three methods for preventing watering out when making raw vegetable complex salads.
4. Discuss the two basic methods for fabricating/cooking potatoes for potato salads. List an advantage and a disadvantage for each method.
5. Describe the procedure for cooking pasta for pasta salads. Explain why refreshing pasta under cold water is not a good idea. Describe the technique for both cooling and flavoring the pasta at the same time.
6. Name two legumes and two grains that might be used in complex side salads, and describe a salad you would make from each.
7. Explain why complex salads made from potatoes, pasta, grains, and legumes need to mellow before their final tasting and correction. Describe how the taste and texture of these salads might change after the mellowing period.
8. Define the term *bound protein salad* and list three examples. List three guidelines that should be followed when making bound protein salads.
9. What three elements must be present to make a complete salad complete? Name and explain the two presentation styles for complete salads. Using your imagination and the information provided in this chapter, name and describe a complete salad of your own creation.
10. Define the term *arranged salad*, and list the three basic elements an arranged salad must have. Give an example of a basic arranged salad.
11. List four guidelines for successful arranged salads.
12. List and describe the five presentation styles used for contemporary arranged salads.

Chapter 6

PREREQUISITES

Before studying this chapter, you should already

- Have read "How to Use This Book," pages xxviii–xxxiii, and understand the professional recipe format.
- Know basic information about seafood and have mastered basic fabrication and cooking methods for it.
- Have basic familiarity with unflavored commercial gelatin and the techniques used in working with it.

Cold Seafood

Cold seafood ranks among the most popular of appetizer foods. Although high-quality chilled seafood is appreciated when served simply, it can also be made into complex cold appetizers that challenge the garde manger's skill and creativity. In hot weather and hot climates, various types of cold seafood are frequently served as entrées as well. Cold seafood presentations are frequently featured on buffets and star as hors d'oeuvres. Thus, in both restaurants and in catering, there are many opportunities to excel in preparing cold seafood dishes.

This chapter focuses on the methods used to properly cook fish and shellfish for cold service and on the specialized techniques necessary to prepare seafood mousses. Seafood mousselines are covered in Chapter 15. In addition to learning about cooked cold seafood dishes, you will also learn to create attractive presentations of raw seafood items and caviars. The recipes in this chapter represent a number of classic cold seafood preparations from the European repertoire as well as some of the most popular North American cold seafood dishes.

After reading this chapter, you should be able to

1. Identify categories of seafood, and select fish and shellfish appropriate for use in cold service.
2. Poach, steam, pan-steam, shallow-poach, and grill fish and shellfish for use in cold service.
3. Prepare fish and shellfish by "cooking" them with acidic ingredients.
4. Prepare seafood mousses and use them to create terrines, timbales, and other formed presentations.
5. Serve raw fish and shellfish in accordance with food safety guidelines.
6. Identify, purchase, and correctly serve caviar.

UNDERSTANDING SEAFOOD CLASSIFICATIONS

A strictly literal definition of the term *seafood* is "foods from the sea." This broad definition technically includes the various plant foods and mineral salts harvested from the oceans and other bodies of salt water, and excludes foods harvested from fresh water. However, here we define the term ***seafood*** to mean "non-mammal animal foods derived from both fresh and saltwater sources." Table 6.1 reviews basic information on seafood classifications.

TABLE 6.1 Seafood Classifications

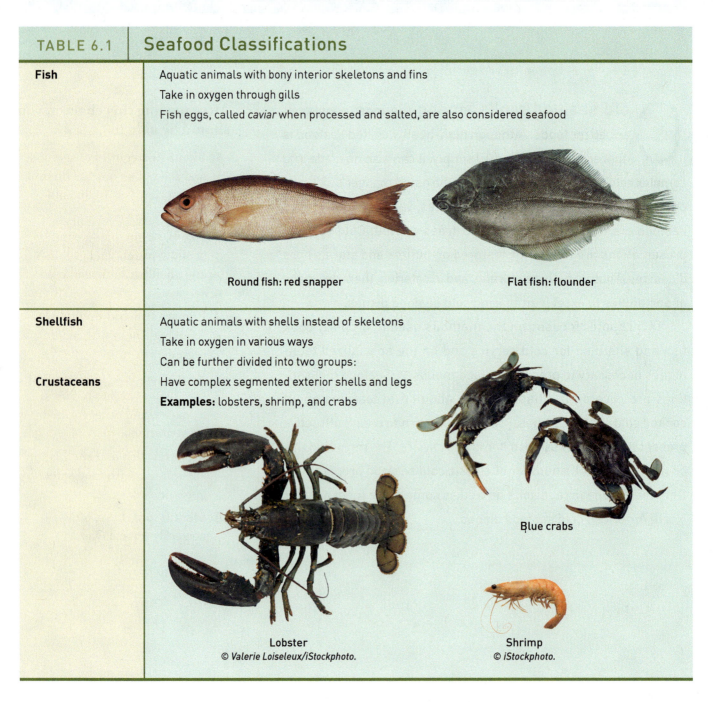

Fish	Aquatic animals with bony interior skeletons and fins Take in oxygen through gills Fish eggs, called *caviar* when processed and salted, are also considered seafood  Round fish: red snapper  Flat fish: flounder
Shellfish	Aquatic animals with shells instead of skeletons Take in oxygen in various ways Can be further divided into two groups:
Crustaceans	Have complex segmented exterior shells and legs **Examples:** lobsters, shrimp, and crabs  Blue crabs  Lobster © *Valerie Loiseleux/iStockphoto.*  Shrimp © *iStockphoto.*

TABLE 6.1 *(Continued)*

<table>
<tr>
<td>Mollusks</td>
<td>
Have simple shell structures (or no shell) and no legs
Can be further divided into three groups:

1. Bivalves: Shellfish with hinged two-section exterior shells
Examples: clams, oysters, mussels, scallops

Cherrystone clams

Blue mussels

St. James River oysters

Scallop in shell
© Georg Hergenhan/iStockphoto.

2. Univalves: Similar to bivalves, but have only one exterior shell section
Example: abalone

Abalone
Courtesy SFB (SeaFood Business).

3. Cephalopods [SEF-ah-low-pods]: Mollusks with tentacles and a defined head
Some, such as squid and cuttlefish, have interior shell-like structures.
Octopus, on the other hand, have no interior shells
Example: Squid

Squid
</td>
</tr>
</table>

TYPES OF COLD SEAFOOD DISHES

In garde manger work it is useful to focus on the preparation and service types of cold seafood because in most cold seafood dishes, items are interchangeable. For example, a cold poached salmon presentation could be made with steelhead trout or striped bass as well.

Shrimp Facts

While more than 300 species of shrimp are used for food throughout the world, four types of warm-water shrimp are important in North American food service:

1. **Pink shrimp:** Small and delicate, with a fine, sweet flavor and firm texture. They are scarce and expensive.
2. **White shrimp:** Available in a full range of sizes and excellent for cold service. They have good, full flavor and a firm texture.
3. **Brown shrimp:** A tough texture better suited to hot preparations; flavor varies.
4. **Tiger shrimp:** Mild to bland in flavor with a soft texture. They are better suited to hot preparations.

Very small shrimp are sometimes called *bay shrimp*, although they are not usually harvested from bays. Large shrimp are often referred to as *prawns*. Shrimp sizes are expressed by count per pound.

Size	Count	Average per 1 lb (450 g)	Average Weight per Piece
Jumbo	U/10	5	3.2 oz (100 g)
	U/12	9	1.77 oz (50 g)
	U/15	14	1.14 oz (33 g)
Large	16/20	18	0.88 oz (24 g)
	21/25	23	0.69 oz (20 g)
Medium	26/30	28	0.57 oz (16 g)
	31/35	33	0.48 oz (14 g)
	36/40	38	0.42 oz (12 g)
Small	41/50	45	0.35 oz (10 g)
	51/60	55	0.29 oz (9 g)
	61/70	65	0.25 oz (7 g)

Cold Seafood Appetizers

Because of its high cost, seafood is often more popular as an appetizer than as a main course. Customers may find that a small appetizer-size portion is more affordable than a large entrée-size portion. Cold seafood appetizers may be served at any time of year.

Seafood Cocktails

A ***seafood cocktail*** consists of chilled seafood tossed or topped with a sauce and typically served in a cocktail glass on a bed of shredded lettuce with a lemon wedge. Shrimp cocktail is the best-known type of seafood cocktail. However, seafood cocktails may be made with crabmeat, lobster meat, crayfish tails, raw oysters, or a mixture of chilled seafood. In some operations, seafood cocktails are served in a ***shrimp cocktail chiller***, which is a stainless-steel or glass presentation vessel. The bottom cup of the chiller holds crushed ice, and the top cup holds the seafood and sauce. Sometimes shrimp are hung from the rim, and only the cocktail sauce is placed in the top cup.

Classic Shrimp Cocktail

The traditional North American ***cocktail sauce*** is based on tomato ketchup and prepared horseradish. Mayonnaise-based sauces are also served with seafood cocktails. Crackers are the typical accompaniment.

Raw Seafood Appetizers

A special category of cold seafood appetizers features fish and shellfish served raw. Various bivalves, such as oysters and clams, are commonly served raw on the half-shell, and specific fish are frequently served as tartares (p. 228) or sashimi (p. 227). Their delicate textures and subtle flavors are considered at their best when not changed by the application of heat, salt, or acid.

Crabmeat Facts

Most dishes featuring crab are made from commercially processed crabmeat. This is because both the labor and waste involved in steaming live crabs and picking the meat are prohibitive. The exception to this is West Coast Dungeness crabmeat, which is sometimes prepared in-house.

Most chefs agree the best commercial crabmeat is Eastern blue crab, handpicked and packed without pasteurization. However, it is both scarce and expensive as well as subject to seasonal availability. Pasteurized crab from the Gulf of Mexico, South America, and Asia has a longer shelf life and is less expensive.

Crabmeat is graded according to the size of the pieces, the color, and the amount of permissible shell content.

- **Colossal lump:** Large, unbroken pieces of white meat from the muscles that control the crab's swimming legs; no shell
- **Jumbo lump:** Slightly smaller pieces than colossal
- **Lump:** Large, clean pieces of white meat with minimal shell
- **Backfin:** White pieces mixed with shredded white meat; minimal shell
- **Special:** Shredded white meat with some brown meat, often with bits of shell
- **Claw meat:** Shredded brown meat from the claws and legs; minimal shell
- **Claw fingers or cocktail claws:** "Lollipops" of claw meat with the claw tips attached to use as handles

Cold Seafood Entrées

Cold seafood entrées are not as common as appetizers. However, in hot weather, they are both refreshing and unusual.

Seafood Presentations for the Cold Buffet

A platter presentation of cold fish or shellfish is frequently planned as the centerpiece of a cold buffet. Many such buffet items are enhanced with aspic, chaud-froid, or mayonnaise collée, covered in Chapter 16.

COOKING METHODS FOR COLD SEAFOOD

Most seafood is tender in texture and must be lightly cooked. It is important to be careful about doneness when preparing seafood to be served cold because carryover cooking occurs during cooling. Another challenge is deciding what cooking method to use. While seafood to be served hot can be prepared by many methods, not all methods produce palatable cold seafood items.

Poaching

Poaching is the gentle cooking method most frequently used for cold seafood. To ***poach*** means to cook a food completely submerged in a *cuisson*, or flavorful poaching liquid, at a moderate to low temperature. For poached seafood, the cooking temperature is usually 180°–200°F (82°–93° C). The *cuisson* should be just hot enough to create steam, form tiny bubbles, and shiver, or have slight surface movement. Cold food added to the *cuisson* will significantly lower the liquid's temperature. For this reason, most chefs bring the *cuisson* to a boil or rapid simmer before adding the food. Once the poaching liquid recovers

The Science of Poaching

In the poaching method, heat is transferred from the heat source to the pan and from the pan into the liquid that surrounds the food being cooked. The poaching liquid consists mostly of water, which transfers the heat into the food. Thus, poaching is based on convection—in this case, the transfer of heat through the movement of liquid.

Low temperature is important to prevent delicate foods from falling apart. In proper poaching, the liquid does not agitate the food because at temperatures at or below 200°F (93°C), the liquid remains relatively still. Boiling creates violent motion because the high level of heat creates enough energy to move the water molecules rapidly. If the liquid is allowed to boil, tender flesh and weak connective tissue that soften due to the cooking process are likely to break apart.

the desired gentle simmer, adjust the heat source to maintain the proper cooking temperature.

Shallow poaching is a technique in which food is simmered, but not completely submerged, in a *cuisson*. In this technique the cooking vessel is usually covered to capture steam that helps to cook the top of the food. Sometimes the food is turned over to ensure even cooking; however, this is not recommended for delicate items, such as fish fillets, that can easily break up from too much handling.

Scallop Facts

In North America, scallops are harvested primarily along the east coast, from Newfoundland to the Carolinas. Scallops more than ¾ in. (1.5 cm) in diameter are called *sea scallops*. Smaller scallops are referred to as *bay scallops*, although few are actually harvested in bays. Most are harvested by dredging, which is an ecologically controversial practice.

Unless otherwise noted, scallops have been treated with phosphates to prevent moisture loss. This practice adds 15–25% water weight to the scallop.

- **Dry-pack scallops** (also called *chemical-free*, or *unsoaked*): No phosphate treatment; firmer texture; more flavorful
- **Day boat scallops:** Dry-pack scallops packed and shipped within 24 hours of harvest; fresher than other scallops
- **Diver scallops:** Hand-harvested dry-pack scallops; no dredging involved

Scallops sizes are expressed in count per pound (450 g): U/10, 10/20, 20/30, 40/80, 80/120, and 120/250.

Cuissons *for Poaching Seafood*

Three standard *cuissons* are used for poaching seafood:

1. Court bouillon: ***Court bouillon*** [KOOR bwee-oh(n)] is a flavorful liquid made by simmering together mirepoix, a bouquet garni, white wine, and water. Sometimes lemon juice is added. Another name for court bouillon is ***nage*** [NAHZH], a term also used to describe a dish in which the *cuisson* is served as a broth or very light sauce along with the seafood.
2. *Fish or shellfish stock*: Flavorful stock imparts its taste to the seafood poached in it. It is frequently used as a component of the sauce with which the poached seafood is served.
3. Brine: ***Brine*** is a solution of salt and water. A brine for cooking seafood is usually made in a ratio of 1 tbsp (15 mL) kosher salt to 1 qt (1 L) water. A brine *cuisson* is especially appropriate for seafood because it approximates the salt concentration of seawater, the natural habitat of the creatures being cooked in it. Because brines contain a significant amount of salt, they add a salty taste to any food cooked in it.

Carryover Cooking

Carryover cooking is an important factor when poaching seafood for cold presentation. Seafood to be served cold will carryover cook for a longer time because it takes time to cool completely. You can prevent overcooking due to carryover cooking by *stopping the cooking process before the desired doneness is achieved and allowing carryover cooking to complete the cooking*. This requires good timing and judgment—especially with seafood—because doneness is not usually determined by internal temperature but rather by touch and appearance.

You should not attempt to stop carryover cooking in seafood by refreshing it (immersing it in an ice bain-marie). Refreshing or shocking is not an appropriate technique for poached foods in general and seafood in particular. Remember that a poached food's taste is enhanced by immersing it in a flavorful liquid. Refreshing it in plain water washes off the flavorful liquid. In addition, foods with porous textures readily absorb water and can quickly become waterlogged.

See the Procedure for Poaching Seafood on the next page for two alternative methods to refreshing in order to stop carryover cooking.

Steaming

Steaming is cooking food in an enclosed space completely surrounded by the vapor produced by water heated to temperatures above 212°F (100°C).

Steam from plain water does not season the food in any way. If a volatile substance such as wine or other alcoholic beverages is added to the steam source, the food will acquire a little of its flavor. Flavor essences from herbs, spices, and aromatics also flavor steamed foods if they are added to the boiling water. This can easily be done in stovetop steaming. It is not possible to flavor steam when using commercial equipment. Instead, seafood is flavored before it is steamed.

Procedure for Poaching Seafood

1. If necessary, fabricate the seafood into portions of equal weight and size.
2. Place enough of the *cuisson* in a nonreactive pan to completely cover the seafood. Bring it to the boil.
3. Prepare an ice bain-marie large enough to accommodate the cooking pan plus an adequate quantity of ice, or set a shallow hotel pan or sheet tray near the stove.
4. Add the seafood to the *cuisson* and wait for the *cuisson* to recover to a bare simmer. Adjust the heat source to maintain the simmer (A).
5. Poach the seafood just under the desired doneness.
6. Cool quickly to stop carryover cooking, using one of the following methods:
   a. Immerse the pan in the ice bain-marie (B). Remove the seafood from the *cuisson* only when it is completely cold. Alternatively, refrigerate the seafood in its *cuisson*.
   b. Remove the seafood from the *cuisson* and place it in one layer in the shallow pan. Moisten it with a little of the *cuisson*, and refrigerate it uncovered. Cover the seafood as soon as it becomes cold.
7. To keep the *cuisson* for further use, bring it to a full, rolling boil and pour it through a fine mesh strainer. Open-pan cool it (preferably in an ice bain-marie), and refrigerate or freeze it.

When steaming seafood to be served cold, be extremely careful with timing. Know the effects of carryover cooking, and stop the steaming process at the proper time to accommodate it. Just as with poaching, refreshing is not a good method for stopping carryover cooking in steamed seafood. Instead, use one of the methods described in the Procedure for Poaching Seafood above.

Pan-Steaming

Pan-steaming is a cooking method in which small, sturdy food items are cooked over high heat in a covered pot or sauté pan with a small amount of liquid that quickly turns into steam. In garde manger work mussels and shrimp are seafood items typically pan-steamed.

Grilling

Because grilling is a harsh, high-heat cooking method, it can be used only for firm-textured seafood. Marinades, and marinade-like basting sauces, are typically used when grilling seafood items. In this case, the marinades are not used to tenderize but rather to flavor the seafood and give it a moist mouthfeel.

Grilled seafood used in cold preparations must be slightly undercooked to compensate for carryover cooking. When the grilling is almost complete, place the seafood in one layer in a shallow pan and refrigerate it uncovered until cold.

"Cooking" with Acid

When we say a food is cooked, we normally mean the food's texture has been changed by the application of heat. Heat acts to tighten a protein food's fibers and make the food firmer. The heat's action also affects the color of the food, gradually changing it from slightly translucent to opaque, and, when red pigments are present, gradually destroying them.

The application of acid has a similar effect on delicate seafood. When tender-textured seafood comes into contact with highly acidic liquids such as citrus juice or vinegar, the liquid quickly penetrates its soft, porous muscle tissue. The acid then changes the protein structure of the seafood's flesh. The seafood acquires a cooked flavor and appearance even though it has not been heated.

Just as with heat, it is possible to overcook seafood with acid. If left in contact with an acid ingredient for too long, seafood becomes mushy, cottony, or rubbery, depending on the structure of its muscle and connective tissues. It also shrinks, losing internal moisture and acquiring a dry mouthfeel.

Many of the world's seafood-eating cuisines include dishes in which seafood is "cooked" with acidic ingredients. Refer to the sidebar on page 210 to learn about some of them. Virtually all seafood preparations based on "cooking" with acid begin the same way.

Procedure for "Cooking" Seafood in Acid

Use this method only for seafood with a tender texture. If applied to tough items, such as large calamari or octopus, the seafood will become too sour to eat by the time it is tenderized by the acid.

1. Trim away all visible silverskin and other connective tissue. Dark-colored deposit fat is usually trimmed off as well.
2. Fabricate the seafood into small pieces of uniform shape so the acidic liquid can penetrate quickly and evenly. The most successful fabrication forms are dice of ½-in. (1-cm) or smaller, and slices ⅛-in. (0.3-cm) to ¼-in. (0.75-cm) thick.
3. Add a small amount of salt to the acidic "cooking" liquid. Salt aids the penetration of the liquid and helps season the seafood. (Do not overly dilute the liquid with other seasonings or oil. The seafood is most efficiently cooked when the liquid consists primarily of the acidic ingredient and salt. Seasonings can be added later, when the "cooking" is complete.)
4. Choose a nonreactive container small enough to keep all of the seafood in contact with the liquid. Add the seafood and stir to thoroughly coat it with the liquid. Refrigerate the seafood. Stir frequently to ensure even "cooking."
5. Carefully monitor the "cooking" time, and observe carefully to determine doneness. Consider the "cooking" time specified in recipe directions as a guideline only. This is because both the strength of your acid ingredient(s) and the texture of your particular seafood item may differ from the products used by the recipe writer. Evaluate the doneness of the seafood by breaking open a piece and observing the color change. You can also evaluate doneness by tasting a bite. Check on the seafood well before the recipe "cooking" time has elapsed, and continue checking until the desired doneness is reached.
6. Drain the seafood as soon as it is sufficiently "cooked." It is often necessary to gently squeeze the acidic liquid out of the seafood mixture.
7. Once the seafood is drained, it can be tossed with oil and other liquid or solid seasonings.
8. Hold seafood "cooked" by acid under refrigeration in the same manner as other cooked seafood.

The scallops on the left are raw. The scallops on the right have been "cooked" by exposure to the acid in the marinade.

BASIC POACHED SHRIMP

Yield:
about 1 lb (500 g) (varies according to size and fabrication)

INGREDIENTS	U.S.	METRIC
Water	1 qt	1 L
White wine	4 fl oz	120 mL
Kosher salt	1 tbsp	15 mL
Whole-spice seafood seasoning	¼ oz	7 g
Frozen headless shell-on shrimp, thawed	1¼ lb	625 g

PROCEDURE

PREPARATION

1. Combine the water, wine, salt, and spices to make the *cuisson*.
2. Proceed according to the Procedure for Poaching Seafood on page 195.
3. Peel the shrimp and return them to the chilled *cuisson* for storage.

HOLDING

Refrigerate in the *cuisson* up to 3 days.

VARIATIONS

POACHED SHRIMP FOR COCKTAIL

Use 16/20 or 21/25 shrimp. When peeling the shrimp, leave on the tail section of the shell.

CLASSIC SHRIMP COCKTAIL

APPETIZER

Portion:
1
Portion size:
4½ oz (130 g)

INGREDIENTS	U.S.	METRIC
Green-leaf lettuce	1 small leaf (about ½ oz)	1 small leaf (about 15 g)
Classic Cocktail Sauce (p. 669)	1½ fl oz	45 mL
Poached Shrimp for Cocktail (p. 197)	6 (about 4½ oz)	6 (about 130 g)
Lemon wedge	1	1
Saltine crackers	3	3
Supplies		
5-in. (12-cm) doily	1	1

PROCEDURE

PLATING

1. Tear the lettuce leaf in half and use the two halves to line the cup of an iced shrimp cocktail chiller.
2. Spoon the cocktail sauce into the cup.
3. Hang the shrimp and lemon wedge on the rim of the chiller.
4. Place the chiller on a doily-lined 6-in. (15-cm) plate. Arrange the crackers on the plate.

VARIATIONS

CLASSIC OYSTER COCKTAIL

Replace the shrimp with 6 freshly shucked raw oysters. Arrange the oysters around the sauce.

CLASSIC CRAB COCKTAIL

Replace the shrimp with 4 oz (120 g) jumbo lump crabmeat mixed with 1½ fl oz (45 mL) Lemon Mayonnaise Sauce for Seafood (p. 43). Omit the cocktail sauce.

SHRIMP COCKTAIL

WITH TWO SAUCES AND SAVORY TUILE

APPETIZER

Portion:
1
Portion size:
4½ oz (130 g), plus garnishes

INGREDIENTS	U.S.	METRIC
Very thin channeled slices of cucumber	1 oz	30 g
Cocktail Sauce (p. 669), in squeeze bottle	1 fl oz	30 mL
Lemon Mayonnaise Sauce for Seafood (p. 43), in squeeze bottle	1 fl oz	30 mL
Poached Shrimp for Cocktail (p. 197)	6 (about 4½ oz)	6 (about 130 g)
Seafood Tuile Spike (p. 698)	1	1
Supplies		
Cocktail napkin	1	1

PROCEDURE

PLATING

1. Line the inside of a 12-fl oz (360-mL) martini glass with the cucumber slices.
2. Holding a squeeze bottle in each hand, squeeze the cocktail sauce and the mayonnaise into the glass at the same time so they pool into the glass side by side.
3. Hang the shrimp on the rim of the glass.
4. Stick the tuile spike upright out of the sauces.
5. Place the glass on a 6-in. (16-cm) plate lined with a cocktail napkin.

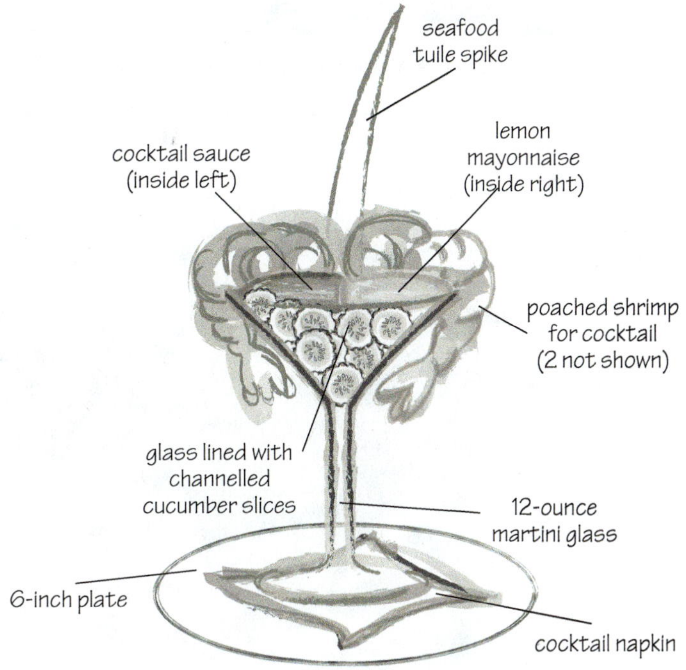

COLD POACHED SALMON

WITH CUCUMBER SALAD AND FINGERLING POTATO SALAD

MAIN COURSE

Portions:
1

Portion Size:
5 oz (150 g) salmon, plus side dishes

INGREDIENTS	U.S.	METRIC
Red-leaf lettuce	I large leaf (about 1 oz)	1 large leaf (about 30 g)
Poached salmon fillet (p. 195)	5 oz	150 g
Vegetable oil	1 tsp	5 mL
Scandinavian Potato Salad (p. 144) made with fingerling potatoes	4 fl oz	180 mL
Cucumber Salad (p. 133)	2 fl oz	60 mL
Lemon Mayonnaise Sauce for Seafood (p. 43)	1½ fl oz	45 mL
Minced parsley	1 tsp	5 mL
Cherry tomato	½	½

PROCEDURE

PLATING

1. Place the lettuce leaf on a cool 12-in. (30-cm) plate.
2. Place the salmon fillet on the lettuce on the front of the plate. Brush it very lightly with oil.
3. Mound the potato salad and the cucumber salad behind the salmon.
4. Nap the salmon with the mayonnaise sauce, allowing it to pool on the lettuce in front of the salmon.
5. Sprinkle a line of parsley across the salmon.
6. Place the cherry tomato half between the salads.

VARIATION

Replace the salmon with steelhead trout, striped bass, or other firm fish fillet.

WHOLE POACHED SALMON

BUFFET PLATTER

Yield:
varies
Portions:
varies
Portion Size:
varies

INGREDIENTS	U.S.	METRIC
Vegetable oil	1 fl oz	30 mL
Court bouillon (p. 194)	2 gal	8 l
Whole salmon, scaled, gutted, gilled	4 to 5 lb	1.75 to 2.25 kg
Curly parsley	2 oz	60 g
Lemon Mayonnaise Sauce for Seafood (p. 43)	1 pt	0.5 L

Note: For a more formal presentation of a whole poached salmon in aspic, refer to pp. 649–650.

PROCEDURE

DAY 1 PREPARATION

1. Remove the rack from a fish poacher. Place the court bouillon in the poacher and bring it to the boil.
2. Brush the poacher rack with half of the vegetable oil.
3. Wash the fish thoroughly, inside and out. Locate the cavity membrane that covers the spinal bone. Cut open the membrane and wash away all traces of blood.
4. Place the fish on its side on the work surface and measure its thickness at the widest point.
5. Place the fish on the rack and lower it into the court bouillon. Watch carefully for the *cuisson* to recover the simmer. Simmer the fish for 8 minutes per inch of thickness (3 minutes per centimeter of thickness).
6. Prepare an ice bain-marie (in a bus tub or food prep sink) that will accommodate the poacher.
7. When the fish is done, remove the poacher from the heat and place it in the ice bain-marie. Cool the fish in its *cuisson* to room temperature, and then refrigerate it in the *cuisson* overnight.

DAY 2 PREPARATION

8. If you wish to save the court bouillon, pass it through a fine strainer into a nonreactive saucepan and bring it to a full, rolling boil. Skim off any foam. Cool it to room temperature in an ice bain-marie and then refrigerate or freeze it.
9. Place a sheet of parchment on the work surface.
10. Remove the fish from the poacher using the rack, and set the rack on the parchment. Use a spatula to release the fish from the rack and slide it onto the parchment.
11. Slit the skin neatly around the tail and behind the gills to release it for removal. Peel off the top skin and discard it. If the fish is very fatty, scrape away the dark deposit fat, leaving a smooth surface of light-colored flesh. Gently turn the fish over. Peel (and scrape) the other side. Blot the cavity dry.
12. Carefully lift the fish onto a 30-in. (75-cm) fish platter so the most attractive side faces up.
13. Brush the fish with the remaining vegetable oil.
14. Camouflage the gill cavity and garnish the tail section with parsley bouquets.
15. Place the mayonnaise in an 18-fl oz (0.5-L) serving bowl.

HOLDING

Refrigerate, loosely covered with plastic film, up to 12 hours.

ASIAN SPICE-CRUSTED TUNA

Portions:
4
Portion size:
6 oz (175 g)

INGREDIENTS	U.S.	METRIC
Fresh ginger, peeled	2 oz	60 g
Minced scallion	½ oz	15 g
Sugar	1 tbsp	15 mL
Japanese soy sauce	2 fl oz	60 mL
Asian sesame oil	2 drops	2 drops
Thick, sashimi-quality tuna steaks, 6 oz (175 g) each	4	4
Coriander seeds, crushed	1 tsp	5 mL
White peppercorns, crushed	1 tsp	5 mL
White sesame seeds	1 tbsp	15 mL
Black sesame seeds	1 tbsp	15 mL
Japanese sansho powder (optional)	1 tsp	5 mL
Cornstarch, sifted	1 oz (about)	30 g (about)
Egg white, beaten to foam	1 oz (1)	30 g (1)
Peanut oil	4 oz (about)	120 mL (about)

PROCEDURE

DAY 1 PREPARATION

1. Juice the ginger in a juice extractor or by forcing it through a garlic press.
2. Combine the ginger juice and pulp, scallions, sugar, soy sauce, and sesame oil to make a marinade.
3. Coat the tuna steaks with the marinade and refrigerate them for 24 hours (A).

A

DAY 2 PREPARATION

4. Combine the spices, sesame seeds and sansho powder in a shallow bowl.
5. Brush the marinade ingredients off the tuna steaks. Dip each steak in the spice mixture. Press on all sides to ensure that the spices adhere. Place the coated tuna on a parchment-lined sheet tray and refrigerate it at least 1 hour (B).
6. Heat a heavy 10-in. (25-cm) sauté pan very hot and add the oil. Sear the tuna steaks about 20 seconds on each side. Remove them to a rack set over a sheet tray, and immediately refrigerate them. Refrigerate uncovered until cold, and then cover them loosely with plastic film.

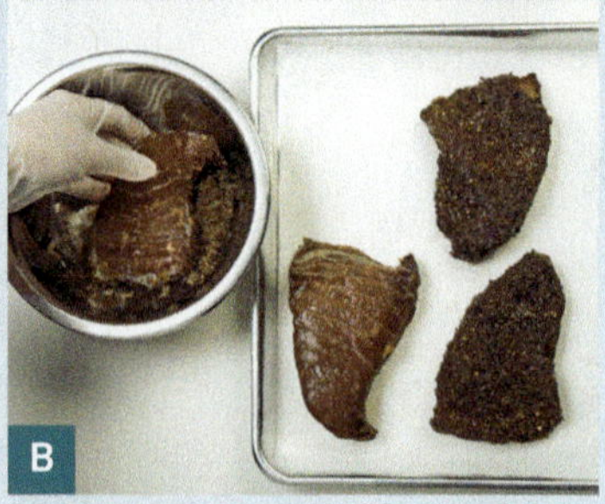
B

HOLDING

Refrigerate up to 24 hours.

PRESENTATION

7. To serve, cut into even ⅜-in. (2-cm) slices.

ASIAN SPICE-CRUSTED TUNA

WITH MANGO SALSA AND COCONUT RICE SALAD

MAIN COURSE

Portion:
1
Portion size:
6 oz

COMPONENTS

as needed Pan coating spray
6 fl oz (240 mL) *Coconut Rice Salad (p. 157)*
1½ fl oz (45 mL) *Mango Salsa (p. 51)*
6 oz (180 g) *Asian Spice-Crusted Tuna (p. 202)*
pinch Sweetened flaked coconut, toasted
1 tbsp (15 mL) Red bell pepper, cut brunoise
1 tbsp (15 mL) Yellow bell pepper, cut brunoise
1 tbsp (15 mL) Scallions, sliced thin on sharp diagonal

PROCEDURE

PLATING

1. Spray the inside of a 6-fl oz (240-mL) pyramid form with pan coating (A). Pack the rice salad into it, and then invert onto the back of a 12-in. (30-cm) plate (B).
2. Slice the tuna on the diagonal (C).
3. Fan the tuna across the front of the plate, propped against the rice salad pyramid (D).
4. Mound the salsa behind the tuna next to the rice salad pyramid.
5. Scatter the peppers and scallions across the tuna slices.
6. Place a pinch of coconut on top of the pyramid.

A

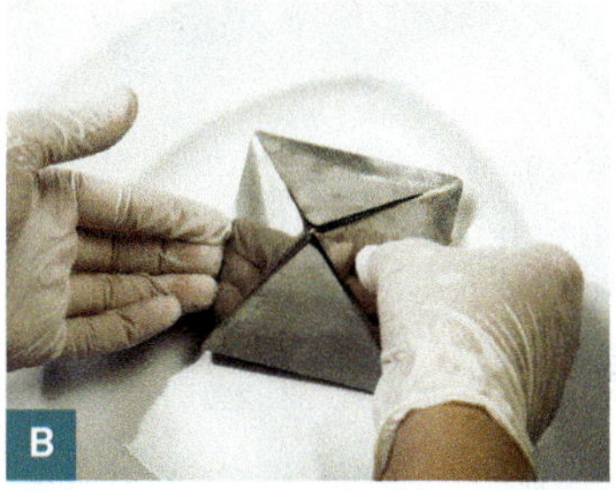
B

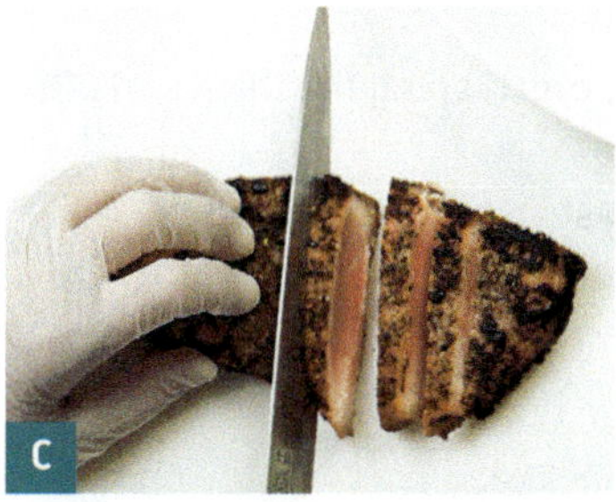
C

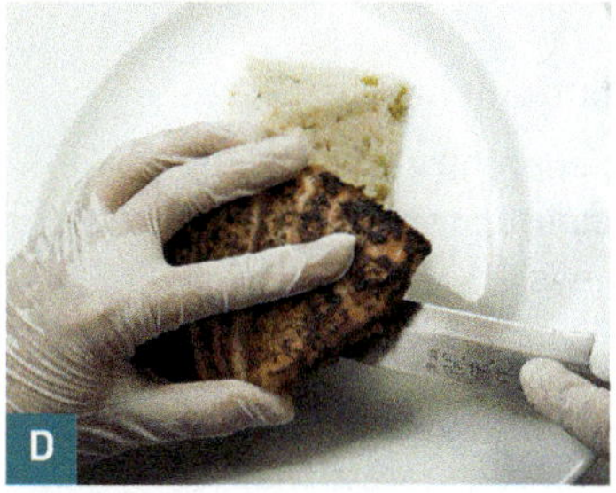
D

SALMON AND STRIPED BASS PINWHEELS

Portions:
4
Portion size:
6 oz (180 g)

INGREDIENTS	U.S.	METRIC
Whole center-cut fillet from a small salmon side (see Note)	1 lb	500 g
Whole center-cut fillet from a striped bass side (see Note)	1 lb	500 g
Fine sea salt	to taste	to taste
Finely ground white pepper	to taste	to taste
Court bouillon (p. 194)	2 qt	2 L
Butter	2 tsp	10 mL
Seafood Aspic for Coating (p. 645), optional	8 fl oz	240 mL
Supplies		
Plain wooden cocktail picks	8–10	8–10

Note: For the pinwheels to have the correct shape, both fish fillets must be the same size.

PROCEDURE

PREPARATION

1. Skin both fish fillets.
2. Use tweezers or clean needlenose pliers to remove all pin bones.
3. Wash the fillets and blot them dry. Place them on a clean cutting board (A).
4. Cut each fillet crosswise into 4 even strips (B).
5. Season the fish with salt and pepper.
6. Fabricate the pinwheels:
   a. Position a salmon strip on the work surface, on its side, with the (shiny) skin side facing you.
   b. Place a striped bass strip on the work surface, on its side, overlapping the thick end of the salmon by ¾ in. (2 cm) (C).
   c. Roll the fish strips into a pinwheel by bringing the salmon strip toward you and the striped bass strip away from you (D). Continue winding the strips around each other to form a disk.
   d. Secure the fish strips together with Cocktail picks (E).
   e. Measure the thickness of the pinwheels.
7. Bring the court bouillon to the boil in a nonreactive pan of the correct size to hold the fish pinwheels submerged in one layer.
8. Cut out a circle of parchment that fits the top of the pan and butter it heavily.
9. Gently place the pinwheels in the court bouillon and press the parchment circle, butter-side down, on their surfaces. Watch carefully, and when the *cuisson* recovers the simmer, poach the pinwheels for 8 minutes per 1 in. (2.5 cm) of thickness.
10. Prepare an ice bain-marie that will hold the sauté pan.
11. When the fish yields to the touch without feeling springy, transfer the pan to the ice bain-marie. Bring the fish and *cuisson* to room temperature and then refrigerate them together until thoroughly cold.
12. Remove the pinwheels from the *cuisson* and blot them dry (F).
13. Place the pinwheels on a rack set over a sheet tray. Remove the picks.

PROCEDURE

OPTIONAL ASPIC COATING

14. If necessary, rewarm the aspic and then stir it in an ice bain-marie until it reaches the consistency of thick syrup.
15. Coat the pinwheels with aspic. Make sure the aspic is not too thick in the crevices. Refrigerate until the aspic is set.
16. Give the pinwheels another coat of aspic and refrigerate until set.
17. Store the pinwheels in a flat plastic container lined with parchment, with the lid tightly closed.

HOLDING

Refrigerate up to 2 days.

A

B

C

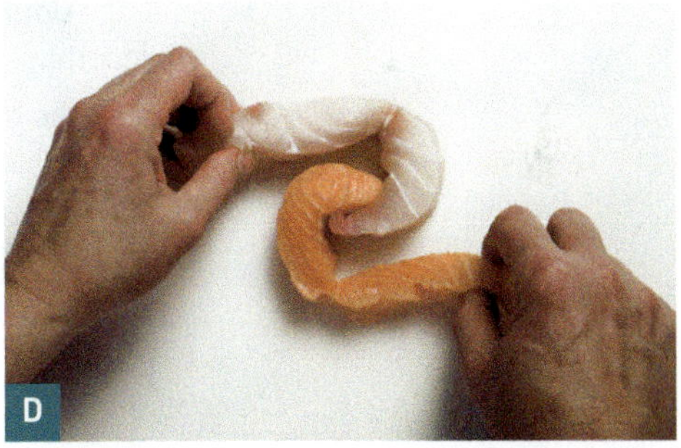
D

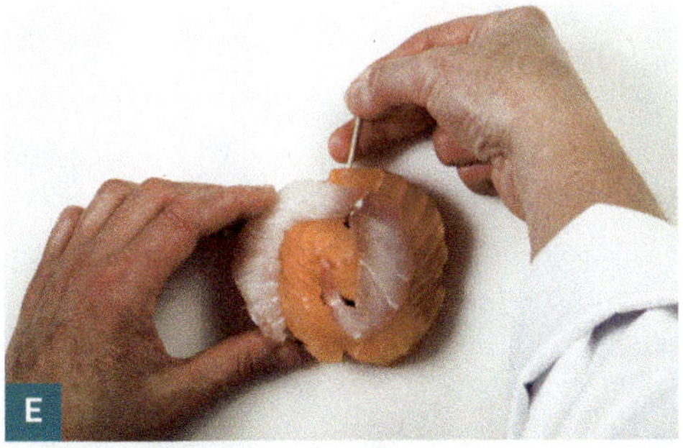
E

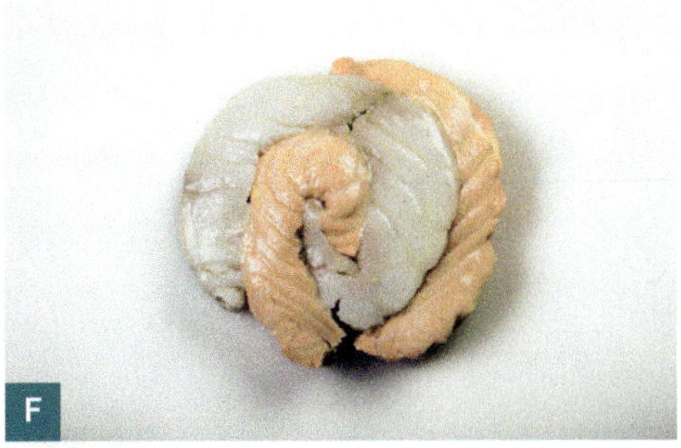
F

CHILLED SALMON AND STRIPED BASS PINWHEELS

WITH SALADE RUSSE

MAIN COURSE

Portions:
1
Portion size:
6 oz (180 g)

COMPONENTS

8 fl oz (240 mL) *Salade Russe (p. 147)*
1 *Salmon and Striped Bass Pinwheel (p. 204)*, 6 oz (180 g)
2 oz (60 g) Haricots verts, blanched *à point* (p. 91), refreshed, blotted dry
2 fl oz (60 mL) *Creamy Vinaigrette (p. 32)*, in squeeze bottle
1 tsp (5 mL) *Beet Oil (p. 687)*, in squeeze bottle
1 Steamed, chilled, peeled baby beet (see Note)

Note: If tiny baby beets are not available, use a large Parisienne scoop to form spheres from a large cooked beet.

PROCEDURE

PLATING

1. Place an entremet ring the same size as the pinwheel in the center of a cool 12-in. (30-cm) plate. Pack the salade russe into the ring (A) and then remove the ring.
2. Set the pinwheel on the salade (B).
3. Arrange the haricots verts in a rope pattern around the base of the salade.
4. Squeeze the vinaigrette around the plate well.
5. Squeeze dots of beet oil around the edge of the vinaigrette.
6. Moisten the beet with a little vinaigrette and place it in the center of the pinwheel.

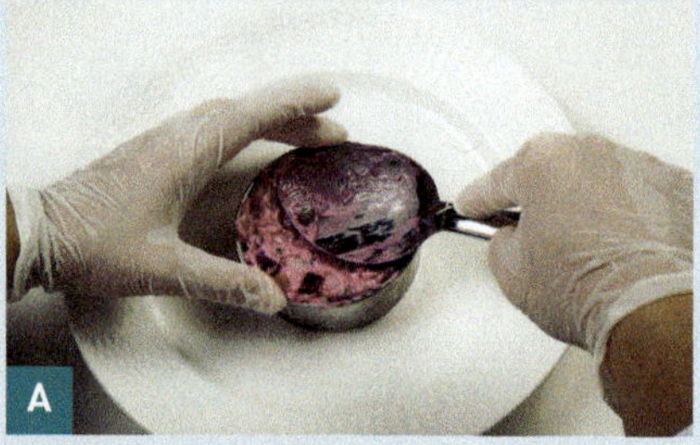
A

B

SEAFOOD MEDLEY BASE

Yield:
about 1 qt (1 L) or 2 lb (960 g)

INGREDIENTS	U.S.	METRIC
Fish Stock (p. 750)	8 fl oz	240 mL
White wine	4 fl oz	120 mL
Water	16 fl oz	480 mL
Minced shallots	1 oz	30 g
Powdered seafood seasoning, such as Old Bay™	1 tsp	5 mL
Bay leaves	2	2
Small lemon, sliced thin	½	½
Peel-on white shrimp (36/40 ct.)	12 oz	360 g
Dry-pack scallops, side muscle trimmed (20/30 ct.)	8 oz	240 g
Small calamari tubes (bodies), cut in ¼-in. (6-mm) rings	8 oz	240 g
Aquacultured mussels, scrubbed and bearded	1 lb	0.5 kg
Topneck clams, scrubbed and soaked in cold water	18	18

PROCEDURE

PREPARATION

1. Combine the stock, wine, water, shallots, seafood seasoning, and lemon in an 8-qt (8-L) nonreactive saucepan with a tight-fitting lid. Bring this *cuisson* to a brisk simmer.
2. Have ready a half-hotel pan set in an ice bain-marie and a perforated half-hotel pan set in a drip pan. Place a triple layer of damp cheesecloth in a strainer set over a bowl.
3. Cook the seafood:
   a. Drop the shrimp into the *cuisson*, cover the pan, and pan-steam (p. 195). Remove the shrimp to the iced hotel pan.
   b. Drop in the scallops, cover the pan, and pan-steam them until barely done. Remove the scallops to the iced hotel pan.
   c. Drop in the calamari, cover the pan, and pan-steam until barely done. Remove the calamari to the iced hotel pan.
   d. Drop in the mussels, cover the pan, and pan-steam just until they open. Remove the mussels to the perforated hotel pan.
   e. Drop in the clams, cover the pan, and pan-steam just until they open. Remove them to the perforated hotel pan.
4. Strain the *cuisson* through the cheesecloth into a bowl. Strain the liquid in the drip pan into the bowl. Wash out the saucepan and pour the strained *cuisson* into it.
5. Reduce the *cuisson* over high heat to about 6 fl oz (180 mL) strong seafood stock. Cool to room temperature.
6. Fabricate the seafood:
   a. Peel and devein the shrimp. Cut each in half lengthwise. Place the shrimp in a freshly sanitized container.
   b. Slice the scallops across the grain. Add them to the container.
   c. Remove the mussels and clams from their shells, and add them to the container along with the calamari.
7. Pour the cooled shellfish stock over the seafood and stir it gently to combine. Gently press the seafood to submerge as much as possible in the stock.

HOLDING

Refrigerate, covered, in an ice-bain-marie up to 2 days.

VARIATION

Vary the seafood as desired. Alter cooking times accordingly.

CALIFORNIA CHILLED SEAFOOD MEDLEY

MAIN COURSE

Portions:
1
Portion Size:
10½ oz (315 g)

COMPONENTS

6 oz (180 g) *Seafood Medley Base (p. 207)*
1½ fl oz (45 mL) *Fresh Tomato Salsa (p. 50)*
¾ oz (22 g) Jícama, cut julienne
2 tsp (10 mL) Ketchup
4 tsp (20 mL) Pure golden olive oil
1½ oz (45 g) Firm-ripe Western avocado, cut in ⅜-in. (1-cm) dice
to taste Fresh lime juice
to taste Kosher salt
2 oz (60 g) Shredded romaine hearts
1 *Tortilla Basket (p. 707)*
1 tsp (5 mL) Chopped cilantro

PROCEDURE

FINISHING

1. Place the seafood medley base, salsa, jícama, ketchup, and olive oil in a work bowl.
2. Place the avocado on top. Sprinkle the avocado with lime juice and salt.
3. Gently mix the medley with the seasonings.

PLATING

4. Place half the romaine on a cool 10-in. (25-cm) plate. Make a well in the center.
5. Set the tortilla basket in the well and place the remaining romaine in it.
6. Spoon the seafood medley into the basket.
7. Sprinkle the cilantro over top.

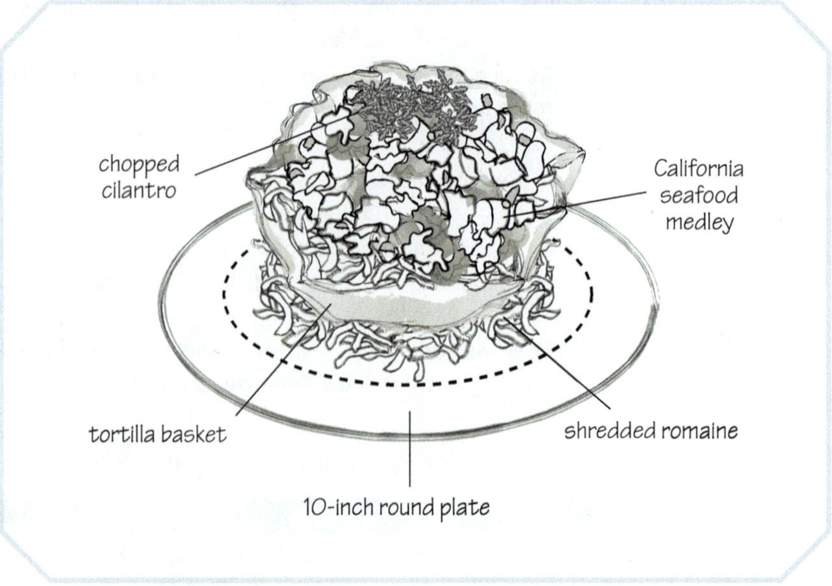

CHILLED ASIAN SEAFOOD IN CRISPY NOODLE NEST

MAIN COURSE

Portions:
1
Portion Size:
8 oz (240 g)

COMPONENTS

6 oz (180 g) *Seafood Medley Base (p. 207)*, drained
1½ fl oz (45 mL) *Asian Vinaigrette (p. 35)*
½ oz (15 g) Jícama, very fine julienne
¼ oz (8 g) Shredded scallions
5 Carrot fish (p. 715), or ½ oz (15 g) blanched and refreshed fine julienne carrots
¼ oz (8 g) Peeled red bell pepper, fine julienne
1½ tsp (8 mL) Chopped cilantro
1½ oz (45 g) Shredded romaine hearts
1 *Crispy Noodle Nest (p. 707)*, 6 in. (15 cm)

PROCEDURE

FINISHING

1. Place the seafood medley base in a bowl and toss it with the vinaigrette, jícama, scallions, carrots, peppers, and cilantro.

PLATING

2. Make a bed of shredded romaine on a cool 10-in. (25-cm). plate. Place the noodle nest in the center and press it to sit firm.
3. Fill the noodle nest with the seafood salad.

SCALLOP SEVICHE BASE

Yield:
14 oz (420 g)
Portions:
4
Portion size:
3½ oz (105 g)

INGREDIENTS	U.S.	METRIC
Fresh lemon juice	2 fl oz	60 mL
Fresh lime juice	2 fl oz	60 mL
Kosher salt	1 tsp	5 mL
Minced shallot	¼ oz	7.5 g
Dry-pack sea scallops (10/20 ct.)	1 lb	0.5 kg

PROCEDURE

PREPARATION

1. Combine the lemon juice, lime juice, salt, and shallot in a nonreactive container and stir the mixture until the salt dissolves.
2. Remove the tough adductor muscle from the side of each scallop. Cut the scallops across the grain into thin slices (A).
3. Toss the scallops with the citrus mixture (B), cover, and refrigerate 1 hour. Stir the scallops gently at 15-minute intervals.
4. Drain the scallops and blot them dry with a clean, lint-free towel. Place them in a freshly sanitized container and refrigerate them until needed.

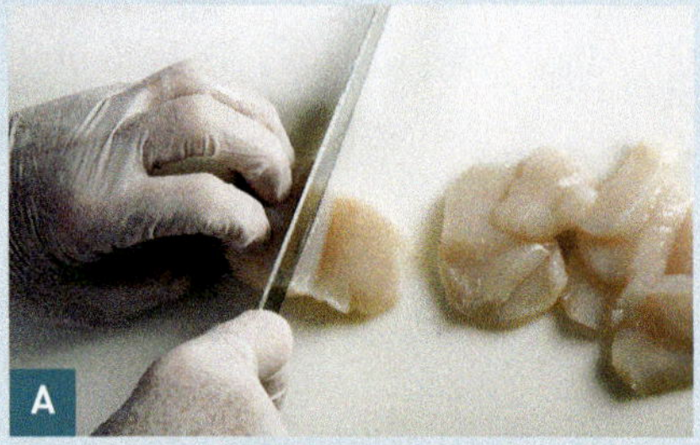
A

B

HOLDING

Refrigerate up to 2 days.

Seafood Dishes Cooked with Acid

In Latin American cuisines, seafood cooked with acid is called ***seviche*** [say-BEE-chay or say-VEE-chay], while in French-speaking cultures it is called ***seviche*** [seh-VEESH]. In the Hawai'ian Islands, a similar preparation is called ***poke*** [POH-kay].

SCALLOP SEVICHE À L'ORANGE

[ah loh-RANZH]

APPETIZER

Portions:
1
Portion size:
4 oz (120 g), plus garnishes

COMPONENTS

1½ tsp (8 mL) Frozen orange juice concentrate, thawed
1 tsp (5 mL) Fresh lemon juice
1 tsp (5 mL) Peeled red bell pepper, cut brunoise
½ tsp (3 mL) Seeded serrano or jalapeño chile, cut brunoise
2 tsp (10 mL) Shellfish glace (optional)
2 tsp (10 mL) Minced orange zest
1 Tbsp (15 mL) Extra-virgin olive oil
3½ oz (105 g) *Scallop Seviche Base (p. 210)*
1 oz (30 g) Spicy micro greens
1 or 2 Small navel orange, *peleé à vif* (p. 87)

PROCEDURE

FINISHING

1. Place the orange juice concentrate, lemon juice, peppers, chile, optional glace, and zest in a bowl. Whisk in the olive oil to make an emulsion.
2. Toss in the seviche base.

PLATING

3. Arrange the micro greens in a ring inside the rim of a cool 10-in. (25-cm) plate
4. Slice the orange thin and arrange the slices in an overlapping ring, leaning against the micro greens (see photo).
5. Mound the seviche in the middle of the plate.

VARIATIONS

SNAPPER SEVICHE ACAPULCO

Replace the scallops in the Seviche Base with perfectly trimmed, thin-sliced red snapper. Replace the orange juice concentrate with tomato juice. Replace the lemon juice with lime juice. Add 2 oz (60 g) diced firm-ripe avocado. Omit the orange and micro greens, and serve in a cocktail glass with shredded romaine and tortilla chips.

POISSON CRU

Replace the scallops in the Seviche Base with equal parts perfectly trimmed, thin-sliced red snapper and sashimi-grade tuna. Replace the lemon juice with lime juice. Add 1 fl oz (30 mL) unsweetened coconut cream. Omit the micro greens and orange, and serve in a half-coconut lined with 2 oz (60 g) purchased seaweed salad or 1 oz (30 g) shredded romaine.

SEAFOOD MOUSSES

A ***mousse*** [MOOSE] consists of a full-flavored base of cooked, puréed food lightened with whipped cream and/or beaten egg whites, served with no further cooking. Sweet dessert mousses are part of the pastry chef's repertoire, while savory mousses are the responsibility of the garde manger department. Mousses are served cold or at cool room temperature, usually in small portions, as appetizers, because they are usually rich as well as light. Mousses made from seafood are among the most popular.

Understanding Mousses

All mousses have two main components:

1. The ***purée base***, which in a savory mousse may consist of cooked or smoked seafood, cooked or smoked poultry, smoked meats, cooked or raw vegetables, or cheese. To ensure proper mixing and achieve a silken texture, the purée base must be very smooth. It must also be full-flavored and highly seasoned, because its flavor is diluted with the addition of the lightening ingredients.
2. ***Lightening ingredients*** (or lighteners) in a savory mousse are whipped cream and/or beaten egg whites. Their purpose is to capture air and give the mousse a light, fluffy texture when incorporated into the purée base.

Many mousses need the addition of a ***stabilizer***, or stabilizing ingredient, in the form of gelatin. A mousse stabilizer gives the purée base enough structure to hold the lighteners and, in some cases, to ensure the mousse will stand alone when unmolded.

Mousse Versus Mousseline

What is the difference between a mousse and a mousseline (covered in Chapter 15)? The terms *mousse* and *mousseline* are based on the French word *mousse*, meaning "froth" or "foam." Mousses and mousselines share qualities of smoothness and lightness. Although the terms are often used interchangeably, a mousse and a mousseline are actually very different preparations.

A mousse is based on a purée of *cooked* meat, poultry, or seafood. This purée base is lightened with whipped cream and/or beaten egg whites. No further cooking is applied. Mousses are always served cold.

A mousseline is based on a purée of *raw* meat, poultry, or seafood. Mousselines are bound with egg, lightened with cream, and then baked or poached. They may be served hot or cold.

Determining Mousse Texture

The desired texture of a mousse depends on its intended use. A mousse formed into a mold, chilled, and then turned out onto a plate as a freestanding item must be firm enough to hold its shape. Mousses packed into oblong terrine forms, chilled, and then sliced must be quite firm. When used in hors d'oeuvre work, mousses used as a filling for pastry shells or canapé bases should be soft enough to be piped from a pastry bag.

Another factor to consider is the temperature at which the mousse will be served. If intended as an à la carte appetizer, plated to order, a mousse can have a softer texture than one that must sit on a buffet table at room temperature for several hours.

The finished texture of a mousse is determined by three factors:

1. *The natural consistency of the purée base.* So lightening ingredients can be added most effectively and keep their volume, the base should be about the thickness of pastry cream. Make adjustments to consistency as follows:
    a. A base made from a starchy vegetable or from a soft, viscous cheese results in a thick, firm mousse. The base may need to be thinned with a liquid to achieve a workable texture.
    b. A base made from firm poached seafood may need additional liquid to be workable enough to be forced through a drum sieve. The liquid may be the seafood's *cuisson*, fish stock, or fish velouté.

c. Watery vegetables are usually loose-textured and benefit from an additional thickening ingredient, such as cream cheese, béchamel sauce, or mayonnaise.

2. *The amount of gelatin added.* Gelatin is added to firm the texture of the finished mousse. The more gelatin is added, the thicker and more stable the final product. However, too much gelatin yields a mousse that is unpleasantly rubbery in texture.

3. *The ratio of purée base to lightening ingredients.* Adding a smaller amount of whipped cream and/or beaten egg white results in a thicker, firmer mousse. Using more makes a softer, less stable mousse.

Food Safety for Mousses

A mousse is a food assembled from precooked ingredients and that receives no further cooking after it is assembled. In addition, a mousse receives a lot of handling and has a lot of surface area exposed to contamination. Many mousses have a highly perishable protein food as their main ingredient, and all contain protein in the form of cream and, sometimes, raw egg whites. Due to these factors, be especially vigilant about food safety when preparing mousses. Before preparing a seafood mousse, review the food safety guidelines below.

Preparing Seafood Mousses

Unless you are using smoked seafood, your first step in preparing a seafood mousse is to cook the seafood. Poaching is the most common method. Steamed seafood may also be used. To ensure a smooth texture and successful structure, trim all visible connective tissue and remove all dark deposit fat, either before or after cooking. Cool the seafood before proceeding.

If using scraps and trimmings of raw or leftover cooked seafood, make sure they are fresh and of good quality. Mousses are particularly susceptible to contamination by harmful microorganisms. A mousse made from substandard ingredients could be a food safety hazard. It will also have poor flavor and texture.

Tips on Folding

When preparing mousses, garde manger chefs utilize techniques and methods borrowed from the pastry kitchen. To incorporate the lightening ingredients into the base, the technique used is ***folding***. This technique is used when one or more ingredients to be mixed together contain air, as do whipped cream and beaten egg whites. The object of folding is to combine the ingredients while retaining as much air as possible.

To properly fold, use a large rubber spatula. Sweep the spatula down the side of the bowl farthest from you and then bring it up under the center of the mixture. Rotate the bowl a quarter-turn and repeat the action (see p. 214). Continue until the mixture appears uniform.

When folding a light, airy substance into a dense, heavy one, you should use a method called ***lightening the base***. In this method, one-fourth to one-third of the light, airy whipped substance is first folded into the heavy substance. This lightens the texture of the base substance and makes it less dense. Then the lightened base is added to the remaining whipped substance and the two are folded together. This results in maximum air retention.

Guidelines for Food Safety in Mousses

- Use pasteurized egg whites only.
- Bring egg whites to room temperature shortly before using them.
- Wear food-service gloves when preparing mousses.
- Work quickly and in small batches.
- Clean and thoroughly sanitize the preparation equipment, especially the grinder or food processor.
- Clean and thoroughly sanitize all molds, forms, or pastry bags and tips used to present mousses.

While the steps to prepare seafood mousses are relatively straightforward, precautions must be taken to ensure a successful result. The procedure for making seafood mousses (and other types of mousse) notes these precautions.

Procedure for Preparing Mousses

1. If you are using gelatin, bloom it as directed on page 633.
2. Break up or dice the cooked, trimmed main ingredient and place it in a freshly sanitized, chilled food processor. If necessary, work in batches.
3. Add the dry and/or liquid seasonings and any thickening ingredients. *Season highly* because the purée base will be diluted with a large amount of the lightening ingredient(s).
4. Grind the base ingredients into a smooth purée. Add any thinning or thickening ingredients through the feed tube while grinding (A).
5. Force the purée through a drum sieve (p. 610) or fine sieve into a large bowl (B).

6. If using granular gelatin, gently heat it in its blooming liquid. If using sheet gelatin, heat it in a small amount of additional liquid until dissolved. Cool the gelatin to room temperature. Do not let the gelatin solidify.
7. Whip the cold heavy cream to soft peaks. If using egg whites, beat the room-temperature egg whites to soft peaks. *Do not overwhip* the cream or egg whites, or the finished mousse will be grainy and may separate. Note: If the mousse includes gelatin, from this point onward you must work quickly and without interruption so it does not resolidify before you have finished.

8. If using gelatin, stir into the purée base (C, D).
9. If using beaten egg whites, immediately fold them in following the tips in the sidebar on page 213 (E).
10. Quickly but gently fold in the whipped cream.
11. Immediately pack the mousse into its form(s) or container.

BASIC SEAFOOD MOUSSE

Yield:
1 lb 2 oz (550 g), about 24 fl oz (700 mL)

INGREDIENTS	U.S.	METRIC
Granular gelatin (see Note)	0.15 oz (1½ tsp)	4.5 g (7.5 mL)
Cold liquid, such as water, fish stock, sherry, Madeira, or dry vermouth	2 fl oz	60 mL
Minced shallots	½ oz	50 g
White wine	3 fl oz	90 mL
Well-trimmed, lightly cooked fish and/or shellfish, room temperature	12 oz	360 g
Salt	to taste	to taste
Finely ground white pepper	to taste	to taste
Fresh lemon juice	to taste	to taste
Fish Stock (p. 750) or *cuisson* from poaching the seafood	2 fl oz	60 mL
Pasteurized egg whites for whipping, room temperature	2 oz	60 g
Heavy cream, very cold	4 fl oz	120 mL

Note: The texture and set of the mousse will vary according to the texture of the seafood items used. The specified amount of gelatin combined with seafood of moderate density yields a mousse that will hold a shape when unmolded. If a soft mousse is desired, decrease or omit the gelatin. If a firm, sliceable mousse is desired, increase the gelatin. Mousse with higher gelatin content must be packed into its form immediately.

PROCEDURE

PREPARATION

1. Combine the gelatin and cold liquid in a metal measuring cup. Set aside until the gelatin blooms (p. 633).
2. Combine the shallots and wine in a small sauté pan and reduce over moderate heat to about 1 fl oz (30 mL). Cool to room temperature.
3. If necessary, cut or break the seafood into ½-in. (1-cm) pieces.
4. Place the seafood in a food processor fitted with the metal blade. Add the cooled shallot mixture, salt, pepper, and lemon juice.
5. Set the cup of gelatin in a pan of hot water and melt it to a syrupy liquid.
6. Grind the seafood to a smooth purée. While the processor is running, pour the fish stock or *cuisson* through the feed tube.
7. Force the purée through a fine sieve into a large bowl.
8. Beat the egg white with a pinch of salt to soft peaks.
9. Whip the cream to soft peaks. Hold at room temperature until needed. Have both the egg whites and the cream ready before the next step, because once the gelatin is added, the mousse must be completed without delay.
10. Mix the dissolved gelatin thoroughly into the seafood purée.
11. Fold half of the egg white into the seafood purée, then fold the lightened purée into the egg whites. Scrape the mixture back into the large bowl.
12. Fold in the whipped cream.
13. Taste and correct the salt, pepper, and lemon juice.
14. Immediately transfer the mousse to a mold or molds. Refrigerate until set.

HOLDING

Refrigerate up to 2 days.

(continues)

VARIATIONS

SALMON MOUSSE

For the seafood, use skinned, well-trimmed, lightly poached salmon. For the gelatin soaking liquid, use Madeira. For a mousse that holds its shape and can be sliced when unmolded, increase the gelatin to 0.25 oz (7.5 g) or 2¼ tsp (11 mL).

HOT-SMOKED SALMON MOUSSE

For the seafood, use skinned, well-trimmed hot-smoked salmon. For blooming the gelatin, use dry vermouth as the cold liquid. Add 1 tsp (5 mL) tomato paste to the salmon when puréeing. (For a mousse that holds its shape and can be sliced when unmolded, increase the gelatin to 0.25 oz (7.5 g) or 2¼ tsp (11 mL).

SHRIMP MOUSSE

For the seafood, use 8 oz (240 g) peeled, deveined cooked shrimp and 4 oz (120 g) well-trimmed, skinless poached white-fleshed fish. For blooming the gelatin, use dry vermouth as the cold liquid. Add 1 tsp (5 mL) tomato paste to the seafood when puréeing. For a mousse that holds its shape and can be sliced when unmolded, increase the gelatin to 0.25 oz (7.5 g) or 2¼ tsp (11 mL).

SPINACH SEAFOOD MOUSSE

For the seafood, use 10 oz (300 g) skinned, well-trimmed poached white-fleshed fish. Add 3 oz (90 g) blanched, refreshed spinach leaves, chopped fine and then puréed, to the fish in the food processor when puréeing. For blooming the gelatin, use dry vermouth as the cold liquid. Increase the gelatin to ⅙ oz (0.17 oz/5 g) or 1¾ tsp (9 mL). For a mousse that holds its shape and can be sliced when unmolded, increase the gelatin to 0.3 oz (9 g) or 2¾ tsp (13 mL).

SAFFRON SEAFOOD MOUSSE

For the seafood, use skinned, well-trimmed poached white-fleshed fish. For blooming the gelatin, use dry sherry as the cold liquid. Add ½ tsp (2.5 mL) powdered saffron or ¾ tsp (4 mL) saffron threads to the wine when making the shallot reduction. For a mousse that holds its shape and can be sliced when unmolded, increase the gelatin to 0.25 oz (7.5 g) or 2¼ tsp (11 mL).

DILLED SALMON MOUSSE WITH RYE CRACKERS

APPETIZER

Portions:
2
Portion size:
4 oz (120 g)

COMPONENTS

½ lb (240 g) *Salmon Mousse (p. 216)*, freshly made and not yet refrigerated
¼ oz (7 g) Minced fresh dill
4 Dill sprigs
8 Grape tomatoes
16 to 20 *Rye Crackers (p. 694)*

Supplies

1 12-in. (30-cm) paper doily

PROCEDURE

PRESENTATION

1. Fold the minced dill into the mousse.
2. Place the mousse in a pastry bag fitted with a large star tip.
3. Pipe the mousse into an 8-fl oz (240-mL) ramekin.

PLATING

4. Line a 12-in. (30-cm) plate with the doily and place the ramekin in the center.
5. Surround the ramekin with dill sprigs and grape tomatoes.
6. Arrange crackers on the plate.

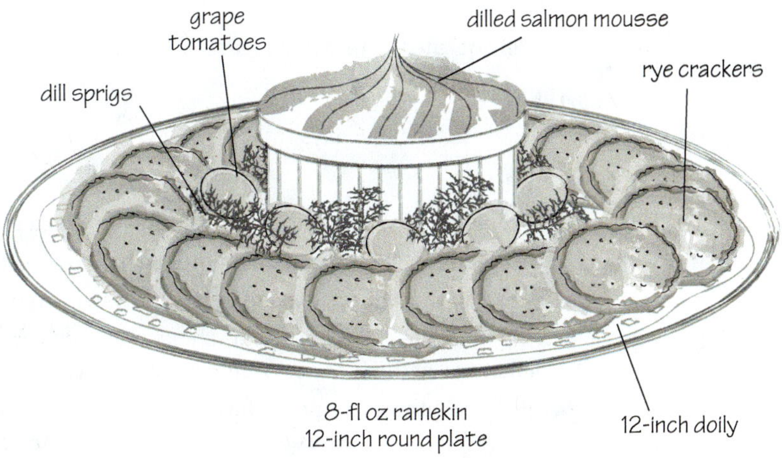

TRIPLE SALMON MOUSSE TRIANGLE TERRINE

Yield:
1 17 × 3½ × 3½-in. (43 × 9 × 9-cm) triangle form, about 2½ lb (1.25 kg)

Portions:
16

Portion size:
about 2 oz (60 g)

INGREDIENTS	U.S.	METRIC
Thin-sliced cold-smoked salmon	10–12 oz	300–360 g
Hot-Smoked Salmon Mousse (p. 216)	8 oz	250 g
Salmon Mousse (p. 216)	1½ lb	750 g
Supplies		
18 × 24-in. (45 × 60-cm) sheet plain acetate	1	1

PROCEDURE

PREPARATION

1. Cut out 3 17 × 3½ × 3½-in. (43 × 9 × 9-cm) strips of acetate. Prepare a terrine weight as described on page 525.
2. Lay a 20-in. (50-cm) length of heavy-duty plastic film on a full sheet tray. Place the hot-smoked salmon mousse in a pastry bag with a very large, round tip. Using heavy pressure, pipe out a cylinder of mousse about 1 in. (3 cm) in diameter and 17 in. (43 cm) long. Wrap the cylinder with the plastic film and roll it on the tray to perfect its shape. Freeze for at least ½ hour, or until solid.
3. Line a 17 × 3½ × 3½-in. (43 × 9 × 9-cm) triangle form with heavy-duty plastic wrap, allowing about 3 in. (8 cm) overhang on all sides. Place a strip of acetate on top of the plastic film on both sides of the form.
4. Line the form with smoked salmon slices, allowing a 2-in. (5-cm) overhang on the long sides. Do not line the short ends.
5. Pack half the salmon mousse into the form. Tap the form on the work surface to force out air pockets.
6. Unwrap the hot-smoked salmon mousse cylinder and place it in the form. Press it gently to push it about ¼ in. (0.5 cm) into the salmon mousse.
7. Pack the remaining mousse into the form and smooth the top . Tap the form on the work surface to force out air pockets.
8. Fold the smoked salmon over the top of the mousse . Place a strip of acetate on top, then fold up the plastic wrap. Place the terrine weight on top.
9. Refrigerate the terrine at least 12 hours.

HOLDING

Refrigerate, uncut, 4 days total.

FINISHING

10. Prepare a tall vessel full of very hot water and a sharp slicing knife.
11. Carefully lift the terrine out of the form onto a cutting board.
12. Unwrap the terrine, leaving the acetate strip on the bottom for support.
13. Dip the knife in the hot water, shake off excess water, and trim about ½ in. (1 cm) from each end of the terrine. Wipe the knife with a clean, damp towel between each cut.
14. Following the same procedure, cut the terrine into thirty-two ½-in. slices (1-cm). As you cut, transfer the slices to a sheet tray lined with parchment.
15. Wrap the sheet tray with plastic film.

HOLDING

Refrigerate 1–2 days.

TRIPLE SALMON MOUSSE TRIANGLES

WITH CUCUMBER FOAM AND TOMATO COULIS

APPETIZER

Portion:
1
Portion Size:
2 oz (60 g), plus garnishes

COMPONENTS

½ oz (15 g) Mild-flavored spring mix
2 *Triple Salmon Mousse Triangle Terrine (p. 218)*, ½-in. (1-cm) slices
2 fl oz (60 mL) *Cucumber Foam (p. 711)*
2 fl oz (60 mL) *Basic Tomato Coulis Sauce (p. 52)*, in squeeze bottle

PROCEDURE

PLATING

1. Place a mound of micro greens on the back left of a cool 10-in. (25-cm) plate.
2. Lean one terrine slice against the greens and prop the other slice against it.
3. Mound the cucumber foam onto the plate to the right of the slices.
4. Squeeze the tomato coulis on the plate well in front of the slices.

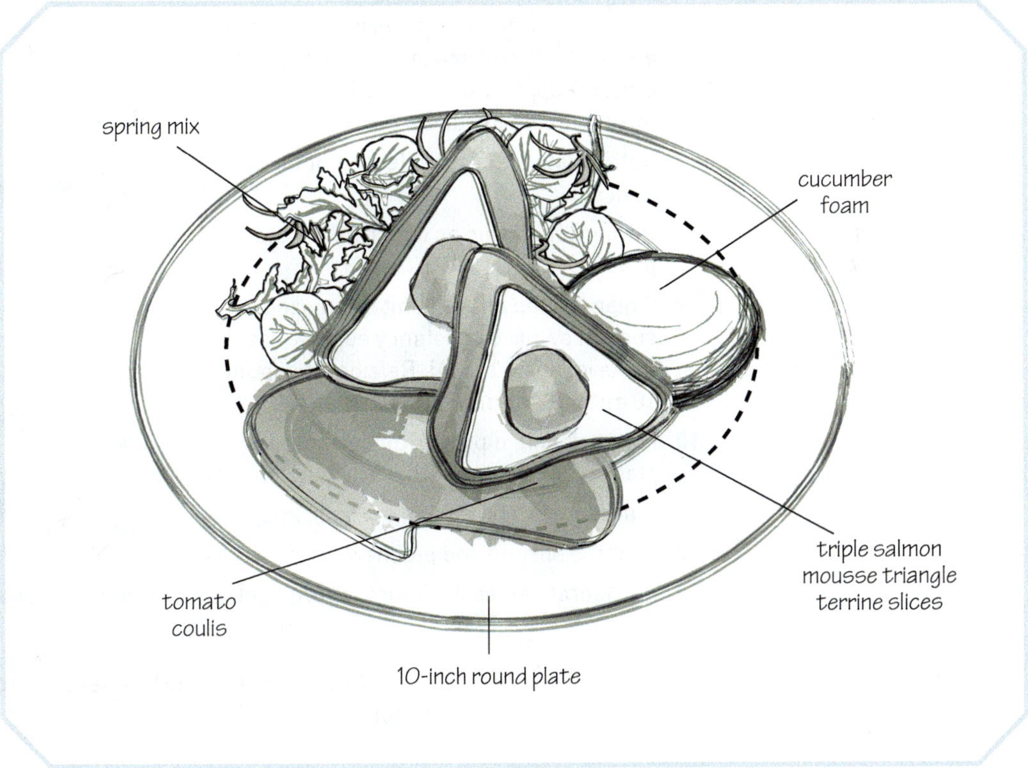

TRICOLOR SEAFOOD MOUSSE CYLINDERS

Yield:
12 4-fl oz (120 mL) cylinders, about 4 oz (120 g) each

INGREDIENTS	U.S.	METRIC
Shrimp Mousse (p. 216)	½ lb	0.5 kg
Spinach Seafood Mousse (p. 216)	½ lb	0.5 kg
Saffron Seafood Mousse (p. 216)	½ lb	0.5 kg
Seafood Aspic for Coating (p. 645)	6 fl oz	180 mL
51/60 ct. cooked, peeled shrimp	12	12
Chervil or parsley pluches	12	12
Supplies		
1¾ × 9-in. (2 × 23-cm) strips of acetate	12	12

PROCEDURE

PREPARATION

1. Place 12 4-fl oz (120- mL) cylinder forms on a sheet tray lined with parchment.
2. Line the sides of the forms with the acetate strips.
3. Place all three mousses in pastry bags fitted with medium plain tips.
4. Fill the forms slightly less than one-third full with the pink-colored shrimp mousse. Tap the tray on the work surface to force out air pockets.
5. Add the spinach mousse as in step 4.
6. Add the saffron mousse as in step 4, leaving a ⅛-in. (0.33-cm) space at the top. Use the pusher supplied with the cylinder form set to smooth the top layer.
7. Refrigerate the form at least 1 hour, or until set.
8. Prepare the aspic as described in step 4 on p. 634.
9. Finish the top of each unit by pouring in enough syrup-consistency aspic to reach the level of the top (A). Refrigerate about 10 minutes, or until almost set.
10. For each unit, dip a shrimp in aspic and place it in the center (B).
11. Place an herb pluche on each shrimp.
12. Coat the shrimp and pluche with syrupy aspic.
13. Refrigerate at least 2 hours, or until set.

A

B

HOLD

Refrigerate, uncovered, up to 24 hours. To hold up to 2 days, add only a light coating of aspic to each unit. Finish prior to serving.

TRICOLOR SEAFOOD MOUSSE
IN CREAMY LEMON VINAIGRETTE

APPETIZER

Portion:
1
Portion Size:
4 oz (120 g)

COMPONENTS

as needed Pan coating spray
1 *Tricolor Seafood Mousse Cylinder (p. 220)*, in its form
2 fl oz (60 mL) *Creamy Vinaigrette (p. 32)*, in squeeze bottle
1 leaf Frisée

PROCEDURE

PLATING

1. Lightly spray the plunger that accompanies the cylinder form set with the pan coating.
2. Place the plunger on the work surface. Lift the cylinder form off its tray using a large, wide spatula. Set the form on the plunger. Gently push the cylinder form downward to release the mousse (see photo at right).
3. Use the spatula and a paring knife to transfer the mousse to the center of a cool 10-in. (25-cm) plate and remove the acetate strip.
4. Squeeze a pool of vinaigrette to the right of the mousse.
5. Place the frisée back left of the mousse.

SEAFOOD SERVED RAW

Seafood restaurants often feature a ***raw bar***, a front-of-house food preparation area where raw shellfish and other chilled seafood items are displayed and plated. Preparing and serving raw seafood presents a number of challenges.

Standards for Serving Raw Seafood

Serving raw seafood requires specific knowledge and special techniques. To successfully include raw seafood on your menu, you must understand the risks involved, and comply with both local and national regulations. The following discussion includes guidelines for both fish and shellfish.

Insist on Absolute Freshness

Seafood is highly perishable. Both its quality and its wholesomeness deteriorate quickly. While freshness is a desirable quality in all foods we serve, a lack of freshness in raw seafood cannot be disguised. Seafood intended for raw consumption must be exceptionally fresh, both for health reasons and for palatability.

Fish are always gutted as soon as possible after being killed, as their internal organs are more perishable than their flesh. However, bivalves such as clams and oysters are eaten in entirety, including their internal organs. For this reason, they must be kept alive until shortly before consumption. Clams, oysters, and mussels are best and safest when opened *within minutes* before eating. At most, opened bivalves can be held refrigerated on ice for an hour or two. If they must be held for more than a few minutes, they should be loosely covered with plastic film to prevent moisture loss. In raw service, opened bivalves should be set out in small quantity and replenished as necessary.

Most fish for raw consumption should not have been previously frozen, However, frozen tuna and yellowtail (hamachi) labeled ***sashimi-grade*** are examples of products that, when properly thawed, retain their flavor and texture and are acceptable for raw service. Frozen, pre-opened bivalves do not retain a palatable texture for serving raw. They are more useful for cooked preparations.

Guidelines for Purchasing Whole Fish

With the exception of frozen, sashimi-grade fish, fish for raw service should be purchased whole. The main reason is that it is easier to determine the freshness of a whole fish than that of a fabricated piece of fish. Look for the following freshness indicators:

- Aroma is fresh, mild, and briny, with no fishy odor.
- Eyes are moist and convex, or bulging, and not dry or sunken.
- Gills are brightly colored and moist, not brown or gray and sticky.
- Scales are shiny and tightly attached, not dull in color and falling off.
- Blood behind the cavity membrane is a bright red or burgundy color, not brown or black.
- Flesh is intact, firm, and springy to the touch, not split open and mushy in texture.

Fabricate Fish Thoroughly and Carefully

For raw service, use only the clean muscle mass of the fish, with little or no connective tissue. Dark deposit fat is usually removed for North American and European service. The manner in which raw fish flesh is fabricated has a large impact on both its flavor and mouthfeel. Fish with no discernable grain and a very fine texture, such as tuna or yellowtail, may be fabricated into blocks or bâtonnets. However, the fillets of most fish species must be sliced paper-thin across the grain in order to melt on the tongue and release their full flavor.

Fish for raw service must be stored on ice both before and after fabrication. Whole, gutted fish should be buried in ice in a drainer box. Fabricated fillets and steaks should be wrapped in airtight plastic bags and buried in ice. Check the ice and empty the drainers twice per day.

The temperature of raw fish also affects its flavor and texture. Raw fish should be served at a temperature cool enough to maintain its firm texture but not so cold as to dull the palate to its subtle flavor. Thin-sliced raw fish comes to room temperature quickly.

Fabricating Bivalves

Staff members assigned to open bivalves must be thoroughly trained in safe procedures. They should be equipped with a stainless-steel ***cutproof glove*** (p. 225). Many states now require by law that such gloves be worn. Keep clam knives and oyster knives in good condition, with backups provided in case of breakage. Do not use paring knives and other standard knives, as they break easily and can slip and cause injuries. If a knife breaks while opening a bivalve, that bivalve must be discarded in case metal fragments have contaminated it.

Use Only Approved Species from Approved Sources

Make sure that seafood for raw service comes from safe and uncontaminated waters. While most ocean fish are safe for raw consumption, freshwater fish are not. Freshwater species may contain parasites that can be transmitted to humans if eaten raw. Some ocean fish, such as swordfish and tropical reef fish, are also prone to parasites. Ocean fish that spend a portion of their lives in fresh water (such as salmon) should also be avoided for raw service.

Bivalves are strongly affected by contaminated water because they are ***filter-feeders***. They take in both oxygen and nutrients by drawing seawater through their system. As they do this, they absorb contaminants. To ensure that bivalves are safe, government regulations require the water from which they are harvested to be regularly tested. Each wholesale container of wild-harvested bivalves must be tagged with the date and place the product was harvested and the name of the person or company that harvested it. To comply with food safety rules, you must keep the tags from your purchases for the length of time specified by local regulations. This helps government officials trace the source of any food-borne illness that may result from eating the shellfish. Because of the risk of contamination, many garde manger chefs prefer to use farm-raised bivalves for both raw and cooked applications (see sidebar, right).

Farm-Raised Shellfish

Aquaculture is the practice of raising seafood in a controlled environment. Seafood produced by aquaculture is also called ***farm-raised*** or *cultivated* seafood. The water in which aquacultured seafood lives is monitored carefully for quality, and the seafood is fed a controlled diet. Today, most bivalve aquaculture operations utilize a ***depuration system*** for enhanced safety and quality. Prior to sale, the mature bivalves are held in tanks of fast-flowing seawater powered by high-pressure pumps for a period of 48 to 72 hours. This flushes out any physical and biological contaminants. Products prepared in this manner are marketed as ***depurated*** *seafood*. The benefits of aquacultured bivalves include consistency of size and enhanced cleanliness and safety.

Guidelines for Raw Seafood Sanitation and Safety

To serve raw seafood that is both safe and delicious, observe these strict standards.

- Sanitize all surfaces that will come into contact with the seafood. Frequently sanitize cutting boards and knives used for raw seafood.
- Store clam and oyster knives in sanitizing solution between uses.
- When opening bivalves, use towels and gloves that are clean and free from strings and lint. Change them frequently.
- If the liquor (interior fluid) from opened bivalves is saved for use in soups and sauces, keep the collection vessel in an ice bath during use. Strain the liquor of grit and shell fragments before using or storing it.

Comply with Warning Regulations

Food-service operations in some areas are required to post warnings about the health risks associated with consuming raw shellfish and other raw food products. Before featuring raw seafood, check local and state regulations.

RAW SHELLFISH SPECIALTIES

Technically, any type of saltwater seafood may be eaten raw as long as it has been harvested from approved waters, is freshly killed, is correctly cleaned and fabricated, and is not of a species likely to contain parasites. However, not all types of shellfish are considered palatable when served raw. Preferences for raw shellfish are cultural. In Hawai'i and in Japan and other Asian countries, a wide range of shellfish is enjoyed raw. European and North American cuisines are more selective, mainly featuring raw bivalves. The following provides information on shellfish that North American chefs are most likely to serve raw.

Raw Oysters

Oysters, once plentiful, have dramatically declined due to overfishing and pollution. Today, they are expensive and considered a luxury. Oysters are bivalves with hard, rough shells of varying shape. The shells have a definitive top and bottom. The bottom shell is more cup-like, while the top shell is flatter. The flesh is very delicate and, when the oysters are fresh, contains a high percentage of fluid. The liquid surrounding the oyster is called oyster ***liquor*** (even though it does not contain alcohol). Oyster liquor is flavorful and should be reserved and used for soups and sauces.

Oysters harvested from more northerly, colder waters have a firm texture and a salty, tangy flavor. Southern oysters are softer in texture and are often less flavorful. Oysters are at their best in the cold months. Northern hemisphere oysters are in season from September through April. However, oysters from the Gulf of Mexico and from other parts of the world are now available year round.

Half-Shell Service

Oysters ***on the half-shell*** are freshly ***shucked*** (opened and the meat removed) and presented in their cup-shaped bottom shells. The procedure for shucking oysters is illustrated at right. Opening fresh oysters to order requires extra turn-out time and skilled labor.

Only freshly shucked oysters can be served raw on the half-shell. *Do not be tempted to serve commercially shucked and packed raw oysters on the half-shell or in any other raw presentation.* Raw oysters served on the half-shell must be very cold to highlight their texture and should be presented on a bed of crushed ice. In traditional oyster service, a lining of seaweed is placed between the ice and the oysters. If seaweed is not packed in with the oysters, a few parsley sprigs or some other greenery can be used to accent the presentation.

Oysters are traditionally served in multiples of six. Seafood restaurants often stock a variety, so a mix of types may be ordered. The server should tell the customer the name of each type on the plate.

While connoisseurs agree that a simple wedge of lemon is the best accompaniment to raw oysters, many North American customers expect a ketchup-horseradish cocktail sauce. In France, ***mignonette*** sauce [meen-yohn-ET], made from white wine, vinegar, and cracked peppercorns, is popular. Bread and butter, oyster crackers, or saltine crackers are the usual accompaniments. A small seafood fork is presented along with the oysters.

North American Oyster Species

North American Eastern oysters (*Crassostrea virginica*) are native to the East Coast. They vary in appearance and flavor, and are categorized by place of origin using various place-names.

European flat oysters (*Ostrea edulis*) today are farm raised. They are often called *Belon oysters*, but that name is properly used only for oysters grown in a specific location in France. Flat oysters have an intense, briny flavor and crisp texture.

Olympia oysters (*Ostrea lurida*) are the only oysters native to the North American west coast. The population was nearly destroyed by pollution and overfishing in the early twentieth century. Today the tiny, flavorful Olympia oyster is raised by aquaculture.

Pacific oysters (*Crassostrea gigas*) are indigenous to the waters around Japan and were introduced to North America's west coast in the 1920s. Most varieties are large in size and vary in flavor and texture.

Kumamoto oysters (*Crassostrea sikamea*) were introduced to the West Coast to replace the endangered Olympia oysters. "Kumas" are small and delicate, with a distinctive flavor.

Alternative Raw Oyster Service

An alternative to half-shell service is freshly shucked raw oysters served as an oyster cocktail (p. 198). The oysters, tossed with lemon juice or a light dressing, are placed in a chilled martini glass on a bed of shredded lettuce. Sometimes a spoonful of cocktail sauce is added or served on the side.

Oyster shooters are also popular. An ***oyster shooter*** is a freshly shucked oyster served in a chilled shot glass topped with a few drops of bottled hot sauce and a half-ounce of frozen vodka. In a brunch-style variation, the oyster is topped with vodka and Bloody Mary mix.

Opening oysters.

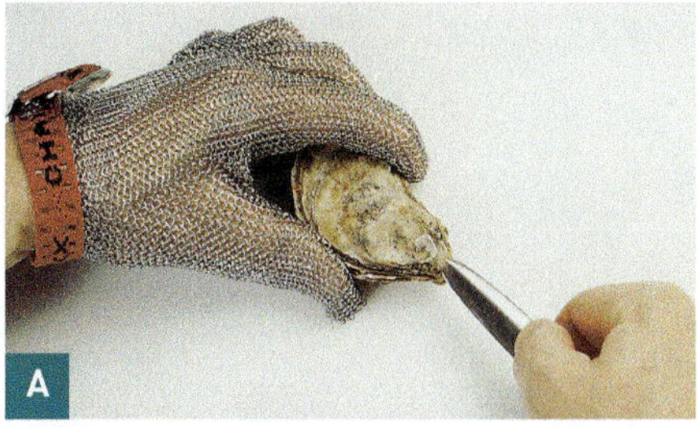

A

Examine the shell to see that it is tightly closed, indicating a live oyster. Rinse the shell under cold running water. Hold the oyster in your left hand, as shown. (Left-handers will hold the oyster in the right hand.) You should hold the oyster with a towel or wear a cut-proof glove to protect your hand. Hold the oyster knife near the tip as shown. Insert the knife between the shells near the hinge.

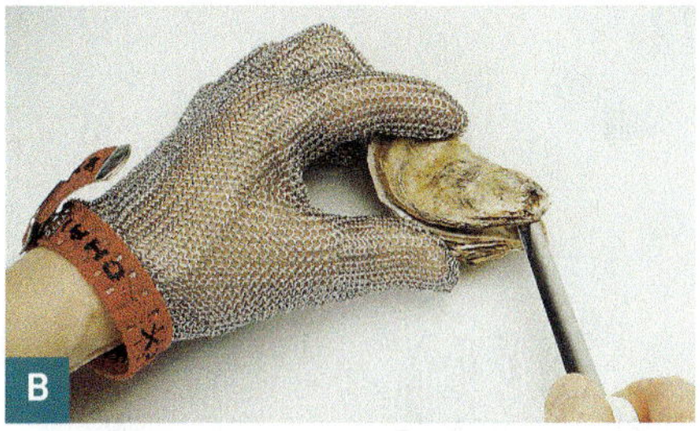

B

Twist the knife to break the hinge.

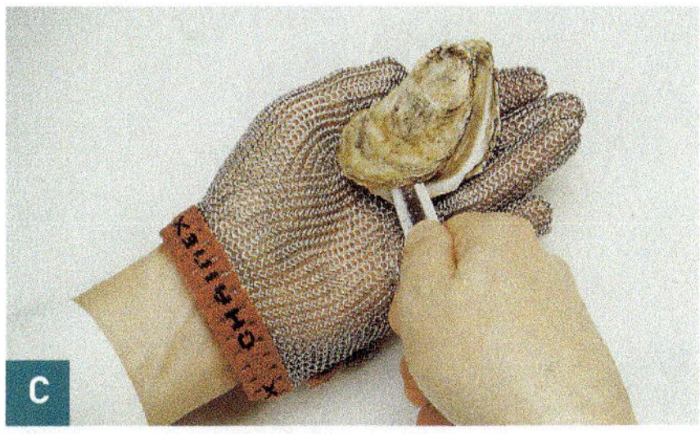

C

Slide the knife under the top shell and cut through the adductor muscle (which closes the shells) near the top shell. Try not to cut the flesh of the oyster, which would lose plumpness as a result. Remove the top shell.

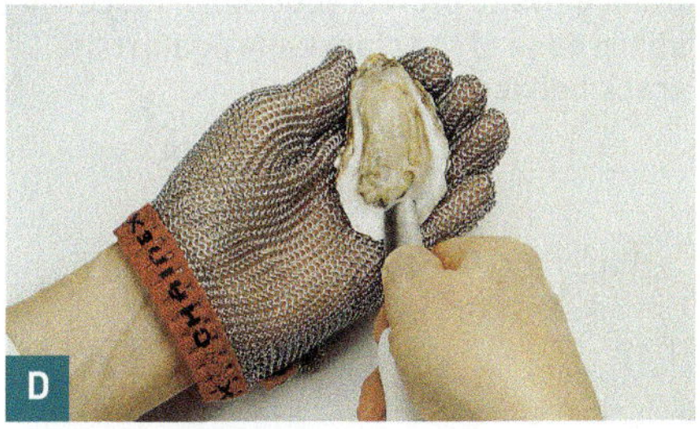

D

Carefully cut the lower end of the muscle from the bottom shell to loosen the oyster. Remove any shell particles from the oyster before serving.

Storing Live Oysters

Refrigerate live oysters in the container in which they were packed. Today, most dealers pack live oysters in cardboard boxes without ice or seaweed. If freshly harvested, oysters keep under refrigeration 5 or 6 days. Discard any open oysters that do not close when prodded or jostled. For prolonged storage, arrange oysters in drainer boxes between layers of damp newspaper. Do not wash or soak oysters in water until just before opening them.

Raw Clams

Raw clams are not as popular as raw oysters and tend to be a regional specialty. Clams on the half-shell are popular in New England and the Mid-Atlantic states, where they are featured on coastal seafood restaurant menus.

Virtually all of the information about purchasing, storing, opening, and serving raw oysters also applies to raw clams. The procedure for shucking clams is illustrated below.

Eastern Hard-Shell Clams

The only widely available clam suitable for serving raw is the Eastern hard-shell clam. These round, light gray clams are native to North America's east coast and have a natural range that extends from Canada to Florida. However, they are now being raised by aquaculture on the West Coast and in Hawai'i.

Eastern hard-shell clams have a crisp, firm texture and a fresh, briny flavor that is more pronounced than that of oysters. They are often served with cocktail sauce or bottled hot sauce as well as lemon wedges.

Opening clams

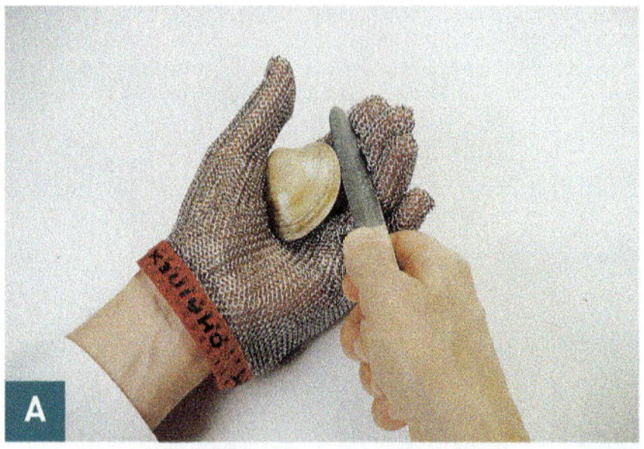

Examine the shell to see that it is tightly closed, indicating a live clam. Rinse the shell under cold running water. Avoid jostling the clam too much, or it will "clam up" tighter. Hold the clam in your left hand as shown (or in your right hand if you are left-handed), with a towel or wear a cut-proof glove to protect your hand. Place the sharp edge of the clam knife against the crack between the shells.

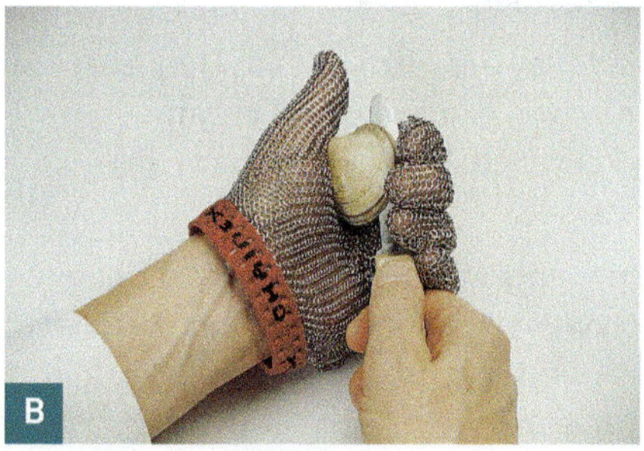

Squeeze with the fingers of the left hand, forcing the knife between the shells.

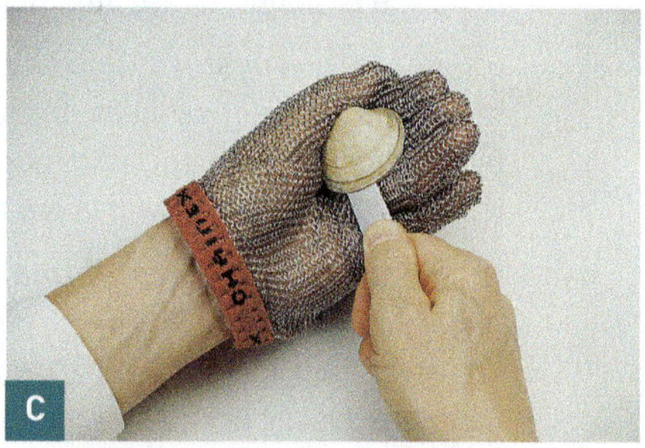

Change the angle of the blade as shown in the illustration and slide the knife against the top shell to cut the adductor muscles (clams have two; oysters have only one). Be careful not to cut or pierce the soft clam.

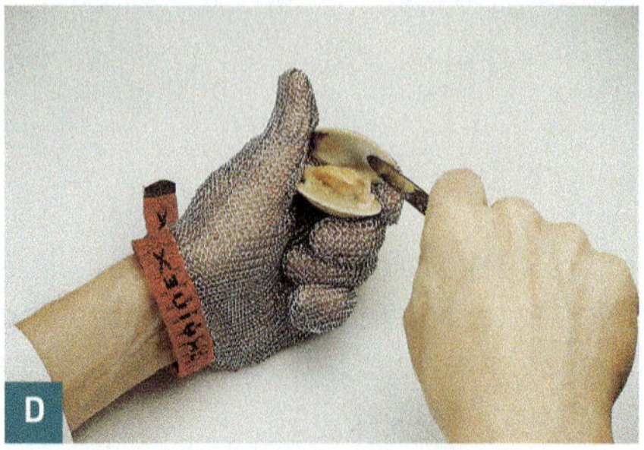

Open the clam and finish detaching the meat from the upper shell.

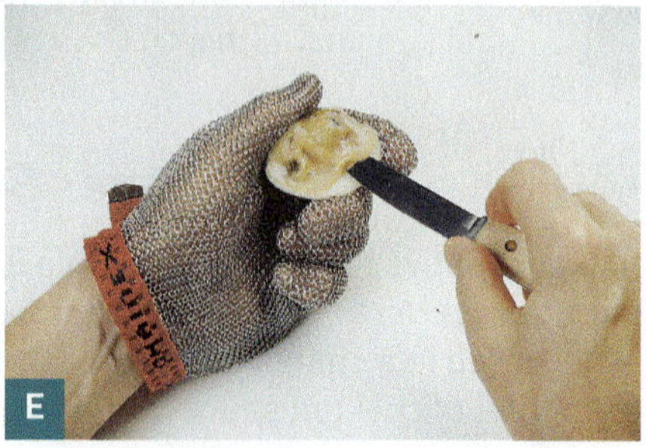

Cut the muscles against the lower shell to loosen the clam completely. Discard the top shell. Remove any shell particles from the clam before serving.

Eastern hard-shell clams are graded by size. The most common market sizes are:

1. Cherrystones, about 2 in. (5 cm) in diameter
2. Topnecks, about 1½ in. (4 cm) in diameter
3. Littlenecks, 1¼ in. (3.5 cm) in diameter or smaller

These size standards change from dealer to dealer, with several intermediate sizes available. When purchasing, specify an exact size in inches and measure the clams when they arrive.

Wild-harvested clams often contain sand or grit, and benefit from being purged. To ***purge***, or remove the sand from clams or other bivalves, place them in a bowl full of brine (3 oz/90 g kosher salt dissolved in 1 gal/4 L cold water) for 20 minutes. Alternatively, place them in a bowl in the sink under fast-running water for 10 minutes.

Raw Geoduck

Geoduck (GOO-ee-duck) is also called ***giant clam***. This huge Pacific clam can weigh up to 9 lb (4 kg), but it is usually harvested at 2–3 lb (1–1.5 kg). Geoducks are of the soft-shell clam variety, and have a long neck that is the primary edible part. To prepare shucked geoduck for raw service, first peel off the coarse, dark-brown sheath from the neck and trim away the membrane and connective tissue. Then slice the neck muscle paper-thin and serve it chilled. It is often served as sashimi.

Raw Mussels

In North America, mussels are almost always served cooked. However, pristinely fresh cultivated mussels from coldwater sources are delicious served raw on the half-shell. Customers who enjoy raw oysters and clams may be pleasantly surprised at an offering of raw mussels.

To open raw mussels, insert a sharp, thin-bladed paring knife at the place where the ***beard***, or hairy filament, protrudes, and draw the knife back toward the hinge. Remove the beard in its entirety, release the mussel from the bottom shell, and then replace it in the shell.

Raw Fish Specialties

In Japan, perfectly trimmed, precisely cut uncooked fish is traditionally eaten plain as sashimi or combined with vinegar-seasoned rice in the form of sushi. There is also a lesser-known tradition of eating raw fish in Italy. Until the late twentieth century, raw fish was not popular in North America. In the late 1970s, when increased travel and globalization led to greater interest in world cuisines, sushi bars became popular in Europe and in certain North American cities. Today, sashimi and sushi and other raw fish dishes appear on menus from coast to coast.

Asian-Inspired Raw Fish Dishes

In Japan, raw fish (and other raw seafood) is served in two distinct types of dish—sashimi and sushi.

SASHIMI

Sashimi consists of meticulously fabricated raw fish and other types of seafood, served simply and with few embellishments. The traditional accompaniments for sashimi are limited to light soy sauce, prepared ***wasabi*** (green horseradish), shredded ***daikon*** (white radish), and sometimes a slice of lemon.

SUSHI

Sushi is a dish consisting of cooked, cooled rice seasoned with vinegar, sugar, and salt, and served with a variety of garnishes. The most popular sushi varieties contain raw fish or other types of raw seafood. However, many types of sushi do not contain raw fish and may not contain any seafood at all.

There are many types of sushi and multiple variations for each type. In Japan, sushi chefs are specialists required to spend years in apprenticeship to a sushi master before being permitted to work on their own. However, simpler types of sushi can be mastered by a dedicated garde manger chef.

In Japanese cuisine, sushi is traditionally prepared à la carte and served immediately. In Western garde manger, sushi is often prepared in quantity and held for service. For this reason, in garde manger it is not always possible to follow traditional Japanese procedures. For example, in classic Japanese cuisine, the rice is cooled just until it is still slightly warm, and it is never refrigerated; sushi items are made to order and served immediately. In Western garde manger, made-up sushi items are held under refrigeration for safety reasons, but only for a short time.

European-Inspired Raw Fish Dishes

In most European countries, raw fish is not a part of traditional cuisine. However, many Europeans discovered raw fish dishes in the late 1970s when French chefs began to experiment with Asian ingredients and cooking methods. However, a little-known, traditional regional specialty of Italy's Adriatic coast features raw fish.

Pesce crudo [peh-shay KROO-doh] is Italian for "raw fish." Pristinely fresh thin-sliced fish is served with a sprinkling of coarse sea salt, a drizzle of extra-virgin olive oil, and a squeeze of lemon. Crusty Italian bread is the only other accompaniment. *Pesce crudo* has recently become popular in North American Italian restaurants and is served as an antipasto, or appetizer.

Two popular European-style raw fish dishes are modern adaptations of raw meat dishes. Carpaccio (p. 261) is now also made with sashimi-grade tuna. The bright red color of the fish is similar to the red color of the raw beef filet. Additionally, tuna tartare is now more frequently found on North American menus than the original beef dish, steak tartare (p. 262).

CLAMS OR OYSTERS ON THE HALF-SHELL

APPETIZER

Portions:
1
Portion size:
6 pieces

INGREDIENTS	U.S.	METRIC
Crushed ice	as needed	as needed
Seaweed or lettuce leaves	as needed	as needed
Cherrystone or topneck clams or shell oysters, chilled	6	6
Cocktail Sauce (p. 669)	1½ fl oz	45 mL
Lemon wedges	2	2
Crisp-crusted bread or dinner rolls	4 oz	120 g
-or-		
Oyster crackers	2 oz	60 g
Butter, softened, in pastry bag with large star tip	1 oz	30 g

PROCEDURE

PLATING

1. Line a deep-edged 12-in. (30-cm) tray with crushed ice. Arrange the seaweed or lettuce leaves on top.
2. Scrub the clams or oysters and open them as illustrated on pages 225 and 226. Place them hinge-side in around the tray.
3. Place the cocktail sauce in a 2-fl oz (60-mL) sauce cup and set it in the center of the tray. Garnish the tray with the lemon wedges.
4. Place the bread, rolls, or crackers in a napkin-lined basket. Pipe the butter into a 1-fl oz (30-mL) ramekin or butter chip and place it in the basket.

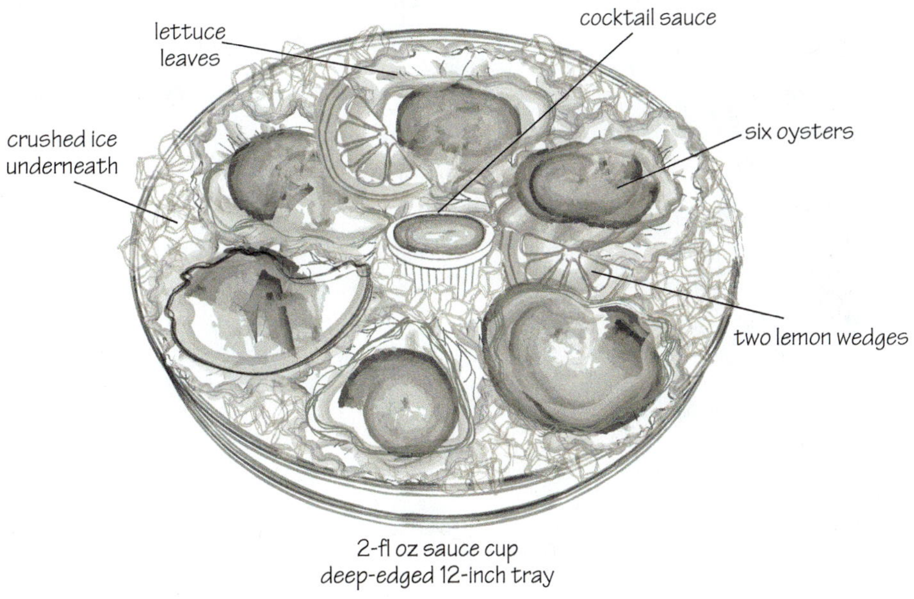

TUNA TARTARE COCKTAIL

APPETIZER

Portions:
1
Portion size:
5 oz (150 g)

INGREDIENTS	U.S.	METRIC
Trimmed sashimi-grade tuna	4 oz	120 g
Minced shallot	¼ oz	7 mL
Minced lemon zest	1 tsp	5 mL
Minced fresh parsley	1 tsp	5 mL
Minced chives	2 tsp	10 mL
Nonpareil capers	2 tsp	10 mL
Dijon mustard	1 tsp	5 mL
Fresh lemon juice	2 tsp	10 mL
Freshly ground white pepper	to taste	to taste
Fine sea salt or kosher salt	to taste	to taste
Extra-virgin olive oil	1 fl oz	30 mL
Bottled hot sauce	dash	dash
Chive tips	1 bouquet	1 bouquet
Freshly Toasted Baguette Croûtons (p. 702)	5 pieces	5 pieces
Supplies		
8-in. (20-cm) doily	1	1

PROCEDURE

FINISHING

1. Cut the tuna into ⅜-in. (1-cm) dice.
2. Toss the tuna with the shallots, zest, minced herbs, capers, mustard, lemon juice, salt, pepper, oil, and hot sauce. Taste and correct the seasonings, balancing them as necessary.

PLATING

3. Mound the tuna mixture in a chilled 8-fl oz (240-mL) martini glass and plant the chive bouquet in it. Place the glass on a doily-lined 8-in. (20-cm) plate.
4. Arrange the croûtons on the plate.

SUSHI

Yield:
about 2½ lb (1.1 kg) rice; garnishes as desired; 24–36 pieces

INGREDIENTS	U.S.	METRIC
Japanese short-grain rice	3 cups	750 mL
Water, cold	3½ cups	875 mL
Sushi vinegar (see Note)	3–4 fl oz	90–120 mL
Garnish	see variations	see variations

Note: Sushi vinegar is commercially available, but it can also be made in the kitchen. Combine 1 pt (500 mL) Japanese rice vinegar, 8 oz (250 g) sugar, and 4 oz (125 g) salt. Heat and stir until the sugar and salt are dissolved. Cool. Store in an airtight bottle.

PROCEDURE

1. Wash the rice in several changes of cold water. Drain well.
2. Put the drained rice in a heavy saucepan and add the measured water. Cover tightly and let stand at least 30 minutes.
3. With the cover in place, set the pan over high heat and bring to the boil. Reduce the heat to medium and let cook until the water is absorbed. If possible, do not remove the cover to check, but listen to the sounds. The bubbling will stop and there will be a faint hissing sound.
4. Reduce the heat to very low and cook another 5 minutes. Then, without removing the cover, remove the pan from the heat and let stand at least 15 minutes. (You now have the basic white rice that is eaten with Japanese meals.)
5. Transfer the rice to a clean mixing bowl.
6. Using a spatula, break up the hot rice to get rid of the lumps. At the same time, fan the rice to cool it.
7. When the rice is slightly warm, begin adding the sushi vinegar. Add a little at a time while mixing gently. The rice is ready when it has a glossy appearance and a very mild taste of the vinegar.
8. Prepare sushi with desired garnish, as detailed in the variations on the next page. The vinegared rice is best if used within 2–3 hours.

(continues)

Selected Sushi Varieties

Nigirizushi: **An oblong mound of vinegared rice topped with sliced raw fish or another topping.**

Norimaki sushi: **Vinegared rice and various fillings rolled in nori (pressed, dried seaweed) and then sliced.**

Kakomi sushi **or** ***gunkan maki:*** **A mound of vinegared rice inside a band of nori that holds loose toppings in place.**

Temaki: **A cone of nori with vinegared rice and filling, also known as a hand-roll.**

Chirashizushi: **A bowl or bento box of vinegared rice topped with an arrangement of raw or cooked items.**

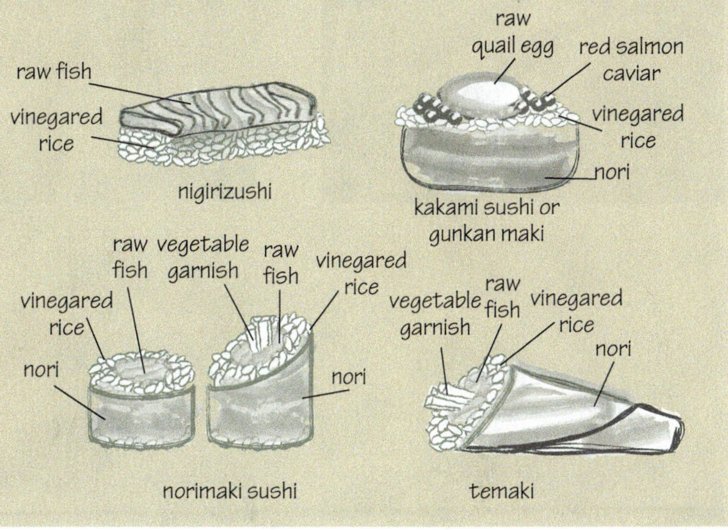

VARIATIONS

NIGIRIZUSHI (FINGER SUSHI)

1. Prepare *wasabi* (green horseradish) by mixing wasabi powder with a little water to form a thick paste. Let stand, covered, a few minutes to allow flavor to develop.
2. Prepare sushi toppings:
   a. Cut very fresh saltwater fish fillets into slices about 1½ × 2½ in. (4 × 6 cm). Tuna, the most popular fish for sushi, and hamachi (yellowtail) are tender and are usually cut about ⅜ in. (1 cm) thick. Other fish are cut thinner.
   b. To prepare shrimp for sushi, insert a bamboo skewer lengthwise between the shell and flesh to keep the shrimp straight during cooking. Poach in salted water until just firm (A). Shell and devein, but keep the tail attached. Butterfly and flatten the shrimp.
3. Have ready a bowl containing 1 pt (500 mL) water mixed with 1 fl oz (30 mL) rice vinegar.
4. Wet your hands with the vinegared water to keep the rice from sticking to them, then pick up about 2 tbsp (30 mL) sushi rice. Shape it into a firm oval about 1½ in. (4 cm) long (B). Pick up a slice of fish or a shrimp in one hand. Dip a finger of the other hand in the wasabi and spread a very small amount on the underside of the fish (C). Drape the fish over the rice, with the wasabi underneath, and press it gently but firmly in place (D, E).

NORIMAKI SUSHI

To make rolled sushi, you need a special bamboo mat called a *sudare* (soo -DAH-ray). Make regular rolls with ½ sheet *nori* seaweed. Thicker rolls require a full sheet. The following examples illustrate the basic techniques, which can be used for a great variety of fillings.

TEKKA-MAKI OR MAGURO MAKI (TUNA ROLL)

1. Cut sushi-grade tuna into bâtonnets; alternatively, cut tuna trimmings into small dice.
2. Place the bamboo mat on the table in front of you, with the bamboo strips horizontal. Put a half-sheet of nori on the mat, smooth side down.
3. Moisten your hand with the vinegar water and spread an even layer of sushi rice, about ¼ in. (6 mm) thick, on the nori, leaving a 1-in. (2.5-cm) border at the far edge.
4. Optional step: Spread a light streak of wasabi from right to left across the middle of the rice.
5. Arrange the tuna in a strip from right to left across the middle of the rice.
6. Lift the edge of the mat closest to you and roll up firmly. This is best done by lifting the mat with the thumbs while holding the filling in place with the fingers (F). Press the roll in the mat gently but firmly to make it tight (G).
7. If you are making the rolls in advance, arrange them on trays, cover, and refrigerate until needed.
8. To cut, wipe the blade of a very sharp knife on a damp towel, then cut the roll in half crosswise. Do not saw the roll but rather cut it cleanly with a single stroke. Wiping the blade on a damp cloth after every cut, cut each half-roll into 3 pieces (H).

A

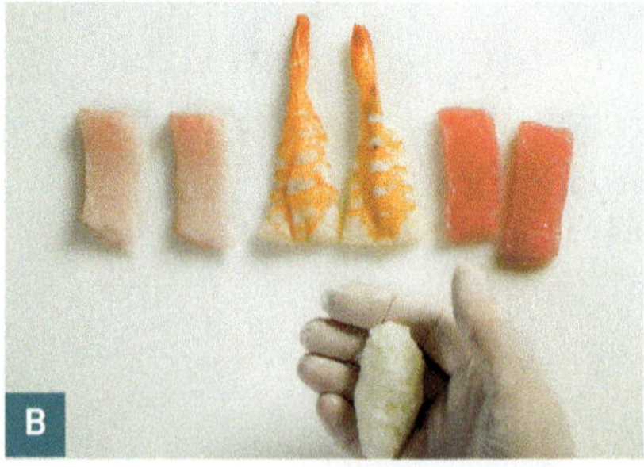
B

C

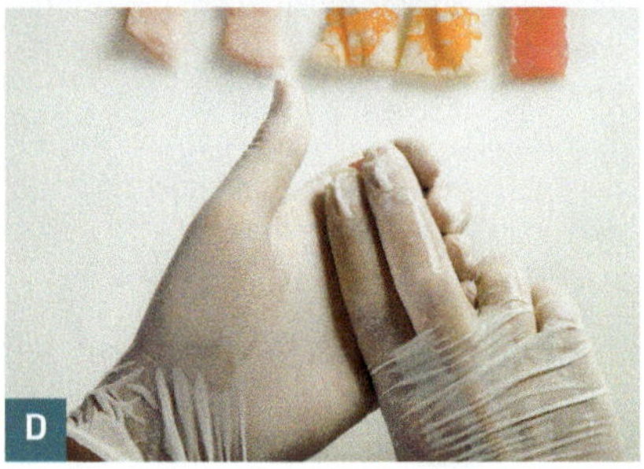
D

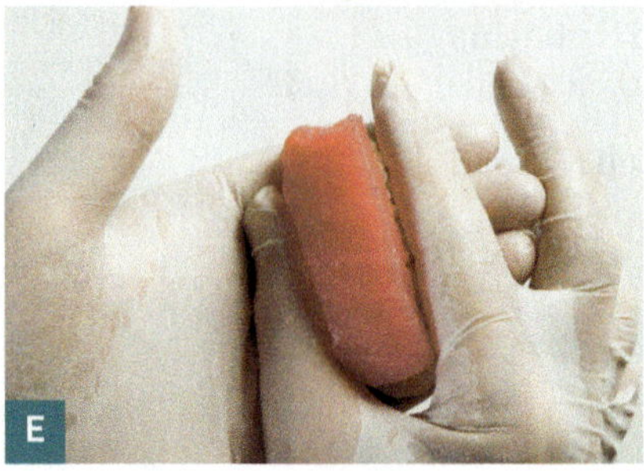
E

F

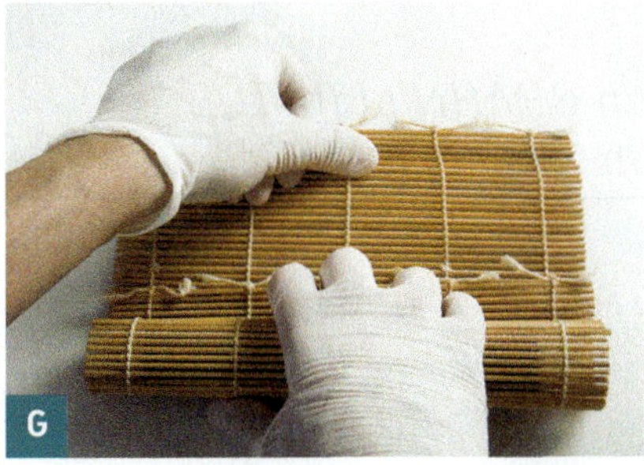

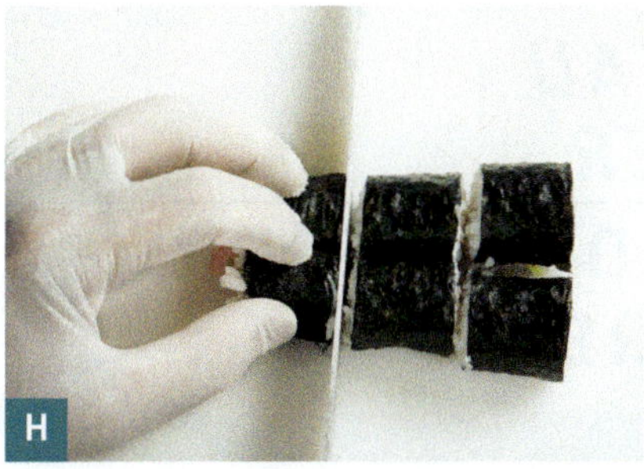

VARIATIONS

CRAB ROLL WITH CUCUMBER AND AVOCADO

1. Have ready the following ingredients for the filling: crabmeat, picked clean of all trace of shell; avocado, cut into thin, short slices and tossed with a little salt and lime juice; and cucumber, cut julienne.
2. Place a full sheet of nori, shiny side down, on the bamboo mat.
3. Wetting the hands with the vinegar water, spread an even layer of sushi rice, about ¼ in. (6 mm) thick, on the nori, leaving a 1-in. (2.5-cm) border at the far edge.
4. Arrange the crab, avocado, and cucumber in a strip from right to left across the middle of the rice (I).
5. Roll, store, and cut as in the above procedure.

SEAFOOD SUSHI ASSORTMENT

The illustration shows a typical presentation of an assortment of seafood sushi, consisting of tuna and hamachi (yellowtail) nigirizushi and tuna and crab rolls. Traditional accompaniments are pickled ginger slices, a dab of wasabi shaped into a rough cone, and soy sauce. The diner makes a dipping sauce by pouring soy sauce into a small dish and mixing in wasabi to taste.

LE GRAND PLATEAU DE FRUITS DE MER

[luh GRAHN plah-TOE duh fwee duh MARE]

DELUXE SEAFOOD PLATTER FOR TWO OR MORE

APPETIZER OR MAIN COURSE

Portions: *2 or more*
Portion Size: *varies*

INGREDIENTS	U.S.	METRIC
Crushed ice	as needed	as needed
Fresh seaweed or kale leaves	as needed	as needed
Lemon crown (p. 716)	1	1
In-shell oysters of choice	6	6
In-shell topneck clams	6	6
Steamed and chilled coldwater lobster, about 1 lb (500 g)	1	1
Poached Shrimp for Cocktail, 21/25 ct. (p. 197)	6	6
Cooked, chilled crab claws of choice	6	6
Lemon, cut into wedges and seeded	½	½
Tomato cup (p. 717)	1	1
Tuna Tartare (p. 230)	5 oz	150 g
Mussels, steamed, chilled, and bearded, on the half-shell	1 lb	0.5 kg
Lemon Mayonnaise Sauce for Seafood (p. 43)	3 fl oz	90 mL
Sauce Mignonette (p. 691)	3 fl oz	90 mL
Salted butter, whipped, room temperature	2 oz	60 g
Country-style white bread	4 oz	60 g
Crisp baguette	4 oz	60 g
Supplies		
10-in. (25-cm) doily or linen napkin	1	1

PROCEDURE

PLATING

1. Assemble the bottom tier:
   a. Fill the bottom tray of a 3-tier seafood stand with crushed ice and line it with seaweed or kale leaves. Place the lemon crown in the center.
   b. Open the oysters and clams, and arrange them around the lemon crown.
   c. Place the tray in the stand.
2. Assemble the middle tier:
   a. Line the middle tray with crushed ice and seaweed or kale.
   b. Cut the lobster in half lengthwise and remove the gills. Crack the claws. Entwine the two halves to make a circle. Place the lobsters in the middle of the tray.
   c. Arrange the shrimp around one side of the tray.
   d. Arrange the crab claws around the other side of the tray.
   e. Garnish with lemon wedges.
   f. Place the tray in the stand.
3. Assemble the top tier:
   a. Fill the tray with crushed ice and line it with seaweed or kale leaves.

PROCEDURE

- b. Fill the tomato cup with tuna tartare and place it in the center of the tray.
- c. Arrange the mussels around the tomato cup.
- d. Place the tray in the stand.

4. Assemble the accompaniments tray:
   - a. Line a 12-in. (30-cm) tray with a doily or linen napkin.
   - b. Place the sauces and butter in 3½-fl oz (100-mL) ramekins and set them in the middle of the tray.
   - c. Slice the country bread thin and arrange it on one side of the tray.
   - d. Slice the baguette in half as for a tartine (p. 336) and then cut the tartines into 1-in. (2.5-cm) pieces. Arrange the baguette pieces on the other side of the tray.

CAVIAR

Caviar is the preserved roe, or eggs, of fish. In Europe, only the roe of certain species of Eurasian sturgeon processed in a special manner can legally be called caviar. In North America, the term is also used to describe the roe of other fish, provided the type of fish is specified. For example, the processed roe of Great Lakes whitefish may be called whitefish caviar. However, when a container is simply labeled *caviar*, its contents must be Eurasian sturgeon caviar and have no other ingredient except salt.

Eurasian Sturgeon Caviar

Eurasian sturgeon caviar is harvested from the Black and Caspian seas, and from their tributary rivers. It ranks as one of the most highly prized and most expensive foods in the world, typically selling for more than $1,000 per pound. To differentiate wild Eurasian sturgeon caviar from other types, we refer to it as *true caviar*.

True caviar has a complex, deeply savory flavor and a unique mouthfeel. Top-grade true caviar is processed with a minimum of salt (2–6%), and is labeled ***malassol***, meaning "little salt" in Russian. Its taste is briny but not excessively salty. One of the most compelling characteristics of true caviar is its mouthfeel, which is very rich from its natural oil content. The individual eggs, called ***berries***, are firm and turgid. They pop when pressed with the tongue, releasing a burst of flavor.

The best true caviar is stored under refrigeration and sold fresh. Amounts less than 4 oz (120 g) are usually packed in glass jars. Larger quantities are packed in specially lined metal tins, the largest of which weighs 2.2 lb (1 kg). True caviar is graded on the basis of color, with 000 allotted to caviar of the palest hue and 0 to the darkest. Connoisseurs believe lighter color indicates finer flavor.

Sometimes, true and other caviars are pasteurized for longer shelf life. However, exposing caviar to heat of any kind changes both its flavor and texture. Pasteurized true caviar is usually just as expensive as the fresh variety, but it is inferior in quality.

Three types of Eurasian sturgeon produce caviar. The caviar product is named after the type of sturgeon from which it is harvested.

1. ***Beluga caviar*** [beh-LOO-gah] consists of large separate berries ranging from pale to dark gray in color. It has a mild, buttery, creamy flavor. Beluga is considered the finest type of caviar and is in the greatest demand.

2. ***Osetra caviar*** [oh-SET-tra] consists of medium-sized berries ranging from the very rare golden color to brown and brownish-black. Osetra has a distinctive nutty flavor.

Why Is Caviar So Expensive?

A number of factors contribute to the high cost of true caviar. Most crucial is that the population of caviar-producing sturgeon has been in decline for more than 100 years. A female European sturgeon must reach a mature age in order to produce roe for caviar. This can take as long as 20 years. The roe must be harvested from the live fish, which then dies without reproducing. Thus the production of caviar contributes to the endangerment of sturgeon species. Pollution and increased marine traffic in traditional sturgeon breeding grounds have accelerated the decline.

High labor costs are involved in processing caviar. Wild sturgeon are difficult to catch, and sturgeon fishing is dangerous. Once caught, the female sturgeon must be slaughtered by hand. The delicate roe must be removed immediately and with extreme care. After the eggs are separated from the roe sacs, they must be washed and drained, inspected and graded by an experienced master grader, and then salted and packed. This entire process must be done by hand.

Although preserved with salt, fresh caviar is highly perishable. It must be kept under constant refrigeration and consumed within a relatively short time of processing.

Demand also increases price. When demand rises, prices rise accordingly.

Finally, virtually all true caviar comes from Russia and Iran, both nations that have had major political differences with the United States. Political affairs, including economic sanctions, have frequently affected the availability of true caviar in the United States.

3. ***Sevruga caviar*** [sev-ROO-gah] consists of tiny, tightly clustered berries ranging from brown to black. It has a strong, assertive flavor.

In addition to these three types, an additional true caviar product is available.

4. ***Pressed caviar*** usually consists of beluga, osetra, and sevruga berries that are over-mature or that have been physically damaged during harvest or processing. The crushed or broken berries are mixed together, salted a little more heavily than intact berries, packed into forms, and compressed under weights. The result is a dense, cakelike caviar mass with a strong flavor and a texture like jam.

Other Types of Caviar

The roe of fish other than Eurasian sturgeon is now processed in the same or similar manner as true caviar. The flavor and mouthfeel of these caviars depends on the type of fish and the processing technique used.

American white sturgeon caviar farmed in the Northwest Pacific is considered the finest of alternative caviars. Similar in quality to true caviar, it is processed with minimal salt and sold fresh. It should be served in the same manner as true caviar.

Paddlefish caviar is farmed in the American West and Midwest. Paddlefish, or spoonbills, are an ancient fish species related to sturgeon. The caviar has medium-sized berries available in gray and golden colors. It has a mild flavor.

Hackleback caviar is harvested from the hackleback sturgeon. It is similar to paddlefish caviar.

Bowfin caviar/choupique [shoo-PEEK] is harvested from a sturgeon-like fish native to the southern Mississippi. It consists of large, dark gray berries that turn red when heated.

Salmon caviar consists of very large, bright red eggs with a jelly-like texture. It has a strong flavor and oily mouthfeel.

Golden whitefish caviar is mostly produced in Montana from freshwater whitefish. It is mild in flavor and has a distinctive, crunchy texture.

Lumpfish caviar is one of the most widely available low-cost caviars. Lumpfish roe is virtually tasteless and used primarily as a garnish. In its natural state this caviar has an unappealing beige-gray color, so it is tinted with food dye by the processor into black, red, and golden varieties. When garnishing foods with dyed lumpfish caviar, you should add it to the food at the last minute because it will eventually bleed color and stain the food it garnishes.

Flying fish roe/tobiko consists of tiny eggs with a firm, crunchy texture and mild flavor. Tobiko, in its natural state, is orange-red in color. Tobiko is also tinted and flavored by the processor.

Capelin roe/masago is similar to tobiko. It is more highly processed than tobiko and often contains artificial sweeteners and flavorings.

The History of Caviar

The history of caviar is a rollercoaster ride of scarcity and plenty, of high demand and oversupply. During the Roman Empire, caviar ranked among the most prized of foods. Caviar was transported on ice from the Black and Caspian seas to Rome, at great cost, and was enjoyed only by the aristocracy. After the fall of Rome, demand fell and caviar became little more than a byproduct of sturgeon fishing. Russian peasants allegedly processed caviar in their kitchens and consumed it by the bowlful. But in the eighteenth century, caviar became a favorite food of Russian czars and Persian princes, and soon all of Europe was paying high prices for it.

In the early 1800s, German immigrants began to harvest and process Delaware River sturgeon caviar and market it to luxury hotels and restaurants in New York City. By the middle of the nineteenth century, America was producing 90% of the world's caviar. But the boom was short-lived. By 1900, the eastern sturgeon population was totally depleted. America's original caviar sturgeon are extinct.

The world turned once again to Russia and Iran, and prices soared. But overfishing, pollution, and political upheaval took their toll on caviar production throughout the twentieth century. Caviar once again became scarce and expensive.

Attempts are being made at sturgeon aquaculture in Europe and North America. Caviar produced in America, harvested from both western sturgeon and related fish species, is once again respected by caviar connoisseurs. Sales of North American caviar equal and often surpass sales of caviar imported from Russia and Iran.

Tarama is the Greek name for a variety of salted and pressed fish roes. Its actual content varies by producer and by country of origin. It is rarely eaten as is but instead is mashed and blended with olive oil, bread, or puréed potatoes.

Bottarga is the Italian name for the salted, pressed roe sac of tuna or gray mullet. It is used as a condiment and is often shaved or grated over pasta or risotto.

Caviar Service

Caviar tastes best served very cold. It is traditional to present caviar on ice. Simply press the container of caviar into a bowl of crushed ice and set the bowl on a plate or tray lined with a linen napkin. The ice may be decorated with parsley sprigs or edible flowers.

Caviar berries are easily crushed or broken when transferred from the original container into another vessel. Further, repeatedly inserting a utensil into a caviar container can contaminate the contents. For these reasons, it is traditional to present caviar in the jar or tin in which it was originally packed. Thus, many chefs choose to order caviar in 1-oz (28-g) jars at a higher per-serving cost rather than store a larger container that has been opened. If you must remove portions of caviar from a container, handle it gently with a disposable plastic spoon and avoid cross-contamination by using a fresh spoon each time. Do not touch the caviar with your fingers.

Caviar is typically served with toast, croûtons, or ***blini*** [BLEE-nee] (p. 755), very small, thin buckwheat pancakes. High-quality fresh caviar—particularly true Eurasian sturgeon caviar—needs no other accompaniment or topping. Its unique taste and texture should not be masked by strong-flavored garnishes. Although lemon wedges are frequently served, the best caviar has its own sweet-salt-acid balance and should be enjoyed as is.

Pressed caviar and other lesser-quality caviars often are served with lemon wedges and small ramekins of chopped hard-cooked egg white, sieved hard-cooked egg yolk, brunoise-cut red onion, and crème fraîche or sour cream.

Caviar is traditionally served with a small spoon made of ivory, bone, horn, or mother-of-pearl. Silver utensils chemically react with the flavor compounds in caviar and impart an unpleasant metallic taste. Utensils made of stainless steel are not considered appropriate for caviar service, even though this metal is nonreactive.

Storing Fresh Caviar

Unopened containers of fresh caviar may be stored at 28°–32°F (–2°–0° C) for two to three weeks without loss of quality. Keep the containers in the refrigerator in a bed of crushed ice in a drainer box. The containers should be turned over at one- or two-day intervals to keep all the berries in contact with the caviar oil.

Cover the surface of an open caviar container with plastic film and keep the container tightly closed. Avoid cross-contamination by using a fresh disposable plastic spoon each time you remove some caviar from the container. An open container of fresh caviar should be used within three days.

Fresh caviar has a clean, briny smell similar to that of the ocean at high tide. It should not smell fishy. The berries, or eggs, should be intact, plump, and separate. The berries should be coated in thick, natural oil. The oil should be smooth and free-flowing and should not appear sticky or tacky. Caviar that does not meet these guidelines cannot be served and should be discarded.

CLASSIC CAVIAR PRESENTATION FOR TWO

APPETIZER

Portions:
2
Portion size:
1 oz

INGREDIENTS	U.S.	METRIC
Crushed ice	as needed	as needed
Caviar	2 oz	(56 g)
Parsley sprigs	½ oz	(15 g)
Seeded lemon wedges	5	5
Freshly *Toasted Baguette Croûtons (p. 702)* or freshly made *Blini (p. 755)*	as needed	as needed

PROCEDURE

PLATING

1. Fill an 8-in. (20-cm) bowl with crushed ice.
2. a. If the caviar is in a 1-oz (28-g) jar, use the jar to make a depression in the center of the ice, then remove the jar.
   b. If the caviar is in a larger volume jar or tin, choose a 1-fl oz (30-mL) ramekin or dip dish and use it to make the depression as in step 2a. Place the ramekin on a scale and tare the scale to 0. Use a fresh, disposable plastic spoon to place 1 oz (28 g) caviar into the ramekin.
3. Arrange the parsley sprigs with the stems in the ice depression and the leaves sticking out.
4. Place the caviar jar or ramekin in the depression.
5. Arrange the lemon wedges on the ice around the caviar.
6. Place a folded linen napkin on a 10-in. (25-cm) plate and set the bowl inside the folds.
7. Arrange the croûtons or blini inside the folds.

DOMESTIC CAVIAR FOR TWO

APPETIZER

Portions:
2
Portion size:
1 oz (28 g)

INGREDIENTS	U.S.	METRIC
Crushed ice	as needed	as needed
Domestic caviar of desired type	2 oz	60 g
Parsley sprigs	2 oz	60 g
Lemon, cut into wedges and seeded	¼	¼
Chopped hard-cooked egg white	½ oz	15 g
Sieved hard-cooked egg yolk	½ oz	15 g
Red onion, cut brunoise	1 oz	30 g
Crème fraîche or sour cream	1¼ fl oz	45 mL
Freshly *Toasted Baguette Croûtons (p. 702)*	8 pieces	8 pieces
Belgian endive, crisped in ice water	8 leaves	8 leaves
Supplies		
12-in. (30-cm) paper doily	1	1

PROCEDURE

PLATING

1. Place the doily on a 14-in. (35-cm) round tray.
2. Fill a 5-in. (12-cm) diameter bowl or shrimp cocktail chiller with crushed ice.
3. a. If the caviar is in a 2-fl oz (60-mL) jar, use the jar to make a depression in the center of the ice, then remove the jar.
   b. If the caviar is in a larger volume jar or tin, choose a 2-fl oz (60-mL) ramekin or dip dish and use it to make the depression as in step 3a. Place the ramekin on a scale and tare the scale to 0. Carefully spoon 2 oz (60 g) caviar into the ramekin.
4. Arrange the parsley sprigs with the stems in the ice depression and the leaves sticking out.
5. Place the open caviar jar or ramekin in the depression.
6. Arrange the lemon wedges on the ice around the caviar.
7. Place the bowl in the center of the tray and surround it with more parsley sprigs.
8. Place the egg white, egg yolk, onion, and crème fraîche in four 1½-fl oz (40-mL) ramekins or dip dishes and arrange the dishes on the tray around the bowl.
9. Arrange the croûtons at 12 o'clock and 6 o'clock.
10. Drain the Belgian endive leaves and blot them dry. Arrange them at 3 o'clock and 9 o'clock.

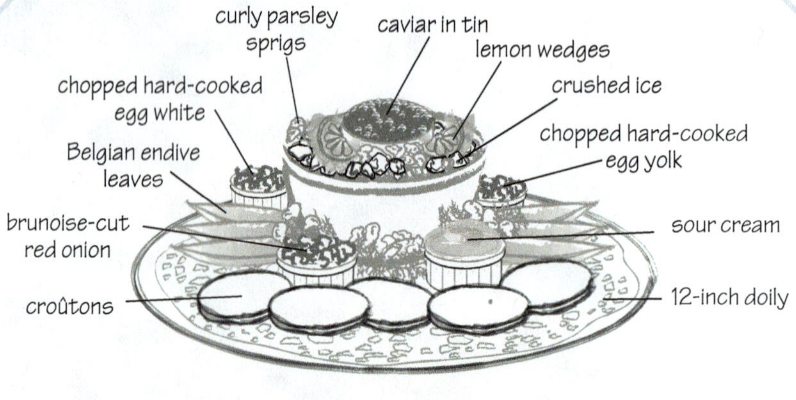

5-inch diameter bowl
4 (1 ½-fl oz) ramekins
14-inch tray

TERMS FOR REVIEW

seafood
seafood cocktail
shrimp cocktail chiller
cocktail sauce
poach
cuisson
shallow poach
court bouillon
nage
brine
carryover cooking
steaming
pan-steaming
seviche
ceviche
poke
mousse
purée base
lightening ingredient
stabilizer
folding
lightening the base
raw bar
sashimi-grade
cutproof glove
filter-feeder
aquaculture
farm-raised
depuration system
depurated
(bivalve) liquor
on the half-shell
shucked
mignonette
oyster shooter
purge
geoduck
giant clam
beard
sashimi
wasabi
daikon
sushi
pesce crudo
caviar
malassol
berries
beluga
osetra
sevruga
pressed caviar
blini

QUESTIONS FOR DISCUSSION

1. List and define the classifications of seafood.
2. Explain how to poach fish or shellfish for cold service. Include in your explanation the three types of *cuisson* used for seafood and how you would handle carryover cooking.
3. Compare and contrast pan-steaming and shallow-poaching.
4. Discuss the concept of "cooking" seafood with acidic ingredients. Explain the science behind this method.
5. Explain how to prepare a seafood mousse. Include in your explanation the basic ingredients ratio and the special techniques needed.
6. Discuss quality and safety standards for serving raw fish and shellfish.
7. Define the term *caviar*. List the four types of true caviar. List several types of domestic caviar.
8. Using your imagination and the information in this chapter, write a recipe for your own signature cold seafood appetizer.

Chapter 7

PREREQUISITES

Before studying this chapter, you should already

- Have read "How to Use This Book," pages xxviii–xxxiii, and understand the professional recipe format.
- Be familiar with standard cuts of meat and poultry.
- Know how to determine tenderness or toughness in a cut of meat or poultry.
- Have mastered basic meat and poultry cooking methods used for hot service.
- Know how to judge the internal doneness of meat and poultry by both touch and temperature.
- Know and observe food safety practices for protein-based foods to be served cold.

Cold Meats

Meats served cold, or at room temperature, are an important element of garde manger work. For the purposes of this chapter, when we refer to *meats* we mean the flesh of both mammals and birds. In other words, we are primarily speaking of beef, lamb, pork, poultry, and game.

Cold cooked meats are the mainstay of the sandwich board and are important elements in the preparation of many complex salads. In high-level garde manger work, such as formal buffets and culinary competitions, cold meat dishes provide an opportunity to create elegant and elaborate presentations. Whether your operation is casual or formal, the preparation of cold meats is an essential skill you must master to become a successful garde manger chef.

After reading this chapter, you should be able to

1. Prepare attractive, profitable deli trays.
2. Roast, grill, and poach meats and poultry for cold presentations.
3. Carve roasted meats and poultry correctly and efficiently.
4. Fabricate cold meats and poultry for use in sandwiches, complex salads, and other garde manger preparations.
5. Prepare cold meats and poultry for formal buffet presentations.

APPLICATIONS FOR COLD MEATS

Cold meats are utilized in many ways within food-service operations.

Cold Meats for Sandwiches

Cold meats are most frequently used as a filling for sandwiches. Sandwiches may be made with industrially produced luncheon meats or with meats cooked in-house. Sandwich making and purchased meats for use in sandwiches are discussed in Chapter 9. In this chapter, we focus on how to roast, poach, and otherwise cook meats to be used in cold sandwiches. In addition, we discuss the various ways in which both types of sandwich meats may be presented.

Deli Trays

A ***deli tray*** can be thought of as a portable do-it-yourself sandwich station. Deli trays usually consist of industrially produced luncheon meats and cheeses sliced thin by machine, garnished with vegetables, and accompanied by spreads and condiments. Offering a variety of high-end, themed deli trays can increase sales and enhance the reputation of your operation. For example, you might list an Italian deli tray featuring coppa ham, mortadella, soppresatta, prosciutto, and provolone cheese accompanied by Italian rolls and condiments.

Hand-Carved Meats

To ***carve*** means to fabricate a large cut of cooked meat into pieces or portions. Today, most cooked meats for sandwiches are carved in the kitchen, out of sight of the guests. However, some buffet operations feature ***carving stations***, or displays at which chefs slice hot or cold meats to order.

When you add the word *hand-carved* to the name of a sandwich or platter, you add the impression of quality. You also imply that the meat in question has been roasted or otherwise cooked in-house. Roast beef, pork, ham, and turkey are the most frequent choices for hand-carved presentation. With few exceptions, tender cuts of beef and pork, such as loin or tenderloin and top round or fresh ham, are used. Cold leg of lamb is also popular in Europe and in some regions of North America.

Until prefabricated, boneless cuts of meat became widely available, large, bone-in roasts were the norm. Today, most meats and poultry are boned out before they are cooked, so carving them is less complicated. However, garde manger chefs still must acquire and practice basic carving skills for both bone-in meats and whole birds. Diagrams for carving a whole fowl and a leg of meat are on page 245.

When carving, look carefully for the meat's grain and cut the meat across the grain to achieve a tender mouthfeel. Slices should be evenly cut and average ⅛–¼ in. (3.5–7 mm) in thickness. Excess fat, all silverskin, and any soft exterior skin of poultry should be trimmed off either before or after slicing.

Cold Meats for Complex Salads

Many of the complex salads featured in Chapter 5 are based on cold cooked meats and poultry. Both the cooking method and the fabrication technique used to prepare meats and poultry depend on the type of salad you are making.

The Changing Role of Cold Meat Dishes

Until the late 1800s, most hotels, restaurants, and affluent homes served a multi-course, hot main meal at noon or during the early afternoon. The evening meal was then based on large joints of meat or whole fowl that had been roasted in the afternoon to be served cold at a later hour, when most of the staff were off duty. Cold sauces, cold vegetable dishes, salads, and breads accompanied these cold meat dishes.

Today, the hot main meal is now eaten in the evening. Cold meats are generally served at lunchtime and are most frequently used as components in sandwiches and salads. Cold meat entrées are featured in upscale box lunches or as part of deluxe picnic baskets.

However, there are still evening occasions for which cold meats are appropriate and welcome. Beautifully displayed roasts of meat and poultry often serve as the centerpiece of a late-evening cold buffet. In restaurants the more complex cold meat dishes, such as mousses and mousselines, make good appetizers and may also be served as light dinner entrées in hot weather.

Guidelines for Making Deli Trays

- Line deli trays with lettuce leaves before placing the meats and cheeses on them. If lettuce is an appropriate addition to the sandwiches, add several layers of lettuce leaves or offer more lettuce on the side.
- Provide about 4 oz (120 g) total meat and 1 oz (30 g) total cheese per serving, plus about 10% extra to ensure all guests will have enough.
- Provide 1–1½ fl oz (30–45 mL) total spreads and condiments per serving. Guests will need a smaller amount of strong-tasting items, such as mustards, and a greater amount of mild-tasting items, such as mayonnaise.
- Separate the slices of meat and cheese, and fold or roll them into attractive shapes before placing them on the tray. This makes the tray look fuller and enables customers to select individual items more easily.
- Slice rolls and breads before service.
- Wrap the deli tray and all accompaniments airtight to prevent drying out or staling. If using a disposable tray, make sure the lid is securely fastened onto it.
- Provide tongs or serving forks for the meats and appropriate utensils for serving the spreads and condiments.

A well-prepared deli tray is attractive and designed for easy service.
Courtesy iStockphoto.

Carving a whole turkey.

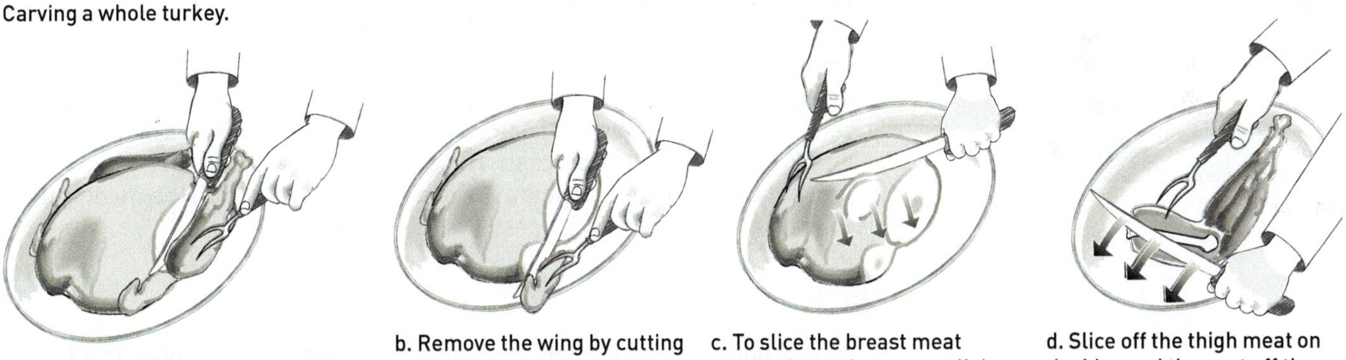

a. Bend back the leg and sever it from the carcass by cutting through the joint.

b. Remove the wing by cutting on the diagonal through the joint.

c. To slice the breast meat across the grain, cut parallel to the breastbone at a slight angle.

d. Slice off the thigh meat on the bias and then cut off the drumstick meat in two or three pieces.

Carving a leg of lamb.

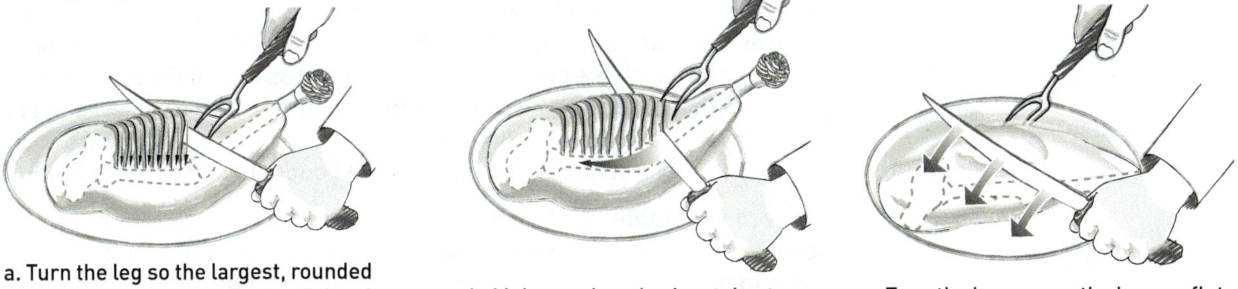

a. Turn the leg so the largest, rounded muscle mass is on top. Begin slicing down to the bone, cutting across the grain and on the bias, until the entire muscle is sliced.

b. Make one long horizontal cut along the bone to free the slices.

c. Turn the leg over so the longer, flat muscle mass is on top. Slice horizontally across the grain down to the bone.

For example, a standard chicken salad is usually made with cold poached chicken cut into medium dice. However, an Asian-inspired California chicken salad might be made with soy-marinated grilled chicken breast that is cooled and then shredded by pulling it into pieces with the grain.

Salads are a good use for leftover cooked meats and poultry. As long as the meat is handled under proper food safety guidelines and used quickly while still fresh, there is no reason it cannot be recycled into a salad.

Cold Meats for Buffet Presentation

Some of the most complex and painstaking work done by a garde manger chef involves preparing large roasts of meat or poultry for a cold buffet. While cooked in the same manner as carving station meats, they are presented in a more elaborate manner. They are included not only as food items but also as decorative centerpieces for the buffet display.

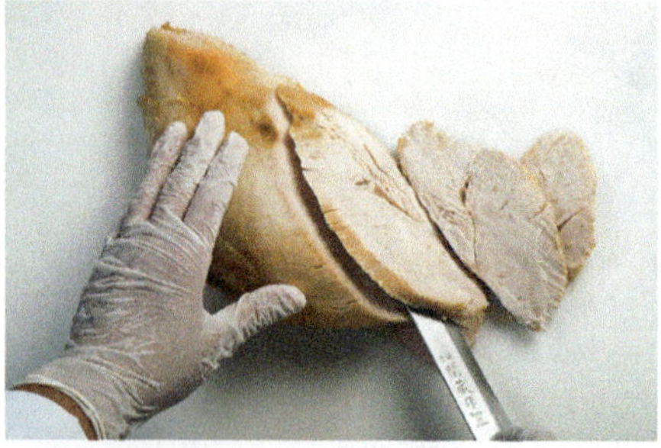

Sequence slicing

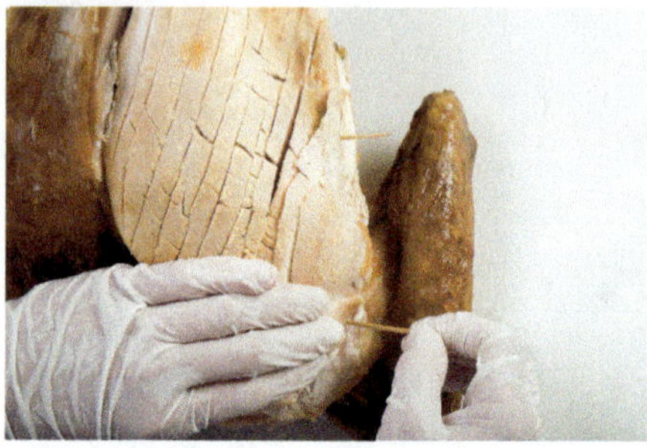

Reassembled slices

To function as a décor item, a roast must remain largely intact and attractive throughout the service. Thus, you should plan ahead to have enough meat both for service and for display. If the buffet is for a smaller number of guests, the chef prepares a large roast and slices one-half to two-thirds of it for service. The remaining section is placed on the platter as the focal point of the presentation. This large, intact section is referred to as the ***grosse pièce*** [gross pee-YEHSS], literally "large piece." For a greater number of guests, an entire small roast might be used as the grosse pièce, and slices from a separate, larger, roast are arranged around it.

When arranged on a platter, with or without a grosse pièce, slices should be arranged in straight or curving lines in an attractive pattern. When the food item being sliced has a tapered shape, the arrangement will look best if the slices are sequenced. ***Sequencing*** means keeping slices in order as they are cut. In other words, as each slice is cut, it is placed directly against or next to the slice cut before it. Sequenced slices can also be reassembled into the original shape of the item before it was sliced.

A special sequencing technique can be used when serving cold roasted fowl, such as turkeys or large roasting chickens. The breast skin is carefully removed from the roasted fowl and reserved intact. The breast meat is then removed from the carcass in two intact pieces. Each breast half is sequence-sliced and reassembled, then replaced on the carcass. The skin is then replaced over it. Although the presentation gives the appearance of a whole roasted fowl, the meat is presliced for the guests to remove easily.

Platter Décor

For formal buffet presentations, garde manger chefs usually choose to add one or more types of décor to cold meat platters:

Herb bouquets are typically placed on the platter or carving board around the base of the roast. They are often tucked into the cavities or over the knuckles of fowl as well. Watercress is the preferred bouquet, as it serves both as décor and as a salad-like accompaniment. Other attractive, sturdy greens, such as frisée and treviso, may be used as well. If the roast is seasoned with a particular herb, decorate the platter with that same herb. Herb bouquets wilt quickly in a warm dining room. If a large roast is on display for several hours, replace its herb bouquets one or more times.

Carved vegetables and fruits are often added to the platter or carving board as decoration. If the meat or poultry is flavored with a fruit essence or is to be served with a fruit sauce, a carved fruit décor item is appropriate. Techniques and procedures for preparing carved vegetables and fruits are covered in Chapter 17.

Procedure for Sequencing Slices

1. If necessary, remove the meat from the carcass or bone framework.
2. Trim and discard deposit fat and surface silverskin.
3. Determine the grain of the meat.
4. If you plan to leave a portion of the meat as a grosse pièce, determine its size and mark the spot where you must stop slicing. The grosse pièce is usually created from the more attractive or larger end of the roast.
5. Begin slicing across the grain from the smaller end. For most cuts of meat, slice on a slight diagonal (see photo). Make sure all slices are the same thickness.

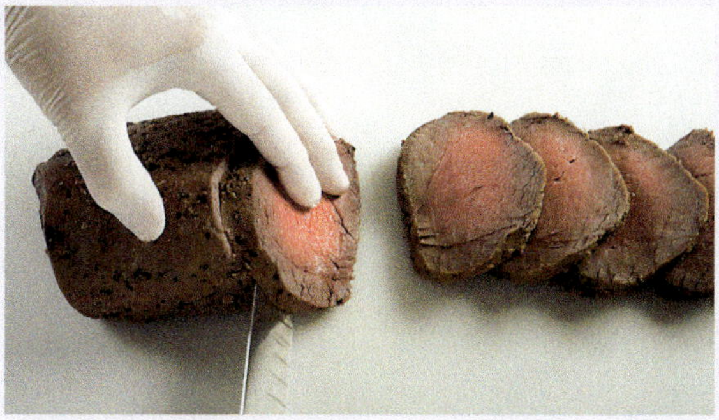

6. After you cut off the first slice, place it on the board or on a work tray with the cut side up.
7. Cut off the second slice and lean it against the first slice, with the newly cut side up.
8. Continue in the same manner until all the meat is sliced or until you have reached the grosse pièce.
9. To place the slices in a sequenced line on a presentation platter, take up the last slice you cut, turn it over, and place it on the platter first, or lean it against the grosse pièce, if used.
10. Place the remaining slices on the platter in reverse order, turning them over and overlapping them, in a straight or curved line. The final slice you place on the platter is the second-to-first slice you cut. Do not use the heel, or first-cut slice.

Attelets are used to create height in the presentation of a cold roast, pâté, or other garde manger item. An ***attelet*** [ah-teh-LAY] is a skewer with an ornamented top. To decorate a roast, thread the attelet with attractive, colorful food items, such as cherry tomatoes and olives, and insert it toward the back of the roast at its tallest point. Page 254 shows an attelet decorating a cold roast filet of beef.

Garnitures are often arranged on a platter of roasted meat or poultry to provide both décor and accompaniment. While the French term *garniture* translates simply as "garnish," in regard to the presentation of cold roasts and other garde manger items, we use the term ***garniture*** [GAHR-nee-tyur] to describe a small, attractive composed food item that is self-contained and freestanding on the platter. The cold roast filet presentation on page 254 includes a garniture of stuffed cherry tomatoes.

Aspic and chaud-froid decoration are the most classic of all décor types. A coating of glimmering clear aspic gelée or ivory-colored chaud-froid not only creates an attractive, elegant presentation but also provides a protective barrier that prevents the meat from drying out. These products and procedures are covered in Chapter 16.

PREPARING COLD MEAT PRODUCTS

Most meats and poultry for cold presentation are cooked by the same basic methods as those intended for hot service. However, a few important principles must be observed.

Principles of Cooking Meats to Be Served Cold

Following these principles results in attractive cold meat dishes with optimal flavor and mouthfeel.

Minimizing Fat

When meats and poultry are served cold, it is important to remove as much visible fat as possible. Customers will tolerate, and may even enjoy, a thin layer of deposit fat on the exterior of a hot roast or around the edges of a sizzling steak, especially if that fat is crisp and well browned. However, when that same fat cools to room temperature it becomes more solid, and when chilled it further solidifies into a dense, slick mass. It feels greasy and slippery on the tongue and, in most Western cultures, is considered unpleasant in texture.

In some preparations, the deposit fat visible on the surface of the meat may be removed before cooking. For example, the fat and fatty skin may be removed from chicken breasts before they are poached. When roasting, however, the layer of deposit fat insulates the meat from the harsh effects of dry-heat cooking. Much of it melts during the roasting process, thus effectively basting the meat as it cooks. The excess fat is then removed after cooking, when the meat is carved or otherwise fabricated for cold service.

It is also necessary to minimize the presence of animal fat in sauces for cold meats. Stocks, jus, and other meat-based cooking liquids used to prepare these cold sauces must be thoroughly defatted.

Seasoning Liberally

Cold temperatures dull the taste buds. Therefore, you must season meats and poultry intended for cold service more highly than you would season the same product for serving hot.

Achieving the Appropriate Internal Temperature

For most people, very rare meat is not palatable when served cold or at room temperature. Red meats cooked well done have an unattractive, gray-brown color that is not appealing on a cold platter or on a buffet presentation. They also harden significantly when chilled and have a cardboard mouthfeel. Therefore, cold preparations of beef, lamb, and game meats should be cooked to a medium-rare or medium doneness. This doneness range has the added advantage of suiting most customers' preference.

Retaining Moisture

Meats and poultry for cold or room temperature service must be cooked ahead of time, cooled, and then held for a time before being served. Often, they are sliced or otherwise fabricated ahead of time as well. Once exposed to the air, their surfaces easily dry out. There are several ways to prevent surface drying and ensure a moist mouthfeel:

1. Once cold meats are carved or otherwise fabricated, baste their surfaces with a small amount of an appropriate stock. (Make sure the stock is thoroughly defatted.)

2. Store poached meat submerged in its *cuisson*, or poaching liquid.

3. Keep prepared platters covered with plastic film until the service begins.

Serving at the Proper Temperature

The optimal temperature for serving cold preparations of meat and poultry is not actually cold. Both meats and poultry are best when served at cool room temperature, 60°–75°F (16°–24°C). Within this temperature range the meat's flavors are most pronounced and its texture has softened slightly, ensuring the best mouthfeel. To achieve the best product, cook meat on the same day it will be served, and then serve it shortly after it reaches room temperature. This requires careful planning and proper timing.

Although cold cooked meats and poultry are better when they have never been refrigerated, it is nonetheless often necessary to cook them ahead of time and refrigerate them. One reason to do so is time management. Another reason is to prepare them to accept aspic, chaud-froid, and other coating sauces. If cooked meats are refrigerated, they should be brought to room temperature before they are served.

Observing Food Safety Procedures

Cold meats and poultry are protein foods that undergo a lot of handling, making them susceptible to contamination by harmful microorganisms. Be especially vigilant about sanitation, and carefully observe food safety procedures.

Cooking Methods for Cold Meats

Of the many methods that can be used to cook meats and poultry, only a few are typically used to prepare them for cold service.

Roasting

The method most frequently used to cook meats and poultry for cold presentation is roasting. Roasting gives meats an attractive, browned exterior.

For cold presentation meats, take into account the additional rise in internal temperature that results from carryover cooking during the longer cooling period. Depending on the size of the item, subtract 2°–5°F (1°–3°C) from the internal temperature normally achieved for hot presentation. For example, if you would normally roast a 5-lb (2.25-kg) chicken for hot service to 160°F (71°C), for cold presentation cook the chicken to an internal temperature of 155°–158°F (68°–70°C).

Procedure for Roasting Meats and Poultry for Cold Presentation

1. Preheat the oven to the specified temperature (Table 7.1). If using a convection oven, set the heat 25°F (14°C) lower.
2. Prepare a shallow roasting pan fitted with a rack and filled with ½–1 in. (1.25–2.5 cm) water or an appropriate stock.
3. If necessary, tie or truss the roast. Season it as desired.
4. Place the roast on the rack and place the pan in the oven.
5. Roast according to one of the methods described in Table 7.1.
6. If desired, baste at intervals with an appropriate stock or other flavorful liquid.
7. Use an instant-read thermometer to test the doneness at the center of the thickest portion of the roast, or where the meat is most dense. Make sure the thermometer probe is not resting against bone or in a fat pocket. Remember to subtract 2°–5°F (1°–3°C) to accommodate carryover cooking during cooling.
8. When the roast is done, remove it to a draft-free location and allow it to cool, uncovered, to an internal temperature of 70°F (21°C).
9. If the pan juices from the roast will be used to prepare a cold sauce, defat them by placing them in a small, deep container, chilling them, and removing the solidified fat that forms on the surface. Alternatively, use a bulb baster or a fat separator.

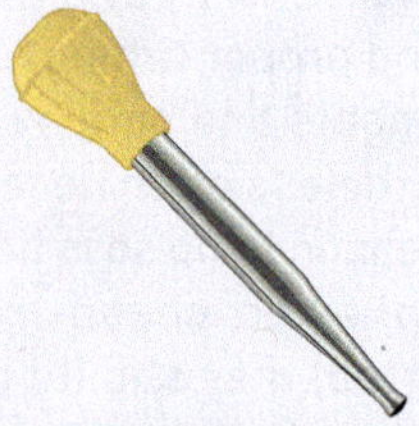
Bulb baster

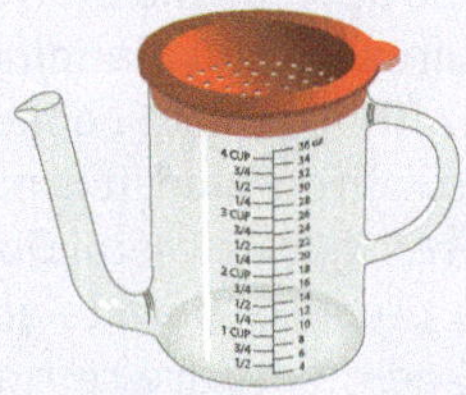
Fat separator

TABLE 7.1 Roasting

Method	Application	Temperature
Low-temperature roasting	Meat roasts, 5 lb (2.25 kg) and up Poultry, 8 lb (3.5 kg) and up	250°–350°F (120°–175°C)
Sear-roasting	Meat roasts, 5–14 lb (2.25–6.4 kg) Poultry, 5–20 lb (2.25–9 kg)	425°F (220°C) for 15–20 min., then finish at 325°–350°F (165°–175°C)
High-temperature roasting	All roasts under 5 lb (2.25 kg)	400°–425°F (200°–225°C)

COLD ROAST TURKEY BREAST

Yield:
about 6 lb (2.75 kg) EP
Portions:
varies
Portion size:
varies

INGREDIENTS	U.S.	METRIC
Hotel turkey breast (whole breast with wings)	12 lb	5.5 kg
Lemons, cut in half crosswise	2	2
Kosher salt	to taste	to taste
Ground white pepper	to taste	to taste
Poultry Stock (p. 749) or water	1 pt	0.5 L
Melted butter	4 fl oz	120 mL

PROCEDURE

PREPARATION

1. Season the turkey by squeezing the lemon juice over all surfaces and sprinkling it with salt and pepper.
2. Follow the Procedure for Roasting Meats and Poultry for Cold Presentation on p. 250, using either the sear-roasting or slow-roasting methods outlined in Table 7.1 on the same page. Roast the turkey to an internal temperature of 155°F (68°C).

HOLDING

Refrigerate, loosely covered, up to 4 days.

VARIATION

COLD ROAST CHICKEN

Replace the hotel turkey breast with a 4–5-lb (2–2.5-kg) roasting chicken. Reduce the amounts of lemon, stock, and butter by one-half.

SLICED AND REASSEMBLED COLD ROAST TURKEY PRESENTATION

BUFFET

Yield:
about 6 lb (2.75 kg) EP
Portions:
varies
Portion size:
varies

COMPONENTS

1 *Cold Roast Turkey Breast (above)*
5–6 fl oz (150–180 mL) *Mayonnaise (p. 41)*, or commercial mayonnaise
6 oz (180 g) Watercress or parsley
1 Large tomato rose (p. 716)

PROCEDURE

FINISHING

1. Free the skin of the turkey breast. Make a shallow slit in the skin, starting just above one wing and proceeding around the front of the breast and then over the wing on the other side.
2. Lift the skin of one side of the breast to expose the meat (A). (Try to keep the skin attached to the breast bone cartilage, but don't worry if the entire breast skin comes away from the meat.)

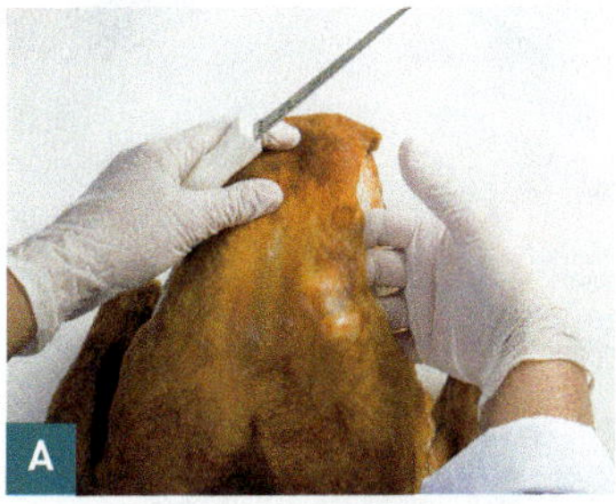
A

(continues)

PROCEDURE *(continued)*

3. Use a flexible boning knife to cut the breast meat away from the carcass in one piece (B).
4. Use a sharp paring knife to remove the cartilage from the breast tender without removing the tender from the breast meat.
5. Cut the breast meat across the grain into even, ¼-in. (0.75-cm) slices (C). Use sequencing (p. 247) to keep the slices in order. Reassemble the breast meat halves into their original shapes.
6. Apply a thin coating of mayonnaise to the turkey carcass where the breast meat halves were removed (D).
7. Replace the breast meat halves in the carcass and press to secure them in place. If necessary, use 1 or 2 toothpicks to hold the meat on the carcass (E)).
8. Use the cutter section of food-service pliers to snip off the exposed ends of the toothpicks (F). Be sure to properly dispose of the toothpick ends.
9. Repeat with the other side of the breast.
10. Replace the skin over the meat and smooth it down. (If the entire breast skin came off in one piece, replace it after both sides of the breast are replaced.)
11. Place the turkey on a 14-in. (35-cm) serving platter.
12. Arrange the watercress or parsley around the turkey.
13. Place the tomato rose in front of the breast.

HOLDING

Cover loosely with plastic wrap and refrigerate up to 4 hours. Bring to cool room temperature before serving.

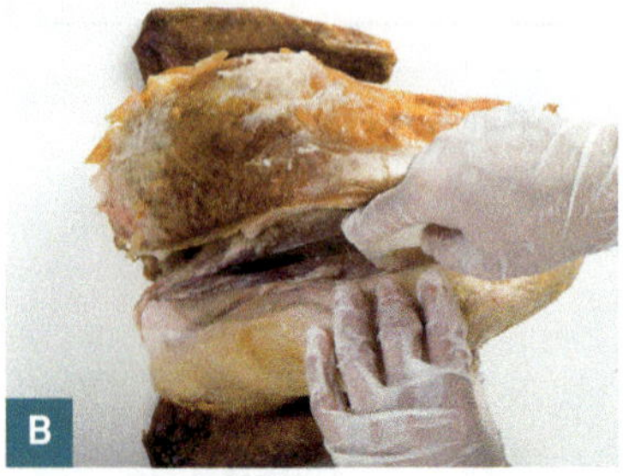
B

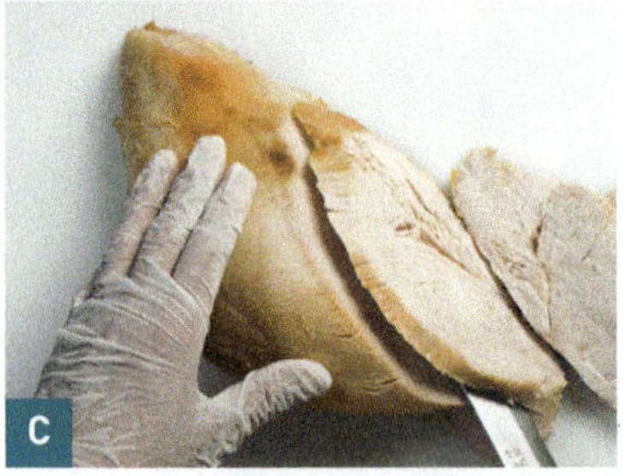
C

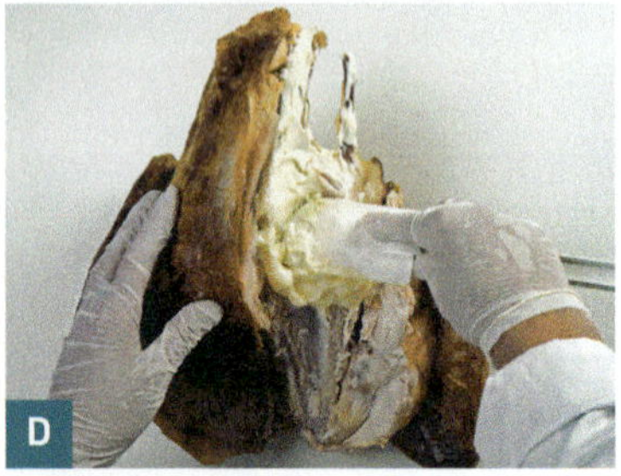
D

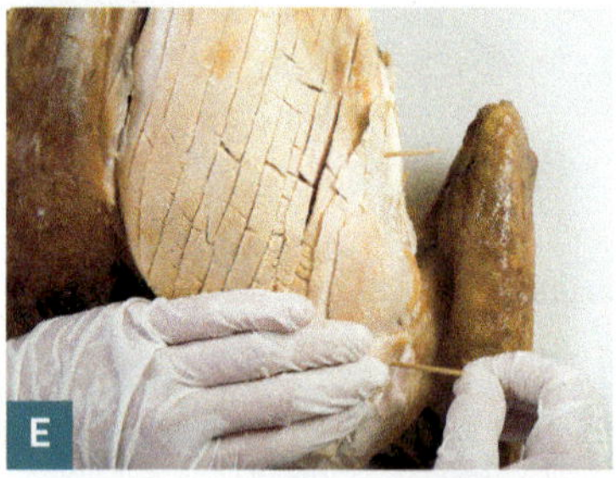
E

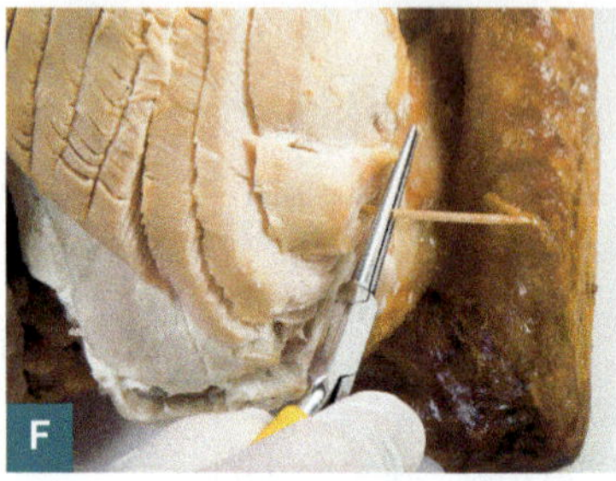
F

COLD ROAST FILET OF BEEF

BUFFET

Yield:
about 3 lb (1.5 kg) EP
Portions:
varies
Portion size:
varies

INGREDIENTS	U.S.	METRIC
Center-cut beef filet (tenderloin)	4 lb	2 kg
Kosher salt	to taste	to taste
Coarsely ground black pepper	to taste	to taste
Pressed or minced and crushed fresh garlic	½ oz	15 g
Pure olive oil (not extra-virgin)	1 fl oz	30 mL
Water	as needed	as needed

PROCEDURE

PREPARATION

1. Trim and discard all silverskin and visible deposit fat from the filet.
2. Combine the salt, pepper, garlic, and oil to make a seasoning paste.
3. Rub the filet with the seasoning paste.
4. Place the filet on a rack set in a roasting pan.
5. Roast to the desired doneness according to the directions in Procedure for Roasting Meats and Poultry for Cold Presentation (p. 250, high-temperature variation).

HOLDING

Hold uncovered at cool room temperature up to 3 hours total. Cover and refrigerate for longer holding, up to 5 days. Bring to cool room temperature before serving.

COLD ROAST FILET PLATTER PRESENTATION

WITH BÉARNAISE MAYONNAISE

BUFFET

Portions:
up to 10, depending on whether the grosse pièce is sliced and served
Portion size:
4 oz (120 g)

COMPONENTS

3 lb EP (1.5 kg EP) *Cold Roast Filet of Beef (above)*, medium rare
2 oz (60 g) Watercress
1 pt (0.5 l) *Béarnaise Mayonnaise (p. 43)*, in pastry bag fitted with medium star tip
1 2 × 3 × ½-in. (5 × 7 × 1-cm) *Sautéed White Bread Croûtons (p. 702)*, toasted and cooled
12 Large cherry tomato crowns (p. 254)
1 Pitted California black olive, blotted dry
1 Cherry tomato
1 Hard-cooked egg crown (p. 254)

PROCEDURE

FINISHING

1. Cut off ½ in. (1 cm) of the filet's smaller end on a slight diagonal and reserve for another use. Following the Procedure for Sequencing Slices (p. 247), cut the filet on the diagonal into six 3-oz (90-g) slices, leaving a grosse pièce about 4 in. (10 cm) long.

(continues)

PROCEDURE *(continued)*

2. Arrange the watercress in a flat bouquet on one end of a 14-in. (35-cm) oval or rectangular platter.
3. Place the croûton in the center of the watercress bouquet.
4. Place the grosse pièce of beef on the croûton with the cut end facing the empty side of the platter.
5. Lean 1 slice of beef against the grosse pièce, and then arrange the remaining slices overlapping a line along the length of the platter.
6. Pipe 6 small dots of béarnaise mayonnaise on either side of the beef slices. Set a cherry tomato crown on each dot and pipe a rosette of mayonnaise on each.
7. Impale the olive and the cherry tomato on an 8-in. (20-cm) attelet (p. 247). Place the egg crown toward the back of the grosse pièce and secure it to the beef with the attelet.
8. Serve the remaining béarnaise mayonnaise in a sauceboat.
9. Provide carving utensils to slice the grosse pièce, if desired.

HOLDING

Hold at cool room temperature no longer than 1 hour. Keep the mayonnaise refrigerated until 15 minutes before service.

Marinades

A ***marinade*** is a fluid mixture that includes vegetable oil, an acidic ingredient such as citrus juice or vinegar, salt, and seasonings such as herbs, spices, and aromatic vegetables. Marinades have two beneficial effects on meats: added flavor and tenderization. The salt and acid in a marinade work as mild tenderizers, because they break down some of the meat fiber and connective tissue. When using tender cuts, the meat is kept in the marinade for only a short period. Skirt steak, hanger steak, and some cuts of beef round are tougher cuts that are marinated for a longer period before grilling.

Grilling

Meats and poultry for grilling are sometimes marinated before they are cooked. If seasoned with a rub (p. 411), the meat is brushed with a little vegetable oil prior to grilling.

In grilling small, thin pieces of food, carryover cooking is not an issue. However, grilled foods cook quickly, and you must be careful not to overcook them. Drying out can be a problem. To preserve moisture and prevent surface drying, brush grilled meats with fresh, uncontaminated marinade, or baste with stock or other flavorful liquid while they are cooling.

Poaching

Lean white meats and white-meat poultry are frequently poached for cold service. Poaching keeps meat moist and imparts the flavor of the *cuisson*, or poaching liquid. The *cuisson* often serves as an ingredient in cold sauces used for cold poached meats. The procedure for poaching both meats and poultry is the same as that for poaching seafood (see pp. 193–195).

VEAL FOR VITELLO TONNATO (vee-TELL-oh tohn-AH-toe)

Yield:
about 2 lb (1 kg) EP

INGREDIENTS	U.S.	METRIC
Whole fresh garlic cloves, peeled	¼ oz	7 g
Firm, high-quality anchovy filets	¼ oz	7 g
Veal top round roast (all one muscle)	2½ lb	1.25 kg
Poultry Stock (p. 749)	1 qt	1 L
White wine	4 fl oz	120 mL
Bouquet garni, in sachet	1	1

Note: When slicing the veal for service, be sure to slice across the grain.

PROCEDURE

PREPARATION

1. Cut the garlic into fine slivers, about ⅛ × ⅛ × ½ in. (3 × 3 × 12 mm).
2. Cut the anchovies into slivers of the same size.
3. Trim all exterior silverskin from the veal roast and discard it or save it for stock making.
4. Bard the roast:
   a. Insert a sharp paring knife ½ in. (12 mm) into the meat.
   b. Press the knife to one side and insert a sliver of garlic into the meat (A). Remove the knife.
   c. Repeat, alternating garlic and anchovy, all over the surface of the meat.
5. Prepare a *cuisson*: Bring the stock to a simmer in a saucepan just large enough to hold the stock and veal.
6. Prepare a double layer of cheesecloth cut just large enough to wrap the roast. Moisten the cheesecloth with cool water and wring it out.
7. Wrap the veal in the cheesecloth and secure it with kitchen string in a butcher's tie (B).
8. Poach the veal in the stock (C) about 20 minutes, or to an internal temperature of 135°F (57°C).
9. Prepare an ice bain-marie large enough to hold the veal pan.
10. Place the veal pan in the ice bain-marie and cool the veal in its *cuisson* to room temperature. Reserve 8 fl oz (240 mL) of the *cuisson* for Tonnato Sauce (p. 43).

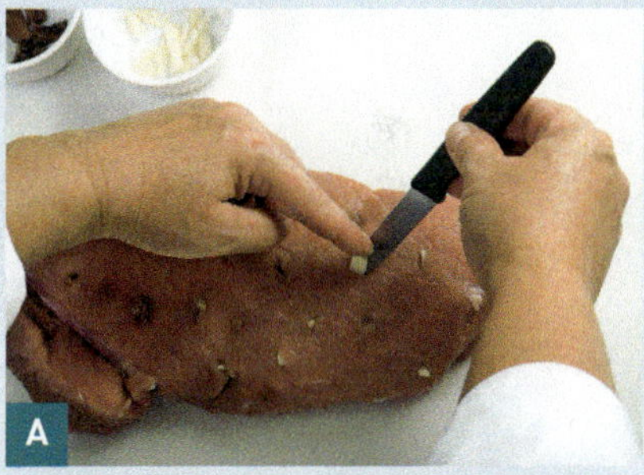
A

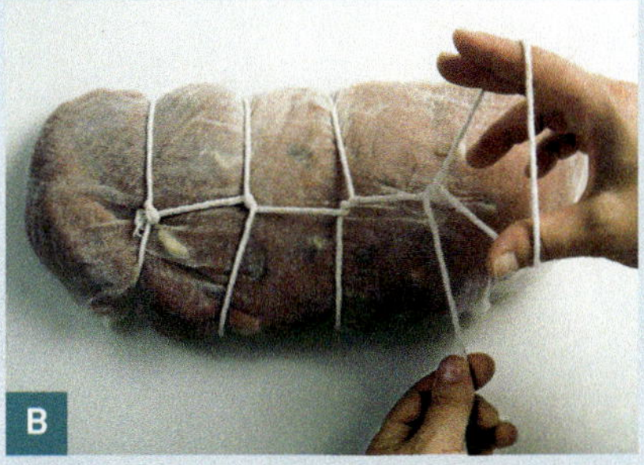
B

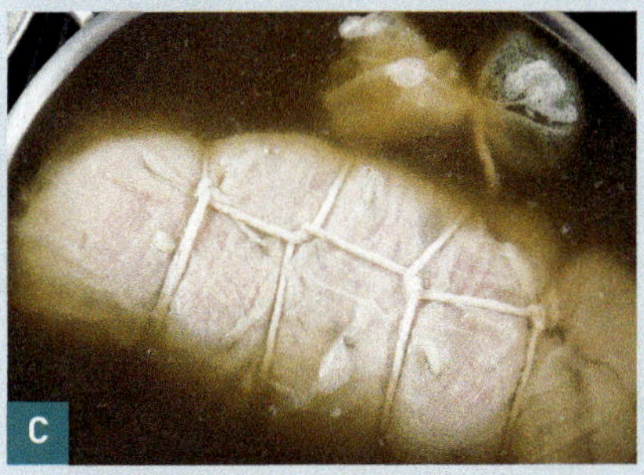
C

HOLDING

Transfer the veal and *cuisson* to a plastic container just large enough to hold the veal completely submerged. Cover and refrigerate up to 5 days.

VITELLO TONNATO

VEAL IN TUNA SAUCE

MAIN COURSE

Portions:
1

Portion size:
5 oz (150 g) veal, plus garnish

COMPONENTS

1 oz (30 g) Spring mix or mild-tasting micro greens
5 oz (150 g) *Veal for Vitello Tonnato (p. 255)*, cut in thin slices across the grain
2 fl oz (60 mL) *Tonnato Sauce (p. 43)*, in squeeze bottle
5-6 Grape tomatoes
¼ oz (7 g) Nonpareil capers

PROCEDURE

PLATING

1. Mound the greens slightly left of center on the back of a cool 10-in. (25-cm) plate.
2. Fan the veal slices in an arc across the front of the plate.
3. Squeeze a band of tonnato sauce across the veal slices.
4. Mound the tomatoes between the greens and the veal.
5. Scatter a line of capers across the veal slices.

COLD PORK LOIN WITH PRUNES AND ARMAGNAC

Yield:
about 2½ lb (1.3 kg)
Portions:
8
Portion size:
5 oz (150 g)

INGREDIENTS	U.S.	METRIC
Pitted prunes	8 oz (12 large)	240 g (12 large)
Armagnac	2 fl oz	60 mL
Water	2 fl oz	60 mL
Firm chicken livers	8 oz	240 g
Clarified butter	½ fl oz	15 mL
Sea salt or kosher salt	to taste	to taste
Center-cut pork loin (one piece)	3 lb	1.5 kg
Egg wash	1 fl oz	30 mL
Ground dried sage	½ tsp	2 mL
Dried thyme	¼ tsp	1 mL
Freshly ground black pepper	1 tsp	6 mL
Poultry Stock (p. 749), plus additional	24 fl oz	0.75 L
Fresh lemon juice	to taste	to taste
Granular gelatin	¼ oz	7 g

PROCEDURE

PREPARATION

1. Place the prunes in a heatproof nonreactive container just large enough to hold them.
2. Combine the Armagnac and water in a saucepan and heat to just under the boil.
3. Pour the mixture over the prunes. Press gently on the prunes to submerge them. Allow the prunes to steep about 20 minutes.
4. Trim the livers of all fat and connective tissue. Separate the lobes. Blot them dry on paper towels.
5. Heat a small sauté pan very hot, add the clarified butter, and sear the livers brown outside, very rare inside. Season with salt. Remove the livers to a sheet tray and place them in the freezer for 10 minutes to firm.
6. Preheat oven to 400°F (200°C).
7. Use a very sharp, flexible boning knife to score the fat side of the pork loin in ¼-in. (6-mm) cross-hatches (A).
8. Insert a larding needle lengthwise through the center of the loin to start an opening (B). Remove it and reinsert it several times to make a cylindrical opening down the center of the roast. Use a boning knife to complete the opening. The hollow cylinder inside the loin should be just large enough to accommodate the prunes.

(continues)

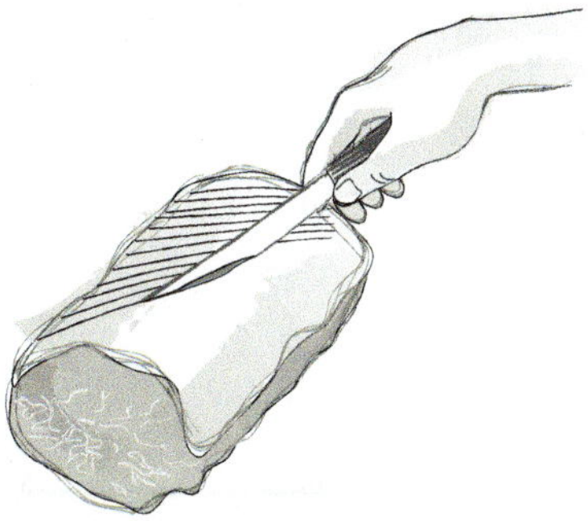

A

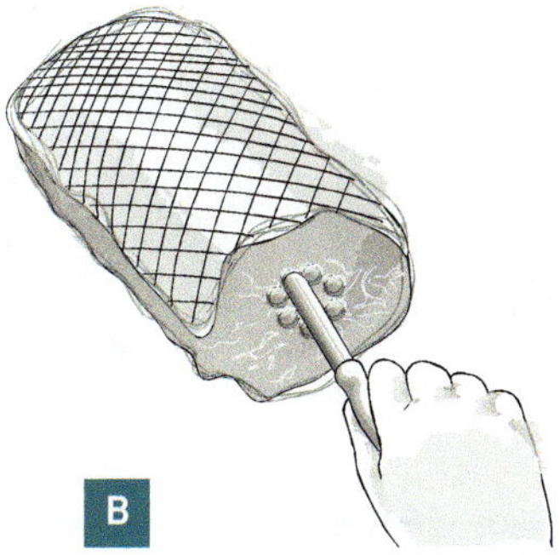

B

PROCEDURE *(continued)*

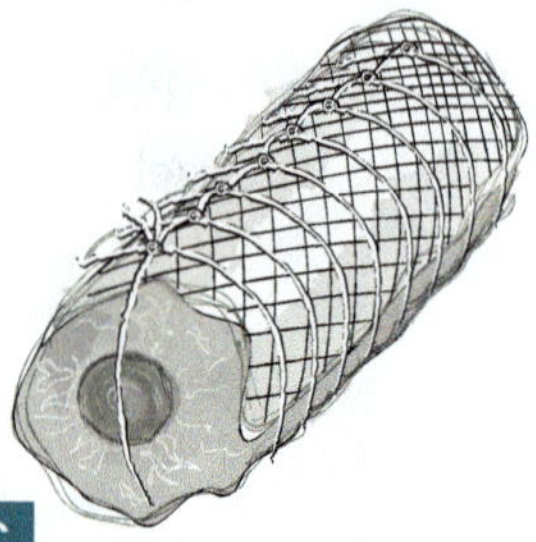

C

9. Drain the prunes and reserve the steeping liquid.
10. Stuff each prune with a piece of liver.
11. Dip each prune into the egg wash and insert it into the opening in the pork loin. Stuff the loin with an even row of prunes.
12. Combine the sea (or kosher) salt, sage, thyme, and pepper to make a seasoning rub.
13. Tie the loin with a butcher's truss to secure its shape (C).
14. Apply an even coating of the seasoning rub to the loin.
15. Place the loin on a rack in a roasting pan. Place about ½-in. (1-cm) water in the bottom of the pan
16. Combine the poultry stock and the prune steeping liquid.
17. Roast the loin about 35 minutes, basting occasionally with the combined stock/prune liquid. Roast to an internal temperature of 150°F (65°C). (Do not insert the thermometer completely into the center of the loin, or you may get a false reading. Make sure the probe is in the meat, not in a prune.)
18. When the pork is done, cool it on the rack to room temperature.
19. Strain the jus (pan juices) into a measuring cup. Spoon off any visible fat from the surface. If necessary, add water or poultry stock to equal 20 fl oz (600 mL).
20. Mix the gelatin with enough cool jus to bloom it (p. 633).
21. Prepare the gelée:
    a. Heat the jus just under the boil.
    b. Season it with salt and a little lemon juice.
    c. Stir in the gelatin and heat just until the gelatin dissolves.
    d. Pour the jus into a quarter-size hotel pan or other flat container. Refrigerate it until it sets into a light gel.
22. Remove the string from the roast.

HOLDING

Refrigerate, covered, up to 5 days.

VARIATION

COLD PORK LOIN WITH PRUNES AND COGNAC

Replace the Armagnac with cognac.

COLD PORK LOIN WITH PRUNES AND ARMAGNAC

SERVED WITH RICE TIMBALE AND CAROTTES RAPÉES

MAIN COURSE

Portions:
1
Portion size:
5 oz (150 g) pork, plus garnish

COMPONENTS

as needed Pan coating spray
5 fl oz (150 mL) *Cool Cucumber Rice Salad (p. 157)*, without cucumbers
2 oz (60 g) Watercress
2 slices *Cold Pork Loin with Prunes and Armagnac (p. 257)*, 2½ oz (70 g) each
½ cup (120 mL) *Carottes Rapées, p. 134*
3 fl oz (90 mL) Gelée from *Cold Pork Loin with Prunes and Armagnac (p. 257)*

PROCEDURE

PLATING

1. Spray the inside of a 5-fl oz (150-mL) timbale form with pan coating. Pack the rice salad into the timbale and turn it out positioned back left on a cool 12-in. (30-cm) plate.
2. Place a bouquet of watercress next to the timbale.
3. Overlap the pork loin slices leaning against the timbale and watercress.
4. Mound the carrottes rapées on top of the timbale.
5. Spoon an arc of gelée across the front of the pork loin slices.

RAW MEAT DISHES

In many of the world's cuisines, raw meat dishes play an important role. For example, in Korea and Southeast Asia, raw beef is featured in salads and snack foods. Chopped raw beef flavored with hot spiced butter is a favorite dish in Ethiopian cuisine. Middle Eastern cuisines boast raw lamb *mezze,* or appetizers. Western cuisines feature only two important dishes in which meat is served uncooked, and in both of these dishes the meat used is beef.

Steak tartare is hand-chopped raw beef filet mixed with raw egg yolk and various spicy seasonings and condiments. Although typically turned out by the garde manger station, in some traditional high-end restaurants steak tartare is prepared tableside. Carpaccio consists of very thin sliced raw beef filet accented with a mustard mayonnaise sauce. Because of the special characteristics of raw red meat, when preparing these dishes, you must carefully follow specific guidelines.

Guidelines for Preparing Raw Meat Dishes

- *Do not serve uncooked pork or poultry* due to the risk of food-borne illness associated with these foods. Only beef, lamb, and farmed venison are considered safe for raw service.
- Use tender cuts only. Even after undergoing the physical tenderization of chopping or slicing, tough cuts are unpleasantly chewy when served raw.
- Keep the meat very cold at all times. This is necessary both for food safety and to keep the meat firm so it will cut well.
- Trim off *all* connective tissue and fat from the meat before chopping or slicing it. If any remains, the meat will be unpleasantly stringy and greasy-tasting.
- Always fabricate the meat by hand. *Do not attempt to chop beef for steak tartare in a meat grinder.* Even a cleaned and sanitized grinder can harbor harmful microorganisms. In addition, a grinder does not create the proper texture.
- For à la carte service, chop or slice the meat to order. For hors d'oeuvre work or buffet service, prepare the meat at the last possible moment, and do not plan to hold the finished dish very long. Chopped or sliced raw meat can easily become contaminated by harmful microorganisms. In addition, exposure to air destroys the red pigments in the meat, causing it to quickly change from an attractive red color to an unattractive shade of brown.
- Add acidic ingredients, such as lemon juice, to raw meat dishes at the last minute before serving. Prolonged contact with acidic ingredients gives the meat a cooked texture and discolors it.
- Use only freshly thawed pasteurized egg yolk in steak tartare.
- Be especially vigilant in your sanitation practices when serving raw meat.
- In some areas, food-service operators are required by law to post warnings about the risks of consuming raw meat. Be sure to know and comply with local regulations.

CARPACCIO (kar-PAH-choh)

APPETIZER

Portions:
1
Portion size:
2½ oz (75 g) beef, plus garnish

INGREDIENTS	U.S.	METRIC
Extra-virgin olive oil, preferably unfiltered artisan	1 fl oz (about)	30 g (about)
Well-trimmed filet of beef (no fat or silverskin; see Note)	2½ oz	75 g
Medium-grind sea salt or kosher salt	to taste	to taste
Anchovy-Mustard Mayonnaise (p. 43), in squeeze bottle	1½ fl oz	45 mL
Nonpareil capers	2 tsp	10 mL
Red onion, cut brunoise	¼ oz	7 g
Micro greens	½ oz	15 g
Freshly *Toasted Baguette Croûtons (p. 702)*	1 oz (6 pieces)	30 g (6 pieces)

Note: For à la carte restaurant service, you would typically slice pieces to order from a large piece of trimmed filet. Precut slices darken due to oxidation.

The History of Carpaccio

Beef Carpaccio was created by the owner of Harry's Bar in Venice in the 1950s. The dish was named after the Italian painter Vittore Carpaccio (1460–1526), because he used a lot of red in his paintings and the fresh-cut raw beef in this dish is a vivid red color. In the 1970s, nouvelle cuisine (p. 5) chefs began to use other meats, as well as fresh tuna, to make this dish. Carpaccio has become so famous around the world that the term is now used for almost any food, including vegetables, served in paper-thin slices.

PROCEDURE

FINISHING AND PLATING

1. Fold a piece of parchment paper lengthwise, open it out, and brush it with a generous coating of olive oil.
2. Use a sharp knife to cut the filet into thin, even slices (A).
3. Lay the slices on the bottom half of the oiled parchment and fold the top over them. Use the smooth side of a meat mallet to gently flatten the meat into paper-thin slices (B).
4. Arrange the filet on a cool 12-in. (30-cm) plate in overlapping concentric circles.
5. Sprinkle the filet with salt.
6. Squeeze a zigzag pattern of anchovy-mustard mayonnaise on the filet.
7. Scatter the capers and onions on the filet.
8. Mound the micro greens in the center of the plate.
9. Serve the croûtons on a separate plate or in a napkin-lined basket.

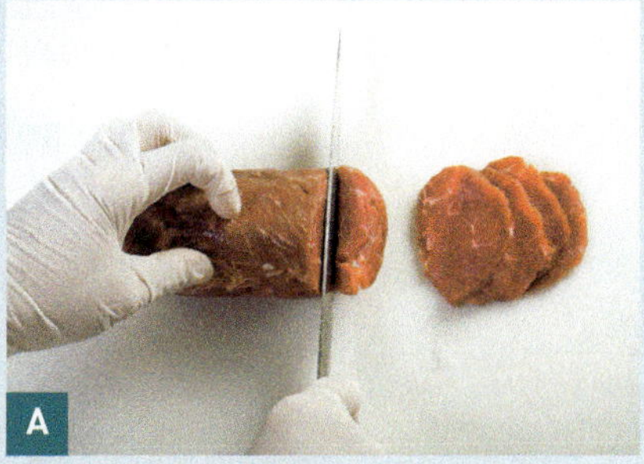
A

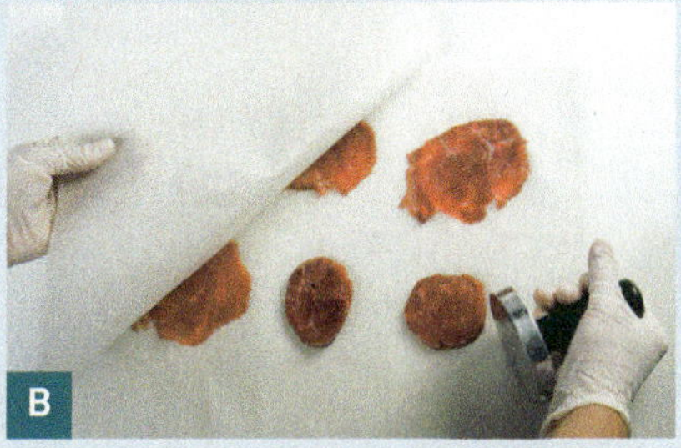
B

STEAK TARTARE

(tahr-TAHR)

APPETIZER OR LUNCH MAIN COURSE

Portions:
1

Portion size:
2½ oz (75 g) beef, plus garnish

COMPONENTS

2½ oz (75 g) Well-trimmed filet (tenderloin) of beef (no fat or silverskin; see Note)
1 fl oz (30 mL) Extra-virgin olive oil, preferably unfiltered artisan, in squeeze bottle
2 tsp (10 mL) Pasteurized egg yolk
to taste Fine sea salt
½ tsp (3 mL) Minced fresh garlic
¼ oz (7 g) Minced red onion
1–2 drops Worcestershire sauce
1–2 drops Bottled hot sauce
½ tsp (3 mL) Minced lemon zest
2 tsp (10 mL) Minced chervil or parsley
to taste Fresh lemon juice
2 tsp (10 mL) Nonpareil capers
to taste Coarsely ground black pepper
2 Grape tomatoes
1 oz (30 g) Micro greens or spring mix
1 oz/30 g (5 pieces) Freshly Toasted Baguette Croûtons (p. 702)

Note: For à la carte restaurant service, you would typically fabricate the beef to order from a large piece of trimmed filet. Precut portions darken due to oxidation.

PROCEDURE

FINISHING AND PLATING

1. Use a very sharp chef knife to fabricate the filet into rough brunoise cuts, and then chop through the brunoise a few times to create a loose, rough-chopped texture.
2. Place the filet in a chilled bowl and use a fork to toss in half the olive oil and the egg yolk, salt, garlic, onion, Worcestershire sauce, hot sauce, lemon juice, zest, and chervil or parsley. Taste and correct the seasoning.

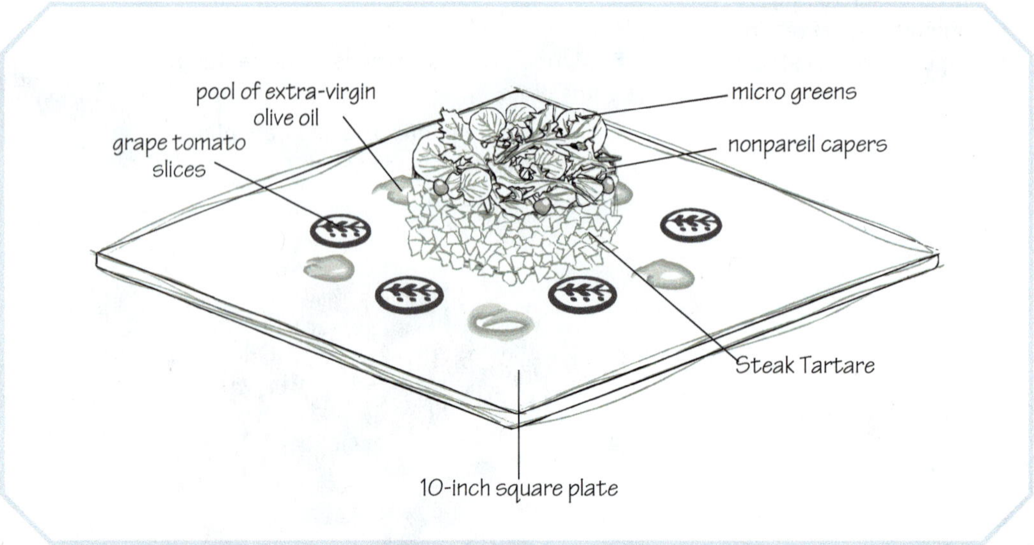

PROCEDURE

3. Brush the inside of a 2½-in. (6-cm) entremet ring with olive oil and place it in the center of a cool 10-in. (25-cm) plate. Pack the tartare mixture into the ring and then remove the ring.
4. Scatter the capers over the tartare and grind some pepper over it.
5. Cut 3 perfect slices from each grape tomato and arrange them around the tartare.
6. Squeeze a dot of olive oil between each tomato slice.
7. Mound the micro greens on top of the tartare.
8. Serve the croûtons on a separate plate or in a napkin-lined basket.

VARIATION

STEAK TARTARE PREPARED TABLESIDE

Chop the filet and place it in a large serving bowl. Arrange the remaining ingredients in ramekins and cruets on a serving tray. Assemble the tartare at tableside to the customer's specifications.

MEAT-BASED MOUSSES

The most frequently prepared meat-based mousses are made from ham, poultry breast, and poultry liver. For basic information on savory mousses, and the procedure for making them, refer to pages 212–214.

Liver Parfaits

Once cooked, cooled poultry livers are puréed with softened butter, the result is a smooth spread that is more rich and dense than a standard liver mousse. Although a preparation such as this sometimes goes by other names, it is most commonly called a liver ***parfait*** [pahr-FAY]. Additional ingredients, such as aromatic vegetables, herbs and spices, spirits, and cream may be added to the mixture.

Liver parfaits are less perishable than liver mousses because they do not contain raw egg whites. Because of their high fat content, liver parfaits freeze well.

Parfaits are served as appetizers much in the same manner as smooth liver pâtés. In fact, liver parfaits are often called *liver pâtés*, although they are not made in the same way (see pp. 542–543) Crackers or bread typically accompany small molded forms or ramekins of liver parfait. Alternatively, liver parfait may be used as an hors d'oeuvre component when piped onto a canapé or into a savory profiterole.

C'est Parfait!

The French word *parfait* literally translates as "perfect." As a culinary term, it has several meanings. In European pastry work, a parfait is a sweet, smooth, custard-like dessert component or a frozen dessert similar to frozen mousse. In America, *parfait* is used to describe a multilayered ice cream dessert presented in a tall glass. In garde manger, *parfait* is the name of a rich, buttery liver spread. It is also used to denote a specific preparation of foie gras, described on page 271.

HAM MOUSSE

Yield:
about 24 fl oz (0.75 L) or 20 oz (600 g)
Portions:
varies
Portion size:
varies

INGREDIENTS	U.S.	METRIC
Granular gelatin	½ oz	15 g
Madeira	2 fl oz	60 mL
Minced shallots	½ oz	15 g
White wine	2 fl oz	60 mL
Strong *Poultry Stock (p. 749)*	2 fl oz	60 mL
Well-trimmed water-added smoked ham	8 oz	240 g
Cream cheese, softened, 80°F (27°C)	2 oz	60 g
Pasteurized egg whites, 70°F (21°C)	4 oz	120 g
Heavy cream, cold 38°F (3°C)	2 fl oz	60 mL
Fine salt	to taste	to taste
Fine ground white pepper	to taste	to taste
Sugar, if needed	to taste	to taste

PROCEDURE

PREPARATION

1. Stir the gelatin into the Madeira and set it aside to bloom (p. 633).
2. Combine the shallots, wine, and stock in a small, nonreactive saucepan. Simmer this mixture about 5 minutes, or until the shallots are soft. Hold it warm.
3. Cut the ham into rough ½-in. (1-cm) cubes and place it in a food processor fitted with the steel blade.
4. Add the cream cheese to the processor with the ham and grind the mixture to a smooth purée.
5. Separately whip the egg whites and cream to soft peaks.
6. Add the gelatin to the shallot liquid and stir until it is dissolved.
7. Turn the processor on and pour the shallot-gelatin liquid through the feed tube in a thin stream.
8. Immediately transfer the ham mousse base into a large bowl.
9. Immediately fold the egg whites into the ham purée, and then fold the whipped cream into it.
10. Taste the mousse and season it with salt, pepper, and a pinch of sugar if needed.
11. Pack into ramekins or aspic-lined molds (p. 644), or place in a pastry bag for piping.

HOLDING

Refrigerate in a freshly sanitized covered container up to 2 days.

POULTRY LIVER PARFAIT

Yield:
12 fl oz (360 g)
or 14 oz (420 g)
Portions:
4
Portion size:
3 fl oz (90 g)
or 3½ oz (100 g)

INGREDIENTS	U.S.	METRIC
Chicken or duck livers	8 oz	240 g
Clarified butter	1 fl oz	30 mL
Salt	to taste	to taste
Fine ground white pepper	to taste	to taste
Minced shallots	½ oz	15 g
White wine	2 fl oz	60 mL
Butter, soft, at 70°F (24°C)	5 oz	150 g
Port, Madeira, or crème de cassis	1 fl oz	30 mL
Fresh lemon juice	to taste	to taste

A

B

C

D

PROCEDURE

PREPARATION

1. Trim the livers of all connective tissue. You will need to separate the lobes to do so, but keep the lobes as intact as possible. Blot the livers dry on paper towels.
2. Heat a sauté pan very hot, add the clarified butter, and sear the livers brown on the outside and very rare inside (A). Season the livers with salt and pepper, and immediately spread them on a cool sheet tray. Place the tray uncovered in the freezer 3–4 minutes—just long enough for them to reach room temperature.
3. Place the shallots and wine in a small sauté pan and reduce to 1 fl oz (30 mL). Cool to room temperature.
4. When the livers have cooled to room temperature, place them in a food processor fitted with the steel blade. Add the shallot mixture, the butter, and the wine or cassis (B). Process to a smooth purée (C).
5. Taste and correct the seasoning, balancing the salt and adding lemon juice to taste.
6. Force the parfait through a drum sieve (p. 18) or fine sieve (D).

HOLDING

Refrigerated up to 5 days, frozen up to 1 month.

PRESENTATION

7. Pack the parfait into the desired forms. Cover the surfaces with plastic wrap or another type of sealing product, such as clarified butter or aspic.

   -or-

   Cool and firm the parfait by stirring it with a rubber spatula in an ice bain-marie until it reaches piping consistency. Transfer the parfait to a pastry bag and proceed immediately to pipe desired shapes.

VARIATION

BRANDIED POULTRY LIVER PARFAIT

Replace the port or Madeira with good-quality brandy. Add the brandy in step 2 (after searing) and flambé the livers by tilting the pan toward the flame until the brandy ignites.

SMOKED TURKEY PARFAIT

Replace the livers with deli smoked turkey, trimmed of all rind. Omit the clarified butter. (There is no need to cook the smoked turkey; begin with step 3.)

DUCK LIVER PARFAIT PYRAMIDS

Portions:
4
Portion size:
3½ oz (90 g)

INGREDIENTS	U.S.	METRIC
Freshly prepared *Poultry Liver Parfait (p. 265)*, made with duck livers and crème de cassis, in pastry bag (no tip needed)	8 fl oz	360 mL
White Poultry Aspic for Coating, (p. 644) optional	12 fl oz	240 mL

PROCEDURE

PREPARATION

1. Pipe the parfait into four 4-fl oz (120-mL) silicone pyramid forms, distributing the parfait evenly among the forms, making them about three-quarters full (A). Level the surfaces with the back of a spoon. Cover with plastic film and freeze at least 2 hours, or until the parfait has hardened.
2. Pop the pyramids out of the forms onto a sheet tray lined with parchment (B).
3. Cover all surfaces of each pyramid with a piece of plastic film.
4. Refrigerate about 6 hours, or until thawed throughout.
5. Optional aspic coating:
   a. Transfer the pyramids to a rack set over a sheet tray lined with parchment.
   b. Apply one or two coatings of aspic as needed (C). Refer to page 643, steps 5 through 7a for coating procedure.

A

B

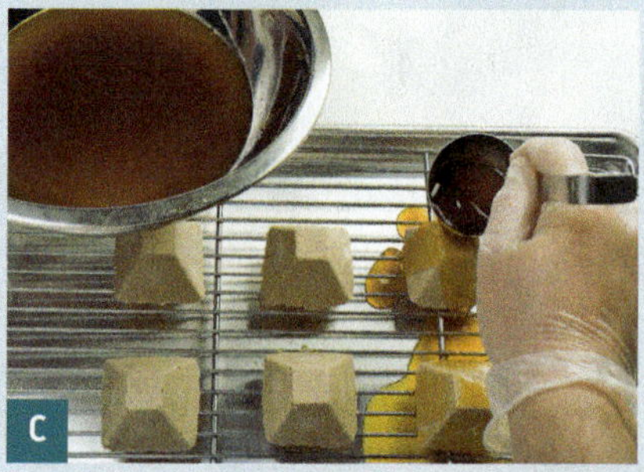
C

HOLDING

Hold uncoated pyramids refrigerated up to 3 days, frozen up to 1 month. Aspic coated pyramids may be refrigerated in a covered container up to 2 days.

DUCK LIVER PARFAIT PYRAMID

WITH CASSIS ESSENCE AND RED CURRANTS

APPETIZER

Portions:
1
Portion size:
3 oz (90 mL)

COMPONENTS

1 fl oz (30 mL) *Cassis Essence (p. 691)*, in squeeze bottle
1 *Duck Liver Parfait Pyramid (p. 266)*, aspic coated or uncoated
½ oz (15 g) Champagne grape or red currant cluster
1 oz/30 g (5 pieces) *Toasted Baguette Croûtons (p. 702)*

PROCEDURE

PLATING

1. Squeeze streaks of cassis essence on a cool 10-in. (25-cm) plate in a decorative fashion.
2. Place the pyramid on the plate slightly left of center.
3. Place the grape or currant cluster on the plate to the right of the pyramid.
4. Serve the baguette croûtons on a separate plate or in a napkin-lined basket.

FOIE GRAS

Foie gras ranks along with caviar and truffles as one of the Western world's most expensive and luxurious foods. The French term *foie gras* literally means "fat liver," and that is a good description. **Foie gras** [FWAH grah] is defined as the enlarged liver of a goose or duck that is the result of accelerated feeding of a high-calorie diet.

When an animal consumes more calories than it expends, the extra calories are converted into fat. Some of this fat is distributed through the interior of its muscles and is evident as marbling. Some of the fat forms on the exterior of the animal's muscles and is visible as deposit fat. However, when geese and ducks consume many calories over a short period, much of the fat also forms within their livers. These grow abnormally large and acquire an unusually pale color. When harvested and correctly prepared, these livers have a delicious, mild, buttery flavor and a rich, smooth mouthfeel.

The Foie Gras Controversy

In recent years, animal rights activists have condemned the production of foie gras as inhumane. The main target of their criticism is the practice of gavage, or force-feeding, which they maintain is harmful to the health of the fowl. They claim the feed tube injures the fowl's throat, some fowl choke during feeding, and the fowls' high-fat diet causes them to contract liver disease. They also protest the practice of confinement production, in which foie gras fowl are kept immobile in small cages to restrict their ability to exercise.

Foie gras producers counter these claims. They maintain that gavage does not injure the fowl's throat or other parts of its digestive system because the esophagus of waterfowl is naturally tough and elastic. In fact, during the gavage period, the birds appear eager to be fed. Dramatic expansion of the liver after accelerated feeding also happens in the wild, when ducks and geese eat massive amounts of food in preparation for migration. This does not typically cause liver disease. Diseased poultry liver would not be fit to eat and would not be legal to sell.

In North America, most foie gras fowl are allowed to range free for the first 12 weeks of life and are confined for fattening only 12 to 18 days. Many artisan producers do not use individual confinement at all and group-pen their fowl during the fattening period.

Many chefs insist on visiting the farms and slaughterhouses where their meats are produced. They know their producers and are familiar with the methods used to produce the foods they serve. In this way, chefs can make an informed decision whether or not to serve foie gras and other controversial foods.

Grade A foie gras
Courtesy Bella Bella Gourmet LLC, West Haven, CT www.bellagourmet.com.

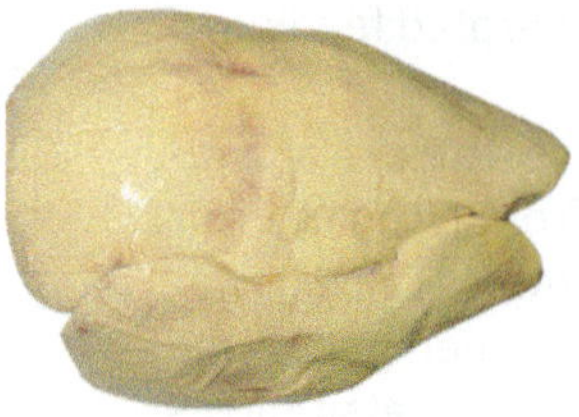

Grade B foie gras
Courtesy Bella Bella Gourmet LLC, West Haven, CT www.bellagourmet.com.

Accelerated feeding of geese and ducks is accomplished by utilizing a method known by the French word **gavage** [gah-VAHJ]. This translates as "force-feeding," although that is not necessarily an accurate description. In traditional gavage, each bird is fed by hand by inserting a funnel-like instrument with a long tube down its throat. Grain, or a mash consisting of grain cooked with water, is placed into the funnel, and it flows through the tube into the bird's esophagus. The amount of grain fed is increased gradually, so by the end of the fattening process, a mature goose is being fed about 4 lb (2 kg) feed per day.

The reasoning behind gavage is not necessarily to force the goose or duck to eat more than it is able to eat but rather to feed a large number of fowl quickly and to make sure all of the birds in the flock receive an equal amount of feed. Today the practice of gavage is widely misunderstood. Misunderstanding is compounded by the fact that, in some operations, foie gras fowl are not maintained in proper conditions and gavage is not practiced in a humane manner (see sidebar, left). However, in North America there are quite a few operations that produce foie gras responsibly. Chefs using foie gras should be familiar with their sources and know how the foie gras is produced.

Fresh Foie Gras

Until recently, virtually all foie gras sold outside its immediate production area was cooked by a processor prior to sale, originally due to the extreme perishability of the product. Even after refrigeration became the norm, most restaurants purchased prepared foie gras because of the difficulty of cooking it correctly. Because foie gras was typically served cold, the processed product was considered perfectly adequate by many.

During the era of nouvelle cuisine, chefs began to serve foie gras hot, slicing and pan-searing raw foie gras to order. Thus, demand was created for **fresh foie gras**, or **foie gras cru**. Most chefs now agree that fresh, domestic foie gras correctly cooked in-house is far superior to processed foie gras in cold presentations as well.

Until the mid-1980s, fresh foie gras had to be flown in from Europe at great cost. Today, duck foie gras is produced in North America and, while not inexpensive, its cost is less prohibitive.

North American fresh duck foie gras is marketed as a whole liver weighing ¾–1½ lb (350–700 g) and consisting of two lobes. After it is harvested, it is removed from pre-chilled carcasses and immediately sealed in vacuum packaging. Fresh duck foie gras is available in three grades:

1. **Grade A Foie Gras** is firm in texture, pale and even in color, and has a rounded oval shape. Grade A foie gras weighs at least 1½ lb (700 g). It has a minimal amount of interior veining, thus yielding large, intact slices. Its firm texture results in a higher melt point, making it less difficult to cook correctly.
2. **Grade B Foie Gras** has a more flattened shape and is smaller than a Grade A liver. It has more interior veining and a lower melt point.

3. **Grade C Foie Gras** is small and may contain visual imperfections. It is usually used for puréed preparations, such as mousses and sauces.

Vacuum-packed foie gras should be carefully inspected upon receipt for freshness and quality, and stored under refrigeration buried in ice to hold it as close to 33°F (1° C) as possible. At that temperature, unopened foie gras can be held up to 1 week.

Preparing Fresh Foie Gras

In garde manger work, foie gras is prepared ahead of time by poaching it or baking it in a pâté or terrine and serving it cold. However, the garde manger department may be asked to clean and season raw foie gras for the hot line as well.

Procedure for Cleaning and Seasoning Fresh Foie Gras

1. Place the opened foie gras in a bowl set under a gentle stream of room-temperature water. Flush the foie gras about half an hour, or until the water runs clear and the foie gras warms enough to become pliable so you can manipulate it without breaking it.
2. Blot the foie gras dry and place it on a freshly sanitized work surface.
3. Slowly and gently pull the two lobes apart (A).
4. Use your fingers or a small, sharp knife to remove any visible membrane and surface blemishes from each lobe (B).
5. Lay each lobe on the worktable so the smooth side is down and the rough side is up. Starting at the narrow, top end of each lobe, slit open the lobe about halfway to the other end and about halfway into its depth (C).
6. Use your fingers and, if necessary, sanitized tweezers or needlenose pliers to remove the interior veins (D). Do so by grasping the thick top part of the vein network and pulling gently while holding back the meat of the liver with the other hand. Your goal is to extract the veins without breaking them and without disturbing the structure of the liver.
7. Sprinkle the interior and exterior of each lobe with the desired seasoning ingredients.
8. Wrap each lobe in plastic film, and then seal the wrapped lobes in a plastic bag.
9. Bury the bag of foie gras in ice and refrigerate 24 hours.

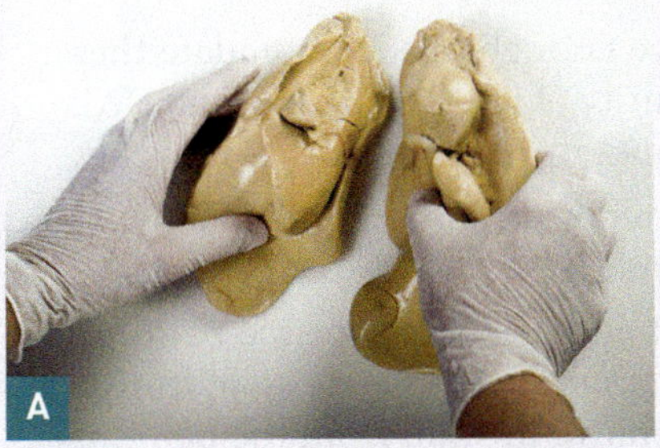
A

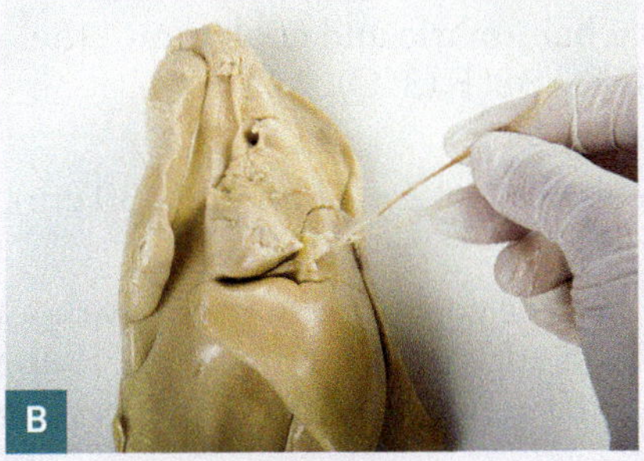
B

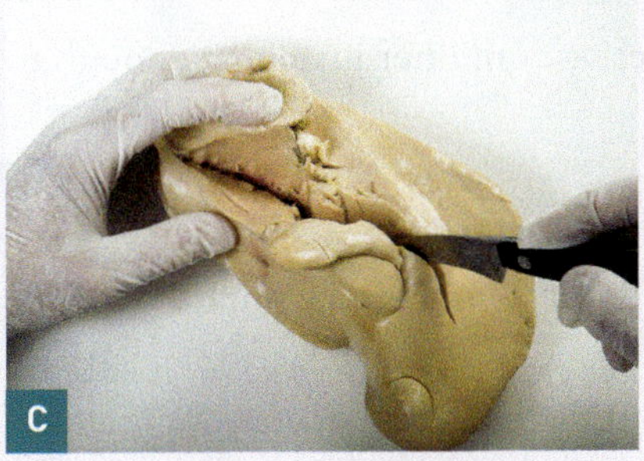
C

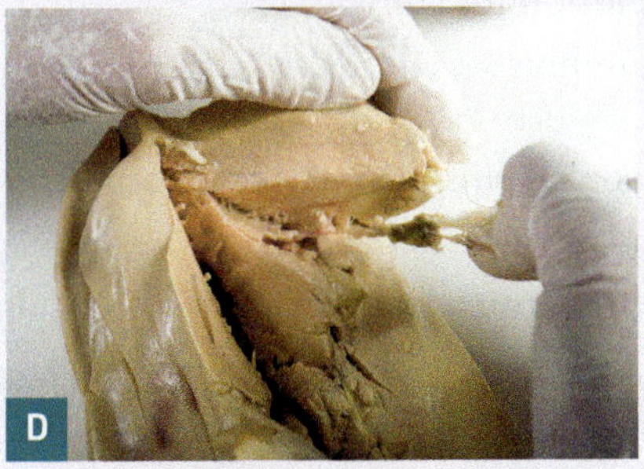
D

Once the foie gras has been cleaned and seasoned, it is ready to cook. Many garde manger chefs believe the best way to experience foie gras is to enjoy it in its most pristine, natural state: simply poached in a flavorful *cuisson* and served at cool room temperature with a minimum of carefully chosen accompaniments.

Procedure for Poaching Fresh Duck Foie Gras

1. Choose a nonreactive saucepan just large enough to hold the foie gras completely submerged in its *cuisson*. Add the *cuisson* and bring it to a bare simmer.
2. Prepare the *torchon* (A):
   a. Moisten a 12 × 12-in. (30 × 30-cm) piece of doubled cheesecloth and lay it on a work surface.
   b. Reassemble the foie gras lobes and place them on the cheesecloth.
   c. Roll the foie gras in the cheesecloth and gently compress it to form as even a cylinder as possible without crushing or breaking the liver.
   d. Tie each end with a piece of kitchen string (A).
   e. Cut 2 or 3 wide bands of cheesecloth and wrap them around the torchon for extra support.
   f. Cut off the excess cheesecloth with scissors, leaving just enough at each end to use as handles with which to pick up the cooked torchon.

A

B

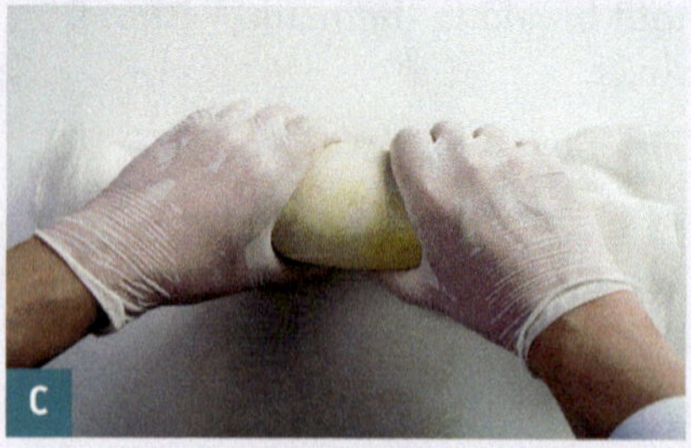
C

3. Prepare an ice bain-marie large enough to accommodate the poaching pan and a large quantity of ice. A large bain-marie is needed to bring down the temperature of the hot pan quickly.
4. Lower the torchon into the simmering *cuisson* and poach it at 200°F (93°C) exactly 90 seconds (see Note).
5. Remove the pan from the heat and place it in the ice bain-marie (B). Hold it there until the temperature of the *cuisson* drops to 180°F (82°C). Immediately remove the pan from the bain-marie and let it stand for exactly 2 minutes.
6. Again place the pan into the ice bain-marie and cool it until the temperature of the *cuisson* reaches 38°F (3°C). Add more ice to the bain-marie as necessary.
7. Lay fresh piece of doubled cheesecloth, 12 × 12 in. (30 × 30 cm), on the worktable.
8. Remove the foie gras torchon from the cooled *cuisson* and, without unwrapping it, lay it on the bottom edge of the cheesecloth, Roll it up in the second cheesecloth while gently but firmly compressing it into a uniform cylinder (C)
9. Prepare the foie gras and *cuisson* for storage:
   a. Transfer the foie gras torchon into a freshly sanitized, nonreactive container just large enough to hold it.
   b. Pour in enough of the cooled *cuisson* to cover it completely.
   c. Cover the container and refrigerate the foie gras.
   d. Pour the remaining *cuisson* into a freshly sanitized container, cover it, and refrigerate it.

Note: The specified poaching and holding times are for a 1½-lb (700-g) Grade A foie gras. If you are poaching a smaller foie gras, reduce the times accordingly. For example, in step 4 poach a 1-lb (500-g) foie gras for 60 seconds and in step 5 let stand for 80 seconds.

Foie gras is extremely delicate in texture. It also has a very high content of solid fat. Because of these two characteristics, it must be poached below the simmer and just long enough to cook it to the desired internal temperature. Your goal is to heat it until the internal fat softens enough to acquire a luscious mouthfeel, but not enough so it liquefies. If the foie gras becomes too hot or is heated for too long, the liquid fat seeps out into the *cuisson* and leaves behind a tasteless, shrunken protein mass.

Foie gras is fabricated in a special way in order to maintain a cylindrical shape that can be cut into attractive, even slices. The cleaned and seasoned lobes are reassembled and then wrapped in a roll of moistened cheesecloth tied with string at either end. When wrapped and poached in this manner, the foie gras is said to be cooked ***en torchon*** [ahn tor-SHAH(N)], and the finished product is called a ***torchon*** [tor-SHAH(N)] of foie gras.

Once fresh foie gras is poached and chilled in its *cuisson,* it is ready to be sliced and served at cool room temperature. The yellow fat that resolidifies on the foie gras should be removed before serving. This fat, and the fat that forms on the chilled *cuisson*, makes a delicious cooking medium for sautéed potatoes and other foods. The *cuisson* used to poach the foie gras is typically used to make a sauce or an aspic gelée to accompany the foie gras.

Wear food-service gloves when handling cooked foie gras to prevent contamination and to keep it from melting and showing fingerprints. After a slice of foie gras is removed from the torchon, the remaining foie gras should be rewrapped and reimmersed in the *cuisson* for storage.

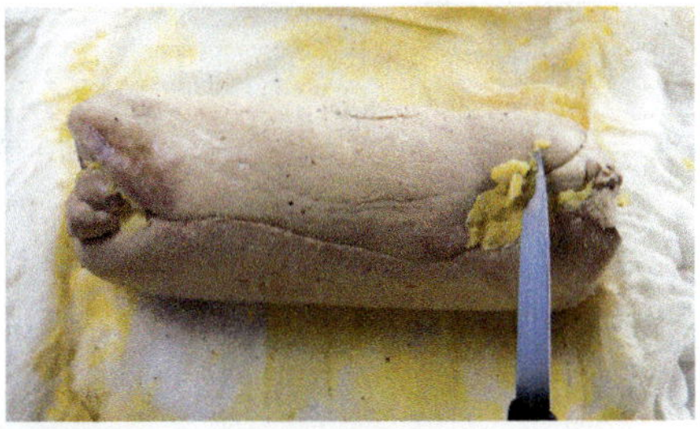
Remove the yellow fat from the foie gras.

Slicing from the torchon of foie gras.

Processed Foie Gras and Foie Gras Products

You may wish to use one of several types of processed foie gras products for some preparations. These products are cooked by the producer and packed in cans or in vacuum packaging. Most are imported from Europe. All are ready to eat as purchased and need no further cooking.

Foie Gras Cuit, Entier [FWA grah kwee ahn-TYAY]: Whole lobes of cooked, seasoned foie gras vacuum-packed and refrigerated or frozen.

Foie Gras Cuit, Morceaux [FWA grah kwee mor-SOH]: Pieces of cooked, seasoned foie gras vacuum-packed and refrigerated or frozen.

Bloc de Foie Gras [BLOCK duh FWA grah]: Foie gras puréed and emulsified with water and then heat-processed in a can. Must be at least 98% total foie gras, and may contain both goose and duck foie gras.

Parfait de Foie Gras [pahr-FAY duh FWA grah]: Puréed and cooked with cream and butter, and then canned and heat-processed. Must contain at least 75% foie gras. Some varieties contain up to 3% truffles.

Pâté or Mousse de Foie Gras: Similar to parfait, but with the addition of chicken livers or unfattened duck livers. May contain as little as 50% foie gras.

COLD POACHED DUCK FOIE GRAS

Yield:
about 12 oz (360 g)
Portion:
6
Portion size:
2 oz (60 g)

INGREDIENTS	U.S.	METRIC
Raw domestic duck foie gras, 1–1½ lb (450–700 g)	1	1
Fine sea salt	to taste	to taste
Finely ground white pepper	to taste	to taste
Best-quality medium-dry Riesling wine	25 fl oz	750 mL
Granular gelatin	as needed	as needed

PROCEDURE

DAY 1

1. Prepare the foie gras according to the Procedure for Cleaning and Seasoning Fresh Foie Gras on p. 269. Season it with the sea salt and pepper.
2. Refrigerate the seasoned, wrapped, iced foie gras 24 hours.

DAY 2

1. Poach the foie gras as directed in the Procedure for Poaching Fresh Duck Foie Gras on p. 270. Use the Riesling as the *cuisson*.
2. Refrigerate the foie gras in its *cuisson* for 24 hours. (The Riesling *cuisson* may be used to make aspic gelée.)

HOLDING

Refrigerate up to 4 days in or out of the *cuisson*.

COOL DUCK FOIE GRAS

WITH RIESLING GELÉE

APPETIZER

Portions:
1
Portion size:
2 oz (60 g)

COMPONENTS

2 oz (60 g) *Cold Poached Duck Foie Gras (above)*
1 fl oz (30 mL) *Riesling Aspic Gelée Jewels (p. 708)*
to taste Coarse fleur de sel or other sea salt
1 oz/30 g (5–6 pieces) Freshly *Toasted Baguette Croûtons (p. 702)*

PROCEDURE

PLATING

1. Wearing food-service gloves, cut a 2-oz (60-g) slice of foie gras (see illustration, p. 271) and place it slightly left of center on a cool 10-in. (25-cm) plate. Immediately return the rest of the foie gras to the refrigerator.
2. Spoon an arc of gelée jewels around the right side of the foie gras.
3. Sprinkle the salt on the left side of the plate.
4. Serve the croûtons on a separate plate or in a napkin-lined basket.

COOL DUCK FOIE GRAS

WITH PLUMS AND PLUM COULIS

APPETIZER

Portions:
1
Portion size:
2 oz (60 g) foie gras, plus garnish

COMPONENTS

2 oz (60 g) *Cold Poached Duck Foie Gras (p. 272)*
1 fl oz (30 mL) *Red Plum Coulis (p. 53)*, in squeeze bottle
to taste Coarse red sea salt or other sea salt
3 slices Thinly sliced ripe plums
1 oz/30 g (5–6 pieces) Freshly *Toasted Baguette Croûtons (p. 702)*

PROCEDURE

PLATING

1. Wearing food-service gloves, cut a 2-oz (60-g) slice of foie gras and place it slightly left of center on a cool 10-in. (25-cm) plate. Immediately return the rest of the foie gras to the refrigerator.
2. Squeeze an arc of plum coulis on the plate to the right of the foie gras.
3. Arrange the plum slices in an overlapping arc on the right of the foie gras.
4. Arrange two mounds of salt on the plate at 1 o'clock and 7 o'clock.
5. Serve the croûtons on a separate plate or in a napkin-lined basket.

TERMS FOR REVIEW

deli tray
carve
carving station
grosse pièce
sequencing
attelet
garniture
marinade
parfait
foie gras
gavage
fresh foie gras
foie gras cru
en torchon
torchon

QUESTIONS FOR DISCUSSION

1. Discuss the changing role of cold meat dishes. When and how were cold meat dishes typically served in the nineteenth century? List and describe three ways cold meats are typically utilized in modern food service.
2. List five guidelines for preparing deli trays.
3. Define the term *hand-carved*, and explain its significance to customers.
4. Draw a diagram showing the procedure for carving a roast chicken.
5. List and describe five decorative elements typically added to a cold meat or poultry platter.
6. Explain *sequencing* as applied to slicing and presenting cold cooked meats. How does the use of a grosse pièce affect slicing and sequencing?
7. Compare and contrast the preparation of meats for hot service and for cold presentation. Include in your discussion six important differences in the preparation and handling of cold meats.
8. Why is it important to minimize fat in meats and poultry to be served cold? List several ways this can be done.
9. What is the preferred temperature range in which cold meats should be served? Explain the reasons for serving cold meats at this temperature.
10. List the guidelines for preparing and serving raw meat dishes.
11. Define *foie gras*, and explain how it is produced.

Chapter

8

PREREQUISITES

Before studying this chapter, you should already

- Have read "How to Use this Book," pages xxviii–xxxiii, and understand the professional recipe format.
- Be proficient at making hot soups.
- Know the procedure for clarifying stocks, and be proficient at doing so.

Cold Soups

In the *Complete Guide to Modern Cookery,* Escoffier states, "The obligation of serving soup very hot is one of the fundamental principles of service from the kitchen." Most soups are meant to be comforting and warming, and some are substantial enough to fill us up. Cold soups are exactly the opposite—they are served chilled, or even iced, as appetizers. Therefore, they are usually featured in the hot summer months, when cold foods are most welcome.

Although most soups are prepared in the hot kitchen and served from the hot line, the garde manger department is responsible for making cold soups. Serving correctly seasoned, well-chilled cold soups is a challenge. It demands a discriminating palate, knowledge of specialized presentation equipment, and attention to detail.

After reading this chapter, you should be able to

1. Prepare semisweet and savory cold soups.
2. Identify appropriate ingredients for cold soups.
3. Modify hot soups for cold service.
4. Maintain cold soups at the proper temperature.
5. Serve cold soups at the proper temperature using both purchased and improvised chilling serviceware.
6. Enhance cold soups with interesting and appropriate garnishes and accompaniments.

UNDERSTANDING COLD SOUPS

Soups are filling and economical. Throughout history, many people traditionally ate soup year-round because it was what they could afford to make. When the weather was too warm to eat hot soup, they served it cold. Thus, cold soups were traditionally a feature of peasant cooking.

Some cold soups are merely hot soups that are chilled before serving. However, there is a category of rustic cold soup made by chopping and pounding a mixture of juicy raw vegetables and enriching them with olive oil or fermented dairy products. These could be prepared by farmers in the fields or by shepherds in the pastures because they required no cooking.

Cold soups were not part of formal cuisine until the twentieth century. In the very hot summer of 1917, Chef Louis Diat of the Ritz Hotel in New York City began serving a cold potato-leek soup in the hotel's elegant formal dining room. He named it *vichyssoise* [vee-shee-SWAHZ] after a fashionable French spa resort. Its success paved the way for other cold soups to find a place on the menus of fine restaurants across North America.

Categories of Cold Soups

Cold soups are divided into three main categories:

1. **Sweet:** Served as dessert and often referred to as ***dessert soup***. Most are based on sweetened fruit purée or a fruit-based syrup. They are often garnished with fruit and may be enhanced with scoops of sorbet or ice cream. As they are dessert items, sweet cold soups *are usually the responsibility of the pastry department.*
2. **Semisweet:** Usually based on fruit, but with several differences from sweet cold soups:
    - *Degree of sweetness.* A semisweet cold soup has less sugar added to it. Sometimes it has no added sugar and relies only on the natural sweetness of the fruit.
    - *Acid balance.* A semisweet cold soup has a strong acid element, giving it a sweet-and-sour taste.
    - *Place in the meal.* Semisweet cold soup is usually served at the beginning of the meal, as an appetizer.
3. **Savory:** Typically served as an appetizer at the beginning of a meal, a savory cold soup should be light in texture, with a refreshing flavor. These soups are meant to stimulate the appetite, not satiate it. Some are simply chilled versions of hot appetizer soups. Others are made from raw ingredients.

Here, we focus on cold soups in the *savory* and *semisweet* categories.

Ingredients for Cold Soups

Ingredients for cold soups should have a low content of semisolid animal-derived fats. A soup containing lots of butter or bacon drippings may have a pleasantly rich mouthfeel when served hot, but it will be greasy and coat the tongue in an unpleasant manner when served cold. All stocks used in making cold soups must be thoroughly defatted (see p. 250, step 9). In addition, butter must be kept to a minimum.

Oils work well in cold soups because they remain fluid at cold temperatures. Flavorful oils, such as extra-virgin olive oil and nut oils, are often used to finish cold soups. These oils give cold soups a rich mouthfeel as well as a distinctive taste.

Very starchy foods must be used in reduced quantity. While some starch is necessary to thicken puréed cold soups, foods with a high starch content, such as potatoes, winter squash, and dried legumes, can make them seem pasty and heavy. For the same reason, roux-based soups are rarely served cold, unless the roux thickening is very light.

Keeping Cold Soups Cold

Cold soups must be served ice cold. A lukewarm soup gives the customers the impression the kitchen has made a mistake.

To ensure that cold soups reach customers at the proper cold temperature:

1. During service turnout, store the soup at as low a temperature as possible. The insert of a sandwich unit or in the refrigerator is usually not sufficient to maintain a really cold temperature. Often, it is necessary to set up an ice bain-marie.
2. Keep the soup covered when not in use.
3. Chill or freeze the cups or bowls in which the soup will be served.
4. Train servers to pick up cold soups promptly so the soup will not warm up waiting in the service window.

In addition to these simple procedures, special serving dishes and garnishes can help maintain cold temperatures.

- *Shrimp cocktail chillers* (essentially miniature ice bain-maries) are the most elegant way to serve cold soups. These must be placed on an underliner plate lined with a napkin or doily to prevent them from slipping and to absorb condensation.
- *Improvised soup chillers* can be constructed by placing a soup cup in a larger cup or bowl full of crushed ice. An underliner plate must be used.
- *Flavored ice cubes* keep a chilled soup cold without diluting its flavor when they melt, and they add both visual and textural appeal. See Chapter 17 for procedures to make flavored ice cubes.

Soup Sips

A recent trend in upscale restaurant and catering service is serving very small portions of soup in tiny serving vessels, such as demitasse cups or shot glasses. This presentation is typically referred to as a **soup sip**. It may be served as a passed hors d'oeuvre or offered as an amuse-bouche. Three sips can also be grouped as a trio or flight to make up a full appetizer portion. Cold soups are especially popular as sips, because they hold their temperature in small quantity better than hot soups do.

Garnishes and Accompaniments for Cold Soups

Cold soups may be enhanced with a variety of garnishes. Minced herbs, beautifully cut vegetables, precisely cut bits of meat or seafood, rosettes or dollops of thickened creams, and many other garnishes are appropriate. In addition, cubes or cutouts of aspic gelée (p. 708) and the flavored ice cubes mentioned above are elegant and unusual cold soup garnishes.

Common accompaniments are croûtons, crackers, bread sticks, or savory pastry items.

Types of Cold Soups

Many cold soups begin as hot soups but are chilled before they are served. Like the hot soups from which they are made, these soups are identified by their thickening method. Other cold soups are not cooked at all.

Chilled Cooked Vegetable Purées

Soups made from vegetables cooked in stock or water and then puréed and chilled are among the most popular cold soups. These soups are thickened by the fiber and starch in the vegetables and do not contain any additional thickeners. When done correctly, this method results in cold soups with a light, pleasant texture. Some are enriched with cream, half-and-half, or crème fraîche.

Jellied Consommés

A consommé made in the classic manner, using plenty of bones and with a pig's foot added for body, sets up into a light gel when chilled. A cold soup prepared in this manner is called a ***jellied consommé***. Today, most recipes call for commercial gelatin instead of the pig's foot. Jellied consommés are often flavored with fortified wines such as dry sherry and Madeira. They are usually served in glass or crystal cups to show off their color and clarity.

Textured Raw Vegetable Soups

Soups made from ground or chopped raw vegetables have a rustic, almost salad-like texture. Most of the vegetable mixture is puréed in a blender or food processor, and then additional vegetables that have been chopped or fabricated into small dice are added. Often, these soups are enhanced with a flavorful oil for seasoning, enrichment, and a glossy appearance. Some textured raw vegetable soups are enriched with sour cream, crème fraîche, or yogurt.

Smooth Raw Vegetable Soups

Smooth soups made from puréed raw vegetables are considered more formal and elegant than their textured counterparts. They are usually made from tender vegetables such as avocadoes, tomatoes, or cucumbers. After they are puréed, they are forced through a food mill or fine mesh sieve to make them perfectly smooth. These soups are often enriched with a dairy product.

Chilled Raw Fruit Purées

These soups are made from ripe fruit that is soft enough to purée smooth without first being cooked. Strawberries, melons, peaches, plums, and mangoes are typical ingredients. If the fruit is at the perfect state of quality and ripeness, no additional sweetening is needed. In fact, the sweetness of the fruit purée is usually such that the flavor of the resulting soup must be balanced with an acid, such as citrus juice. If sweetening is needed, a fluid sweetener such as simple syrup or honey is typically used. After puréeing, these soups are sieved to achieve smoothness. They may be finished with precision-cut fruits, thickened creams, or other appropriate garnishes. They may be garnished with a tart sorbet.

Cooked Fruit Soups

Fresh fruits with firm or mealy textures when ripe, such as pears and apricots, are cooked first in liquid. Dried fruits are also made into cold soups by cooking them. The cooking liquid is usually a light syrup made from sugar and water, fruit juice, or wine. Because of the sugar present in the cooking liquid, the flavor of these soups usually must be balanced with a strong acid. Otherwise, they would be too sweet to be served as a first course. Cooked fruits soups are sometimes puréed but are often left chunky and are lightly thickened with a cornstarch or arrowroot slurry, or tapioca.

Preparing Cold Soups

Some important factors must be taken into consideration when preparing cold soups, and some special techniques used to deal with these factors.

Achieving the Proper Texture

Liquids thickened with vegetable fiber or starch are thinner at hot temperatures but become thicker when chilled. Also, a well-made stock becomes gelatinous when it is cold. To maintain a pleasant, lightly nappé consistency in cold soups, you must compensate for this thickening effect.

If you are serving a normally hot soup cold, a good general rule is to decrease the amount of thickening ingredient in the formula by about 20%. For example, if the ratio of carrot to stock in a hot carrot purée soup is 1 lb (500 g) to 1 gal (4 L), decrease the amount of carrots to about 13 oz (400 g). This is a general guideline, and individual soups may have different requirements. You may still need to thin the soup after it has become cold.

Puréed soups made from raw fruit also thicken over time due to the jelling action of the fruit's pectin content. Check their texture after an hour or two in the refrigerator. If they thicken too much, thin with fruit juice, water, or another appropriate liquid. After you thin the soup, readjust its flavor balance as well.

Seasoning Accurately

A food that tastes properly seasoned when hot often tastes flat after it is chilled. This is especially true for cold soups. While you should season your soup with salt and most other flavorings while it is cooking, you cannot accurately evaluate its final seasoning until it is thoroughly chilled.

Most recipe formulas in this text recommend kosher salt for seasoning. However, coarse kosher salt does not dissolve quickly in cold liquids. Use fine salt for the final seasoning of a cold soup because it dissolves more quickly, enabling you to determine the correct seasoning without waiting for it to dissolve.

Quick Chilling

An ice bain-marie alone is sufficient to cool small amounts of cooked soup. However, when quick-chilling large quantities of hot soup, you should use a cooling paddle along with an ice bain-marie to chill the soup even more quickly. (This is a good procedure to follow when cooling a large amount of any hot liquid because it shortens the time the product spends in the temperature danger zone [TDZ].) Quick-chilling cold soups also allows you to make final adjustments to the texture and flavor of the final product in a timely manner. If you rely on room-temperature cooling followed by refrigerator cooling, it is easy to forget to make the necessary final adjustments in texture and seasoning.

Serving Cold Soups

It is important to match the style of a cold soup with the style of the rest of the menu. Many cold soups have a casual feeling and are appropriate as a starter before grilled meats, salad entrées, and other simple summer foods. Others, such as jellied consommés and cream-enriched purées, are elegant and technically complex, and may be served as the first course of a formal meal. No matter when cold soups are served, be sure to hold and serve them at the proper temperature.

RECIPES

VICHYSSOISE *(vee-shee-SWAHZ)*

Yield:
about 2½ qt (2.4 L)
Portions:
8
Portion size:
10 fl oz (300 mL)

INGREDIENTS	U.S.	METRIC
Leeks	1½ lb	750 g
Butter	2 oz	60 g
Peeled russet potato, ½-in. (1-cm) dice	8 oz	240 g
Kosher salt	to taste	to taste
Defatted *Poultry Stock (p. 749)*	1½ qt	1.5 L
Half-and-half	6 fl oz	180 mL
Additional defatted poultry stock	as needed	as needed
Fine salt	to taste	to taste
Fresh lemon juice	to taste	to taste
Finely ground white pepper	to taste	to taste

PROCEDURE

PREPARATION

1. Cut off the dark green leaves of the leeks and, if desired, reserve them for stock. Cut off the root ends. Slit the leeks lengthwise and open them under cool running water to remove any dirt. Shake the leeks dry and chop them coarse.
2. Heat the butter in a heavy pot and sweat the leeks over low heat without browning them, about 8 minutes or until they are soft.
3. Add the potatoes and some salt. Stir to coat them with butter.
4. Add the stock and bring it to a simmer. Cook the soup, stirring occasionally, about 20 minutes, or until the vegetables are very tender.
5. Purée the soup with an immersion blender, or cool slightly and purée in a food processor.
6. Force the soup through a fine mesh sieve into a freshly sanitized, nonreactive container.
7. Add the half-and-half and correct the salt.
8. Place the container in an ice bain-marie and stir the soup occasionally to chill it.
9. If necessary, correct the thickness with more stock to achieve a light nappé consistency texture.
10. Taste and correct the seasoning balance with fine salt and lemon juice. Season lightly with pepper.

HOLDING

Refrigerate up to 5 days. Freeze up to 1 month.

VARIATIONS

CARROT VICHYSSOISE

Replace half of the potatoes with carrots.

LOBSTER VICHYSSOISE

Replace the poultry stock with Shellfish Stock (p. 750). Garnish each serving with ½ oz (15 g) steamed, chilled diced lobster.

VICHYSSOISE
WITH POTATO TUILE

APPETIZER

Portions:
1
Portion size:
10 fl oz (300 mL)

COMPONENTS

10 fl oz (300 mL) *Vichyssoise (p. 280)*
2 tsp (10 mL) Minced fresh chives
1 *Potato Tuile (p. 697)*

Supplies
1 8-in. (20-cm) doily

PROCEDURE

PLATING

1. Ladle the vichyssoise into a chilled 12-fl oz (360-mL) soup plate.
2. Sprinkle the chives on the soup's surface.
3. Place the bowl on a doily-lined 9-in. (23-cm) plate.
4. Place the potato tuile on the rim of the soup plate.

CHILLED MINTED PEA PURÉE

Yield:
about 2½ qt (2.4 L)
Portions:
8
Portion Size:
10 fl oz (300 mL)

INGREDIENTS	U.S.	METRIC
Butter	2 oz	90 g
Minced yellow onions	6 oz	180 g
Fresh or frozen shelled peas	4 oz	120 g
Sugar snap peas, stringed and chopped	8 oz	240 g
Defatted *Poultry Stock (p. 749)*	1½ qt	1.5 L
Kosher salt	to taste	to taste
Fine salt	to taste	to taste
Half-and-half, cold	6 fl oz	180 mL
Additional defatted poultry stock	as needed	as needed
Coarsely chopped mint leaves	⅛ oz (2 tsp)	4 g (10 mL)

PROCEDURE

PREPARATION

1. Heat the butter in a large pot and add the onion. Sweat the onion over low heat about 1 minute, or until it is soft but not brown.
2. Add the peas and snap peas, the stock, and some kosher salt.
3. Bring the stock to the boil and continue cooking the soup at a rapid boil, stirring often, just until the peas are tender.
4. Place a freshly sanitized, nonreactive container in an ice bain-marie.
5. As soon as the vegetables are tender, drain off and reserve most of the stock.
6. Place the solids into a blender or food processor fitted with the steel blade. Purée the vegetables, adding just enough of the cooking stock through the top opening to make a smooth purée.
7. Immediately scrape the purée into the container in the ice bain-marie. Add the remaining stock and the half-and-half.
8. Stir the soup often to cool it as quickly as possible.
9. When the soup is cold, adjust the texture to a light nappé with additional stock if necessary.
10. Correct the seasoning with fine salt and stir in the chopped mint.

HOLDING

Refrigerate in a covered container up to 5 days.

CHILLED MINTED PEA PURÉE

WITH PEA SHOOTS

APPETIZER

Portions:
1
Portion size:
10 fl oz (300 mL)

COMPONENTS

10 fl oz (300 mL) *Chilled Minted Pea Purée (p. 282)*
½ fl oz (15 mL) *Creamy Cold Carrot Soup (p. 288)*, in squeeze bottle
¼ oz (7 g) Pea shoots

Supplies

1 Cocktail napkin or 4-in. (10-cm) doily

PROCEDURE

PLATING

1. Prepare a shrimp cocktail chiller or a chilled 12-fl oz (360-mL) soup cup set into a larger cup of crushed ice.
2. Ladle the soup into the top cup.
3. Squeeze a ring of ⅜-in. (1.5-cm) dots of carrot soup around the edge of the pea purée (A) and use a knife to create a string of hearts pattern (see p. 715) (B).
4. Place a tangle of pea shoots in the center of the soup's surface.
5. Set the bowl on an underliner plate lined with a cocktail napkin or doily.

A

B

CHILLED ROASTED TOMATO SOUP

Yield:
2½ qt (2.4 L)
Portions:
8
Portion Size:
10 fl oz (300 mL)

INGREDIENTS	U.S.	METRIC
Vine-ripe tomatoes	3 lb	1.5 kg
Whole yellow onion	6 oz	180 g
Whole, peel-on garlic cloves	1 oz	30 g
Extra-virgin olive oil	4 fl oz	120 mL
Kosher salt	to taste	to taste
White wine	4 fl oz	120 mL
Defatted *Poultry Stock (p. 749)*	1 qt	1 L
Fresh basil	1 oz	30 g
Additional defatted poultry stock	as needed	as needed
Balsamic vinegar	to taste	to taste

PROCEDURE

PREPARATION

1. Core the tomatoes and cut them in half horizontally.
2. Preheat a broiler to high heat. Preheat an oven to 400°F (200°C).
3. Brush a half-hotel pan with olive oil. Salt the flesh of the tomatoes and place them flat side down in the pan. Drizzle with half the remaining oil.
4. Peel and quarter the onion. Peel the garlic and remove the root ends.
5. Brush another hotel pan with oil and place the onion and garlic in it. Drizzle with the remaining oil and season with salt.
6. Broil the tomatoes until they are blistered and lightly charred. Cool.
7. Bake the onions and garlic 12–15 minutes, or until they begin to char.
8. Add the wine to the onions and garlic, cover the pan with foil, and continue to bake about 20 minutes more, or until the vegetables are tender.
9. Chop the vegetables coarse and place them in a heavy, nonreactive saucepan. Scrape all of the oil and juices from the two hotel pans into the saucepan. Add the stock and the basil. Bring to a rapid simmer and cook, stirring occasionally, about 15 minutes, or until the vegetables are soft.
10. Force the soup through a food mill into a freshly sanitized, nonreactive container.
11. Place the container in an ice bain-marie and stir occasionally until the soup is cold.
12. If necessary, thin the soup with additional stock.
13. Season the soup with balsamic vinegar and fine salt to achieve a tangy but balanced flavor.

HOLDING

Refrigerate in the covered container up to 3 days. (For longer holding, do not add the vinegar. Season the soup with vinegar just before serving it.)

VARIATION

CHILLED GOLDEN TOMATO SOUP

Replace the red tomatoes with yellow tomatoes.

CHILLED ROASTED TOMATO SOUP

WITH BASIL CRÈME FRAÎCHE AND PARMESAN TUILE

APPETIZER

Portions:
1
Portion size:
10 fl oz (300 mL)

COMPONENTS

10 fl oz (300 mL) *Chilled Roasted Tomato Soup (p. 284)*
1 *Parmesan Tuile (p. 696)*
½ fl oz (15 mL) *Crème Fraîche (p. 567)*
2–3 Basil leaves

Supplies
1 Cocktail napkin or 4-in. (10-cm) doily

PROCEDURE

PLATING

1. Prepare a shrimp cocktail chiller or a chilled 12-fl oz (360-mL) soup cup set into a larger cup of crushed ice.
2. Ladle the soup into the top cup.
3. Break the tuile into thirds and float the pieces in the center of the soup's surface.
4. Spoon the crème fraîche on the tuile pieces.
5. Roll up the basil leaf and chiffonnade it. Scatter the chiffonnade basil on the soup's surface.
6. Place the chiller on an underliner plate lined with a cocktail napkin or doily.

PROVENÇAL COLD PEPPER AND FENNEL PURÉE

Yield:
2½ qt (2.4 L)
Portions:
8
Portion size:
10 fl oz (300 mL)

INGREDIENTS	U.S.	METRIC
Red bell peppers	2 lb	1 kg
Extra-virgin olive oil	8 fl oz	240 mL
Whole peeled garlic cloves	1 oz	30 g
Trimmed fennel bulb, chopped coarse (reserve the fronds for garnish)	10 oz	300 g
Kosher salt	to taste	to taste
Defatted *Poultry Stock (p. 749)*	2 qt	2 L
Additional defatted poultry stock	as needed	as needed
Fine salt	to taste	to taste
Fresh lemon juice	to taste	to taste
Finely ground white pepper	to taste	to taste

PROCEDURE

PREPARATION

1. Roast the peppers according to the procedure on page 109.
2. Place the olive oil and whole garlic cloves in a nonreactive pan over low heat. Cook very slowly until the garlic is light golden. Stir occasionally.
3. Add the fennel and a little salt and stir to combine with the garlic. Cook over low heat until the fennel begins to soften.
4. Add the stock and simmer about 20 minutes.
5. Peel and clean the peppers according to the procedure on page 109. Chop the pepper flesh fine.
6. Add the peppers to the soup and simmer 5 minutes more.
7. Pour the soup through a strainer and reserve the broth.
8. Purée the solids in a blender or food processor, adding just enough of the broth to make a smooth purée.
9. Scrape the purée into a freshly sanitized, nonreactive container set in an ice bain-marie.
   Whisk in the remaining broth. Correct the thickness with additional stock as necessary.
10. Taste and balance the seasonings with fine salt and lemon juice. Season with pepper.

HOLDING

Refrigerate up to 5 days. Do not freeze.

VARIATION

COLD PEPPER AND CELERY PURÉE

Replace the fennel with celery. If a fennel-like flavor is desired, flavor the soup with a few drops of Pernod.

COLD PEPPER AND FENNEL PURÉE

WITH HERBES DE PROVENCE CROÛTONS

APPETIZER

Portions:
1
Portion size:
10 fl oz (300 mL)

COMPONENTS

10 fl oz (300 g) *Provençal Cold Pepper and Fennel Purée (p. 286)*
½ oz (15 g) *Herbes de Provence Croûton Cubes (p. 703)*
pinch Chopped fennel fronds

Supplies
1 Cocktail napkin or 4-in. (10-cm) doily

PROCEDURE

PLATING

1. Prepare a shrimp cocktail chiller or a chilled 12-fl oz (360-mL) soup cup set into a larger cup of crushed ice.
2. Ladle the purée into the top cup.
3. Top with the fennel fronds and croûtons.
4. Place the chiller on a 5-in. (12-cm) underliner plate lined with a cocktail napkin or doily.

COLD CURRIED CARROT SOUP

Yield: *2½ qt (2.4 L)*
Portions: *8*
Portion size: *10 fl oz (300 g)*

INGREDIENTS	U.S.	METRIC
Butter	2 oz	60 g
Minced yellow onion	6 oz	180 g
Minced garlic	½ oz	15 g
Madras curry powder	1 tbsp	15 mL
Chopped carrots	12 oz	360 g
Defatted *Poultry Stock (p. 749)*	1½ qt	1.5 L
Kosher salt	to taste	to taste
Half-and-half	8 fl oz	240 mL
Additional defatted poultry stock	as needed	as needed
Sugar	to taste	to taste
Fine salt	to taste	to taste

PROCEDURE

PREPARATION

1. Heat the butter in a nonreactive pan. Add the onion and garlic. Sweat them, partially covered, about 2 minutes, or until they are soft but not browned.
2. Add the curry powder and stir 10–20 seconds, or until fragrant.
3. Add the carrots and stir until they are well combined with the onions and curry.
4. Add the stock and some kosher salt, bring to the simmer, and cook about 20 minutes, or until the carrots are very soft.
5. Pour the soup through a strainer and reserve both solids and broth.
6. In a blender or food processor purée the solids, adding just enough broth through the top opening to make a thick purée.
7. Scrape the purée into a bowl and whisk the remaining broth back into it.
8. Force the soup through a fine sieve into a freshly sanitized, nonreactive container set in an ice bain-marie.
9. Whisk in the cream.
10. Stir the soup until it is cold.
11. Adjust the texture with more stock if necessary. Correct the salt and, if necessary, add a little sugar.

HOLDING

Refrigerate up to 5 days. Freeze up to 1 month.

VARIATIONS

CREAMY COLD CARROT SOUP

Omit the curry powder.

COLD CARROT-ORANGE SOUP

Omit the curry powder. Replace the half-and-half with 6 fl oz (180 mL) orange juice. Garnish with peeled orange segments and chiffonnade orange zest.

COLD CURRIED COCONUT CARROT SOUP

Replace the half-and-half with thick, unsweetened coconut milk or unsweetened coconut cream.

COLD CURRIED CARROT SOUP

WITH TOASTED COCONUT AND ALMONDS

APPETIZER

Portions:
1
Portion size:
10 fl oz (300 mL)

COMPONENTS

10 fl oz (300 mL) *Cold Curried Carrot Soup (p. 288)*
¼ oz/7 g (1 tbsp/30 mL) Toasted shredded coconut
¼ oz/7 g (1 tbsp/30 mL) Toasted sliced almonds
pinch Minced chives or scallion greens

Supplies

1 Cocktail napkin or 4-in. (10-cm) doily

PROCEDURE

PLATING

1. Prepare a shrimp cocktail chiller or a chilled 12-fl oz (360-mL) soup cup set into a larger cup of crushed ice.
2. Ladle the carrot soup into the top cup.
3. Arrange the coconut and almonds on the soup's surface and place a dot of chives in the center.
4. Place the chiller on an underliner plate lined with a cocktail napkin or 4-in. (10-cm) doily.

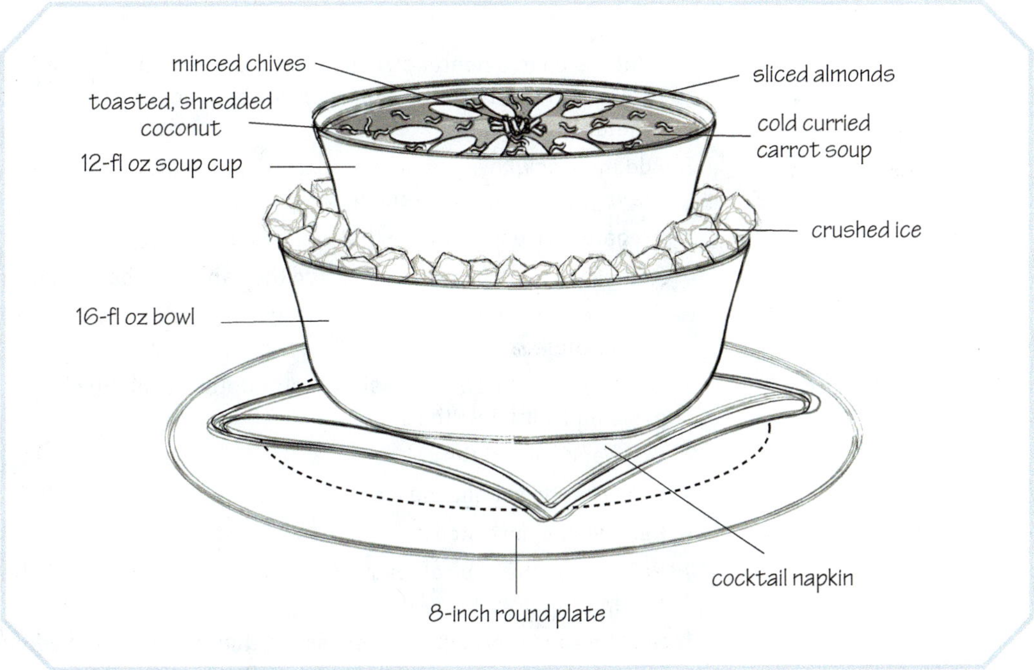

MINESTRONE FREDDO

(meen-eh-STROH-neh FRED-doh)

COOL ITALIAN VEGETABLE SOUP

Yield:
2½ qt (2.4 L)
Portions:
8
Portion size:
10 fl oz (300 mL)

INGREDIENTS	U.S.	METRIC
Extra-virgin olive oil	2 fl oz	60 mL
Peeled carrots, ¼-in. (0.5-cm) dice	4 oz	120 g
Peeled celery, ¼-in. (0.5-cm) dice	2 oz	60 g
Coarsely chopped yellow onion	2 oz	60 g
Trimmed green beans, ¼-in. (0.5-cm) lengths	4 oz	120 g
Peeled turnips, ¼-in. (0.5-cm) dice	3 oz	90 g
Kosher salt	to taste	to taste
Minced garlic	½ oz	15 g
Defatted, light-bodied *Poultry Stock* *(p. 749)*	1½ qt	1.5 L
Thyme	2 sprigs	2 sprigs
Rosemary	1 sprig	1 sprig
Cooked, drained cannellini beans	3 fl oz	90 mL
De-seeded zucchini, ¼-in. (0.5-cm) dice	4 oz	120 g
Filet of tomato, ¼-in. (0.5-cm) dice	4 oz	120 g
Ditalini or other short soup pasta	2 oz	60 g
Fine salt	to taste	to taste
Additional defatted, light-bodied poultry stock	as needed	as needed
Fresh lemon juice or white wine vinegar	to taste	to taste

PROCEDURE

1. Heat the oil in a nonreactive saucepan and add the carrot, celery, onion, green beans, turnips, and some salt. Cook over low heat about 5 minutes, stirring often, until the vegetables begin to soften. Add the garlic and stir a few seconds more.
2. Add the stock, thyme, and rosemary. Bring to the boil and cook at a brisk simmer until the vegetables are just tender.
3. Prepare an ice bain-marie that will hold the soup pan.
4. Remove the pan from the heat. Add the cannellini beans, zucchini, and tomato.
5. Place the pan in the ice bain-marie and stir occasionally until the soup reaches room temperature.
6. Boil the pasta in 2 qt (2 L) salted water until it is slightly firmer than al dente. Drain the pasta and stir it into the soup.
7. Taste and correct the salt.
8. If necessary, change the ice so the soup quickly chills to 38°F (3°C).
9. Remove the herb stems.
10. Refrigerate the soup at least 12 hours before serving so the flavors mellow and the pasta softens slightly.
11. Stir the soup thoroughly. If necessary, thin the soup with additional stock. Taste and correct the seasoning, adding more salt and some lemon juice or vinegar if necessary.

HOLDING

Refrigerate in a freshly sanitized, covered container up to 4 additional days.

VARIATIONS

Replace any vegetable with another, similar vegetable. Vary the herbs and seasonings as desired.

MINESTRONE FREDDO AL PESTO *(ahl PAY-stoh)*

COOL SUMMER VEGETABLE SOUP WITH BASIL PESTO

APPETIZER

Portions:
1
Portion size:
10 fl oz (300 mL)

COMPONENTS

10 fl oz (300 mL) *Minestrone Freddo (p. 290)*
1 fl oz (30 mL) *Pesto alla Genovese (p. 688)*
2 Fresh basil leaves

PROCEDURE

PLATING

1. Stir the minestrone well to distribute the vegetables in the broth. Ladle the minestrone into a cool 10-in. (25-cm) soup plate.
2. Place the soup in a microwave oven and heat it for a few seconds only, just to bring it to room temperature.
3. Spoon the pesto into the center of the soup.
4. Cut the basil leaves chiffonnade and sprinkle them on the soup's surface.

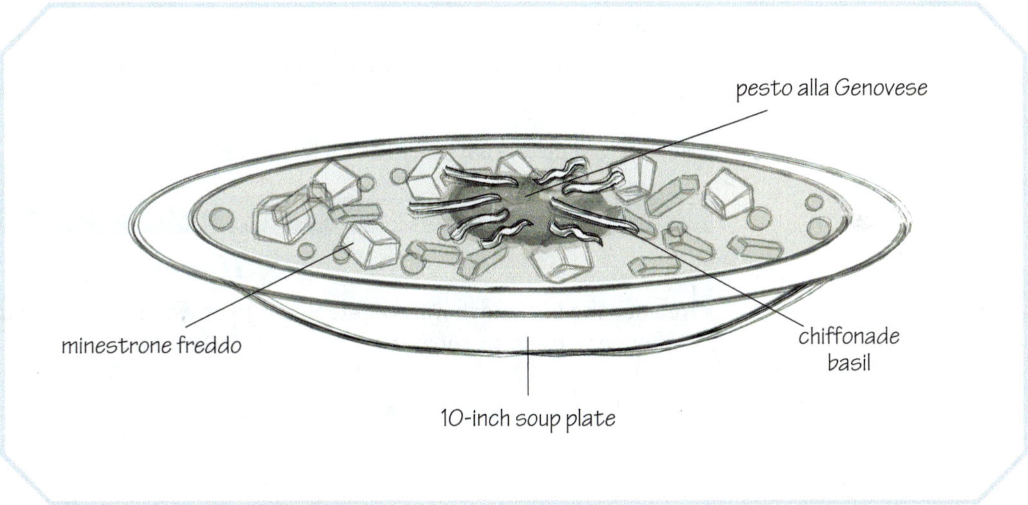

COLD BORSCHT

Yield:
2½ qt (2.4 L)
Portions:
8
Portion size:
10 fl oz (300 mL)

INGREDIENTS	U.S.	METRIC
Bland vegetable oil	1 fl oz	30 mL
Beets, peeled and grated	1½ lb	750 g
Yellow onion, quartered and sliced fine	8 oz	240 g
Kosher salt	to taste	to taste
Defatted *Brown Beef Stock (p. 751)*	1 qt	1 L
Water	1 qt	1 L
Fresh thyme	2 sprigs	2 sprigs
Bay leaf	1	1
Fresh lemon juice	to taste	to taste
Fine salt	to taste	to taste

PROCEDURE

PREPARATION

1. Place the oil, beets, onion, garlic, and a little salt in a large, nonreactive saucepan and sweat them over low heat about 5 minutes. Do not allow the vegetables to brown.
2. Add the stock, water, thyme, and bay leaf. Partially cover and simmer about 40 minutes, or until the vegetables begin to disintegrate and the soup is reduced to about 2½ qt (2.4 L).
3. Run the soup through a food mill into a freshly sanitized, nonreactive container set in an ice bain-marie. Stir until cold.
4. Correct the seasoning with lemon juice and fine salt.

HOLDING

Refrigerate up to 5 days. Freeze up to 1 month.

VARIATION

SCHAV

Replace the beef stock with vegetable broth or water. Omit the bay and thyme. Add 2 oz (60 g) chiffonnade fresh sorrel at the end of step 3. Garnish with sour cream and chiffonnade fresh sorrel.

COLD BORSCHT

WITH SOUR CREAM, DILL, AND BAGEL CRISP

APPETIZER

Portions:
1
Portion size:
10 fl oz (300 mL)

COMPONENTS

10 fl oz (300 mL) *Cold Borscht (p. 292)*
½ fl oz (15 mL) Sour cream, in pastry bag with large star tip
1 Very thin lemon slice
1 tbsp Minced fresh dill
1 *Bagel Crisp (p. 702)*

Supplies

1 8-in. (20-cm) doily

PROCEDURE

PLATING

1. Stir the borscht thoroughly and ladle it into a chilled 12-fl oz (360-mL) soup plate.
2. Float the lemon slice in the center of the soup's surface.
3. Pipe a rosette of sour cream on the lemon.
4. Sprinkle the dill onto the soup.
5. Place the bowl on a doily-lined 9-in. (23-cm) plate and set the bagel crisp on the rim.

CONSOMMÉ MADRILÈNE

(mahd-ree-LEN)

JELLIED BEEF CONSOMMÉ WITH MADEIRA AND TOMATO

Yield:
2½ qt (2.4 L)
Portions:
8
Portion size:
10 fl oz (300 mL)

INGREDIENTS	U.S.	METRIC
Brown Beef Stock (p. 751), cold	3 qt	3 L
Fresh thyme	2 sprigs	2 sprigs
Vine-ripe tomato, chopped	10 oz	300 g
Minced yellow onion	8 oz	240 g
Minced carrot	4 oz	120 g
Minced celery	4 oz	120 g
Egg whites	6 oz (6)	180 g (6)
Madeira	2 fl oz	60 mL
Granular gelatin (see steps 2 and 3)	¾ oz	21 g
Kosher salt	to taste	to taste
Fresh lemon juice	to taste	to taste

PROCEDURE

PREPARATION

1. Remove all fat from the surface of the stock.
2. Evaluate the natural gel of the stock to determine how much gelatin it will need. If it is strongly gelled when cold, decrease the gelatin by 25%. If it is liquid when cold, increase the gelatin by 25%.
3. Clarify the stock, using the thyme, tomato, mirepoix, and egg whites as the raft ingredients. (See procedure on p. 748.) When clarification is complete, you should have 2½ qt (2.5 L) clear stock. If you have a different yield, adjust the amount of gelatin accordingly.
4. Season the clarified stock with salt. Remember to salt it generously, as it will take extra time to adjust the seasoning after it has chilled.
5. Stir the gelatin into the Madeira and allow it to bloom.
6. Stir the gelatin into the hot stock until it is completely dissolved.
7. Add lemon juice to taste and reevaluate the salt.
8. Transfer the consommé to a freshly sanitized, nonreactive container set in an ice bath. Stir it at intervals until cold. The consommé should thicken to a light, pourable gel.
9. Taste again for seasoning. If the consommé needs more salt or lemon, heat it to dissolve the salt and then chill it again.

HOLDING

Refrigerate, covered, up to 5 days.

VARIATION

SEAFOOD MADRILÈNE

Replace the beef stock with Shellfish Stock (p. 750). Replace the Madeira with dry vermouth.

CONSOMMÉ MADRILÈNE

WITH TOMATO FILETS

APPETIZER

Portions:
1
Portion size:
10 fl oz (300 mL)

COMPONENTS

8 fl oz (240 mL) *Consommé Madrilène (p. 294)*
8 or 10 Peeled tomato décor shapes (p. 715)
½ tsp (5 mL) Fine diagonal-cut chives

Supplies

1 8-in. (20-cm) doily

PROCEDURE

PLATING

1. Prepare a shrimp cocktail chiller or a chilled 10-fl oz (360-mL) soup cup set into a larger cup of crushed ice.
2. Place consommé and décor shapes in the cup in alternating layers.
3. Place a dot of chives in the center of the soup's surface.
4. Place the chiller on a doily-lined 8-in. (20-cm) plate.

VARIATION

SEAFOOD MADRILÈNE SIPS

Replace the Consommé Madrilène with Seafood Madrilène (p. 294). Serve in 3-fl oz (90-mL) shot glasses. Omit the tomato filet and doily. For each serving, layer in ⅛ oz (3 g) each lump crabmeat and diced bay shrimp. Pipe a tiny rosette of crème fraîche on the surface of each sip and top with small dollops of red and black caviar.

Seafood Madrilène Sips

GAZPACHO BASE

Yield:
2½ qt (2.4 L)
Portions:
8
Portion size:
10 fl oz (300 mL)

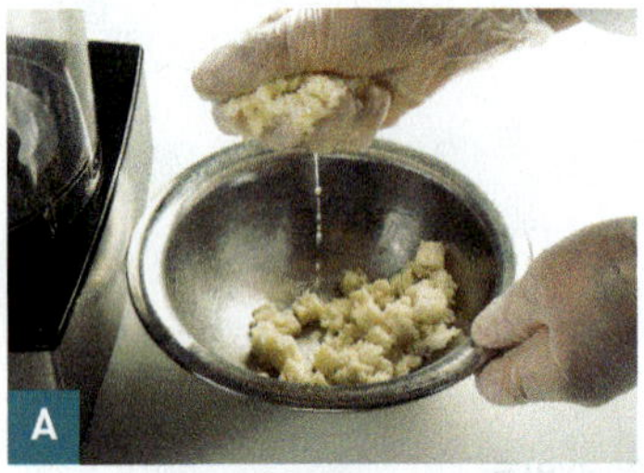
A

B

C

D

INGREDIENTS	U.S.	METRIC
Crustless, firm white bread	2 oz	60 g
Water	as needed	as needed
Vine-ripe tomato concassé	2 lb	1 kg
Peeled and seeded cucumber, chopped coarse	10 oz	300 g
Peeled sweet onion, chopped coarse	3 oz	90 g
Cleaned green bell pepper, chopped coarse	5 oz	150 g
Very fresh garlic cloves, peeled	½ oz	15 g
Canned tomato juice	20 fl oz	600 mL
Extra-virgin olive oil	4 fl oz	120 mL
Kosher salt	to taste	to taste
Red wine vinegar	to taste	to taste
Additional tomato juice or water	as needed	as needed

PROCEDURE

PREPARATION

1. Soak the bread in water to cover for 10 minutes.
2. Squeeze the water out of the bread (A) and crumble the bread into a food processor (B).
3. Add the tomatoes, cucumbers, onions, and peppers to the processor and grind to a coarse purée (C).
4. Force the garlic through a garlic press into the processor.
5. Turn the processor on and immediately pour in the tomato juice (D) and olive oil. Process just until combined and smooth. Do not overprocess to a foamy consistency.
6. Season the soup with salt and vinegar.
7. Transfer to a freshly sanitized, nonreactive container and refrigerate about 1 hour to mellow.
8. If necessary, thin the soup with additional tomato juice or water. Taste and correct the seasoning balance with salt and/or vinegar.

HOLDING

Refrigerate, covered, up to 12 hours only.

VARIATIONS

GOLDEN GAZPACHO

Replace the red tomatoes with yellow tomatoes.

WHITE GAZPACHO

Omit the tomatoes and peppers. Increase the cucumbers to 2 lb (1 kg). Add 2 oz (60 g) almond flour or finely ground blanched almonds. Add 8 oz (240 g) peeled white grapes. To serve, garnish with diced white grapes and toasted, slivered almonds.

GAZPACHO

WITH GARLIC CROÛTONS AND SURPRISE ICE CUBE

APPETIZER

Portions:
1
Portion size:
10 fl oz (300 mL)

COMPONENTS

10 fl oz (300 mL) *Gazpacho Base (p. 296)*
⅛ oz/3 g (1 tbsp/15 mL) Brunoise cucumber
⅛ oz/3 g (1 tbsp/15 mL) Brunoise green bell pepper
⅛ oz/3 g (1 tbsp/15 mL) Brunoise tomato filet
⅛ oz/3 g (1 tbsp/15 mL) Brunoise sweet onion
⅛ oz/3 g (1 tbsp/15 mL) Chopped scallions
1 *Consommé Ice Cube (p. 712),* made without chives
½ oz (15 g) *Garlic Croûton Cubes (p. 703)*

Supplies

1 Cocktail napkin

PROCEDURE

PLATING

1. Ladle the gazpacho base into a chilled 12-fl oz (360-mL) soup plate.
2. Sprinkle the vegetable garnishes into the soup.
3. Place the ice cube in the center of the soup.
4. Place the croûtons in a small ramekin or dip dish.
5. Place the napkin in the center of a 12-in. (30-cm) plate.
6. Place the soup plate on the napkin and set the ramekin on the right side of the plate.

CHILLED AVOCADO SOUP

Yield:
2½ qt (2.4 L)
Portions:
8
Portion size:
10 fl oz (300 mL)

INGREDIENTS	U.S.	METRIC
Western avocados, slightly softer than firm-ripe	1½ lb (4)	720 g (4)
Fresh lime juice	1 fl oz	30 mL
Kosher salt	to taste	to taste
Defatted *Poultry Stock (p. 749)*, cold	1½ qt	1.5 L
Additional defatted poultry stock	as needed	as needed
Half-and-half	8 fl oz	240 mL
Fine salt	to taste	to taste
Additional lime juice	to taste	to taste

PROCEDURE

PREPARATION

1. Cut the avocados in half, remove the pits, and scoop the flesh into a blender or food processor. Pour the lime juice on top, add a little salt, and blend smooth. Add just enough cold stock to release the blade and achieve a pourable texture.
2. Transfer the purée to a bowl set in an ice bain-marie and whisk in the remaining stock to achieve a light nappé consistency. Whisk in the half-and-half.
3. Correct the seasoning with fine salt and lime juice.
4. Transfer the soup to a freshly sanitized container, place plastic wrap directly on the soup's surface, cover with the lid, and refrigerate.

HOLDING

Refrigerate 6 hours only.

VARIATIONS

CHILLED AVOCADO SOUP WITH VODKA AND CAVIAR

To each serving add ½ fl oz (15 mL) chilled vodka. Garnish with ¼ oz (7 g) red tobiko or salmon caviar set on a toasted, cooled croûton.

CHILLED AVOCADO-MANGO SOUP

Replace 1 of the 4 avocados with 6 fl oz (180 mL) mango purée. Garnish with toasted shredded coconut and diced mango.

CHILLED AVOCADO SOUP

WITH SALSA, SOUR CREAM, AND TORTILLA CHIPS

APPETIZER

Portions:
1

Portion size:
10 fl oz (300 mL)

COMPONENTS

10 oz (300 mL) *Chilled Avocado Soup (p. 298)*
6 to 8 Plain tortilla chips
½ fl oz (15 mL) Sour cream, in pastry bag with medium star tip
1 fl oz (30 mL) *Fresh Tomato Salsa (p.50)*

Supplies

1 Cocktail napkin

PROCEDURE

PLATING

1. Ladle the avocado soup into a chilled 12-fl oz (360-mL) soup cup and set it in a larger cup of crushed ice. Alternatively, use a shrimp cocktail chiller.
2. Float one of the tortilla chips on the surface. Pipe a circle of sour cream on the chip.
3. Gently spoon the salsa into the circle.
4. Place the napkin in the center of a 10-in. (25-cm) oval plate. Place the soup on the left and mound the tortilla chips on the right.

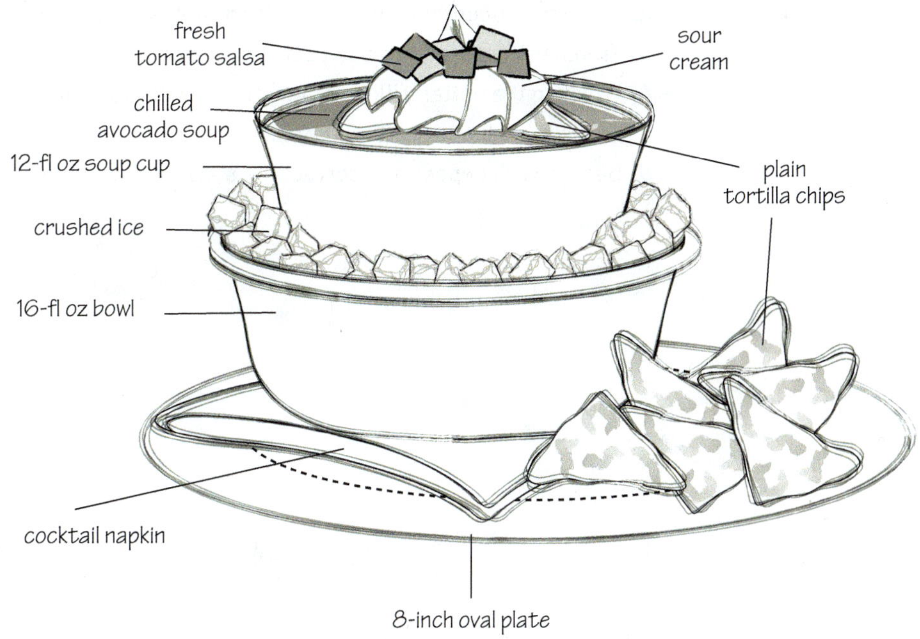

CHLODNIK

(HLOD-neek)

COLD CUCUMBER SOUP

Yield:
2½ qt (2.4.L)
Portions:
8
Portion size:
10 fl oz (300 mL)

INGREDIENTS	U.S.	METRIC
Firm cucumbers, cold	4 lb	2 kg
Kosher salt	to taste	to taste
Minced very fresh garlic	¾ oz	25 g
Minced white of scallion	4 oz	120 g
Plain whole-milk yogurt	10 fl oz	300 mL
Buttermilk	20 fl oz	600 mL
Ice water	as needed	as needed
Minced fresh dill	½ oz	15 g
Minced green scallion	3 oz	90 g
Finely ground white pepper	to taste	to taste
Fine salt	to taste	to taste
White wine vinegar	to taste	to taste

PROCEDURE

PREPARATION

1. Prepare the cucumbers:
   a. Peel the cucumbers and trim the ends.
   b. Cut the cucumbers in half lengthwise and scrape out the seeds.
   c. Grate the cucumbers coarse.
   d. Mix the cucumbers with a generous amount of kosher salt.
   e. Place the salted cucumbers in a strainer set over a bowl and drain for 15 minutes.
   f. Press the cucumbers to remove as much moisture as possible.
2. Place the cucumbers, garlic, scallion whites, and yogurt in a blender and purée smooth.
3. Transfer the purée to a bowl set in an ice bain-marie.
4. Whisk in the buttermilk and enough ice water to achieve a light nappé consistency.
5. Stir in the dill and scallion greens.
6. Season with pepper and correct the seasoning with fine salt and vinegar.

HOLDING

Refrigerated up to 6 hours only.

CHLODNIK

WITH GARLIC CROÛTONS

APPETIZER

Portions:
1
Portion size:
10 fl oz (300 mL)

COMPONENTS

10 fl oz (300 mL) *Chlodnik (p. 300)*
⅛ oz/3 g (1 tbsp/15 mL) Minced fresh dill
½ oz (15 g) *Garlic Croûton Cubes (p. 703)*
as needed Freshly ground black pepper

Supplies

1 Cocktail napkin or 5-in. (15-cm) doily

PROCEDURE

PLATING

1. Ladle the chlodnik into a chilled 12-fl oz (360-mL) soup cup set in a larger cup of crushed ice. Alternatively, use a shrimp cocktail chiller.
2. Sprinkle the dill on the soup's surface.
3. Mound the croûtons on top.
4. Line an 8-in. (20-cm) plate with a cocktail napkin or doily and place the bowl on it.

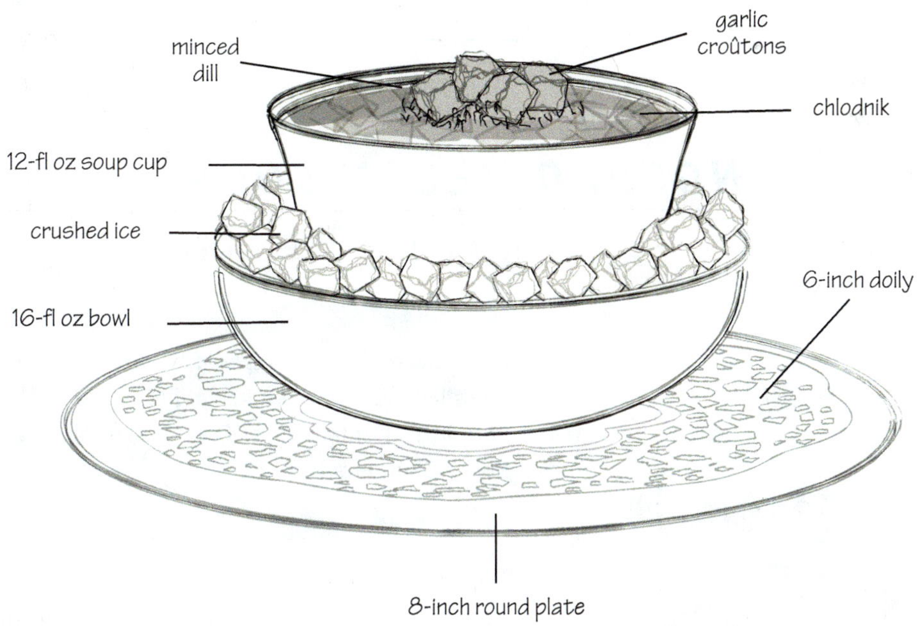

COLD GINGERED MELON SOUP

Yield:
2½ qt (2.4 L)
Portions:
8
Portion size:
10 fl oz (300 mL)

INGREDIENTS	U.S.	METRIC
Peeled fresh ginger, rough ½-in. (1-cm) dice	3 oz	90 g
Large limes	3	3
Peeled, diced honeydew melon	2 lb	1 kg
Moderately sweet Riesling wine	25 fl oz	750 mL
Ice water	as needed	as needed
Additional lime juice	to taste	to taste

PROCEDURE

PREPARATION

1. Juice the ginger in a juice extractor or force it through a garlic press.
2. Zest the limes and mince the zest extremely fine. Juice the limes.
3. Combine the melon, lime juice and zest, ginger juice, and 8 fl oz (240 mL) wine in a food processor. Purée it smooth.
4. Transfer the melon purée to a freshly sanitized, nonreactive container and stir in the remaining wine to achieve a light nappé consistency.
5. Chill the soup 2–3 hours.
6. Correct the texture and seasoning by adding ice water and more lime juice as needed.

HOLDING

Refrigerate up to 2 days.

VARIATION

Vary the type of melon as desired.

COLD GINGERED MELON SOUP

WITH LIME SORBET AND MELON PEARLS

APPETIZER

Portions:
1
Portion size:
10 fl oz (300 mL)

COMPONENTS

10 oz (300 mL) *Cold Gingered Melon Soup (above)*
2 fl oz (60 mL) *Lime Sorbet (p. 713)*
1 oz (30 g) Cantaloupe or Crenshaw-melon, ⅜-in. (1-cm) parisiennes
pinch Chiffonnade mint

PROCEDURE

PLATING

1. Ladle the soup into a chilled 12-fl oz (360-mL) soup plate.
2. Use a quenelle scoop or two spoons to place a quenelle of sorbet in the center of the plate.
3. Scatter the melon parisiennes around the sorbet.
4. Sprinkle the mint around the sorbet.

HUNGARIAN COLD CHERRY SOUP

Yield:
2½ qt (2.4 L)
Portions:
8
Portion size:
10 fl oz (300 mL)

INGREDIENTS	U.S.	METRIC
Pitted sour cherries, fresh or IQF (individually quick frozen)	1¼ lb	600 g
Water	1½ qt	1.5 L
Sugar	12 oz	360 g
Cherry brandy	2 fl oz	60 mL
Cornstarch	1 tbsp	15 mL

PROCEDURE

PREPARATION

1. Combine the cherries, water, and sugar in a nonreactive saucepan. Bring to the simmer and cook, stirring occasionally, 20 minutes, or until the cherries are soft.
2. Mix the cherry brandy into the cornstarch to make a slurry.
3. Taste the soup and add more sugar if it seems too tart.
4. Bring the soup to the boil and whisk in the cornstarch slurry to achieve a light nappé consistency.
5. Transfer the soup to a freshly sanitized, nonreactive container set it in an ice bain-marie. Stir occasionally until cold.

HOLDING

Refrigerate up to 7 days.

HUNGARIAN COLD CHERRY SOUP

WITH YOGURT AND TOASTED HAZELNUTS

APPETIZER

Portions:
1
Portion size:
10 fl oz (300 mL)

COMPONENTS

10 fl oz (300 mL) *Hungarian Cold Cherry Soup (p. 303)*
1 fl oz (30 mL) Thick whole-milk yogurt, in pastry bag with large star tip
⅛ oz (1 tbsp) Toasted, crushed hazelnuts
pinch Chiffonnade mint

PROCEDURE

PLATING

1. Stir the cherry soup well to distribute the cherries. Ladle 10 fl oz (300 mL) soup into a chilled 12-fl oz (360-mL) soup plate.
2. Pipe a rosette of yogurt into the center of the soup.
3. Scatter the hazelnuts and mint around the yogurt.

CHILLED SPICED SCANDINAVIAN FRUIT SOUP

Yield:
2½ qt (2.4 L)
Portions:
8
Portion size:
10 fl oz (300 mL)

INGREDIENTS	U.S.	METRIC
Dry red wine	25 fl oz	750 mL
Water	1 qt	1 L
Sugar	8 oz	240 g
Dried apricots, ⅜-in. (1-cm) dice	4 oz	120 g
Dried cherries	4 oz	120 g
Golden raisins	4 oz	120 g
Cinnamon sticks	2	2
Cloves	6	6
Cornstarch	2 tbsp	30 mL
Water	2 fl oz	60 mL

PROCEDURE

PREPARATION

1. Combine the wine and 1 qt (1 L) water in a large, nonreactive saucepan. Add the sugar and dissolve it over low heat.
2. Add the apricots, cherries, raisins, cinnamon, and cloves. Simmer, uncovered, 30 minutes, or until the fruit is tender.
3. Stir the cornstarch into 2 fl oz (60 mL) water until completely mixed. Stir the starch mixture into the soup, raise the heat, and boil just until lightly thickened and clear.
4. Transfer the soup to a freshly sanitized, nonreactive container placed in an ice bain-marie. Stir occasionally until cold.

HOLDING

Refrigerate up to 1 week.

VARIATION

Vary the dried fruits as desired. Replace the red wine with a fruit beer, such as raspberry lambic.

CHILLED SPICED SCANDINAVIAN FRUIT SOUP

WITH SOUR CREAM

APPETIZER

Portions:
1
Portion size:
10 fl oz (300 mL)

COMPONENTS

10 fl oz (300 mL) *Chilled Spiced Scandinavian Fruit Soup (p. 304)*
1 tbsp (15 mL) Sour cream, in pastry bag with large star tip

PROCEDURE

PLATING

1. Stir the fruit soup well to evenly distribute the fruit. Ladle 10 fl oz (300 mL) soup into a chilled 12-fl oz (360-mL) soup plate.
2. Pipe a rosette of sour cream into the center of the soup.

TERMS FOR REVIEW

dessert soup
soup sip
jellied consommé

QUESTIONS FOR DISCUSSION

1. List the three main categories of cold soup. Describe the two categories typically prepared by the garde manger department.
2. Explain why ingredients for cold soups must not contain significant amounts of animal fat.
3. List three examples of cooked soups served cold. Explain how these soups are prepared.
4. In what ways do the consistency and seasoning of a hot soup change when the soup is chilled? What steps would you take to ensure your cold soups have proper consistency and seasoning?
5. List three examples of cold soups made from raw ingredients. Explain how these soups are prepared.
6. Explain how you would keep cold soups properly chilled on the service line.
7. Describe the special presentation serviceware used to keep cold soups properly chilled while being served and eaten. Describe a special type of garnish that keeps cold soups chilled while being eaten.
8. Using your imagination and the information you learned in this chapter, write a recipe for your own signature cold soup. Include garnishes and accompaniments in your recipe.

Chapter

9

PREREQUISITES

Before studying this chapter, you should already

- Have read "How to Use This Book," pp. xxviii–xxxiii, and understand the professional recipe format.
- Have mastered the preparation of bound protein salads covered in Chapter 5.
- Have mastered the preparation of cold meats and poultry covered in Chapter 7.
- Know basic sanitation procedures for products served raw.
- Know state and local regulations for food-service glove use.

Garde Manger Sandwiches

What do people reach for when they don't have time for a sit-down meal? When they're on the go, customers need something quick, neat, and easy to eat. Luckily, today's wide repertoire of interesting and delicious sandwiches offers plenty of choices.

The garde manger department concentrates mainly on cold sandwiches. However, well-equipped garde manger stations often include countertop heating equipment used to prepare heated sandwich items, such as panini and heated deli sandwiches.

To be successful, your sandwich menu should contain not only the classic sandwiches everyone knows and loves but also feature unique signature sandwiches that make your operation stand out from the competition. The information in this chapter gives you the skills needed to correctly prepare standard sandwiches as well as to offer sandwiches of your own creation.

After reading this chapter, you should be able to

1. Name the four elements of a basic sandwich, and explain the functions of each.
2. List and describe the six basic sandwich construction types, and explain the principles of sandwich construction.
3. Properly use the tools and equipment found in a modern sandwich station.
4. Become proficient at both plated and tray presentation of sandwiches.
5. Correctly package sandwiches for box lunches and to-go service.
6. Set up and maintain an efficient sandwich station.
7. Correctly prepare the most popular North American cold sandwiches as well as the hot sandwiches typically prepared in the garde manger station.
8. Combine food items and ingredients to make successful new sandwich creations.

UNDERSTANDING SANDWICHES

The History of the Sandwich

The custom of making food portable by layering, folding, or rolling it in some form of bread dates as far back in history as bread itself. Our modern sandwich, however, is named after the eighteenth-century British statesman John Montague, the fourth Earl of Sandwich. According to food history legend, the earl was a fanatical card player who hated to interrupt his card games even for meals. He ordered his cooks to place slabs of meat between two slices of buttered bread so he and his guests could eat with one hand while playing cards with the other. The "sandwich" became all the rage among the British upper classes. Even though he didn't invent it, the Earl of Sandwich made the sandwich both popular and respectable.

In this chapter, we focus on full-size cold sandwiches, which are classified into six basic types. We look at the planning and set-up of the garde manger sandwich station and learn to use specialized equipment that makes sandwich preparation faster and easier. Then we learn the techniques necessary to quickly and efficiently prepare these sandwiches to order for à la carte service as well as ahead of time for buffets, trays, and box lunches. Finally, we learn to prepare the types of hot sandwiches that are part of the garde manger station's menu.

THE FOUR BASIC SANDWICH ELEMENTS

Virtually all sandwiches are constructed from four basic elements:

1. Bread
2. Spread
3. Filling
4. Internal garnishes

The bread and filling are the essential elements. In fact, the earliest sandwiches consisted of bread and filling only—and some people still prefer such sandwiches. However, without a spread, most sandwiches have a dry mouthfeel, and without internal garnishes they lack textural contrast. Most modern sandwiches include all four basic elements.

The four basic elements of a sandwich: bread, spread, filling, and internal garnishes

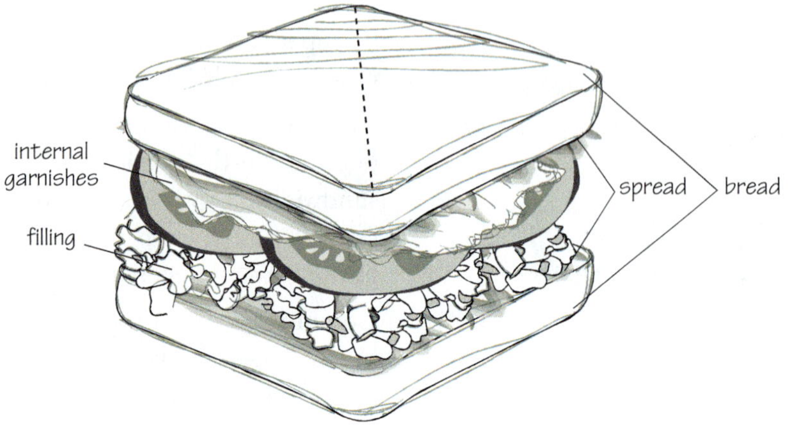

Breads for Sandwiches

The majority of sandwiches are made with ***leavened breads***, which are made with yeast. These breads have a soft, porous interior, called the ***crumb***, and a firm or crisp exterior, called the ***crust***. Because ***unleavened breads*** do not contain yeast to make them rise, they have a flat shape and are also called ***flatbreads***. Some leavened breads are fabricated to give them a flat appearance as well. These are called ***yeasted flatbreads***.

The primary function of bread as a sandwich element is to encase the filling and enable it to be eaten neatly out of hand. It greatly affects the flavor and mouthfeel of a sandwich, and it also contributes to food cost. The bread product you choose for sandwich making must fulfill five requirements.

It must be:

1. Firm and sturdy enough to hold the filling without falling apart.
2. Tender and moist enough so it doesn't make the sandwich tough or dry.
3. Fresh, not stale or dried out.
4. Priced to fit your budget.
5. Shaped and sized to ensure proper portion control and minimize waste.

Bread Market Forms

Breads are classified into four basic market forms:

1. **Industrial bread products:** Manufactured by large, industrial producers and marketed to consumers on a regional or national level. Industrial breads are generally bland in flavor, and both their crust and crumb are quite soft. They are usually pre-sliced.
2. **Commercial bread products:** Made by small to midsize local or regional bakeries and marketed to both food-service and retail stores. Commercial breads are made in many styles ranging from light, Italian-type crisp-crusted breads to sturdy American loaves to hearty German potato breads and ryes. Commercial bread loaves may be ordered either unsliced or pre-sliced. Pullman loaves (photo p. 312) are often available. Commercial rolls are available in various sizes determined by weight.
3. **Frozen par-bake bread products:** Many varieties are available. Frozen par-bake bread products have been through all of the normal steps in bread production. They are baked until they reach their full size and proper interior temperature but are removed from the oven before they acquire a golden brown color. Once cooled, they are boxed and frozen. Before they can be used, they must be baked for a short period to crisp and color the crust and bring the interior crumb to a temperature of 140°F (60°C)—see sidebar, page 313.
4. **Artisan bread products:** While the term ***artisan bread*** has no exact definition, in general we give that name to breads made in small batches by traditional processes and from natural ingredients. Artisan breads are often made from whole-grain flours and leavened with sourdough starters. They are available from small specialty bakeries usually located in urban or affluent suburban areas. Many artisan breads are not baked in pans but rather shaped for baking directly on the oven hearth or deck.

Types of bread slices by flour type and flavor. Top row from left: multigrain, white pan loaf, marble rye, whole wheat, olive loaf. Bottom row from left: raisin swirl, pumpernickel, and Jewish rye

Breads by Flour Type and Flavor

Breads are primarily classified according to the type of flour from which they are made. Once that classification is determined, breads can also be categorized by non-flour flavorings added to the dough. The breads listed in Table 9.1 are among the most popular for sandwich making.

TABLE 9.1 Breads by Flour Type and Flavor

Flour and Flavor Type	Characteristics
White	Bread most often used for sandwiches; neutral flavor complements virtually any filling. Many textural variations and production types exist. Find a firm white bread with a full, honest wheat flavor.
Fat-enriched white	Fine-textured crumb is made rich with butter or other fats and sometimes eggs. Sometimes used for tea sandwiches and canapés, and grilled/pressed sandwiches.
Whole wheat	Earthy, nutty taste complements more rustic, full-flavored fillings. Some have high sugar content—often made with honey, maltose, or molasses. Sweet taste may clash with the intended filling, spread, or garnishes.
Rye	Standard bread for many deli-type sandwiches. Excellent with German-style smoked sausages and pungent cheeses. Made from rye flour mixed with white flour for lighter texture, milder flavor. Traditional artisan ryes are made with sourdough cultures have a tangy flavor. Commercial ryes include souring agents to simulate sourdough taste. Some are flavored with caraway seeds, both within the crumb and as topping.
Pumpernickel	Made mostly from dark rye flour. Acquires a dark brown color from the addition of molasses and caramel coloring. Tangy taste comes from the sourdough leavening process or souring agents. Firm texture and full flavor needs equally strong-flavored filling.
Marble rye	Swirled appearance comes from white and dark rye doughs rolled together. Makes attractive, eye-catching sandwiches.
Multigrain	Partially made of white flour and flours derived from grains such as rye, spelt, kamut, corn, and other specialty grains. Often includes whole or crushed grains and seeds within the dough. Some are made by the sourdough process. Popular with health-conscious customers.
Tea breads and other quick breads	Leavened with baking powder and/or baking soda instead of yeast. Most are sweet because of high proportion of sugar or honey in formulas. Dense and moist, they often incorporate nuts and dried fruit. Category includes biscuits, soda bread, and corn bread, commonly used for hot breakfast sandwiches.
Herb	Usually these yeasted white breads are made with chopped fresh herbs added.
Olive	Italian or French bread with pitted olives added; similar product is made with sun-dried tomatoes.
Nut	These sweet or nonsweet yeast breads are made with chopped nuts added.
Raisin	This is white or whole wheat bread, and often made with cinnamon rolled into dough. Usually a breakfast bread but it makes interesting sandwiches combined with complementary fillings.

Bread Fabrication Types

Breads can be shaped or formed in hundreds of ways. Table 9.2 describes popular bread fabrication types for sandwiches.

TABLE 9.2 Bread Types

Category/Description	Market Form	Baking Method
Loaves Large units sold by weight and marketed by size Cut into slices to make sandwiches	Oblong pan loaf is most cost-effective. Standard pan loaves 8 in. (20cm) in length and 12–16 oz (340 g–0.5kg) in weight are common. Longer 12-in. (30-cm), 2-lb (1-kg) food-service loaf yields less waste per loaf because of higher crumb-to-crust ratio.	Normal pan loaves are baked in open pans; top expands outward and upward in classic mushroom top.
	Pullman loaves yield many slices, exactly square. Makes more uniform sandwiches; preferred for food-service use.	Baked in 12-in. (30-cm) closed pans that give the finished bread a uniform rectangular shape.
	Hearth loaves not supported on the side have rounded or freeform shape. Generate significant waste.	Not baked in pans but rather made into various shapes and baked on oven floor.
Baguettes (bah-GETS) Long, narrow loaves with crisp crust and light, airy, elastic crumb French in origin Today, *baguette* refers to all long, narrow breads, whether French, Italian, or North American.	Standard baguette is 24 in. (60 cm) long and about 2½ in. (6.25 cm) in diameter. Large surface area, lean formula means they stale quickly. Round or diagonal slice is called a ***croûton***, used to make canapés (p. 368) and in other preparations.	Sometimes baked in special form that supports cylindrical shape
Rolls Small, single-serving units Available in many shapes and sizes Many designed to accommodate specific fillings, i.e., cylindrical hot dog rolls, round hamburger rolls Often preferred over bread slices because shape neatly contains fillings, and high ratio of crust to crumb prevents sandwiches from becoming soggy Economical; portion-controlled by bakery, yield little waste	Sandwich rolls normally weigh 3–4 oz (90–120 g) each. 1½–2 oz (45–60 g) dinner rolls are frequently used to make small sandwiches for sandwich trays. Weight depends on heaviness of ingredients. Inquire about size before you purchase and, if possible, get a sample to test. Two main categories, depending on the texture of crust: 1. hard 2. soft	Baked on trays
Croissants (kwa-SAHN) Originated in France, where they are eaten at breakfast In North America, often split and used as a sandwich bread with various fillings	Croissants are buttery, multilayered crescent rolls.	Baked on tray

(continues)

TABLE 9.2 Bread Types *(continued)*

Category/Description	Market Form	Baking Method
Pita Most common North American name for various yeasted flatbreads Became popular as a sandwich bread in 1970s To make sandwiches, cut pitas in half, open into a pocket, stuff with a spread, filling, and garnishes. Larger, no-pocket pitas used for wrapping sandwich fillings	Standard pitas are about 6 in. (15 cm) in diameter, round, and hollow. Available in white and whole wheat varieties.	Conveyor oven
Bagels Unique bread rolls formed into a doughnut-like shape. True bagels are made with strong flour and low water content and have a dense, chewy texture.	Jewish-style delicatessens serve authentic smaller, firm-textured bagels split and filled with cream cheese and smoked salmon. Today's larger, softer commercial bagels may encase virtually any food, including such unusual fillings as ham and Swiss cheese or even cheeseburger patties.	Boiled before baking, resulting in a distinctive chewy texture
Flour Tortillas Originated in northern Mexico	Thin and pliable when fresh, they are rolled around various fillings to make the popular wrap sandwiches.	Griddle baked
Lavash (lah-VAHSH) Middle Eastern; also known by other names	Unleavened wheat flour flatbreads of various origin but similar in flavor, texture, appearance. Lavash are available in white or whole wheat. Colored and flavored varieties are sold.	Griddle baked
Focaccia (foh-KAH-chya), **Ciabatta** (chyah-BAH-tah) Italian yeast breads	Focaccia has a close grain and is relatively firm. Ciabatta is puffy, with lots of holes in the crumb. Both are now made into square rolls specifically intended for sandwiches. Both may be cut into sandwich-size pieces and split horizontally to hold sandwich fillings.	Formed into flat shapes before baking on trays

Types of bread by fabrication type. Top row, from left: pullman loaf, baguette, homestyle loaf, batard, sub roll, and hearth loaf. Middle row, from left: Cuban loaf, kaiser roll, hot dog roll, New England hot dog roll, hamburger roll, ciabatta roll, and steak roll. Bottom row, from left: naan, flour tortillas, wheat wrap, and pita.

Guidelines for Storing Sandwich Bread and Rolls

- To prevent drying, do not store any bread product near heat-producing equipment such as ovens or refrigeration compressors.
- To prevent rapid staling, do not store any bread product in the refrigerator.
- Store soft-crusted breads and rolls wrapped in plastic film or in sealed plastic bags at cool room temperature. Do not store in a dark, closed cabinet. Inspect for mold before each service.
- If soft-crusted bread products must be kept longer than 1–2 days, wrap tightly and freeze.
- Store crisp-crusted bread products intended for same-day service at cool room temperature. Keep in micro-perforated bags specially manufactured to prevent drying and surface contamination while allowing moisture to escape. Alternatively, store in closed cartons or in open plastic containers covered with kitchen towels.
- If crisp-crusted bread products must be kept for longer periods, wrap tightly and freeze.
- Thaw frozen bread products unwrapped on a rack at room temperature. Once they are completely thawed and free of surface moisture, immediately proceed with wrapping or recrisping.
- Place soft-crusted breads and rolls in sealed plastic bags as soon as they are completely thawed. Do not refreeze.
- To recrisp crisp-crusted breads and rolls, place them on a rack set on a sheet tray and bake in a preheated 400°F (200°C) oven just until the crusts regain their original crispness and until the bread reaches an interior temperature of 140°F (60°C). Cool to room temperature on the rack. Use within a few hours. Do not refreeze.

Spreads for Sandwiches

A ***sandwich spread*** is a liquid or paste-like dressing usually applied to the bread element of the sandwich. Sandwich spreads are intended to fulfill several functions:

- Form a liquid-resistant barrier that prevents a moist filling from seeping into the bread and making it soggy.
- Add moisture and a rich, smooth mouthfeel to sandwiches having less moist fillings.
- Help the sandwich hold together by acting as a kind of glue, binding the bread, filling, and internal garnishes to one another.
- Add a particular flavor or combination of flavors to the sandwich.
- Add a particular color to the sandwich's visual effect.

In à la carte service, the choice of spread is often left to the customer, who specifies it when ordering. There are some classic sandwiches in which a particular spread, such as mayonnaise on a BLT or Russian dressing on a corned beef special, is dictated by tradition.

Butter

Until the availability of commercial mayonnaise in 1920, butter was North America's most commonly used sandwich spread, and it remains popular in some areas today. Butter is often used when making small sandwiches, such as tea sandwiches and canapés (p. 368). It has a high proportion of fat that remains semisolid at room temperature and that solidifies when refrigerated. This makes it a good moisture barrier.

Butter must be at room temperature to have a spreadable consistency. Many chefs whip butter to make it spread more easily and to give it greater volume. This can be an effective technique. However, whipped butter is more perishable than unwhipped.

Butter flavored with seasonings, condiments, or other ingredients is called a ***compound butter***, or ***composed butter***. Compound butters (p. 562) can be effective and delicious as spreads on full-size sandwiches, although they are most commonly used for canapés.

Mayonnaise

Mayonnaise is one of North America's most popular sandwich spreads. Its rich mouthfeel and tangy flavor enhance almost any cold sandwich. Mayonnaise for sandwiches may be flavored with many of the same ingredients as composed butters.

Prepared Mustards

Prepared mustard is made by grinding mustard seeds into a fine powder and then moistening the powder with a liquid, such as wine or vinegar, until it becomes a spreadable paste. Mustard may be made from yellow mustard seeds, brown mustard seeds, or a combination of the two. While most types of mustard are completely smooth, some have a coarse or grainy texture because they contain crushed or whole seeds.

The sharp, tangy flavor of prepared mustard complements many sandwich fillings. Mustard is particularly suited for use on smoked meats and poultry. It is especially appropriate on German and Jewish deli-style sandwiches, such as those made with dried sausages, pastrami, and liverwurst. When terrines (p. 516) and rillettes (p. 457) are used as sandwich fillings, mustard is the traditional choice of spread.

Table 9.3 describes the types of commercially prepared mustard.

TABLE 9.3 Commercially Prepared Mustards

Mustard Type	Characteristics
Yellow	Mild flavor and smooth, light texture Although made from yellow mustard seeds, its bright yellow color comes from turmeric.
Brown	Robust flavor resulting from a proportion of brown mustard seeds. Thick and somewhat coarse texture
Dijon	Possibly the world's best-known mustard; true Dijon is made in and around the town of Dijon, France. Formula includes white Burgundy wine. Two main types: 1. Smooth, golden, moderately sharp "original" blend. 2. Grainy, brown, tangy "ancienne" (ahn-SYEHN) variety. There are flavored Dijon mustards as well as pungent "extra strong" varieties.
Dijon-style	Lower-cost imitations of true French Dijon mustard Select with care, as they vary widely in taste and texture
English	Smooth, pale golden in color, and very pungent
German	May be golden or brown, and often includes beer Most are strong and boldly flavored.
Flavored	Varieties include tarragon, green peppercorn, honey, and caraway.

Cheese Spreads

Virtually any soft-textured cheese may be used as a sandwich spread. Cream cheese is most commonly used for bagel sandwiches and for sweet and savory tea sandwiches. Soften by bringing it to room temperature and lighten by whipping before use. Cream cheese is often flavored with minced herbs, citrus zest, and even minced seafood, chopped nuts, or fruit preserves. Soft-textured natural cheeses enhanced with flavorings, such as Boursin, make delicious, if costly, sandwich spreads.

Vegetable Purées and Fresh Salsas

A wide variety of vegetable purées and vegetable salsas are appropriate for use as sandwich spreads. Examples include:

- Red Bell Pepper Purée (p. 54)
- Bean purées, such as Hummus (p. 118)
- Herb purées, such as Pesto alla Genovese (p. 688)
- Eggplant purées, such as Baba Ghanouj (p. 119)
- Olive spreads, such as Tapenade (p. 52)
- Fresh tomato salsas (p. 50)

These are best used on sandwiches made to order. Because these mixtures are largely water based, and some also contain vegetable oil, they quickly make sandwich bread and rolls soggy.

Ketchups, Relishes, and Processed Salsas

Tomato ketchup is a popular sandwich spread more closely associated with hot sandwiches but sometimes used on cold sandwiches, such as those made with meatloaf. House-made ketchups (p. 669) have a distinctive signature flavor.

Relishes are sweet and tangy fine-cut pickles often made from cucumbers but also made from other vegetables, such as corn and peppers (p. 669).

Southwestern-style bottled tomato salsa is available in many varieties and can also be made in-house.

Flavored Oils and Vinaigrettes

Vegetable oil flavored with garlic, dried herbs, spices, and vinegar is often used to dress the roll and vegetable garnishes of the Italian-style sandwiches known in North America as subs, hoagies, or po'boys. Garde manger chefs can expand on this by using a variety of flavored oils, such as those in Chapter 17, and vinaigrettes, such as those in Chapter 2. With a few exceptions, oils and vinaigrettes must be added to sandwiches at the last minute before serving. Sandwiches that include oil-based dressings can quickly become soggy, and the oil may seep out and make them unpleasant to hold.

Sandwich Fillings

The filling is the heart of the sandwich and is considered its main ingredient. In fact, the portion size of a particular sandwich is expressed as the weight of its filling. For example, a "4-oz (120-g) turkey sandwich" actually weighs much more if placed on a scale. In this case, the additional weight of the bread, spread, and internal garnishes is understood.

A sandwich filling may consist of a single ingredient or a combination of ingredients. Most sandwich fillings are animal protein foods such as meats, poultry, seafood items, cheeses, and eggs. However, sandwiches that conform to vegan dietary guidelines are becoming more popular.

North American customers perceive a sandwich to be a good value if there is a high ratio of filling to bread. The filling portion for a standard sandwich is 4 oz (120 g). In general, a well-made sandwich affords the diner an equal amount of filling and bread in each bite. However, overstuffed sandwiches, or those having much more filling than bread, are popular in some areas.

Deli Meats

The most widely used sandwich fillings in North America are industrially processed deli meats. Garde manger chefs have a huge assortment of boiled or smoked hams, smoked poultry, roast beef, roast pork, cured meats such as corned beef and spiced beef, turkey breast, compressed chicken breast, salamis and bolognas, and various loaf products, such as olive or pickle, to choose from. These range in quality from budget to deluxe, and are priced accordingly. If deli meats are to be featured on the sandwich menu, the preparation area must include an electric slicing machine. See page 323 for guidelines for preparing and storing deli meats.

House-Made Cooked Meats and Poultry

There are several advantages to preparing sandwich meats from scratch. By choosing from the full range of raw products you can offer unusual fillings, such as roast lamb or grilled duck. Each product can be seasoned to achieve a unique flavor. Beef and lamb can be roasted to a desired doneness. Products from organic sources and prepared in-house can be marketed as "all natural." If your operation features roasted meats and poultry as hot entrées, you can use the resulting leftovers as sandwich fillings. Refer to Chapter 7 for procedures and guidelines for preparing meats and poultry to be used in sandwiches and other cold dishes.

Although house-made cooked meats and poultry may be sliced on a slicing machine, offering these items in hand carved form results in thicker, more natural-looking slices that add perceived value to the sandwich.

Bacon

Many cold sandwiches, such as club sandwiches and BLTs, feature cooked sliced bacon as part of their fillings. Bacon makes three important contributions to a cold sandwich:

1. Cooked crisp, it adds textural interest.
2. High in fat, it adds richness.
3. Its salty flavor helps season the sandwich. (Keep salt content in mind when seasoning other ingredients in a sandwich containing bacon.)

To ensure a crisp product that is tender enough to yield easily to the bite, use thin-sliced bacon. In quantity cooking, bacon slices are laid flat on a sheet tray and baked in a moderate oven until nearly crisp. The fat is poured off and the bacon is then laid out on paper towels to drain and become crisp.

Cheese

Any of the semisoft and firm cheeses may be sliced and used as sandwich fillings, either alone or in combination with other ingredients. Deli cheeses are specially fabricated for use on an electric slicing machine. They yield slices of consistent shape with little waste. Most deli cheeses are mild in flavor. All are similar in texture.

To make more interesting specialty sandwiches, choose from the world of natural cheeses intended for table use. These include domestic and imported commercial cheeses as well as artisan cheeses, discussed in Chapter 14. They come in a wide variety of shapes and textures. Most must be sliced by hand, and many require special slicing techniques. To achieve thin, even slices you may need to partially freeze them or use a special tool called a cheese plane (p. 584). Hard cheeses, such as Parmesan, may be scraped into shards or curls with a vegetable peeler. Crumbly cheeses, such as Roquefort and feta, can be broken apart and sprinkled onto the sandwich.

Seafood

While many hot sandwiches are based on seafood fillings, only a few cold sandwiches are based on seafood. Most are made with seafood fabricated into bound protein salads, such as tuna salad, shrimp salad, and lobster salad.

Smoked and cured seafood is featured in some sandwiches, particularly in small sandwiches such as canapés. Smoked salmon is an elegant filling whose bright pink color adds eye appeal. Smoked trout and smoked bluefish are interesting alternatives. Kippered salmon and herring, sardines, and smoked oysters are among other seafood products that can be used in sandwiches. The preparation of cured and smoked seafood is covered in Chapter 12.

Bound Protein Salads

Salads made from meats, poultry, and seafood bound with a thick mayonnaise dressing are among the most popular sandwich fillings in North America. Chicken salad, turkey salad, tuna salad, shrimp or crab salad, and egg salad are favorites. Salads bound with thick, emulsified vinaigrettes make interesting sandwich fillings as well.

When bound protein salads are intended for use as sandwich fillings, both the protein ingredient and the vegetables must be cut quite small, or even chopped or ground. Otherwise, large chunks of food will prevent the sandwich from staying together properly, and the filling will fall out of the bread.

Bound protein salads are covered in detail in Chapter 5.

Vegetable and Vegetarian Fillings

Until quite recently, vegetarians at the sandwich counter were pretty much limited to cheese sandwiches. Those following vegan diets had to settle for peanut butter and jelly. Today, most delis, sandwich shops, and restaurants now offer a respectable selection of meatless sandwich fillings. One of the most popular consists of cool grilled vegetables served with or without cheese. Spreads such as hummus (p. 118) and baba ghanoush (p. 119), if made thick and applied generously, make good vegetarian sandwich fillings as well. Nut butters and fruit leathers make interesting alternatives to peanut butter and jelly. Food processing companies specializing in vegan foods offer soy-based "turkey," "bacon," and other meat substitutes that can be used for vegetarian sandwiches.

Internal Garnishes

When we speak of a garnish for a sandwich, we must differentiate between an external garnish and an internal garnish.

An ***external garnish*** is a piece of food served outside the sandwich rather than included inside it. Examples are a pickle spear placed on the plate next to the sandwich and an olive on a cocktail pick stuck into the top of the sandwich. Sometimes a side dish, such as coleslaw or potato chips, served on the plate along with the sandwich, is considered an external garnish.

An ***internal garnish*** is part of the sandwich and enclosed within the bread (except, of course, in open-face sandwiches made with a single bread slice). In North America, the most common internal sandwich garnishes are lettuce leaves and tomato slices, although there are many others.

Internal garnishes are meant to add contrasting texture and mouthfeel to the sandwich. In addition, they should complement the flavor of the sandwich and add to its overall taste. Finally, the internal garnishes should be attractive to look at and add color and visual texture to the composition of the sandwich.

Lettuce

Iceberg lettuce is often the best lettuce choice when a crunchy texture is desired. However, other types of lettuce are more flavorful and are perceived by customers to be of higher quality. Romaine and green-leaf lettuces are popular, although many other types can be used (see p. 59). Make sure the lettuce is well dried before using it, or you risk a soggy sandwich. For most cold sandwiches, lettuce leaves are used whole or torn in half during assembly. Shredded lettuce is used for subs and wraps.

Tomatoes

Tomatoes are an indispensable element in many popular sandwiches such as clubs and BLTs. Sandwiches that include tomatoes are best featured when local tomatoes are in season. However, many customers want tomatoes on their sandwiches year-round. Although they are expensive, high-quality vine-ripe tomatoes add value to your sandwiches.

Fabricate fresh tomatoes at the last possible minute before serving to keep them firm and attractive, and prepare only the amount you estimate is needed for one service. A folded paper towel at the bottom of the container absorbs excess moisture and prevents drippy sandwiches. Because tomatoes taste best at room temperature, hold them out of refrigeration during service. However, in this case they must be covered tightly and used with 1–2 hours. Leftover tomatoes may be recycled for cooking.

Onions

Many people love the crisp, pungent bite of raw onion on their sandwiches. In recent years, a number of sweet onion varieties, such as Vidalia, Maui, and Walla Walla, have come onto the market. These onions are preferred for raw use in both salads and sandwiches because of their mild flavor and crisp, tender texture. Red onions add an attractive color.

Onions served raw must be firm and fresh and show no signs of softening or spoilage. They should be peeled and fabricated close to serving time and stored under refrigeration in tightly closed containers to prevent flavor change. Fabricated onions left over from the sandwich service should be recycled into use for cooked items.

Most cold sandwiches require raw onions fabricated into thin slices. Chopped onions are not good for most cold sandwiches because they fall out easily. Some cooked onion products, such as Red Onion Confiture (p. 682), make interesting additions to cold sandwiches.

Other Garnishes

In addition to lettuce, tomato, and onion, many other garnishes may be used to enhance sandwiches of all kinds. Here are a few ideas for internal sandwich garnishes:

- Cucumber pickles
- Pickled peppers (sweet or hot)
- Sliced radishes
- Sliced cucumbers
- Sprouts and micro greens
- Roasted peppers
- Grilled vegetables
- Fresh herbs
- Coleslaw
- Sauerkraut
- Sliced fruits
- Toasted nuts
- Hard-cooked eggs (sliced or chopped)

TYPES OF SANDWICHES

Today's repertoire of sandwich types is much wider than in the past. This is due, in part, to the influence of international cuisines, and also to the creations of contemporary sandwich cooks and garde manger chefs. While the classic cold sandwiches remain as popular as ever, new forms are emerging every day.

Sandwiches can be categorized into six basic construction types:

- Simple sandwiches
- Double-decker and multi-decker sandwiches
- Open-face sandwiches
- Long roll sandwiches
- Pocket sandwiches
- Wrap sandwiches

Simple Sandwiches

A ***simple sandwich*** consists of two slices of bread with the spread, filling, and internal garnishes between them. No matter how many layers of filling or how many internal garnishes a sandwich might contain, if there are only two slices of bread, a sandwich is considered a simple sandwich. Sandwiches made with horizontally split rolls are also called *simple sandwiches.*

Another term that could describe a simple sandwich is a ***single-decker sandwich***. In sandwich terminology, the construction of a traditional sandwich is compared to the construction of a ship: The bottom bread slice is like a floor; the filling is like the living space; and the top slice is like a ceiling. The configuration as a whole is referred to as a *deck*.

Double-Decker Sandwiches

If you begin building a simple sandwich having one deck, but then go on to place another layer of filling on top of the ceiling slice and then top that filling with a third slice of bread, you have made a ***double-decker sandwich***. As in building

The History of the Dagwood

In the 1930s cartoon strip *Blondie*, the character Dagwood Bumstead was repeatedly pictured raiding the refrigerator in the middle of the night and making huge, unwieldy sandwiches stacked high with outlandish combinations of ingredients. The strip created a fad for overstuffed multi-decker sandwiches that became known as Dagwoods.

A simple or single-decker sandwich

A club sandwich or double-decker sandwich

a ship, you could continue adding decks to make a triple- or even quadruple-decker sandwich. Sandwiches having more than one deck are sometimes called ***multi-decker sandwiches***.

The most famous double-decker sandwich is the ***club sandwich***. A classic club sandwich has a lower deck consisting of sliced roast turkey or chicken and an upper deck consisting of bacon, lettuce, and tomato. It is made on toasted white bread spread with mayonnaise. Today, many variations are made on this classic. Sometimes turkey salad or chicken salad is used; other meats, such as ham or roast beef, may be substituted. Cheese may be added. In the 1980s, Chef Anne Rosenzweig popularized the luxurious lobster club sandwich. Contemporary chefs sometimes replace the bacon with pancetta or frizzled prosciutto.

Open-Face Sandwiches

An open-face sandwich

An ***open-face sandwich*** is a single slice of bread topped with a spread, filling ingredients, and garnishes. In other words, an open-face sandwich is a sandwich without a lid. One reason to leave off the top slice of bread is to allow the attractive fillings and garnishes to be seen. Another is to make the sandwich less filling.

Many open-face sandwiches are meant to be eaten with a knife and fork, especially those with hot or semiliquid toppings. Very small open-face sandwiches, called *canapés*, are considered hors d'oeuvres. These are covered in Chapter 10.

Long Roll Sandwiches

A simple long roll sandwich

Sandwiches made with long, narrow French and Italian breads can be constructed in two different ways. If the rolls are split completely in half horizontally and then filled, the result is a ***simple long roll sandwich***. This construction type works well with solid slices of filling ingredient and internal garnishes that are fabricated in large pieces. It is less successful with small-cut, loose ingredients, such as bound protein salads and shredded lettuce, because the long, narrow shape of the sandwich makes it difficult to keep the filling from falling out.

To make a ***hollowed long roll sandwich***, the roll is slit along one side, opened out, and flattened into a canoe shape. Breads having a dense, firm interior are further hollowed by removing and discarding some of the crumb. After the roll is spread, filled, and garnished, it is then closed around the filling. This results in a sort of bread tube encasing the filling ingredients. Long roll sandwiches assembled in this manner stay together better and are easier to eat.

Italian Sandwiches

A hollowed long roll sandwich

The ***Italian sandwich*** is probably the best-known long roll sandwich. Throughout North America it is also known variously as a ***hero***, ***hoagie***, ***submarine***, ***grinder***, or ***po'boy***. The original version consists of Italian-style deli meats and cheeses, shredded lettuce, tomatoes, and onions on a long, crisp-crusted roll. Early versions were dressed with olive oil, while mayonnaise has since become a popular alternative. Internal garnishes, such as sweet or hot pickled peppers, fresh or roasted peppers, olives, or fresh or dried herbs, may be added. There are many regional variations on the original Italian sandwich theme. Heated Italian sandwiches prepared by the toasted sandwich procedure are called ***oven grinders***. In addition, modern sandwich shops offer nontraditional fillings such as tuna salad, roast turkey, and even corned beef. Asian grocers now offer Italian-style sandwiches made with ingredients such as Chinese sausages and kim chee.

How Italian Sandwiches Got Their Names

The Italian sandwich came to North America with the great wave of southern Italian immigration in the last decades of the nineteenth century. Italian-American workers asked for antipasto-style meats and vegetables sold in mom-and-pop grocery stores to be encased in bread so they could take their dinners to work, and the Italian sandwich was born.

- In Philadelphia, the sandwiches were a favorite of the naval shipyard workers at Hog Island. Both the workers and their sandwiches were called *hoggies*, but the sandwich eventually became known as the *hoagie*.
- In New London, Connecticut, grocery stores made footlong Italian sandwiches for the workers at the Groton submarine base during World War II. The workers decided the sandwiches resembled submarines, and they were soon called by that name.
- During a transit strike in 1929, a New Orleans restaurant began selling inexpensive long roll sandwiches to the "poor boys" on the picket lines, and soon the sandwiches became known as *po'boys*.

Pocket Sandwiches

Pocket sandwiches are made with yeasted flatbreads that are fabricated and baked in a way that gives them a hollow center. Pita bread is the most common product used, although flatbreads of other ethnic origin are now becoming available. To assemble a pocket sandwich, the bread is cut in half and opened up to form two pouches, or pockets. The interior walls of the bread are moistened with the spread of choice, and the filling and garnishes are stuffed inside.

A pocket sandwich

Wrap Sandwiches

Thin, pliable flatbreads may be rolled with or around a filling and internal garnishes to make ***wrap sandwiches***. There are two ways to roll wraps: pinwheel-style (p. 345) and burrito-style (p. 347). Wraps are cut crosswise into two or more pieces before serving. In low-calorie or low-carbohydrate cooking, wrap sandwiches are sometimes made with lettuce leaves rather than a bread product as the wrapper.

Burrito-style wrap sandwich

MAKING SANDWICHES

Because they are such a commonplace food, sandwiches are sometimes disregarded when chefs write recipes, design turnout stations, and train cooks. However, while anyone can make a sandwich, not everyone can make a good sandwich—and make it fast. À la carte sandwich preparation in a busy foodservice operation requires organization, special techniques, speed, and good hand skills.

An important skill is the ability to use two hands at the same time. An experienced sandwich cook reaches for the bread with one hand while reaching for the spread squeeze bottle with the other. He or she applies the spread to the bread while reaching for the filling meats with the first hand, and so on. Two-handed sandwich assembly depends on the proper station set-up.

The Sandwich Station

In small operations with varied menus, there is usually only one garde manger area responsible for salads and cold appetizers (and, often, dessert turnout) as well as sandwiches. In such stations, the sandwich ingredients and equipment must be integrated with those used for the other dishes served. In large operations, an entire station may be dedicated to sandwiches. Sandwiches are the main menu items in delis and sandwich shops, so the stations in them are planned expressly for sandwich production.

No matter the size of the station, the fast and efficient production of cold and heated sandwiches requires a well-planned set-up that includes the equipment listed in Table 9.4.

TABLE 9.4 Sandwich Station Equipment

Equipment Type	Use
Salad/sandwich units	Refrigeration units specially designed for efficient assembly of cold foods (see p. 12).
Pans and inserts	Designed to fit into the top sections of salad/sandwich units Available in both stainless-steel and food-service-grade plastic
Electric slicing machine(s)	Quickly and evenly slices deli meats and cheeses in varying degrees of thinness Used in the sandwich turnout station if no designated sandwich prep area is available, or if meats are to be sliced to order
Electric bread slicers	Used in high-volume sandwich operations using in-house baked breads or bakery breads not available sliced
Countertop ovens	May be used in cold sandwich station to warm filling ingredients such as pastrami or roast beef Also used to heat or brown sandwiches such as toasted subs or tuna melts
Panini grills or clamshell grills	Countertop heating units that brown sandwiches top and bottom while compressing them
Scales	Necessary for portion control of meat and cheeses. Digital scales are preferred for accuracy.
Multi-tip squeeze bottles	Fast and effective tools for applying most sandwich spreads
Portion scoops or dishers	For bound protein salads and thick spreads
Shakers	For applying salt and pepper, dried herbs and spices, and grated cheese
Spatulas (straight and offset) and rubber scrapers	For thick spreads
Deli wrap and patty paper	To wrap sandwiches for take-out and to separate portions of sliced meats and cheeses
Sandwich picks	Used to hold sandwiches together Also used for identification purposes (see guidelines box, p. 323)
Knives	Serrated knives to slice artisan breads to order and for slitting and slicing rolls Utility knives for slicing tomatoes and other internal garnishes Chef knives for cutting sandwiches
Cutting boards	Included in the construction of sandwich/salad units Additional boards may be needed for slicing breads or for hand-carved roasted meats or poultry
Food-service gloves	Must be worn when handling ready-to-eat foods

Mise-en-Place

A well-planned and complete mise-en-place is essential for à la carte sandwich service. Sandwiches are usually ordered during lunch service, when most customers have limited time. In addition, customers perceive them to be quick to order. Garde manger chefs who are well prepared ensure the time between the order and the arrival of the food at the table is brief.

Guidelines for Preparing Sandwiches

- Slice enough deli meats and cheeses for the day's service. Portion fillings ahead of time. Place the proper portion scoop near each container of bound protein salad.
- Clean and fabricate all garnishes. When fabricating items portioned by count, make sure each is of the correct size. Pre-portion when possible.
- Prepare all spreads and place in appropriate containers. Place oils and semiliquid spreads in multi-tip squeeze bottles. Whip or soften butters and semisolid spreads.
- Slice breads and rolls.
- Arrange ingredients in assembly-line fashion. Place items in such a way that you can use two hands at the same time.
- Use color-coded sandwich picks or other appropriate markers to identify orders. For example, you could use yellow frill picks for a ham sandwich with mustard and clear frill picks for one with mayonnaise.
- Have plates, baskets, wrappers, or take-out containers at hand.

Quantity Sandwich Production

As a garde manger chef in a large operation, you may be asked to fill an order for several hundred box lunches, or you may need to prepare sandwich trays for a buffet. In these situations, it is more efficient to create an assembly line set-up on a long worktable. Place the prepared sandwich ingredients on the table in order of use, beginning with the bread product and ending with the trays or wrapping materials. Place the necessary tools at the appropriate places along the line. You can then begin assembling the sandwiches quickly and efficiently, whether working alone or in a production line with other staff members. Refrigerate the assembled sandwiches within a half-hour.

Packaging Sandwiches for Take-Out and Catering

Sandwiches are ordered to go more often than any other type of food. Because sandwiches must be neat and easy to eat, it is important that they arrive at their destination in good shape. Even the most delicious sandwich is ruined if it falls apart while being transported. Customers don't appreciate soggy, oily wrappers and leaky condiment containers.

Wrapped Sandwiches

Most take-out sandwiches are wrapped in some sort of paper product. The advantage of wrapping sandwiches is that tight wrapping holds them together even if they are jostled during transport. For presentation purposes, some operations place sandwiches in containers rather than wrapping them. In this case, the sandwiches containers must be boxed or stacked securely in heavy paper bags to stay level during transport.

The first step in properly wrapping sandwiches is to have the correct supplies. Sandwiches of different construction require different wrapping techniques. Refer to the illustrations on this page to learn professional wrapping techniques.

The four steps to wrap a square sandwich:

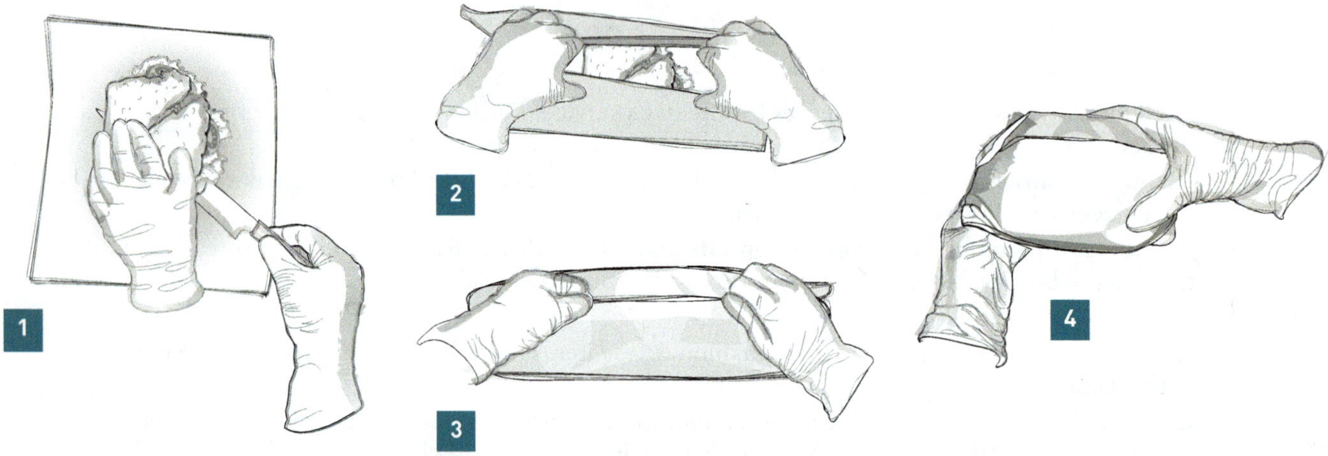

The four steps to wrap a long roll sandwich:

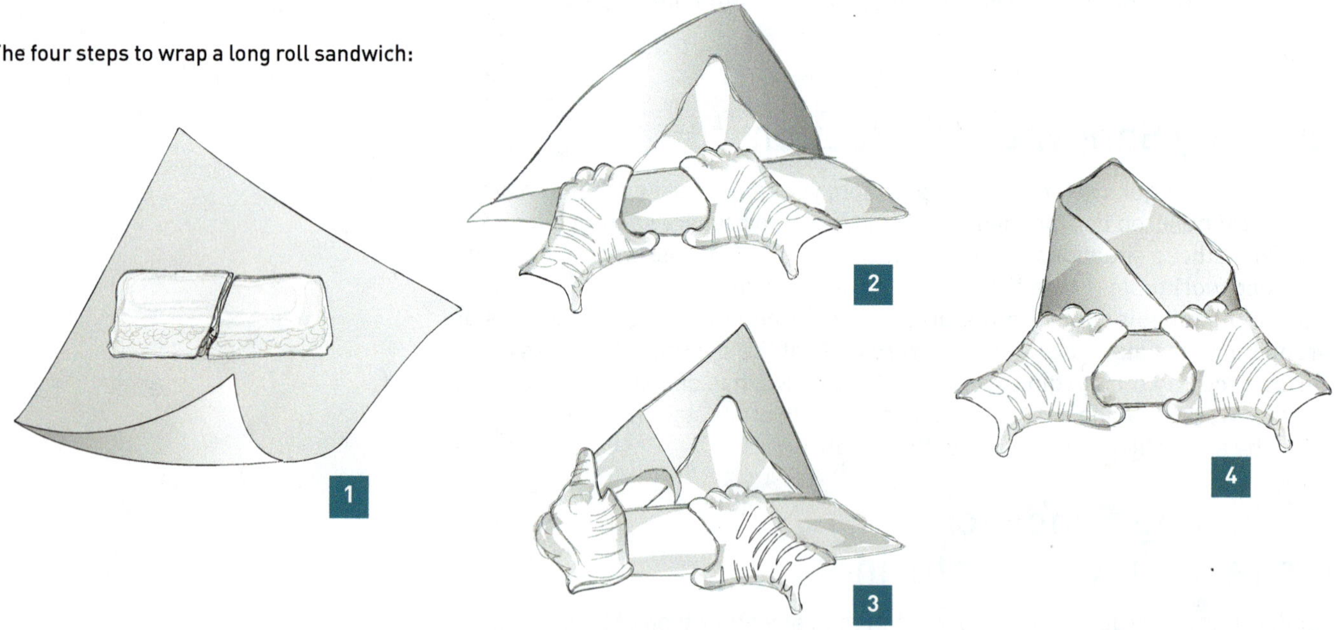

Box Lunch Sandwiches

The main element of most box lunches is some sort of cold sandwich. Most sandwiches for box lunches are prepared and wrapped in the same way as for take-out, but with one difference: Because box lunches are usually stored for some time before being eaten, sandwich spreads and condiments are usually left off the sandwich and packaged separately in small, lidded soufflé cups. Unless you are sure the box lunches will be kept under refrigeration at all times, do not use mayonnaise or other foods that have a high risk of spoilage. Alternatively, provide commercial condiment packets.

Along with the sandwich and its condiments, a box lunch should also contain at least one type of side dish, such as one of the side salads covered in Chapter 5, and a simple dessert, such as fresh fruit or a cookie. Include disposable napkins and appropriate utensils as well.

Sandwich Trays

For catering, sandwiches are arranged on durable or disposable trays in an attractive presentation. For successful sandwich trays, it is essential to construct the sandwiches neatly and securely. Plan sandwich trays to consist of an assortment that will suit virtually all guests. Offer a variety of fillings, including at least one vegetarian option. To afford guests a wider variety of choices, cut full-size sandwiches in half or into smaller sections and secure with cocktail picks. Alternatively, use half-size sandwich rolls. Pack sandwich spreads and other condiments separately, and be sure to supply the proper utensils for applying them.

Sandwich Sanitation

Cold sandwiches are subject to a lot of handling and are not cooked before they are served. Many contain mayonnaise, an especially risky ingredient. It is important to observe all general food safety guidelines when preparing and serving cold sandwiches. In addition, some food safety procedures apply especially to sandwiches.

Guidelines for Sandwich Food Safety

- Wear food-service gloves when preparing sandwiches. Change gloves frequently, and always put on fresh gloves after handling dirty dishes or trash.
- Do not allow a counterperson making sandwiches to handle money.
- Wipe knives with sanitizer solution between each task.
- Keep perishable fillings, spreads, and garnishes refrigerated during the service, and keep the lid of the sandwich/salad unit closed when not in active use.
- Wash and sanitize the tops of squeeze bottles after each service. Empty, wash, and sanitize squeeze bottles on a regularly scheduled basis, at least once per week.

SANDWICH PROCEDURES AND RECIPES

Each of the six construction types of sandwich has its own method of assembly. After you have mastered the procedure for a particular type, you can apply it to virtually any combination of fillings and internal garnishes.

Simple Sandwiches

Procedure for Assembling Simple Sandwiches

Simple sandwich construction:

1. Place 2 slices of bread, cooled toast, or a split roll on a cutting board.
2. Apply the spread to both slices in a thin, even layer extending to the edges of the bread (A).
3. Place the filling ingredient(s) on 1 piece of bread (B) or the bottom of the roll. If applicable, fluff the filling ingredients, and then distribute them in an even layer extending to the edges of the bread.
4. Place the internal garnish ingredients on top of the filling in an even layer extending to the edges of the bread (C).
5. Place the remaining bread slice or the top of the roll on the filling, and press gently to firm and compact the sandwich.
6. If necessary, secure with sandwich picks.
7. Using a sharp chef's knife, cut the sandwich as desired (D).
8. Slide the blade of the knife under the sandwich pieces, place your hand on top of the sandwich to hold it on the knife, and lift the sandwich onto the plate or into the wrapper (E).
9. If applicable, wrap the sandwich using the proper method for the sandwich type.
10. Add the appropriate external garnishes.

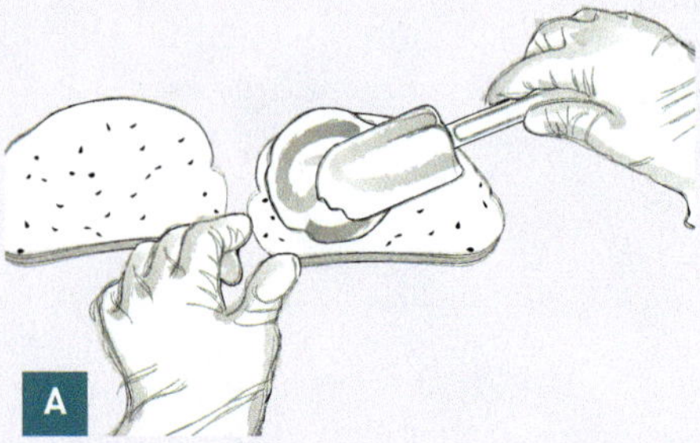
A

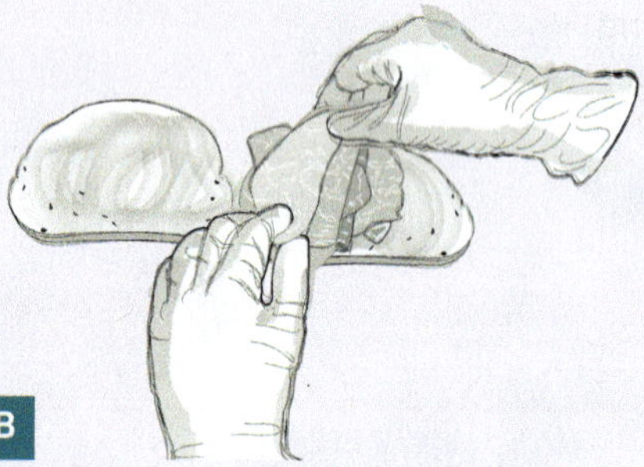
B

C

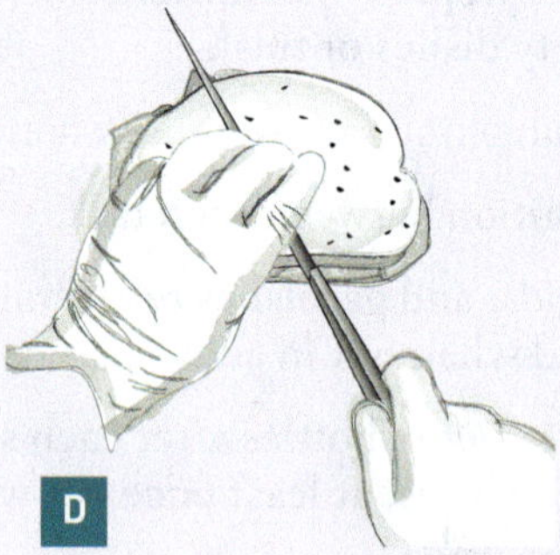
D

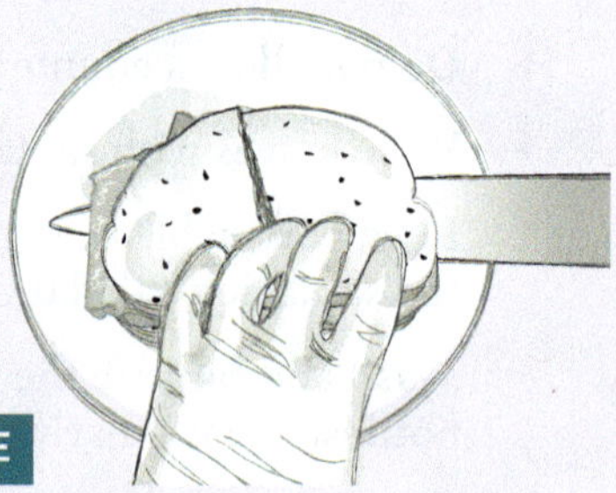
E

HAND-CARVED TURKEY ON WHITE OR WHOLE WHEAT

LUNCH MAIN COURSE

Yield:
1 sandwich, 4 oz (120 g) filling

COMPONENTS

2 slices (2 slices) Firm white or whole wheat bread
1 fl oz (30 mL) *Mayonnaise (p. 41)*, or commercial mayonnaise
4 oz (120 g) Hand-sliced *Cold Roast Turkey Breast (p. 251)*
to taste Kosher salt
to taste Freshly ground black pepper
1 leaf (¼ oz/7 g) Green-leaf lettuce or romaine lettuce
3 slices (1½ oz/45 g total) Vine-ripe tomato

Supplies

2 Sandwich picks

PROCEDURE

FINISHING

1. Prepare according to the Procedure for Assembling Simple Sandwiches (p. 326), placing the lettuce on the bottom.
2. Secure with sandwich picks.
3. Cut in half on the diagonal.

PLATING

4. Place the sandwich on a cool 8-in. (20-cm) round plate.

VARIATIONS

THANKSGIVING TURKEY SANDWICH

Reduce the turkey to 3½ oz (100 g) and add ½ oz (15 g) cooked bread stuffing, warmed to room temperature. Replace half the mayonnaise with jellied cranberry sauce.

HAND-CARVED ROAST BEEF WITH HORSERADISH SAUCE

Replace the bread slices with a Kaiser roll. Replace the turkey with 4 oz (100 g) cold hand-sliced roast beef. Replace the tomato with thin-sliced red onion. Replace the mayonnaise with Creamy Horseradish Sauce (p. 45).

HAND-CARVED TURKEY AND SMOKED GOUDA

Reduce the turkey to 3½ oz (100 g) and add ½ oz (15g) sliced smoked Gouda cheese.

HAND-CARVED ROAST BEEF AND SWISS

Replace the turkey with 3½ oz (100g) cold hand-sliced roast beef. Add ½ oz (15 g) sliced Swiss cheese and thin slices of sweet onion. Replace half the mayonnaise with brown or Dijon mustard.

CORNED BEEF SPECIAL

LUNCH MAIN COURSE

Yield:
1 sandwich, 4 oz (120g) filling

COMPONENTS

2 slices Jewish rye bread or marble rye
1 fl oz (30 mL) *Russian Dressing (p. 43)*
4 oz (120 g) Thin-sliced *Jewish Corned Beef (p. 421)*
3 fl oz (90 mL) *Creamy Coleslaw (p. 135)*, well drained

External Garnish
1 (1 oz) (30 g) Jewish half-sour pickle spear, blotted dry

Supplies
2 Frilled sandwich picks

PROCEDURE

FINISHING

1. Prepare according to the Procedure for Assembling Simple Sandwiches (p. 326), but apply the Russian dressing to the bottom bread slice only. Add the coleslaw as an internal garnish.
2. Secure with sandwich picks.
3. Cut in half.

PLATING

4. Place the sandwich in the center of a cool 8-in. (20-cm) round plate. Place the pickle across the top of the sandwich.

VARIATIONS

SMOKED TURKEY SPECIAL

Replace the Jewish corned beef with deli smoked turkey breast.

LIVERWURST ON RYE

Prepare as for corned beef on rye, but replace the Jewish corned beef with liverwurst. Add thin-sliced sweet onion.

CORNED BEEF ON RYE

Replace the Russian dressing with brown mustard applied to both bread slices. Omit the coleslaw, or place it on the plate as an external garnish.

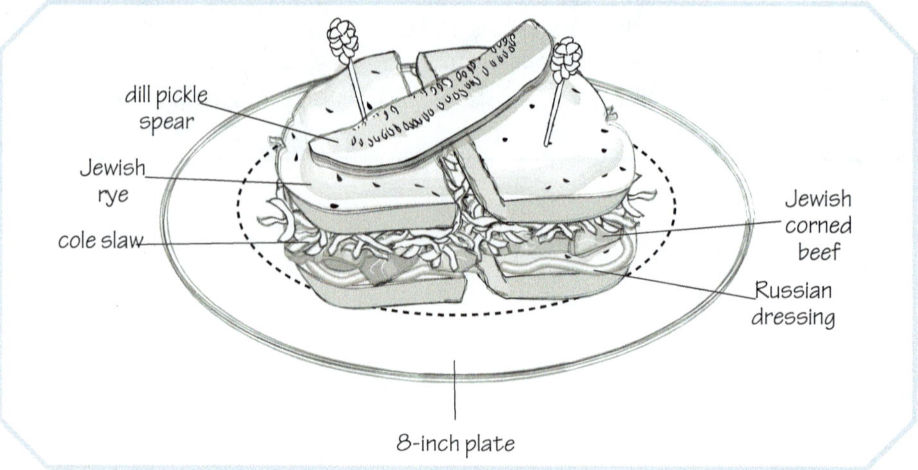

CHICKEN SALAD ON A KAISER ROLL

LUNCH MAIN COURSE

Yield:
1 sandwich, 4½ oz (125 g) filling

COMPONENTS

1 Kaiser roll
1 fl oz (30 mL) *Mayonnaise (p. 41)*, or commercial mayonnaise
4½ oz (125 g) *Classic Chicken Salad (p. 159)*, made with chopped chicken
1 leaf (¼ oz/7 g) Green-leaf lettuce or romaine lettuce
3 slices (1½ oz/45 g total) Vine-ripe tomato

External Garnish
2 Pimiento-stuffed olives

Supplies
2 Frilled sandwich picks

PROCEDURE

FINISHING

1. Prepare according to the Procedure for Assembling Simple Sandwiches (p. 326), but apply the mayonnaise to the top of the roll only.
2. Impale an olive on each sandwich pick and secure the sandwiches with the picks.
3. Cut in half.

PLATING

4. Place in the center of a cool 10-in. (25-cm) round plate.

VARIATIONS

TURKEY SALAD ON A KAISER ROLL

Replace the chicken salad with Turkey Salad (p. 159).

TUNA SALAD ON A KAISER ROLL

Replace the chicken salad with Traditional Tuna Salad (p. 161).

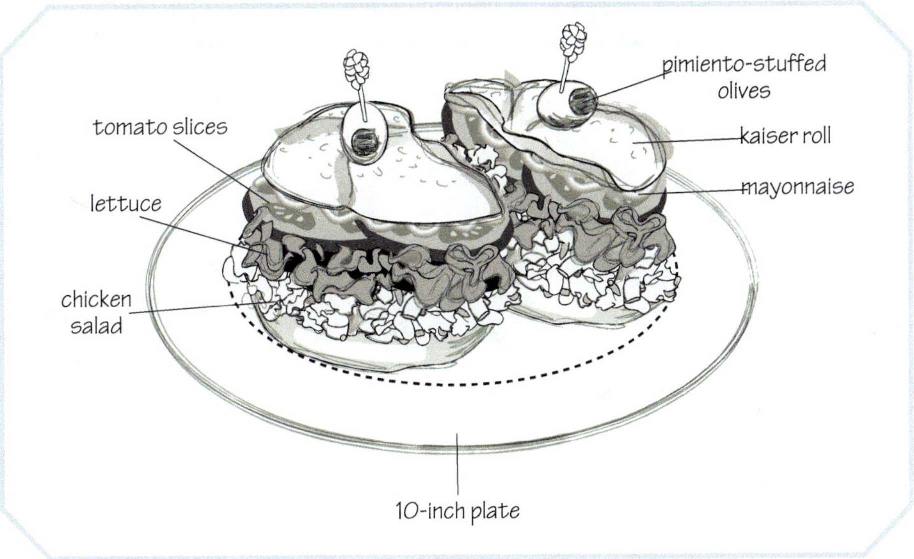

SMOKED SALMON ON A BAGEL

LUNCH MAIN COURSE

Yield:
1 sandwich, 2 oz (60 g) salmon and 2 oz (60 g) cream cheese filling

COMPONENTS

1 Bagel (plain, poppy seed, or onion)
2 oz (60 g) Whipped cream cheese
2 oz (60 g) Sliced smoked salmon
1 slice (¼ oz/7 g) Red onion
3 slices (1½ oz/45 g total) Vine-ripe tomato

Supplies

2 Plain sandwich picks

PROCEDURE

FINISHING

1. Slice the bagel in half.
2. Toast the bagel and allow it to cool.
3. Spread each bagel half with cream cheese.
4. Fluff the salmon on the bagel bottom.
5. Separate the onion into rings and place on the salmon.
6. Arrange the tomato slices on the onion.
7. Place the bagel top on the sandwich and press gently.
8. Secure with sandwich picks.
9. Cut in half.

PLATING

10. Place in the center of a cool 8-in. (20-cm) round plate.

VARIATIONS

Replace the smoked salmon with any of the following: lox, kippered salmon, smoked whitefish, chub, smoked trout.

Add chopped dill or chopped scallions to the cream cheese.

ROAST PORK WITH PROVOLONE ON CIABATTA ROLL

LUNCH MAIN COURSE

Yield:
1 sandwich, 4 oz (120 g) pork and cheese filling)

COMPONENTS

1 (3 oz/90 g) Ciabatta roll or bread section
3 fl oz (90 mL) *Roasted Peppers in Garlic Oil (p. 688)*
3½ oz (100 g) Sliced roast pork loin, prepared as the filet on p. 253, roasted to 150°F (65°C)
½ oz (15 g) Sliced sharp provolone cheese
¼ oz (7 g) Arugula, cleaned

External Garnish

2 Pitted black olives

Supplies

2 Sandwich picks

PROCEDURE

FINISHING

1. Split the roll or bread section.
2. Spoon half the peppers and their oil onto the bottom of the roll.
3. Fluff the pork and place it on the roll bottom.
4. Fold the cheese and place it on the pork.
5. Place the arugula on the cheese.
6. Spoon the remaining peppers onto the arugula.
7. Drizzle the remaining oil onto the cut side of the roll top.
8. Place the roll top on the sandwich and press gently.
9. Secure the sandwich with the picks.
10. Cut in half.
11. Impale the olives on the picks.

PLATING

12. Place the sandwich on a cool 10-in. (25-cm) round plate.

VARIATIONS

ROAST PORK WITH PESTO ON CIABATTA ROLL

Replace the roasted peppers with 1 fl oz (30 mL) Pesto alla Genovese (p. 688).

GRILLED TUNA ON CIABATTA ROLL

Replace the pork and provolone with a 4 oz (120 g) grilled and cooled tuna steak.

GRILLED VEGETABLES, PESTO, AND PROVOLONE ON CIABATTA ROLL

Replace the pork with 3 oz (90 g) Grilled Summer Vegetable Medley (p. 108). Replace the roasted peppers with 1 fl oz (30 mL) Pesto alla Genovese (p. 688).

Double-Decker Sandwiches

Procedure for Assembling Double-Decker (Club) Sandwiches

1. Toast 3 bread slices and allow to cool upright or on a rack so they stay crisp.
2. Place the cooled slices in a row on a cutting board.
3. Apply a thin layer of mayonnaise to all 3 slices (A).
4. Place a lettuce leaf on the left bread slice.
5. Place the primary filling ingredient on the lettuce (B).
6. Place the second bread slice on top of the filling ingredient spread-side down (C), and press gently.
7. Apply a thin layer of mayonnaise to the top of the second bread slice of the sandwich (D).
8. Place slices of cooked and cooled bacon on top of the bread slice (E).
9. Place another lettuce leaf and tomato slices on top (F).
10. Place the remaining bread slice, spread-side down, on top, and press gently.
11. Secure with 4 sandwich picks (G).
12. Cut diagonally into quarters (H).
13. Place on the plate in a pinwheel arrangement with center points facing upward (I).
14. Add external garnish(es).

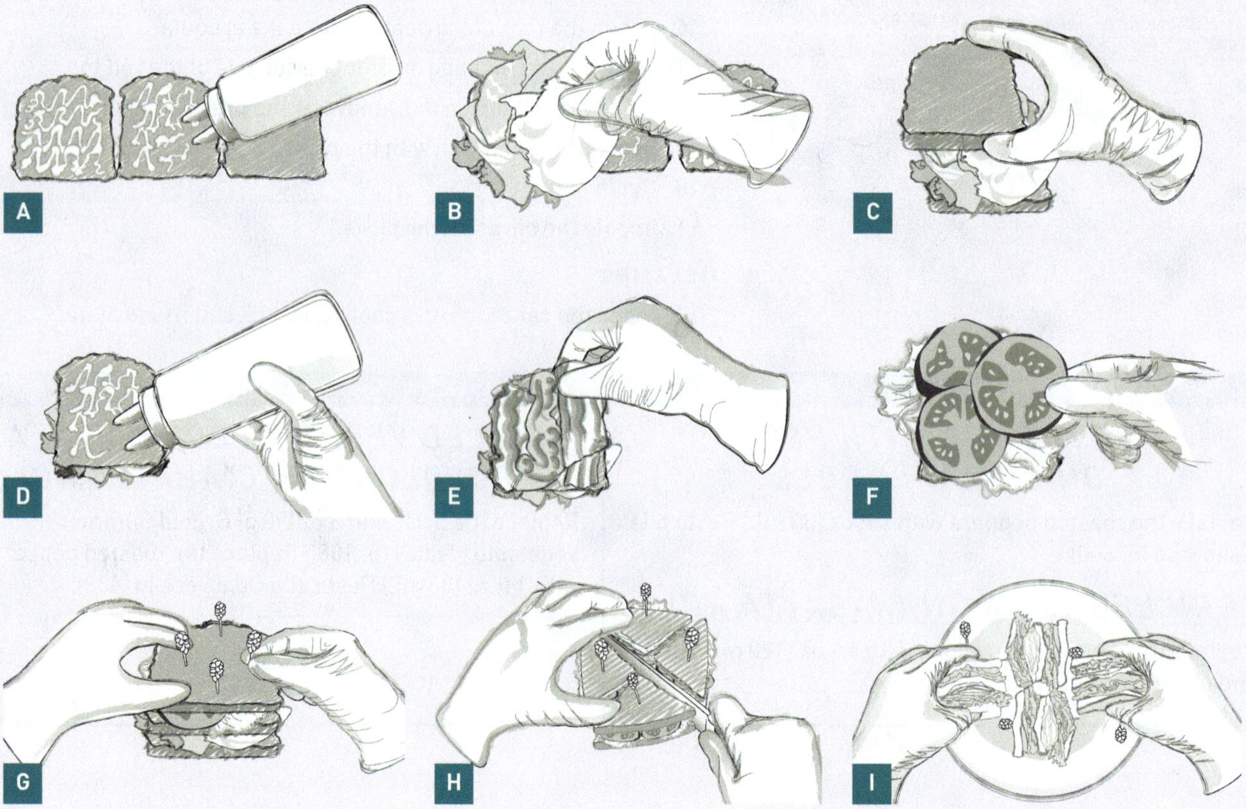

CLASSIC CLUB SANDWICH

LUNCH MAIN COURSE

Yield:
1 sandwich,
3½ oz (100 g) chicken or turkey,
½ oz (15 g) bacon

COMPONENTS

3 slices (3½ oz/115 g total) Firm white Pullman bread
1½ fl oz (45 mL) *Mayonnaise (p. 41)*, or commercial mayonnaise
2 leaves (½ oz/15 g) Iceberg or leaf lettuce
3½ oz (100 g) Sliced *Cold Roast Chicken* or *Turkey Breast (p. 251)*
to taste Kosher salt
to taste Freshly ground black pepper
½ oz (15 g) Crisp-cooked and cooled thin-sliced bacon (cooked weight)
3 slices (1½ oz/45 g total) Vine-ripe tomato
1 (½ oz/15 g) *Dill Pickle* spear *(p. 675)*, cut in half

External Garnish
½ oz (15 g) Potato chips

Supplies
4 Sandwich picks

PROCEDURE

FINISHING

1. Prepare according to the Procedure for Assembling Double-Decker (Club) Sandwiches (p. 332).

PLATING

2. Plate according to the Procedure for Assembling Double-Decker (Club) Sandwiches (p. 332).
3. Place the pickle spear halves on the plate between the sandwich sections.
4. Pile the potato chips in the center of the sandwich.

VARIATIONS

CALIFORNIA CLUB

Add 3 slices firm-ripe, chilled avocado to the top deck.

COBB CLUB

Prepare a California Club, but reduce the chicken to 3 oz (90 g) and add ½ oz (15 g) crumbled blue cheese to the bottom deck.

LOBSTER CLUB

Replace the toasted bread slices with a ciabatta roll split into thirds. Substitute handmade, thick Lemon Mayonnaise (p. 43) for the plain mayonnaise. Substitute Boston lettuce for the iceberg or leaf lettuce. Replace the chicken with steamed and chilled sliced lobster tail meat.

The Origin of the Club Sandwich

Food historians debate the club sandwich's origin. Some authorities credit the sandwich to the chefs of the Saratoga Club, a hotel and casino that opened in 1894 at Saratoga Springs, New York. Others trace its origin to the club cars on passenger trains, whose chefs were supposedly inspired by double-decker freight cars. A recipe for the club sandwich first appeared in the 1906 edition of Fanny Farmer's *Boston Cooking-School Cook Book.*

Open-Face Sandwiches

Procedure for Assembling Open-Face Sandwiches

1. Place 1 bread slice or toast slice on a cutting board.
2. Apply the spread in an even layer (A).
3. Place the filling on the sandwich (B) and press gently.
4. Cut the sandwich as desired.
5. Top the sandwich pieces with the garnish ingredients (C).

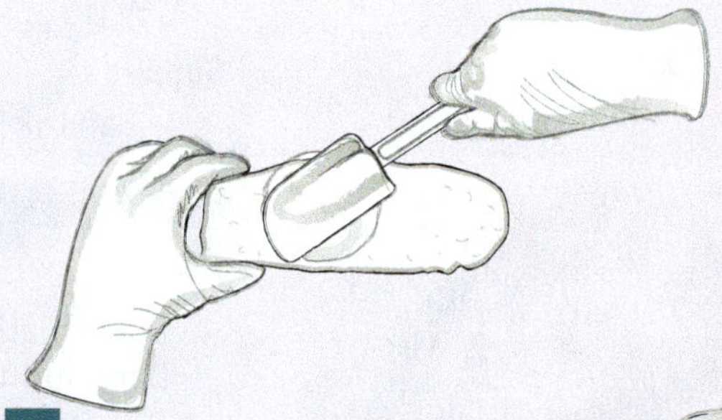

A

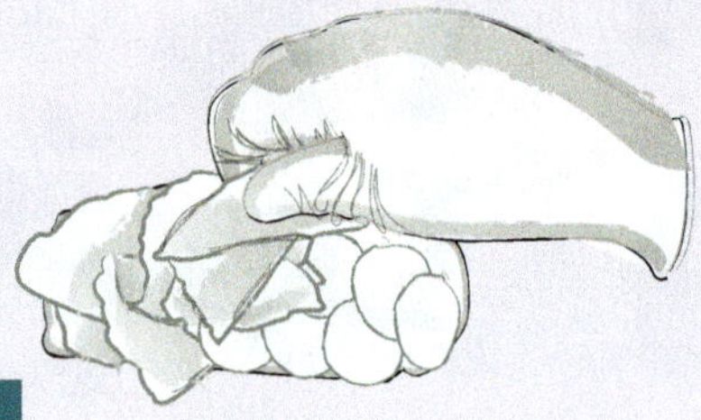

B

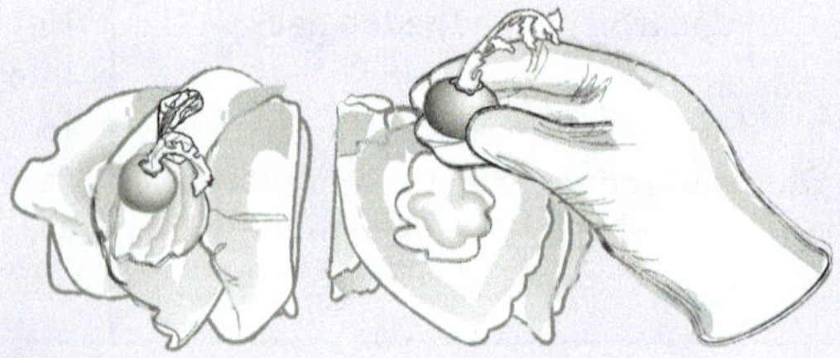

C

OPEN-FACE EGG SALAD ON BLACK BREAD

LUNCH MAIN COURSE

Yield:
1 sandwich, 4–5 oz (120–150 g) filling

COMPONENTS

1 slice (1½ oz/45 g) Pumpernickel bread
4 oz to 5 fl oz (120 g to 150 mL) *Traditional Egg Salad (p. 162)*
4 thin slices (1¾ oz/50 g total) Small vine-ripe tomato
to taste Kosher salt
to taste Freshly ground black pepper
½ fl oz (15 mL) *Mayonnaise (p. 41)*, or commercial mayonnaise, in pastry bag fitted with star tip
1 sprig Dill

PROCEDURE

FINISHING

1. Place the bread on a cutting board.
2. Spread the egg salad on the bread and smooth the edges.
3. Cut the sandwich into quarters.
4. Press a tomato slice onto each piece of the sandwich and season with salt and pepper.
5. Pipe a rosette of mayonnaise onto each tomato.
6. Stick a pluche of dill in each rosette.

PLATING

7. Using a large, wide spatula, transfer the sandwich to a cool 8-in. (25-cm) plate.

VARIATIONS

DILLED SHRIMP SALAD ON BLACK BREAD

Replace the egg salad with Scandinavian Shrimp Salad made with chopped shrimp (p. 160).

TARRAGON CHICKEN SALAD ON FOCACCIA

Replace the pumpernickel with a 5 × 5 in. (12 × 12 cm) square focaccia. Replace the egg salad with Tarragon Chicken Salad made with chopped chicken (p. 159). Replace the dill sprig with a tarragon sprig.

TARTINE AUX JAMBON-RADIS-BEURRE

(tahr-TEEN oh zhahm-boh rah-dee BURR)

FRENCH HAM AND RADISH OPEN-FACE SANDWICH

LUNCH MAIN COURSE

Yield:
1 sandwich,
3 oz (90 g) filling
plus 2 oz (60 g)
substantial spread

COMPONENTS

¼ (3 oz/120 g) Crisp baguette, room temperature (see step 1)
2 fl oz (60 mL) Whipped butter, room temperature, in pastry bag with large star tip
6–8 (2 oz/60 g) French white-tipped radishes or other mild radishes with tops
3 oz (90 g) Thin-sliced smoked ham

PROCEDURE

FINISHING

1. To make a tartine from a whole baguette: Place the baguette on a cutting board and, using a serrated knife, cut it in half crosswise. Holding the knife parallel to the board, cut one of the halves in half lengthwise. Place 1 tartine crumb-side up on the board. Reserve the remaining bread for other purposes.
2. Pipe 1½ oz (45 g) butter onto the tartine and spread it across the surface.
3. Reserve 2 radishes with tops for garnish. Remove the tops from the remaining radishes and slice them thin.
4. Arrange the radish slices on the butter and gently press them down.
5. Fluff the ham slices and arrange on the radishes in a ruffle.
6. Cut the sandwich in half widthwise.
7. Pipe a rosette of butter in the center of each tartine half. Press a garnish radish onto each rosette.

PLATING

8. Place the sandwich on a cool 10-in. (25-cm) plate.

VARIATION

TARTINE AU PARFAIT DE FOIE

(tahr-TEEN oh pahr-FAY duh FWA)

FRENCH LIVER PÂTÉ OPEN-FACE SANDWICH

Replace the butter with 3 oz (90 g) Poultry Liver Parfait (p. 265). Omit the ham. Omit the radishes. Garnish with Cornichon Fans (p. 408) and thin slices of red onion.

GRILLED DUCK AND WHITE BEAN SALAD TARTINE

LUNCH MAIN COURSE

Yield:
1 sandwich,
3 oz (90 g) filling plus
2 oz (60 g) spread

Tartines

A ***tartine*** is a flat piece of bread prepared for the purpose of topping it with a spread, such as butter, butter and jam, or liver parfait. The name *tartine* is also given to the resulting open-face sandwich. Although a tartine can be made with any slice of bread, in practice it is most often based on a piece of baguette cut in half horizontally.

If you have a baguette that is round in cross-section, cut it in half lengthwise by holding the knife perpendicular to the cutting board, making two halves with equal amounts of top and bottom crust. However, many if not most baguettes are more flattened rather than round, so this method is not practical, as the tartines would tip onto their sides. Cut the loaf in half lengthwise by holding the knife parallel to the cutting board.

COMPONENTS

¼ Crisp baguette, room temperature (see step 1)
2 oz (60 g) *Tuscan White Bean Salad (p. 153)*, mashed
1 oz (30 g) Chiffonade radicchio
3 oz (90 g) Grilled rare duck breast, cooled to room temperature
to taste Kosher salt
1 large Pitted green olive
⅛ oz or 1 tbsp (3 g/15 mL) Brunoise yellow bell pepper
¼ bunch watercress

PROCEDURE

FINISHING

1. Prepare a tartine as directed in step 1 of French Ham and Radish Open-Face Sandwich (p. 336).
2. Spread the tartine with the bean salad.
3. Sprinkle with the radicchio.
4. Slice the duck breast on a sharp diagonal.
5. Arrange the duck slices in an overlapping pattern down the length of the tartine. Season with salt.
6. Cut the tartine in half on the diagonal and reassemble it.
7. Arrange the olives and yellow pepper brunoise in a lengthwise pattern down the length of the tartine.

PLATING

8. Place on a cool 10-in. (25-cm) oval plate.
9. Arrange a bouquet of watercress behind the tartine.

VARIATION

GRILLED BEEF AND TOMATO CONFIT TARTINE

Replace the bean salad with Tomato Confiture (p. 689). Replace the radicchio with arugula. Replace the duck with rare-grilled beef filet. Omit the olive.

Long Roll Sandwiches

Procedure for Assembling Hollowed Long Roll Sandwiches

1. Place a long roll or length of baguette on a cutting board.
2. Cut off and discard about ½ in. (1 cm) of the bread heels.
3. Slit the roll open on the more rounded of the two sides.
4. Open the roll into a flat canoe shape.
5. If necessary, pull out and discard some of the bread's crumb to hollow it (A).
6. Apply flavored oil or spread to the entire interior surface of the roll (B).
7. Arrange one-third of the filling ingredients (usually the sliced cheese) in an overlapping layer that covers the entire interior surface of the roll (C).
8. Place the interior garnishes in the roll (D).
9. Moisten with flavored oil and/or add dry seasonings.
10. Fluff the remaining filling meats and arrange them in an overlapping layer on top of the garnishes. Tuck the sides down into the roll (E).
11. Close the roll around the filling and squeeze gently to compress the sandwich (F).
12. Secure the sandwich with picks or roll in deli paper.
13. Cut on the diagonal into 2 or 3 pieces (G).
14. Place on a plate.

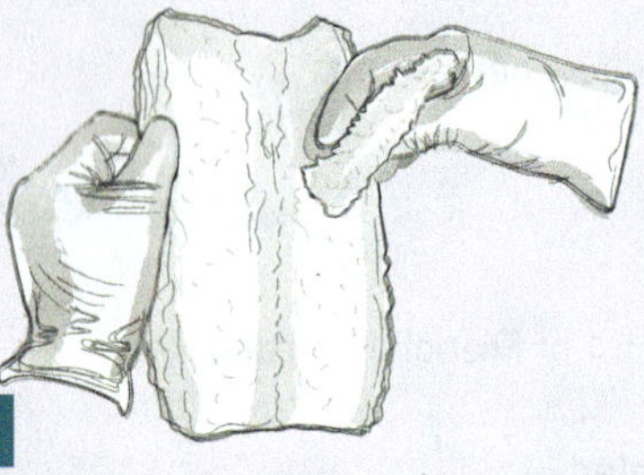
A

B

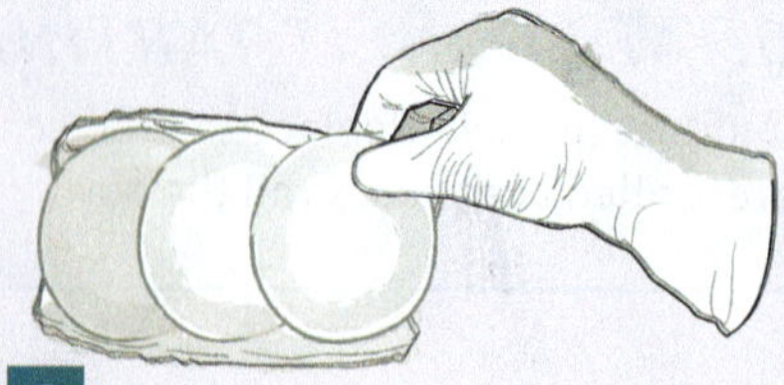
C

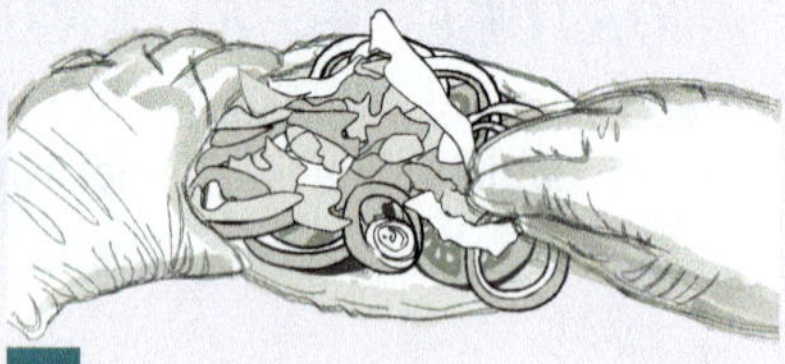
D

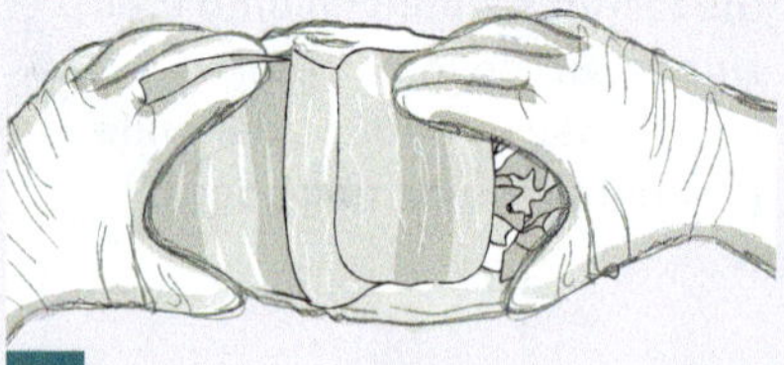
E

F

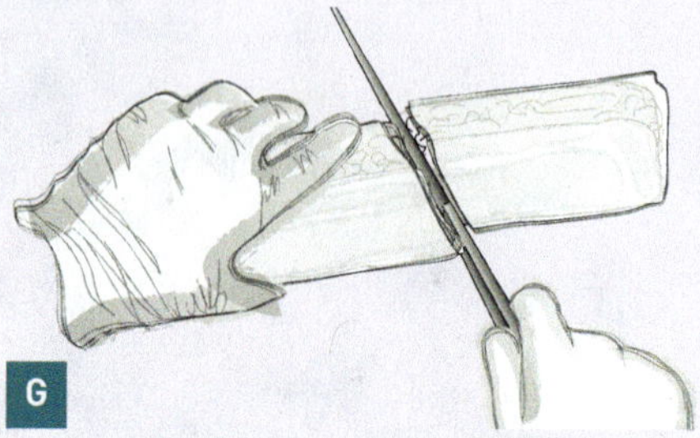
G

ORIGINAL ITALIAN SANDWICH (HERO, HOAGIE, SUB)

LUNCH MAIN COURSE

Yield:
1 sandwich,
4 oz (120 g) meat and cheese filling

COMPONENTS

1 8-in. (20-cm) crisp-crusted long roll or ⅓ baguette
1 fl oz (30 mL) *Balsamic Vinaigrette (p. 33)*, in multi-tip squeeze bottle
1 oz (30 g) Sharp provolone cheese, sliced
1½ oz (45 g) Shredded iceberg lettuce
¼ oz (7 g) Thin-sliced onion
2 slices (1 oz/30 g total) Vine-ripe tomato, halved into semicircles
1 tbsp (15 mL) Hot or sweet pickled peppers
1½ oz (45 g) Sliced boiled ham
1½ oz (45 g) Sliced Genoa salami

Supplies

2 Frilled sandwich picks

PROCEDURE

FINISHING

1. Prepare according to the Procedure for Assembling Hollowed Long Roll Sandwiches (p. 338). Apply half the dressing to the roll and half to the internal garnish. Include the pickled peppers in the sandwich or serve on the side.

PLATING

2. Place on a cool 10-in. (25-cm) plate.

VARIATIONS

ITALIAN MARKET SANDWICH

Reduce the dressing to ½ fl oz (15 mL) and apply to the roll only. Replace the deli meats with 1 oz (30 g) each sliced prosciutto, capicola, sopressata, and mortadella. Add 3 fl oz(90 mL) Roasted Peppers in Garlic Oil (p. 688) to the internal garnishes.

TURKEY HOAGIE OR HERO

Replace the Italian dressing with Mayonnaise (p. 41) or commercial mayonnaise. Replace the meats with 3 oz (90 g) sliced deli turkey breast.

HEARTLAND SUBMARINE SANDWICH

LUNCH MAIN COURSE

Yield:
1 sandwich,
4 oz (120 g) meat and cheese filling

COMPONENTS

1 8-in. (20-cm) roll or ⅓ baguette
1 fl oz (30 mL) *Mayonnaise (p. 41)*, or commercial mayonnaise
1 oz (30 g) Sliced mild provolone cheese
1 oz (30 g) Sliced boiled ham
1 oz (30 g) Sliced cooked salami
1 oz (30 g) Sliced bologna
3 slices (1½ oz/45 g total) Vine-ripe tomato
2 thin slices (½ oz/15 g total) Sweet onion
3 thin rings (1 oz/30 g total) Green bell pepper
3 slices (½ oz/15 g total) Sweet or dill pickle

Supplies

2 Frilled sandwich picks

PROCEDURE

FINISHING

1. Prepare according to the Procedure for Assembling Simple Sandwiches (p. 326).

PLATING

2. Plate according to the Procedure for Assembling Simple Sandwiches (p. 326).

VARIATIONS

ROAST BEEF SUBMARINE

Replace the ham, salami, and bologna with 3 oz (90 g) sliced deli roast beef.

MIXED CHEESE SUBMARINE

Replace the ham, salami, and bologna with 1 oz (30 g) each sliced Swiss, Monterey Jack, and Colby cheddar cheeses.

TERRINE DE CAMPAGNE ON BAGUETTE

[tair-EEN duh kahm-PAHN (yuh)]

LUNCH MAIN COURSE

Yield:
1 sandwich,
4 oz (120 g) filling

COMPONENTS

1 8-in. (20-cm) crisp baguette, at room temperature
1 fl oz (30 mL) Dijon mustard
4 oz (120 g) *Terrine de Campagne (p. 534)*, sliced thin
2 thin slices (½ oz/15 g) Red onion
4 Cornichon pickles, sliced thin

PROCEDURE

FINISHING

1. Prepare according to the Procedure for Assembling Simple Sandwiches (p. 326). Cut on the diagonal into three even pieces.

PLATING

2. Place on a cool 10-in. (25-cm) oval plate.

VARIATIONS

Replace the terrine de campagne with any rustic terrine or pâté, or with Rillettes (p. 462).

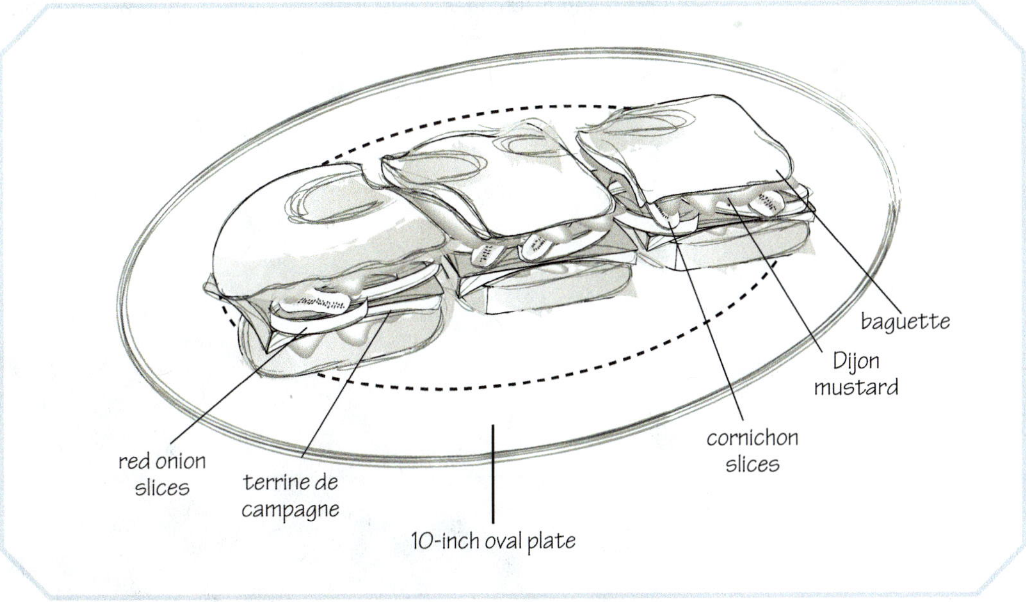

LOBSTER ROLL

LUNCH MAIN COURSE

Yield:
1 sandwich,
6 fl oz (180 mL)
or about 5 oz (150 g)
filling

COMPONENTS

1 New England–style Frankfurter Roll (p. 312)
½ fl oz (15 mL) Clarified butter
6 fl oz (180 mL) *Classic Lobster Salad (p. 160)*
2 tsp (10 mL) Minced parsley
½ oz (15g) Cooked, shelled, lobster claw (optional)

Supplies

1 Cocktail napkin
1 sheet Deli paper

PROCEDURE

FINISHING

1. Brush the sides of the roll with clarified butter and place on a sizzle pan.
2. Toast the roll in a hot countertop oven until the sides are golden brown.
3. Cool the roll 1–2 minutes.
4. Open the roll and flatten it slightly.
5. Scoop in the lobster salad and press gently to firm it into the roll.
6. Sprinkle the salad with a line of parsley.
7. Place the optional lobster claw on top and press to secure.

PLATING

8. Line a sandwich basket first with the napkin, then with deli paper, and then place the lobster roll in it.

Pocket Sandwiches

Procedure for Assembling Pocket Sandwiches

1. Warm the pocket bread in a countertop oven until it softens and becomes pliable.
2. Place the bread on a cutting board and cut it into 2 half-circles. Allow to cool 1–2 minutes.
3. Open each half and apply the spread to both sides of the interior of each pocket (A).
4. Place the internal garnishes in the pockets. Arrange them to rest against the walls of the pockets, leaving space for the filling in between.
5. Place the filling in the pockets (B, C). If sliced deli meats are used, fluff the meats before placing in the pockets.
6. Stand the pockets upright in a paper-lined sandwich basket (D), or prop one against another on a plate.

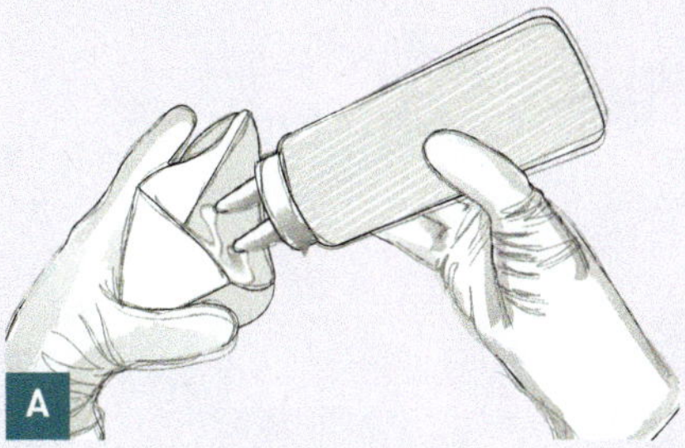
A

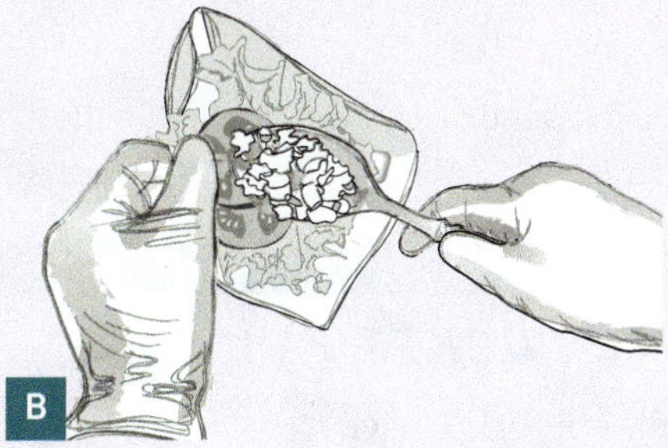
B

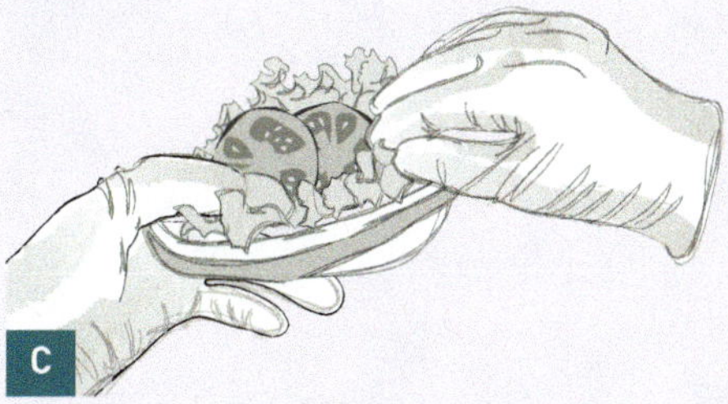
C

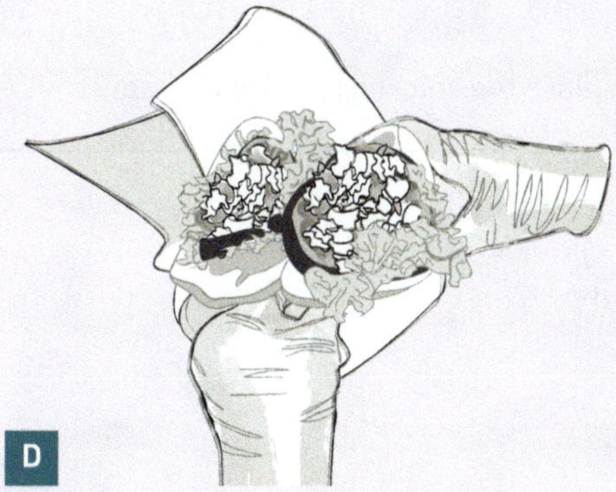
D

CHICKEN SALAD PITA POCKET

LUNCH MAIN COURSE

Yield:
1 sandwich, 5 fl oz (150 mL), or about 4 oz (120 g) filling

COMPONENTS

1 6-in. (15-cm) white or whole wheat pita bread
1 fl oz (30 mL) *Mayonnaise (p. 41)*, or commercial mayonnaise
2 leaves (½ oz/15 g total) Green-leaf lettuce
4 thin slices (1½ oz/45 g total) Vine-ripe tomato
5 fl oz (150 mL) *Classic Chicken Salad (p. 159)*, made with chopped chicken

Supplies

1 sheet Deli paper

PROCEDURE

FINISHING

1. Prepare according to the Procedure for Assembling Pocket Sandwiches (p. 343).

PLATING

2. Line a sandwich basket with deli paper and prop the sandwich halves upright in the basket.

VARIATION

TUNA SALAD PITA POCKET

Replace the chicken salad with Traditional Tuna Salad (p. 161).

GRILLED LAMB PITA POCKET

LUNCH MAIN COURSE

Yield:
1 sandwich,
3 oz (90 g) filling

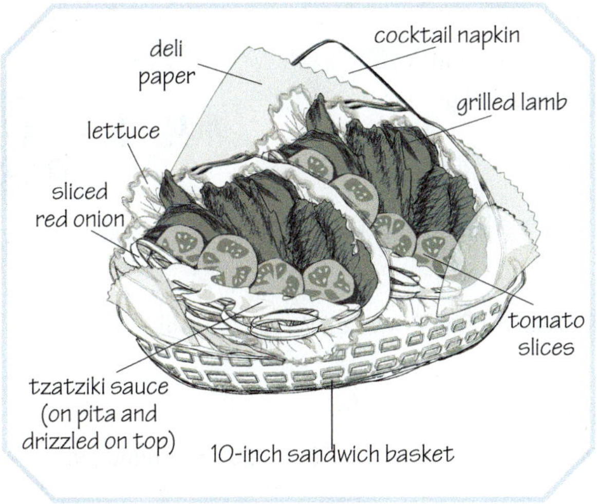

COMPONENTS

1 6-in. (15-cm) white or whole wheat pita bread
2 fl oz (60 mL) *Tzatziki Sauce (p. 47)*
2 leaves (½ oz/15 g total) Green-leaf lettuce
4 thin slices (1½ oz/45 g total) Vine-ripe tomato
2 thin slices (½ oz/15 g total) Red onion
3 oz (90 g) Grilled lamb leg, cooled and sliced
to taste Kosher salt

Supplies

1 Cocktail napkin
1 sheet Deli paper

PROCEDURE

FINISHING

1. Prepare according to the Procedure for Assembling Pocket Sandwiches (p. 343). Apply half the sauce to the pocket interior and drizzle the remaining sauce onto the lamb.

PLATING

2. Line a sandwich basket first with the napkin, then with deli paper, and then prop the sandwich halves upright in the basket.

Wrap Sandwiches

Procedure for Assembling Pinwheel Wraps

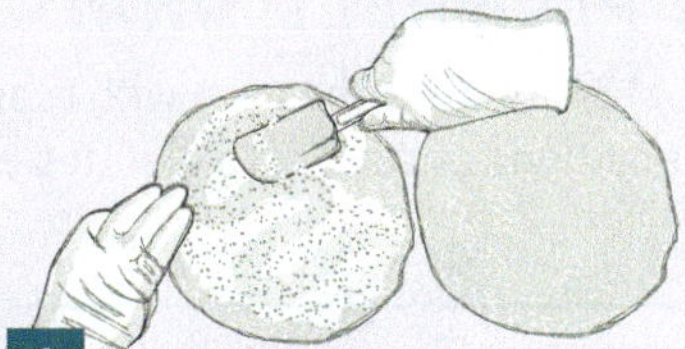
A

B

1. Place 2 10-in. (25-cm) round or square flatbreads on a cutting board.
2. Apply the spread to the upper surfaces of the flatbreads in an even layer extending to ½ in. (1 cm) from the edges (A).
3. Move the flatbreads together so that one overlaps the other by about 3 in. (7 cm).
4. Place the filling ingredients on the flatbreads in a flat, even layer.
5. Scatter on the garnish ingredients (B).
6. Roll the flatbreads to tightly enclose the filling and garnishes (C).
7. Secure shut with 2 or 3 sandwich picks.
8. Cut on the diagonal into 2 or 3 sections (D).
9. Prop the sections against one another on a plate (E).

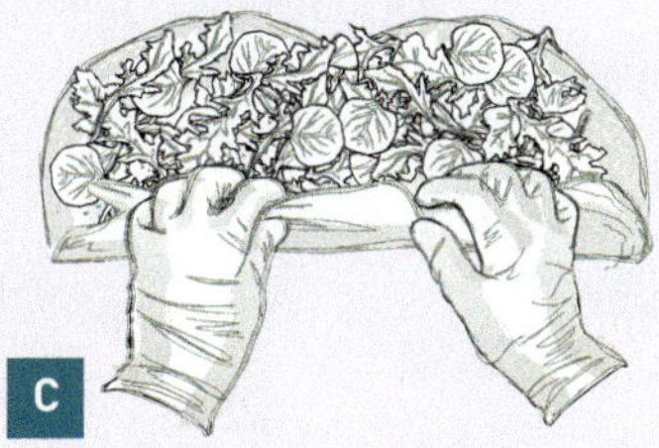
C

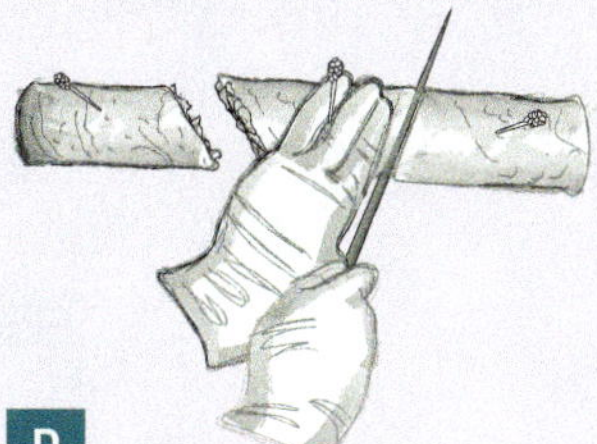
D

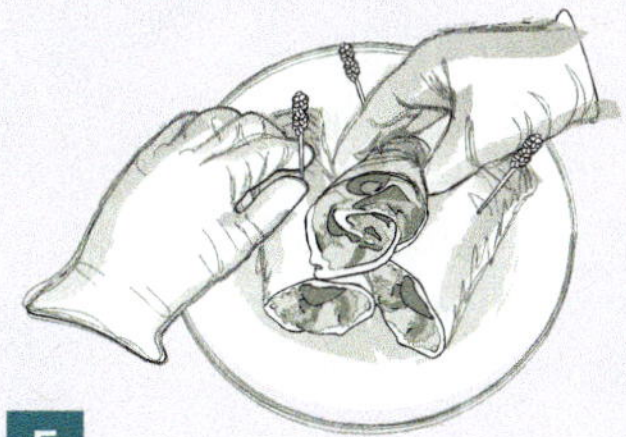
E

PROVENÇAL CHEESE, HAM, AND TOMATO WRAP

LUNCH MAIN COURSE

Yield:
1 sandwich, about 5 oz (150 g) cheese and meat filling

COMPONENTS

2 10-in. (25-cm) flour tortillas or lavash breads
3 oz (90 mL) *Garlic-Herb Cheese Spread (p. 594)*, room temperature
2 oz (60 g) Julienne smoked ham
1½ oz (45 g) Vine-ripe tomato, drained and diced small
1½ oz (45 g) Provençal mesclun or spring mix salad greens

Supplies

3 Frilled sandwich picks

PROCEDURE

FINISHING

1. Prepare according to the Procedure for Assembling Pinwheel Wraps (p. 345).
2. Cut into 3 sections.

PLATING

3. Arrange the sections propped against one another on a cool 10-in. (25-cm) round plate.

VARIATIONS

CHEDDAR-BEEF PINWHEEL WRAP

Replace the garlic-herb cheese spread with room-temperature Mustard Butter (p. 563). Scatter 2 oz (60 g) sharp yellow cheddar cheese over the tortillas. Replace the ham with 4 oz (120 g) grilled, cooled sliced skirt steak or other beef steak. Add ¼ oz (7 g) diced red onions. Replace the mesclun with shredded romaine.

MIDDLE EASTERN VEGETARIAN PINWHEEL WRAP

Replace the garlic-herb cheese spread with Hummus (p. 118). Replace the ham with roasted red and yellow bell pepper strips. Add ¼ oz (7 g) chopped scallions and ½ oz (15 g) pitted and halved oil-cured olives.

Procedure for Assembling Burrito-Style Wraps

1. Select a 12-in. (30-cm) flour tortilla or lavash bread. If necessary, warm it in a countertop oven to make it flexible.
2. Place the flatbread on a cutting board.
3. Apply the spread in an even layer to within ½ in. (1 cm) of the edge (A).
4. Arrange the filling ingredients horizontally in a roughly 4 × 10-in. (10 × 25-cm) rectangle slightly forward of center on the flatbread (B).
5. Arrange the internal garnishes in a smaller rectangle on top of the filling (C).
6. Lift the bottom edge of the flatbread over the filling and tuck it under the far edge of the filling (D). Pull back to form the bread and filling into a roll.
7. Fold in the edges of the flatbread on either side (E).
8. Roll the sandwich (F).
9. Secure shut with 2 sandwich picks.
10. Cut the sandwich into 2 sections (G).
11. Place on a plate (H).

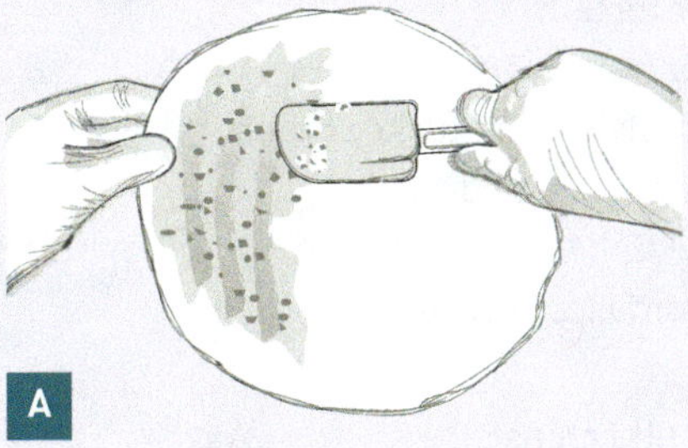

A

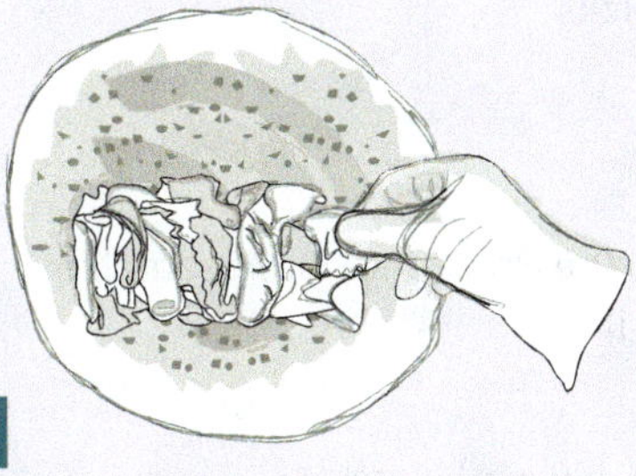

B

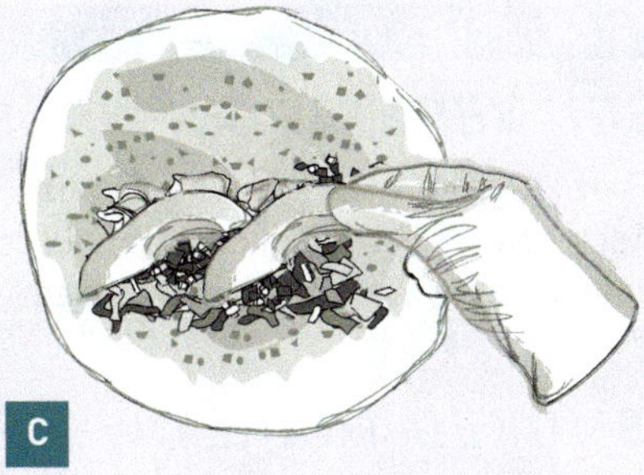

C

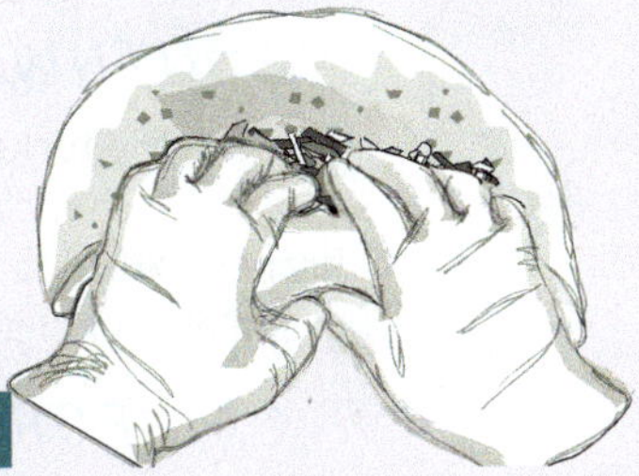

D

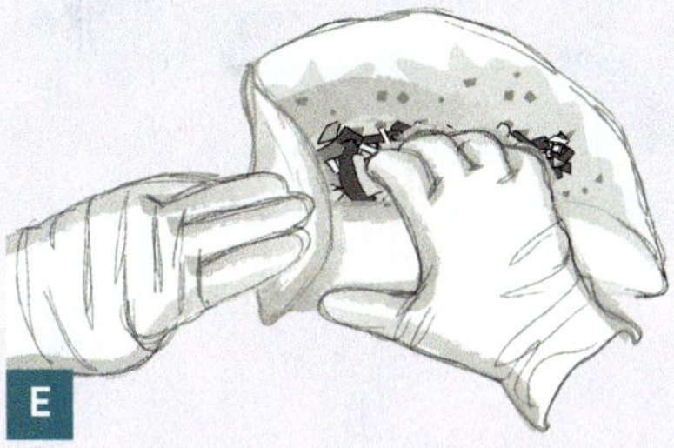

E

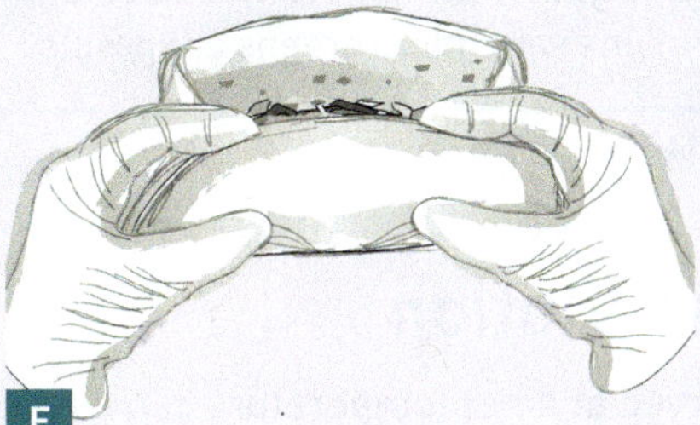

F

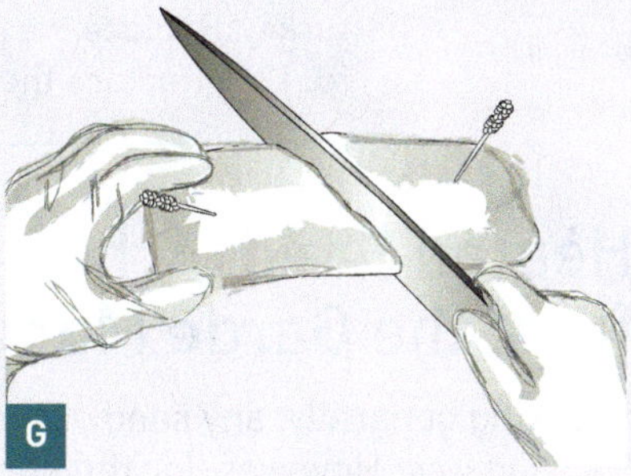

G

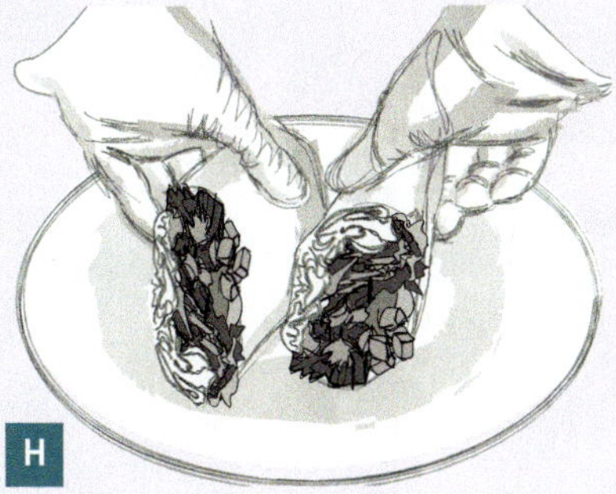

H

SOUTHWESTERN TURKEY WRAP

LUNCH MAIN COURSE

Yield:
1 sandwich, 4 oz (120 g) meat filling

COMPONENTS

1 12-in. (30-cm) flour tortilla
2 fl oz (60 mL) *Chipotle Mayonnaise (p. 43)*
4 oz (120 g) Sliced deli-style roast turkey breast
1½ oz (45 g) Diced avocado, chilled
4 fl oz (120 mL) *Pico de Gallo (p. 51)*
1 oz (30 g) Shredded romaine lettuce

External Garnish

1 oz (30 g) Plain tortilla chips

Supplies

2 Frilled sandwich picks

PROCEDURE

FINISHING

1. Prepare according to the Procedure for Assembling Burrito-Style Wraps (p. 347).

PLATING

2. Place on a cool 12-in. (30-cm) plate.
3. Garnish with the tortilla chips.

VARIATIONS

SOUTHWESTERN VEGETARIAN WRAP

Replace the turkey with 1 oz (30 g) cool cooked pinto beans, 1 oz (30 g) cool cooked black beans, 1 oz (30 g) cool cooked corn kernels, ½ oz (15 g) julienne jícama, and ¼ oz (7.5 g) toasted green pumpkin seeds.

CALIFORNIA SMOKED TURKEY WRAP

Replace the chipotle mayonnaise with Roasted Red Pepper Mayonnaise (p. 43). Replace the turkey with deli-style smoked turkey. Replace the pico de gallo with Tomato-Basil Salad (p. 136). Replace the romaine with micro greens or sprouts.

Heated Sandwiches from the Garde Manger Station

Speaking generally, any sandwich served at a hot temperature can be called a *hot sandwich*. However, for the purposes of this text, it is necessary to distinguish between hot-temperature sandwiches that must be prepared by the hot line and those that can be prepared by the garde manger station.

Unlike the garde manger station, the hot line is outfitted with equipment for cooking raw sandwich fillings, such as hamburger patties and boneless chicken breasts, to order. In this text, we call sandwiches made from such ingredients *hot sandwiches*. However, another type of hot sandwich is made from pre-cooked or ready-to-eat ingredients. In this text, we call these ***heated sandwiches***.

In many food-service operations, both hot sandwiches and heated sandwiches are turned out by the hot line. However, as you have learned, some garde manger stations are equipped with countertop heating units that enable garde manger chefs to turn out heated sandwiches. This takes some of the pressure off the hot line and simplifies preparation by keeping all precooked ingredients, such as deli meats, in one place.

There are three basic types of heated sandwiches.

1. Heated-filling sandwiches
2. Toasted sandwiches
3. Pressed sandwiches

Heated-Filling Sandwiches

Heated-filling sandwiches begin by baking the filling ingredients in a countertop oven. (Some operations use a microwave; however, this is not recommended, as it can easily dry out or overcook the filling ingredients.) The hot filling is then added to the bread product, and the sandwich is assembled.

Procedure for Making Heated-Filling Sandwiches

1. Preheat a countertop oven (or standard oven) to 400°F (200°C).
2. Arrange the sandwich filling on the oven tray or on a sizzle plate in the shape of the bread product to be used (A). Fluff deli meats for best mouthfeel. Do not add cheese at this time.
3. Bake the filling until hot.
4. If using cheese, arrange cheese slices on top of the meat and return to the oven just until melted.
5. Apply the spread to the bread product (B).
6. Use a spatula to transfer the hot filling to the bread product (C).
7. Add the internal garnishes.
8. Close the sandwich (D) and, if necessary, secure it with sandwich picks.
9. Cut the sandwich as desired (E).
10. Place the sandwich on a plate and add any external garnishes.

A

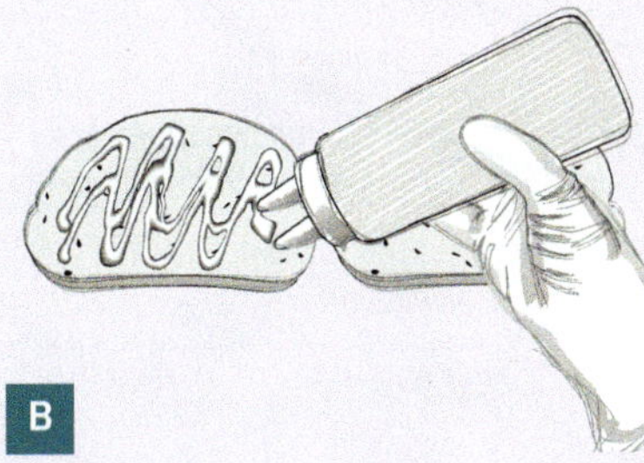
B

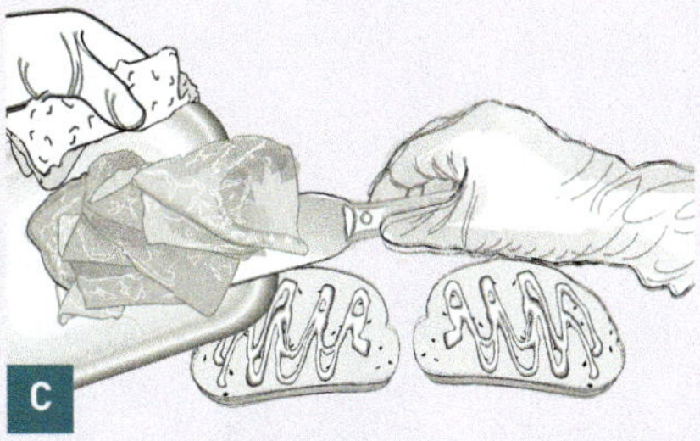
C

D

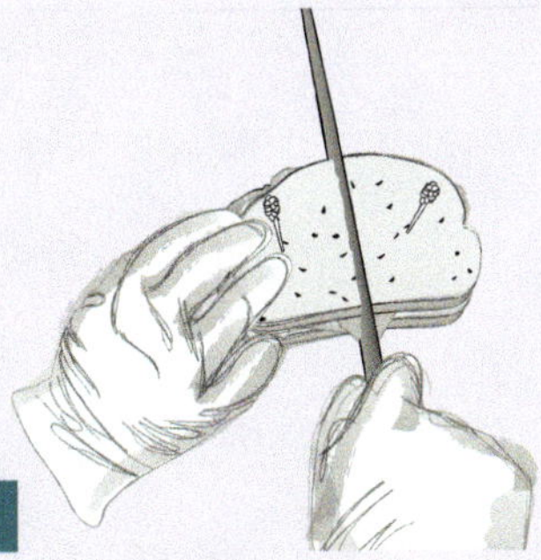
E

HOT PASTRAMI SANDWICH

LUNCH MAIN COURSE

Yield:
1 sandwich,
5 oz (120 g) filling

COMPONENTS

5 oz (150 g) Pastrami, sliced thin
2 slices (2½ oz/75 g total) Jewish rye bread
½ fl oz (15 mL) Prepared brown mustard

External Garnish

1 spear (1 oz/30 g) Jewish sour or half-sour pickle

Supplies

2 Frilled cocktail picks

PROCEDURE

FINISHING AND PLATING

1. Prepare according to the Procedure for Making Heated-Filling Sandwiches (p. 349).

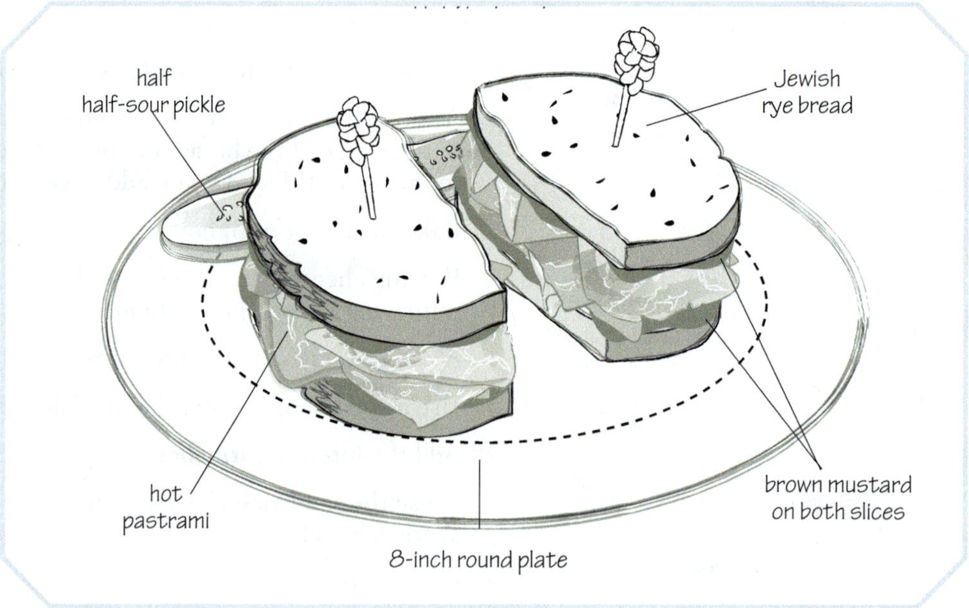

Toasted Sandwiches

A ***toasted sandwich*** may begin as a simple sandwich, a hollowed long roll sandwich, or an open-face sandwich. Most include some type of cheese. To make a toasted sandwich, the bread product is spread and the filling ingredients are added to the open bread product. The sandwich is then heated in a countertop oven. Once the sandwich filling is hot and the cheese is melted, raw garnishes, such as lettuce and tomato, are added, and then, in most cases, the sandwich is closed.

Procedure for Making Toasted Sandwiches

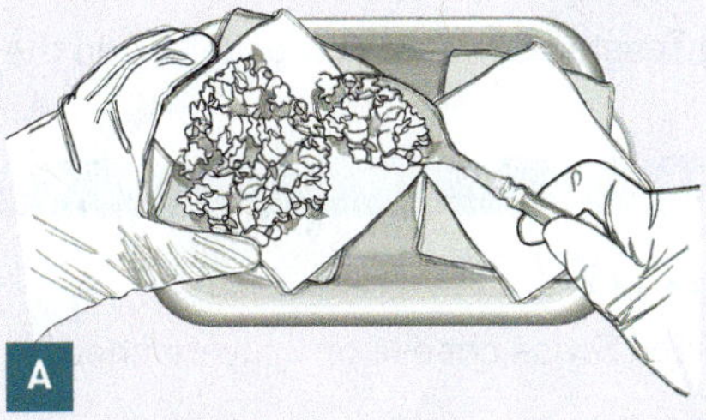

A

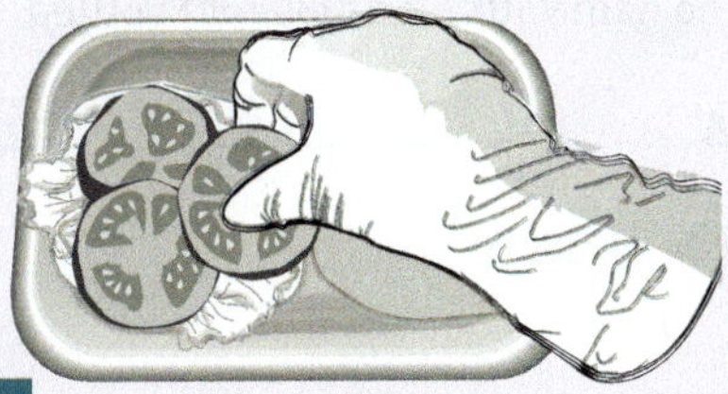

B

C

1. Preheat a countertop oven or standard oven to 400°F (200°C).
2. Apply the spread and fillings to the sandwich according to its type, but leave off any raw internal garnishes. If using deli meats, fluff them for best mouthfeel.
   a. If making a simple sandwich, divide the filling between the 2 pieces of bread product. If using cheese, place it underneath the fillings (A).
   b. If making an open-face sandwich or a hollowed long roll sandwich, place the cheese under or between the other filling ingredients.
3. Place the sandwich on a sizzle plate and put it in the oven.
4. Bake the sandwich until the filling is hot and the cheese, if any, is melted.
5. Remove the sandwich from the oven.
6. Add the raw internal garnishes (B).
7. Unless making an open-face sandwich, close the sandwich (C) and press gently to firm it.
8. If necessary, secure the sandwich closed with sandwich picks. Cut the sandwich as desired.
9. Place the sandwich on a plate and add any external garnishes.

HOT HAM AND CHEESE

LUNCH MAIN COURSE

Yield:
1 sandwich,
4 oz (120 g) filling

COMPONENTS

1 (2½ oz/75 g) Kaiser roll, split
½ fl oz (15 mL) *Mayonnaise (p. 41)*, or commercial mayonnaise
½ fl oz (15 mL) Prepared brown mustard
3½ oz (100 g) Deli boiled ham, sliced thin
½ oz (15 g) Processed American cheese, sliced
3 (½ oz) (15 g) Sweet pickle slices

PROCEDURE

FINISHING AND PLATING

1. Prepare according to the Procedure for Making Toasted Sandwiches (p. 351). Add the pickles after baking.

VARIATIONS

HOT HAM AND SWISS

Replace the American cheese with deli-style imported Swiss cheese or Gruyère cheese.

HAM BARBECUE

Omit the mayonnaise, mustard, and cheese. Toss the ham with 1 fl oz (30 mL) bottled barbecue sauce before baking.

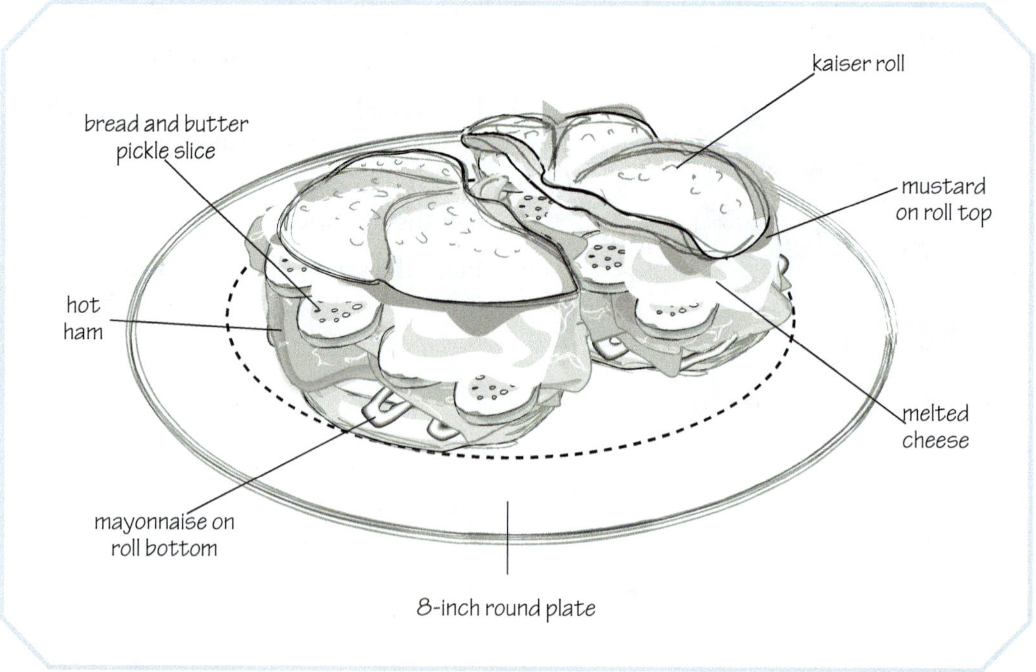

TUNA MELT

LUNCH MAIN COURSE

Yield:
1 sandwich,
4 oz (120 g) total filling

COMPONENTS

1 (2½ oz/75 g) Kaiser roll, split
½ fl oz (15 mL) Prepared yellow mustard
3½ fl oz (100 mL) *Traditional Tuna Salad (p. 161)*
½ oz (15 g) Deli Swiss cheese, sliced
1 leaf (½ oz/15 g) Iceberg or romaine lettuce
3 slices (1½ oz/45 g) Vine-ripe tomato

External Garnish
3 (½ oz/15g) *Dill Pickles (p. 675),* sliced

PROCEDURE

FINISHING AND PLATING

1. Prepare according to the Procedure for Making Toasted Sandwiches (p. 351).

VARIATION

CHEDDAR-TUNA MELT

Replace the Swiss cheese with thin-sliced sharp yellow cheddar cheese.

OPEN-FACE SMOKED TURKEY, APPLE, AND CHEDDAR SANDWICH

LUNCH MAIN COURSE

Yield:
1 sandwich,
4 oz (120 g) meat and cheese filling

COMPONENTS

2 slices (2 oz/60 g total) Whole wheat or multigrain artisan bread
1½ fl oz (45 mL) *Mayonnaise (p. 41)*, or commercial mayonnaise
3 oz (90 g) Deli-style smoked turkey breast, sliced
2 oz (60 g) Red Delicious apple, julienne
1 oz (30 g) Sharp yellow cheddar cheese, sliced thin

External Garnishes
2 (½ oz/15 g total) Red Delicious apple, thin wedges
2 pluches Flat-leaf parsley

PROCEDURE

FINISHING

1. Preheat a countertop oven or standard oven to 400°F (205°C).
2. Toast the bread slices.
3. Place on a sizzle plate and spread with the mayonnaise.
4. Fluff the smoked turkey and place on the toast slices.
5. Sprinkle with the julienne apple.
6. Place the cheese slices in an even layer on top.
7. Bake the sandwich halves until the filling is hot and the cheese is melted.

PLATING

8. Use a wide spatula to transfer the sandwich halves to a warm 10-in. (25-cm) plate.
9. Garnish each half with an apple wedge and a parsley pluche.

VARIATION

OPEN-FACE HAM, APPLE, AND GRUYÈRE SANDWICH

Replace the smoked turkey with sliced deli smoked ham. Replace the cheddar with thin-sliced Gruyère cheese.

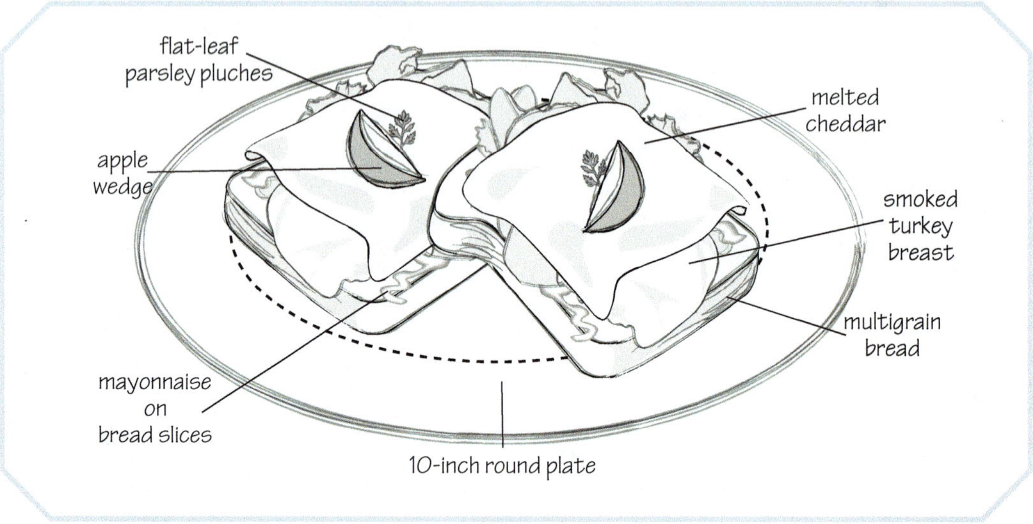

Pressed Sandwiches

A ***pressed sandwich*** is a simple sandwich that is griddle-baked between the hot plates of a countertop appliance called a sandwich press or panini grill or, in Spanish, a ***plancha***.

The plates of a sandwich press have several functions. As the hot plates contact the top and bottom bread slices, they toast the bread by direct heat. The heat of the plates is transmitted into the interior of the sandwich and melts the filling ingredients, which almost always include cheese. Finally, the pressure exerted by the plates compresses the sandwich and makes it compact and neat to eat.

Sturdy greens, such as spinach or arugula, are sometimes used as internal garnishes. If a pressed sandwich is to contain moist ingredients, such as tomatoes, they should first be blotted dry on paper towels or drained in some other manner. Many pressed sandwiches are made with precooked or otherwise processed vegetables, such as roasted peppers or sun-dried tomatoes.

In South Florida, sandwich shops have specialized in the Cuban variety of pressed sandwich since the late 1800s. But it was the introduction of the Italian pressed sandwich, or *panino,* in the early 1990s that made pressed sandwiches popular throughout North America.

> **Panini.** In Italian, the word ***panino*** literally translates as "little bread," or roll. It also refers to any sandwich, hot or cold. A *panino* made in a sandwich press is known as a *panino caldo,* or hot panino. By the 1980s, these became known worldwide simply as *panini*. A *panino* may be filled with just about any combination of ingredients.
>
> **Cuban sandwiches.** Cuban exiles who moved to South Florida began making a pressed sandwich known as a ***Cubano*** (koo-BAH-no), or ***Cuban sandwich***. It is made on Cuban bread, a crisp-crusted, lard-enriched loaf shaped like a thick, flat baguette. A Miami *Cubano* is spread with butter and brown mustard and filled with ham, roast pork, Swiss cheese, and sliced dill pickles. A Tampa *Cubano* also includes Genoa salami and, sometimes, mayonnaise.

Featuring Cuban sandwiches or panini on your sandwich menu can boost sales and distinguish your operation from its competition. It can also be quite profitable. Although the initial cost of purchasing a sandwich press or panini grill is significant, typically the machine soon pays for itself through increased revenue. Customers will pay more for the same sandwich ingredients when the sandwich made from them is hot, crisp, and cooked before their eyes.

Procedure for Making Pressed Sandwiches

A

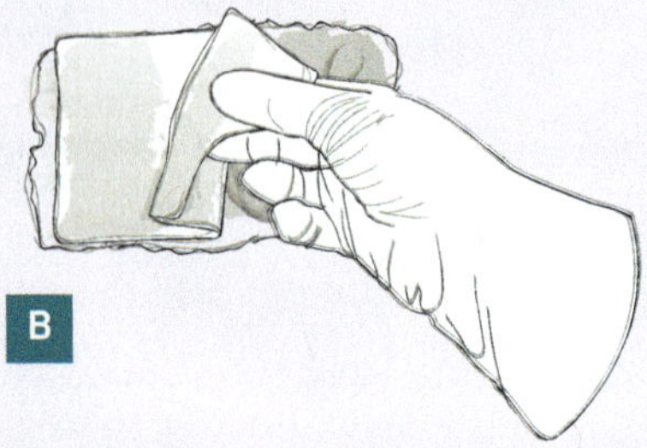

B

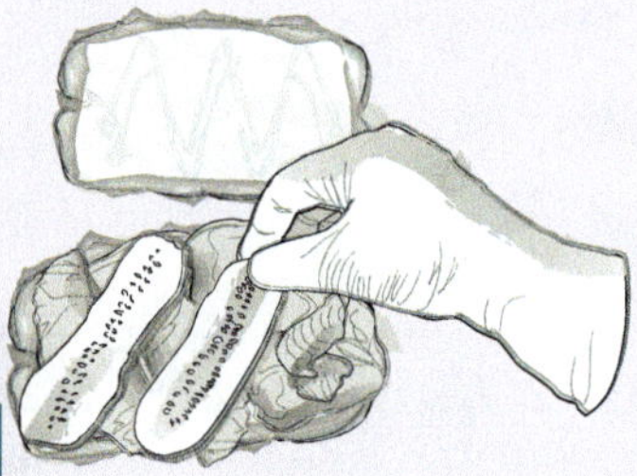

C

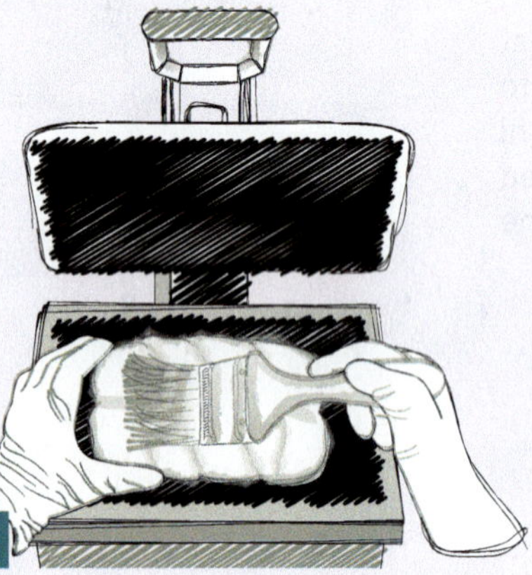

D

1. Preheat a sandwich press.
2. Holding a serrated knife parallel to the board, slice a long roll or a section of baguette in half lengthwise. Alternatively, use 2 slices of bread.
3. Apply the spread(s) to the inside of both the top and the bottom of the bread product in an even layer (A).
4. Divide the cheese in half and place a layer of cheese on both top and bottom (B). Press each to make the cheese adhere to the bread.
5. Fluff the remaining filling ingredients and place them on the bottom of the roll.
6. Arrange the internal garnishes on top of the filling (C).
7. Close the sandwich and press gently to help it hold together.
8. Brush the bottom of the sandwich with oil or clarified butter.
9. Place the sandwich on the bottom plate of the grill.
10. Quickly brush the top of the sandwich with oil or clarified butter (D) and close the press.
11. Bake until the exterior of the roll is crisp and the filling is hot and melted.
12. Transfer the sandwich to a cutting board and cut in half on the diagonal.
13. Place on a plate, or wrap for take-out.

CROQUE MONSIEUR

[kroak ms-YEU]

FRENCH HOT HAM AND CHEESE SANDWICH

LUNCH MAIN COURSE

Yield:
1 sandwich,
4 oz (120 g) meat and cheese filling

COMPONENTS

2 slices (2½oz/75 g) Firm white sandwich bread
½ fl oz (15 mL) Dijon mustard
1½ oz (45 g) Gruyère cheese, sliced thin or planed
2½ oz (75 g) Smoked ham, sliced thin
½ fl oz (15 mL) Clarified butter

External Garnish

1 Cornichon fan (p. 402)

PROCEDURE

FINISHING

1. Prepare according to the Procedure for Making Pressed Sandwiches (p. 356).

PLATING

2. Place on an 8-in. (20-cm) plate.
3. Garnish with the cornichon fan.

VARIATION

CROQUE MADAME

Replace the ham with sliced turkey breast.

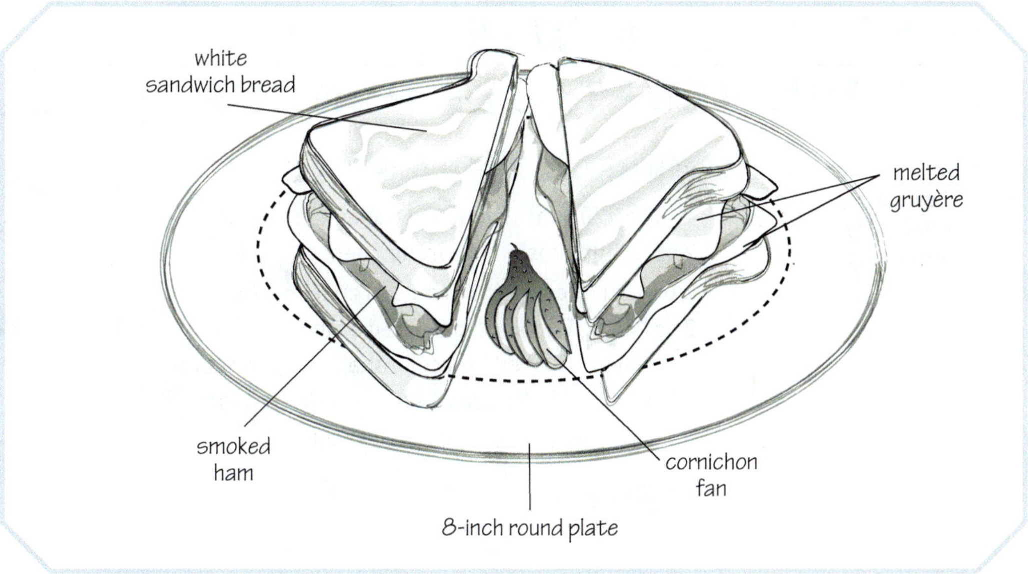

MIAMI CUBANO

LUNCH MAIN COURSE

Yield:
1 sandwich,
4 oz (120 g) meat and cheese filling

COMPONENTS

1 3-oz (90-g) or 8-in. (20-cm) Cuban bread or other baguette-type bread section
½ oz (15 g) Butter, softened
½ fl oz (15 mL) Prepared brown mustard
1½ oz (45 g) Swiss cheese, sliced thin
1 oz (30 g) Deli smoked ham, sliced thin
1½ oz (45 g) Roast pork loin, prepared as the filet of beef on p. 253, sliced thin
½ fl oz (15 mL) Clarified butter
1 oz (60 g) Sandwich-style sour pickles, sliced

PROCEDURE

FINISHING AND PLATING

1. Prepare according to the Procedure for Making Pressed Sandwiches (p. 356).
2. Include the pickles as an internal garnish.

VARIATION

TAMPA CUBANO

Replace the butter with mayonnaise. Decrease the ham to ½ oz (15 g). Add ½ oz (15 g) thin-sliced Genoa salami.

PANINO GIARDINIERE

[jar-dee-NYAIR-eh]

GARDEN VEGETABLE PANINO

LUNCH MAIN COURSE

Yield:
1 sandwich,
6 oz (180 g) total filling

COMPONENT

1 8-in. (20-cm) section of Italian long bread
2 oz (60 g) Fresh mozzarella cheese
¼ oz (7 g) Reggiano Parmesan cheese, planed
2 oz (60 g) Eggplant, prepared as in *Grilled Summer Vegetable Medley (p. 108)*
1 oz (30 g) Cooked broccoli rabe, chopped coarse
2 fl oz (60 mL) *Roasted Peppers in Garlic Oil (p. 688)*
½ fl oz (15 mL) Pure golden olive oil

PROCEDURE

FINISHING AND PLATING

1. Prepare according to the Procedure for Making Pressed Sandwiches (p. 356).

VARIATION

Replace any or all of the vegetables with other appropriately prepared vegetables.

BRESAOLA, FONTINA, AND ARUGULA PANINO

LUNCH MAIN COURSE

Yield:
1 sandwich,
4 oz (120 g) meat and cheese filling

COMPONENTS

1 3-oz (90-g) or 8-in. (20-cm) section of Italian long bread
2 oz (60 g) Italian Fontina cheese, chilled and planed
2 oz (60 g) *Bresaola (p. 432)*, sliced thin
1 oz (30 g) Arugula leaves
½ fl oz (15 mL) Pure golden olive oil

PROCEDURE

FINISHING AND PLATING

1. Prepare according to the Procedure for Making Pressed Sandwiches (p. 356).

VARIATIONS

PROSCIUTTO, ASIAGO, AND RADICCHIO PANINO

PROSCIUTTO, MOZZARELLA, AND FIG PANINO

SOPPRESSATA, MOZZARELLA, AND BROCCOLI RABE PANINO

PANCETTA, GORGONZOLA, AND TOMATO PANINO

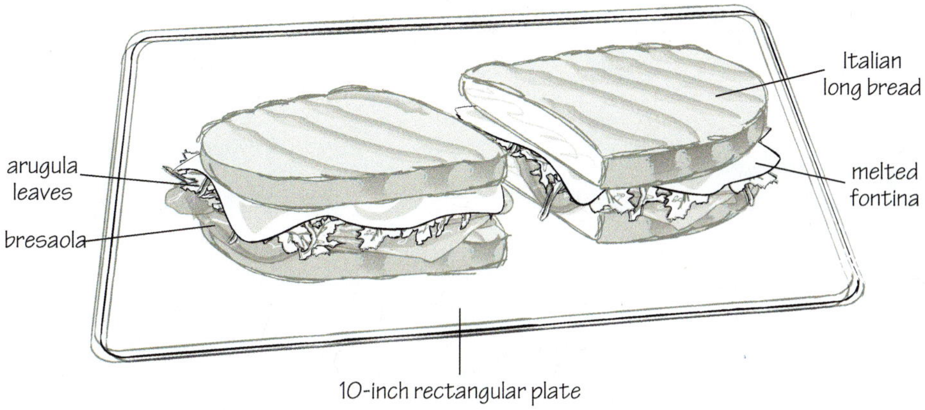

SANTA FE SMOKED TURKEY PANINO

LUNCH MAIN COURSE

Yield:
1 sandwich,
4 oz (120 g) meat and cheese filling

COMPONENTS

2 slices (2½ oz/75 g total) Firm white sandwich bread
1 fl oz (30 mL) *Chipotle Mayonnaise (p. 43)*
2 oz (60 g) Monterey Jack cheese, sliced thin
2 oz (60 g) Deli smoked turkey, sliced thin
1 oz (30 g) Bottled tomato salsa
1 oz (30 g) Jícama, julienne
½ fl oz (15 mL) Clarified butter

PROCEDURE

FINISHING AND PLATING

1. Prepare according to the Procedure for Making Pressed Sandwiches (p. 356).

VARIATION

CALIFORNIA SMOKED TURKEY PANINO

Replace the white bread with multigrain bread. Replace the chipotle mayonnaise with an herbed mayonnaise. Replace the salsa with sun-dried tomatoes. Replace the jícama with radish sprouts.

TERMS FOR REVIEW

leavened bread
crumb
crust
unleavened bread
flatbread
yeasted flatbread
artisan bread
sandwich spread
compound/composed butter
external garnish
internal garnish
simple sandwich
single-decker sandwich
double-decker sandwich
multi-decker sandwich
club sandwich
open-face sandwich
simple long roll sandwich
hollowed long roll sandwich
Italian sandwich
hero
hoagie
submarine
grinder
po'boy
oven grinder
pocket sandwich
wrap sandwich
tartine
heated sandwich
toasted sandwich
pressed sandwich
plancha
panino (pl. panini)
Cubano
Cuban sandwich

QUESTIONS FOR DISCUSSION

1. List five requirements for choosing bread for sandwich making.
2. List four flour types or bread flavors, and suggest an appropriate spread, filling, and garnish for each.
3. Discuss the guidelines for storing sandwich breads and rolls. Explain how you would put them into practice.
4. List three functions of sandwich spreads, and name a spread that is particularly effective at fulfilling each.
5. List and describe the six sandwich construction types.
6. Discuss sanitation guidelines for sandwiches.
7. Name and describe the two types of heated sandwich that are often turned out in the garde manger station. Give an example of each.
8. Draw a plan for a garde manger sandwich station. Include a list of equipment needed for your station.
9. Using your imagination and the information you have learned in this chapter, create your own signature cold or heated sandwich.

Chapter 10

PREREQUISITES

Before studying this chapter, you should already

- Understand the professional recipe format outlined in "How To Use This Book," pp. xxviii–xxxiii.
- Be proficient in preparing the cold meats, cold seafood, cold vegetables, and complex salads that are components of many hors d'oeuvres.

Cold Hors d'Oeuvres

Hors d'oeuvres are miniature works of art. Each piece of a skillfully made hors d'oeuvre creation is strikingly designed, beautifully garnished, and full of flavor.

Cocktail parties and receptions at which hors d'oeuvres are served are among the most important events for any garde manger staff. Whether the party is large or small, the skills and knowledge necessary to present delicious and memorable hors d'oeuvres remain the same. This chapter gives you a basic foundation in this important facet of garde manger work.

After reading this chapter, you should be able to

1. List the six requirements for successful hors d'oeuvres.
2. Identify foods frequently used for hors d'oeuvre preparations.
3. List and describe the five basic construction types of hors d'oeuvres.
4. Prepare a variety of cold hors d'oeuvres.
5. List and explain the four elements of hors d'oeuvre tray design.
6. Present hors d'oeuvres attractively on various types of serviceware.

UNDERSTANDING HORS D'OEUVRES

In North America, an ***hors d'oeuvre*** [or DERV] is a small, attractive piece of savory food meant to be picked up and eaten with the fingers. For this reason, hors d'oeuvres are often called *finger foods*. Hors d'oeuvres are usually served on trays or platters rather than on individual plates. They are primarily served at cocktail parties or receptions, although they also may be offered at a dinner party before the guests are seated at the table.

Stationary hors d'oeuvres
Courtesy iStockphoto.

Two types of service are used for hors d'oeuvres:

1. ***Butler service***, in which trays of hors d'oeuvres are carried from person to person by servers. Hors d'oeuvres served in this manner are also called ***passed hors d'oeuvres***.
2. ***Buffet service***, in which trays of hors d'oeuvres are placed on one or more tables. Hors d'oeuvres served in this manner are also called ***stationary hors d'oeuvres***. Buffet planning and service, including buffet hors d'oeuvres, is covered in Chapter 18.

Characteristics of Hors d'Oeuvres

There are many types of hors d'oeuvres, made from virtually any food. As diverse as they may be, correctly made hors d'oeuvres all have a number of traits in common.

Successful hors d'oeuvres are:

- Small, consisting of one or two bites only
- Self-contained and neat to eat
- Attractive and eye-catching
- Special or unusual
- Savory, not sweet
- Full-flavored and well seasoned

Beyond these characteristics, just about anything goes. Many of the salads, spreads, vegetables, meats, seafood preparations, cheeses, pastry products, and charcuterie items throughout this book can be used to make hors d'oeuvres. You can combine these ingredients in many ways to create an ever-changing repertoire. For example, you can stuff a poached artichoke bottom with crab salad and top it with a cut-out star of roasted pepper. Pâtés and terrines can be sliced and served on toast points. Cheese spreads or mousses may be piped onto croûtons or into pastry shells. Your options are endless.

Hors d'oeuvres are often classified into two broad categories according to the temperature at which they are served.

1. ***Cold hors d'oeuvres*** are served cold, cool, or at room temperature. They are the focus of this chapter.
2. ***Hot hors d'oeuvres*** are usually turned out by the hot kitchen because they require cooking equipment not normally found in a garde manger station. Like hot sandwiches, however, hot hors d'oeuvres are divided into those cooked to order and those cooked ahead of time and then simply

reheated, called ***heated hors d'oeuvres***. These may be turned out by the garde manger department, providing it has the proper equipment to do so. In some operations, the garde manger department may be asked to prepare hot hors d'oeuvres and send them to the hot kitchen for finishing and service.

TYPES OF HORS D'OEUVRES

In addition to dividing hors d'oeuvres into the two main categories of hot and cold, chefs also group them by construction type. There are five major hors d'oeuvre construction types:

1. Stuffed
2. Wrapped and rolled
3. Picked and skewered
4. Pastry
5. Canapé

Some hors d'oeuvres fall into more than one category. For instance, a cube of melon wrapped in prosciutto is usually secured with a cocktail pick. Thus, it is both a wrapped item and a picked item. Similarly, many items served on a pastry base (pastry hors d'oeuvres) are nearly identical to items served on a toast base (canapés). What is important is recognizing the basic construction categories and using them to create a well-balanced selection for your customers.

Stuffed Hors d'Oeuvres

When a small piece of food is stuffed and attractively garnished, it is called a ***stuffed hors d'oeuvre***. Some foods have natural cavities that are perfect for stuffing. Artichoke bottoms (p. 113) and the whites of halved hard-cooked eggs are good examples. Other foods must be hollowed to be stuffed. Cooked baby beets and new potatoes, for example, may be hollowed with a parisienne scoop. When preparing this type of hors d'oeuvre, it is often necessary to cut off a slice of the hors d'oeuvre's base so it remains stable on the tray.

Here are some popular foods that can be stuffed as cold hors d'oeuvres:

- Mushrooms, cooked or marinated
- Baby pattypan squash, steamed and chilled
- Cherry tomatoes
- Baby beets, steamed and chilled, or pickled
- Slender cucumbers, cut into boats or cups
- Jalapeño chiles, roasted and peeled
- Artichoke bottoms, cooked
- Large pitted olives
- Large grapes

Hors d'Oeuvre Terminology

The French term *hors d'oeuvre* literally translates as "outside of the work," the reference being to a work of art, not work as in performing a task. In this case, the work of art is the meal. So, an hors d'oeuvre is a food served outside of, or apart from, other dishes served in a meal.

The term *hors d'oeuvre* is used differently in Europe than in North America. In France and in much of Europe, *hors d'oeuvre* denotes a small amount of plated food served at the table and eaten with a knife and fork. (In North America, such a dish is usually called an *appetizer* or *starter*.) In France, the hors d'oeuvre is typically served before the first formal course in a lengthy menu.

The French term for a finger food (that North Americans would call an hors d'oeuvre) is ***amuse-bouche*** [ah-mooz BOOSH], which literally translates as "a thing that amuses the mouth." Confusingly, North American chefs and restaurateurs have begun using this term to denote a small plated appetizer served as a complimentary, or free, offering before the first course of a restaurant meal.

The word *hors d'oeuvre* has been part of the English language for more than a hundred years. In French, the term has no final *s* to form the plural, but in English the final *s* is both written and pronounced.

Stuffed hors d'oeuvres

- Celery, cut into boats
- Belgian endive leaves
- Large pasta shells or rigatoni, cooked and refreshed
- Pullet eggs and quail eggs

Wrapped and Rolled Hors d'Oeuvres

Wrapped hors d'oeuvres consist of a food item or filling encased in a thin sheet of another food item. Virtually any food can be wrapped, and there are many kinds of wrappers.

Rolled hors d'oeuvres consist of foods layered together and then rolled into a cylinder. These are frequently called by their French name, ***roulades*** [roo-LAHDS]. When the cylinder is cut crosswise into pieces, the resulting slices have a spiral or pinwheel appearance. Sometimes roulades have a bread element, as in a wrap sandwich.

Here are some foods that can be used as wrappers to be filled, or that can be layered and rolled, to make cold hors d'oeuvres:

- Thick-sliced cold cuts
- Pliable sliced cheeses
- Roasted peppers
- Soft-textured lettuce leaves
- Cabbage, Swiss chard, and kale, blanched and refreshed
- Pasta sheets, cooked and refreshed
- Moist, crustless bread, sliced thin
- Flour tortillas
- Lavash

Wrapped and rolled hors d'oeuvres

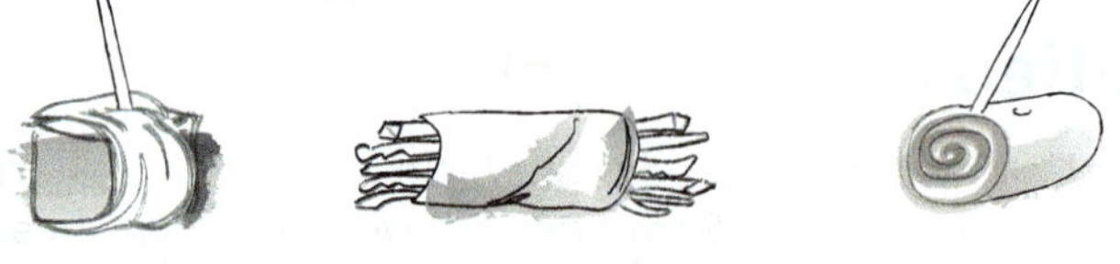

Spoons and Sips

In the 1980s, some chefs began to challenge the accepted concept of hors d'oeuvres and expand the repertoire to include non-traditional items. Contemporary chefs now create hors d'oeuvres by placing tiny portions of food, such as mousses, bound protein salads, and hot food items, on attractive silver spoons or Asian-style ceramic spoons and garnishing them in the same manner as canapés. The filled spoons are arranged on trays and passed to guests by servers. A second server follows along behind the first to collect the used spoons. This type of hors d'oeuvre is called a ***spoon hors d'oeuvre***, or simply a *spoon*.

Both hot and cold soups are now presented as hors d'oeuvres as well. Tiny portions of soup are served in demitasse cups or shot glasses and passed to guests in the same manner as spoon hors d'oeuvres. This type of soup hors d'oeuvre is known as a ***sip***.

Picked and Skewered Hors d'Oeuvres

Foods too moist or oily to be eaten neatly with the fingers can served on a cocktail pick. They are called ***picked hors d'oeuvres***. Foods dry enough to be held directly in the fingers but meant to be dipped in a sauce are also served on picks. If two or three pieces of food are threaded onto a cocktail pick or bamboo skewer, the result is called a ***skewered hors d'oeuvre*** or an ***hors d'oeuvre kebab***.

Virtually any bite-size food can be picked or skewered. This list includes some of the most popular:

- Marinated vegetables
- Cubed cheeses
- Cheese balls
- Cubed hams, sausages, and other charcuterie items
- Chilled seafood
- Cold, cubed meats and poultry

Picked/skewered hors d'oeuvres

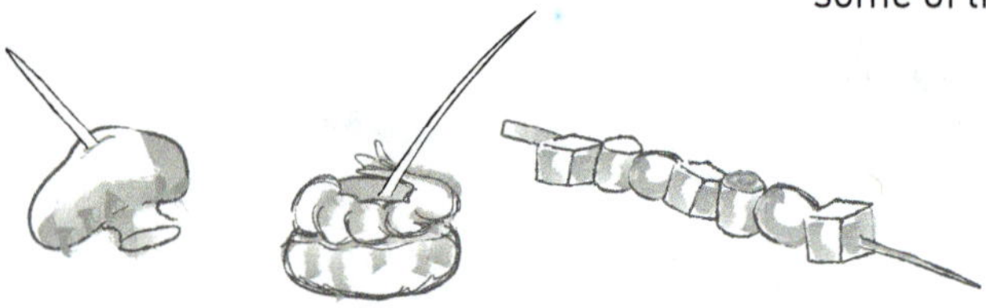

Pastry Hors d'Oeuvres

Hors d'oeuvres based on pastry are among the most versatile. Hundreds of kinds of ***pastry hors d'oeuvres*** are made from several kinds of pastry. Table 10.1 lists the most popular pastries or doughs.

TABLE 10.1 Most Popular Pastry Doughs for Hors d'Oeuvres

Pastry Type	Description
Flaky	Unleavened dough based on flour and butter, shortening, or lard. When baked, it is crisp, brittle, and flaky.
Pâte brisée [PAHT bree-ZAY]	Unleavened dough based on flour and butter, shortening, or lard. When baked, it is tender and crumbly, and it holds moist fillings without becoming soggy.
Puff pastry or pâte feuilletée [PAHT foy-ye-TAY]	Steam-leavened dough based on flour and butter or manufactured fat. When baked, it rises to many times its original height and has many flaky layers.
Phyllo (also filo) [FEE-low]	Paper-thin manufactured dough based on flour. Brushed with butter and layered before baking. When baked, it becomes crisp, golden, and buttery. Originally part of Greek cuisine and now universally used for hors d'oeuvres and desserts.
Feuille de brik [foy duh BREEK]	Paper-thin rounds of manufactured dough based on flour. It is used in the same manner as phyllo, but it is sturdier and easier to handle. May be fried as well as baked. A Moroccan pastry that became popular among French chefs in the 1980s; it has been discovered by North American chefs and is now available from specialty purveyors.
Batters	Thin, pourable forms of pastry dough. Savory forms can become bases or containers for hors d'oeuvre fillings: Crêpes [kreps], thin, unleavened pancakes, can be made in miniature and used to wrap a filling. Blini [BLEE-nee], miniature yeasted buckwheat pancakes, are traditionally topped with caviar. Fritter batter can be formed into crispy little tartlets with a rosette iron. Batter for tuile cookies can be made without sugar and formed after baking into cups and tubes.

Various fillings can be wrapped in pastry and then baked. Pastry can be formed into shells, filled, and baked. Or shells can be ***blind baked***, or baked empty, and then filled.

Pastry hors d'oeuvres

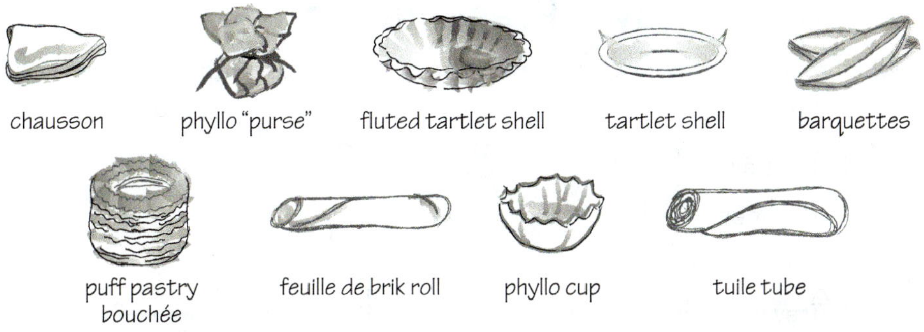

Crudités

Crudités [kroo-dee-TAY(s)] are raw or very lightly cooked vegetables served chilled and accompanied by dips. The term *crudités* is derived from the French word *cru,* meaning "raw." The term came into wide use in North America in the 1970s, when health-conscious diners requested lighter and lower-calorie foods at cocktail parties. Today, crudités remain popular, especially when baby vegetables and specialty vegetables are included in the assortment and when unusual sauces and dips accompany them. The preparation and presentation of crudités is covered in Chapter 4.

Canapés

Without question, canapés are *the* classic hors d'oeuvres. In fact, when most people think of hors d'oeuvres, it is some type of canapé that comes to mind.

Canapés are miniature open-face sandwiches. The French word *canapé* literally translates as "bed" or "sofa." This term refers to the piece of bread, toast, or flat pastry that is the bed, or base, on which the other ingredients are placed. On top of that base, a canapé has two other elements: a filling, and a garnish.

In addition to the bread-like base, canapés can include virtually any other savory ingredient. Because canapés are a type of open-faced sandwich, many of the sandwich ingredients listed in Chapter 9 are appropriate for making them. However, canapés are expected to be elegant and impressive, so you often see luxury foods such as smoked salmon, shrimp, caviar, beef filet, or the more refined charcuterie products as fillings. Canapés that include these expensive ingredients usually don't break your food cost budget because you use very little of them on each piece. Canapé garnishes must be tiny, attractive, and completely edible.

Canapés are prepared in two basic construction types and require specific techniques. This specialized information is presented beginning on p. 401 in the recipe section of this chapter.

PRESENTING HORS D'OEUVRES

No other food demands as much attention to presentation as hors d'oeuvres. In addition to being beautiful in and of themselves, hors d'oeuvres must also be presented artistically.

Serviceware for Hors d'Oeuvres

The serviceware you choose for your hors d'oeuvres can add a great deal to the presentation. The vessel used for presenting hors d'oeuvres is generally referred to as a *tray,* although many other types of serviceware may be used. Table 10.2 lists some serviceware items that can be used for hors d'oeuvres presentation.

The Four Elements of Hors d'Oeuvre Presentation

Whether using a tray, platter, or even a basket or bento box, there are four basic design elements.

1. The tray
2. The liner
3. The hors d'oeuvres
4. Tray décor

All four elements should combine to create a design that is pleasing to the eye. In addition, it must be easy for the guests to pick up the hors d'oeuvres and easy for the cooks or servers to refill the trays.

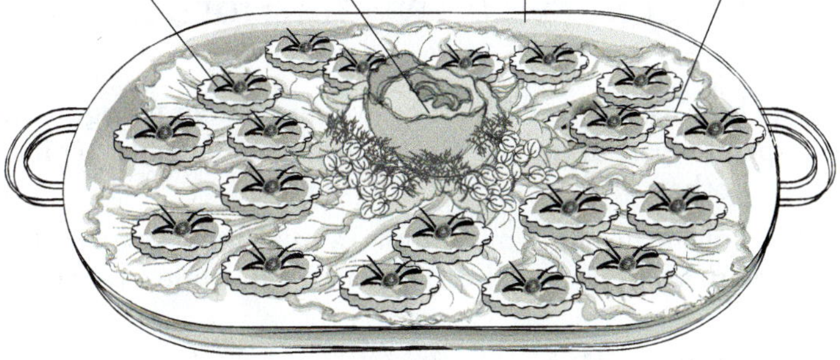

The four elements of tray design

TABLE 10.2 Serviceware for Hors d'Oeuvre Presentation

Type	Details
Trays made of silver plate	This is a classic presentation of formal hors d'oeuvres. These trays are available in rounds, ovals, and rectangles of various sizes. They must be polished to a bright shine with silver polish or a salt-and-vinegar paste. Make sure silver pieces have no smudges or fingerprints. Hors d'oeuvres are not placed directly on the silver; a liner (p. 370) must be used.
Trays made of stainless steel	These are a budget version of silver plate trays. Most details that pertain to silver also apply to stainless ware.
Ceramic platters	These are large, flat dishes made of china, stoneware, or porcelain. Platter colors can enhance presentation. Hors d'oeuvres may be placed directly onto this type of platter. Ceramic platters are usually used for buffet presentation rather than butler service.
Glass platters	Clear and frosted glass platters can make stunning presentations. They are fragile and can become safety hazards if broken or chipped. *These should never be used for butler service*, as they might be dropped and broken.
Baskets	Their rustic appearance at a casual affair can make a pleasing presentation. Flat and deep baskets may be used, depending on the type of hors d'oeuvre. Baskets are always lined.
Lacquerware trays and bento boxes	These are particularly appropriate for Asian-inspired hors d'oeuvres.
Presentation mirrors	Canapés and other hors d'oeuvres with a dry, non-greasy bottom surface may be presented on mirrors for buffet/stationary service only. Use square, rectangular, round, or oval shapes with rounded or beveled edges. *Do not use straight-edge mirrors for hors d'oeuvre presentation, as their sharp edges are a safety hazard.* *Do not use framed mirrors, as they cannot be properly sanitized.*

The Tray

Choose a tray that is appropriate in style and design for both the event and the hors d'oeuvres it will display.

Guidelines for Choosing the Correct Service Tray for Hors d'Oeuvres

- The tray must be large enough to hold the hors d'oeuvres without crowding them or piling them on top of one another (unless doing so is a specific part of the design). Guests must be able to pick up a single hors d'oeuvre without disturbing any others.
- The shape of the tray determines the shape of the design. For example, a round tray suggests that the hors d'oeuvres should be arranged in concentric circles, or a bull's-eye pattern, while a rectangular tray suggests parallel rows.
- The rim of the tray forms the frame of your design and should complement the color of both the hors d'oeuvres and the liner. Neither the hors d'oeuvres nor the décor should extend onto the rim.
- If the hors d'oeuvres are to be passed, the combined weight of the tray and the hors d'oeuvres should not be so heavy that it will be difficult for a server to carry.

The Liner

Most hors d'oeuvre trays are lined, or covered, before the hors d'oeuvres are placed on them. Liners can be made of cloth, paper, or food.

Linen table napkins: Starched white linen table napkins are the classic tray liner. Linen is used only if the hors d'oeuvres have bases that are dry and not greasy.

Disposable paper doilies: Paper doilies are the practical choice for lining trays because they are disposable and inexpensive. Most paper doilies are round, although rectangular doilies may be ordered. While white is the preferred color, colored doilies can be effective in enhancing the presentation. Greaseproof glassine doilies are recommended for oily foods and fried foods.

Liner leaves: Large, perfect liner leaves of lettuce, kale, and other leafy vegetables are used to line trays for cold hors d'oeuvres that benefit from contact with a moist surface. The leaves are arranged in an attractive pattern on the tray and then flattened to provide a level surface for the hors d'oeuvres to rest on. Canapés, pastry hors d'oeuvres, and other crisp items should not be presented on liner leaves, as they become soggy from contact.

Aspic: For a formal presentation, trays and platters can be lined with very stiff aspic (p. 644). This creates a smooth, shiny surface ranging in color from pale golden to rich brown. Pour cool liquid aspic on a tray placed level in the refrigerator. Once the aspic is set, décor, such as herb pluches or vegetable cut-outs, can be placed on top and then a second layer of aspic added.

Dealing with Doilies

Paper doilies are stamped out of multiple sheets of paper with a die. This compresses them together, and they can be difficult to separate, especially when in a hurry. It is a good idea to estimate the number of doilies needed for a particular event and separate them ahead of time. Separate doilies away from the food preparation area to avoid "doily dandruff," or loose chads of paper, getting into the food and posing a physical hazard.

When ready to line a tray with a paper doily, make sure to place it right-side up. If you look closely at a doily you will notice it has a face side, with a raised pattern, and a bottom side. Doilies should always be used face-side up.

The Hors d'Oeuvres

The hors d'oeuvres are the stars of your presentation. Thus, their appearance should not be overwhelmed by the tray liner or by the décor item(s). Make sure the hors d'oeuvres are the focal point of your design.

Guidelines for Presenting Hors d'Oeuvres

- Each hors d'oeuvre should be identical to the others of its kind in size, shape, and garnish. When you order ingredients for hors d'oeuvres, give detailed product specifications as to size, and order extra to compensate for those items that are too big or too small. Careful fabrication is also necessary. Use a ruler or a template to make sure all cuts are consistent.
- Make sure all hors d'oeuvres of the same kind are garnished exactly the same.
- For most events, *serve trays consisting of one type of hors d'oeuvre.* This gives the tray a professional appearance. It also saves time during service, because guests will not linger over the tray trying to decide which hors d'oeuvre to choose. Only for very small groups should you serve mixed trays.
- When serving mixed trays, keep all one type of hors d'oeuvre together in a row or section. Do not mix the hors d'oeuvres in a random arrangement on the tray.
- Place hors d'oeuvres on trays in neat rows, concentric circles, or blocks with even spacing between pieces. Make sure guests can pick up one individual hors d'oeuvre without touching another.

Tray Décor

In hors d'oeuvre work, the culinary term ***décor*** [day-KOR] is defined as a food item added to a tray or platter to add visual appeal (Chapter 18 discusses décor in detail).

While many hors d'oeuvres are colorful and attractive enough to need no additional décor, the addition of thoughtfully chosen tray décor can add strong visual impact to your presentation. Appropriate tray décor particularly enhances hors d'oeuvre items that lack color.

Tray décor can also add height to a low presentation. Many canapés are flat, and their presentation benefits from a plume of greenery or a tall fruit or vegetable carving. Make sure, though, that the tray décor is stable and will not topple when the tray is moved or passed.

SERVING HORS D'OEUVRES

For many cocktail parties and receptions, hors d'oeuvres are passed or served butler-style. The typical guest is holding a beverage in one hand and has limited ability to deal with the food being served. It is up to the servers to ensure that the guests can enjoy the hors d'oeuvres without undue effort, and that all guests are served equally. The garde manger chef should be ready to guide servers in giving correct hors d'oeuvre service.

When hors d'oeuvres are served buffet-style, the general rules of buffet service apply (Chapter 18).

Cocktails and Aperitifs

In North America, hors d'oeuvres are most frequently served at cocktail parties, where they accompany cocktails. A ***cocktail*** is an alcohol beverage made by mixing a spirit, or strong alcohol, such as whiskey, vodka, or rum, with a non-alcohol beverage such as carbonated water, soda pop, or fruit juice. A modern cocktail can also consist of two or more spirits mixed together without a non-alcohol component, as in a martini or Manhattan.

A more European approach to pre-dinner beverages is to serve an ***apéritif*** [ah-pair-ih-TEEF]. This is a drink based on table wine or a fortified wine such as sherry or vermouth. In fact, light-bodied white table wines, sparkling wines, and dry sherry are considered perfect apéritifs in their own right. However, most apéritifs consist of a wine-like beverage with a slightly sweet flavoring mixed into it.

Guidelines for Butler Service

- The server should announce the name of each hors d'oeuvre as it is presented. Make sure the server knows the hors d'oeuvre's main ingredients. If the hors d'oeuvre contains possible food allergens, their presence should be mentioned.
- Try to arrange more than one access point to the event room so servers can reach both ends of the room with full trays. If this is not possible, instruct servers to periodically hold full trays overhead while passing through the crowd so the guests at the back of the room may be served first.
- Offer a paper cocktail napkin along with each hors d'oeuvre served. Fan the cocktail napkins to make each napkin easy to grasp.
- Servers should frequently pass through the event room with empty trays to collect used napkins, cocktail picks, etc.
- Hors d'oeuvre trays should be returned to the kitchen for straightening and refilling before they are completely empty and at any time they begin to look wilted or untidy.

Creating New Hors d'Oeuvres

Even in a book dedicated solely to hors d'oeuvres, it would be impossible to include every hors d'oeuvre and all variations. In addition to the hors d'oeuvres that are part of North American and European cuisines, thousands more hors d'oeuvre-type foods are featured in world cuisines. Garde manger chefs are creating new hors d'oeuvres every day, often by combining ingredients from various world cuisines and fusing those techniques with Western ingredients. Another way to create a new hors d'oeuvre is to miniaturize a favorite main dish food, as in Mini Beef Wellingtons or Mini Crabcake Sandwiches.

If you understand the requirements for successful hors d'oeuvres and have a solid knowledge of the five hors d'oeuvre construction types, you can develop a repertoire of interesting and delicious hors d'oeuvres of your own creation.

RECIPES

Most of the recipes in this chapter were chosen to represent one of the five hors d'oeuvre construction types. Some fit into more than one category. Others fit no category but are popular enough to stand alone. While we focus primarily on cold hors d'oeuvres, there are recipes for a few heated hors d'oeuvres that would typically be turned out by the garde manger station using a countertop oven.

In addition to recipes for canapés, information on constructing canapés and procedures for both construction types are presented at the end of this section.

SEAFOOD SEASHELLS

HORS D'OEUVRE

Yield:
24 pieces

INGREDIENTS	U.S.	METRIC
Cucumber	4 oz	120 g
Medium-size pasta seashells	26–30 (about 12 oz)	26–30 (about 360 g)
Kosher salt	to taste	to taste
Basic Seafood Mousse (p. 215)	12 fl oz (about 10 oz)	360 mL (about 300 g)
Orange tobiko caviar	½ oz	15 g
Décor		
Lettuce leaves	5–6 leaves (3 oz total)	5–6 (90 g total)
Carrot tumbleweed (p. 716; prepare first)	1	1

PROCEDURE

PREPARATION

1. Peel the cucumber, cut it in half lengthwise, and scrape out the seeds. Cut the cucumber brunoise. Salt the cucumber and roll it in a clean kitchen towel to drain.
2. Prepare the pasta:
   a. Bring 1 gal (4 L) water to the boil and salt it heavily.
   b. Place a colander in a large bowl set in a food prep sink. Fill the bowl with cold water.
   c. Boil the pasta, stirring occasionally, to an al dente texture.
   d. Use a spider or slotted spoon to lift the pasta out of the water and into the colander. Refresh the pasta for 30 seconds, then lift the colander and drain the pasta.
   e. Transfer the pasta to a sheet tray lined with a kitchen towel. Turn the pasta shells so the openings face downward and all the water drains out.
   f. When the shells are drained, turn them over so the hollow sides face up.
3. Assemble the stuffed shells:
   a. Place 1 tsp (5 mL) cucumber in each shell.
   b. Place the seafood mousse in pastry bag fitted with a medium star tip. Fill each shell with mousse and place it on a sheet tray lined with parchment.
   c. Use kitchen tweezers to place a dot of tobiko in one end of each shell. Cover the tray with plastic wrap (see Note).

HOLDING

Refrigerate up to 24 hours.

PRESENTATION

4. Arrange the service tray:
   a. Line a 14-in. (35-cm) tray with the lettuce leaves.
   b. Place the carrot chrysanthemum in the center of the tray.
   c. Arrange the shells on the tray.

Note: If service is within an hour of preparation, you may place the stuffed shells directly on the lined and decorated service tray and hold it refrigerated.

CUCUMBER CUPS WITH DILLED CRAB AND SHRIMP

HORS D'OEUVRE

Yield:
24 pieces

INGREDIENTS	U.S.	METRIC
Long, slender English cucumbers, 6 oz (180 g)	2	2
Kosher salt	to taste	to taste
Small shrimp (51/60 ct. recommended)	about 12 oz (24 pieces)	about 360 g (24 pieces)
Court bouillon (p. 194)	1 pt	0.5 L
Fresh lemon juice	to taste	to taste
Classic Crab Salad (p. 160)	1 pt	0.5 L
Décor		
Slender English cucumber	2 oz (1½-in. section)	60 g (4-cm section)
Fresh dill	2 oz	60 g

PROCEDURE

PREPARATION

1. Fabricate the cucumbers:
   a. Peel the cucumbers and trim the ends.
   b. Cut the cucumbers crosswise into 24 ¾-in. (2-cm) sections.
   c. Using a parisienne scoop, hollow each section to make a shallow cup (see photo).
   d. Salt each section lightly, making sure to evenly salt the interior of each cup.
   e. Line a sheet tray with paper towels. Place the cucumbers hollow-side down on the paper towels to drain. Place the tray in the refrigerator.

2. Prepare the garnishes:
   a. Poach and chill the shrimp in the court bouillon as directed on page 195.
   b. Shell the shrimp and season them with lemon juice and salt.
3. Prepare the filling: Mince 1 tbsp (30 mL) of the décor dill and mix it with the crab salad.
4. Assemble the cucumber cups:
   a. Blot each cucumber cup dry with paper towels.
   b. Fill each cup with crab salad.
   c. Top each cucumber cup with a shrimp.
5. Place the cucumber cups on a sheet tray lined with a clean, dry, lint-free kitchen towel. Cover the tray with plastic wrap and refrigerate it (see Note).
6. Prepare the tray décor:
   a. To make the plinth, use a channeling tool to cut decorative grooves in the 1½-in. (2.5-cm) cucumber section.

PROCEDURE

b. Set the cucumber plinth on the work surface, on end, and insert a paring knife in the seed core. Twist the knife to create a deep, conical hole.

c. Blot the plinth dry and clean up any loose seeds.

d. Make a bouquet out of the remaining dill and force the stems down the hole in the cucumber section so the dill forms a plume.

HOLDING

Refrigerate up to 6 hours.

PRESENTATION

7. Arrange the platter:

   a. Place the décor plinth/plume in the center of the tray.

   b. Place the cucumber cups on the tray in an attractive pattern.

Note: If service is within an hour of preparation, you may omit step 5. Place the cucumber cups and décor directly on the service tray, and hold it refrigerated.

PESTO TUNA-STUFFED CHERRY TOMATOES

HORS D'OEUVRE

Yield:
24 pieces

INGREDIENTS	U.S.	METRIC
Large cherry tomatoes	24 (1 pt)	24 (0.5 L)
Kosher salt	to taste	to taste
Pine nuts	½ oz	15 g
Minced garlic	1 tsp	5 mL
Fresh basil leaves, chopped fine	½ oz	15 g
Grated lemon zest	2 tsp	10 mL
Mayonnaise (p. 41), or commercial mayonnaise	4 fl oz	120 mL
Canned white tuna in water	7 oz	220 g
Oil-cured black olives	3 (½ oz total)	3 (15 g total)
Décor		
Curly parsley, washed and dried	2–3 oz	60–90 g

PROCEDURE

PREPARATION

1. Fabricate the tomatoes:
   a. Cut ¼ in. (0.6 cm) off the stem end of each tomato.
   b. Use the small end of a parisienne scoop to remove the seeds and veins of the tomato, leaving a hollow shell.
   c. Lightly salt the inside of each tomato and place it upside down on a sheet tray lined with paper towels. Place the tray in the refrigerator.
2. Prepare the filling:
   a. Combine the pine nuts, garlic, basil, and lemon zest in a small mortar or wet-dry spice mill. Grind to a rough paste. Stir in the mayonnaise.
   b. Drain the tuna thoroughly and break it up into small flakes. Mix the pesto mayonnaise with the tuna. Taste and correct the seasoning.
3. Prepare a sheet tray lined with crumpled parchment paper that will hold the tomatoes upright without rolling around (see Note).
4. Stuff each tomato with the pesto tuna, mounding the filling on top and rounding it neatly. Place the tomatoes upright on the sheet tray. Cover the tray with plastic wrap and refrigerate it (see Note).
5. Halve and pit the olives and cut them into 24 triangular garnishes. Place the garnishes in a container and set it on the tray.

HOLDING

Refrigerate up to 24 hours.

PROCEDURE

PRESENTATION

6. Remove the large stems from the parsley and make a bed of parsley on a 14-in. (35-cm) tray.
7. Place an olive triangle on top of each tomato and place it on the tray. (The parsley should hold the tomatoes upright.)

Note: If service is within 1–2 hours of preparation, you may omit step 3 and place the tomatoes directly on the parsley-lined service tray, and hold it refrigerated.

VARIATIONS

TARRAGON CRAB-STUFFED CHERRY TOMATOES

Replace the pine nuts, garlic, lemon zest with 2 tbsp (30 mL) chopped fresh tarragon. (Do not grind it; just mix it with the mayonnaise.) Replace the tuna with 6 oz (180 g) crabmeat. Replace the olive garnish with tiny stars cut out of pimiento or roasted red bell pepper.

CHERRY TOMATOES STUFFED WITH DILLED EGG SALAD

Replace the filling ingredients with 10 oz (300 g) Dilled Egg Salad (p. 162). Replace the olive garnish with tiny pluches of dill.

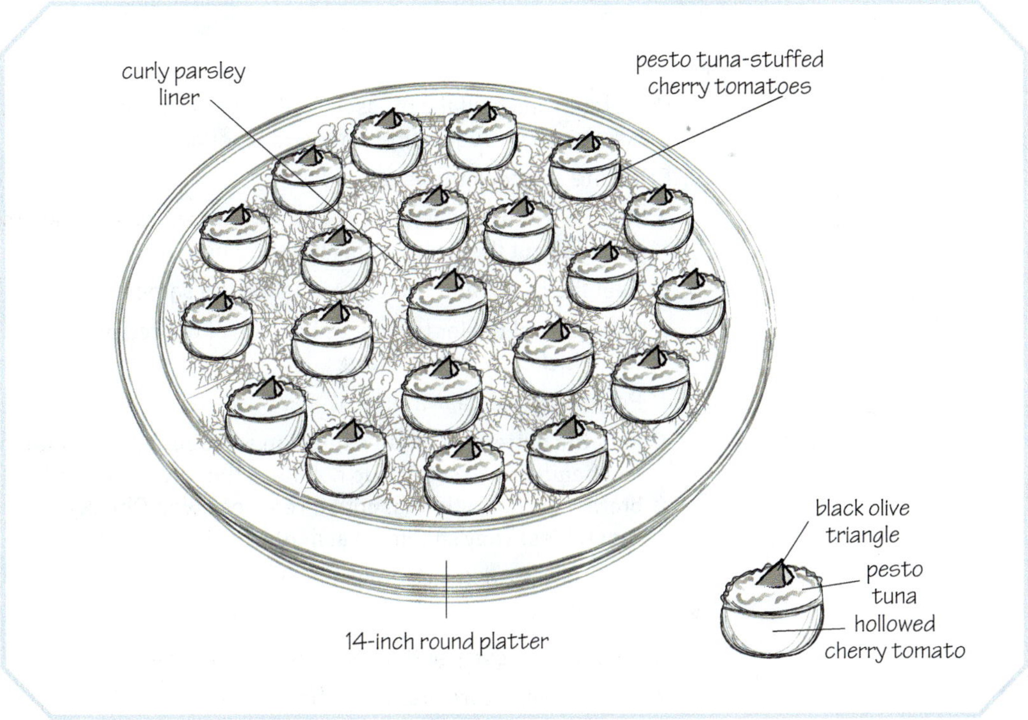

CHILLED MUSSELS WITH MUSTARD SAUCE

HORS D'OEUVRE

Yield:
24 pieces–30 pieces

INGREDIENTS	U.S.	METRIC
Large farm-raised mussels	2 lb	1 kg
White wine	4 fl oz	120 mL
Minced garlic	¼ oz	7 g
Leek, whole	12 oz	360 g
Carrot, whole	6 oz	180 g
Red bell pepper, cleaned	6 oz	180 g
Butter	½ oz	15 g
Miami Mustard Sauce (p. 44)	7 fl oz	210 mL
Minced parsley	1 tbsp	15 mL
Red bell pepper, peeled and cut brunoise	2 tbsp	30 mL
Décor		
Romaine lettuce leaves	5–6 (1½ oz total)	5–6 (45 g total)
Leek chrysanthemum (p. 716; prepare first, as scallion brush)	1	1
Red hot pepper lilies (p. 716; prepare first)	3	3

PROCEDURE

PREPARATION

1. Pan-steam and chill the mussels in the wine and garlic as directed on p. 195. Strain the mussel broth through a fine sieve and reserve it.
2. Fabricate and cook the vegetables:
   a. Cut the white part of the leek in half and separate the layers. Wash them thoroughly and then cut them into ½-in. (1.25-cm) fine julienne.
   b. Peel the carrot and cut it into julienne the same size as the leeks.
   c. Use a swivel peeler to remove the skin of the red bell pepper and cut it into julienne a little thicker than the others.
   d. Prepare an ice bain-marie.
   e. Melt the butter in a small sauté pan and sauté the vegetables over moderate heat until just beginning to soften. Do not allow them to brown. Add a few ounces of the mussel broth and cook, stirring, until it reduces away. Check the texture and seasoning of the vegetables. They should be al dente and lightly salty.
   f. Cool the pan in the ice bain-marie.
3. Prepare the mussels:
   a. Shell the mussels and reserve the bottom shell of each.
   b. Remove any beard filaments that remain on the mussels.
   c. Remove the muscle remnants from the reserved shells.
   d. Rinse the shells, blot them dry, and place them on a sheet tray lined with parchment.
   e. Divide the vegetable mixture among the shells and top each with a mussel. Cover the tray with plastic wrap and refrigerate it (see Note).

PROCEDURE

HOLDING

Refrigerate up to 24 hours.

PRESENTATION

4. Nap each mussel with mustard sauce.
5. Sprinkle parsley and brunoise red bell pepper on each mussel.
6. Line a 14-in. (35-cm) tray with the romaine leaves.
7. Place the leek chrysanthemum in the center of the tray and arrange the red hot pepper lilies around it.
8. Place the mussels on the tray with the rounded ends facing the rim.

Note: If service is within an hour of preparation, you may place the mussels directly on the lined and decorated service tray and hold it refrigerated.

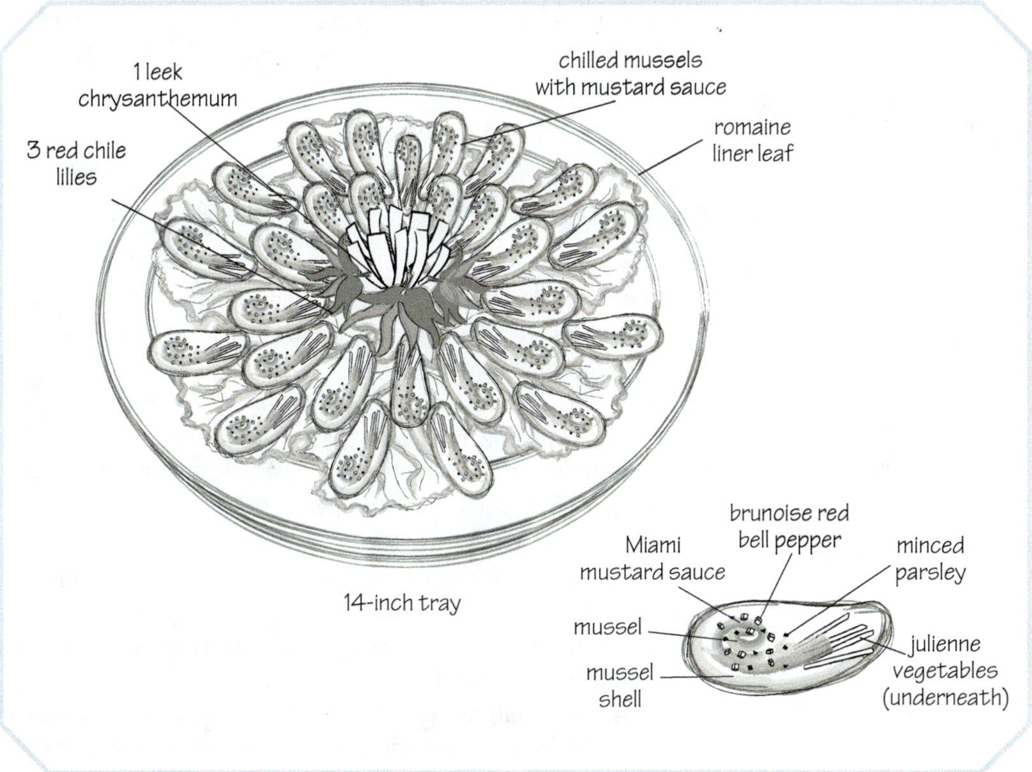

STUFFED QUAIL EGGS IN BABY BEETS

HORS D'OEUVRE

Yield:
24 pieces

INGREDIENTS	U.S.	METRIC
1-in. (2.5-cm) diameter baby beets (or 12 canned baby beets)	12 pieces (10 oz total)	12 pieces (300 g total)
Red wine vinegar	4 fl oz	120 mL
Kosher salt	to taste	to taste
Sugar	2 tbsp	30 mL
Boston lettuce (see Note)	3 heads (14 oz total)	3 heads (420 g total)
Eggs	2	2
Quail eggs	12	12
Mayonnaise (p. 41) or commercial mayonnaise	2 fl oz	60 mL
Dijon mustard	2 tsp	10 mL
Anchovy paste	½ tsp	3 mL
Tiny dill or curly parsley pluches	24	24

Note: Only about one-third of the lettuce will actually be used for this recipe.

PROCEDURE

PREPARATION

1. Cook and fabricate the beets (if using canned beets, begin with step 1f):
   a. Preheat a pressure steamer and place a drip pan in the bottom. Alternatively, prepare a stovetop steamer.
   b. Scrub the beets under cool water and place them in a perforated hotel pan.
   c. Steam about 2 minutes in the pressure steamer or 8 minutes in the stovetop steamer, until tender. (Cooking times will vary depending on your equipment.)
   d. Open-pan cool to room temperature.
   e. Peel the beets.
   f. Cut the beets in half widthwise. Use a parisienne scoop to hollow a shallow depression on the cut surface of each beet.
   g. Toss the beets with the vinegar, salt, and sugar. Cover and marinate at room temperature at least 20 minutes.
2. Separate the lettuce leaves and select 24 small, cup-shaped leaves of appropriate size to hold the beets. Wash these leaves and roll them in a towel. Refrigerate until needed. (Reserve the remaining leaves for another use.)
3. Prepare the eggs:
   a. Cook the large eggs in simmering water for about 8 minutes, then add the quail eggs to the pan. Cook about 4 minutes more.
   b. Refresh the eggs under cold water and carefully shell them.
   c. Cut the eggs in half widthwise, being careful to keep the quail egg whites in presentable form for stuffing.
   d. Carefully remove the yolks from the whites and press the yolks through a strainer into a bowl. Reserve only the quail egg whites for stuffing. Discard the large egg whites.
   e. Whisk the mayonnaise, mustard, and anchovy paste into the sieved egg yolks. Taste and correct the seasoning.
   f. Transfer the yolk mixture to a pastry bag fitted with a small star tip.

PROCEDURE

4. Assemble the hors d'oeuvres:
   a. Pipe a dot of yolk mixture into the center of each lettuce cup and place the lettuce cups on a sheet tray lined with parchment (see Note).
   b. Fill each quail egg by piping a rosette of yolk mixture in its cavity and on its cut surface (A).
   c. Garnish each quail egg with a tiny pluche of dill or parsley.
   d. Drain the beets and blot them dry on paper towels.
   e. Pipe a tiny dot of yolk mixture in each beet cavity.
   f. Place a stuffed quail egg in the depression made in each beet (B).
   g. Place each beet into a lettuce cup. Cover the tray with plastic wrap and refrigerate it (see Note).

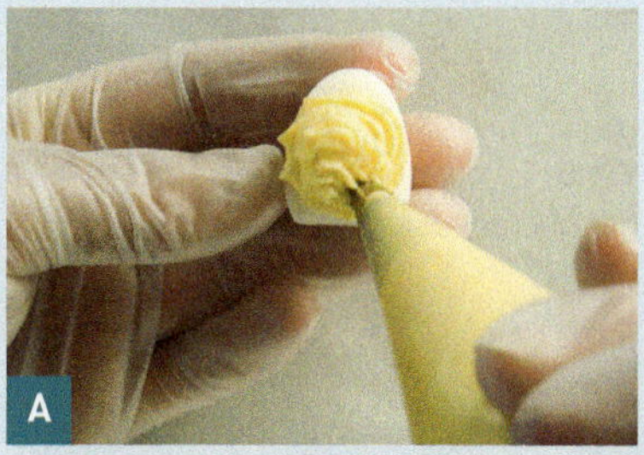
A

B

HOLDING

Once assembled, refrigerate no longer than 3 hours. For longer holding, stop preparation after step 3 and refrigerate the ingredients separately up to 2 days.

PRESENTATION

5. Blot the bottom of the filled lettuce cups on a clean kitchen towel and place them on a deviled egg dish or serving tray.

Note: If service is within an hour of preparation, you may place the hors d'oeuvres directly on the plate and hold it refrigerated.

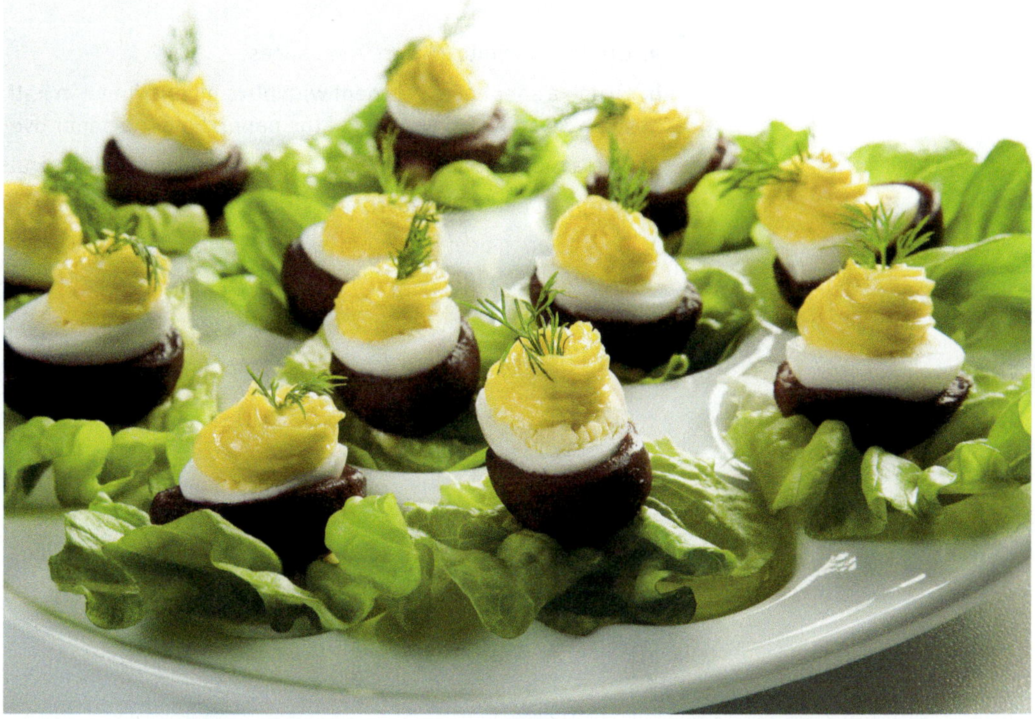

ASPARAGUS IN CARPACCIO [kar-PAH-choh]

HORS D'OEUVRE

Yield:
24 pieces

INGREDIENTS	U.S.	METRIC
Eye round or filet of beef (see Note)	1 lb	0.5 kg
Asparagus	24 stalks (1¼ lb total)	24 stalks (0.6 kg total)
Long, slender carrot, peeled	1 (4 oz)	1 (120 g)
Extra-virgin olive oil	½ fl oz	15 mL
Anchovy Mayonnaise (p. 43)	8 fl oz	240 mL
Grated Reggiano Parmesan cheese	2 oz	60 g

Note: You typically incur some waste in cutting correct-size slices of beef. About 12 oz (360 g) is used actually for the hors d'oeuvres. A lower percentage of waste occurs when preparing a larger number of hors d'oeuvres.

PROCEDURE

PREPARATION

1. Trim off and discard all exterior fat and silverskin from the beef. Place the beef in a freezer about 30 minutes to firm it enough so it can be sliced very thin.
2. Prepare the asparagus:
   a. Bring a saucepan of water to the boil. Prepare an ice bain-marie.
   b. Snap off and discard the tough butt ends of the asparagus.
   c. Peel the asparagus.
   d. Blanch the asparagus *à point* (p. 91) and refresh it.
   e. Blot it dry.
3. Prepare carrot ribbons:
   a. Using a swivel peeler, shave off 12 long, horizontal ribbons of carrot.
   b. Cut each ribbon in half.
4. Fabricate the beef:
   a. Cut the beef into 24 thin, even slices.
   b. Brush a sheet of parchment with olive oil and fold it in half. Open it out again and lay the beef slices on one half of the paper. Fold the paper over to cover the beef.
   c. Use a meat mallet to gently flatten the slices into thin ovals.
5. Assemble the hors d'oeuvres:
   a. Spread each beef slice with an even layer of anchovy mayonnaise, extending the mayonnaise almost to the edges.
   b. Sprinkle with parmesan.

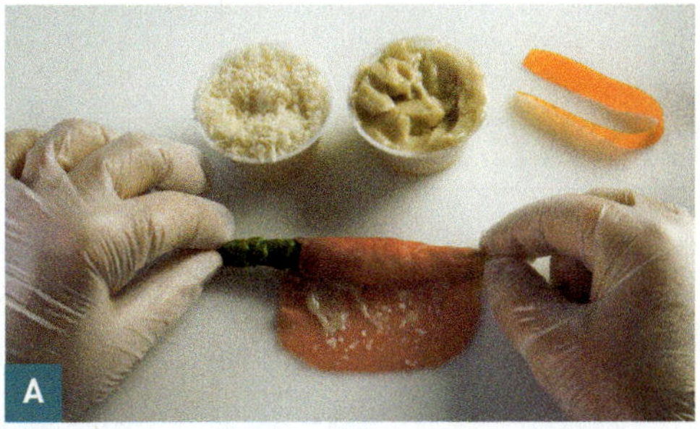

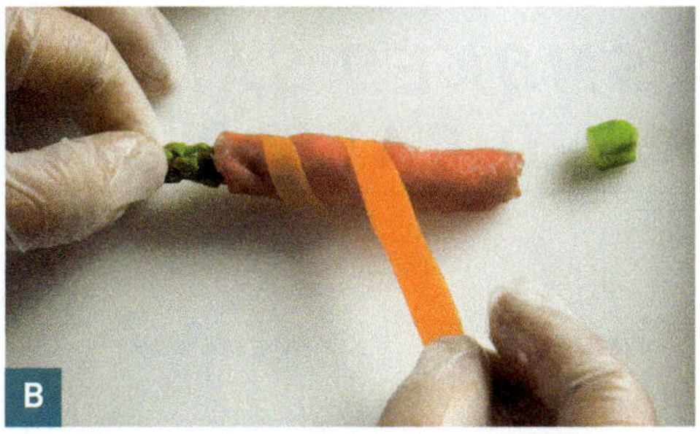

PROCEDURE

c. Place an asparagus spear across one short end of each slice and roll it in the beef in such a way that the asparagus tip is visible on one end (A). Trim off the butt end even with the edge of the beef.

d. Wrap a piece of carrot ribbon around each asparagus roll (B).

e. Place the asparagus rolls on a sheet tray lined with parchment. Cover the tray with plastic wrap and refrigerate it (see Note).

HOLDING

Refrigerate up to 24 hours.

PRESENTATION

6. Arrange the asparagus rolls on a rectangular serving tray.

Note: If service is within an hour of preparation, you may place the hors d'oeuvres directly on the lined and decorated tray and hold it refrigerated.

VARIATION

ASPARAGUS IN PROSCIUTTO

Replace the beef with thin-sliced prosciutto. Do not oil or pound the prosciutto. Replace the anchovy mayonnaise with Garlic-Herb Cheese Spread (p. 594). Omit the parmesan and carrot ribbons.

SMOKED SALMON AND CAVIAR BLINI BASKETS

HORS D'OEUVRE

Yield:
24 pieces

COMPONENTS

Décor

1 Tomato rose (p. 716), prepare first
3 sprigs (½ oz/15 g total) Watercress

Ingredients

24 *Blini (p. 755)* freshly baked 2-in. (5-cm)
6 oz (180 g) Thin-sliced smoked salmon, pulled into shreds
4 fl oz (120 mL) Thick *Crème Fraîche (p. 567)*, in pastry bag fitted with small star tip
2 oz (60 g) Black caviar
24 4-in. (10-cm) Scallion ties (p. 715)

PROCEDURE

PRESENTATION

1. Arrange the décor:
   a. Place the tomato rose in the center of a 14-in. (35-cm) round serving tray.
   b. Arrange the parsley sprigs around it to resemble leaves.
2. Quickly assemble the blini baskets and arrange them on the tray:
   a. Place a scallion tie on a sanitized work surface and place a blini, best side down, on top of it.
   b. Place a line of smoked salmon down the center of the blini perpendicular to the scallion tie.
   c. Pipe a small line of crème fraîche on the salmon.
   d. Use the tip of a paring knife to place a row of caviar on top of the crème fraîche.
   e. Have a helper bring the edges of the blini together over the filling. Use the scallion tie to secure the blini closed (see photo).
   f. If necessary, trim the ends of the tie with scissors.

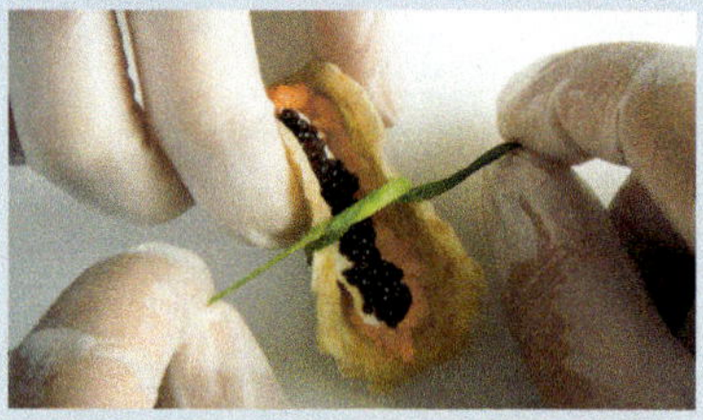

VARIATION

SMOKED TROUT BLINI BASKETS

Replace the tomato rose with a red Apple Bird (p. 717). Replace the smoked salmon and caviar with 7 oz (210 g) smoked trout. Using 2 oz (60 g) julienne tart apple, add some julienne apple on top of the crème fraîche.

CURRIED CHICKEN BOUCHÉES

HORS D'OEUVRE

Yield:
24 pieces

COMPONENTS

Décor

3 Greaseproof doilies, one 10-in. (25-cm) and two 8-in. (20-cm)
1 oz (30 g) curly parsley or micro greens
1 Apple Bird (p. 717)

Ingredients

24 1½-in. (3-cm) *Puff Pastry Bouchées (p. 704)*, freshly baked and cooled or commercial
16 fl oz/480 mL (about 14 oz/420 g) *Curried Chicken Salad (p. 159)* (chop all ingredients fine, omit the currants, season strongly)
8 oz (24 g) Red apple
1 fl oz (30 mL) Lemon juice
24 Tiny chervil or parsley pluches

PROCEDURE

PRESENTATION

1. Line a 14-in. (35-cm) oval tray with the doilies. Arrange the parsley in the center and place the apple bird on top.
2. Fill each bouchée with curried chicken salad.
3. Cut the apple into very thin slices, then cut pointed arcs from the ends of the slices. Immediately coat the arcs with lemon juice.
4. Stick an apple arc upright in each bouchée and place a pluche in front of it.
5. Arrange the bouchées on the tray.

VARIATIONS

DILLED SHRIMP SALAD BOUCHÉES

Replace the curried chicken salad with Scandinavian Shrimp Salad (p. 160). Replace the apple arc with a tiny cooked shrimp. Replace the chervil pluche with a dill pluche.

BOUCHÉES OF LIVER PARFAIT

Replace the curried chicken salad with Poultry Liver Parfait (p. 265). Pipe the parfait into the bouchées using a pastry bag fitted with a star tip.

BOUCHÉES OF SALMON MOUSSE

Replace the curried chicken salad with Salmon Mousse (p. 216). Pipe the mousse into the bouchées using a pastry bag fitted with a star tip. Replace the apple arc with a tiny rose formed of smoked salmon. Replace the chervil pluche with a dill pluche.

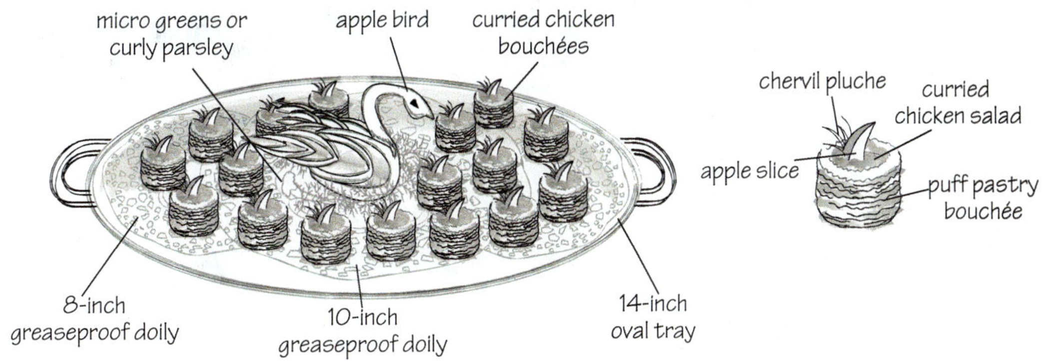

RILLETTES EN ROULADE [ree-YET awn roo-LAHD]

HORS D'OEUVRE

Yield:
24 pieces–30 pieces

INGREDIENTS	U.S.	METRIC
Crêpes (p. 754) 5-in. (12-cm)	6	6
Mustard Mayonnaise (p. 43)	3 fl oz	90 mL
Rillettes de Tours (p. 462), warmed, drained, and cooled or variation	12 fl oz (about 10 oz)	360 mL (about 300 g)
Chopped sweet onion	3 oz	90 g
Small cornichons each sliced into 6 perfect disks	4	4
Brunoise-cut yellow bell pepper	24 pc (½ oz)	24 pc (15 g)
Small dice red bell pepper	24 pc (1 oz)	24 pc (30 g)
Supplies		
Frilled cocktail picks	24	24

PROCEDURE

PREPARATION

1. Assemble the roulades:
   a. Place the crêpes, best side down, on a sanitized work surface and spread them with mustard mayonnaise, leaving a small amount for garnishing.
   b. Scatter the rillettes evenly on the surface of the crêpes and press down so they adhere.
   c. Sprinkle the onion over the rillettes and press to firm.
   d. Roll each crêpe into a tight roulade and place the roulades on a sheet tray lined with parchment. Cover the roulades and put the tray in the refrigerator for about 20 minutes, or until the roulades are firm.
2. Use a sharp knife to trim the ends of the roulades and cut them into 1-in. (2.5-cm) lengths.
3. Garnish each roulade:
   a. Impale a piece of yellow bell pepper and red bell pepper on a cocktail pick.
   b. Place a cornichon disc on the non-seam side of a roulade section and stick the cocktail pick through it into the roulade.
   c. Place the garnished roulade lengths on a parchment-lined sheet tray, cover with plastic wrap, and refrigerate (see Note).

HOLDING

Refrigerate up to 6 hours.

PROCEDURE

PRESENTATION

5. Arrange the roulades in straight, even rows on a 14-in. (35-cm) rectangular tray or presentation mirror.

Note: If service is within an hour of preparation, you may place the hors d'oeuvres directly on the lined and decorated tray and hold it refrigerated.

VARIATION

SMOKED CHICKEN ROULADES

Replace the rillettes with shredded Hot-Smoked Chicken (p. 446 or commercial).

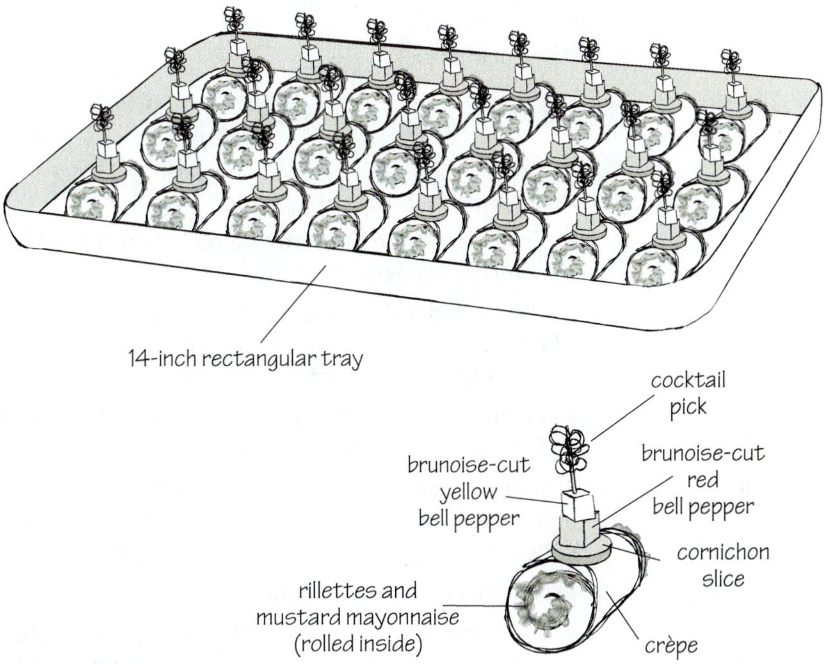

ANTIPASTO PINWHEELS

HORS D'OEUVRE

Yield:
24 pieces

INGREDIENTS	U.S.	METRIC
7-oz (210-g) red bell peppers	4 (28 oz total)	4 (840 g total)
Kosher salt	to taste	to taste
10-in. (25-cm) flour tortillas	2	2
Anchovy Mayonnaise (p. 43), thick	4 fl oz	120 mL
Thin-sliced sharp provolone cheese, room temperature	2 oz	60 g
Thin-sliced Genoa salami	1 oz	30 g
Arugula leaves or fresh basil leaves, chiffonnade	½ oz	15 g
Décor		
Bouquet of curly parsley or fresh basil leaves	½ oz	15 g
Supplies		
Plain cocktail picks	24	24

PROCEDURE

PREPARATION

1. Roast and fabricate the peppers:
   a. Prepare roasted peppers as directed on page 109. Open each pepper to clean it, but keep the peppers intact.
   b. Place the peppers on a sheet tray lined with doubled paper towels and salt them lightly. Turn the peppers over, salt the new top surface, and place a doubled layer of paper towels on top of them.
   c. Place another sheet tray on top of the peppers, and place a 2-lb (1-kg) weight on it. Refrigerate the peppers at least 20 minutes.
2. Just before you are ready to assemble the pinwheel roulades, pass the tortillas briefly under the broiler to soften them and make them pliable. Do not allow them to brown or stiffen. Cool the tortillas to room temperature and proceed.
3. Assemble the pinwheel roulades:
   a. Place the softened, cooled tortillas on a cutting board. Measure 1¼ in. (3 cm) in from the top and bottom, and then cut off the rounded tops and bottoms to make rectangles with rounded sides measuring about 5¼ × 8 in. (13 × 20 cm).
   b. Spread each tortilla rectangle with a thin layer of anchovy mayonnaise.
   c. Arrange a thin, even layer of provolone cheese on the rectangles, cutting and patching as necessary.
   d. Arrange a thin, even layer of salami on top of the cheese, cutting and patching as necessary.
   e. Spread a thin layer of anchovy mayonnaise on the salami.
   f. Arrange an even layer of roasted peppers on the mayonnaise, cutting and patching as necessary.
   g. Sprinkle the arugula or basil on the peppers in an even layer (A).
   h. Starting with the bottom edge, roll the tortillas and their toppings into tight roulades (B).
   i. Wrap each roulade in plastic film and place on a sheet tray lined with parchment. Refrigerate the roulades 20 minutes.

PROCEDURE

4. Remove the plastic film from the roulades. Place them on the cutting board seam-side down. Trim the rounded ends. Cut each roulade into 12 pinwheel slices, ½ in. (1.25 cm) thick (C).
5. Insert a cocktail pick into the side of each pinwheel, holding it closed at the seam.
6. Place the finished pinwheels on the sheet tray, cover the tray with plastic film, and refrigerate it (see Note).

HOLDING

Refrigerate up to 6 hours.

PRESENTATION

7. Arrange the pinwheels on a 14-in. (35-cm) round serving tray, overlapping, in a concentric circle, with the cocktail picks all pointing in the same direction.
8. Place the herb bouquet in the center of the tray.

Note: If service is within an hour of preparation, you may place the hors d'oeuvres directly on the tray and hold it refrigerated.

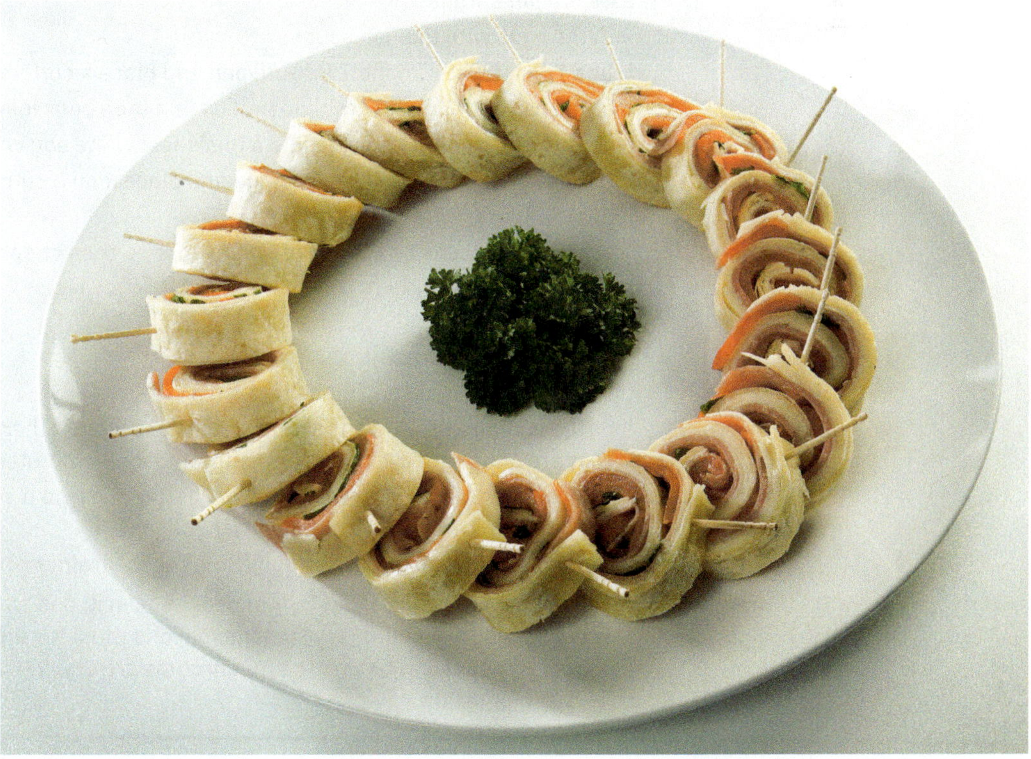

CHICKEN AND SHIITAKE MUSHROOM SUMMER ROLLS

HORS D'OEUVRE

Yield:
24 pieces

INGREDIENTS	U.S.	METRIC
Eggs	2	2
Thai or Vietnamese fish sauce	½ fl oz	15 mL
Peanut oil	1 fl oz	30 mL
Water	1 pt	0.5 L
Dried shiitake mushrooms	1 oz	30 g
Peanut oil	1 fl oz	30 mL
Sugar	1 tsp	5 mL
Japanese soy sauce	½ fl oz	15 mL
Asian roasted sesame oil	2 drops	2 drops
Cooked, shredded chicken breast	1 pt (about 10 oz)	0.5 L (about 300 g)
Asian Vinaigrette (p. 35)	4 fl oz	120 mL
7-in.(18-cm) round rice paper wrappers	24	24
Carrot, very fine julienne	4 oz	120 g
Scallions, shredded	2 oz	60 g
Sriracha sauce (optional)	1 fl oz	30 mL
4-in. (10-cm) Scallion ties (p. 715)	24	24
Nonstick pan coating	as needed	as needed
Décor		
Red chile lily (p. 716; prepare first)	1	1
Scallion brush (p. 716; prepare first)	1	1

PROCEDURE

PREPARATION

1. Prepare omelet shreds:
   a. Beat the eggs with the fish sauce.
   b. Heat a 12-in. (30-cm) nonstick sauté pan and place a cutting board near the stove.
   c. Coat the pan with ¼ fl oz (7 mL) peanut oil and then pour in half the egg mixture.
   d. Swirl the pan to spread the egg into a thin sheet. (The egg will set almost immediately.)
   e. Roll the egg sheet into a loose roulade and place it on a cutting board.
   f. Repeat with the remaining oil and egg.
   g. Cut the egg roulades crosswise into long shreds, then chop through the shreds a few times to make rough, 2-in. (5-cm) lengths.
2. Prepare mushroom shreds:
   a. Bring the water to the boil.
   b. Rinse the mushrooms and place them in a very small bowl.
   c. Pour the boiling water over the mushrooms and weight them down with a small plate so they are submerged. Soak the mushrooms for 20 minutes, or until softened.
   d. Drain the mushrooms, reserving the liquid. Remove and discard the stems. Rinse the mushroom caps and cut them into rough julienne.
   e. Strain the mushroom liquid through a fine mesh strainer or coffee filter.
   f. Heat a sauté pan, heat ½ fl oz (15 mL) peanut oil in it, and sauté the mushrooms about 30 seconds. Add the sugar, soy, sesame oil, and mushroom liquid. Stir and toss until the liquid is reduced away and the mushrooms are dry. Remove from the heat and cool to room temperature.

PROCEDURE

4. Toss the chicken with the Asian vinaigrette. Refrigerate until needed.
5. Prepare 1 or 2 rice paper wrappers at a time:
   a. Place the rice paper wrappers on a freshly sanitized work surface. Brush the top surfaces with cold water (A). Turn the papers over and brush the other side.
   b. Allow the papers to soften and become translucent. Brush with more water only if necessary.

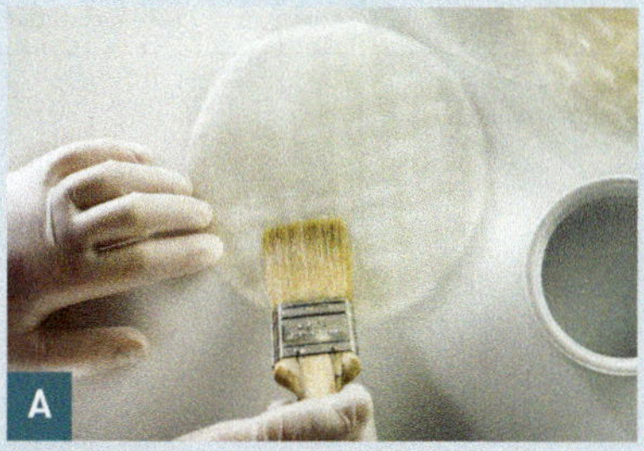
A

6. Assemble the summer rolls 1 or 2 at a time:
   a. Place a horizontal line of carrot and scallion across a wrapper about 1 in. (2.5 cm) away from the edge nearest you and ½ in. (1.25 cm) from the side edges.
   b. Place a line of mushrooms on top of the carrots and scallions.
   c. Place a line of chicken on top of the mushrooms.
   d. Squeeze a few small dots of the optional sriracha onto the chicken. (This sauce is spicy-hot.)
   e. Begin rolling the wrapper around the filling, and then fold the wrapper's sides over the filling (B). Continue rolling the wrapper around the filling into a tight cylinder.
   f. Decorate the summer roll with a scallion tie, tied around the middle of the cylinder.

B

7. Line a sheet tray with parchment and spray it very lightly with pan coating (see Note).
8. Transfer the summer rolls to the tray. Do not allow them to touch one another, or they will stick together. Cover the rolls with a clean, damp, lint-free towel, then wrap the tray with plastic film. Refrigerate the tray.

HOLDING

Refrigerate up to 24 hours.

PRESENTATION

10. Arrange the summer rolls on a 14-in. (35-cm) square or rectangular serving tray.
11. Place the red chile lily and scallion brush on a corner of the tray.

Note: If service is within 1–2 hours of preparation, you may omit steps 7 and 8. Place the summer rolls directly on the service tray, cover it, and hold it refrigerated.

VARIATIONS

Replace the chicken with diced, cooked shrimp, julienne Asian roast pork, or julienne pressed tofu.

TROPICAL SEAFOOD SKEWERS WITH MANGO DIP

HORS D'OEUVRE

Yield:
24 pieces

INGREDIENTS	U.S.	METRIC
Peeled fresh pineapple	12 oz	360 g
Red bell pepper	6 oz	180 g
Large scallions	4	4
51–60 ct. white shrimp in shell	1 lb	0.5 kg
Bay scallops	8 oz	240 g
Minced garlic	⅛ oz	3 g
Minced shallot	¼ oz	7 g
Chopped cilantro	1 tbsp	15 mL
Minced flat-leaf parsley	1 tbsp	15 mL
Minced lime zest	1 tbsp	15 mL
Minced orange zest	1 tbsp	15 mL
Seeded and minced Scotch bonnet chile	1–2 tsp	5–10 mL
Sugar	1 tsp	5 mL
Kosher salt	2 tsp	10 mL
Fresh lime juice	1 fl oz	30 mL
Fresh orange juice	1 fl oz	30 mL
Sugar	1 tsp	5 mL
Corn oil or peanut oil	3 fl oz	90 mL
Spicy Mango Sauce (p. 53)	8 fl oz	240 mL
Décor		
9 × 9-in. (23 × 23-cm) squares banana leaf (or 4–5 romaine leaves)	3	3
Supplies		
5-in. (12-cm) bamboo skewers	24	24

PROCEDURE

PREPARATION

1. Fabricate the produce:
   a. Cut the pineapple into 48 ½-in. (1.25-cm) cubes. Place it in a bowl with all of its juices.
   b. Cut the red bell pepper into 48 ⅜-in. (1-cm) cubes.
   c. Cut the solid white parts of the scallions into 48 ¼-in. (0.6-cm) lengths. Reserve the green parts.
2. Fabricate and marinate the seafood:
   a. Peel and devein the shrimp.
   b. Trim the tough side muscles from the scallops and discard them.
   c. Combine the remaining ingredients (except the mango sauce) and the juice from the pineapple in a nonreactive container to make the marinade. Taste the marinade and correct the seasoning.
   d. Mix the shrimp and scallops with the marinade, cover the container, and refrigerate them at least 30 minutes and no more than 1 hour.
3. Cook the seafood:
   a. Preheat a charcoal or gas grill very hot.

PROCEDURE

b. Thread the shrimp and scallops onto 1 or 2 metal skewers each.
c. Grill the seafood skewers about 30 seconds on each side, or until lightly marked and just cooked through.
d. Immediately transfer the skewers to the sheet tray and place the tray in the refrigerator for about 15 minutes, or until the seafood is cold.
e. Carefully remove the seafood from the metal skewers.

4. Assemble the hors d'oeuvre skewers:
   a. Place a pineapple cube on a bamboo skewer and slide it about halfway up the skewer's length.
   b. Add a red bell pepper square and push it against the pineapple cube.
   c. Add a scallion length and push it against the pepper.
   d. Place a scallop in the curl of a shrimp and stick the two together on the skewer. Push them against the pepper.
   e. Repeat, adding another pineapple cube, another pepper square, another scallion, and another scallop-in-a-shrimp. Adjust the food on the skewer so the skewer's point is covered and about 2½-in. (6-cm) of the handle is exposed.
   f. Place the seafood skewers back on the sheet tray, cover it with plastic film, and refrigerate it (see Note).

PRESENTATION

5. Arrange the tray:
   a. Line a 14-in. (35-cm) tray with the banana leaves or romaine leaves.
   b. Place a 10-fl oz (300-mL) ramekin in the center and fill it with the mango sauce.
   c. Arrange the seafood skewers, handle out, around the tray.

Note: If service is within 1–2 hours of preparation, you may omit step 4f. Place the skewers directly on the service tray, cover it, and hold it refrigerated.

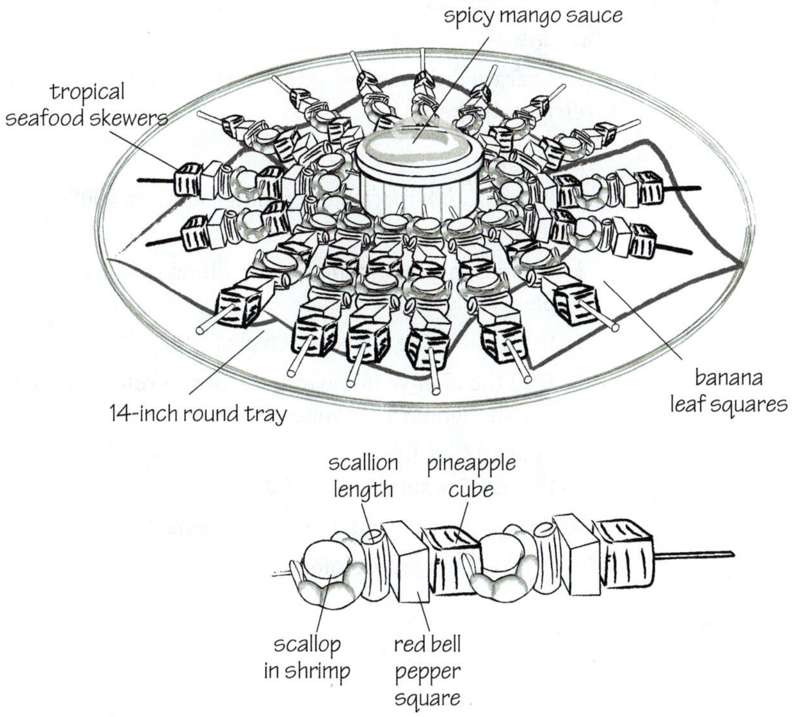

CHÈVRE AND SUN-DRIED TOMATO PROFITEROLES

HORS D'OEUVRE

Yield:
24 pieces

INGREDIENTS	U.S.	METRIC
Sun-dried tomatoes	1 oz	30 g
Cream cheese, room temperature	5 oz	150 g
Full-flavored goat cheese, room temperature	5 oz	150 g
Chopped fresh basil leaves	½ oz	15 g
Hors d'Oeuvre Profiterole Shells (p. 706)	24	24
Décor		
12-in. (30-cm) white doily	1	1
Tomato rose (p. 716)	1	1
Flat-leaf parsley sprigs	3	3
Grape tomatoes, each sliced to make 4 rounds	6	6
Tiny basil leaves	24	24

PROCEDURE

PREPARATION

1. Soak the sun-dried tomatoes about 20 minutes in boiling water to soften them and remove some of the salt. Drain the tomatoes and squeeze them dry.
2. Fabricate the sun-dried tomatoes into brunoise cuts.
3. In a mixer fitted with the paddle attachment, beat together the cream cheese, goat cheese, sun-dried tomatoes, and basil.
4. Transfer the cheese mixture to a pastry bag fitted with a small plain tip. Hold at cool room temperature no longer than 2 hours. If holding longer, instead place the cheese in a covered container and refrigerate it.

HOLDING

Refrigerate the cheese mixture up to 5 days. Freeze the profiteroles up to 1 month. (Do not refrigerate them.)

FINISHING AND PRESENTATION

5. If necessary, recrisp the profiteroles in a 400°F (200°C) oven and cool them to room temperature.
6. If necessary, bring the cheese filling mixture to room temperature and put it in the pastry bag.
7. Cut a slit in the side of each profiterole.
8. Pipe the cheese filling into the profiteroles through the slit. Use a paper towel or clean, dry kitchen towel to wipe off any filling visible on the exterior.
9. Line a 14-in. (35-cm) tray with the doily. Place the tomato rose in the center and arrange the parsley sprigs around it.
10. Garnish each profiterole with a tomato slice and a basil leaf.
11. Arrange the profiteroles on the tray.

VARIATIONS

GARLIC-HERB CHEESE PROFITEROLES

Replace the goat cheese mixture with Garlic-Herb Cheese Spread (p. 594).

LIPTAUER CHEESE PROFITEROLES

Replace the goat cheese mixture with Liptauer Cheese (p. 595). Replace the basil leaf garnish with parsley or chervil pluches.

LIVER PARFAIT PROFITEROLES

Replace the goat cheese mixture with Poultry Liver Parfait (p. 265). Replace the grape tomato slice garnish with sliced red grapes. Replace the basil leaf garnish with parsley or chervil pluches.

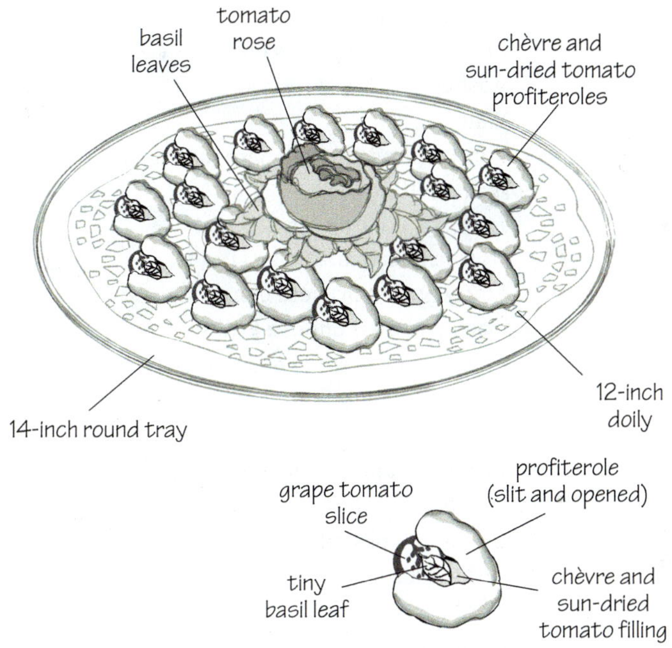

ASSORTED MINI-QUICHES: HAM AND CARAMELIZED ONION, LORRAINE, SPINACH AND GOAT CHEESE, CRAB AND CAVIAR

HORS D'OEUVRE

Yield:
48 pieces

INGREDIENTS	U.S.	METRIC
1½-in. (4-cm) *Hors d'Oeuvre Pastry Shells* (p. 705 or commercial)	48	48
Ham and Caramelized Onion Filling		
Butter	1 oz	30 g
Finely chopped yellow onion	10 oz	300 g
Kosher salt	to taste	to taste
Water	as needed	as needed
Full-flavored smoked ham, brunoise	2 oz	60 g
Lorraine Filling		
Bacon (p. 451), or commercial slab bacon, brunoise	2 oz	60 g
Finely grated Gruyère cheese	4 oz	120 g
Spinach and Goat Cheese Filling		
Full-flavored goat cheese, frozen	2 oz	60 g
Butter	½ oz	15 mL
Minced shallots	1 tbsp (¼ oz)	15 mL (7 g)
Cooked chopped spinach	4 oz	120 g
Crab and Caviar Filling		
Crabmeat, picked over	3 oz	90 g
Red tobiko caviar	1 oz	30 g
Custard		
Eggs	2	2
Half-and-half	12 oz	360 mL
Finely ground white pepper	to taste	to taste

PROCEDURE

PREPARATION

1. Arrange the tartlet shells on a sheet tray lined with parchment in 4 rows of 12 shells each.
2. Prepare the ham and caramelized onion filling:
   a. Place the butter, onions, and salt in a 12-in. (30-cm) nonstick pan and cook them over low heat, stirring often, until the onions wilt and begin to brown. Add water as needed to deglaze the pan and keep the color even. When the onions are a rich caramel brown, cook them dry and correct the salt. Cool the onions to room temperature.
   b. Divide the ham among 12 tartlet shells and top with the onions.
3. Prepare the Lorraine filling:
   a. Place the bacon in a small nonstick sauté pan over low heat.
   b. Fry the bacon slowly until it renders out most of its fat and becomes slightly crisp.
   c. Pour the bacon and fat through a strainer set in a bowl. Discard the fat or reserve it for another use.
   d. Divide the bacon among 12 of the shells and top with the Gruyère.

PROCEDURE

4. Prepare the spinach and goat cheese filling:
   a. Cut the goat cheese into 12 cubes and place a cube in each of 12 tartlet shells.
   b. Heat the butter in a small sauté pan, add the shallots, and sauté a few seconds, or until fragrant. Add the spinach and a pinch of salt. Sauté until the liquid reduces away and the spinach is well seasoned. Cool to room temperature.
   c. Flatten the thawed goat cheese into the shells and top with the spinach.
5. Prepare the crab and caviar filling:
   a. Divide the crabmeat among the remaining 12 tartlet shells.
   b. Place the caviar on top.
6. Preheat an oven to 325°F (162°C).
7. Prepare the custard: Whisk the eggs until well beaten, then whisk in the half-and-half. Season the custard mixture with salt and white pepper.
8. Strain the custard mixture and pour it into a 16-oz (0.5-L) squeeze bottle.
9. Slowly and carefully fill each tartlet shell with custard mixture. Do not allow the custard to overflow the shells. Wait a few minutes for the custard mixture to settle and then top off the shells as necessary.
10. Bake the mini-quiches 15–20 minutes, or until the custard is set and the tops are golden.
11. Cool the quiches to room temperature.

HOLDING

Hold at cool room temperature up to 2 hours. If necessary, refrigerate up to 24 hours.

FINISHING AND PRESENTATION

12. If necessary, rewarm the quiches in a standard or countertop oven.
13. Arrange the mini-quiches in neat, even rows on one or more square or rectangular serving trays. Each row should contain only one type of quiche.

VARIATIONS

Vary the quiche fillings as desired. Fillings must be fully cooked or ready to eat, full-flavored, fabricated into small size, and not be so moist as to dilute the custard.

SCALLOP SEVICHE IN PHYLLO CUPS

[sev-EE chay or seb EE chay]

HORS D'OEUVRE

Yield:
24 pieces

INGREDIENTS	U.S.	METRIC
Chives (see Note)	1 bunch (3 oz total)	1 bunch (90 g total)
Scallop Seviche Base (p. 210), made with small diced scallops	1 lb	0.5 kg
Extra-virgin olive oil	2 fl oz	60 mL
Tomato puree	1 tbsp	15 mL
Fresh lemon juice	to taste	to taste
Small, firm grape tomatoes	8	8
Phyllo Cups (p. 706)	24	24
Chiffonnade romaine hearts	2 oz	60 g

Note: Only a small amount of the chives will be used; reserve the rest for another use.

PROCEDURE

PREPARATION

1. Line up the tips of the chives even and cut off a ¾-in. (2-cm) length from the bunch. You will need about 72 chive tips. (If you do not have enough pointed tips, cut the remaining bunch of chives on a very sharp diagonal to create pointed ends, and then cut ¾-in. (2-cm) lengths from them.)
2. Mix the seviche base with the olive oil, tomato purée, and lemon juice.

HOLDING

Hold the seviche and chives in the refrigerator for no more than 6 hours. Hold the phyllo cups at cool room temperature in a tightly sealed plastic container up to 24 hours.

FINISHING AND PRESENTATION

3. Cut each tomato into 3 oval slices, discarding the ends.
4. Assemble the phyllo cups:
   a. Line the bottom of each phyllo cup with a bed of chiffonnade romaine.
   b. Fill each with lined phyllo cup with a heaping tablespoon (20 mL) seviche.
   c. Lean a cherry tomato slice against the side of each cup's rim.
   d. For each phyllo cup, bundle together 3 chive tips and stick them through the tomato to stand upright out of the cup.
5. Place the phyllo cups in neat, even rows on a presentation mirror.

VARIATIONS

POISSON CRU IN PHYLLO CUPS

Replace the seviche with Poisson Cru (p. 211).

TUNA TARTARE IN PHYLLO CUPS

Replace the seviche with Tuna Tartare (p. 230). Add a tiny avocado wedge dipped in lemon juice to the garnish.

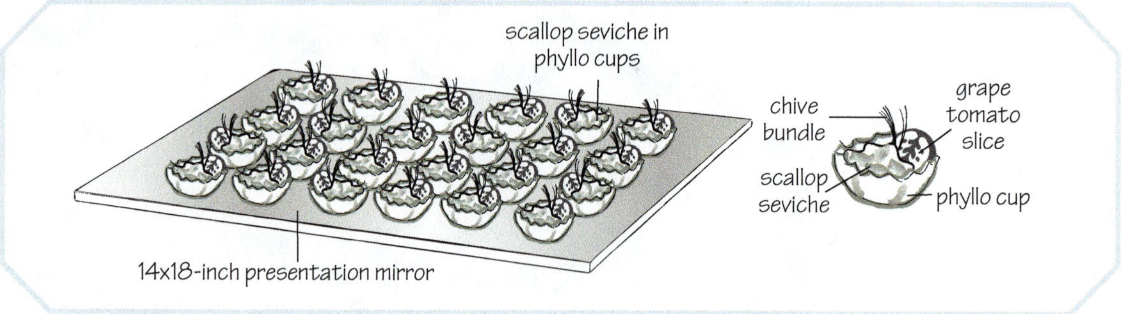

PREPARING CANAPÉS

As you learned earlier in this chapter, canapés are miniature open-face sandwiches having three basic elements:

- A *base* consisting of bread, toast, or sometimes a flat pastry shape
- A *filling* or *topping* consisting of a spread or complex salad, or a spread topped with a solid ingredient
- A *garnish* or garnishes

Canapés are a special type of hors d'oeuvre whose preparation requires skill and attention to detail. Of all hors d'oeuvres, they demand the greatest precision.

Canapé Shapes and Sizes

Canapés should be bite-sized, or two-bite-sized at most. Their dimensions usually range from 1 to 1½ in. (2.5 to 4 cm) across or in diameter, with 2 in. (5 cm) being the largest acceptable size. Canapés may be cut with a knife into squares, diamonds, triangles, or long rectangles called *fingers*. Alternatively, they may be punched out with cutters into rounds, crescents, hearts, and other decorative shapes. When preparing canapés, a clean, freshly sanitized ruler is an essential piece of equipment.

Canapé Garnishes

In addition to the bread-like base and the filling or topping, most canapés are finished with a small garnish item. Many foods are attractive enough to be used as canapé garnishes in their natural form. In addition to these natural-looking garnishes, you may also use ***hors d'oeuvre cutters*** (p. 16) to punch diamonds, hearts, stars, and other shapes out of colorful foods such as roasted red peppers and slices of ham. When planning a canapé garnish, remember that the garnish food must complement the flavor of the canapé as well as make it look attractive. For some very formal canapés, the fillings and garnishes are coated with clear aspic.

To achieve a neat, professional look, make sure the garnishes you place on your canapés are all exactly uniform in size, shape, and color. Canapé garnishes can be glued to the filling with a dot or rosette of a complementary spread.

Constructing Canapés

There are two basic methods for constructing canapés:

- Slab construction method
- Individual construction method

Slab Construction

The slab construction method uses large, thin, horizontal slices of crustless bread cut from Pullman loaves (p. 311) or other pan loaves. The slices are prepared as illustrated on page 400. The bread slabs are first covered with a thin, even layer of the designated spread. When mass-producing large numbers of slab canapés, it is fast and efficient to apply the spread with a speed icer, or a pastry bag fitted with a large basketweave tip, as illustrated on page 400. After they are spread, the slabs are then topped with the designated filling and cut into pieces of the desired shape. With this method you can make many canapés at one time. Although the slab method is fast and efficient, it does create some waste because it results in scraps. This is especially true when the canapés are punched out with a cutter. You should not use the slab method if the spread or filling is costly.

Preparing bread for slab construction.

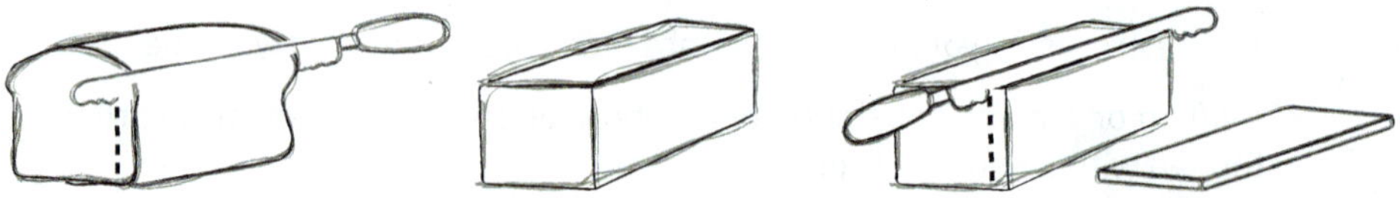

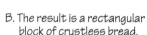

A. Use a serrated knife to remove all crust.

B. The result is a rectangular block of crustless bread.

C. Slice the bread into wide, thin slabs.

Procedure for Constructing Canapés by the Slab Method

A

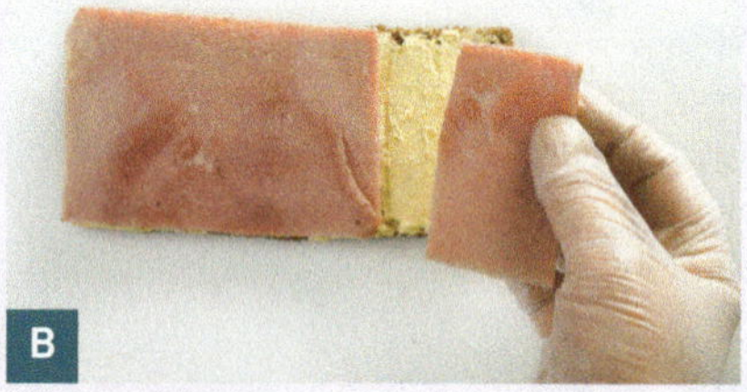

B

C

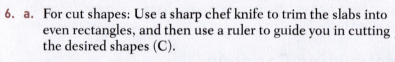

1. Prepare bread slabs as shown above. As you work, keep the slabs covered with damp towels to prevent drying.
2. If the canapés are to be based on toast, place the bread slabs on a rack set in a sheet tray and bake in a hot oven or broil until golden brown on both sides. Cool to room temperature pressed between two racks to flatten them.
3. Apply a thin, even layer of spread to the bread slabs, making sure the spread extends to the edges. Use a speed icer, or pastry bag fitted with a large basketweave tip, to apply the spread (A), then smooth it with an offset spatula.
4. Apply the filling or topping to the slabs in a thin, even layer, making sure the filling extends to the edges or slightly beyond (B). Press gently to firm.
5. Place the filled or topped slabs on a sheet tray, cover with plastic wrap, and refrigerate or freeze until the spread is firm enough to cut neatly.
6. a. For cut shapes: Use a sharp chef knife to trim the slabs into even rectangles, and then use a ruler to guide you in cutting the desired shapes (C).

   b. For punched-out shapes: Punch out with a sharp cutter and discard the scraps.
7. Using a large offset spatula, transfer the canapés to a sheet tray lined with parchment. Place them in neat, even rows.
8. Use food-service tweezers to apply the garnish(es) to the canapés. If there are multiple garnishes, use the production line method. In other words, place all of the bottom garnishes on all of the canapés first, then place all of the middle items, then all of the top items. Do not complete the garnishing of one canapé at a time, as this is not efficient.
9. Wrap the sheet tray in plastic film and refrigerate the canapés until you are ready to place them on their serving trays.

Individual Construction

The individual construction method is used when the canapés are based on croûtons or slices of baguette, or on pastry shapes. It may also be used for shapes cut from pan loaf slabs. The individual method is slower and less efficient than the slab method. It should be used for pan loaf canapés only if the spread or filling ingredients are so costly that a even small amount of waste would substantially increase food cost.

Procedure for Constructing Canapés by the Individual Method

1. If necessary, cut or size the filling items to fit the bases.
2. a. If using Pullman or loaf bread, prepare bread slabs. If using baguette, slice it into rounds or ovals of the desired thickness.
   b. If the canapé is to be based on toasted bread, place the bread slabs or baguette slices on a rack set on a sheet tray and bake in a hot oven or broil until golden brown on both sides. To prevent curling, weight with another rack.
3. If using pan loaf slabs, cut or punch out into desired shapes.
4. Using a small offset spatula, apply a thin, even layer of spread to each individual canapé base. Place each base on a parchment-lined sheet tray as it is completed.
5. Apply the filling ingredients to each individual canapé base.
6. Apply the garnishes to the canapés using the production line method, described in step 8 of the Procedure for Constructing Canapés by the Slab Method (p. 400).
7. Wrap the sheet tray in plastic film and refrigerate the canapés until you are ready to place them on their serving trays.

Bruschette

Bruschette (broo-SKET-teh) are a special type of canapé that originated with Italian cuisine. The name ***bruschetta*** (singular form) comes from the Italian word *bruscare,* meaning "to cook over coals." The original bruschette were made by toasting thick slices of rustic bread over the coals of a wood fire, giving them a smoky taste. The warm toast slices were then rubbed with crushed garlic cloves and finally drizzled with extra-virgin olive oil. These are bruschette in their purest form.

Today bruschette are most frequently topped with vegetable salads dressed with olive oil, including peeled, diced tomatoes; roasted peppers; braised, chopped broccoli rabe; cooked dried beans; or chopped sautéed mushrooms. Bruschette can also be topped with thin-sliced cured meats and sausages, such as prosciutto and salami. They are less frequently topped with seafood or seafood salads. Cheese toppings are a recent innovation.

HAM AND CORNICHON CANAPÉS

HORS D'OEUVRE

Yield:
42 pieces

INGREDIENTS	U.S.	METRIC
Crustless rye bread slabs, 3 × 7 × ⅛-in. (7 × 17 × 0.3-cm) each	2	2
Mustard Butter (p. 563), room temperature	6 fl oz	180 mL
Deli-style smoked ham, cut in 2 slices, 3 × 7 × ⅛-in. (7 × 17 × 0.3-cm) each	4 oz	120 g
Cornichon fans, see photo	48	48

PROCEDURE

PREPARATION

1. Follow the Procedure for Constructing Canapés by the Slab Method (p. 400), spreading the two bread slabs with 5 fl oz (150 mL) of the mustard butter. It is important to spread the butter to the very ends of the bread slabs
2. Arrange the ham slices on the slabs and press gently to help them adhere. If necessary, you may piece slices together to cover the bread slabs.
3. Place the remaining mustard butter in a pastry bag fitted with a small round tip and hold at room temperature while the spread and filled slabs harden in the freezer.
4. Trim the edges of the slabs, then cut each slab into 21 1 × 1-in. (2.5 × 2.5-cm) squares.
5. Pipe a small dot of mustard butter near one corner of each square.
6. Place a cornichon fan on each square, pressing the base of the fan into the butter (see photo).

HOLDING

Cover with plastic film and refrigerate up to 4 hours.

PRESENTATION

7. Arrange the canapés in straight, neat rows on a 14 × 20-in. (35 × 50-cm) rectangular tray or presentation mirror.

VARIATIONS

ROAST BEEF AND HORSERADISH CANAPÉS

Replace the rye bread with firm white bread. Replace the mustard butter with cream cheese flavored with horseradish. Replace the ham with medium-rare roast beef. Replace the cornichons with thin slices of grape tomato and diagonal-cut scallions.

SMOKED TURKEY AND RASPBERRY CANAPÉS

Replace the rye bread with firm white or whole wheat bread. Replace the mustard butter with Raspberry Butter (p. 563). Replace the ham with deli smoked turkey. Replace the cornichons with a fresh raspberries and chervil pluches.

SMOKED SALMON AND DILL BUTTER CANAPÉS

Replace the rye bread with pumpernickel bread. Replace the mustard butter with Dill Butter (p. 563). Replace the ham with thin-sliced smoked salmon (you will need to piece the irregular salmon slices together on the slabs). Replace the cornichons with dill pluches.

WALNUT AND SMOKED TURKEY PARFAIT CANAPÉS

HORS D'OEUVRE

Yield:
40 pieces

INGREDIENTS	U.S.	METRIC
Crustless firm white bread slabs, 3 × 7 × ⅛-in. (7 cm × 17 × 0.3-cm) each, toasted and cooled	4	4
Smoked Turkey Parfait (p. 265), room temperature	12 fl oz	360 mL
Minced parsley, dried by wringing in a towel	1 cup	240 mL
Strained English sweet mango chutney, such as Major Grey's	7 fl oz	210 mL
Small walnut halves, toasted and cooled	40	40

PROCEDURE

PREPARATION

1. Follow the Procedure for Constructing Canapés by the Individual Method (p. 401), spreading with the parfait and using a 1⅜-in. (3.5-cm) round cutter to punch out 40 rounds.
2. Roll the edges of the rounds in the minced parsley and tap off any excess.
3. Spoon 1 tsp (5 mL) chutney in the center of each round.
4. Press 1 walnut half on each canapé.

HOLDING

Cover with plastic film and refrigerate up to 4 hours.

PRESENTATION

5. Arrange the canapés on a 16-in. (40-cm) round presentation mirror or other tray.

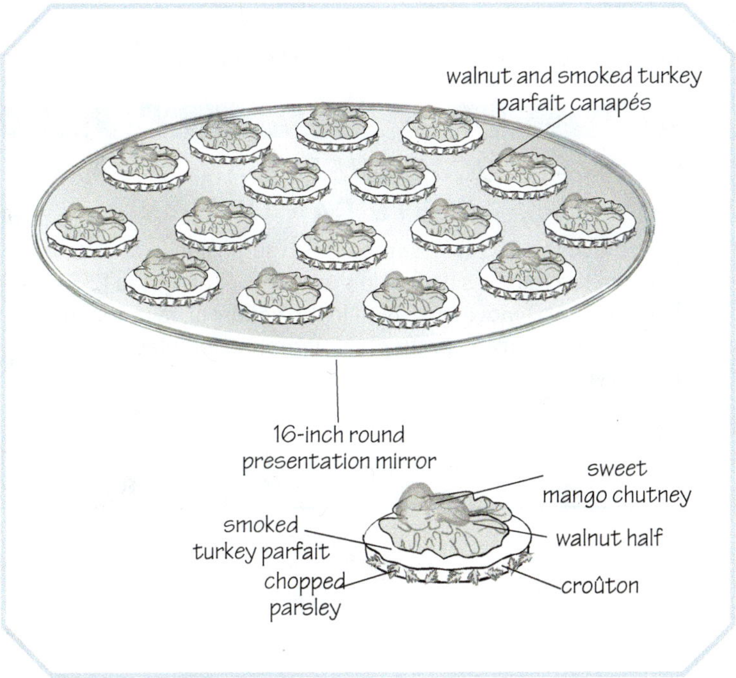

VARIATIONS

LIVER PARFAIT AND SHALLOT CANAPÉS

Replace the smoked turkey parfait with Poultry Liver Parfait (p. 265). Replace the parsley with minced chives. Omit the chutney and walnuts. Press a slice of pink shallot onto the parfait. Pipe a small rosette of mayonnaise on the shallot slice. Place a round of scallion on the rosette.

SALMON MOUSSE AND SMOKED SALMON CANAPÉS

Replace the white toast with 2 3 × 7 × ⅛-in. (7 cm × 17 × 0.3-cm) crustless pumpernickel bread slabs. Replace the smoked turkey parfait with Salmon Mousse (p. 216). Freeze the slabs and then cut into triangles. Garnish each triangle with a small smoked salmon rose made in the same way as a tomato rose and a dill pluche.

ROQUEFORT AND FLAME GRAPE CANAPÉS

HORS D'OEUVRE

Yield:
40 pieces

INGREDIENTS	U.S.	METRIC
Roquefort cheese, room temperature	10 oz	300 g
Cream cheese, room temperature	10 oz	300 g
Small Flame (or other seedless red-skinned) grapes	20 (2 oz total)	20 (60 g total)
Firm white bread slabs, 3 × 7 × ⅛-in. (7 cm × 17 × 0.3-cm) each, toasted and cooled	4	4
Micro green or parsley pluches	40	40

PROCEDURE

PREPARATION

1. Prepare Roquefort spread:
   a. Place the Roquefort and cream cheese in a mixer fitted with the paddle attachment. Blend on medium speed until combined.
   b. Place the Roquefort spread in a pastry bag fitted with a medium star tip.
2. Cut the grapes lengthwise into 80 slices, 1/16-in. (0.15-cm) thick. Discard the end pieces.
3. Using a 1⅜-in. (3.5-cm) round cutter, punch 40 rounds out of the toast slabs.
4. Pipe a rosette of Roquefort spread onto each toast round.
5. Stick 2 grape slices upright out of the center of each rosette.
6. Using food-service tweezers, stick a micro greens or parsley pluche in front of the grapes on each canapé.

HOLDING

Cover with plastic film and refrigerate up to 2 hours.

PRESENTATION

7. Arrange the canapés on a 14-in. (35-cm) round serving tray or presentation mirror.

VARIATIONS

LIPTAUER CHEESE CANAPÉS

Replace the Roquefort spread with Liptauer Cheese (p. 595). Replace the grapes with radishes. Replace the chervil with chive tips.

PORT WINE CHEDDAR AND APPLE CANAPÉS

Replace the Roquefort spread with Port Wine Cheddar (p. 593). Replace the grapes with a red-skinned apple cut into tiny wedges.

GOAT CHEESE AND PESTO CANAPÉS

Replace the Roquefort spread with soft fresh goat cheese. Make the rosettes hollow in the center. Place ½ tsp (2.5 mL) Pesto alla Genovese (p. 688) in the center of each rosette. Replace the grapes with grape tomatoes. Replace the chervil with basil.

STEAK TARTARE CANAPÉS

HORS D'OEUVRE

Yield:
about 40 pieces

INGREDIENTS	U.S.	METRIC
Firm white bread slabs, 3 × 7 × ⅛ in. (7 × 17 × 0.3 cm) each, toasted and cooled	4	4
Whipped unsalted butter, room temperature	4 fl oz	120 mL
Steak Tartare (p. 262)	20 oz	600 g
Extra-virgin olive oil	1 tbsp	15 mL
Minced chives	1 tbsp	15 mL

PROCEDURE

PREPARATION

1. Using a 1⅜-in. (3.5-cm) round cutter, punch 40 rounds out of the toast slabs.
2. Spread each toast round with a thin, even layer of butter. Place the rounds on a sheet tray lined with parchment.
3. Refrigerate 10 minutes, or until the butter is firm.
4. Using a #80 (½ fl oz/15 mL) portion scoop, place a mound of steak tartare on each toast round.
5. Gently flatten each mound of steak tartare so it covers the toast round and adheres to it.
6. Brush the steak tartare with a light coating of olive oil.
7. Place a tiny dot of chives in the center of each canapé.

HOLDING

Cover with plastic film and refrigerate no longer than 2 hours.

PRESENTATION

8. Arrange the canapés on a 14 × 20-in. (35 × 50-cm) rectangular or oval presentation mirror.

VARIATIONS

TUNA TARTARE CANAPÉS

Replace the steak tartare with Tuna Tartare (p. 230).

CRAB SALAD CANAPÉS

Replace the plain whipped butter with Maître d'Hôtel Butter (p. 563). Replace the steak tartare with Classic Crab Salad (p. 160). Omit the olive oil. Replace the chives with red tobiko caviar.

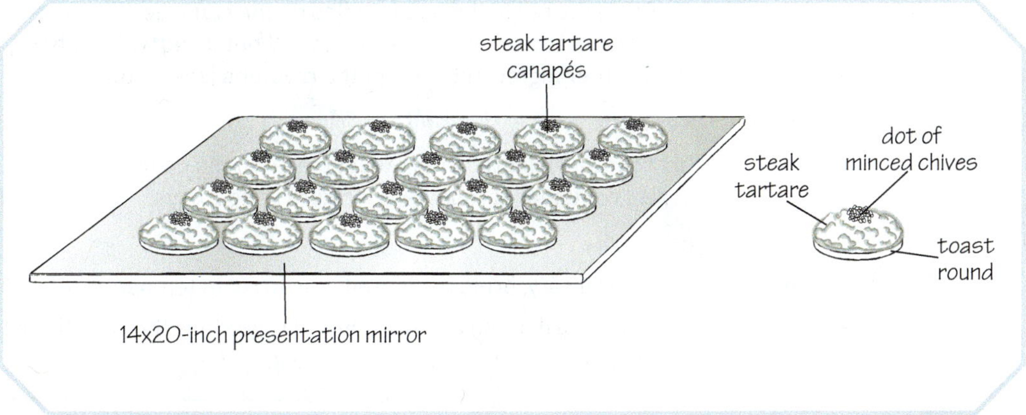

ITALIAN SAUSAGE AND PEPPER BITES

HORS D'OEUVRE

Yield:
24 pieces

INGREDIENTS	U.S.	METRIC
Sweet Italian Sausage (p. 499), or commercial Italian sausage, in rope form	1 lb	0.5 kg
Olive oil	½ fl oz	15 mL
Firm, high-quality white bread, unsliced	6 oz	180 g
Red bell peppers, 7 oz (210 g) each	3	3
Yellow bell pepper, 7 oz (210 g) each	1	1
Marinara sauce, cold	2 fl oz	60 mL
Décor		
12-in. (30-cm) greaseproof doily	1	1
Red chile lily (p. 716)	1	1
Curly parsley sprigs	3	3

PROCEDURE

PREPARATION

1. Cook the sausage:
   a. Poach the sausage as directed in the Procedure for Poaching Sausages, steps 1–6, on page 493.
   b. Add the olive oil to a heated sauté pan and sauté the sausages until the casings are golden brown.
   c. Cool the sausages to room temperature on a rack, and then cover and refrigerate them until they are cold.
2. Prepare the croûtons:
   a. Slice the bread thin.
   b. Toast the bread light golden brown and then cool it on a rack.
   c. Use a round cutter to punch out discs of toast the same diameter as the sausage.
3. Fabricate, roast, and peel the peppers as directed in the Procedure for Roasting Peppers on page 109.
4. Trim the ragged ends of the sausages. Cut the sausage into 24 ⅜-in. (1.25-cm) slices. Place the slices on a sheet tray lined with parchment.
5. Use the round cutter to punch out 24 circles of roasted red bell pepper. Use a ½-in. (1-cm) star-shaped hors d'oeuvre cutter to punch out 24 yellow bell pepper stars.
6. Place the red bell pepper circles on the sausage slices, then place the yellow pepper stars on the circles. Cover the tray. If not using within 1 hour, refrigerate the sausage and all other ingredients except the croûtons (see Note).

HOLDING

Refrigerate all ingredients except the croûtons up to 2 days. Hold the croûtons in a tightly sealed container at room temperature up to 2 days.

PRESENTATION

7. If necessary, bring the ingredients to room temperature.
8. Place the doily on a 14-in. (35-cm) tray. Place the chile lily in the center of the tray and arrange the parsley sprigs around it.

PROCEDURE

9. Spread each croûton with a dab of marinara sauce and top with a garnished sausage slice.
10. Arrange the sausage and pepper bites on the tray.

Note: If service is within an hour of preparation, you may place the assembled hors d'oeuvres directly on the lined and decorated service tray, cover it, and hold it refrigerated.

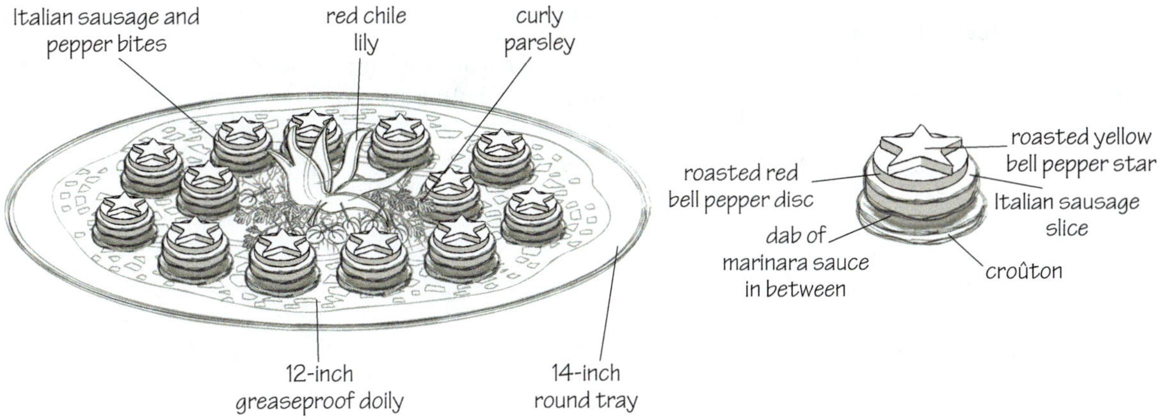

TERMS FOR REVIEW

hors d'oeuvre
butler service
passed hors d'oeuvre
buffet (hors d'oeuvre) service
stationary hors d'oeuvre
cold hors d'oeuvre
hot hors d'oeuvre
heated hors d'oeuvre
amuse-bouche
stuffed hors d'oeuvre
wrapped hors d'oeuvre
rolled hors d'oeuvre
roulade
spoon hors d'oeuvre
sip
picked hors d'oeuvre
skewered hors d'oeuvre
hors d'oeuvre kebab
pastry hors d'oeuvre
blind bake
crudités
canapé
décor
cocktail
apéritif
hors d'oeuvre cutters
bruschetta

QUESTIONS FOR DISCUSSION

1. List the six characteristics of successful hors d'oeuvres.
2. List the five major construction types of hors d'oeuvres and describe each type.
3. Discuss the options available to garde manger chefs in selecting presentation ware for both passed and stationary hors d'oeuvres.
4. List the four elements of hors d'oeuvre tray design. Explain how these four elements work together to make a successful presentation.
5. Discuss guidelines for butler service of hors d'oeuvres.
6. List the three elements of a canapé and give examples of each.
7. List and describe the two methods of canapé construction.
8. Using your imagination and the information you have learned in this chapter, write a recipe for a cold hors d'oeuvre of your own creation.

Chapter 11

PREREQUISITES

Before studying this chapter, you should already

- Have read "How to Use this Book," pp. xxviii–xxxiii, and understand the professional recipe format.
- Know how to accurately scale up and scale down recipe formula amounts.
- Know how to accurately weigh ingredients using both a spring scale and a digital scale.
- Be able to correctly fabricate various cuts of meat, poultry, and seafood.
- Be able to create and maintain accurate records of the times and temperatures involved in food production.

Cured and Smoked Foods

Our ancestors, faced with the challenge of preserving meats, poultry, and fish in the days before refrigeration, used several methods of preserving food that were handed down from generation to generation. Of these, the most basic method is curing with salt. The art of smoking is also a preserving technique that dates to prehistoric times. Today, smoking is used not so much for its preservative qualities as for the flavors it gives to some of our favorite foods.

In this chapter, we also take a brief look at another time-honored food preservation technique adapted here to modern dishes: sealing cooked foods from the air by covering them with a layer of fat. This technique is used with both cured and uncured meats.

After you read this chapter, you should be able to

1. Explain the scientific principles involved in curing foods.
2. Prepare the two basic types of curing compounds, and use nitrite/nitrate curing mixes safely and effectively.
3. Identify appropriate meats, poultry, and seafood for curing, and choose the most appropriate curing compounds for each.
4. Use both the dry cure and brine cure methods to cure meats, poultry, and seafood.
5. Describe the results when wood smoke is applied to cured foods.
6. Explain the science of smoking.
7. Select smoking equipment appropriate for your operation's product list, sales volume, and budget.
8. Prepare smoked products by both the hot smoking and cold smoking methods.
9. Prepare various types of confit and other traditional and modern foods sealed in fat.

UNDERSTANDING CURING

The History of Charcuterie

This chapter begins our discussion of charcuterie, a specialized discipline within the garde manger profession. Chapters 12 and 13 also focus on charcuterie topics.

The word *charcuterie* is derived from the French words *chair*, meaning "flesh," and *cuit*, meaning "cooked." This term dates from the late Middle Ages in Europe. As the feudal aristocracy became less powerful, and an urban middle class began to develop. In towns and cities, cooks and other artisans begin opening shops, and organized themselves into guilds. Similar to modern trade associations, medieval guilds developed the apprenticeship system and controlled the production and prices of goods.

The guilds encouraged specialization, and strictly defined the types of products and services a particular trade was permitted to offer. Within the culinary guilds, for example, artisans who sold raw food products were not permitted to sell cooked foods. The sale of raw meat products was restricted to the *boucher*, or butcher. Cooked meats were sold by the *charcutier*, or seller of cooked flesh. Thus, **charcuterie** is the preparation of cooked meat products, today referring specifically to cured and smoked products, sausages, and pâtés.

To ***cure*** means to treat a food with salt, making it less hospitable to bacteria, molds, and other harmful microorganisms and thus delaying spoilage. Virtually all foods, including vegetables and cheeses, can be preserved with salt. The information presented here broadly pertains to all types of animal flesh, including domestic meat, wild game meat, domestic poultry and game birds, and various types of fish and shellfish. We refer to all of these as *meat*.

How Curing Works

Harmful organisms such as bacteria and molds need water to live and grow. Because salt is strongly attracted to water, it acts as a food preservative by making water unavailable to bacteria in two ways:

1. *Salt applied to the surface of a food removes much of the water from it.* Heavily salt a piece of meat or fish and let it stand. Soon it will be sitting in a puddle of its own juices.
2. *Some salt is absorbed into the food.* This salt bonds strongly with the remaining moisture in the food so it cannot be absorbed and used by microorganisms.

As a result, meats cured with salt keep longer than unsalted meats.

In addition to helping foods last longer, the curing process also changes their texture. Salt makes foods denser and more fine-grained than in their original state. Some cured foods undergo further drying after the cure is complete. As the drying process continues, these cured products become even denser in texture, smaller in size, and lighter in weight, and their flavor becomes more concentrated.

Today, many foods are cured under refrigeration, and most are stored in the refrigerator after the cure is complete. Therefore, today less salt is used in curing mixtures and, thus, modern cured meats are less salty than traditional cured meats.

Types of Cured Foods

Cured foods are prepared and served in several ways.

- Some are ready to eat as soon as the curing process is complete. Gravlax, or cured salmon, is an example.
- Some cured foods are cooked, typically by the consumer, after they are cured. Pancetta, or Italian unsmoked bacon, is an example.
- Other cured foods are dried after they are cured or during the curing process. Some of these are then eaten in their dry form without any cooking. Jerky, prosciutto, and dry sausages, such as salami and soppressata, are examples of this category.
- Other cured and dried foods are fully or partially rehydrated by soaking them in water before they are eaten. This also removes some of the salt. These foods are usually cooked after they are soaked. Salt cod and the country hams of the American South are good examples.
- Some cured foods are further preserved by cooking and storing them in fat after they are cured. Confit (p. 457) is an example.

- Some meats and poultry are lightly cured to season them before they are grilled or roasted. These cures are for flavor only and, while they will slightly increase refrigerated holding times, do not preserve the foods to which they are applied.
- Finally, curing is the first step in smoking.

Curing Compounds

A ***curing compound*** (sometimes simply called a *cure*) is a salt-based mixture of ingredients that usually contains flavoring ingredients, such as sugar, spices, and herbs. Some cures include additional preserving agents as well. There are two ways in which a curing compound can be applied to foods.

Dry Cures

As the name implies, a ***dry cure*** is based on dry salt and other dry ingredients that are ground or pulverized into a granular or powdered form. A dry cure is sometimes called a ***rub*** because the dry salt and seasonings are rubbed into the meat.

Plain, granular salt is the simplest dry cure of all. However, using salt alone as a curing agent can result in a harsh taste, and it does not impart any special flavoring to the food. Thus, sugar, spices, herbs, and other dry flavorings are usually mixed into a dry cure.

Dry cures are applied to the surface of most meats, poultry, or fish by rubbing or massaging them into the flesh. Because they take time to penetrate, the product is usually refrigerated, or held in temperature-controlled, humidity-controlled cooling rooms, during the curing process.

When a food item having a low water content is treated with a dry cure and then hung or stored in a perforated container, the item remains relatively dry. However, if a food item treated with a dry cure has a high water content and the item is stored in a solid container, the dry curing compound typically dissolves in the liquid it draws from the food and eventually becomes a brine.

Brine Cures

When salt is dissolved in water, the resulting liquid is called a ***brine***. (Seawater is a naturally occurring brine.) When salt is dissolved in water to make a curing medium, the resulting liquid curing compound is called a ***brine cure***, also called a ***wet cure***. A brine with a high ratio of salt to water is referred to as a *strong brine*, while a brine with a low ratio of salt to water is called a *weak brine*.

Brine cures usually contain other ingredients, such as sugar, spices, herbs, and other flavorings. Today, a brine cure that has a strong acidic component is called a ***pickle***; in the past, this term was used for any brine.

Most brines are prepared at room temperature. However, some brines are heated in order to dissolve the salt more quickly and to more thoroughly extract the flavors of whole spices and aromatic vegetables. These mixtures are called ***cooked brines***. They are always brought to room temperature, or cooler, before they are applied to foods.

A brine cure can be applied to foods in several ways:

- Immerse the food in the brine.
- Inject the brine into the flesh with a food injector.
- Pump the brine into the flesh through the arteries.

Often a combination of these methods is used.

The Science of Curing

Salt enters the cells of a cured product through the process of osmosis. It preserves the product by inhibiting the growth of harmful microorganisms in foods by dehydrating them to the point where the microorganisms are destroyed or their growth is dramatically slowed.

In brine curing, ***osmosis*** occurs when there is an unequal balance between the high salt concentration outside and the low concentration inside the meat cells. The salty water outside attracts water from inside the meat in an effort to equalize the concentration. Some of the highly salty external fluid is then reabsorbed through the cell walls of the meat, making the meat cells saltier. As curing progresses, the salty brine gradually penetrates farther and farther into the interior of the meat, passing from cell to cell, until it reaches the center. At this point, the cure is complete. In addition to the salt, any other flavorful substances dissolved in the brine permeate the meat.

When a dry cure is used on meat, the process of osmosis is basically the same, but it happens more slowly and yields different results. When the dry salt comes in contact with the meat's moist exterior, it slowly dissolves in the meat's fluids and thus creates a small amount of very strong brine. However, osmosis occurs much more slowly because there is far less exterior fluid than when a true fluid brine is applied. As a result, meat that has been dry-cured is less moist and has a denser texture than meats that have been brine-cured.

INGREDIENTS FOR CURED FOODS

Before you attempt to prepare the recipes in this chapter, you must know and understand the ingredients used for curing. If you make a mistake, such as using the wrong preservation ingredient, you can cause serious harm to your customers. In addition to curing ingredients, this section also discusses the variety of food ingredients that can be cured.

Curing Ingredients

The most important curing ingredient is salt. However, many other ingredients are also used as part of a curing mix.

Salt

For general curing, most charcutiers and garde manger chefs use a medium-grind refined salt. Medium-grind salts are preferred because they are easy to handle, dissolve quickly in a brine without excessive caking, and can be applied evenly to meat when used in a dry cure. ***Refined salts*** undergo a manufacturing process that removes all minerals other than sodium chloride. ***Natural salts*** are not refined, and they contain other minerals as well as sodium chloride.

Kosher salt is a refined salt processed into medium-size, flaky particles that dissolve quickly in water to make brines and in dry cures coat and penetrate meat in a gentle, even manner.

Sea salt is an unrefined, natural salt made by evaporating seawater in man-made lagoons or by mechanical processes. The result is a salt that varies in both flavor and color depending on the source and, thus, the additional minerals found in it. Although medium-grind sea salt is best for curing, often only fine and coarse grinds are available. Pulverize coarse sea salt to a medium consistency in a mortar.

Fine-grind table salt should not be used for dry curing because its fine texture makes even application difficult and because it can impart a harsh flavor. More important, all industrially produced fine table salts include anticaking agents, and some contain iodine. Both of these additives can interfere with the curing process.

Nitrate/Nitrite Mixes

Centuries ago, people discovered that salts derived from certain sources preserved meat better and for a longer time. Early twentieth-century scientists discovered this was due to the presence of ***sodium nitrite*** ($NaNO_2$) and/or ***sodium nitrate*** ($NaNO_3$) in the salt.

Today both industrial food producers and artisan charcutiers use these chemicals in cured foods for two main reasons: preservation and color. While most cured products are now stored under refrigeration, the addition of nitrites and nitrates increases the safety factor, effectively preventing serious foodborne illnesses such as botulism. In addition, nitrites and nitrates give cured foods a subtle flavor and an attractive pink color that most consumers have come to expect. While it is possible to make bacon, sausages, and other cured products without the use of nitrites and nitrates, the resulting product will look and taste different from the norm.

Because of modern sanitation and refrigeration, today's cured products contain far less nitrite/nitrate content than in the past. The amount of nitrites or nitrates needed to cure a given amount of meat is very small—so small, in fact, that it is extremely difficult to accurately measure and handle them in pure form. For this reason, nitrites and nitrates are mixed with sodium chloride to create a product that has enough volume to be measured and handled easily. Because the resulting mixture looks exactly like plain salt, it is tinted pink with food coloring so it will not be mistaken for salt and used incorrectly. This mixture is referred to as a ***pink cure*** or a ***tinted curing mix (TCM)***. Two types of tinted curing mix are available for curing:

1. Based on nitrites, ***Prague Powder #1*** [PROG] is a mixture of 6% sodium nitrite and 94% sodium chloride plus a small amount of red food coloring. The more frequently used of the two types, Prague Powder #1 is often simply referred to as ***curing salt*** or tinted curing mix (TCM), although there are other, very different, mixtures that are also TCMs.
2. Based on nitrites and nitrates mixed together, ***Prague Powder #2*** is a mixture of roughly 6% sodium nitrite and 94% sodium chloride, but with a fraction of a percent of sodium nitrate added. Red food coloring is also included to tint the mixture pink.

Although they are similar, these two mixtures have different ingredients and are used for different products and curing procedures. *They are not interchangeable.*

The amount of nitrites and nitrates to be used in a cure for a given amount of meat depends on several factors, such as:

- Type of meat
- Type of cure
- Length of curing time

Cure Accelerators

Cure accelerators are used to assist in the curing process and to help the curing compound penetrate into meats more quickly. They help retain the attractive pink color desired in cured products and also aid in flavor development. The United States Food and Drug Administration (USDA) permits the use of these cure accelerators in cured foods:

- Ascorbic acid (vitamin C)
- Sodium ascorbate
- Sodium erythorbate

It is important to remember that cure accelerators are used *in addition* to nitrites and nitrates, not in place of them.

Sugars

Both brine cures and dry cures usually include some form of sugar. Granular sugars can be used in both brines and dry cures, while liquid sugars are used in brine cures only.

The primary reason sugar and other sweeteners are used is for flavor. A touch of sugar balances the salty flavor of lightly cured foods. Stronger-flavored sweeteners, such as maple sugar and molasses, can counteract the harshness of the highly concentrated salt found in strongly cured products like hams and bacon.

The Nitrosamine Question

Foods containing nitrites or nitrates, when subjected to high heat, form substances called ***nitrosamines***. Under certain circumstances, nitrosamines are known to cause cancer in laboratory animals. However, not all cured products carry the same risk of nitrosamine development. In foods cured with nitrites only, the nitrites break down relatively quickly and are not present in significant quantity by the time the food is cooked and eaten. Nitrates break down more slowly and can remain present in some foods when they are served. That is why bacon, which is often fried or baked at a relatively high temperature, should not be cured with nitrates. However, most products cured with nitrates are eaten raw and so are not exposed to high heat.

In order to protect the health of their customers, charcutiers and garde manger chefs who prepare foods with curing compounds containing nitrites and nitrates must be careful to use them in the proper amounts and to monitor curing times diligently.

Because of the concern about nitrosamines, some manufacturers market nitrate- and nitrite-free cured meat products that they label "uncured." This is, of course, inaccurate, as these products *are* cured with a salt mixture.

The presence of sugar also adds to the perception of moistness in cured foods that might otherwise seem dry. Brown sugar and syrup-like sugars, such as honey and corn syrup, are ***humectants***, or substances that aid in retaining moisture. Corn syrup and dextrose are less sweet than other sugars and thus can be used in higher concentration. They contribute to moisture without making products taste overly sweet. Choose from these types of sugar:

- Granulated white sugar
- Brown sugar (light or dark)
- Maple sugar
- Dextrose
- Caramelized sugar
- Corn syrup (light or dark)
- Honey
- Molasses
- Maple syrup
- Cane syrup
- Sorghum syrup

Mixed Pickling Spice

Curing brines, vinegar-based pickling liquids, and *cuissons* for seafood are frequently seasoned with a combination of whole or crushed spices and dried herbs. Traditionally, these mixtures were prepared individually to suit the preparation and the taste of the cook. In the early twentieth century, spice companies began marketing proprietary blends, called "mixed pickling spice." Today some commercial blends contain sulfites, chemicals used for their preservative qualities but that may cause allergic reactions in some people.

Instead of purchasing commercial mixed pickling spice, you can prepare your own. Follow this formula or vary it to your taste.

1 cinnamon stick, crushed
1 nutmeg, crushed
6 allspice, crushed
4 cloves, crushed
2 tbsp (30 mL) coriander seeds
2 tbsp (30 mL) black peppercorns
2 tsp (10 mL) yellow mustard seeds
1 tsp (5 mL) brown mustard seeds
1 tbsp (15 mL) dill seeds
2 tsp (10 mL) crushed red pepper
6 bay leaves, broken into bits or chopped

To use, tie in a sachet or steep in liquid and then strain out.

Herbs, Spices, and Other Flavorings

Virtually any herb, spice, aromatic vegetable, or seasoning used in cooking may be used in a curing compound. For example:

- Dried herbs may be used in both dry cures and brines, while fresh herbs are used in brine cures.
- Dried and pulverized aromatics, such as granulated onion and garlic, are often used in dry cures.
- Ground or crushed spices are used in both dry cures and brines. If using whole spices, the brine should be heated just under the boil in order to release and infuse the flavors into the liquid. If you do so, bring the brine back to refrigerator temperature before applying it to the food item you wish to cure.
- Condiments such as prepared mustard, Worcestershire sauce, and soy sauce may be used in brine cures.
- Vinegar is added to a brine to give the cured product a tangy taste and to increase is preservative power. When vinegar is added to a brine, the brine is called a *pickle*.

Water

The water used to make a brine cure can affect the success of the product being cured. Unwanted chemicals and trace metals in tap water can create off-flavors and interfere with the curing process. It is advisable to use filtered or distilled water for making brines.

Foods To Be Cured

In general, cuts of meats with a substantial amount of internal fat are better suited to curing. The drying action of the cure can make very lean meats taste unpleasantly dry. Thus, pork makes a more succulent cured product than beef or venison. Fish with a higher amount of oil within the muscles has a richer mouthfeel when cured. If cured foods are to be smoked after curing, it is even more important to start with a rich, high-fat meat.

When choosing a cut of meat, be aware of both muscle size and structure. Single, large muscles (such as pork loin or beef tenderloin) have ideal structure, but they are costly and can have a dry mouthfeel if not handled correctly. Large cuts with fewer, larger muscles within the muscle bundle, such as fresh ham or top round, are good choices. These contain less connective tissue than cuts having many small muscles within them. Cuts with less internal connective tissue yield a product that is easy to slice thin and even, a desirable characteristic in most cured foods.

Pork

Pork is the preferred basic ingredient in traditional charcuterie products because of its fine grain, its sweet, neutral flavor, and its plentiful, clean-tasting fat. Virtually every part of a hog can be cured in one form or another. In some of these products, such as prosciutto and pancetta, curing is the sole preservation method. Others, such as American country hams and European hams and Canadian and American bacon, are smoked after they are cured. Smaller cuts and cuts that contain lots of connective tissue can be ground or puréed and made into various types of cured sausages.

Beef, Veal, Mutton, and Lamb

Although red meats are less frequently used in charcuterie work, excellent products may be produced by curing them. With rare exceptions, the costly, tender parts of red meat animals are not cured. The top round of beef may be prepared by either brine curing or dry curing, after which it is air-dried. The plate and brisket of beef are brine-cured to make corned beef. The tough cuts of mutton and lamb are most frequently ground and made into cured sausages, as are the tough cuts of veal.

Game Meats

The characteristic leanness of game meats makes them less than desirable for curing. Cured game meat products, such as venison jerky, are associated with frontier cooking and today are eaten mostly by hikers, climbers, and other outdoors enthusiasts (although, in some areas, jerky of all kinds is growing in popularity as a snack food). When tough cuts of game are ground and mixed with sufficient ground pork fat, they can be made into delectable cured sausages.

Poultry and Game Birds

Chicken, duck, turkey, goose, and game birds may all be cured. Most are cured as a preliminary step before they are smoked. Poultry can be cured in whole bird form or as cut-up parts. Whole birds and legs are usually brine-cured because their complicated shape and varying thickness make it difficult for a dry cure to penetrate them evenly.

Fish and Shellfish

The fabrication of fish to be cured varies according to size. Very small fish, such as sardines and anchovies, are scaled and gutted but usually left whole for curing. Larger fish are butterflied or cut into fillets. The skin is typically left on to provide support for the tender flesh.

Both lean-fleshed fish and oily fish are traditionally preserved by curing. Lean fish become very dry and salty once cured. These fish are soaked in several changes of fresh water to rehydrate them and remove some of the salt and then cooked by a moist method. After being cured, oily fish are usually eaten raw or are smoked.

Shellfish items require a very light cure. Mollusks and crustaceans are usually cured in a light brine for a short period only. Often, an acidic ingredient is added to the cure for flavor, as in pickled oysters or pickled shrimp. Some cured shellfish is lightly smoked as well.

CURING PROCEDURES

Whether following a recipe or developing a new cured product, first examine and evaluate the food item at hand to make necessary judgments and adjustments.

Evaluating Meats, Poultry, and Fish for Curing

Before you proceed with the curing of an item, consider its size and weight, its shape and surface area, and the texture of its flesh. Each of these considerations helps determine the type of cure, the strength of the cure, and duration of the curing time. Here are factors to consider when beginning a cure:

- Larger/heavier food items need more curing compound, while smaller/lighter items need less curing compound.

Guidelines for Cured Foods Safety

- *Maintain strict standards of sanitation.* Because many cured products are held in the temperature danger zone (TDZ) for longer than is safe for fresh items, it is important to maintain the lowest possible level of bacteria and other harmful microorganisms in the product. Thoroughly sanitize every surface and utensil that will come into contact with the cure or the product to be cured. *Always* wear food-service gloves when handling cures and food products. Do not reuse a brine or dry cure that has come into contact with raw food because it has been contaminated with bacteria from the raw food.
- *Be extra careful when measuring ingredients for cured foods.* Make sure to use the type of salt specified. Always weigh the salt rather than measure by volume. If you are using a TCM, make certain it is the correct type. Use a precision digital scale when weighing small amounts of ingredients, particularly TCMs. If the food to be cured is not exactly the weight specified in the recipe, make sure to correctly adjust the ratio of curing compound to food by scaling up or down.
- *Maintain strict temperature controls.* Keep the foods to be cured in the refrigerator until you need them. Fabricate them quickly, in small batches, and return them to the refrigerator when fabrication is complete. Make sure brine cures are at room or refrigerator temperature when they are applied to foods. While foods are curing, be diligent about keeping them at the temperature specified in the recipe. Use accurate, sanitized thermometers to monitor temperatures, and avoid fluctuations in temperature.
- *Always use nonreactive materials, such as plastic or stainless steel, when curing.* Aluminum pans can react with the salt in the dry cure or brine, causing discoloration of the product and interference with the curing process.
- *Be sure to observe the correct curing times and techniques.* Do not attempt to take shortcuts. There is no way to hurry a cure. Make sure to perform the specified maintenance steps throughout the curing time.

- Thick, compact food items with less surface area require a longer curing time. Thin, flat food items that have greater surface area require less curing time.
- Foods with a delicate texture and a loose, open grain require less dry curing compound or a weaker brine. Foods that are firm and dense require more dry curing compound or a stronger brine.
- Irregularly shaped food items are not well suited to a dry cure because they have nooks and crannies that make even application difficult. Instead, such items are usually cured in a brine. Because a brine cure is fluid, it flows evenly around all surfaces and cavities and penetrates the flesh quickly and evenly.

The Four Phases of the Curing Process

Curing comprises four phases: fabrication, cure application, cure penetration, and drying. Table 11.1 describes these four distinct phases.

TABLE 11.1 Four Phases of the Curing Process

Phase	Description	Preparation
1. Fabrication	The meat is prepared to receive the cure.	Fabrication may include some or all of these procedures: Meats may be boned, trimmed, butterflied, or rolled/trussed. Poultry may be boned, skinned, butterflied, disjointed, or left whole; poultry is not trussed before curing. Fish is always scaled, gilled, and gutted before curing; fish may be filleted, butterflied, cut into steaks, headed, or left whole, with the skin usually left on. Shellfish is fabricated in various ways according to type and size. After fabrication, the product is washed and blotted dry.
2. Cure Application	Curing compound is applied to the meat.	Application methods vary according to type of cure (dry or brine) and product being cured, and are covered in detail for each type of cure later in this chapter.
3. Cure Penetration	The meat is left in contact with the curing compound for a specific length of time.	For most modern products, cure penetration occurs under refrigeration. Some products require maintenance during cure penetration, while others are simply left alone to cure.
4. Drying	Whether the cure is a brine or a dry cure, when cure penetration is complete, the exterior of the product will be wet. Thus, it is necessary to air-dry the surface of the cured meat.	If residue of a dry curing compound is still clinging to the meat, it is brushed off or washed off before drying. Cured meats are placed on a rack or hung from hooks or rods. A drip pan is placed underneath to catch any fluids the meat exudes during the drying period. Air-dry under refrigeration or in a cool, temperature-controlled, humidity-controlled drying room. A fan may be directed on the products to speed the process.

The Pellicle

Air-drying cured products gives them a translucent, tacky skin called a ***pellicle***. The pellicle has four functions:

1. It forms a protective coating that keeps microorganisms and physical contaminants from contacting the meat during storage or further processing.
2. It prevents the meat from excessive drying during storage or further processing.
3. It prevents wrapping materials from sticking to the meat during storage.
4. In cured meats to be smoked, the pellicle captures the smoke's flavors and passes them into the meat's interior. The pellicle also captures and holds the pigments present in the smoke, giving the smoked product an attractive burnished color.

For most cured foods, the drying period is short (a few hours to overnight), usually just long enough for successful pellicle formation. Then they are wrapped for refrigerated storage or subjected to further processing, such as smoking.

Some cured foods are subjected to lengthy air-drying after pellicle formation. Prosciutto and bresaola are air-dried for weeks, until the exterior is leathery and the interior has a supple, velvety texture. Other cured foods, such as salt cod and beef jerky, are air-dried until leathery throughout.

BRINE CURING

Various ways a brine cure can be applied to meats, poultry, and seafood follow.

Immersion Brining

Immersion brining is a technique in which food is placed in a sanitized, nonreactive container and immersed in brine. This works best for small items or larger items with a lot of surface area. It also works well for whole poultry items. To be successful, all parts of the meat must be completely covered in brine. Most brine curing is done under refrigeration. The length of the cure depends on the strength of the brine and the size, shape, and texture of the meat.

Internal Brining

Large cuts of meat, as well as smaller cuts with a compact shape and little surface area, cannot be brine-cured by the immersion method alone. It takes too long for the brine to penetrate from the outside to the center, and harmful microorganisms can grow to a dangerous level. For this reason, the cure must be applied to both the inside and the outside of the meat. Applying brine to the inside of the meat is called ***internal brining***. It can be done in two ways:

1. ***Injection brining***: Forcing the brine through a needle directly into the muscle structure of the meat. For even application, the needle is inserted at key points all over the item, as shown on page 420.
2. ***Arterial brining***: Forcing the brine into the arteries in a front or hind leg primal cut. The brine travels through the arteries, into the smaller blood vessels, and finally into the muscle structure of the meat (see p. 420 and, for greater detail, p. 454).

These methods are usually used in conjunction with immersion brining to ensure the fastest and most even penetration of the brine cure.

Procedure for Immersion Brining

1. Fabricate the meat as specified in the recipe, with attention to consistency in size, shape, and surface area. If necessary, truss the meat to ensure consistency. Refrigerate the meat until you are ready to proceed.
2. Select a nonreactive container large enough to hold the food and brine. Sanitize the container and its lid. Sanitize all other utensils that will come into contact with the food.
3. a. Standard brine: Thoroughly mix together the salt, cool water, and other brine ingredients in the sanitized container. Make sure the salt dissolves completely.
   b. Cooked brine: Thoroughly mix together the salt, cool water, and other brine ingredients in a nonreactive pan. Bring the mixture to a boil, lower the heat, and simmer only until the salt is dissolved. Cool to room temperature. Pour the brine into the sanitized container.
4. Blot away any fluids from the exterior (and cavity) of the meat.

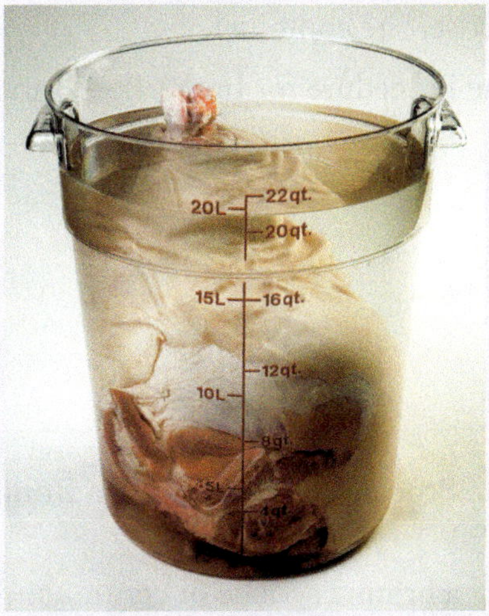

Immersion brining of ham. This ham is shown before weighting to submerge it completely.

5. Place the meat in the brine and, if necessary, weight it with a plate, lid, or other flat, heavy, nonreactive object that is safe for food contact. Cover the container.
6. Refrigerate the meat in the brine for the time specified in the recipe.
7. When the specified time is complete, remove the meat from the brine. To test the cure, cut a small slit into the center of the meat and make sure the brine has fully penetrated to the center. If the cure is complete, the texture and color will be the same throughout.
8. Drain the meat and air-dry it by the specified method and at the specified temperature.
9. After the pellicle has formed, wrap the food or proceed with additional processing.

Equipment for Internal Brining

Industrial producers use large, electrically powered machinery to force brine into meats in various ways. Artisan producers perform these methods by hand with a ***food injector***. Several types of food injector are available:

- ***Brining syringe***: A stainless-steel cylindrical chamber with a large needle and a plunger. The brine is drawn up through the needle into the chamber by suction and then forced into the meat.
- ***Continuous-feed brine pump***: A plastic cylinder with a large needle and a plunger. One end of a flexible plastic tube is connected to the cylinder near the needle. The other end of the tube is inserted in a container of brine. When the plunger is pumped, it creates suction that draws the brine into the cylinder and out through the needle into the meat or an artery.

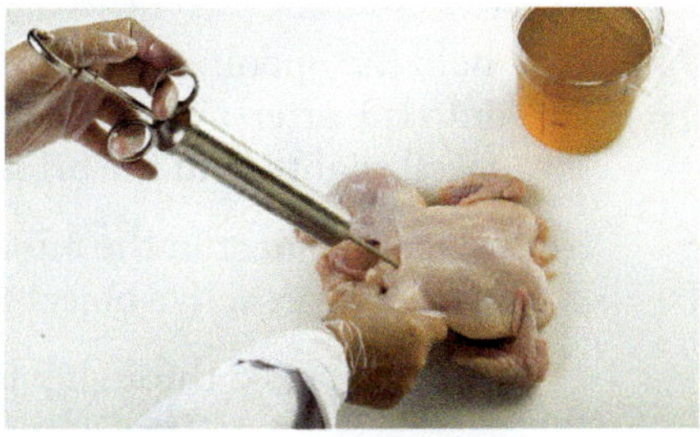
Brining syringe in use

Procedure for Artisan Injection Brining

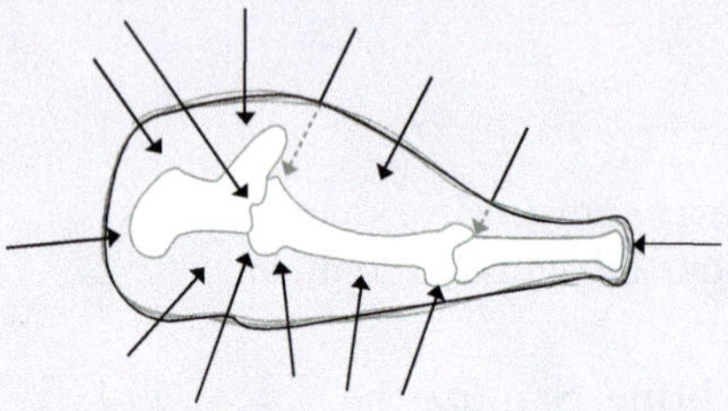

Key injection points for meats

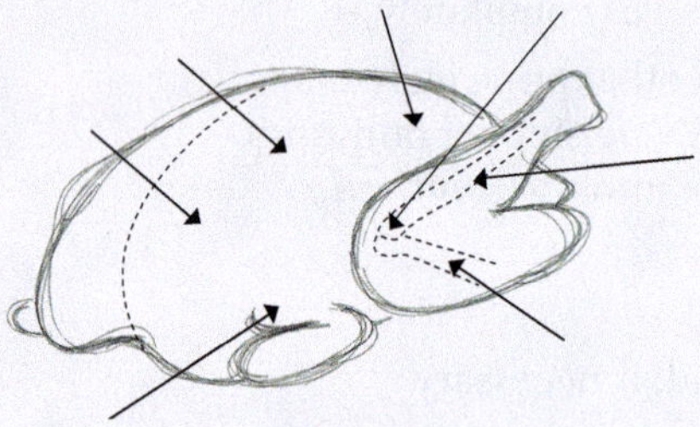

Key injection points for poultry

1. Follow steps 1 through 4 in the Procedure for Immersion Brining on page 419.
2. Thoroughly sanitize all parts of a brining syringe or continuous-feed brine pump fitted with a medium-gauge needle.
3. If necessary, strain any solid matter out of the brine that will go into the injector.
4. Weigh the meat to be brined. Weigh enough brine to equal 10% of the weight of the meat.
5. Inject the brine into the meat, spacing the points of injection evenly over the surface of the meat and penetrating as deeply as possible. When injecting bone-in meats and whole poultry, be sure to inject the key contact points near the joints, as illustrated at left.
6. Immerse the meat in the remaining brine and, if necessary, weight it with a plate, lid, or other flat, heavy, nonreactive object that is safe for food contact. Cover the container.
7. Follow steps 6 through 9 in the Procedure for Immersion Brining.

Procedure for Artisan Arterial Brining

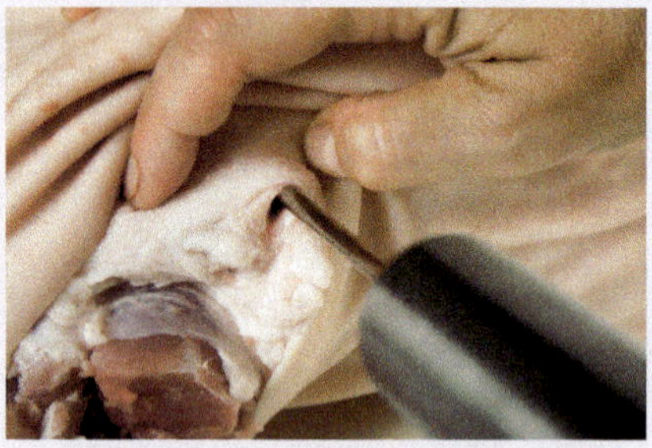

Needle going into femoral artery of a ham

1. Follow steps 1 through 4 in the Procedure for Immersion Brining on page 419.
2. Thoroughly sanitize all parts of a brining syringe or continuous-feed brine pump fitted with a large, heavy-gauge needle.
3. If necessary, strain any solid matter out of the brine that will go into the syringe or pump.
4. Weigh the meat to be brined. Weigh out enough brine to equal 10% of the weight of the meat.
5. Locate the opening of the brachial or femoral artery in the meat, as illustrated at left. Insert the needle into the artery and hold the opening of the artery closed around the base of the needle. Slowly pump or inject the brine into the artery. When the brine has penetrated throughout the muscles of the meat, the meat will swell slightly and the brine will begin to back up and flow out of the opening of the artery.
6. Place the meat in the remaining brine and, if necessary, weight it with a plate, lid, or other flat, heavy, nonreactive object that is safe for food contact. Cover the container.
7. Follow steps 6 through 9 in the Procedure for Immersion Brining.

JEWISH CORNED BEEF

Yield:
about 4 lb (2 kg) EP

Corning

In the past, curing was also called *corning*, as in corned beef. This dates from the days when salt was typically sold in large granules the size of a wheat grain. In those days, the general term for grain was *corn*. People commonly referred to "a corn of salt" in the same way we today refer to "a grain of salt."

Thus, to apply salt to meat was to *corn* it.

INGREDIENTS	U.S.	METRIC
Brine		
Distilled or filtered water	1 gal	4 L
Kosher salt	8 oz	240 g
Light brown sugar	2 oz	60 g
Light corn syrup	3 oz	90 g
Mixed pickling spices (p. 414)	1½ oz	45 g
Prague Powder #1	½ oz	15 g
Beef brisket, first or second cut	6 lb	3 kg
Whole peeled garlic cloves	2 oz	60 g
Thinly sliced onion	6 oz	180 g
Thinly sliced carrot	3 oz	90 g
Thinly sliced celery	3 oz	90 g
Whole peeled garlic cloves, smashed	1½ oz	45 g
Mixed pickling spices (p. 414)	½ oz	15 g

PROCEDURE

DAY 1: FABRICATION AND CURE APPLICATION

1. Sanitize all equipment that will come into contact with the brine or the meat.
2. Combine the water, salt, brown sugar, corn syrup, first quantity of pickling spices, and Prague Powder #1 in a nonreactive pan. Stir well and bring to the boil to dissolve the salt and sugar. Cool to room temperature and then refrigerate until cold.
3. Trim away all but ½ in. (1 cm) of surface fat from the meat. Weigh the meat.
4. Chop the first quantity of garlic and place it in a blender. Place a strainer across the top of the blender and strain in just enough cold brine to release the blades. Purée the garlic to a smooth paste, then strain in more brine to make a pourable liquid. Re-blend, then pour the garlic liquid back into the brine. Stir well.
5. Weigh out enough brine to equal 10% of the weight of the meat.
6. Inject the meat evenly with the weighed brine.
7. Place the meat in a nonreactive pan or curing tub just large enough to hold it and the remaining brine. Place a flat, nonreactive plate or lid on the meat to hold it submerged. Cover the container and place it in the refrigerator.

DAYS 2–6: CURE PENETRATION

8. Allow the meat to cure in the brine for 5 days.

AIR-DRYING

9. Remove the meat from the brine and rinse it thoroughly in cool water.
10. Place the meat on a rack set over a hotel pan and refrigerate it, uncovered, for 24 hours.

COOKING

11. Place the onion, carrots, celery, second quantity of garlic cloves and pickling spice, and corned beef in a nonreactive pan and add enough water to cover the meat. Bring to a simmer and poach the meat about 2 hours, or until it is fork tender. (The corned beef is now ready for hot service. However, for most garde manger uses it will be served at room temperature or cold.)
12. Remove the corned beef to a nonreactive storage container and pour enough broth over it to cover it completely. Open-pan cool the corned beef in its broth. Cover and refrigerate the corned beef as soon it cools to room temperature.

(continues)

PROCEDURE *(continued)*

HOLDING

Refrigerate up to 2 weeks.

FINISHING

13. Remove the corned beef from its broth and blot it dry.
14. Slice the corned beef thin across the grain and serve as desired.

VARIATION

IRISH-AMERICAN CORNED BEEF

Omit the Prague Powder. Omit all of the garlic. Reduce holding time to 1 week.

PICKLED HERRING

Yield:
about 1 lb (500 g) EP

Pickling

The term *pickle* is an old-fashioned word for grain. Like "corn," it was also used to describe the salt used for curing. So, to pickle a food was to cure it with salt. When vegetables such as cucumbers or cabbage are cured in a salt brine, desirable bacterial action causes them to ferment and turn sour. Over time, the term *to pickle* became most closely associated with these sour preserved vegetables. Today, when we speak of foods cured in a pickling solution, we usually mean there is also vinegar in the brine, as in pickled herring.

INGREDIENTS	U.S.	METRIC
Skin-on herring fillets	1½ lb	750 g
Kosher salt	2 oz	60 g
Distilled or filtered water, cold	½ gal	2 L
Kosher salt	10 oz	300 g
Distilled or filtered water	10 oz	300 mL
Sugar	4 oz	120 g
White wine vinegar (5–6% acidity)	10 oz	300 mL
Bay leaves	4	4
Mixed pickling spices (p. 414)	2 tbsp	30 mL
Peeled carrots, sliced into thin rounds	2 oz	60 g
Red onion, peeled and cut into medium-thick rings	4 oz	120 g

PROCEDURE

DAY 1: FABRICATION AND FIRST CURE APPLICATION

1. Sanitize all equipment that will come into contact with the fish or brine ingredients.
2. Using tweezers or needlenose pliers, remove all pin bones from the fish.
3. In a nonreactive container, dissolve 2 oz (60 g) salt in ½ gal (2 L) distilled water. Soak the fish fillets in the water at cool room temperature for 30 minutes.
4. Drain the fish and blot it dry.
5. Place a thin layer of the remaining salt in a ninth-hotel pan or other small, nonreactive container. Place 1 or 2 fish fillets, skin-side down, on the salt and cover with more salt. Continue layering fish and salt, ending with the last fish fillets skin-side up and covering them with salt. Press to firm the fillets into the salt. Cover the container and place it in the refrigerator.

DAYS 2–6: FIRST CURE PENETRATION

6. Refrigerate for 5 days. The salt will turn into a brine when it mixes with the fluids that exude from the fish. Check periodically to see that the fillets are submerged in the brine, and, if not, weight them.

DAYS 6–7: SOAKING

7. Remove the fish from the brine and rinse it under cool water.
8. Place the fish in a nonreactive pan and cover it with cold water and a lid. Allow to soak in the refrigerator 2 days, changing the water twice per day.

DAY 8: SECOND CURE APPLICATION

9. To make the pickling brine, combine 10 oz (300 mL) distilled water, the sugar, vinegar, bay, pickling spices, and carrots in a nonreactive pan. Bring to a boil and remove from the heat. Cool to room temperature and then refrigerate until cold.

PROCEDURE

10. Sanitize a nonreactive container just large enough to hold all the combined ingredients.
11. Drain the fish and blot it dry. Cut each fillet crosswise into 1-in. (2.5-cm) slices.
12. Using a slotted spoon, remove the carrots and bay leaves from the pickling brine and reserve them.
13. Layer the fish, onions, carrots, and bay leaves in the sanitized container. Pour the pickling brine over the fish and vegetables. Make sure the brine evenly penetrates the spaces around the ingredients. Cover the container and place it in the refrigerator.

DAYS 9–14: SECOND CURE PENETRATION

14. Refrigerate for 5 days.

HOLDING

Refrigerate up to 3 weeks.

VARIATION

CREAMED HERRING

Reduce the amount of pickling brine water and vinegar by 2 fl oz (60 mL) each. Add 4 fl oz (120 mL) sour cream to the pickling brine at the end of step #9. Reduce the holding time to 1 week.

PICKLED HERRING

WITH BEETS AND CUCUMBERS

APPETIZER

Portion:
1

Portion size:
3 oz (90 g) drained pickled herring, plus some of the pickled vegetables

COMPONENTS

1 Boston lettuce leaf
4 slices (1½ oz/45 g) *Roasted Beets (p. 107)*
3 slices (1 oz/30 g) English cucumber
3 oz (90 g) *Pickled Herring (p. 422)*, drained, with vegetables
1 oz (30 g) Unsalted butter, room temperature, in butter dish or ramekin
2 oz (60 g) Thin-sliced pumpernickel bread cut into attractive shapes

PROCEDURE

PLATING

1. Place the lettuce leaf in the center of a cool 10-in. (25-cm) plate.
2. Alternate the beet and cucumber slices at the back of the leaf.
3. Mound the herring and its vegetables in the center of the leaf.
4. Serve the pumpernickel and butter in a basket or on a side plate.

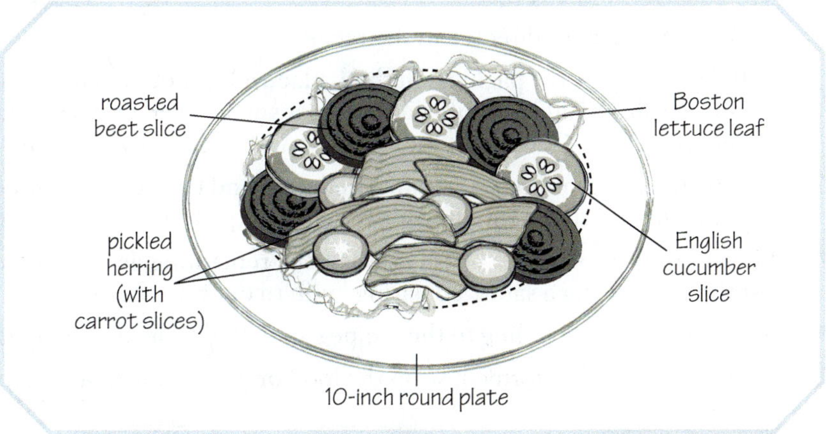

DRY CURING

The manner in which a dry cure is applied to a food item depends on the size and weight of the food and the amount of dry curing compound necessary to accomplish the cure. There are two basic methods for applying a dry cure: rubbing and packing.

Rubbing Method

Small, flat items that need only a light cure are coated with a thin layer of the dry cure compound. It is massaged into the meat to ensure an even coating and to jump-start penetration. Once rubbed, the food may be stored in a plastic bag or nonreactive container with a tight-fitting lid. Moisture released from the food combines with the dry cure and creates a highly concentrated brine. As it cures, the food should be turned over one or more times to ensure even penetration.

Large items are coated with the dry cure compound in the same way. However, after the initial coating, they are rubbed with additional dry cure compound at carefully monitored intervals throughout the duration of the cure. Each rub adds another layer of dry cure compound that replaces the layer absorbed into the meat's interior. The fluids released from the meat are drained off each time more curing compound is applied.

If a cut of meat to be cured has a protruding bone, such as the shank end of a ham, special care must be taken to prevent spoilage in that critical area. The end of the bone must first be exposed and scraped clean of all meat. The dry cure compound must be packed firmly into the crevices where the bone protrudes from the meat and also into the bone's hollow center.

Procedure for Dry Curing

1. Fabricate the meat to be cured, with attention to consistency in size, shape, and surface area as much as possible. Note the average weight of the individual pieces. Refrigerate the meat until you are ready to proceed.
2. Prepare the dry cure compound. If using a premade compound, stir it well to ensure it is evenly mixed.
3. Sanitize all equipment that will come into contact with the meat.
4. Blot away any fluids from the exterior of the meat.
5. Massage an even layer of dry cure compound onto all surfaces of the meat in the amount and thickness specified in the recipe.
6. a. Wrap the meat as directed in the recipe.
   b. If dry curing by the packing method, place a layer of dry cure compound in the bottom of the curing tub and add the rubbed meat in a single layer, or in even layers with layers of compound between them. Cover with more compound. Weight the contents of the tub and cover.
7. Cure the meat according to the specified time and temperature. If necessary, post a maintenance schedule for additional rubbing or overhauling (p. 425).
8. When curing is complete, brush or wash any remaining dry cure compound off the meat's surface. Test the cure, using a sanitized paring knife to cut into the center as described on page 419, step 7.
9. Air-dry the meat according to the recipe's specified time and temperature.
10. After the pellicle has formed, wrap the food or proceed with additional processing.

Packing Method

The packing method often begins in the same way as the rubbing method. After the meat is rubbed with a dry cure compound, it is placed into a nonreactive container, called a ***curing tub***, lined with a shallow layer of additional dry cure compound. The meat is added to the tub in a single layer, and more of the dry cure compound is added to the tub in sufficient quantity to completely cover the meat. Often, additional layers of meat and compound are added. When all of the meat is completely covered, it must be weighted to compress the meat and force fluids out. The amount of weight needed for a particular food item depends on its density and the desired result. The tub is covered and stored in the refrigerator for the duration of the cure. The meat is periodically turned and its position in the tub is rotated, a procedure called ***overhauling***.

AIR-DRIED BEEF JERKY

Yield:
about 8 oz (240 g)
Portions:
16
Portion size:
½ oz (15 g)

INGREDIENTS	U.S.	METRIC
Top round of beef, preferably a single muscle	1½ lb	750 g
Kosher salt	½ oz	15 g
Granulated garlic	1 tsp	5 mL
Granulated onion	1½ tsp	8 mL
Finely ground white pepper	¼ tsp	2 mL
Finely ground black pepper	¼ tsp	2 mL
Ground dry sage	¼ tsp	2 mL

PROCEDURE

DAY 1: FABRICATION AND CURE APPLICATION

1. Trim away all fat, silverskin, and connective tissue from the beef.
2. Place the beef in a freezer for about 30 minutes to firm the texture for slicing.
3. Combine the remaining ingredients to make the dry curing compound.
4. Slice the beef across the grain into even ⅛-in. (0.33-cm) slices (A). Cut the slices into 1-in. (2.5-cm) strips.
5. Lay the strips on a sheet tray and sprinkle on *half* of the dry cure compound (B). Turn the strips over and sprinkle with the remaining compound. Transfer the strips to a plastic bag along with any curing compound that remains on the tray. Place the bag in the refrigerator.

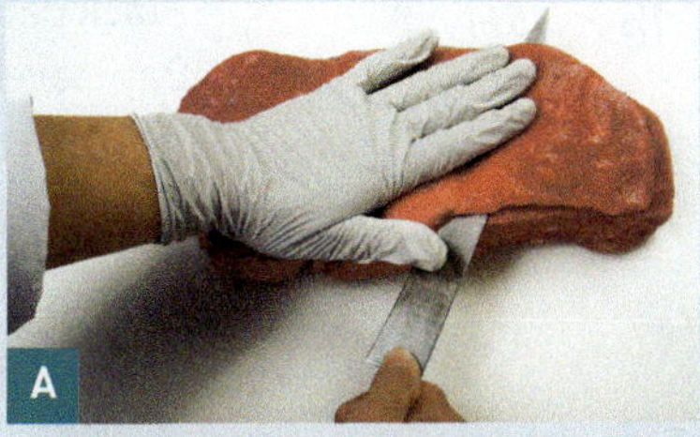

A

B

DAY 2: CURE PENETRATION

6. Refrigerate for 24 hours.

DAY 3: AIR-DRYING

7. Place the beef strips in a single layer on the rack of a food dehydrator or on a cooling rack (C).

C

(continues)

PROCEDURE *(continued)*

8. If room temperature will drop lower than 70°F (21°C) overnight, set the dehydrator to 80°F (27°C). If room temperature will remain above 70°F (21°C), turn on the dehydrator fan. Place the rack in the dehydrator and dry the beef for 24 hours.

   Alternatively, set the rack in a turned-off gas oven with only the pilot flame for heat. Place a drip pan at least 6 in. (15 cm) below the rack. (Place a sign on the oven door to prevent anyone from turning it on.) Dry the beef for 24 hours.

9. When finished, the beef will be dark in color, completely dry and stiff, and have a leathery texture. Place it in a sealed container.

HOLDING

Store at cool room temperature up to 3 months.

VARIATIONS

TEX-MEX BEEF JERKY

Replace the white and black peppers with 1 tbsp (15 mL) Texas-style chili powder.

NEW MEXICO BEEF JERKY

Replace the white and black peppers with 1 tbsp (15 mL) ground dried pure red New Mexico chile.

DUCK "PROSCIUTTO"

Yield:
about 1 lb (450 g) EP
Portions:
10
Portion size:
1½ oz (45 g)

INGREDIENTS	U.S.	METRIC
Moulard duck breast halves, skin on	1½ lb (2 pieces)	675 g (2 pieces)
Kosher salt	1 lb	450 g
Juniper berries	10	10
Black peppercorns	1 tbsp	15 mL
Bay leaves, chopped coarse	2	2
Whole peeled garlic cloves	1 oz	30 g
Chopped fresh sage leaves	½ oz	15 g

PROCEDURE

DAY 1: FABRICATION AND CURE APPLICATION

1. Trim the edges of the duck skin so it is even with the meat. Using a very sharp knife, score the skin of the duck breasts in a ⅛-in. (0.33-cm) cross-hatch pattern. Do not cut into the meat.
2. Pour half the salt into a sixth-hotel pan or other nonreactive container just large enough to hold the duck breast halves in one layer. Smooth the salt into an even layer.
3. Place the duck breasts on the salt at least ½ in. (2 cm) apart and cover them with the remaining salt. Place another sixth-pan on top and press the pans together. Place the pans in the refrigerator.

DAY 2–3: CURE PENETRATION

4. Allow the duck breasts to cure in the refrigerator for 36 hours.

DAYS 3–13: SEASONING AND AIR-DRYING

5. Remove the duck breasts from the salt and rinse them thoroughly under cold water. Blot them dry.
6. Place the remaining ingredients in a small mortar and grind to a rough powder.
7. Evenly coat the duck breasts with the seasoning powder and massage it in.
8. Wrap each duck breast in a single layer of cheesecloth and tie the ends with kitchen string. Make a loop at one end of each packet so you are able to hang it.
9. Hang the duck breasts in the refrigerator, preferably in front of the circulation fan, for 10 days.

PROCEDURE

10. Unwrap one of the duck breasts and check the cure by squeezing it. The duck breast should feel firm throughout. (If the center still feels squishy, rewrap the duck breast and continue to air-dry for several more days.)
11. Wrap the duck breasts in butcher paper and place them in a loosely closed plastic bag.

HOLDING

Refrigerate up to 3 weeks.

DUCK "PROSCIUTTO"

WITH BALSAMIC GLAZE AND FIG JAM

APPETIZER

Portion:
1

Portion size:
1½ oz (45 g) duck, plus garnish

COMPONENTS

1 oz (30 g) Mild-flavored micro greens
¼ fl oz (8 mL) *Balsamic Vinaigrette (p. 33)*
1½ oz (45 g) *Duck "Prosciutto" (p. 426)*, sliced thin
1½ fl oz (45 mL) *Fig Jam (p. 683)*, in squeeze bottle
½ fl oz (15 mL) *Balsamic Glaze (p. 690)* or commercial, in squeeze bottle
3 oz (90 g) Crusty Italian bread

PROCEDURE

PLATING

1. Toss the micro greens with the vinaigrette.
2. Mound the micro greens on the back center of a cool 10-in. (25-cm) plate.
3. Ruffle the "prosciutto" on the plate in an arc around the micro greens.
4. Squeeze flourishes of fig jam on the plate around the greens and "prosciutto," as illustrated below.
5. Squeeze drops of the balsamic glaze among the flourishes.
6. Serve the bread in a basket lined with a linen napkin.

VARIATIONS

DUCK "PROSCIUTTO" WITH SHAVED PARMESAN AND BALSAMIC GLAZE

Omit the fig jam. Drizzle the "prosciutto" with extra-virgin olive oil and use a cheese plane to shave ½ oz (15 g) Reggiano Parmesan over it.

DUCK "PROSCIUTTO" WITH MELON

Replace all ingredients except the duck "prosciutto" with thin-sliced ripe honeydew and cantaloupe.

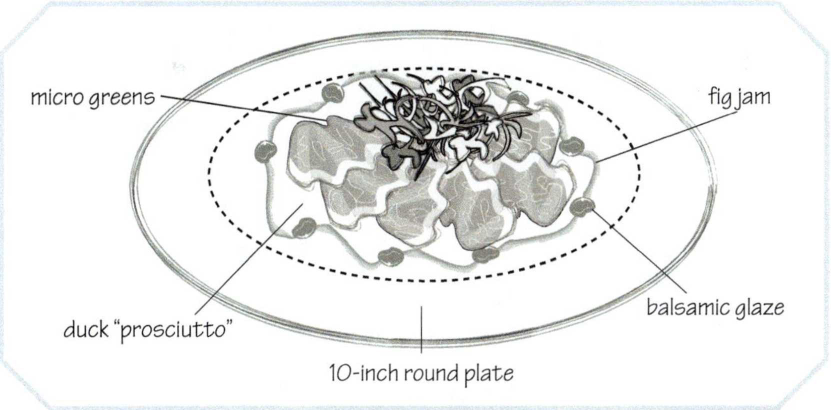

SALT COD

Yield:
about 1¾ lb (750 g) dry weight
Portions:
vary
Portion size:
varies

INGREDIENTS	U.S.	METRIC
Skinless fresh cod fillet	2½ lb	1.25 kg
Kosher salt	15 oz	450 g

PROCEDURE

DAY 1: FABRICATION, CURE APPLICATION, AND CURE PENETRATION

1. Trim off any shreds of skin remaining on the fish. Using tweezers or needlenose pliers, remove any pin bones.
2. Using a ruler, measure and note the maximum thickness of the fillet in inches (cm). To calculate the necessary hours of curing time, multiply the inches by 22 (or the centimeters by 8.25). For example, a fillet that is ¾-in. thick needs 16½ hours curing time because $0.75 \times 22 = 16.5$. Metric example: A fillet that is 2 cm thick needs 16½ hours curing time because $2 \times 8.25 = 16.5$.
3. Wash the fish in cool water and blot it dry with a clean towel.
4. Place a large piece of cheesecloth in a 2-in. (5-cm) deep, perforated half-hotel pan, and allow the cheesecloth to drape 6 in. (15 cm) over the sides.
5. Place half of the salt on the cheesecloth in the shape of the fillet.
6. Place the cod fillet on top of the salt and cover it with the remaining salt.
7. Fold one long end of the cheesecloth over the fillet and then roll it up into a flat bundle. Tie the ends closed with kitchen string.
8. Place the perforated pan in a 4-in. (10-cm) half-hotel pan and refrigerate the fish in the pan, uncovered, for the proper number of hours as calculated in step 2.

DAY 2–10: AIR-DRYING

9. Check the cure as described on page 419, step 7. If the cure is complete, the texture and color will be the same throughout the fillet. (If the cure is not complete, return to the refrigerator and continue curing for several more hours.) Unwrap the fish and wash off the surface salt. Blot the fish dry with a clean towel.
10. Lay a flat piece of cheesecloth on a rack set over a sheet tray. Place the fish on top. Place the tray in a refrigerator or walk-in cooler as close to the fan as possible in a location with good air circulation. Allow the fish to air-dry, uncovered, up to 8 days. When the drying process is complete, the fish will have a milky color and be firm throughout.
11. Loosely wrap the fish in butcher paper or parchment and place it in a sealed plastic bag.

HOLD

Refrigerate up to 4 months.

POACHED SALT COD

Yield:
about 2¼ lb (1 kg)
Portions:
vary
Portion size:
varies

INGREDIENTS	U.S.	METRIC
Salt Cod (p. 428) or commercial	1¾ lb	750 g
Court bouillon (p. 194)	1 qt	1 L
Lemon	½	½

PROCEDURE

DAY 1: FINISHING

1. Place the cod in a bowl and cover it with cold water. Refrigerate the cod in the water for 24 hours, changing the water every 3–4 hours. For overnight soaking, place the bowl in a food preparation sink under a thin stream of cold water.

DAY 2: FINISHING

2. Bring the court bouillon to a simmer in a nonreactive pan just large enough to hold the cod completely submerged.
3. Poach the cod about 20 minutes, or until it is tender throughout.
4. Serve immediately or open-pan cool in the court bouillon.

HOLD

Refrigerate the cod in a freshly sanitized, covered container, submerged in the court bouillon, up to 4 days.

The History of Buried Salmon

Burial was one of man's earliest techniques for food preservation because the earth is much cooler underground than at the surface. Primitive hunters and fishermen discovered they could keep food for a longer period by salting it, wrapping it in leaves, and then burying it in the ground. This kept it cold and protected it from insects and animals as well. When the people needed the food, they simply dug it up.

In Scandinavian countries, salmon fishermen traditionally cured their catch with a combination of salt, sugar, and wild herbs, wrapped it in leaves, and then buried the fish in the ground for the duration of the cure. They called this *gravad lax*, or *gravlax* (p.430), literally "buried salmon." Today we use a similar cure, but instead of burying the fish we cure it in the refrigerator.

GRAVLAX

Yield:
about 6 lb (3 kg) EP
Portions:
48
Portion size:
2 oz (60 g)

INGREDIENTS	U.S.	METRIC
Salmon fillet, skin on	8 lb (2 4-lb sides)	4 kg (2 2-kg sides)
Fresh lemon juice	4 fl oz	120 mL
Aquavit (optional)	2 fl oz	60 mL
Kosher salt	12 oz	360 g
Sugar	6 oz	180 g
Cracked black pepper	¼ oz	7 g
Fresh dill leaves and stems, chopped coarse	1½ oz	45 g

PROCEDURE

DAY 1: FABRICATION AND CURE APPLICATION

1. Place the salmon sides on a cutting board skin-side down. Using tweezers or needlenose pliers, remove the pin bones (A), following the anatomy of the fish and being careful not to shred the flesh.
2. Wash the salmon sides in cool water to remove any scales or debris. Blot it dry with a clean towel.
3. Place a large piece of cheesecloth on your work surface and place the salmon sides, skin-side down, on the cheesecloth.
4. Sprinkle the salmon flesh evenly with the lemon juice and aquavit, if you are using it.
5. Mix the salt, sugar, and pepper to make the dry cure compound.
6. Spread the dry cure compound on the flesh of the salmon sides, applying less on the smaller ends (B).
7. Place the dill on the sides and press it down (C).
8. Fold the sides together, flesh to flesh.
9. Wrap the doubled sides tight in the cheesecloth (D).
10. Place a 2-in. (5-cm) deep perforated hotel pan in a 4-in. (10-cm) deep solid hotel pan. Place the salmon in the pan and drape the top loosely with plastic film. Place a solid hotel pan on top of the plastic-covered fish and fill the top pan with 10 lb (5 kg) evenly placed weights.
11. Place the pan in the refrigerator for 24 hours.

A

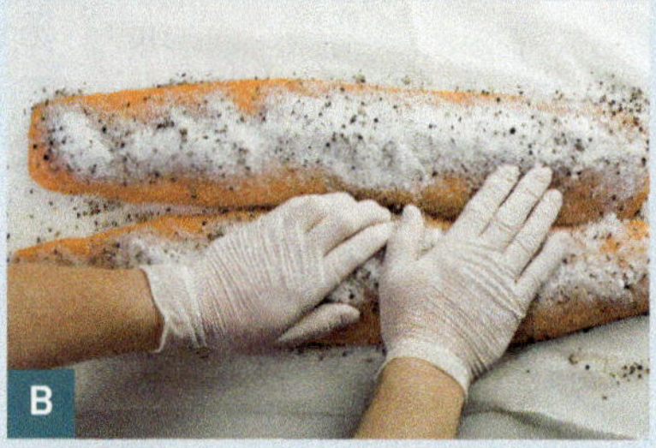
B

C

D

DAY 2: CURE PENETRATION AND MAINTENANCE

12. Take the pans out of the refrigerator and remove the weighted pan and the perforated pan holding the salmon.
13. Turn the salmon over and replace the plastic film.
14. Drain the liquid from the bottom pan and rinse it out.
15. Replace the perforated pan in the drip pan, cover with fresh plastic film, and replace the weighted pan on top.
16. Refrigerate for 24 more hours.

DAY 3: CURE PENETRATION AND MAINTENANCE

17. Repeat the Day 2 maintenance steps.

PROCEDURE

DAY 4: CURE PENETRATION AND MAINTENANCE

18. Repeat the Day 2 maintenance steps.

DAY 5: AIR-DRYING

19. Check the cure by pressing gently on the salmon. The flesh should feel firm throughout. If the cure is complete, unwrap the salmon and brush off the cure. (If the center still feels squishy, rewrap the salmon and continue to cure for 1 more day.)
20. Place the gravlax, skin-side down, on a rack set over a drip pan and air-dry it, unwrapped, in the refrigerator for 3 hours.
21. Wrap the salmon sides individually in butcher paper or parchment.

HOLD

Refrigerate up to 5 additional days.

VARIATION

To make a smaller amount of gravlax, use 1 4-lb (2-kg) salmon side cut in half crosswise. Scale down the other ingredients by multiplying by 0.67.

GRAVLAX

WITH MUSTARD SAUCE

APPETIZER

Portion:
1
Portion size:
2 oz (60 g) gravlax, plus garnish

COMPONENTS

2 oz (60 g) *Gravlax (p. 430)*
1½ fl oz (45 mL) *Miami Mustard Sauce (p. 44)*
¾ oz (20 g) Finely chopped sweet onion
1 Cherry tomato
1 Dill sprig
2 oz (60 g) Danish sour rye bread slices or baguette croûtons

PROCEDURE

FINISHING

1. Use a very sharp, flexible slicing knife to carve paper-thin slices off the gravlax sides. Starting at the tail end of each fillet piece, hold the knife crosswise to the fillet and almost parallel to the cutting board with the blade angled down. Slice on the bias (see photo at right).

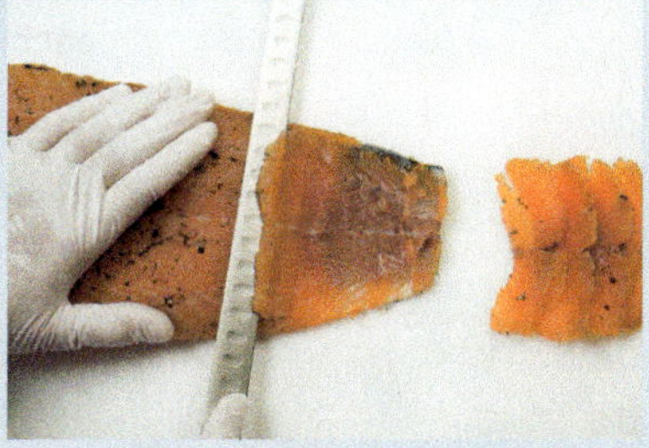

PLATING

2. Place the mustard sauce in a small dip dish and place it slightly left of center on a cool 10-in. (25-cm) plate.
3. Arrange the tomato and onions in the back center of the plate.
4. Arrange the sliced gravlax on the plate in a ruffle.
5. Stick the sprig upright behind the onions.
6. Serve the bread or croûtons in a basket lined with a napkin.

BRESAOLA

(bres-ah-AW-lah)

NORTHERN ITALIAN AIR-DRIED BEEF

Yield:
about 2 lb (1 kg) EP
Portions:
30
Portion size:
about 1 oz

INGREDIENTS	U.S.	METRIC
Beef eye-round roast	1 (3 lb)	1 (1.5 kg)
Fresh thyme leaves	¼ oz	7 g
Fresh rosemary leaves, chopped fine	¼ oz	7 g
Juniper berries, crushed	¼ oz	7 g
Freshly ground black pepper	¼ oz	7 g
Sugar	2 oz	60 mL
Prague Powder #2	4 g	4 g
Kosher salt	1 oz	30 g

PROCEDURE

DAY 1: FABRICATION AND FIRST CURE APPLICATION

1. Sanitize all equipment that will come into contact with the meat or dry cure compound.
2. Trim away all fat and silverskin from the eye round. If the diameter of the eye round is larger than 3 in. (8 cm), wrap it in plastic film and have a helper pull firmly on either end of the meat while you gently flatten the meat with a mallet on all sides (A). Continue until you achieve a long cut of meat that is 3 in. (8 cm) in diameter.

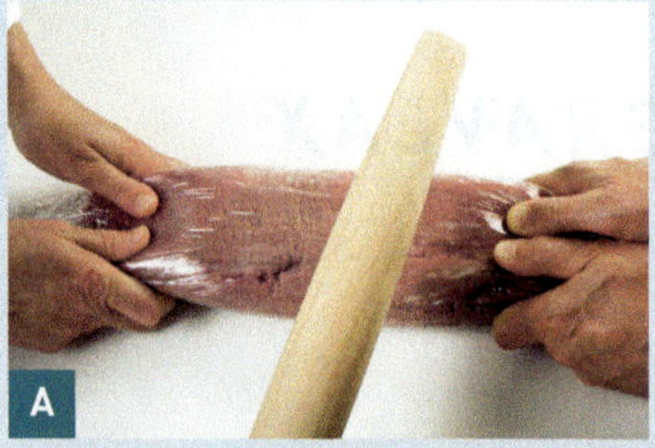

3. To make the dry cure compound, place *half* the total herbs, spices, sugar, Prague Powder #2, and salt in a small mortar and grind to a powder.
4. Remove the plastic film and sprinkle the meat with an even coating of the dry cure compound (B). Massage it into the meat.

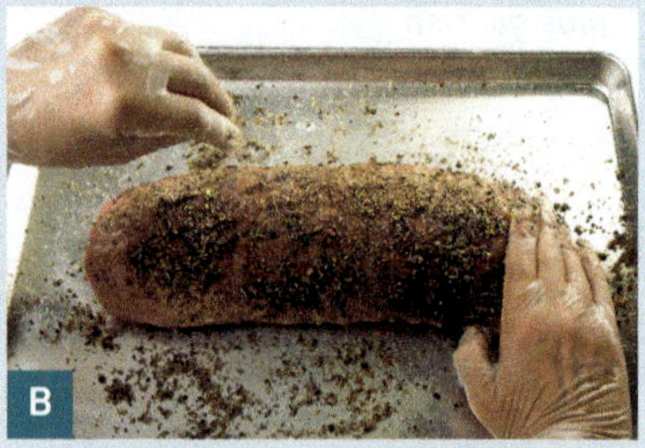

5. Place the meat in a plastic bag and tie it shut. Refrigerate the meat.

DAYS 2–8: FIRST CURE PENETRATION

6. Refrigerate the meat for 7 days, turning the bag each day.

DAY 9: SECOND CURE APPLICATION

7. Remove the beef from the bag and drain off the liquid. Using the remaining dry cure ingredients, repeat steps 1 through 5, placing the beef in a fresh bag.

DAYS 10–18: SECOND CURE PENETRATION

8. Refrigerate for 7 more days, turning the bag daily.

DAYS 19–40: AIR-DRYING

9. Drain the beef, rinse it under cool water to remove the dry cure ingredients, and blot it dry. Using kitchen string, tie the meat tight in a butcher's truss (p. 433) and make a loop at one end so you can hang the beef.
10. Hang the beef in the refrigerator over a drip pan, preferably in front of the circulation fan, for 1 month.

C

PROCEDURE

DAY 41: FINISHING

11. Cut down the bresaola and check the cure as described on page 419, step 7. When the cure is complete, the exterior will be dry and leathery (C) and the interior supple and smooth. If white mold has developed on the exterior, scrub it off with a vegetable brush under cold running water and blot the bresaola dry.
12. To serve, slice paper-thin with an electric slicer.

BRESAOLA

WITH ARUGULA AND PARMESAN

APPETIZER

Portion:
1

Portion size:
1½ oz (45 g) bresaola, plus garnish

COMPONENTS

1 oz (30 g) Arugula leaves, cleaned and thoroughly dried
1½ oz (45 g) *Bresaola (p. 432)*, sliced very thin
1 fl oz (30 mL) Extra-virgin olive oil, in squeeze bottle
½ fl oz (15 mL) *Balsamic Glaze (p. 690)*, in squeeze bottle
½ oz (15 g) Reggiano Parmesan cheese, shaved from the block
3 oz (90 g) Rustic Italian bread

PROCEDURE

PLATING

1. Arrange a bed of arugula leaves on a cool 10-in. (25-cm) plate.
2. Ruffle a circle of bresaola on top of the leaves, reserving a few slices for the center garnish. Roll the reserved slices into a loose "rose" and arrange it in the center.
3. Drizzle the bresaola with olive oil.
4. Squeeze dots of balsamic glaze around the edge of the plate well.
5. Use a cheese plane to shave slivers of Parmesan on top.
6. Serve the bread in a basket lined with a linen napkin.

PANCETTA

(pahn-CHET-tah)

ITALIAN UNSMOKED BACON

Yield:
2 rolls, about 4 ½ lb (2.25 kg) each

INGREDIENTS	U.S.	METRIC
Whole pork belly, skin on	1 (10 lb)	1 (5 kg)
Kosher salt	8 oz	240 g
Granulated sugar	1 oz	30 g
Light brown sugar	1 oz	30 g
Cracked black pepper	2 oz	60 g
Juniper berries, crushed	½ oz	15 g
Large bay leaves, crushed	7	7
Dried thyme leaves	1 tsp	5 mL
Crushed dried rosemary leaves	1 tsp	5 mL
Large cloves garlic, pushed through a press or crushed	2 oz	60 g
Prague Powder #1	¼ oz	7 g

PROCEDURE

DAY 1: FABRICATION AND CURE APPLICATION

1. Using a long, flexible knife, remove the rind (skin) from the pork belly.
2. Using a meat mallet, flatten the thicker parts of the belly to make it as even in thickness as possible.
3. Cut the pork belly in half widthwise.
3. Mix the remaining ingredients to make the dry cure compound.
4. Apply an even coating of the dry cure compound to the entire surface of each pork belly half. Massage the compound into the meat.
5. Place the meat in a hotel pan or plastic curing tub and cover it tight with plastic film or a lid. Place the pan in the refrigerator.

DAYS 2–11: CURE PENETRATION

6. Refrigerate the pork belly for 10 days. Overhaul every 2 days by turning the belly over. Wrap with fresh plastic film each time.

DAY 12: FABRICATION

7. Rinse the pork belly pieces under cool water and blot dry with a clean towel.
8. Starting at a short end, roll each belly half into a tight cylinder and, using kitchen string, secure it with a butcher's truss.
9. Hang the pancetta rolls in the refrigerator in front of the circulation fan. Place a drip pan underneath.

DAYS 13–26: AIR-DRYING

10. Allow the pancetta rolls to air-dry undisturbed for 2 weeks.

DAY 27: FINISHING

11. Cut the pancetta rolls down from their position in the refrigerator and wrap them in butcher paper or parchment. Place the wrapped pancetta in a plastic bag for storage. The pancetta is now ready to be sliced and pan-fried or used in pasta or other preparations.

HOLDING

Refrigerate up to 2 weeks, or freeze up to 3 months.

INTRODUCTION TO SMOKED FOODS

To flavor any food with smoke, all you need is a fuel that burns and creates the smoke and an enclosed area in which to trap the smoke. In small to mid-size smoking equipment, this enclosed area is called a ***smoke box*** or ***smoking chamber***. In the past, it was common to build an entire structure, called a ***smokehouse***, to enclose the smoke. Industrial producers have large smokehouses, as well.

Whether the equipment is large or small, the process is simple. When the fuel is ignited, the chamber fills with smoke. The food is suspended in the chamber, where it remains enveloped in a cloud of smoke for a designated period of time. The temperature in the chamber and the type of fuel used to create the smoke are important factors that determine the characteristics of the final product. Smoke changes food in several ways:

- The smoke's aroma penetrates the food.
- The flavor compounds in the smoke permeate the food.
- Pigments present in the smoke are transferred to the food's exterior and darken its color.
- Certain chemicals found in the smoke enhance its preservation.

The Importance of Curing Before Smoking

Smoking can be thought of as a finishing touch that adds flavor to foods and aids in preserving them. But smoking alone does not adequately preserve protein foods. That is why *meats, poultry, and seafood are always cured before smoking.* Properly curing protein foods in a brine or with a dry cure compound before smoking them reduces the number of microorganisms to a safe level, and prevents their growth and reproduction both during and after the smoking period.

Curing before smoking also improves the texture and flavor of the final product in two ways:

1. Curing accompanied by proper air-drying forms a pellicle that prepares the food to more fully accept the smoke.
2. Curing seasons the meat with the flavors we associate with smoked foods.

Curing before smoking does not necessarily apply to smoke-roasting and barbecuing, which are more properly considered cooking methods because they take place at higher temperatures that destroy harmful microorganisms. However, a light cure enhances the flavor of these foods and is recommended.

The Science of Smoking

Smoke contains more than 200 naturally occurring chemical components, all of which affect foods in various ways. Some of these chemicals are known to have beneficial effects on food, while others may actually be harmful to eat in high concentration. Although these questionable chemicals may be considered toxic to humans, they are also toxic to the harmful microorganisms that cause spoilage and food-borne illnesses, which is why smoke is a mild preservative. See the sidebar on page 437 for information on carcinogens in smoked products.

INGREDIENTS

Foods for Smoking

When choosing a food to be smoked, consider the strength of the item's inherent flavor, the strength of the cure to be applied, and the ultimate product's intended use. These factors help determine the type of wood to use, the flavoring ingredients to add to the smoke, the amount of smoke to use, and the length of the smoking time.

Meats, poultry, and fish are the most common foods to be smoked. Shellfish items, such as oysters or shrimp, are occasionally smoked. In general, foods with a high fat content are better for smoking.

Some cheeses are treated with smoke to enhance their flavor. Probably the best-known smoked cheeses are smoked gouda from the Netherlands and domestic smoked cheddars. We discuss smoked cheeses in Chapter 14.

Today, certain fruits and vegetables are also flavored with smoke. Contemporary chefs produce smoked fruits and vegetables as garnishes, condiments, and side dishes. Unlike meats, fruits and vegetables need not be cured before they are smoked.

Woods for Smoking

The flavor imparted by the smoking process depends on the type of wood burned to create the smoke. Not all woods are suitable. Soft-textured woods burn too quickly and produce too much soot and ash. The wood of evergreen trees contains strong resins that impart an unpleasant taste. Trees subjected to heavy doses of pesticides or that grow in soil heavily treated with herbicides should not be used. Pressure-treated wood should *never* be burned for smoking, as it contains dangerous chemical compounds, including arsenic.

The woods most frequently used come from hardwood trees. Some types of hardwood are much more fragrant and produce a more flavorful smoked product than others. Tradition is also a factor. The smoked meats of the American South are usually flavored with hickory wood, while the smoked fish of the American Pacific Northwest and Canadian West are smoked over alder. The prized hams of Westphalia in Germany hang in beechwood smoke.

Table 11.2 is a list of commercially produced woods for smoking available throughout North America.

TABLE 11.2 | Woods Commonly Used for Smoking

Type of Wood	Description	Smoke Flavor
Fruitwoods	Apple and cherry are the most widely available fruitwoods. In some areas you may find pear, peach, and even citrus woods.	The flavor marries well with light meats such as pork and poultry. Also good with fish.
Hickory	This regional favorite is essential for the true taste of classic Southern barbecue.	Hickory produces an unmistakable, bold flavor ideal for robust cuts of pork such as hams, bellies, butts, and ribs.
Maple	Favored in New England, the Mid-Atlantic, and Canada's Maritime Provinces.	Its sweet flavor is traditionally applied to sugar-cured American and Canadian bacon, but it also works well with poultry.
Mesquite	A scrub wood used in the American Southwest for smoke-roasting and grilling.	Use carefully, as prolonged application can give a bitter flavor to foods.
Oak	Several varieties are favored for both smoke-roasting and cold smoking.	Black Jack oak is distinctively flavored and is prevalent in the Deep South and in northern Florida, where it often replaces hickory.
Peat	The traditional smoking fuel of Ireland and Scotland. Peat is actually partially decayed moss and other vegetation. It requires no soaking.	Peat produces a distinctive flavor found in Irish and Scottish smoked salmon and Irish hams.

Wood Aging

Green wood, or wood from freshly harvested trees, burns slowly and creates a lot of smoke, both desirable qualities for smoking. However, it is difficult to ignite and maintain at the burn. It also creates storage problems, especially if it must be kept indoors. Because it is moist, it can easily mold or attract insects.

Aged wood, or **seasoned wood**, has been stored away from moisture and insects for at least a year after harvest. It is dry throughout and can be stored safely indoors. To create a sufficient amount of smoke, soak in water before use.

Wood Market Forms

Wood for smoking is available is several fabrication forms. The form you choose to use depends on the manufacturer's specifications provided with your smoker.

Split logs are used in large commercial and industrial smokers and outdoor smokehouses.

Wood blocks are rough-cut cubes of wood, roughly 2 × 2 in. (5 × 5 cm) in size. They contain both bark and interior wood.

Wood chips are small, flat pieces of wood and bark.

Sawdust is used in some smokers. It burns quickly and needs frequent restoking.

Flavorings for Smoking

Other ingredients may be used to impart interesting flavors and aromas to smoked foods. These ingredients are usually moistened and then placed on top of the smoking wood. As they heat up and begin to smolder, their volatile flavor compounds are released into the smoke and give a special taste to the food. A few of the many flavoring ingredients that may be used to flavor smoked foods are:

- Grapevine clippings
- Fennel stalks
- Peanut shells
- Herb branches and stems
- Whole spices
- Fruit peels
- Tea leaves
- Acorn hulls
- Cornhusks and corncobs

The Carcinogen Question

In the mid-twentieth century, scientists discovered that substances found in wood smoke—and, thus, in foods prepared by smoking them—cause cancer in laboratory animals. However, it is important to recognize that modern smoked foods are subjected to a relatively light application of smoke, so the concentration of toxins is very small. The USDA has ruled that the amount of carcinogenic substances present in modern industrial and artisan smoked products is so low they can be considered safe. Health officials do, however, counsel consumers to limit the amount of smoked products they consume to one or two servings per week.

SMOKING TEMPERATURES

The texture of smoked products and, to a lesser extent, their flavor and appearance, are determined by the temperature at which they are smoked. The temperature factor is so important that we use temperature to name the two basic types of smoking and to describe the products that result from them:

1. Cold smoking
2. Hot smoking

Cold Smoking

In ***cold smoking***, foods are held at temperatures below 100°F (38°C) during the application of smoke. A temperature range of 80°–90°F (26°–32°C) is ideal. At these temperatures, there is not enough heat to denature the protein structure of the flesh, so there is little change in texture or appearance. Cold-smoked foods are appreciated not only for their smoky flavor but also for their smooth, supple texture and unique mouthfeel.

Because of their special texture, most cold-smoked foods are not cooked for service but, instead, are presented as is, at cool room temperature. They are usually carved into paper-thin slices. There are three reasons for this:

1. The thin slices showcase the products' attractive, translucent appearance.
2. Thin slicing takes into account the powerful flavors of the cure and the smoke. When cold-smoked foods are sliced thin, these flavors are distributed evenly on the tongue so the taste does not overwhelm the palate.
3. Because connective tissues have not been broken down by heat, many smoked products would be too chewy if cut into thick slices.

Hot Smoking

In ***hot smoking***, foods are surrounded by smoke at temperatures between 150° and 200°F (65°C and 93°C). Most are brought to an internal temperature of 165°F (75°C). At this temperature, the texture and appearance of the food changes. Fish changes from translucent to opaque and takes on a visibly flaky texture. Meat also becomes opaque. Its texture becomes smoother and, in most products, more tender. Fat, as in bacon and on the surface of hams, becomes firmer in texture and changes in color from white to ivory. The outer surfaces of these foods darken not only due to the pigments in the smoke but also from Maillard browning and caramelization. Thus, hot smoking produces foods with smoky flavors and cooked textures.

Some hot-smoked foods are served as is, at cool room temperature. Other hot-smoked foods are customarily reheated for service, although they are safe to eat without doing so.

EQUIPMENT FOR SMOKING

The type and size of smoking equipment you choose depends on the kinds of products you wish to produce, the volume of product you expect to generate, the space available to accommodate the equipment, and your budget. No matter which type of equipment you plan to use, your smoker will have three basic features:

1. A heat source
2. A smoking chamber
3. A ventilation/circulation system

Heat Source

A smoker's heat source serves to ignite the fuel and maintain it at the proper temperature to smolder. In more technologically advanced smokers, the heat source is powered by electricity, and the amount of heat produced is controlled with an external dial. Simple smokers, as well as smokers improvised from covered grills, use burning fuel as their heat source. Charcoal smokers and smokers improvised from charcoal grills use charcoal slabs or briquettes as the heat source. With skill and patience, you can manipulate the coals to burn at very low temperatures. However, maintaining low temperatures for long periods is tricky and time-consuming. On a gas grill it is easy to control the amount of heat, but few gas grills can be set to temperatures lower than 200°F (93°C). Chefs limited to these types of smokers typically restrict their production to hot-smoked items.

Units designed for cold smoking have their heat source in an external fuel box connected to the smoking chamber by a pipe or tube. This keeps much of the heat out of the smoking chamber. However, if the smoking chamber is not equipped with refrigeration, the temperature inside can still climb to temperatures unsuitable for cold smoking, so these units must be carefully monitored. Only large commercial smokers have refrigerated chambers.

Smoking Chamber

Smoking requires an enclosed area that contains the smoke. This area is generally boxlike in shape and thus is often called a smoke box. In some domestic smokers, the smoke is contained in a cylindrical chamber. The smoking chamber must contain one or more racks to hold the food. Larger smokers are fitted with equipment for hanging foods from rods or hooks.

Ventilation/Circulation System

Ventilation is necessary to control the amount of smoke that comes into contact with the food. While you can, to some extent, control the amount of smoke from the heat source, it is faster and easier to control smoke by venting it, or letting it out of the chamber through adjustable openings. All commercial and domestic smokers are equipped with vents. However, many improvised smoking setups are not. With these, your only option is to prop the lid open and monitor the amount of smoke inside.

For even smoke penetration and good appearance, the smoky air must circulate properly around the food. In simple smokers, the circulation of the smoke is generated by the draw from the vents. More advanced smokers are equipped with fans that move the smoke around the interior of the smoking chamber more efficiently.

In addition to creating ventilation within the smoker itself, *you must be certain to provide adequate external ventilation* when using any type of smoker indoors.

Types of Smokers

Table 11.3 describes the types of smokers available.

Small Equipment for Smoking

Most commercial and domestic smokers are equipped with the racks, rods, and hooks to suspend foods in them. You may wish to purchase additional items. Some chefs improvise with tools and equipment already present in their kitchens.

Smoker Safety

When any type of carbon fuel is burned, the result is a number of byproducts, among them harmful gases such as carbon monoxide. If you were to breathe these harmful gases in high concentration, you would quickly become sick. However, gases are not the only danger inherent in the smoking process. The smoke that gives foods a tantalizing aroma, wonderful flavor, and beautiful color also contains substances known to cause cancer when ingested in high concentration. Thus, people who regularly breathe in high amounts of smoke are at risk of developing lung cancer. Because it produces harmful gases and smoke, place your smoker where both will be drawn away from the air people breathe. In a commercial kitchen, the smoker is placed or installed under an exhaust system hood, and the exhaust system must always be in operation when the smoker is in use.

TABLE 11.3 Type of Smokers

Type of Smoker	Description
Commercial/industrial convection smoker with temperature-controlled chamber and external fuel box	Suitable for both hot and cold smoking. It can also function as an air-drying chamber for cured foods and as a food dehydrator.
Commercial convection smoker with external fuel box (electric)	Well suited to hot smoking and can be used for cold smoking with the use of an ice pan. When cold smoking, carefully monitor the chamber's internal temperature and replace the melted ice frequently.
Domestic convection smoker with external fuel box (electric)	This smaller and more affordable smoker can maintain a lower internal temperature than other domestic smokers with internal fuel boxes. To successfully cold smoke, use an ice pan to lower the temperature inside the chamber.
Domestic convection smoker with internal fuel box (electric)	Because the fuel box is located in the bottom of the smoking chamber, the temperature inside the chamber typically rises well above 100°F (38°C). This makes it unsuitable for cold smoking. If connected to a food dehydrator, the two units together can be used for cold smoking.
Domestic smoker (electric)	Has no fan or temperature control system. It relies on venting to adjust both circulation and internal temperature.
Gas grill converted for smoking	To use a propane gas grill for smoking, place the fuel directly on the ceramic briquettes on one side of the grill and maintain the lowest possible heat under them. Place the food on the top rack on the other side of the grill and close the lid. Control the smoke and heat by propping open the lid as necessary. Use outdoors only.
Charcoal grill converted for smoking	To use for smoking, place charcoal slabs or briquettes on one side of the fire pan, ignite them, and allow them to burn down to a low glow. Place the fuel on them. Place the food on the top rack on the other side of the grill. Close the lid. Use the vents on the lid to control the smoke and heat. Use outdoors only.

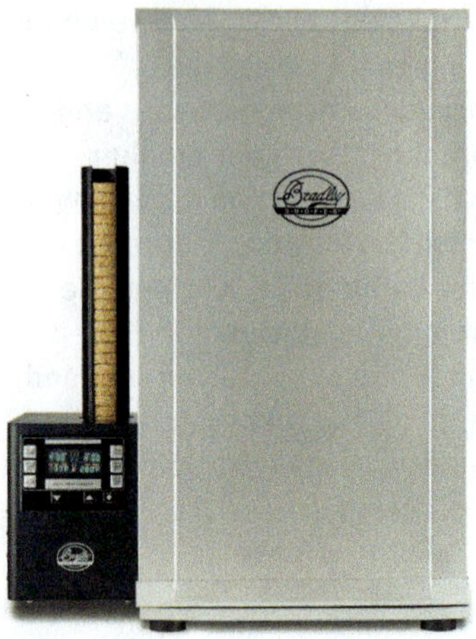

Domestic convection smoker with external fuel box (electric) *© Bradley Smoker, Inc.*

Others use nonfood-service sources, such as the hardware store, to purchase smoking hardware. If you do, make sure all equipment coming into contact with food is made of a food-grade material.

THE SMOKING PROCEDURE

While the procedure for smoking is relatively simple and straightforward, preparing superb smoked products is a skill that takes time and experience to develop. Creating a product that is firm and moist, with just the correct balance of cure and smoke, is the goal. Successful smoking requires careful observation, attention to detail, judgment, and patience.

Your smoked product will only be as safe and as good as the cured product on which it is based. *Follow all curing procedures carefully and correctly before smoking.*

Procedure for Smoking

1. Fabricate and cure the food to be smoked. (Curing procedures appear earlier in this chapter.) Make sure air-drying and pellicle formation are complete before beginning the smoking process.
2. Twenty-four hours before beginning the smoking process, select the wood that will be used as fuel. Estimate the amount of wood needed and include about 10% extra. Place the fuel in a nonreactive container, cover it with cold water, weight it with a nonreactive lid, and allow it to soak at room temperature until needed. (Sawdust and some other types of fuel need no soaking.)
3. Drain the wood and place the correct amount on the heat source. If using hardwood logs or charcoal briquettes as fuel, make the fire and allow it to burn down to the specified temperature. Open the vent(s) to create a draft. Position the racks or other hardware in an appropriate configuration to accommodate the food to be smoked. Close the door.
4. Turn on the electric or gas heat source to the temperature specified in the recipe. Allow smoke to build in the smoking chamber.
5. Quickly place the cured food in the smoking chamber and close the door. (If using an ice pan, add it when placing the food in the chamber.)
6. Adjust the vents and temperature control as necessary to maintain the specified smoking temperature within the chamber.
7. Set a timer as needed for rotation, smoke adjustment, refueling, re-icing, or any other maintenance steps. Reset the timer each time for the duration of the smoking process.
8. After smoking is complete, air-dry the smoked products on racks (or hanging) over a drip pan at the specified temperature for the specified amount of time.
9. Spread any unused soaked wood on a tray. Place in the sun or in a warm, nonhumid place to dry for reuse.
10. Wrap the smoked products in butcher paper and refrigerate.

RECIPES

CHERRY-HONEY HOT-SMOKED TROUT

Yield:
24 3-oz (90 g) fillets

INGREDIENTS	U.S.	METRIC
Boned and butterflied whole brook trout or rainbow trout, 10 oz (300 g) each	12	12
Filtered or distilled water	1 gal	4 L
Kosher salt	1 lb 4 oz	600 g
Mild clover honey	5 fl oz	150 mL
Mixed pickling spices (p. 414)	1 oz	30 g

Supplies

Cherrywood (fabrication type and amount specified by smoker manufacturer)

PROCEDURE

DAY 1: FABRICATION, CURE APPLICATION, AND CURE PENETRATION

1. Remove the heads from the trout (see Note). Using kitchen tweezers or needlenose pliers, remove the pin bones.
2. Wash the trout and blot them dry.
3. Place the trout in a single layer in plastic container or hotel pan just large enough to hold them. Refrigerate the trout.
4. Combine the water, salt, honey, and spices in a stainless-steel pan. Bring to the boil, stirring occasionally. Remove the brine from the heat, cool it to room temperature, and then refrigerate it to 38°F (3°C). Alternatively, cool the pan in an ice bain-marie.
5. Pour the cold brine over the trout (A), cover with plastic wrap, and place another container or pan on top to gently weight the trout and keep it submerged in the brine. Place the containers in the refrigerator.
6. Allow the trout to cure 8–10 hours.
7. Place the wood in a container, cover it with tap water, and weight it to keep it submerged. Soak at room temperature at least 24 hours.

A

B

C

DAY 2: AIR-DRYING AND SMOKING

8. Drain the trout and gently rinse it under cool water.
9. Place the trout skin-side down, in a single layer, on the smoker rack set over a sheet tray (B). Place the rack uncovered in the refrigerator.
10. Air-dry the trout 8 hours.
11. Place the soaked wood in the smoker, set the temperature controls to 200°F (93°C), and wait for a full build of smoke.
12. Place the trout in the smoker (C) and smoke it for 1–1½ hours, or until it reaches an internal temperature of 145°F (63°C).

D

PROCEDURE

13. Cool to room temperature (D).
14. Individually wrap each trout in butcher paper or parchment, then place all of the wrapped trout in an open plastic bag.
16. Refrigerate.

HOLDING

Refrigerate up to 2 weeks. Do not freeze.

Note: Heads may be refrigerated or frozen for use in stock.

VARIATIONS

NORTHWOODS HOT-SMOKED TROUT

Replace the honey with light brown sugar. Add to the brine ¼ oz (7 g) juniper berries and 6 oz (180 g) thinly sliced onions. Optionally, replace the cherrywood with maple wood.

SOUTHWEST-STYLE MESQUITE HOT-SMOKED TROUT

Replace the honey with light brown sugar. Replace the pickling spices with ¼ oz (7 g) coriander seed, ¼ oz (7 g) cumin seed, ½ oz (15 g) black peppercorns, 4 bay leaves, 1 tsp (5 mL) dried oregano, and 6 chiles de arbol or other small dried red chiles. Replace the cherrywood with mesquite.

CHERRYWOOD-SMOKED TROUT

WITH CHERRY-PEAR CHUTNEY

APPETIZER

Portion:
1
Portion size:
2½ oz (70 g) trout, plus garnishes

COMPONENTS

1 Red-leaf lettuce leaf
1 (3 oz/120 g) Fillet of *Cherry-Honey Hot-Smoked Trout (p. 442)*
1 fl oz (30 mL) *Cherry-Pear Chutney (p. 681)*
5–6 Baguette croûtons
3 slices (½ oz/15 g) Firm-ripe red pear

PROCEDURE

PLATING

1. Place the lettuce leaf on a cool 10-in. (25-cm) plate.
2. Carefully remove the skin from the trout fillet. Place the fillet across the front of the plate.
3. Mound the chutney on the lettuce behind the trout..
4. Fan the croûtons from 12 to 4 o'clock.
5. Fan the pear slices on the right side of the trout.

VARIATIONS

NORTHWOODS HOT-SMOKED TROUT WITH HORSERADISH CREAM

Replace the chutney with Horseradish Cream (p. 45). Garnish with 1 oz (30 g) brunoise-cut red onion.

SOUTHWEST-STYLE MESQUITE HOT-SMOKED TROUT WITH SWEET CORN SALSA

Replace the chutney with Sweet Corn Salsa (p. 51). Add a ½-oz (15 g) rosette sour cream.

PACIFIC NORTHWEST HOT-SMOKED SALMON

Yield:
about 3 lb (1.5 kg)

INGREDIENTS	U.S.	METRIC
Kosher salt	1¾ lb	875 g
Light brown sugar	1 lb	500 g
Filtered or distilled water	5 qt	5 L
Bay leaves	6	6
Coriander seeds	¼ oz	7 g
Black peppercorns	⅛ oz	3 g
Wild Pacific salmon fillet, skin on	4 lb	2 kg
Dark rum	8 fl oz	240 mL
Light brown sugar	5 oz	150 g
Kosher salt	¼ oz	7 g

Supplies

Alder or cherrywood (fabrication type and amount specified by smoker manufacturer)

PROCEDURE

DAY 1: FABRICATION AND CURE APPLICATION

1. To make the brine, combine the salt, sugar, water, bay leaves, coriander seeds, and peppercorns in a stainless-steel pan. Bring to the simmer to dissolve the salt and sugar. Cool to room temperature and then refrigerate until cold.
2. Wash the salmon to remove any scales. Blot it dry.
3. Using kitchen tweezers or needlenose pliers, remove any pin bones. Cut the salmon into 4-oz (120-g) pieces, about 2 × 5 in. (5 × 12 cm) and as uniform in size as possible. Refrigerate the salmon until needed.
4. Sanitize a deep half-hotel pan or plastic container just large enough to hold the salmon in one layer.
5. Blot the salmon dry of any fluids and place it in one layer in the container. Pour the brine over the salmon, making sure it is completely submerged. Cover the container and place it in the refrigerator.
6. Cure the salmon 6–8 hours.
7. To make the glaze, combine the rum, brown sugar, and salt in a small saucepan and bring to the simmer to dissolve the sugar and salt. Cool to room temperature.
8. Make a slit in the thickest piece of salmon and check the cure. If the cure is complete, the color and texture of the flesh will be the same throughout. If the cure is not complete, continue curing a few hours longer.
9. Remove the salmon from the brine and rinse it in cold water. Blot it dry.
10. Place the salmon skin-side down on a rack set over a drip pan. Paint the top and sides of the salmon pieces with *half* the glaze. Place it in the refrigerator, preferably near the circulation fan.
11. About 4 hours later, apply the remaining glaze to the salmon. Allow it to air-dry about 4 hours longer.
12. Place the smoking wood in a container and cover it with tap water. Weight it with a lid. Soak the wood at room temperature for at least 24 hours.

DAY 2: AIR-DRYING AND SMOKING

13. Allow the salmon to air-dry 12–24 hours.
14. Place the soaked wood in the smoker, set the temperature controls to 180°F (82°C), and wait for a full build of smoke.
15. Place the salmon skin-side down on smoking racks and load it into the smoker. Open all the vents to maintain as low a temperature as possible.

The History of Kippered Salmon

Salmon cured in a brine or a dry curing compound and then hot smoked is often called *kippered*. Food historians cite two different origins of this term. In English slang of the nineteenth and early twentieth centuries, a bed was called a *kip*, and *to kip* meant "to lie down in bed." It is possible the term *kipper* was applied to fish laid down in a bed of salt. Other possible sources for the term are the Middle English word *kypre* and the Old English word *cypera*, meaning "copper colored." This could refer to the bronzed color hot smoking gives to the exterior of pink-fleshed fish.

PROCEDURE

16. Smoke the salmon 45 minutes–2 hours, or until the thickest piece reaches an internal temperature of 138°F (58°C).
17. Cool the salmon to room temperature and then refrigerate it, uncovered, until it is cold.
18. Individually wrap each piece in butcher paper or parchment and then place the packages in an open plastic bag. Alternatively, vacuum-seal each piece.

HOLDING

Refrigerate up to 2 weeks. Do not freeze.

VARIATIONS

PEPPER-CRUSTED HOT-SMOKED SALMON

Replace the dark rum and brown sugar in the glaze with light rum and white sugar. After the second glaze application, press 1½ tsp (7 mL) cracked black peppercorns into the top and sides of each piece.

PACIFIC NORTHWEST HOT-SMOKED STEELHEAD TROUT

Replace the salmon with 2 steelhead trout fillets, 2½ lb (1.2 kg) each, pinned and cut into 10 4-oz (120 g) pieces.

PACIFIC NORTHWEST SMOKED SALMON

WITH SAUCE SUÉDOISE

APPETIZER

Portion:
1
Portion size:
3½ oz (105 g) salmon, plus garnish

COMPONENTS

1 Red-leaf lettuce leaf
1 piece (3½ oz/105 g) *Pacific Northwest Hot-Smoked Salmon (p. 444)*
1 (4 oz/120 g) Small Red Delicious apple
2 fl oz (60 mL) *Sauce Suédoise (p. 42)*
5 Toasted baguette croûtons

PROCEDURE

PLATING

1. Place the lettuce leaf on a cool 10-in. (25-cm) plate.
2. Peel the skin off the salmon. Place the salmon diagonally, from 2 to 7 o'clock, on the leaf.
3. Cut off the top 3rd of the apple and use a parisienne scoop to carve out a 2 fl oz (60 mL) hollow, creating an apple "cup." Fabricate the remaining apple into julienne cuts.
4. Fill the apple "cup" with the sauce Suédoise and place it behind the salmon.
5. Fan the croûtons from 1 to 4 o'clock.
6. Mound the julienne apple between the salmon and the croûtons.

VARIATION

PEPPER-CRUSTED HOT-SMOKED SALMON WITH MUSTARD MAYONNAISE

Replace the Pacific Northwest hot-smoked salmon with Pepper-Crusted Hot-Smoked Salmon. Replace the apple cup with a cucumber cup (p. 717). Replace the sauce Suédoise with Mustard Mayonnaise (p. 43).

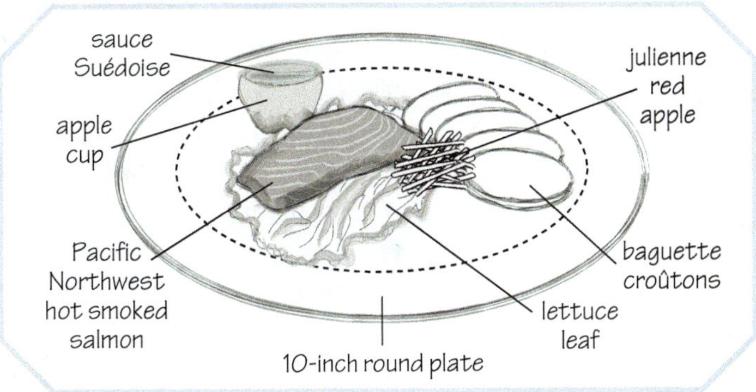

HOT-SMOKED CHICKEN

Yield:
about 5 lb (2.25 kg) with bone and skin, about 3 lb (2.25 kg) trimmed meat

Portions:
4

Portion size:
one-half chicken, about 1¼ lb (0.5 kg) bone-in

INGREDIENTS	U.S.	METRIC
Filtered or distilled water	1½ gal	6 L
Kosher salt	12 oz	360 g
Sugar	6 oz	180 g
Fresh lemon juice	4 oz	120 mL
Cracked black peppercorns	1 oz	30 g
Crushed garlic cloves	1 oz	30 g
Sliced onions	4 oz	120 g
Fresh tarragon	2 bunches	2 bunches
Fryer chickens, 3 lb (1.4 kg) each	2	2

Supplies

Choice of fruitwood (fabrication type and amount as specified by the smoker manufacturer)

PROCEDURE

DAY 1: FABRICATION AND CURE APPLICATION

1. To make the brine, place the water, salt, sugar, lemon juice, peppercorns, garlic, onions, and tarragon in a large stainless-steel pan. Bring to a simmer to dissolve the salt and sugar. Cool the brine and then refrigerate it until it is cold.
2. Sanitize a nonreactive container large enough to hold the chickens and brine. Sanitize its lid and a plate or other nonreactive object to use as a weight.
3. Remove the giblet pack from the cavity of the chickens. Remove any traces of liver that remain attached to the backbones. Trim away any excess skin and fatty deposits from the chickens, taking special care not to cut skin away from the breast, leg, and thigh areas.
4. Rinse the exterior and cavity of the chickens under cool running water. Pat dry inside and out.
5. Weigh each chicken and calculate 10% of its weight.
6. Strain enough brine to equal 10% of each chicken's weight and place it in a freshly sanitized food injector.
7. Following the diagram on page 420, inject the brine into each chicken at the key injection points (A).
8. Place the chickens in the container and cover it with the remaining brine. Place the plate on top to keep them completely submerged (B). Cover the container and place it in the refrigerator.

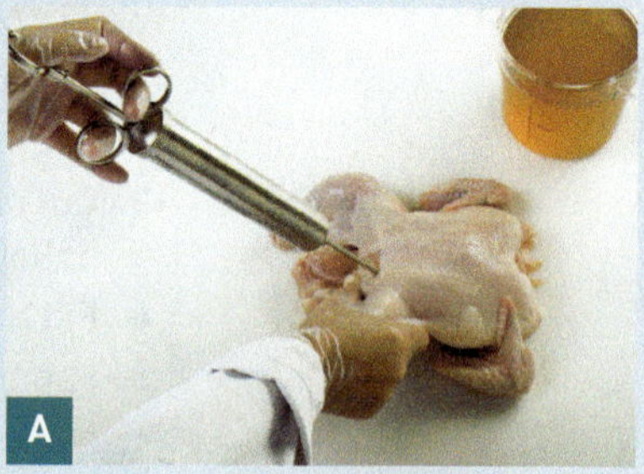
A

DAYS 1–2: CURE PENETRATION

9. Allow the chickens to cure for 24 hours.

DAYS 2–3: AIR-DRYING

10. Remove the chickens from the brine and rinse them, inside and out, under cool running water. Blot them dry.
11. Place the chickens on a rack set over a drip pan. Place the pan in the refrigerator.
12. Air-dry the chickens for 24 hours.

B

PROCEDURE

13. Place the wood in a container, cover it with tap water, weight the wood to submerge it, and soak at least 24 hours.

DAY 4: SMOKING AND FINISHING

14. Place the soaked wood in the smoker, set the temperature controls to 180°F (82°C), and wait for a full build of smoke.
15. Truss the chickens by an approved method. Place the chickens breast-side up on the smoker rack.
16. Smoke the chickens for 12 hours to an internal temperature of 160°F (71°C) taken in the thigh.
17. Remove the smoked chickens from the smoker and place them on a rack set over a drip pan. Cool to room temperature. (The smoked chicken is at its best served within 2 hours after reaching room temperature.)
18. Wrap each chicken loosely in butcher paper or parchment, then place each package in an unsealed plastic bag. Refrigerate.

HOLDING

Refrigerate up to 1 week.

VARIATIONS

HOT-SMOKED TURKEY BREAST

Replace the chickens with a 6-lb (2.8 kg) boneless turkey breast. Increase the curing time to 48 hours. Increase the smoking time to 12 hours.

CHINESE TEA-SMOKED CHICKEN

Replace the brine with a Chinese brine consisting of 3 qt (3 L) filtered or distilled water, 1 qt (1 L) Chinese light soy sauce, 1 qt (1 L) brewed black tea, 3 whole star anise pods, 1 bunch crushed scallions, and 8 oz (240 g) crushed and chopped fresh ginger. Cover the smoking wood with 8 oz (240 g) leaf black tea that has been soaked in water for 2 hours.

SMOKED CHICKEN

WITH TARRAGON MAYONNAISE

MAIN COURSE

Portion:
1

Portion size:
one-half chicken, 1¼ lb (0.5 kg) bone-in, plus accompaniments

COMPONENTS

1¼ lb (0.5 kg) *Hot-Smoked Chicken (p. 446)*, half
½ (2 oz/60 g) Plum tomato
6 fl oz (180 mL) *French Potato Salad (p. 145)* or other cold starch accompaniment
1 fl oz (30 mL) *Creamy Tarragon Mayonnaise (p. 43)*, made without half-and-half
2 oz (60 g) Salad greens of choice
1 fl oz (30 mL) *American Cider Vinaigrette (p. 32)*

PROCEDURE

FINISHING

1. If working with a whole chicken, remove the trussing string and cut it in half through the breastbone and backbone without damaging the skin. Wrap and store one of the chicken halves and proceed with the other one.
2. Fabricate the chicken half as follows, taking care not to damage the skin.
   a. Separate the leg from the chicken.
   b. Cut the leg through the joint into a thigh and drumstick.

(continues)

PROCEDURE *(continued)*

c. Chop the knuckle off the drumstick, making a clean break of the bone. If necessary, chop a small slice off the other end so the drumstick will sit upright.

d. Remove the thigh bone from the thigh.

e. Remove the breast meat from the bones.

f. Slice the breast on the diagonal, keeping the slices together in the shape of the breast.

3. If necessary, place the chicken in a microwave oven and heat it a few seconds only to bring it just to room temperature.
4. Use a parisienne scoop to hollow out the plum tomato, making a tomato "cup."

PLATING

5. Mound the potato salad on the back right of a cool 12-in. (30-cm) plate.
6. Prop the drumstick upright, with the bone up, against the left side of the potato salad and place the thigh in front of it. Fan the chicken breast across the front of the plate leaning against the thigh.
7. Fill the plum tomato "cup" with the tarragon mayonnaise and place it to the left of the thigh.
8. Toss the salad greens with the vinaigrette and mound them on the back left of the plate.

VARIATIONS

SMOKED TURKEY BREAST WITH TARRAGON MAYONNAISE

Replace the Hot-Smoked Chicken with 5 oz (150 g) sliced Hot-Smoked Turkey Breast (p. 447).

TEA-SMOKED CHICKEN WITH ASIAN SALADS

Replace the Hot-Smoked Chicken with Tea-Smoked Chicken. Replace the accompaniments with Asian Cucumber Salad (p. 133) and Chinese-Style Peanut Noodle Salad (p. 150). Replace the tarragon mayonnaise in the tomato cup with Wasabi Soy Dip (p. 690) in a cucumber cup (p. 717).

ALSATIAN-STYLE HOT-SMOKED PORK LOIN

Yield:
about 4½ lb (2 kg)

INGREDIENTS	U.S.	METRIC
Distilled water	1 gal	4 l
Prague Powder #1	1¼ oz	37 g
Sugar	8 oz	240 g
Kosher salt	12 oz	360 g
Juniper berries, crushed	1 oz	30 g
Black peppercorns	½ oz	15 g
Fresh sage	½ oz	15 g
Fresh thyme	½ oz	15 g
Thinly sliced onion	6 oz	180 g
Crushed garlic	1 oz	30 g
Boneless pork loin, fat and silverskin on	5 lb	2 kg
Gewürztraminer or other fruity, floral-scented wine	25 fl oz	750 mL

Supplies

Oak wood (fabrication type and amount as specified by the smoker manufacturer)

PROCEDURE

DAY 1: BRINE APPLICATION AND PENETRATION

1. To make the brine, place the distilled water, Prague Powder, sugar, salt, juniper berries, pepper, sage thyme, onion, and garlic in a large stainless-steel pan. Bring the liquid to a simmer to dissolve the salt and sugar. Cool to room temperature and then refrigerate until cold.
2. Score the pork loin: Using a sharp boning knife, cut a ¼-in. (0.5-cm) cross-hatch pattern through the fat and silverskin and extending ⅛ in. (0.33 cm) into the meat beneath them. (Refer to page 257.)
3. Place the pork loin in heavy-duty 2-gal (8-L) plastic bag and place it in a large bowl. Pour the brine into the bag and seal it. Weight the pork loin with a plate to keep it submerged. Place it in the refrigerator.

DAYS 2–4: CURE APPLICATION

4. Cure in the refrigerator for 72 hours.

DAYS 4–5: FLAVORING WITH WINE

5. Remove the pork loin from the brine and rinse it thoroughly under cool water. Blot it dry.
6. Check the cure by cutting a slit into the center. If the cure is complete, the color and texture of the flesh will be the same throughout. If the cure is not complete, continue curing for another day.
7. Place the pork loin in another plastic bag and place it in a bowl. Pour the wine into the bag, seal, and weight it. Make sure the pork is completely surrounded by the wine.

DAYS 5–6: AIR-DRYING

8. Remove the pork from the wine and blot it dry.
9. Place the pork on a rack set over a drip pan. Place in the refrigerator, preferably near the circulation fan.
10. Air-dry, uncovered, 24 hours.
11. Place the wood in a container, cover it with tap water, weight the wood to submerge it, and soak at least 24 hours.

DAY 6: SMOKING AND FINISHING

12. Place the soaked wood in the smoker, set the temperature to 180°F (82°C), and wait for a full build of smoke.

(continues)

PROCEDURE *(continued)*

13. Place the pork, fat-side up, on the smoker rack.
14. Smoke the pork loin 2–3 hours, or to an internal temperature of 155°F (68°C).
15. Remove the pork loin from the smoker and cool it to room temperature on a rack set over a drip pan.
16. Wrap the pork loin in butcher paper or parchment.

HOLDING

Refrigerate up to 2 weeks.

VARIATIONS

CANADIAN BACON

Omit the juniper and onion from the brine. Replace the pork loin with pork loin eye. Reduce the curing time to 48 hours. Omit the wine. Replace the oak with maple. Reduce the smoking time to 2 hours.

SMOKED PORK CHOPS

Prepare Canadian bacon, but replace the pork loin eye with eight 7-oz (200-g) center-cut rib pork chops. Reduce the curing time to 24 hours. Reduce the smoking time to 1 hour.

ALSATIAN PORK LOIN

WITH MUSTARD AND PICKLED PLUMS

MAIN COURSE

Portion:
1
Portion size:
4 oz pork, plus garnish

COMPONENTS

4 oz (120 g) *Alsatian-Style Hot-Smoked Pork Loin (p. 449)*, sliced thin
½ oz (15 g) Mesclun (p. 62)
3 halves (1½ oz/45 g) *Pickled Prune Plums (p. 677)*, drained
½ fl oz (15 mL) Dijon mustard, in squeeze bottle
3 oz (90 g) French baguette or other crisp-crusted white bread
1 oz (30 g) Whipped unsalted butter

PROCEDURE

PLATING

1. Arrange the pork loin slices in an overlapping circle on a cool 12-in. (30-cm) plate, leaving a 2-in. (5-cm) space in the center and at least a ½-in. (1-cm) space inside the plate rim.
2. Place a bed of the mesclun in the center and arrange the plums on it.
3. Pipe flourishes of mustard around the edge of the plate well.
4. Serve the bread in a basket and the butter in a butter chip or dip dish.

VARIATION

ALSATIAN PORK LOIN WITH CHERRY-PEAR CHUTNEY

Replace the pickled plums with Cherry-Pear Chutney (p. 681).

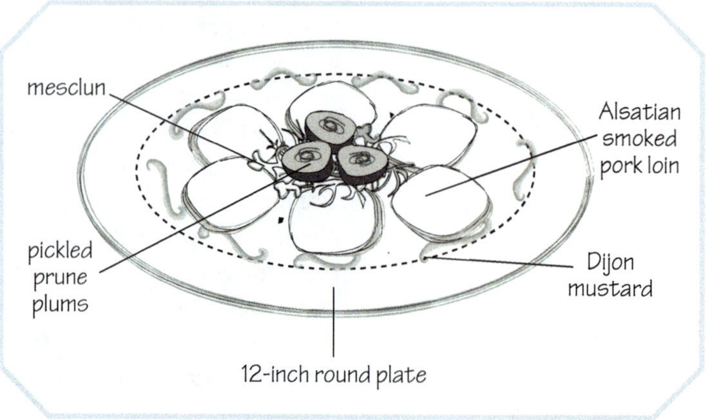

BACON

Yield:
about 9 lb (4.3 kg)

INGREDIENTS	U.S.	METRIC
Whole pork belly, skin (rind) on, about 10 lb (4.8 kg)	1	1
Prague Powder #1	0.8 oz	24 g
Sugar	3 oz	90 g
Kosher salt	4 oz	120 g

Supplies

Hickory (fabrication type and amount as specified by the smoker manufacturer)

PROCEDURE

DAY 1: CURE APPLICATION

1. Weigh the pork belly. If its weight is more or less than 10 lb (4.8 kg), adjust the formula for the curing compound ingredients accordingly.
2. Cut the belly in half widthwise.
3. Mix the Prague Powder, sugar, and salt to make the curing compound.
4. Rub the curing compound onto all surfaces of the pork belly.
5. Place one half of the belly skin-side down in a 4-in. (10-cm) half-hotel pan. Place the other half of the pork belly skin-side-up on top of the other half.
6. Wrap the pan tight with plastic film and place it in the refrigerator.

DAYS 2–9: CURE PENETRATION

7. Allow to cure for 8 days, overhauling (turning) every 2 days.

DAYS 9–10: AIR-DRYING

8. Remove the pork bellies from the pan and rinse them thoroughly under cool water.
9. Using a bacon hook, hang the pork bellies in the refrigerator over a drip pan for 24 hours.
10. Place the wood in a container, cover it with tap water, weight the wood to submerge it, and soak it at least 24 hours.

DAY 11: SMOKING AND FINISHING

11. Place the soaked wood in the smoker, set the temperature to 180°F (82°C), and wait for a full build of smoke.
12. Hang the pork bellies in the smoker, or place them on racks, skin-side down, in the smoker.
13. Smoke the bellies 2–3 hours, or to an internal temperature of 165°F (73°C).
14. Remove the bacon from the smoker and cool it to room temperature by hanging or on a rack set over a drip pan.
15. Wrap each slab of bacon in butcher paper or parchment and refrigerate.

HOLDING

Refrigerate up to 2 weeks or freeze up to 3 months. Remove rind before slicing.

VARIATIONS

PEPPERED BACON

Between steps 14 and 15 press ½ oz (15 g) cracked black peppercorns in an even layer all over the flesh side of the bacon.

SUGAR-CURED BACON

Replace the granulated sugar with 8 oz (240 g) brown sugar.

HONEY-CURED BACON

Replace the granulated sugar with 16 fl oz (500 mL) full-flavored dark honey.

MAPLE-CURED BACON

Replace the granulated sugar with 8 oz (240 g) maple sugar. Replace the hickory with maple wood.

Procedure for Cooking Artisan Bacon

1. Using a sharp, flexible slicing knife, remove the rind from the bacon (see Note 1).
2. By hand or machine, slice the bacon into strips ranging from 1⁄16 in. (1.5 mm) to ⅛ in. (3 mm) thick.
3. To prevent curling, score the bacon slices. To do so, cut ⅛-in. (3-mm) notches at 1–1½-in. (2.5–4-cm) intervals on the side where the rind was removed.
4. If cooking the bacon in the oven, preheat a standard oven to 325°F (162°C).
5. Lay the bacon strips, slightly overlapping, in a cold sauté pan or on a sheet tray.
6. Place the sauté pan over moderate heat, or put the sheet tray in the oven.
7. Cook the bacon at a moderate temperature until most of its fat renders out and it is golden brown. If cooking bacon in a sauté pan, turn it halfway through the cooking time.
8. Pour off the bacon drippings (see Note 2). Drain the bacon on paper towels placed on a sheet tray.

Note 1: *Bacon rinds may be used to flavor broths, soups, sauces, and simmered vegetables.*
Note 2: *Bacon drippings may be used for frying, in savory baked goods, and in simmered vegetables.*

CLASSIC COLD-SMOKED SALMON

Yield:
about 8 lb (3.9 kg)

INGREDIENTS	U.S.	METRIC
Skin-on salmon sides, 4½ lb (2.2 kg) each	2	2
Kosher salt	12 oz	360 g
Light brown sugar	5½ oz	165 g
Ground white pepper	3 tsp	15 mL
Ground allspice	1 tsp	5 mL
Ground bay leaves	1 tsp	5 mL

Supplies

Fruitwood (fabrication type and amount as specified by smoker manufacturer)

PROCEDURE

DAY 1: FABRICATION AND CURE APPLICATION

1. Using kitchen tweezers or needlenose pliers, remove the pin bones from the salmon.
2. Wash the salmon and blot it dry.
3. Mix the salt, sugar, pepper, allspice, and bay leaves to make the curing compound.
4. Place half of the curing compound in the bottom of a hotel pan.
5. Place the salmon sides skin-side down close together on the curing compound. Coat the flesh of the salmon with the rest of the curing compound.
6. Cover the salmon with plastic wrap and place another pan on top. Add about 2 lb (1 kg) weight to the pan.
7. Place the pan in the refrigerator.

DAYS 2–3: CURE PENETRATION

8. Cure at least 36 hours. The dry cure will draw fluids out of the salmon and form a brine.

DAYS 3–4: AIR-DRYING

9. Remove the salmon from the brine, rinse it under cool water, and blot it dry.
10. Place the sides flesh-side up on a rack set over a drip pan.
11. Refrigerate the salmon, uncovered, for 24 hours.
12. Place the wood in a container, cover it with tap water, and weight it to keep it submerged. Soak at room temperature at least 24 hours.

PROCEDURE

DAY 4: COLD SMOKING AND FINISHING

13. Place the soaked wood in the smoker, set the temperature to 70°F (20°C), and wait for a full build of smoke.
14. Place the salmon on the smoker rack, skin-side up, and place it in the smoker.
15. Smoke at 70°F (20°C) 5–6 hours.
16. Wrap each salmon side in butcher paper or parchment paper and refrigerate.

HOLDING

Refrigerate up to 3 weeks. Rewrap in fresh paper once per week. Do not freeze.

VARIATIONS

IRISH-STYLE COLD-SMOKED SALMON

Replace the light brown sugar with granulated sugar. Omit the spices. Use peat as the fuel.

CLASSIC SMOKED SALMON PLATTER

APPETIZER

Portion:
1
Portion size:
3 oz salmon, plus garnishes

COMPONENTS

1 Green-leaf lettuce leaf
1 Small lemon basket (p. 717)
1½ oz (45 g) *Crème Fraîche (p. 567)* or commercial
6 Baguette croûtons
3 oz (90 g) *Classic Cold-Smoked Salmon (p. 452)*, sliced as illustrated on p. 431
1 oz (30 g) Red onion, brunoise-cut
½ oz (15 g) Nonpareil capers, drained
4 Thin lemon wedges

PROCEDURE

PLATING

1. Place the lettuce leaf on a cool 12-in. (30-cm) oval plate.
2. Fill the lemon basket with the crème fraîche and place it on the back center of the plate.
3. Fan 3 croûtons on either side of the lemon basket.
4. Arrange the smoked salmon in a ruffle across the front of the plate.
5. Scatter the onions and capers across the salmon.
6. Arrange the lemon wedges in front of the croûtons.

VARIATION

IRISH SMOKED SALMON PLATTER

Replace the lemon basket with a small tomato crown (p. 716). Replace the crème fraîche with a rosette of whipped, salted butter piped onto the crown and garnished with a parsley pluche. Replace the croûtons with Irish brown bread or other firm, moist whole wheat bread.

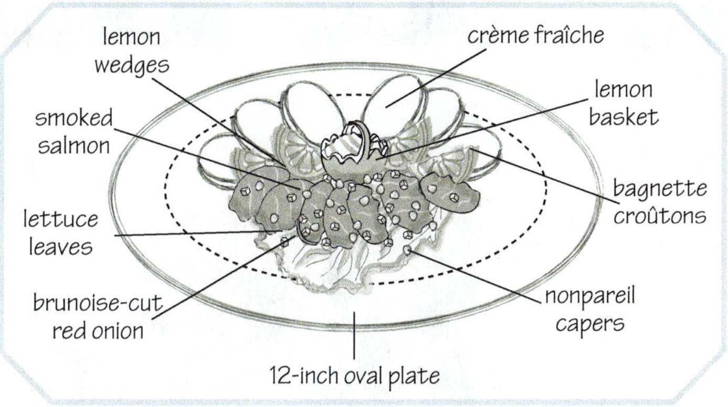

OLD-FASHIONED SMOKED HAM

Yield:
1 13-lb (6-kg) bone-in ham, about 9 lb (4 kg) EP

INGREDIENTS	U.S.	METRIC
Bone-in pork leg or fresh ham, 16 lb (8 kg)	1	1
Distilled or filtered water	3 gal	12 L
Kosher salt	2 lb	1 kg
Light corn syrup	1 lb	0.5 kg
Dark brown sugar	8 oz	240 g
Prague Powder #2	6.5 oz	195 g

Supplies

Hickory wood (fabrication type and amount as specified by the smoker manufacturer)

PROCEDURE

DAY 1: FABRICATION AND CURE APPLICATION

1. To make the brine, place the water, salt, corn syrup, sugar, and Prague Powder in a large stainless-steel pan. Bring the liquid to a simmer to dissolve salt and sugar. Cool the brine to room temperature and then refrigerate it until cold.
2. Measure 3 to 5 inches from the shank end of the ham (depending on its size and shape). Using a chef knife, cut through the skin and score the meat down to the bone (A). Remove the meat from the shank bone by scraping and cutting to leave the bone clean (B).
4. Weigh the meat and calculate 10% of that weight.
5. Fill a brining mechanism with an amount of brine equal by weight to 10% of the weight of the meat.
6. Sanitize a nonreactive container just large enough to hold the meat and the brine. Sanitize its lid and a plate or other nonreactive object to be used as a weight.
7. Find the large artery located near the shank bone (C). Inject about half of the measured brine into the ham through the artery (D). Inject additional brine into the artery at the opposite end (E). The meat is sufficiently filled with brine when it begins to swell and the brine begins to back up in the pump or injector.

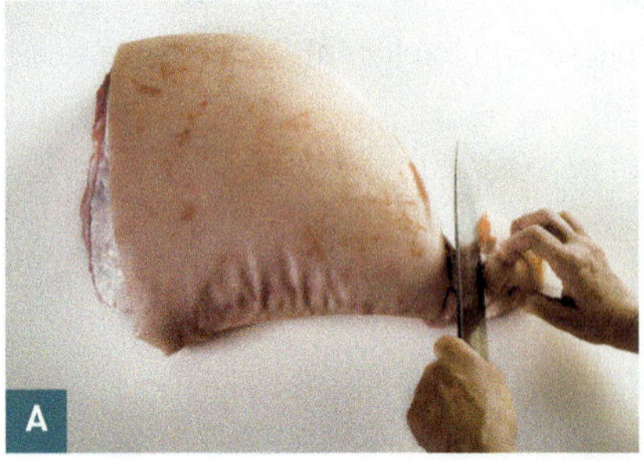
A

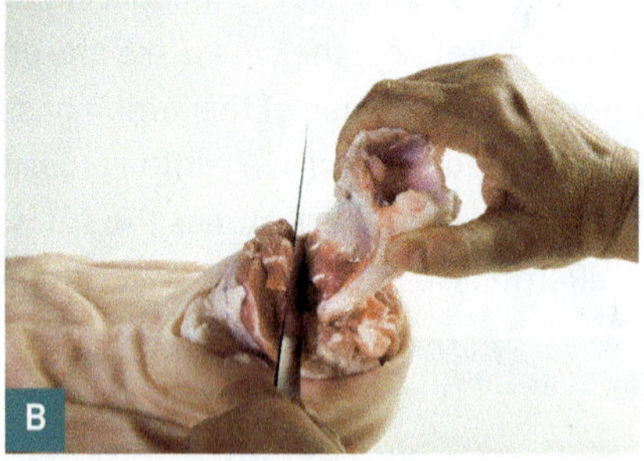
B

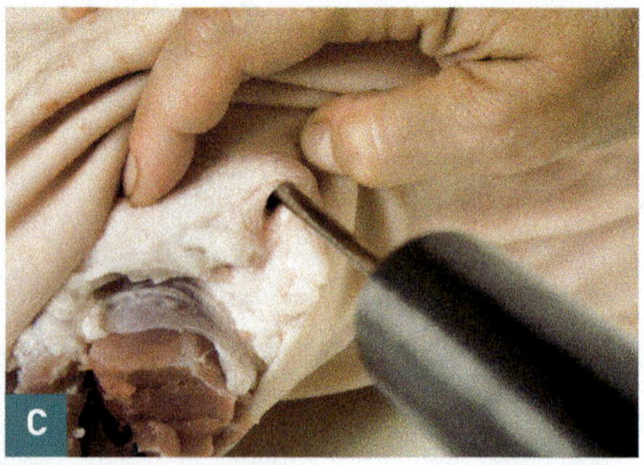
C

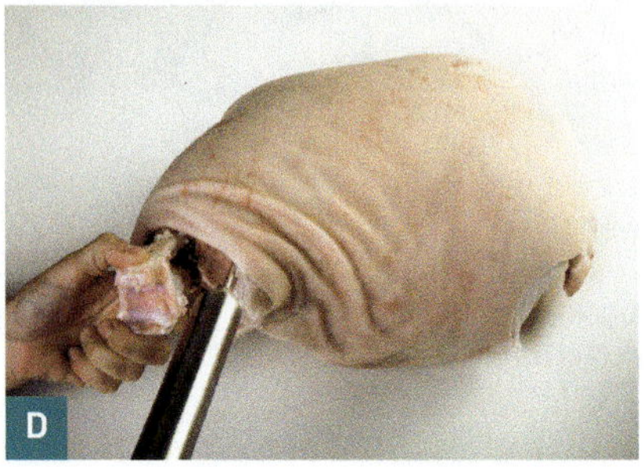
D

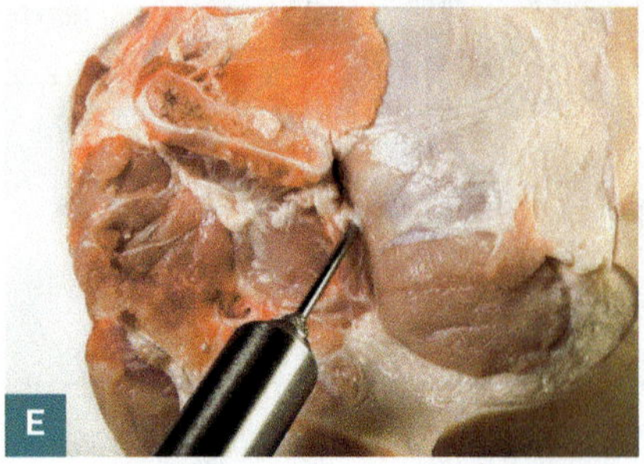
E

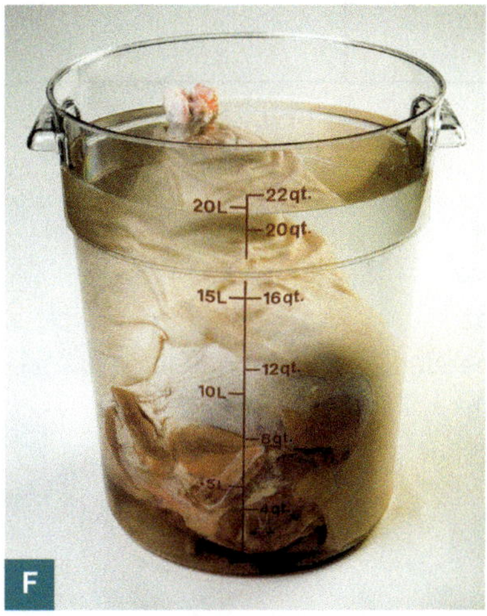

F

PROCEDURE

8. Place the injected meat in the sanitized container and pour the brine over it (F). Place the plate or other weight on top to keep the meat submerged.
9. Cover the container and place it in the refrigerator.

DAYS 2–8: CURE APPLICATION

10. Allow the meat to cure for 8 days.

DAYS 9–10: AIR-DRYING

11. Remove the meat from the brine and rinse it in cool water.
12. Place the meat in a sanitized container and cover it with cold water. Cover the container and refrigerate for 2 hours.
13. Place the wood in a container, cover it with tap water, weight the wood to submerge it, and soak at least 24 hours.
14. Blot the ham with a clean towel. Place the meat on a rack set over a drip pan and place it in the refrigerator, preferably near the circulation fan.
15. Air-dry the meat, uncovered, for 24 hours.

DAY 11: SMOKING AND FINISHING

16. Place the soaked wood in the smoker, set the temperature to 180°F (82°C), and wait for a full build of smoke.
17. Place the meat on the smoker rack and put it in the smoker.
18. Hot-smoke for 12 hours, or until the meat reaches an internal temperature of 150°F (65°C).
19. Remove the smoked ham from the smoker and cool it to room temperature on a rack set over a drip pan.
20. Store the ham in a sanitized hotel pan covered with clean, dampened towels.

HOLDING

Refrigerate up to 2 weeks. Change the ham to a fresh pan and cover with fresh damp towels every 3 days.

BOURBON AND BROWN SUGAR–GLAZED BAKED HAM

BUFFET PRESENTATION

Yield:
about 13 lb (6 kg),
about 9 lb (4 kg) EP
Portions:
about 35
Portion size:
4 oz (120 g)

INGREDIENTS	U.S.	METRIC
Bourbon whiskey	8 fl oz	240 mL
Light brown sugar	12 oz	360 g
Water	as needed	as needed
Old-Fashioned Smoked Ham (p. 455)	13 lb	6.5 kg
Whole cloves	to taste	to taste

PROCEDURE

PREPARATION

1. Preheat a standard oven to 350°F (175°C).
2. In a small saucepan, combine the bourbon, brown sugar, and enough water to make a thick paste.
3. Bring the mixture to a simmer to dissolve the sugar. Cool to room temperature.
4. Place the ham in a clean hotel pan or roasting pan.
5. Using a sharp, flexible boning knife, remove the rind from the ham. Leave an even ⅜-in. (0.1-cm) layer of fat on the ham's surface. With the same knife, score the fat on the ham's surface in a ½-in. (1-cm) diamond cross-hatch pattern.
6. Insert cloves in the ham's surface at evenly spaced intervals.
7. Coat the surface of the ham with the bourbon mixture.
8. Place the ham in the oven and bake about 2 hours, or until it reaches an internal temperature of 150°F (65°C). (The ham may be served hot.)
9. For a cold buffet, cool the ham to room temperature.

VARIATION

PINEAPPLE-GLAZED HAM

Replace the bourbon and water with canned pineapple juice. Glaze the ham. Dip small canned pineapple rings in clarified butter and place them at evenly spaced intervals on the ham's surface. Insert the cloves in the center of the pineapple rings.

FOODS PRESERVED IN FAT

In addition to curing and smoking, another time-honored method of food preservation is to protect foods from contamination by sealing them in a layer of fat. This method is still in use today because of the unusual and delicious products that result from it.

Fats traditionally used for this process are animal fats that have been melted and released from their surrounding connective tissue by a process called ***rendering***. This process converts the solid fat of animal tissue to ***semisolid fat***, which is solid when chilled, soft at room temperature, and liquid when heated.

When semisolid fat is melted, poured over hot cooked food in a container so it covers the food completely, and then cooled until the fat is solid, the result is an airtight seal that protects the food from airborne microorganisms. Before the days of refrigeration, this was an important method of preserving meats.

Today, we use this technique for three categories of foods:

1. ***Confits*** [kon-FEE]: Foods that are first cured and then cooked and sealed in fat.
2. ***Rillettes*** [ree-YET]: Foods that are cooked in a flavorful, fatty liquid, shredded, and then sealed in fat. Rillettes are seasoned with salt but not cured.
3. *Terrines:* Foods that are sometimes sealed in their baking pans with their own and additional fat.

In this section we take a look at the first two of these categories. The third, terrines sealed with fat, is covered in Chapter 13.

> **The History of Potted Meat**
>
> Traditional British cooking uses much the same method of sealing foods in fat as the French confit. In colonial and pioneer days, freshly slaughtered pork was preserved by curing it with salt, cooking it in lard, and then sealing it in the cooking fat. It was then stored in large earthenware vessels called *pots*. For this reason the confit method is called *potting* in English, and the resulting product is called ***potted meat***. A similar technique is applied to shrimp and other seafood, except clarified butter is used instead of lard.

Confits

To be safely preserved by sealing in fat, foods must be very low in microorganisms before they are sealed. In addition, they must have a low water content because liquids promote bacterial growth and because liquids can break the seal as they accumulate. Curing helps achieve both of these goals.

The Confit Process

There are three stages in the preparation of confit meats:

1. *Curing:* Meat is first treated with a dry cure. Because modern confit products are cured and stored under refrigeration and are not intended for extended storage, confit cures need not contain nitrite/nitrate curing mixes. A small amount of Prague Powder #1 may be used to enhance the color of the final product, although confits made without Prague Powder are more common. Because confit foods are fabricated into relatively small pieces, curing time is short.
2. *Cooking in fat*: The cured meat is poached in melted semisolid fat. The cooking process must be slow and gentle, and must not exceed 200°F (93°C). It may be done on the stovetop or in the oven. The meat must be completely submerged in fat at all times. The cooking process is complete when the meat is meltingly tender. A knife or skewer inserted into its center should meet no resistance. The time required to achieve this texture varies with the type of meat and size of the pieces. When the cooking process is complete, the confit is ready to be cooled and chilled in a storage container, completely covered by its cooking fat.

3. *Mellowing:* For confit to develop its full flavor and best texture, it must be held under refrigeration about 1 week. This action is called **mellowing**. It is important that the fat be in contact with all the meat's surfaces and that no air spaces remain in the container in which it is stored. During this time the flavors of the cure become more complex, and some of the flavors that were transmitted into the fat are reabsorbed into the meat. Once the mellowing period is complete, the confit is ready to eat. It can be held in the fat, under refrigeration, 2–3 weeks, or it may be frozen up to 3 months.

Procedure for Making Confit

A

1. Prepare the dry curing compound as specified in the recipe.
2. Trim and fabricate the meat as specified in the recipe.
3. Apply the cure to the meat in an even coating, massaging it in thoroughly.
4. Place the meat in a freshly sanitized container (A). Weight it with a sanitized, nonreactive lid or other food-service object and cover the container. Refrigerate it for the specified curing time.
5. Check the cure by making a slit into the center of a piece of meat. If the cure is complete, the color and texture will be uniform throughout. If the cure is not yet complete, return the meat to the refrigerator and continue the curing process 1–2 days longer.

B

6. If necessary, render solid fat to yield enough semisolid fat to completely cover the meat.
7. Preheat an oven or food warming unit to 180°F (82°C).
8. Melt the semisolid fat over low heat.
9. Rinse the curing compound off the meat and blot it dry. Place the meat in a brazier or deep hotel pan just large enough to comfortably hold the total volume of meat and fat.

C

10. When the fat reaches 200°F (93°C), pour or ladle it over the meat, making sure all pieces are submerged (B). On a stove burner, quickly bring the fat and meat to 200°F (93°C). Cook in the oven or warming unit, making sure the temperature stays between 180°F (82°C) and 200°F (93°C). Cook the meat for the length of time specified in the recipe, or until it is very tender when tested with a knife.
11. Sanitize the container and lid to be used to store the confit, as well as all utensils to be used.
12. Remove the confit from the heat and allow it to cool slightly. Using a slotted spoon or spider, transfer the meat to the container.
13. Pour or ladle the hot fat over the meat (C). Be sure to use the melted fat only, not the juices that remain on the bottom of the pan. (These juices can be saved for other uses, such as cooking beans.) Make sure the meat is completely submerged and that no air spaces remain between the pieces.
14. Open-pan cool the confit to room temperature, cover it, and refrigerate it.
15. Allow the confit to mellow in the refrigerator 1 week.

Recycling the Fat

To prepare a confit item for eating, it is removed from the surrounding fat and is usually heated so that much of the residual fat clinging to it melts off. The fat that remains after the confit is served can be reused to prepare future batches. To be reused safely, the fat must be heated to 165°F (73°C), strained through a fine sieve, and open-pan cooled as quickly as possible. After it is poured into a freshly sanitized container, cover and freeze until needed. It can be reused once or twice more, depending on the strength of the cure to which the meat was subjected. If the fat becomes too salty, it can be diluted with fresh, unused semisolid fat.

Confit fat may also be used as a frying medium. Frying in confit fat gives food a spicy, savory flavor. It is particularly suited to sautéing or pan-frying potatoes.

Types of Confit

CONFIT OF GOOSE AND DUCK

Classic confits are made with goose and duck. Because of the high demand for fresh duck and goose breast today, usually the legs of ducks and geese are the parts preserved as confit.

Confit duck and goose legs have a soft, succulent texture and a rich, meaty flavor similar to that of the best hams. The cure used on modern confit products is mild, and they are only slightly salty. Their flavor also depends on the type and amount of herbs and spices used in the cure.

CONFIT OF PORK

Pork butt, or pork shoulder, is the traditional meat used for pork confit. The shoulder is cut into large cubes, about 3 in. (8 cm) in size. It is cured and then simmered in lard.

An extraordinary dish can be made by processing a whole loin of pork by the confit method. A boneless pork loin is first cured and then poached in lard. It may be served hot, but it is even more delicious served at room temperature in thin slices, in the same manner as a fine ham.

CONFIT VEGETABLES

Confit vegetables are fabricated, salted and drained, and then simmered in vegetable oil until their liquid evaporates. They are then stored in the oil. Confit vegetables are covered in Chapter 17 on page 668.

CONFIT DE CANARD [kon-FEE duh kan-AHR]

DUCK CONFIT

Yield:
6 duck legs, 8 oz (240 g) each about 36 oz (1 kg) boneless, skinless meat

INGREDIENTS	U.S.	METRIC
Kosher salt	1 oz	30 g
Minced garlic	¼ oz	7 g
Quatre Épices (p. 519)	2 tbsp	30 mL
Dried thyme	1 tsp	5 mL
Ground bay leaf	¼ tsp	1 mL
Duck legs, 12 oz (360 g) each	6	6
Rendered poultry fat and/or pork lard	1½ qt	1.5 L

PROCEDURE

Please refer to the Procedure for Making Confit (p. 458) for additional information and photos.

DAY 1: FABRICATION AND CURE APPLICATION

1. To make the curing compound, place the salt, garlic, spices, thyme, and bay leaf in a small mortar or spice grinder and grind to a powdery paste.
2. Trim excess fat and ragged skin tags from the duck legs. Chop off the knuckle of each leg in a clean cut, leaving no bone chips.
3. Wash the duck legs and blot them dry.
4. Coat the duck legs with the curing compound and massage it in thoroughly.
5. Place the duck legs in a freshly sanitized, nonreactive container. Place a layer of plastic film on them and weight them with another hotel pan.

DAYS 1–3: CURE PENETRATION

6. Place the pan in the refrigerator and cure the duck legs 48 hours.

DAY 3: COOKING

7. Preheat an oven or food warmer unit to 180°F (82°C).
8. Rinse the duck legs under cool running water and blot them dry.
9. Melt the fat over low heat.
10. Place the duck legs in a saucepan or deep hotel pan just large enough to hold them and the melted fat. Ladle the melted fat over the duck legs, making sure they are completely submerged. Heat quickly to 200°F (93°C).
11. Place the pan in the oven or warming unit and cook the duck legs below the simmer about 6 hours. When done, the meat will have shrunk significantly and the drumstick bone will be exposed. The meat will be very tender and give no resistance to a knife inserted in it.
12. Open-pan cool the confit and fat to room temperature.
13. Transfer the confit and fat to a freshly sanitized container. (If cooked in a hotel pan, refrigerate in the pan.)
14. When the confit and fat are completely cold, cover the container.

DAYS 3–10: MELLOWING

15. Allow the confit to mellow in the refrigerator 1 week.

HOLDING

Refrigerate undisturbed up to 3 weeks. After the fat seal is disturbed, hold refrigerated up to 5 days longer.

(Variations on next page)

VARIATIONS

MEXICAN CONFIT OF DUCK

Replace the herbs and spices in the curing compound with 2 tsp (10 mL) chile de arbol powder (or other pure red chile powder), 1 tsp (5 mL) ground cumin, ¼ tsp (1 mL) ground anise seeds, ⅛ tsp (0.5 mL) ground cinnamon, 2 tsp (10 mL) dried oregano, 1 tsp (5 mL) ground black pepper, and ⅛ tsp (0.5 mL) ground bay leaf.

ASIAN-INSPIRED CONFIT OF DUCK

Replace the herbs and spices in the curing compound with 2 tsp (10 mL) finely ground white pepper and 2 tsp (10 mL) five-spice powder. Add to the cure 1 oz (30 g) peeled fresh ginger forced through a garlic press.

CONFIT OF PORK

Replace the duck legs with 5 lb (2 kg) pork butt cut into 3-in. (8-cm) cubes. Use all pork lard.

DUCK CONFIT

WITH WALNUT MESCLUN SALAD

APPETIZER

Portion:
1

Portion size:
8 oz (240 g) duck confit, plus garnish

COMPONENTS

1 leg Confit de Canard (p. 460)
2 oz (90 g) Mesclun (p. 62)
1½ fl oz (45 mL) Walnut Vinaigrette (p. 32)
2 Baguette Croûtons (p. 702)
¼ oz (7 g) Toasted walnut pieces
⅛ oz (3 g) Edible flower petals (optional)

PROCEDURE

FINISHING

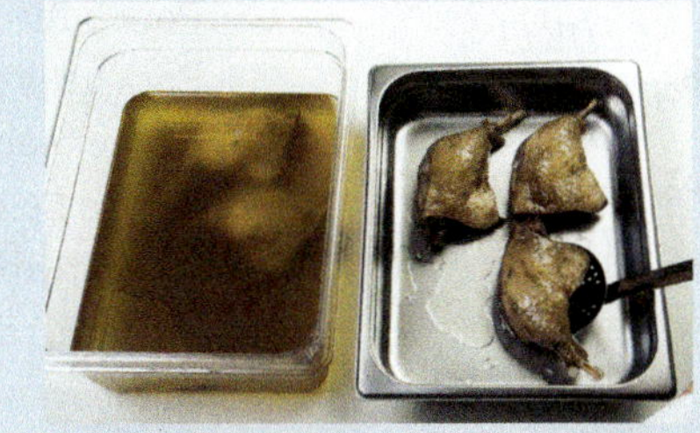

1. Preheat a countertop oven to 400°F (200°C).
2. If necessary, warm the fat surrounding the duck leg and remove it intact from the fat (see photo at right).
3. Using a paper towel, blot the surface fat from the duck leg without damaging the skin.
4. Place the duck leg on a sizzle plate, skin-side up, and place it in the oven.
5. Heat the duck about 15 minutes, or until sizzling hot.
6. Transfer the duck leg to a rack set over a drip pan and cool it slightly.
7. Toss the mesclun with the vinaigrette.

PLATING

8. Place a bed of mesclun on a cool 10-in. (25-cm) plate.
9. Set the croûtons on the mesclun and place the duck leg on top of them.
10. Sprinkle the walnuts and optional nasturtium petals on the mesclun.

VARIATIONS

MEXICAN CONFIT OF DUCK WITH BORDER SALAD

Replace the traditional duck confit with Mexican Confit of Duck (above). Replace the salad ingredients with a bed of shredded romaine hearts tossed with American Cider Vinaigrette (p. 32), cooked pinto beans, and cooked corn kernels.

ASIAN CONFIT OF DUCK ON RICE NOODLE SALAD

Replace the traditional duck confit with Asian-Inspired Confit of Duck (above). Replace the salad ingredients with soaked and drained rice noodles tossed with Asian Vinaigrette (p. 35) and crisp-cooked julienne vegetables.

Rillettes and Other Uncured Foods Sealed in Fat

In addition to true confit products, there is a separate but related category of foods sealed in fat after being cooked in a liquid. Although they are seasoned with salt and other flavorings, they are not cured before they are cooked. While these foods have a longer refrigerated shelf life than if they were not sealed in fat, they do not have the extended keeping qualities of confit.

Some of these foods are sealed, stored, and used in the same manner as confit. For example, cooked pork cubes or cooked pork sausage patties are layered into a sterilized container, covered with hot lard, and then cooled and chilled. When it is needed, the product is removed from the fat, reheated, and eaten. While these foods were commonly prepared and eaten in the days before refrigeration, they are less common today.

Rillettes is the French name for cooked, shredded meats preserved in fat. In rillettes and similar fat-sealed charcuterie products, the fat is meant to be eaten along with the meat it surrounds. Rillettes are typically made from pork shoulder or poultry legs sealed with pork lard or rendered poultry fat. Seafood rillettes or potted shrimp are sealed with butter. These products could be considered substantial spreads, as they are usually eaten on bread, toast points, or crackers.

RILLETTES DE TOURS *[ree-YET duh TOOR]*

PORK SPREAD AS MADE IN TOURS

Yield:
about 2 lb (1 kg), 5 c (1¼ L)
Portions:
8
Portion size:
5 fl oz (150 mL)

INGREDIENTS	U.S.	METRIC
Pork butt	2½ lb	1.2 kg
Pork belly (rind removed)	½ lb	240 g
Kosher salt	1 tbsp	15 mL
Quatre Épices (p. 519)	1 tbsp	15 mL
Dried thyme	1 tsp	5 mL
Dried tarragon	2 tsp	10 mL
Bay leaves	4	4
Peeled garlic cloves, crushed	½ oz	15 g
White Poultry Stock (p. 749)	1 qt	1 L
Pork lard, preferably artisan quality	4 oz	120 g
Onion, whole or in one piece	6 oz	180 g
Pork lard, melted and cooled	8 oz	240 g
–or–		
White Poultry Aspic for Coating (p. 644), cooled to a syrupy texture	16 oz	480 g
Flat-leaf parsley pluches (optional)	8	8

PROCEDURE

DAY 1: FABRICATION AND PRE-SEASONING

1. Cut the pork butt into 1½-in. (4-cm) cubes. Cut the pork belly into ½-in. (1-cm) cubes.
2. Blanch the meats:
   a. Place the pork butt and belly in a large pan and cover them with cold water.
   b. Place the pan on a stove burner and bring the water just under the boil.
   c. Immediately pour the pork and water into a colander set in a food prep sink.
   d. Rinse the pork under cold running water and blot dry.

PROCEDURE

3. Mix together the salt, spices, thyme, tarragon, and bay leaves.
4. Toss the dry spice mix and the garlic with the pork.
5. Place the pork in a plastic bag or covered container and refrigerate 24 hours.

DAY 2: COOKING

6. Preheat a standard oven or food warming unit to 275°F (135°C).
7. Place the pork in a heavy pan just large enough to hold it comfortably. Add the stock, onion, and half the lard.
8. Place the pan on a stove burner and quickly bring the stock to the simmer. Taste the stock and add salt as needed to make the liquid taste slightly saltier than you would season a soup.
9. Transfer the pan to the oven or food warmer. Cook the pork under the simmer 4–5 hours. Check at 1-hour intervals and, if necessary, add enough boiling water to keep the pork submerged. When done, the meat will be fork-tender.
10. Open-pan cool the pork and broth to room temperature. (For fastest cooling, set the pan in an ice bain-marie.)
11. Refrigerate the pan for several hours, or until all of the fat has risen to the surface.
12. Break a hole in the fat at one side of the pan to release the broth. Pour the broth into a sauté pan. Pack the fat into a measuring cup and allow it to warm to room temperature. Remove and discard the onion, garlic, and bay leaves.
13. Reduce the broth over high heat to ½ cup (120 mL). Cool it to room temperature.
14. Wearing food-service gloves, pull the pork apart into short shreds. Measure the pork's volume. You should have close to 4½ cups (4.5 mL) tightly packed pork.
15. Place the pork in the bowl of a mixer fitted with the paddle attachment. Add ½ cup (120 mL) room-temperature fat. On low speed, mix the pork and fat while adding the cooled broth in a thin stream.
16. Taste and correct the seasoning if necessary.
17. Pack the rillettes into 8 freshly sanitized 6-oz (180-mL) ramekins or into a freshly sanitized 1½-qt (1.5-L) stoneware crock. Refrigerate until cold.
18. Seal the rillettes with cooled melted lard or aspic. If using aspic, place a parsley pluche on the surface of each serving and seal with more aspic.

DAYS 2–4: MELLOWING

19. Allow the rillettes to mellow in the refrigerator 2 days.

HOLDING

Refrigerate lard-sealed rillettes up to 2 weeks or freeze up to 1 month. Refrigerate aspic-sealed rillettes up to 5 days.

VARIATIONS

RILLETTES DU MANS

[ree-YET doo MAN]

Replace half the pork butt with duck leg meat or goose leg meat.

RILLETTES D'ORLÉANS

[ree-YET dor-lay-AWN]

Replace half the pork butt with rabbit leg and shoulder meat.

RILLETTES GARNI

APPETIZER

Portion:
1
Portion size:
5 fl oz (150 mL) rillettes, plus garnish

COMPONENTS

5 oz (150 mL) 1 ramekin *Rillettes de Tours (p. 462)* or its variations
1½ oz (45 g) Mesclun or spring mix (p. 62)
¾ fl oz (22 mL) *Classic French Vinaigrette (p. 32)*
2 oz (60 g) Vine-ripe tomato
3 Cornichon fans (p. 402)
½ oz (15 g) Niçoise olives
3 oz (90 g) Crisp baguette or French-style dinner rolls

PROCEDURE

PLATING

1. Place the ramekin of rillettes on the left side of a cool 12-in. (30-cm) oval plate.
2. Toss the greens with the vinaigrette and mound them on the back of the plate.
3. Cut the tomato into 3 wedges and fan them against the greens.
4. Fan the cornichons in front of the tomatoes.
5. Mound the olives between the tomatoes and cornichons.
6. Serve the bread in a basket lined with a linen napkin.

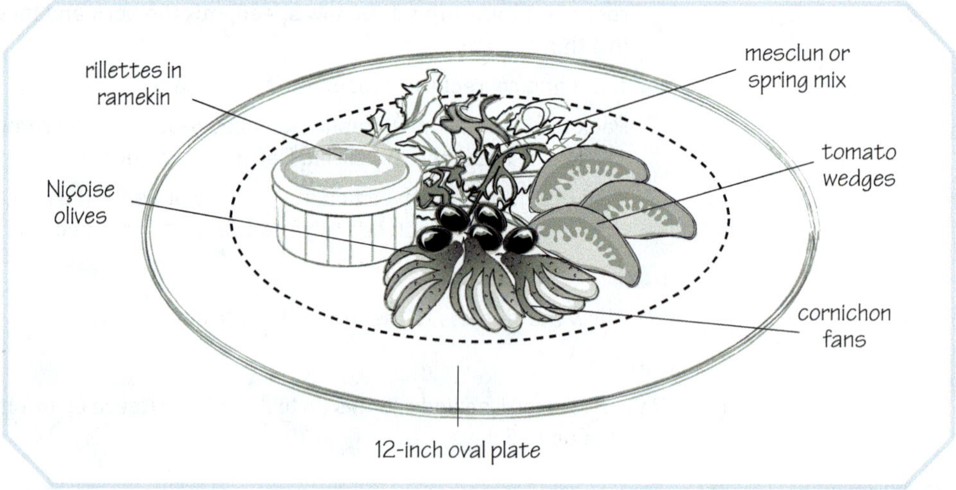

POTTED SHRIMP

APPETIZER

Portions: *8*

Portion size: *5 fl oz (150 mL)*

INGREDIENTS	U.S.	METRIC
Mixed pickling spice	½ oz	15 g
Kosher salt	2 tsp	10 mL
White wine	4 fl oz	120 mL
Lemon	½	½
36–40 ct. raw white shrimp (or shrimp of other sizes)	2 lb	1 kg
Unsalted butter	1 lb	0.5 kg
Ground mace	pinch	pinch
Grated lemon zest	2 tsp	10 mL

PROCEDURE

DAY 1: PREPARATION

1. To make the *cuisson*, place the pickling spice, salt, and wine in a sauté pan. Squeeze in the lemon juice and drop in the lemon half.
2. Cover the sauté pan and place it over high heat. Just as the *cuisson* comes to the boil add the shrimp, stir once, and immediately cover the pan. Remove the pan from the heat and allow the shrimp to pan-steam in their own heat 5 minutes.
3. Set a strainer over a small stainless-steel saucepan. Pour the shrimp into the strainer and reserve the strained *cuisson* in the pan.
4. Spread the shrimp on a sheet tray to cool to room temperature.
5. Peel the shrimp and reserve the shells.
6. Reserve 8 perfect shrimp for garnish.
7. Chop the remaining shrimp into rough ¼-in. (0.5-cm) dice. Place them in a container and refrigerate until needed.
8. Rough chop the shells and add them to the pan with the *cuisson*. Place the butter in the pan and set the pan on a low burner.
9. When the butter is melted, continue to keep the pan on low heat until the bubbling stops, signifying that the water in the *cuisson* and shells has evaporated. Do not allow the butter to darken.
10. Strain the shrimp butter into a bowl set in an ice bain-marie. Stir the butter over the ice with a rubber scraper until it begins to thicken. Stir in the mace and lemon zest, and then stir in the shrimp and any liquid that has accumulated around it. Taste and correct the seasoning, adding salt and/or lemon juice if needed.
11. Pack the shrimp mixture into 8 freshly sanitized 6-oz (180-mL) ramekins. Press a garnish shrimp into the surface of each ramekin. Cover each ramekin with plastic film.

DAYS 1–2: MELLOWING

12. Allow the potted shrimp to mellow in the refrigerator 24 hours.

HOLDING

Refrigerate up to 5 days.

VARIATION

POTTED LOBSTER

Replace the shrimp with 2 steamed lobsters, 1¼ lb (600 g) each. (Do not cook the lobsters in the *cuisson*.) Use only the soft, flexible shells for the butter.

TERMS FOR REVIEW

(to) cure
charcuterie
curing compound
dry cure
rub
brine
brine cure
wet cure
pickle
cooked brine
osmosis
refined salt
natural salt
kosher salt
sea salt
sodium nitrite
sodium nitrate
pink cure
tinted cure mix (TCM)
Prague Powder #1
curing salt
Prague Powder #2
cure accelerator
nitrosamines
humectant
pellicle
immersion brining
internal brining
injection brining
arterial brining
food injector
brining syringe
continuous-feed brine pump
(to) corn
curing tub
overhauling
smoke box
smoking chamber
smokehouse
green wood
aged wood
seasoned wood
cold smoking
hot smoking
rendering
semisolid fat
confit
rillettes
potted meat
mellowing

QUESTIONS FOR DISCUSSION

1. Explain the principle of curing foods with salt.
2. List and describe the two types of nitrite/nitrate curing mixtures, and explain how each type works.
3. Explain the food safety risks associated with the use of nitrite/nitrate curing mixtures.
4. List five safety precautions you would take when curing foods.
5. List and explain the four phases of the curing process.
6. Name a food product made by brine curing only. List the ingredients in its cure, explain how it is prepared, and describe its flavor and texture characteristics.
7. Name a food product made by dry curing only. List the ingredients in its cure, explain how it is prepared, and describe its flavor and texture characteristics.
8. Explain why all meats, poultry, and seafood to be smoked must first be cured to ensure food safety.
9. Discuss the health risks inherent in consuming smoked foods.
10. List the three basic features all smokers must have. Explain the function of each.
11. Discuss the safety issues posed by smoking equipment, and list the precautions you would take when installing large, or small smokers in your operation.
12. Explain the difference between confit of pork and pork rillettes.

Chapter 12

PREREQUISITES

Before studying this chapter, you should already

- Have read "How to Use This Book," pages xxviii–xxxiii, and understand the professional recipe format.
- Have read Chapter 11, "Cured and Smoked Foods," and have achieved a thorough understanding of salt curing (p. 410) and nitrite/nitrate curing mixes (p. 412).
- Be able to identify primal meat cuts and have mastered basic meat fabrication.

Sausages

A **well-made sausage** is nothing less than a masterpiece. Each type of sausage has its own unique mouthfeel and distinctive flavor. Some are mild and subtle, while others are strong and aggressive. All are expressions of the culinary magic that happens when you mix meat, fat, and salt.

The art of making fine sausages has come down to us through the ages and is part of most of the world's cuisines. You can find equally exquisite products in a French charcuterie, in a German *delikatessen,* and in the retail stores of North America's growing number of artisan sausage makers. With good instruction, study, and practice, you can create fine artisan sausages, too.

After reading this chapter, you should be able to

1. List and describe the four basic types of ground meat sausages and the two basic types of emulsified sausages.
2. Correctly and safely use meat grinders, planetary mixers, food processors, and sausage stuffers.
3. Prepare sausage products according to food safety guidelines.
4. Successfully prepare ground meat forcemeats and puréed forcemeats.
5. Use various types of natural and manufactured casings to prepare encased sausages.
6. Finish sausages by poaching and hot-smoking, cold-smoking, and drying.

UNDERSTANDING SAUSAGES

The term ***sausage*** refers to a mixture of seasoned ground meat and fat. Once prepared, this mixture can be further processed into many products of varying form, shape, and production method.

The sausage is both humble and noble. Sausages were originally created to use the trimmings and excess fat that resulted from butchering meat. After the large, tender cuts were removed from the carcass, the smaller, tougher pieces that remained were chopped or ground in order to tenderize them. The resulting mixture was then seasoned with spices and salt, both for flavor and to preserve it. In fact, the English word *sausage* is derived from the Latin word *salsus,* a term denoting salted products.

Most sausages are regarded as modest, casual fare because they were originally made from scraps. Today they are still frequently made from inexpensive, tough cuts of meat that have lots of fat and connective tissue but lots of flavor, too. In sausage making, the skill of the maker is the most important element. In fact, sausage making is considered the highest form of the charcutier's art. From a limited selection of meats, fats, and seasonings, a sausage specialist can create scores of kinds of sausages because the basic concept of sausage making is open to unlimited variation.

The History of Sausage

Primitive hunters were masters at utilizing every part of the animals they killed. Bones and horns became tools, hides became clothing and shelter, and the pouch-like stomachs and other internal organs became vessels for transporting, storing, and cooking food. Early on, humans discovered that meat cured with salt lasts longer than it does when fresh, and that salt preserves meat most quickly when the meat is chopped or ground. By packing salted ground meat into animal intestines, early humans created our first easily portable processed foods.

Most food historians believe modern sausage making began in Sumeria, in today's Middle East, around 3000 BCE. The practice eventually spread north and west into the Mediterranean region and then into Europe. Sausage making reached East

(continues next page)

THE ANATOMY OF A SAUSAGE

At its most basic level, sausage is a simple product. A sausage has only three basic elements: the forcemeat, the casing, and the internal garnish(es). Of these, two are optional.

The Forcemeat

In its simplest form, sausage is a mixture of highly seasoned ground meat and fat combined in a special way to create both protein development (p. 486) and emulsfication. Such a mixture is called a ***forcemeat***, whether used for sausage or for another preparation. This name is given to ground meat and fat mixtures because they are often forced, or stuffed, into casings or other types of edible containers. The French culinary term for forcemeat is ***farce***. (In French, this word can refer to nonmeat stuffings as well. The French verb *farcir* [far SEER] means "to stuff.")

Sometimes a sausage forcemeat is sold as is, without being forced into a casing. However, most sausage forcemeats are encased, or stuffed into a casing.

The Casing

Casings are long, flexible tubes that encase, or surround, the forcemeat of most sausage products. ***Natural casings*** are the inner lining of the intestines and other parts of the digestive tract of various meat animals. ***Manufactured casings*** are also available in several materials and sizes.

The casing performs six important functions in a sausage:

1. The casing is a built-in container that aids in portion control.
2. The casing holds the sausage together during cooking.
3. The particular type of casing used helps distinguish one sausage from another and is an important element in defining traditional sausage styles.
4. The casing adds visual appeal to a sausage, especially when the sausage is cooked by a dry method such as frying or grilling, or when it is smoked. When cooked in this manner, the casing turns an appealing brown color and, when grilled, it exhibits attractive grill marks.
5. The casing adds textural interest to the sausage. Each time you bite into a properly cooked sausage made in a high-quality natural casing, you experience a pleasant "snap" as your teeth break through the casing and into the juicy, tender interior.
6. The casing is the site of pellicle formation (p. 417) in sausages that will be smoked.

A few sausage products are wrapped in caul fat instead of casings. ***Caul fat*** is a thin, tender membrane with a lacy pattern of fat that surrounds the stomach and intestines of hogs and sheep.

The Internal Garnish

Sometimes small cubes or pieces of food are mixed into the ground forcemeat of a sausage. When the sausage is cooked or dried, these pieces of food remain visible. When the sausage is eaten, they contribute to its mouthfeel. In addition, they can add a distinctive flavor. Such food items are called ***internal garnishes***.

In traditional sausage making, internal garnishes were limited to cubes of tender meat or fat, or occasionally bits of truffle or pistachio nuts, in a smooth, refined sausage. Today's garnishes include nuts, dried fruits, and cubes of cheese. While the use of internal garnishes is optional, their addition makes sausages more interesting to eat and can set your product apart from the competition.

Asia early in history, or it may have developed there independently. Chinese writings mention a Mongolian lamb and goat sausage as early as the sixth century BCE.

Sausage making came of age with the European medieval guilds and the development of charcuterie. France, Italy, and Germany are all renowned for their sausages. Poland and other Eastern European nations have venerable sausage-making traditions as well. Spain and Portugal developed their own styles of sausage and transplanted them to Latin America. English bangers and breakfast sausages are beloved in British-influenced countries, and North America now has its own favorite sausages. While the twentieth century saw the rise of industrial sausage making, artisan sausages are growing in popularity in the twenty-first century. Contemporary chefs are creating new sausage varieties, some with ingredients as unusual as seafood and vegetables.

TYPES OF SAUSAGE

In garde manger, the most useful way of categorizing sausages is based on production methods. We first divide sausages into two large categories:

- ***Standard-grind sausages*** are made of forcemeats ground to varying degrees of fineness or coarseness in a meat grinder.
- ***Emulsified sausages*** are made of forcemeats puréed to a smooth texture.

Within each of these groups, we further classify sausages by their preservation method.

Standard-Grind Sausages

Sausages made from ground-meat forcemeats include most of our familiar textured sausages, ranging from fresh breakfast links to firm, aged salamis.

Different methods of curing and preservation yield three main categories of standard-grind sausage.

Sausage varieties
© *iStockphoto.*

1. ***Fresh sausages*** are made from ground meat and fat seasoned with salt and other ingredients. They are meant to be eaten within a day or two after preparation, although they may be frozen for extended storage. Most fresh sausages have a coarse texture. Examples are American Italian sausage and breakfast sausages. Fresh sausages may be sold raw or cooked.
2. ***Cured and hot-smoked sausages*** are smoked at a temperature between 170°F (76°C) and 200°F (93°C). This temperature range is high enough to cook them. Even though they are fully cooked by the smoking process, they are held within the temperature danger zone (TDZ) for a long enough time that harmful microorganisms can possibly grow in them. For this reason, curing always precedes smoking. Curing also helps retain an attractive pink color in the sausages' interiors. Hot-smoked sausages are ready to eat when they emerge from the smoker. However, they are usually quick-chilled in a water bath and then refrigerated until needed. They may be served cold or reheated for service by almost any method. Smoked kielbasa is an example.
3. ***Cured and dried sausages*** are made from ground meat and fat preserved with a dry curing compound containing salt, other seasonings, and a nitrite/nitrate curing mix such as Prague Powder #2. The curing compound is necessary because these sausages are traditionally held within the temperature danger zone (TDZ), usually at 60°F (15°C), for a lengthy period while they dry. After the forcemeat is stuffed into the casings, the sausages are air-dried in a temperature- and humidity-controlled area until the cure is complete. Although the bodies of these sausages begin as a coarse-ground forcemeat, the texture becomes firm and smooth by the time they are ready to eat. The effect of drying causes the sausages to shrink in size and their flavor to become intense and concentrated. The nitrite/nitrate mix gives them a beautiful, rosy color. Dried sausages can be divided into two subcategories:
   - ***Unsmoked dried sausages*** are, as the name says, dried without smoking. Most unsmoked dried sausages are eaten as is, with no cooking. Examples are salami and soppressata.

     Fermented sausages are a special category of cured and dried sausages. They are traditionally made with dairy products in the forcemeat. The inclusion of milk solids makes possible the growth of a beneficial bacterial culture that develops despite the presence of the cure. The result is a slight souring that gives these sausages their characteristic, tangy flavor.
   - ***Cured and cold-smoked sausages*** are prepared in the same manner as cured and dried sausages, but after they are encased and before they are dried they are smoked at a temperature below 100°F (37°C). Properly cured and cold-smoked sausages are safe to eat with no further cooking. However, they are usually used as flavoring meats, typically added to dishes while they are cooking. Examples are andouille and Spanish chorizo.

Spanish chorizo
© *iStockphoto.*

Emulsified Sausages

Emulsified sausages are made from meats and fat puréed together rather than ground. Thus, they have a smooth texture. Because all sausages are made from forcemeats, which are emulsions by definition, technically all could be called emulsified sausages. However, sausages made with puréed forcemeats are almost completely dependent on emulsion both for their smooth texture and to hold them together. That is why they are specially singled out as "emulsified." (Standard-grind sausages are more dependent on protein development (p. 486) than on emulsification for their texture and structure.)

Emulsified sausages are the most difficult to prepare. They require skill and attention to detail, particularly with respect to the temperatures maintained during their preparation. After a puréed, emulsified forcemeat is stuffed into its casing, the resulting sausage is gently poached in water or another flavorful liquid in order to set the emulsion and make the sausage firm enough for storage or further processing. Emulsified sausages are ready to eat after poaching, but they are usually quick-chilled in a water bath and then stored or processed further. There are two basic types:

1. ***White or fresh emulsified sausages*** do not contain a nitrite/nitrate curing mix. They are meant to be eaten as quickly as possible after poaching and chilling and can be held under refrigeration only a day or two. They are called "white" because they contain no nitrite/nitrate mix to develop a pink color in the meat. Weisswurst is an example.

2. ***Cured emulsified sausages*** contain nitrite/nitrate curing mixes. Most but not all cured emulsified sausages are hot smoked either before or after they are poached. Smoking gives the casing an attractive brown color, while the curing mix makes the interior pink. An example of unsmoked, cured, emulsified sausage is classic Italian mortadella (see sidebar on p. 508).

   Some emulsified sausages, such as frankfurters, are given only a light smoking. When eating these sausages, you might not even notice the flavor of smoke. Others are more heavily smoked, such as German bologna. While the smoking process acts as a mild preservative on the exterior of these sausages, they are still relatively perishable and should be kept under refrigeration. Most types can be refrigerated several weeks.

Weisswurst
© iStockphoto.

INGREDIENTS

The days of making sausages from scraps are long gone. Industrial producers and artisan charcutiers who specialize in sausages purchase exactly the cuts of meat they need for their products. However, there is no reason not to cut food costs by reserving fresh, high-quality trimmings of meat and fat in the freezer and adding them to meats purchased specifically for sausage making

The quality of the meat and fat used in the forcemeat determines the basic flavor of the finished sausage product. Do not, however, confuse "quality" with tenderness. Except for some internal garnishes, there is no need to use tender cuts for sausage making because the great majority of sausages are made from ground or puréed meat. The effect of grinding and puréeing is to break up the meat's connective tissue and cut its firm protein chains. This makes tough meat tender.

Quality standards for sausage meat refer to flavor, texture, and fat content. In general, well-exercised free-range animals fed a rich and varied diet produce firm, flavorful meat and lots of pure, clean-tasting fat. Although the seasonings used in a sausage forcemeat are important, it is the meat that can make the flavor of a sausage extraordinary. Using high-quality meat will make your sausages stand out.

Meats and Poultry for Sausages

Pork is the primary meat used in charcuterie work, including sausage making. Most sausages made from pork are cooked before they are eaten, so standard pork may be used to make them. If you plan to make a cured and dried sausage or a cured and smoked sausage that will not be cooked to a temperature above 140°F (60°C), you should purchase certified pork. ***Certified pork*** has been frozen for a time-temperature period proven to destroy the pathogens that cause trichinosis. Alternatively, you may treat pork in-house to destroy the trichina parasite by holding it frozen below 5°F (–15°C) for 20 days.

Many popular sausages are based on beef. However, their formulas may contain pork fat. If you wish to prepare sausages without pork, you may choose from a variety of traditional sausage styles developed by cultures that do not eat pork. In addition, you may choose to modify existing sausage formulas to use poultry instead of pork. Turkey sausages have become popular in recent years due to the growing number of North Americans who avoid eating pork. All poultry sausages must be cooked to an interior temperature of 160°F (71°C).

In the 1970s, nouvelle cuisine chefs began preparing specialty sausages made of seafood. These sausages are covered in Chapter 15.

The following meats and poultry are used for sausage making. Suggested cuts are included for each type.

Fats for Sausages

The fat component of a forcemeat is as important, if not more important, than the meat. In many sausage preparations, fat is used in high proportion, often equaling the weight of the meat. Fat content of most traditional sausages is generally 30–50% of the total weight.

Pork Fat

Pork fat is the preferred fat for sausage making. The clean flavor and light texture of pork fat make it the ideal vehicle for absorbing flavors and creating a rich, luscious mouthfeel. Even sausages that do not contain pork meat benefit from pork fat. In fact, the only case in which another fat is normally substituted for pork fat is when religious or cultural considerations make pork unacceptable as a sausage ingredient.

The location of fatback, jowl fat, and suet on a hog.

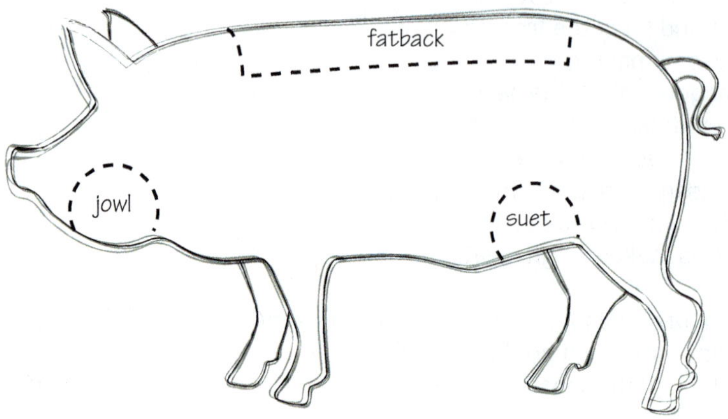

Pork fat is available in three basic market forms.

FRESH PORK FATBACK

The layer of fat deposited between the back muscles of a hog and its skin is called ***fatback***, or sometimes ***backfat***. Because modern, industrially raised hogs are much leaner than those of the past, the fat yield on a commercial slab of fatback can be as low as 75%. Often, more than one-quarter of the slab's weight is the skin, or ***pork rind***, which must be removed before the fatback is used.

The majority of fatback produced in North America is salted at the processing plant as a means of preserving it. This product is called **salt fatback**. It is easily identifiable by its grainy texture and by the grains of salt visible on its surface. *Salt fatback should not be used for sausage making or other charcuterie work* for two reasons:

1. The large amount of salt that has penetrated the fatback will alter the salt-to-solids ratio in a forcemeat and can cause any food with which it comes into contact to become oversalted.
2. The salt's preservative action draws out much of the fatback's water content and changes its texture.

When ordering pork fatback for charcuterie work, *be sure to specify fresh, unsalted fatback.*

PORK JOWL FAT

Jowl fat is a dense, pure white deposit fat located in the head of the hog. It is considered the finest fat on the carcass. There is very little of it per carcass, so it can be difficult to acquire. Jowl fat is specified in some sausage formulas. However, any other good-quality pork fat may be substituted.

PORK SUET

Suet [SOO-et] is the deposit fat that forms around an animal's kidney. Pork suet is considered a very pure form of pork fat. It is sometimes specified for use in high-quality sausage forcemeats. Suet has a slightly lower water content than fat from elsewhere on the hog carcass. It is not as widely available as fatback because there is less of it in each carcass. Note: When suet is rendered (p. 457), the result is called ***leaf lard***. This term, however, is often used to denote high quality in any lard.

PORK TRIM FAT

The hog carcass yields a significant amount of random interior fat. This is the fat deposited between the various muscles in the animal's body. To distinguish it from fatback and suet, it is generally called ***trim fat***. Trim fat can be purchased from purveyors who break down their own carcasses and/or primal cuts. This fat is lower in cost than fatback, jowl fat, and suet. However, trim fat usually contains a significant amount of connective tissue that must be trimmed away. This type of fat may produce unsightly and unpalatable strings and lumps when ground for use in forcemeats.

Beef and Veal Fat

The fat of mature steers is ivory in color. It has a stronger taste than pork fat and thus it gives forcemeat products a distinctive flavor. Beef suet, or kidney fat, is considered the cleanest, lightest-tasting fat on the carcass. The fat of calves, or veal fat, is lighter in color and flavor. Both beef fat and veal fat are used in beef sausages.

Poultry Fat

The fat from chicken, turkey, and duck carcasses is used in poultry sausages. While it has good flavor, it is soft in texture and can be difficult to grind. A solution is to freeze the fat before grinding it. If there is pork fat in your formula, mix the frozen poultry fat with the pork fat before grinding. *Do not use rendered poultry fat in a forcemeat.* Its melt temperature and emulsification properties are different from those of raw fat, and it will not yield a successful product.

Flavorings for Sausages

There is no limit to the flavorings you can add to a sausage forcemeat. Salt is always included in a sausage mixture, not only for flavor but also for its preservative qualities. As in curing, kosher salt is most frequently used, although natural salts (p. 412) may also be used.

Sugar is an important element in many sausages. The sweet taste of sugar balances the flavor of salt and any nitrite/nitrate curing mixes used in the forcemeat. Sugar products and other sweeteners also act as humectants (p. 414), and thus add moisture to sausages.

Dextrose is a powdered glucose sweetener often added to sausage forcemeats. Because it is very finely milled, it dissolves easily in forcemeats. A high proportion of dextrose can be added to a forcemeat without affecting its flavor balance because it is significantly less sweet than sucrose. Sausages containing dextrose have an exceptionally moist mouthfeel because dextrose is a strong humectant.

Virtually any other seasoning ingredient may be added to a sausage forcemeat. Both solid and liquid seasonings are frequently used. In fact, liquid ingredients are desirable because they contribute moistness to the finished product and help create the forcemeat emulsion.

When developing your sausage menu, employ different seasonings according to personal taste and the preferences of customers. Varying flavorings can give sausages a seasonal touch or an ethnic flavor. For example, adding sage and dried mushroom powder to a sausage makes it seasonal to fall, while flavoring a lamb sausage with oregano, mint, and red wine gives it a Greek flair.

Synthetic souring agents reproduce the flavors produced by the action of bacteria in traditionally fermented sausages. The best-known brand is Fermento™. Today, these products are often used because they are faster and safer than relying on natural fermentation.

Here are some ideas for sausage flavoring ingredients:

- Salt (kosher or natural)
- Sugar products (granulated sugar, brown sugar, maple sugar, maple syrup, cane syrup, sorghum syrup, molasses, corn syrup, dextrose, etc.)
- Fruit juices
- Wines, beers, and spirits
- Vinegar
- Condiments and prepared sauces
- Herbs, dried or fresh
- Ground or cracked spices
- Pulverized dried seasonings, such as dried mushroom powder or granulated garlic
- Fresh or cooked onions, garlic, shallots
- Chopped vegetables, cooked and raw
- Citrus zest
- Fermento™

Internal garnishes add flavor as well as texture. As with seasonings, thoughtfully chosen internal garnishes can lend a seasonal or ethnic feeling to a sausage product. Here are some options for internal garnishes:

Dried fruits

Cooked fresh fruits

Cooked or raw vegetables

Nuts

Firm or hard cheeses

Fresh, cured, or smoked meats

Solid fat

Secondary Binders

Some sausages require additional ingredients to help their basic forcemeats bind together and to give them a firm, cohesive structure. These are called ***secondary binders***. Secondary binders for sausages are usually starchy ingredients or protein enhancers, including:

Bread crumbs

Nonfat dried powdered milk

Eggs or egg products

Soy protein concentrate

Bacterial Cultures

Some traditional cured and dried sausages rely on a high acid content for preservation. One way to lower the pH of a sausage is through the action of a beneficial ***acid-loving bacterial culture***. The beneficial bacteria feed on the sugars in the sausage forcemeat and produce lactic acid as a waste product. The production of acid aids preservation because of the varying acid tolerances of different types of bacteria. Although the beneficial acid-loving bacteria can thrive in the acidic environment they create, harmful bacteria cannot. Thus, the sausage is preserved as well as flavored. Bactoferm ™ F-RM-52 is a laboratory-produced culture frequently used in preparing dried sausages.

Sausage Casings

The casing of a sausage determines its size and shape, and it fulfills several other important functions outlined on page 471. There are two basic types of casings: natural and manufactured.

Natural Casings

Natural casings are derived from the digestive systems of animals. They may be used in their original shape, or they may be fabricated by sewing them together to make them larger in diameter.

Natural casings are preferred by charcutiers for four main reasons:

1. They give sausages an attractive, natural appearance.
2. They have natural elasticity and, thus, make it easier to encase the forcemeat. When used for dried sausages, natural casings shrink along with the forcemeat as it dries so the sausage looks well formed.

3. Natural casings accept the color and flavor of smoke better than synthetic casings.
4. Most important, natural casings give sausages a superior mouthfeel no matter what cooking method is used. It is the pleasant snap you experience when biting through a firm but tender natural casing that makes artisan sausage products so appetizing.

Here is a list of the most frequently used natural casings:

Sheep casings: small intestines, ¾–1⅛ in. (18–28 mm) in diameter (very delicate)

Hog casings: small intestines, 1³⁄₁₆–1½ in. (30–38 mm) in diameter

Hog middles: large intestines, about 2¼ in. (55–60 mm) in diameter

Hog bung: end of large intestine, more than 2 in. (50 mm) in diameter

Beef rounds: small intestines, about 1¾ in. (43–46 mm) in diameter (tightly curled)

Beef middle: large intestine, about 2½ in. (60–65 mm) in diameter

Beef bung cap: appendix, 4¾ in. (120 mm)

Natural casings are processed at the slaughterhouse. When taken from the carcass, they are cleaned by flushing water through them and by scraping off impurities.

Natural casings are sold in two market forms: salt-packed and pre-flushed.

SALT-PACKED CASINGS

In this traditional market form, casings are wrapped in bundles, called ***hanks***, of a specific length. They are then packed in dry salt or in a heavy brine to preserve them. Salting slows bacterial growth and keeps the casings from sticking together. Although they are salt-preserved, these casings should nonetheless be stored in the refrigerator or frozen.

Salt-packed natural casings must be flushed to rid them of excess salt and soften them before they can be used. Follow the procedure below:

Procedure for Flushing Salt-Packed Casings

1. Measure the needed length of casings into a bowl and set the bowl in a food preparation sink under a gentle stream of cold water about 30 minutes.
2. Cleanse the casings' interior by slipping one end over the lip of the faucet and allowing cold water to flow through it.
3. Hold the prepared casings refrigerated in water until they are needed.

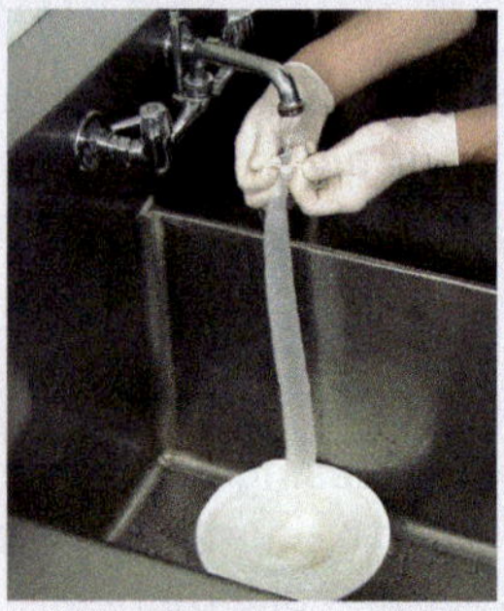

Flushing casings
© The Sausage Maker, Inc.

PRE-FLUSHED CASINGS

Natural casings are now available in pre-flushed form, either loose or in plastic tubs. They are packaged in a liquid preservative that keeps them softened for immediate use.

Manufactured Casings

The high demand for sausage products and the limited availability of natural casings has led to the development of a variety of manufactured casings.

COLLAGEN CASINGS

Collagen is a protein substance found in the skin, flesh, and connective tissue of animals. Today, collagen derived from cattle hides is used to make **collagen casings**. After the collagen is extracted, it is first processed to make it firm and flexible, and then it is extruded into precisely uniform tubes. These casings are manufactured in the same sizes as natural casings. Some are tinted with food coloring to appear smoked. Collagen casings are strong and easy to handle. However, their strength also means they can be tough to bite. To make them as tender as possible, they should be soaked for 24 hours before use. Collagen casings readily take on the color and flavor of smoke and can shorten a sausage's required smoking time. Although they cannot be considered natural, collagen casings are made from an animal product and, so, are both edible and perishable.

SYNTHETIC CASINGS

Synthetic casings may be made from plastic or plant fiber. They are available in various sizes and colors. Some are lined with protein and/or spice mixtures. This type of casing is not edible and, so, is used for sausages that are peeled before they are eaten.

Guidelines for Sausage Safety and Sanitation

- Thoroughly sanitize cutting boards, knives, and any other tools used for fabricating sausage ingredients.
- Because meats for sausage are touched often and are handled by many workers, all should wash hands frequently during the preparation of forcemeats.
- Wear food-service gloves when stuffing and forming fresh sausages that will not be cooked in-house, and when finishing dried sausages.
- Meat grinders, food processors, mixers, and sausage stuffers have many ridges, perforations, and tight spaces that are difficult to properly clean and inspect. You often must use special cleaning equipment, such as a bottle brush and toothpicks, to remove particles of food from them. These machines and their many parts must be sanitized both before and after use.
- Sterilize perforation equipment, such as knives or teasing needles used to puncture holes in sausages, by boiling them at least 5 minutes. Use them immediately after sterilization.
- Both the presence of large amounts of fat and the wetness that results from moistening and showering sausages can cause slippery floors. Workers must wear nonskid shoes and mop up spills as soon as they occur.
- To avoid accidents from machinery, use the guards and other safety devices. Always stop the grinding or mixing mechanism when loading and scraping down, and unplug the machine during cleaning. Be careful when handling blades, and never leave them soaking where they are not clearly visible.

EQUIPMENT FOR SAUSAGE MAKING

Mass producers of sausage products use large, industrial machinery that can process thousands of pounds of sausage in an hour. Artisan charcutiers and garde manger chefs use several varieties of commercial and domestic equipment to accomplish the same tasks, although in smaller batches and at a slower rate. Industrial, commercial, and domestic equipment all work in the same basic ways.

Grinding Equipment

Different types of machinery are used to produce forcemeats of two different textures.

Meat Grinders

Meat grinder
© *The Sausage Maker, Inc.*

The best way to reduce meat into small, precisely shaped particles is to cut the meat with a rotating knife as it is pushed through a die by a corkscrew-shaped part called a ***worm***. A ***die*** is a plate that has multiple openings of a particular shape and size. These openings determine the size and shape of the resulting particles. A machine that processes meats in this manner is called a ***meat grinder***, and the process of using it is called *grinding*.

Meat grinders are equipped with round dies having openings of different sizes. The three standard die sizes are:

Coarse (3/8 in./1 cm)

Medium (1/4 in./6 mm)

Fine (1/8 in./3 mm)

Two basic types of electrically powered grinders are available. One is a freestanding grinder with its own power source (p. 498, photo C). The other option is a grinder attachment that fits onto an electric mixer. Hand-operated grinders, such as the one shown at left, may be used for small batches.

Meat grinders are the preferred equipment for making coarse- and medium-textured sausages. A good grinder with a sharp blade is the only machine capable of producing the cleanly cut, separate meat and fat particles that give such sausages their pleasantly rough, rustic mouthfeel.

Parts of a meat grinder clockwise from top: sausage horn, collar, worm, fine die, blade, coarse die, and grinder housing

Rotation Choppers

Rotation choppers work by spinning meat and other foods in a horizontal circular motion that brings the meat into periodic contact with vertically rotating blades. These machines cut meat into random shapes rather than precise, granular pieces. As the meat passes repeatedly through the blades, the random shapes become smaller and smaller. Because both the rotation and the chopping happen quickly, the operator has little control over the size of the resulting particles. For this reason, rotation choppers are not preferred for grinding coarse- and medium-textured forcemeats. They are, however, excellent at breaking down meats and fat into smooth purées, such as those required for emulsion sausages and mousselines.

Rotation choppers, commonly called *buffalo choppers*, also have an attachment hub, like that found on mixers, that accepts meat grinder attachments.

Food Processors

When fitted with a stainless-steel grinding blade, a food processor reduces meat into randomly shaped particles similar to those produced by rotation choppers. However, with these machines you can more easily control the size of the resulting meat particles by pulsing the machine on and off. Even so, when attempting to achieve a coarse grind you will not have as good a result as you will using a meat grinder. Food processors are best suited to puréeing. Capacity, however, is a drawback. Even with a large processor, most sausage formulas must be prepared in batches.

Mixing Equipment

The old-fashioned method of mixing forcemeats was to work them by hand, much like kneading bread. For small batches of medium- or coarse-textured forcemeats, you may opt to use the hand method as well. However, most chefs now use electric mixing equipment to do this work.

Electric Mixers

A standard ***planetary mixer*** is most commonly used for mixing forcemeats. These mixers are called "planetary" because the arm of the mixer causes the attachment to revolve around the mixer bowl while the attachment itself rotates. When fitted with the paddle attachment, these mixers quickly and efficiently develop protein (explained on p. 486) and create the emulsion necessary for a successful forcemeat.

Commercial floor mixers or stand mixers are used for preparing large batches of sausage, while for small batches a countertop mixer can be used.

Encasement Equipment

Once the preparation of the sausage forcemeat is complete, the mixture is ready to be encased, or stuffed into the casings.

Sausage-Stuffing Machines

Encasement is most efficiently accomplished with a ***sausage stuffer***. All sausage stuffers work in the same basic way. The forcemeat is placed in a chamber that has a ***pressure plate*** at one end and a ***nozzle*** at the other end. The nozzle is fitted with a ***sausage horn*** of the correct diameter to accommodate a particular type of casing The casing is fed onto the horn; its end may be secured shut. When force is applied to the pressure plate, the sausage is ***extruded*** through the nozzle and horn and into the casing.

Pressure for extruding the forcemeat into the casing is applied with a hand-operated crank or an electric motor, depending on the model of stuffer. (A hand-operated sausage stuffer appears in the photos on p. 499.) Large producers use electrically powered stuffers that have continuous-feed action.

Meat-Grinder/Sausage-Stuffer Attachments

Meat grinders can do double duty as sausage stuffers. To convert a grinder to a stuffer, simply replace the grinder blade and die with a nozzle and stuffer tube. The completed forcemeat is loaded into the grinder chamber, and the combined action of the tamper and the worm forces the sausage into the casing.

Blade Maintenance

To achieve proper consistency in both ground and puréed products, the blades in all of your grinding equipment must be kept razor-sharp. Unfortunately, these blades cannot be sharpened in-house and must be sent out for professional sharpening. The manufacturer of your equipment may offer sharpening services or may have a website or hotline that can lead you to a service in your area.

In a busy operation, it is a good idea to purchase a second blade or set of blades that can be used while the others are out for sharpening.

Pastry Bag and Tip

If you want to encase a small batch of a smooth, delicate forcemeat, you can use a pastry bag fitted with a large, plain tip. To make cleanup faster and easier, you may line a standard plastic or canvas bag with a disposable plastic pastry bag. However, it is still necessary to wash and sanitize the outer bag after it is used.

Small Equipment for Sausage Making

These small equipment items and supplies are frequently used when making sausages:

Kitchen string is used for tying off sausages and for hanging sausages to smoke or dry.

A ruler is necessary for measuring sausages to ensure uniform length. Use only a plastic ruler that can be sanitized.

Casing clips and clip pliers are used to close the ends of sausage casings.

Hog rings and a hog ring tool are used to close the ends of large natural and synthetic casings.

A ***teasing needle*** (p. 510) is used to puncture tiny holes in the casing of a filled sausage in order to release air bubbles and prevent the sausage from bursting during cooking.

THE FOUR PHASES OF SAUSAGE PRODUCTION

There are four distinct phases in sausage preparation.

1. *Grinding* reduces meats and fat to small particles. (Puréeing, which is a slightly different action from grinding, is included in this phase and also accomplishes the mixing process.)
2. *Mixing* is a process that includes both protein development and emulsification. The production of bulk fresh sausage is complete after the mixing phase.
3. *Encasing* is the process of stuffing the forcemeat into the casing. The production of encased fresh sausages is complete after the encasement phase.
4. *Finishing* procedures are the final production steps for various sausages. The basic procedures are cooking, smoking (both hot and cold), and drying. These procedures may be done singly or in combination.

The first two of these phases are steps in the production of all forcemeats, whether for sausages or other charcuterie products.

Grinding Forcemeats

Grinding (or puréeing) is the first step in preparing a sausage (or other) forcemeat.

Preparation for Grinding

Before you proceed to the actual grinding process, you must take several steps to ensure the meat and fat will grind properly.

MAINTAINING COLD TEMPERATURES

All of the ingredients and equipment for forcemeats should be kept very cold at all times. This is necessary for proper grinding and for creating and maintaining an emulsion.

Guidelines for Maintaining Proper Forcemeat Temperatures

- Have all meats and fat to be diced for a forcemeat at refrigerator temperature when you begin working on them.
- Place meats and fat in an ice bain-marie as you complete their fabrication.
- Keep the fabricated mixture cold while you are mixing it with the seasonings and curing mix. If you are pre-seasoning, keep the meats refrigerated during the seasoning period.
- Be sure liquids to be added to the forcemeat are ice-cold.
- Work as quickly as possible, work in small batches, and keep any ingredients not being actively worked on in the refrigerator.

MAINTAINING CORRECT RATIOS

When preparing forcemeats, you must maintain the proper ratio of one ingredient to another in order to achieve a successful product. You must consider the following three ratios.

The Lean Meat:Fat Ratio

The ratio of lean meat to fat is crucial to the success of a forcemeat. For most standard-grind sausage forcemeats, the minimum ratio of lean meat to fat is 70:30. Many of the best sausages have a 50:50 ratio.

When determining this ratio, evaluate the fat content of the lean meat component you are using. If it has a large amount of exterior fat, the fat should be trimmed away before the meat is weighed so the ratio is not compromised. If necessary, the trimmed fat can be used as part of the forcemeat's fat component.

The Liquid:Fat Ratio

The ratio of liquid to fat is also important to the success of a forcemeat. It is the liquid content of the forcemeat that makes a sausage juicy (and that prevents a compressed terrine or pâté from tasting dry). The amount of liquid you add is directly dependent on the amount of fat the forcemeat contains.

An important purpose of the fat in a forcemeat is to hold its liquid in emulsion. If you change the fat content, you must change the amount of liquid that goes into the mixture.

Liquid:fat ratios vary from product to product. In standard-grind sausages, the liquid amount is low. Emulsified sausages (and mousselines, Chapter 15) require a higher amount of liquid.

The Cure:Solids Ratio

The combined weight of the meat and fat in a forcemeat is called the forcemeat's ***solids component***. The ratio of salt, and especially the ratio of nitrite/nitrate curing mixtures, added to a forcemeat's solids component is very important. The proportion of salt/cure mix to meat and fat depends on the type and duration of the cure. For accuracy, amounts of salts and nitrite/nitrate curing mixes are always weighed, never determined by volume.

PRE-SEASONING

Many charcutiers and garde manger chefs choose to devote extra time to ***pre-seasoning*** the meats and fat to be used in a forcemeat. Pre-seasoning allows the salt and other seasonings to evenly and deeply penetrate the fiber of the meats and fat. To pre-season, mix the fabricated cubes or strips of meat and fat with their intended spices, herbs, flavorings, salt, and nitrite/nitrate cure mix at least 24 hours in advance of grinding and mixing

When a sausage (or terrine or pâté) is to have an internal garnish of cubed raw meat, the meat cubes are usually pre-seasoned as well. Sometimes garnish ingredients are pre-seasoned with a marinade, which not only seasons meats but also tenderizes them. Cubes of fat are pre-seasoned with salt both to make them flavorful and to tenderize them by starting the breakdown of their solid components prior to cooking.

Grinding Standard-Grind Forcemeats

For sausages and other forcemeat products to have the proper texture, the meats and fat must be ground to the consistency specified in the recipe's procedure.

Guidelines for Grinding Forcemeats in a Meat Grinder

- Make sure the grinder blade is sharp.
- Chill all grinder parts in the freezer, or in an ice bath, before beginning to grind.
- Cut meats and fat into pieces that will easily pass through the grinder feed tube. Do not force the meat into the grinder.
- Keep the meats to be ground in an ice bain-marie. Receive the ground meats into an ice bain-marie as well.
- Begin with the coarsest die. Continue to grind through progressively smaller dies until you achieve the specified texture.
- Make sure the worm, blade, and die are properly seated in the grinder and that the collar (round part that holds the die in place) is screwed on tight.
- If you have followed all the other guidelines, yet the meat or fat does not come out of the grinder in clean, separate granules but instead looks like a purée, there is probably connective tissue wrapped around the worm or clogged in the blade or die. (This may also be the result of a dull blade or of improper fabrication.) Take apart the grinding mechanism and clear it.
- To clear the last bits of meat or fat from the grinder, push a piece of bread through it.

To achieve the proper texture when grinding, both the meat and the fat must be very cold. Always start the grinding process with the coarse die. If a finer grind is desired, regrind the coarse-ground meat through progressively smaller dies until it is ground to the desired texture. If you try to force large pieces of meat through a fine die without first grinding them through the coarser dies, the meat's fibers will be squashed rather than cleanly cut. In addition, the power necessary to push the large pieces of meat through the small die can cause the grinder mechanism to heat up. The higher temperature can begin to break down some of the meat's collagen and melt the liquid fat out of the solid fat. Both squashing and heating produce ground meat that has a greasy, puréed texture, a condition called ***smear***. Smear can also be caused by a dull grinder blade or by excessive connective tissue clogging the worm or the blade and interfering with the grinding process.

5:4:3 Forcemeats

Many traditional emulsified sausages are based on a formula known as the ***5:4:3 ratio***. This means 5 parts meat to 4 parts fat to 3 parts water, all expressed as weight. Most water in the formula appears in the form of crushed ice. The ice aids in keeping the forcemeat very cold while it is being puréed. When done correctly, the puréeing action of the machinery melts the ice at the precise time the emulsion is completed. In addition to the primary bind created by the protein development and the emulsion of fat and water, most 5:4:3 forcemeats contain a secondary binder, such as dry milk powder.

Puréeing Emulsified Forcemeats

Puréed emulsified forcemeats are used for making emulsified sausages and mousselines. They are much more challenging to prepare than ground-meat forcemeats. They are more dependent on emulsification than on protein development and are extremely temperature-sensitive. If the temperature rises just a few degrees too high at a particular phase in the mixing, the emulsion may break and your product will have an unpleasant grainy texture.

Because of the action of the machines used for puréeing, *emulsified forcemeats are mixed during the grinding/puréeing phase. Thus, no additional mixing is needed.* However, because the meats and fat are reduced to a paste, it is difficult to judge when they are sufficiently mixed. In fact, they can easily become overmixed. If this happens, there is no visible clue. You can detect overmixing or a broken emulsion only in a poach-test sample or in the finished product. Puréed forcemeats that are overmixed will be tough and rubbery due to excess protein development. A rubbery texture can also be the result of not adding enough liquid to the emulsion. If this happens, it is difficult to repair the damage; in most cases, your product is ruined.

The ingredients ratios in emulsified sausage forcemeats vary according to the type of sausage and the particular recipe you are using. Many emulsified sausages are prepared with the 5:4:3 ratio explained in the sidebar at right.

Guidelines for Making Puréed Emulsified Forcemeats

When preparing emulsified forcemeats, follow the directions given in the recipe you are using. The techniques you use will vary according to the type of equipment you are using.

- Make sure the chopper or processor blade is sharp.
- Chill all removable parts in the freezer, or in an ice bath, before beginning to purée.
- When using a rotation chopper, pay very close attention to the appearance of the product, and stop the machine as soon as the forcemeat reaches the proper consistency.
- When using a food processor, work in batches. Measure carefully and make sure all the proper ratios are maintained for each batch.

Mixing Forcemeats

A separate mixing step is necessary only for standard-grind forcemeats. This is because emulsified forcemeats are thoroughly mixed during the puréeing process, and therefore no further mixing is necessary. The following discussion, then, applies only to standard-grind forcemeats.

Once the meats and fat of a standard-grind forcemeat are properly ground, they must be thoroughly mixed. Additional seasonings may be added during mixing. However, mixing has a more important function than merely combining the ingredients. To ensure proper texture and mouthfeel, it is not enough to simply combine the forcemeat ingredients. They must also be mixed to create a successful bind, as explained below. This is particularly important for medium- and coarse-ground forcemeats made with a meat grinder.

During the grinding phase, note that the particles of meat and fat as they come from the grinder do not naturally stick together. If you were to go on to season and cook a forcemeat such as this—ground but not fully mixed—the resulting product would be loose and crumbly in texture and have a grainy mouthfeel. However, when properly mixed and with the right amount of liquid added, the meat and fat particles cling to each other. In other words, they bind together.

This clinging state is called the forcemeat's ***bind***. The action of mixing meat, fat, and liquid is called the forcemeat's ***primary bind***, because it is the most important way to keep a forcemeat bound together. A well-bound forcemeat will have a pleasant, firm-yet-tender texture and a juicy mouthfeel. Two essential factors contribute to bind: protein development and emulsification.

The Science of Protein Structure Development

Meat muscle structure consists of parallel, elongated muscle cells (called *myofibers*) encased in continuous layers of connective tissue. When the meat is ground and salt is added, the muscle structure is changed and the proteins are made partly soluble. These solubilized proteins then interact and create a network, called *continuous protein network development* or *protein structure development*. (A similar form of development occurs when kneading bread, and the result is the formation of gluten.)

The netlike structure that results from protein development provides the structure necessary to hold the emulsion of fat and liquid that is taking place within the forcemeat at the same time.

Protein Development

The physical action of mixing together the lean meat particles and the fat particles in a raw forcemeat causes protein structure development, more simply called ***protein development***. When this occurs, the separate particles of meat and fat in the mixture bond together in a network. This causes the mixture to change in appearance from a group of separate particles into a tight, cohesive mass. The appearance of the meat mixture changes from red-and-white specks to a more uniform pink color. The texture changes from loose and crumbly to smooth and sticky.

Emulsification

Although the terminology may be confusing, you must remember that both standard-grind forcemeats and emulsified forcemeats are emulsions, as explained on page 487. A forcemeat is a mixture of meat particles, fat particles, and water-based liquids. As you have learned, fat and water do not normally stay evenly mixed but, using proper procedures, you can combine them into an emulsion.

Some of the liquid in forcemeats comes from the lean meat fibers. In many recipes, additional water, ice chips, or liquid seasonings are added. Because of a sausage's high fat content, proper mixing of the forcemeat results in an emulsion that can hold a substantial amount of water. This is one reason why well-made sausages and other forcemeat products have a juicy mouthfeel. However, there is a limit to the amount of liquid a forcemeat can hold in emulsion. If you try to add too much liquid, the emulsion will break, the liquid will be released, and the resulting product will have a dry and grainy mouthfeel.

Machines such as rotation choppers and food processors mix emulsified forcemeats at the same time as puréeing them. That is why the liquid ingredients are added as the puréeing occurs. *Puréed emulsified forcemeats do not need additional mixing* because the action of the machine creates the primary bind as it reduces the meat into particle form. Be careful not to overmix to avoid a rubbery texture. Follow the instructions in the recipe procedure carefully, and add the seasonings and liquids at the proper time. If you run the machine for too long, the protein may become too developed, and the resulting forcemeat will have a rubbery texture.

The Science of Forcemeat Emulsions

At the same time protein development occurs, the action of mixing squeezes the lean meat particles and causes them to release a certain amount of their internal moisture. The same mixing action softens and further breaks down the structure of the fat particles, releasing some of the fluid components of the fat. As the forcemeat is mixed, the water present in the meat is able to mix with the fluid fat and remain distributed within it.

The action of mixing breaks up particles and droplets into smaller and smaller increments, so the two ingredients are able to mix evenly. The protein net described in the sidebar on page 486 creates a framework that helps stabilize the emulsion.

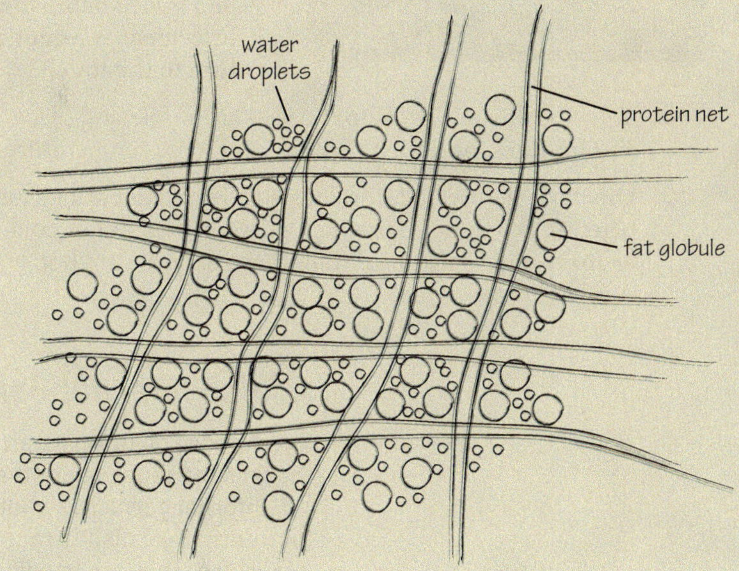

SECONDARY BINDERS

In some products, the forcemeat mixture needs additional ingredients to help the meat and fat bind together and to stabilize the emulsion. These are usually starch or protein ingredients, as listed on page 477 for sausages (and on page 537 for terrines and pâtés). Such an ingredient is called a *secondary binder*. In standard-grind forcemeats, these are added during the mixing process.

Poach-Testing Forcemeats

When all seasonings are added and the protein development and emulsification of the forcemeat is complete, test and evaluate both its texture and flavor before proceeding to the next step in your preparation. This should be done every time you make any type of forcemeat, whether you are using a new formula or one that is familiar to you. It is far better to discover your forcemeat is poorly seasoned or lacks fat while it is still in the mixer bowl than to realize your cooked sausage or terrine lacks flavor or has a dry mouthfeel.

To properly evaluate the flavor and texture of a forcemeat, it must be cooked and cooled to room temperature before you taste it. Poaching in plastic wrap is the best cooking method to use because it neither adds nor removes any flavors or fat content. The procedure for performing a ***poach test*** is on the next page.

Procedure for Poach-Testing Forcemeats

1. Have ready a small pan of simmering water and an ice bain-marie.
2. Form 1–1½ oz (30–45 g) of the cold forcemeat into a rough cylinder about the size of a breakfast sausage. Place it on a square of plastic wrap and roll it up. Twist both ends; if desired, tie with kitchen string.
3. Place the forcemeat in the simmering water and place a small lid or a folded damp towel on it to keep it submerged. Poach the forcemeat at a gentle simmer for about 1 minute, or until it feels firm to the touch.
4. Transfer the forcemeat to the ice bain-marie and place the lid or towel on top. Allow it to chill for 1–2 minutes, or until it reaches cool room temperature.
5. Unwrap the forcemeat and taste it. Evaluate both its taste and its mouthfeel. Take into consideration whether the finished product will be served hot or cold. Forcemeat products to be served cold should be more highly seasoned than those to be served hot.

Adding Internal Garnishes

The purpose of internal garnishes is to add visual, textural, and flavor appeal to the finished sausage or other forcemeat product.

Internal garnishes should be attractively and precisely cut. Meats and fat for internal garnishes must be tender and clean of all connective tissue and impurities. They are usually seasoned separately and with different seasoning ingredients than the forcemeat. They are often pre-seasoned.

Internal garnishes are added at the end of the mixing process, after the primary bind is achieved and after any secondary binders are incorporated. They must be small enough to not interfere with the forcemeat's bind and must not protrude through the casing or make the surface of the encased sausage rough or lumpy.

Often, a basic sausage forcemeat is prepared in large quantity and then divided into batches. Each batch is then mixed with different internal garnishes. In this way, one basic sausage recipe can be modified to yield two or three kinds of sausages.

General Procedure for Making Standard-Grind Forcemeats

1. Prepare a meat grinder and an electric mixer, as well as all other necessary equipment and supplies. Be sure to sanitize all equipment that will come into contact with the forcemeat, and keep it very cold.
2. Trim all fats and lean meats, and fabricate them to the proper size to fit the grinder. Weigh them and make sure you have the correct amounts for the formula. If not, adjust the formula accordingly. Refrigerate the fats and meats.
3. Fabricate any internal garnishes as specified and refrigerate them.

4. Weigh the dry seasoning ingredients and mix them together.
5. Weigh or measure the seasoning ingredients for the internal garnishes and mix them together.
6. Season the internal garnishes. Refrigerate them.
7. Mix together the fats and meats with the dry seasoning ingredients. (Note: Some recipes specify keeping the meats and fats separate so they can be ground separately.) Refrigerate them. (If you are pre-seasoning, refrigerate for 24 hours.)
8. Prepare an ice bain-marie to receive the ground meat.
9. Grind the forcemeat ingredients as indicated in the recipe. Always start with the coarsest die and progress through finer dies until the specified texture is achieved.
10. Transfer the ground-meat mixture to a mixer fitted with an ice bain-marie.
11. Mix on moderate speed, adding very cold liquid ingredients in a slow stream to build the emulsion and achieve the primary bind. Add secondary binders if specified in the recipe.
12. Perform a poach test.
13. If necessary, adjust the formula.
14. Mix in any internal garnishes.
15. Proceed with further processing, or refrigerate immediately.

General Procedure for Making Puréed Emulsified Forcemeats

1. Prepare a meat grinder and a food processor or rotation chopper, as well as all other necessary equipment and supplies. Be sure to sanitize all equipment that will come into contact with the forcemeat, and keep it very cold.
2. Trim all fats and lean meats, and separately fabricate them to the proper size for the grinder. Weigh them and make sure you have the correct amounts for the formula. If you have more or less than specified, adjust the formula accordingly. Refrigerate the fats and meats in separate pans.
3. Fabricate any internal garnishes as specified and refrigerate them.
4. Weigh the dry seasoning ingredients for the forcemeat. Sift the dry milk powder and place it in a covered container in the freezer for later use in step 13. (If you will need to work in batches, divide the milk powder accordingly.)
5. Mix the remaining dry seasonings with the lean meat only. Return the meat to the refrigerator. If you wish to pre-season, refrigerate it for 24 hours.
6. Weigh or measure the seasoning ingredients for the internal garnishes and mix them together.
7. Season the internal garnishes. Refrigerate them.
8. Grind the fat, starting with the coarsest die and progressing to the finest die. Spread the fat in a thin layer on a sheet tray and place it in the freezer until the exterior is crunchy with ice crystals.
9. Grind and partially freeze the seasoned meat in the same way.
10. If you are making a large amount of forcemeat in a food processor, at this point you must divide all ingredients into batch quantities.

(continues)

(continued)

11. Place the partially frozen meat in the processor bowl or the pan of the rotation grinder. Add the crushed ice and cold liquid seasonings. Grind until thoroughly puréed, with no visible ice chips. The purée should remain below 30°F (–1°C) during this step.
12. Continue to grind until the purée reaches 40°F (4°C).
13. Immediately add the partially frozen fat and continue to purée. The temperature will drop and then begin to climb. Get the dry milk powder out of the freezer.
14. At 45°F (7°C), add the dry milk powder and continue to purée until the forcemeat reaches 58°F (14°C).
15. Immediately refrigerate the forcemeat.
16. Perform a poach test.
17. If necessary, adjust the formula.
18. Mix in any internal garnishes.
19. Refrigerate immediately, and hold only as long as necessary to prepare for encasement and finishing.

Encasing

When the grinding and mixing phases of a standard-grind sausage forcemeat are complete, the resulting product is called ***bulk sausage***. When it is cooked, there is nothing to hold it together other than the bind. Bulk sausage is cooked by sautéing using moderate heat. If it is stirred while it is cooked, it comes apart into crumbles that can be used in stuffings, pasta sauces, and composed dishes such as lasagna and casseroles.

Bulk sausage may also be portioned and formed into cakes, called ***sausage patties***. These are usually pan-fried over moderate heat. In a classic French preparation, sausage patties are wrapped in caul fat and pan-fried or baked. Sausage patties prepared in this manner are called ***crépinettes***.

While bulk sausage and sausage patties are frequently used, most medium- and coarse-ground sausage forcemeats, and all puréed emulsified sausage forcemeats, are encased, or forced into casings.

The process of encasing, or stuffing a forcemeat into a casing, is called ***encasement***. One goal when encasing sausages is to evenly fill the casings with enough forcemeat so they are plump and attractive but not so full they burst during cooking or other handling.

Whenever possible, encasing should immediately follow mixing. The texture of a cold, freshly mixed forcemeat is soft and slippery without being greasy. When you grasp a handful of freshly prepared forcemeat and squeeze it, it will squirt freely through your fingers. At this texture it will also flow freely through the stuffer and into the casing. If a forcemeat is refrigerated for any length of time after mixing, it hardens and becomes more difficult to encase. If you must refrigerate a forcemeat before encasing it, you may need to beat it in a mixer fitted with an ice bain-marie so it recovers its former texture.

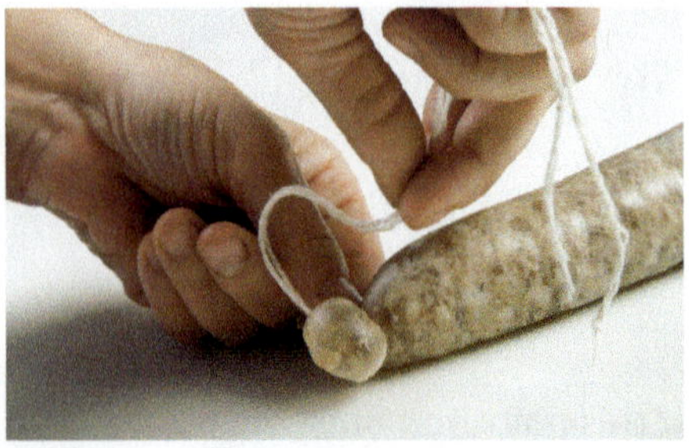

Bubble tie used for closing sausage casings

Many encased sausages are twisted or tied off into specific lengths with kitchen string. A ***bubble tie*** creates a double seal with an air pocket between the seals. If it is necessary to expel air from the sausage, the first seal can be loosened and the bubble can be pricked open without compromising the seal.

Procedure for Encasing Sausages

1. Cut the casings into manageable lengths, usually about 6 ft (2 m), or the length specified in your recipe. Flush and soak the casings as described on page 478 at least 30 minutes, or overnight for collagen casings.
2. Sanitize and chill the parts of the sausage stuffer that will come into contact with the sausage forcemeat.
3. Have ready the ruler, string, clips, pliers, and any other small equipment you will need. Prepare a sanitized container for the encased sausages. Sterilize the teasing needle or knife by boiling it 5 minutes and holding it in the boiling water.
4. Assemble the stuffer and fill it with cold forcemeat, tamping the meat firmly to press out any air pockets. Attach the correct sausage horn for the size of casing you are using. Lubricate the horn and the work surface with cold water.
5. Slip one end of the casing onto the sausage horn and work the remaining casing onto the horn. Leave about 6 in. (15 cm) of casing hanging off the end.

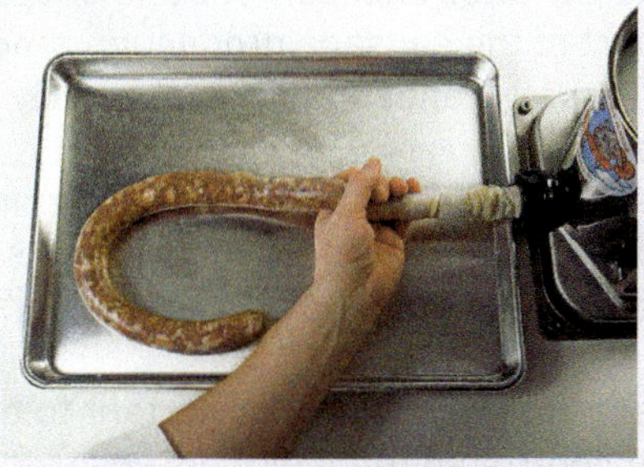

6. Support the end of the casing with one hand. Apply pressure with the stuffer so the forcemeat is extruded through the horn and into the casing. Use the supporting hand to help the casing move smoothly and evenly off the horn and to maintain an even fill. Take care to fill the casing to the proper tautness without over- or underfilling it. Leave about 6 in. (15 cm) of empty casing at the fill end.
7. Fabricate the sausage into the desired length, using the appropriate materials for closing or tying off.
8. Shape the sausages as specified in the recipe.
9. Prick the casing at even intervals with a sterilized teasing needle or knife to release air.
10. Place the sausages in the sanitized container and immediately refrigerate them. Alternatively, proceed immediately with further processing.

TRADITIONAL SAUSAGE SHAPES

Sausage formed in a casing without further fabrication is called ***rope sausage***. Sausage ropes are usually formed into long, cylindrical ***coils***. A sausage rope may be cut to a specific length and then tied into a loop. Sausages shaped in this manner are called ***ring sausages***. Or, sausage ropes may be tied or twisted into short lengths called ***sausage links***. A rope of links may be doubled and twisted into a ***sausage chain***. Sausages made in large-diameter casings are shaped like logs.

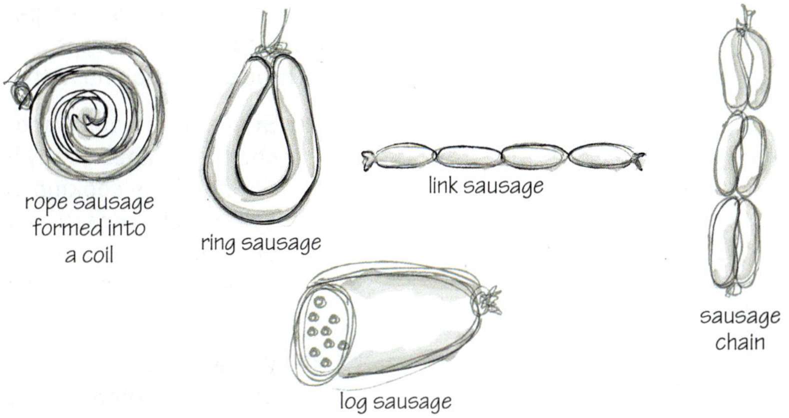

Finishing

Except for fresh sausages that are sold raw and cooked by the consumer, sausages must be finished after they have been encased. There are six basic methods for finishing sausages. Four of these methods involve precooking the sausages, and two involve drying (without cooking):

- Precooking methods
  - Poaching
  - Steaming
  - Poaching or steaming followed by cold-smoking
  - Hot-smoking
- Drying methods
  - Cold-smoking and drying
  - Drying without smoking

Precooked Sausages

Many sausages are cooked immediately after encasement and shaping. This precooking, or primary cooking, is part of the sausage production process and differs from the secondary cooking (actually reheating) that is done by the consumer at the time the sausage is served.

The purpose of precooking sausages is to raise their internal temperature high enough to set the emulsion and to destroy internal bacteria. The sausages must be heated to an internal temperature of 150°F (65°C), or 160°F (71°C) for sausages containing poultry.

Because sausage forcemeats are emulsions, it is important to apply the cooking heat to them in a gentle and controlled manner. This ensures that the fat component melts slowly and that the proteins will denature, or change, gradually. This treatment yields a sausage with a rich, juicy mouthfeel. Applying harsh, high heat methods to sausages tightens the proteins too quickly, breaks the emulsion, and results in a dry, grainy product. A similar result occurs if the sausages are cooked to too high an internal temperature. This is one reason why raw sausages should not be broiled or grilled at high temperatures and should never be allowed to boil.

Another reason not to cook encased sausages with high heat is to avoid bursting the casing. When the forcemeat is first exposed to the heat of cooking, it swells and releases steam. If this happens too quickly, the sausage forcemeat expands faster than the casing and the casing can burst open. This can happen even if the casing has been perforated with a skewer or teasing needle. (Overstuffed casings can burst even with proper cooking.)

Three basic cooking methods are used by sausage producers:

- Steaming is a quick and efficient cooking method for sausages. Steaming cooks sausages gently but very quickly and with high heat. Therefore, the timing of the cooking process must be exactly right. The fast action of commercial pressure steamers makes it difficult to judge the doneness of sausage products. Therefore, we do not recommend steaming as a sausage-cooking method for anyone who is just beginning to learn about sausage making.
- While it is slower and more time-consuming, poaching is the preferred cooking method for beginning charcutiers. One benefit is that you can observe and touch your product during the cooking process. Another is

that the slower action of poaching allows you the time to make necessary adjustments.

For some sausages, poaching or steaming are followed by a brief period of cold smoking to add both color and flavor.

- Hot smoking is the finishing method for many medium- and coarse-ground sausages. Before foods are smoked (either hot-smoked or cold-smoked), they must be air-dried for a short period, usually 6–24 hours. Do not confuse this procedure with the drying used to finish uncooked sausages.

Procedure for Poaching Sausages

1. Fill a brazier or braising table with enough water or court bouillon to cover the sausages to be poached. Bring the water to the simmer over high heat.
2. Prepare a pan of ice water large enough to hold the finished sausages.
3. Set a rack over a sheet tray or prepare equipment with which to hang the sausages over a drip pan.
4. If the sausages were not perforated during production, sterilize a teasing needle or knife and perforate them.
5. Place the sausages in the water and watch carefully until the water recovers to a bare simmer. If the sausages float, gently weight them with a folded towel or lid.
6. Once the simmer is recovered, immediately lower the heat and poach the sausages at a bare simmer until they reach an internal temperature of 150°F (65°C), or 160°F (71°C) for poultry sausages. Cooking time will vary according to the type and size of the sausages.

7. Immediately transfer the sausages to the ice water. Chill 5–10 minutes, or until the sausages reach an internal temperature of 70°F (21°C).
8. Drain the sausages at room temperature on the rack, or by hanging them, for no longer than 30 minutes.
9. Wrap and refrigerate the sausages or immediately proceed with further processing, such as smoking.

Procedure for Hot-Smoking Sausages

1. Soak the desired smoking wood in water overnight or as directed by the manufacturer.
2. Place the fresh or poached, chilled sausages on a rack set over a drip pan and set them in the refrigerator. Alternatively, hang them in the refrigerator over a drip pan. Refrigerate the sausages at least 6 hours, or until their exterior surfaces are shiny and tacky (see discussion of pellicle formation, p. 418).
3. Prepare a smoker with the desired wood. Set the smoker to 180°F (82°C) and allow it time to preheat and build smoke.

(continues)

(continued)

4. If the sausages were not perforated during production, sterilize a teasing needle or knife and perforate them.
5. Hang the sausages from smoke sticks or rods and place them in the smoker.
6. Smoke for the designated period, or until the sausages reach an internal temperature of 150°F (65°C), or 160°F (71°C) for poultry sausages.
7. Shortly before the end of the smoking period, prepare a pan of ice water large enough to hold the sausages. Prepare a rack set over a sheet tray or equipment for hanging the sausages over a drip pan.
8. Immerse the sausages in the ice water until they reach an internal temperature of 40°F (5°C).
9. Drain the sausages on the rack or by hanging them for no longer than 30 minutes.
10. Immediately wrap and refrigerate the sausages.

Dried Sausages

Sausages preserved with salt and nitrite/nitrate curing mixes and that are not subjected to heat are finished by drying. Because these sausages are not cooked, their production is considered the most challenging of all charcuterie items. Their success depends on many factors. To achieve a safe and delicious uncooked, dried sausage product you must utilize the correct grind, the correct type and amount of curing compound, the correct casing size, and proper fabrication methods. Many of these sausages also rely on internal fermentation for both flavor and preservation. In addition, all types require the proper temperature and the proper level of humidity while they are being smoked and/or dried. Careful observation is essential during the drying period, and maintenance may be needed. Strict attention to sanitation is necessary throughout all of these processes.

Dried sausages fall into two categories: unsmoked sausages and sausages that are cold-smoked before drying. Although care and attention to detail are essential, the first three steps in preparing these sausages are relatively simple. The challenges arise in the finishing processes that occur after the sausages are encased. For the small producer, the greatest challenge is in creating and maintaining the proper environment for the finishing processes. For cold-smoked sausages, a smoker that maintains temperatures under 90°F (32°C) is required. For all dried sausages, a drying chamber that maintains the proper humidity and temperature is essential for making a safe product.

COLD-SMOKING SAUSAGES BEFORE DRYING

The procedure for cold-smoking sausages is the same as the procedure for hot-smoking sausages, except the temperature inside the smoker is kept at 90°F (32°C) or lower (see the Procedure for Hot-Smoking Sausages on p. 493). So they do not absorb excess liquid, cold-smoked sausages to be dried are not immersed in ice water to cool them. Instead, they are showered or rinsed under a spray of cold water to lower their internal temperature to 60°F (15°C). The sausages are then hung to dry.

Procedure for Cold-Smoking Sausages

1. Soak the desired smoking wood in water overnight or as directed by the manufacturer.
2. Place the fresh or poached, chilled sausages on a rack set over a drip pan and set them in the refrigerator. Alternatively, hang them in the refrigerator over a drip pan. Refrigerate the sausages at least 6 hours, or until their exterior surfaces are shiny and tacky (pellicle formation, p. 417).
3. Prepare a smoker with the desired wood. Set the smoker to below 90°F (32°C). Allow time for the smoker to preheat and build smoke.
4. If the sausages were not perforated during production, sterilize a teasing needle or knife and perforate them.
5. Hang the sausages from smoke sticks or rods and place in the smoker.
6. Smoke for the designated period, or until the sausages take on the desired color, no longer than 2 hours.
7. Rinse cold-smoked sausages under a spray of cold water to lower their internal temperature to 60°F (15°C).
8. Drain the sausages on the rack or by hanging them.
9. Immediately wrap and refrigerate sausages that will not be further dried.

–or–

If preparing cold-smoked sausages that will be dried, transfer them to the drying chamber.

DRYING SAUSAGES

The difficulty in successfully preparing dried sausages is in creating the proper environment for drying them.

The area in which sausages are dried is called a ***drying chamber***. A drying chamber is an enclosed area in which the sausages are kept under correct conditions for drying. To ensure even drying, the sausages are usually tied with kitchen string or netting and are hung suspended from hooks or rods. Alternatively, they may rest on racks made of nonreactive metal.

Four conditions are necessary for proper drying:

- Good air circulation
- Darkness
- Controlled temperature
- Controlled humidity

Of these, the two most important factors you must control are temperature and humidity.

Temperature

The ideal temperature for drying sausages is 60°F (15°C). For small producers, the best method is to dedicate a refrigerator as a drying chamber and use it for drying purposes only. To operate it near 60°F (15°C), turn its temperature control dials up as high as possible, and place a thermometer inside. If you are using an older refrigerator, or one previously used to store cheese, scrub it thoroughly with a strong bleach solution to prevent the growth of undesirable molds.

An option for larger-scale production is to create a drying room by equipping a small room with an air-conditioning unit set to 60°F (15°C). Windows must be blacked out to create darkness. Install a thermometer and monitor it frequently. Add a fan to increase air circulation.

It is possible to dry sausages in a general-use walk-in refrigerator. Hang the sausages in the warmest section, usually near the door. Monitor the sausages carefully and perform frequent maintenance. Be aware that microorganisms present on other foods stored in the walk-in may compromise your sausages, so your success rate will be lower than when using a dedicated drying chamber.

Humidity

Humidity is a factor when attempting to dry a sausage product. If you attempt to dry sausage in a too dry environment, its casing will quickly dry and harden, and lose its permeability. This is called ***case hardening.*** When case hardening occurs, moisture is trapped within the sausage, which then does not dry properly. The result is a sausage that is dry outside and decayed inside.

On the other hand, if the environment is too humid, the sausage will not dry at all and will spoil.

A humidity range of 60–70% is ideal for drying sausages. To monitor humidity, place a hygrometer in the drying chamber. The humidity in a drying chamber can be increased by placing one or more pans of brine in the drying chamber. (The salt in the brine prevents the growth of harmful molds in the water.) If possible, place the brine pan in front of the circulation fan. If you have constructed a drying room, increase humidity with a humidifier or decrease it with a dehumidifier, whichever is necessary.

The physical process of drying sausages is simple in the correct environment. Hang the sausages in the drying chamber over a drip pan, and monitor them daily during the drying period. The following guidelines will help you head off possible problems and correct any that develop nevertheless.

Guidelines for Drying Sausages

- Maintain strict sanitation standards when preparing sausages for drying. Wear food-service gloves when handling drying sausages, and change gloves for each product you handle.
- Weigh each individual sausage at the beginning of the drying process and keep weight records for each sausage.
- Monitor your sausages daily. Remove your glove to check the texture of the casings. The casings should feel moist and have a matte finish.
- If you suspect that case hardening is beginning to occur (the casings begin to look shiny and feel dry or brittle), spray the sausages with a fine mist of weak brine daily for the first week of drying.
- You may see mold developing on your sausages. Powdery white mold is beneficial to sausages and should not be removed. Fuzzy mold, or molds of any color other than white, are harmful and should be removed as soon as they appear. To do so:

a. Remove the moldy sausages from the drying chamber and discard any kitchen string tied around them.

b. Clean and sanitize all surfaces of the drying chamber. Replace the brine pan with a freshly sanitized brine pan.

c. Scrub the sausages with a strong brine, using a new, clean, plastic mesh pad. Discard the pad after using it.

d. Put on fresh food-service gloves. Blot the sausages dry with paper towels and tie them with fresh string.

e. Return the sausages to the drying chamber.

- Judge the doneness of dried sausages by one of these three methods:

a. Weight test: The recipe should indicate the sausages' finished weight. In general, dried sausages lose about 30% of their original weight.

b. Touch test: Squeeze the sausage firmly and judge by feel. A fully dried sausage is firm throughout and does not feel squishy in the center. (To get a sense of how a properly dried sausage feels, squeeze a whole store-bought salami.)

c. Slice test: Cut off a 2-in. (5-cm) end of your sausage and look at the interior. The cross section you have revealed should be smooth and shiny. It should be a uniform deep rose color from the edges to the center, with no difference in texture. If the sausage does not look right, there are two possibilities:

If the sausage appears raw in the center but otherwise looks and smells good, the drying process is not complete. Brush the cut surface with strong brine and rehang the sausage for further drying.

If you see a grayish ring on the outside of the slice with soft, purple-red texture inside, your sausage has suffered from case hardening and the accompanying decay, and it should be discarded. The sausage should also be discarded if it has a bad smell or shows any other indications of decay.

Storing Uncooked Sausages

When the drying period is complete, both cold-smoked dried and unsmoked dried sausages should be wrapped loosely in butcher paper or parchment paper. Plastic film is not recommended because it holds in moisture and promotes the growth of mold. Both types of uncooked sausages will keep in the refrigerator for several weeks and often may be held for several months, as long as they are left intact and not cut open.

Cold-smoked sausages to be used as flavoring meats in cooked dishes may be frozen for longer storage. Before freezing, enclose the butcher paper package in a plastic bag to prevent freezer burn.

Dried sausages to be eaten raw should not be frozen, because freezing causes a grainy texture and a loss of flavor.

RECIPES

BASIC FRESH PORK SAUSAGE

Yield:
5 lb 10 oz (2.8 kg)

INGREDIENTS	U.S.	METRIC
Chilled lean pork butt	3 lb	1.5 kg
Chilled fresh pork fatback with no rind	2 lb	1 kg
Kosher salt	2 oz	60 g
Seasonings (see variations)	as specified	as specified
Chilled water or other liquid	8 oz	250 mL
Casings (desired type)	as needed	as needed

PROCEDURE

DAY 1: FABRICATION AND PRE-SEASONING

1. Cut the pork into about 2-in. (5-cm) dice.
2. Cut the fat into about 2-in. (5-cm) dice.
3. Mix the meat, fat, and the seasonings in a non-reactive container (A).
4. Cover the meats and refrigerate for 24 hours.

A

DAY 2: GRINDING, MIXING, AND ENCASING

5. Spread the cured meat in a thin layer on a sheet tray and set the tray, uncovered, in a freezer about ½ hour, or until the exterior of the cubes stiffens slightly. Do not allow the meat to freeze solid.
6. Chill all parts of the grinder that will contact the meat (B). Refrigerate a mixer bowl and the paddle attachment.

B

7. Grind the meat mixture through the coarse die into a bowl placed in an ice bain-marie (C).
8. Grind the mixture through the medium die into the bowl.
9. Place the meat in the chilled mixer bowl. Using the chilled paddle, mix the ground meat on low speed for 2 minutes.
10. Turn the machine speed to medium power and slowly add the chilled liquid in a thin stream (D).

C

D

E

F

G

PROCEDURE

11. Blend the forcemeat until the liquid is completely absorbed and the mixture is smooth and sticky.
12. Perform a poach test (E).
13. Make any necessary adjustments to the forcemeat.
14. Use the forcemeat as bulk sausage, or encase the sausage as described on page 491, using the type of casing and the desired shaping method (F, G).
15. Place the sausage in a freshly sanitized, covered container or in plastic bags.

HOLDING

Refrigerate up to 2 days, or freeze up to 3 months.

VARIATIONS

SAGE BREAKFAST SAUSAGE

For seasonings, use ⅛ oz (4 g) dried ground sage, 1⁄16 oz (2 g) dried thyme, ⅛ oz (4 g) granulated onion, and ⅓ oz (10 g) freshly ground black pepper. Form into patties or encase in sheep casings tied into 3-in. (8-cm) lengths.

SWEET ITALIAN SAUSAGE

For seasonings, use ½ oz (15 g) freshly ground black pepper, ½ oz (15 g) crushed fennel seeds, ⅛ oz (4 g) dried oregano, ¼ oz (7.5 g) granulated onion, ½ oz (15 g) granulated garlic, ½ oz (15 g) sweet Spanish paprika, ½ oz (15 g) crushed fennel seeds, and ½ oz (15 g) dextrose. Use 4 fl oz (125 mL) red wine and 4 fl oz (125 mL) water as the liquid. Encase in hog casings and form into a coil.

HOT ITALIAN SAUSAGE

Prepare sweet Italian sausage, but replace the sweet paprika with hot Hungarian paprika. Add ⅛ oz (4 g) crushed dried red chile. Use 2 fl oz (60 mL) red wine vinegar and 6 fl oz (190 mL) water as the liquid.

ITALIAN SAUSAGE WITH SPINACH AND PROVOLONE

Prepare sweet Italian sausage and add 8 oz (250 g) cooked, finely chopped spinach and 8 oz (250 g) brunoise-cut sharp provolone cheese in step 13.

FRESH KIELBASA

For seasonings, use 1 oz (30 g) freshly ground black pepper, ½ oz (15 g) dried marjoram, and 2¾ oz (85 g) minced fresh garlic. For the liquid, use lager beer. Encase in hog casings and tie off into 6-in. (15-cm) links.

FRESH BRATWURST

Replace half the pork with veal. For seasonings, use ½ oz (15 g) finely ground white pepper, ¼ oz (7.5 g) ground dried sage, ⅛ oz (4 g) ground mace, and ⅛ oz (4 g) ground dried ginger. Grind through the fine die. Use 1 beaten egg and 8 fl oz (250 g) heavy cream as the liquid.

BASIC FRESH POULTRY SAUSAGE

Yield:
5 lb 7 oz (2.7 kg)

INGREDIENTS	U.S.	METRIC
Chilled, well-trimmed dark meat of poultry	3½ lb	1.75 kg
Chilled fresh pork fatback with no rind	1 lb	0.5 kg
Chilled, well-trimmed raw poultry fat	½ lb	250 g
Kosher salt	1¾ oz	55 g
Seasonings (see variations)	as specified	as specified
Chilled water or other liquid	6 oz	190 mL
Casings (desired type)	as needed	as needed

PROCEDURE

DAY 1: FABRICATION AND PRE-SEASONING

1. Cut the poultry into about 2-in. (5-cm) dice.
2. Cut the fats into about 1-in. (2.5-cm) dice.
3. Mix the poultry and the seasonings in a nonreactive container.
4. Cover the poultry and refrigerate for 24 hours.
5. Mix the fats in a plastic bag and refrigerate until needed.

DAY 2: GRINDING, MIXING, AND ENCASING

6. Spread the seasoned poultry in a thin layer on a sheet tray and set the tray, uncovered, in a freezer about ½ hour, or until the exterior of the cubes stiffens slightly. Do not allow it to freeze solid.
7. Repeat step 6 with the fats.
8. Refrigerate all parts of the grinder that will contact the meat. Refrigerate a mixer bowl and the paddle attachment.
9. Grind the poultry through the coarse die into a bowl placed in an ice bain-marie. Grind it again through the medium die.
10. Grind the fat first through the coarse die into the bowl, then through the medium and fine dies.
11. Place the poultry and fats in the chilled mixer bowl. Using the chilled paddle, mix the force-meat on low speed 2 minutes.
12. Turn the machine speed to medium power and slowly add the chilled liquid in a thin stream.
13. Blend the forcemeat until the water is completely absorbed and the mixture is smooth and sticky.
14. Perform a poach test.
15. Make any necessary adjustments to the forcemeat.
16. Use the forcemeat as bulk sausage, or encase the sausage using the type of casing and the desired shaping method.
17. Place the sausage in a freshly sanitized, covered container or in plastic bags.

HOLDING

Refrigerate up to 2 days or freeze up to 3 months.

VARIATIONS

CALIFORNIA CHICKEN SAUSAGE

Use chicken leg and thigh meat and chicken fat. Steep 2 oz (60 g) brunoise-cut sun-dried tomatoes in 4 oz (125 mL) heated sweet white wine. For seasonings, use ½ oz (15 g) finely ground white pepper, 1 oz (30 g) minced shallots, ½ oz (15 g) minced fresh garlic, and 2 oz (60 g) chopped fresh basil. For the liquid, use the chilled wine (from soaking the tomatoes) and 2 oz (60 mL) extra-virgin olive oil. Add the steeped tomatoes and 3 oz (90 g) brunoise-cut California black olives in step 15. Encase in hog casings and tie off into 6-in. (15-cm) links.

(Variations continue on next page)

VARIATIONS

SOUTHWEST CHICKEN AND CHEDDAR SAUSAGE

Use chicken leg and thigh meat and chicken fat. For seasonings, use ½ oz (15 g) finely ground white pepper, ½ oz (15 g) ground dried pure New Mexico chile, ¼ oz (7 g) ground dried sage, 1 oz (30 g) minced shallots, ½ oz (15 g) minced fresh garlic, and 2 oz (60 g) chopped cilantro. For the liquid, use dry white wine. Add 6 oz (180 g) brunoise roasted and peeled New Mexico green chile and 6 oz (180 g) brunoise sharp white cheddar cheese in step 15. Encase in hog casings and tie off into 6-in. (15-cm) links.

DUCK, WILD RICE, AND DRIED CHERRY SAUSAGE

Use duck leg and thigh meat and duck fat. Steep 2 oz (60 g) quartered dried cherries in 4 fl oz (140 mL) heated ruby port. For seasonings, use ½ oz (15 g) freshly ground black pepper, ¼ oz (7.5 g) dried tarragon, 2 oz (60 g) minced shallots, ½ oz (15 g) minced fresh garlic, and ¼ oz (7.5 g) ground dried ginger. For the liquid, use 1 beaten egg and the chilled port. Add 4 oz (125 g) cooked wild rice and the dried cherries in step 15. Encase in hog casings and tie off into 6-in. (15-cm) links.

In addition to these variations, basic fresh poultry sausage may be prepared in many of the variations given for Basic Fresh Pork Sausage on page 498.

BASIC FRESH LAMB SAUSAGE

Yield:
5 lb 10 oz (2.8 kg)

INGREDIENTS	U.S.	METRIC
Chilled, well-trimmed lamb shoulder	3½ lb	1.75 kg
Chilled, well-trimmed beef or veal fat	1½ lb	0.75 kg
Kosher salt	2 oz	62 g
Seasonings (see variations)	as specified	as specified
Chilled water or other liquid	8 oz	250 mL
Casings (desired type)	as needed	as needed

PROCEDURE

Prepare as for Basic Fresh Pork Sausage, page 498.

VARIATIONS

MERGUEZ

[mair-GEZ]

For the seasonings, use ¼ oz (7.5 g) freshly ground black pepper, ½ oz (15 g) sweet Spanish paprika, ½ oz (15 g) ground dried ginger, ¼ oz (7.5 g) toasted and freshly ground cumin, ⅛ oz (4 g) cayenne, ⅛ oz (4 g) crushed dried red chile, 1 oz (30 g) minced fresh garlic, and 1½ oz (45 g) minced flat-leaf parsley (A). For the liquid, use a light red wine. Add 8 oz (250 g) brunoise roasted and peeled red bell pepper in step 15. Encase in sheep casings and form into a coil (B).

A

B

LOUKANIKA

[loo-kan-EE-ka]

For the seasonings, use ¼ oz (7.5 g) freshly ground black pepper, ¼ oz (7.5 g) ground bay leaf, ¹⁄₁₆ oz (2 g) ground cloves, ¼ oz (7.5 g) cayenne, 2 oz (60 g) minced shallot, and 1 oz (30 g) minced fresh garlic. For the liquid, use a light red wine. Add 1 oz (30 g) each chopped flat-leaf parsley and fresh oregano and 2 oz (60 g) finely grated orange zest in step 15. Form into 3-oz (90-g) patties and wrap in caul fat.

SAUCISSON À L'AIL

[soh-see-SOHN ah LIE]

FRENCH GARLIC SAUSAGE

Yield:
7¾ lb (3.8 kg)

INGREDIENTS	U.S.	METRIC
Kosher salt	2 oz	60 g
Prague Powder #1	¼ oz	7 g
Dextrose	½ oz	15 g
Finely ground white pepper	½ oz	15 g
Ground dry mustard	¼ oz	8 g
Boneless pork butt	3 lb	1.5 kg
Well-trimmed beef chuck	1½ lb	0.75 kg
Fresh pork jowl fat or fresh pork fatback with no rind	2 lb	1 kg
Minced fresh garlic	1½ oz	45 g
Crushed ice	¾ lb	360 g
Nonfat dry milk powder	2 oz	60 g
Cleaned and prepared beef middle casings in 15-in. (40-cm) lengths	8 ft	2.5 m

PROCEDURE

DAY 1: FABRICATION AND PRE-SEASONING

1. To make the curing compound, mix the salt, Prague Powder, dextrose, pepper, and mustard. Divide the mixture in half.
2. Cut the pork into 1-in. (2.5-cm) dice.
3. Mix the pork with half the curing compound and ¾ oz (22 g) garlic. Place it in a covered, nonreactive container and refrigerate 24 hours.
4. Cut the beef into 1-in. (2.5-cm) dice.
5. Mix the beef with the remaining curing compound and garlic. Place it in a covered, nonreactive container and refrigerate 24 hours.
6. Cut the fat into 1-in. (2.5-cm) dice, spread on a sheet tray, cover, and refrigerate.

DAY 2: GRINDING, MIXING, AND ENCASING

7. Freeze the grinder parts, the bowl and blade of a commercial-size food processor, a large stainless-steel bowl, and a hotel spoon.
8. Place the pork fat in the freezer about 30 minutes, or until the exterior is crusted with ice crystals.
9. Set up the grinder and place an ice bain-marie under the grinder head.
10. Using the coarse die plate, grind the chilled, seasoned pork. Refrigerate it.
11. Grind the semifrozen pork fat through the coarse, medium, and fine dies. Refrigerate it.
12. Grind the beef through the coarse, medium, and fine dies. Refrigerate it.
13. Place the chilled ground beef in the chilled processor bowl. Add the crushed ice and immediately begin processing. Use an instant-read thermometer to monitor the temperature of the beef as it rises from 30°F to 40°F (–1°C to 5°C).
14. Immediately add the ground fat and process until the temperature reaches 45°F (7°C).
15. Immediately add the nonfat dry milk and process until the temperature reaches 58°F (14°C).
16. Transfer the beef forcemeat to the chilled bowl set in the ice bain-marie and fold in the coarsely ground pork.

PROCEDURE

17. Perform a poach test.
18. Evaluate and make necessary corrections.
19. Encase the sausage to make 12-in. (30-cm) lengths. Clip or tie off.
20. Hang the sausages over a drip pan in the refrigerator.

DAY 3: DRYING

21. Allow the sausages to dry, undisturbed, 24 hours.

DAY 4: FINISHING

22. Sterilize a teasing needle or skewer and perforate the sausages at 2-in. (5-cm) intervals.
23. Bring enough water to cover the sausages to a simmer in a brazier. Poach the sausages at a bare simmer to an internal temperature of 150°F (65°C) (see photo).
24. Prepare a pan of ice water.
25. Refresh the sausages until they reach an internal temperature of 38°F (3°C).
26. Blot the sausages dry with paper towels.
27. Wrap the sausages in butcher paper and refrigerate.

HOLDING

Refrigerate up to 6 days, or wrap in plastic and freeze up to 2 months.

RING BOLOGNA

Yield:
6 lb (3 kg)

INGREDIENTS	U.S.	METRIC
Kosher salt	2 oz	60 g
Prague Powder #1	¼ oz	7.5 g
Dextrose	½ oz	15 g
Brown sugar	½ oz	15 g
Granulated garlic	¼ oz	7.5 g
Granulated onion	½ oz	15 g
Finely ground white pepper	¼ oz	7.5 g
Finely ground caraway seeds	⅛ oz	4 g
Finely ground nutmeg	⅛ oz	4 g
Well-trimmed beef chuck	2½ lb	1.2 kg
Fresh pork jowl fat or fresh pork fatback with no rind	1¾ lb	840 g
Crushed ice	1½ lb	720 g
Nonfat dry milk powder	3½ oz	105 g
Beef middle casing, cut into 18-in. (45-cm.) lengths	9 ft	2.75 m
Supplies		
Kitchen string	as needed	as needed
Fruitwood (fabrication type and amount as specified by the smoker manufacturer)	as needed	as needed

PROCEDURE

DAY 1: FABRICATION, GRINDING AND MIXING, ENCASEMENT

1. Freeze the grinder parts and the bowl and blade of a commercial-size food processor.
2. To make the curing compound, mix the salt, Prague Powder, dextrose, brown sugar, garlic, onion, pepper, caraway, and nutmeg.
3. Cut the beef into ½-in. (1.25-cm) dice and mix it with the curing compound. Refrigerate it.
4. Cut the fat into ½-in. (1.25-cm) dice and spread on a sheet tray. Freeze about 15 minutes, or until the exterior is crusted with ice crystals.
5. Set up the grinder and place an ice bain-marie under the grinder head.
6. Grind the semifrozen pork fat through the coarse, medium, and fine dies. Refrigerate it.
7. Grind the beef through the coarse, medium, and fine dies. Refrigerate it.
8. Place the chilled ground beef in the chilled processor bowl. Add the crushed ice and immediately begin processing. Use an instant-read thermometer to monitor the temperature of the beef as it rises from 30°F to 40°F (–1°C to 4°C)
9. Immediately add the ground fat and process until the temperature reaches 45°F (7°C).
10. Immediately add the nonfat dry milk and process until the temperature reaches 58°F (14°C). Refrigerate the forcemeat.
11. Perform a poach test. Evaluate and make necessary corrections.
12. Encase the sausage to make 18-in. (45-cm) lengths. Keep the fill just a little looser than normal. Tie off each end with a bubble tie. Form each length into a ring and tie the ends together.
13. Hang the rings over a drip pan in the refrigerator.

DAYS 1–2: DRYING

14. Allow the rings to dry, undisturbed, 24 hours.
15. Soak the wood in water to cover at room temperature for 24 hours.

DAY 2: SMOKING AND FINISHING

16. Follow steps 23–29 in the Smoked Kielbasa recipe on page 505.

HOLDING

Refrigerate up to 6 days, or wrap in freezer paper and freeze up to 2 months.

SMOKED KIELBASA

Yield:
6½ lb (3 kg)

INGREDIENTS	U.S.	METRIC
Kosher salt	2 oz	60 g
Prague Powder #1	⅜ oz	11 g
Dextrose	¼ oz	7 g
Finely ground white pepper	½ oz	15 g
Ground dry mustard	¼ oz	7 g
Chilled boneless pork butt	2½ lb	1.2 kg
Minced fresh garlic	1 oz	30 g
Chilled, well-trimmed beef top round	1½ lb	720 g
Chilled fresh pork jowl fat or fresh pork fatback with no rind	1½ lb	720 g
Crushed ice	¾ lb	360 g
Nonfat dry milk powder	2 oz	60 g
Cleaned and prepared beef round casing, cut into 15-in. (40-cm) lengths	as needed	as needed
Supplies		
Hog rings or kitchen string	as needed	as needed
Oak (fabrication type and amount as specified by the smoker manufacturer)	as needed	as needed

PROCEDURE

DAY 1: FABRICATION AND PRE-SEASONING

Follow steps 1 through 6 in the French Garlic Sausage recipe on page 502.

DAY 2: GRINDING, MIXING, AND ENCASING

Follow steps 7 through 20 in the French Garlic Sausage recipe on pages 502–503.

DAY 3: DRYING

21. Allow the kielbasa to dry, undisturbed, 24 hours.
22. Soak the wood in water to cover at room temperature for 24 hours.

DAY 4: SMOKING AND FINISHING

23. Prepare a smoker to 180°F (82°C).
24. Sterilize a teasing needle or skewer and perforate the kielbasa at 2-in. (5-cm) intervals.
25. Hang the kielbasa in the smoker and smoke about 2 hours to achieve a rich brown color.
26. Bring enough water to cover the kielbasa to a simmer in a brazier or braising table. Poach the kielbasa at a bare simmer to an internal temperature of 150°F (65°C).
27. Shower the kielbasa under a spray of cold water until it reaches an internal temperature of 38°F (3°C).
28. Blot the kielbasa dry with paper towels.
29. Wrap the kielbasa in butcher paper and refrigerate it.

HOLDING

Refrigerate up to 6 days, or wrap in plastic and freeze up to 2 months.

ARTISAN SAUSAGE PLATTER

WITH THREE MUSTARDS

BUFFET

Portions:
12
Portion size:
4 oz (125 g)

COMPONENTS

5 to 6 Red-leaf lettuce leaves
3 oz (90 g) French Dijon mustard
3 oz (90 g) *Honey Mustard (p. 673)*
3 oz (90 g) *Green Peppercorn Mustard (p. 674)*
1 lb (0.5 kg) *Saucisson à l'Ail (p. 502)*
1 lb (0.5 kg) *Ring Bologna (p. 504)*
1 lb (0.5 kg) *Smoked Kielbasa (p. 505)*
as needed Assorted French breads and German rye breads

PROCEDURE

PLATING

1. Line a 14-in. (35-cm) tray with the lettuce leaves.
2. Fill 3 small ramekins with the mustards. Place the ramekins in the center of the tray.
3. Cut the sausages on the diagonal into ¼-in. (0.6-cm) slices.
4. Arrange each sausage in overlapping rows on one-third of the tray.
5. Slice the breads and arrange them in a basket lined with a linen napkin.

HOLDING

Cover the sausage tray with plastic film and refrigerate up to 24 hours. Cut the bread just before serving

MINI-MORTADELLA

Yield:
5¼ lb (2.5 kg)

INGREDIENTS	U.S.	METRIC
Finely ground white pepper	⅓ oz	10 g
Sweet Hungarian paprika	2 tsp	10 mL
Ground nutmeg	2 tsp	10 mL
Ground coriander	1 tsp	5 mL
Ground cloves	¼ tsp	1 mL
Ground bay leaf	½ tsp	2 mL
Granulated onion	1 tsp	5 mL
Granulated garlic	½ tsp	2 mL
Prague Powder #1	¼ oz	7 g
Kosher salt	1½ oz	45 g
Dextrose	½ oz	15 g
Well-trimmed pork butt	1 lb	480 g
Trimmed veal top round	1 lb	480 g
Fresh pork jowl fat or fresh pork fatback with no rind	1 lb 5 oz	630 g
Additional fresh pork fatback with no rind	¼ lb	120 g
Black peppercorns	⅓ oz	10 g
Shelled pistachio nuts	3 oz	90 g
Crushed ice	1 lb	480 g
White wine, very cold	4 fl oz	120 mL
Nonfat dry milk powder	2⅓ oz	70 g
Beef middles, prepared and cut into 16-in. (40-cm) lengths	4 ft	1 m
Supplies		
Oak or fruitwood (fabrication type and amount as specified by the smoker manufacturer)	optional	optional

PROCEDURE

DAY 1: FABRICATION AND PRE-SEASONING

1. Combine the white pepper, paprika, nutmeg, coriander, cloves, bay, onion, and garlic. Label the container "seasoning mix."
2. To make the curing compound, combine the Prague Powder, half the salt, and the dextrose. Add half the seasoning mix, stir well, and label the container "curing compound."
3. Complete the seasoning mix by stirring in the remaining salt.
4. Cut the pork and veal into 1-in. (2-cm) cubes. In a nonreactive container, mix the pork and veal with the curing compound. Cover and refrigerate for 24 hours.
5. Cut 1 lb 5 oz (0.6 kg) fat into 1-in. (2-cm) dice. Spread the fat on a sheet tray, cover the tray, and refrigerate it.
6. Fabricate the additional pork fatback into brunoise cuts.
7. Bring about 2 qt (2 L) water to the boil. Prepare a small bowl of ice water.
8. Place the peppercorns in a very small, heatproof container and pour about ½ cup (120 mL) boiling water over them. Allow the peppercorns to steep overnight.
9. Place the pistachios in a bowl and pour about 3 cups (0.75 L) boiling water over them. Drain the pistachios in a strainer and refresh them by immersing the strainer in the ice water. Lift the pistachios out of the water and place them on a clean, lint-free kitchen towel. Rub the pistachios gently in the towel to remove the skins.

(continues)

Mortadella

Classic mortadella sausage originated in Bologna, Italy. It became so popular that it was widely copied throughout the country. Much mortadella is made in the traditional Bologna style, but other localities developed their own style.

Although most Italian mortadella is not smoked, one regional specialty is lightly smoked (as is the version included here). It is this variety that became widely copied in North America, where it was given the name of the city that first made it, Bologna.

PROCEDURE *(continued)*

10. Drop the brunoise fatback into the remaining boiling water, lower the heat to a bare simmer, and poach about 2 minutes, or until tender. Drain the fatback, cool it to room temperature, and refrigerate it.

DAY 2: GRINDING AND MIXING, ENCASEMENT, CURING

11. Freeze the grinder parts, the bowl and blade of a commercial-size food processor, a large stainless-steel bowl, and a hotel spoon.
12. Place the pork fat in the freezer about 30 minutes, or until the exterior is crusted with ice crystals.
13. Set up the grinder and place an ice bain-marie under the grinder head.
14. Grind the chilled, seasoned pork and veal through the coarse, medium, and fine dies. Refrigerate it.
15. Grind the semifrozen pork fat through the coarse, medium, and fine dies. Refrigerate it.
16. Place the chilled meat in the chilled processor bowl. Add the crushed ice, wine, and seasoning mix. Begin processing immediately. Use an instant-read thermometer to monitor the temperature of the meat as it rises from 30°F to 40°F (-1°C to 4°C).
17. Immediately add the ground fat and process until the temperature reaches 45°F (7°C).
18. Immediately add the nonfat dry milk and process until the temperature reaches 58°F (14°C). Refrigerate the forcemeat.
19. Perform a poach test.
20. Evaluate and make necessary corrections.
21. Transfer the forcemeat to the frozen bowl set in the ice bain-marie and fold in the brunoise pork fat, drained and blotted peppercorns, and pistachios.
22. Encase the forcemeat to make 14-in. (35-cm) lengths, and clip or tie off.
23. Hang the mortadellas over a drip pan in the refrigerator for 24 hours.

DAY 3: POACHING

24. Sterilize a teasing needle or knife and perforate the mortadellas at 2-in. (5-cm) intervals.
25. Bring enough water to cover the mortadellas to a simmer in a brazier or braising table. Place the mortadellas in the water and keep them submerged by weighting them with a lid. Poach the mortadellas at a bare simmer to an internal temperature of 150°F (65°C).
26. Prepare a large bowl of ice water.
27. Refresh the mortadellas in the ice water until they reach an internal temperature of 38°F (3°C)
28. Blot the mortadellas dry with paper towels. If you do not plan to smoke them, wrap the mortadellas in butcher paper and refrigerate them.
29. If you plan to smoke them, hang the mortadellas over a drip pan in the refrigerator overnight to form a pellicle.
30. If smoking, soak the wood in water to cover at room temperature overnight.

DAY 4: OPTIONAL COLD-SMOKING AND FINISHING

31. Prepare a smoker set to 80°F (26°C).
32. Hang the mortadellas in the smoker and smoke them 1–2 hours, or until the desired exterior color is achieved.
33. Shower the mortadellas under a spray of cold water until they reach an internal temperature of 38°F (3°C).
34. Blot the mortadellas dry with paper towels.
35. Wrap the mortadellas in butcher paper and refrigerate them.

HOLDING

Refrigerate up to 6 days.

SOPPRESSATA

[sop-press-AH-tah]

ITALIAN DRY-CURED SAUSAGE

Yield:
11 ½ lb (5.5 kg)

INGREDIENTS	U.S.	METRIC
Fresh pork fat back	2½ lb	1.2 kg
Boneless pork butt	8 lb	3.85 kg
Bactoferm™ F-Rm-52	1½ oz	45 g
Distilled water	4 oz	120 g
Kosher salt	3 oz	90 g
Prague Powder #2	½ oz	15 g
Sugar	½ oz	15 g
Nonfat dry milk powder	4½ oz	135 g
Dextrose	1 oz	30 g
Finely ground white pepper	½ oz	15 g
Minced garlic	½ oz	15 g
Crushed dried red pepper	¼ oz	7 g
White wine	3½ fl oz	105 mL
14-in. (35-cm) hog middles, soaked and rinsed	2	2
Supplies		
Hog rings or kitchen string	as needed	as needed

PROCEDURE

DAY 1: FABRICATION, GRINDING AND MIXING, ENCASEMENT

1. Freeze the grinder parts. Prepare an ice bain-marie. Freeze the mixer bowl and paddle attachment.
2. Cut the fatback into 1-in. (2-cm) dice. Spread it on a sheet tray and place in the freezer about 30 minutes, or until the exterior is crusted with ice crystals.
3. Cut the pork shoulder into 1-in. (2-cm) dice and partially freeze as you did with the fat.
4. Grind the fatback through the coarse and medium dies into the ice bain-marie.
5. Grind the pork through the coarse die into the ice bain-marie.
6. Refrigerate the fat and pork.
7. Dissolve the Bactoferm in the distilled water.
8. Put the ground meat into the chilled mixer fitted with the paddle attachment. Place the ice bain-marie underneath.
9. Add the Bactoferm water and the remaining ingredients. Mix on low speed about 2 minutes to thoroughly blend in the seasonings.
10. Perform a poach test.
11. Evaluate and make necessary corrections.
12. Encase the sausages (A, B) and tie them (C).

A

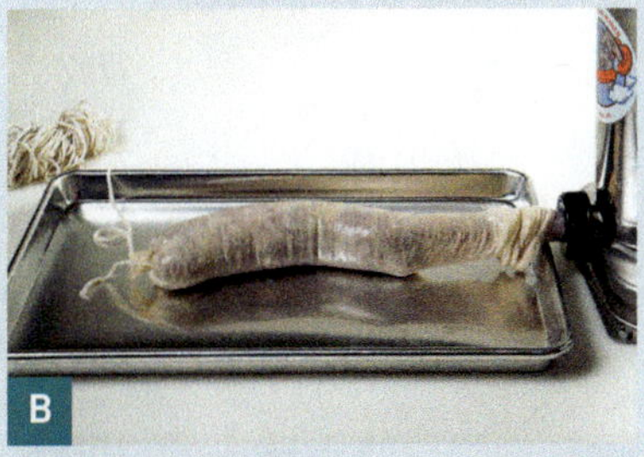
B

C

(continues)

PROCEDURE *(continued)*

13. Sterilize a teasing needle or knife and perforate the sausages at 1-in. (2-cm) intervals (D).
14. Hang the sausage for 12 hours at 85°F (29°C) to activate the bacteria in the Bactoferm (E).

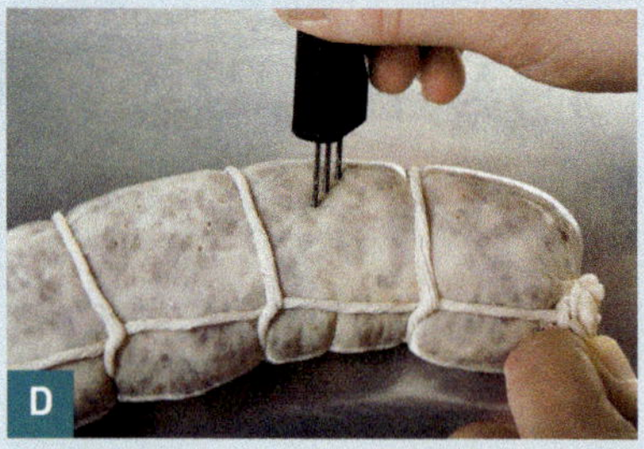

DAYS 2–24: AIR-DRYING

15. Prepare a drying chamber at 60°F (15°C) with 60% humidity.
16. Hang the sausages over a drip pan and allow them to air-dry 24 days (F). To maintain the sausages, follow the guidelines on page 496.

HOLDING

Continue to hold the sausages in the drying chamber up to 1 month. Alternatively, wrap in butcher paper and refrigerate up to 2 months.

ITALIAN SAUSAGE PLATTER

WITH ROASTED PEPPERS AND OLIVES

BUFFET

Portions:
12
Portion size:
4 oz (125 g) sausage, plus garnish

COMPONENTS

1¼ lb (625g) *Sweet Italian Sausage (p. 499)*
8 oz (250 g) Kale leaves
12 fl oz (360 mL) *Roasted Peppers in Garlic Oil (p. 688)*
8 oz (250 g) Assorted Italian olives
1 lb (500 g) *Mini-Mortadella (p. 507)*
1 lb (500 g) *Soppressata (p. 509)*
as needed Italian bread

Supplies
as needed Plain cocktail picks

PROCEDURE

PREPARATION

1. Preheat a gas or charcoal grill to moderate heat.
2. Perforate the Italian sausage at 2-in. (5-cm) intervals.
3. Grill the sausage slowly, turning it as necessary, until it reaches an internal temperature of 150°F (65°C) and is lightly browned. Cool to room temperature.
4. Refrigerate the sausage at least 2 hours.

PLATING

5. Line an 18-in. (45-cm) tray with the kale leaves.
6. Mound the peppers in the center of an 8-in. (20-cm) shallow bowl. Place the bowl in the center of the tray. Arrange the olives around the rim of the bowl.
7. Thinly slice the mini-mortadella. Roll each slice tight and place it on one-third of the tray.
8. Cut the sweet Italian sausage on the diagonal into ¼-in. (0.5-cm) slices. Arrange it on one-third of the tray.
9. Cut the soppressata on the diagonal into ¼-in. (0.5-cm) slices. Arrange it on one-third of the tray.
10. Place the cocktail picks in a small container.
11. Slice the bread and place it in a basket lined with a linen napkin.

HOLDING

Cover with plastic wrap and refrigerate up to 6 hours. Bring to cool room temperature before serving. Slice the bread just before serving.

TERMS FOR REVIEW

sausage(s)
forcemeat
farce
casing(s)
natural casings
manufactured casings
caul fat
internal garnish(es)
standard-grind sausage
emulsified sausage
fresh sausage
cured and hot-smoked sausage
cured and dried sausage
unsmoked dried sausage
fermented sausage
cured and cold-smoked sausage
white or fresh emulsified sausage
cured emulsified sausage
certified pork
fatback/backfat
pork rind
salt fatback
jowl fat
suet
leaf lard
trim fat
dextrose
synthetic souring agent
secondary binder
acid-loving bacterial culture
hank(s)
collagen casing
synthetic casing
worm
die
meat grinder
rotation chopper
planetary mixer
sausage stuffer
pressure plate
nozzle
sausage horn
extrude
casing clip
hog ring
teasing needle
solids component
pre-season(ing)
smear
5:4:3 ratio
bind
primary bind
protein development
poach test
bulk sausage
sausage patty
crépinette
encasement
bubble tie
rope sausage
coil
ring sausage
sausage link
sausage chain
drying chamber
case hardening

QUESTIONS FOR DISCUSSION

1. List and describe the three basic elements of a sausage. Which are optional?
2. List the six functions of a sausage casing.
3. Compare and contrast the four types of standard-grind sausages.
4. List and describe the two types of emulsified sausages.
5. Discuss sausage safety. Include precautions you would take to ensure your customers are safe from food-borne illness. Include ways in which you would keep yourself and your staff safe from accidents.
6. List and describe the four phases of sausage production.
7. Define the term *forcemeat*. Explain four concepts or techniques that are important when making a good forcemeat.
8. List five guidelines for successful use of a meat grinder.
9. Explain the scientific principles behind protein structure development and forcemeat emulsification.
10. Why are some sausages pre-cooked at the point of production? List the two recommended ways to cook sausages this way and describe each method in detail, including recommended internal temperatures.
11. List and explain five guidelines for drying sausages. List three ways to determine whether the drying process is complete.

Chapter 13

PREREQUISITES

Before studying this chapter, you should already

- Have read "How to Use This Book," pages xxviii–xxxiii, and understand the professional recipe format.
- Know basic meat and poultry cuts, and be proficient at fabricating them.
- Be familiar with various spices, and know how to toast and grind whole spices.
- Be proficient at clarifying stock.
- Have read Chapter 11, "Cured and Smoked Foods," and understand the use of curing mixtures.
- Have read Chapter 12, "Sausages," know the various types of pork fat, and be proficient at preparing standard-grind forcemeats.
- Know how to work with gelatin if you will be preparing pâtés en croûte, or have read ahead to Chapter 16, "Aspic and Chaud-Froid," pages 632–635.

Pâtés, Terrines, and Charcuterie Specialties

The pâté and its country cousin, the terrine, are both forcemeats prepared in the shape of a loaf or log. The repertoire of traditional pâtés and terrines ranges from elegant and sophisticated to rough and rustic. They can be made of virtually any meat, and take a variety of forms. Bold-flavored, coarse-textured terrines are served in hearty slabs with piquant accompaniments. Exquisite pâtés are rich and smooth, enrobed in shimmering aspic under their golden crusts. Thus, these foods can be as appropriate at a picnic as they are at a formal dinner.

With the knowledge and skills you acquire from this chapter, you will be able to create pâtés, terrines, and other charcuterie specialties that appeal to a wide range of customers and are appropriate on any menu.

After reading this chapter, you should be able to

1. List and describe the five basic types of pâté.
2. List and describe the four elements of pâté construction.
3. Identify and safely use the proper equipment for pâté production.
4. Prepare pâté forcemeats.
5. Correctly assemble various types of pâté.
6. Cook pâté products to the proper internal doneness and finish them appropriately according to type.
7. Prepare complementary sauces, condiments, and accompaniments for pâtés.
8. Present finished pâté products for both plated service and platter service.

PÂTÉS AND TERRINES

A ***pâté*** [pah-TAY] is a forcemeat baked in a pastry crust and usually served cold. This technical, culinary definition is the one generally accepted among chefs and food-service professionals worldwide. However, to the average North American consumer, the definition is much broader, encompassing pâtés with and without crusts as well as spread-like mixtures and cold seafood mousselines (p. 612). Today, the term *pâté* can even include loaflike cold vegetable preparations.

In this chapter, we use the term *pâté* when generally referring to meat- and poultry-based pâté products of all kinds—with and without crusts. When specifying a crusted pâté we use the term *pâté en croûte*, and when specifying a pâté without a crust we use the term *terrine*.

Today, the art and craft of making pâtés has become one of the most specialized forms of food production.

With the proper equipment and a sound understanding of the principles of the craft, you can produce world-class pâtés and terrines that will set your operation apart from the ordinary.

The History of the Word *Pâté*

The term *pâté* is derived from the French word *pâte* [PAHT], or "paste." This word has two applications in culinary French: 1. a paste created by grinding or pulverizing a food substance, as in *pâte d'amandes*, or almond paste; and 2. a flour-and-water paste, or pastry, as in *pâte sucrée*, or sugar pastry. Confusion arises when food historians attempt to explain the origin of the term. Does the "paste" refer to the ground-up meat, or does it refer to the pastry in which the meat is wrapped?

According to most chefs and food authorities, the correct name for a ground meat mixture baked in a crust is *pâté en croûte*, and the full and proper term for a ground meat mixture baked in an earthenware dish is *pâté en terrine*. Therefore, it is safe to assume the word *pâté* refers to a meat paste.

Types of Pâtés

Today there are five basic types of pâtés:

1. ***Pâté en croûte:*** a forcemeat baked inside a crust of pastry dough. Most are made with a fine-grind or smooth forcemeat and contain one or more internal garnishes. The space that forms between the crust and the forcemeat after baking and cooling is filled with aspic (p. 635).

2. ***Terrine:*** a forcemeat baked in a form or vessel without a pastry crust. The vessel is traditionally lined with pork fatback or caul fat (p. 522) to protect and insulate the forcemeat. Many terrines are made from a coarse-grind forcemeat and have a rustic texture. Others are made from a medium-grind forcemeat. Terrines may include internal garnishes.

3. ***Galantine*** and ***ballottine:*** forcemeats wrapped in poultry skin or meat.

   A *galantine* consists of a poultry-based forcemeat wrapped in the skin of a fowl. It is normally formed into a large, cylindrical shape. In modern galantines, the skin is usually lined with a thin layer of poultry breast meat, and the interior forcemeat is made from the leg meat and additional pork and pork fat. Internal garnishes are usually added to the forcemeat. The assembled galantine is poached in poultry stock.

   Ballottines are the subject of controversy among charcutiers and garde manger chefs. Some believe *ballottine* is just another name for a galantine. Other sources assert that a ballottine is a forcemeat wrapped in a butterflied, flattened piece of meat, and is never made with poultry. See the sidebar on page 529 for more information on the controversy.

4. ***Pâté roulade*** (or *pâté en roulade*): assembled and cooked in the same way as a galantine, but not wrapped in a poultry skin. Slices of cooked or raw meat, ham, or even leafy vegetables form its wrapper. It is also wrapped in plastic film and then poached.

5. ***Mousseline pâté***: The smoothest and most refined form of pâté is made from an emulsion of puréed raw meat, eggs, and cream. When a mousseline is formed into a loaf or log, cooked, and cooled, it can be sliced in the same manner as a terrine. Mousselines are covered in Chapter 15.

The Four Elements of Pâté Construction

Most pâtés have four basic elements:

1. ***Forcemeat:*** All pâtés begin with a forcemeat. This emulsified mixture of ground meat and fat makes up the body of the pâté.
2. ***Internal garnishes:*** pieces of food placed within the forcemeat to add texture, flavor, and visual interest. Internal garnishes are added to pâté forcemeats in two ways (listed on p. 521). By varying the internal garnishes, a charcutière or garde manger chef can make several products out of one basic forcemeat.
3. ***Liners*** and ***wrappers:*** A pâté forcemeat is usually contained in some form of *wrapper* or *liner*. Only mousselines are not wrapped or lined, although they may be encased in a colorful vegetable wrapper for an attractive presentation.
4. ***Sealers:*** In times past, after a pâté product was baked and cooled, it was sealed with a semisolid fat to preserve it. This practice is still sometimes used, although modern pâtés and terrines are more often sealed with aspic (p. 523) for presentation purposes. Lard, rendered poultry fat, butter, and aspic are used as pâté sealers.

The four elements of pâté construction

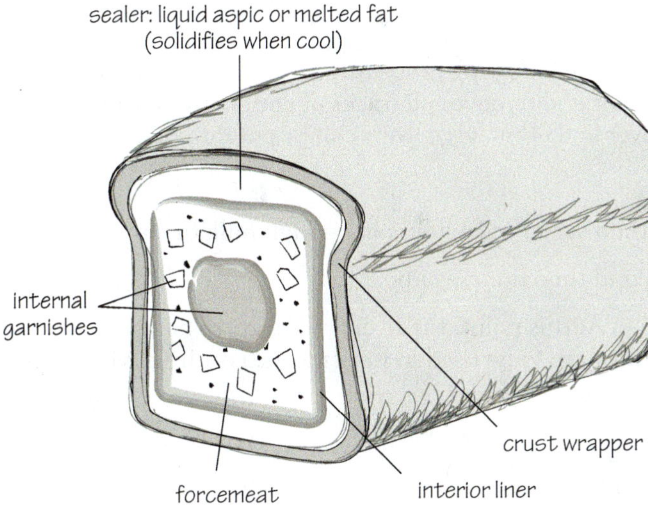

Ingredients

Meats and Poultry for Pâté Forcemeats

Most of the meats, fats, and seasonings covered in Chapter 12 are also used for pâtés. However, there are several requirements to consider when choosing the ingredients for pâté forcemeats. Pâtés are meant to be pale in color, firm-textured, and subtly flavored. Beef and lamb are *never* used in traditional pâtés because of their strong flavor, but poultry and game meats are often used. Liver, which is rarely used in North American sausages, is frequently used in pâtés (see sidebar on p. 518). In addition, pâtés are likely to be made with a mixture of meats. Within this mixture, one meat is considered primary and the rest secondary.

The History of Pâtés

By the late Middle Ages, the European aristocracy was living well. Each noble wanted to appear wealthier and more sophisticated than his peers. This set the stage for the humble sausage to become the aristocratic pâté.

By the end of the Middle Ages, garde manger chefs had developed the technique of creating a rich and smooth emulsion of meat and meat fat to make the kind of pâté forcemeat still in use today. Kitchen assistants hand-chopped and then pounded meats and fat in gigantic mortars. These old-style pâtés contained a high proportion of salt, alcohol, and spices.

Once prepared, a way was needed to contain the forcemeat while it cooked. One solution was to wrap it in pastry and bake it in the bread oven. Forcemeats prepared in this manner became known as *pâtés en croûte.* Another was to wrap the forcemeat in a poultry skin and poach it, making a product called a *galantine.*

With the development of towns and cities and the beginning of the medieval guilds, the art of making pâtés passed to the charcutiers. When the pastry chefs' guild objected to charcutiers using pastry for their pâtés, the charcutiers began baking pâté forcemeats in earthenware dishes called *terrines,* from the Latin *terra,* or "earth." These were called *pâtés en terrine,* a term later shortened to *terrines.*

The ***primary meat*** must total more than half the pâté forcemeat's weight. It is this meat that gives the pâté its name. For example, the primary meat in the forcemeat for a duck pâté is duck. In some pâtés, the primary meat may be the only lean meat included in the forcemeat. In this case, the remainder of the forcemeat's composition is made up of pork fat.

Secondary meats are meats added to a pâté forcemeat. They are used for a number of reasons. One is to add a rich mouthfeel to a forcemeat made from a lean primary meat. Both pork and liver are used for this purpose. Another reason is to lighten the color of the finished product. Chicken and turkey breast meat are good for this. Finally, inexpensive secondary meats are added for economy, to stretch more expensive game meats or veal.

In most cases, the forcemeat component of a pâté is made from tough cuts. The tender cuts are generally reserved for internal garnishes or to line the skins of galantines.

Following is a list of meats and poultry frequently used in pâté forcemeats:

- Pork
- Veal
- Game meats
- Chicken
- Turkey
- Duck
- Wildfowl
- Poultry livers
- Pork liver
- Calf's liver

Procedure for Preparing Poultry Livers for Forcemeats

When poultry livers are to be added to forcemeats, the following procedure gives good results, especially for finer forcemeats, because it makes the flavor milder and removes all traces of connective tissue. (For coarse terrines, this procedure is often skipped.) Pork liver and other large livers can be cut into pieces and prepared the same way.

1. Rinse the livers in cold water, drain, and then soak for 24 hours in enough milk to cover.
2. Drain and rinse thoroughly in cold water, and then drain again.
3. Remove all visible fat and connective tissue. At this point, the livers are ready to be used whole as internal garnish for pâtés and terrines. If they are to be used in forcemeats, continue with steps 4 and 5.
4. Blend the livers in a blender until liquid.
5. Strain through a fine-mesh strainer to remove all traces of connective tissue.

Fats for Pâté Forcemeats

FRESH PORK FAT

Various forms of pork fat are traditionally used in pâté making. These fats are discussed at length in Chapter 12 on pages 474–475. If information on pork fat is not fresh in your mind, refer to these pages before proceeding to make pâtés.

CHICKEN FAT AND TURKEY FAT

The solid fat of chickens and turkeys is useful in charcuterie products based on poultry. However, these fats are not widely available because poultry processing plants either use the fat in their own products or send it directly to other industrial food processors. While you may be able to order solid chicken or turkey fat from a butcher or local processor, it is more likely you will need to save these fats from the carcasses you use for meat.

DUCK FAT

Solid duck fat may be purchased from specialty purveyors whose main products are duck and duck foie gras. Many charcutiers and garde manger chefs derive duck fat from butchering whole Long Island or Muscovy ducks, both of which are high in fat.

Seasonings for Pâté Forcemeats

The amount and type of seasonings used in forcemeats are among a pâté product's most distinctive features. One reason for the high seasoning is that the finished product is served at a cool temperature, which tends to dull the taste buds. Although today's pâtés no longer need the high salt content and heavy spicing used in the past for preservation, the seasoning must still be quite bold.

SALT

Salt is crucial to the flavor of a well-seasoned pâté. Coarse-grain kosher salt is recommended for seasoning pâté marinades and cures and for the direct seasoning of pâté forcemeat mixtures. However, a special flavor can be achieved by using premium natural salts.

SPICES

The distinctive taste of spices is one of the defining flavors of a pâté. Freshly ground spices are recommended. Before preparing the forcemeat, toast, grind, and strain the spices specified in the formula. If you must use pre-ground spices, make sure they are fresh and flavorful.

Traditional pâté spices include black pepper, white pepper, dry ginger, nutmeg, mace, cloves, juniper, and allspice. Contemporary choices include paprika, cayenne, anise, fennel seed, and a wide range of Asian and Meso-American spices used in new-style world cuisines pâtés.

Charcutiers and garde manger chefs who make pâtés on a regular basis often prepare pre-ground seasoning mixtures based on spices. The best-known pre-ground pâté spice blend is a mixture called ***quatre épices*** [KAT-ray-piece] (see sidebar). For convenience, dried herbs and other dry seasonings are often mixed into pâté spice blends as well. Once ground, these blends must be tightly wrapped and stored in the freezer for no longer than one month. Stir the mixture thoroughly before you use it.

HERBS

A variety of herbs is also used to season pâté forcemeats. Herb leaves and sprigs may be used to flavor and decorate the exterior of terrines as well.

Dried herbs are quite potent and concentrated in flavor and must be used cautiously. When evaluating the flavor of dried herbs added directly to the forcemeat, allow sufficient hydration time before sampling.

Fresh herbs are also added to pâté forcemeats. In general, fresh herbs are less concentrated in flavor than dried. However, their intensity of flavor varies dramatically according to the conditions under which they were grown.

Fat-to-Lean Ratios for Pâté Forcemeats

In traditional European formulas for pâté forcemeats, the ratio of fat to lean meat ranges from 35:75 to 40:60. However, if you are using today's very lean American pork or a large amount of lean game meat, you may need to increase the ratio to 50:50 to achieve a firm texture and rich mouthfeel.

To determine whether the fat-to-meat ratio of a raw pâté forcemeat is correct, it is necessary to poach-test a sample using the method described on page 531 in step 11. Only by tasting a cooked, cooled sample can you determine how the finished pâté will taste and feel in the mouth.

Quatre Èpices

One of the best-known spice blends used in pâté making is called *quatre épices,* or "four spices." The blend's composition varies. Some modern blends actually contain as many as nine or ten spices. The original four spices in this famous blend were most likely pepper, dry ginger, nutmeg, and cloves. However, allspice is frequently added or substituted for the cloves.

CONTEMPORARY QUATRE ÉPICES

1 oz (30 g)	finely ground white pepper
1/2 oz (15 g)	ground dried ginger
1/2 oz (15 g)	ground nutmeg
1/4 oz (7.5 g)	ground allspice

Fresh herbs add color and can create a stunning visual impact if used as part of an interior garnish. A high proportion of fresh herbs in a pâté forcemeat can shorten its holding time.

Gratin Forcemeats

An optional technique when preparing a pâté forcemeat is to pan-sear and then immediately chill a portion of the lean meat before grinding it. Such a mixture is called a ***gratin*** [grah-TAN] ***forcemeat***. The browning of proteins that occurs when the meat is seared adds a deep, complex flavor to the finished product. When preparing a gratin forcemeat, take care to sear the exterior of the meat without fully cooking it. However, even careful searing of a forcemeat component more or less weakens the forcemeat emulsion. Therefore, gratin forcemeats usually contain a strong secondary binder, such as a *panade* (p. 521).

AROMATIC VEGETABLES

Aromatic vegetables such as minced shallots and garlic add complexity to the flavor of a pâté forcemeat. Other aromatics commonly added to pâté forcemeats include citrus zest, reconstituted dried mushrooms or powdered dried mushrooms, and, in modern world cuisines' pâté variations, fresh ginger and chiles.

MEAT GLAZES

Many chefs add *glace de viande* (meat glaze) or *glace de volaille* (poultry glaze) to enhance and deepen the flavor of their pâtés. These also contribute highly concentrated proteins that aid in the emulsion of the pâté forcemeat.

ALCOHOLIC BEVERAGES

Table wines, fortified wines, and spirits are traditional ingredients in pâté forcemeats. Alcohol was originally included in pâtés because its antiseptic qualities aided in preservation. Today, it adds distinctive flavors much prized in fine pâté products.

Table wines add complex flavors to both pâté forcemeats and internal garnishes. Before adding a table wine to a pâté forcemeat, reduce it slowly by gentle heating. This removes the alcohol and most of the wine's volatile acids, and concentrates its flavor. Red wines also need reduction to concentrate color. If used unreduced, most inexpensive red wines give an unattractive magenta color to meats. Reduction darkens red wines to an attractive burgundy color. Reduced wines must be cooled to room temperature before being added to the meat.

Fortified wines, such as port, sherry, and Madeira, are added straight into pâté products with no reduction. Their sugar content adds a note of sweetness.

Spirits, such as brandy, cognac, Armagnac, and Calvados, are among the most traditional of alcohols added to pâté forcemeats and marinades. However, there is a wide range of spirits from which to choose, including American and British whiskeys and the clear liquors. When chosen appropriately, fruit *eaux-de-vie* (colorless, nonsweet fruit alcohols) and fruit cordials can support a flavor theme and lend a subtle sweetness. Spirits for pâtés may be added straight or flambéed to remove their alcohol content.

NITRITE CURING MIX

Many charcutiers add a small proportion of Prague Powder #1 (p. 413), or nitrite curing mix, to pâté forcemeats to prolong storage and preserve color.

Secondary Binders and Extenders for Pâté Forcemeats

While the primary bind in any pâté forcemeat is the emulsion created by the mixture of fat and meat, many forcemeats acquire a better texture with the addition of another, secondary, binding element. These ***secondary binders*** consist of protein ingredients and starch ingredients. The starch binders also function as extenders, adding low-cost bulk to the forcemeat mix. Secondary binders used in pâté forcemeats include:

- Raw eggs
- Flour
- Panades (see sidebar)

Panades

A ***panade*** [pah-NAHD] or ***panada*** [pah-NAH-dah] is a soft, smooth, starchy mixture used to bind and extend a pâté forcemeat. The most commonly used panades are:

- Bread crumbs soaked in milk or water
- A thick purée of cooked rice or cooked potato
- Pâte à choux dough (with or without the egg)

Ingredients for Pâté Internal Garnishes

The modern charcutier can choose from a wide variety of food categories when internally garnishing a pâté product. Here are some:

- Cured and smoked meats
- Nuts
- Dried fruits and vegetables
- Truffles
- Marinated raw meats and poultry
- Seasoned livers

Raw meats and poultry or livers are sometimes seared to add both flavor and an attractive brown color to the finished pâté product. These are called ***gratin garnishes***.

The ratio of internal garnish to pâté forcemeat may be quite low, such as a handful of pistachios scattered throughout a pork and veal pâté. Sometimes the ratio is very high, where the forcemeat is little more than a binder for the garnishes.

Internal garnishes are applied to pâtés in two ways:

1. ***Random garnishes***: A simple way to add internal garnishes is to mix pieces of the garnish food into the forcemeat before it is packed into the pâté form. These are called *random garnishes* because, in the finished product, they appear scattered randomly throughout the loaf. Foods used as random garnishes are usually fabricated into cubes or chunks or, if small, left in their natural shapes.

2. ***Inlay garnishes***: A more precise way to apply an internal garnish is to arrange the garnish food in a specific pattern while packing the forcemeat into its form, a method called *inlay garnishing*. *Inlay garnishes* are often fabricated into long cylinders or strips. Some central inlay garnishes are left whole, such as truffles or poultry livers. When the finished product is sliced, the inlay garnish ingredients appear as a colorful mosaic within each slice. To ensure the inlays adhere to the forcemeat and the pâté slices neatly and remains intact, inlay ingredients are usually dusted with a light coating of gelatin or powdered egg whites before they are added.

Random and inlay garnishes

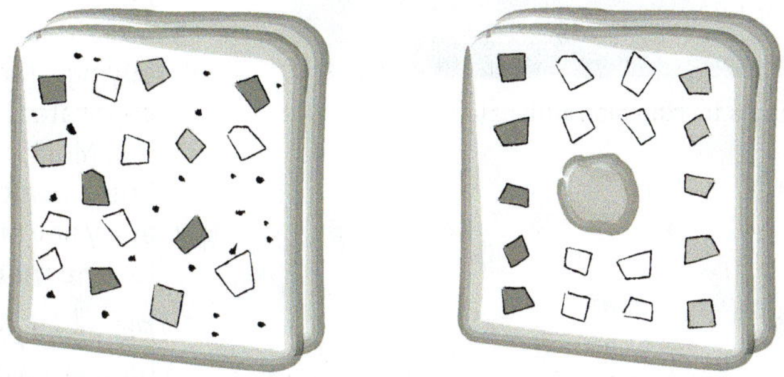

random garnishes (mixed into forcemeat before packing into form)

inlay garnishes (placed into forcemeat while packing into form)

Wrappings and Linings for Pâtés

PASTRY DOUGH WRAPPERS FOR PÂTÉS EN CROÛTE

The pastry dough used to wrap a pâté en croûte is called **pâte à pâté** [paht ah pah-TAY] in French, meaning "pastry for pâté." These doughs must be sturdy enough to hold up to heavy forcemeats and the steam, juices, and rendered fat they produce. Thus, the proportion of fat in a standard dough formula is usually decreased to create a stronger structure. Dough choices include:

- Pâte brisée, made with lard or vegetable shortening
- A milk-enriched biscuit-type dough
- A lightly yeasted, lard-enriched bread dough

The thickness to which the dough is rolled depends on the size of the pâté and the weight of the forcemeat; 3⁄16 in. (0.4 cm) to 1⁄4 in. (0.6 cm) are good general thicknesses for pâté work. The dough is usually sealed and glazed with egg wash, and one or more vents are placed in the top to release steam. Formulas for basic pâté pastry doughs appear on pages 753–754.

LINERS FOR TERRINES

When making traditional terrines, it is necessary to cover the interior of the terrine form with a fat-based lining material. This provides good insulation against harsh heat and prevents the forcemeat from sticking to the form. You can choose from a number of liner fat options.

Fresh pork fatback is the preferred lining fat for most terrines. Nothing equals pork fatback for insulating and basting a terrine forcemeat. Its smooth, dense texture and slow, even melting ensure that the forcemeat wrapped in it remains moist and evenly cooked. However, fatback used for lining terrines must be fabricated into long, wide, even slices, 1⁄8-in. (0.3-cm) thick, to line the terrine mold thoroughly and efficiently. To prepare fatback in this manner you need an electric slicing machine with a very sharp blade. To slice neatly and evenly, the fatback must be very cold. Leave the rind intact for the safety guard to grip.

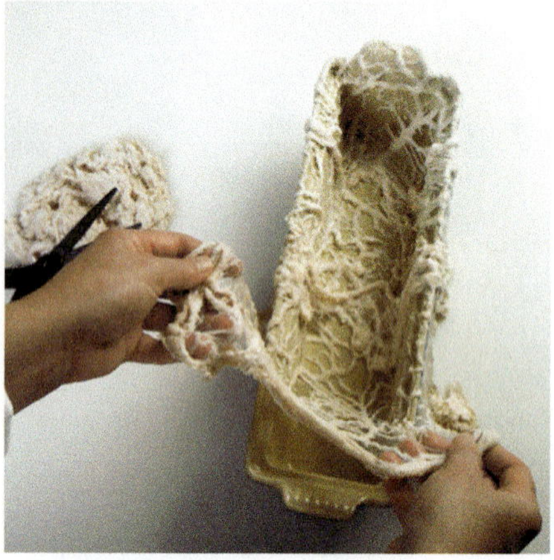

Lining a terrine dish with caul fat

Caul fat (also called **lace fat**) is a thin yet remarkably strong membrane that encases the stomach and intestines of hogs and other animals. Embedded in the surface of this membrane is a lacy pattern of deposit fat. Caul fat is used as liner for the forms and dishes in which terrines are baked. (It is also sometimes used to wrap sausage forcemeats.)

Garde manger chefs who do not have access to a slicing machine like to use caul fat because it is a ready-made wrapper that requires virtually no fabrication. Although it is generally sold frozen in large quantities, buying a large amount is not a problem. Thaw it under cold running water, separate it into sheets, and wrap the sheets individually before refreezing. Most caul fat is lightly salted to preserve it. Before using caul fat as a liner, soak it in cool water to freshen it and remove excess salt. Trim away any strings, tangles, and thick areas before using the sheets to line terrine molds.

Bacon or pancetta is the usual liner choice of amateur cooks because both are widely available in pre-sliced form. However, the assertive taste of these products can overwhelm the flavor of a delicate forcemeat. They are best teamed with bold, rustic forcemeats, particularly those that include liver.

Dry-cured meats such as ham, prosciutto, or bresaola may be used as liners for modern pâté roulades and molded terrines. Because they lack the substantial fat content of the fat-based liners, these products do not work well as insulators and should not be used for traditional baked terrines. However, they make colorful and tasty wrappings for forcemeats to be poached in plastic. These meats can also be used as a lining inside the dough of a pâté en croûte.

Vegetables, such as sturdy lettuce leaves, mild-flavored cabbage, kale, and blanched leeks, may be used as liners for modern poached or steamed terrines. In addition, thin, even slices of root vegetables may be arranged in a colorful pattern around the outside of such terrines. Vegetable liners are more perishable than meat-based liners.

Sealer Ingredients for Pâtés and Terrines

When a pâté en croûte has finished baking and cooling, there is a gap between the forcemeat and the crust. This gap must be sealed so the crust remains on the forcemeat when the pâté is sliced. Similarly, when a terrine bakes and cools, a gap remains between the meat and the dish. In addition, the top surface of the terrine is exposed to air. These gaps and exposed surfaces must be sealed if the terrine is to keep for the longest time possible.

ASPIC SEALER FOR PÂTÉS EN CROÛTE

For pâtés en croûte, modern charcutiers use flavorful, crystal-clear aspic to fill the gap and adhere the crust to the forcemeat.

The aspic must be firm enough to slice neatly but not be so firm that it has a rubbery mouthfeel. Clarified beef, veal, and poultry stocks are the usual bases for these aspics. The strength and quality of the stock and the purity of the clarification are important elements in producing an attractive and flavorful sealer aspic. Sealer aspics are frequently flavored with fortified wines, such as port or Madeira, that complement the flavors of the forcemeat and internal garnishes.

Sealing a pâté en croûte with liquid aspic

SEALERS FOR TERRINES AND OTHER PÂTÉ PRODUCTS

Lard is the traditional material used to seal terrines for extended storage. See page 527 for the procedure.

Aspic may be used to seal a terrine for attractive presentation in its dish, as explained in the procedure on page 527.

For a more formal presentation, slices of pâté en croûte or terrine are sealed with a thin coating of aspic and then arranged on individual plates or a serving tray. The aspic prevents the slices from drying out and gives each piece an attractive, shiny appearance. See the procedure on page 557 for an illustration for coating pâté slices.

North America Discovers Pâtés

By the late 1960s, both the British and North Americans were discovering the pleasures of French charcuterie—and of pâtés and terrines in particular. The 1964 World's Fair in Flushing, New York, reintroduced Americans to French cuisine at the French Pavilion, a fine-dining restaurant sponsored by the French government. A few of the French Pavilion chefs stayed on in Manhattan to open restaurants, and soon other French chefs opened charcuteries serving the same pâtés and terrines found in France. The words *charcuterie, pâté,* and *terrine* entered the American vocabulary, and fine-dining restaurant menus across the continent soon featured some form of pâté. Before long, pâté products made in North America by large-scale producers could be purchased in cheese shops and specialty groceries as well.

EQUIPMENT FOR PÂTÉ PRODUCTION

Equipment for Grinding and Puréeing

Pâté forcemeats are prepared in the same manner as sausage forcemeats. Therefore, the same equipment is used for grinding and puréeing both. Refer to Chapter 12, pages 480–482, for equipment information and photos.

Pâté and Terrine Forms

Today's charcutiers can choose from a variety of vessels in which to bake both pâtés en croûte and terrines. The following choices are most common for commercial food service:

Pâté en Croûte Forms

Traditional pâté en croûte forms are made of French tin and have removable sides. These sides ensure easy removal of the pâté once it is baked, cooled, and filled with aspic.

Modern pâté en croûte forms are rectangular, have hinged sides, and are made of stainless steel. Charcutiers also bake pâtés en croûte in stainless-steel triangle forms and tunnel forms.

From top to bottom: Stainless-steel triangle form, enameled cast-iron terrine, porcelain terrine, stainless-steel collapsible pâté en croûte form

Terrines

The original forms used for baking forcemeats without pastry crusts were earthenware—that is, pottery dishes made of clay. Earthenware terrines are still made in France, and antique earthenware terrines can be found as well. While both traditional and beautiful, these cannot be used in commercial food service because they do not meet HACCP sanitation guidelines. Ceramic forms of heavy porcelain have largely taken their place. An even more popular type of terrine form is made of heavy enameled cast iron. These vessels are attractive enough to be used as presentation dishes for casual buffets. If your operation does not have terrine forms, you may use heavy, food service-grade loaf pans instead.

Traditional terrine forms have lids that are used during baking. If you must use loaf pans without lids for baking terrines, cover them with three or four layers of heavy-duty aluminum foil.

The forcemeats for most terrines are not ground fine or puréed smooth but instead consist of medium- to coarse-grind meat. A forcemeat of this consistency contains a significant amount of air. If steps are not taken to remove air, a finished terrine will have a crumbly consistency that lends poor mouthfeel and that results in the terrine not slicing properly. In addition, air pockets provide an environment for bacterial growth, resulting in faster spoilage.

To force out the air, the terrine must be weighted after it comes out of the oven, and as it cools and chills. Weighting compacts a terrine, making it slightly smaller in volume. However, weighting results in a smooth, dense texture that feels luscious in the mouth. Weighted terrines slice neatly and keep longer. To date, terrine manufacturers do not supply weighting equipment, so the charcutier and garde manger chef must improvise.

The most efficient way to weight a terrine uses a weighting plate in combination with a heavy object. To acquire a weighting plate, have a building supply store fabricate a piece of Plexiglas® or Lexan® that exactly fits the top opening of the terrine form. The sanitized weighting plate is placed on the cooked, covered forcemeat, and then a heavy object, such as a #5 can, is placed on top. For most terrines, a weight of about 2 lb (1 kg) is sufficient. The weighting plate ensures the pressure of the weighting object is evenly distributed over the terrine.

Another option is to wrap bricks in foil and use them for weights. However, bricks do not exactly fit the shape of most terrine forms, and thus the pressure exerted on the cooked forcemeat may be uneven. In addition, bricks cannot be sanitized, and you must be extremely careful to keep them covered at all times.

PREPARING PÂTÉS AND TERRINES

Because both sausages and pâtés begin with forcemeats, the initial preparation of pâtés is the same as sausages. Thus, you should review the information on the preparation of forcemeats in Chapter 12, pages 482–490.

While there are hundreds of formulas for pâté forcemeats, and while many pâtés have their own specific preparation requirements, the following steps can be used as general guidelines for preparing pâté products.

Procedure for Making Terrines

1. Prepare the pre-seasoning marinade(s) and/or cure(s) for the primary meat, secondary meats, and internal garnishes.
2. Fabricate the primary and secondary meats: Keeping them cold at all times, trim these meats, and weigh out the correct amounts. Cut the meats into pieces that will easily fit into the grinder.
3. Pre-season the primary and secondary meats as directed. Refrigerate overnight or longer.
4. Fabricate the fat, keeping it cold at all times. If using pork fatback, remove the rind and weigh out the correct amount. Cut it into pieces that will easily fit into the grinder. Refrigerate.
5. Trim all of the internal garnish meats thoroughly. Fabricate them into the desired shapes. Pre-season them as directed. Refrigerate them overnight or longer.
6. Prepare all other internal garnish ingredients as directed in the recipe.
7. Prepare the fat being used for the lining. Refrigerate.
8. Set up a grinder with chilled parts. Place an ice bain-marie under the grinder head.
9. Grind the meats as directed in the recipe. Refrigerate them.
10. Grind the fat as directed. Refrigerate it.
11. Fit a mixer with a chilled paddle attachment.
12. Mix the forcemeat: Beat together the meats and fat on medium speed. Add the seasonings and any binder ingredients. Refrigerate the forcemeat in the mixer bowl.
13. Preheat an oven to the specified temperature.
14. Poach-test the forcemeat as directed on page 488.
15. Evaluate the sample and make necessary corrections. If necessary, do another poach test.
16. Mix the random internal garnishes into the forcemeat so they are evenly distributed. Refrigerate.
17. Assemble the terrine:
    a. Line the terrine mold with the prepared lining fat, allowing about 3 in. (7 cm) overhang all around.
    b. Pack the forcemeat into the lined form, adding the inlay internal garnishes as directed. The forcemeat should more than fill the form, extending above its rim.
    c. Tap the form on the work surface to expel any air pockets.
    d. Fold the liner over the top of the forcemeat in an even layer. Trim any excess.
    e. Place herb leaves or sprigs on top as directed.
18. Cover the terrine with a piece of parchment and then with a triple layer of foil folded up around the lip of the dish to prevent wicking (p. 611).
19. Cover the terrine dish with its lid, if it has one. Set the dish in a hotel pan and pour in enough hot water to come halfway up the sides of the terrine dish.
20. Bake the terrine for the time specified in the recipe or to the specified internal temperature, usually 155°F (68°C).

21. Remove the terrine from the oven in its pan and put it in a cool place. Remove the lid, if any, but do not remove the foil. Place the weighting plate (p. 525) on the surface and set a heavy object, about 2 lb (1 kg), on top. Cool to room temperature.
22. Transfer the weighted terrine to a clean sheet tray and refrigerate it for at least 48 hours to mellow.
23. If desired, seal the terrine with aspic or lard. Procedures follow.

Procedure for Sealing a Terrine with Lard for Long Storage

1. Melt sufficient pork lard to cover the top of the terrine to its rim. Cool it to 100°F (38°C).
2. Wearing food-service gloves, remove the foil and parchment from the terrine.
3. Ladle the lard over the terrine, filling it to the rim.
4. Refrigerate, uncovered, until the lard hardens.
5. Wrap the entire terrine dish in several layers of plastic film and refrigerate it.

Procedure for Sealing a Terrine with Aspic

1. Wearing food-service gloves, remove the terrine from its dish. Scrape off all the congealed fat and meat gelée from its surfaces.
2. Wash and dry the terrine dish and replace the terrine in it.
3. Cool the aspic by stirring constantly in an ice bath until it achieves a texture similar to that of thick syrup.
4. Slowly ladle the aspic over the terrine. Tap the terrine on the work surface to force out air pockets.
5. Refrigerate until the aspic sets.
6. Apply surface décor (see p. 715), if desired.
7. Remelt and cool the remaining aspic to a syrupy consistency.
8. Cover the surface and décor with another thin coat of aspic.
9. Refrigerate at least 2 hours before serving.

Procedure for Making Pâtés en Croûte

1. Prepare the pâte pastry dough and refrigerate it.
2. Follow steps 1 through 16 in the Procedure for Making Terrines (p. 526), omitting step 7 and step 16 if no random internal garnishes are specified in your recipe.
3. Roll out the dough and line a collapsible pâté en croûte form with it, leaving the specified amount of dough overhanging the edges of the form. Use egg wash to seal the interfaces where two dough pieces meet. This technique is illustrated on page 555.
4. Cut out a dough lid and dough décor and refrigerate them until needed.
5. If lining the dough with thin-sliced meat, do so, allowing enough overhang to cover the top once the forcemeat is packed.
6. Pack the forcemeat into the form, adding inlay garnishes as directed in your recipe. Tap the form on the work surface to force out air pockets. The forcemeat should more than fill the form, extending above its rim.
7. Fold up the optional meat liner to cover the forcemeat, and then fold up the dough edges. Egg wash the edges.
8. Place the pastry lid on top of the forcemeat, tucking it in at the sides of the form.
9. Use a small, round cutter to punch one or more vent holes in the dough lid, cutting through the optional meat liner. Leave the cutter in the dough to prevent it from warping. Alternatively, place foil chimney(s) in the vent hole(s).
10. Brush the pastry lid with egg wash and apply the pastry décor. Egg wash the décor.
11. Place the assembled pâté on a parchment-lined sheet tray and refrigerate it for 1 hour to rest the pastry.
12. Preheat an oven to the specified temperature, usually 400°F (200°C).
13. Bake the pâté for 20 minutes to set the pastry, and then lower the temperature to 325°F (160°C). Continue baking until the pâté reaches the desired internal temperature, usually 150°–155°F (65°–68°C). If the lid gets too dark, shield it with a loose cover of foil.
14. Remove the pâté from the oven and cool it to room temperature on its pan.
15. Refrigerate the pâté for 24 hours.
16. Seal the pâté:
    a. Prepare the appropriate aspic for sealing the pâté. Cool it to a syrupy consistency in an ice bath (see pp. 634–635).
    b. Place a funnel in the vent hole(s) and ladle in the aspic. Tilt the form so the aspic penetrates throughout the spaces between the crust and the forcemeat. Fill until the aspic reaches the level of the top crust.
17. Refrigerate the sealed pâté for 24 hours.
18. Release the pâté from the form:
    a. Remove the form's pins or supports.
    b. Run a thin-bladed knife between the crust and the sides of the form, gently pulling on the form to drop the sides and release the pâté neatly from the crust.
    c. Run an offset spatula under the bottom crust to release it from the bottom of the form.

GALANTINES, BALLOTTINES, AND PÂTÉ ROULADES

Both galantines and ballottines consist of forcemeats wrapped in skin or meat prior to being cooked.

Pâté roulades are modern interpretations of galantines and ballottines. The poultry skin is replaced by a decorative liner, and the lined forcemeat is wrapped in heavy-duty plastic film before it is poached.

Galantine or Ballottine?

Most food historians believe the culinary term *galantine* is derived from the archaic French word *galine*, meaning "chicken," and is related to the modern Spanish word for chicken, *gallina*. If this is the true linguistic root of the term, it is safe to assume that a galantine should be made from a chicken, or at least from some kind of fowl.

The term *ballottine* is also frequently used to describe a poultry forcemeat cooked in a poultry skin. However, this term is derived from the French *ballot*, or "bundle," and so is more generic than *galantine*. Thus, it can refer to any kind of wrapped forcemeat.

Preparing Galantines and Ballottines

Here we discuss both galantines and ballottines under the single term *galantine*, although the information pertains to both.

Galantines have a reputation for being difficult to prepare. They require good knife skills, patience, and attention to detail, as well as a thorough knowledge of forcemeat preparation.

To produce a fine galantine, start with the highest-quality poultry you can find. You normally need more than one fowl to prepare a galantine. You need a large fowl, such as a roasting chicken, to provide a skin wrapper large enough to encase the forcemeat. This is called the galantine's ***primary fowl***.

No matter how large a fowl is used as the primary fowl, there is not enough meat on its carcass to fill the skin. The breast meat of the primary fowl is most often used to line the skin. This means only the leg and thigh meat are available for grinding. Therefore, you need additional poultry meat to make the forcemeat. This is called the ***secondary poultry***. For secondary poultry, purchase legs and thighs, breast meat, or an additional whole bird.

Fine-ground pork fat is also added to galantine forcemeat. It contributes richness and binding qualities without obscuring the flavor of the poultry.

Galantines are usually enhanced with internal garnishes. These may include any of the items listed on page 521.

When forming a galantine, roll it tight enough so it stays together and slices well, but not so tight that it bursts when cooking. A galantine must be poached gently at a bare simmer and not allowed to boil. In addition to the risk of bursting, if a galantine is cooked at too high a temperature the emulsion breaks and the fat is released. This results in a dry, grainy mouthfeel.

Although preparing a galantine is exacting and challenging work, by carefully following the steps listed on page 530 as well as the directions in your chosen recipe, you can prepare a delicious and professional-looking galantine that will please and impress your customers.

Procedure for Making Galantines and Ballottines

1. Prepare the poultry skin wrapper:
   a. Remove the skin from the primary fowl in one intact piece to use as a wrapper. (Begin by cutting vertically along the backbone.)
   b. Trim the skin to a neat rectangle of the size specified in your recipe.
   c. Line a half-sheet tray with plastic film and lay a doubled sheet of dampened cheesecloth on top of the film. Place the chicken skin on it, outside down.
   d. Freeze the skin for a few minutes, or until it hardens.
   e. Scrape off any deposit fat and remove any connective tissue. Refrigerate the skin.
2. Finish fabricating the primary fowl carcass:
   a. Remove the breast meat intact, to use for the lining.
   b. To prepare the lining, slice the breast meat into ¼-in. (0.5-cm) slices across the grain. Place them between two sheets of buttered parchment and pound them thin and even. Refrigerate in the parchment.
   c. Remove the leg and thigh meat, and trim it thoroughly. Refrigerate it.
   d. Use the bones, scraps, and gizzard to make a stock to use as a *cuisson*. (The liver may be added to the forcemeat ingredients or used as an internal garnish.)
3. Fabricate the remaining internal garnish meats and pre-season them as directed in the recipe. Refrigerate them.
4. Trim, weigh, and fabricate the secondary poultry and other meats to fit into the grinder. Pre-season as directed. Refrigerate.
5. Trim, weigh, and fabricate the fat to fit in the grinder. Refrigerate.
6. Grind all of the forcemeat ingredients as directed by the recipe.
7. In a mixer, beat together the ground meats, fat, secondary binder(s), and seasonings to make the forcemeat. Refrigerate.
8. Perform a poach test. Taste the sample and make necessary adjustments.
9. Mix the random garnishes into the forcemeat so they are evenly distributed. Refrigerate the forcemeat.
10. Assemble the galantine as directed in your recipe (and as illustrated on pp. 549–551):
    a. Sprinkle powdered gelatin on the skin wrapper.
    b. Place the pounded breast meat on the skin in one even layer, leaving 1 in. (2.5 cm) skin exposed at the far end. Season as directed and sprinkle with gelatin.
    c. Spread the forcemeat evenly on the liner meat, leaving the skin exposed at the far end. Sprinkle the exposed skin generously with gelatin.
    d. Place the inlay garnish in a horizontal line across the middle of the forcemeat.
    e. Roll the galantine into a firm cylinder.
    f. Wrap the galantine firmly in the cheesecloth and plastic film. Tie with kitchen string at each end.

11. Poach the galantine in a *cuisson* to an internal temperature of 155°F (68°C).
12. Open-pan cool the galantine in its *cuisson* to room temperature.
13. Refrigerate the galantine in the *cuisson* at least 24 hours to mellow it.

Variation: Pâté Roulade

Follow the procedure for galantines, but use slices of cooked or raw meat, leafy vegetables, or other items as a wrapper. Place a sheet of plastic film on a half-sheet pan as in step 1c above (omit the cheesecloth). Arrange the selected wrapper on the film. Continue assembling the roulade as indicated in the procedure above, beginning with step 10c. Roll and wrap in plastic. Poach and cool as in the basic procedure.

Roasted Galantines and Ballottines

Roasting is an alternative cooking method for galantines and ballottines. The advantage of roasting is the attractive brown color it gives the skin. Before roasting, the poultry skin must be sewn closed with a trussing needle and kitchen string. Place the galantine on a bed of mirepoix and roast at 350–400°F (175°–200°C) to an internal temperature of 155°F (68°C). After cooling, wrap the galantine and refrigerate at least 24 hours to mellow.

STORING AND PRESENTING PÂTÉS

Storage

Most pâté products, once sealed as in the preceding procedures, have a relatively long refrigerated shelf life. A terrine untouched in its dish easily keeps in the refrigerator for a month, while an uncut, aspic-sealed pâté en croûte lasts at least two weeks.

It is only when you cut it open that a pâté becomes vulnerable to airborne or handler-borne microorganisms. Once a pâté product is cut open, it must be served within a few days. So, if you plan to prepare pâtés and terrines ahead of time and store them for extended periods, it is better to make more, smaller pâtés rather than fewer, larger ones.

Although you can freeze uncooked pâté forcemeat and even freeze an uncooked, assembled terrine, *you cannot successfully freeze a cooked pâté*. Freezing a cooked pâté turns the fluid component of the cooked meat particles into ice crystals. When the pâté is thawed, these ice crystals melt and the forcemeat emulsion breaks. The cooked meat particles shrink and dry out. The result is a watery pâté with an unpleasantly grainy texture.

Presentation Styles

Pâtés, terrines, and galantines may be presented on a platter for buffet service or individually portioned for plate service.

Platter Presentation

A well-crafted pâté en croûte, terrine, galantine, or roulade is often the centerpiece of a garde manger display. For classic platter presentation, about two-thirds of the pâté is sliced, and the remaining third of the pâté loaf is placed at the head of the platter as a ***grosse pièce*** (p. 246), or focal point of the presentation. The pâté slices are then arranged on the platter. The uncut portion of the pâté contributes height to a presentation that would otherwise be flat. Even more height can be achieved by impaling the pâté loaf with an ***attelet*** (ah-tel-LAY), or decorative skewer. In formal presentations, both the slices and the cut surface of the pâté loaf are coated with aspic. The platter is additionally decorated with edible greenery, appropriate fruit or vegetable décor, and, sometimes, diced aspic. Condiments, accompaniments, and bread are presented on the side.

Plate Presentation

Plated presentation can range from simple and rustic to elaborate and formal. In simple, traditional presentations, one or two slices of pâté are plated with a liner leaf or herb sprig garnish, a condiment, and perhaps a simple or composed salad accompaniment. For more formal plates, the slices may be coated with aspic, and the accompaniments may be more elaborate. Contemporary plate presentations may feature geometrically shaped individual pâtés, layered and molded salads, and décor items such as fancifully shaped savory tuiles and plate painting with herb oils and vinegar glazes.

En Terrine Presentation

For casual service, a terrine may be served in the same dish in which it was baked, a service style called ***en terrine presentation***. It may be sealed with aspic, as described on page 527, or left plain. In either case, the terrine must be removed from the dish, scraped clean of fat, and the dish washed and dried before the terrine is replaced in it.

Country terrine presented in an enameled cast-iron terrine dish—a casual presentation

En terrine service invites diners to cut a hefty slice and serve themselves. Thus a small, sharp knife is typically stuck into the terrine. Accompaniments are served in bowls, crocks, and baskets on the side.

Pâté Accompaniments

Good bread is the essential accompaniment for pâtés. Some diners will eat the pâté with a knife and fork and nibble on the bread to cleanse the palate between bites. Others like to place a morsel of pâté on a piece of bread and eat the two together like a miniature open-face sandwich. Because pâtés are basically French in origin, crisp baguettes and other French-type breads are most appropriate. Smooth, spreadable pâtés are sometimes served with crackers.

Because they are dense, rich, and have a high fat content, pâté products are traditionally accented with foods that are tart and crunchy. However, the strong flavors of such condiments may overpower more subtle and refined pâtés. For this type of pâté, you may wish to serve an accompaniment that has a milder, less sharp flavor. Following are some ideas for pâté accompaniments.

- Flavored mustards
- Cumberland sauce
- Anglo-Indian chutneys
- Mayonnaise sauces
- Relishes
- Fruit or vegetable salsas
- Reduced vinegar glazes
- Pickled vegetables
- Vegetables dressed in vinaigrette
- Vegetable slaws
- Mesclun and micro greens salads

PÂTÉ RECIPES

TERRINE DE CAMPAGNE [tair-EEN duh kahm-PAHN(yuh)]
COUNTRY TERRINE

Yield:
1 1½-qt (1.5-L) terrine, about 4 lb (2 kg)
Portions:
16 appetizer servings
Portion size:
about 4 oz (120 g)

INGREDIENTS	U.S.	METRIC
Internal garnish		
Trimmed pork loin cut into ⅜-in. (1-cm) cubes	5 oz	150 g
Madeira	1 oz	30 mL
Cognac	1½ tsp	7.5 mL
Dried thyme	pinch	pinch
Freshly ground black pepper	to taste	to taste
Kosher salt	to taste	to taste
Forcemeat		
Lean pork butt	2½ lb	1.25 kg
Trimmed chicken livers	4 oz	125 g
Minced garlic	¾ oz	21 g
Minced shallots	2 oz	60 g
Fresh, unsalted pork fatback with no rind	1 lb	500 g
Eggs	2	2
Freshly ground white pepper	⅛ oz	4 g
Freshly ground black pepper	⅛ oz	4 g
Ground ginger	⅛ oz	4 g
Ground cloves	½ tsp	2.5 mL
Dried thyme	1 tbsp	15 mL
Dried tarragon	2 tsp	10 mL
Kosher salt	1¼ oz	37 g
Internal garnish and liner		
Trimmed smoked ham, cut in ⅜-in. (1-cm) cubes	3 oz	90 g
Caul fat	1 5-oz sheet	1 150-g sheet
Bay leaves	3	3

PROCEDURE

DAY 1: FABRICATION AND PRE-SEASONING

1. Marinate the pork loin cubes in the Madeira, cognac, pinch of thyme, and salt and pepper to taste in a nonreactive container. Cover and refrigerate 2 hours.
2. Cut the pork butt into 1-in. (2.5-cm) cubes and place them in a nonreactive container.
3. Pour the marinade off the pork loin cubes and onto the pork butt cubes. Mix well and cover the container.
4. Refrigerate the large and small pork cubes 24 hours.

DAY 2: PREPARATION

5. Sanitize the grinder parts and chill them in the refrigerator. Prepare an ice bain-marie and set two backup bowls in the refrigerator. Chill a mixer bowl and paddle attachment.
6. Keeping all ingredients and equipment very cold, grind the forcemeat ingredients:
   a. Grind half the large pork cubes through the coarse die of the grinder into the ice bain-marie. Refrigerate the coarse-ground meat.

A

B

C

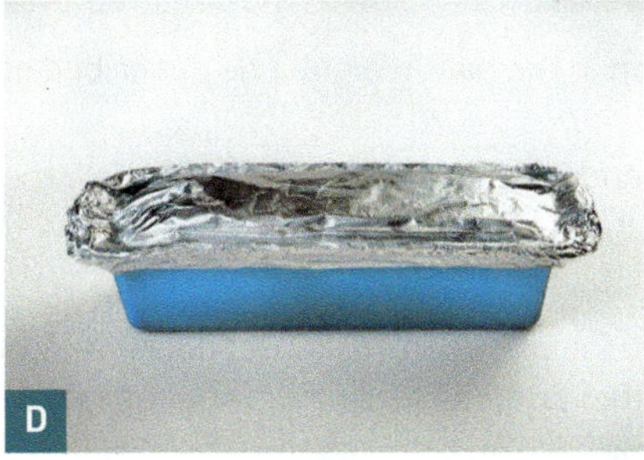
D

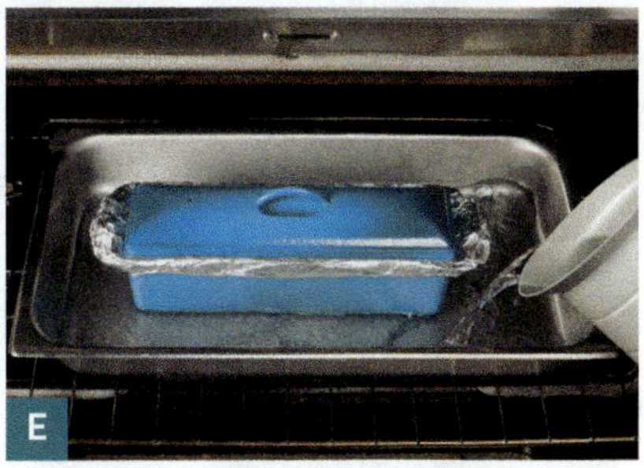
E

PROCEDURE

b. Grind the pork fat through the coarse die into the ice bain-marie and refrigerate it.

c. Grind the remaining large pork cubes through the coarse die into the bain-marie. Place the livers, garlic, and shallots on top of it and refrigerate the bowl.

d. Change to the fine die and grind the pork fat through the fine die *twice*.

e. Grind the pork-liver mixture into the ground pork fat.

7. Place the coarse- and fine-ground meats in a chilled mixer bowl and attach a chilled paddle. Begin beating on moderate speed, then add the eggs and remaining seasonings (except the bay leaves). Beat 3–4 minutes, or until the mixture becomes sticky and homogenous.
8. Poach-test a sample as described on page 488. Correct the fat and seasonings if necessary.
9. Beat in the marinated pork cubes and ham.
10. Preheat an oven to 375°F (200°C).
11. Assemble the terrine:

    a. Rinse the caul fat and trim it to fit a 1½-qt (1.5-L) terrine form.

    b. Line the pan with the caul fat, leaving a 2-in. (5-cm) overhang (A).

    c. Pack in the forcemeat (B). Tap the terrine form on the work surface to force out air pockets.

    d. Wrap the caul fat over the forcemeat and tuck in the edges (C).

    e. Arrange the bay leaves on top.

    f. Place a piece of parchment on the surface of the forcemeat. Cover the terrine with a triple layer of foil, crimping the edges of the foil so water will not wick up into the pans (D). If the terrine has a lid, place it on top.

12. Place the terrine in a deep hotel pan filled with enough hot water to come about 2 in. (5 cm) up its sides (E). Bake the terrine for about 1 hour, or until the forcemeat tests to an internal temperature of 150°F (65°C).

(continues)

F

G

PROCEDURE *(continued)*

13. Remove the terrine from the oven in the pan. Weight it as described on page 527 (F). Cool to room temperature.
14. Leave the weight on the terrine and put it in the refrigerator. Allow the terrine to mellow at least 48 hours before serving it.

HOLDING

Refrigerate unopened up to 2 weeks. Once the terrine is cut open, it may be refrigerated up to 5 additional days. (If sealed with melted lard, the terrine may be refrigerated up to 4 weeks.)

FINISHING

15. When ready to serve, scrape off the solidified fat (G), run a knife between the terrine and the dish, and gently turn the terrine out of the dish. Scrape away any remaining fat. Note: Remove the bay leaves before serving.

VARIATIONS

TERRINE GRANDMÈRE
[grahn-MARE]
GRANDMOTHER'S TERRINE

Replace the Madeira with 2 oz (60 mL) reduced red wine. Replace all of the chicken livers and 12 oz (340 g) of the lean pork butt with trimmed pork liver. Replace 4 oz (120 g) of the pork fatback with trimmed smoked bacon.

TERRINE DE LAPIN AUX PRUNEAUX
[duh lah-PAN oh proon-OH]
RABBIT TERRINE WITH PRUNES

Replace the Madeira with port and the cognac with Armagnac. Replace the pork loin and ham with rabbit saddle meat. Replace the pork butt with trimmed rabbit meat. Add 2 oz (60 g) quartered pitted prunes soaked in Armagnac to the forcemeat.

TERRINE DE CAMPAGNE

WITH MUSTARD AND CORNICHONS

APPETIZER

Portion:
1

Portion size:
4 oz (120 g) terrine, plus garnish

COMPONENTS

1 ¼ oz (7 g) Romaine lettuce leaf
4 oz (120 g) *Terrine de Campagne (p. 534)*, in 2 slices
¼ oz (7 g) Vine-ripe tomato wedge
3 ½-oz (15-g) Small cornichon pickles
½ fl oz (15 mL) Dijon mustard, in squeeze bottle
3 oz (90 g) Crisp baguette or other French bread

PROCEDURE

PLATING

1. Place the romaine leaf on the back left of a cool 10-in. (25-cm) plate.
2. Overlap the terrine slices on the leaf in the center of the plate.
3. Arrange the tomato wedge on the right of the slices and fan the cornichons in front of it. Squeeze a dab of mustard in front of the cornichons.
4. Serve the bread in a basket lined with a linen napkin.

CHECKERBOARD TERRINE OF PORK AND VEAL

Yield:
1 1½-qt (1.5 L) terrine, about 4 lb (2 kg)
Portions:
16 appetizer servings
Portion size:
4 oz (120 g)

INGREDIENTS	U.S.	METRIC
Panade		
Crustless firm white bread	3 oz	90 g
Half-and-half	3 fl oz	90 mL
Internal garnishes		
Pork tenderloin	14 oz	420 g
Veal top round, in one piece	1 lb	500 g
Fresh pork fatback, with no rind	1¼ lb	625 g
White wine	4 fl oz	125 mL
Minced shallots	1 oz	30 g
Minced garlic	¼ oz	7 g
Bay leaves	4	4
Fresh thyme	2 sprigs	2 sprigs
Kosher salt	to taste	to taste
Quatre épices (p. 519)	small pinch	small pinch
Forcemeat		
Trimmed lean pork butt (see step 3)	1 lb (about)	500 g (about)
Quatre épices (p. 519)	¼ oz	7 g
Caul fat	1 5-oz sheet	1 150-g sheet
Prague Powder #1 (optional)	¼ tsp (0.04 oz)	1.25 mL (1.2 g)
Heavy cream	2 fl oz	60 mL
Cognac	½ fl oz	15 mL
Egg white	1	1

PROCEDURE

DAY 1: FABRICATION AND PRE-SEASONING

1. Prepare the panade:
   a. Tear the bread into large crumbs and place in a small container.
   b. Mix in the half-and-half and cover the container. Refrigerate at least 1 hour.
2. Prepare the internal garnishes:
   a. Trim and discard all silverskin from the pork tenderloin. Fabricate from it 4 long rods of meat measuring ¼ × ¼ × 11 in. (0.6 × 0.6 × 28 cm). If the piece of meat is not long enough, fabricate enough shorter pieces to put together into four 11-in. (28-cm) rods. Cut all the trim meat into 1-in. (2.5-cm) dice and reserve it.
   b. Fabricate the veal in the same way.
   c. Fabricate the pork fatback in the same way, but place all remaining trim fat in a plastic bag in the refrigerator.
   d. You should now have 4 rods of pork, 4 rods of veal, and 4 rods of fatback. Place these in a nonreactive container.
   e. Mix together the white wine, shallots, garlic, bay leaves, thyme sprigs, a big pinch of salt, and a small pinch of quatre épices. Pour this mixture over the meat rods and mix it to coat the meat thoroughly. Cover and refrigerate the internal garnishes 1 hour.

PROCEDURE

3. Prepare the forcemeat ingredients:
   a. Mix together the pork tenderloin cubes and veal cubes (left from preparing the garnish) and weigh them. Cut enough of the lean pork butt into 1-in. (2.5-cm) dice to total 1½ lb (0.75 kg) mixed meat.
   b. Cut 1 lb (0.5 kg) of the remaining pork fatback into 1-in. (2.5-cm) dice and add it to the mixed meat.
   c. After 1 hour of marinating the internal garnish meat rods, drain the marinade from it and add the marinade to the mixed meat. Return the drained internal garnishes to the refrigerator. Add the remaining quatre épices and 1 tbsp (15 mL) salt to the mixed meat. Mix the seasonings into the meat, cover it, and refrigerate it overnight.

DAY 2: GRINDING AND MIXING

4. Sanitize the grinder parts and chill them in the refrigerator. Prepare an ice bain-marie. Chill a mixer bowl and paddle attachment.
5. Trim any ragged edges from the caul fat and soak it in cold water at least 20 minutes.
6. Drain the marinade from the garnish meats and the forcemeat meats into a small sauté pan. Pick out and discard the herbs. Reduce the marinade to a thin glaze over moderate heat. Cool the glaze to room temperature.
7. Keeping all ingredients and equipment very cold, grind the forcemeat ingredients:
   a. Mix the panade and the reduced marinade into the forcemeat ingredients.
   b. Grind the forcemeat ingredients through the coarse die of the grinder into the ice bain-marie.
   c. Change to the fine die and grind the forcemeat ingredients through it *twice*.
8. Mix together the cream and the optional Prague Powder #1.
9. Place the meats in a chilled mixer bowl and attach a chilled paddle. Begin beating on moderate speed, then add the cognac and cream. Beat 3–4 minutes, or until the mixture becomes sticky and homogenous.
10. Poach-test a sample as described on page 488, and correct the fat and seasonings if necessary.

DAY 2: ASSEMBLY AND BAKING

11. Preheat an oven to 375°F (200°C).
12. Beat the egg white with 1 tbsp (15 mL) water.
13. Blot the garnish meat rods dry with a paper towel and toss them with the egg white.
14. Drain the caul fat and blot it dry with a clean kitchen towel.
15. Line a 1½-qt (1.5-L) terrine form with caul fat, allowing about 3-in. (8-cm) overhang.
16. Press a ½-in. (1-cm) layer of forcemeat into the bottom of the terrine.
17. Arrange 1 pork rod, 1 fatback rod, and 1 veal rod down the length of the terrine form and press them gently into the forcemeat so they stay in place.
18. Add another ½-in. (1-cm) layer of forcemeat and smooth it level.
19. Arrange another 3 internal garnish rods down the length of the terrine. This time, alternate colors as shown in the cross-section diagram on page 540.
20. Continue with the remaining garnishes and forcemeat, alternating colors each time, to make a checkerboard pattern.
21. Tap the terrine form on the work surface to firm the layers and force out air pockets.
22. Wrap the caul fat over the forcemeat and tuck in the edges.
23. Place a piece of parchment on the surface of the forcemeat. Cover the terrine with a triple layer of foil, crimping the edges of the foil so water will not wick up into the pans. If the terrine has a lid, place it on top.

(continues)

PROCEDURE *(continued)*

24. Place the terrine in a deep hotel pan filled with enough hot water to come 2 in. (5 cm) up its sides. Bake the terrine about 1 hour, or until the forcemeat tests to an internal temperature of 150°F (65°C).
25. Remove the terrine from the oven in the pan and weight the terrine. Cool to room temperature.
26. Leave the weight on the terrine and put it in the refrigerator. Allow the terrine to mellow at least 48 hours before serving it.

HOLDING

Refrigerate unopened up to 2 weeks. Once the terrine is cut open, it may be refrigerated up to 5 additional days. (If sealed with melted lard, the terrine may be refrigerated up to 4 weeks.)

VARIATION

Replace the internal garnish meats with other meats, such as smoked ham, smoked turkey, poached tongue, pork loin, etc.

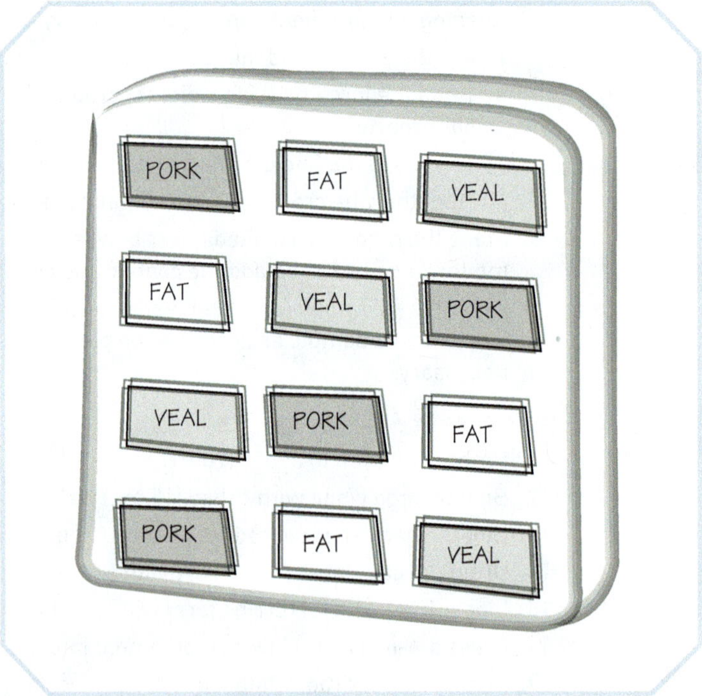

CHECKERBOARD TERRINE OF PORK AND VEAL

WITH MICRO GREENS AND RED PLUM COULIS

APPETIZER

Portions:
1

Portion size:
4 oz (120 g), plus garnish

COMPONENTS

½ oz (15 g) Micro greens
½ fl oz (15 mL) *Lemon Vinaigrette (p. 34)*
4 oz (120 g) *Checkerboard Terrine of Pork and Veal (p. 538)*
1½ fl oz (45 mL) *Red Plum Coulis (p. 53)*, in squeeze bottle
3 oz (90 g) Crisp baguette or other French bread

PROCEDURE

FINISHING AND PLATING

1. Toss the micro greens with the vinaigrette and mound them on the back left of a cool 10-in. (25-cm) plate.
2. Place the terrine slice against the greens in the center of the plate.
3. Squeeze a pool of coulis on the right front of the plate.
4. Serve the bread in a basket lined with a linen napkin.

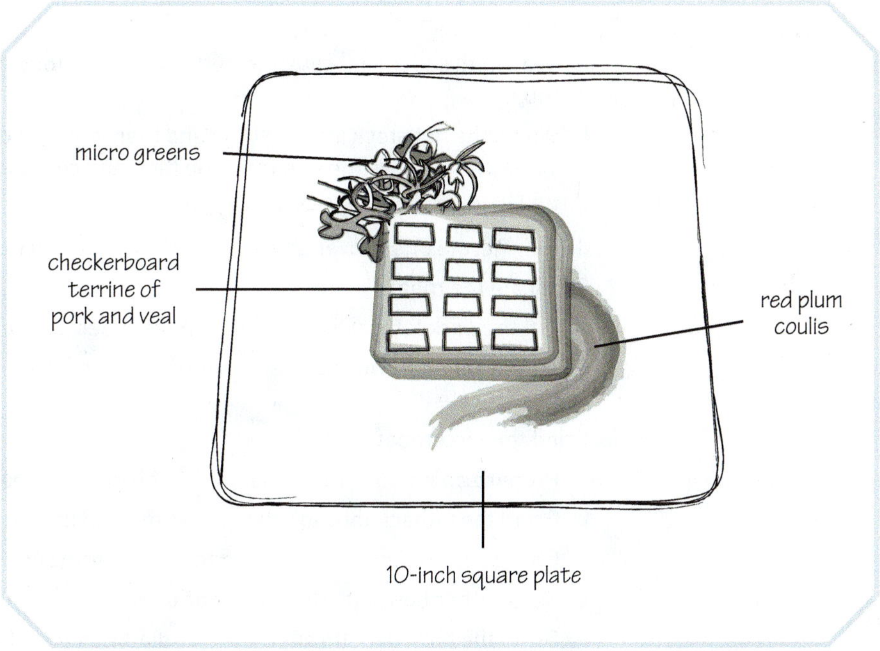

DANISH LIVER PÂTÉ WITH BACON

Yield:
1 1½-qt (1.5 L) terrine, about 4 lb (2 kg)
Portions:
16 appetizer servings
Portion size:
about 4 oz (120 g)

INGREDIENTS	U.S.	METRIC
Panade		
Unsalted butter	1 oz	30 g
All-purpose flour	1 oz	30 g
Strong brown veal stock or beef stock, hot	4 fl oz	120 mL
Crème fraîche	8 oz	240 g
Eggs	2	2
Anchovy paste	2 tsp	10 mL
Forcemeat		
Pork fatback, with no rind, very cold	14 oz	400 g
Pork liver, very cold	1½ lb	0.75 kg
Fine salt	2 tsp	10 mL
Ground cloves	½ tsp	0.25 mL
Ground ginger	2 tsp	10 mL
Green peppercorns, drained	2 tsp	10 mL
Canned pimientos, drained and blotted, brunoise	2 tbsp	30 mL
Smoked bacon, sliced thin	1½ lb	0.75 kg

PROCEDURE

PREPARATION

1. Prepare the panade:
   a. In a small saucepan, cook the butter and flour together 30 seconds to make a white roux.
   b. Whisk the hot stock into the roux and then whisk in the crème fraîche. Simmer briskly 1 minute. Remove the pan from the heat and cool the panade to room temperature.
   c. Whisk in the eggs and anchovy paste.
   d. Refrigerate or stir over an ice bain-marie until very cold.
2. Fabricate the meat:
   a. Cut the pork fatback into 1-in. (2.5-cm) cubes and refrigerate it.
   b. Trim all connective tissue and tubes from the liver and cut it into 1-in. (2.5-cm) cubes. Refrigerate it.
3. Grind the forcemeat:
   a. Prepare an ice bain-marie set under the grinder head.
   b. Grind the fatback through the coarse die into the ice bain-marie.
   c. Change to the fine die and grind the fatback through it *twice*. Refrigerate it.
   d. Set another bowl into the bain-marie under the grinder head.
   e. Grind the pork liver through the fine die *twice* into the ice bain-marie.
   f. Force the pork liver through a fine sieve and refrigerate it.
4. Preheat an oven to 375°F (200°C).
5. Mix the forcemeat:
   a. Place the bowl of ice under the bowl of a mixer fitted with the paddle attachment.
   b. Mix together the pork fat, liver, panade, salt, cloves, and ginger on medium speed 3 minutes, or until thick and uniform in color.

PROCEDURE

   c. Perform a poach test as directed on page 488. Taste and make necessary corrections.
   d. On low speed, stir in the green peppercorns and pimientos.

6. Assemble the terrine:
   a. Line the terrine form with bacon slices, allowing about 3-in. (7-cm) overhang on all sides (A).
   b. Fill the terrine with the forcemeat (B). Tap the terrine on the work surface to force out any air bubbles. Fold the bacon to encase the top of the forcemeat (C).
   c. Place a piece of parchment on the top of the forcemeat. Cover the terrine with a triple layer of foil, crimping the edges of the foil so water will not wick up into the pans. If the terrine has a lid, place it on top.
7. Place the terrine in a deep hotel pan filled with enough hot water to come 2 in. (5 cm) up its sides. Bake the terrine 1½ hours, or until the forcemeat tests to an internal temperature of 150°F (65°C).
8. Remove the terrine from the oven, in its pan, and compress the terrine with 1 lb (0.5 kg) weight. Cool to room temperature.
9. Leave the weight on the terrine and put it in the refrigerator. Allow the terrine to mellow at least 2 days before serving it.

HOLDING

Refrigerate unopened up to 10 days. Once the terrine is cut open (D), it may be refrigerated up to 5 additional days.

VARIATIONS

DANISH CHICKEN LIVER PÂTÉ WITH BACON

Replace the pork liver with chicken livers.

TRUFFLED DUCK LIVER PÂTÉ

Replace the pork liver with duck livers. Omit the green peppercorns and pimientos and add 1 oz (30 g) brunoise truffles or truffle peelings to the forcemeat. Replace the bacon with pork fatback sliced into large, thin sheets.

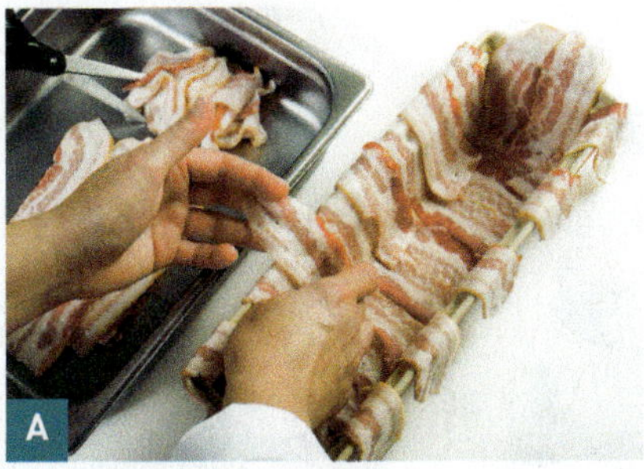
A

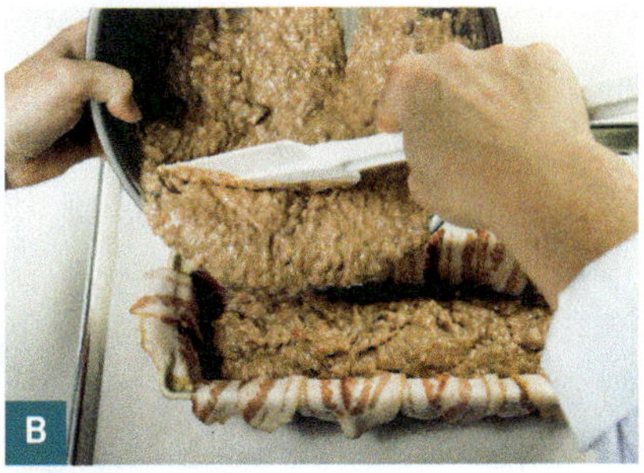
B

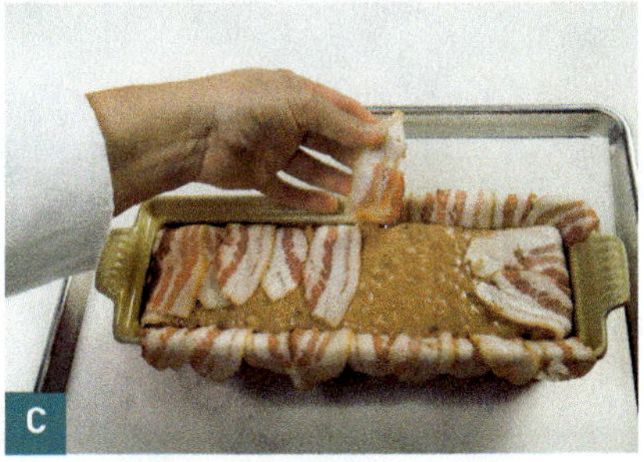
C

D

DANISH LIVER PÂTÉ

WITH PICKLED ONIONS

APPETIZER

Portions:
1
Portion size:
4 oz (120 g) pâté, plus garnish

COMPONENTS

3 1-oz (30-g) Slices light rye bread
4 oz (120 g) *Danish Liver Pâté (p. 542)*, in 2 slices
1 oz (30 g) *Pickled Pearl Onions (p. 676)*, drained well
1 tbsp (15 mL) *Delicate White Poultry Aspic (p. 644)*
1 sprig Fresh dill

PROCEDURE

PLATING

1. Toast the rye bread slices and cool them to room temperature on a rack.
2. Overlap the pâté slices in the center of a cool 10-in. (25-cm) plate.
3. Arrange the onions to the back right of the pâté.
4. Spoon the aspic on the plate to the left front of the pate slices.
5. Stick the dill sprig upright behind the onions.
6. Cut off the crusts of the rye toast slices and cut each slice into 4 triangle-shaped toast points.
7. Serve the rye toast points on a doily-lined 6-in. (15-cm) plate.

PROVENÇAL TERRINE OF RABBIT

Yield:
about 2 lb (1 kg)
Portions:
18
Portion size:
2 oz (60 g)

INGREDIENTS	U.S.	METRIC
Forcemeat base		
Skinless, boneless rabbit meat	10 oz	300 g
Boneless pork loin	5 oz	150 g
Pork fatback, no rind	8 oz	240 g
Finely ground white pepper	⅛ oz	4 g
Quatre épices (p. 519)	¼ oz	7 g
Kosher salt	⅛ oz	4 g
Panade		
Crustless firm white bread	3 oz	90 g
Heavy cream	2 fl oz	60 mL
Vegetable liner		
Green Swiss chard leaves	12 oz	360 g
Remaining ingredients		
Egg white, cold	1	1
Minced shallots	¼ oz	7 g
Heavy cream, cold	6 fl oz	120 mL
Sweet white vermouth, cold	1 fl oz	30 mL
Powdered gelatin	as needed	as needed
Smoked ham, sliced thin	12 oz	360 g

PROCEDURE

DAY 1 FABRICATION AND PRE-SEASONING

1. Remove all fat and silverskin from the meats.
2. Cut the meats and fat into ½-in. (5-cm) cubes. Place them in a nonreactive container.
3. Mix the pepper, quatre épices, and salt with the meats and cover the container. Refrigerate for 24 hours.
4. Prepare the panade: Break up the bread into coarse crumbs and mix with 2 fl oz (60 mL) heavy cream. Cover and refrigerate 24 hours.

DAY 2 GRINDING AND MIXING

5. Prepare the vegetable liner:
   a. Prepare a large pot of boiling water and an ice bath for refreshing.
   b. Blanch the Swiss chard leaves a few seconds just to wilt them. Immediately refresh the chard leaves, drain them, and blot them dry in clean, lint-free kitchen towels.
6. Freeze the grinder parts, a mixer bowl, and the paddle attachment. Prepare an ice bain-marie.
7. Grind the forcemeat:
   a. Place the ice bain-marie under the grinder head.
   b. Grind the meat and fat cubes through the coarse die into the ice bain-marie.
   c. Grind the mixture through the fine die *twice*.
8. Mix the forcemeat:
   a. Transfer the forcemeat to the mixer bowl set over the ice bain-marie.
   b. Add the egg white, shallots, and panade.

(continues)

PROCEDURE *(continued)*

c. Mix on moderate speed until the forcemeat is homogenous and sticky.

d. Raise the speed to high and add the remaining cream and vermouth in a thin stream.

e. Perform a poach test as directed on page 488. Taste and make necessary corrections.

DAY 2: ASSEMBLING AND BAKING

9. Line an 18-in. (45-cm) triangle form with plastic film. Make sure the film is smooth and unwrinkled.
10. Trim any thick veins from the chard leaves.
11. Line the form with overlapping chard leaves. Leave about 2 in. (5 cm) overhang. Sprinkle with a light, even coating of gelatin.
12. Line the form again with the ham, leaving 2 in. (5 cm) overhang (A). Sprinkle lightly with gelatin.
13. Pack in the forcemeat. Tap the form on the work surface to firm the forcemeat and force out any air pockets.
14. Fold the ham over the top surface, then fold the chard leaves (B). Finally, fold the plastic film over the top.
15. Cover the form with a double layer of foil and fold up the edges to prevent wicking.
16. Place the form in a large roasting pan or fish poacher and fill the pan with hot water to reach about 2 in. (5 cm) up the sides of the form.
17. Bake the terrine 30 to 40 minutes, or until it reaches an internal temperature of 155°F (68°C).
18. Remove the pan from the oven and place it on a rack. Place a weighting plate or another pan on top of the terrine and top it with a 2-lb (1-kg) weight. Cool to room temperature.
19. Refrigerate the terrine, still under weight, at least 24 hours.

HOLDING

Refrigerated, unopened, up to 7 days. Once cut (C), refrigerate up to 2 days longer.

VARIATIONS

PROVENÇAL TERRINE OF CHICKEN

Replace the rabbit meat with a mixture of light and dark meat chicken.

A

B

C

PROVENÇAL TERRINE OF RABBIT

WITH BEET SALAD

APPETIZER

Portions:
1

Portion size:
2 oz (60 g) terrine, plus garnish

COMPONENTS

2 slices *Provençal Terrine of Rabbit (p. 545)*, 2 oz (60 g) each
1 oz (30 g) *Roasted Beets in Mustard Vinaigrette (p. 140)*, made with julienne beets
1½ tsp (7 mL) *Beet Oil (p. 687)*, in squeeze bottle
1½ tsp (7 mL) *Bright Green Basil Oil (p. 686)*, in squeeze bottle

PROCEDURE

PLATING

1. Place the terrine slices upright on the left side of a cool 10-in. (25-cm) rectangular plate.
2. Mound the beets on the right side of the plate.
3. Squeeze a decorative drizzle of beet oil on the plate.
4. Squeeze a decorative drizzle of basil oil on the plate.

GALANTINE DE POULARDE [gah-lahn-TEEN duh poo-LARD]

GALANTINE OF CHICKEN

Yield:
about 4 lb (2 kg)
Portions:
16
Portion size:
4 oz (120 g)

INGREDIENTS	U.S.	METRIC
Chicken, liner, and fat fabrication		
Free-range roaster chicken, with giblets	1 (5 lb)	1 (2.25 kg)
Free-range fryer chicken, with giblets	1 (2½ lb)	1 (1.15 kg)
Butter, cold	½ oz	15 g
Kosher salt	to taste	to taste
Finely ground white pepper	to taste	to taste
Powdered gelatin	as needed	as needed
Pork fatback, no rind	10 oz	300 g
Gratin garnish		
Firm, pale chicken livers, preferably free-range	6 oz	180 g
Clarified butter	1 fl oz	30 mL
Kosher salt	to taste	to taste
Finely ground white pepper	to taste	to taste
Minced shallots	1 oz	30 g
Glaze		
Madeira	6 fl oz	180 mL
Poultry Stock (p. 749)	6 fl oz	180 mL
Shelled pistachios	2 oz	60 g
Finishing the forcemeat		
Egg whites, very cold	2	2
Quatre épices (p. 519)	⅛ oz	4 g
Kosher salt	¼ oz	7.5 g
Minced fresh tarragon leaves	½ oz	15 g
Truffles or truffle peelings, cut brunoise	½ oz	15 g
Smoked ham, ¼-in. (0.6-cm) dice	2 oz	60 g
Powdered gelatin	as needed	as needed
Poultry Stock (p. 749)	1 gal	4 L
Fresh tarragon	6 sprigs	15 g

PROCEDURE

FABRICATION

1. Prepare the chicken skin wrapper:
   a. Remove and discard the tail of the roaster chicken.
   b. Cut apart the wings between the double-bone sections and the wingettes.
   c. Cut apart the legs between the thighs and drumsticks.
   d. Place the chicken breast-down on a work surface and slit the skin from the neck to the tail.
   e. Use your fingers to separate the skin from the meat in one piece. When necessary, use a flexible knife to assist in removing the skin (A).
   f. Refrigerate all meat, bones, and giblets. (Reserve bones and gizzard for stock.)
   g. Place the chicken skin on a cutting board and trim it into an 8 × 12-in. (20 × 30-cm) rectangle.

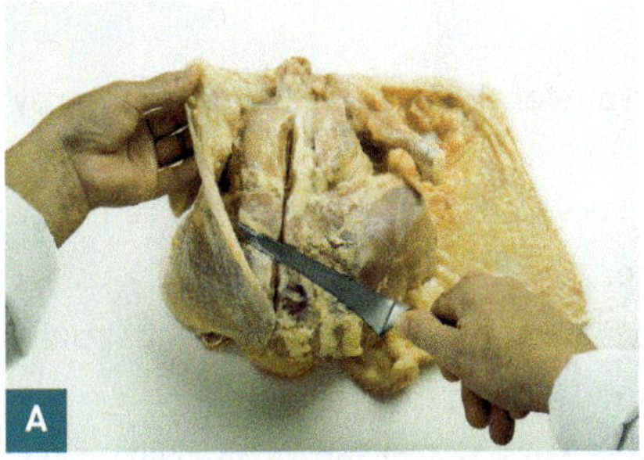
A

B

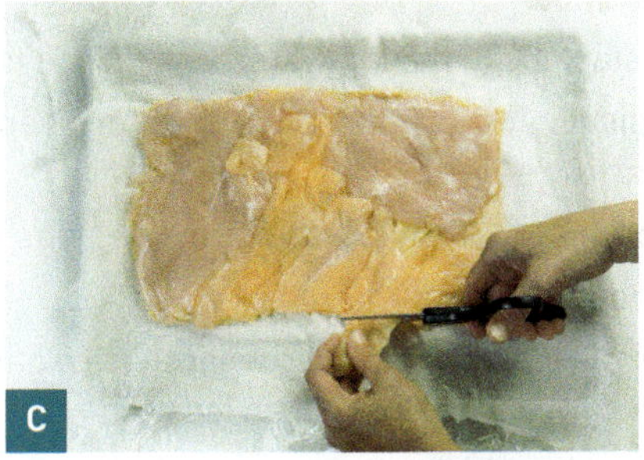
C

D

PROCEDURE

h. Line a half-sheet tray with plastic film and lay a doubled 16 × 18-in. (40 × 45 cm) sheet of dampened cheesecloth on top of the film. Place the chicken skin on it, outside down.

i. Freeze the skin for a few minutes, or until it hardens.

j. Scrape off any deposit fat and remove any connective tissue. Refrigerate the skin.

2. Remove the breast meat from both chickens. Remove the breast tenders from the breast meat and remove the tendons from them. Refrigerate the tenders in a large bowl.

3. Prepare the wrapper liner:

a. Fold a sheet of parchment in half lengthwise, open it up, and rub it with butter.

b. Starting with the roaster breasts, cut the chicken breasts across the grain into large slices about ¼-in. (0.6-cm) thick.

c. Lay the breast slices on the bottom half of the parchment and fold the top over them.

d. Use the smooth side of a meat mallet to gently flatten the breast meat to an even ⅛-in. (0.3-cm) thickness (B). Season it with salt and white pepper.

e. Sprinkle the skin with a very light dusting of gelatin.

f. Arrange the breast meat slices on the chicken skin and trim any excess (C).

4. Remove all the remaining meat from both chickens. Trim the meat of all connective tissue and cut it into 1-in. (2.5-cm) cubes. Add the chicken cubes and any remaining breast meat to the bowl with the breast tenders. Weigh the meats. You will need 1 lb (0.5 kg) chicken meat for the forcemeat. Return the meat to the refrigerator.

5. Cut the fatback into 1-in. (2.5-cm) cubes and refrigerate it.

PREPARATION

6. Prepare the gratin garnish:

a. Trim all connective tissue from the chicken livers and blot them dry on paper towels.

b. Heat a 10-in. (25-cm) nonstick sauté pan very hot.

c. Add the clarified butter and sear the chicken livers brown outside but still raw inside (D). Season them with salt and pepper.

(continues)

PROCEDURE *(continued)*

d. Immediately transfer the livers to a half-sheet tray and set them in the freezer for 10 minutes.

e. Transfer the livers from the freezer to the refrigerator.

7. Prepare the glaze:

a. Add the shallots, Madeira, and 6 oz (180 mL) poultry stock to the pan and deglaze it.

b. Reduce the liquid almost to a glaze (E).

c. Cool the glaze to room temperature and refrigerate it.

8. Prepare the pistachios:

a. Blanch the pistachios in boiling water 20 seconds and drain them in a colander.

b. Transfer the pistachios to a clean, lint-free towel and rub them gently with the towel to begin removing the skins.

c. Pick out the bright green pistachios from the skins and reserve them (F).

9. Grind the forcemeat:

a. Refrigerate the grinder parts and prepare an ice bain-marie. Refrigerate the bowl and blade of a food processor. Prepare an ice bath with a large bowl placed in it.

b. Grind the fat and the chicken meat through the coarse die of the grinder into the bain-marie.

c. Transfer the meats into a food processer fitted with the cold bowl and blade. Add the egg whites, quatre épices, glaze, and ¼ oz (7 g) salt. Pulse a few times to combine the meats, binder, and seasonings.

d. Turn on the processor and quickly add the cream in a fast stream (G). Add the tarragon. Purée no longer than 30 seconds total.

e. Perform a poach test. Taste and make necessary corrections.

f. Scrape the forcemeat into the iced bowl and stir in the pistachios, truffles, and ham to distribute them evenly (H). If you are not immediately proceeding to step 10, refrigerate the forcemeat.

ASSEMBLY

10. Sprinkle the breast meat wrapper liner with a very light dusting of gelatin.

E

F

G

H

I

J

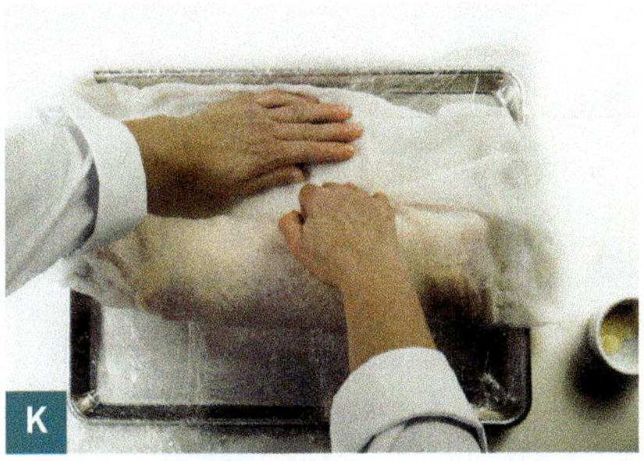
K

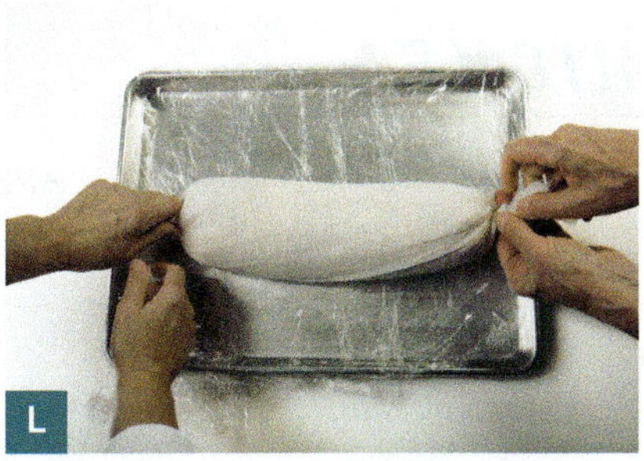
L

M

PROCEDURE

11. Spread the forcemeat evenly on the breast meat, leaving a margin of exposed skin on the far side (I).
12. Sprinkle the chilled, seared chicken livers very lightly with gelatin and arrange them lengthwise in a row down the center of the forcemeat (J).
13. Starting with the long side nearest you, use the cheesecloth to roll the skin and forcemeat into a firm cylinder with the livers exactly in the center (K). The long edges of the forcemeat should meet each other with no skin inside the roulade. The skin on the far side of the roulade should overlap and adhere to the outside of the skin wrapper.
14. Roll the sealed roulade firmly in the cheesecloth and tie the ends with kitchen string (L).
15. Cut 3 wide bands of cheesecloth and tie them around the galantine for extra support (M).
16. Refrigerate the galantine.

POACHING

17. Prepare the *cuisson*:
    a. Place 1 gal (4 L) poultry stock in an 18-in. (45-cm) nonreactive fish poacher. Add enough water to fill it two-thirds full.
    b. Bring the *cuisson* to the boil and add the tarragon sprigs.
18. Place the galantine on the poacher rack and lower it into the *cuisson*.
19. Return the *cuisson* to a bare simmer and poach the galantine 40 minutes, or until it reaches an internal temperature of 155°F (68°C).
20. Remove the poacher from the heat and place it on a rack. Cool to room temperature.
21. Refrigerate the galantine in the *cuisson* at least 24 hours.
22. Remove the galantine from the *cuisson*. De-fat the *cuisson* and reserve it for preparing aspic. (Depending on the strength of the original stock, it may need to be reduced.)
23. Cut off the cheesecloth wrapper and discard it. If not serving the galantine immediately, wrap it in fresh cheesecloth and return it to the refrigerator.

HOLDING

Refrigerate up to 2 weeks unopened. Once cut, refrigerate 3 days longer.

VARIATION

GALANTINE DE CANETON
[gah-lahn-TEEN duh kan-eh-TON]
GALANTINE OF DUCKLING

Replace the chickens with 2 ducklings, 4 lb (2 kg) each. (You will need to overlap the skins to make a large enough rectangle. Replace the chicken livers with duck livers. Replace the Madeira with 6 oz (180 mL) orange juice. Replace the lemon zest with orange zest.

GALANTINE OF CHICKEN

WITH TARRAGON MAYONNAISE

APPETIZER

Portions:
1
Portion size:
4 oz (120 g) galantine, plus garnish

COMPONENTS

1 1½-in. (4-cm) *Cucumber Cup (p. 717)*
1 fl oz (30 mL) *Creamy Tarragon Mayonnaise Sauce (p. 43)*, see Note, in pastry bag fitted with star tip
½ oz (15 g) mild-flavored micro greens
4 oz (120 g) *Galantine de Poularde (p. 548)*, in 2 slices
2 fl oz (60 mL) *Madeira Poultry Aspic Jewels (p. 708)*
3 oz (90 g) Crisp baguette or other French bread

Note: Prepare Creamy Tarragon Mayonnaise Sauce without the half-and-half.

PROCEDURE

PLATING

1. Fill the cucumber cup with a rosette of tarragon mayonnaise and place it on the back left of a cool 10-in. (25-cm) plate.
2. Mound the micro greens next to the cup.
3. Overlap the galantine slices leaning on the micro greens.
4. Scatter an arc of aspic jewels on the plate to the right of the galantine slices.
5. Serve the bread in a basket lined with a linen napkin.

PÂTÉ DE GIBIER [pah-TAY duh zheeb-YAY]

GAME PÂTÉ

Yield:
1 12 × 2 × 3-in. (30 × 5 × 7.5 cm) pâté, about 2 lb (1 kg)
Portions:
10
Portion size:
about 3 oz

INGREDIENTS	U.S.	METRIC
Meats and stock		
Venison shoulder or leg meat	12 oz	360 g
Bone-in rabbit, with giblets	1¼ lb	600 g
Bone-in pheasant, with giblets	1 lb	500 g
Pork fatback, no rind	6 oz	180 g
Ingredients for stock (p. 751)	as needed	as needed
Garnish marinade		
White wine	3 fl oz	90 mL
Minced shallots	½ oz	15 g
Fresh tarragon, crushed	2 sprigs	2 sprigs
Kosher salt	to taste	to taste
Finely ground white pepper	to taste	to taste
Forcemeat marinade		
Red wine	8 fl oz	240 mL
Crushed garlic	⅛ oz	4 g
Crushed juniper berries	⅛ oz	4 g
Bay leaves	2	2
Panade		
Crustless firm white bread	2 oz	60 g
Half-and-half	2 oz	60 mL
Forcemeat		
Cognac	½ oz	15 mL
Quatre épices (p. 519)	1½ tsp	7 mL
Freshly ground black pepper	1 tsp	5 mL
Prague Powder #1	¼ tsp	1.25 mL
Kosher salt	to taste	to taste
Assembly and finishing		
Flour	as needed	as needed
Pâte à Pâté (p. 753)	1 lb	0.5 kg
Smoked ham, very thin sliced	3 oz	90 g
Powdered gelatin	as needed	as needed
Egg wash (1 egg plus 1 tbsp water)	2½ fl oz	75 mL
Aspic (made from game bones)	12 fl oz	360 mL

PROCEDURE

DAY 1: FABRICATION

1. Trim excess silverskin from the venison and cut it into 1-in. (3-cm) cubes. Place the venison in a nonreactive container and refrigerate it.
2. Bone out the rabbit, keeping the saddle meat intact in two long strips. Place the bones in a bowl and refrigerate them.
3. Trim the rabbit liver and add it to the venison container.
4. Remove all silverskin from the rabbit saddle strips. Place the saddle strips end to end on the cutting board and measure their length. (The saddle strips will be used as a central inlay garnish.) Place them in a nonreactive container, and refrigerate them.
5. Cut the remaining rabbit meat into 1-in. (3-cm) cubes and add it to the venison container.
6. Skin and bone out the pheasant. Add the pheasant bones to the rabbit bones.
7. Trim the pheasant liver and add it to the venison container.

(continues)

PROCEDURE *(continued)*

8. If the rabbit saddle strips do not equal 11 in. (27 cm) in length, fabricate enough pheasant breast in a similar shape to make up the remaining 11 in. (27 cm) inlay. Add this garnish meat to the container with the saddles.
9. Cut the remaining pheasant breast into ⅜-in. (1-cm) dice. Add the dice to the container with the saddle strips.
10. Place the remaining pheasant meat in the container with the venison.
11. Cut the fatback into 1-in. (2.5-cm) cubes, place it in a plastic bag, and refrigerate it.
12. Remove all traces of internal organs from the bones and wash them under cool running water until the water runs clear.
13. Follow the recipe on page 751 to make stock from the bones. When completed, open-pan cool the stock and refrigerate it.

DAY 1: PRE-SEASONING AND MAKING PANADE

14. To marinate the rabbit saddle garnish meats, add the white wine, shallots, tarragon, salt, and white pepper to them and mix well. Cover and refrigerate.
15. To make the forcemeat marinade, place the red wine, garlic, juniper berries, and bay leaves in a small, nonreactive sauce pan and reduce the wine very slowly over low heat to about half its original volume. Cool the wine to room temperature.
16. Pour the red wine marinade over the meats in the venison container, season the meats with salt, and mix well. Cover and refrigerate.
17. Make the panade: Tear the bread into crumbs and mix it with the half-and-half. Cover and refrigerate the panade.

DAY 2: GRINDING AND MIXING

18. Prepare an ice bain-marie. Refrigerate the grinder parts and the bowl and paddle of a mixer.
19. Drain the marinades from the garnish meats and the venison mixture into a small, nonreactive sauce pan. Pick out the solid ingredients. Reduce the marinades almost to a glaze. Cool the pan in the ice bain-marie until the glaze is cold.
20. Place the ice bain-marie under the grinder head.
21. Grind the pork fatback through the coarse die and refrigerate it.
22. Grind the venison mixture through the coarse die and refrigerate it.
23. Grind the fatback through the fine die *twice*.
24. Grind the venison mixture through the fine die *twice*.
25. Mix the forcemeat:
    a. Place the ground fat, ground venison, marinade glaze, cognac, and panade in the mixer bowl. Mix together the quatre épices, pepper, Prague Powder #1, and salt, and sprinkle the mixture over the meats.
    b. Place the ice bain-marie under the mixer bowl.
    c. Beat the forcemeat on medium speed 3 minutes, or until it is homogenous and sticky.
    d. Perform a poach test as directed on page 488. Taste and make any necessary corrections.
    e. On low speed, mix in the pheasant cubes.

DAY 2: ASSEMBLING AND BAKING

26. Dust a sanitized work surface with flour and roll out the pastry about ⅛ in. (0.33 cm) thick. Cut out the dough liner and lid (A). If you plan to decorate the pâté, cut out décor shapes and refrigerate them.
27. Fit the dough into a 12 × 3 × 2-in. (30 × 7 × 5-cm) collapsible-sided pâté form.Make sure the dough is fitted completely into the corners without stretching it. Trim the edges of the dough (B).
28. Line the dough with ham (C).

A

B

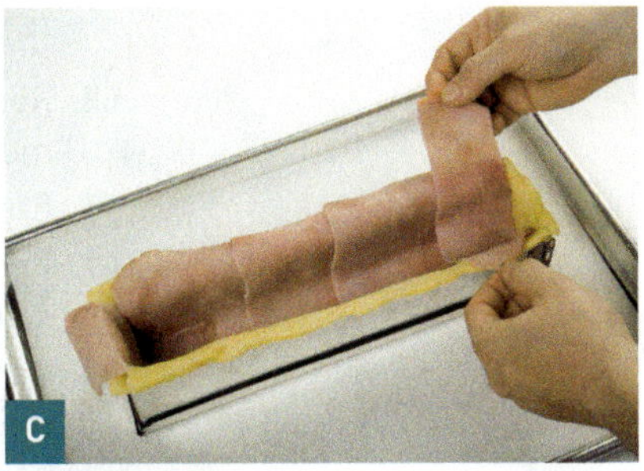
C

D

E

F

PROCEDURE

29. Press half the forcemeat into the pastry-lined form.
30. Dust the inlay garnish meats with a thin, even coating of gelatin on all surfaces.
31. Arrange the inlay meats down the center of the forcemeat and press them gently so they stay in place (D).
32. Pack the remaining forcemeat into the form. There should be enough forcemeat to mound up about ¾-in. (2-cm) above the rim. Smooth the top of the forcemeat and tap the form on the work surface to force out any air pockets.
33. Wrap the ham up over the top of the forcemeat.
34. Fold the edges of the pastry dough over the forcemeat and brush them with egg wash. Place the lid on top of the forcemeat and tuck it down inside the edges of the pan.
35. Egg-wash the top of the pâté and, if using them, apply and egg-wash the décor shapes (E).
36. Using a ½-in. (1.25-cm) round cutter, punch out a vent hole at each end of the pâté's pastry top. Make and insert an aluminum foil chimney in each vent hole. Alternatively, leave in the cutters during baking.
37. Refrigerate the pâté 1 hour.
38. Preheat an oven to 400°F (200°C). Line a sheet tray with foil and place a sheet of parchment on top of the foil.
39. Place the pâté on the double-lined tray and place it in the oven. Bake the pâté 20 minutes.
40. Lower the heat to 325°F (160°C) and continue baking another 40 minutes, or until it reaches an internal temperature of 150°F (65°C). If the crust seems to be browning too much, shield it with a loose covering of foil.
41. Remove the pâté from the oven and place the form on a cooling rack. Cool to room temperature.
42. Refrigerate the pâté at least 24 hours.

FINISHING

43. If necessary, warm the aspic until it melts and then stir it in an ice bain-marie until it cools to the consistency of honey.
44. Remove the chimneys from the pâté crust and insert a large pastry tube tip or funnel in one of the vent holes. Slowly ladle in the aspic until it becomes visible under the crust (F). If necessary, move the funnel to the other vent for even application of aspic.

(continues)

PROCEDURE *(continued)*

45. Refrigerate the pâté at least 24 hours, or until the aspic is fully set and the pâté is mellowed.
46. Run a paring knife between the pâté's pastry crust and the pâté form to loosen it.
47. Remove the pins from the form and open out its side panels.
48. Carefully remove the pâté's bottom crust from the form (G). If it sticks, use an offset spatula to help release it.
49. If you are not serving the pâté immediately, wrap it in plastic film and refrigerate it.

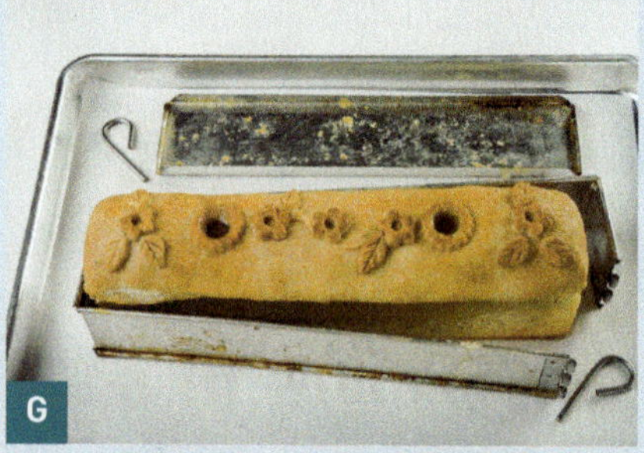
G

HOLDING

Refrigerate unopened up to 10 days. Once cut, refrigerate up to 5 days longer.

VARIATIONS

PÂTÉ CHASSEUR
[pah-TAY shah-SUR]
HUNTER'S PÂTÉ

Vary the game meats in the formula as desired. Replace the tarragon with rosemary and thyme. Hydrate ½ oz (15 g) dried cèpes or porcini mushrooms in boiling water, fabricate them in brunoise cuts, and add them to the forcemeat.

PÂTÉ MAISON
[pay-TAY may-SOHN]
HOUSE PÂTÉ

Replace the game meats in the forcemeat with lean pork butt. Replace the rabbit saddles with chicken or duck livers. Replace the diced pheasant with smoked tongue or ham.

GAME PÂTÉ
WITH CUMBERLAND SAUCE

BUFFET APPETIZER

Portions:
6 to 10, depending on whether the grosse pièce is served

Portion size:
3 oz (150 g) pâté, plus garnish

COMPONENTS

1 2 lb (0.5 kg) *Pâté de Gibier (p. 553)*
2 qt (2 L) *White Poultry Aspic for Coating (p. 644)*
½ lb. (0.25 kg) Fresh red currants or red champagne grapes
8 fl oz (240 mL) *Cumberland Sauce (p. 692)*

PROCEDURE

PRESENTATION

1. Slice the pâté :
   a. Decide which end of the pâté is most attractive for use as the grosse pièce.
   b. Trim away a ½-in. (1-cm) piece of crust and meat from the opposite end.
   c. Beginning at the trimmed end, use a serrated knife or electric slicing knife to cut 6 even slices, each slightly less than 1 in. (2.5 cm) thick. As you cut, place each slice on a rack set over a sheet tray.

PROCEDURE

d. Carefully prop the grosse pièce, cut face upward, in a loaf pan or other small container.

e. Refrigerate the grosse pièce and the tray of pâté while you prepare the aspic.

2. Follow the procedure on page 643 to coat the pâté slices (see illustration) and the cut face of the grosse pièce with aspic.

3. Follow the procedure on page 650, step 4, to coat the surface of a 30-in. (75-cm) fish platter or other long, narrow tray with aspic.
4. Place the grosse pièce on one end of the platter and arrange the pâté slices in an overlapping row down the length of the platter.
5. Break the currants or grapes into clusters and decorate the platter with them.
6. Serve the Cumberland sauce in a sauceboat.

TERMS FOR REVIEW

pâté
pâté en croûte
terrine
galantine
ballottine
pâté roulade
mousseline pâté
forcemeat
internal garnish
wrapper
liner
sealer
primary meat
secondary meat
gratin forcemeat
quatre épices
secondary binder
panade/panada
gratin garnish
random garnish
inlay garnish
pâte à pâté
caul fat/lace fat
primary fowl
secondary poultry
grosse pièce
attelet
en terrine presentation

QUESTIONS FOR DISCUSSION

1. List and describe the five basic types of pâté.
2. List the four basic elements of pâté construction, describe their functions, and give examples of each.
3. List the five types of seasonings used in pâté forcemeats, and give some examples of each.
4. List the two forms of internal pâté garnishes, and give examples of each. Explain the two ways in which an internal pâté garnish may be added.
5. Describe the general procedure for making a terrine.
6. Describe the general procedure for making a pâté en croûte.
7. How would you judge the doneness of a pâté product?
8. What is the purpose of weighting many pâté products?
9. Discuss the storage of various pâté products, including special preservation techniques and keeping times. Describe the effect of freezing on cooked pâté products.
10. Discuss the presentation of various pâté products. Include both platter and plated presentations and the appropriate décor, garnishes, and accompaniments for each.
11. Write a recipe for your own signature pâté creation.

Chapter 14

PREREQUISITES

Before studying this chapter, you should already

- Have read "How to Use This Book," pages xxviii–xxxiii, and understand the professional recipe format.
- Have a sound knowledge of sanitation procedures, especially as related to protein foods.
- Know how to calibrate and use an instant-read or probe thermometer.

Cheese and Other Dairy Products

Dairy products, and the many foods made from them, are important elements in the garde manger repertoire. Fresh cream and various types of fermented or soured creams are widely used as ingredients in cold sauces, salad dressings, and cold soups. Both plain and flavored butters are used as spreads and fillings. Fresh soft cheeses may be used in the same way. Cream is also used to lighten mousses, mousselines, and custards. Firm and hard cheeses are frequently used in hors d'oeuvres and salads, and they are featured ingredients in sandwiches. Finally, cheeses of all types are enjoyed in their own right when they are presented as cheese platters for receptions or parties—or, in the classic manner, as a cheese course served between the main course and the dessert of a formal meal.

The information in this chapter will enable you to identify commercial dairy products and correctly use them in garde manger applications. In addition, you will find techniques and recipes for making your own signature dairy products in-house.

After reading this chapter, you should be able to

1. Select fresh milks and creams according to their milk-fat content, and make knowledgeable decisions when substituting one for another.
2. Prepare whipped butter and compound butters.
3. Explain the process of fermentation as it applies to fermented dairy products.
4. Use commercial fermented dairy products in various cold preparations.
5. Produce fermented dairy products in-house.
6. List and explain the five steps in the cheese-making process.
7. Produce fresh cheeses in-house.
8. Correctly store and handle various types of cheese.
9. Prepare attractive, well-balanced cheese platters and cheese boards.
10. Develop a cheese menu for a restaurant or catering operation.

FRESH DAIRY PRODUCTS

Dairy products are foods made from milk. In its natural state, milk is a highly perishable food because it is high in proteins and contains a lot of water. Both of these characteristics make foods susceptible to microorganisms. However, not all microorganisms are harmful. Some microorganisms create good changes in foods. These are called ***beneficial microorganisms***.

Dairy products that have not been changed by beneficial microorganisms are called ***fresh dairy products***. Here, "fresh" has a specialized meaning other than "not old." Of course, we want most of our dairy products to be fresh in the usual sense, as well. Milk, cream, and butter are fresh dairy products.

Pasteurization and Homogenization

In North America, the vast majority of milk and other dairy products are subjected to both pasteurization and homogenization at the dairy.

Pasteurization is the process of heating milk to a specific temperature for a specific period in order to destroy harmful microorganisms that could cause food-borne illness. The process is named after Louis Pasteur, the French scientist who invented it in 1862.

Milk that has not been pasteurized is called ***raw milk***. Raw milk may be purchased from farms and at certain retail outlets, such as health food stores. The sale of raw milk is strictly regulated, and regulations vary from state to state. Know your local health codes before attempting to use raw milk in a food-service operation.

Homogenization is a method used to maintain the fat-water emulsion in dairy products and thus keep them from separating. Homogenization involves forcing milk or cream through very fine holes under high pressure (much like spraying water through a screen). This process breaks the milk-fat globules into very tiny droplets. This maintains the emulsion by making it difficult for the droplets to re-join and separate out of the water phase.

Milk

Milk is a nutritious fluid produced by female mammals in order to feed their newborn offspring. In North America, when we speak of milk we are usually referring to cow's milk. However, the milk of goats and sheep is frequently used to make cheeses and other dairy products. In other countries, people also consume the milk of camels, water buffaloes, yaks, and even horses. For the purposes of this text, when we refer to milk we mean cow's milk unless specified otherwise. However, much of the information on cow's milk pertains to other types of milk as well.

Milk consists of water, milk fat, and milk solids. In milk and most other dairy products, these three elements are combined in an emulsion.

- *Water* is the component that makes milk fluid.
- ***Milk fat*** consists of both saturated and unsaturated fats. Because it is the major component of butter, milk fat is often called ***butterfat***. Milk fat has a golden color. In combination with white-colored milk solids, milk fat gives milk its off-white color. The higher concentration of milk fat found in cream gives cream an ivory color, while the very high proportion of milk fat in butter makes butter yellow. Dairy products are often classified by the percentage of milk fat they contain. Refer to Table 14.1 on page 561 to learn the milk-fat content of various dairy products and to the sidebar on page 578 for information on the milk-fat content of cheeses.
- ***Milk solids*** is the collective name given to the remaining components in milk. These components include proteins, minerals, salts, and milk sugar, called ***lactose***. The protein ***casein*** is an important emulsifier found in milk solids. Milk solids contain white pigments that give milk its white color. In addition, milk solids contribute most of the flavor to milk and other dairy products. The protein in milk solids makes most dairy products quite perishable.

The ratio of water, milk fat, and milk solids in milk as it comes from the cow varies significantly according to the breed of cow, the season of the year, and the quality of the cows' feed. In North America, commercially produced milk is blended at the dairy to a specific ratio of 88 percent water, 3.5 percent milk fat, and 8.5 percent milk solids to yield a consistent product. This product is called ***whole milk***.

Commercial dairies remove milk fat from whole milk to produce milks that have a lower fat content than standard whole milk. These products are called ***reduced-fat milks***, listed below whole milk in Table 14.1. Reduced-fat milks are rarely used in standard garde manger work. However, they are important ingredients in low-fat cuisine and special-needs cooking.

Cream

If milk from the cow is allowed to cool, undisturbed, under refrigeration for several hours, most of the lighter milk-fat globules partially separate out of the milk's watery base. This thick, rich liquid rises to the top of the container and is called ***cream***. Like milk, cream is an emulsion. However, it has a higher ratio of milk fat to water than milk does.

To produce milk for drinking, most of the cream is removed from the milk. Cream is used and sold separately. Modern dairy processors control the milk-fat content of cream to make various types of creams, such as half-and-half, light cream, (light) whipping cream, and heavy (whipping) cream. In many applications, such as sauces, dips, and salad dressings, these products are interchangeable. For example, the only differences that result from substituting half-and-half for heavy cream in a dip or salad dressing are a lighter texture and a leaner flavor. However, in some applications, such as mousses and mousselines, this substitution would result in a failed product. When making complex dishes, you must know the milk-fat content of the dairy products you are using and understand the food science behind the preparation you are making before you attempt a substitution. See Table 14.1 for the fat content of various creams.

TABLE 14.1	Milk-Fat Content of Fresh Dairy Products
Butter	80% or higher
Heavy cream	36% or higher
Whipping cream	30–36%
Light cream	18–30%
Half-and-half	10–18%
Whole milk	3.5%
2% low-fat milk	2%
1% low-fat milk	1%
Skim milk	less than 0.5%

Whipped Cream

Cream having a fat content of 30 percent or higher is able to capture and hold air when whipped at a cold temperature. Whipped cream may be prepared by hand with a bowl and whip, or in a mixer fitted with the whip attachment. In addition, cream may also be whipped by forcing nitrous oxide gas into it, as with a whipped cream dispenser. While sweet whipped cream is usually associated with dessert preparation, unsweetened whipped cream is used in garde manger work when making mousses and sauces.

Butter

When rich, high-fat cream is brought to room temperature and then churned, or agitated, its emulsion begins to break. The water and the golden-colored milk fat in the cream begin to separate. The substance that remains when most of the watery fluid is drained away from the milk fat is called ***butter***. Some of the milk solids that were present in the cream remain in the butter, and these contribute much of butter's flavor. A small percentage of water remains in the butter as well. The composition of standard butter is roughly 80 percent milk fat, 5 percent milk solids, and 15 percent water. These components remain combined in an emulsion called ***whole butter***.

Whole butter is a ***semisolid fat***. Semisolid fats are temperature sensitive. Butter is hard when frozen, firm when refrigerated, pliable at cool room temperature (60°–70°F/15°–21°C), and soft at warm room temperature (70°–80°F/21°–26°C), and it melts between 92° and 98°F (33° and 36°C). The melt temperature of butter is significant because it is lower than the internal temperature of the human body. Thus, butter "melts in your mouth."

At room temperature, whole butter has rich, pleasant mouthfeel without tasting greasy or waxy. Thus, in most applications this is the temperature at which it should be served.

When whole butter is held slightly above its melt point for a time, the milk fat separates out of emulsion. If the water and milk solids are removed, the resulting product is called ***clarified butter***. Clarified butter has limited use in garde manger preparations.

Unsalted butter is also called ***sweet butter***, although no sweeteners are added to it. Salt was traditionally added to butter as a preservative. In North America and some other parts of the world, ***salted butter*** is preferred as a table butter because people like its slightly salty taste on bread and toast. Food-service operations generally purchase unsalted butter because it is more versatile and can be used in both baking and cooking.

European butters are now available from specialty purveyors. They have a higher milk-fat content and, correspondingly, a lower water content than domestic butter. In addition, some farms and small independent dairies have begun making old-fashioned ***artisan butter*** from raw, lightly fermented cream. Such artisan butters have a deep, golden color, rich mouthfeel, and a full, tangy flavor.

Whipped Butter

Due to its high fat content, soft, room-temperature butter captures and holds air when whipped. When butter is softened and beaten until light and fluffy in an electric mixer fitted with the whip attachment, the resulting product is called ***whipped butter***.

Decorative Butter Shapes

The soft texture of whipped butter enables it to be piped from a pastry bag to make attractive shapes. Butter is usually piped through a large star tip to make rosettes, either in ramekins or butter chips, or directly onto a plate or sheet tray. More elaborate butter shapes, such as roses, may be piped with specialized tips borrowed from the pastry department. When chilled, the butter holds its shape.

Compound Butters

Softened butter may be flavored with a variety of ingredients, both savory and sweet. Flavored whole butter is called a ***compound butter***, also called ***composed butter*** or *beurre composé*. The preparation of compound butters usually begins with whipping the butter. This softens its texture and makes it less dense, so it can accept more flavoring ingredients. Flavoring ingredients, including salt, are usually added to taste. There is no limit other than taste to adding solid ingredients to a compound butter. However, even whipped butter can accept only a limited amount of liquid ingredients (such as lemon juice) because it is an emulsion that already contains water. If you try to add too much liquid ingredient to a compound butter, the liquid will cease to blend into the butter and the finished product may weep beads of liquid or appear curdled.

Assorted compound butters in ramekins

In garde manger work, compound butters are primarily used as spreads for sandwiches and canapés. Ideas for compound butters are listed in Table 14.2.

Table 14.2: Sweet and Savory Compound Butters

Add these ingredients to 8 oz (240 g) softened, unsalted, whipped butter:

Orange Butter	6 tbsp (90 mL) minced orange zest, 4 tbsp (60 mL) honey, pinch fine salt, 1 tbsp (15 mL) orange juice concentrate, 1 tbsp (15 mL) fresh lemon juice
Cinnamon-Honey Butter	6 tbsp (90 mL) honey, ½ tsp (2.5 mL) ground cinnamon, pinch fine salt, 1 tbsp (15 mL) fresh lemon juice
Maple-Walnut Butter	¼ cup (60 mL) pure maple syrup, 1 tbsp (15 mL) walnut oil, pinch fine salt, 1 tbsp (15 mL) fresh lemon juice
Raspberry Butter	½ cup (120 mL) raspberry preserves, pinch fine salt, 1 tbsp (15 mL) fresh lemon juice
Maitre d'Hôtel Butter	4 tbsp (60 mL) minced lemon zest, 1 tsp fine salt (5 mL), ½ tsp (2.5 mL) ground white pepper, ½ cup (120 mL) minced parsley, 2 tbsp (30 mL) minced shallot, 4 tbsp (60 mL) fresh lemon juice
Escargot Butter	2 tbsp (30 mL) minced lemon zest, 1 tsp (5 mL) fine salt, ½ tsp (2.5 mL) ground white pepper, ½ cup (120 mL) minced parsley, 2 tbsp (30 mL) minced fresh garlic, 3 tbsp (45 mL) fresh lemon juice
Provençal Butter	2 tbsp (30 mL) minced lemon zest, 2 tbsp (30 mL) minced orange zest, 1 tsp (5 mL) fine salt, ½ tsp (2.5 mL) ground white pepper, 2 tbsp (30 mL) minced fresh oregano, 2 tbsp (30 mL) minced fresh rosemary, 4 tbsp (60 mL) minced fresh basil, 3 tbsp (45 mL) fresh lemon juice
Dill Butter	2 tbsp (30 mL) minced lemon zest, 1 tsp (5 mL) fine salt, ½ tsp (2.5 mL) ground white pepper, ½ cup (120 mL) minced fresh dill, 2 tbsp (30 mL) fresh lemon juice
Mustard Butter	2 tbsp (30 mL) minced lemon zest, ½ tsp (2.5 mL) fine salt, ½ tsp (2.5 mL) ground white pepper, ¼ cup (60 mL) Dijon mustard, pinch sugar

FERMENTED DAIRY PRODUCTS

A ***fermented dairy product*** is a food or beverage that begins as fresh milk or cream but is changed in several ways by the action of a beneficial bacterial culture. ***Fermentation*** is the process by which a bacterial culture creates changes in a food or beverage. Most fermented dairy products are made in commercial dairies, but they may also be prepared in-house by the garde manger department.

This section begins with basic information on the process of fermentation and concludes with descriptions of the most popular fermented dairy products.

Dairy Fermentation

Milk comes into contact with bacteria from many sources, beginning with the exterior of the cow's healthy teats and udder and continuing with human hands, storage vessels and utensils, and even the air in the barn and dairy. Some of these bacteria are harmful, and some are not. In fact, when certain bacteria invade milk and cream, after a time the result is a totally different food product that is not only palatable but also delicious and healthful.

A group of beneficial bacteria purposely added to a food product is called a ***culture***, and the process of adding it is called ***culturing***. Beneficial bacteria change milk and cream into different products through the process of fermentation. Fermentation is a complex process. This simple explanation gives you a basic idea of how it works.

Dairy bacteria need to live within a certain temperature range, and they thrive between 70° and 90°F (21° and 32°C). In dairy product fermentation, the beneficial bacteria begin to eat various substances in the milk, primarily the lactose. When an organism eats, it produces waste. The primary waste products of dairy fermentation bacteria are carbon dioxide (CO_2) gas and lactic acid. As the bacteria grow and reproduce, more and more CO_2 and lactic acid are produced. These substances produce five important changes in the milk, changes that you can see and/or taste.

1. *Bubbling* is the result of CO_2 gas produced by dairy bacteria. You can see this bubbling during fermentation when you are making the product. However, you do not see bubbling in the finished product because fermentation has stopped.
2. *Souring* is the result of increased levels of lactic acid produced by dairy bacteria during fermentation. The resulting fermented dairy product has a pleasant, tangy taste.
3. *Thickening* occurs because lactic acid changes the protein structure within the milk. This process is called **coagulation** (see the sidebar below).
4. *Preservation* is an important result of fermentation. Active-culture fermented dairy products keep longer than fresh dairy products because the presence of large numbers of beneficial bacteria prevents the growth of undesirable, harmful bacteria. All fermented dairy products keep

The Science of Coagulation

Both acids and enzymes denature, or change, the structure of milk proteins. In cheese making, lactic acid waste from the culture's bacterial action causes milk proteins to unravel into long strands that then bond together in a net-like form. This protein net captures the liquid content of the milk and sets up into a protein gel. This process is called *coagulation*. The coagulation of milk by beneficial bacteria results in a thickened texture ranging from syrupy to custardy, depending on the product.

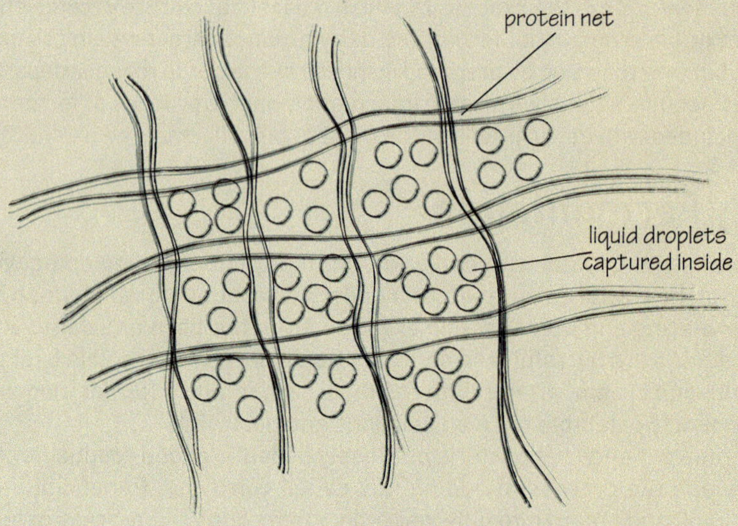

Protein Net Capturing Liquid

well because their higher acid content discourages growth of non-acid-loving bacteria.

5. *Increased digestibility* is another important quality of fermented dairy products. The primary food of dairy bacteria is lactose, or milk sugar, which is difficult for some people to digest. During fermentation, dairy bacteria consume lactose, effectively removing much of it from the finished product. Thus, fermented dairy products are easier to digest. People who are ***lactose intolerant***, or cannot digest milk sugar, may be able to eat fermented dairy products but cannot consume fresh dairy products.

Types of Fermented Dairy Products

The final flavor and texture of a fermented dairy product depends on the type of milk used and the type of culture introduced to it. Milks of varying milk-fat content, in combination with different cultures, produce a wide array of fermented dairy products.

Cultured buttermilk is made from skim milk and a culture specific to North America. It has a light, slightly thickened, but pourable texture and a tangy flavor. Widely used in North American baking, in garde manger work it is used in salad dressings and dips. (Traditional buttermilk is made from the thin liquid that remains after butter is made. This liquid was left at room temperature to thicken and sour by fermentation through the action of ambient bacteria. It is not produced by commercial dairies.)

Yogurt is made from milks of varying fat content. Whole-milk yogurt is rich and creamy, and it often has an even thicker, creamier layer on the top. Low-fat yogurt and nonfat yogurt are often treated with additional milk solids and natural and artificial thickeners. Plain, unflavored yogurt is appropriate for most garde manger work. It is frequently used to replace sour cream or crème fraîche in low-fat cooking. Yogurt culture is native to the Middle East and the Caucasus.

Kefir [kef-FEER] is a milk beverage traditional to the Caucasus area that has become popular in North America. It is fermented by both a bacterial culture and a yeast culture specific to the Caucasus. As its popularity grows, kefir will likely be used in much the same way as buttermilk.

Sour cream is a thick, custardy product made from light cream and a specific North American culture. It has a mildly tangy taste. Standard sour cream has a milk-fat content of about 18 percent. Low-fat sour cream usually contains natural and artificial thickeners to approximate the texture of full-fat sour cream.

Crème fraîche [krem FRESH] is a rich, thick, fermented dairy product made from creams of varying milk-fat content and a culture originating in France. It has a tangy, nutty flavor.

Most commercially made fermented dairy products are pasteurized after fermentation is complete. This process stops further fermentation and keeps the product from overfermenting to the point of spoilage. Unpasteurized or "live culture" products are also available.

Making Fermented Dairy Products

The only ingredients necessary to prepare a fermented dairy product are milk (or cream) and the proper culture. Dairy cultures can be derived from a batch of

Active-Culture Dairy Products

When a dairy product undergoes fermentation, the beneficial bacteria added to it are alive. Under the correct, warm conditions they consume lactose, create beneficial waste products, and soon begin multiplying to create more and more bacteria. When the action of these bacteria has created the desired changes—typically souring and thickening—the product is refrigerated to slow the bacterial action and keep the product in the desired state. At this point the bacteria are still alive, but their activity is suppressed by the cold temperature. A product such as this is called an active-culture or live-culture dairy product.

In order to ensure a longer shelf life and a consistent product, industrial dairy producers destroy a fermented dairy product's bacterial culture through pasteurization once the desired product characteristics are achieved. Thus, most purchased sour cream, yogurt, and other commercial dairy products no longer contain their original culture. However, growing public awareness of the health benefits of dairy bacteria has led to consumer demand for active-culture fermented dairy products, and they are becoming more widely available.

"live culture" product or purchased in dehydrated form. Dehydrated cultures are also known as laboratory cultures. They are the most reliable type of culture, producing consistent results. The recipes in this text were prepared with laboratory cultures purchased from a commercial source.

Raw milk produces the best result in house-made fermented products. However, standard pasteurized milk can be cultured as well. Depending on the temperature in your kitchen and the type of culture you use, it normally takes about 24 hours to prepare a finished batch.

Procedure for Making Fermented Dairy Products

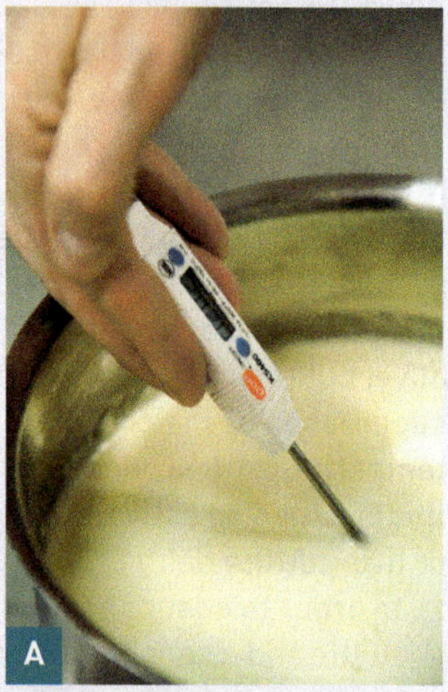
A

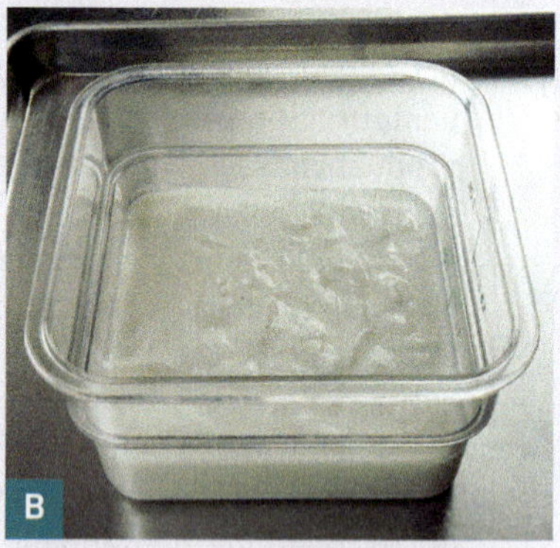
B

C

1. Use only nonreactive equipment, such as stainless-steel pans and plastic containers. Sanitize all equipment that will come into contact with the milk and the finished product.
2. If necessary, preheat a food warming box to the specified temperature.
3. Carefully measure all ingredients. Use an accurate digital scale to weigh small quantities of powdered laboratory cultures.
4. Over moderate heat, bring the milk or cream to the specified temperature. Be sure to use an accurate thermometer (A).
5. Turn off the heat and stir in the culture.
6. Transfer the milk to a container and cover it loosely with plastic film. Allow the milk to stand at the specified temperature for the specified amount of time. If necessary, hold the milk in the warming box to maintain the correct temperature until souring and thickening are complete (B).
7. To make a thicker product:
   a. Line a strainer or colander with a double layer of cheesecloth. Place the strainer in a bowl.
   b. Spoon the product into the cheesecloth.
   c. Gather the corners of the cheesecloth and tie it into a bag using kitchen string. Leave enough string to hang the bag.
   d. Place the bowl on a lower shelf in the refrigerator and suspend the bag from the rack above it (C). Allow the product to drain until the desired thickness is achieved.

RECIPES

CRÈME FRAÎCHE

Yield:
1 qt (1 L)

INGREDIENTS	U.S.	METRIC
Half-and-half or light cream	1 qt	1 L
Crème fraîche culture (C-33), see Note	1 packet	1 packet

Note: The culture used in developing this recipe was purchased from New England Cheesemaking Supply Company.

PROCEDURE

DAY 1: PREPARATION

1. Follow steps 1–6 in the Procedure for Making Fermented Dairy Products on page 566. Bring the half-and-half to 86°F (30°C) and allow it to culture at 70°F (21°C) for 24 hours.

DAY 2: PREPARATION

2. After 24 hours, the product will have thickened to the texture of soft-serve ice cream and have a slightly tangy taste. It may be used at this point. However, to achieve a full, nutty flavor and thick texture, refrigerate the crème fraîche and hold 24 hours longer.

HOLDING

Refrigerate up to 10 days.

WHOLE-MILK YOGURT

Yield:
1 qt (1 L)

INGREDIENTS	U.S.	METRIC
Whole milk	1 qt	1 L
Dry milk powder	½ oz	15 g
Yogurt culture (Y4), see Note	1 packet	1 packet

Note: The culture used in developing this recipe was purchased from New England Cheesemaking Supply Company.

PROCEDURE

DAY 1: PREPARATION

1. Follow steps 1–6 in the Procedure for Making Fermented Dairy Products on page 566. Add the milk powder in step 2. Bring the milk to 86°F (30°C) and allow it to culture at 80°F (26°C) for 24 hours.

DAY 2: PREPARATION

2. After 24 hours, the product should have a texture similar to custard. It is ready to use.
3. To make a thicker yogurt, follow step 7 in the Procedure for Making Fermented Dairy Products. Hang the yogurt for several hours, or until the desired consistency is reached.

HOLDING

Refrigerate up to 10 days.

VARIATIONS

LOW-FAT YOGURT

Replace the whole milk with 2 percent milk.

GOAT'S-MILK YOGURT

Replace the whole milk with goat's milk.

YOGURT CHEESE (LABNI)

Prepare yogurt. Follow step 7 in the Procedure for Making Fermented Dairy Products. Hang the yogurt 24–48 hours, or until the desired thick consistency is achieved.

SPINACH-YOGURT DIP WITH BAGEL CRISPS

BUFFET APPETIZER

Yield:
1 pt (0.5 L)
Portions:
8
Portion size:
2 fl oz (60 mL)

INGREDIENTS	U.S.	METRIC
Fresh spinach	1 lb	0.5 kg
Clarified butter	1 oz	30 g
Minced shallots	1 oz	30 g
Minced garlic	¼ oz (1 tbsp)	7 g (15 mL)
Kosher salt	to taste	to taste
Ground black pepper	to taste	to taste
Grated nutmeg	pinch	pinch
Thick *Whole-Milk Yogurt (p. 567)* or commercial	10 fl oz	300 mL
Cherry tomato halves	½ oz (3)	15 g (3)
Bagel Crisps (p. 702)	12 oz	360 g
Supplies		
14-in. (35-cm) greaseproof doily	1	1

PROCEDURE

PREPARATION

1. Bring 1 gal (4 L) water to the boil. Prepare a bowl of ice water for refreshing.
2. Stem and devein the spinach.
3. Wash the spinach thoroughly in several changes of cold water and drain it.
4. Blanch the spinach for a few seconds to wilt it, and then refresh it until cold.
5. Drain the spinach well and squeeze it dry.
6. Chop the spinach fine.
7. Heat a nonstick sauté pan and add the clarified butter. Add the shallots and garlic, and then add the spinach, salt, pepper, and nutmeg. Sauté until the spinach is dry and well coated with the butter and seasonings. Cool to room temperature.
8. Mix the yogurt with the spinach.
9. Taste and correct the seasoning.

HOLDING

Refrigerate in a freshly sanitized, covered container up to 5 days.

PRESENTATION

10. Place the dip in an 18-fl oz (0.5-L) serving bowl.
11. Garnish the dip with the cherry tomato halves.
12. Place the bowl on a 14-in. (35-cm) tray lined with a doily.
13. Arrange the bagel crisps around the dish.

VARIATIONS

ROASTED PEPPER SPINACH-YOGURT DIP

Decrease the spinach to 12 oz (360 g) and add ⅓ cup (80 mL) chopped roasted red bell pepper (p. 109).

SPINACH-YOGURT DIP IN BREAD BOWL

Omit the bagel crisps. Cut the top off a 16-oz (0.5-kg) French bread boule (round), and hollow it to form a bowl. Place the bowl on the tray and fill it with dip. Arrange 6-oz (180 g) baguette slices around the bread bowl and provide a steak knife so guests can cut the bread bowl into pieces.

THREE-ONION SOUR CREAM DIP WITH CHIPS

BUFFET APPETIZER

Yield:
1 pt (0.5 L)
Portions:
8
Portion size:
2 fl oz (60 mL)

INGREDIENTS	U.S.	METRIC
Red onion, rough brunoise-cut	4 oz	120 g
Kosher salt	to taste	to taste
Sugar	1 tbsp	15 mL
Red wine vinegar	1 fl oz	30 mL
Water	2 fl oz	60 mL
Minced fresh chives	1 oz	30 g
Dehydrated fried onion flakes	½ oz (¼ cup)	15 g (120 mL)
Kosher salt	to taste	to taste
Sour cream	12 fl oz	360 mL
Potato Chips (p. 700), other chips or crackers, or vegetables as prepared for crudités (p. 89)	about 12 oz	about 360 g
Supplies		
14-in. (35-cm) greaseproof doily	1	1

PROCEDURE

PREPARATION

1. Combine the red onion, salt, sugar, vinegar, and water in a small, nonreactive pan. Bring to the simmer and reduce the liquid, stirring constantly with a heatproof rubber spatula until the onions are dry. Do not allow the onions to brown. Cool to room temperature.
2. Combine the red onion mixture, chives, onion flakes, salt, and sour cream. Place in a freshly sanitized covered container and refrigerate at least 3 hours.
3. Taste and correct the seasoning.

HOLDING

Refrigerate up to 5 days.

PRESENTATION

4. Place the dip in an 18-fl oz (0.5-L) serving bowl.
5. Set the bowl on a 14-in. (35-cm) tray lined with a doily.
6. Arrange the chips or vegetables around the dish.

CHEESE

Like other dairy products, cheese begins with milk. The goal of the cheese maker is to separate the milk solids and the milk fat from the water in order to create a firm, compact, and relatively dry food mass. When this separation occurs, the milk is said to ***curdle***. The resulting solid food, consisting mainly of milk solids and milk fat, is called ***curds***. The watery liquid is called ***whey***. When curds are drained of whey and compacted together, they become ***cheese***—specifically, ***fresh cheese***.

At the most basic level, the flavor of curds, and of the cheese made from them, depends on the characteristics of the milk that was curdled. Six factors influence the characteristics of milk.

1. *The type of animal* that gives the milk. Cow's milk, goat's milk, and sheep's milk are most commonly used, and all have distinctive flavors.
2. *The animal's breed.* Certain breeds of milk-giving animals produce a high volume of milk, but their milk is often less rich in milk fat and blander in flavor. Other breeds produce less milk, but that milk is often richer and more flavorful.
3. *The location.* The area where the animals are grazed greatly affects the taste of the cheese. In French, this effect is called *le goût de terroir* (the taste of the soil), or simply, *terroir* (tare-WAH).
4. *The season.* Milk that is the result of animals grazing on green-grass summer pasture with flowers and herbs creates cheese with fuller and more complex flavors, while milk from animals eating dry winter fodder produces cheese that is less flavorful.
5. *The amount of milk fat present in the milk.* Many artisan cheeses are made from milk just as it comes from the cow. This milk typically contains about 4 percent milk fat; in some artisan-owned herds, milk-fat percentages may be as high as 6 percent. The listed milk-fat content of cheeses made from this type of whole, unprocessed milk usually ranges from 40 to 50 percent (see sidebar, p. 578). Other cheeses are made from milk that has had some of the cream removed. These cheeses have correspondingly lower milk-fat content. Yet other cheeses are made from milk to which additional cream has been added and, therefore, have higher milk-fat content.
6. *Whether the milk is pasteurized or not.* Refer to the sidebar on page 560 for a discussion of the effects of pasteurization in cheese making.

Table 14.3 identifies cheese producer classifications.

A Cheese by Any Other Name

The Latin word *caseus* means "curds" or "cheese." From this root we derive many of the modern European words for cheese. It became the Saxon word *kasi,* which became *cese* in Old English, and finally *cheese* in modern English. The German word *käse* comes from the same Saxon root. The Spanish *queso* and Portuguese *queijo* also reflect the Latin *caseus.* However, the Italian *formaggio* and the French *fromage* are both derived from the Latin *forma,* meaning "form" or "mold," reflecting the manner in which curds are formed into cheese. ***Fromage*** [froh-MAZH] is an important word to remember because it is part of the names of many cheeses.

Classifying Cheeses

Because there are so many cheeses, and because the process of cheese making is complex, it is difficult to place cheeses in tidy classifications. There are several ways to classify cheeses, such as by country of origin, by type of milk used, by texture, and by type of production process. Thus, each cheese may fall into several categories. For example, Roquefort can be classified as a French cheese, a sheep's-milk cheese, and a firm cheese as well as a blue cheese.

Classifying cheeses by texture can be a useful system, but it may create confusion because the way in which texture is perceived is subjective. Where do we draw the line between soft and semisoft? Or between semifirm and firm? Adding to this confusion is that the ripening and aging processes change the texture of cheeses.

TABLE 14.3 Cheese Producer Classifications

Classification	Production	Characteristics
Farmstead Cheeses	Produced on a single farm, from milk produced only by herds raised on that particular farm. Made largely by hand using traditional methods. Made from milk produced without the use of hormones or antibiotics. Many do not use chemical herbicides or pesticides on their grazing land. Some certified as organic. In Europe and Great Britain, farmstead cheeses may be made from raw milk.	Farmstead cheeses exhibit great character and individuality and are among the most expensive of cheeses.
Artisan Cheeses	Made largely by hand using traditional methods; not necessarily produced on a farm. May be made from milk from various farms that are usually local and typically follow organic guidelines.	Although the quality of artisan cheeses varies, most are well made and interesting.
Co-op cheeses	Made in small factories owned collectively by a group of local farmers. Only milk from co-op members is used in producing co-op cheeses; member farmers are involved in monitoring the cheese-making process.	Co-op cheeses are considered the best among factory cheeses.
Factory cheeses	Natural cheeses produced on a large scale with milk collected from many sources.	Factory cheeses vary widely in character and quality.
Industrial cheeses	Manufactured using nontraditional heat processes and may contain sweeteners, vegetable gums, vegetable oil, and stabilizers.	Industrial chesses include pasteurized process cheeses, cheese spreads, and other cheese "foods."

A better way to classify cheeses is according to their production process. Thus, we list cheeses under the categories listed on pages 576 to 580. Cheeses having special production processes are sub-classified according to those processes. Cheddar and *pasta filata* (p. 574) cheeses are good examples.

Some types of cheese have distinctive qualities that trump all other characteristics, including production process. Goat cheese is generally considered its own category because its definitive goaty taste is its most noticeable flavor characteristic. Goat cheeses are frequently referred to by their French name, ***chèvre*** [SHEV]. Blue cheese is also a category in its own right because of the distinctive flavor and appearance created by various "blue" cultures.

The Cheese-Making Process

Thousands of cheeses are made throughout the world. In fact, it is truly amazing that so many distinctive kinds of cheese can be produced from little more than milk. Although at its most basic level the cheese-making process is similar for all cheeses, even small variations in the basic process can produce great differences. Thus, each type of cheese is unique.

Cheese production consists of five steps:

1. Culturing and curd formation
2. Curd consolidation
3. Forming
4. Ripening
5. Aging

Fresh cheeses require only the first three steps. Some cheeses are not aged.

Step 1: Culturing and Curd Formation

The first step in cheese making involves two processes that usually occur almost simultaneously.

CULTURING

Most modern cheeses begin when the milk is cultured. This process is virtually the same as in the production of fermented dairy products (p. 566), but the specific cultures used are different. The cheese maker heats the milk to a temperature ranging from 80° to 90°F (21° to 32°C) and adds a selected laboratory dairy culture to begin fermentation.

The acid that results from culturing begins the coagulation and curdling processes. Thus, the culturing process is sometimes called ***acidification***. As the bacterial culture does its work, the milk begins to coagulate, gradually thickening into a custard-like mass called ***clabber***. The amount of time needed for culturing ranges from less than an hour to several days, depending on the type of culture and the result the cheese maker desires.

The acid produced by culturing not only starts coagulation but also creates a pleasant, slightly sour taste in the milk. This contributes to the final flavor of the cheese, adding a tangy note. In cheeses that will be ripened, the culture remains alive and thriving inside the cheese during the ripening process, and it continues to influence the final flavor.

CURD FORMATION (CURDLING)

The cheese maker's goal is to remove the water component from milk in order to create a solid food product. This is done by a process called ***curdling***, which can be thought of as a continuation of the coagulation process. In curdling, the protein nets formed by coagulation begin to tighten and eventually expel the liquid they once held. Refer to the sidebar on page 574 for the science of curdling.

Culturing initially thickens the milk by coagulating it. If the culturing process is allowed to continue for a lengthy period, the culture will eventually curdle the milk. However, by the time milk is curdled by a culture, it contains a high level of lactic acid resulting in an unpleasantly sour product. To initiate curdling without excessive souring, after the culturing has progressed to a given point an additional, non-acid-producing curdling agent is added. The traditional cheese-curdling agent is ***rennet***, a substance that contains the enzyme ***rennin***. Rennet was originally derived from the stomach lining of young ruminant animals, such as cows and goats. Today food scientists create vegetable-based rennet as well.

How Pasteurization Affects Cheeses

In North America, virtually all of the milk that is sold for fresh consumption and that is made into commercial fermented dairy products and cheese has been pasteurized. U.S. regulations forbid the use of raw milk in commercial cheeses that will be aged for fewer than 60 days. Although the widespread practice of pasteurization has unquestionably benefited the health and well-being of milk drinkers, it is not beneficial to fine cheese making.

While pasteurization kills harmful bacteria, it also destroys beneficial bacteria and vital flavor-producing enzymes. Although today's cheese makers are able to coagulate and flavor their curds with laboratory cultures after pasteurization, when the milk is pasteurized, the true local character of the resulting cheese is destroyed.

Artisan cheese makers and knowledgeable chefs believe small producers should be permitted to hand-craft farmstead cheeses on their own premises from raw milk produced by their own certified herds. To be certified for raw milk production in the United States, a dairy herd is subject to 20 strict standards regulating feed, water, pasture management, herd management, sanitation, and veterinary care. The risk of contamination under such controlled circumstances is very low.

Rennin curdles milk more quickly and more gently than lactic acid, and does so without excessive souring. In some cheeses, the total curdling time is only half an hour. Other cheeses require two or more hours. When curdling is complete, the milk separates into a smooth, creamy-white curd mass floating on top of thin, yellow-green whey. At this point the curds are said to be *set*.

Step 2: Curd Consolidation

Once the curd is set, it still contains some watery whey. To drain the remaining whey from the curds, the next step is cutting them. While the curd mass is still floating on the whey, the cheese maker slices through it. This increases the surface area of the curd mass, allowing more whey to drain out of it. Small, fine-cut curds produce firm, dry cheeses, while curds that are left large and more intact produce softer, moister cheeses.

To achieve a very firm textured cheese, curds are heated to temperatures above 100°F (37°C). This causes the protein net to contract even further and forces out almost all of the residual whey.

After cutting, the curds may be lifted out of the whey, or the whey may be drained off the curds.

At this point, salt is usually added to the curds. Salt may be added at other times during the cheese-making process as well. Sometimes salt is added earlier, stirred into the milk along with the culture or rennet. Additional salt may be rubbed onto the exterior of a cheese after it is formed. No matter when it is added, salt is an important element in cheese. Not only does it add to the flavor of the cheese, it also affects the rate of whey drainage and slows bacterial action. In aged cheeses, salt aids the dehydration process and prevents spoilage.

Other flavorings, such as herbs, spices, wines, and spirits, may be added at this point. The plant-derived coloring agent ***annatto*** may be added to the curds in order to give the cheese an attractive yellow-gold color. An additional bacterial culture may be added at this time as well.

The Science of Curdling

If certain enzymes (such as rennin) are introduced into cultured milk, the protein net created by the culture begins to shrink and tighten. This process is called *curdling*. When curdling occurs, the liquid captured with the net is squeezed out and the protein strands bond together into clumps, or curds, that contain much of the milk solids and milk fat. The expelled watery liquid is called *whey*.

Step 3: Forming

The third step is to pack the curds into forms. For traditional cheese types, the size and shape of the form is dictated by custom—and, in some countries, by law. If the cheeses are not legally regulated, they are formed as the cheese maker chooses. Some forms have openings or perforations to allow further drainage. Many cheeses are weighted during forming in order to press out additional moisture. Other cheeses are further cut, stacked, or otherwise manipulated to achieve a particular texture and mouthfeel. Some cheeses, such as cheddar, are wrapped in cheesecloth during forming. Once they are packed into their final form, most cheeses are turned frequently during the forming period to ensure an even shape and consistency.

A few special cheeses are formed in a different manner. To make these cheeses, heated curds are stretched and kneaded like bread dough or taffy and then shaped by hand into free-form spheres or twists. These cheeses are grouped as a special fresh cheese category: string cheese or ***pasta filata*** [PAH-stah fee-LAH-tah], in Italian. Fresh mozzarella is a well-known cheese made by the *pasta filata* method.

Once curds are drained and formed—even casually and loosely formed by spooning them into a tub—they become fresh cheese.

Step 4: Ripening

All types of cheese begin as fresh cheese. The next stage for most cheeses is ***ripening***, a series of changes that occur in a cheese due to the action of bacteria, molds, and enzymes. Ripening must occur under controlled conditions of humidity and temperature. Cheeses were originally ripened in caves. Today, cheese-ripening rooms, or ***cheese vaults***, are engineered to create cavelike conditions of high humidity, moderate temperature, and darkness.

At the beginning of the ripening process, beneficial microorganisms are fewer and the changes in the cheese are slight. At this stage, a cheese is often referred to as a ***young cheese***. During the ripening process, microorganisms multiply and produce compounds that contribute to flavor, aroma, color, texture, and mouthfeel. While ripening, a cheese can change dramatically, often changing from firm, white, and mild-tasting to soft, creamy-yellow, and pungent, becoming a ***mature cheese***.

Three factors influence ripening.

1. *The type of microorganisms* introduced makes each cheese ripen in a distinctive manner. For example, a bacterial culture creates a totally different result than a mold culture.

2. *The water content* of a cheese largely influences how quickly it ripens. Firm cheeses having relatively low water content ripen slowly and, under proper conditions, may be stored for long periods without spoiling. Soft cheeses having high water content ripen quickly and also spoil quickly.

3. *The manner in which microorganisms are introduced into the cheese.* Some cheeses ripen only from the action of the original microorganisms added to the curds. Other cheeses, such as many blues, have cultures injected into the interior of the cheese after it is formed. Both of these processes are called ***interior ripening***. Still others ripen due to the action of additional microorganisms applied to the surface. This is called ***surface ripening***. Surface-ripening cheeses acquire an edible rind, called the ***bloom***, which has a distinctive textured feel and appearance.

Step 5: Aging

Aging is the extended storage of a fully ripened firm cheese, under proper conditions, in order to change and improve it. Aging can be considered an extension of the ripening process because it occurs under the same or similar conditions of controlled temperature and humidity. In fact, when looking at a cheese or even tasting one, *it is impossible to determine the exact point at which ripening ceases and aging begins.* However, at some point, the microorganisms in the cheese become inactive because of increased lactic acid and decreased moisture. In theory, that is when the ripening process ends.

After ripening ceases, the cheese continues to change, but these changes are caused almost entirely by dehydration and by the action of enzymes. Increased dehydration results in shrinkage, or additional loss of weight and volume. Shrinkage changes the texture of the cheese from firm to hard. Loss of moisture also concentrates the flavor of the cheese. At the same time, enzymes continue to make the flavors fuller and more complex.

This final step in the cheese-making process is done to some, but not all, cheeses. It is the choice of the cheese maker whether or not to age a particular firm cheese. Usually the best specimens of their type are selected for aging.

Only firm cheeses having low moisture content are aged; their lower water content slows the action of the microorganisms within them and thus prevents spoilage.

Types of Fresh, Cured, and Aged Cheeses

The following discussion relates production methods to some of the best-known cheeses. It covers cheeses in these categories:

- Fresh cheeses
- Soft surface-ripened cheeses
- Firm interior-ripened cheeses
- Hard, aged cheeses

Cheeses made by unique methods, such as cheddar, are also discussed.

Fresh Cheeses

Fresh cheeses have a mild, fresh-milk taste that is simple and uncomplicated. They vary in texture from very soft and spoonable (cottage cheese) to firm (feta cheese). Most *pasta filata* cheeses belong in the category of fresh cheeses as well.

TABLE 14.4 Selected Fresh Cheeses

Soft, Spoonable Cheeses		
Fromage frais/ Fromage blanc	France	cow's milk
Petit-Suisse	France	cow's milk
Dry-curd cottage cheese	U.S.	cow's milk
Pot cheese	U.S./U.K.	cow's milk
Ricotta	Italy/U.S.	cow's milk
Mascarpone	Italy/U.S.	cow's milk
Cream-Added Cheeses		
Creamed cottage cheese	U.S.	cow's milk
Cream cheese	U.S.	cow's milk
Neufchâtel	France/U.S.	cow's milk
Gervais	France	cow's milk
Flavored Fresh Cheeses		
Alouette (garlic-herb)	France	cow's milk
Boursin (garlic-herb)	France	cow's milk
Pasta Filata Cheeses		
Mozzarella	U.S./Italy	cow's milk
Buffala mozzarella	Italy	water buffalo's milk
String cheese	Middle East	cow's milk
Semifirm, Crumbly Textured Cheeses		
Farmer's cheese	U.S./U.K.	cow's milk
Queso fresco, queso blanco	Spain/Latin America	cow's milk
Feta	Greece/U.S.	cow's milk
Fresh Chèvres		
Banon (leaf-wrapped)	France	goat's milk
Valençay	France	goat's milk
Montrachet	France	goat's milk
Coated chèvres	France/U.S.	goat's milk

Because they are very mild to bland in flavor, most fresh cheeses are not served as table cheeses but rather are used in cooking and as the base of cheese spreads or sauces. The exception to this rule is fresh goat cheeses, which are flavorful enough to be enjoyed in their own right. Table 14.4 lists selected fresh cheeses.

Fresh cheeses, left to right: string cheese, queso blanco, cream cheese, ricotta, fresh chèvre, fresh mozzarella, and Boursin

Firm Interior-Ripened Cheeses

Most of the world's cheeses fall into the very broad category of firm interior-ripened cheeses. Many cheese experts further divide this category of cheeses into semisoft and semihard cheeses. While the textures of firm cheeses vary, a simple way to describe them is to say that, at maturity, they are firm enough to slice neatly but not so firm that they are difficult to slice. Firm cheeses acquire this texture from pressing, from the internal changes that occur during ripening, and from the mild dehydration that occurs during the ripening period.

Most firm cheeses gradually acquire a leathery or hard natural rind that protects the interior from invasion by additional microorganisms. Natural rinds are permeable. In other words, they allow a limited amount of air to pass through them and also allow gases to escape from the interior of the cheese. Thus, rind formation slows weight loss and shrinkage but does not adversely affect the ripening process. The rinds of some firm cheeses are washed, or basted, with a flavorful liquid, such as wine or beer, as they form. However, this washing is meant only to add flavor and to slow dehydration. It does not directly affect ripening.

Firm cheeses with natural rinds ripen slowly and remain at a mature level for relatively long periods. The term **curing** is often used to describe the slow ripening of firm cheeses. Some mature cheeses are coated with wax.

Some of the best-known firm cheeses are made by special processes.

Cheddar cheeses acquire their unique texture through two special processes. During curd consolidation, the curds are cut into slabs. The slabs are stacked on top of one another to exert pressure and squeeze moisture from them. During the draining period, the slabs are rearranged several times. Finally, the curd slabs are milled, or ground into pieces. The tiny curd pieces are salted and then packed into forms and weighted. This process, called **cheddaring**, creates a special texture unique to cheddar cheeses. Some cheddars are colored a rich, golden yellow by the addition of annatto. Both the special flavor and tangy-tingly mouthfeel of cheddar cheese are the result of the particular culture added to it combined with the effects of the cheddaring process. Cheese connoisseurs refer to this flavor as **sharp**. Sharpness increases as the cheese becomes more mature.

Swiss cheese is a generic term used for a type of firm cheese with a distinctive, nutty flavor and supple texture. Most Swiss-type cheeses have a distinctive appearance due to the presence of **eyes**, or holes, in the body of the cheese. These are caused by pockets of CO_2 gas resulting from bacterial activity during ripening. The size of the eyes varies as well. Swiss cheeses that have no eyes are called **blind**.

Firm cheeses, top row from left: Morbier, domestic cheddar, Italian Fontina. Bottom row from left: Tilsit, baby Gouda, Emmenthaler

Fat Content of Cheese

The listed fat content of cheese usually refers to the percent of solids. In other words, if a cheddar cheese, for example, is labeled "50% fat," this means the cheese would be 50 percent fat if all the moisture were removed. In fact, the cheese may have a moisture content of about 40 percent, and its actual fat content may be about 30 percent of the total.

Blue cheeses are treated with one of two types of penicillium molds. In some blues, the mold culture is mixed with the curds before they are formed. Other blue cheeses are ***inoculated***, or injected with the culture. The action of the penicillium molds gives the cheese a distinctive veined or mottled appearance. The color of the veining is not actually blue but rather ranges from gray-green to almost black. Blues differ from other firm cheeses in that they undergo very little draining and are not pressed. Thus, they are on the soft side of firm and have a relatively high moisture content. The mold culture gives blue cheeses a sharp, pungent flavor that is offset by the rich and creamy texture.

Although most of the common blue cheeses are firm cheeses, soft-ripening blue cheeses are also made (see below).

Soft Surface-Ripening Cheeses

Many European cheeses and North American artisan cheeses are made by the soft surface-ripening method. Most of the mild-flavored soft surface-ripening cheeses are further classified by milk-fat content.

Single-cream cheeses have about 50 percent milk fat. The best-known and most popular of these cheeses are Brie and Camembert, mild-flavored cheeses originating in France. Because of worldwide demand, much French Brie and Camembert is factory produced for export and is made with pasteurized milk. True artisan and farmstead Bries and Camemberts, made with raw milk and natural cultures, are vastly different and far superior.

Soft surface-ripening cheeses, top row from left: Brie de Meaux, l'Explorateur, Taleggio. Bottom row, from left: Camembert, l'Edel de Clairon

Double-cream cheeses are richer than single-cream cheeses, at about 60 percent milk fat. Most double-cream cheeses are identified as such on the label, as in "60% Brie."

Triple-cream cheeses have a milk-fat content of 70 percent or higher. These cheeses are almost as rich as butter. L'Explorateur is one of the best-known French triple creams.

Some soft surface-ripening cheeses are classified by additional culturing, or by the type of milk used to make them, such as the following:

Soft-ripening blue cheeses have blue veining in the paste and a surface culture bloom. Saga Blue is a widely available soft-ripening blue cheese.

Soft-ripening chèvres are goat cheeses made with a surface culture. Bûcheron is an excellent soft-ripening chèvre.

Washed-rind strong cheeses, clockwise from left: Époisses, Livarot, Limburger, and Reblochon

Washed-Rind Strong Cheeses

Some of the world's greatest cheeses are soft surface-ripening cheeses that are washed with brine, wine, or spirits as they ripen. Washing is intended to encourage the action of certain desirable bacteria and discourage others. A cheese treated in this manner is called a *washed-rind cheese*. Because of their strong flavor and aroma, these cheeses can be called ***washed-rind strong cheeses***.

Washed-rind strong cheeses develop a powerful, deeply savory, very earthy flavor and an aroma to match. Cheese connoisseurs call this combination of flavor and

Guidelines for Handling Soft Surface-Ripening Cheeses

All types of soft surface-ripening cheeses ripen quickly and are fully ripe after only a few weeks. The challenge is purchasing them at a manageable stage of ripeness, serving them at their peak of ripeness, and marketing them so they sell quickly.

- Decide whether you wish to purchase soft surface-ripening cheeses when they are just ripe or fully ripe, or whether you prefer to purchase underripe cheeses and ripen them yourself.
- When ordering, specify to your cheesemonger exactly the stage of ripeness you want. When beginning your cheese sales program, you may need to request samples to ensure your dealer understands your product specifications. Keep in mind that many dealers offer only underripe cheeses because they do not wish to risk loss from spoilage. Be aware that once a soft surface-ripening cheese is cut open, it will no longer continue to ripen. Over time, it will simply spoil.
- When you receive soft surface-ripening cheeses, open the boxes or wrappers and inspect the cheeses top and bottom. Make sure they are at the ripeness stage you specified. Wear food-service gloves when handling cheeses, and change gloves between types. Smell them to detect any ammonia odor, which indicates deterioration. If you are not sure whether a cheese is spoiled, bring it to room temperature and check it again.
- To determine ripeness by touch, gently grasp the cheese in its wrapper. Squeeze gently to feel the interior texture, moving in toward the center. If ripe, the cheese will feel soft throughout. If underripe, you will feel a firm core that begins somewhere near the outer edge of the cheese and extends into the center. As ripening progresses, the core becomes smaller, and eventually you will not be able to detect a core at all.
- Store ripe cheeses under refrigeration in their original packaging. Store in the warmest part of the walk-in or in a specially designated refrigerator at about 38°F (3°C). Do not stack them too high or set heavy objects on top of them. Turn the cheeses at least every other day, and inspect often.
- To ripen an intact soft surface-ripening cheese, hold it on a perforated tray in its wrapper at cool room temperature, between 60° and 70°F (15° and 21°C). Check ripeness every 12 hours and turn the cheese after each inspection. Refrigerate it when it reaches the ripeness you desire.

aroma *barnyard* or *stinky feet*. A cheese having these characteristics is called a strong cheese, or ***fromage fort*** in French. Connoisseurs consider these cheeses the most delicious of all.

Hard Cheeses

Hard cheeses can be defined as aged cheeses having a texture that makes them difficult to cut by hand with a standard knife. Large chunks of hard cheese are cut with a special double-handled cheese knife called a ***guillotine*** [GHEE-oh-teen], or may be broken with a ***cheese pick***. Large whole wheels of hard cheese are often halved and quartered with an electric saw.

All hard cheeses may be served as part of a cheese selection and eaten in the same manner as other cheeses. However, many are typically grated and used as an ingredient or topping for cooked foods. Following are among the best-known types.

Hard cheeses, top row from left: Parmigiano-Reggiano and Caerphilly. Bottom row from left: aged Gouda, Pecorino Romano, dry jack

Aged cheeses are particular specimens of a firm cheese that have been subjected to extended aging. The dehydration that results from long aging gives them their hard texture. Aged cheeses have the same basic flavor as the firm cheese type from which they were made, but that flavor is much more intense. Examples are aged cheddars and aged Goudas.

Grana cheeses take their name from their granular, or grainy, texture. Grana cheeses are often aged for two years or longer. Parmesan and Romano cheeses are well-known examples.

Cheeses Classified by Flavor Characteristics

Blue cheeses, clockwise from top left: Stilton, Cabrales, Roquefort, and Bleu d'Auvergne.

Blue Cheeses

This distinctive group of cheeses acquires a special flavor from the action of a penicillium culture. This beneficial mold typically creates blue veining, clearly visible streaks or blotches in colors that can be described as blue-gray or gray-green. Penicillium culture may be mixed with the curds before forming, or may be injected into the formed cheese. Additional pungent flavor is the result of bacterial cultures.

Most blue cheeses fall into the production category of firm interior-ripened cheeses. This type of blue does not form a hard rind and, thus, is relatively perishable. Cheeses made by the soft surface-ripening production process may be inoculated with penicillium cultures to create soft surface-ripened blues.

Goat cheeses, top row from left: Bucheron, Humboldt Fog, Valençay. Bottom row from left: Banon and herbed button chèvres.

Goat Cheeses, or Chèvres

As the name implies, goat cheeses are made from goat's milk. Because goat's milk is subjected to virtually every cheese production method, goat cheeses are available in many forms. You can choose from fresh, firm interior-ripened, soft surface-ripened, and hard goat cheeses—even goat's milk blues.

Smoked Cheeses

Natural smoked cheeses are firm cheeses that have been subjected to cold smoking after or in place of aging. When done with discretion, smoking imparts a light smoke flavor but also causes subtle changes in the cheese's volatile flavor compounds. (Do not confuse natural smoked cheeses with firm or processed cheeses flavored with liquid smoke.)

Cheese Character Factors

All fine distinctive cheeses derive their characteristics from nine basic factors:

1. The type and breed of animal giving the milk.
2. The *terroir*, or surroundings, in which the animals were raised.
3. The milk-fat content of the milk.
4. The particular combination of culture and rennet used in curd formation.
5. The quantity of salt used, and the optional addition of other flavorings and coloring.
6. The physical production methods used, including curd consolidation methods, amount of drainage and pressing, and forming methods.
7. The use of additional bacterial and mold cultures after forming.
8. Ripening time and conditions.
9. Optional aging.

Storing Cheeses

The following guidelines will help you store fresh, firm, and hard cheeses.

Guidelines for Standard Cheese Storage

- Store bulk cheeses in the warmest part of the walk-in refrigerator. This is usually the area nearest the door, where the temperature is near 38°F (3°C).
- Store cheeses as far away from produce as possible. Bacteria and molds that are beneficial to cheeses may cause produce to spoil.
- After opening a shrink-wrapped firm or hard cheese, remove the original packaging and rewrap the cheese tightly in two layers of plastic film.
- Use new plastic film each time a bulk cheese is opened and cut.
- If white surface mold appears on a large piece of cheese, trim off and discard at least ½ in. (1 cm) of the cheese's surface on all sides. The interior cheese is safe to serve. If blue mold veining extends into the interior of a non-blue cheese, discard the entire cheese.
- Store feta and fresh mozzarella in covered tubs submerged in cool water. Change the water at regular intervals, preferably every other day.
- Do not attempt to freeze table cheeses. The texture of most cheeses is destroyed when they are frozen. If freezing is the only alternative to spoilage, plan to use the cheese in cooking or as part of a potted cheese or cheese spread.

Guidelines for Storing Soft Surface-Ripening and Artisan Cheeses

- Soft surface-ripening cheeses and other fine farmstead or artisan cheeses require specific storage conditions and special attention. The cultures in these cheeses are more active, and thus these cheeses need the correct conditions of temperature, humidity, and air flow in order to remain at their best.
- If possible, dedicate a separate refrigerator for fine cheese storage. Set the controls to maintain a temperature of 50°F (10°C). Monitor temperature with an external thermometer. Place one or more pans of water in the refrigerator to create the highest humidity possible, optimally between 80 and 90 percent. Change the water daily.
- Store soft surface-ripening cheeses in the packaging in which they were purchased. Once cut, protect the cut surfaces with deli paper, butcher paper, or parchment, and then close the original wrapper over top. If the cheese arrived in a wooden or paper carton, keep it in the carton as long as possible and as space allows. Turn over the cheeses every other day. Small pieces may be wrapped in butcher paper or parchment and then placed inside a loosely closed plastic bag. Do not wrap soft surface-ripening cheeses in plastic film, as this smothers them and results in spoilage.
- Whole, intact natural-rind cheeses need no wrapping. Store them in the refrigerator on a rack to ensure even respiration and air circulation. Turn over these cheeses every week.
- After firm natural-rind cheeses are cut open, cover only the cut surfaces with plastic wrap. Secure the wrap with masking tape or kitchen string. Wrap small pieces of natural-rind cheese in butcher paper or parchment and then place them inside a loosely closed plastic bag.
- Blue cheeses should be stored in their original foil wrapper as long as possible. You may rewrap them in fresh foil if necessary. Store most blue cheeses at cooler temperatures than other fine cheeses, preferably between 42° and 45°F (5° and 7°C).
- Cheeses whose surfaces are drying out may be moistened by wrapping them in a clean, very damp towel for 24 hours. Repeat with a fresh towel at 24-hour intervals if necessary.

Serving Cheese

Presenting a thoughtfully chosen selection of fine cheeses at their peak of perfection presents many challenges for the garde manger chef.

Planning a Cheese Menu

Planning a cheese menu involves assembling a collection of cheeses that is balanced in type, texture, flavor, and appearance. In general, you should offer at least one cheese representing each production type. Refer to Table 14.5 for a list of cheese types and recommended choices within each type. Fresh chèvres, listed in Table 14.4, should also be considered. An alternative is to offer a flight of cheeses showcasing the differences and similarities within one cheese production type.

When tasting cheeses, it is wise to taste the milder, more subtle cheeses first and then proceed in order of strength to the most powerful flavors. Cheese boards and cheese platters should be arranged in this order.

The Cheese Board

A traditional cheese board is made of unfinished hardwood. However, modern food-service guidelines prohibit the use of wood, so garde manger chefs find other attractive surfaces instead. Clean, unstained white plastic cutting boards are acceptable for use as cheese boards. A marble slab makes a more elegant presentation.

Cheese Service Styles

Cheese may be presented in various service styles.

BUFFET AND PASSED CHEESE SERVICE

For casual affairs, standard firm cheeses may be cubed and served on cocktail picks. This lends itself to passed, or butler, service. Alternatively, cheeses may be sliced and arranged on trays on the buffet table. Standard cheeses may be accompanied by mustards, sweet chutneys, and other sauces or condiments. Crackers are an appropriate accompaniment.

Soft surface-ripening cheeses and other fine cheeses demand a more formal presentation. These cheeses are typically arranged on a cheese board in whole form or in large wedges or blocks. When offering a cheese board, you must provide appropriate service ware for cutting or slicing the cheese. Cheese service utensils are illustrated on page 584. Artisan breads are the correct accompaniment, although in North America crackers are also served. Do not offer flavored breads or crackers with fine cheeses, as these mask the flavors of the cheese.

In self-service buffets, customers choose and portion their own cheeses. This can lead to unattractive and unusable leftovers and significant waste. You may wish to provide a staff member to portion and serve expensive cheeses.

RESTAURANT CHEESE SERVICE

Today, more North Americans are ready to enjoy a cheese course after the entrée in the European manner. One way to market fine cheeses is to include one or more cheese assortments on the dessert menu. Offering flights of cheese is a good sales tool. Cross-merchandising cheese and wine is also a helpful strategy. For example, you might list a wine pairing on your cheese menu while suggesting a cheese pairing on the wine list.

To present a cheese cart, place an attractive cheese board on a *gueridon* [GARE-ee-don], or service trolley, and instruct servers to present the cart to each table after the entrée plates are removed. The captain or server can suggest cheeses and coordinate wine sales to enhance the cheeses.

Preparing Cheese for Service

The texture, aroma, and flavor of cheese are all best at room temperature, between 65° and 75°F (18° and 23°C). Therefore, for buffet service you must plan ahead. You must cut and present your cheeses far enough ahead of time so they warm to room temperature just before they are needed but not so far ahead that they become too warm. Overwarm firm cheeses can acquire an oily appearance, and very ripe soft surface-ripening cheeses can ooze out of their rinds and collapse. Keep cheese presentations covered loosely with plastic film while they are warming. Add perishable décor items, such as cut fruit and Apple Birds (p. 716), at the last minute.

Serving room-temperature cheese is a challenge in à la carte food service, because cheese must normally be stored under refrigeration until it is ordered. If cheese sells quickly, you may hold at room temperature the amount of cheese you estimate you will need during the service. If cheese sales are sporadic, encourage diners to order cheese platters at the beginning of the meal so the cheese can be plated early and thus be at the proper temperature when it is needed. Also, if you can store soft-ripening cheeses in their own refrigerator at 50°F (10°C), as explained above, they will be closer to proper serving temperature at all times.

Launch a Flight

In North American food service, a ***flight*** is a group of sample servings having something in common. This term dates from the 1980s when newly popular wine bars began offering customers 2-fluid-ounce servings of three or four different wines for one price. These themed samples became known as "flights of wine," although it is unclear why. The wines in a flight are selected to illustrate a theme, such as wines made from a particular grape, or from a particular growing area.

Today chefs serve flights of food, as well. For example, a garde manger chef might offer a flight of cold soups (all made with spring vegetables), or a flight of cheeses (all made from goat's milk). Flights give your customers variety and help to educate them about food.

Guidelines for Preparing Cheese for Service

- Cut cheese while it is cold. Cold cheese slices more neatly, and the remaining block or wheel of cheese maintains a better shape. Be sure to allow enough time for the cheese to reach room temperature before it is served.
- Wear food-service gloves when handling cheeses. This prevents contamination. It also helps prevent the cheese from softening under the heat of your hands, and it prevents fingerprints. To avoid cross-contamination, change gloves before you begin working with another type of cheese.
- Use a clean, freshly sanitized knife when cutting cheeses. Wipe the knife blade with a clean, damp towel between cuts. To avoid cross-contamination, wash and sanitize the knife before you begin working with another type of cheese.
- Use a portion scale to ensure proper and consistent portion sizes.
- Unless they are very large, most round cheeses should be cut into wedges. Make sure each wedge has a proper ***nose***, or point. Logs of cheese are cut into disks, or ***buttons***. Large cheeses that are sold in cut blocks are fabricated into long, thin, slabs. It is customary to leave some rind on the cheese, whether it is meant to be eaten or not. The rind helps identify the cheese and is part of its visual appeal. Very soft, fresh cheeses may be scooped or formed, or served in crocks or ramekins.
- When working with soft surface-ripening cheeses having edible blooms, cut the cheese in such a way that each portion has an equal amount of bloom.
- When presenting a cheese platter or board, use appropriate markers to identify each cheese. When serving a cheese plate, the server should name the cheeses when the plate is presented and suggest the tasting order. Advise buffet customers of the tasting order by numbering the cheese tags.
- Make sure to provide proper utensils for cheese service. A short, sharp knife or cheese plane is appropriate for firm and hard cheeses. Fresh cheeses and soft surface-ripening cheeses may be served with a dinner knife or a spreading knife. Sliced firm cheeses should be served with small tongs or a fork.
- The classic presentation of fine cheeses is simple: properly cut cheeses on a plain board, marble slab, or plate. You may add color to a cheese plate or platter by including fresh fruit, whole or sliced. Sliced fruit should be treated with acidulated water.

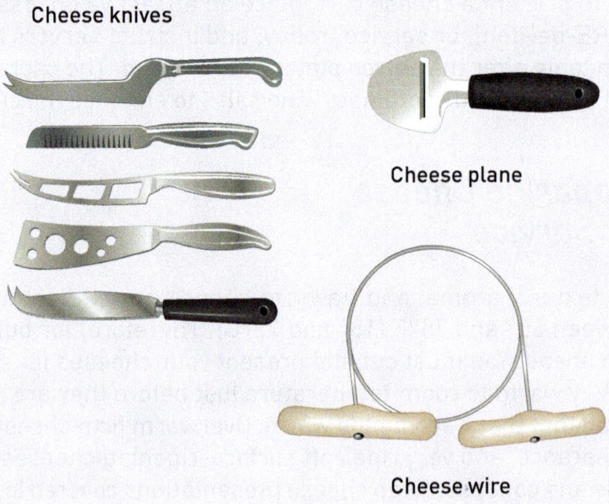

Table 14.5 represents only a small portion of the vast number of cheeses from which you can choose. When composing a cheese board or cheese plate, include at least one selection from each category.

TABLE 14.5 Selected Table Cheeses by Type

Firm Cheeses (includes semisoft and semihard cheeses)		
Beaufort	France	cow's milk
Bel Paese	Italy	cow's milk
Butterkäse	Germany	cow's milk
Caerphilly	U.K.	cow's milk
Cantal	France	cow's milk
Edam	Netherlands	cow's milk
Emmental	Switzerland	cow's milk
English Farmstead Cheddar	U.K.	cow's milk
Fontina Val d'Aosta	Italy	cow's milk
Gouda	Netherlands	cow's milk
Graviera	Greece	cow's milk
Grunländer	Germany	cow's milk
Gruyère	France, Switzerland	cow's milk
Halloumi	Cyprus	goat's/sheep's milk
Havarti	Denmark	cow's milk
Lappi	Finland	cow's milk
Leerdammer	Netherlands	cow's milk
Manchego	Spain	cow's milk
Morbier	France	cow's milk
Teleme Jack	U.S.	cow's milk
Tillamook Cheddar	U.S.	cow's milk
Tilsit	Germany	cow's milk
Tomme de Savoie	France	cow's milk
Wensleydale	U.K.	cow's milk
Soft Surface-Ripening Mild Cheeses (includes mountain cheeses and some washed-rind cheeses)		
Brie de Meaux/de Melun	France	cow's milk
Camembert	France	cow's milk
Chaource	France	cow's milk
L'Explorateur (triple cream)	France	cow's milk
Neufchâtel	France	cow's milk
St Nectaire	France	cow's milk
Taleggio	Italy	cow's milk
Toma	Italy	cow's milk
Vacherin Mont d'Or	France	cow's milk
Soft Surface-Ripening and Washed-Rind Strong Cheeses		
Époisses	France	cow's milk
Gubbeen	Ireland	cow's milk
Liederkrantz	U.S.	cow's milk
Limburger	Belgium, Germany	cow's milk
Livarot	France	cow's milk
Maroilles	France	cow's milk
Munster	France (Alsace)	cow's milk
Pont l'Eveque	France	cow's milk
Reblochon	France	cow's milk

(continues)

TABLE 14.5 | Selected Table Cheeses by Type *(continued)*

Goat Cheeses/Chèvres (includes firm and soft surface-ripening cheeses; refer to Table 14.4 for fresh goat cheeses)		
Banon (fresh)	France	goat's milk
Cabécou (soft/surface ripening)	France	goat's milk
Crottin de Chavignol (firm)	France	goat's milk
Garrotxa (hard)	Spain	goat's milk
Geitost or Gjetost (firm)	Norway	goat's and cow's milk
Humboldt Fog (soft surface-ripening)	U.S.	goat's milk
Valençay (soft surface-ripening)	France	goat's milk
Blue Cheeses (includes firm, hard, and soft surface-ripening cheeses		
Bleu d'Auvergne (soft surface-ripening)	France	cow's milk
Cabrales (firm)	Spain	cow's/goat's/sheep's milk
Danish Blue (firm)	Denmark	cow's milk
Fourme d'Ambert (soft surface-ripening)	France	cow's milk
Gorgonzola (firm)	Italy	cow's milk
Rogue River Blue (firm)	U.S.	cow's milk
Roquefort (firm)	France	sheep's milk
Saga Blue (semisoft)	Denmark	cow's milk
Stilton (firm)	U.K.	cow's milk
Hard Cheeses		
Aged Gouda	Netherlands	cow's milk
Asiago	Italy	cow's milk
Caerphilly	U.K.	cow's milk
Dry Jack	U.S.	cow's milk
Pecorino Romano, de Sarda	Italy	sheep's milk
Parmigiano-Reggiano	Italy	cow's milk
Smoked Gouda (natural)	Netherlands	cow's milk

Making Fresh Cheeses

Fresh cheeses are relatively quick and simple to make. Most well-equipped kitchens already contain most of the implements needed to make them. They require no special storage space or storage equipment because they are meant to be used within a few days of being made. Once you find a local source for milk and mail-order sources for cultures and rennet, you can make fresh cheeses as part of your regular production routine.

Ingredients

MILK AND CREAM

Raw milk makes the best cheese for two reasons. First, raw milk has a more complex, better flavor than blended commercial dairy milk. Second, raw farm milk that has not been pasteurized or homogenized produces smoother, more cohesive curds, and it yields a higher volume of curds than commercial milk. To ensure food safety, purchase raw milk only from certified herds. You may additionally choose to heat the milk to pasteurization temperature during the cheese-making process.

Raw cream is much harder to find than raw milk. However, industrially produced whipping cream and heavy cream may be used to boost the milk-fat content of raw milk when necessary.

If raw milk products are not available, or if you choose not to use them, acceptable fresh cheese may be made from pasteurized milk as well.

CHEESE CULTURES

Bacterial cheese cultures are available from many sources. Reculturable cultures are activated by the presence of milk and warmth, then are stored and used again to make subsequent batches of cheese. Because this type of culture requires time, attention, and storage space, it is not recommended for food-service operations. For efficiency and accuracy, most garde manger chefs use ***direct-set cultures***. Direct-set cultures are used as is, from the packet, and cannot be reused.

One way that cultures are classified is by their heat tolerance. The two primary cultures used for making fresh cheeses are classified in this way:

Direct-set mesothermic culture is used for cheeses cultured and curdled at moderate temperatures, usually 80°–90°F (26°–32°C). (*Meso* means "medium.") Most fresh cheeses are made with mesothermic cultures.

Direct-set thermophilic culture is used for cheeses that are heated above 100°F (37°C). Mozzarella and other *pasta filata*–type cheeses are made with thermophilic cultures.

In addition to these primary cultures, cheese labs offer additional preconsolidation cultures specific to particular cheeses. These cultures may include rennet as well as bacteria. Other, more complex bacteria and mold cultures are used for applying to cheeses that will be ripened.

RENNET

Commercial rennet is derived from three sources. Each type may be available in several forms.

Animal rennet is derived from the stomach lining of calves. It coagulates milk proteins by means of rennin. It is available in liquid and powdered forms.

Vegetable rennet is derived from a variety of plants. It coagulates by means of various plant enzymes. It is usually in tablet form. Cheeses made with vegetable rennet are suitable for vegetarian diets.

Microbial rennet consists of enzymes derived from either fungi or bacteria. Fungal rennet is strictly vegetarian. Bacterial rennet is genetically engineered from animal sources. The most widely available brand of bacterial microbial rennet is marketed under the trade name Chymostar™.

Rennets made by various producers are of different strengths. Thus, it is difficult to specify the required amount of rennet in a cheese formula. The best course of action is to follow the instructions on the rennet package or bottle.

ACIDIFIERS

A few fresh cheeses are curdled solely through the use of acidic ingredients.

Citric acid is a powdered acid used to make mozzarella and ricotta.

Tartaric acid is a powdered acid used to make mascarpone.

SALT

Although you can buy special flaked cheese salt, any fine-texture, non-iodized salt is suitable for fresh cheeses.

CALCIUM CHLORIDE

Pure calcium chloride is a natural chemical sold in powdered form. It is used when making fresh goat cheese to achieve a firmer curd set. When dissolved in the water used to store mozzarella, it helps prevent the cheese from acquiring a sticky, pasty texture under prolonged storage.

WATER

In many areas, tap water has a high mineral content and may have a high pH. Urban and suburban tap water is treated with chlorine and may also contain fluoride. All of these chemicals can interfere with the use of acidifiers and have an adverse affect on rennet and cheese-making cultures. Thus, when using water to dissolve dry rennet or acidifiers, it is better to use distilled water or bottled water.

Equipment

Because of the acidity of cultured milk, all pots and pans used to heat milk for cheese making must be nonreactive. In commercial food service, this generally means stainless steel. In addition, strainers, ladles, forms, and other utensils must be nonreactive.

Cheesecloth is used to drain and hang cheese and fermented dairy products. Food-service-grade cheesecloth is preferred over domestic because its greater width allows you to work with larger pieces.

The only specialized equipment necessary for making fresh cheeses is perforated cheese forms. Forms are used to drain, press, and shape firm-textured fresh cheeses such as farmer cheese and *fromage frais*. You can purchase plastic cheese forms from the cheese-making supply companies. Alternatively, you can improvise a cheese form by drilling holes in the bottom of a durable plastic food container. Once in the form, the cheesecloth-wrapped curds are pressed with a small plate or lid weighted with a heavy object.

When preparing fresh cheeses and fermented dairy products, it is essential to maintain strict standards of sanitation. If undesirable microorganisms come into contact with the milk you are culturing, your culture will be contaminated. If this happens, your product will not have the correct characteristics for its type, and it may spoil much more quickly. Be sure to use a sanitizing solution on countertops and to wear food-service gloves. Even if the equipment you plan to use is clean on the shelf, take the time to run it through a sanitizing dishwasher or soak it in sanitizing solution before you begin to make cheese.

Improvised cheese form with drainage holes

Procedure for Making Fresh Cheeses (non-*pasta filata* fresh cheeses)

1. Use only nonreactive equipment, such as stainless-steel pans and plastic containers. Sanitize all equipment that will come into contact with the milk and the finished product.
2. If necessary, preheat a food warming box to the specified temperature.
3. Carefully measure all ingredients. Use an accurate digital scale to weigh small quantities of culture powders.
4. If desired, pasteurize the milk:
   a. Place the milk in a pan over moderate heat and bring it to 145°F (62°C).
   b. Hold the milk at 145° (62°C) for 30 minutes by placing it in a food warming cabinet. Alternatively, hold the milk on a low flame and monitor its temperature frequently. Do not allow the heat to rise above 145°F (62°C).
5. Curdle the milk:
   a. Remove the milk from the heat source and cool it to the specified culturing temperature. If using a food warming cabinet, lower its temperature as specified.
   b. Stir in the culture or acidifier.
   c. Hold the milk at the specified culturing temperature by placing it in a food warming cabinet. Alternatively, hold the milk on a low flame and monitor its temperature frequently. Do not allow the temperature to change up or down.
   d. If necessary, prepare the rennet by crushing the tablet and dissolving it in water.
   e. If using rennet, stir it into the cultured milk.
   f. Hold the milk at the specified temperature for the specified time. When curdling is complete, there will be a thick curd mass floating on thin liquid whey (A).
6. Consolidate the curds:
   a. Line a strainer or form with dampened cheesecloth and set it over a bowl or pan.
   b. Spoon the curds into the strainer (B) or form (C). Allow them to drain for the specified times and at the specified temperatures.
7. Optionally, press the curds:
   a. Wrap the cheesecloth around the curds.
   b. Place the sanitized form lid or a sanitized plate plate on the curds and set the desired weight on top of them.
   c. Refrigerate for the specified length of time.

RECIPES

FROMAGE BLANC/FROMAGE FRAIS

Yield:
about 1 lb (0.5 kg)

INGREDIENTS	U.S.	METRIC
Whole milk, preferably raw	1 gal	4 L
Direct-set *fromage blanc* culture (C-20), see Note	1 packet	1 packet
Non-iodized fine salt (optional)	to taste	to taste

Note: The culture used in developing this recipe was purchased from New England Cheesemaking Supply Company.

PROCEDURE

PREPARATION

1. Follow steps 1, 2, and 3 in the Procedure for Making Fresh Cheese on page 589.
2. To culture and curdle the milk, follow steps 5a–c of the procedure. Heat the milk to 72°F (22°C) and hold at that temperature 24–36 hours, or until a very soft curd forms.
3. Follow step 6 of the procedure. Using a strainer, drain the cheese in the refrigerator at least 4 hours for a spoonable consistency and up to 12 hours to form a soft block.

HOLDING

Refrigerate up to 1 week.

MASCARPONE

Yield:
about 1 lb (0.5 kg)

INGREDIENTS	U.S.	METRIC
Heavy cream	1 qt	1 L
Powdered tartaric acid	¼ tsp	1 mL
Distilled or bottled water	1 tbsp	15 mL

PROCEDURE

PREPARATION

1. Heat the cream to 180°F (92°C).
2. Dissolve the tartaric acid in the water.
3. Remove the cream from the heat and stir in the acid solution.
4. Allow to stand at room temperature until the curd forms.
5. Pour into a cheesecloth-lined strainer set over a bowl.
6. Drain in the refrigerator 12–14 hours.

HOLDING

Refrigerate in a freshly sanitized covered container up to 5 days.

FARMER CHEESE/QUESO FRESCO

Yield:
about 1 lb (0.5 kg)

INGREDIENTS	U.S.	METRIC
Whole milk, preferably raw	2 gal	8 L
Direct-set mesophilic cheese culture (C-101), see Note	1 packet	1 packet
Vegetable rennet tablet	½	½
Distilled or bottled water	2 fl oz	60 mL
Non-iodized fine salt (optional)	to taste	to taste

Note: The culture used in developing this recipe was purchased from New England Cheesemaking Supply Company.

PROCEDURE

PREPARATION

1. Follow the Procedure for Making Fresh Cheeses on page 589.
   a. Culture the milk at 85°F (29°C) for 30 minutes.
   b. Allow the rennet to work at 85°F (29°C) 30 minutes–1 hour.
   c. For a sliceable consistency, press the cheese with a 5-lb (2-kg) weight in the refrigerator for 12 hours.

HOLDING

Refrigerate up to 1 week.

FRESH COW'S-MILK MOZZARELLA

Yield:
about 12 oz (340 g)

INGREDIENTS	U.S.	METRIC
Vegetable rennet tablet	¼	¼
Distilled or bottled water	2 fl oz	60 mL
Whole milk, preferably raw	1 gal	4 L
Powdered citric acid	2 tsp	10 mL
Non-iodized fine salt	¼ cup	60 mL

PROCEDURE

PREPARATION

1. Crush the rennet tablet and dissolve it in the water.
2. Begin warming the milk over moderate heat. Stir in the citric acid.
3. When the milk reaches 88°F (31°C), stir in the rennet solution.
4. Continue stirring over moderate heat until the milk reaches 105°F (40°C). At that temperature, curds will form (A).
5. Immediately remove the pan from the heat and scoop out the curds with a spider or perforated lifter. Place the curds in a bowl (B).
6. Return the pot to the heat and stir in the salt. Bring the whey to 185°F (85°C) and hold it at that temperature.
7. Put on a pair of clean, heatproof rubber gloves and form the hot curds into a ball of cheese (C).
8. Place the cheese in the spider and lower it into the whey for about 10 seconds (D).
9. Return the curd ball to the bowl and knead it like bread dough for about 30 seconds.
10. Return the curd ball to the whey and heat it for 10 seconds more.
11. Return the cheese to the bowl, and knead again. Pull on the cheese and try to stretch it like taffy (E). If the cheese will stretch and is pliable and shiny, form it into large or medium size balls, a twisted braid, bite-size balls (*bocconcini*), or other desired shape. If it does not stretch, repeat heating in whey and kneading until the correct consistency is achieved.
12. Place the cheese in the bowl, cover it with a clean, wet towel, and cool it to room temperature.

A

B

C

D

E

PROCEDURE

13. Use immediately, or place the cheese in a freshly sanitized covered container submerged in cool water.

HOLDING

Refrigerate up to 1 week.

Potted Cheese Variations

Garde manger chefs frequently find themselves with odds and ends of cheese that are damaged, dried out, or too small to serve. A traditional use for such cheese scraps is ***potted cheese***, a mixture of natural cheese, flavorings, and a moistening ingredient such as butter or a flavorful liquid. Such mixtures are typically packed into sterilized crocks, sealed with melted butter, and stored in a cool place to mellow. (Refer to the sidebar on page 457, about potted meats.) Potted cheese is served as a spread with bread or crackers. Here are some traditional and modern ideas for potted cheese.

Grind the ingredients together in a food processor fitted with the steel blade. Pack into freshly sanitized ramekins or crocks. Mellow in the refrigerator at least 2 days before serving. For long keeping, sterilize the containers and seal the surfaces with melted, cooled clarified butter.

PLOUGHMAN'S CHEDDAR

8 oz (240 g) sharp English cheddar, 3 oz (90 g) butter at 70°F (21°C), ¼ oz (15 g) minced shallots, 1 fl oz (30mL) dark beer. Serve with brown bread and pickled onions.

PORT WINE CHEDDAR

8 oz (240 g) extra-sharp cheddar, 3 oz (90 g) butter at 70°F (21°C). Remove two-thirds of the mixture and reserve it. Add 1 fl oz (30 mL) best-quality ruby port wine to the remaining cheese and process smooth. Place the port cheese mixture in a piping cone or pastry bag. Swirl the port cheese into the remaining cheese while packing. Serve with white bread or plain crackers.

POT DE FROMAGE FORT ALSACIEN

8 oz (240 g) rindless European Munster or Liederkrantz, 1 oz (30 g) minced shallot, 2 tsp (10 mL) minced garlic, 1 tbsp (15 mL) caraway seeds, 2 fl oz (60 mL) marc or vodka. Serve with a crisp baguette.

POT DE FROMAGE ILE DE FRANCE

8 oz (240 g) rindless Brie or other soft-ripening cheese, 2 oz (60 g) butter at 70°F (21°C), 2 fl oz (60 mL) medium-sweet sherry. Serve with a crisp baguette.

RED, WHITE, AND BLUE POTTED CHEESE

Steep 1 oz (30 g) quartered dried cherries in 2 oz (60 mL) warmed ruby port wine. Grind 6 oz (180 g) strong-flavored blue cheese with 2 oz (60 g) cream cheese at 70°F (21°C). Add the cooled port. Swirl 3 oz (90 g) cream cheese at 70°F (21°C) and the cherries into the blue cheese mix while packing. Serve with wheatmeal biscuits or plain crackers of choice.

GARLIC-HERB CHEESE SPREAD

APPETIZER

Yield:
12 oz (360 g)
Portion:
6
Portion size:
2 oz (60 g)

INGREDIENTS	U.S.	METRIC
Fromage Blanc (p. 590)	12 oz	360 g
Half-and-half or *Crème Fraîche (p. 567)*, optional	1–2 fl oz	30–60 mL
Granulated garlic	2 tsp	10 mL
Minced parsley	1 tbsp	15 mL
Minced chives	1 tbsp	15 mL
Minced thyme leaves	1 tsp	5 mL
Minced fresh tarragon	1 tbsp	15 mL
Fine sea salt	to taste	to taste
Finely ground white pepper	to taste	to taste
Baguette croûtons or plain crackers	10–12 oz	300–360 g

PROCEDURE

PREPARATION

1. Place the *fromage blanc* in a food processor fitted with the steel blade.
2. If necessary, thin it by processing in the half-and-half or crème fraîche.
3. Add the remaining ingredients and process to a smooth paste.
4. Taste and correct the seasoning.
5. Transfer to a freshly sanitized container and refrigerate at least 2 hours to mellow.
6. Taste and evaluate the seasoning, and make necessary corrections.

HOLDING

Refrigerate, covered, up to 1 week. Bring to room temperature before serving.

PRESENTATION

7. Pack into a 14-fl oz (420-mL) crock or six 2-fl oz (60-mL) ramekins.
8. Serve with croûtons or crackers.

LIPTAUER CHEESE

BUFFET APPETIZER

Yield:
18 oz (0.5 kg)
Portion:
6
Portion size:
3 oz (90 g)

INGREDIENTS	U.S.	METRIC
Farmer Cheese (p. 591)	10 oz	300 g
Very sharp cheddar or asiago cheese, finely grated	2 oz	60 g
Crème fraîche	2 oz	60 g
Minced shallot	1 oz	30 g
Minced nonpareil capers	2 tsp	10 mL
Chopped caraway seeds	1 tsp	5 mL
Anchovy paste	1 tsp	5 mL
Dijon mustard	1 tsp	5 mL
Hungarian sweet paprika	pinch	pinch
Dark beer	1–2 fl oz	30–60 mL
Chopped fresh parsley	¼ oz	8 g
Pumpernickel or other black bread, sliced thin	12–14 oz	360–400 g

PROCEDURE

DAY 1 PREPARATION

1. Grind together the cheeses and crème fraîche in a food processor fitted with the steel blade.
2. Add the shallot, capers, caraway, anchovy paste, mustard, and paprika. Pulse to blend.
3. Thin the mixture to a spreadable consistency with the beer.
4. Taste and correct the seasonings.
5. Refrigerate the cheese in a freshly sanitized, covered container for 24 hours.

DAY 2 PREPARATION

6. Bring the cheese to room temperature.
7. Taste and correct the seasoning.
8. Pack the cheese into a 20-fl oz (0.6-L) crock and garnish the top with parsley.
9. Place the crock on a 12-in. (30-cm) serving plate and surround it with the pumpernickel slices.

MARINATED MOZZARELLA BOCCONCINI

(bok-kon-CHEE-nee)

APPETIZER

Yield:
1 lb (0.5 kg)
Portions:
varies
Portion size:
varies

INGREDIENTS	U.S.	METRIC
Chopped fresh garlic	½ oz	15 g
Crushed dried red pepper	1 tbsp	15 mL
Dried basil	2 tsp	10 mL
Dried oregano	1 tsp	5 mL
Dark green extra-virgin olive oil	8 fl oz	240 mL
Fresh Cow's-Milk Mozzarella (p. 592) bocconcini or commercial	1 lb	0.5 kg
Red wine vinegar	to taste	to taste
Kosher salt	to taste	to taste

PROCEDURE

PREPARATION

1. Combine the garlic, pepper, herbs, and oil in a small saucepan and place the pan over low heat.
2. Heat the oil to 150°F (65°C). Stir in the salt.
3. Cool the oil to room temperature.
4. Blot the mozzarella dry on paper towels and place it in a freshly sanitized container just large enough to hold it snug.
5. Pour in the oil, making sure to scrape in all the seasonings.
6. Place the lid on the container and turn it upside down for a moment to coat the mozzarella evenly with the oil.
7. Refrigerate at least 24 hours.

HOLDING

Refrigerate up to 1 week.

FINISHING AND PRESENTATION

8. Toss each portion with a few drops of red wine vinegar before serving.
9. Use as part of an antipasto or in a complex salad.

COATED CHÈVRE BOULETTES

GARLIC-HERB, LEMON-PEPPER, AND PAPRIKA

APPETIZER

Yield:
18 pieces,
1 oz (30 g) each

INGREDIENTS	U.S.	METRIC
Firm, fresh chèvre	18 oz	0.5 kg
Granulated garlic	to taste	to taste
Dried parsley	1 tbsp	15 mL
Dried tarragon	1 tbsp	15 mL
Dried thyme	pinch	pinch
Minced lemon zest	2 tbsp	30 mL
Cracked black pepper	to taste	to taste
Hungarian sweet paprika	to taste	to taste
Baguette croûtons or plain crackers	12–16 oz	360–500 g

PROCEDURE

PREPARATION

1. Wearing food-service gloves, divide the chèvre into 16 portions, 1 oz (30 g) each. Form each portion into a ball, or *boulette.*
2. Prepare Garlic-Herb Boulettes:
   a. Sprinkle 6 boulettes with granulated garlic.
   b. Mix the dried parsley, tarragon, and thyme on a tray.
   c. Roll the boulettes in the herbs to coat them evenly.
3. Prepare Lemon-Pepper Boulettes:
   a. Sprinkle the lemon zest and pepper evenly on a tray.
   b. Roll 6 boulettes in the lemon zest and pepper to coat them evenly.
4. Prepare Paprika Boulettes:
   a. Sprinkle the paprika on a tray.
   b. Roll the remaining 6 boulettes in the paprika to coat them evenly.

HOLDING

Refrigerate in a flat, covered box lined with parchment, in a single layer, up to 1 week.

PRESENTATION

5. Arrange the desired number of boulettes on a serving platter.
6. Serve the croûtons or crackers on a plate or in a napkin-lined basket.

ROQUEFORT MOUSSE

Yield:
about 18 fl oz (0.5 L)
Portions:
6
Portion size:
3 fl oz (90 mL)

INGREDIENTS	U.S.	METRIC
Granular gelatin	1 tbsp	15 mL
White port wine	2 fl oz	60 mL
Roquefort cheese, room temperature	8 oz	240 g
Heavy cream, cold	4 fl oz	120 mL

PROCEDURE

PREPARATION

1. Mix the gelatin with the port in a small, heatproof cup. Let stand about 10 minutes to bloom.
2. Place the cup of gelatin mixture into a small pan of simmering water and heat the gelatin to melt it.
3. Crumble the cheese into a food processor fitted with the steel blade. Process it to a purée, then add the gelatin mixture through the feed tube. Scrape the cheese into a bowl.
4. Whip the cream to soft peaks.
5. Fold the whipped cream into the Roquefort mixture in thirds.
6. Immediately pack the mixture into six 3-fl oz (90-mL) silicone forms.
7. Freeze until firm, about 2 hours.
8. Pop the mousses out of the forms onto a sheet tray lined with parchment. Cover the surface of each mousse with plastic film.

HOLDING

Refrigerate up to 3 days. Freeze up to 1 month. Bring to cool room temperature before serving.

ROQUEFORT MOUSSE

WITH GRAPES AND VERJUS ESSENCE

APPETIZER OR CHEESE COURSE

Portions:
1
Portion size:
3 fl oz (90 mL), plus accompaniments

COMPONENTS

1 *Roquefort Mousse (p. 598)*, made in a 3-fl oz (90-mL) pyramid form
2 fl oz (60 mL) *Verjus Essence (p. 691)*, in squeeze bottle
1 oz (30 g) Micro greens of choice
2 oz (60 g) Peeled Red Flame grapes
5 Freshly toasted baguette croûtons

PROCEDURE

PLATING

1. Place the Roquefort mousse in the center of a cool 10-in. (25-cm) plate.
2. Squeeze a flourish of verjus essence on the plate to the right of the mousse.
3. Mound the micro greens to the back left of the mousse.
4. Arrange the grapes in an arc to the right of the mousse.
5. Serve the croûtons on a side plate or in a napkin-lined basket.

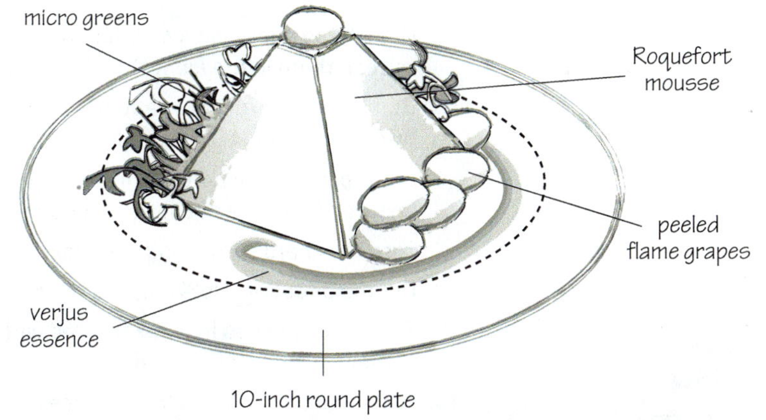

PROVENÇAL CHÈVRE AND VEGETABLE TERRINE

Yield:
1 3½×4×12-in. (9×10×30-cm) terrine

Portions:
16

Portion size:
4 oz (120 g)

INGREDIENTS	U.S.	METRIC
Green beans, trimmed	6 oz	180 g
Swiss chard, with stems	12 oz	360 g
Artichoke bottoms (p. 113), see Note	6 oz	180 g
Fresh lemon juice	to taste	to taste
Kosher salt	to taste	to taste
Roasted red bell peppers (p. 109)	6 oz	180 g
Tangy, ripened chèvre, at 70°F (21°C)	1 lb	0.5 kg
Cream cheese, at 70°F (21°C)	12 oz	360 g
Fine salt	to taste	to taste
Colossal California pitted black olives, well drained	12	12
Chopped fresh basil	2 tbsp	30 mL

Note: If using frozen artichoke bottoms, thaw before using.

PROCEDURE

PREPARATION

1. Bring about 1 gal (4 L) water to the boil and prepare a bowl of ice water.
2. Blanch the beans *à point* (p. 91) and refresh them. Blot them dry. Cut the beans into ⅜-in. (1-cm) lengths.
3. Remove the stems from the Swiss chard and peel them. Cut into ⅜-in. (1-cm) pieces.
4. Blanch the chard leaves about 30 seconds to soften them and then immediately refresh them in the ice water. Drain and blot dry.
5. Blanch the chard stems about 20 seconds or until tender and refresh in the ice water. Drain and blot dry.
6. Cut the artichoke bottoms into rough ⅜-in. (1-cm) dice. Taste and evaluate the texture. If they are not already tender, blanch and refresh them and blot them dry.
7. Toss the chard stems and artichoke pieces with a little lemon juice and salt.
8. Cut the peppers into ⅜-in. (1-cm) squares.
9. Place the cheeses in a mixer fitted with the paddle attachment. Blend them together on moderate speed.
10. Taste and add salt and lemon juice if needed.
11. Remove about 2 oz (60 g) of the cheese mixture from the mixer bowl and mix the basil into it. Place the basil cheese in a piping cone or pastry bag fitted with a small round tip.
12. Fill the olives with the basil cheese and reserve them.
13. Add all vegetable except the olives to the cheese mixture and pulse the mixer just to distribute the vegetables evenly throughout the mixture.
14. Line a 3½×4×12-in. (9×10×30-cm) terrine form with plastic wrap, allowing about 3 in. (8 cm) overhang on all sides.
15. Lay the chard leaves vein side up on the work surface and remove the thick part of the center veins to make the leaves flat and even (A).
16. Line the terrine form with the chard leaves, leaving about 2-in. (5-cm) overhang on all sides (B).

A

B

PROCEDURE

17. Pack half of the vegetable-cheese mixture into the terrine form. Tap it on the work surface to force out any air pockets.
18. Arrange the olives in a row down the center of the terrine form.
19. Pack in the remaining cheese and tap the terrine on the work surface to force out air pockets.
20. Fold the overhanging leaves over the surface of the terrine to encase the filling.
21. Fold the plastic wrap over top.
22. Place a terrine weight on the surface.
23. Refrigerate at least 6 hours.

HOLDING

Refrigerate, uncut, up to 5 days. Once cut, refrigerate 2 additional days only.

FINISHING

24. Use a heated thin-bladed knife to cut slices of the terrine. Wipe the knife blade between slices.

PROVENÇAL CHÈVRE AND VEGETABLE TERRINE

WITH TOMATO VINAIGRETTE

APPETIZER

Portions:
1
Portion size:
4 oz (120 g), plus garnish

COMPONENTS

1 *Provençal Chèvre and Vegetable Terrine (p. 601)* ¾-in. (2-cm) slice
3 fl oz (90 mL) *Basic Tomato Coulis Sauce (p. 52)*, seasoned with red wine vinegar, in squeeze bottle
1 oz (30 g) Provençal mesclun mix or other spicy greens mix
3 Oil cured black olives or Niçoise olives
5 *Croûtons (p. 702)* of choice

PROCEDURE

PLATING

1. Place the terrine slice slightly left of center on a cool 10-in. (25-cm) plate
2. Squeeze a pool of tomato coulis around the terrine slice.
3. Mound the mesclun at the back left corner of the terrine slice.
4. Arrange the olives on the coulis to the right of the terrine slice.

WARM BAKED BRIE WITH ENGLISH CHUTNEY AND WALNUTS

BUFFET APPETIZER OR CHEESE COURSE

Yield:
16–20 oz (0.5–0.6 kg)
Portions:
varies
Portion size:
varies

INGREDIENTS	U.S.	METRIC
Walnut pieces	6 oz	180 g
Baby Brie, 12–14 oz (350–400 g), 7–8 in. (17–20 cm) in diameter	1	1
Egg wash	1 fl oz	30 mL
Bottled English chutney, such as Major Grey's	8 fl oz	240 mL
Wheatmeal biscuits or other unsalted crackers	10–12 oz	300–360 g

PROCEDURE

PREPARATION

1. Chop the walnuts coarse.
2. Place them in a sieve and sift out the tiny particles.
3. Paint the edge and top of the Brie with egg wash and coat it with the walnuts. Press firmly so they adhere.
4. Place the Brie on a 12-in. (30-cm) round, heatproof serving platter and refrigerate it, uncovered, at least 1 hour.

HOLDING

Refrigerate, loosely covered with plastic film, up to 3 days.

FINISHING AND PRESENTATION

5. Preheat an oven to 400°F (204°C).
6. Place the tray of Brie in the oven and bake about 12 minutes, or until the nuts are crisp and the cheese is warm in the center.
7. Spoon the chutney onto the center of the Brie.
8. Arrange the biscuits around the Brie.
9. Serve on a hot tray or under warming lights.

VARIATIONS

PECAN-CRUSTED BRIE WITH PEACH CHUTNEY

Replace the walnuts with pecans. Replace the mango chutney with Peach Chutney (p. 681).

PASTRY-WRAPPED BRIE WITH POACHED PEARS

Omit the walnuts and chutney. Encase the Brie with an ⅛-in. (0.1-cm) thick sheet of commercial puff pastry. Decorate the top with puff pastry cutouts if desired. Bake until the pastry is puffed and golden. Serve with Port Poached Pears (p. 99) on the side.

TERMS FOR REVIEW

pasteurization
raw milk
homogenization
dairy product
beneficial microorganism
fresh dairy product
milk
milk fat
butterfat
milk solids
lactose
casein
whole milk
reduced-fat milk
cream
butter
whole butter
semisolid fat
clarified butter
unsalted/sweet butter
salted butter
artisan butter
whipped butter
compound/composed butter
fermented dairy product
fermentation
culture
culturing
coagulation
lactose intolerant
curdle
curds
whey
cheese
fresh cheese
fromage
chèvre
acidification
clabber
curdling
rennet
rennin
annatto
pasta filata
ripening (of cheese)
cheese vault
young cheese
mature cheese
interior ripening
surface ripening
bloom
aging (of cheese)
curing (of cheese)
cheddaring
sharp
eyes
blind
(to) inoculate
washed-rind strong cheese
fromage fort
hard cheese
guillotine
cheese pick
aged cheese
grana cheese
natural smoked cheese
flight
nose
button
direct-set culture
potted cheese

QUESTIONS FOR DISCUSSION

1. List the three basic components of milk. Explain the characteristics of each component, and describe how each component affects the quality of milk.
2. List the nine most widely available fresh dairy products in order of milk-fat content, from highest to lowest.
3. Explain the process of fermentation as it applies to fermented dairy products. List the five changes fermentation causes in milk.
4. Explain the differences between buttermilk, sour cream, crème fraîche, kefir, and yogurt.
5. Name and describe the two parts of the first step in cheese making. What ingredient is typically used for the first part? What ingredient is typically used for the second part?
6. Describe the processes that change a newly formed fresh cheese into a firm interior-ripening cheese. Give an example.
7. Describe the processes that change a newly formed fresh cheese into a soft surface-ripening cheese. Give an example.
8. Describe the processes that change a firm interior-ripening cheese into an aged cheese. Give an example.
9. Discuss the effects of pasteurization on milk to be made into cheese. Include in your discussion the types of cheese producers and how pasteurization pertains to them.
10. Write a cheese menu for a restaurant or catering operation.

Chapter 15

PREREQUISITES

Before studying this chapter, you should already

- Have read "How to Use This Book," pages xxviii–xxxiii, and understand the professional recipe format.
- Be proficient in fabricating meats, poultry, and seafood.
- Have read Chapter 12, "Sausages," understand the principles behind meat emulsions, and be proficient at preparing forcemeats.
- Have read Chapter 13, "Pâtés and Terrines," and be proficient at assembling and baking forcemeats.

Mousselines

Silky-smooth and light as air, a properly made mousseline is considered a test of the truly skilled chef. Served hot or cold, mousselines lend themselves to many presentation styles. Their delicate texture and subtle flavors appeal to the most demanding gourmets.

Mousselines were developed during the classical cuisine period, when they required many hours of intensive labor to prepare. Today, mousselines are still an important part of the garde manger repertoire. Fortunately, however, the availability of modern tools means they can be prepared more quickly and easily. Nevertheless, a good mousseline still demands careful ingredient selection and preparation, careful attention to mixing and cooking procedures, and an understanding of how mousselines work.

After studying this chapter, you should be able to

1. List the primary ingredients in mousselines and explain their functions.
2. Select proper meat, poultry, and seafood items for use in mousselines.
3. Prepare and cook mousselines.
4. Serve cold mousseline items correctly, and select appropriate sauces and garnishes for them.

INTRODUCTION TO MOUSSELINES

A ***mousseline*** is a light-textured, puréed forcemeat made of raw fish, shellfish, poultry, liver, or meat. While mousseline forcemeats are similar in many ways to other forcemeats you have studied, they differ in several important ways as well. These differences are explained in the following section.

Mousseline forcemeats may be poached or baked. In garde manger work, they are then cooled and chilled before they are served. However, they may also be served hot. Whether served hot or cold, mousselines are extremely versatile.

An individual cold mousseline may be unmolded onto a plate and served as an appetizer accompanied by a cold sauce. Mousselines may also be prepared in the form of a terrine, in which case they are sliced for service and presented in the same manner as the terrines in Chapter 13.

UNDERSTANDING MOUSSELINE FORCEMEATS

In order to successfully prepare mousselines—and to troubleshoot a mousseline that is not looking successful—it is essential to have a basic understanding of what happens when mousselines are mixed and cooked. The structure of a mousseline depends on two interconnected processes: emulsion and protein coagulation.

The Mousseline Emulsion

The preparation of a mousseline begins with creating a meat emulsion. As you recall, a culinary emulsion is a mixture of fat and a water-based liquid. In the emulsion of a mousseline forcemeat, most of the fat is derived from the fat content of the heavy cream. Most of the water is contributed by the water content of the meat and of the cream. The emulsion is created when the seafood, poultry, or meat is properly puréed and a thin stream of cream, just a little at a time, is whipped in.

Before food processors were invented, mixing mousselines was a two-step procedure. First the protein was very finely ground by hand or in a grinding machine, and then the ground mixture was placed in a mixer so the cream could be whipped into it. However, you can accomplish both tasks in a food processor, as described in the Procedure for Mixing and Testing Mousseline Forcemeats on page 611. To make a large amount of mousseline forcemeat, you can use a rotation chopper.

To make a successful mousseline forcemeat, the ingredients must be very cold. This is needed both to keep the milk fat from separating out of the cream and to prevent certain meat proteins from breaking down too quickly.

The emulsion that forms when you properly mix mousseline forcemeat ingredients functions primarily to hold the raw ingredients together as the mousseline's protein structure is being created. As the mousseline cooks, coagulation becomes the primary structure builder.

Protein Coagulation

Two types of protein coagulation form the structure of a mousseline.

Meat Proteins and the Primary Bind

Although it begins as an emulsion, a mousseline forcemeat is primarily held together, or bound, by the process of protein coagulation. The most important protein ingredient in a mousseline is the seafood, poultry, or meat. When puréed into very fine particles, the muscle tissue fibers in the meat are broken down, and the proteins they contain are released. The protein-based connective tissue that surrounds the fibers is also broken down. We call these proteins ***meat proteins***, whether the substance we are working with is meat, poultry, or seafood. Grinding enables these meat proteins to coagulate more quickly than when the meat is left intact. When the forcemeat is cooked and the proteins coagulate, they form a protein gel that makes up the primary structure of the mousseline.

Because the coagulation of meat proteins is the primary factor that holds the forcemeat together, the protein ingredient is called the ***primary binder***. The structure created by grinding or puréeing the primary binder ingredient is called the ***primary bind***. For a mousseline to hold together, you must grind and mix the primary binder correctly and choose the correct type of protein. Some types of seafood, poultry, and meat contain more usable meat proteins than others. The ingredients section beginning on page 608 gives information on the types of protein foods most suitable for mousselines.

Egg Proteins and the Secondary Bind

After it is puréed, a mousseline forcemeat's primary meat protein binder is diluted with a large quantity of cream. Because of this, the primary bind may not remain strong and stable. To strengthen the structure, you normally need to include an additional type of protein in the form of eggs. The additional coagulation of egg proteins helps create needed structure. Thus, in a mousseline, eggs function as a ***secondary binder***, and the structure formed by the coagulation of egg proteins is called the ***secondary bind***. Eggs are included with the meat protein as it is being puréed. The particular type of protein used for the mousseline determines whether whole eggs or egg whites are a better choice.

Whole eggs are composed of both egg yolks and egg whites. Egg whites consist almost totally of protein. They begin coagulating at about 140°F (60°C), and create a strong protein gel. Egg yolks contain a high proportion of fat and a lower proportion of protein. They begin coagulating at about 150°F (65°C) and create a weaker gel. The proportion of egg white and egg yolk added to a mousseline forcemeat is a factor in determining its structure as well as its flavor and color.

Cream Acting as the Lightener

After the meat protein is puréed and the egg added, the next step is to add the cream. In addition to the high proportion of milk fat in the cream helping form the mousseline's emulsion, the milk fat also gives the mousseline a rich, creamy mouthfeel. However, the most apparent function of the cream is to make the mousseline forcemeat light in texture. For this reason, the cream is referred to as the ***lightener***. The water in the cream dilutes the protein gel and, thus, loosens the mousseline's bind.

The amount of cream that should be added to a particular mousseline depends on a number of factors. These include the strength of the primary and secondary binders and the desired texture of the finished mousseline.

INGREDIENTS FOR MOUSSELINES

Although meat and poultry can be used to make mousselines, seafood mousselines are by far the most popular.

Seafood

Many kinds of seafood are ideal for making mousselines because they have a soft, tender muscle structure that is high in the proper type of meat proteins.

The following seafood items are listed in the general order of bind strength, with the first-listed items being those that create the strongest primary bind.

- Scallops
- Lobsters
- Shrimp
- White-fleshed fish
- Salmon

While you can prepare a seafood mousseline using only one kind of seafood, it is common to use a mixture of seafood items. This is done not only to yield interesting flavor combinations but also to improve the mousseline's bind. For example, strongly binding scallops are frequently added to a salmon mousseline that might be too soft if made from salmon alone.

Meats and Poultry

The meat of young animals is the proper choice for mousselines because it is rich in connective tissue proteins. These meats are recommended for use in mousseline forcemeats:

- Fryer chicken breast
- Duckling breast
- Breast of young game birds
- Loin of veal
- Top round of veal
- Calf or chicken liver

Eggs

Seafood items that create a stronger bind need a less powerful secondary binder ingredient. Therefore, they are often bound with lower-protein whole

Guidelines for Meats Used in Mousselines

- Use tender cuts from young animals.
- Use only pale-colored meats. If red meats were to be used in a mousseline forcemeat, the resulting product would have an unappetizing gray-brown color.
- The meat must be raw. *Do not attempt to make a mousseline forcemeat with cooked meat.* The protein in cooked meat has already coagulated and thus cannot contribute to mousseline structure.
- Use meat having little or no interior fat.
- Trim the meat completely free of deposit fat. Solid animal fat is not included in mousseline forcemeats.

eggs or egg yolks. Meats that create a weaker bind often must be bound with high-protein egg whites to give them more structure. While your mousseline must contain enough secondary binder ingredient to hold it together, be careful not to add too much. Mousselines that have too much egg white added are tough and rubbery.

Cream

In order that the fat content is high enough to create a strong emulsion, you must use heavy cream having 36 percent milk fat or higher. The cream must be fresh and smooth, and show no signs of curdling or acidity.

Seasonings and Flavorings

You must season your mousseline forcemeat with enough salt and other flavorings to give it a good taste but not so heavily as to mask the basic flavor of the seafood or meat. Some flavorings, such as saffron and tomato paste, add color as well as flavor. Whatever seasonings and flavorings are used, they must not mar the smooth texture of the mousseline. Spices, herbs, and aromatics must be minced extremely fine. Vegetables must be puréed and then reduced (moisture cooked off) so as not to dilute the forcemeat.

In addition to salt, finely ground white pepper is commonly used to flavor mousselines. Here are additional suggestions for mousseline seasonings and flavorings.

- Minced citrus zest
- Minced shallots
- Minced fresh herbs
- Ground saffron or a saffron infusion
- Pale-colored fortified wines, such as sherry and Madeira
- Vegetable pastes and purées

The Science of Heat and Mousseline Structure

When proteins are heated, they gradually change form. They first bond to each other in a netlike structure that captures and holds moisture. Then they begin to shrink and tighten. Because of this, meats and other protein foods are firmer when cooked than when raw. As the protein network shrinks, it squeezes out some of the moisture.

Because a raw mousseline mixture is a soft paste rather than a solid piece of fish or meat, we rely on the bonding quality of proteins to change the paste into a solid food. The main proteins are ***myofibers*** and ***collagen***. When the temperature inside the mousseline mixture reaches about 120°F (48°C), the myofiber proteins start to coagulate and bond to each other, forcing out moisture. Most of this moisture, however, remains trapped in the protein network. As the temperature continues to rise, the collagen molecules also shrink and bond to each other.

The mousseline achieves its optimal structure at 140°–150°F (60°–65°C). Its protein structure is now solid, but the proteins have not shrunk so much that they have forced out much moisture. At this point the mousseline is smooth, moist, and flavorful. However, if it is heated to too high a temperature or for too long a time, the proteins shrink to the point where much of the moisture is forced out. The result is a grainy, crumbly protein mass surrounded by watery liquid.

Meat proteins forming a net

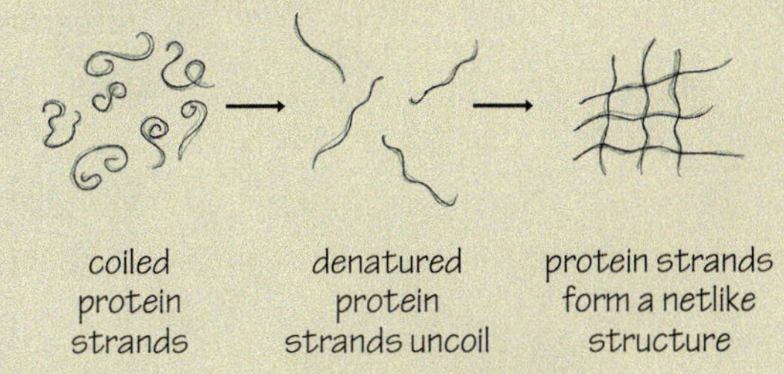

Proper coagulation and over-coagulation

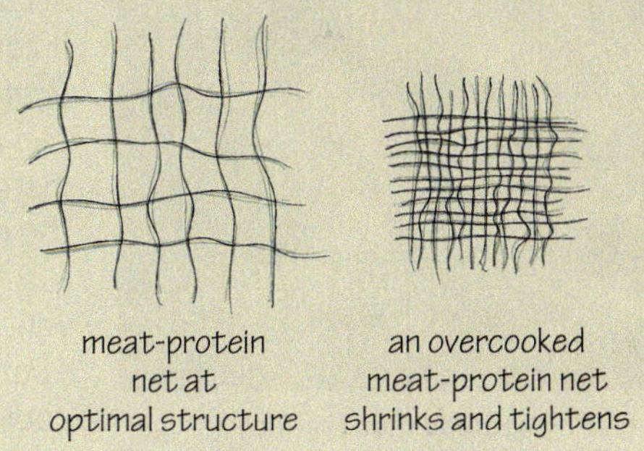

PREPARING MOUSSELINE FORCEMEATS

You must follow several important procedures and observe certain precautions in order to achieve a superior mousseline.

Fabrication and Straining for Smoothness

Because smoothness is of the utmost importance in a mousseline, it is important that the seafood, poultry, or meat intended

Seafood mousseline being forced through a tamis

for mousselines be free of fat and connective tissue. Poultry and meat may have large amounts of both internal and external connective tissue and may have visible deposit fat. Trim these ingredients carefully.

Once the meat protein is puréed with the eggs, cream, and other ingredients, the resulting forcemeat is forced through a ***tamis*** [tam-EE], or fine-mesh drum sieve, to remove any last trace of solid animal fat or connective tissue.

Temperature Requirements

Keep all ingredients ice-cold at all times. Thoroughly chill all equipment that will come into contact with the ingredients, and keep the seafood, poultry, or meat, and other ingredients in the refrigerator or in an ice bain-marie. Work in small batches, and proceed as quickly as possible.

Mixing Procedure

When making a mousseline forcemeat, mix the ingredients in the proper order. The meat protein, egg, and flavorings are first ground together in a food processor. Only when these ingredients have been reduced to a fine, smooth purée can you add the cream. The cream must be added gradually, in a thin stream, through the feed tube while the machine is running. *If you do not follow this procedure, the emulsion may break.*

Stop the processor as soon as the cream is fully incorporated into the puréed meat. An overprocessed mousseline can become tough and rubbery when cooked. In addition, overprocessing can incorporate too much air and make a mousseline unpleasantly loose and puffy in texture.

Evaluating the Bind

Both the desired bind of the forcemeat and the resulting density of the finished mousseline depend on its intended use. A mousseline preparation that is meant to be unmolded and sliced must be more solid and tightly bound. For poached quenelles or for small, individual mousselines that will be unmolded, a medium bind is desired. Mousselines that will be used as fillings, and ones that will be served in cups or ramekins, can be made very light and soft.

The texture of a finished mousseline depends on the ratio of binding ingredients to lightening ingredients. Here is a basic ingredients ratio for mousseline forcemeats:

BASIC MOUSSELINE FORMULA

1 lb (0.5 kg) meat

1½ oz (45 g) egg whites

12 fl oz (360 mL) heavy cream

This is a basic, general formula. This ratio of ingredients must be adjusted to accommodate the meat protein contents of various seafoods, poultry, and meats. It can also be adjusted to create mousselines of varying textures. In general, *the lightener ingredients work against the binder ingredients, and vice versa*. For example, if you wanted to change the formula of a soft chicken mousseline filling to instead make a firm, sliceable chicken terrine, you would need to either increase the egg whites or decrease the cream.

Poach testing seafood mousseline forcemeat

When you have finished mixing a mousseline forcemeat recipe that is new to you, cook off a small sample in order to evaluate its bind. Cooking and tasting a sample helps you evaluate the seasoning, as well. The most efficient way to cook a forcemeat sample is to wrap a small cylinder of forcemeat in plastic film and poach it. This procedure is called a ***poach test***.

Procedure for Mixing and Testing Mousseline Forcemeats

1. Chill the bowl and blade of a food processor. Have all ingredients very cold.
2. Thoroughly trim the protein ingredient of all fat and connective tissue and, if necessary, cut it into 1-in. (2.5-cm) dice. Place the fabricated protein in an ice bain-marie as you work.
3. Weigh the protein ingredient and, if necessary, divide it and the other ingredients into batches that will fit into your food processor without overloading it. Keep it on ice as you do so.
4. Place the chilled protein ingredient in the chilled processor along with a measured amount of cold eggs/egg whites and seasonings. Purée them just until smooth.
5. With the blade running, stream a measured amount of very cold heavy cream through the feed tube. Purée the mixture only until the cream is incorporated.
6. Remove a 1-oz (30-g) sample of mousseline and place the processor bowl in the refrigerator.
7. Perform a poach test on your sample (see p. 610).
8. Taste the sample and make any corrections needed.
9. Force the mousseline through a tamis set over an ice bain-marie.
10. Transfer the finished mousseline forcemeat to a container and place it on ice or in the refrigerator.
11. If necessary, proceed with additional batches, maintaining the correct formula. Combine the batches when complete.
12. Refrigerate the completed mousseline forcemeat.

Cooking Mousselines

Mousseline forcemeats need moist, low heat in order to turn out smooth and tender. They may be baked in a form or shaped into quenelles and poached.

Molded mousselines and mousseline-based terrines are baked at low temperatures in a hot bain-marie, or water bath. They are always covered, usually with parchment and then aluminum foil, to prevent the top surface from drying out or browning. With any foil covering, care must be taken to prevent wicking. Molded mousselines are generally cooked to an internal temperature of 145°F (62°C), or until they are just set. They then reach a final internal temperature of about 150°F (65°C) through carryover cooking.

Quenelles are delicate ovals of mousseline poached in barely simmering water or in a *cuisson* (see p. 193). Quenelles are typically served hot, although they are occasionally presented cold. The doneness of quenelles is usually judged by touch. When cooked through, a quenelle is lightly springy and does not squash under light pressure.

Storing Mousselines

Once it has cooled to room temperature, a mousseline must be immediately refrigerated. Like pâtés, mousselines acquire a better flavor and texture after 24 hours of mellowing.

The holding time for a cooked mousseline varies with the perishability of the main ingredient. Mousselines made from seafood or liver must be used within about 48 hours, while a chicken mousseline may be kept under refrigeration up to five days.

Wicking

Wicking occurs when the foil covering of a baking dish extends into the water bath in which the dish is placed. As the product bakes, water is drawn up under the foil and seeps into the interior of the dish. Excess wicking can interfere with the ingredients ratio in a mousseline (or custard) and cause it to become loose and grainy. To prevent wicking, fold the foil covering up to create a cap that seals tight but does not touch the water.

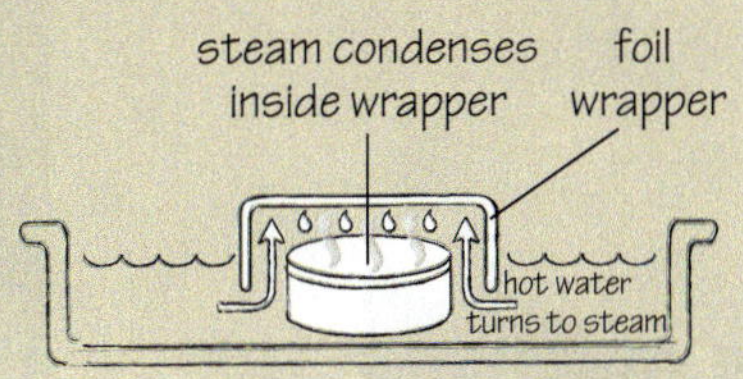

Presenting Cold Mousselines

Sometimes mousselines are intended to be reheated by the hot kitchen and served as hot appetizers. However, many are served cold. Mousseline-based terrines are sliced and served in the same manner as pâtés, either in platter or plate presentation. Individual mousselines are plated. In either case, they are usually served with a sauce and one or more garnishes, and sometimes with additional accompaniments.

SEAFOOD MOUSSELINE FORCEMEAT

Yield:
about 1½ qt (1.5 L) or 2 lb (1 kg)

INGREDIENTS	U.S.	METRIC
White wine	4 oz	120 mL
Minced shallots	½ oz	15 g
Perfectly trimmed raw fish, shrimp, lobster, scallops, etc., cold	1 lb	0.5 kg
Fine salt	to taste	to taste
Finely ground white pepper	to taste	to taste
Fish glace or shellfish glace (optional)	1 tsp	5 mL
Egg whites, cold	2 oz	60 g
Heavy cream, very cold	1 pt	0.5 L

PROCEDURE

PREPARATION

1. Place a food processor bowl and steel blade in the freezer.
2. Combine the wine and shallots in a small sauté pan and reduce over moderate heat to 1 tbsp (15 mL) liquid. Set the pan in an ice bain-marie until the liquid is cold.
3. If necessary, cut the seafood into 1-in. (2.5-cm) dice.
4. Mix the mousseline:
    a. Place the cold reduction, the seafood, and the salt, pepper, glace, and egg whites in the processor. Pulse a few times to grind and combine the ingredients.
    b. Turn on the processor and reduce the ingredients to a smooth purée without over grinding.
    c. Immediately pour the cream in through the feed tube in a thin stream (A).The finished mixture should be light, fluffy, and homogenous.
5. Perform a poach test (B) as directed on page 610.
6. Make necessary adjustments to the texture and seasoning using the information on pages 610 and 611.
7. Force the mixture through a tamis or fine-mesh sieve (C) into a bowl set in an ice bain-marie.
8. Proceed with a recipe or transfer to a freshly sanitized, covered container. Refrigerate until needed.

HOLDING

Refrigerate up to 12 hours.

A

B

C

CONFETTI SEAFOOD SAUSAGES

Yield:
about 2 lb (1 kg)
Portions:
10
Portion size:
3 oz (90 g)

INGREDIENTS	U.S.	METRIC
Blanched and refreshed brunoise-cut carrot	1 oz	30 g
Blanched and refreshed tiny peas or brunoise-cut peeled asparagus stems	1½ oz	45 g
Pimento or roasted and peeled red bell pepper (p. 109), brunoise-cut	1½ oz	45 g
Truffle peelings, drained, blotted dry, brunoise-cut (optional)	¼ oz	7 g
Egg white	½ fl oz	15 mL
Fine salt	to taste	to taste
Seafood Mousseline Forcemeat (p. 612), very cold	1½ qt	1.5 L
Hog sausage casing, prepared as directed on p. 478	6 ft (about)	2 m (about)

PROCEDURE

PREPARATION

1. Spread the vegetables on a clean, lint-free kitchen towel and blot them very dry.
2. Beat the egg white to foam and add the salt. Stir in the vegetables and toss to coat them with the egg white.
3. Fold the vegetables and the truffle peelings into the forcemeat.
4. Stuff the casing using a pastry bag and large round tip as directed on page 482. (If preparing a large quantity, it is more efficient to use a sausage stuffer.) Do not stuff the casings too full or they will burst when cooked.
5. Use kitchen string to tie off the sausage into 3-oz (90-g) links, each about 4 in. (10 cm) long. Refrigerate at least 1 hour.
6. Use a sterilized teasing needle (photo, p. 510) or pin to perforate the sausages at 1-in. (2.5-cm) intervals.
7. Bring a large pan of water to the simmer. Prepare a bowl of ice water.
8. Poach the sausages at a bare simmer, covered with a clean damp towel to keep them submerged. Poach about 10 minutes, or until the sausages reach an internal temperature of 140°F (60°C).
9. Immerse the sausages in the ice water and place the towel on top to keep them submerged. Refresh until cold.
10. Remove the sausages from the ice bain-marie and blot them dry. Wrap in butcher paper or parchment.

HOLDING

Refrigerate up to 3 days. May be frozen after step 5 for 1 month.

Seafood Sausages

Seafood sausages are sautéed in clarified butter and served hot, usually with a butter sauce, cream reduction sauce, or light tomato sauce. They are typically prepared by the garde manger department and turned out by the hot line.

SEAFOOD TURBANS

Portions:
10
Portion size:
3 oz (90 g)

INGREDIENTS	U.S.	METRIC
Butter, room temperature	½ oz	15 g
Skinless salmon fillet	8 oz	240 g
Skinless striped bass or red snapper fillet	8 oz	240 g
Sea salt or kosher salt	to taste	to taste
Finely ground white pepper	to taste	to taste
Fresh lemon juice	to taste	to taste
Fresh chives	¼ oz	7 g
Fresh tarragon	¼ oz	7 g
Cooked shrimp, small dice	4 oz	120 g
Seafood Mousseline Forcemeat (p. 610), made with 75% white-fleshed fish and 25% sea scallops	3 cups, about 1 lb	240mL, about 0.5 kg

PROCEDURE

PREPARATION

1. Preheat a standard oven to 300°F (150°C).
2. Butter ten 3-fl oz (90-mL) nonstick hemisphere forms (see Note). Place the forms on a sheet tray.
3. Carefully remove all pin bones, connective tissue, and dark fat deposits from the salmon and striped bass. Cut the fish on the diagonal into very thin, wide slices. Cut the slices into rough triangles about 2 × 2 × 2-in. (5 × 5 × 5-cm). You need 20 salmon triangles and 20 bass triangles.
4. Line each form with alternating triangles of fish (A). Overlap the fish triangles by about ⅛ in. (0.3 cm) to compensate for shrinkage.

A

5. Sprinkle the fish with lemon juice, salt, and pepper.
6. Mince the herbs and mix with the shrimp and about ½ cup (120 mL) of the mousseline.
7. Assemble the turbans:
   a. Pack each lined hemisphere form half full of mousseline.
   b. Divide the shrimp mixture into 10 equal portions and place a portion in the center of each hemisphere (B).
   c. Pack in the remaining mousseline. Press gently to firm the mixture into the forms.

B

8. Cover the hemisphere forms with a silicone pad or buttered parchment. Tap the tray firmly on the work surface to force out any air pockets.
9. Place the tray in the oven and pour about ½ in. (1 cm) very hot water into the tray under the hemisphere forms. Bake 30–35 minutes, or until the mousseline is very slightly puffed and just set in the middle.
10. Carefully remove from the oven without spilling the hot water. Place the tray on a rack. If you used a silicone pad on top, remove it and replace it with a sheet of parchment.
11. Cool the turbans to room temperature.
12. Refrigerate the turbans at least 4 hours, or until cold.

PROCEDURE

13. Wearing food-service gloves, carefully remove the turbans from the forms (C).
14. Place the turbans in a flat, parchment-lined plastic box or on a parchment-lined sheet tray. Cover the surface of each turban with a square of plastic film, and then put the lid on the box or wrap the sheet tray in plastic film.

C

HOLDING

Refrigerate up to 24 hours. For longer holding, do not remove from the forms, and refrigerate up to 3 days.

Note: If using a silicone form with 24 compartments to prepare only 10 units, space the turbans across the entire surface of the form.

SEAFOOD TURBAN

WITH SAFFRON RICE SALAD AND MICRO GREENS

MAIN COURSE

Portion:
1
Portion size:
6 oz (180 g), plus accompaniments

COMPONENTS

3 oz (90 g) *Saffron Rice Salad (p. 157)*
1 *Seafood Turban (p. 614)*
½ oz (15 g) Mild-flavored micro greens
3 fl oz (90 mL) *Basic Tomato Coulis Sauce (p.52)*, seasoned with red wine vinegar, in squeeze bottle
1 Poached and peeled 36–40 ct. shrimp

PROCEDURE

PLATING

1. Select an entremet ring of the same size as the base of your turban. Place it in the center of a cool 12-in. (30-cm) plate, pack it with the rice salad, and remove the ring.
2. Place the turban on top of the rice with its best side facing the front of the plate.
3. Squeeze the tomato coulis into the plate well.
4. Arrange the micro greens around the turban.
5. Place a shrimp on top of the turban.

SPRING VEGETABLE SEAFOOD TERRINE

Yield:
1 11½ × 3½ × 3½-in. (29 × 9 × 9-cm) terrine, about 3 lb (1.35 kg)

INGREDIENTS	U.S.	METRIC
Leeks	12 oz	360 g
Sugar snap peas	4 oz	120 g
Thick asparagus	5 oz	150 g
Granular gelatin	¼ oz	7 g
Cooked artichoke bottoms (p. 113 or frozen)	4 oz	120 g
Egg white	1 oz	30 g
Madeira	½ fl oz	15 mL
Fine salt	to taste	to taste
Pan coating spray	as needed	as needed
Seafood Mousseline Forcemeat (p. 612), made with equal parts shrimp, scallops, and fish	1 qt (about 1¾ lb)	1 L (about 0.75 kg)

PROCEDURE

PREPARATION

1. Preheat an oven to 300°F (150°C).
2. Bring a large pot of water to the boil. Prepare a bowl of ice water. Line a full sheet tray with clean, dry, lint-free towels. Prepare a terrine weight (p. 541).
3. Cut the dark green leaves off the leeks and reserve for another use. Cut off the roots and discard them. Slit the leeks lengthwise to the center, separate the layers, and rinse them.
4. Blanch the leeks until they are fork-tender, then immediately refresh them in ice water. Remove and blot dry on the towel.
5. Peel the carrots and cut them into ¼ × ¼ × 5½-in. (0.6 × 0.6 × 14-cm) bâtonnets. You will need 8 perfect bâtonnets.
6. Snap the ends off the snap peas and string them if necessary.
7. Peel the asparagus and cut each spear into 5½-in. (14-cm) lengths. (Reserve the tips for another use.) You will need 8 spears.
8. Cut the artichokes into ⅜-in. (1-cm) dice.
9. Separately blanch each type of vegetable *à point* (p. 91). (Do not allow the vegetables to remain crisp, or the terrine will not slice correctly.) Immediately refresh each vegetable when done. Drain the vegetables and blot them dry on the towel-lined tray.
10. Beat the egg white and Madeira to foam and add a little salt.
11. Assemble the terrine:
    a. Spray the inside of a 48-oz (1.4-L) 11½ × 3½ × 3½-in. (29 × 9 × 9-cm) terrine with pan coating. Line the terrine with heavy-duty plastic film, allowing a 4-in. (10-cm) overhang on all sides.
    b. Sprinkle the leeks with a light, even coating of granular gelatin. Use the leeks to line the terrine, gelatin-side up, overlapping them by about ¼ in. (0.6 cm). Allow about 3 in. (8 cm) of overhang on the long sides and 1½ in. (4 cm) of overhang on the short sides.
    c. Pack a ¾-in. (2-cm) layer of mousseline forcemeat into the terrine. Tap the terrine on the work surface to force out any air pockets.
    d. Dip the asparagus into the egg white wash and arrange the spears in 4 evenly spaced lengthwise rows. Press the vegetables gently into the mousseline forcemeat to keep them in place.
    e. Repeat steps c and d, using the carrots.

PROCEDURE

f. Repeat steps c and d, using the snap peas.

g. Repeat steps c and d, using the artichoke dice and ending with a layer of mousseline forcemeat. Tap the terrine sharply on the work surface to force out air pockets.

h. Fold the leeks up and over the mousseline forcemeat, starting with the short ends.

i. Wrap the plastic film up and around the top of the terrine and put on the lid. If the terrine has no lid, use a triple layer of foil folded to avoid wicking (p. 611).

12. Set the terrine on a rack in a deep hotel pan and add hot water to a level two-thirds up the side of the terrine.

13. Bake the terrine for 35 minutes, or to an internal temperature of 140°F (60°C).

14. Remove the lid of the terrine and weight the top (see photo, p. 552). Cool the terrine in the pan to room temperature.

15. Refrigerate the weighted terrine at least 12 hours.

HOLDING

Refrigerate uncut up to 4 days total. Once cut, use within 2 days.

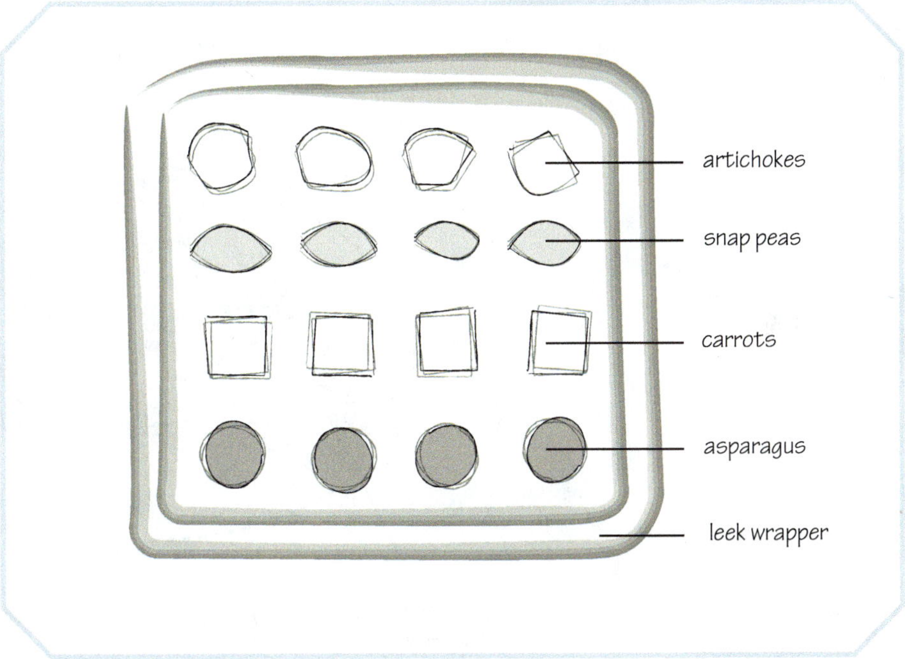

SPRING VEGETABLE SEAFOOD TERRINE

PLATE PRESENTATION

APPETIZER

Portion:
1
Portion size:
4 oz (120 mL), plus garnishes

COMPONENTS

5 3-in. (8-cm) asparagus spears, peeled, blanched *à point*, and refreshed
1 slice *Spring Vegetable Seafood Terrine (p. 616)*, ½-in. (1.25-cm) thick and about 4 oz (120 g)
2 fl oz (60 mL) *Lemon Mayonnaise Sauce for Seafood (p. 43)*, in squeeze bottle
1 Small carrot tumbleweed (p. 716)

PROCEDURE

PLATING

1. Arrange the asparagus spears on a cool 10-in. (25-cm) plate with the butt ends in the center and the tips fanned from 11 o'clock to 2 o'clock.
2. Place the terrine slice slightly front center, leaning on the butt ends of the asparagus.
3. Squeeze a pool of mayonnaise sauce around the right side of the terrine.
4. Place the carrot tumbleweed against the lower left corner of the terrine.

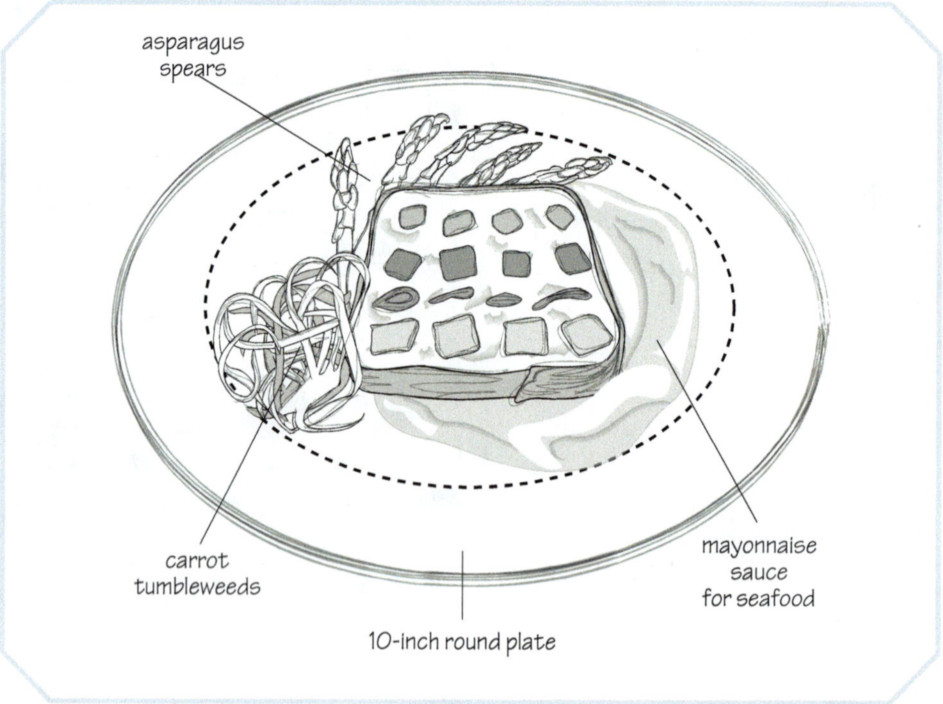

SPRING VEGETABLE SEAFOOD TERRINE

PLATTER PRESENTATION

BUFFET APPETIZER

Portions:
12–16, including unsliced section of terrine

Portion size:
3–4 oz (90–120 mL)

COMPONENTS

1 *Spring Vegetable Seafood Terrine (p. 616)*
1½ qt (1.5 L) *Seafood Aspic for Coating (p. 645)*, optional
1 oz (30 g) Mild flavor microgreens or parsley
3 Carrot tumbleweeds (p. 716)
3 cups (240 mL) *Lemon Mayonnaise Sauce for Seafood (p. 43)*

PROCEDURE

PRESENTATION

1. Cut the terrine into about six ½-in. (1.5-cm) slices, leaving a *grosse pièce* (p. 246) about 4 in. (10 cm) in length. Wipe the knife with a clean, damp towel between cuts. Reserve the heel slice (the first slice) as a prop for use in step 3.
2. If using aspic, coat the terrine and platter:
   a. Lay out the slices and the *grosse pièce* on a rack set on a sheet tray lined with parchment.
   b. Coat the *grosse pièce* and the slices as directed on page 643. Refrigerate until the aspic is set.
   c. Coat the well of a 14 × 20-in. (35 × 50-cm) rectangular platter with the remaining aspic. Refrigerate it on a level shelf until set.
3. Place the *grosse pièce* on one end of the platter. Cut the heel piece into a wedge-shaped prop and place it against the cut end of the *grosse pièce*. Lean the first slice against the prop, then overlap the remaining slices in a line down the length of the platter.
4. Arrange the micro greens and carrot tumbleweeds around the *grosse pièce*.
5. Serve the mayonnaise sauce on the side.

HOLDING

Refrigerate, uncovered, up to 6 hours

TRIANGLE TERRINE OF LOBSTER

Yield:
1 19×3×3×3½-in. (48×8×8×9-cm) triangle form, about 3 lb (1.5 kg)

Portions:
18 to 36

Portion size:
1⅓ to 2⅔ oz. (40 to 80 g)

INGREDIENTS	U.S.	METRIC
Live coldwater lobsters, preferably female, 1½ lb (700 g)	3	3
White wine	2 fl oz	60 mL
Trimmed dry-packed sea scallops, cold	4 oz (see Note)	120 g
Trimmed white fleshed fish, cold	4 oz (see Note)	120 g
Minced shallots	⅓ oz	10 g
Fine salt	to taste	to taste
Finely ground white pepper	to taste	to taste
Egg whites, cold	1½ oz	45 g
Heavy cream, cold	8 fl oz	240 mL
Minced chives	½ oz	15 g
Egg whites, beaten to foam	1 oz	30 g
Large savoy cabbage leaves	8	8
Granular gelatin	¼ oz	7 g

Note: Purchase a few oz (g) extra fish and scallops in case lobster yield is low. If presenting the terrine for buffet service, cut off and reserve the most attractive lobster head and tail section. Prepare as illustrated on page 718.

PROCEDURE

PREPARATION

1. Steam 2 of the lobsters for 25 minutes, or until just cooked through.
2. Bury the lobsters in ice and chill until cold.
3. Extract the meat from the remaining raw lobster:
    a. Place a cutting board inside a full sheet tray and place the remaining live lobster on it. Kill the lobster by plunging a chef knife into its head section just behind the first joint.
    b. Break the lobster open and remove all of the meat. Reserve the light-green tomalley and dark-green coral, if any (the coral turns red when cooked).
    c. Reserve the fluids from the cutting board and sheet tray. (Also reserve the soft, pale-colored shells for making stock.)
4. Chill the bowl and blade of a food processor. Prepare a bowl of ice water.
5. Weigh the raw lobster meat, coral, and tomalley. The total should be 8 oz (240 g) of raw lobster. If the raw lobster is underweight, make up the difference with additional scallops and/or fish to total 1 lb (0.5 kg) raw seafood when the lobster is combined with the scallops and fish.
6. Cut the raw lobster, scallops, and fish into 1-in. (2.5-cm) pieces and combine them in a bowl along with the coral and tomalley. Refrigerate until thoroughly cold.
7. Prepare the shallots and wine as directed in step 2 of Seafood Mousseline Forcemeat (p. 612).
8. Follow steps 4 through 7 of Seafood Mousseline Forcemeat to prepare a lobster mousseline forcemeat using the mixed raw seafood, shallots, salt, pepper, 1½ oz (45 mL) egg white, lobster fluids, and cream. Refrigerate the mousseline forcemeat until you are ready to pack the form.
9. Remove the meat, coral, and tomalley from the cooked lobsters (see Note). Cut the tail and claw meat into 1-in. (2.5-cm) chunks. Fabricate the scrap meat into rough brunoise cuts. Crumble the coral and tomalley.
10. Preheat a standard oven to 300°F (150°C). Prepare a terrine weight (p. 541).
11. Fold the brunoise lobster, crumbled roe, and tomalley into the mousseline forcemeat. Refrigerate it.
12. Mix the 1-in. (2.5-cm) lobster chunks with 1 oz (30 mL) egg whites, chives, salt, and pepper. Refrigerate.

PROCEDURE

13. Bring at least 1 gal (4 L) salted water to the boil.
14. Blanch the cabbage leaves for 30 seconds and refresh them in the ice water. Drain and blot them dry.
15. Lay the cabbage leaves flat on a cutting board and remove the thick center veins. Sprinkle the leaves with a light, even coating of powdered gelatin.
16. Assemble the terrine:
    a. Line a 19 × 3 × 3 × 3½-in. (48 × 8 × 8 × 9-cm) triangle form with heavy-duty plastic film. Allow about 2 in. (5 cm) overhang on the long sides.
    b. Line the form with the cabbage leaves, gelatin-side up, overlapping the pieces by about 1 in. (2.5 cm) (see photo). Allow 2 in. (5 cm) of cabbage to overhang on the long and short sides.
    c. Pack half the lobster mousseline forcemeat into the form. Tap it on the work surface to force out any air pockets.
    d. Arrange the lobster pieces in a row down the center of the form.
    e. Pack the remaining mousseline forcemeat into the form and tap out air pockets.
    f. Fold the overhanging cabbage leaves up around the top of the terrine.
    g. Fold the plastic wrap up and over the top of the terrine.
17. Place the form in a deep hotel pan. Add hot water to the pan to a level two-thirds up the sides of the form.
18. Bake the terrine 25 minutes, or to an internal temperature of 145°F (52°C).
19. Weight the terrine (see photo, p. 552). Cool it in the water to room temperature.
20. Refrigerate the weighted terrine 24 hours.

HOLDING

Refrigerate the uncut terrine up to 4 days total. Once cut, use within 2 days.

TRIANGLE TERRINE OF LOBSTER

PLATE PRESENTATION

APPETIZER

Portion:
1
Portion size:
2⅔ oz (80 g)

COMPONENTS

1 oz (30 g) Watercress
2 slices *Triangle Terrine of Lobster (p. 620)*, ½ in. (1.25 cm) and 1⅓ oz (40 g) each
2 fl oz (60 mL) *Lemon Mayonnaise Sauce for Seafood (p. 43)*, in squeeze bottle

PROCEDURE

PLATING

1. Place a bouquet of watercress on the back left of a cool 10-in. (25-cm) plate.
2. Lean a terrine slice against the watercress and overlap the other slice against the first.
3. Squeeze a pool of mayonnaise sauce in the plate well to the right and in front of the terrine slices.

TRIANGLE TERRINE OF LOBSTER

PLATTER PRESENTATION

BUFFET APPETIZER

Portions:
18 to 36
Portion size:
⅓ to 2⅔ oz. (40 to 80 g)

COMPONENTS

1 *Triangle Terrine of Lobster (p. 620)*
1 qt (1 L) *Seafood Aspic for Coating (p. 645)*, optional
1 set Lobster head and tail décor (p. 718)
2 oz (60 g) Watercress
36 Cherry tomatoes, large, hollowed and drained
12 fl oz (360 mL) *Cool Cucumber Rice Salad (p. 157)*, see Note
¼ oz (7 g) Minced chives
40 fl oz (1.2 L) *Lemon Mayonnaise Sauce for Seafood (p. 43)*

Note: The quantity of rice salad needed depends on the size of the cherry tomatoes. You may need more or less than the quantity indicated. Not all 36 garnitures will fit on the platter without crowding. Plan to replenish or serve separately.

PROCEDURE

FINISHING AND PRESENTATION

1. Unmold the terrine onto a cutting board.
2. Use a sharp knife to trim off the ends. Wipe the knife with a clean, damp towel between cuts. Cut the terrine into 36 perfect ½-in. (1.25-cm) slices.
3. If you choose to glaze the slices with aspic, place them on a rack set over a clean, grease-free full sheet tray. Proceed as directed on page 643, using the seafood aspic. Refrigerate the glazed slices until needed.
4. Place the lobster head on the far end of a 36 × 10-in. (90 × 25-cm) oval fish platter or presentation mirror. Surround it with watercress.
5. Arrange the terrine slices, overlapping slightly, in an *S* pattern down the length of the mirror. End with the lobster tail decorated with watercress. Refrigerate the platter.
6. Fill each cherry tomato with cucumber rice salad, mounding the rice on top. Place a dot of chive on top of each one.
7. Arrange the stuffed tomatoes along each side of the terrine slices.
8. Serve the mayonnaise sauce in a sauce boat.

HOLDING

Refrigerate, loosely covered with plastic film, up to 6 hours.

HERBED CHICKEN MOUSSELINES

Yield:
10 3 fl oz (90 mL) ramekins, about 2 lb (1 kg)
Portions:
10
Portion size:
3 oz (90 g)

INGREDIENTS	U.S.	METRIC
Butter	½ oz	15 g
Minced shallots	1 oz	30 g
White wine	3 fl oz	90 mL
Poultry Stock (p. 749)	4 fl oz	120 mL
Boneless, skinless chicken breast, preferably free-range	1 lb	0.5 kg
Egg whites, cold	2	2
Kosher salt	2 tsp	10 mL
Finely ground white pepper	to taste	to taste
Heavy cream, cold	14 fl oz	0.5 mL
Minced fresh chervil	¼ oz	7 g
Minced thyme leaves	⅛ oz	3.5 g
Minced chives	¼ oz	7 g
Minced tarragon	¼ oz	7 g
Grated lemon zest	2 tsp	10 mL

PROCEDURE

PREPARATION

1. Preheat an oven to 325°F (160°C).
2. Place the bowl and blade of a food processor in the freezer.
3. Butter the interior of ten 3-fl oz (90-mL) ramekins. Line the bottom of each with a circle of buttered parchment. Prepare a buttered parchment circle to fit the top of each ramekin. Prepare a square of doubled aluminum foil to fit the top of each ramekin.
4. Prepare an ice bain-marie.
5. Place the shallots, wine, and stock in a nonreactive pan and reduce the liquid almost to a glaze. Place the pan in the ice until the glaze is cold, then replace the bain-marie bowl.
6. Trim every trace of fat, silverskin, and connective tissue from the chicken breast. Cut it into 1-in. (2.5-cm) cubes. As you work, place the chicken cubes in the ice bain-marie to keep them very cold.
7. Place the chicken cubes, egg whites, salt, pepper, and glaze in the processor and grind the mixture to a smooth purée. With the processor running, quickly pour in the cream in a thin stream. Stop the processor as soon as the cream is incorporated.
8. Perform a poach test as directed on page 610. Taste and make necessary corrections.
9. Force the mousseline through a tamis or fine-mesh sieve into a clean bowl set in the ice bain-marie.
10. Wrap the herbs in the corner of a clean, dry, lint-free kitchen towel and wring them dry.
11. Mix the herbs and lemon zest into the mousseline to distribute them evenly.
12. Fill the ramekins with the mousseline. Tap each one on the work surface to force out any air bubbles. Smooth the top surface of each.
13. Place a parchment circle, buttered side down, on the surface of each ramekin. Cover the ramekins with foil, folding the edges up to prevent wicking, as illustrated on page 611.
14. Place the ramekins in a half-hotel pan and fill the pan with hot water to within ½ in. (1.25 cm) of the top of the ramekins. Do not allow the water to touch the foil caps.
15. Bake the mousselines about 20 minutes, or until they are just set (see Note).
16. Remove the pan from the oven and place it on a rack. Cool the mousselines to room temperature. Pour out the water and refrigerate the mousselines at least 6 hours.

HOLDING

Refrigerate up to 5 days.

(continues)

PROCEDURE *(continued)*

FINISHING

17. To unmold the mousselines, uncover them and run a knife around the edges to release them from the ramekins. Turn out the mousselines onto a parchment-lined tray or onto the service plate. Peel off the parchment. Serve with an appropriate sauce and garnish.

Note: The mousselines may be unmolded and served hot at this point, or may be cooled and chilled as in step 15 and then reheated to be served hot.

VARIATIONS

MOUSSELINE OF CHICKEN WITH WILD MUSHROOMS

Replace the herbs with 1 oz (30 g) dried cèpes or porcini mushrooms reconstituted in hot Madeira, then chopped, sautéed in butter, and chilled.

MOUSSELINE OF CHICKEN WITH LEEKS AND CARROTS

Line the sides of the ramekins with ribbons of very tender, pale-green poached leek. Omit the chervil, thyme, and chives. Stir in by hand 6 fl oz (180 mL) well-seasoned brunoise-cut poached carrots sautéed in butter until dry and then chilled.

HERBED CHICKEN MOUSSELINE

WITH TARRAGON SAUCE

APPETIZER

Portion:
1

Portion size:
3 oz (90 g) mousseline, plus accompaniments

COMPONENTS

1 Large Boston lettuce leaf
1 *Herbed Chicken Mousseline (p. 623)*, cool room temperature
1½ fl oz (45 mL) *Creamy Tarragon Mayonnaise Sauce (p. 43)*, in squeeze bottle
½ Cherry tomato
½ fl oz (15 mL) Unsweetened whipped cream or crème fraîche, in pastry bag fitted with star tip
3 1-in. (2.5-cm) chive tips
1 Chervil pluche
1 Thyme pluche
1 Tarragon pluche

PROCEDURE

PLATING

1. Place the lettuce leaf in the center of a cool 10-in. (25-cm) plate and gently flatten it.
2. Unmold the mousseline and place it slightly back center on the leaf. Be sure to remove the parchment liner.
3. Squeeze the mayonnaise into the leaf in an arc to the right front of the mousseline.
4. Place the tomato on the mayonnaise next to the mousseline.
5. Pipe a small rosette of whipped cream on top of the mousseline.
6. Gather the chive tips and herb pluches into a tiny bouquet and stick it upright in the rosette.

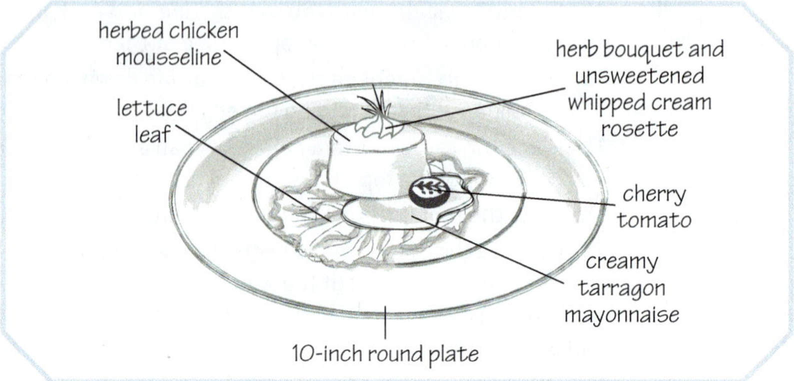

DUCK MOUSSELINE WITH JUNIPER

Yield:
1 1½-qt (1.5 L) terrine, about 3 lb (1.4 kg)
Portions:
16 to 32
Portion size:
1½ to 3 oz (45 to 90 g)

INGREDIENTS	U.S.	METRIC
Juniper berries, crushed	¼ oz	7 g
Fresh rosemary, crushed	1 sprig	1 sprig
Black peppercorns, crushed	⅛ oz	3.5 g
Shallots, thin slices	½ oz	15 g
Kosher salt	to taste	to taste
Gin	4 fl oz	120 mL
Skinless, boneless duck breast	1 lb	500 g
Pale, firm duck livers	¾ lb	350 g
Butter, at cool room temperature	8 oz	240 g
Egg whites, cold	2	2
Egg yolk, cold	1	1
Kosher salt	¼ oz	7 g
Heavy cream, cold	12 fl oz	360 g

PROCEDURE

DAY 1: FABRICATION AND PRE-SEASONING

1. Combine the juniper, rosemary, peppercorns, shallots, salt, and gin in a nonreactive container.
2. Trim off every bit of fat and connective tissue from the duck breasts. Cut them into 1-in. (2.5-cm) cubes. Place them in the container with the gin mixture.
3. Trim off the fat and connective tissue from the livers, blot them dry, add them to the gin mixture, and mix to coat the duck and livers with seasonings.
4. Cover the container and refrigerate it 24 hours.

DAY 2: PREPARATION

1. Preheat an oven to 325°F (160°C).
2. Moisten the inside of a 1½-qt (1.5-L) terrine form with cold water and pour out the excess. Line the terrine with plastic film, making sure the film is smooth and unwrinkled. Leave an overhang of about 3 in. (8 cm) on each side. Place the terrine in a half-hotel pan. Have ready a piece of doubled foil to cover the terrine form.
3. Prepare the forcemeat:
   a. Freeze grinder parts and the bowl and blade of a food processor.
   b. Place the butter in a mixer fitted with the whip attachment and beat it on medium speed to lighten it. Hold at cool room temperature until needed.
   c. Drain the gin mixture from the duck meat and livers. Pick out and discard the solid ingredients. Wipe the meat and livers clean of seasoning debris.
   d. Prepare an ice bain-marie set under the grinder head.
   e. Grind the duck meat through the coarse die into the ice bain-marie.
   f. Grind the duck meat through the fine die into the ice bain-marie twice.
   g. Place the duck meat, livers, egg whites and yolk, and ¼ oz (7 g) kosher salt in the processor and grind the mixture to a smooth purée. With the processor running, quickly add the cream in a thin stream.
   h. Transfer the forcemeat to a bowl and fold in the butter until no trace of it remains visible.
   i. Take out a 1-oz (60-g) sample and place the bowl in the refrigerator.
   j. Perform a poach test as directed on page 610. Taste and make necessary corrections.
4. Force the mousseline through a tamis or fine-mesh sieve into an ice bain-marie.
5. Pack the mousseline into the terrine form. Tap the form on the work surface to force out any air bubbles.

(continues)

PROCEDURE *(continued)*

6. Fold the plastic wrap up over the top surface of the mousseline. Cover it with the doubled foil. Fold the edges up to prevent wicking (p. 611).
7. Fill the pan with hot water to within ½ in. (1.25 cm) of the top of the form. Do not allow the water to touch the foil.
8. Bake the terrine about 1 hour, or until it reaches an internal temperature of 150°F (65°C). It will appear slightly puffed and set firm to the touch.
9. Remove the pan from the oven and place it on a rack. Weight the terrine (see photo, p. 552). Cool to room temperature.
10. Refrigerate the weighted terrine at least 24 hours.

HOLDING

Refrigerate, unopened, up to 10 days. Once opened, refrigerate up to 3 days longer.

VARIATION

MOUSSELINE DE CANARD AU PORTO

[oh PORT-oh]

Omit the juniper and rosemary. Replace the gin with red port wine. Add 1 fl oz (30 mL) additional red port wine along with the cream in step 3g.

JUNIPER-SCENTED DUCK MOUSSELINE

WITH ASPIC JEWELS

APPETIZER

Portion:
1
Portion size:
3 oz (90 g) mousseline, plus garnish

COMPONENTS

2 slices *Duck Mousseline with Juniper (p. 625)*, 1½ oz (45 g) each
1 sprig Fresh rosemary
1½ fl oz (45 mL) *Madeira Poultry Aspic Jewels (p. 708)*
5 Thin, freshly toasted baguette croûtons

Supplies

1 6-in. (15-cm) paper doily

PROCEDURE

PLATING

1. Overlap the mousseline slices diagonally across the center of a cool 10-in. (25-cm) plate.
2. Place the rosemary sprig to the left of the mousseline slices.
3. Spoon a mound of aspic jewels to the right of the mousseline slices.
4. Serve the croûtons on a doily-lined 8-in. plate.

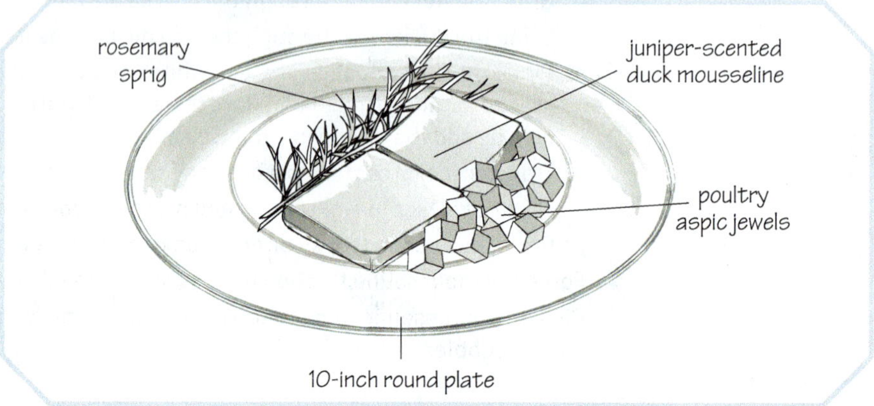

POULTRY MOUSSELINE DOMES WITH PRUNES AND ARMAGNAC

Portions:
12
Portion size:
3 oz (90 g)

INGREDIENTS	U.S.	METRIC
Boneless, skinless chicken breast, preferably free-range	12 oz	360 g
Boneless, skinless duck breast	7 oz	210 g
Large duck liver	2 oz	60 g
Kosher salt	to taste	to taste
Freshly ground white pepper	to taste	to taste
Armagnac	3 fl oz	90 mL
Large pitted prunes	6	6
Vegetable oil	½ fl oz	15 mL
Minced shallots	1 oz	30 g
Egg whites, cold	2	2
Heavy cream, very cold	8 fl oz	240 mL
Powdered dehydrated egg whites	pinch	pinch
White Poultry Aspic for Coating (p. 644)	1 qt	1 L

PROCEDURE

DAY 1: FABRICATION AND PRE-SEASONING

1. Remove all fat, silverskin, and connective tissue from the chicken breast. Cut it into ½-in. (1.25-cm) cubes and season it with salt and pepper. Place it in a plastic bag and refrigerate.
2. Remove all fat, silverskin, and connective tissue from the duck breast and liver. Separate the liver into 2 lobes. Separate the tender from the breast meat, remove the tendon, and add the tender to the chicken.
3. Place the whole duck breast and liver in a nonreactive container. Season them with salt and pepper and moisten them with 1 oz (30 mL) Armagnac. Cover and refrigerate 24 hours.
4. Place the prunes in a small container, cover them with the remaining Armagnac, cover the container, and hold at cool room temperature 24 hours.

DAY 2: PREPARATION

1. Preheat a standard oven to 325°F (160°C).
2. Freeze a food processor bowl and blade.
3. Place a 3-fl oz (90-mL) multiple hemisphere silicone mold on a sheet tray. Alternatively, line the insides of twelve 3-fl oz (90-mL) individual hemisphere forms with plastic film. If using freestanding forms, crumple foil into a hotel pan to support them without tipping. Set the molds firmly into the foil. Prepare 12 doubled squares of aluminum foil to fit the opening of each form.
4. Heat a nonstick pan very hot, add the oil, and sear the duck breast to brown its exterior, keeping the interior raw. Immediately place the duck breast, uncovered, in the freezer for about 20 minutes so it becomes firm enough to slice very thin.
5. Blot the liver, then sear the 2 lobes in the same way as the duck breast. Refrigerate them, uncovered, to cool.
6. Drain the Armagnac from the prunes and put it in the freezer.
7. Prepare the mousseline:
   a. Place the chicken, shallots, ⅛ oz (3.5 g) salt, pepper, and egg whites in the processor.
   b. Grind the chicken mixture to a smooth purée. With the processor running, quickly add the cream and Armagnac in a thin stream.
   c. Take out a ½-oz (15-g) sample and place the processor bowl in the refrigerator.

(continues)

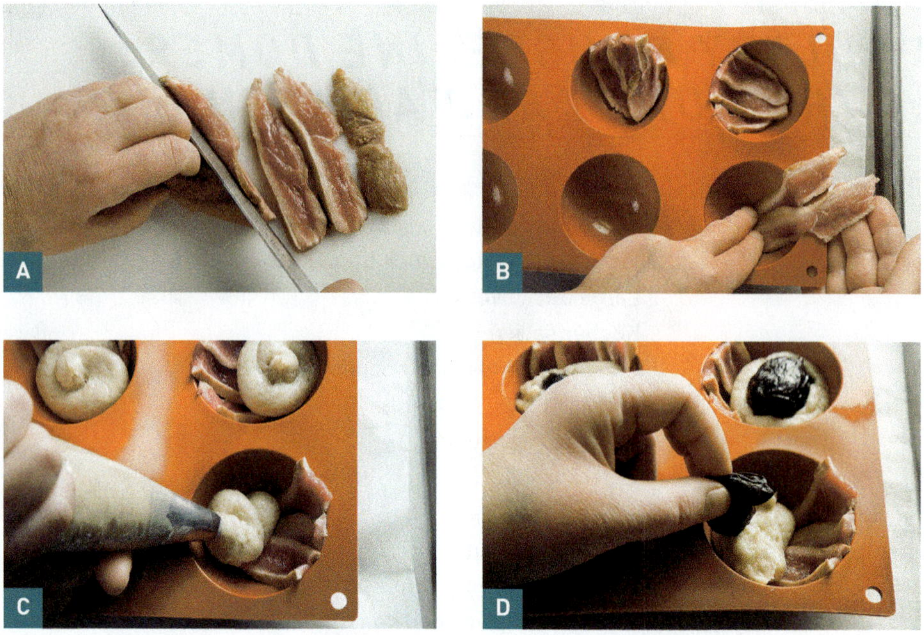

PROCEDURE *(continued)*

d. Perform a poach test as directed on page 610. Make necessary corrections.

e. Force the mousseline through a tamis or fine-mesh sieve.

f. Transfer the mousseline to a pastry bag fitted with a large round tip.

g. Slice the duck breast on a sharp diagonal to make 18 thin oblong slices (A). Reserve the end pieces for another use.

h. Cut each lobe of the liver into 3 pieces. Stuff each prune with a piece of liver.

8. Assemble the domes:

   a. Fan 3 slices of duck breast on the sides of each mold (B).

   b. Pipe in enough mousseline to fill the mold one-quarter full (C).

   c. Place a stuffed prune in each form (D).

   d. Fill the forms with the remaining mousseline.

   e. Tap the forms on the work surface to firm the mousseline and force out air pockets.

   f. Cover the silicone mold with a silicone mat. If using individual forms, cap each form with doubled foil, crimping up the edges to prevent wicking (p. 611).

   g. Pour enough hot water into the pan to come halfway up the sides of the forms.

9. Bake the mousselines about 25 minutes, or until they reach an internal temperature of 140°F (60°C).

10. Remove the pan from the oven, set another pan across the tops of the mousselines, and evenly distribute objects totaling about 2-lb (1-kg) weight across the surface of the pan. Cool to room temperature.

11. Refrigerate under weight at least 4 hours.

12. Unmold the domes onto a rack set over a sheet tray and glaze with two coats of aspic as directed on page 643.

HOLDING

Refrigerate in a freshly sanitized, lidded container up to 5 days.

ARMAGNAC POULTRY MOUSSELINE

WITH RED PLUM COULIS

APPETIZER

Portion:
1
Portion size:
1 3 oz (90 g) dome, plus garnish

COMPONENTS

½ Large, firm-ripe redskin plum, pitted (about 2 oz or 60 g)
1 *Poultry Mousseline Dome with Prunes and Armagnac* *(p. 627)*
1½ fl oz (45 mL) *Red Plum Coulis* *(p. 53)*, in squeeze bottle

PROCEDURE

FINISHING AND PLATING

1. Cut a ¼-in. (1-cm) slice from the cut surface of the plum and place it on a cutting board. Cut the remaining plum into ⅜-in. (1-cm) dice.
2. Use an offset spatula to place the mousseline dome on the plum slice. Cut a wedge equal to ¼ of its volume out of the dome/plum slice.
3. Use the offset spatula to place main section of dome/plum slice slightly left center on a cool 10-in. (25-cm) plate. Place the smaller wedge to its right.
4. Squeeze an arc of plum sauce around the dome pieces.
5. Scatter the plum dice on the plate.

TERMS FOR REVIEW

mousseline
meat protein
primary binder
primary bind
secondary binder
secondary bind
lightener
myofiber
collagen
tamis
poach test
quenelle
wicking

QUESTIONS FOR DISCUSSION

1. Explain the process of emulsification that sets up the initial structure of a mousseline. Include in your explanation the techniques, temperatures, and ingredients involved.
2. Explain the process of meat protein coagulation that creates a mousseline's final structure.
3. Why must all ingredients be kept cold when you are making a mousseline? Describe how to keep a mousseline forcemeat cold while you are working on it.
4. Explain what is meant by *primary bind* and *secondary bind*. What ingredients create the primary bind? the secondary bind?
5. What is the main purpose of heavy cream in a mousseline?
6. What characteristics make a particular cut or type of meat or poultry appropriate for use in mousselines? What characteristics make a particular fish or seafood item appropriate?
7. Describe the basic procedures for mixing and testing mousseline forcemeats.
8. At what general temperature are mousselines cooked? Why? What two cooking methods are used for cooking mousselines? Describe these methods as applied to mousselines.
9. Compare and contrast mousselines and mousses.
10. Discuss ways in which mousselines can be formed and presented for cold service. Include in your discussion choices for sauces, garnishes, and other accompaniments.

Chapter 16

PREREQUISITES

Before reading this chapter, you should already

- Have read "How to Use This Book," pages xxviii–xxxiii, and understand the professional recipe format.
- Have read Chapter 6, "Cold Seafood," and Chapter 7, "Cold Meats," and know how to prepare these foods for cold service.
- Be proficient at preparing and clarifying stock.
- Be proficient at preparing velouté and demi-glace sauces.

Aspic and Chaud-Froid

Coating cold foods with aspic and chaud-froid and enhancing their appearance with attractive, artistically designed edible décor are among the most challenging aspects of garde manger work. Stunning aspic and chaud-froid presentations are frequently the focal points of formal buffets, and they are important elements of culinary competitions.

The information in this chapter will help you understand the multiple processes involved in aspic and chaud-froid artistry. The knowledge and skills you acquire from studying this chapter, combined with practice and careful attention to detail, will enable you to create aspic and chaud-froid presentations that are both beautiful and delicious.

After reading this chapter, you should be able to

1. Use granular gelatin to properly gelatinize liquids into preparations of varying consistencies.
2. Prepare aspics, chaud-froid sauces, and mayonnaise collée.
3. Set up an efficient aspic and chaud-froid workspace.
4. Prepare various foods for coating.
5. Prepare and fabricate vegetables, fruits, and herbs for surface décor.
6. Coat foods with aspic, chaud-froid, and mayonnaise collée, and decorate them with attractive designs.
7. Prepare various dishes that are bound or molded with aspic, chaud-froid, and mayonnaise collée.

THE CHALLENGE OF ASPIC AND CHAUD-FROID WORK

Aspic and chaud-froid work is considered an advanced topic because it involves many preparation skills. First of all, the foods to be coated must be properly prepared, whether they are roasted, poached, or cooked by some other method. Making good coating sauces requires knowledge of several basic preparations you should have already learned. For example, you must be able to make a strong, well-balanced stock and clarify it properly. Correctly and efficiently applying coating sauces to foods requires skill in handling gelatin products. Creating and arranging the customary décor items on and around the coated items demands precision cutting and an artistic eye.

If you have studied the preceding chapters in this text and practiced the techniques presented in them, you should be ready to master the art of aspic and chaud-froid work. Let's begin by learning about the elements used in this challenging facet of garde manger work.

Understanding Coating Sauces

A ***coating sauce*** is a dressing for cold food that is fluid when warm but sets up into a gel when chilled. Aspic and chaud-froid are the two most important coating sauces used in the formal presentation of cold foods. A third coating sauce, called *mayonnaise collée*, is frequently used in place of chaud-froid. While all three contain gelatin, they are otherwise quite different in composition.

Aspic is clarified, seasoned stock with the addition of gelatin.

Chaud-froid [show-FWAH] is a cream velouté sauce or demi-glace sauce with the addition of aspic.

Mayonnaise collée [may-oh-NEZ koh-LAY] consists of thick mayonnaise and aspic.

Coating sauces gel because they contain a high proportion of gelatin. The original coating sauces made during the classical cuisine period gelled naturally. This is because traditional stocks were made with a high proportion of bones, meat, and connective tissue and were simmered for many hours. Today, most garde manger chefs use standard stocks of lighter consistency to make these sauces. Therefore, it is necessary to ***fortify***, or strengthen, the gelatin content by adding commercial gelatin.

When liquid gelatin is chilled, it quickly sets up and becomes firm. This enables a gelatin-rich sauce to adhere instantly to any piece of cold food with which it comes into contact. When this happens, the food's surface is sealed by the sauce. The application of a coating sauce protects foods from drying out and from contamination. If the coating sauce is properly prepared, it also contributes good flavor, a moist mouthfeel, and a smooth, shiny, attractive appearance.

Understanding Gelatin

Gelatin is a nearly colorless, nearly flavorless water-soluble substance derived from ***collagen***, an animal protein found in bones, cartilage, connective tissue, and hides. Collagen is extracted from these products by simmering them in water. When collagen combines with water in the correct way, it forms a protein net that captures the water and forms a ***protein gel***. When chilled, this gel appears as a solid, translucent, jelly-like mass. When heated, it is a thick, syrup-consistency liquid.

In the early twentieth century, industrial food producers perfected a way to remove the water from liquid gelatin and purify it of most of its meat flavor and odor. This product is called ***unflavored dry gelatin***. (There are also sweetened, flavored gelatin powder products, the best-known of which is Jell-O™. However, in this text when we refer to *gelatin*, we always mean "unflavored dry gelatin.")

Blooming Gelatin

Unflavored dry gelatin must be rehydrated before it is used. This is called ***blooming***. When the gelatin comes into contact with cool water or a water-based liquid, it absorbs the liquid and expands. Thus, when you rehydrate gelatin you are said to ***bloom*** it.

After blooming, the gelatin is usually mixed with additional liquid that is warm enough to completely dissolve it. When this liquid is then chilled, the protein gel forms, and the liquid is said to have *set*. The degree of firmness to which the liquid gels is called its ***set***.

Gelatin is available in two market forms. Each form requires a different blooming procedure.

GRANULAR GELATIN

To make ***granular gelatin***, liquid gelatin is dehydrated and ground into fine granules. This product is also called ***gelatin powder***. For food service, granular gelatin is sold in bulk containers usually weighing 1 lb (454 g). For domestic use, gelatin is sold in boxes of packets, each packet weighing ¼ oz (7 g).

Granular gelatin is bloomed by mixing it with a cold liquid in a ratio of roughly 1 part gelatin to 4 parts liquid by volume. The liquid can be water, stock, or a low-acid fortified wine. Granular gelatin reaches full bloom in about 10 minutes. At full bloom, the gelatin mixture appears as a solid, rubbery, grainy mass.

Once bloomed, granular gelatin may be added directly to hot liquid and stirred until it dissolves. You can also melt bloomed granular gelatin by placing its container in a hot bain-marie.

Granular gelatin produced in North America is consistent in bloom strength. This basic ratio is a good general guideline to use when determining how much granular gelatin to use:

¼ oz (7 g) or 2¼ tsp (11mL) sets 2 cups (0.5 L) liquid to a medium-consistency gel or set

Acidic ingredients and high amounts of salt decrease gelling power, while sugar and dairy products increase it. The enzymes present in raw pineapple, papaya, passion fruit, melons, ginger, kiwifruit, and figs interfere with the gelling process. These fruits must be cooked to at least 185°F (85°C) before adding them to the mixture to be gelatinized.

Granular gelatin (and some lesser-quality sheet gelatins) produces a slight yellow coloration and a barely perceptible meat odor in products in which it is used. These qualities are not as much of an issue in garde manger as they are in the pastry kitchen. Recipes in this text that utilize gelatin specify granular gelatin because it is less expensive and more widely available than sheet gelatin.

SHEET GELATIN

Sheet gelatin is extracted by the same method as granular gelatin, but it is dried in a different way. The liquid gelatin is poured into very shallow trays, dehydrated into a filmlike layer, and then cut into rectangular pieces. The result is very thin, brittle sheets of translucent gelatin. It is also called ***leaf gelatin***. Sheet gelatin is used more commonly in Europe than in North America.

Many culinary texts and other cooking authorities state that sheet gelatin and granular gelatin are interchangeable, weight for weight. This is not necessarily the case. European sheet gelatin is available in three strengths. When using sheet gelatin, refer to the manufacturer's specifications to determine the necessary ratio of gelatin to liquid.

Sheet gelatin can be stirred directly into hot liquid and dissolves quickly. It can also be bloomed by soaking it in 5 to 6 times its weight of very cold water.

Preparing and Using a Gelatinized Liquid

Gelatin is used to thicken, or ***gelatinize***, a liquid. Its preparation is a four-step process.

Step 1: Determine the Gelatin-to-Liquid Ratio

The first step in gelling a liquid is determining how much gelatin to use. The basic ratio of granular gelatin to liquid specified on page 633 creates a medium-consistency set. If you want to achieve a softer, more delicate set, decrease the gelatin amount. Conversely, if you want a firmer set, increase the gelatin amount.

Additional factors come into play when determining gelatin amount. In making acidic gelatin salads, a higher ratio of gelatin to liquid is needed. The original thickness of the mixture you want to gelatinize is also a factor in determining the amount of gelatin to use. If you are attempting to gel a sauce, such as a velouté or demi-glace, you will need less gelatin because the sauce was already thickened during the sauce-making procedure.

Step 2: Bloom the Gelatin

Bloom, or rehydrate the gelatin according to the type you are using or according to the recipe you are following.

Step 3: Dissolve the Bloomed Gelatin in the Liquid

Even after it has been bloomed, dry gelatin is still not completely rehydrated. When you mix it into the liquid, the gelatin is still visible. The liquid must be heated in order to thoroughly dissolve the gelatin. Stir the liquid so the gelatin does not fall to the bottom of the pan and scorch.

Protein gels are weakened by high heat or prolonged heating. Therefore, do not boil the gelatinized liquid nor hold it at a high temperature for a long time. Heat the liquid to 180°F (82°C) and hold it there until the gelatin is no longer visible.

Step 4: Cool the Gelatinized Liquid to Working Consistency

Cooling gelatinized liquid to working consistency.

Once the gelatin is dissolved, the liquid is ready to be cooled. The efficient way to do this is to pour the gelatinized liquid into an ice bain-marie. Stir constantly so it cools evenly. (If you do not stir it, it will set along the surface of the bowl before the rest of the liquid sets.) Stir slowly and gently so as not to incorporate air bubbles, which would mar the smooth texture of the final product when it sets. While the gelatinized liquid is cooling, carefully watch its changing consistency.

For every preparation there is a particular gel consistency at which the gelatinized liquid must be used. This is called its ***working consistency***. In general, the gelatinized liquid must be thick enough to stick to a food item but not so thick that it forms lumps. Many recipe directions specify gelatinized liquid cooled until "***syrupy***," which means a consistency similar to that of maple syrup. A gelatinized liquid cooling in an ice bain-marie changes texture very quickly and can go from syrupy to set in just a few seconds. The trick is to remove the bowl from the ice at precisely the right time.

If the gel sets up too quickly, you can remelt it and then cool it once again. If you are careful, you may reheat the gelatinized liquid in the stainless-steel bowl you used for the ice bain-marie. Simply hold the bowl over the stove burner with a dry, folded towel and stir it until it melts.

Once a gelatinized liquid is at the proper consistency, it must be used immediately. The gelatinized liquid may be poured over a chilled food item, to which it will stick. Alternatively, a small food item may be dipped into it. The food is then refrigerated until the gel sets up. A gelatinized liquid can also be used to line a form, plate, platter, or tray.

ASPIC

Aspic is a translucent, gelatinized coating that adds sparkle and shine to the products it enhances. It was originally used to form a protective barrier on foods that were set out on buffet tables for lengthy periods. Aspic has several culinary names. In French it is called ***aspic gelée*** [ahss-PEE(K) zhe-LAY]. In English its correct, full name is ***aspic jelly***, although in North America the name is usually shortened to simply *aspic*. In classical cuisine, true *aspic gelée* begins with ***gelée de viande*** [zhe-LAY duh VYAHND], or ***meat jelly***.

Meat jelly is the term used to describe stocks and meat-cooking juices that have enough natural gelatin to gel when chilled. However, these cannot be called aspics until they are clarified and seasoned. Seasoning is important because, unless you are creating a showpiece for visual display only, the aspic should add flavor to the food as well as color and shine.

Meat aspics are classified both by color and by the type of stock with which they are made. For example, a brown aspic made from beef stock could be called *brown beef aspic*. Some alternative aspics not based on stock are now part of the garde manger repertoire.

White poultry aspic is made from white chicken stock, turkey stock, or stock made from white-fleshed game birds. Although it is called *white*, properly made white poultry aspic has an attractive golden color.

White seafood aspic is made from fish stock, shellfish stock, or a mixture of both.

Brown aspic is made from brown stock. Classically, this stock is made from a mixture of veal and beef parts. Because of the high cost of veal bones, many chefs now prepare brown stock from only beef bones and meat. Brown aspic can also be prepared from brown poultry or game bird stock.

Meatless aspic is made from wine, fruit juices, vegetable juices, *cuissons*, or a combination of these ingredients. They are called *meatless* because they are not based on stock. However, as gelatin is a meat product, the term *meatless aspic* is not technically correct unless a vegetable-based gelling agent is used (see the sidebar at right.

Vegetable-Based Gelling Ingredients

Agar-agar is a gelling ingredient made from red algae or seaweed. It is also known as *kanten* or *China grass*. Culinary agar-agar is extracted from the plant, dried, and sold in strips or powdered form. Agar-agar is traditionally used in Asian desserts and is sold primarily in Asian markets.

Carrageenan is a jelling ingredient processed from several species of seaweed. It is used primarily in industrial food processing and is present in many ice creams, frozen drinks, sauces, and processed meat products.

Preparing Aspic

There are four steps in the preparation of aspic.

Step 1: Obtain the Stock

Begin with a strong, well-made stock. Taste and evaluate the stock to ensure it is of the proper strength and clarity. If you prepare the stock yourself—especially a brown stock—start at least one day ahead, as it is a lengthy procedure. It must be strained, chilled, and thoroughly defatted before it can be used to prepare aspic.

If you are making a meatless aspic, you will need to prepare the base liquid.

Step 2: Clarify the Stock

Once you have obtained a well-made, full-flavored stock for aspic work, your next step is to ***clarify*** it, or make it clear. Clarifying removes impurities such as fat, scum, and meat or vegetable particulate matter through the process of protein coagulation. The primary protein ingredient used for clarification is egg whites. (A recipe for clarified stock appears in the Appendix on p. 748.)

The transparency of aspic is one of its key characteristics. This is referred to as its ***clarity***, or clearness. To achieve proper clarity, perform the clarification process correctly and carefully. The process reduces the amount of unclarified stock you started with, sometimes by as much as 20 percent. Thus, if you need 1 qt (1 L) aspic, you must start with at least 40 fl oz (1.25 L) stock.

Step 3: Season the Clarified Stock

Season the correct amount of clarified stock with salt and, if desired, additional flavorings. It is best to add salt while the clarified stock is still warm so the salt dissolves quickly. However, you should add other seasonings, and taste and evaluate the stock, at room temperature or slightly colder, because that is the temperature at which the aspic will be served.

The seasonings must not destroy clarity. For example, do not add ground pepper because the flecks of pepper will mar the crystal-clear appearance of the final product. Instead, add solid seasonings during the clarification process.

Seasonings added after clarification is complete are usually liquid seasonings. Here are some ideas for aspic seasonings.

Fortified wines, such as port, sherry, Madeira, and vermouth

Liqueurs, such as Grand Marnier and crème de cassis

Citrus juices

Clear vegetable juices

Step 4: Add the Gelatin

The final task is to add the proper amount of gelatin. The amount of gelatin you add depends on the use for which the aspic is intended.

Aspics are used for three basic purposes at three gel strengths.

Delicate aspic is used as a spoonable garnish and in making jellied consommés. It contains a low proportion of gelatin.

Aspic for coating is used to glaze cold foods. It is also used as a finish coat added over a previous coating of chaud-froid or mayonnaise collée.

Aspic at this strength is added to velouté and demi-glace sauce to make chaud-froid. It contains a moderate proportion of gelatin, the same as the basic ratio you have already learned.

Aspic for slicing is used to line forms such as timbales, ring molds, and silicone forms. It also is used to bind the ingredients for aspic-based terrines. Aspic for this purpose must hold its shape at cool room temperature and must cut cleanly with a hot, sharp knife. It contains a high proportion of gelatin. However, it must not be tough or rubbery.

When adding gelatin to the clarified, seasoned stock, follow the steps for gelatinizing a liquid listed on page 634.

CHAUD-FROID

Chaud-froid is an opaque coating sauce used to mask foods. To **mask** means to cover a food in such a way that its surface is no longer visible. For this reason, the two opaque coating sauces, chaud-froid and mayonnaise collée, are also called ***masking sauces***.

The French name *chaud-froid* literally means "hot-cold," referring to the fact that the sauce is made hot but served cold. This term dates from the early classical cuisine period, when cooked foods often sat on a table for a long time. When hot foods cooked in these sauces cooled, the rich, thick sauces set up into a gel and thus enveloped the foods in a smooth, tasty coating.

The term *chaud-froid* actually has two meanings: It describes a dish of food coated in chaud-froid sauce and also the coating sauce itself.

Today, chaud-froid sauce is primarily used for coating previously cooked and cooled foods and, thus, is prepared separately. While the original chaud-froid sauces contained egg yolks, modern garde manger chefs usually omit the yolks for handling and food safety reasons. Like aspics, chaud-froid sauces are classified both by their color and by the stock that was used to make their base sauce.

White poultry chaud-froid sauce is a velouté sauce made from chicken stock or other white poultry stock, enriched with heavy cream and fortified with poultry aspic.

White seafood chaud-froid sauce is a velouté sauce made from fish stock or shellfish stock, enriched with heavy cream and fortified with seafood aspic.

Brown chaud-froid sauce is a demi-glace sauce made from brown veal, beef, or game stock, fortified with brown aspic. Caramelized sugar is often added to this sauce in order to deepen its color. Brown chaud-froid is used less frequently than white chaud-froid.

Tinted chaud-froid sauces are a more recent development. White chaud-froid sauces are simmered with an ingredient that adds its color to the sauce. Examples are spinach (green), beets (magenta), and saffron (yellow). The coloring ingredient must be strained out of the sauce before it is used.

The History of Chaud-Froid

According to Philéas Gilbert, an early-twentieth-century chef and food writer, chaud-froid foods were popularized by the Maréchal de Luxembourg, a French aristocrat. In 1759, at the start of a grand banquet at his Château de Montmorency, the Maréchal was suddenly called away to the royal council. The banquet went on without him. However, the chefs saved portions of each dish for their employer and reheated them for him when he returned late that night. Only one dish could not be reheated—a creamy fricassee of chicken that had been finished with egg yolks. The chefs rightly reasoned that if such a sauce were to be reheated, it would curdle. So the dish was presented to the Maréchal cold, enveloped in its thick, gelatinous sauce. Due to the preserving qualities of the gelatin, this dish survived the wait far better than the other foods, and the Maréchal pronounced it delicious—so delicious, in fact, that he demanded that it be served at all future banquets. The next time it was served, the dish was presented as a *refroidi*, or "cooled dish." However, the Maréchal insisted that it be called a *chaud-froid*, as defined by the Maréchal, meaning "first hot, then cold."

Preparing Chaud-Froid Sauce

The preparation of chaud-froid sauce requires the combination of two stock-based products. It is a multistep procedure.

Step 1: Obtain the Stock

As for aspic, chaud-froid preparation begins with making or obtaining a good stock. The information on stock for aspic on page 636 also applies to chaud-froid.

Step 2: Prepare the Base Sauce

Next, prepare the velouté or demi-glace sauce that forms the base of the chaud-froid preparation. For high-quality sauce chaud-froid, you must start with a base sauce that is full-flavored, smooth, and of the proper nappé consistency.

It is best to prepare the base sauce at least one day ahead and refrigerate it overnight before modifying it. The flavor of most sauces improves with mellowing time. The rest also allows any excess fat that might be in the sauce to rise to the surface and solidify for easy removal. The presence of fat in a base sauce for chaud-froid work may cause the finished sauce to be grainy and have a poor mouthfeel.

If you are able to requisition the sauces you need from the hot kitchen, taste and evaluate them and make any adjustments you believe are necessary.

Step 3: Prepare the Aspic

The best and most efficient way to gelatinize the base sauce is by adding aspic to it. While it is true that you can simply thin the base sauce with stock and then add bloomed gelatin to it, this method does not produce the best appearance. The clarity of the aspic adds shine to a chaud-froid sauce.

Preparing the aspic does not actually constitute extra work because virtually all chaud-froid coatings are finished with an aspic glaze. Remember to prepare enough aspic to fortify your sauce as well as to apply as the aspic finish coat.

The aspic you use to gelatinize the sauce must be of the same flavor type as the sauce. For example, poultry aspic is added to a poultry-based velouté. The best-looking brown chaud-froid sauces are made by adding brown aspic to demi-glace. However, if you have no other need for brown aspic and will be using a white poultry aspic for glazing, the poultry aspic may be added to the demi-glace instead.

Step 4: Add the Aspic (and Cream)

Next, combine the base sauce and aspic. Adding aspic to a base sauce for coating work fortifies it, or makes it stronger. This ensures it will properly cling to the food. Your goal is to achieve a smooth, glossy coating just thick enough to mask the food's surface but not so thick as to appear gloppy or to make too heavy a coating. Keep in mind that the base sauce already contains a thickener (the roux) and a certain amount of gelatin (from the stock with which it was made). Depending on the sauce you are using, you may need to use more or less aspic than your formula specifies. Always start by adding less aspic than the formula calls for, and test the chaud-froid by chilling it and pouring it onto a cold plate or over a cold piece of food. If it seems too thin, you can add more aspic. If your chaud-froid sauce is too thick, thin it with additional clarified stock.

White chaud-froid sauces contain cream as well as sauce and aspic. The cream is usually added to the sauce at the same time as the aspic. When combining sauce, aspic, and cream, all of the elements are combined and then heated just under the boil. The sauce must be stirred constantly to mix the ingredients and prevent scorching on the bottom of the pan.

Step 5: Strain

The final step in preparing chaud-froid sauce is to strain it through a fine-mesh sieve. This removes any lumps that may have formed during storage of the base sauce or during preparation. However, if you are preparing the chaud-froid ahead of time, for later use, there is no point in straining it, as you must strain it again just before using it for coating.

MAYONNAISE COLLÉE

The French word *coller* means "to stick" or "to adhere." Thus, mayonnaise collée is a mayonnaise sauce that has had gelatin added to it so it will stick to food and form a coating. The basic ratio for preparing mayonnaise collée is:

2 parts thick mayonnaise to 1 part aspic for coating, measured by volume

However, as when preparing chaud-froid sauce, you should test the consistency of the sauce as described on page 638.

The strength of the aspic you use determines the thickness of the finished mayonnaise collée. For coating, aspic of moderate strength is used. If a strong aspic, such as Aspic for Slicing (variations, pp. 644 and 645), is added to mayonnaise, the result is a mayonnaise collée that will gel enough to bind a salad. Strong mayonnaise collée may be placed in a pastry bag and piped into decorative borders, rosettes, or other shapes.

If you have both mayonnaise and aspic on hand, mayonnaise collée is quick and easy to prepare. Today, most garde manger chefs use commercial mayonnaise for mayonnaise collée because it safer to use for display at room temperature. It is also more temperature-stable and will not break if the aspic added to it is a little too warm.

To obtain an attractive, ivory-colored mayonnaise collée, only pale-colored aspics should be used. For the best results, have the mayonnaise at room temperature and the aspic melted and cooled to a syrupy consistency. When combining the mayonnaise and aspic, avoid whipping air into the mixture. Simply stir the two ingredients together until well blended.

If both the mayonnaise and the aspic used have been correctly seasoned, there is no need to further season the mixture. However, mayonnaise collée is sometimes flavored and colored with additional ingredients. It may be tinted with colorful foods such as tomato coulis, spinach purée, or saffron.

ASPIC AND CHAUD-FROID WORK

There is almost no limit to the types of cold foods that may be coated with aspic or chaud-froid. In general, foods that are naturally colorful and attractive are coated with aspic only. For example, the bright pink flesh of a cold poached salmon is typically glazed with clear seafood aspic, while a pale-colored striped bass is usually masked with white seafood chaud-froid.

Both large and small cold food items are coated with aspic and chaud-froid. A large, whole roasted turkey breast or baked ham may be coated with chaud-froid.

These items are then sliced for service. Small fish roulades or pork medallions may be coated and arranged on a platter for individual service. Sometimes a platter of coated foods contains both a large food item, or *grosse pièce* (p. 246), for display as well as a number of individual pieces meant for consumption.

Garnitures for both coated and uncoated cold foods are frequently glazed with aspic to add shine, to keep them intact, and to prevent them from drying out.

Steps in Basic Coating and Decorating Work

Coating foods with aspic and chaud-froid or mayonnaise collée is a multi-step procedure that is usually done over a period of two or more days. Here are the basic steps necessary to achieve a typical finished dish.

1. Fabricate, cook, and chill the food items to be coated.
2. Prepare the coating sauces.
3. Prepare the surface décor items.
4. Skin, trim, or otherwise prepare the food to receive the coating.
5. Apply one or more base coats to the food item.
6. Apply the surface décor items to the food item.
7. Apply an aspic finish coat to the food item.
8. Add décor to the plate or presentation platter.

Let's first look at the decorative food items used on coated foods. This reflects the way in which the work proceeds. In doing the actual work of coating and decorating, the décor design is planned well ahead of time, and the décor items are prepared before the coating work begins.

SURFACE DÉCOR FOR ASPIC AND CHAUD-FROID WORK

A coating of aspic or chaud-froid presents a smooth, neutral background on which the garde manger chef can apply décor items. Décor applied to the surface of a coated food is called ***surface décor*** in order to distinguish it from décor items used elsewhere in the presentation. It is also called ***flat decor***.

To look attractive and professional, the surface decoration of an aspic or chaud-froid piece must be carefully thought out and planned on paper before the actual decorating begins. Many chefs work out their designs in colored pencil on a parchment paper template cut to the exact dimensions of the food item they plan to decorate. The most successful décor designs are balanced, symmetrical, and proportioned to the size of the food they enhance.

Surface décor must be edible and is meant to be eaten along with the coated food. These décor items are usually crafted from vegetables. Some can be used as is, without cooking. Others must be blanched and refreshed to soften them and improve their flavor. Thin-sliced roasted or steamed beets may be used for surface décor. However, they will quickly begin to bleed color into the surrounding coatings. Skilled garde manger chefs can take advantage of color bleeding to create unusual effects. Paper-thin slices of fruit are occasionally used for surface décor when their flavors are appropriate to the dish. Truffles and black olives add dramatic contrast when placed on a white or pale background. Hard-cooked egg white provides contrast when used with brown chaud-froid.

Vegetables used for surface décor are cut into decorative shapes. By combining shapes and colors, a garde manger chef can create intricate geometric designs or realistic natural motifs. The preparation of surface décor items for aspic and chaud-froid work, and the tools used to prepare them, are covered in Chapter 17. Become familiar with this information before continuing to prepare decorated coated foods.

After surface décor is applied to the coated item, a final glaze, or coating, of light-colored aspic must be applied. This finish glaze holds the surface décor in place and protects it from drying out. Here are guidelines for planning and executing surface décor.

Guidelines for Making Aspic and Chaud-Froid Surface Décor

- When planning a design, take into account the natural shape and position of the food item you are decorating. For example, the breast of a whole chicken requires a vertical pear shape, while a whole poached salmon requires a horizontal oval.
- Geometric patterns and simple nature motifs are the best choices for beginners. Realistic representations are difficult and should be attempted only by experienced decorators.
- Simplicity is the key to elegance. The best designs are based on one main element that serves as a focal point.
- Use no more than two or three supporting elements, and arrange them to lead the eye to the focal point.
- Create groupings that consist of odd numbers. In other words, arrange elements in groups of three, five, and seven rather than groups of two, four, and six.
- Limit your use of color to no more than three or four choices.
- Include a border in your design to make it look finished.
- Make sure all décor items are precisely cut and that like items are consistent in size.
- Make sure surface décor items are dry before using them. Lay out décor items on paper towels to blot them dry.
- Wear food-service gloves while applying décor items.
- Use freshly sanitized food-service tweezers to apply small décor items.
- To help them stick, dip décor items in syrupy aspic immediately before applying them to the surface.
- Place décor items precisely where you want them. Once a décor item is placed, it is very difficult to move it without marring the coating. Repairing a marred coating is virtually impossible. Often your only option is to remove all décor items and add a complete additional coating.
- If three-dimensional items are to be added, dip them in thick aspic and allow the aspic to set before applying them.
- Once the décor items are applied, carefully add a finish coat of light-colored aspic to protect them from drying out.

Coating and Decorating Procedures

Now you are ready to learn about the coating and decorating procedure in depth. Aspic and chaud-froid work requires a great deal of organization. Here are guidelines that will help you set up an organized workspace.

Guidelines for Setting Up an Aspic and Chaud-Froid Workspace

- Have plenty of room to work. You need a large, empty worktable dedicated only to the task at hand.
- Clear enough space in a nearby refrigerator to accommodate your food item(s) and the serving platter(s).
- Assemble your complete equipment mise en place before beginning. All equipment must be clean and grease-free. Double-check the cleanliness of sheet trays and racks so they do not contaminate the excess coating sauces that drip onto them.
- Place a bus tub for used equipment on the undershelf of your worktable.
- Have plenty of ice on hand for cooling your coating sauces.
- If your work area is far from the stove, you may wish to set up a ***rechaud*** [RAY-show], or portable butane burner, on your worktable for rewarming coating sauces.
- Have all coating sauces, décor items, and other ingredients ready and close at hand.
- Place your design template in a page protector, or cover it with plastic film, to keep it clean for future use.

As you progress through the multiple steps of the procedure, be neat, and clean up as you go. Keep excess coating sauces free of contaminants and reserve them for future use. As you finish with a piece of equipment, remove it from your work surface to the bus tub. A clean and orderly workspace makes the job faster and easier.

Other Applications for Coating Sauces

In addition to their use as a coating substance, aspic, chaud-froid, and mayonnaise collée may be used for other purposes.

- Aspic may be poured into a flat container, chilled until set, and cut into cubes or other shapes for use as garnish or décor (p. 708).
- Aspic may be used to coat the interior of timbales or other forms to ensure that the contents turn out neatly and to provide a shiny, protective exterior coating once the timbales are unmolded (pp. 646 and 661).
- Aspic may be used to bind the layers of a vegetable or seafood terrine (p. 653).
- Aspic is used to finish a pâté en croûte (p. 571).
- Aspic may be used as a seal on the surface of pâtés presented en terrine, and on the surface of parfaits, mousses, or other foods presented in crocks, ramekins, or forms (p. 220).
- Aspic or mayonnaise collée may be used to bind a complex salad so it can be formed and unmolded (p. 661).
- Aspic, chaud-froid, or mayonnaise collée may be used to line a plate or platter, as illustrated on page 660.

Procedure for Coating and Decorating Foods with Aspic and Chaud-Froid

1. Place the cooked, thoroughly chilled food item(s) on a cutting board.
2. If necessary, remove trussing strings and other support structure from the food item(s).
3. Trim the food item(s) as necessary for a neat, even appearance. Remove poultry or fish skin according to your design plan. Blot the surfaces dry with a clean, lint-free towel.
4. Transfer the food item(s) to a rack set over a sheet tray.
5. If necessary, melt and strain the coating sauce that will be used for the first coat.
6. Use a ladle to stir the coating sauce over an ice bain-marie until it reaches syrupy consistency.
7. a. Ladle the coating sauce over the food item, allowing the excess to drip onto the tray (see Note). Use a small offset spatula to push the sauce into uncoated spaces around the bottom edges.

   –or–

   b. Use dipping forks to dip small food items into the coating sauce. Replace the foods on the rack.
8. Refrigerate the food item(s) until the first coat is set.
9. Remove any aspic or chaud-froid burrs (see sidebar) by touching them with a hot knife blade.
10. If a second coat is needed, repeat steps 5 through 9.
11. Use sanitized food-service tweezers to dip the décor items into syrupy aspic and arrange them on the coated food.
12. Melt the aspic for the finish coat.
13. Use a ladle to stir the aspic over an ice bain-marie until it reaches syrupy consistency.
14. Change to a clean sheet tray and repeat step 7, using the aspic.
15. Refrigerate the coated item(s) until set.
16. Remove burrs with a hot knife blade.

Note: Aspic, chaud-froid, or mayonnaise collée that has dripped through the rack onto the sheet tray may be scraped up, melted, and reused as long as it has not been contaminated by other foods.

Removing Burrs

After a food item is coated and set, there may be drips or tags of set coating sauce visible on the food's surface. These are called ***burrs***. You can remove a burr by heating a knife blade very hot over a gas flame and touching the blade to the burr. The burr will quickly melt away.

Procedure for Coating Forms with Aspic

A

B

1. Prepare a hotel pan or bus tub filled with enough crushed ice to hold the form(s) you intend to use.
2. Press the form(s) into the ice to the level of their rims.
3. If necessary, wipe the inside(s) of the form(s) completely dry with a clean, lint-free towel.
4. If necessary, melt the aspic and cool it in an ice bain-marie to syrupy consistency.
5. Fill a form to the top with aspic and allow the aspic to solidify on the bottom and sides of the form 10–20 seconds, depending on the desired thickness of the coating (A).
6. Pour the aspic back into the ice bain-marie bowl (B).
7. Evaluate the thickness of the coating. If it is too thin, repeat the process. If the coating is too thick, melt it out and repeat the process, leaving the form in the ice for less time.
8. Continue this process to coat the remaining forms.

WHITE POULTRY ASPIC FOR COATING

Yield:
1 qt (1 L)

INGREDIENTS	U.S.	METRIC
Clarified Stock for poultry *(p. 748)*, warm	1 qt	1 L
Kosher salt	to taste	to taste
Madeira or other pale color fortified wine	2 fl oz	60 mL
Granular gelatin (see Note)	1 oz	30 g
Fresh lemon juice, strained	to taste	to taste

Note: To use sheet gelatin, follow manufacturer's bloom ratios or perform a kitchen test.

PROCEDURE

PREPARATION

1. Season the stock to taste with kosher salt.
2. Bloom the gelatin in the Madeira.
3. Add the bloomed gelatin to the stock. Heat the stock, stirring gently to dissolve the gelatin completely.
4. Set the stock in an ice bain-marie. Stir gently, without forming air bubbles, until the aspic reaches a syrupy consistency. The aspic is now ready for use. Alternatively, refrigerate, covered, for later use.

HOLDING

Hold at cool room temperature up to 3 hours. Refrigerate up to 5 days.

VARIATIONS

DELICATE WHITE POULTRY ASPIC

Decrease the gelatin to ½ oz (15 g).

WHITE POULTRY ASPIC FOR SLICING

Increase the gelatin to 2 oz (60 g).

BROWN MEAT ASPIC FOR COATING

Yield:
1 qt (1 L)

INGREDIENTS	U.S.	METRIC
Clarified Stock for brown beef and/or veal *(p. 748)*, warm	1 qt	1 L
Kosher salt	to taste	to taste
Granular gelatin (see Note)	1 oz	30 g
Ruby port or other fortified wine	2 fl oz	60 mL
Fresh lemon juice, strained	to taste	to taste

Note: To use sheet gelatin, follow manufacturer's bloom ratios or perform a kitchen test.

PROCEDURE

PREPARATION

1. Season the stock to taste with kosher salt.
2. Bloom the gelatin in the port.
3. Add the bloomed gelatin to the stock. Heat the stock, stirring gently to dissolve the gelatin completely.
4. Set the stock in an ice bain-marie. Stir gently, without forming air bubbles, until the aspic reaches a syrupy consistency. The aspic is now ready for use. Alternatively, refrigerate, covered, for later use.

HOLDING

Hold at cool room temperature up to 3 hours. Refrigerate up to 5 days.

VARIATIONS

DELICATE BROWN MEAT ASPIC

Decrease the gelatin to ½ oz (15 g).

BROWN MEAT ASPIC FOR SLICING

Increase the gelatin to 2 oz (60 g).

SEAFOOD ASPIC FOR COATING

Yield:
1 qt (1 L)

INGREDIENTS	U.S.	METRIC
Clarified Stock for fish or shellfish *(p. 748)*, warm	1 qt	1 L
Kosher salt	to taste	to taste
Dry sherry or other pale-color fortified wine	2 fl oz	60 mL
Granular gelatin (see Note)	1 oz	30 g
Fresh lemon juice, strained	to taste	to taste

Note: To use sheet gelatin, follow manufacturer's bloom ratios or perform a kitchen test.

PROCEDURE

PREPARATION

1. Season the stock to taste with kosher salt.
2. Bloom the gelatin in the sherry.
3. Add the bloomed gelatin to the stock. Heat the stock, stirring gently to dissolve the gelatin completely.
4. Set the stock in an ice bain-marie. Stir gently, without forming air bubbles, until the aspic reaches a syrupy consistency. The aspic is now ready for use. Alternatively, refrigerate, covered, for later use.

HOLDING

Hold at cool room temperature up to 3 hours. Refrigerate up to 5 days.

VARIATIONS

DELICATE SEAFOOD ASPIC

Decrease the gelatin to ½ oz (15 g).

SEAFOOD ASPIC FOR SLICING

Increase the gelatin to 2 oz (60 g).

OEUFS EN GELÉE [OOF ahn zheh-LAY]
JELLIED EGGS

Yield:
4 servings

INGREDIENTS	U.S.	METRIC
White Poultry Aspic for Slicing (p. 644), see Note	1 qt	1 l
Leek décor teardrops (p. 715)	40	40
Tomato décor disks (p. 715)	40	40
Soft-poached eggs, stored in ice water	4	4

Note: You will not use the full amount of aspic. About 10 fl oz (300 mL) will remain and can be utilized for another purpose.

PROCEDURE

PREPARATION

1. Follow the Procedure for Coating Forms with Aspic on page 644 to coat four 4-fl oz (120-mL) brioche forms with a 3/16-in. (0.5-cm) coating of aspic.
2. Remelt the aspic to syrupy consistency.
3. Use sanitized food-service tweezers to quickly dip a leek décor teardrop into the syrupy aspic, and then place it, upside down, lying against one of the curved flutes of the form. Repeat to place a teardrop in each of the flutes.
4. Use tweezers to dip and place a tomato décor disk on the surface of the aspic at the point of each teardrop (A).
5. Bring the aspic to a syrupy consistency and ladle ½ fl oz (15 mL) into each form (B). Be careful not to disturb the décor items. Refrigerate the forms until set.
6. Use a slotted spoon to remove the eggs from the water onto a clean, lint-free towel. Use sanitized scissors to trim the eggs into rounded shapes (C).
7. Place an egg, rounded side down, into each form.
8. Bring the aspic back to syrupy consistency and ladle it over the eggs to fill the forms (D). Refrigerate at least 1 hour, or until set.

A

B

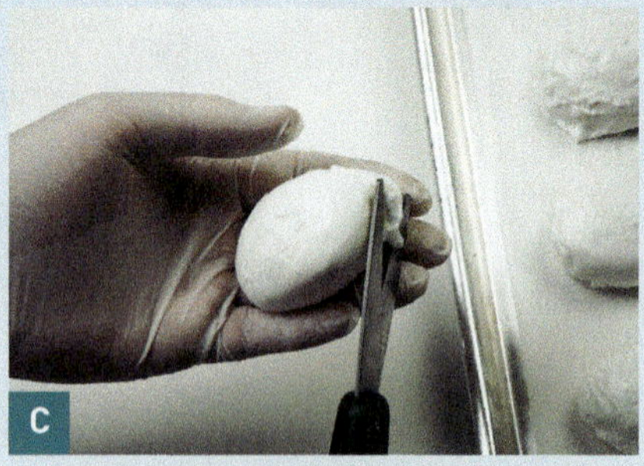
C

D

HOLDING

Refrigerate the forms, covered with plastic film, up to 3 days.

FINISHING

To unmold:

9. Remove the plastic film and place a square of parchment on the surface of each filled form.
10. Set a sheet tray on top of the forms.

PROCEDURE

11. Grasp both trays and flip them over. Remove the new top tray.
12. Wet a clean towel in very hot water and wring it out.
13. Place the hot towel on the forms for a few seconds, or until the aspic softens slightly.
14. Remove the forms from the oeufs en gelée.

HOLDING

Refrigerate, uncovered, up to 8 hours.

VARIATION

SEAFOOD OEUFS EN GELÉE

Replace the White Poultry Aspic with Seafood Aspic for Slicing (p. 645). Use a 6-fl oz (180 mL), 3¼-in. (8-cm) diameter cylinder silicone form. Replace the leek décor teardrops with diamonds of the same size as the disks. Arrange the décor items in an alternating pattern around the rim of the form, as shown on page 648.

OEUF EN GELÉE

WITH HAM AND MAYONNAISE

LUNCH MAIN COURSE

Portion:
1
Portion size:
1 egg plus
1 oz (30 g) ham

COMPONENTS

1 oz (30 g) Smoked ham, sliced ⅜ in. (1 cm) thick
1 *Oeuf en Gelée (p. 646)*
½ oz (15 g) Micro greens or watercress leaves
2 fl oz (60 mL) Thick *Mayonnaise (p. 41)*, in pastry bag fitted with a small star tip
4 oz (120 g) Crisp baguette

PROCEDURE

PLATING

1. Use a 3-in. (8-cm) round cutter to make a 3-in. (8-cm) disk of ham.
2. Use an offset spatula to lift the jellied egg onto the ham disk, then lift the two together onto the center of the plate.
3. Surround the egg with the micro greens.
4. Pipe a star border of mayonnaise around the egg.
5. Serve the baguette on a separate plate or in a napkin-lined basket.

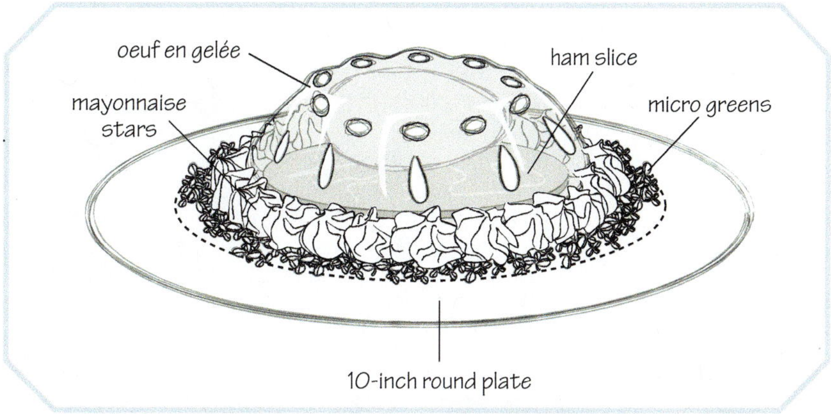

OEUF EN GELÉE

WITH COOL GRILLED TUNA AND TONNATO SAUCE

LUNCH MAIN COURSE

Portion:
1

Portion size:
1 egg, 3 oz (90 g) tuna, plus sauce and garnish

COMPONENTS

3 fl oz (90 mL) *Tonnato Sauce (p. 43)*
1 oz (30 g) Micro greens
1 Thin, rare-grilled tuna medallion, 2½ oz (75 g)
1 *Seafood Oeuf en Gelée (p. 647)*
4 oz (120 g) Crisp baguette

PROCEDURE

PLATING

1. Pool the tonnato sauce in the well of a cool 10-in. (25-cm) plate.
2. Arrange a 4-in. (10-cm) bed of micro greens in the center of the plate.
3. Use an offset spatula to lift the jellied egg onto the tuna medallion, then lift the two together onto the bed of greens.
4. Serve the baguette on a separate plate or in a napkin-lined basket.

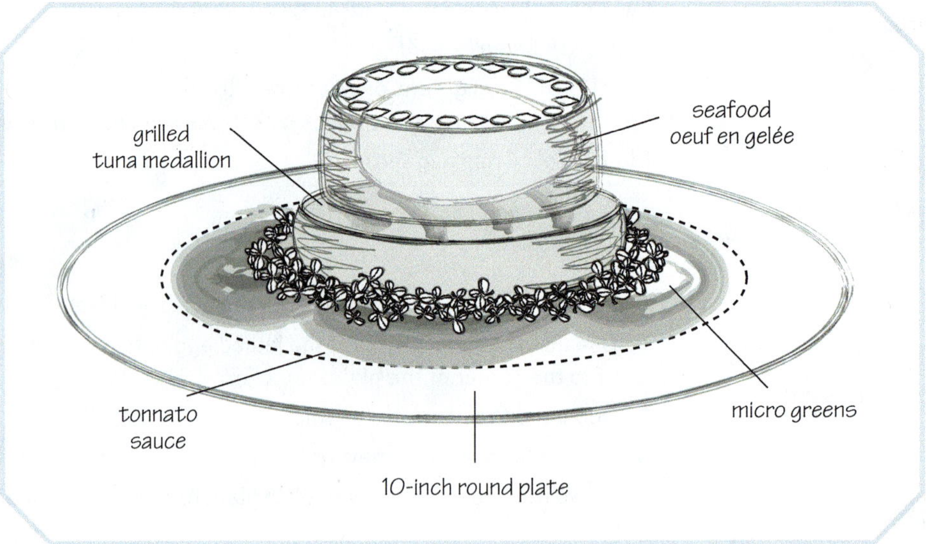

WHOLE POACHED SALMON IN ASPIC

BUFFET MAIN COURSE OR APPETIZER

Yield:
about 3 lb EP (1.5 kg)
Portions:
8
Portion size:
6 oz (180 g)

INGREDIENTS	U.S.	METRIC
Whole Poached Salmon (p. 201), without oil or garnishes	1	1
Seafood Aspic for Coating (p. 645)	3 qt	3 L
⅛-in. (3-mm) Pimiento or tomato décor disks	66	66
¼-in. (6-mm) Leek décor diamonds	45	45
¼-in. (6-mm) Pimiento or tomato décor disk	1	1
¾-in. (2-cm) Egg white décor teardrops	7	7
½-in. (1.25-cm) Egg white décor teardrops	14	14
Leek décor strings	3 or 4	3 or 4
⅝-in. (1.5-cm) Egg white décor disk	1	1
Pitted black olive	1 slice	1 slice
Mayonnaise Collée (p. 660)	1 qt	1 L
Lemon Mayonnaise Sauce for Seafood (p. 43)	1 pt	0.5 L
Basic Tomato Coulis Sauce (p. 52)	1 pt	0.5 L

Note: Décor items are illustrated on p. 715.

PROCEDURE

PREPARATION

1. Obtain a long, oval fish platter of the correct size to hold the salmon. Make sure it is completely clean, dry, and grease-free. Create a perfectly level space in the refrigerator and place the fish platter in it to chill. Make additional room in the refrigerator for a sheet tray large enough to hold the salmon.
2. Place the salmon, best side up, on a rack set over a clean, grease-free sheet tray. Blot the surface dry with paper towels.
3. If necessary, rewarm the aspic to melt it, and then stir it in an ice bain-marie until it reaches a syrupy consistency.
4. Without removing the platter from the refrigerator, ladle a ⅛-in. (3-mm) layer of aspic onto it. Wait about 10 minutes, or until the aspic is set.
5. Use sanitized food-service tweezers to place 60 pimiento or tomato décor dots around the perimeter of the aspic on the fish platter, as illustrated in the blueprint drawing. (Remember to reserve 2 of the dots for decorating the salmon.)
6. Rewarm the aspic, cool it to a syrupy texture, and ladle a finish coat of aspic over the dots. Return the platter to the refrigerator.
7. Follow the Procedure for Coating and Decorating Foods with Aspic and Chaud-Froid (p. 643) to coat and decorate the salmon, as illustrated in the blueprint.
8. Carefully place the salmon on the fish platter.
9. Melt the mayonnaise colleé in a warm bain-marie.
10. Prepare a pastry bag fitted with a large star tip.
11. Stir the mayonnaise colleé in an ice bain-marie until it has the consistency of firm whipped cream. Quickly transfer it to the pastry bag, and pipe a shell border around the salmon.
12. Refrigerate the salmon platter until it is needed.

(continues)

PROCEDURE *(continued)*

13. Place the sauces in sauce bowls or serving dishes and refrigerate until needed.

HOLDING

Refrigerate, uncovered, up to 8 hours.

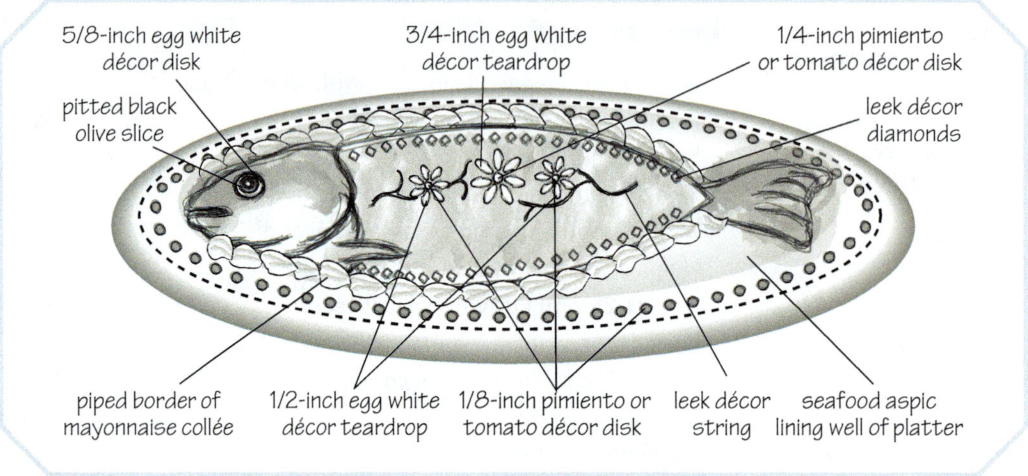

JAMBON PERSILLÉ *[zham-BOH(N) pare-see-YAY]*

PARSLEYED HAM

Yield:
16 fl oz (0.5 L)
Portions:
4
Portions size:
4 fl oz (120 mL)

INGREDIENTS	U.S.	METRIC
Smoked ham	1 lb	0.5 kg
Roasted red bell pepper (p. 109), brunoise-cut	2 oz	60 g
Minced parsley	1 oz	30 g
White Poultry Aspic for Slicing (p. 644)	6–8 fl oz	180–240 mL

PROCEDURE

PREPARATION

1. Trim the ham of all fat and connective tissue. Cut it into rough ⅜-in. (1-cm) dice.
2. Place a grease-free 16-fl oz (0.5-L) loaf pan or four 4-fl oz (160-mL) individual single-portion forms in crushed ice, as illustrated on page 644.
3. If necessary, melt the aspic and set the bowl in an ice bain-marie. Stir the aspic over the ice until it thickens past the syrupy stage and will hold a cube of ham without the ham cube sinking. Immediately fold in the ham, roasted peppers, and parsley.
4. Immediately pour the mixture into the pan or forms.
5. Refrigerate, uncovered, until set: 2–3 hours for the loaf, 1–1½ hours for the forms.

HOLDING

Refrigerate, loosely covered, up to 5 days.

PRESENTATION

6. To turn out, invert the pan or forms onto the serving platter or plates. Wet a clean towel with very hot water, wring it out, and set it on the pan or forms until the aspic is released.
7. Decorate or garnish as desired.

VARIATION

JAMBON PERSILLÉ PYRAMIDS

Use a 4-fl oz (120-mL) pyramid silicone form.

ASPIC-GLAZED ARTICHOKE BOTTOMS WITH SALMON MOUSSE

Yield:
6 garnitures or appetizer components

INGREDIENTS	U.S.	METRIC
2-in. (5-cm) diameter cooked artichoke bottoms (p. 113, or frozen and thawed)	6	6
Seafood Aspic for Coating (p. 645)	1 pt	0.5 L
Salmon Mousse (p. 216), in pastry bag with medium star tip	10 fl oz	300 mL
Frozen petite peas, thawed	2 oz	60 g
Chervil or flat-leaf parsley pluches	6	6
Salmon caviar or other red caviar	¼ oz	7 g

PROCEDURE

PREPARATION

1. Blot the artichoke bottoms dry with paper towels and place them on a rack set over a clean, grease-free sheet tray.
2. Melt and cool a small amount of the aspic as directed in the Procedure for Coating and Decorating Foods with Aspic and Chaud-Froid (p. 643).
3. Brush the inside of the artichoke bottoms with a light coating of aspic and place them in the refrigerator about 5 minutes, or until the aspic is set.
4. Pipe a rosette of salmon mousse into each artichoke bottom.
5. Blot the peas dry on paper towels. Use sanitized food-service tweezers to place a border of peas around the rim of each artichoke bottom, as illustrated on page 652.
6. Stick a pluche on top of each mousse rosette. Place a pearl or dot of caviar at the base of each pluche.
7. Follow the Procedure for Coating and Decorating Foods with Aspic and Chaud-Froid to glaze each artichoke bottom with 2 coatings of aspic. Make sure the pluches are fully coated with aspic.

HOLDING

Refrigerate, uncovered, up to 8 hours.

VARIATION

ARTICHOKE BOTTOM PRINTANIÈRE

[pran-tawn-YAIR]

Replace the Seafood Aspic with White Poultry Aspic for Coating (p. 644). Replace the Salmon Mousse with fine-diced *à point* blanched carrots mixed with aspic. Mound some of the carrots into each artichoke bottom in a cone shape, and refrigerate until set. After adding the border of petite peas, arrange ¾ in. (2 cm) *à point* blanched asparagus tips around the carrots in tepee fashion. Omit the pluches and the caviar.

SALMON MOUSSE ARTICHOKE BOTTOM

WITH SAUCE AURORE AND ASPARAGUS TIPS

APPETIZER

Portion:
1
Portion size:
about 5 oz (150 g), plus sauce and garnish

COMPONENTS

1 *Toasted Baguette Croûton (p. 702)*, freshly toasted, 2-in. (5-cm)
1 *Aspic-Glazed Artichoke Bottom with Salmon Mousse (p. 651)*
2 fl oz (90 mL) *Sauce Aurore (p. 42)*, in squeeze bottle
½ fl oz (15 mL), or as needed, *Bright Green Parsley Oil (p. 686)*
9 1-in. (2.5-cm) asparagus tips, blanched *à point* and refreshed

PROCEDURE

PLATING

1. Place the croûton in the center of a cool 10-in. (25-cm) plate.
2. Place the aspic-glazed artichoke bottom on the croûton.
3. Squeeze a pool of sauce aurore around the artichoke bottom to fill the plate well.
4. Squeeze decorative flourishes of parsley oil around the edge of the plate well.
5. Arrange the asparagus tips around the artichoke bottom.

VARIATION

ARTICHOKE BOTTOM PRINTANIÈRE

Replace the Aspic-Glazed Artichoke Bottom with Salmon Mousse with an Artichoke Bottom *Printanière* (p. 651). Replace the Sauce Aurore with thin Mayonnaise (p. 41). Replace the asparagus tips with dots of Beet Oil (p. 687).

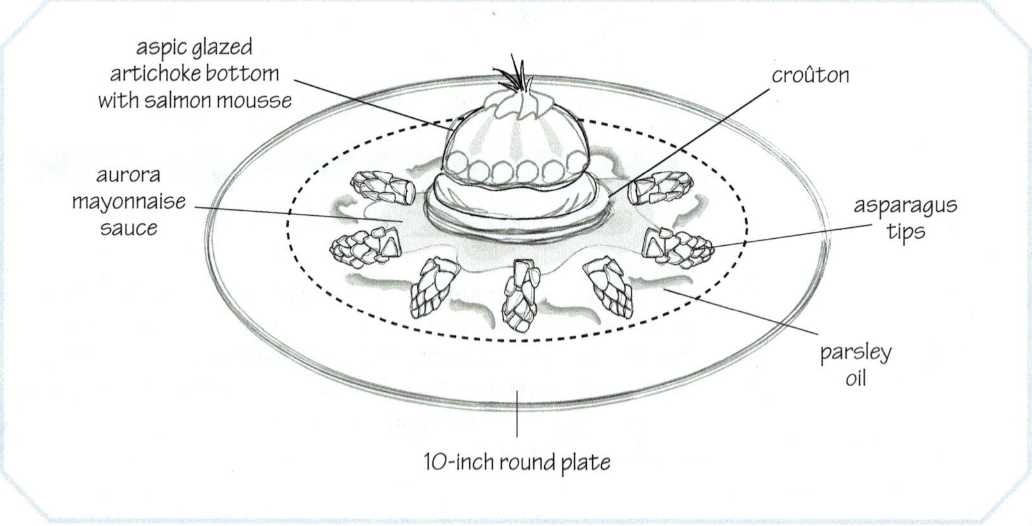

CONFETTI VEGETABLE TERRINE

Yield:
about 2½ lb (1.15 kg)
Portions:
12
Portion size:
¾-in. (1.9-cm) slice, about 3½ oz (105 g)

INGREDIENTS	U.S.	METRIC
White Poultry Aspic for Slicing (p. 644)	20 fl oz	0.6 L
À point blanched and refreshed green beans, cut in ¼-in. (0.6-cm) lengths	2 oz	60 g
À point blanched and refreshed peeled asparagus spears, cut in ¼-in. (0.6-cm) lengths	2 oz	60 g
À point blanched and refreshed or frozen and thawed peas	2 oz	60 g
À point blanched and refreshed ¼-in. (0.6-cm) diced carrots	2 oz	60 g
À point blanched and refreshed ¼-in. (0.6-cm) diced rutabaga or turnip	2 oz	60 g
À point blanched and refreshed ¼-in. (0.6-cm) diced artichoke bottom	2 oz	60 g
¼-in. (0.6-cm) squares roasted red bell pepper (p. 109) or pimiento	2 oz	60 g
¼-in. (0.6-cm) squares peeled tomato flesh	2 oz	60 g
Scallions, thin sliced	½ oz	15 g
Fresh thyme leaves	1/16 oz (1 tsp)	5 mL
Chopped fresh tarragon leaves	⅛ oz (1 Tbsp)	15 mL

PROCEDURE

PREPARATION

1. Place a 1½-qt (1.5-L) terrine form in the freezer at least 15 minutes.
2. If necessary, melt the aspic and cool it in an ice bain-marie to syrupy consistency.
3. Ladle a ⅜-in. (0.9-cm) layer of aspic into the terrine and place the terrine in the refrigerator for a few minutes, or until the aspic is set.
4. Spread all of the vegetables on clean, lint-free towels and blot them with more towels so they are completely dry.
5. Place the terrine form on the work surface close at hand.
6. Remelt the remaining aspic and cool it slightly thicker than syrupy to a consistency where it will hold a piece of vegetable suspended in it. Immediately fold in the remaining vegetables, scallions, and herbs (A).
7. Immediately pour the mixture into the terrine form (B). Tap the form on the work surface to firm it and force out air pockets.
8. Refrigerate the terrine for 2 hours, or until set.

A

B

HOLDING

Refrigerate, covered, up to 5 days.

FINISHING

9. Unmold the terrine:
   a. Run a knife around the edges of the terrine.
   b. Invert the terrine form on a cutting board.

(continues)

PROCEDURE *(continued)*

c. Wrap the terrine form in clean, hot, damp towels about 5 minutes, or until the terrine is released from the form. If the terrine form is made of metal, you may carefully warm it with a torch to release the terrine.

d. Heat a sharp, thin-bladed knife with a torch or over a gas flame and cut the terrine into ¾-in. (1.8-cm) slices.

e. Use a wide offset spatula to transfer the slices to a flat container lined with parchment. Keep the slices in one layer. Cover the container with its lid.

HOLDING

Refrigerate up to 2 days, but no longer than 5 days total.

VARIATIONS

Vary the vegetables and herbs as desired.

SEAFOOD CONFETTI VEGETABLE TERRINE

Replace the Poultry Aspic with Seafood Aspic for Slicing (p. 645). Use only half the weight of each vegetable, and add 2 cups (0.5 L) mixed cooked seafood, such as diced shrimp, diced scallops, flaked salmon, or lump crabmeat.

CONFETTI VEGETABLE TERRINE

WITH LEMON MAYONNAISE

APPETIZER

Portion:
1
Portion size:
5 oz (150 g), plus garnish

COMPONENTS

3 ⅜-in. (1-cm) slices *Confetti Vegetable Terrine (p. 653)*
2 sprigs Watercress, stems trimmed
1 tbsp (15 mL) *Mayonnaise (p. 41)*, made with lemon juice, in pastry bag with large star tip

PROCEDURE

PLATING

1. Overlap the terrine slices diagonally on a cool 10-in. (25-cm) plate.
2. Arrange the watercress at the back right corner.
3. Pipe a rosette of lemon mayonnaise to the right of the terrine slices.

TOMATO ASPIC

Yield:
24 fl oz (0.7 L)

INGREDIENTS	U.S.	METRIC
Granular gelatin	⅓ oz	10 g
Water	2 fl oz	60 mL
Vodka, or additional water	1 fl oz	30 mL
Canned tomato juice	20 fl oz	600 mL
Minced yellow onion	1 oz	30 g
Celery seeds	1 tsp (⅛ oz)	5 mL (3 g)
Dried tarragon	1 tsp (1/16 oz)	5 mL (2 g)
Cracked black peppercorns	1 tsp (⅛ oz)	5 mL (3 g)
Bottled hot sauce	dash	dash
Red wine vinegar	to taste	to taste
Kosher salt	to taste	to taste

PROCEDURE

PREPARATION

1. Place the gelatin in a small container and mix in the water and vodka. Allow the gelatin to bloom about 10 minutes at room temperature, or until softened.
2. Combine the tomato juice, onion, celery seeds, tarragon, and peppercorns in a nonreactive saucepan. Steep over very low heat about 15 minutes.
3. Place the desired form(s) on a sheet tray and refrigerate until cold.
4. Stir the gelatin into the tomato juice mixture until it is completely dissolved.
5. Remove the tomato juice mixture from the heat and season with hot sauce, vinegar, and salt.
6. Strain the mixture though a fine sieve or cheesecloth into an ice bain-marie.
7. Stir the tomato aspic until it reaches a syrupy consistency, then immediately pour it into the chilled forms.
8. Refrigerate until set. (Set time varies according to the size of the forms used.)

HOLDING

Refrigerate, covered, up to 5 days. Protein additions, such as seafood, shorten holding time accordingly.

VARIATIONS

TOMATO ASPIC SAVARINS

Use six 4-fl oz (120-mL) savarin forms.

SHRIMP TOMATO ASPIC

In step 7, allow the aspic to become thick enough to hold a small piece of food. Immediately fold in ¼ cup (60 mL) brunoise-cut peeled cucumber and 1 cup (240 mL) tiny cooked, peeled shrimp. Quickly pour into the forms.

CONFETTI TOMATO ASPIC

In step 7, allow the aspic to become thick enough to hold a small piece of food. Immediately fold in ¼ cup (60 mL) each brunoise-cut peeled cucumber and yellow bell pepper, thawed frozen petit peas, and ¼-in. (6-mm) lengths of *à point* blanched and refreshed green beans. Quickly pour into the forms.

TOMATO ASPIC SAVARIN

WITH SHRIMP SALAD

APPETIZER OR LUNCH MAIN COURSE

Portion:
1
Portion size:
about 6 oz (180 g), plus garnish

COMPONENTS

1 *Tomato Aspic Savarin (p. 655)*
3 fl oz (90 mL) *Classic Shrimp Salad (p. 160)*, made with 51–60 ct. shrimp
½ oz (15 g) Micro greens or spring mix
1 tsp (5 mL) Minced parsley
3 oz (90 g) Crisp baguette

PROCEDURE

PLATING

1. Invert the savarin form holding the tomato aspic savarin in the center of a cool 10-in. (25-cm) plate. Place a hot, damp towel on the form to release the savarin.
2. Use a 3-fl oz (90-mL) portion scoop to place a scoop of shrimp salad in the center of the savarin.
3. Place a dot of minced parsley on top of the shrimp salad.
4. Arrange the greens around the savarin.
5. Serve the baguette on a separate plate or in a napkin-lined basket.

VARIATIONS

CONFETTI TOMATO ASPIC WITH MAYONNAISE

Replace the savarin with a 4-fl oz (120 mL) ramekin of Confetti Tomato Aspic. Replace the shrimp salad with ½ fl oz (15 mL) thick mayonnaise (p. 41) piped in a rosette on top.

SHRIMP TOMATO ASPIC WITH MAYONNAISE

Replace the savarin with a 4-fl oz (120-mL) ramekin of Shrimp Tomato Aspic (p. 655). Replace the shrimp salad with ½ fl oz (15 mL) thick mayonnaise (p. 41) piped in a rosette on top. Garnish the top with a medium-size cooked, peeled shrimp.

WHITE POULTRY CHAUD-FROID

Yield:
1 qt (1 L)

INGREDIENTS	U.S.	METRIC
Velouté Sauce (Poultry or Fish) for poultry *(p. 752)*	16 fl oz	0.5 L
White Poultry Aspic for Slicing (p. 644)	12 fl oz	360 mL
Heavy cream	4 fl oz	120 mL

PROCEDURE

PREPARATION

1. Place the velouté in a heavy saucepan and bring it to the simmer.
2. Stir in the aspic and cream. Simmer just until the aspic melts and the mixture is well blended.
3. Pour the chaud-froid through a fine strainer into an ice bain-marie for immediate cooling and use. To hold briefly for later use, strain it into a hot bain-marie.

HOLDING

Hold in the hot bain-marie up to 3 hours. If the chaud-froid is allowed to become cold, it will form lumps and must be strained after heating.

VARIATION

WHITE SEAFOOD CHAUD-FROID

Replace the poultry velouté with 16 fl oz (0.5 L) seafood velouté. Replace White Poultry Aspic for Slicing with 12 fl oz (360 mL) Seafood Aspic for Slicing (p. 645).

BROWN CHAUD-FROID

Yield:
1 qt (1 L)

INGREDIENTS	U.S.	METRIC
Demi-Glace (One-Step Method) (p. 752)	16 fl oz	0.5 L
Brown Meat Aspic for Coating (p. 645)	16 fl oz	0.5 L

PROCEDURE

PREPARATION

1. Place the demi-glace in a heavy saucepan and bring it to the simmer.
2. Stir in the aspic. Simmer just until the aspic melts and the mixture is well blended.
3. Pour the chaud-froid through a fine strainer into an ice bain-marie for immediate cooling and use. To hold briefly for later use, strain into a hot bain-marie.

HOLDING

Hold in the hot bain-marie up to 3 hours. If the chaud-froid is allowed to become cold, it will form lumps and must be strained after heating.

CHICKEN BREASTS CHAUD-FROID

BUFFET MAIN COURSE

Portions:
6
Portion size:
5 oz (150 g), plus garnish

INGREDIENTS	U.S.	METRIC
Poached boneless, skinless chicken breasts, 5 oz (150 g) each, chilled	6	6
White Poultry Chaud-Froid (p. 657)	1½ pt	0.75 L
Leek décor strings (p. 715)	as needed	as needed
Leek décor bells (p. 715)	30	30
Leek décor tulip leaves (p. 715)	6	6
White Poultry Aspic for Coating (p. 644)	1 qt	1 L
Madeira Poultry Aspic Jewels (p. 708)	1 cup	240 mL

PROCEDURE

PREPARATION

1. Trim the chicken breasts of all visible fat and membrane. Use sanitized scissors to trim the edges into neat, even, uniform shapes. Blot the chicken breasts dry with paper towels and place them on a rack set over a clean, grease-free sheet tray.
2. Coat the chicken breasts with the chaud-froid, decorate them with the leek décor, and finish-coat them with the aspic as directed in the Procedure for Coating and Decorating Foods with Aspic and Chaud-Froid (p. 643 and illustrated in the blueprint below).
3. Place a 20-in. (50-cm) oval or rectangular platter in the refrigerator.
4. Melt and cool the remaining aspic to syrupy consistency. Pour enough aspic onto the platter to line it. Keep in the refrigerator at least 15 minutes, or until set.
5. Arrange the chaud-froid chicken breasts on the aspic-lined platter. Mound the aspic jewels around them.

HOLDING

Refrigerate, uncovered, up to 8 hours.

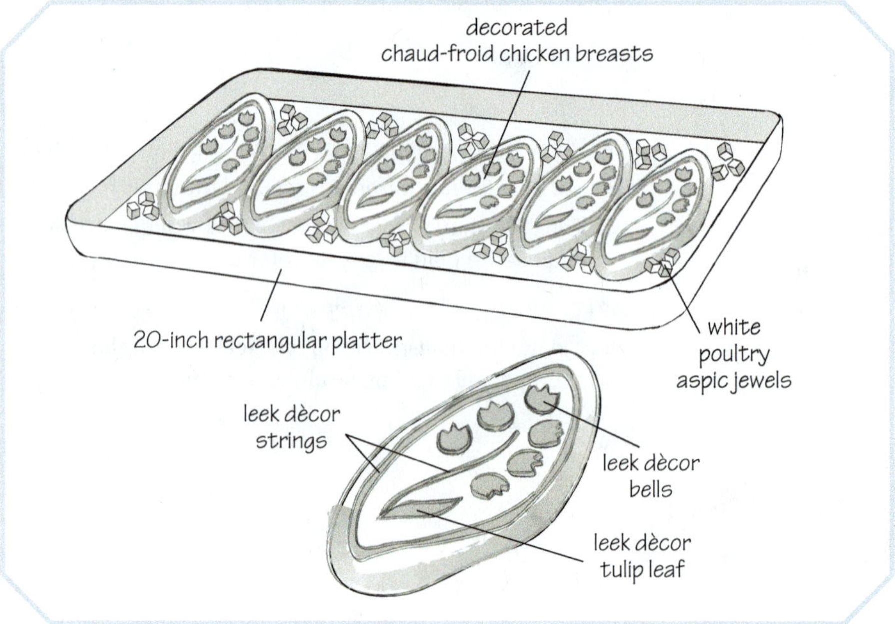

WHOLE ROAST CHICKEN CHAUD-FROID

BUFFET
MAIN COURSE

Yield:
about 2 lb (1 kg) EP
Portions:
varies
Portion size:
varies

INGREDIENTS	U.S.	METRIC
Cold Roast Chicken (p. 251)	1	1
Poultry Liver Parfait (p. 265), cold	about 6 oz	about 180 g
White Poultry Chaud-Froid (p. 657)	1 qt	1 L
White Poultry Aspic for Coating (p. 644)	1 qt	1 L
⅛-in. (3-cm) Black truffle or black olive décor disks	36	36
¼-in. (6-cm) Turnip disks	2	2
¾-in. (2-cm) Carrot décor teardrops	16	16
Rutabaga flower	1	1
⅜ in. (1-cm) Leek décor diamonds	14	14
Leek décor tulip stems and leaves	as needed	as needed
Watercress	2 oz	60 g

Note: Décor is illustrated on p. 715.

PROCEDURE

PREPARATION

1. Remove the trussing from the chicken. Blot dry all over with paper towels.
2. Remove the breast skin. Trim off all visible fat and membranes to leave a perfectly smooth surface of breast meat.
3. Fill the cavity between the two breast lobes with the liver parfait and smooth the surface (A).
4. Place the chicken on a rack set over a clean, grease-free sheet tray. Mask, or cover, the surface of the chicken breast with plastic film to protect it from aspic drips.
5. Obtain an oval platter large enough to hold the chicken. Place it perfectly level in the refrigerator.
6. If necessary, melt and strain the chaud-froid. Coat the platter with a thin layer of chaud-froid (B), and then hold the remaining chaud-froid in a hot bain-marie. Stir it occasionally until you are ready to use it.
7. If necessary, melt the aspic and cool it to syrupy consistency.
8. Coat only the skin-covered legs and wings of the chicken with aspic. Refrigerate the chicken until the aspic is set, then remove the plastic film.
9. Insert parchment strips between the chicken breast and legs. Follow the Procedure for Coating and Decorating Foods with Aspic and Chaud-Froid to coat the chicken breast only (C). Decorate as illustrated (D).
10. Decorate the platter as illustrated in the finished dish photo.
11. Finish-coat the entire chicken with aspic (E).

(continues)

A

B

C

D

E

PROCEDURE *(continued)*

12. Finish-coat the platter décor with aspic.
13. Carefully place the chicken on the chaud-froid–coated platter.
14. Arrange a bouquet of watercress between the drumstick knuckles.

HOLDING

Refrigerate, uncovered, up to 24 hours.

VARIATIONS

CHAUD-FROID CHICKEN AND HER FLOCK

Prepare 3-oz (90 g) oval-shaped poached chicken cutlets. Secure each cutlet to a same-size Toasted Baguette Croûton (p. 702) with thick mayonnaise or Poultry Liver Parfait (p. 265). Chaud-froid-coat, decorate, and aspic-glaze each cutlet in the same manner as the chicken breast, but in miniature. Impale small grape tomatoes on white frilled cocktail picks and stick them into the back of each cutlet. Arrange the coated cutlets surrounding the Whole Chaud-Froid Chicken on a large, coated platter.

WHOLE ROAST DUCK IN BROWN CHAUD-FROID

Replace the chicken with a 5-lb (2.25 kg) cold roast duck. Replace the White Poultry Chaud-Froid with Brown Chaud-Froid for veal (p. 657). Replace the truffle décor shapes with egg white décor shapes (p. 715).

MAYONNAISE COLLÉE

Yield:
2 qt (2 L)

INGREDIENTS	U.S.	METRIC
White Poultry Aspic for Coating (p. 644) or *Seafood Aspic for Coating (p. 645)*	1 pt	0.5 L
Commercial mayonnaise	1½ qt	1.5 L
Clarified Stock for poultry or seafood *(p. 748)*	as needed	as needed

PROCEDURE

PREPARATION

1. If necessary, melt the aspic and cool it to syrupy consistency.
2. Combine the mayonnaise and aspic in a hot bain-marie with water no hotter than 180°F (82°C). Whisk until smooth.
3. Test the consistency of the mayonnaise collée by coating a plate and refrigerating it until set.
4. If necessary, thin the mayonnaise collée with consommé to achieve the desired set.

HOLDING

Hold at 180°F (82°C) in the hot bain-marie, whisking occasionally, up to 2 hours. If the mayonnaise collée is refrigerated, it may need to be strained after melting.

VARIATION

STRONG MAYONNAISE COLLÉE

Use Aspic for Slicing (p. 645).

MOLDED SALADES RUSSES [sah-LAHD ROOCE]

Yield:
1 qt (1 L)
Portions:
6
Portion size:
5 fl oz (150 mL)

INGREDIENTS	U.S.	METRIC
White Poultry Aspic for Coating (p. 644), see Note	1 qt	1 L
Salade Russe (p. 147), without mayonnaise	1 qt	1 L
Strong Mayonnaise Collée (p. 660)	8 fl oz	240 mL

Note: You will not use the full amount of aspic. About 10 fl oz (300 mL) will remain and can be utilized for another purpose.

PROCEDURE

PREPARATION

1. Follow the Procedure for Coating Forms with Aspic on page 644 to coat six 5-fl oz (150-mL) ramekins with a ³⁄₁₆-in. (0.5-cm) coating of aspic.
2. Remelt the aspic to syrupy consistency.
3. If necessary, melt and cool the mayonnaise collée to slightly thicker than syrupy consistency.
4. Quickly combine the salade russe ingredients and fold in the mayonnaise collée to bind them. Pack the salade into the aspic-lined forms. Refrigerate about 30 minutes, or until set.

HOLDING

Cover with plastic film and refrigerate up to 3 days.

VARIATIONS

Almost any mixed complex salad may be molded in this manner. Prepare an appropriately flavored mayonnaise collée to suit the ingredients, and use an appropriately flavored aspic to coat the form. For example, to mold a seafood salad, use seafood aspic in both the mayonnaise collée and to coat the mold. Most vegetable salads use poultry aspic. However, to make a vegetarian salad, you may gelatinize vegetable broth with a vegetable-based gelatin and mix it with mayonnaise to make a vegetarian mayonnaise collée. Use a vegetable-based aspic to coat the form.

SALADE RUSSE

WITH SHRIMP

LUNCH MAIN COURSE OR APPETIZER

Portion:
1
Portion size:
5 oz (150 g), plus garnish

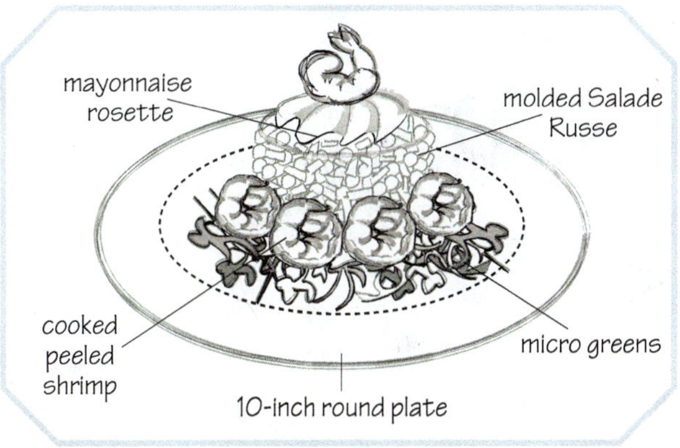

COMPONENTS

1 *Molded Salade Russe (p. 661)*
1 oz (30 g) Micro greens of choice, or shredded romaine hearts
8 Cooked, peeled 31–35 ct. shrimp
1 fl oz (30 mL) *Mayonnaise (p. 41)*, in pastry bag with medium star tip

PROCEDURE

PLATING

1. Invert the salade Russe, in its form, in the center of a cool 10-in. (25-cm) plate. Unmold as directed in Tomato Aspic Savarin on page 656.
2. Surround the base of the salade Russe with the greens.
3. Arrange 7 of the shrimp upright around the salade Russe.
4. Pipe a rosette of mayonnaise on top of the salade Russe and stick the remaining shrimp upright out of it.

WHOLE HAM IN MAYONNAISE COLLÉE

Yield:
about 6 lb (2.75 kg) EP

INGREDIENTS	U.S.	METRIC
8-lb (3.6-kg) fully-cooked, bone-in, shank-end smoked ham	1	1
Mayonnaise Collée (p. 660)	1 qt	1 L
Leek décor ribbon for tulip stem	1	1
Ham décor tulip	1	1
Large leek décor tulip leaves	2	2
¼-in. (0.6-cm) Carrot décor disks	2	2
¾-in. (2-cm) Rutabaga décor petals	16	16
Leek décor strings for grape flower stems	2	2
Red Flame grapes, each cut into 5 oval slices	2	2
⅛-in.(0.3-cm) Leek décor disks	70	70
Strong Mayonnaise Collée (p. 660)	1 pt	0.5 L
White Poultry Aspic for Coating (p. 644)	2 qt	2 L
Supplies		
Cutlet frill for ham bone (p. 718)	1	1

Note: Décor is illustrated on p. 715.

PROCEDURE

PREPARATION

1. Use a boning knife to remove all of the ham's rind, leaving a smooth surface throughout.
2. French the shank bone: Cut a slit around the bone about 3 in. (8 cm) from the end. Scrape the meat off the bone, leaving 3 in. (8 cm) clean, exposed bone. Wrap the bone in foil.
3. Place the ham on a rack set over a clean, grease-free sheet tray. Mask the cut end of the ham with a piece of plastic film.
4. Place an oval platter larger enough to hold the ham perfectly level in the refrigerator.
5. If necessary, melt and strain the mayonnaise collée. Coat the platter with a thin layer of mayonnaise collée, and then hold the remaining mayonnaise collée in a hot bain-marie with water no hotter than 180°F (82°C). Stir occasionally until you are ready to use it.
6. Follow the Procedure for Coating and Decorating Foods with Aspic and Chaud-Froid (p. 643) to coat with strong mayonnaise collée only the side surfaces of the ham. Do not coat the cut face of the ham.

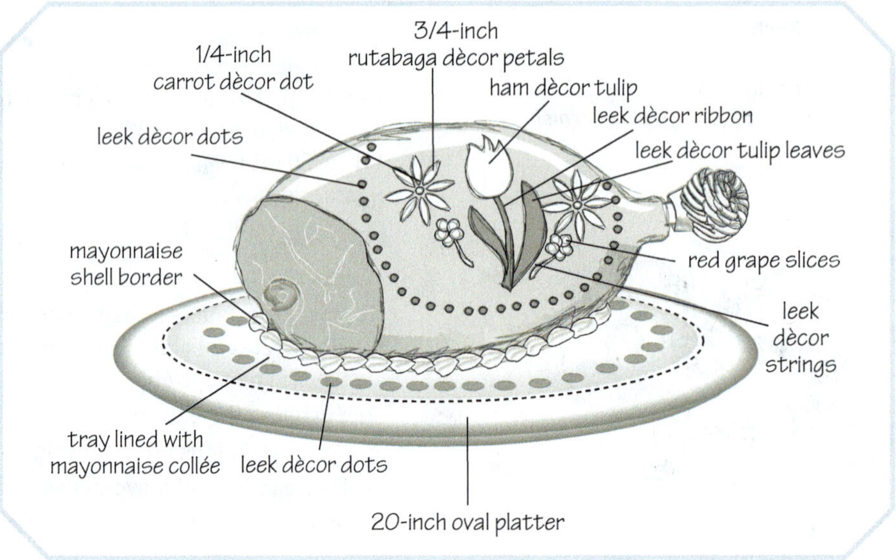

PROCEDURE

7. Decorate the ham. Reserve 40 leek décor dots for the platter.
8. Finish-coat the entire ham, including the face, with aspic.
9. Carefully place the ham on the mayonnaise collée–coated platter.
10. If necessary, melt the strong mayonnaise collée and cool it to piping consistency. Immediately place it in a pastry bag fitted with a medium star tip and pipe a shell border around the base of the ham.
11. Remelt the remaining aspic and cool it to syrupy texture. Use sanitized food-service tweezers to dip the remaining leek décor dots in the aspic and arrange them around the shell.
12. Quickly place the aspic in a squeeze bottle and squeeze a drop of aspic on each dot.

HOLDING

Refrigerate, uncovered, up to 24 hours.

FINISHING

13. Cover the aluminum foil–wrapped shankbone with the cutlet frill.

TERMS FOR REVIEW

coating sauce
aspic
chaud-froid
mayonnaise collée
fortify
gelatin
collagen
protein gel
unflavored dry gelatin
blooming
(to) bloom
set
granular gelatin
gelatin powder
sheet gelatin
leaf gelatin
gelatinize
working consistency
syrupy
aspic gelée
aspic jelly
gelée de viande
meat jelly
meatless aspic
clarify
clarity
(to) mask
masking sauce
surface décor/flat décor
rechaud
burr

QUESTIONS FOR DISCUSSION

1. List and describe the three basic coating sauces used in garde manger work. Explain at least one way you would use each of these sauces.
2. Compare and contrast the two market forms of unflavored dry gelatin. Which of these is typically used for garde manger work in North America? Why is it preferred?
3. What term is frequently used to describe the rehydration process for unflavored dry gelatin? Explain how this process is accomplished for each of the gelatin market forms.
4. List and describe the four steps in preparing and using a gelatinized liquid. Give the basic ratio of granular gelatin to liquid you would use to achieve a medium set.
5. List and describe the four steps in preparing an aspic.
6. Translate the French term *chaud-froid*. List the two meanings of the culinary term *chaud-froid*. Describe the primary application for chaud-froid sauce in modern garde manger work.
7. List the five steps in the preparation of chaud-froid sauce.
8. Define *mayonnaise collée*. How it is made, and how and when it is used?
9. Discuss surface décor for coated foods. Explain what it is made of and how it is prepared. List and describe some of the tools used to create it.
10. How you would set up a workspace for aspic and chaud-froid work? Include the equipment and food ingredients you need as well as the amount of space and the preferred particular location in the kitchen.
11. List the eight basic steps in coating and decorating work.
12. List and describe at least four applications for aspic, chaud-froid, and mayonnaise collée other than coating the surface of large and small food items.

Chapter 17

PREREQUISITES

Before studying this chapter, you should already

- Have read "How to Use This Book," pages xxviii–xxxiii, and understand the professional recipe format.
- Be proficient at rolling out and making up pastry products.
- Have mastered basic aspic techniques.

Condiments, Embellishments, and Décor

The perfect accompaniment or décor item can transform an ordinary dish into an extraordinary one. As a garde manger chef, you will frequently face the challenge of completing your product or presentation with a food that complements it both visually and in taste.

This chapter offers an array of condiments, accompaniments, advanced garnishes, and food décor techniques you can use throughout your garde manger career. Once you have mastered these basics, you can go on to make your own signature condiments and design unique décor items that reflect your talent and creativity.

After reading this chapter, you should be able to

1. Prepare ketchups, mustards, pickles, relishes, chutneys, and other condiments, and use them to complement a range of foods.
2. Prepare handmade crackers, chips, croûtons, and pastry cases for garde manger applications.
3. Make aspic garnishes and décor items.
4. Be proficient at basic fruit and vegetable carving.
5. Prepare savory ices and foams.
6. Be proficient at basic plate painting.
7. Create a simple ice sculpture.

FINISHING TOUCHES

Adding "a little something" to a presentation can be as easy as spooning a dollop of mustard onto a pâté plate or crowning a bowl of guacamole with a fan of tortilla chips. It can also be as challenging and time-consuming as arranging hundreds of tiny vegetable flowers on a chaud-froid creation. In all of these examples, the main food item is enhanced with a smaller, secondary food item.

In garde manger work, finishing touches are divided into three main categories: condiments, garnishes, and décor.

1. A ***condiment*** is an assertively flavored food added to or served along with a dish. Its main function is to enhance the flavor of the food with which it is served. Some condiments are also attractive and add visual appeal. For example, many condiments have bold colors. Others have interesting shapes or textures, or are fabricated into precise, good-looking cuts. Ketchups, mustards, relishes, and chutneys are examples of condiments.

2. A ***garnish*** is a small piece of food added to a presentation to provide a finishing touch. Garnishes must fulfill two main functions: to make the dish more attractive, and to make it taste better. Thus, a garnish is meant to be eaten. Some garnishes are simple, such as a dot of minced parsley placed on an hors d'oeuvre or a few cherry tomatoes arranged around a salad. Other garnishes are more elaborate.

   To distinguish more elaborate garnishes from simpler ones, in this text we call fancy, ornate garnishes ***embellishments***. Embellishments can add real drama to a plate or platter. For example, a spiral-shaped parsnip chip or a choux paste trellis adds height and visual interest to a complex salad presentation. The most complex and elaborate garnishes are actually miniature composed dishes, called ***garnitures***. These are served along with a larger main dish in order to make its presentation more attractive.

3. ***Décor*** means "decoration." In the culinary sense, *décor* refers both to small food décor items and large *pièces montées*.

   a. A ***décor item*** is a small piece of food added to a platter presentation to make it more attractive. While décor items must be edible, their main purpose is visual. Many are not meant to be eaten and, therefore, are inappropriate for plated presentations. Décor items also differ from garnishes in that they are frequently quite elaborate and require a lot of labor to create and present.

   b. A ***pièce montée*** is a large decorative food item. This French term literally translates as "mounted piece," and it means an object that rises or is elevated. *Pièces montées* are typically tall and frequently set up on risers so they can be seen as the focal point of a display. All must be made of edible materials, but while some are meant to be eaten, others are not. Large chaud-froid–coated and decorated food items, fruit and vegetable carvings, and ice sculptures are examples of modern *pièces montées*.

Mastering the preparation of condiments and embellishments and becoming proficient at décor work will make your products stand out from the competition.

Designing Cold Food Platters

Begin planning your platter design by drawing a sketch. Divide your platter into six or eight equal parts, as shown in the diagrams. This gives you equally spaced markers to use as guides.

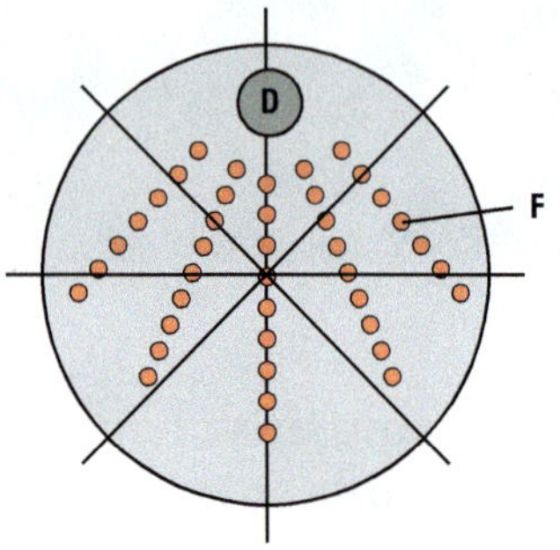

A décor item (D) usually provides the focal point for a formal platter presentation. It captures the eye, and leads the eye to the food items (F) that flow from it in graceful lines.

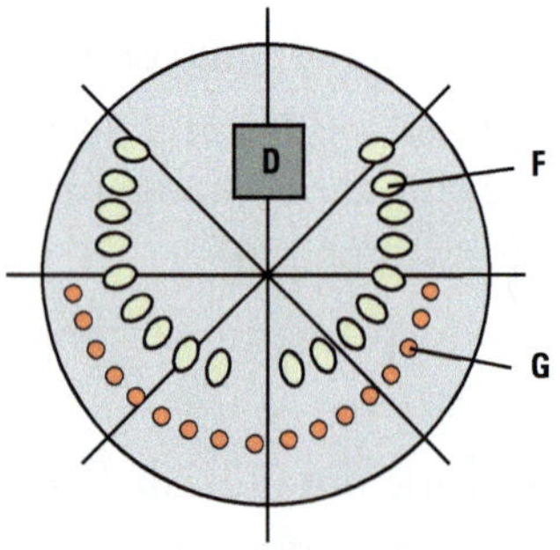

Garnitures (G) provide an additional design element, here repeating the semi-circular pattern established by the placement of the food items (F) around the décor item (D).

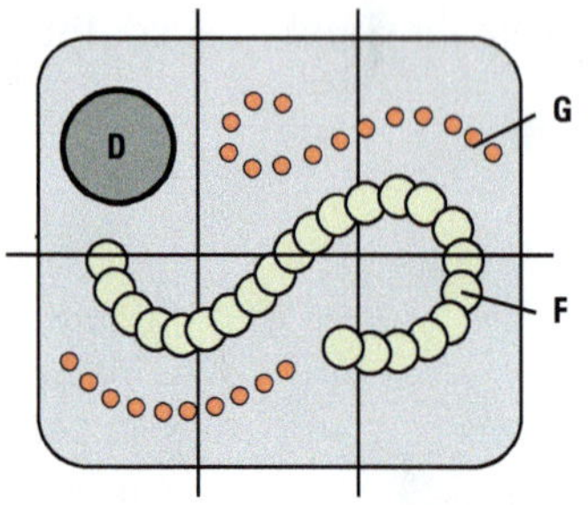

Create movement in your design by curving or angling the lines of both food items (F) and garnitures (G). Place the taller décor item (D) toward the back.

CONDIMENTS

One of the first recorded condiments was garum, a sauce made from fermented fish that was a feature of the cuisine of the Roman Empire. Today, condiments are as varied as the cuisines that produce them. Many modern condiments considered thoroughly North American have their roots in cuisines from around the world.

All condiments have in common a strength and boldness of flavor. They are typically sour, sweet, salty, spicy, or spicy-hot. Many include a combination of these basic tastes. Condiments enliven the flavors of milder-tasting foods. However, they should not be used in such large quantity that they mask or overwhelm the flavor of the foods they are paired with.

Many condiments are fluid, like sauces, but are classified separately from sauces for two reasons. First, they have strong, assertive flavors and are served in very small amounts. Second, they are prepared separately from the foods they accompany.

Fluid condiments may be poured over foods like sauces. Sometimes they are used to glaze foods as they are cooking. Saucelike condiments are also frequently served on the side, presented in little dishes, to be spooned onto foods in small dabs.

Other condiments are not fluid. Instead, they are thick pastes or consist of chunks or pieces of food. These are usually placed on the plate alongside the foods they accompany.

Condiments can be divided into a number of categories. Here is a list of the most common condiment types, with brief descriptions.

Mustards enhance an artisan sausage platter.

Ketchup, also spelled catsup, is a thick, smooth, saucelike condiment seasoned with onions, vinegar, and aromatic spices. When North Americans think of ketchup, they usually envision tomato ketchup. However, there are other types of ketchup made from other main ingredients. In the United Kingdom and its former colonies, mushroom ketchup is popular.

Prepared mustards are thick, smooth pastes made from ground mustard seeds and an acidic ingredient such as vinegar or sour wine.

Pickles are foods preserved in an acidic liquid, such as a vinegar solution, or in a fermented brine or other salted mixture. Modern pickles are usually based on vegetables or fruits.

Relishes are almost too varied to define. In its broadest meaning, *relish* refers to any piquant or refreshing food item used to enhance a dish or a meal. A platter of crisp, chilled raw vegetables, pickles, and olives is called a *relish tray*. When speaking of a *finishing touch relish*, we mean a mixture of chopped vegetables or fruits that has a tangy, acidic flavor. In North America, the most familiar relishes are cooked and heat-processed, such as sweet pickle relish or corn relish. Many traditional relishes have fanciful names, such as chow-chow or piccalilli. Chefs also prepare tangy uncooked mixtures of chopped or diced fresh vegetables and fruits to accompany cold meats, poultry, and seafood. Sometimes these mixtures are referred to as *salsas*, but they are more correctly called *fresh relishes* because they are chunky in texture, not pourable.

Compotes consist of a mixture of fresh and/or dried fruits simmered in sugar syrup. Compotes used in garde manger work are semisweet and frequently contain vinegar or spices.

In Search of Flavor

Garde manger chefs use special techniques to flavor liquids for making condiments and sauces.

To ***steep*** means to soak a flavorful ingredient, usually in hot water or a water-based liquid, in order to release its flavors. After it is steeped, the once-flavorful ingredient is discarded and the liquid retained. For example, to make tea, you steep tea leaves in water just under the boil.

To ***infuse*** means nearly the same thing as to steep. However, infusing may be done either hot or at room temperature. In culinary usage, this term more commonly refers to flavoring oils or vinegars, but it can be used for water-based liquids as well. An ***infusion*** is the fluid that results when infusing is compete. For example, the beverage tea is an infusion. Basil oil and garlic vinegar are also infusions.

To ***reduce*** means to boil or simmer a flavorful liquid in order to evaporate some of its water content and concentrate its flavor. A ***reduction*** is the result of reducing. Reductions are thicker in consistency and stronger in flavor than the original liquid. Mixtures that include stock are frequently used for reductions. Water-based infusions are sometimes reduced to strengthen their flavor as well. A reduction is sometimes called an essence.

Cooked chutneys consist of fruits and/or vegetables simmered with sugar, salt, vinegar, aromatic vegetables, and South Asian spices. They may be chunky or relatively smooth. Cooked chutneys are the type most frequently used in garde manger work.

Raw chutneys consist of herbs, soft textured vegetables, or soft, ripe fruits ground into a purée. They are seasoned with spices and raw chiles, and are frequently spicy-hot. Most raw chutneys are quite perishable and should be prepared just before service.

Jams and ***confitures*** are thick, rough-textured condiments made by cooking fruits or vegetables until they are highly reduced. Vegetable jams and confitures are typically made of vegetables that have a naturally high sugar content, such as onions and carrots. The long, slow cooking brings out the natural sugars present in the vegetables, so these mixtures are slightly sweet. Lemon juice, wine, or vinegar is often added to balance their flavors, as is salt.

Flavored vinegars are made by steeping or soaking herbs, spices, or aromatic vegetables in vinegar to create a flavorful infusion. The flavoring ingredients may be left in the vinegar for use or may be strained out and discarded.

Flavored oils may be prepared in the same way as flavored vinegars. Alternatively, they may be prepared by puréeing a flavorful ingredient with the oil. Once the oil has absorbed the flavor and color of the purée, you may strain it or use it as is. Thick, purée-style flavored oils are frequently used to accent plate presentations and for plate painting.

Vegetables preserved in oil, such as roasted peppers or grilled eggplant, are used as condiments. The oil in which they were preserved may be used as their dressing or used alone as a condiment it its own right.

Dipping sauces are highly seasoned liquid condiments. Dipping sauces may be thin or thick.

Glazes are flavorful, lightly sweetened liquids brushed or basted onto foods as they cook. To stick to the food, they must be moderately thick in texture. They are typically made by reducing flavorful liquids until they are thickened, or by thickening liquids with a cornstarch slurry.

Essences are highly reduced flavorful liquids. Essences may be used for plate painting, which provides visual interest, and as a powerful flavor element.

There are hundreds of kinds of condiments and many variations within each type.

TOMATO KETCHUP

Yield:
8 fl oz (240 mL)

INGREDIENTS	U.S.	METRIC
Water	8 fl oz	240 mL
Canned diced tomatoes in juice	16 fl oz	0.5 L
Minced yellow onion	1¼ oz	35 g
Cider vinegar	1½ fl oz	45 mL
Brown sugar	1 oz	30 g
Kosher salt	1 tbsp	15 mL
Dry mustard	1 tsp	5 mL
Sweet Hungarian paprika	½ tsp	3 mL
Ground allspice	¼ tsp	1 mL
Freshly ground black pepper	½ tsp	3 mL
Ground cloves	pinch	pinch

PROCEDURE

PREPARATION

1. Combine the ingredients in a small, nonreactive saucepan. Bring to the simmer.
2. Cook the mixture about 30 minutes, or until thickened and reduced by half. Stir the mixture occasionally. Scrape the bottom of the pan to prevent sticking and scorching.
3. Use an immersion blender to purée the mixture. Alternatively, force it through a food mill or sieve.
4. Stirring constantly, continue to reduce the mixture over moderate heat until the desired thickness is reached. Remember that the ketchup will thicken as it cools.
5. Correct the seasoning to achieve a salt-sugar-vinegar balance.
6. Open-pan cool to room temperature.
7. For best flavor, refrigerate at least 24 hours before using.

HOLDING

Refrigerate in a freshly sanitized squeeze bottle or covered, nonreactive container up to 2 weeks.

VARIATIONS

SPICY TEX-MEX KETCHUP

Add 1 oz (30 g) seeded, minced jalapeño chiles in step 1.

TOMATO-PEPPER KETCHUP

Replace 8 fl oz (240 mL) tomato with 12 fl oz (360 mL) roasted and peeled red bell pepper (p. 109).

COCKTAIL SAUCE

Add to the finished, cooled ketchup 3 tbsp (90 mL) prepared horseradish, 1 tbsp (30 mL) minced lemon zest, and fresh lemon juice to taste.

MUSHROOM KETCHUP

Yield:
8 fl oz (240 mL)

INGREDIENTS	U.S.	METRIC
Fresh mushrooms	1½ lb	0.75 kg
Kosher salt	1 tbsp	15 mL
Dried boletus mushrooms (porcini)	1 oz	30 g
Boiling water	8 fl oz	240 mL
Chopped shallots	6 oz	180 g
Minced garlic	¼ oz	7 g
Cider vinegar	1 fl oz	30 mL
Cold water	8 fl oz	240 mL
Ground cloves	¼ tsp	1 mL
Ground mace	½ tsp	3 mL
Ground ginger	½ tsp	3 mL
Anchovy paste	1 tsp	5 mL
Bay leaves	2	2
Madeira	2 fl oz	60 mL
Fine ground black pepper	¼ tsp	1 mL

PROCEDURE

DAY 1: PREPARATION

1. Wipe the fresh mushrooms clean with a damp towel. Slice the mushrooms paper-thin on a mandoline or with the fine slicing blade of a food processor.
2. Combine the sliced fresh mushrooms with the salt in a nonreactive container. Cover and refrigerate 24 hours.
3. Rinse the dried mushrooms and place them in a small container. Cover them with the boiling water and let stand at room temperature at least 1 hour and up to 24 hours.

DAY 2: PREPARATION

4. Drain the liquid off the sliced fresh mushrooms and reserve it. (The mushrooms will have turned dark brown, and the liquid will be almost black).
5. Place the sliced mushrooms in a food processor fitted with the grinding blade.
6. Drain the liquid off the boletus mushrooms and pass it through a fine-mesh sieve or dampened cheesecloth. Rinse the boletus mushrooms and squeeze them dry. Add them to the processor.
7. Add the shallots and garlic to the processor and grind the vegetables into a coarse purée. With the motor running, add the boletus soaking liquid through the feed tube. Add enough of the fresh mushroom liquid through the tube to make a loose purée.
8. Scrape the mushroom mixture into a large, nonreactive saucepan. Stir in the remaining mushroom liquid, vinegar, water, spices, and bay leaves.
9. Cook the mushroom mixture, uncovered, at a bare simmer about 1 hour, or until it is reduced by about half. If necessary, add more water to keep the mixture from sticking and scorching.
10. Remove the bay leaves and discard them. Purée the mixture smooth with an immersion blender. Alternatively, run it through a sieve or food mill.
11. Rinse the pan and return the ketchup to it along with the Madeira and the pepper. Reduce the ketchup, stirring often, to a thickness resembling that of tomato ketchup. Test the thickness by placing a spoonful on a cool plate. It should not release any watery liquid. If it does, reduce the ketchup further.

PROCEDURE

12. Taste and correct the salt and vinegar balance.
13. Open-pan cool the ketchup to room temperature.
14. For best flavor, refrigerate at least 24 hours before using.

HOLDING

Refrigerate in a freshly sanitized squeeze bottle or covered container up to 2 weeks.

The History of Ketchup

During the 1500s and 1600s, Europe was a crossroads of cuisines as returning explorers brought back new foods from around the globe. Europeans discovered and adopted ingredients and dishes from Asia, Africa, and the Americas. One of the foods they found in Asia was a thick, salty sauce—much like modern Chinese oyster sauce—made by cooking down aromatic vegetables seasoned with fermented fish. The Malay word, perhaps borrowed from Cantonese, for this condiment is *ke-chap* or *ke-tsiap*.

The English soon began preparing similar condiments based on their own native foods but seasoned with South Asian spices such as cinnamon and cloves. The name of this sauce was spelled *catchup*. In the 1600s, catchup was made from mushrooms, walnuts, oysters, and anchovies.

English colonists in the Americas adapted this preparation to local ingredients. Blueberry catchup and cranberry catchup were among the results. When the tomato was finally accepted as a food in the early 1800s, it became a favorite base ingredient for catchup, now often spelled *ketchup*. By 1837, a thin, watery version of tomato ketchup was being commercially produced and marketed. Ketchup acquired its present-day flavor and texture through improvements made by H.J. Heinz. Today, the Heinz brand is the foremost name in ketchup, and in most of the world, *ketchup* means "tomato ketchup."

In modern North American cooking, ketchup is not only a condiment but also an ingredient. It is used in cocktail sauce, in barbecue sauces, and even in Chinese-American stir-frys.

DIJON-STYLE MUSTARD

Yield:
about 8 fl oz (240 mL)

INGREDIENTS	U.S.	METRIC
White wine	12 fl oz	360 mL
Bay leaves, crumbled	2	2
Juniper berries	6	6
Minced shallots	1 oz	30 g
Minced garlic	¼ oz	7 g
Dry mustard	2 oz	60 g
Cool water	4 fl oz	120 mL
White wine vinegar	1 fl oz	30 mL
Honey	1 fl oz	30 mL
Kosher salt	1 tsp	5 mL

PROCEDURE

PREPARATION

1. Place the wine, bay leaves, juniper, shallots, and garlic in a small, nonreactive saucepan. Bring to the simmer and reduce by half.
2. Place the mustard in a small, nonreactive bowl. Whisk in a thin stream of cool water to make a moderately thick paste.
3. Cover the bowl and allow the mustard to hydrate and develop flavor at least 15 minutes.
4. Strain the wine reduction and discard the solids.
5. Whisk the wine reduction into the hydrated mustard and then scrape the mixture back into the saucepan. Add the honey and salt.
6. Simmer the mustard over low heat about 5 minutes, stirring constantly, until it thickens slightly and the flavors marry.
7. Open-pan cool to room temperature.
8. Transfer the mustard to a freshly sanitized, covered, nonreactive container.
9. Refrigerate at least 24 hours.

HOLDING

Refrigerate in a freshly sanitized, covered container up to 1 month.

VARIATION

ANCIENNE-STYLE MUSTARD

Pour 1 cup (240 mL) boiling water over 1 oz (30 g) brown mustard seeds and steep for 24 hours. Drain the mustard seeds and grind them to a coarse paste in a mortar. Add the ground mustard seeds in step 5.

BASIC PREPARED MUSTARD

Yield:
about 8 fl oz (240 mL)

INGREDIENTS	U.S.	METRIC
Dry mustard	2 oz	60 g
Cool water	5 fl oz (about)	150 mL (about)
White wine vinegar	1 fl oz	30 mL
Fine salt	1 tsp	5 mL
Sugar	1 tsp	5 mL

PROCEDURE

PREPARATION

1. Place the mustard powder in a small, nonreactive bowl. Whisk in a thin stream of cool water to make a moderately thick paste.
2. Cover the bowl and allow the mustard to hydrate and develop flavor at least 15 minutes.
3. Whisk in the vinegar, salt, and sugar. Add more water as needed to achieve the desired consistency.

HOLDING

Refrigerate in a freshly sanitized, covered container up to 1 month.

VARIATIONS

YELLOW MUSTARD

Decrease the vinegar to ½ fl oz (15 mL). Add 1 tsp (5 mL) turmeric in step 3.

CHINESE-STYLE MUSTARD

Replace the white wine vinegar with rice vinegar. Add pickled ginger pickling liquid to taste.

HONEY MUSTARD

Yield:
8 fl oz (240 mL)

INGREDIENTS	U.S.	METRIC
Dijon mustard or *Dijon-Style Mustard (p. 672)*	5 fl oz	150 mL
Honey	3 fl oz	90 mL

PROCEDURE

PREPARATION

1. Combine the mustard and honey and whisk until smooth.
2. Taste and adjust the balance as desired.

HOLDING

Store in a freshly sanitized, covered, nonreactive, container at cool room temperature up to 2 weeks.

GREEN PEPPERCORN MUSTARD

Yield:
8 fl oz (240 mL)

INGREDIENTS	U.S.	METRIC
Green peppercorns in brine	1 oz	30 g
Dijon mustard or *Dijon-Style Mustard (p. 672)*	6½ fl oz	200 mL
Sugar	½ oz	15 g

PROCEDURE

PREPARATION

1. Drain the peppercorns and reserve the brine.
2. Chop the peppercorns coarse and place them in a bowl.
3. Blend in the mustard and sugar.
4. Cover the bowl and hold at cool room temperature at least 20 minutes.
5. Taste and correct the flavor balance. Add a little peppercorn brine for a sharper flavor and thinner consistency.

HOLDING

Store in a freshly sanitized, covered, nonreactive container up to 1 month.

HOME-STYLE COOKED MUSTARD

Yield:
about 8 fl oz (240 mL)

INGREDIENTS	U.S.	METRIC
Dry mustard	1½ oz	45 g
Cool water	4 fl oz	120 mL
Egg	1	1
Egg yolk	1	1
Kosher salt	1 tsp	5 mL
Sugar	½ oz	15 g
Cider vinegar	3 fl oz	90 mL
Honey	½ fl oz	15 mL

PROCEDURE

PREPARATION

1. Place the mustard in a small, nonreactive bowl. Whisk in a thin stream of cool water to make a moderately thick paste.
2. Cover the bowl and allow the mustard to hydrate and develop flavor at least 15 minutes.
3. Beat the egg and yolk in a stainless-steel bowl until well mixed and fluffy. Whisk in the mustard and the remaining ingredients.
4. Place the bowl over a pan of simmering water and whisk about 5 minutes, or until the mustard thickens and reaches 150°F (65°C).
5. Open-pan cool the mustard and place it in a freshly sanitized, covered, nonreactive container.

HOLDING

Refrigerate up to 1 week.

VARIATION

PUB-STYLE BEER MUSTARD

Replace the sugar and honey with 1 oz (30 g) dark brown sugar. Replace 2 oz (60 mL) of the cider vinegar with lager beer. Replace the remaining cider vinegar with malt vinegar.

DILL PICKLES

Yield:
about 2 lb EP (1 kg)

INGREDIENTS	U.S.	METRIC
Unwaxed Kirby cucumbers	3 lb	1.5 kg
Filtered or distilled water	2 qt	2 L
Kosher salt	3 oz	90 g
Cider vinegar	5 fl oz	150 mL
Dill seeds	½ oz	15 g
Crumbled bay leaves	¼ oz	7 g
Crushed dried red pepper	¼ oz	7 g
Black peppercorns	¼ oz	7 g
Coriander seeds	¼ oz	7 g
Peeled garlic cloves	3 oz	90 g
Powdered alum (optional; see Note)	¼ tsp	1 mL
Fresh dill	4 oz	120 g

Note: Alum contributes to crunchy texture.

PROCEDURE

PREPARATION

1. Wearing food-service gloves, scrub the cucumbers thoroughly with a new nylon scrubbing pad. Trim the ends and any spots or bruises. If the cucumbers are small, they may be left whole. Otherwise, cut the cucumbers lengthwise into quarters or spears.
2. To make the brine, combine the water, salt, and vinegar in a nonreactive saucepan and begin heating it.
3. Clean and sanitize a plastic container just large enough to hold the pickles upright with about 3 in. (8 cm) headroom. Clean and sanitize the lid. Place the container, its lid, and tongs in a pressure steamer for 5 minutes, or immerse them in boiling water for 10 minutes, to sterilize them.
4. Bring the brine to a boil and make sure the salt is dissolved.
5. Wearing food-service gloves, pack the cucumbers upright and snug into the hot container.
6. Pour the boiling brine over the cucumbers. There should be enough to cover them by at least 1 in. (2.5 cm). Reserve the remaining brine.
7. Scatter the spices and garlic cloves over the surface of the brine.
8. If using the alum, sprinkle it on top and stir it into the brine with the sterilized tongs.
9. Use the sterilized tongs to push the dill sprigs, and with them the spices, between the cucumbers, submerging them in the brine.
10. Place the container in a hotel pan and set the lid on top. Do not seal the lid shut.
11. Cool the unused brine, place it in a covered container, and refrigerate it.
12. Store the pickles in a cool, dark place, 55°–65°F (13°–18°C), and allow them to ferment up to 10 days. The brine will begin to bubble and may overflow the container. Monitor the pickles daily, and, if the brine threatens to go below the level of the pickles, top them off with more boiled, cooled brine.
13. For half-sours, stop the fermentation before the bubbling stops, at a sourness of your liking. Taste a pickle after 5 days and check its flavor. (Sterilize any utensil you use to handle the pickles.) Stop fermentation by refrigerating the pickles.
14. For full-sours, wait until the bubbling stops, then refrigerate the pickles.

HOLDING

Refrigerate up to 2 months.

PICKLED PEARL ONIONS

Yield:
1 pt (0.5 L)

INGREDIENTS	U.S.	METRIC
Red or white pearl onions	1 lb	0.5 kg
White wine vinegar	8 fl oz	240 mL
Sugar	2 oz	60 g
Bay leaves	2	2
Small dried red chile	1	1
Fresh thyme	⅛ oz (2 sprigs)	4 g (2 sprigs)
Peppercorns	1/16 oz (6)	2 g (6)
Kosher salt	1 tbsp	30 mL
Filtered or distilled water	as needed	as needed

PROCEDURE

PREPARATION

1. Trim the root ends of the onions and cut an *X* in each.
2. Blanch the onions 10–12 seconds and immediately refresh them. Drain and blot dry on towels.
3. Cut off the stem ends of the onions and slip off their skins.
4. Put the onions in a nonreactive saucepan just large enough to hold them with about 1 in. (3 cm) of room to spare.
5. Add the vinegar, sugar, herbs and spices, salt, and enough water to just cover the onions.
6. Bring the pickling liquid to a simmer and stir gently until the sugar dissolves.
7. Cook the onions at a bare simmer to *à point* texture.
8. Transfer the onions to a freshly sanitized, nonreactive container just large enough to hold them.
9. Cool the pickling liquid to room temperature and pour it over the onions. Cover the container and refrigerate at least 24 hours.

HOLDING

Refrigerate up to 1 month.

VARIATIONS

PICKLED RED ONIONS

Replace the pearl onions with 1 qt (1 L) or about 1 lb (0.5 kg) thin-sliced red onions.

PICKLED VEGETABLES

Any firm vegetable or mixture of vegetables may be pickled in the same way. Fabricate the vegetables into uniform sizes. (Green vegetables will turn olive green from the acid in the pickling liquid.)

QUICK PICKLED GRAPES

Yield:
about 1 qt (1 L)

INGREDIENTS	U.S.	METRIC
Red Flame grapes or other table grapes	1 lb	0.5 kg
Japanese rice vinegar	8 fl oz	240 mL
Cider vinegar	4 fl oz	120 mL
Sugar	4 oz	120 g
Kosher salt	1 tbsp	15 mL
Bay leaves	6	6

PROCEDURE

PREPARATION

1. Remove the grapes from their stems.
2. Wash the grapes in cool running water and drain them well.
3. Blot the grapes completely dry on clean, lint-free towels.
4. Place the grapes in a freshly sanitized, nonreactive container just large enough to hold them with about 1 in. (3 cm) of headroom.
5. To make the pickling liquid, bring the remaining ingredients to the boil. Stir once or twice to ensure the sugar dissolves.
6. Taste the pickling liquid and, if necessary, adjust the sweet-acid-salt balance.
7. Pour the hot pickling liquid over the grapes. Let stand, uncovered, 24 hours.

HOLDING

Cover and refrigerate the grapes in their pickling liquid up to 24 hours longer. For additional keeping time, drain the grapes and hold up to 2 days longer. The pickling liquid may be brought to the boil and used again.

VARIATION

PICKLED PRUNE PLUMS

Replace the grapes with halved and pitted Italian prune plums. Increase pickling time to 4 days.

SWEET AND TANGY CUCUMBER RELISH

Yield:
1 qt (1 L)

INGREDIENTS	U.S.	METRIC
Unwaxed Kirby cucumbers	3 lb	1.5 kg
Peeled yellow onions, quartered	12 oz	360 g
Cored and seeded red bell peppers, cut brunoise	12 oz	360 g
Kosher salt	1 oz	30 g
Cider vinegar	8 fl oz	240 mL
Light brown sugar	3 oz	90 g
Turmeric	1 tsp	5 mL
Yellow mustard seeds	1 tsp	5 mL
Ground allspice	¼ tsp	1 mL
Ground cinnamon	¼ tsp	1 mL
Ground cloves	¼ tsp	1 mL
Ground ginger	¼ tsp	1 mL

PROCEDURE

DAY 1: PREPARATION

1. Trim the ends off the cucumbers. Cut them in half lengthwise and scrape out the seeds.
2. Run the cucumbers and onions through a meat grinder fitted with the coarse die. (Do not grind them in a food processor. If a meat grinder is not available, chop the vegetables by hand.)
3. Place the cucumber mixture, peppers, and salt in a nonreactive container and mix them thoroughly. Cover the container with a clean kitchen towel and allow the mixture to stand at cool room temperature at least 12 hours and up to 24 hours.

DAY 2: PREPARATION

4. Transfer the cucumber mixture to a large sieve and press firmly to remove as much liquid as possible.
5. Place the drained cucumber mixture in a nonreactive saucepan with the remaining ingredients. Stir thoroughly, cover, and bring to the boil.
6. Uncover the pan and cook at a rapid boil 10 minutes.
7. If the relish appears too watery, ladle off some of the liquid.
8. Taste the relish and correct the salt-sugar-vinegar balance.
9. Open-pan cool.
10. Place the relish in a freshly sanitized, nonreactive container. Cover and refrigerate at least 2 weeks before using.

HOLDING

Refrigerate up to 3 months.

CORN RELISH

Yield:
about 1 qt (1 L)

INGREDIENTS	U.S.	METRIC
Raw fresh corn kernels	12 oz	360 g
Fine chopped green or white cabbage	6 oz	180 g
Chopped yellow onions	4 oz	120 g
Fine diced red bell peppers	4 oz	120 g
Fine diced seeded jalapeño chiles	4 oz	120 g
Kosher salt	2 tbsp	30 mL
Dry mustard	1 tbsp	15 mL
Celery seed	1 tsp	5 mL
Sugar	8 oz	240 g
Cider vinegar	10 fl oz	300 mL

PROCEDURE

PREPARATION

1. Combine all ingredients in a nonreactive saucepan.
2. Cover and bring to the boil.
3. Stir the mixture and leave the pan partially covered. Cook at a lively simmer, stirring occasionally, 30 minutes.
4. Taste and adjust the sugar-salt-acid balance if necessary.
5. Open-pan cool to room temperature and place in a freshly sanitized, nonreactive container. Place a small plate or other nonreactive object on the relish and press down on it to keep the relish submerged in its pickling liquid.
6. Refrigerate at least 1 week before serving.

HOLDING

Refrigerate up to 2 months.

ANGLO-INDIAN MANGO CHUTNEY

Yield:
1 pt (0.5 L)

INGREDIENTS	U.S.	METRIC
Unripe mangoes	2 lb	1 kg
Kosher salt	½ oz	15 g
Turmeric	1 tsp	5 mL
Peeled, minced fresh ginger	4 oz	120 g
Chopped yellow onions	6 oz	180 g
Chopped fresh green chile (Asian or Serrano)	1 oz	30 g
Raisins	3 oz	90 g
Brown sugar	8 oz	240 g
Cider vinegar	8 oz	240 mL
Cloves	6	6
Cardamom pods	12	12
Coriander seeds	1 tbsp	15 g
Fenugreek seeds	2 tsp	10 mL
Crushed cinnamon stick	1	1
Crumbled bay leaves	2	2
Crumbled dried red Asian chiles	1 or 2	1 or 2
Water	as needed	as needed

PROCEDURE

DAY 1: PREPARATION

1. Peel the mangoes and cut the flesh away from the seeds. Cut the mango flesh into ½-in. (1-cm) dice.
2. Mix the mango dice with the salt and turmeric in a nonreactive container. Cover loosely with plastic film and let stand at cool room temperature about 24 hours.

DAY 2: PREPARATION

3. Combine the mangoes and their liquid with the ginger, onion, chile, raisins, brown sugar, and vinegar in a nonreactive saucepan. Bring the mixture to the boil.
4. Prepare a spice sachet: Wrap the spices in one layer of cheesecloth and tie the sachet with string. Cut off excess cheesecloth and string.
5. Add just enough water to cover the mango mixture. Add the sachet. Bring to the simmer and cook, stirring occasionally, about 15 minutes, or until the mangoes are tender and the syrup around them thickens.
6. Remove the sachet.
7. If necessary, remove the mangoes from the syrup, boil it down, and then return the mangoes to it.
8. Open-pan cool to room temperature.

HOLDING

Refrigerate in a freshly sanitized, covered container up to 2 weeks.

CHERRY-PEAR CHUTNEY

Yield:
1 pt (0.5 L)

INGREDIENTS	U.S.	METRIC
Minced fresh ginger	½ oz	15 g
Dried cherries	2 oz	60 g
White wine	4 fl oz	120 mL
Sugar	6 oz	180 g
Broken cinnamon stick	½	½
Cloves	6	6
Cardamom pods	10	10
Coriander seeds	1 tsp	5 mL
Peeled firm pears, cut in ⅜-in. (1-cm) dice	1 lb	0.5 kg
Water	as needed	as needed
Fresh lemon juice	to taste	to taste

PROCEDURE

PREPARATION

1. Combine the ginger, cherries, wine, and sugar in a nonreactive saucepan. Bring the mixture to the boil.
2. Prepare a spice sachet: Wrap the spices in one layer of cheesecloth and tie the sachet with string. Cut off excess cheesecloth and string.
3. Add the pears and spice sachet to the pan. Add just enough water to cover the pears. Bring to the simmer and cook, stirring occasionally, about 15 minutes, or until the pears are tender and the syrup around them thickens. If necessary, remove the pears from the syrup, boil it down, and then return the pears to it.
4. Remove the sachet.
5. Open-pan cool to room temperature.

HOLDING

Refrigerate in a freshly sanitized, covered container up to 2 weeks.

VARIATIONS

APPLE-RAISIN CHUTNEY

Replace the dried cherries with raisins. Replace the pears with tart cooking apples.

PEACH CHUTNEY

Omit the cherries. Replace the pears with 1½ lb (0.75 kg) peeled, pitted, diced peaches.

Understanding Chutneys

In the many regional cuisines of India and other South Asian countries, cold sauces, relishes, and jamlike condiments are used to accent snacks, appetizers, salads, and kebabs. Although they have specific names in many South Asian languages, they can be roughly grouped under the generic Hindi term *chatni.* Most are raw sauces made from fresh herbs, aromatic vegetables or fruits, and fresh chiles, although some are cooked.

In the nineteenth century, British government officials stationed in India grew fond of these condiments and wished to bring them home to Britain. They discovered that only the sweet-spicy, long-cooked fruit chutneys could be transported overseas without spoiling. The most popular of these, a sweet mango chutney that includes onions, ginger, and raisins, was mass-produced in Britain under the name Major Grey's Chutney™. For many years, this was the only type of chutney widely known in the West. Today, many Western chefs are discovering the wide spectrum of chutneys that South Asian cuisines have to offer.

RED ONION CONFITURE

Yield:
about 8 fl oz (240 mL)

INGREDIENTS	U.S.	METRIC
Safflower oil or corn oil	2 fl oz	60 mL
Red onions, peeled, halved, and sliced thin	1 lb	0.5 kg
Bay leaves	2	2
Kosher salt	to taste	to taste
Red wine	2 fl oz	60 mL
Water	as needed	as needed
Maraschino cherry juice	to taste	to taste
Fresh lemon juice	to taste	to taste
Fine ground white pepper	to taste	to taste

PROCEDURE

PREPARATION

1. Warm the oil over moderate heat in a large, nonreactive sauté pan. Stir in the onions, bay leaves, salt, and the wine.
2. Cover the pan and sweat the onions over low heat, stirring occasionally, until the onions are wilted but not browned. Use a heatproof rubber spatula to scrape up the pan glaze, and add water as needed to prevent sticking.
3. When the onions are very soft, uncover the pan and add just enough cherry juice to heighten the red color of the onions. Stir over moderate heat until all the liquid evaporates and the onions just begin to sizzle.
4. Remove the bay leaves and balance the flavor with lemon juice and salt. Season with pepper.
5. Open-pan cool to room temperature.

HOLDING

Refrigerate in a freshly sanitized, covered container up to 2 weeks.

FIG JAM

Yield:
about 1 pt (0.5 L)

INGREDIENTS	U.S.	METRIC
Tart cooking apples	8 oz	240 g
Sugar	12 oz	360 g
Ripe figs	8 oz	240 g
Fresh lemon juice	to taste	to taste

PROCEDURE

DAY 1: PREPARATION

1. Peel and core the apples. Cut them into ½-in. (1-cm) dice. Place the apples in a nonreactive container and mix them with the sugar.
2. Wash the figs and remove the fibrous stem ends. Cut the figs into ½-in. (1-cm) dice. Mix the figs with the apples.
3. Cover the container loosely with plastic film. Let stand at cool room temperature 24 hours.

DAY 2: PREPARATION

4. Transfer the mixture and all its juices to a heavy, nonreactive saucepan. Cover and bring to the simmer.
5. Uncover and cook at a lively simmer, stirring often, about 20 minutes, or until the mixture is thick and reduced. For the last few minutes of cooking, scrape the bottom of the pan with a heatproof rubber spatula to avoid sticking and scorching.
6. Taste the jam and season with lemon juice if needed.
7. Open-pan cool to room temperature.

HOLDING

Refrigerate up to 1 month in a freshly sanitized, covered container.

Procedure for Infusing Flavored Vinegars and Oils

1. Prepare the flavoring ingredients as appropriate:
   a. Wash and thoroughly dry bouquets of fresh herbs.
   b. Tie dried herbs and spices in a sachet.
   c. Peel and lightly crush aromatic vegetables.
   d. Slice citrus fruits thin, or peel off zest in wide bands.
2. Sanitize a nonreactive container and its lid.
3. Place the flavoring ingredients in the container.
4. Heat the vinegar or oil to 200°F (93°C) and immediately pour it into the container.
5. Place the lid partially on the container and allow the flavoring ingredients to steep at cool room temperature 24–48 hours.
6. Strain the vinegar or oil through doubled cheesecloth into another, smaller, sanitized container, and cover with a sanitized lid.

IDEAS FOR FLAVORED VINEGARS

LEMON-THYME VINEGAR

Infuse 2 oz (60 g) fresh thyme sprigs and the zest of 2 lemons in 1 pt (0.5 L) white wine vinegar.

TARRAGON VINEGAR

Infuse 3 oz (90 g) fresh tarragon sprigs in 1 pt (0.5 L) white wine vinegar.

RASPBERRY VINEGAR

Infuse 1 pt (0.5 L) raspberries in 1 pt (0.5 L) Japanese rice wine vinegar heated to 120°F (48°C).

Infused vinegar
© *iStockphoto.*

SPICY GARLIC-OREGANO RED WINE VINEGAR

Infuse 2 oz (60 g) crushed, peeled garlic cloves, 1 oz (30 g) fresh oregano sprigs, and 2–3 small dried red chiles in 1 pt (0.5 L) red wine vinegar.

GINGER VINEGAR

Infuse 3 oz (90g) finely sliced fresh ginger in 1 pt (0.5 L) Japanese rice wine vinegar.

HOT PEPPER VINEGAR

Infuse 3 oz (90 g) sliced fresh banana peppers or long hot green chiles in 1 pt (0.5 L) cider vinegar.

IDEAS FOR INFUSED FLAVORED OILS

ROSEMARY-GARLIC OIL

Infuse 2 oz (60 g) fresh rosemary sprigs and 1 oz (30 g) crushed, peeled garlic cloves in 1 pt (0.5 L) extra-virgin olive oil.

CITRUS OIL

Infuse the zest (in strips) of 2 oranges and 1 lemon in 1 pt (0.5 L) safflower oil.

PAPRIKA OIL

Infuse 1 oz (30 g) sweet Hungarian paprika in 8 fl oz (240 mL) pure golden olive oil.

SPICE TRADE OIL

Infuse 2 cinnamon sticks, ¼ whole nutmeg, 8 cardamom pods, 2 cloves, 2–3 small dried red chiles, 1 tsp (5 mL) black peppercorns, 2 peeled and lightly crushed garlic cloves, and ½ oz (15 g) sliced fresh ginger in 1 pt (0.5 L) pure golden olive oil.

ASIAN SCALLION-GINGER OIL

Infuse 6 oz (180 g) minced scallions and 4 oz (120 g) minced fresh ginger in 10 fl oz (300 mL) peanut oil. Add 1 tsp (5 mL) kosher salt and 2–3 drops Asian sesame oil. Cool and refrigerate. Do not strain.

Procedure for Making Puréed Herb Oils

A

B

C

D

1. Place herb leaves or sprigs in a strainer. Blanch them by dipping them in rapidly boiling water for 1 second. Immediately refresh them in ice water.
2. Drain the herb leaves, spread them on clean, lint-free paper towels, and roll them up to dry them thoroughly (A).
3. Chop the herbs coarse.
4. Place the chopped herbs in a food processor fitted with the steel blade.
5. With the blade running, pour in the oil in a thin stream (B).
6. For strongest flavor and color:
   a. Transfer the mixture to a freshly sanitized container.
   b. Cover and refrigerate 24 hours.
   c. Bring the herb-oil mixture to room temperature.
7. Set a strainer in a bowl and line it with doubled cheesecloth.
8. Pour the herb-oil mixture into the cheesecloth-lined strainer (C).
9. Allow the oil to drain through the cheesecloth about 10 minutes.
10. Pick up the edges of the cheesecloth and squeeze as much oil out of the herbs as possible (D). Discard the herbs.
11. Transfer the oil to a freshly sanitized squeeze bottle.

BRIGHT GREEN BASIL OIL

Yield:
8 fl oz (240 mL)

INGREDIENTS	U.S.	METRIC
Fresh basil leaves	3 oz	90 g
Flat-leaf parsley leaves	1 oz	30 g
Extra-virgin olive oil	8 fl oz	240 mL

PROCEDURE

PREPARATION

1. Follow the Procedure for Making Puréed Herb Oils on page 685.
2. Transfer to a freshly sanitized squeeze bottle.

HOLDING

Best if used immediately. May be refrigerated up to 2 days, but the oil will gradually lose color and fresh flavor. Bring to room temperature before serving.

VARIATIONS

BRIGHT GREEN CHIVE OIL

Replace the basil and parsley with fresh chives.

BRIGHT GREEN CHERVIL OIL

Replace the basil and parsley with fresh chervil.

BRIGHT GREEN PARSLEY OIL

Replace the basil with 4 oz (120 g) flat-leaf parsley.

BRIGHT GREEN TARRAGON OIL

Replace the basil and parsley with fresh tarragon. Replace the olive oil with safflower oil.

BRIGHT GREEN MINT OIL

Replace the basil and parsley with fresh mint. Replace the olive oil with safflower oil.

RED BELL PEPPER OIL

Yield:
8 fl oz (240 mL)

INGREDIENTS	U.S.	METRIC
Roasted, peeled, and chopped red bell peppers (p. 109)	8 fl oz	240 mL
Pure golden olive oil	8 fl oz	240 mL
Salt	to taste	to taste

PROCEDURE

PREPARATION

1. Combine the peppers and oil in a small saucepan and heat to 120°F (48°C).
2. Set the pan in a hot bain-marie and hold the mixture at 120°F (48°C) 30 minutes.
3. Cool the mixture to room temperature.
4. Follow steps 4–11 of the Procedure for Making Puréed Herb Oils on page 685.
5. Season with salt.

HOLDING

Best if used immediately. May be refrigerated up to 2 days, but will gradually lose color and fresh flavor. Bring to room temperature before serving.

VARIATIONS

RED BELL PEPPER GARLIC OIL

Replace 1 oz (30 g) peppers with 1 oz (30 g) chopped fresh garlic.

YELLOW BELL PEPPER OIL

Replace the roasted red bell peppers with roasted yellow bell peppers. When roasting the peppers, be careful not to allow them to discolor.

ORANGE BELL PEPPER OIL

Replace the roasted red bell peppers with orange bell peppers. When roasting the peppers, be careful not to allow them to discolor.

CARROT OIL

Replace the red bell peppers with grated carrots. Season to taste with fresh lemon juice.

BEET OIL

Replace the red bell peppers with grated raw red beets. Season to taste with red wine vinegar.

TOMATO OIL

Replace the red bell peppers with vine-ripe tomato concassé that has been squeezed dry of moisture. Add 1 tbsp (15 g) tomato paste in step 3.

PESTO ALLA GENOVESE *(pay-stoh ah la jay-no-VAY-say)*
GENOA BASIL PASTE

yield:
1 pt (0.5 L)

INGREDIENTS	U.S.	METRIC
Chopped fresh basil leaves	4 oz	120 g
Pine nuts	½ oz	15 g
Grated Reggiano Parmesan cheese	1 oz	30 g
Chopped fresh garlic	½ oz	15 g
Extra-virgin olive oil	6 fl oz	180 mL
Kosher salt	to taste	to taste

PROCEDURE

PREPARATION

1. Place the basil, pine nuts, cheese, and garlic in a food processor fitted with the steel blade.
2. Turn the processor on and pour the olive oil through the feed tube in a thin stream to make a thick purèe.
3. Season the pesto with salt.

HOLDING

Refrigerate in a small, freshly sanitized container, with plastic wrap directly on the surface of the pesto, up to 24 hours. Freeze up to 1 month.

VARIATIONS

TRADITIONAL PESTO ALLA GENOVESE
Prepare the pesto by pounding it to a rough paste in a mortar.

PARSLEY PESTO
Replace the basil leaves with flat-leaf parsley.

ROASTED PEPPERS IN GARLIC OIL

Yield:
1 lb (0.5 L), plus flavored oil

INGREDIENTS	U.S.	METRIC
Extra-virgin olive oil	6 fl oz	180 mL
Very fresh garlic, minced	1 oz	30 g
Salt	to taste	to taste
Roasted red bell peppers (p. 109)	8 oz	240 g
Roasted yellow bell peppers (p. 109)	8 oz	240 g

PROCEDURE

PREPARATION

1. Combine the oil and garlic in a freshly sanitized, nonreactive container just large enough to hold the peppers. Season it generously with salt and allow to mellow at cool room temperature about 30 minutes.
2. Fabricate the peppers as desired.
3. Mix the peppers with the garlic oil.
4. Cover the container and mellow at room temperature 1 hour.

HOLDING

Refrigerate up to 1 week. Bring to room temperature before serving.

DRIED TOMATOES IN OIL

Yield:
about 8 oz (240 g), plus flavored oil

INGREDIENTS	U.S.	METRIC
Firm plum tomatoes	1½ lb	0.75 kg
Kosher salt	to taste	to taste
Pure golden olive oil	4–6 oz	120–180 mL

PROCEDURE

DAY 1: PREPARATION

1. Core the tomatoes and cut them in half lengthwise.
2. Place the tomatoes on a sheet tray, cut surfaces up, and sprinkle them generously with salt. Let stand at cool room temperature 1 hour.
3. Line another sheet tray with paper towels and place the tomatoes on it, cut surfaces down. Allow to drain at cool room temperature 1 hour.
4. Prepare a food dehydrator by setting a drip pan on the bottom rack. Pull out enough racks to hold the tomatoes in a single layer.
5. Arrange the tomatoes, cut surfaces up, on the dehydrator racks and brush them lightly with about 1 fl oz (30 mL) of the oil.
6. Dehydrate the tomatoes on the lowest heat setting 2–3 days. When properly dehydrated, the tomatoes will feel leathery to the touch and show no moisture when squeezed.

FINAL DAY: PREPARATION

7. Toss the tomatoes with the remaining oil and pack them into a freshly sanitized, nonreactive container.

HOLDING

Hold at cool room temperature up to 1 week. Refrigerate up to 3 months.

VARIATION

TOMATO CONFIT

Peel the tomatoes by blanching and refreshing before cutting them in half, salting, and draining. Arrange the tomatoes snug in one tight layer in a half-hotel pan and drizzle with the oil. If desired, add peeled garlic cloves and herb sprigs. Bake at 200°F (100°C) for about 2 hours until flattened and semi-dry.

PREPARED WASABI

Yield:
varies

INGREDIENTS	U.S.	METRIC
Powdered wasabi	½ oz	15 mL
Water	as needed	as needed

PROCEDURE

PREPARATION

1. Place the powder in a small bowl and mix in just enough water to make a smooth paste.
2. Cover the bowl and allow the wasabi to develop and hydrate 20 minutes.
3. Adjust the texture as desired by adding more water.

HOLDING

Store at cool room temperature up to 1 week. Refrigerate indefinitely. Bring to room temperature before using.

WASABI SOY DIP

Yield:
8 fl oz (240 g)

INGREDIENTS	U.S.	METRIC
Thick *Prepared Wasabi (p. 689)*	1 fl oz	30 mL
Japanese or light Chinese soy sauce	6 fl oz	180 mL
Liquid from pickled ginger	1 fl oz	30 mL

PROCEDURE

PREPARATION

1. Place the wasabi in a small bowl. Whisk in the soy sauce and pickled ginger liquid.

HOLDING

Hold at cool room temperature up to 4 hours. Refrigerate in a freshly sanitized, covered container up to 1 week. Bring to room temperature and shake or stir well before using.

BALSAMIC GLAZE

Yield:
4 fl oz (120 mL)

INGREDIENTS	U.S.	METRIC
Standard balsamic vinegar	8 oz	240 mL
Sugar	1 oz	30 g

PROCEDURE

PREPARATION

1. Combine the vinegar and sugar in a small, nonreactive saucepan.
2. Stir the mixture over low heat until the sugar dissolves.
3. Reduce the mixture by half very slowly over low heat.
4. Open-pan cool.

HOLDING

Refrigerate in a freshly sanitized squeeze bottle or nonreactive container up to 1 month.

SOY GLAZE

Yield:
8 fl oz (240 mL)

INGREDIENTS	U.S.	METRIC
Japanese or light Chinese soy sauce	4 fl oz	120 mL
Honey	2 fl oz	60 mL
Poultry Stock (p. 749)	3 fl oz	90 mL
Fresh lemon juice or lime juice	to taste	to taste

PROCEDURE

PREPARATION

1. Combine the soy, honey, and stock in a nonreactive saucepan and bring the mixture to a full, rolling boil.
2. Cool to room temperature.
3. Add lemon or lime juice to taste.

HOLDING

Refrigerate in a freshly sanitized container up to 3 days.

VERJUS ESSENCE

Yield:
about 4 fl oz (120 mL)

INGREDIENTS	U.S.	METRIC
Strong, defatted *Brown Beef and/or Veal Stock (p. 751)*	8 fl oz	240 mL
Red or white verjus (p. 23)	4 fl oz	120 mL
Kosher salt	to taste	to taste

PROCEDURE

PREPARATION

1. Combine the stock and verjus in a nonreactive saucepan.
2. Simmer the mixture over low heat until it is reduced by two-thirds and has the consistency of light syrup. During the last few minutes of cooking, stir and scrape the bottom of the pan with a heatproof rubber spatula to prevent sticking and scorching.
3. Season with salt.
4. Open-pan cool.

HOLDING

Refrigerate in a freshly sanitized squeeze bottle up to 1 week.

VARIATIONS

BALSAMIC ESSENCE

Replace the verjus with balsamic vinegar.

ORANGE ESSENCE

Replace the verjus with 8 fl oz (240 mL) orange juice.

POMEGRANATE ESSENCE

Replace the verjus with 2 fl oz (60 mL) pomegranate juice.

CASSIS ESSENCE

Replace the verjus with 2 fl oz (60 mL) crème de cassis liqueur.

CARROT ESSENCE

Replace the stock and verjus with 12 fl oz (360 mL) carrot juice made by processing carrots in a juice extractor.

SAUCE MIGNONETTE

Yield:
about 5 fl oz (150 mL)
Portions:
4
Portion size:
1¼ fl oz (about 35 mL)

INGREDIENTS	U.S.	METRIC
Crushed black peppercorns	¼ oz	7 g
Minced shallots	½ oz	15 g
Red wine vinegar	4 fl oz	120 mL
Salt	pinch	pinch

PROCEDURE

1. Combine all ingredients in a nonreactive container.
2. Refrigerate at least 30 minutes.

HOLDING

Refrigerate in a covered, nonreactive container up to 2 days.

CUMBERLAND SAUCE

Yield:
about 1 pt (0.5 L)

INGREDIENTS	U.S.	METRIC
Dry mustard	2 tsp	10 mL
Ground dried ginger	1 tsp	5 mL
Ground cloves	pinch	pinch
Orange juice	6 fl oz	180 mL
Minced shallots	½ oz	15 g
Minced golden raisins	2 oz	60 g
Red currant jelly	4 fl oz	120 mL
Cornstarch	1 tbsp (about)	15 mL (about)
Water	as needed	as needed
Minced orange zest	2 tbsp	30 mL
Minced lemon zest	1 tbsp	15 mL
Red port wine	4 fl oz	120 mL

PROCEDURE

PREPARATION

1. Place the mustard, ginger, and cloves in a small, nonreactive saucepan. Whisk in the orange juice in a thin stream. Add the shallots, raisins, and currant jelly.
2. Bring the mixture to a simmer and cook about 5 minutes, or until the raisins are very soft. Add water if the mixture becomes too thick.
3. Make a thick slurry with the cornstarch and a little water.
4. Add the zests and port to the saucepan and bring to a full boil. Immediately whisk in just enough cornstarch slurry to lightly thicken the sauce to light nappé. (Remember that it will thicken slightly when it cools.) Boil for a few seconds until the sauce is translucent.
5. Open-pan cool the sauce.
6. Taste and correct the sweet-acid balance if necessary.

HOLDING

Refrigerate in a freshly sanitized, covered container up to 2 weeks.

EMBELLISHMENTS

Embellishment has its roots in the Latin word *bellus*, meaning "beautiful." We use this word to refer to the wide variety of garnishes more elaborate than the typical sprig of parsley or slice of lemon.

Some embellishments can be grouped into categories. Others defy categorization and are in a class by themselves. Some contemporary chefs are merging the art of cooking with industrial food science to create foams, "airs," and encapsulations, all used as fanciful embellishments on plate presentations.

Here, we discover some traditional and contemporary embellishments to enhance plate presentations. They are divided into the following categories:

- Crackers, chips, and croûtons
- Pastry containers and accents
- Aspics, foams, and ices

Crackers, Chips, and Croûtons

Dishes that are soft and spreadable are enhanced by a thin, crisp accompaniment such as crackers or chips. Many favorite hors d'oeuvres and appetizers depend on a base of toasted or sautéed bread, properly called croûtons, for structure. Without croûtons there would be no canapés or bruschette, and no crunchy counterpoint to salads and cold vegetables.

Crackers are small, dry, savory pastries similar to cookies in shape and size, but made with little or no sugar. Like cookies, crackers may be fabricated by rolling and cutting, or by the refrigerator method (see Cheddar Cheese Thins, p. 695).

Savory tuiles [TWEEL] are thin baked wafers made from batters, cheese, or potatoes.

Straws are long, thin strips of puff pastry topped with cheese or other flavorings, twisted into an attractive shape, and baked crisp and golden.

Chips are thin slices of a sturdy or starchy vegetable deep-fried or baked until crisp. They are usually flavored with salt and other seasonings once cooked. In Great Britain and former colonies, they are called *crisps*.

Croûtons are small, thin slices of bread toasted or sautéed crisp. The name is derived from the French word *croûte*, meaning "crust." Original croûtons were exactly that: leftover crusts of bread softened in soup or rubbed with garlic and tossed along with simple salads. Today, some croûtons contain a proportion of crust, as those made by slicing baguettes. However, many modern croûtons are crustless. In North America, cubes of bread are toasted or sautéed to make salad croûtons.

Crackers Versus Biscuits

The small, crunchy, unsweetened pastries we know as *crackers* were originally created as a less perishable replacement for bread.

In the seventeenth through the nineteenth centuries, travelers needed a bread product too dry to harbor mold growth. For long sea voyages, bakers prepared lean and sturdy pastry dough, rolled it out thin, cut it into small pieces, and baked it at a normal temperature until done. Then the pieces were returned to a low oven and baked until thoroughly crisp and dry. These small, lean pastries were called *biscuits* because they were baked twice (in French, *bis* means "twice" and *cuit* means "cooked"). In Britain, both sweet cookies and savory crackers are still called *biscuits*.

North Americans began calling savory biscuits *crackers*, probably to distinguish them from softer, sconelike biscuits.

BASIC ROLLED AND CUT CRACKERS

Yield:
number of pieces varies according to size and thickness, about 12 oz (360 g)

INGREDIENTS	U.S.	METRIC
All-purpose flour	10 oz	300 g
Fine salt	1½ tsp	8 mL
Butter, cold	1½ oz	45 g
Water, ice-cold	2 fl oz (about)	60 mL (about)
Flour for rolling	as needed	as needed
Egg wash	as needed	as needed

PROCEDURE

PREPARATION

1. Preheat an oven to 400°F (200°C). Line a sheet tray with parchment.
2. Combine the flour and salt on the work surface.
3. Use a pastry scraper to cut the butter into the flour until the butter pieces are barely visible.
4. Scrape the flour mixture into a bowl.
5. Use a fork to toss the flour mixture as you drizzle in the water.
6. Use your hand to gather the dough together. The dough should be just moist enough to hold together. Knead only one or two strokes to complete the mixing.
7. Form the dough into a disk and wrap it in plastic film. Refrigerate at least 20 minutes (or up to 24 hours).
8. Dust the work surface with flour and roll out the dough to an even ⅛-in. (3-mm) thickness, or thinner.
9. Use a fluted pastry wheel, pizza cutter, or shaped cutter to fabricate the crackers.
10. Transfer the crackers to the sheet tray with a pastry scraper.
11. Brush the crackers with a light coating of egg wash.
12. Dock the crackers by pricking them with a sharp fork in an even pattern.
13. Apply the desired topping (see variations).
14. Bake the crackers 8–12 minutes, depending on size and thickness, or until golden brown.
15. Cool the crackers on a rack to room temperature.

HOLDING

Store in a tightly sealed container at cool room temperature up to 1 week.

VARIATIONS

HERBED CRACKERS

Add 2 tbsp (30 mL) finely minced mixed fresh herbs in step 5. Top with coarse salt.

GARLIC-ONION CRACKERS

Add 1 tsp (5 mL) granulated garlic and 2 tsp (10 mL) granulated onion in step 1. Top with 2 tbsp (30 mL) dehydrated shredded onions that have been rehydrated in water and squeezed dry.

SESAME CRACKERS

Add 2 drops Asian sesame oil in step 5. Top with white sesame seeds.

RYE CRACKERS

Replace half of the flour with light rye flour. Top with caraway seeds.

WHOLE WHEAT CRACKERS

Replace half of the flour with whole wheat flour. Top with wheat germ.

CHEDDAR CHEESE THINS

Yield:
number of pieces varies according to size and thickness, about 12 oz (360 g)

INGREDIENTS	U.S.	METRIC
Extra-sharp aged white cheddar, grated fine	6 oz	180 g
Butter, softened	2 oz	60 g
Fine salt	½ tsp	3 mL
Cayenne powder	pinch	pinch
Sifted all-purpose flour	4 oz	120 g
White wine	1–2 tbsp	15–30 mL
Egg wash	as needed	as needed

PROCEDURE

PREPARATION

1. Place the cheese, butter, salt, and cayenne in a mixer fitted with the paddle attachment.
2. Cream the mixture on medium speed until well blended.
3. Add the flour and pulse the paddle just until the dough comes together. Add the wine as you pulse.
4. Transfer the dough to a sheet of parchment and form it into a short cylinder about 2 in. (5 cm) in diameter. Roll the dough cylinder in the parchment.
5. Refrigerate the dough about 1 hour, or until firm enough to slice.
6. Preheat an oven to 400°F (200°C). Line a sheet tray with parchment.
7. Use a sharp, thin-bladed knife to cut the dough cylinder into even ⅛-in. (3-mm) slices.
8. Place the slices on the sheet tray.
9. Bake about 8 minutes, or until golden.
10. Cool the thins on a rack.

HOLDING

Store in a tightly sealed container at cool room temperature up to 1 week.

VARIATIONS

CHEDDAR-DILL THINS

Add 2 tbsp (30 mL) minced fresh dill in step 3.

SPICY GREEN CHILE THINS

Add 2 tbsp (30 mL) finely chopped, seeded Serrano chiles in step 3.

CHEDDAR-WALNUT THINS

Add ¼ cup (60 mL) finely chopped walnuts in step 3.

BLUE CHEESE–WALNUT THINS

Replace the cheddar with strong-flavored blue cheese and add ¼ cup (60 mL) finely chopped walnuts in step 3. Extra flour may be needed depending on the moisture content of the cheese.

PARMESAN THINS

Replace the cheddar cheese with Reggiano Parmesan cheese. Extra wine may be needed.

PARMESAN TUILES

Yield:
varies according to size, about 8 3-in. (8-cm) tuiles

INGREDIENTS	U.S.	METRIC
Shredded domestic parmesan cheese	3 oz	90 g

PROCEDURE

PREPARATION

A

1. Preheat an oven to 400°F (200°C).
2. Line 2 or more sheet trays with silicone mats. Set a cooling rack on another sheet tray.
3. Sprinkle a thin, 3-in. (8-cm) disk of cheese on one of the trays (A) as a test batch.
4. Bake about 5 minutes, or until the cheese is melted and brown around the edges.
5. Use an offset spatula to scrape the tuile off the mat (B) and onto the cooling rack. When cool, the tuile should have a crisp texture. If it is soft, bake the remaining tuiles longer or make the disks thinner.
6. Repeat with the remaining cheese, working with as many disks at a time as you can handle.

B

HOLDING

Store in a tightly sealed container at cool room temperature up to 1 week.

VARIATION

PARMESAN ROLL-UPS

As you remove each hot tuile from the mat, quickly flip it over and roll it around a dowel or the handle of a wooden spoon to make a cylinder. You can pipe savory creams and mousses into the roll-ups.

POTATO TUILES

Yield:
varies according to size, about 8 3-in. (8-cm) tuiles

INGREDIENTS	U.S.	METRIC
Russet potato, 10 oz (300 g)	1	1
Kosher salt	to taste	to taste
Beaten egg	1 fl oz	30 mL
Melted clarified butter	2 fl oz	60 mL

PROCEDURE

PREPARATION

1. Preheat an oven to 400°F (200°C).
2. Line 2 or more sheet trays with silicone mats. Set a cooling rack on another sheet tray.
3. Peel the potato, wash it under cold water, and blot it dry on a clean, lint-free towel.
4. Grate the potato into long shreds into the towel.
5. Pick up the corners of the towel and wring all the water from the potato.
6. Place the potato in a bowl, season it generously with salt, and mix in the egg.
7. Sprinkle a 3-in. (8-cm) disk of potato on one of the trays as a test batch. Brush the disk with a thin coating of clarified butter.
8. Bake about 5 minutes, or until the potato tuile is golden brown and darker brown around the edges.
9. Use an offset spatula to scrape the tuile off the mat and onto the cooling rack. When cool, the tuile should have a crisp texture. If it is soft, bake the remaining tuiles longer or make the disks thinner.
10. Repeat with the remaining potato mixture, working with as many disks at a time as you can handle.

HOLDING

Store in a tightly sealed container at cool room temperature up to 12 hours.

BASIC SAVORY TUILES

Yield:
varies according to size, about 8 3-in. (8-cm) tuiles

INGREDIENTS	U.S.	METRIC
Rice flour	3 oz	90 g
All-purpose flour	½ oz	15 g
Sugar	1 tsp	5 mL
Fine salt	½ tsp	2.5 mL
Egg whites, room temperature	3 oz	90 mL
Heavy cream, room temperature	2 fl oz	60 mL
Butter, melted and cooled	2 fl oz	60 mL
Flavorings (see variations)	to taste	to taste

PROCEDURE

PREPARATION

1. Combine the flours, sugar, and salt in a small bowl.
2. Whisk in the egg whites one at a time.
3. Whisk in the cream and then the butter.
4. Stir in the flavorings.
5. Cover and refrigerate at least 30 minutes (or up to 24 hours).
6. Preheat an oven to 400°F (200°C).
7. Line 2 or more sheet trays with silicone mats. Set a cooling rack on another sheet tray.
8. Use a plastic stencil or work freehand to spread the tuile paste in a thin disk on one of the trays as a test batch.
9. Bake about 8 minutes, or until the tuile is lightly brown around the edges.
10. Use an offset spatula to scrape the tuile off the mat and onto the cooling rack. When cool, the tuile should have a crisp texture. If it is soft, bake the remaining tuiles longer or make the disks thinner.

 –or–

 Form the tuile as desired and allow to cool.
11. Repeat with the remaining batter, working with as many tuiles at a time as you can handle.

HOLDING

Store in a tightly sealed container at cool room temperature up to 1 week.

VARIATIONS

SAVORY SESAME TUILES

Add 1 tsp (5 mL) paste-style chicken base and 1 tbsp (15 g) black sesame seeds in step 4. Shape as desired.

SEAFOOD TUILE SPIKES

Add 1 tsp (5 mL) paste-style seafood base in step 4. Make a 5-in. (12.5-cm) spike template. Use the template to shape spike tuiles as shown on page 199.

ONION-BEER TUILE SPIRALS

Replace the cream with flat beer. Add 1 tsp (5 mL) granulated onion in step 4. Use a ⅜-in. (1-cm) basketweave tip and pastry bag to pipe out the batter into 8-in. (20-cm) strips. When the tuile strips come out of the oven, quickly flip each one over with the spatula and wrap it in a spiral shape around a ½-in. (1-cm) dowel.

CHEESE STRAWS

Yield:
30 straws

INGREDIENTS	U.S.	METRIC
Frozen puff pastry sheet, 10 × 16 in. (25 × 40 cm), thawed in the refrigerator	1	1
Egg wash	1 fl oz	30 mL
Reggiano Parmesan cheese, grated fine	4 oz	120 g
Sweet paprika	to taste	to taste

PROCEDURE

PREPARATION

1. Preheat an oven to 400°F (200°C). Line a sheet tray with parchment.
2. Place the pastry sheet on a cutting board. Use a sharp chef knife to trim about ⅛ in. (0.3 cm) from all sides. Do not drag the knife as you cut. Instead, press straight down to make each cut.
3. Brush the pastry sheet with a thin, even coating of egg wash.
4. Sprinkle the cheese onto the pastry in a thin, even layer. Press the cheese into the pastry to help it adhere.
5. Dust the pastry very lightly with paprika.
6. Cut the pastry into ½ × 10-in. (1 × 25-cm) strips, pressing straight down with the knife.
7. Place the cutting board in the refrigerator about 15 minutes, or until the pastry becomes firm and cold.
8. Pick up each pastry strip and twist it (A) Space the cheese straws about 1 in. (3 cm) apart on the sheet tray.
9. Bake about 10 minutes, or until golden (B).
10. Cool on a rack.

A

B

HOLDING

Store in a tightly sealed container at cool room temperature up to 1 week.

VARIATIONS

POPPY SEED CHEESE STRAWS

Replace the paprika with poppy seeds and press to help them adhere.

SESAME STRAWS

Omit the cheese. Sprinkle with sesame seeds and press to help them adhere.

SALT STRAWS

Omit the cheese. Sprinkle with coarse pretzel salt.

EVERYTHING STRAWS

Mix together dehydrated onion flakes, dehydrated garlic flakes, sesame seeds, caraway seeds, and poppy seeds. Sprinkle on the puff pastry and press to adhere.

CRISP-FRIED VEGETABLE CHIPS

Yield:
varies, about 12 oz (360 g)

INGREDIENTS	U.S.	METRIC
Russet potatoes, sweet potatoes, plantains, taro, yams, or other starchy vegetables	1 lb	0.5 kg
Vegetable oil or frying compound	as needed	as needed
Popcorn salt or fine salt	as needed	as needed

PROCEDURE

FIRST DAY: PREPARATION

1. Sanitize a nonreactive container and its lid. Fill it halfway with cool water.
2. Scrub and peel the vegetables. Immerse them in the water as you work.
3. Set up a mandoline or electric slicer. Cut the vegetables into even slices, 1⁄16–1⁄8 in. (1.5–3 mm) thick. (For standard chips, cut crosswise. For elongated chips, slice lengthwise.) Place the vegetables in the water as soon as they are cut. Make sure the slices are separate and not sticking to each other.
4. Cover the container and refrigerate the vegetable slices in the water at least 24 hours and up to 48 hours.

SECOND DAY: PREPARATION

5. Preheat a fryer to 425°F (215°C). Set a perforated hotel pan into a deep hotel pan.
6. Drain the vegetable slices thoroughly. Spread them out on clean, lint-free kitchen towels and roll in the towels to absorb water.
7. Lower the fryer basket and scatter in a few vegetable slices. Deep-fry the slices until golden. Lift the basket, shake off excess oil, and gently slide the chips into the hotel pan.
8. Repeat with the remaining slices.
9. Sprinkle the chips lightly with salt while they are still warm.

HOLDING

Store in a tightly sealed container lined with paper towels at cool room temperature up to 3 days.

VARIATION

Carrot Chips, Parsnip Chips, Beet Chips, Elephant Garlic Chips, and chips made from other nonstarchy vegetables: Do not soak in water. Simply fabricate and fry at 375°F (190°C).

SAVORY BAKED FRUIT CHIPS

Yield:
varies,
about 12 pieces

INGREDIENTS	U.S.	METRIC
Firm, sweet apples or underripe pears	2	2
Vegetable oil	½ oz	15 mL

PROCEDURE

PREPARATION

1. Preheat an oven to 375°F (190°C). Line a sheet tray with a silicone mat.
2. Use an apple corer to punch out the cores of the apples or pears.
3. Use a mandoline or electric slicer to cut the fruit into even 1/16-in. (2-mm) lengthwise slices.
4. For use as an embellishment, choose only the large slices that show the shape of the fruit. Lay these slices on the silicone mat and brush them with a very light coating of oil. Turn them over and brush the new tops with oil.
5. Bake the fruit slices about 20 minutes, or until they have lost most of their moisture. If they are not yet crisp, continue to bake, checking them at 5-minute intervals.
6. Transfer the fruit chips to a cooling rack and cool to room temperature.

HOLDING

Store in a tightly sealed container, with parchment between layers, at cool room temperature up to 3 days.

VARIATION

BAKED VEGETABLE CHIPS

Zucchini, chayote, winter squashes, kohlrabi, young turnips, and other firm, high-moisture vegetables may be baked in the same manner. Baking times differ. Salt them lightly while warm.

TOASTED BAGUETTE CROÛTONS

Yield:
varies according to size and volume of bread; about 24 pieces

INGREDIENTS	U.S.	METRIC
Firm baguette	6 oz	180 g

PROCEDURE

PREPARATION

1. Preheat a broiler to high heat.
2. Use a serrated knife to cut the baguette into even ¼-in. (6-mm) slices. (You can cut the baguette into rounds, or slice it on the diagonal to make ovals.)
3. Place the slices on a rack set over a sheet tray.
4. Broil the baguette slices a few seconds until golden brown.
5. Turn the slices and broil the other sides until golden brown.
6. Cool to room temperature on the rack.

HOLDING

Store in a tightly sealed container at cool room temperature up to 24 hours.

VARIATIONS

BUTTER-TOASTED BAGUETTE CROÛTONS

Brush both sides of the baguette slices with clarified butter before broiling.

OIL-TOASTED BAGUETTE CROÛTONS

Brush both sides of the baguette slices with pure golden olive oil before broiling.

BAGEL CRISPS

Use an electric slicing machine to prepare ⅛-in. (3-mm) slices of day-old bagels. Brush both sides of the bagel slices with clarified butter before broiling. Optionally, sprinkle with garlic salt while still warm.

SAUTÉED WHITE BREAD CROÛTONS

Yield:
varies according to size

INGREDIENTS	U.S.	METRIC
Unsliced firm white sandwich bread, crust removed	5–10 oz	150–300 g
Clarified butter or pure golden olive oil	2–6 fl oz	60–180 mL

PROCEDURE

PREPARATION

1. Prepare a rack set over a sheet tray.
2. Use a serrated knife to cut the bread into even ¼-in. (6-mm) slices. Fabricate into the desired shapes.
3. Heat a sauté pan over moderate flame. Add a thin layer of butter or oil and place the croûtons in the pan in one layer. Sauté until the bottoms are golden brown. Add more butter or oil around the edges as necessary.
4. Turn the croûtons over and sauté the new bottoms in the same manner.
5. Cool the croûtons on the rack to room temperature.

HOLDING

Store in a tightly sealed container at cool room temperature up to 24 hours.

(Variations on next page)

VARIATIONS

ROUND CROÛTONS FOR CANAPÉS

Use a round cutter to punch out disks 1–2-in. (2.5–5-cm) in diameter.

CROÛTONS FOR LEEKS

Cut out 2 × 5-in. (5 × 12-cm) rectangles. Trim the corners on the diagonal to make lozenges.

CROÛTON FLEURONS

(floo-RON)

Use a fluted, crescent-shape cutter to punch out fleurons, or fluted crescents, of the desired size.

SAUTÉED CROÛTON CUBES

Yield:
about 6 oz (180 g) or 1 pt (0.5 L)

INGREDIENTS	U.S.	METRIC
Unsliced firm white sandwich bread, crust removed	8 oz	240 g
Pure golden olive oil	3–4 fl oz	90–120 mL
Flavorings (see variations for suggestions)	to taste	to taste
Kosher salt	to taste	to taste

PROCEDURE

PREPARATION

1. Use a serrated knife to cut the bread into ½-in. (1-cm) cubes or any desired size.
2. Heat the oil in a sauté pan over low heat. If using solid flavorings, such as crushed garlic or bay leaves, add them to the oil.
3. Add the bread cubes and stir them to coat each with oil.
4. Cook over low heat, stirring occasionally, about 10 minutes, or until the croûton cubes are rich golden brown.
5. If using ground seasonings, such as dried herbs, add them during the last few seconds of cooking. Cool to room temperature in the pan.
6. Season the croûton cubes lightly with salt.

HOLDING

Store in a tightly sealed container at cool room temperature up to 48 hours.

VARIATIONS

GARLIC CROÛTON CUBES

Add 2 large peeled, crushed garlic cloves in step 2. Remove them before storing the croûtons.

HERBES DE PROVENCE CROÛTON CUBES

Prepare Garlic Croûton Cubes, and then add 2 tsp (10 mL) Herbes de Provence in step 5.

PARMESAN CROÛTON CUBES

Prepare plain or Garlic Croûton Cubes. Decrease the salt, and toss in ½ oz (15 g) finely grated Reggiano Parmesan when the cubes are almost cool.

Pastry Containers and Accents

The use of pastry to contain both sweet and savory foods dates to the Roman Empire and flourished in the Middle Ages. In Chapter 13, you learned about foods that are encased in pastry before they are cooked. Here we focus on pastry cases that are baked before they are filled.

Various types of nonsweet pastry can be used as containers for a range of savory preparations. Many are filled with hot food and served hot, a responsibility of the hot kitchen. Most have cold applications as well. For example, a puff pastry bouchée can be filled with either hot creamed chicken or cold chicken salad.

Nonsweet pastries can also be formed into decorative shapes and used as accent pieces to garnish savory plate presentations. Often, these decorations are made of scraps that remain after fabricating pastry containers or pastry desserts. Using pastry scraps creatively minimizes waste and lowers food costs.

Assorted pastry cases. Clockwise from top left: puff pastry bouchée, phyllo cup, hors d'oeuvre profiterole shell, hors d'oeuvre pastry barquette, and hors d'oeuvre pastry tartelet.

In most operations the garde manger department does not actually make the pastry used for pastry containers and accents. If your operation has a separate bakeshop, you may be able to requisition doughs, prebaked items, or fully baked items from the pastry chefs. However, with the exception of puff pastry, basic garde manger doughs are not difficult to make and should be in your repertoire of skills. As an alternative to making doughs in-house, you may purchase them. High-quality commercial pastry is available for purchase in three basic forms.

Frozen pastry doughs are available in both block form and in sheets. Thaw under refrigeration before using.

Prefabricated pastry shapes need only to be baked and cooled before serving. Many can be baked directly from the freezer.

Fully baked pastry containers and accent pieces are ready to use. For best texture, crisp them in a hot oven and then cool them before using.

To serve pastry items with the best flavor and mouthfeel, purchase products labeled "all butter" or that have a high percentage of butter in their formulas. Avoid products made solely with hydrogenated fats, as they have poor flavor and are under study as a possible health risk.

Formulas for most basic pastry doughs needed to complete these recipes are presented in this text's Appendix. Alternatively, use basic dough formulas of your choice. For recipes specifying puff pastry, choose a high-quality, commercial dough product.

PUFF PASTRY BOUCHÉES [boo-SHAY]

Yield:
12 pieces

INGREDIENTS	U.S.	METRIC
Commercial puff pastry, thawed in the refrigerator	½ sheet	½ sheet
Water	as needed	as needed

PROCEDURE

PREPARATION

1. Preheat an oven to 400°F (200°C). Line a half-sheet tray with parchment.
2. Using a 1½-in. (4-cm) fluted round cutter, cut 24 disks from the puff pastry sheet.
3. Use a 1-in. (2.5-cm) plain round cutter to punch ring-shaped perforations inside 12 of the disks. Do not remove the centers.

PROCEDURE

4. Moisten the edges of the solid disks with a little water.
5. Place the perforated disks on top of the solid disks and press gently to help the disks adhere.
6. Refrigerate 15 minutes.
7. Bake the bouchées about 10 minutes, or until puffed and golden brown.
8. Cool the bouchées to room temperature.
9. Remove the inside pastry disk and pull out any dough shreds to make hollow cups.

HOLDING

Store loosely covered with plastic film at cool room temperature up to 8 hours. May be frozen after step 5 up to 1 month.

VARIATIONS

PUFF PASTRY VOL-AU-VENTS

[vohl-oh-VAWN]

Use a 3-in. (8-cm) cutter for the disks and a 2-in. (5-cm) cutter to punch out the centers.

PUFF PASTRY FLEURONS

[floo-RON]

Use a fluted, crescent-shape cutter to punch out fleurons, or fluted crescents, of the desired size. Brush the tops only with a light coating of egg wash. Bake about 8 minutes, depending on size.

HORS D'OEUVRE PASTRY SHELLS

Yield: *varies according to size*

INGREDIENTS	U.S.	METRIC
Flour for dusting	as needed	as needed
Pâte Brisée (p. 753), refrigerated at least 20 minutes	8 oz	240 g

PROCEDURE

PREPARATION

1. Preheat an oven to 400°F (200°C). Line a sheet tray with parchment.
2. Dust the work surface with flour and roll out the dough very thin, about 1⁄16 in. (1.5 mm) thick.
3. You will need 2 tartlet or barquette forms for each unit. Line half of the forms with the pastry dough.
4. Press another form inside the pastry to sandwich the dough between two forms. Place the filled forms upside down on the sheet tray. (Baking the pastries upside down helps prevent the dough from sinking down into the form while baking.)
5. Refrigerate the shells at least 20 minutes.
6. Bake the shells 8–12 minutes, depending on size. Bake until crisp and golden brown. If necessary, remove the top form and return the shells to the oven for 1 minute or less to complete the browning.
7. Cool the shells on a rack to room temperature.

HOLDING

Store in a tightly sealed container with parchment between layers at cool room temperature up to 24 hours. May be frozen after step 4 up to 1 month.

HORS D'OEUVRE PROFITEROLE SHELLS

Yield:
varies according to size, about 48 pieces

INGREDIENTS	U.S.	METRIC
Choux Paste (p. 754)	1 lb	0.5 kg
Egg wash	as needed	as needed

PROCEDURE

PREPARATION

1. Preheat an oven to 400°F (200°C). If you are preparing multiple batches, preheat a separate oven to 225°F (100°C). Line a sheet tray with parchment.
2. Place the choux paste in a pastry bag fitted with a ⅜-in. (1-cm) round tip.
3. Pipe a dot of choux paste under the parchment on each corner of the sheet tray to hold the parchment in place.
4. To make 1¼-in. (3-cm) shells, pipe out ¾-in. (2-cm) spheres spaced evenly on the tray.
5. Brush each sphere with egg wash.
6. Bake at 400°F (200°C) about 10 minutes, or until puffed and golden brown.
7. Lower the oven temperature to 225°F (100°C), or move the tray to the low oven. Bake at low temperature about 20 minutes more, or until the shells are crisp and dry.
8. Cool to room temperature on a rack.

HOLDING

Store in a tightly sealed container at cool room temperature up to 48 hours. May be frozen up to 1 month. Recrisp in a hot oven and then cool to room temperature before using.

VARIATION

CHOUX PASTE ACCENT ITEMS

Pipe out spirals, corkscrews, trellises, or any desired shapes. Various tips may be used. Items may be sprinkled with spices, seeds, salts, etc. Baking times vary according to size.

PHYLLO CUPS

Yield:
24 pieces

INGREDIENTS	U.S.	METRIC
Clarified butter	4 fl oz	120 mL
Fresh phyllo dough	3 sheets	3 sheets

PROCEDURE

PREPARATION

1. Preheat an oven to 400°F (200°C).
2. Brush a light coating of butter in the cups of a 24-unit, 1½ oz (45 mL) mini-muffin tin.
3. Prepare 105 individual phyllo squares:
   a. Remove the number of phyllo sheets you need. Keep these sheets stacked together.
   b. Use scissors to cut the stacked sheets into thirty-five 3-ply squares, each measuring 2½ × 2½ in. (6 × 6 cm). This will yield 105 individual squares. (You will have some trim waste on the edges and may have up to 9 extra squares when finished.) Keep the phyllo squares covered with a damp towel as you work.
4. Make the phyllo cups:
   a. Place 1 phyllo square on the work surface and brush it lightly with butter (A).
   b. Place another single square on top (B) and brush it with melted butter.

A

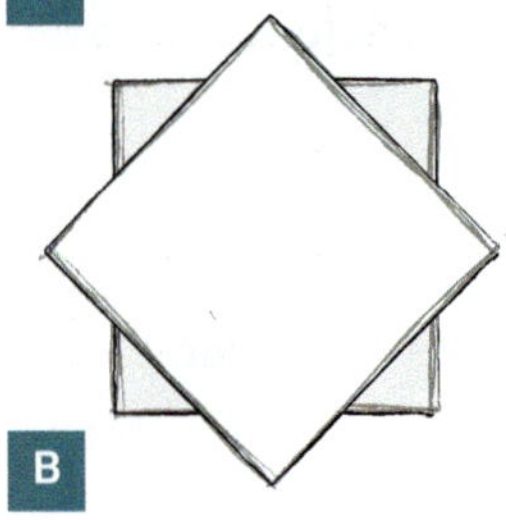

B

C

D

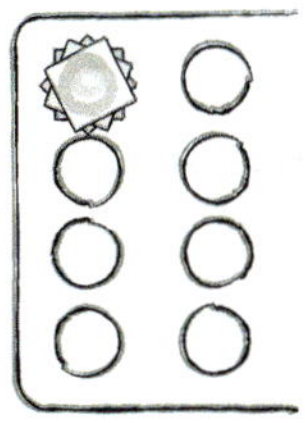

E

PROCEDURE

c. Place a third square (C) and brush with butter.
d. Add a final square to make a 4-layer pointed circle (D). Brush with butter
e. Press the pointed phyllo circle into one of the mini-muffin cups (E).
f. Repeat to make 24 phyllo cups.

5. Bake the phyllo cups about 5 minutes, or until golden.
6. Cool to room temperature.
7. Carefully lift the phyllo cups out of the muffin tin.

HOLDING

Store in one layer in a tightly sealed flat plastic container lined with paper towels. Hold at room temperature. Best used within a few hours.

VARIATION

PHYLLO SQUARES

Cut phyllo to the desired size. Proceed through step 4c, but stack the phyllo sheets to make squares. Place each square stack on a sheet tray lined with parchment, and place a second sheet tray on top. Bake until golden.

CRISPY NOODLE NEST

Yield:
1 4-in. (10-cm) nest

INGREDIENTS	U.S.	METRIC
Dry rice vermicelli noodles	½ oz	15 g
Vegetable oil or frying compound	as needed	as needed

PROCEDURE

PREPARATION

1. Preheat a fryer to 400°F (200°C). Line a sheet tray with paper towels.
2. Break the noodles into lengths of about 2 in. (5 cm).
3. Dip a 4-in. (10-cm) *nid-de-pommes* (potato-nest basket) tool into the hot oil and shake off the excess.
4. Line the bottom of the tool with the noodles and fit the top into place.
5. Immerse the noodles in the oil and fry about 8 seconds, or until they puff up. Do not allow the noodles to acquire any color.
6. Release the noodle nest upside-down onto the paper towels and allow to drain.

HOLDING

Hold, uncovered, on the paper towels up to 8 hours.

VARIATIONS

To make nests of other sizes, select 2 metal strainers of the desired size. Dip the strainers in hot oil, line one with broken noodles, fit the second strainer on top, and fry as in the basic recipe.

CRISPY NOODLE BED

Instead of using the *nid-de-pommes* tool, place the noodles in a strainer and dip it into the hot oil. When plating, form the noodles by hand into a bed on the plate.

TORTILLA BASKET

Replace the rice vermicelli noodles with an 8-in. (20-cm) flour tortilla. To make the tortilla pliable enough to fit in the strainers, briefly warm it on an ungreased griddle or sauté pan. Fry the tortilla until it is very light golden in color.

Aspics, Foams, Ices, and Plate Painting

This section covers both classic and innovative embellishments made from thickened liquids.

Aspic Garnishes and Décor Items

When enough gelatin is added to an aspic that it becomes firm enough to slice, it can function as both garnish and décor. Firm aspic may be cut freehand into cubes or punched out into shapes with cutters. A mound of glittering aspic cubes beautifully complements a slice of pâté or terrine, and it can also dress up an aspic or chaud-froid platter presentation. Aspic ***fleurons*** (floo-RON), or fluted crescents, are usually used to decorate platters.

Procedure for Making Aspic Garnishes and Décor Items

1. Choose a flat pan of the correct size to hold the aspic at the desired depth. (Test the pan size by pouring in a measured amount of water.) Make sure it is thoroughly clean and grease-free.
2. Line the pan with a sheet of acetate.
3. Find a shelf in the refrigerator that will hold the pan level.
4. Prepare Aspic for Slicing as directed on pages 644 and 645.
5. Strain the aspic into the pan to remove all bubbles.
6. Place the pan in the refrigerator and chill it until the aspic is set.
7. Lift out the aspic on its acetate sheet.
8. Cut the aspic into the desired shapes with a knife or decorative cutter.
9. Use a small offset spatula to loosen and remove the aspic décor items.

MADEIRA POULTRY ASPIC JEWELS

Yield:
about 1 qt (1 L)

INGREDIENTS	U.S.	METRIC
White Poultry Aspic for Slicing (p. 644), made with Madeira	1 qt	1 L

PROCEDURE

PREPARATION

1. Follow the Procedure for Making Aspic Garnishes and Décor Items, above.
2. Cut the aspic into ⅜-in. (1-cm) dice.

HOLDING

Refrigerate on the acetate sheet, loosely covered with plastic film, up to 24 hours.

VARIATION

RIESLING ASPIC GELÉE JEWELS

Replace the Madeira with a slightly sweet Riesling wine.

Foams

A culinary ***foam*** is an aerated liquid—in other words, a liquid filled with air. Whipped cream and beaten egg whites are examples of culinary foams. Until recently, the use of culinary foams as garnishes was limited to pastry chefs.

Garde manger chefs have begun to experiment with savory foams. Those based on heavy cream behave much in the same way as whipped cream. However, if the savory liquid is low in fat, the cream mixture may not have a high enough proportion of fat to hold air for long. When air is forced into such liquids, they are likely to develop large, delicate bubbles that break and disappear quickly. In order to create more stable savory foams, it is necessary to do one of two things:

1. Use a different type of gas and apply it under pressure, or
2. Add a specialized form of protein to the base liquid.

Pressurized canister

PRESSURIZED CANISTERS

Pressurized canisters are used to make whipped cream by forcing nitrous oxide into heavy cream. The pressure within the can is released by pressing a lever, and fluffy whipped cream is forced out.

Garde manger chefs have begun foaming both savory flavored creams and noncream liquids. Cream-based savory foams are relatively stable and can be held under refrigeration in a pastry bag. Low-fat savory foams are less stable. However, they are able to maintain their shape on a plate for a reasonable period—at least long enough to pump them onto a plate and send them to the table.

The base liquids for savory foams must be strong in flavor and highly seasoned. This is true for two reasons: They are served cold, and they are diluted with a lot of air.

Procedure for Making Savory Foams in a Pressurized Canister

1. Chill the base liquid and canister.
2. Open the pressurized canister and pour the base liquid into the chamber.
3. Close the canister top.
4. Insert the charger by screwing it into the charger aperture. You will hear a hissing noise as the gas enters the chamber. (Use the proper number of chargers for your canister. Do not attempt to add additional pressure beyond manufacturer recommendations.)
5. To release the foam, shake the canister, point the nozzle at the plate and press the lever.
6. Refrigerate the filled canister when not in use.

CREAMY SWEET CORN FOAM

Yield:
about 1 qt (1 L)

INGREDIENTS	U.S.	METRIC
Large ears fresh sweet corn, shucked	2	2
Heavy cream	1 pt	0.5 L
Salt	to taste	to taste
Sugar	to taste	to taste
Finely ground white pepper	to taste	to taste
Supplies		
Nitrous oxide charger	per manufacturer	per manufacturer

PROCEDURE

PREPARATION

1. Cut the kernels off the corncobs and reserve the cobs.
2. Place the corn kernels in a food processor.
3. Use the back of a knife to scrape all the remaining pulp and juice from each corncob. Add them to the processor.
4. Purée the corn.
5. Combine the corn and heavy cream in a saucepan and bring the mixture to a bare simmer. Remove from the heat and allow to steep at room temperature 30 minutes.
6. Strain the corn mixture through a double layer of damp cheesecloth. Squeeze out as much liquid and pulp as possible.
7. Season the corn cream highly with salt, and add sugar as necessary, depending on the sweetness of the corn. Season with pepper.
8. Chill the corn cream in the refrigerator or an ice bain-marie.
9. Follow the Procedure for Making Savory Foams in a Pressurized Canister (p. 709).

HOLDING

Store the filled canister in the refrigerator up to 3 days.

GELATIN-STABILIZED FOAMS

When a thin, low-fat base liquid is fortified with a protein gel, it acquires enough structure and elasticity to hold air. Thus, it can be successfully whipped into a foam. ***Gelatin-stabilized foams*** are relatively stable. They can be prepared in a pressurized canister or in an electric mixer.

The basic formula for gelatin stabilized foams is:

¼ oz (7 g) granular gelatin : 12 fl oz (360 mL) liquid

CUCUMBER FOAM

Yield:
about 1 qt (1 L)

INGREDIENTS	U.S.	METRIC
Fresh, unwaxed cucumbers (see Note)	1 lb	0.5 kg
Fine sea salt	to taste	to taste
Midori liqueur	½ fl oz	15 mL
Fresh lime juice	to taste	to taste
Granular gelatin, bloomed in 1 fl oz (30 mL) water	¼ oz	8 g
Supplies		
Nitrous oxide charger	per manufacturer	per manufacturer

Note: The flavor of this preparation depends almost entirely on the quality of the cucumbers. Try to use freshly harvested local cucumbers.

A

B

PROCEDURE

PREPARATION

1. Scrub the cucumbers thoroughly and trim the ends. Cut the cucumbers in half lengthwise and scrape out the seeds. Cut the cucumbers into 1-in. (3-cm) chunks.
2. Place the cucumbers in a blender with a little salt. Blend to a purée.
3. Strain the purée through a double layer of dampened cheesecloth and squeeze out as much juice as possible.
4. Measure out 12 fl oz (360 mL) cucumber juice. Add the Midori. Balance the flavor with lime juice, season highly with salt, and add the bloomed gelatin. Stir over barely simmering water until the gelatin dissolves.
5. Refrigerate the cucumber mixture and a pressurized canister until cold.
6. Fill the canister with the cucumber mixture (A) and pressurize the canister with the charger.

HOLDING

Refrigerate up to 12 hours.

7. Shake the canister and dispense the cucumber foam as desired (B).

VARIATION

CUCUMBER FOAM MADE IN A MIXER

Follow the Procedure for Making Gelatin-Stabilized Savory Foams in a Mixer, below.

Procedure for Making Gelatin-Stabilized Savory Foams in a Mixer

1. Place two-thirds of the liquid in the freezer just long enough to become very cold.
2. Bloom the gelatin with the remaining liquid in a small, heatproof container.
3. Melt the bloomed gelatin by placing the container in a hot bain-marie until the gelatin is completely dissolved.
4. Place the liquid gelatin in a mixer fitted with the whip attachment.
5. Begin to whip the gelatin on low speed. On low speed, whip in the very cold liquid in a thin stream until all of it is incorporated.
6. Whip on medium-high speed about 5 minutes, or until a large mass of foam forms on the surface of the liquid.
7. Turn off the mixer and allow the foam to stabilize 5 minutes more.
8. Lift the foam off the liquid.

Savory Ices

Adding a frozen component to a garde manger preparation creates an element of surprise. Savory frozen products are divided into still-frozen ice cubes and churn-frozen sorbets.

Savory ice cubes are nothing more than highly seasoned liquids frozen in ice cube trays. When added to cold soups, they maintain an icy temperature without diluting the soup's flavor as they melt.

Savory sorbets consist of semisweet syrups, vegetable juices, or fruit juices frozen in an ice cream machine. Contemporary savory sorbets are frequently used as elements in complex plate presentations. They add both flavor and visual interest to cold soups and keep them cold without diluting them. A tiny scoop of savory sorbet served in a savory tuile cone makes a show-stopping hors d'oeuvre.

CONSOMMÉ ICE CUBES WITH CHIVES

Yield:
varies, standard ice cube tray yields 12 1½-fl oz (45-mL) cubes

INGREDIENTS	U.S.	METRIC
Clarified Stock for poultry *(p. 748)*	1 pt	0.5 L
Fresh chives, cut in very fine rings	1 oz	30 g

PROCEDURE

PREPARATION

1. Place an ice cube tray in the freezer until very cold.
2. Place the consommé in a bowl in the freezer. Stir the consommé at 10-minute intervals until it has frozen to a slushy consistency.
3. Mix the chives with the slushy consommé and then immediately pack the consommé into the ice cube tray.
4. Freeze solid.

HOLDING

Seal the ice tray in plastic wrap and freeze up to 1 month. Alternatively, transfer the ice cubes to a plastic bag.

LEMON-THYME SORBET

Yield:
about 1 pt (0.5 L)

INGREDIENTS	U.S.	METRIC
Sugar	6 oz	180 g
Distilled or filtered water	10 fl oz	300 mL
Fine minced lemon zest	1 tbsp	15 mL
Fresh lemon thyme leaves or fresh thyme	¼ oz	7 g
Fresh lemon juice	4 fl oz	120 mL
Sorbet stabilizer (optional)	0.15 oz	5 g
Thyme leaves (optional)	additional	additional

PROCEDURE

PREPARATION

1. Combine the sugar and 4 fl oz (120 mL) water in a saucepan and bring the mixture to the boil to dissolve the sugar and create a syrup.
2. Remove the syrup from the heat and add the zest and thyme. Cool to room temperature.
3. Stir the lemon juice and sorbet stabilizer into the syrup. Add the remaining water.
4. Pour the syrup through a fine sieve or cheesecloth to remove the zest and thyme leaves.
5. If possible, test the syrup's sugar concentration with a hydrometer or saccharometer. It should read 16°–18° Baumé or 30°–32.5° Brix. If the reading is low, add more simple syrup. If the reading is high, dilute the syrup with more water.
6. Chill the syrup in the refrigerator or by stirring it in an ice bain-marie.
7. Freeze the syrup in an ice cream machine according to the manufacturer's directions.
8. Add the optional additional thyme leaves when the sorbet is almost finished freezing.
9. Pack the sorbet into a freshly sanitized, chilled container. Place a piece of plastic film directly on its surface and cover the container with its lid.
10. Place the sorbet in a freezer about 1 hour, or until firm.

HOLDING

Store in a 0°F (–17°C) freezer up to 1 week. Transfer to a 28°F (–2°C) dipping cabinet at least 1 hour before serving.

VARIATIONS

LIME SORBET

Replace the lemon juice and zest with lime juice and zest. Omit the thyme leaves.

PORT WINE SORBET

Replace the lemon juice with 10 fl oz (300 mL) good-quality ruby port wine. Omit the zest and thyme leaves. Balance the flavor with a little lemon juice to taste.

Measuring Sugar Concentration

The amount of sugar present in a liquid affects the way it freezes. You can measure the sugar concentration of your sorbet syrup with an instrument called a hydrometer, or saccharometer. Sugar concentration is expressed in degrees on the Brix scale or on the Baumé scale (which technically measures specific gravity). Test the syrup at room temperature (68°F or 20°C).

TOMATO SORBET

Yield:
about 1 qt (1 L)

INGREDIENTS	U.S.	METRIC
Vine-ripe *Basic Tomato Coulis Sauce (p. 52)*	8 fl oz	240 mL
Canned tomato juice	8 fl oz	240 mL
Fresh lemon juice	2 fl oz	60 mL
Red wine vinegar	1 fl oz	30 mL
Sugar	2 oz	60 g
Fine sea salt	to taste	to taste
Sorbet stabilizer	0.12 oz	4 g

PROCEDURE

PREPARATION

1. Combine all ingredients except the stabilizer in a nonreactive saucepan. Heat to 120°F (48°C). Stir the mixture to combine the ingredients and blend the flavors.
2. Cool to room temperature.
3. Strain the mixture through a double layer of dampened cheesecloth and squeeze out as much pulp and juice as possible.
4. Taste. Correct the sweet-salt-acid balance by adding salt, sugar, or vinegar as needed.
5. Stir in the stabilizer.
6. Chill the sorbet base in the refrigerator or by stirring it in an ice bain-marie.
7. Freeze the base in an ice cream machine according to the manufacturer's directions.
8. Pack the sorbet into a freshly sanitized, chilled container. Place a piece of plastic film directly on its surface and cover the container with its lid.
9. Place the sorbet in a freezer about 2 hours, or until firm.

HOLDING

Store in a 0°F (−17°C) freezer up to 1 week. Transfer to a 28°F (−2°C) dipping cabinet at least 1 hour before serving.

VARIATIONS

TOMATO-BASIL SORBET

Add 1 oz (30 g) chopped fresh basil leaves at the end of churn freezing in step 7.

YELLOW TOMATO SORBET

Replace the red tomatoes with yellow tomatoes. Replace the canned tomato juice with juice extracted from yellow tomatoes.

Plate Painting

Plate painting can be described as the art of using sauces to create images on a plate. One way to think about plate painting is that the plate is the canvas and the sauces are the paint.

Cold sauces and a variety of fluid condiments are used to embellish garde manger plate presentations. Coulis and purées, mayonnaise sauces, glazes, essences, and flavored oils are among the many preparations that can be used. Specialized equipment is needed: squeeze bottles, droppers, piping cones, and pastry bags and tips.

For plate painting to be successful, sauces and condiments must be of the correct texture. In general, they must be fluid enough to flow freely from their container, yet solid enough to stay in place on the plate. *When two sauces are used together, they must be of the same texture, consistency, and weight in order to hold their shapes.* The exception to this rule is sauces for flooding. ***Flooding*** is a plate painting technique in which a thicker sauce is used to form a border that contains a thinner sauce, as in step 7 of Asian Crab, Shrimp, and Cucumber Salad on page 184.

While the purpose of plate painting is to create visual interest, do not forget that flavor comes first. You should not add an accent sauce to a plate just because the color looks good on it. The flavor of the sauce must complement the food and its primary sauce.

Zigzags

String of hearts

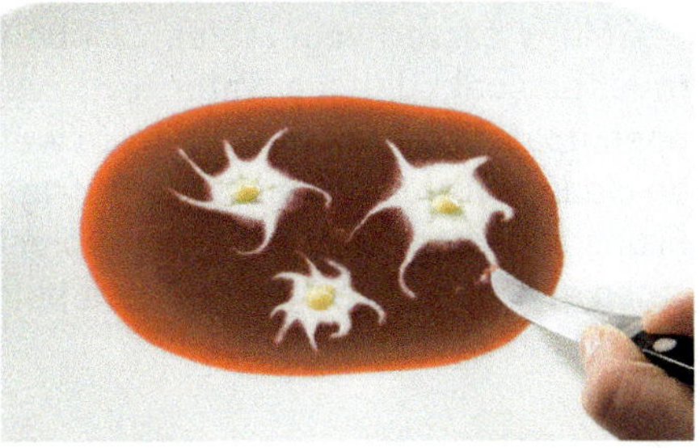
Starbursts

Houndstooth

DÉCOR

Décor work is of prime concern to garde manger chefs specializing in buffet work. Small décor items beautify platter presentations and, when applied directly to foods, yield visual masterpieces. Large décor items, or *pièces montées*, become the focal point for a buffet table or station and can establish the theme of the buffet.

Flat Décor Items for Aspic and Chaud-Froid Work

Most flat décor items are made from vegetables because they are our most colorful foods. Before they can be cut into the necessary shapes, they must be fabricated into thin, flat slabs and are typically cooked in some way. Most are blanched and refreshed. Be sure the vegetables are thoroughly dry before proceeding.

Garde manger chefs use specialized tools for carving vegetables (p. 16).

Flat décor items:
Column 1, top to bottom: small and large leek diamonds, leek tulip, leek ribbon, leek or scallion string or tie, hard-cooked egg white disk (on leek square)

Column 2, top to bottom: peeled and unpeeled tomato disks, carrot flower variation with rutabaga center, rutabaga flower variation with carrot center, rutabaga flower variations with carrot centers

Column 3, top to bottom: peeled and unpeeled tomato triangles, rutabaga butterfly, carrot fish with rutabaga eye, carrot flower variations (first made with carrot teardrops) with rutabaga centers, rutabaga flower variation (made with rutabaga petals) with black olive center

Column 4, top to bottom: carrot club, diamond, heart, spade; black olive disks, rutabaga tulip with leek stem and leaves

Thai Fruit Carving

Experts agree the world's most elaborate and intricate food décor is created by Thai chefs specializing in fruit and vegetable carving. Once a skill reserved for ladies of the Thai aristocracy, fruit and vegetable carving now can be practiced by anyone with the time and talent to learn it. Books, CDs and videos, and classes are available in this venerable, high-skill craft.

© iStockphoto.

Carved Fruits and Vegetables

Fruit and vegetable carving is an art that requires years of practice to master. This text offers an introduction to the art of food carving. Using the correct tools, and with diligent practice, you can become proficient at the basic carved décor presented in this chapter.

Carving sets made from food-grade materials are necessary to achieve the most intricate patterns. Some chefs use stencils to aid in creating elaborate designs, while others carve freehand and judge by eye.

Many carved vegetables can be prepared well in advance. In fact, some must be soaked in ice water for several hours in order for them to bloom, or open up. Some may remain in ice water until needed. Others can be mounted on clean Styrofoam boards and refrigerated under damp towels up to 24 hours. Fruits and vegetables that are subject to enzymatic browning should be fabricated at the last possible moment before service, and their cut surfaces should be treated with lemon juice.

Cucumber Hedge

Lemon Crown

Carved Vegetable Décor:
Top row, left to right: cucumber flourish, carrot tumbleweed, turnip rose in lettuce leaf

Second row, left to right: cucumber butterfly, radish tulip, lemon basket filled with fresh herbs

Third row, left to right: carrot tulip, radish rose, tomato rose with watercress leaves, red chile lily

Bottom row, left to right: scallion brush, turnip and asparagus calla lily, double-ended scallion brush

Note: With the exception of the cucumber items and the tomato rose, all décor items require 1 hour soaking in ice water after fabrication.

Procedure for Carving an Apple Bird.

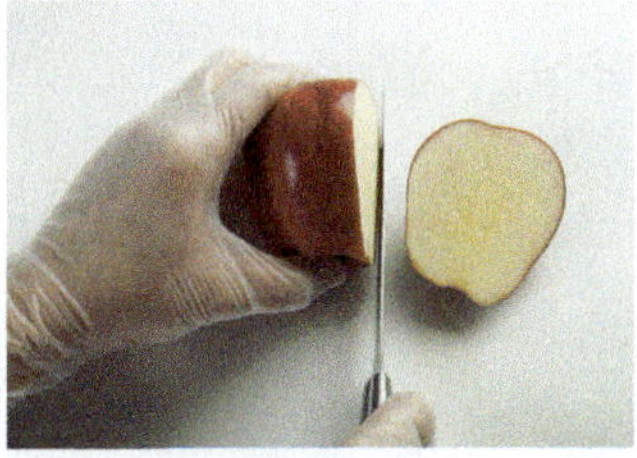

A. Cut off about ¼ of the apple's flatter side and coat the cut surface with lemon juice.

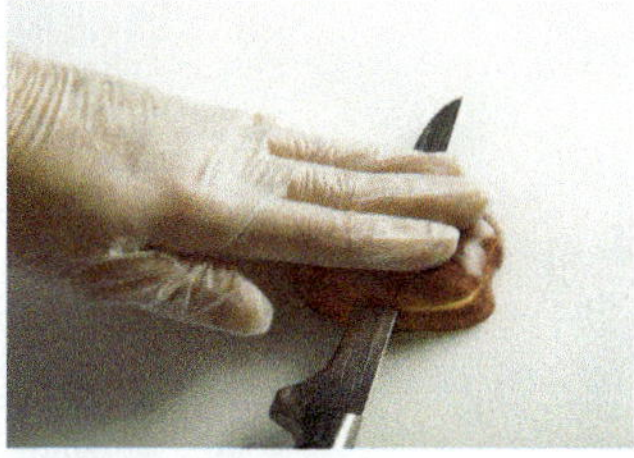

B. Fabricate an even ¼ in. slab from the cut piece of apple and coat all surfaces with lemon juice. Reserve the resulting rounded piece of apple.

C. From the apple slab, fabricate the bird's head and neck.

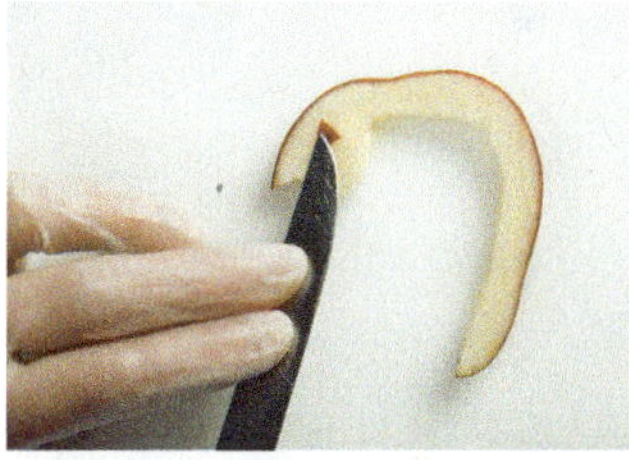

D. Cut two tiny triangles of red apple from the reserved rounded piece. Using the tip of a paring knife, press the triangles into either side of the bird head to make eyes.

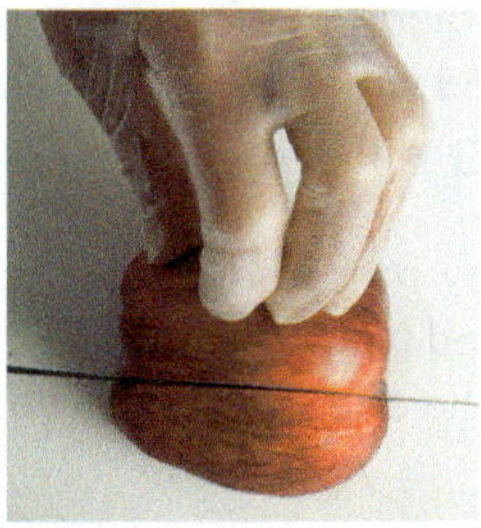

E. To begin a wing, make a vertical cut on one side of the apple.

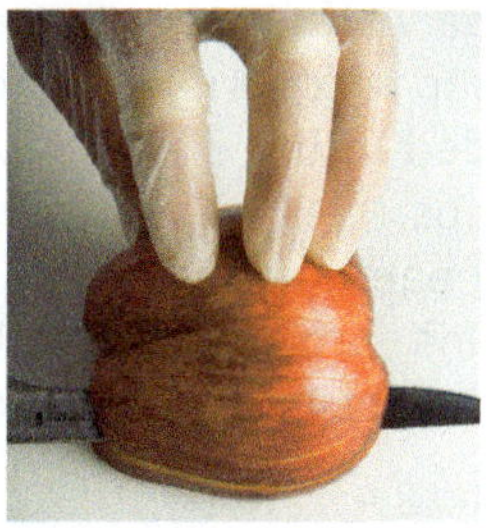

F. Make a series of vertical and horizontal cuts to create layers that will pull out to form the wing.

G. When cut correctly, the wing sections will slide back to form an elegant wing. If the décor bird will be viewed from one side only, make the wing and tail sections slightly off-center.

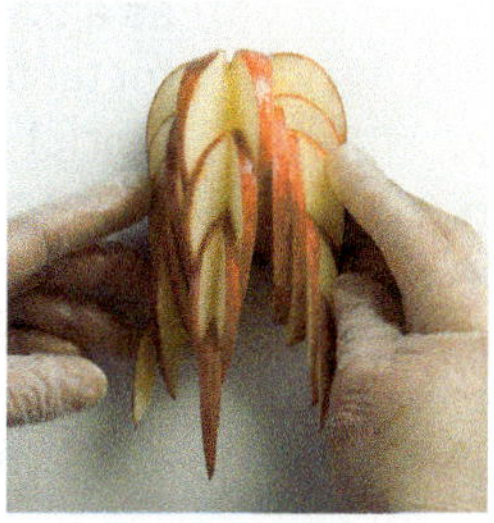

H. Repeat, making a wing on the left side of the apple and a tail in the center.

I. Cut a wedge in the front of the apple and insert the head and neck.

Cucumber Cup Procedure.

A. Pare the skin from the cucumber.

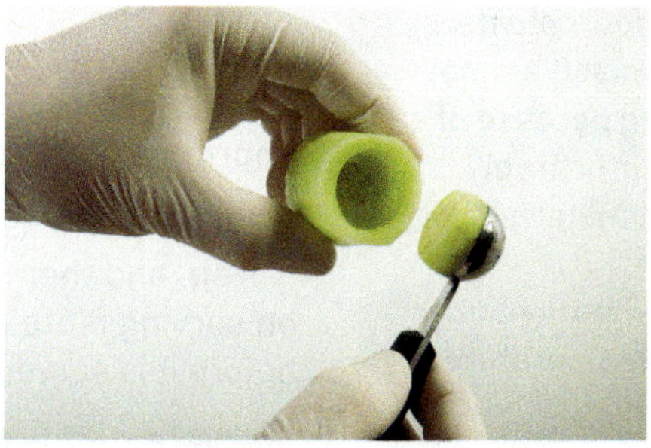

B. Using a parisienne scoop, hollow out the cucumber to create a cup.

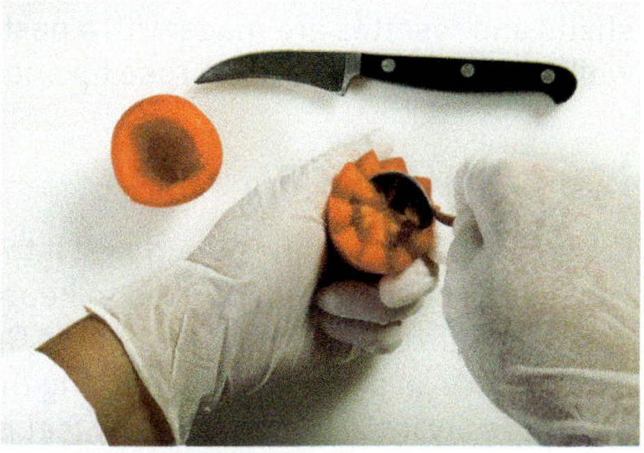

Preparing a tomato cup.

Miscellaneous Fabricated Items

Lobster head and tail décor

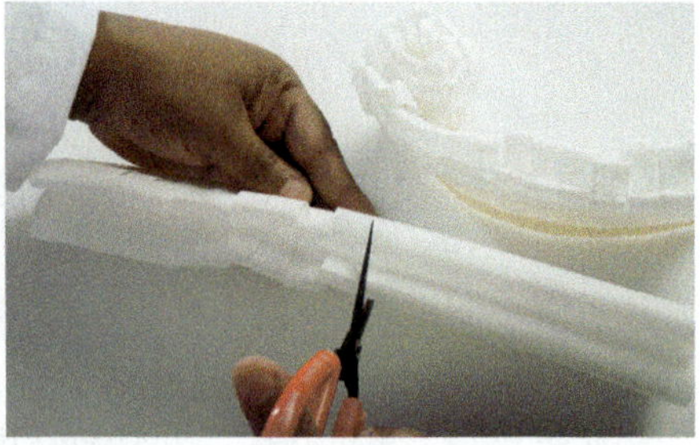

Cutlet frill

Fruit Displays

A fruit display can be as simple as a basket of fruit on a sideboard or as elaborate as a towering holiday *pièce montée*. Artfully constructed displays often involve metal frames or Styrofoam forms to which fruit is attached with picks or wires. Florist's greenery may be included in the display along with other nonfood elements such as ribbons and props.

Although not intended to be eaten, fruits on display must be fresh and unblemished. A display that contains shriveled or discolored fruit does not present a good appearance. Maintain a strict inspection schedule and replace part or all of the display as necessary.

Fat Carvings

The impulse to create sculpted images out of malleable materials is as old as human civilization. The idea of playing with food to create works of art is a part of almost every culinary culture.

In the classic cuisine period, European chefs were challenged to create elaborate *pièces montées* from a variety of edible materials. Semisoft animal fats were a natural choice for sculpting because of their pure white or ivory color and their firm yet malleable texture. The two traditional materials for fat sculpting are butter and tallow.

Butter sculpture is successful only when the butter can be kept very cold, at refrigerator temperatures. Thus, it is rarely used for table displays.

Tallow is a special kind of semisoft fat rendered from the deposit fat found in certain areas of sheep and cattle carcasses. It has a higher melt point than butter and remains firm at temperatures as high as 65°F (18°C). Over time, the composition of tallow has been altered to give it more stability. Industrial fats are added to achieve a higher melt point, longer keeping qualities, and lower cost. Malleable sculpting tallow or hard casting tallow, which is formulated to be melted and poured into molds, can now be purchased.

Butter Décor

Garde manger decorative arts include forming and sculpting butter into attractive shapes. Most butter décor is used as ***table butter***, the butter that accompanies the bread served at meals. Table butter is often brought to room temperature and whipped for greater volume and to maintain a softer, more spreadable texture when cold. It can be presented in several ways:

Pressed butter is packed into a butter chip or ramekin and chilled. Before it becomes completely firm it is sometimes imprinted with a decorative butter press.

Molded butter is packed into decorative silicone forms, frozen, and then popped out of the forms. It is then placed on serving plates and brought to refrigerated temperature before it is served.

Shaped butter is formed into decorative shapes with scoops and butter curlers. More elaborate butter décor items are piped with a pastry bag and tube tip. Instructions for piped décor shapes appear in cake decorating manuals. Butter shells and rosettes are made with a pastry bag and star tip, while butter roses require a rose tip and rose nail.

Ice Sculptures

From the classic cuisine period well into the twentieth century, huge ice blocks were used to keep dining rooms and banquet halls cool during hot weather. Garde manger chefs used this ice as a means of expressing their creativity, turning necessity into art. Today, many feel no important buffet is complete without an ice sculpture as its focal point.

Guidelines for Ice Carving Safety

Practicing the art of ice carving can be dangerous as well as challenging. Following these guidelines will keep everyone safe while ice sculpting.

- Always wear safety goggles when working on ice. Flying ice chips or a broken power tool can cause serious eye injuries.
- Lift ice blocks and sculptures from a crouching position so the strain of lifting is on your legs and not on your back. Use a cart to transport the ice block rather than carrying it in your arms.
- If you do not have ice tongs, wear work gloves to avoid slipping and to protect your hands from the cold.
- Carve on a nonskid surface and wear nonskid shoes. Keep the floor clear of ice chips and puddles of water.
- Make sure all electrical cords and power tools are in good repair. Keep power tools off the floor and away from water.
- Do not use a gas-powered chainsaw. The smoke and fumes from the motor can discolor the ice and give it an unpleasant smell.

Traditional Ice Sculpture

For centuries, the garde manger chef used the same tools as the artisan stone sculptor and wood carver: handsaws, hammers and chisels, and picks. Some contemporary artisan ice sculptors still swear by these traditional tools.

Modern Ice Sculpture

In the 1970s, ice sculptors began using power tools to make sculpting faster and easier. The introduction of lightweight electric chain saws and an array of electric woodworking tools in the 1980s revolutionized ice carving.

Purchasing and Storing Ice Blocks for Carving

Most small and midsize food-service operations purchase ice blocks from a local manufacturer or distributor. A typical manufactured ice block measures 40 × 20 × 10 in. (100 × 50 × 25 cm). When ordering, make sure to specify ***clear ice*** for carving. This is ice produced by a special method that keeps it from clouding as it freezes.

Ice should arrive wrapped in plastic. Keep it in the freezer until you are ready to temper it. Keep the original plastic wrapper intact to prevent ***sublimation***, a form of dehydration in which ice changes directly into vapor. Ice stored uncovered for long periods can simply evaporate, losing its shape and becoming brittle. Store ice on a rubber mat. If you store it on cardboard, moisture from melting during shipping can cause the cardboard to stick to the freezer floor or to the ice.

Procedure for Basic Ice Sculpting

1. Prepare a life-size template (see Note) of your design on butcher paper. If your sculpture will be seen from the back, prepare a template for the back as well.
2. Attach the template to the ice block at least 12 hours before you plan to work on it. In the walk-in freezer, unwrap your ice block. Use water misted from a spray bottle to moisten the ice and create a surface to which the template will stick. Take care to apply it correctly the first time. You will not be able to adjust the placement because the paper will immediately stick to the ice.
3. Use an ice pick or die grinder to trace the outline of your design onto the ice. Rewrap the ice block in its plastic covering.
4. Temper the ice block by placing it in a walk-in refrigerator for about 12 hours without unwrapping it. Refer to the sidebar below to learn why tempering is important.
5. Test the temper of the ice block by placing a piece of paper against one of the sides. If it slides on the surface freely without sticking, the ice is sufficiently tempered.
6. Prepare a shaded outdoor carving area and assemble your mise-en-place. Set up a sturdy plastic or wooden stand on which to place the ice block. Set up a table for your tools. Obtain a broom and snow shovel to keep the ice out from underfoot. If using power tools, make sure there is a grounded outlet and a heavy-duty extension cord. Have safety goggles and a plastic apron on hand.
7. Use a cart to transport your ice block to the carving area. Unwrap the ice block and place it on the stand.
8. To begin carving, use a hammer and chipper combined with a handsaw—or an electric chainsaw—to remove large pieces of ice outside the area of your design. The goal is to achieve the design in rough form only.
9. As the design form emerges, change to finer tools.
10. If desired, finish the sculpture by rubbing it with a towel soaked in hot water, or apply a heat gun.
11. Carefully transfer the sculpture to a self-draining tray set on a cart.
12. Wheel the sculpture to the display area, or return it to the walk-in freezer for storage.
13. If you are storing the sculpture in the freezer for more than a few hours, wrap it in heavy-duty plastic to prevent sublimation. Do not wrap it before the surface is solidly frozen, or the plastic wrap will stick to it.
14. Transport the sculpture to the display area far enough in advance so it will re-temper before the display event begins. At 70°F (21°C), a sculpture usually tempers clear in 2 hours.

Note: Many skilled ice sculptors work freehand, without a template. If you plan to sculpt freehand, omit steps 1 through 3.

The Science of Tempering and Thermal Shock

The molecular structure of ice consists of many differently shaped crystals. Although not visible to the eye, this structure changes as the ice becomes warmer or colder. The ice actually expands and contracts, depending on its interior temperature. If this happens slowly, the pressure within the ice adjusts itself and the ice remains strong and solid.

If the temperature of the ice changes quickly, its molecular structure is compromised. When an ice block is suddenly brought from below freezing temperatures to room temperature or higher, its molecular structure changes rapidly. The ice block is subjected to uneven internal pressures. At room or warmer temperatures, the surface warms much faster than the interior.

When subjected to sudden changes of temperature, ice is said to undergo ***thermal shock***. In this condition, it easily cracks or splits under the pressure of sculpting. Ice sculptors ***temper*** ice by moving it from the freezer to refrigerator temperature about 12 hours before working on it. Tempering also changes the appearance of the ice, giving it greater clarity.

Molded Ice Sculptures

Operations with ample freezer storage but without a skilled ice sculptor can prepare molded ice sculptures.

Single-use ice molds are filled with water and placed in the freezer until the water is frozen solid. Then the mold is cut away from the ice.

Reusable ice molds are manufactured in sections that seal during filling and freezing, and then come apart so the sculpture can be removed.

Ice-molding machines use glycol to rapidly freeze the water inside the molds.

Functional Ice Sculptures

Many ice sculptures are created and displayed solely as works of culinary artistry. However, their traditional function is to keep foods cold. Ice sculptures can be designed as vessels for serving food or beverages. For example, ice sculpture punch bowls are popular. Perhaps the most useful and decorative version is a hollow boat or clamshell used to display chilled seafood. Ice sculptures can also function as lanterns. A hollow design is sculpted, and candles or outdoor-rated electric lights are placed within it.

TERMS FOR REVIEW

condiment
garnish
embellishment
garniture
décor
décor item
pièce montée
ketchup
prepared mustard
pickle
relish
(to) steep
(to) infuse
infusion
reduce
reduction
compote
cooked chutney
raw chutney
jam
confiture
flavored vinegar
flavored oil
vegetables preserved in oil
dipping sauce
glaze
essence
cracker
savory tuile
straw
chip
croûton
fleuron
(culinary) foam
pressurized canister
gelatin-stabilized foam
savory ice cube
savory sorbet
plate painting
flooding
tallow
table butter
pressed butter
molded butter
shaped butter
clear ice (for carving)
sublimation
thermal shock
(to) temper (ice)

QUESTIONS FOR DISCUSSION

1. Define the term *condiment.* List at least five condiment categories, and give an example of each.
2. Explain the term *embellishment.* How does an embellishment differ from a garnish?
3. Explain the differences between a cracker, a chip, and a croûton. How are these embellishment items used? How should they be stored?
4. List and describe at least three types of pastry containers used in garde manger work. Give an example of how each might be used. As a garde manger chef in a large food-service operation, what are your options for obtaining pastry containers? In a small operation, what are your options?
5. Discuss the use of aspic garnishes and décor items. Give an example of an aspic plate garnish. Give an example of an aspic platter garnish.
6. Discuss the use of savory ices and foams. Describe the two types of savory ices, and give an example of each. Describe the two types of savory foams, and explain how each is prepared.
7. Explain the concept of plate painting. What is meant by the expression "flavor comes first"? Draw pictures of typical plate painting designs.
8. Discuss food décor. How does it differ from food garnish?
9. What is a *pièce montée*? Discuss the history of *pièces montée*. How are they used today?
10. What type of ice is used for ice sculpting? Why is it important to temper ice for ice sculpting? Explain how you would prepare an ice block for sculpting.
11. List six safety guidelines for ice sculpting.

Chapter

18

PREREQUISITES

Before studying this chapter, you should already

- Have read Chapters 1 through 17 of this text and thoroughly understand the fundamentals of garde manger work.
- Have a sound understanding of food-service mathematics and be proficient at recipe costing.

Buffets and Food Bars

You may have heard the saying, "We eat with our eyes." While this is so for all types of food, it is especially true for buffets. No other type of service showcases the garde manger chef's decorative talents more fully than the formal buffet. Moreover, buffet food must taste as good as it looks. In addition to the all-important visual aspect, buffets demand detailed planning and careful craftsmanship, both hallmarks of top-level garde manger work.

Food bars are a new type of buffet primarily featured in midlevel restaurants and retail establishments. Much of the same planning and decorative skills used in buffet work is needed to operate a successful food bar.

In this chapter, you will learn the professional techniques and strategies needed to plan, cost, set up, and maintain buffets and food bars. After studying this chapter, you can combine all the topics covered in previous chapters and utilize your knowledge of garde manger ingredients and techniques to design a cold buffet as the grand finale of your garde manger course.

After reading this chapter, you should be able to

1. Plan a successful garde manger buffet menu.
2. Use backwards planning to write food preparation lists for buffet work.
3. Calculate food quantities for buffets.
4. Determine the per-person food cost of a buffet menu and price the menu according to an established food cost percentage.
5. Schedule the staffing for various types of buffets.
6. Set up self-service buffets, attended buffets, and action buffets.
7. Utilize various serving pieces, structure props, and food-based and nonfood visual props to create attractive buffet displays.
8. Work as part of a team to plan, present, and break down a cold foods buffet.
9. Plan and operate a safe and successful food bar.

UNDERSTANDING BUFFETS

A ***buffet*** [boo-FAY] is a type of service in which a variety of dishes are arranged in an attractive display from which guests choose the foods they wish to eat. Buffets are purchased on a ***prix fixe*** [pree FEEKS] basis, meaning guests are able to consume as much as they wish for one set price.

The traditional buffet configuration is a long table, or line of tables, on which the food platters are attractively arranged. This is known as a ***buffet line***. The buffet line is divided into ***buffet stations***, or sections that feature a particular type of food, such as appetizers, salads, seafood, and carved meats. Guests approach the buffet line from a designated starting point and proceed along the line as they choose the food items they want. Today, buffet planners use many configurations for buffet setup.

Buffets were originally created to feed a large number of people quickly and efficiently with a small number of servers. Traditional buffets featured cold foods only and thus were solely the responsibility of the garde manger department. However, modern buffets typically include both cold and hot food items.

Some buffets are elegant and formal, while others are simple and casual. The most successful buffets have a theme, a topic discussed on page 729.

Buffets may be large, sometimes consisting of 50, 60, or even 100 different dishes. They may also be small, including only six or seven offerings. To meet customer expectations, a buffet must offer a variety of choices and convey a feeling of plenty. The number of dishes offered corresponds to the number of customers to be served, typically one main course per a minimum of 20 guests. Thus, for very small groups, buffets are not cost-effective.

In North America, buffets are frequently featured at hotels and large restaurants and are an important element of catering. Caterers prefer buffet service for events because they require fewer servers and most dishes can be prepared ahead of time. Hotels—particularly casino hotels—have become famous for large, elaborate buffets. In fact, many hotels maintain a permanent ***established buffet*** always available to guests. Restaurants may offer buffets for special occasions, such as Mother's Day, when a high volume of business is expected. In such cases, a buffet allows the restaurant to serve more customers faster and more efficiently than their usual à la carte service.

Buffet Service Styles

Although the buffet is a major style of service in its own right, today there are several ways to present and serve buffet foods. We can identify three basic buffet service styles:

1. Self-service buffets
2. Attended or served buffets
3. Action buffets

Each of these service styles has advantages and disadvantages.

The History of the Buffet

The buffet was created as a way to give large numbers of people access to food throughout an extended period. Here is a brief timeline.

Middle Ages: When sizable groups of people were expected to dine, hosts ordered large joints of roasted meats, whole roasted fowls, and platters of cold foods to be laid out on narrow tables placed along the walls. Because this type of table was called a *buffet*, the service style became known as *buffet service*.

The 1700s: Buffets were served at parties and balls as well as at wakes and funerals. During the classic cuisine period of French cooking, the chefs of the aristocracy presented elaborate buffets consisting of hundreds of costly dishes and decorated with fantastic *pièces montées*.

The mid-1800s: Buffets were instituted in railway stations and on steamships. Thus, they are frequently associated with travel accommodations.

The late 1800s–early twentieth century: Grand hotels made buffets famous, offering lavish displays of elegant and costly foods. Blocks of ice, often carved into elaborate shapes, were used to keep the buffet foods cold. Chafing dishes, tabletop food warmers, allowed buffet planners to add a limited number of hot items to the previously all-cold-foods buffet. Caterers soon began to emulate hotel buffets for private parties, weddings, and other events.

Soon after the steam table was invented in 1897, it was adapted for commercial buffets. Cafeterias were installed in factories, schools, and hospitals throughout North America. In order to keep prices affordable, cafeterias served low-cost foods and priced them individually. Modern cafeterias offer a wider range of choices than old-style cafeterias.

The mid-twentieth century: Portable refrigeration units specially designed for buffet service once again revolutionized the buffet, making possible new buffet concepts. In the 1960s, restaurants began installing salad bars and invited guests to create their own salads. Before long, the simple salad bar was transformed into the all-purpose food bar, eventually offering a wide variety of cold and hot foods.

Meanwhile, buffets were getting larger and, in some cases, less expensive as well. In 1946, proprietor Herb McDonald of the El Rancho Casino in Las Vegas turned the buffet into a powerful marketing tool. McDonald created the prototype of the low-cost, high-value "mega-buffet" in order to attract gamblers to his casino.

Late twentieth century to the present: Buffets are now often equipped with both cold and hot action stations, at which chefs prepare foods to order in front of the guests' eyes. Today there is a buffet for every occasion and for every budget. Low-cost, family-style buffet restaurants provide cheap, quick meals for workers and shoppers. Elegant, elaborate buffets are served at weddings and other formal events.

Self-Service Buffets

Traditional buffets are self-service. In a ***self-service buffet***, all food platters are placed within easy reach of the customers, and an appropriate serving utensil is placed on a small tray or plate in front of each platter. Guests serve themselves as much or as little as they want of whichever food items they choose.

When setting up a self-service buffet, it is essential to prepare and set out ***food identification placards***, or small signs that indicate the name of each dish. Guests prefer to know what they are eating, and they don't like surprises. If a dish contains a potential allergen, such as nuts or shellfish, this information should be noted on the placard.

One advantage of self-service buffets is that they can be set up in a double-line configuration. A ***double buffet line*** is set up so guests can access the food from both sides of the table. This configuration doubles the number of guests that can pass along the food line at one time. Thus, a double line is twice as fast as a single line. A double-line buffet is illustrated on page 732.

The main advantage of a self-service buffet is that it requires minimal labor. Because the guests do the serving, there is no need to pay staff members to serve. However, some service staff members must still be on hand.

One disadvantage of self-service buffets is that they can quickly become messy and look unappealing. For this reason, at least one server should be assigned to frequently tidy up the table(s). In addition, food platters must be monitored and replaced or replenished when necessary. The server on duty must make sure the platters on the buffet remain attractive and at least half full.

Another disadvantage of self-service buffets is that they are slow. Most guests are not skillful at putting food onto their plates and take a lot of time to do so. They may be unfamiliar with some of the foods presented on the buffet and hesitate when serving themselves. Thus, it takes more time for a crowd to get through a self-service buffet line than through a line that has servers.

The biggest disadvantage of self-service buffets is that they offer no real means of portion control. In a self-serve situation, guests are free to take large portions of their favorite foods. Unfortunately, these favorites typically tend to be the most expensive items on the buffet. Later in this chapter you will learn some portion-control strategies for setting up buffet lines and stations.

Attended or Served Buffets

Today, many buffets are staffed with servers. These are called ***attended buffets*** or ***served buffets***. In this type of buffet, several servers are stationed behind the buffet table(s). The servers are equipped with appropriate serving utensils. Customers indicate which food items they want, and the servers place a portion of those foods onto the customers' plates. Attended buffets are advantageous in many ways. The only disadvantage of attended buffets is their higher labor costs relative to self-service buffets.

Portion control is the biggest advantage of the attended buffet. Another advantage is speed of service. Buffet servers are experienced in portioning and plating foods, so the buffet line moves more quickly. Servers are less likely to make a mess and are trained to clean up drips and spills as they happen. Thus, an attended buffet looks neat and attractive throughout the service. Servers who remain stationed at the buffet table are constantly aware of how much food remains on the platters and can call for replenishments in a timely manner.

Customer interaction is another advantage of attended buffets. While food identification placards are always helpful, they are less important when servers are present to identify the buffet dishes. Well-trained, knowledgeable servers can greatly enhance your guests' experience. For example, if a cheese display is staffed by a server who is well-informed about the various cheeses, guests can be directed to the types of cheese they will like best.

Although paying additional staff members to serve at buffets increases labor costs, these costs may be more than offset by many advantages.

Action Buffets

Modern buffets frequently include special buffet stations where certain types of food preparation are performed before the customers' eyes. These are called ***action stations***. A buffet that includes one or more action stations is called an ***action buffet***.

At an action buffet, customers can chat with the chefs and learn interesting facts about the food and the operation. At many action stations, the food being prepared can be customized to each guest's personal preference. For example, when a customer visits a sushi action station, he confers with the chef about his order. The sushi chef is able to make a sushi item that contains the customer's favorite fillings and can leave out ingredients the customer dislikes. On a breakfast buffet, an omelet action station allows guests to order omelets cooked to the doneness they prefer and filled with the ingredients of their choice. This is service customers remember and tell their friends about.

Action stations can be quite cost effective because they generate almost no waste. Because action station dishes are prepared to order, there are no leftovers. As long as the ingredients are kept properly chilled and free from contamination, they may be returned to general use after the buffet is over.

Action stations must be staffed with appropriate personnel, typically from the culinary staff rather than the service staff. Action station cooks must be experienced at the task they are assigned to perform because they will be working in a situation that presents many distractions. They must look well groomed and act professionally at all times. They must know and observe sanitation rules because they can be seen at all times while they work. Because they will be interacting with customers, action station cooks must be polite and friendly.

The type of staff member just described typically draws a higher rate of pay than the average line cook or server. However, the higher labor cost for action station personnel is balanced by the higher price that can be charged for an action buffet.

Ideas for garde manger action stations appear in the suggested menus section on pages 741–742.

Combination Buffets

Experienced garde manger chefs frequently combine two or even all three of the basic buffet service styles to create an unusual and memorable buffet. For example, a self-service hors d'oeuvre buffet might be set up near the entrance to the buffet room or in a foyer. The main buffet table may be attended. As a grand finale, the chef might plan a dessert action station, such as an ice cream sundae bar or a Bananas Foster station. Buffets that combine service styles are called ***combination buffets***.

A combination buffet may also include service styles other than buffet service. For example, a formal buffet might begin with butler service hors d'oeuvres and end with banquet service desserts.

The Five Phases of Buffet Work

Professional buffet work involves five distinct phases:

Phase 1: Planning

Phase 2: Food preparation

Phase 3: Setup

Phase 4: Service

Phase 5: Breakdown

Phase 1: Planning

Planning is the most important phase of buffet work and crucial to its success. Buffet planning is an involved procedure and can take a lot of time. Many details must be worked out:

- The theme must be identified.
- The menu must be designed to meet the customers' expectations and offer sufficient variety.
- Food preparation must be organized.
- The physical layout of the buffet and its service strategy must be carefully planned.

No matter how delicious the food is, if the buffet table is not set up for proper flow, if the platters are hard to reach and the food is difficult to put on the plates, or if there is no procedure for replenishing the empty platters, guests will not enjoy the event.

To begin the work of planning a buffet, you need the following information about the event:

- The date
- Its start and end times
- The occasion or purpose
- Type of clientele attending
- Number of guests being served
- Per-person price or designated per-person food cost
- Service fees, if any, to be charged
- Special requests or restrictions regarding the food to be served

These facts determine whether or not the buffet planning should go forward. For example, the proposed date may conflict with another event already booked. The head count may be too high for your operation to accommodate or too low to be cost-effective as a buffet. The price the client is willing to pay may be too low to be profitable within your quality standards. Sometimes these problems can be overcome through rescheduling or negotiation.

Once these details are found satisfactory, planning can begin. The information affects the type and amount of food you will serve, the layout of the buffet room, line(s), and stations, and the number of staff you will need.

Buffet planning can be divided into ten tasks that must be done in order:

Step 1: Establishing the theme

Step 2: Planning the menu

Step 3: Designing the buffet line and/or stations

Step 4: Choosing the props

Step 5: Writing serving equipment lists

Step 6: Designing the room layout

Step 7: Writing food prep lists

Step 8: Scheduling staff

Step 9: Writing food order lists

Step 10: Planning the service strategy

Let's examine each of these steps.

STEP 1: ESTABLISHING THE THEME

The ***buffet theme*** is the concept, or basic idea, of the buffet, and should be clear and instantly recognizable. The theme dictates almost all creative choices when planning the buffet. The buffet theme drives the menu, the style of food presentation used for the dishes, the appearance of the buffet line or stations, the decorations and props used on the stations and in the buffet room—even the music, if any, played during the buffet event.

Most buffet themes are based on a concept that directly involves food. Some are as simple as a type of meal service. Thus, the theme of a breakfast buffet is "morning foods." Often, the theme of a buffet is chosen to suit the tastes of the guest of honor. If the birthday honoree loves pasta, then an Italian theme is the right choice for the birthday party buffet. Holiday themes are popular and can focus on traditional holiday food. Thus, on or near St. Patrick's Day an Irish food buffet is appropriate, while an all-American menu is perfect for the Fourth of July.

Not all buffet themes are food-focused. When this is the case, try to plan some elements of the food to support the theme. For example, if the buffet is for a garden club social, make flowers the theme. To support the theme, use floral-patterned linen, create a chaud-froid showpiece with a floral motif, and garnish some of the dishes with edible flowers.

A buffet's theme should suit the tastes of the clientele and be compatible with the season and time of day. Ignoring this advice can result in unhappy customers. For example, it is unwise to plan a Bavarian sauerkraut and sausage lunch buffet for a group of women in July or to offer a cold soup and salad dinner buffet to a football team in November.

The theme of a buffet should complement the concept, décor, and style of the food-service operation hosting it. For example, a Texas barbecue buffet is inappropriate for a formal French restaurant. Likewise, it would be difficult for a casual, roadhouse-style restaurant to properly present a formal European buffet.

Finally, the type of menu the theme demands must be within the abilities of the culinary staff. No matter how much your customer might want a Thai cuisine buffet, if you and your staff know little about Asian cooking you should definitely suggest another theme.

STEP 2: PLANNING THE MENU

Buffet menu planning is a complex task. Planning successful menus of any kind requires a broad knowledge of the culinary arts and years of practical experience. Entire books are written on the subject of menu planning, and culinary schools offer complete courses of study on it. Clearly you cannot learn all there is to know about planning buffet menus from reading a few paragraphs here. However, as you begin to explore buffet work, the guidelines (p. 731) can help you.

In most cases, your menu must be approved before you can go on to the remaining planning steps. If the buffet has been ordered by a client, you or your representative will meet with the client and review the menu. If the buffet is internally generated, you will likely meet with the owner or manager of your operation. Be prepared for questions, and be flexible about making changes if requested to do so.

STEP 3: DESIGNING THE BUFFET LINE AND/OR STATIONS

Once your menu is approved, you can begin to plan the layout of the buffet menu dishes. First, determine whether the dishes will be laid out on a single buffet line or whether to break up the display into multiple lines and/or stations. Once that is determined, you can plan the layout of the dishes on the line(s) and stations. In making these determinations, you have two major goals.

1. To make the food look as attractive as possible
2. To ensure the guests are served quickly and efficiently

Buffet Lines

The traditional model for buffets is the buffet line. A buffet line can be straight, as in a row of rectangular tables. Rectangular tables can also be arranged in a *U*-shape, *V*-shape, or other pattern. Curved tables can be used to create a horseshoe or serpentine buffet line. Buffet line configurations are illustrated on pages 732 and 733. The speed and efficiency of a buffet line depends on its configuration, its contents, and whether it is attended or self-service. As a general rule, you can expect a standard, single buffet line to accommodate 50 to 70 guests per hour. If you expect a larger crowd or need to feed your guests more quickly, you can set up two or more identical lines. These lines can be in separate sections of the room or connected in mirror image. The illustration of the horseshoe buffet configuration on page 732 shows a mirror-image buffet line. Self-service buffets can be set up as double lines.

When planning your buffet line, you must create and maintain ***flow***. In other words, the food containers on the buffet line must be set up in a logical order for service. Foods typically eaten first, such as appetizers and salads, should appear first on the line. Main dishes and accompaniments come next. If there is only one buffet line for the entire meal, desserts appear last. However, most buffet planners set up desserts separately from the savory buffet. If identification placards are used, they should be placed to avoid confusion and so they stay clean. A single large décor item, such as a *pièce montée* or an ice carving, is typically placed in the center of the line. If there are more than one décor piece, space them symmetrically along the line, with the tallest piece in the center.

The order in which dishes are arranged on the buffet line can help establish portion control. For example, you should place less expensive foods, such as bread and salads, at the beginning of the line or section, and more expensive items, such as seafood and meats, toward the end. When plates are nearly full, there is less room for costly items. Using smaller plates helps control portion sizes as well. Another way to control portion size is to provide only small serving spoons and serving tongs.

Guidelines for Successful Buffet Menu Planning

- *The menu should support the theme of the buffet.* Each dish should reflect the theme. Including dishes that do not support the theme dilutes your concept and creates confusion for your customers. For example, you should not add a Mexican guacamole appetizer to a French cuisine buffet just because you like guacamole.
- *The menu must have broad appeal.* In other words, the dishes you serve on your buffet must satisfy a wide variety of people with differing taste preferences. The larger the buffet, the more diverse its customer base will be. You must strike a balance between dishes that are new and unusual and those that are familiar and comforting.
- *Make sure the menu fits the budget.* A buffet must be planned to be profitable. You will have been given a per-person food cost limit (or you will have determined the proper food cost as a percentage of the menu price), and you must stay within it. By the time you are given the responsibility of planning a buffet, you should have a solid background in food-service mathematics, and thus know how to cost your recipes and how to determine correct quantities to be served. Before you submit your buffet menu for approval, *you must accurately cost the recipes for all dishes served on your buffet, determine the total cost of the buffet foods, and calculate the correct per-person cost.* If your per-person cost is over limit, you must revise your menu. Refer to pages 742–744 for information on determining quantities and buffet food costing.
- *Offer variety.* A good way to start planning your menu for variety is to choose a main dish from each of the major protein groups. For example, plan a red meat dish, a white meat dish, a poultry dish, a seafood dish, and a vegetarian main dish. Make sure their sauces and garnitures are varied. Build your side dishes around the main dishes using the same model. Finally, choose your appetizers from each of the main appetizer production types. In other words, plan one or two salads, a charcuterie item, a seafood item, a dairy item, and one or more pastry items.
- *Avoid repetition.* Do not use important ingredients more than once. For example, if you plan to present a whole poached salmon as an entrée, don't choose smoked salmon as an appetizer. If you are serving a whole baked ham, don't use ham mousse on your canapés.
- *Serve foods that are easy to eat.* For seated buffets, this is less important because guests will be provided with chairs and place settings. Nonetheless, foods that require special tools (such as seafood crackers or steak knives) or that require a lot of attention (such as bone-in Cornish hens or whole artichokes) are not appropriate for buffets. Standing buffets offer limited seating, at best, and many guests find it necessary to eat standing up or perched on the arm of a sofa. In this case, serve only fork foods that are easy to eat with one hand. For more information, refer to the sidebar on page 736.
- *Consider the visuals.* The appearance of the dishes on a buffet is a major part of its success. Vary the color of your foods and the size and shape of dishes to create visual interest. Alternate low, flat presentations, such as terrine slices fanned on a presentation mirror, with tall, vertical presentations, such as a crudité basket.
- *Make sure you have the proper serving equipment.* For example, if you do not have a 30-in. (75-cm) fish platter, it is unwise to add a whole poached salmon to the menu. The same holds true for showpieces. If you do not have a self-draining ice sculpture display tray, you will have to rent one or forego the ice sculpture.
- *Serve what you know.* A buffet is not the best place for experimentation. On a buffet, your dishes will be on display to scores or even hundreds of people. Each guest will see and taste virtually all of your work. Thus, the majority of the dishes should be items you and your staff have successfully prepared in the past. If you add one or two new dishes, have a backup plan if one of the new items does not meet your standards.

On all buffet tables, stacks of plates are the first item on the line. If flatware and napkins are to be placed on the buffet line, they should be the last items. There is no need for customers to carry these items down the line as they are taking or being served food.

Single-line buffet configuration

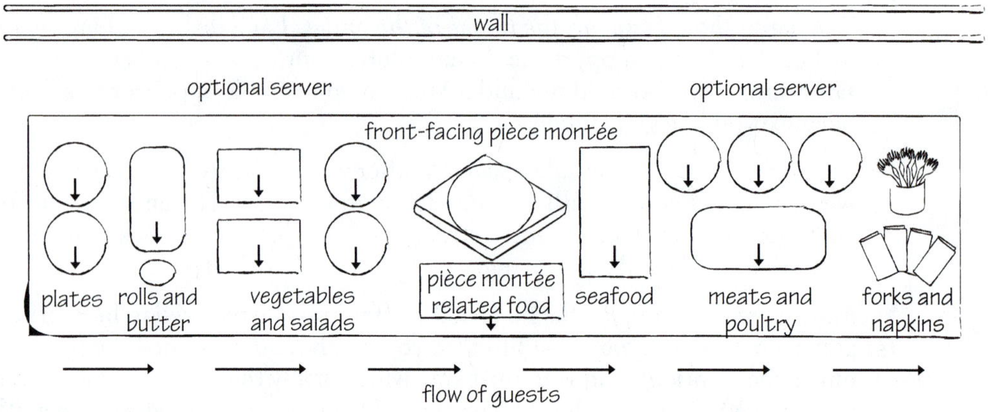

Double-line buffet configuration

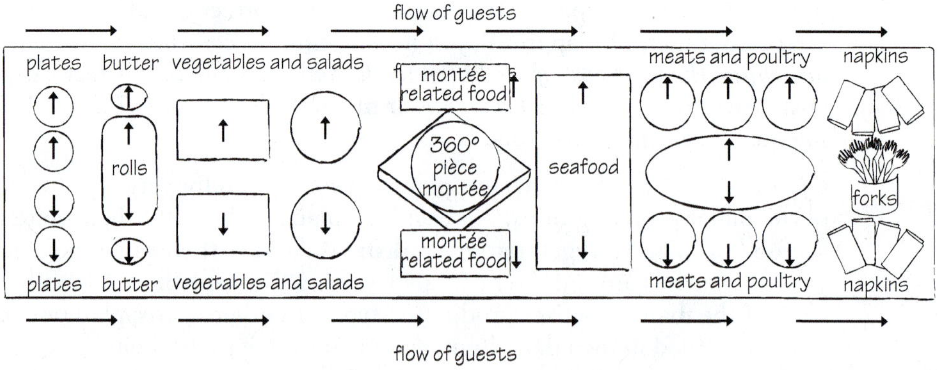

Horseshoe buffet configuration

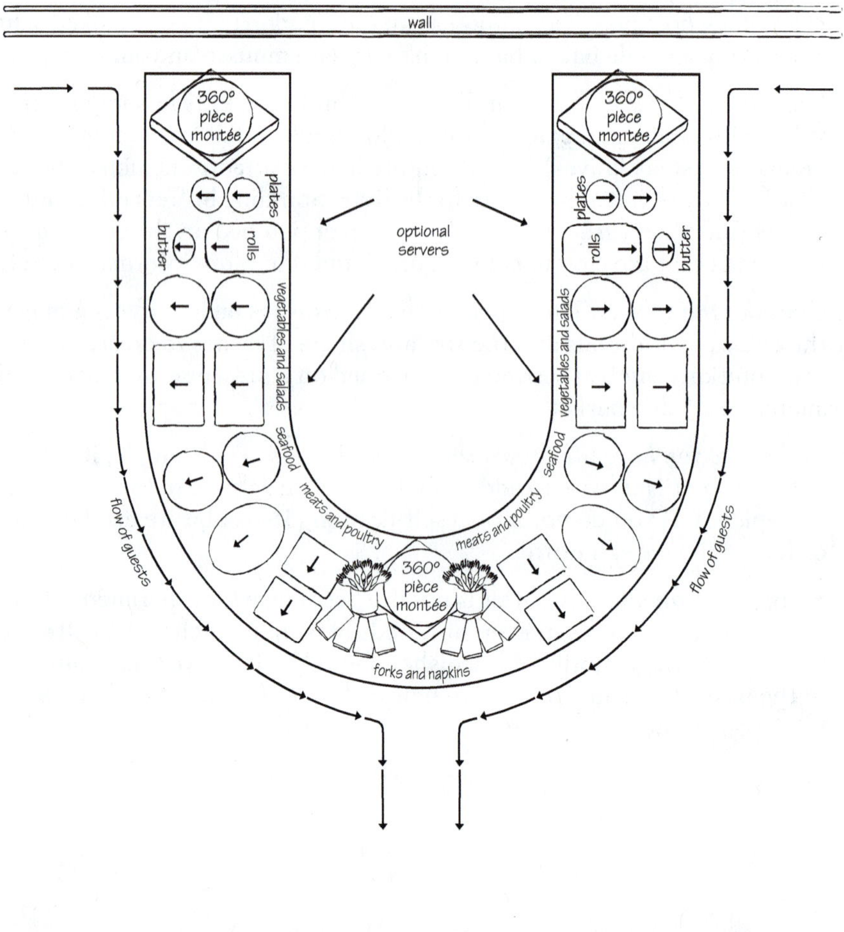

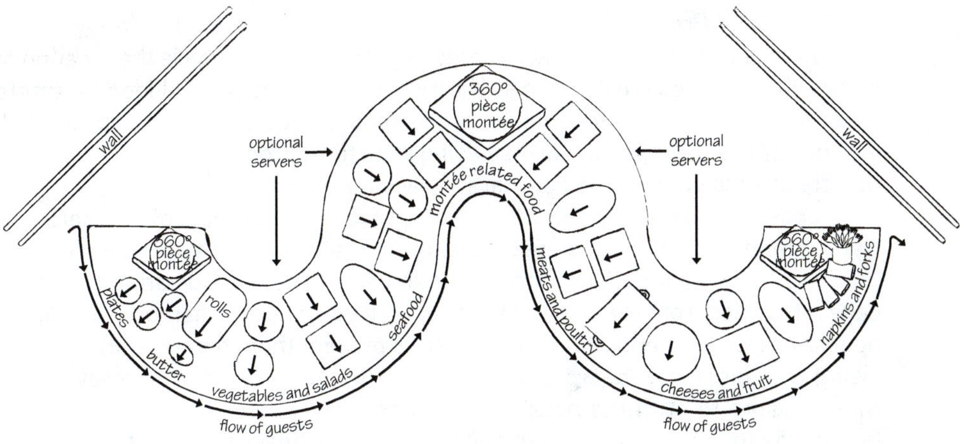

Serpentine buffet configuration

Buffet Stations

The modern trend in buffet planning is to set up small, separate buffet stations in place of, or in addition to, the standard buffet line. When one or more smaller stations are used in addition to a main buffet line, they are referred to as ***satellite stations***. Satellite stations take some of the pressure off the main buffet line and keep guests occupied when the main buffet line is crowded.

Separate stations have several advantages. The biggest advantage of placing various stations around the buffet area is the avoidance of long lines. Rather than waiting for many minutes to access the food, guests instead can stroll around the room and visit the stations that offer their favorite dishes. They can ignore the stations that feature foods not to their taste. Stations are generally simpler to maintain and easier to replenish than long buffet lines. Stations create movement in the buffet area and stimulate conversation among the guests.

Buffet stations may be self-service, attended, or action stations. A station should have its own mini-theme and, thus, feature all one type of food. For example, a raw bar station consists of oysters and clams on the half-shell, and sometimes cold cooked seafood, presented on ice. A raw bar might be self-service and consist of pre-opened shellfish, or it might be an action station featuring a chef opening shellfish to order. A sushi station features various types of seafood and vegetable sushi. The sushi might be pre-made, or a sushi chef can make sushi to order. Action stations that include cooking involve the hot line staff, while cold action stations are operated by the garde manger staff.

To speed service at very large buffets, you can set up duplicate stations at each end of the buffet area.

Buffet Line Maps and Station Maps

The best way to plan the layout of your buffet lines and stations is to make maps. Buffet maps are identical in concept to service line maps. Refer to page 14 for an explanation of food-service mapmaking. To become buffet line maps, the buffet line configurations on pages 732 and 733 need only to have platters labeled with specific dishes.

When you are satisfied that you have properly organized the line(s) and/or stations, and the order in which the buffet dishes will be arranged on them, you can proceed to planning the props and serving equipment. Step 4 and Step 5 go hand in hand and are typically done simultaneously.

STEP 4: CHOOSING THE PROPS

The most attractive buffets utilize props as well as food items to create visual interest. Buffet props fall into two categories:

1. Structural
2. Visual

Pre-Plating

An effective serving strategy for delicate items that are difficult to portion is to use ***pre-plating***. In this service style, small, individual portions of a special food are placed on little plates, or in little cups, that are lined up on the buffet in a symmetrical pattern. Pre-plating is especially effective for appetizers, particularly the costly or high-labor items the chef wants to showcase. High-end food-service equipment suppliers now offer tiny plates, cups, and glasses made of both durable and disposable materials.

Structural Props

One of the most important elements of buffet visual design is the creation of height. Buffet tables are flat, and so are most platters and trays of food. To create visual interest and ensure that all of the food can be seen and appreciated, elevate some of your serving dishes using structural props. ***Structural props*** are objects used to support food platters and visual props.

Food-service equipment suppliers sell food service–approved risers and tiered stands designed to elevate food presentations. However, you can save money by purchasing Styrofoam blocks to use as risers. You can also borrow cake turntables from the pastry department. If you do so, remember to plug the apertures in their stands with plastic film to prevent them from turning. Improvising with *clean* cardboard boxes is a time-honored practice. However, you must be sure to stuff the boxes with newspaper and secure them shut with heavy tape to prevent them from collapsing under heavy food platters. Improvised structural props should not be visible. For appearance and sanitation, cover them with clean tablecloths, linen napkins, or fabric.

Visual Props

Visual props are decorative items placed on a buffet line or station to make it more attractive and to support the buffet theme. The most traditional visual props are food-based showpieces, or pièces montées. Large and elaborate food centerpieces were a hallmark of classical cuisine beginning with Carême, and they are still appropriate on formal buffets today. Pastry structures, bread sculptures, arrangements of both natural and carved fruits and vegetables, and ice sculptures are all classic visual props that enhance any buffet. If your garde manger team has the skill, resources, and time to create such showpieces, you should certainly plan to include them in your design. Customers who order theme buffets frequently pay large sums of money for custom-made showpieces that reflect their chosen theme.

Nonfood items are also used as visual props. Floral arrangements are sometimes used on buffet lines, although they are not traditional. If flower arrangements are used, they should be composed of scentless flowers. Strong floral scents interfere with the aroma of the food.

Table linens and skirting can be considered props when they support the theme. For example, red-and-white checkered tablecloths set the mood for an Italian-American pasta buffet. You can use fabric other than table linen for buffet tables. For example, the structural props on a Mexican buffet might be covered with colorful serapes.

Whimsical props that reflect the buffet theme add fun and visual interest to casual buffets. For example, you could use miniature straw bales, cowboy hats, and a pony saddle as props on a Western ranch–themed barbecue buffet. Nets, buoys, and lobster traps enhance the mood of a seafood buffet.

Props can be scavenged from thrift and antique stores, borrowed from friends and fellow employees, or rented from food stylists or theatrical property houses. Some clients are enthusiastic about supplying appropriate props for the buffets they order. Of course, props for use on the buffet table must be thoroughly clean and should not come into contact with the food.

STEP 5: WRITING SERVING EQUIPMENT LISTS

Once you have identified the order in which you will arrange your dishes on the buffet line(s) and/or stations, make sure you have the necessary serving vessels and utensils. The importance of matching each dish with the most appropriate serving vessel cannot be overestimated. The shape, color, and size of the serving piece can make or break the visual appeal of a dish. For example, slices of pale white seafood terrine "disappear" on a white ceramic platter but stand out boldly on a black lacquer tray. Serving platters must be the proper size to comfortably hold the food. Platters should not appear crowded, nor should they look sparse and skimpy.

The custom of presenting huge platters heaped with large amounts of food is no longer in style. The main reason is sanitation—primarily, the danger of holding foods within the temperature danger zone (TDZ) for long periods. It is safer to serve smaller amounts of food on smaller platters and to replace or replenish the platters more frequently.

Many types of food presentation vessels and equipment are used in buffet work. Most of the trays, bowls, platters, and presentation mirrors illustrated and discussed in previous chapters are used in buffet presentation. For items that must be kept consistently cold, such as shellfish and mayonnaise-bound salads, you should use ***iced presentation trays***, ***ice-filled chafing dishes***, or portable refrigeration. For hot items, you can use electric ***warming trays*** and ***heat lamps***, and ***chafing dishes*** of various types.

Serving utensils are almost as important as serving vessels. Without the appropriate serving tools, it will be difficult to get the food onto the plates quickly and neatly. If utensils are too large, portions will likely be too large as well. Do not use kitchenware utensils on a buffet line. They are too large for most purposes and do not have the formal, finished look of serviceware.

Buffets also involve tables, chairs, plates, flatware, glasses, napkins, and all of the other items necessary to serve a meal. This type of equipment is usually handled by the service staff.

When planning a buffet, you must plan and secure your serving equipment by making lists. To secure the serving pieces you already have in-house, you must write an equipment pull list. A ***pull list*** not only allows you to plan what you need but also reserves those items and prevents other divisions from taking them at the last minute. Post your pull list where staff from other departments can see it. Large operations have computerized equipment inventories. By placing an item on your computerized pull list, you effectively remove it from the available inventory.

If your operation does not have all of the serving equipment you need, you must rent it or buy it. In this case, you will write an order list.

STEP 6: DESIGNING THE ROOM LAYOUT

Now that you know how many buffet lines and/or stations you need, and how those lines and stations will be organized, you can plan the layout of the buffet room(s). Your layout depends primarily on the size and shape of the room. Therefore, you need a floor plan that includes entrances, exits, traffic patterns, and barriers such as support pillars. Hotels, catering halls, and other party venues can sometimes supply blueprints or printed floor plans. Otherwise, you must do your own sketches at the site. Use a tape measure, and try to draw the floor plan to scale. Graph paper, or computer software, is helpful.

Once you have an accurate floor plan, sketch in your buffet lines and stations. Lines and stations must be easy for both the guests and the service staff to access. Try to keep food lines and stations reasonably close to the kitchen for efficient setup, replenishment, and breakdown. If any of your serving equipment requires electricity, plan its station near an electrical outlet, and make sure electrical cords do not pose a safety hazard. Make sure your lines do not block active doorways or emergency exits. Similarly, be sure not to block obvious traffic patterns. If the room includes table-and-chair seating, or other nonfood elements such as a lecture podium, stage, or dance floor, you must work around these features.

Buffet room layout

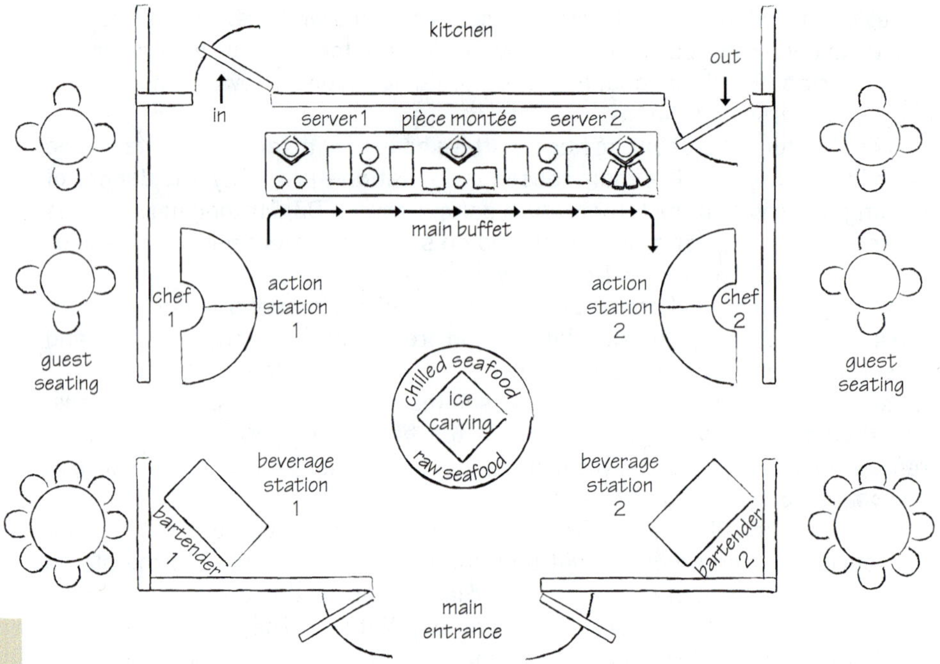

Seated Buffets Versus Standing Buffets

A ***seated buffet*** includes table-and-chair seating with a place setting for each guest. They are more comfortable for guests and are typical of high-end, formal buffets. Tables and chairs take up a lot of space, so seated buffets are usually offered in large venues, or outdoors. In this service, the tables are usually pre-set with flatware, napkins, glasses, condiments such as salt and pepper, and, often, coffee service items. Thus, the only dinnerware on the buffet line is the plates.

A ***standing buffet*** is any buffet that does not include a table place setting for every guest. Although some tables and chairs may be provided, many guests will not be able to sit down at a table; rather, they will have to hold their plate in one hand and eat with the other hand. Therefore, the foods served at a standing buffet must be fork foods. ***Fork foods*** are precut into bite-size pieces or tender enough to be cut with the side of a fork.

You must also keep flow in mind when placing your lines and stations within the buffet room. Guest traffic should flow freely and logically from the entrance to the bar area to the hors d'oeuvre stations. Traffic should also flow logically from the main buffet line to the seating areas. Server traffic should flow efficiently between the kitchen and the lines and stations. Establishing kitchen "in" and "out" doors aids flow and helps avoid accidents.

STEP 7: WRITING FOOD PREP LISTS

A food-service ***prep list*** is a step-by-step plan for completing a number of food preparation tasks. Writing prep lists for your buffet event is little different from writing prep lists for the day-to-day food preparation at your food-service job or in your culinary school production classes. By now you should be able to write clear, concise, and easy-to-follow prep lists both for your own use and for others to follow.

The one real difference between à la carte service prep lists and buffet prep lists is that a buffet typically requires several days of preparation work. To plan the food preparation for your buffet event, you will need to space the workload over a number of days. Therefore, you should write one list for each day's prep work. Planning multiple days' prep lists has the added issue of food perishability. The more perishable dishes and components must be prepared closer to the event date, while the less perishable can be prepared further in advance. The holding instructions in professional recipes are helpful in determining how far ahead the recipes can be prepped.

In order to successfully plan multiple days' prep lists, you should use backwards planning. ***Backwards planning*** is a strategy that enables planners to create a logical flow of preparation work by first focusing on the date of an event and then working backwards to assign tasks to the appropriate days.

On the day of the event, time management is crucial. One or two days before the event, you should backwards-plan the hours of Day 1 from the event start time to the start of the workday. For example, for a 6:00 P.M. dinner buffet, the period between 5:00 P.M. and 6:00 P.M. is Hour 1, the time between 4:00 P.M. and 5:00 P.M. is Hour 2, and so forth.

Procedure for Backwards-Planning Buffets

1. Write a complete master list of all individual food preparation tasks that must be accomplished for the entire event. Using the professional recipe format and understanding modular cooking enables you to break down complex dishes into individual tasks.
2. Decide how many days in advance you must begin preparation.
3. Assign a time priority to each task. In other words, for each component or master recipe, decide how far ahead it can be prepared. For example, a country terrine can be prepared a week in advance and held under refrigeration. Assign that task the number 7, meaning seven days ahead. The horseradish cream for the cold roast beef must be made on the same day as the event. Assign that task the number 1, meaning the day of the event. Complex foods with several components must be broken down into individual component recipes. For example, unbaked pastry shells for mini-quiches can be prepared two weeks ahead of time and frozen. But the shells can be filled and baked only on the day of the event. If you discover that too many dishes need last-minute work, you may need to rethink your menu. If you feel there is too much to do each day, add more work days to your plan or obtain extra help.
4. Prepare an individual prep list sheet for each workday leading up to the event, which is Day 1. Be sure to place the actual date as well as the day number on each sheet. Copy the individual tasks from your master list onto the appropriate daily list. For efficiency, you may wish to assign specific tasks to the specific staff members who are most skilled at them. Note their names next to the tasks they are assigned to perform.
5. Post the prep lists in the kitchen, in calendar order. Be sure to make photocopies of your lists as backup.

Plan to have the buffet completely set up, all food preparation complete, and the kitchen clean and in order fully one hour before the event start time. Hour 1 should be a rest hour. You and your staff need this hour to catch your breath, grab something to eat, and clear your heads. Nothing is worse than having to scramble to finish the buffet setup as guests are walking in the door.

STEP 8: SCHEDULING STAFF

Go over your daily prep lists and decide how many kitchen staff members you will need to work on each day's tasks. In the real world, your staff will also have to perform their normal daily tasks as well. Schedule the appropriate number of staff members on each prep day. If you need a particular staff member to perform a special task, make sure he or she is available on the day the task must be done.

When you plan the staff scheduling for the day of the event, make sure you budget for enough help. Unexpected problems always crop up, so plan to have at least one extra pair of hands. Remember that if you have culinary staff working an action station during the buffet event, those staff members will not be available in the kitchen and must be replaced. It is a good idea to schedule at least one staff member to be on call on the day of the event in case a scheduled staff member is absent.

Noncidinary service staff is usually scheduled by the service department. You must work with the service director to make sure the service end of the buffet is properly staffed.

STEP 9: WRITING FOOD ORDER LISTS

Now that the menu and food preparation lists are finished, you know exactly what ingredients and products are needed on which days. During the planning phase, while costing the menu, you determined the necessary food quantities. You will now base your orders on those quantities. If the menu or the head count has changed, you must make the necessary adjustments.

Both food perishability and storage space are issues to consider when writing your order lists. For example, a frozen steamship round of beef can be ordered and received several weeks in advance, providing you have the freezer space. However, fresh seafood should not be held more than a day or two. Apply the backwards planning technique to writing food order lists. For example, you can plan to receive your steamship round on Day 14, begin thawing it in the refrigerator on Day 5, and roast it on Day 2 for cold service on Day 1, the day of the event. In contrast, fresh crabmeat should come in on Day 2 to be made into crab salad on Day 1.

STEP 10: PLANNING THE SERVICE STRATEGY

The final step is to plan your service strategy. If you have action stations, you must decide which staff member will work each station. If culinary staff are serving attended buffet line(s), assign each to a place on the line. If service staff are serving, meet with the service manager and determine which servers are working each station. Make sure each server has a copy of the menu so he or she is knowledgeable about the dishes being served.

If the buffet service will extend over several hours, schedule an additional staff member to act as roundsperson. A ***roundsperson*** is a staff member capable of performing all the buffet service and action station duties. The roundsperson's job is to relieve individual staff members when they need to leave their posts.

To ensure a successful event, food runners and buffet maintenance persons are also needed. A ***food runner*** is responsible for monitoring the buffet line and stations and replenishing or replacing the platters. A ***buffet maintenance server*** keeps the line(s), stations, guest tables, and room clean and orderly. For a small buffet, one person can usually cover both these tasks. Large buffets may require several staff members for each job.

Pencil staff names and corresponding service jobs onto your buffet room layout in the appropriate places.

Phase 2: Buffet Food Preparation

If your experience is primarily in restaurant cooking, you will discover that preparing food for a buffet is somewhat different than preparing food for à la carte service. You may be working with larger amounts of food than usual. You will be creating foods for platter presentation rather than plate presentation. You will likely be asked to prepare items that are not on the regular menu and that may be more elaborate or of a different ethnic origin.

Because cold foods are an important element in traditional buffets, scheduling for a buffet results in a heavier workload for the garde manger department. In addition, the garde manger team may be asked to create a showpiece and/or several decorative food items. These items take extra time.

Label food components for a buffet clearly and carefully. This helps ensure they are not mistakenly used for the regular service. Store buffet event foods separately, if possible.

Proper planning is the key to successful buffet food preparation. If you have thorough and clearly written prep lists, if adequate staffing has been scheduled, and if ingredients and food products have been correctly ordered to arrive on the proper days, the food preparation will be orderly and efficient.

Phase 3: Setup

For a large buffet, the setup of the buffet line(s) and stations starts several days ahead of the event.

In most operations, the service staff sets up the buffet tables and adds the skirting and table linens. They are in charge of setting up the beverage stations as well. They also set the customer tables, if used. Servers place the plates at the beginning of the lines and on the stations—also the flatware and napkins, if called for.

The culinary staff arranges the food platters and their structure props on the buffet tables. They set up the action stations with the necessary food preparation equipment.

The decoration of the buffet tables is often done jointly. On every staff there is someone who has the artistic ability needed to create a pleasing design effect. Work with that person to create the best possible buffet display.

The buffet room should be completely set up at least an hour before the event start time. The placement of highly perishable food items and filling the chafing dishes with pans of hot food are the only tasks that should be left to the last minute.

Phase 4: The Service

In catering, the event is considered "the show" because it has many of the same elements as a musical or theatrical performance. Thus, the service is frequently called ***showtime***. Showtime begins when the first guest enters the buffet room, and it does not end until the last guest walks out the door. During showtime, the entire service staff is on view and the kitchen staff is on alert. Thus, showtime demands a high standard of professionalism.

For a buffet—or any other type of catered event—the success of the service is directly related to the quality of the planning. When the planning has been done correctly and thoroughly, the service phase is easy and fun.

During the service, the main responsibility of the kitchen staff is to keep the food platters replaced or replenished. Service staff should be trained to call for more food as soon as a platter is half empty. To replace a platter, the food runner brings a full, fresh platter of the same dish, and removes the half-empty platter. Platters should not be removed from the buffet table until the replacement has arrived. Doing so leaves a gap in the line. When customers see a gap, they perceive that they have missed out on something. To replenish a platter, the runner brings a pan of the same food item and refills the platter from the pan. Replenishment is more time-consuming than replacement and can be messy. In high-level cold buffet work, replenishment is rarely done.

At the beginning of the buffet service, the customers are hungry. Guests who arrived early will be lined up and waiting for food service to begin. Therefore, food platters become depleted much more quickly at the start of the event. At the beginning of a large buffet, you should have a full backup platter of each item ready to go out at a moment's notice. As soon as that platter leaves the kitchen, you should start to assemble another. As the buffet service wears on, platter replacement slows down.

Phase 5: Breakdown

Breakdown is the removal and storage of leftover buffet food, disassembly of the buffet line(s) and stations, and general cleanup. The breakdown phase applies to both the kitchen and to the buffet room.

Kitchen breakdown can begin toward the end of the buffet event, when the service reaches the point where no more platter replacement or replenishment

A Springtime Lunch Buffet

Stuffed Quail Eggs in Baby Beets (p. 380)

Spinach and Goat Cheese Mini-Quiches (p. 396)

Smoked Trout Blini Baskets (p. 384)

Whole Poached Salmon in Aspic (p. 649)

Spring Vegetable Seafood Terrine (p. 619)

Whole Ham in Mayonnaise Collée (p. 662)

Galantine of Chicken
with Tarragon Mayonnaise (p. 552)

Spring Vegetable Crudités (p. 89)

Spring Greens with Raspberries and
Raspberry Vinaigrette (p. 75)

Baguettes

Charcuterie Display

Rillettes de Tours (p. 462)

Checkerboard Terrine of Pork and Veal (p. 538)

Danish Liver Pâté with Bacon (p. 542)

Game Pâté with Cumberland Sauce (p. 556)

Herbed Chicken Mousselines
with Tarragon Sauce (p. 624)

Bourbon and Brown Sugar-Glazed Baked Ham (p. 456)
with Mustard Mayonnaise (p. 43)

Saucissons à l'Ail (p. 502)

Carrottes Rapées (p. 134)

French Lentil Salad (p. 154)

Creamy Green Bean Salad (p. 139)

Chioggia Beets in Lemon Vinaigrette (p. 140)

Baguettes, Artisan Rye Bread,
and Assorted Crackers (p. 694)

is likely to be needed. At this point, the kitchen staff can begin storing unserved food and cleaning up.

In the buffet room, the timing of breakdown is more problematic. When a buffet has been served to a unified group of invited guests, breakdown of the savory buffet line(s) and stations can begin when it appears all guests have been served and have had a chance to return for second helpings. A good rule of thumb is to start breaking down when the line or station has not been visited for at least 30 minutes. In some situations, such as a continuously operating, established buffet, the lines and stations are expected to remain staffed and open until a certain time, whether guests are eating or not. The dessert buffet line and the coffee station should remain open and presentable until the last guest leaves the building.

If line and station breakdown is permitted while guests are still in the buffet room, it is important to perform these duties quietly and unobtrusively. The broken-down tables must remain clean and attractive. Linens and skirting must not be removed while guests are present.

LEFTOVERS

It is the responsibility of the chef in charge to determine which, if any, leftover buffet dishes should be retained for reuse. Considerations here include the time-temperature factor, likelihood of contamination, and whether the food will be of use for the next event or regular service.

Hot foods must be quickly open-pan cooled and then immediately placed in sanitized containers, covered, labeled, and refrigerated. If it is late and the kitchen staff is ready to leave, you can use an ice bain-marie to hasten cooling. Cold foods should be immediately wrapped, labeled, and refrigerated. If time allows, it is a good idea to break foods down into usable components before they are stored. For example, when a whole roast turkey is brought back to the kitchen, you should carve the remaining meat off it and store the meat in an appropriate container. The carcass can be chopped, bagged, and saved for making stock.

At the end of a buffet event, everyone is tired, and breakdown can be a chore. Nonetheless, it is important that breakdown be done correctly and completely. If budget allows, you can schedule a small team to arrive toward the end of the event to finish the food management and clean up the kitchen.

Buffet Menus

Each menu presented here has been planned to illustrate the principles of buffet planning and execution covered in this chapter. In addition, the menus showcase the techniques and skills you have mastered in your classes. Some of the menus focus on a particular garde manger specialty. Others represent a particular season or theme.

Antipasto Buffet

Insalata di Frutti de Mare (p. 163)

Insalata Caprese (p. 180)

Beet Carpaccio (p. 181)

Italian Potato Salad (p. 145)

Farfalle and Artichoke Salad (p. 151)

Tuscan White Bean Salad (p. 153)

Salumeria Platter: Soppressata (p. 509)
and Mini-Mortadella (p. 507)

Vitello Tonnato (p. 256)

Duck Prosciutto (p. 426) with Melon

Salad of Italian Greens
with Balsamic Vinaigrette (p. 33)

Assorted Italian Breads and Rolls

Asian-Inspired Buffet

Chicken and Shiitake Mushroom Summer Rolls (p. 390)

Maguro Norimaki Sushi with Wasabi Soy Sauce (p. 232)

Asian Crab, Shrimp, and Cucumber Salad (p. 184)

Asian Spice-Crusted Tuna with Mango Salsa (p. 203)

Chinese Tea-Smoked Chicken (p. 447)

Asian-Inspired Confit of Duck (p. 461)

Chinese-Style Peanut Noodle Salad (p. 150)

Asian Cucumber Salad (p. 133)

Autumn Buffet

Oysters on the Half-Shell (p. 229)

Pacific Northwest Hot-Smoked Steelhead Trout (p. 445)
with Horseradish Cream (p. 45)

Rillettes en Roulade (p. 386)

Minnesota Turkey and Wild Rice Salad (p. 165)

Cold Pork Loin with Prunes and Armagnac (p. 257)

Whole Roast Duck in Brown Chaud-Froid (p. 660)

Game Pâté with Cumberland Sauce (p. 556)

Roasted Beets in Mustard Vinaigrette (p. 140)

Green Bean and Roasted Red Pepper Salad (p. 139)

Salad of Autumn Fruits
with Pomegranate Seeds (p. 171)

Apple and Cheddar Platter
with Walnuts (p. 125)

Seven-Grain Bread and Pain de Campagne

Summer Buffet

Tuna Tartare in Phyllo Cups (p. 398)

Bouchées of Salmon Mousse (p. 385)

Classic Lobster Salad (p. 160)

Chaud-Froid Chicken and Her Flock (p. 660)

Cold Roast Filet of Beef (p. 253)
with Bearnaise Mayonnaise (p. 43)

Provençal Terrine of Rabbit with Beet Salad (p. 547)

Two-Color Tomato Basil Salad (p. 137)

Green Beans Vinaigrette (p. 139)

Fruit Kebabs with Minted Yogurt Sauce (p. 124)

Sourdough Rolls

Buffet Calculations

When you are ready to plan and present your garde manger buffet, you must perform a number of calculations. One of the most important tasks is calculating how much food will be needed to serve your guests. In order to have the right amount of food, you must understand how to do basic quantity calculations. Your worst nightmare is running out of food! But if you prepare too much food and cannot sell it to other customers, your buffet will not be profitable—and may actually incur a loss.

When planning your menu, you may be required to stay within a specific food cost percentage. Or, you may be asked to come up with a menu and establish its per-person price. Both require food costing and other calculations.

Following is a brief review of information that will help you plan a profitable buffet.

Determining Food Quantities

At first glance, determining food quantities for a catered event seems simple and straightforward: To calculate the amount of cooked food required, simply multiply the portion size by the projected number of guests. In banquet planning, this is typically the only calculation needed. So, for example, if you are serving 6 oz (168 g) baked salmon fillets to 100 guests, simply multiply 6 oz (168 g) (portion size) by 100 (number of guests). Thus, you need 600 oz (1680 g) or 37½ lb (16.80 kg) salmon fillets. Determining portion size is easy for banquet and à la carte service because customers consume only one item per course, and that item is portion-controlled in the kitchen.

Buffet portioning is more complicated. Buffet guests have many choices and typically consume several items per course. Not all guests choose to eat all items. Portions are not controlled, and thus vary. Guests take more of items they like, and less of others. However, the portions they take are typically much smaller than standard portions. Finally, buffets require more food because they must look abundant. The last person to pass through the buffet line must have as many food choices as the first person to visit it.

In calculating buffet food quantities, start with some averages. In North America, the average dinner entrée portion is a 5–6-oz (140–168-g) cooked edible portion. The average appetizer portion is a 3–4-oz (84–112-g) cooked edible portion. Taking into account an additional 4 oz (112 g) of side dishes, the average person eats 12–14 oz (336–392 g) of food for dinner. A typical lunch is 8–10 oz (224–280 g). Breakfast is the most difficult meal to project because some people eat very little in the morning and others eat quite a lot.

Starting with these averages, factor in some other information. Accurately determining food quantities for buffets involves knowing about your clientele and making generalizations. For example, men typically eat more than women, and young adults eat more than elderly people. People tend to eat more in the winter and less in the summer. Physical activity, such as a golf outing before the buffet, makes people eat more. Use this information to adjust quantities from the norm. Remember to also plan a ***cushion***, or safety factor, of extra food into your quantity calculation. Depending on the policy of the operation, a buffet cushion may be as high as 25 percent.

The cost of the cushion is considered part of the food cost. This is why buffets are usually priced higher than banquets. These calculations will help you determine food quantities for buffets:

1. *Divide the projected per-person food consumption ounces (grams) by the number of entrèes you plan to serve.* For example, if each person is projected to consume 6 oz (168 g) of entrée foods, and you plan to offer six

Calculating Buffet Entrée Purchasing Quantities

ENTRÉE MENU

poached salmon fillet
grilled chicken breast
hot-smoked pork loin
roast beef filet
steamed shrimp
tortellini salad
= 6 entrèes

GUEST COUNT

100 guests, mixed age and gender

CONSUMPTION PROJECTION

each guest is projected to eat 6 oz (168 g) of entrée foods

PRELIMINARY CALCULATIONS

6 oz (168 g) / 6 entrées = 1 oz (28 g) of each entrée food needed per guest

1 oz (28 g) entrée food x 100 guests = 100 oz (2800 g) of each entrèe food

ADDING CUSHION (25%)

100 oz (2800 g) x 1.25 = 125 oz (3500 g) of each entrèe food

CONVERTING TO POUNDS (KILOGRAMS)

125 oz /16 oz = 7.81 lb or 7¾ lb (3500 g /1000 g = 3.5 kg)

ENTRÈE FOOD ORDER LIST

7¾ lb (3.5 kg) skinless salmon fillet

7¾ lb (3.5 kg) skinless, boneless chicken breast

7¾ lb (3.5 kg) boneless pork loin

7¾ lb (3.5 kg) trimmed filet of beef

7¾ lb (3.5 kg) peeled and deveined shrimp

7¾ lb (3.5 kg) frozen tortellini

entrées, you can project that each person will consume 1 oz (28 g) of each of the six entrées:

6 oz (168 g) / 6 = 1 oz (28 g)

2. *Multiply the amount of each dish to be consumed by one person by the number of guests.* If you expect 100 guests who will each eat 1 oz (28 g) of each dish, you can project the group will consume 100 oz (2800 g) of each of the six entrée dishes:

1 oz (28 g) x 100 = 100 oz (2800 g)

3. *Factor in the cushion (25 percent).* If you project the group will consume 100 oz (2800 g) of each dish, multiply 100 oz (2800 g) by 1.25. Thus, it is safe to prepare 125 oz (3500 g) of each dish:

100 oz (2800 g) x 1.25 = 125 oz (3500 g)

4. *For ordering purposes, convert ounces (grams) to pounds (kilograms).*

125 oz (3500 g) / 16 oz (1000 g) = 7.81 lb or 7¾ lb (3.5 kg)

5. *Calculate appetizers, side dishes, and breads in the same manner.*

Of course, certain food items will require additional calculations to compensate for trim waste and weight loss incurred during cooking. For these foods, you should consult an AP/EP (as purchased/edible portion) chart. To simplify the buffet calculation process, the example at right uses raw products having virtually no waste or weight loss.

Costing Menu Items and Décor items

Once you know how much of each menu item you need to prepare, determine the food cost of each item by adding the cost of all of its ingredients. To cost a complex menu item with many components, first cost the recipe for each component. If time does not allow you to properly cost all recipes, at least calculate the cost of the main ingredients to project an approximate cost.

If food décor items that add to the cost of the buffet are included, determine their cost as well. For example, if you plan to decorate your buffet with a bread sculpture or fruit display, you must calculate its food cost in the same manner as the dishes that will be eaten.

Determining Total Buffet Food Cost

Add the costs of all dishes and food décor items to determine the total buffet food cost.

Determining Per-Person Food Cost

To determine the per-person food cost, divide the total food cost by the number of guests. Let's say you determined the total buffet food cost to be $436. If you are serving 100 guests, the per-person food cost is $4.36. ($4.36 / 100 = $4.36).

MANAGING FOOD COST

If you have a food cost limit and your food cost is too high, you have two alternatives:

1. Shop around for better food prices.
2. Replace some of the more expensive dishes with ones that cost less to prepare.

Determining Per-Person Food Cost

poached salmon fillet	$ 65.90
grilled chicken breast	$ 35.50
hot-smoked pork loin	$ 53.00
roast beef filet	$ 95.75
steamed shrimp	$ 49.65
tortellini salad	$ 26.60
rolls and butter	$ 18.50
vegetable salad	$ 22.30
green salad	$ 26.80
cheese board	$ 42.00
	$436.00

$436.00 / 100 guests = $4.36 per-person food cost

If your food cost is lower than your limit, you will make a better profit. However, for increased customer satisfaction, you may decide to upgrade some dishes or add extra items.

Pricing the Buffet

per-person food cost: $4.36

pre-determined food cost percentage: 22%

$4.36 / 0.22 = $19.82

price rounded to an even number: $20.00 per person

Pricing the Buffet

If asked to price the buffet menu you have planned, determine the desired food cost percentage. Most operations have an established food cost for various types of service. Buffet food costs usually range from 18 to 28 percent.

To determine the per-person price for your buffet, divide the per-person food cost by the food cost percentage expressed as a decimal. For example, at a 22 percent food cost, a buffet with a per-person food cost of $4.36 is priced at $19.82. ($4.36 / 0.22 = $19.82). You typically round up or down to an even number, so this buffet might be priced at $20.00 per person.

FOOD BARS

Understanding Food Bars

A ***food bar*** is a relatively new form of self-service buffet in which prepared foods are kept on permanent display in specialized equipment. Early food bars featured cold foods only. Today, many operations offer both cold and hot food bars. The history of food bars is included in the sidebar on buffet history on page 725.

While many eat-in restaurants feature food bars, they are becoming even more popular in take-out operations. Take-out food bars are now found in supermarkets, convenience stores, delis, transportation stations, and institutions such as schools and large businesses. In recent years, food bars have been added to cafeterias, in many cases entirely replacing the traditional service-style cafeteria line.

Retail food bar
© *iStockphoto.*

The difference between a food bar and a buffet is often blurry. Traditionally, buffets are temporary, but food bars are permanent. Most food bars feature built-in equipment that is often plumbed in with water and wired in with electricity. Small, portable food bars also exist. In a hotel or catering hall, a traditional buffet line may remain set up for months or even years, but it is typically composed of movable tables and portable equipment. However, hotels, casinos, and other large food-service operations that offer established buffets now have built-in buffet lines.

One difference between food bars and buffets is that food bars are always casual. While food bar equipment is constructed to be eye-catching and attractive, they are not designed for formal events. In contrast, many high-end buffets are extremely formal, using fine linen, silver serviceware, and the best china.

The biggest difference between a buffet and a food bar is that, while buffets have several service options, food bars are specifically designed and used for self-service. Food bar units are always equipped with sneeze guards (p. 745) and other sanitation safeguards necessary when displayed food is handled by the public.

Food bars are one of the fastest-growing segments of North American food service. They are popular with customers because they are fast and inexpensive, and they offer a wide variety of choices. Thus, garde manger chefs should be familiar with both food bar operations and the equipment used for food bars.

Food Bar Equipment

Modern food bars are self-contained units equipped with everything needed to display self-service foods attractively and safely. Food bars range from small, semiportable units 6 feet in length to huge built-in bars extending for many yards. Manufacturers offer modular fittings that can be used to convert their food bars to different uses. For example, food bars in restaurants are fitted with plate holders, while food bars in supermarkets have racks that hold take-out containers.

All food bars are designed with features that protect food from public contamination. The most visible form of protection is sneeze guards. A ***sneeze guard*** is a clear Plexiglas® panel suspended over or in front of the food display to protect it. Some food bars have additional food covers, primarily for hot foods.

Food bars are divided into cold bars, hot bars, and combination hot-and-cold bars. Cold food bars typically display a variety of salads. The traditional salad bar consists of large containers of leafy greens, an assortment of toppings, and wells for dressings. A cold appetizer bar displays complex salads, cold cuts, cheeses, and other composed cold dishes. Hot steam table bars display soups, casserole-type dishes such as lasagne or macaroni and cheese, and stewlike foods in sauces. Dry hot bars are used for fried fish, fried chicken, and similar crisp-textured foods.

Salad bar
© iStockphoto.

Operating a Food Bar

Because a food bar is a specialized form of buffet, much of the information about buffets pertains to food bars as well. Like buffets, all food bars have a theme, even one as simple as "salad fixings" or "take-out food." However, many high-end food bars have distinct and recognizable themes. For example, a Spanish restaurant might offer a tapas bar, while an Italian restaurant might feature an antipasto bar. A specialty food store might offer a charcuterie bar. Within the parameters of your operation, be creative with the choices on both hot and cold bars.

Food Bar Menu Planning

Menu planning for food bars is similar to menu planning for buffets. However, because food bars are, by definition, self-service, you cannot include items that require carving or other forms of skilled portioning. Most of the guidelines for buffet menu planning on page 731 also apply to food bar menus. While the visual appeal of the foods you display in a food bar is not as crucial as on a buffet, offerings must still be colorful and attractive. Variety is essential because it is one of the main attractions of a food bar.

Determining Food Bar Food Costs

Food cost is a major issue in food bar planning. Food cost parameters are much lower for a food bar than for a restaurant or catering buffet. The typical food bar cost percentage is 15–20 percent.

One problem with food bars is that all dishes presented in a particular bar are sold at the same price. If more expensive items are chosen more often than less expensive items, the food bar will not make a good profit. Therefore, an important safeguard for a food bar menu planner is to maintain a sales mix. A ***sales mix*** is a costing tool that reports the sales volume of each menu item expressed as a percentage of total sales. In à la carte food sales, where items are priced separately, a sales mix is easy to determine by reviewing cash register or computer reports. However, food bar items are not priced individually. To run a sales mix you must physically keep track of sales by monitoring replenishments. Your goal is to sell more of the inexpensive items and fewer of the more costly items. You can use placement to influence sales. For example, if you place expensive foods in the back row of pans, they are less likely to be taken. Place inexpensive foods, or foods you want to move, in the front.

Just as in buffet planning, use a station map to plan the setup of a food bar. Try to keep standard items in the same position from day to day. Repeat customers appreciate being able to locate their favorite items quickly.

Food Bar Sanitation and Safety

Because food bars are exposed to the general public, and because they hold foods for extended periods, they pose significant risk of contamination by food-borne pathogens. For this reason, chefs who operate food bars must be especially vigilant about observing food safety and sanitation guidelines. Hot bars pose the additional risk of causing burns. Many of the food safety practices you already follow also apply to food bars. These guidelines are specific to cold and hot food bar food safety.

Guidelines for Food Bar Safety

1. When setting up a food bar for service, turn it on at least 30 minutes before the food is placed into it. Make sure proper temperature is reached before loading in food.
2. Place all foods in clean, freshly sanitized pans at the beginning of each service day. When replacing foods, also use a fresh pan.
3. Thoroughly chill foods below 41°F (5°C) before placing them in a cold bar, and thoroughly heat hot foods above 135°F (57°C) before placing them in a hot bar. These units are designed to maintain temperature, not to chill or heat foods.
4. Do not fill food bar pans more than three-quarters full.
5. Use a sanitized probe thermometer to monitor the temperature of food bar foods every two hours. Post a monitoring schedule, and train staff to record the temperatures on it.
6. If a food bar unit is not holding the proper temperature, immediately remove all food from it and call a repair service.
7. Never combine food from a used pan with food from a fresh pan. Instead, transfer small amounts of food from used pans into smaller containers.
8. Keep sneeze guards in place, and clean them frequently.
9. Do not use spray cleaner on or around a food bar. Instead, moisten a towel with the cleaning solution and wipe around the food. Do not allow chemical cleaners to come into contact with food.
10. Make sure each food bar item has its own sanitized serving utensil. Place sanitized serving utensils in the food bar pans with handles facing out. Replace utensils with freshly sanitized utensils regularly.
11. Train staff to monitor customer behavior at the food bar. Insist that parents control their children. If you believe a customer has contaminated a food item, immediately remove and discard it.
12. Make sure warning signs are posted on potentially dangerous hot bar areas.
13. Know and observe your local food safety regulations.

TERMS FOR REVIEW

buffet
prix fixe
buffet line
buffet station
established buffet
self-service buffet
food identification placards
double buffet line
attended buffet
served buffet
action station
action buffet
combination buffet
buffet theme
flow
satellite station
pre-plating
structural prop
visual prop
iced presentation tray
ice-filled chafing dish
warming tray
heat lamp
chafing dish
pull list
seated buffet
standing buffet
fork food
prep list
backwards planning
roundsperson
food runner
buffet maintenance server
showtime
breakdown
cushion
food bar
sneeze guard
sales mix

QUESTIONS FOR DISCUSSION

1. List and describe the three basic buffet service styles. Explain the advantages and disadvantages of each. Describe a combination buffet.
2. List the five phases of buffet work. Which is most important? Why?
3. List, in order, the ten steps in buffet planning.
4. Discuss buffet themes. Include in your discussion the ways in which the theme of a buffet affects all other elements.
5. List and explain at least five of the guidelines for successful buffet menu planning.
6. Write a menu for a six-item buffet and draw a line map for it.
7. Discuss the advantages of presenting separate buffet stations. List the additional advantages of action stations.
8. Explain the difference between structural props and visual props. How are structural props used? What functions do visual props fulfill?
9. Calculate the entrée food quantities needed for a four-entrée buffet for 200 guests.
10. You have planned a buffet menu having a total food cost of $237. You expect to serve 50 guests, and the specified food cost percentage is 22 percent. Calculate the per-person price of your buffet.
11. List and explain at least six food bar safety and sanitation guidelines.

Appendix: Basic Preparations

CLARIFIED STOCK

Yield:
about 1 gal (4 L)

INGREDIENTS	U.S.	METRIC
Lean beef, white meat chicken, or white-fleshed fish, ground	1 lb	500 g
Finely chopped onion	8 oz	250 g
Finely chopped celery	4 oz	125 g
Finely chopped carrot	4 oz	125 g
Egg whites	8 oz	250 g
Canned tomatoes, crushed (for beef)	8 oz	250 g
or		
Lemon juice (for chicken or fish)	1 tbsp	15 mL
Parsley stems, chopped	6–8	6–8
Dried thyme	pinch	pinch
Bay leaf	1	1
Whole cloves	2	2
Peppercorns, crushed	½ tsp	2 mL
Defatted *Brown Beef and/or Veal Stock (p. 751)*, *Poultry Stock (p. 749)*, or *Fish Stock (p. 750)*, cold	5 qt	5 L

PROCEDURE

PREPARATION

1. Combine the beef, chicken, or fish, onion, celery carrot, egg whites, tomatoes or lemon juice, herbs, and spices in a tall, heavy stockpot. Mix the ingredients vigorously with a wooden paddle or a heavy whip.
2. Add about 1 pt (500 mL) cold stock and stir well. Let stand about 30 minutes.
3. Gradually stir in the remaining cold stock. Be sure the stock is well mixed with the other ingredients.
4. Set the pot on moderately low heat and let it come to a simmer very slowly. Stir occasionally.
5. When the simmering point is approaching, stop stirring.
6. Move the pot to lower heat and simmer very slowly about 1½ hours. Do not stir or disturb the raft that forms on top.
7. Push aside the raft and very carefully ladle the stock through a fine-mesh sieve lined with several layers of cheesecloth.

HOLDING

Open-pan cool and refrigerate in a freshly sanitized, covered container up to 5 days. Freeze up to 3 months.

POULTRY STOCK

Yield:
about 2 gal (8 L)

INGREDIENTS	U.S.	METRIC
Raw poultry bones	10 lb	5 kg
Water, cold	as needed	as needed
Lemon	½	½
Peeled, diced onions	2 lb	1 kg
Peeled, diced carrots	1 lb	0.5 kg
Diced celery	1 lb	0.5 kg
Bay leaves	2	2
Black peppercorns	2 tsp	10 mL
Dried thyme	½ tsp	2 mL
Parsley stems	4–5	4–5
Clove	1	1

PROCEDURE

PREPARATION

1. Remove the skin and fat from the poultry bones. Carefully remove any bloody organs, especially hearts and livers (check backs for bits of liver still attached to the body cavity). Wash the poultry bones in several changes of cool water.
2. Place the bones in a stockpot and add cool water to cover by 2 in. (5 cm). Bring just under the boil.
3. Skim off the scum.
4. Squeeze in the lemon juice and drop in the lemon.
5. Add the onions, carrots, and celery.
6. Tie the herbs and spices in a cheesecloth sachet and add them.
7. Adjust the heat to simmer. Do not allow to boil.
8. Simmer 2 to 3 hours, adding water as needed to keep the water level just above the bones.
9. Strain the stock into a freshly sanitized container and discard the solids.
10. Rapid-cool the stock in an ice bain-marie or cold running water sink bath.

HOLDING

Refrigerate up to 4 days; may be frozen up to 3 months. (Allow the fat layer to remain on the stock until needed; once the fat layer is broken, completely remove all fat.)

FISH STOCK

Yield:
about 1 gal (4 L)

INGREDIENTS	U.S.	METRIC
Non-oily fish frames	8 lb	4 kg
Butter	2 oz	60 g
Chopped onion	8 oz	240 g
Finely chopped carrot	4 oz	120 g
Finely chopped celery	4 oz	120 g
Mushroom trimmings (optional)	2–4 oz	60–120 g
White wine	8 fl oz	240 mL
Water, cold	1 gal (about)	4 L (about)
Bay leaf	1	1
Fresh thyme (optional)	2 sprigs	2 sprigs
Parsley stems	3–4	3–4
Black peppercorns	½ tsp	3 mL

PROCEDURE

PREPARATION

1. Carefully clean the frames of all internal organs, gills, and blood, slitting the cavity membrane near the spine and removing all blood underneath. If the frames are large, chop them into 3 or 4 pieces each. Wash the frames under cold running water until the water runs clear. Drain and shake dry.
2. Melt the butter in a brazier, add the onions, carrots, celery, and the fish frames, cover the pan, and sweat over low heat about 5 minutes, or until the raw smell is gone and the bones are opaque.
3. Add the white wine, cover the brazier, and steam over moderate heat 5 minutes more.
4. Uncover the brazier and allow the steam to escape. Add cold water to cover the frames by ½ in. (1 cm) and bring just under the boil.
5. Skim the scum and push down the bones to compact them. Tie the bouquet garni ingredients in a cheesecloth sachet and add them. Simmer 20–30 minutes.
6. Strain the stock into a freshly sanitized container.
7. Rapid-cool the stock in an ice bain-marie or cold running water sink bath.

HOLDING

Refrigerate up to 4 days; may be frozen up to 3 months.

VARIATION

SHELLFISH STOCK

Replace the fish frames with soft, flexible crustacean shells. Add trimmings from scallops if desired.

BROWN BEEF AND/OR VEAL STOCK

Yield:
about 2 gal (8 L)

INGREDIENTS	U.S.	METRIC
Corn oil	2 fl oz	60 mL
Beef and/or veal marrow bones, sawed into 3-in. (8-cm) lengths, knuckles cracked	6 lb	3 kg
Beef and/or veal shank, plate or bottom round, trimmed of fat, cut into 2-in. (5-cm) cubes	4 lb	2 kg
Water, cold	as needed	as needed
Yellow onions, unpeeled, quartered	2 lb	1 kg
Carrots, unpeeled, cut in 1-in. (3-cm) pieces	1 lb	0.5 kg
Celery, cut in 1-in. (3-m) pieces	1 lb	0.5 kg
Tomato purée	4 fl oz	120 mL
Bay leaves	4	4
Black peppercorns	1 tbsp	30 mL
Dried thyme	½ tsp	3 mL
Parsley stems	4–5	4–5
Cloves, small	2	2

PROCEDURE

PREPARATION

1. Preheat an oven to 400°–425°F (200°–220°C).
2. Brush a sheet tray with the oil. Wipe off the bones and meat with a damp paper towel and place on the tray.
3. Roast the bones and meat in the preheated oven about 40 minutes, or until well browned.
4. Drain the fat from the sheet tray into a bowl. Place the bones in a stockpot and add cool water to cover by 4 in. (10 cm). Place the stockpot over high heat and monitor it until just under the boil.
5. Deglaze the sheet tray with a little more water and add the deglazings to the pot.
6. Place the onions, carrots, and celery on the sheet tray and mix them with just enough of the beef/veal fat to coat them lightly.
7. Roast the vegetables about 20 minutes, or until browned.
8. Skim the scum from the stock and adjust the heat to a simmer.
9. Add the browned vegetables and the tomato purée.
10. Tie the remaining ingredients in a cheesecloth sachet and add them to the pot.
11. Simmer about 5 hours, adding water as needed to keep the water level just above the bones.
12. Strain the stock into a freshly sanitized container and discard the solids.
13. Rapid-cool the stock in an ice bain-marie or cold running water sink bath.

HOLDING

Refrigerate up to 4 days; may be frozen up to 3 months. (Allow the fat layer to remain on the stock until needed; once the fat layer is broken, completely remove all fat.)

VARIATION

BROWN GAME STOCK

Replace the beef/veal bones and meat with raw game bones and game meat. Deglaze the pan with 1 cup (240 mL) red wine; add 1 tbsp (30 mL) juniper berries to the bouquet garni ingredients.

VELOUTÉ SAUCE (POULTRY OR FISH)

Yield:
about 1 gal (4 L)

INGREDIENTS	U.S.	METRIC
Clarified butter	8 oz	250 g
Bread flour	8 oz	250 g
Poultry Stock (p. 749) or *Fish Stock (p. 750)*, hot	5 qt	5 L
Salt	to taste	to taste

PROCEDURE

PREPARATION

1. Heat the butter in a heavy saucepot, add the flour, and stir to make a blond roux.
2. Whisk the hot stock into the roux in a thin stream.
3. Simmer about 1 hour, stirring and skimming occasionally.
4. Season with salt.
5. Strain before using.

HOLDING

Open-pan cool and immediately refrigerate in a freshly sanitized, covered container up to 5 days. Strain after reheating.

DEMI-GLACE (ONE-STEP METHOD)

Yield:
about 1 gal (4 L)

INGREDIENTS	U.S.	METRIC
Medium-diced onions	1 lb	500 g
Medium-diced celery	8 oz	250 g
Fine-diced carrot	8 oz	250 g
Clarified butter	8 oz	250 g
Bread flour	8 oz	250 g
Brown Beef and/or Veal Stock (p. 751), thoroughly defatted and then heated	2½ gal	10 L
Canned tomatoes, diced or crushed	6 oz	180 g
Bay leaf 1 small	1 small	
Dried thyme	¼ tsp	1 mL
Parsley stems	6–8	6–8

PROCEDURE

PREPARATION

1. In a large saucepan sauté the onions, celery, and carrots in the butter until browned.
2. Add the flour and stir over moderate heat to make a brown roux.
3. Whisk in *half* the stock and then add the tomato.
4. Enclose the bay, thyme, and parsley in a cheesecloth sachet and add it to the sauce.
5. Simmer about 2 hours, stirring and skimming occasionally.
6. Strain into another saucepan, pressing on the solids.
7. Return the sauce to the simmer and stir in the remaining stock.
8. Cook, stirring and skimming occasionally, until the sauce reaches a nappé consistency, is translucent, and is reduced to about 1 gal (4 L).
9. Strain.
10. Season with salt.

HOLDING

Open-pan cool and immediately refrigerate in a freshly sanitized, covered container up to 5 days. Freeze up to 3 months. Strain after reheating.

PÂTE BRISÉE
UNSWEETENED DOUGH

yield:
about 20 oz (600 g)

INGREDIENTS	U.S.	METRIC
Unsalted butter, room temperature	2 oz	60 g
Lard or shortening, room temperature	2 oz	60 g
Fine salt	½ tsp	3 mL
Eggs, beaten	1 oz	30 g
Fresh lemon juice	1 tsp	5 mL
Pastry flour	12 oz	360 g
Water, cold	as needed	as needed

PROCEDURE

PREPARATION

1. Place the butter, lard or shortening, salt, egg, and lemon juice in a mixer fitted with a paddle. Stir on low speed just to combine.
2. Add the flour and pulse on low speed just until mixed into a cohesive but not sticky dough. Add water only if necessary.
3. Wrap in plastic film and refrigerate at least 30 minutes.

HOLDING

Refrigerate up to 24 hours. May be frozen up to 3 months.

PÂTE À PÂTÉ
PASTRY DOUGH FOR PÂTÉ

yield:
1 lb 12 oz (860 g)

INGREDIENTS	U.S.	METRIC
All purpose flour	1 lb	500 g
Butter, cold	4 oz	120 g
Lard, cold	4 oz	120 g
Salt	1½ tsp	8 mL
Egg, cold	1	1
Water, cold	3 fl oz	90 mL
Additional water	as needed	as needed

PROCEDURE

PREPARATION

1. Place the flour in a food processor.
2. Cut the butter and lard into 1-in. (3-cm) chunks and add them to the processor.
3. Pulse until the fats are well blended into the flour and no lumps remain.
4. Beat together the egg and 3 fl oz (90 mL) water, then pulse it in through the feed tube to make a medium-firm dough. Add more water only if necessary.
5. Form the dough into a thick rectangle and wrap it in plastic film.
6. Refrigerate the dough at least 30 minutes.

HOLDING

Refrigerate up to 24 hours, or freeze up to 1 month.

PÂTE À CHOUX
CHOUX PASTE

yield:
about 2 lb (1 kg)

INGREDIENTS	U.S.	METRIC
Milk	8 fl oz	240 mL
Water	8 fl oz	240 mL
Salt	1 tsp	5 mL
Sugar	2 tsp	10 mL
Unsalted butter, medium dice	8 oz	240 g
All-purpose flour	8 oz	240 g
Eggs	8 oz	240 g

PROCEDURE

PREPARATION

1. Combine the milk, water, salt, sugar, and butter in a saucepan. Bring just to the boil.
2. Immediately add the flour and beat vigorously until the flour becomes a solid mass.
3. Lower the flame, then beat until smooth and shiny and pulling away from the pan.
4. Transfer to a mixer fitted with the paddle attachment. Beat at moderate speed until cooled to 140°F (60°C).
5. Add the eggs, one at a time, beating only until thick and shiny.
6. Transfer to a pastry bag fitted with the appropriate tip.

HOLDING

Store at cool room temperature up to 2 hours.

CRÊPES

Yield:
varies,
about 36 crêpes

INGREDIENTS	U.S.	METRIC
All-purpose flour	8 oz	250 g
Salt	1 tsp	5 g
Eggs	6	6
Milk	1 pt	500 mL
Browned butter	1½ oz	50 g
Oil	as needed	as needed

PROCEDURE

PREPARATION

1. Whisk together the flour, salt, and eggs, then add the milk in a thin stream to make a smooth batter, about the consistency of heavy cream.
2. Strain the batter through a fine sieve and whisk in the browned butter.
3. Cover with plastic wrap and set aside to rest at least 30 minutes at room temperature.
4. Heat a crêpe pan and brush with oil. Add some batter, swirl to coat the pan, and pour excess batter back into the bowl. Cook until the edges are brown and the bottom is golden. Flip over and cook a few seconds longer.
5. Transfer the crêpe to a cooling rack. Repeat to make additional crêpes.

HOLDING

Stack crêpes with deli tissue or parchment squares between them, then wrap in plastic film. Refrigerate up to 3 days, or freeze up to 1 month.

BLINI

Yield:
varies according to size, about 24 2-in. (5 cm) pancakes

INGREDIENTS	U.S.	METRIC
Fresh yeast	½ oz	15 g
Water, 100°F (38°C)	2 fl oz	60 mL
Sugar	pinch	pinch
Milk	12 fl oz	480 mL
Sugar	1 oz	30 g
All-purpose flour	5 oz	150 g
Water, lukewarm	as needed	as needed
Egg yolks	3	3
Salt	1 tsp	5 mL
Buckwheat flour	8 oz	240 g
Egg whites, room temperature	3	3
Melted and cooled clarified butter	1 fl oz	30 mL
Additional clarified butter for the griddle	as needed	as needed

PROCEDURE

DAY #1: PREPARATION

1. Dissolve the yeast in the 100°F (38°) water with a pinch of sugar and let stand until bubbly.
2. Combine the milk and 1 oz (30 g) sugar in a saucepan, heat just to scalding, and then cool to room temperature.
3. Place the all-purpose flour in a bowl and stir in the yeast mixture and cooled milk to make a sponge, or thick batter. If necessary, add lukewarm water to achieve the proper consistency.
4. Cover the bowl with a towel and allow to ferment in a warm place 12 hours.

DAY #2: PREPARATION

5. Beat the yolks, salt, and buckwheat flour into the sponge along with enough water to create a medium-thick batter. Rest in a warm place 30 minutes to 1 hour.
6. Preheat a well-seasoned griddle to medium-high heat. Place a sheet tray fitted with a rack next to the griddle. Have a heatproof pastry brush and a clean, damp towel at hand.
7. Beat the egg whites to soft peaks. Fold the whites and 1 fl oz (30 mL) clarified butter into the batter.
8. Bake the blini:
   a. Brush a film of clarified butter onto the griddle.
   b. Use a ½-oz (15-mL) portion scoop or ladle to drop batter onto the griddle (or use a different size measure to make blini of the desired size). Griddle-bake until large bubbles appear on the surface of the blini.
   c. Turn the blini over and bake until golden on both sides.
   d. Transfer the baked blini to the rack and cover with the towel.

HOLDING

Hold in a warm place, covered with the towel, up to 3 hours.

Bibliography

C

Child, Julia, Louisette Bertholle, and Simone Beck. *Mastering the Art of French Cooking.* New York: Knopf, 1967.

Claiborne, Craig, and Pierre Franey. *Classic French Cooking.* New York: Time-Life, 1970.

Corriher, Shirley O. *Cookwise: The Hows and Whys of Successful Cooking.* New York: William Morrow, 1997.

Cottenceau, Marcel, Jean-François Deport, and Jean-Pierre Odeau. *The Professional Charcuterie Series.* 2 vols. New York: Van Nostrand Reinhold, 1991.

Culinary Institute of America. *Garde Manger: The Art and Craft of the Cold Kitchen*, 3rd ed. Hoboken, NJ: John Wiley & Sons, 2008.

D

David, Elizabeth, *French Provincial Cooking*. Harmondsworth, England: Penguin, 1960.

——, *Summer Cooking*. Foreword by Molly O'Neill. New York: New York Review of Books, 2002.

E

Escoffier, Auguste. *The Complete Guide to the Art of Modern Cookery.* H. L. Cracknell and R. J. Kaufmann, trans. Hoboken, NJ: John Wiley & Sons, 2003.

G

Garlough, Robert, and Angus Campbell. *Modern Garde Manger: A Global Perspective*. Clifton Park, NY: Thomson Delmar Learning, 2006.

Gisslen, Wayne. *Professional Cooking,* 7th ed. Hoboken, NJ: John Wiley & Sons, 2011.

Greenberg, Jan. *Hudson Valley Bounty: A Guide to Farms, Fine Foods, and Open-Air Markets*. Lee, MA: Berkshire House, 1996.

Grigson, Jane. *Charcuterie and French Pork Cookery.* London: Grub Street, 2001.

H

Hazan, Marcella. *The Classic Italian Cookbook.* New York: Knopf, 1976.

——. *More Classic Italian Cooking.* New York: Knopf, 1978.

K

Kamman, Madeleine. *In Madeleine's Kitchen.* New York: Collier, Macmillan, 1984.

——. *The New Making of a Cook: The Art, Techniques, and Science of Good Cooking*. New York: William Morrow, 1997.

Keller, Thomas, Susie Heller, and Deborah Jones, *The French Laundry Cookbook*, 2nd ed. New York: Artisan, 1999.

Kinsella, John, and David T Harvey, *Professional Charcuterie: Sausage Making, Curing, Terrines, Pâtés*. New York: John Wiley & Sons, 1993.

L

Lewis, Edna. *In Pursuit of Flavor.* Charlottesville: University of Virginia Press, 2000.

Lesem, Jeanne. *The Pleasures of Preserving and Pickling*. New York: Knopf, 1975.

M

McGee, Harold. *On Food and Cooking: The Science and Lore of the Kitchen*. New York: Charles Scribner's Sons, 2004.

McNair, James. *Cold Cuisine.* San Francisco: Chronicle, 1988.

Montagné, Prosper. *Larousse Gastronomique: The Encyclopedia of Food, Wine, and Cookery*. New York: Crown, 1961.

N

North American Meat Processors Association. *The Poultry Buyer's Guide: Chicken, Turkey, Duck, Goose, Game.* Hoboken, NJ: John Wiley & Sons, 2004.

——. *The Meat Buyer's Guide: Beef, Lamb, Veal, Pork, and Poultry.* Hoboken, NJ: John Wiley & Sons, 2007.

R

Richter, Henry. *Dr. Richter's Fresh Produce Guide.* Apopka, FL: Try-Foods International, 2000.

Rombauer, Irma S., and Marion Rombauer Becker. *Joy of Cooking.* Indianapolis/New York: Bobbs-Merrill, 1980.

Ruhlman, Michael, and Brian Polcyn. *Charcuterie: The Craft of Salting, Smoking, Curing.* New York: W.W. Norton, 2005.

S

Schmidt, Arno. *Chef's Book of Formulas, Yields, and Sizes,* 2nd ed. New York: John Wiley & Sons, 1996.

Sonnenschmidt, Frederick H., and Jean F. Nicolas. *The Professional Chef's Art of Garde Manger*, 5th ed. New York: John Wiley & Sons, 1993.

T

Trager, James. *The Food Chronology: A Food Lover's Compendium of Events and Anecdotes, from Prehistory to the Present*. New York: Henry Holt, 1995.

W

Willan, Anne. *La Varenne's Paris Kitchen.* New York: William Morrow, 1981.

——. *French Regional Cooking.* New York: William Morrow, 1981.

Wolfert, Paula. *The Cooking of South-West France.* Garden City, NY: Doubleday, 1983.

Glossary

5:4:3 emulsion The ratio of ingredients on which many traditional emulsified sausages are based—5 parts meat to 4 parts fat to 3 parts water, all expressed as weight.

A

À la carte service When customers order dishes individually from the menu, and the dishes are prepared to order.

À la Grecque [ah lah GREK] A classic *cuisson* that includes salt, acidic ingredients, and vegetable oil to cook and preserve vegetables at the same time, giving them a slightly pickled and tangy taste.

À point [ah PWAN] Literally, "to the point." In vegetables, cooked to a tender texture.

Acetic acid A clear odorless organic acid found in vinegar

Acetous fermentation When combined with oxidation, changes the alcohol in the wine into acetic acid.

Acidification When acid that results from culturing begins the coagulation and curdling processes.

Acid-loving bacterial culture A type of bacteria that thrives in a high acid medium.

Action buffet Includes one or more action stations.

Action station Buffet station where certain types of food preparation are done before the customers' eyes.

Aged cheese Firm cheese that has been subjected to extended aging.

Aged wood Wood that has been stored away from moisture and insects for at least a year after harvest.

Aging Extended storage of a fully ripened firm cheese, under proper conditions, in order to change and improve it.

Al dente [ahl DAYN-tay] Literally, "to the tooth." Although it is usually used to describe pasta, North American chefs apply this term to vegetables as well. Al dente vegetables are cooked just enough to lose their raw taste while retaining their crunchy texture.

Amuse-bouche [ah-mooz BOOSH] Literally, "a thing that amuses the mouth." A small, savory portion of food served before a meal.

Annatto Coloring agent derived from plants.

Anthocyanins Pigments found in purple and purple-red vegetables.

Anthoxanthins Pigments found in most white vegetables.

Apéritif [ah-pair-eh-TEEF] An alcoholic drink served before a meal to stimulate the appetite.

Aquaculture The practice of raising seafood in a controlled environment. Seafood produced by aquaculture is also called *farm-raised* or *cultivated* seafood.

Arranged presentation Dressed or seasoned elements placed on a plate or platter individually.

Arranged salad A complex salad consisting of several separate food elements placed on the plate in a precise, planned design.

Arterial brining Forcing a brine into the arteries in a front or hind leg primal cut.

Artichoke bottom The fleshy base section of an artichoke.

Artichoke heart The cup-shaped edible portion of the artichoke, consisting of the bottom and the tender, edible interior leaf bases.

Artisan A skilled craftsperson who makes products primarily by hand using traditional methods.

Artisan bread Breads made in small batches, by traditional processes, and from natural ingredients.

Artisan butter Contains a higher milk fat content and, correspondingly, a lower water content than domestic butter.

Artisan foods High-quality food products made by traditional methods.

Aspic Clarified, seasoned stock with the addition of gelatin.

Aspic gelée [ahss-PEEK zhe-LAY] In English, aspic jelly.

Aspic jelly English term for a transluscent, clarified stock that is fortified with gelatin.

Attelet [ah-tel-LAY] Skewer with an ornamented top.

Attended buffet Servers are stationed behind the buffet table(s); also called a *served buffet*.

B

Baby greens Young, immature leaves of standard lettuces and other salad greens.

Back of the plate The part of the plate intended to be placed farthest from the diner.

Backfat Fat deposited between the back muscles of a hog and its skin. Also called *fatback*.

Backwards planning A strategy that enables planners to create a logical flow of preparation work by first focusing on the date of an event and then working backward to assign tasks to appropriate days.

Bain-marie: A container used for keeping foods either cold or hot by suspending them over iced or hot water.

Ballottine Forcemeat wrapped in a butterflied, flattened piece of meat. It is never made with poultry.

Banquet service Plated foods served to large numbers of guests at one time. Dishes are typically plated ahead of time but may be sauced and garnished at the last minute.

Barquette Literally, "small boat" in French. A boat-shaped miniature pastry shell used for hors d'oeuvres or petits fours.

Beard Hairy filament protruding from a mussel.

Bedded presentation Salads placed on a bed, or layer, of salad greens.

Bed of greens A simple salad used as a component of a complex salad.

Beluga caviar [beh-LOO-gah] Consists of large, separate sturgeon eggs ranging from pale to dark gray in color, with a mild, buttery, creamy flavor. Beluga is considered the finest type of caviar and is in the greatest demand.

Beneficial microorganism One that creates good changes in foods.

Berries Individual fish eggs.

Bind In mixing forcemeats, meat and fat particles cling to each other with the right amount of liquid added, creating a bind.

Bivalve Shellfish with hinged, two-section exterior shells.

Blanc [BLAHN] (1) White; (2) Flour and water slurry added to acidulated water to prevent certain foods from discoloring during cooking.

Blanching Boiling a food for a short period to partially or fully cook it to a firm texture, to remove skins or peels, or to stop enzymatic browning and remove undesirable strong flavors from vegetables.

Blind Describes Swiss cheese that does not have eyes.

Blind bake Pastry shell baked empty and then filled.

Blini [BLEE-nee] Very small, thin buckwheat pancakes.

Bloom (1) Edible outer rind of cheese; (2) When gelatin comes into contact with cool water or a water-based liquid, it rehydrates, absorbing the liquid and expanding.

Blooming To rehydrate gelatin.

Boiling Cooking food completely submerged in water at 212°F (100°C).

Bolted State of extreme overmaturity in which a lettuce or other type of green develops long, thick stems, grows tall, and is often tough, with a strong, bitter flavor.

Bouchée From the French word for "mouth." A miniature vol-au-vent, or hollow cylindrical puff pastry cup used for hors d'oeuvres or petits fours.

Bound Main food items glued together with a thick dressing.

Bound protein salad Composed primarily of diced meat, poultry, or seafood mixed with a thick dressing.

Break When a vinaigrette or mayonnaise separates out of emulsion.

Breakdown Removal and storage of leftover buffet food, disassembly of the buffet line(s) and stations, and general cleanup. The break-down phase applies to both the kitchen and the buffet room.

Brine Solution of salt and water; when salt is dissolved in water to make a curing medium, the resulting liquid curing compound is called a *brine cure* or a *wet cure*.

Brine cure Brine used as a curing compound.

Brining syringe Stainless-steel cylindrical chamber with a large needle and a plunger.

Broken mayonnaise When a properly emulsified mayonnaise comes apart and the oil and liquid separate.

Broken vinaigrette When the oil and vinegar separate.

Bruschetta (broo sket ta) A slice of toasted Italian bread served as an appetizer, usually rubbed with garlic and moistened with olive oil, often served with additional toppings.

Bubble tie When tying off sausages with kitchen string, this creates a double seal with an air pocket between the ties.

Buffet [boo-FAY] Type of service with a variety of dishes arranged in an attractive display from which guests choose the foods they wish to eat.

Buffet or **stationary hors d'oeuvres** Hors d'oeuvre trays presented on small tables.

Buffet line Traditional buffet configuration; a long table, or line of tables, on which the food platters are arranged in a row.

Buffet maintenance server Staffperson who keeps the line(s), stations, guest tables, and room clean and orderly.

Buffet station Sections that feature a particular type of food, such as appetizers, salads, seafood, carved meats, and so on.

Buffet theme Concept, or basic idea, of the buffet, which should be clear and instantly recognizable.

Bulk sausage A complete forcemeat.

Burr Drips or tags of set coating sauce visible on a food's surface.

Butler service Trays of hors d'oeuvres carried from person to person by servers. Hors d'oeuvres served in this manner are also called passed hors d'oeuvres.

Butter Substance that remains when most of the watery fluid is drained away from milk fat.

Button Disk that results when a log of cheese is cut crosswise.

C

Cafeteria service and **food bar service** Specialized forms of buffet service that utilize permanently installed heating and refrigeration equipment.

Canapé A piece of bread, toast, or flat pastry that is the bed, or base, upon which the other ingredients are placed.

Carême [kah-REM], **Marie-Antoine** Innovator of European cuisine. Carême rose to culinary stardom around 1800. Although he worked exclusively as a cook in aristocratic households, his writings influenced restaurant cooking as well. He is most famous for his *pièces montées*, or elaborately constructed food centerpieces. Classic garde manger presentations of carved fruits and vegetables, aspic and chaud-froid work, and ice carvings owe their beginnings to the work of Carême.

Carotenoid Pigment found in orange and orange-red vegetables.

Carryover cooking When foods continue to cook by internal heat after removal from heat source.

Carve To fabricate a large cut of cooked meat into pieces or portions.

Carved vegetables and **fruits** Often added to the platter or carving board as decoration.

Carving station Display at which chefs slice hot or cold meats to order.

Case hardening Occurs when moisture is trapped within a sausage and it does not dry out properly.

Casein (1) Protein found in milk and other dairy products; (2) An important emulsifier found in milk solids.

Casing Long, flexible tubes that encase, or surround, the forcemeat of most sausage products

Casing clip Used to secure shut the ends of sausage casings.

Catering Serving large numbers of guests with a pre-planned menu of dishes.

Caught emulsion The point when a developing mayonnaise forms a ribbon and the oil can be added more quickly and whipped more gently.

Caul or **lace fat** Thin yet remarkably strong membrane that encases the stomach and intestines of hogs and other animals. It is used as a liner for the forms and dishes in which terrines are baked.

Caviar Preserved roe, or eggs, of fish. In order to be called *caviar*, the product must be roe from Eurasian sturgeon and have no other ingredient except salt.

Cellulose The fiber in cell walls. Cellulose, together with the water and pectin within the cells, determines a vegetable's texture.

Cephalopods [SEF-ah-low-pods] Mollusks with tentacles and a defined head.

Certified organic produce Fruits and vegetables grown without the use of chemical fertilizers, pesticides, and herbicides. Must come from a USDA-certified farm.

Certified pork Pork frozen for a time-temperature period proven to destroy the pathogens that cause trichinosis.

Ceviche [seh-VEESH] French version of a seafood dish "cooked" with acid.

Chafing dish Hot bain-marie unit used to keep food hot on a buffet line.

Chaud-froid [show-FWAH] Cream velouté sauce or demiglace sauce with the addition of aspic.

Chausson [show-SOHN] Flaky pastry turnover.

Cheddaring Process used in making cheddar cheese; involves cut curd, salted and packed into forms and weighted.

Cheese (fresh cheese) Forms when drained curds are compacted together.

Cheese pick Short, pointed knife used for hard cheeses.

Cheese vault Room engineered for cave-like conditions of high humidity, moderate temperature, and darkness.

Chèvre Goat cheese.

Chip Thin slice of a sturdy or starchy vegetable deep-fried or baked until crisp.

Chlorophyll Pigment found in green vegetables.

Choke Crown of inedible, fibrous spines found in the center of an artichoke.

Clabber A custardlike mass of soft curds.

Clarified butter Pure butterfat; whole butter from which all water and milk solids are removed.

Clarify Remove impurities such as fat, scum, and meat or vegetable particulate matter, from stock through the process of protein coagulation.

Clarity Quality of translucence in properly clarified stock.

Classical cuisine A style of cooking based on the work of French chefs from Carême to Fernand Point that strongly influenced both European and North American cuisines through the 1960s.

Clear ice Ice produced by a special method that keeps it from clouding as it freezes. Used for carving.

Club sandwich The most famous double-decker sandwich.

Coagulation Tightening and consolidation of the protein structure within milk, eggs, and other protein foods.

Coating sauce A dressing for cold food that is fluid when warm and that sets up into a gel when chilled.

Cocktail Chilled seafood tossed or topped with a sauce, and typically served in a cocktail glass.

Cocktail sauce Based on tomato ketchup and prepared horseradish.

Coil Rope sausage formed into a spiral shape.

Cold hors d'oeuvre Categorized by temperature, a cold hors d'oeuvre is served cold, cool, or at room temperature.

Cold smoking The process of holding foods at temperatures below 100°F (37°C) during the application of smoke.

Cold vegetable dish Whole, intact cold vegetables, or a single type of cold vegetable.

Collagen Animal protein found in bones, cartilage, connective tissue, and hides.

Collagen casing Derived from cattle hides.

Combination buffet One that combines various service styles.

Commercial pop-up toaster Works in the same manner as domestic toasters.

Commercial toaster oven Takes the place of both a toaster and a convection oven.

Complete salad Provides a complete and balanced meal, comprised of starch, vegetable, and protein items.

Complex salad Consists of meats, poultry, seafood, or vegetables other than leafy greens.

Complex side salad Used primarily as a side dish.

Compote Fruits stewed or cooked in syrup.

Compound butter or **composed butter** Whipped whole butter seasoned with salt and other seasonings such as pepper, fresh herbs, or lemon.

Condiment An assertively flavored food added to or served along with a dish. Its main function is to enhance the flavor of the food with which it is served.

Confit [kon-FEE] Food that is first cured and then cooked and sealed in fat.

Confiture Thick, rough-textured condiments made by cooking fruits or vegetables until they are highly reduced.

Continental cuisine The combination of classical French cuisine with North American ingredients and taste preferences. Later, it incorporated Italian cuisine elements as well.

Continuous-feed brine pump Plastic cylinder with a large needle and a plunger.

Continuous phase In an emulsion, the liquid into which the droplets are dispersed.

Conveyor toaster Works continuously and discharges the finished toast directly onto the work surface.

Cooked brine Heated to dissolve the salt more quickly and to more thoroughly extract the flavors of whole spices and aromatic vegetables.

Cooked chutney Fruits and/or vegetables simmered with sugar, salt, vinegar, aromatic vegetables, and South Asian spices.

Cooked salsa Typically made from tomatoes, onions, garlic, and chiles. May contain natural and artificial thickeners, stabilizers, and preservatives.

Corn To apply salt to meat.

Coulis [koo-LEE] Puréed sauce made from a vegetable or fruit.

Countertop convection oven Used for toasting croûtons needed for canapé bases and to accompany dips and spreads, and for toasting sandwiches and heating slices of quiche and other savory pastries.

Court bouillon [KOOR bwee-oh(n)] Flavorful liquid made by simmering together mirepoix, a bouquet garni, white wine, and water.

Cracker Small, dry, savory pastry similar to a cookie in shape and size, but made with little or no sugar.

Cream The fatty fluid that rises to the top when milk is allowed to cool, undisturbed, under refrigeration for several hours.

Crépinette Sausage patty wrapped in caul fat and pan-fried or baked.

Crisping Replacing some lost moisture, and also firming the texture, of most vegetables by immersion in ice water after they are peeled and fabricated.

Crudités (kroo-dee-TAY) Classic French raw or very lightly cooked vegetable dish served chilled and accompanied by dips.

Crumb The soft, porous interior of bread.

Crust The crisp exterior of bread.

Crustacean Sea animal with complex segmented exterior shells and legs.

Croûton Small, thin slice of bread toasted or sautéed until crisp.

Cuban sandwich A pressed sandwich originally made by Cuban exiles living in South Florida.

Cubano [koo-BAH-no] Another name for a Cuban sandwich.

Cuisson [kwee-SOH(N)] French culinary term for a flavorful poaching liquid.

Cull To separate decayed or spoiled produce from undamaged produce.

Culture Beneficial bacteria purposely added to a food.

Culturing Process of adding a beneficial bacteria.

Curdle To separate the milk solids and the milk fat from the water in milk to create a firm, compact, and relatively dry food mass, curds.

Curdling A continuation of the coagulation process. In curdling, the protein nets formed by coagulation begin to tighten, and eventually expel the liquid they once held.

Curds The solid food element that results from curdling; consists mainly of milk solids and milk fat.

Cure To treat a food with salt, making it less hospitable to bacteria, molds, and other harmful microorganisms, and thus delaying spoilage.

Cure accelerator Used to assist the curing process and help the curing compound penetrate meats quickly.

Cured and cold-smoked sausage Ground meat and fat preserved with a dry curing compound containing salt, other seasonings, and a nitrite/nitrate curing mix such as Prague Powder #2; smoked at temperatures under 100°F (37°C).

Cured and dried sausage Made from ground meat and fat preserved with a dry curing compound containing salt, other seasonings, and a nitrite/nitrate curing mix such as Prague Powder #2; air-dried.

Cured and hot-smoked sausage Prepared in the same manner as cured and dried sausages, then encased and smoked at a temperature above 100°F (37°C).

Cured and smoked emulsified sausage Smooth pureed sausage that contains nitrite/nitrate curing mixes and is hot smoked either before or after poaching.

Curing (of cheese) Term used to describe the slow ripening of cheese.

Curing compound A mixture, based on salt, that usually contains flavoring ingredients such as sugar, spices, and herbs (sometimes simply called a *cure*).

Curing salt Also known as tinted curing mix; mixture of 6% sodium nitrite and 94% sodium chloride plus a small amount of red food coloring.

Curing tub Nonreactive container in which foods are layered with a dry curing compound.

Cushion Safety factor of extra food built into your quantity calculation.

Cutproof glove Flexible stainless-steel glove used when shucking bivalves.

D

Daikon White radish.

Dairy product Food made from milk.

Decay The natural progression of ripening in which the fruit or vegetable flesh softens to a mealy or mushy texture and finally disintegrates.

Décor [day-KOR] A small food item placed on a tray or platter to add visual appeal; also large decorative items.

Deli tray Portable do-it-yourself sandwich station.

Depurated Describes farm-raised mature bivalves held in tanks of fast-flowing seawater powered by high-pressure pumps for 48 to 72 hours to remove impurities.

Depuration system Tanks in which bivalves are depurated.

Dessert soup Based on sweetened fruit purée or a fruit-based syrup.

Dextrose Powdered glucose sweetener.

Die Plate with multiple openings of a particular shape and size.

Dipping sauce A highly seasoned fluid condiment.

Direct-set culture Cheese-making culture used as is, from the packet, just once.

Dispersed phase In an emulsion, the liquid component that is broken into small droplets.

Double-decker sandwich A sandwich having one deck, then another layer of filling on top of the ceiling slice, and finally a third slice of bread on top.

Double-service line At a buffet, a front line and a back line that run parallel to each other.

Dressing A sauce usually used to enhance salads; sometimes used on sandwiches and as a dip.

Dry cure Based on dry salt and other dry ingredients that are ground or pulverized into a granular or powdered form. A dry cure is sometimes called a rub because the dry salt and seasonings are rubbed into the meat.

Drying chamber Enclosed area in which sausages are kept under correct conditions for drying.

E

Edible flowers Flowers raised specifically as food to avoid the risk of contamination by herbicides and pesticides.

Embellishment Fancy or elaborate garnish.

Emulsified sausage Forcemeat puréed and almost completely dependent on emulsion both for smooth texture and to hold it together.

Emulsified vinaigrette A dressing that coats salad greens and other ingredients evenly and uniformly.

Emulsifier An ingredient that keeps a mixture in emulsion for an indefinite period.

Emulsion Uniform mixture of two normally unmixable substances.

En terrine presentation Terrine served in the same dish in which it is baked.

En torchon Foie gras fabricated in a cylindrical shape that can be cut into attractive, even slices. The cleaned and preseasoned lobes are reassembled and then wrapped in a roll of moistened cheesecloth tied with string at each end. When wrapped and poached in this manner, the foie gras is said to be cooked *en torchon*, and the finished product is called a torchon of foie gras.

Encasement Process of stuffing a forcemeat into a casing.

Escoffier [eh-SKOFF-yay], **Georges-Auguste** A pivotal and influential chef who simplified French cuisine in the late 1800s and early 1900s. He identified the basic cold sauces used in garde manger work and named the many garnitures used in cold foods presentation. He also created the brigade system still used in large kitchens today. He recognized garde manger as a specialized type of work significantly different from hot foods cooking, and he physically separated the garde manger station from the hot line. He placed meat and poultry fabrication within the responsibilities of the garde manger department.

Essence Highly reduced, flavorful liquid based on stock.

Established buffet A buffet that is permanent and always available to guests.

Ethylene gas As fruit ripens, the ethylene gas it produces triggers several enzymatic processes.

External garnish A piece of food served outside a sandwich rather than inside it.

Extra-virgin olive oil Top grade of virgin olive oil.

Extrude To push a substance through an opening.

Eyes Holes in the body of a cheese caused by pockets of CO_2 gas resulting from bacterial activity during ripening.

F

Failed mayonnaise When the watery ingredients and the oil do not successfully emulsify.

Family-style banquet service Food served on platters to each table; guests are expected to serve themselves.

Farce French culinary term for forcemeat. The French verb *farcir* [far SEER] means "to stuff."

Farm-raised Seafood produced by aquaculture.

Fatback Fat deposited between the back muscles of a hog and its skin. Also called *backfat*.

Fermentation The process by which a bacterial culture creates changes in a food or beverage.

Fermented dairy product Food or beverage that begins as fresh milk or cream but that is changed in several ways by the action of a beneficial bacterial culture.

Fermented sausage Traditionally made with dairy products in the forcemeats, which adds a slight souring that gives these sausages their characteristic tangy flavor.

Filter-feeder Bivalve that takes in both oxygen and nutrients by drawing large amounts of seawater through its system, thus absorbing high levels of contaminants when they are present.

Fish Aquatic animals with bony interior skeletons and fins that take in oxygen through gills.

Flat presentation Includes salads assembled from sliced solid foods as well as salads made from spreads, dips, and purées. Usually presented on an oversized plate, this type of salad sometimes appears as though the food elements were applied to the plate with a brush or palette knife.

Flatbread Unleavened bread or leavened bread fabricated to give it a flat appearance.

Flavonoids Two types of pigments: anthocyanins and anthoxanthins.

Flavored oil Prepared by steeping a flavorful ingredient in oil, or by puréeing a flavorful ingredient with the oil.

Flavored vinegar Made by steeping or soaking herbs, spices, or aromatic vegetables in vinegar to create a flavorful infusion.

Fleuron Crescent-shaped garnish, or its cutter.

Flight A group of sample servings having something in common, for example, wine or cheese.

Flooding Plate painting technique in which a thicker sauce is used to form a border that contains a thinner sauce.

Florets Crown pieces of broccoli or cauliflower, favored for their unique shape and texture.

Flow A logical and fluid progression of movements; food containers on the buffet line or in a station must be set up in a logical order for service.

Foam An aerated liquid.

Foie gras [FWAH grah] The enlarged liver of a goose or duck, the result of accelerated feeding of a high-calorie diet.

Foie gras cru Fresh, uncooked foie gras.

Folding A method of combining ingredients while retaining as much air as possible.

Food bar A relatively new form of self-service buffet in which prepared foods are kept on permanent display in specialized equipment.

Food identification placards Small signs that indicate the name of each dish on a buffet or food bar.

Food injector Machinery that forces brine into meats in various ways. Commercial machines are powered by electricity; artisan producers inject food by hand.

Food runner Staff person responsible for monitoring a buffet line and stations and for replenishing or replacing the platters.

Forcemeat Mixture of highly seasoned ground meat and fat blended in a special way to create both protein bind and emulsion.

Fork foods Those that are pre-cut into bite-size pieces, or foods tender enough to be cut with the side of a fork.

Fork-tender Describes cold vegetable and fruit preparations cooked to complete tenderness, such that they can be cut with the side of a fork.

Fortify To add commercial gelatin to a stock to make a coating sauce.

Fresh dairy product A dairy product unchanged by beneficial microorganisms.

Fresh foie gras Raw foie gras.

Fresh salsa Made from tomatoes or other soft, juicy vegetables or fruits that have not been cooked, other than sometimes a brief blanching in order to remove the skins.

Fresh sausage Ground meat and fat seasoned with salt and other ingredients, meant to be eaten within a day or two of preparation.

Fromage [froh MAZH] Derived from the Latin *forma*, meaning form or mold, reflecting the manner in which curds are formed into cheese.

Fromage fort Strong cheese with powerful, deeply savory flavors and aroma.

Front of the plate Part of the plate intended to be placed nearest to the diner.

Fruit The reproductive organ, specifically the ovary, of a seed plant.

Fruit salad A salad based on fresh fruit, although other ingredients may be included.

Fusion cuisine The result of the adoption of international ingredients into garde manger work, which expanded the garde manger repertoire. Garde manger chefs began adding soy sauce and sesame oil to classic vinaigrette formulas. Japanese sushi and sashimi prompted experimentation with raw seafood. Mexican-style salsas took their place alongside classic relishes and vegetable coulis. Spare Asian plate presentations were emulated.

G

Galantine Poultry-based forcemeat wrapped in the skin of a fowl.

Garde manger [gahrd mahn-ZHAY] (1) The person in charge of cold foods preparation and preservation; (2) The department in which cold foods are prepared and stored; (3) The craft, or profession, of cold foods preparation.

Garnish A small piece of food added to a plate presentation to provide a finishing touch.

Garniture Miniature composed dish, used as garnish or décor, that is self-contained and freestanding on the platter.

Gavage [gah-VAHJ] Force feeding, as in feeding geese and ducks intended to yield foie gras. In traditional gavage, each bird is fed manually by inserting a funnel-like instrument with a long tube down its throat.

Gelatin Nearly colorless, nearly flavorless water-soluble substance derived from collagen.

Gelatin powder Another name for granular gelatin.

Gelatin-stabilized foam A thin, low-fat base liquid fortified with a protein gel that acquires enough structure and elasticity to hold air.

Gelatinize Using gelatin to thicken a liquid.

Gelée de viande [zhe-LAY duh VYAHND] Meat jelly.

Geoduck (GOO-ee-duck) Pacific clam that can weigh up to 9 lb (4 kg) but is usually harvested at 2–3 lb (1–1.5 kg). Also called *giant clam*. Only the "neck" is eaten.

Giant clam Another name for geoduck.

Glaze Flavorful, lightly sweetened liquids brushed or basted onto foods as they cook.

Grana cheese A grainy textured chese often aged for two years or longer.

Granular gelatin Liquid gelatin, dehydrated and ground into fine granules.

Gratin [grah-TAN] **forcemeat** To pan-sear and then immediately chill a portion of lean meat before grinding it for forcemeat.

Gratin garnish An internal garnish that is pan-seared before being added to a forcemeat.

Green wood Wood from freshly harvested trees, burns slowly and creates a lot of smoke.

Grinder Toasted long roll sandwich.

Grinder collar Holds the grinder blade and die together on the machine.

Grinder knife or **blade** Four-sided blade that lies flush against the die.

Grosse pièce [gross pee-YEHSS] Literally, "large piece." A section of a cooked roast is placed on the platter as the focal point of the buffet presentation.

Guacamole A dip made from avocadoes.

Gueridon [GEH-ree-don] Service cart.

Guillotine Double-handled cheese knife.

H

Handing off Cooperation between the hot side and the cold side, meant to enhance a menu.

Hank Casings wrapped in bundles.

Hard cheese Aged cheeses having a texture that makes them difficult to cut by hand with a standard knife.

Healed end Tough, dry area where a vegetable was cut during harvesting.

Heat lamp External heating device that can be set up on a buffet line to keep foods warm.

Heated hors d'oeuvre One that was cooked ahead of time and then is reheated for service.

Heated sandwich A sandwich made from pre-cooked or ready-to-eat ingredients that is warmed for service.

Heirloom Vegetable or fruit grown from seeds handed down from past generations.

Herb bouquets Typically placed on the platter or carving board around the base of a roast.

Hero New York version of an Italian long roll sandwich.

Hoagie Philadelphia version of the Italian long roll sandwich.

Hog ring Used to secure shut the ends of large natural and synthetic casings.

Hollowed long roll sandwich A long roll is slit along one side, opened out, and flattened into a "canoe" shape. Excess crumb is removed.

Homogenization Method used to maintain the fat-water emulsion in dairy products and thus keep them from separating.

Hors d'oeuvre [or DERV] In North America, a small, attractive piece of savory food meant to be picked up and eaten with the fingers.

Hors d'oeuvre cutters Very small cutters of various shapes used to punch out garnishes and décor.

Hors d'oeuvre kebab Two or three pieces of food are threaded onto a cocktail pick or onto a bamboo skewer.

Hot hors d'oeuvres Usually turned out by the hot kitchen because they require cooking equipment not normally found in a garde manger station.

Hot smoking Procedure in which foods are surrounded by smoke at temperatures between 150°F and 200°F (65° and 93°C).

Humectant Substance that aids in retaining moisture without making products taste overly sweet—brown sugar and syruplike sugars, such as honey and corn syrup, for example. Corn syrup and dextrose are less sweet than other sugars and can be used in higher concentration.

Hydroponics The practice of growing plants in water-based nutrient solutions, normally in climate-controlled greenhouses.

I

Ice-filled chafing dish A pan set inside a pan filled with ice to keep food cold.

Iced presentation tray Used for items that must be kept consistently cold, such as shellfish and mayonnaise-bound salads.

Immersion brining Technique in which food is placed in a sanitized, nonreactive container and submerged in brine.

Infuse Virtually the same as to steep. However, infusing may be done either hot or at room temperature. In culinary usage, this term is more commonly used when referring to flavoring oils or vinegars, but it can also be used for water-based liquids.

Infusion The fluid that results when infusing is compete.

Injection brining Forcing the brine through a needle directly into the muscle structure of the meat.

Inlay garnish Garnish food arranged in a specific pattern while packing the forcemeat into its form.

Inoculate To inject a cheese with a culture.

Institutional cooking Food service for large groups of repeat customers, as in college cafeterias or hospital service. Institutional feeders must offer a large variety of food choices. They may utilize a menu cycle, a sequence of menus that changes daily over an established number of days before reverting to the first menu and beginning the cycle again.

Interior ripening Culture is injected into the interior of a cheese after it is formed.

Internal brining Applying a liquid cure to the inside of the meat.

Internal garnish (1) Sandwich enhancement enclosed within the bread; (2) Pieces of food placed within a forcemeat to add texture, flavor, and visual interest.

Italian long roll sandwich Combination of Italian-style meats, cheeses, and vegetables on a long roll.

J

Jam Preserve or confiture.

Jellied consommé (1) Consommé made in the classic manner, with plenty of bones and a pig's foot added for body, that sets up into a light gel when chilled; (2) A similar cold soup prepared with commercial gelatin.

Jowl fat Dense, pure white deposit fat located in the head of the hog.

Jumbo asparagus Very thick, with a fibrous skin on the lower part of the stalk that must be removed to ensure even cooking.

Jus [ZHOO] Cooking liquid derived from a roast.

K

Ketchup A thick, smooth, saucelike condiment seasoned with onions, vinegar, and aromatic spices.

Kosher salt Refined salt processed into medium-size, flaky particles that dissolve quickly in water; used to make brines and, in dry cures, to coat and penetrate meat in a gentle, even manner.

L

Lactose Type of sugar found in milk.

Lactose intolerant Cannot digest milk sugar.

La Varenne [lah vah-REN], **Pierre-François de la** Considered the founder of modern French cuisine. He is credited as the first to use roux as a thickener, and he refined the technique of dough lamination to make an early form of puff pastry. He lightened and simplified European cooking, and popularized fresh vegetables and herbs. In 1651, La Varenne wrote an important cookbook, *La Cuisinier François*, which contains recipes still in use today.

Leaf gelatin Another name for sheet gelatin.

Leaf lard (1) Rendered suet; (2) Any high-quality lard.

Leavened bread Breads made with yeast.

Lecithin Found in egg yolks, it is the most effective emulsifier.

Lightening the base Method used when folding a light, airy substance into a dense, heavy one.

Lightener or **lightening ingredient** Added to a heavier, base substance to give it a less heavy texture, as cream in a mousseline.

Line map Defines the boundaries of each station in the garde manger department and indicates which menu items are turned out from each.

Liner Used to contain a forcemeat.

Liner leaf One or two lettuce leaves placed under a complex salad or other food.

Living greens Lettuces packaged with their root ball submerged in a shallow well of water.

Liquor In a bivalve, the liquid surrounding the flesh. It does not actually contain alcohol.

M

Manufactured casings Man-made tubes available in several materials and sizes, used in sausage making.

Marinade Fluid mixture that always includes vegetable oil, an acidic ingredient such as citrus juice or vinegar, salt, and seasonings such as herbs, spices, and aromatic vegetables.

Mask To cover a food in such a way that its surface is no longer visible.

Masking sauce Opaque coating sauce.

Mature cheese As cheese ripens, the microorganisms multiply and produce various compounds that contribute to flavor, aroma, color, texture, and mouthfeel. While ripening, a cheese can change dramatically, often changing from firm, white, and mild-tasting to soft, creamy-yellow, and pungent, becoming a mature cheese.

Mayonnaise collée [may-oh-NEZ koh-LAY] Coating sauce composed of thick mayonnaise and aspic.

Meat grinder Machine that processes meats into particles.

Meat protein Its coagulation contributes to a forcemeat's bind.

Meatless aspic Gelatinized liquid made from wine, fruit juices, vegetable juices, *cuissons*, or a combination of these.

Mellowing period The time given to allow the aromatic ingredients in a food to release their volatile oils, and the flavors to marry.

Mesclun A mixture of baby lettuces, young arugula, and immature red chicory that originated in Provence, a region of southern France.

Micro greens The stem and the first true leaves that form after a plant has sprouted.

Microwave oven Has limited use on the garde manger line, because microwave heating has adverse effects on bread and pastry items.

Mignonette A sauce made from wine, vinegar, and cracked peppercorns.

Milk A nutritious fluid produced by female mammals in order to feed their newborn offspring.

Milk fat Consists of both saturated and unsaturated fats. Because it is the major component of butter, milk fat is often called *butterfat*.

Milk solids The components of milk other than fat and water, including milk proteins, lactic acid, and white pigments.

Mixed presentation Complex salad in which all elements are mixed together.

Molded butter Decorative presentation in which butter is shaped in silicone forms.

Molded presentation Foods compressed into attractive shapes by pressing them into a food service–grade form.

Mollusk Sea animal with simple shell structure and no legs.

Malassol Literally, "little salt," in Russian; top-grade true caviar processed with a minimum of salt.

Mounded presentation A selection of complex salads arranged together on a plate in separate piles.

Mousse [MOOSE] A full-flavored base of cooked, puréed food lightened with whipped cream and/or beaten egg whites, and served with no further cooking.

Mousseline A light-textured, puréed forcemeat made of raw fish, shellfish, poultry, liver, or meat. Cooked before serving hot or cold.

Mousseline pâté Smoothest and most refined form of pâté, made from an emulsion of puréed raw meat, eggs, and cream.

Multi-decker sandwich Sandwiches having more than one "deck" or layer.

Mycoderma aceti Microscopic organism introduced into wine that causes additional acetous fermentation and results in vinegar.

Myofiber Protein in a mousseline that coagulates and bonds to others.

N

Nage [NAHZH] Describes a dish in which the *cuisson* is served as a broth or light sauce along with the seafood.

Nappé Describes a liquid of consistency thick enough to coat a cool, clean metal spoon yet thin enough to flow on the plate.

Natural casings Inner lining of the intestines and other parts of the digestive tract of various meat animals, used as sausage casing.

Natural salts Unrefined salts that contain other minerals as well as sodium chloride.

Natural smoked cheese A firm cheese that has been subjected to cold-smoking after or in place of aging.

Neutral mayonnaise Basic mayonnaise having no assertive flavors.

Nitrosamines Foods containing nitrites or nitrates, when subjected to high heat, form these substances. Under certain circumstances, nitrosamines are known to cause cancer in laboratory animals.

Nose Point of a cheese wedge.

Nouvelle cuisine Literally, "new cooking." In the 1970s chefs developed a fresher, lighter, and more imaginative style of French cooking, inspired by guidelines later called "The Ten Commandments of Nouvelle Cuisine." One influence on the garde manger chef was the new practice of plating food in the kitchen. Previously, most high-level French restaurants sent food to the table in platter presentation, to be portioned onto plates by servers. Now, garde manger chefs began to create intricate plate presentations that included individual food portions formed in molds.

Nozzle The part of a meat grinder that attaches the sausage horn.

O

O'clock A directive indicating a specific place on the perimeter of the plate well that corresponds to the numeral placement on a standard clock.

On the half-shell Freshly shucked oyster (opened and meat removed) presented in its cup-shaped bottom shell.

Open-face sandwich A single slice of bread topped with a spread, filling ingredients, and garnish.

Osetra caviar [oh-SET-tra] Medium-sized sturgeon eggs ranging from the very rare golden color to brown and brownish-black. Osetra has a distinctive, nutty flavor.

Osmosis Salt enters the cells of a cured product through the process of osmosis, which occurs when there is an unequal balance between the amount of salty, fluid brine outside the meat cells and the amount of unsalty fluid.

Oven grinder A heated Italian sandwich prepared by the toasted sandwich procedure.

Overhauling Turning a curing item to make sure the cure is applied evenly.

Overshelf A shelf unit designed to attach to a worktable or refrigeration unit.

Oyster shooter Freshly shucked oyster served in a chilled shot glass topped with a few drops of bottled hot sauce and a half-ounce of frozen vodka.

P

Panade [pah-NAHD] or **panada** [pah-NAH-dah] A soft, smooth, starchy mixture used to bind and extend a pâté forcemeat.

Panino (pl. panini) (1) Literally, "little bread," or roll; (2) In Italy, any sandwich, hot or cold; (3) A sandwich grilled in a sandwich press (In Italy, known as a *panino caldo*, or hot panino. By the 1980s, such sandwiches became known worldwide simply as *panini*.)

Panini grill A countertop appliance with with a hinged hot plate used to make a pressed sandwich.

Pan-steaming Cooking food in very little liquid in a covered pan on a stove burner.

Parfait [pahr-FAY] Literally, "perfect." (1) In European pastry work, a parfait is a sweet, smooth, custardlike dessert component or a frozen dessert similar to frozen mousse; (2) A multilayered ice cream dessert presented in a tall glass; (3) In garde manger, a rich, buttery liver spread; (4) A specific preparation of foie gras.

Passed or **butler service** Attractively arranged platters or trays of single-bite portions of food passed or carried around the service area where guests are standing or informally seated away from tables.

Passed hors d'oeuvres Trays of hors d'oeuvres carried from person to person by servers. Also called *butlered hors d'oeuvres*.

Pasta filata [PAH-stah fee-LAH-tah] Cheeses made by heating curds and then stretching and kneading them like bread dough or taffy.

Pasteurization Process of heating milk to a specific temperature for a specific period in order to destroy harmful microorganisms that could cause food-borne illnesses.

Pastry hors d'oeuvres Hors d'oeuvres based on pastry.

Pâté [pah-TAY] (1) Forcemeat baked in a pastry crust, usually served cold; (2) Today, any pâté product, encrusted or not.

Pâte à pâté The pastry dough used to wrap a pâté en croûte.

Pâté en croûte Forcemeat baked inside a crust of pastry dough.

Pâté roulade Assembled and cooked in the same way as a galantine, but not wrapped in a poultry skin.

Pelée à vif [peh-LAY ah VEEF] Literally, "skinned alive." To pare away tough skin and, on citrus fruits, the underlying pith.

Pellicle Translucent, tacky skin caused by air-drying cured products.

Pencil asparagus Slender shoots of asparagus with a diameter about the size of a pencil.

Permanent or **stable emulsion** An emulsion with a high percentage of emulsifying ingredients that remains emulsified indefinitely.

Pesce crudo [peh-shay KROO-doh] Italian for "raw fish."

Physical tenderization Tenderizing meat without the use of chemicals, usually by pounding or grinding.

Picked hors d'oeuvre Small piece of food speared with a cocktail pick.

Pickle Brine cure with a strong acidic component.

Pico de gallo Chunky tomato relish.

Pièce montée [PYESS mon-TAY] Literally, "mounted piece." A large decorative food item, frequently tall or elevated.

Plancha Griddle or sandwich press.

Pink cure Also known as Tinted Curing Mix or TCM.

Planetary mixer A mixer with an arm that causes the beating attachment to revolve around the mixer bowl while the attachment itself rotates.

Plant pigments The source of color in vegetables.

Plate painting The art of using sauces to create images on a plate.

Plate rim The raised outer edge of a plate. It serves as the frame for the composition created when the food is arranged on the plate.

Plate well The main part of the plate inside the rim.

Plinth Square or rectangular block that serves as a base.

Pluches [PLOOSH] Tiny herb leaves.

Po'boy New Orleans sandwich served on a long roll.

Poach To cook a food completely submerged in a *cuisson* [kwee-SOH(N)], or flavorful poaching liquid, at low temperature.

Poaching *à blanc* To cook in *a blanc*, or poaching liquid consisting of water, oil, lemon juice, salt, and a flour slurry. Used to poach vegetables susceptible to discoloration.

Poaching à la Grecque To cook in a classic *cuisson* that includes salt, acidic ingredients, and vegetable oil that both cooks and preserves vegetables at the same time.

Poach test To cook a sample of forcemeat for tasting and evaluation.

Pocket sandwich Sandwich made in yeasted flatbreads that are fabricated and baked in a way that gives them a hollow center.

Point, Fernand [fair-nahn PWAN] French chef credited with the transition to nouvelle cuisine. This new and radically different style of French cooking emerged in the late 1960s and became world-famous in the early 1970s. Point's culinary philosophy included seeking simplicity and perfection in all of his dishes, openly sharing knowledge and techniques, and seeking new ideas.

Poke [POH-kay] Hawai'ian seafood dish "cooked" with acid.

Polar Molecule having a positive charge on one end and a negative charge on the other.

Pork rind or **skin** Removed before the fatback is used.

Potted cheese A mixture of natural cheese, flavorings, and a moistening ingredient, such as butter or a flavorful liquid.

Potted meat Preserved meat cured with salt, cooked in lard, and then sealed in the cooking fat.

Pre-plating Portioning buffet foods onto small plates. Effective serving strategy for delicate items that are difficult to portion.

Pre-seasoning Mixing fabricated cubes or strips of meat and fat with spices, herbs, flavorings, salt, and nitrite/nitrate cure mix at least 24 hours in advance of grinding and mixing.

Prep list A step-by-step plan for completing a number of food preparation tasks.

Prepared mustard A thick, smooth paste made from ground mustard seed and an acidic ingredient such as vinegar or sour wine.

Pressed butter Butter that is packed into a butter chip or ramekin and chilled. Before it becomes completely firm it is imprinted with a decorative butter press.

Pressed caviar Dense, cakelike caviar mass with a strong flavor and a jamlike texture.

Pressed sandwich A type of heated sandwich cooked between two hot metal plates.

Pressure canister Used to make whipped cream or savory foams by forcing nitrous oxide into a liquid.

Pressure plate Helps move forcemeat through the chamber of a grinder or stuffer.

Pressure steamer Device for cooking food completely surrounded by water vapor at 212°F (100°C) or higher, in a sealed chamber that prevents the release of steam pressure.

Primary bind (1) The action of mixing meat, fat, and liquid for a forcemeat; (2) Structure created by grinding or puréeing the primary binder ingredient.

Primary binder Main ingredient mixture that causes a forcemeat to hold together.

Primary fowl Large fowl, such as a roasting chicken, that provides a skin wrapper large enough to encase a forcemeat.

Primary meat Must total more than half of the pâté forcemeat's weight.

Prix fixe [pree FEEKS] Guests consume as much as they wish for one set price.

Prague [PROG] **Powder #1** Cure containing only sodium nitrite.

Prague [PROG] **Powder #2** Cure containing sodium nitrite and sodium nitrate.

Proprietary greens mix Brand-name mixture of salad greens.

Protein gel Collagen, when combined with water in the correct way, forms a protein net that captures the water.

Protein structure development When meat is ground and salt is added, the muscle structure is changed and the proteins are made partly soluble. These solubilized proteins then interact to create a network that holds the mixture together.

PSI Pounds per square inch, the unit in which pressure is measured.

Pull list The list of in-house equipment written to secure the serving pieces needed for a buffet. This not only allows planning for what is needed but also reserves those items and prevents other divisions from taking them at the last minute.

Purée A smooth, cohesive substance created by grinding solid ingredients into a paste.

Purée base A smooth, thick, full-flavored, and highly seasoned mixture typically lightened with cream or beaten egg white to make a mousse, mousseline, or soufflé.

Purge To remove the sand from clams or other bivalves.

Q

Quatre épices (KAT ray-PEECE) One of the best-known spice blends used in making pâté, typically consisting of white pepper, ground ginger, nutmeg, and allspice.

Quenelle Delicate oval of mousseline poached in barely simmering water or a *cuisson*.

R

Rancid Describes the acrid odor and rank, nasty flavor acquired by oil and other fats when they spoil.

Random garnish Pieces of the garnish food mixed into a forcemeat before it is packed into the pâté form.

Raw bar Front-of-house food preparation area where raw shellfish and other chilled seafood items are displayed and plated.

Raw Chutney Herbs and soft-textured vegetables or soft, ripe fruits ground into a purée and seasoned with spices and raw chiles.

Raw milk Milk that has not been pasteurized.

Rechaud [RAY-show] Portable butane burner.

Recovery time The time it takes to regain the original cooking temperature when a cold or room-temperature food is added to a hot cooking medium.

Reduce To boil or simmer a flavorful liquid in order to evaporate some of its water content and concentrate its flavor.

Reduced-fat milk Milk from which milk fat has been removed to yield a product with a lower fat content than standard whole milk.

Reduction The result of reducing; also called an *essence*.

Refined salts Salt from which all minerals other than sodium chloride were removed by a manufacturing process.

Refresh To quickly and efficiently stop the process of carryover cooking in steamed and blanched foods by immediately placing them into a large vessel full of ice water after cooking.

Relish Refers to any piquant or refreshing food item that is used to enhance a dish or a meal.

Rendering The cooking process that melts and releases fats from their surrounding connective tissue.

Rennet A curdling agent derived from the stomach lining of young ruminant animals.

Rennin Enzyme found in rennet.

Ribbon The stage when mayonnaise visibly thickens to the point of clinging to the blades of the whisk or forming thick bands on the surface when it falls back into the bowl.

Rillettes [ree-YET] Foods cooked in a flavorful, fatty liquid, shredded, and then sealed in fat. Seasoned with salt, but not cured.

Ring sausages Sausage rope cut to a specific length and then tied into a loop.

Ripe fruit When a fruit has reached perfection and gone through the six important changes that occur during the ripening process.

Ripening (1) Process by which a mature fruit completes its life cycle; (2) Series of changes that occur in a cheese due to the action of bacteria, molds, and enzymes.

Rolled hors d'oeuvres Foods layered together and then rolled into a cylinder.

Room service Foods on covered plates are placed on trays or carts for delivery on premises.

Rope sausage Formed in a casing without further fabrication; usually formed into long, cylindrical coils.

Rotation chopper Works by spinning meat and other foods in a horizontal circular motion that brings the meat into periodic contact with vertically rotating blades.

Roulade [roo-LAHD] A food rolled into a cylindrical shape.

Roundsperson Staff member capable of performing all buffet service and action station duties.

Rub A dry seasoning mixture.

Rust Bruising or brown discoloration on lettuce.

S

Sales mix A report that compares the popularity of menu items expressed as a percentage of total sales.

Salsa fresca Rough sauce made from tomatoes or other soft, juicy vegetables or fruits that have not been cooked.

Salt fatback Fatback salted at the processing plant as a means of preserving it.

Salted butter Butter that is processed with salt.

Sandwich press Specialized heating unit designed for making panini and Cuban sandwiches; see *panini grill*.

Sandwich spread A liquid or pastelike dressing usually applied to the bread element of the sandwich.

Sandwich/salad unit and **pizza prep table** Refrigeration units designed with refrigerated cabinets below and a cold bain-marie configuration on top.

Sashimi Raw fish and other types of seafood, served simply and with few embellishments.

Sashimi-grade A quality standard that describes tuna, yellowtail snapper and other seafood items that are suitable for serving raw.

Satellite Station Smaller buffet stations used in addition to the main buffet line.

Sauce A fluid accompaniment to solid food.

Sausage A mixture of seasoned ground meat and fat. The word is derived from the Latin word *salsus*, denoting salted products.

Sausage chain Rope of links doubled and twisted.

Sausage horn Tube whose diameter corresponds with that of a particular type of casing that is threaded onto it. Used for encasement.

Sausage link Sausage ropes tied or twisted into short lengths.

Sausage patty Bulk sausage formed into cakes of varying weights.

Sausage stuffer A machine for encasing sausage.

Savory cold soup A light-textured soup with a refreshing flavor served as an appetizer at the beginning of a meal. Some are chilled versions of hot appetizer soups. Others are made from raw ingredients.

Savory ice cube Highly seasoned liquid frozen in an ice cube tray. When added to a cold soup, it helps retain temperature without diluting flavor when it melts.

Savory sorbet Semisweet syrup, vegetable juice, or fruit juice frozen in an ice cream machine.

Savory tuile [TWEEL] Very thin, baked wafer made from batter, cheese, or potato.

Seafood Non-mammal animal foods derived from both fresh and saltwater sources.

Sea salt Unrefined, natural salt made by evaporating seawater in man-made lagoons or by mechanical processes.

Seafood cocktail Chilled seafood tossed or topped with a sauce; typically served in a cocktail glass on a bed of shredded lettuce with a lemon wedge.

Sealer After a pâté product is baked and cooled, it is filled and/or coated to preserve it. The traditional sealer was a semisolid fat. Modern pâtés and terrines are usually sealed with aspic.

Seasoned wood Also known as aged wood.

Seated buffet Includes table-and-chair seating with a place setting for every guest.

Secondary bind In forcemeats, structure formed by the coagulation of egg proteins.

Secondary binder The additional protein needed to strengthen the structure of a mousseline, usually eggs. The secondary binder helps the meat and fat bind and stabilizes the emulsion.

Secondary meat Additional type of meat added to a pâté forcemeat.

Secondary poultry Additional poultry meat needed to make the forcemeat of a galantine.

Self-service buffet Guests serve themselves as much or as little as they want of whichever food items they choose to take.

Semisolid fat Fat that is solid when chilled, soft at room temperature, and liquid when heated—for example, whole butter.

Sequencing Keeping slices in order as they are cut.

Service line A row of large food-service equipment units selected and arranged for the fast and efficient turn-out of food. Service lines may be single or double.

Set The degree of firmness to which a liquid gels.

Seviche [say-VEE-chay] Latin-American seafood dish "cooked" with acid.

Sevruga caviar [sev-ROO-gah] Tiny, tightly clustered sturgeon eggs ranging in color from brown to black, with a strong, assertive flavor.

Shallow-poaching Cooking food partially submerged in the cooking liquid in a covered pan.

Shaped butter Butter that is formed into decorative shapes with scoops, butter curlers, or pastry bags and tips.

Sharp Tangy flavor and unique mouthfeel of cheddar cheese.

Sheet gelatin Product made by pouring liquid gelatin into very shallow trays, dehydrating it into a filmlike layer, and then cutting it into rectangular pieces.

Shellfish Aquatic animals with shells instead of skeletons.

Shocking Another name for refreshing.

Showtime The period between the moment the first guest enters a buffet room and the moment the last guest leaves.

Shrimp cocktail chiller A stainless-steel or glass presentation vessel in which the serving cup rests in a bowl of crushed ice.

Shucked Fresh bivalve oyster that is opened, the meat detached from the shell, and presented in the cup-shaped bottom shell.

Simple long roll sandwich A long roll that is split completely in half horizontally and then filled.

Simple salad The combination of leafy greens tossed with a vinaigrette dressing, with minimal garnishes.

Simple sandwich A sandwich of two slices of bread with the spread, filling, and internal garnishes between them.

Single-decker sandwich A simple sandwich, having only two slices of bread.

Single-service line One row of equipment with a pickup window situated above one or more of the equipment units.

Sip Short for *soup sip*.

Skewered hors d'oeuvres Two or three pieces of food threaded onto a cocktail pick or bamboo skewer. Also called *hors d'oeuvre kebabs*.

Slurry A mixture of raw starch and cold liquid used for thickening.

Smear Describes ground meat with a greasy, puréed texture. Caused by dull grinder blades, improper trimming, and overheating.

Smoke box Enclosed area in which smoke is trapped.

Smokehouse A structure used as a smoking chamber.

Smoking chamber Smoke box.

Socle [SOCK-l] A molded base; shapes vary.

Solids component Combined weight of the meat and fat in a forcemeat.

Soup sip Very small portion of soup in small serving vessel, such as a demitasse cup or shot glass, passed to guests in the same manner as spoon hors d'oeuvres. This is a recent trend in upscale restaurant and catering service.

Spears A classic presentation for broccoli in which the vegetable is fabricated into pieces consisting of both peeled stem and crown.

Sneeze guard Clear Plexiglas panel suspended over or in front of a food display to protect it.

Sodium nitrate A preservative found in Prague Powder #2.

Sodium nitrite The preservative found in Prague Powder #1.

Spoon hors d'oeuvres Tiny portions of food, such as mousses, bound protein salads, and hot food items, served on attractive silver spoons or Asian-style ceramic spoons and garnished in the same manner as canapés.

Spring mix Blend of virtually any baby greens or specialty greens.

Sprouts The first shoots produced from a plant seed, harvested before any true leaves form.

Stabilizer An ingredient that gives a mousse's purée base enough structure to hold the lighteners and, in some cases, to stand alone when unmolded.

Standard-grind sausage Forcemeats ground in a meat grinder to varying degrees of fineness or coarseness.

Standing buffet Any buffet that does not include a table place setting for every guest.

Station A portion of a service line dedicated to turning out one particular type of preparation.

Stationary hors d'oeuvres Trays of hors d'oeuvres placed on one or more tables.

Station map Document listing the components of each dish the station must turn out and indicating the proper place to store each of these components.

Steaming To cook food completely surrounded by water vapor at a temperature of 212°F (100°C) or higher, but without pressure.

Steep To soak a flavorful ingredient, usually in hot water or a water-based liquid, in order to release its flavors.

Straw Long, thin strip of puff pastry topped with cheese or other flavorings, twisted into an attractive shape, and baked crisp and golden.

Structural props Objects used to support food platters and visual props on a buffet table.

Stuffed hors d'oeuvre A small piece of food that is filled with a complementary ingredient and attractively garnished.

Sublimation A form of dehydration in which ice changes directly into vapor.

Submarine sandwich Connecticut version of the long roll Italian sandwich.

Succession blanching Blanching several types of vegetable in the same water, beginning with mild-flavored vegetables and proceeding in order of flavor strength.

Suet [SOO-et] The deposit fat that forms around an animal's kidney.

Surface décor Décor applied to the surface of a coated food.

Surface ripening Process by which the exterior of certain cheeses are sprayed with a culture, acquiring an edible outer rind, called the *bloom*, which has a distinctive texture and appearance.

Surface tension The phenomenon wherein surface water molecules cling tightly to each other and form a kind of elastic sheet.

Sushi Based on cooked, cooled rice seasoned with vinegar, the most popular and well-known types of this Japanese dish are garnished with raw fish or other types of raw seafood.

Sweet butter Contains no salt.

Sweet cold soup Served as dessert and often referred to as *dessert soup*.

Synthetic casing Tubes for sausage encasement made from plastic or plant fiber.

Synthetic souring agent Reproduces the flavors produced by the action of bacteria in traditionally fermented sausages.

Syrupy Describes the consistency of a cooled gelatinized liquid—similar to that of maple syrup.

T

Table butter Butter that accompanies the bread served at meals.

Take-out or **take-away service** Foods packed in disposable containers for pickup or delivery. Picnic baskets and box lunches are variations of this service style.

Tallow Semisoft fat rendered from the deposit fat found in certain areas of sheep and cattle carcasses.

Tamis [tahm-EE] Fine-mesh drum sieve.

Tamper Tool that pushes meat through a grinder; also called a *pusher*.

Tartine A French open-faced sandwich.

Teasing needle Tool used to puncture tiny holes in the casing of a filled sausage in order to release air bubbles and prevent the sausage from bursting during cooking.

Temper To move ice from the freezer to refrigerator temperature approximately 12 hours before working on it. Tempering gives ice greater clarity and stability.

Temporary or **unstable emulsion** An emulsion having a low percentage of emulsifying ingredients and thus prone to separating after time.

Terrine Forcemeat baked in a form or vessel without a pastry crust.

Thermal shock The condition of ice subjected to sudden changes of temperature; shocked ice easily cracks or splits under the pressure of sculpting.

Tight mayonnaise Mayonnaise that is overthickened and oily. Extremely tight mayonnaise has an unpleasant greenish color and feels greasy on the tongue.

Tinted cure mix (TCM) Curing compound tinted pink with food coloring so it will not be mistaken for salt and used incorrectly. Also called a *pink cure*.

Toasted sandwich The bread product is spread and the filling ingredients are added to the open bread product. The sandwich is then heated in a countertop oven.

Torchon Foie gras cylinder wrapped in cheesecloth then poached.

Tossed salad Green salad mixed or topped with a variety of brightly colored vegetable garnishes, typically served with the diner's choice of dressing, usually a vinaigrette or a dairy- or mayonnaise-based dressing. Tossed salads function as a light starter eaten before a substantial entrée. Served in large portions, they may be called *dinner salads* and served as a light entrée.

Trim fat Fat deposited between the muscles of an animal's body.

Turgid Describes a perfectly fresh salad green having moisture-filled cells. The leaf edges show no signs of softening, flattening, or disintegration.

U

Undercounter refrigeration units Refrigeration units that provide workspace on top, which makes them more useful on a service line than upright units.

Unflavored dry gelatin Liquid gelatin that has been dehydrated and purified to remove most of its meat flavor and odor.

Univalve A shellfish similar to a bivalve, but with one exterior shell section only.

Unleavened bread Breads made without yeast.

Unsmoked sausage Type of dried sausage.

V

Vegetable Plant part that is prepared and served as a savory (nonsweet) food.

Verjus Fresh juice of unripe wine grapes.

Vinaigrette A mixture of vegetable oil, salt, and vinegar. An emulsified vinaigrette contains an emulsifying ingredient and is mixed in a special way so that the oil and vinegar stay mixed together.

Virgin olive oil Made completely from olives and extracted by physical processes that do not include heat or chemicals.

Visual props Decorative items placed on a buffet line or station to make it more attractive and to support the buffet theme.

W

Warming tray An electrically heated, flat serving vessel used to keep food warm during service.

Wasabi Green horseradish.

Washed-rind strong cheese A cheese washed with brine, wine, or spirits as it ripens.

Water out To exude moisture.

Waxed produce Fruits and vegetables that are coated by commercial growers with a thin coat of edible wax to combat moisture loss.

Wet cure Brine used as a curing compound; also called *brine cure*.

Whey Watery liquid left after the removal of milk solids and milk fat.

Whipped butter When butter is softened and beaten until light and fluffy in an electric mixer fitted with the whip attachment.

White or **fresh emulsified sausage** Smooth-texture sausage *not* treated with a nitrite/nitrate curing mix so as *not* to develop a pink color in the meat.

Whole butter Standard butter composed roughly of 80 percent milk fat, 5 percent milk solids, and 15 percent water. These components remain combined in an emulsion.

Whole milk Milk blended at the dairy to a ratio of 88 percent water, 3.5 percent milk fat, and 8.5 percent milk.

Wicking Problem that occurs when the foil covering of a baking dish extends down into the water bath in which the dish is placed. Water is drawn up into the dish itself, diluting or otherwise marring the food.

Working consistency The gel consistency at which a gelatinized liquid must be used to coat foods.

Worm The spiral-shaped mechanism that pushes meat into the die of a grinder; also called the *auger*.

Wrap sandwich Thin, pliable flatbread rolled with or around a filling and internal garnishes.

Wrapped hors d'oeuvre Food item or filling encased in a thin sheet of another food item.

Wrapper Used to contain a forcemeat.

Y

Yeasted flatbread Leavened breads that are fabricated to give them a flat appearance

Young cheese At the beginning of the ripening process, beneficial microorganisms are fewer and the changes in the cheese are slight. At this stage, a cheese is often referred to as a young cheese.

Subject Index

D

E

F

G

Recipe Index

D

E

F

G

H

I

Q

R

S

T

U

V

W

Y